Praise for *A World of Ideas*

"In my opinion, the most important factor is choosing a book that will make [students] think. If they cannot think, they cannot write. This book is really focused on that aspect of learning, and I have had great success with my students in teaching from the diverse spectrum of authors contained."
— JENNIFER C. PHILPOT, *Eastern Kentucky University*

"I continue to use *A World of Ideas* because I believe in the concept that good writing is more than style and because students, deep down, hunger for substance."
— GERALD MCCARTHY, *San Antonio College*

"There is no other text available that can equal this one in providing an intellectual basis for your course."
— THOMAS L. WILMETH, *Concordia University*

"I like the fact that the readings are challenging, informative, thought provoking, historically important, and models of exemplary writing. I think the readings contribute to helping students understand how their world and country have evolved, and they give students helpful perspectives with which to evaluate their goals, responsibilities, and values—in addition to stimulating their thinking and writing."
— MARTHA WILLOUGHBY, *Pearl River Community College*

"*A World of Ideas* is a thought-provoking blend of traditional and contemporary essays that allows students to participate in conversations they've inherited by confronting the original thinkers and theorists. It's not stuffy, but neither is it easy. This anthology is an excellent tool to introduce students to what college-level discourse should be all about."
— BRANDY MCKENZIE, *Clark College*

"All in all a wonderful guide to the classic and modern ideas that shape the way we think."
— JOSH LEDERMAN, *Emmanuel College*

"Simply the greatest freshman English teaching text. I can't tell you how many students thank me and say, 'I will never sell it back.'"
— JOHN FREDERICK, *Santa Monica College*

EIGHTH EDITION

A WORLD OF IDEAS

ESSENTIAL READINGS FOR COLLEGE WRITERS

LEE A. JACOBUS

University of Connecticut

BEDFORD/ST. MARTIN'S
Boston ◆ *New York*

For Bedford/St. Martin's

Senior Developmental Editor: Maura Shea
Production Editor: Katherine Caruana
Production Supervisor: Andrew Ensor
Marketing Manager: Molly Parke
Cover Design: Donna Lee Dennison
Text Design: Anna Palchik
Copyeditor: Mary Lou Wilshaw-Watts
Photo Research: Linda Finigan
Cover Art: Brian Dettmer, *Today's World.* Modified book. Courtesy Packer
    Schopf Gallery.
Composition: Macmillan Publishing Solutions
Printing and Binding: Haddon Craftsmen, an RR Donnelley & Sons Company

President: Joan E. Feinberg
Editorial Director: Denise B. Wydra
Editor in Chief: Karen S. Henry
Director of Marketing: Karen R. Soeltz
Director of Editing, Design, and Production: Marcia Cohen
Assistant Director of Editing, Design, and Production: Elise S. Kaiser
Managing Editor: Elizabeth M. Schaaf

Library of Congress Control Number: 2008937680

Manufactured in the United States of America.

4   3   2   1
g   f   e

For information, write: Bedford/St. Martin's, 75 Arlington Street, Boston,
MA 02116   (617-399-4000)

ISBN-10: 0-312-38533-1
ISBN-13: 978-0-312-38533-0

PREFACE

Among the pleasures of editing *A World of Ideas* are the discussions I have had over the years with students and teachers who have used the book in their writing classes. A student once wrote to tell me that the book meant a great deal to her and that her experience with it impelled her to wonder what originally inspired me to assemble the first edition. I explained that my teaching of first-year writing has always inclined toward ideas that serious writers and thinkers have explored and contemplated throughout the ages; early on, I could not find a composition reader that introduced students to the important thinkers whose writing I believe should be basic to everyone's education. As a result of that need, *A World of Ideas* took shape and has continued to grow and develop through eight editions, attracting a wide audience of teachers and students who value the thought-provoking ideas that affect the way we interpret the world.

In preparing the eighth edition of *A World of Ideas,* I have benefited, as usual, from the suggestions of hundreds of users of earlier editions. The primary concern of both teachers and students is that the book remain centered on the tradition of important ideas and on the writers whose work has had a lasting influence on society. To that end, I have chosen writers whose ideas are central to our most important and lasting concerns. A new edition offers the opportunity to reevaluate old choices and make new ones that expand and deepen what has always been the fundamental purpose of this composition reader: to provide college students in first-year writing courses with a representative sampling of important ideas examined by men and women who have shaped the way we think today.

The selections in this volume are of the highest quality. Each was chosen because it clarifies important ideas and can sustain discussion and stimulate good writing. Unlike most composition readers, *A World of Ideas* presents substantial excerpts from the work of each of its authors. The selections are presented as they originally appeared;

only rarely are they edited and marked with ellipses. They average fifteen pages in length, and their arguments are presented completely as the authors wrote them. Developing a serious idea in writing takes time and a willingness to experiment. Most students are willing to read deeply into the work of important thinkers to grasp their ideas better because the knowledge yielded by the effort is so vast and rewarding.

A Text for Readers and Writers

Because students perceive writers such as Plato and Thoreau as serious and important, they take the writing course more seriously: they learn to read more attentively, think more critically, and write more effectively. But more important, this may be a student's only opportunity to encounter the thinkers whose ideas have shaped civilization. No other composition reader offers such a comparable collection of important readings along with the supportive apparatus students need to understand, analyze, and respond to them.

Classic Readings.   *A World of Ideas* draws its forty-seven selections from the writing of some of the world's most important thinkers. Those writers with selections that remain from the seventh edition are Lao-tzu, Niccolò Machiavelli, Jean-Jacques Rousseau, Thomas Jefferson, Hannah Arendt, Marcus Tullius Cicero, Frederick Douglass, Henry David Thoreau, Elizabeth Cady Stanton, Martin Luther King Jr., John Rawls, Adam Smith, Karl Marx, John Kenneth Galbraith, Robert B. Reich, Plato, Sigmund Freud, Carl Jung, Howard Gardner, Francis Bacon, Charles Darwin, Rachel Carson, Stephen Jay Gould, Michio Kaku, Aristotle, Friedrich Nietzsche, Iris Murdoch, Mary Wollstonecraft, and Virginia Woolf.

A Focus on Eight Great Ideas.   *A World of Ideas'* unique structure highlights seminal ideas as developed by great thinkers throughout history and facilitates cross-disciplinary comparisons. Each of the eight parts of the book focuses on one great idea—government, justice, the individual, wealth and poverty, mind, nature, ethics and morality, and gender and culture. Part introductions ground students in the history of each idea and connect the philosophies of individual writers.

"Evaluating Ideas: An Introduction to Critical Reading."   This introduction demonstrates a range of methods students can adopt to participate in a meaningful dialogue with each selection. This

dialogue—an active, questioning approach to texts and ideas—is one of the keys to critical reading. In the introduction, a portion of Machiavelli's "The Qualities of the Prince" is presented in annotated form, and the annotations are discussed for their usefulness in understanding this essay and in helping students develop their own annotations while reading the other essays in the book. The introduction encourages students to mark what they think are the most interesting and important ideas in an essay and highlight or underline all sentences that they might want to quote in an essay of their own.

Selection Headnotes. Each selection is preceded by a detailed headnote on the author's life and work and by comments about the primary ideas presented in the reading. The most interesting rhetorical aspects of the selection are identified and discussed to help students see how rhetorical techniques can achieve specific effects.

Prereading Questions. To emphasize critical thinking, reading, and writing, prereading questions precede every selection. The content of the selections is challenging, and these prereading questions can help students in first-year writing courses overcome minor difficulties in understanding the author's meaning. These brief questions are designed to help students focus on central issues during their first reading of each selection.

Extensive Apparatus. At the end of each selection is a group of discussion questions designed for use inside or outside the classroom. "Questions for Critical Reading" focus on key issues and ideas and can be used to stimulate general class discussion and critical thinking. "Suggestions for Critical Writing" help students practice some of the rhetorical strategies employed by the author of a given selection. These suggestions ask for personal responses, as well as complete essays that involve research. A number of these assignments, labeled "Connections," promote critical reading by requiring students to connect particular passages in a selection with a selection by another writer, either in the same part of the book or in another part. The variety of connections is intriguing—Lao-tzu with Machiavelli, Rawls with Rousseau, Smith with Jefferson, Emerson with Fromm, Rousseau with Durkheim and Lévi-Strauss, Ortega y Gasset with Becker, Freud with Greer, Leopold with Nietzsche and Murdoch, Darwin with Fukuyama, and many more.

"Writing about Ideas: An Introduction to Rhetoric." This appendix explains how a reader can make annotations while reading critically and then use those annotations to write effectively in response to the

ideas presented in any selection in the book. The appendix relies on
the annotations of the Machiavelli selection illustrated in "Evaluating
Ideas: An Introduction to Critical Reading." A sample student essay
on Machiavelli, using all the techniques taught in the context of reading and writing, gives students a model for writing their own material. In addition, this section helps students understand how they can
apply some of the basic rhetorical principles discussed throughout
the book.

Instructor's Resource Manual.   I have prepared an extensive
manual, *Resources for Teaching A WORLD OF IDEAS*, that contains
further background on the selections, examples from my own classroom responses to the selections, and more suggestions for classroom
discussion and student writing assignments. Sentence outlines for the
selections—which have been carefully prepared by Michael Hennessy,
Carol Verberg, Ellen Troutman, Ellen Darion, and Jon Marc Smith—
can be photocopied or downloaded from the book's companion Web
site, **bedfordstmartins.com/worldofideas**, and given to students.
The idea for these sentence outlines came from the phrase outlines
that Darwin created to precede each chapter of *On the Origin of
Species*. These outlines may be used to discuss the more difficult selections and to provide additional guidance for students. At the end
of the manual, brief bibliographies are provided for all forty-seven
authors. These bibliographies may be photocopied or downloaded
and distributed to students who wish to explore the primary selections in greater depth.

New in the Eighth Edition

The eighth edition offers a number of new features to help students engage and interact with the texts as they learn to analyze
ideas and develop their own thoughts in writing.

New Essential Readings.   The selections in *A World of Ideas*
explore the key ideas that have defined the human experience and
shaped civilization. Of the forty-seven selections (one more than in
the seventh edition), eighteen are new to the eighth edition includ-
ing works by Carl Becker, José Ortega y Gasset, Ralph Waldo
Emerson, W. E. B. Du Bois, Ruth Benedict, Erich Fromm, Emile
Durkheim, Andrew Carnegie, Steven Pinker, V. S. Ramachandran,
Francis Fukuyama, Aldo Leopold, Peter Singer and Jim Mason,
John Stuart Mill, Margaret Mead, Claude Lévi-Strauss, Germaine
Greer, and René Descartes.

Two New Foundational Ideas.   The selections in the two new parts on "The Individual" and "Gender and Culture" cover considerable historical periods and attitudes toward their subjects. Both these new sections contain ideas that affect every one of us in a number of important ways. The concept of the individual, for example, is in many ways modern—highly developed beginning in the late seventeenth century, flourishing in the eighteenth-century's Age of Enlightenment, and continually discussed throughout the nineteenth and twentieth centuries by writers featured here including Ralph Waldo Emerson, W. E. B. Du Bois, and Ruth Benedict. The second new part, "Gender and Culture," approaches the concepts of masculine and feminine from a cultural perspective, including important works by John Stuart Mill, Margaret Mead, Claude Lévi-Strauss, and Germaine Greer.

New "Visualizing" Feature Encourages Students to Apply Great Ideas to Great Works of Art.   Immediately preceding the selections in each part, a well known painting is accompanied by a commentary that places the work historically and aesthetically, and prepares students to make thoughtful connections between the work and the thinkers that follow. For example, Visualizing Gender and Culture features Mary Cassatt's painting *In the Loge* along with a brief caption and a discussion of the work's exploration of gender roles. The **"Seeing Connections"** questions that follow each of the readings ask students to relate a given text back to the work of art. Other featured works of art include but are not limited to: Eugène Delacroix's *Liberty Leading the People* for Visualizing Government, Caspar David Friedrich's *Wanderer Above the Sea of Fog* for Visualizing the Individual, and Salvador Dalí's *The Persistence of Memory* for Visualizing the Mind.

More "Connections" Questions.   Throughout the book students are asked to make connections and comparisons between writers within the same great idea topic and between writers in different great idea topics.

Increased Coverage of Argument.   The "Writing about Ideas: An Introduction to Rhetoric" section at the back of the book now provides brief coverage of the three most common approaches to argument: Classical, Toulmin, and Rogerian. Additionally, many of the suggestions for critical reading and critical writing which follow each selection in the book highlight the basic elements of a writer's argument and ask students to make arguments of their own.

A Fully Updated Companion Web Site Provides Students with More Ways to Explore the World of Ideas. At **bedfordstmartins .com/worldofideas,** students will find links to full-text documents of historical and philosophical interest, and more information on each selection's author and his or her ideas. Instructors will find the helpful Instructor's Manual, which includes a sentence outline for every selection.

Acknowledgments

I am grateful to a number of people who made important suggestions for earlier editions, among them Shoshana Milgram Knapp of Virginia Polytechnic and State University and Michael Hennessy of Texas State University–San Marcos. I want to thank Jon Marc Smith of Texas State University–San Marcos and Chiara Sulprizio of the University of Southern California for assisting with the Instructor's Manual for the eighth edition. I also remain grateful to Michael Bybee of Saint John's College in Santa Fe for suggesting many fascinating pieces by Eastern thinkers, all of which he has taught to his own students. Thanks to him, this edition includes Lao-tzu.

Like its predecessors, the eighth edition is indebted to a great many creative people at Bedford/St. Martin's, whose support is invaluable. I want to thank Charles Christensen, former president, whose concern for the excellence of this book and whose close attention to detail are truly admirable. I appreciate as always the advice of Joan E. Feinberg, president, and Denise Wydra, editorial director, whose suggestions were timely and excellent. Nancy Perry, editor in chief, New York; Karen Henry, editor in chief, Boston; and Steve Scipione, executive editor, offered many useful ideas and suggestions as well, especially in the early stages of development, and kept their sharp eyes on the project throughout. My editor, Maura Shea, is the professional's professional. Her guidance, her sensibility, and her commitment to this project from the beginning have been an inspiration for me as I have worked to make this edition the best yet. She is creative, smart, and the perfect editor for this and other projects we have worked on together. Assisting her were a number of hard-working individuals including Erin McGhee, Kate Mayhew, and Britt Hansen. Katherine Caruana, production editor, also helped with innumerable important details and suggestions. Mary Lou Wilshaw-Watts, copyeditor, improved the prose and watched out for inconsistencies. Thanks also to several staff members and researchers: Diane Kraut cleared text permissions, Donna Dennison found the cover art and designed the cover, and Linda Finigan secured all the new photographs. In earlier editions, I had help from Sarah Cornog, Rosemary Winfield, Michelle Clark, Professor Mary W. Cornog, Ellen Kuhl, Mark Reimold, Andrea Goldman, Beth Castrodale, Jonathan Burns, Mary Beth McNulty, Beth Chapman, Mika De Roo, and Greg Johnson. I feel I had a personal relationship with each of them. I also want to thank the students— quite a few of them—who wrote me directly about their experiences in reading the first seven editions. I have attended carefully to what they told me, and I am warmed by their high regard for the material in this book.

Earlier editions named hundreds of users of this book who sent their comments and encouragement. I would like to take this opportunity to thank them again. In addition, the following professors were generous with criticism, praise, and detailed recommendations for the eighth edition: D. Michelle Adkerson, Nashville State Community College; Robert Alexander, Point Park University; Jonathan Ausubel, Chaffey College; Michael Bloomingburg, Eastern Kentucky University; Norma Darr, Long Beach City College; David Elias, Eastern Kentucky University; Susan Gorman, Massachusetts College of Pharmacy and Health Sciences; James Kenkel, Eastern Kentucky University; Kay Kolb, University of Texas–Permian Basin; Leslie Layne, Lynchburg College; Josh Lederman, Emmanuel College; Katherine Liesener, Emmanuel College; Yaroslav Malyuta, University of Texas at Arlington; Gerald McCarthy, San Antonio College; Brandy McKenzie, Clark College; Agnetta Mendoza, Nashville State Community College; Sean P. Murphy, College of Lake County; Courtney L. Novosat, Emmanuel College; Jennifer C. Philpot, Eastern Kentucky University; Ron Schwartz, Pierce College; Danny F. Shears, University of San Francisco; Michele Singletary, Nashville State Community College; Scott Votel, Emmanuel College; Martha Willoughby, Pearl River Community College; and Thomas L. Wilmeth, Concordia University.

I want to mention particularly the past experiences I had visiting Professor Elizabeth Deis and the faculty and students of Hampden-Sydney College in connection with their writing and humanities programs. Professors James Kenkel and Charlie Sweet were gracious in welcoming me to Eastern Kentucky University for workshops and classes using *A World of Ideas*. These were delightful and fruitful experiences that helped me shape the book. I am grateful to all who took part in these workshops.

TO THE STUDENT

When the first edition of *A World of Ideas* was published, the notion that students in first-year composition courses should be able to read and write about challenging works by great thinkers was a radical one. In fact, no other composition reader at the time included selections from such important thinkers as Hannah Arendt, Marcus Tullius Cicero, Ralph Waldo Emerson, Karl Marx, Plato, Charles Darwin, or Mary Wollstonecraft. I had expected a moderate response from a small number of people. Instead, teachers and students alike sent me a swarm of mail commending the book for the challenge it provided and the insights they gained.

One of the first letters I received was from a young woman who had read the book after she graduated from college. She said she had heard of the thinkers included in *A World of Ideas* but in her college career had never read any of their works. Reading them now, she said, was long overdue. Another student wrote me an elaborate letter in which he demonstrated that every one of the selections in the book had been used as the basis of a *Star Trek* episode. He sagely connected every selection to a specific episode and convinced me that whoever was writing *Star Trek* had read some of the world's most important thinkers. Other students have written to tell me that they found themselves using the material in this book in other courses, such as psychology, philosophy, literature, and history, among others. In many cases, these students were the only ones among their peers who had read the key authors in their discipline.

Most of the time you will have to read the selections in *A World of Ideas* more than once. Works by influential thinkers, such as Jean-Jacques Rousseau, John Rawls, W. E. B. Du Bois, Adam Smith, Sigmund Freud, Francis Bacon, Iris Murdoch, and Ruth Benedict, can be very challenging. But do not let the challenge discourage you. In "Evaluating Ideas: An Introduction to Critical Reading," I suggest methods for annotating and questioning texts that are designed to help you keep track of what you read and to help you master the material. In addition, each selection is accompanied by a headnote on the author's life and work, comments about the primary ideas presented in the selection, and a host of questions to help you overcome minor difficulties in understanding the author's meaning. Some students have written to tell me that their first reading of the book was off-putting, but most of them have written later to tell me how they eventually overcame their initial fear that the selections would be too difficult for them. Ultimately, these students agreed with me that this material is important enough to merit their absolute attention.

The purpose of *A World of Ideas* is to help you learn to write better by giving you something really significant to think and write about. The selections not only are avenues into some of the most serious thought on their subjects but also are stimulating enough to sustain close analysis and to produce many good ideas for writing. For example, when you think about the law, it helps to know where our sense of justice comes from. "The Defense of Injustice" by Cicero, the first selection in the "Justice" part, is a brilliant argument against justice. It is so brilliant that one almost buys his ideas. But he is a clever orator and is merely testing us because he was one of Rome's champions of justice. Henry David Thoreau's "Civil Disobedience" draws a line between the law and the justice that sometimes sees beyond the law. Elizabeth Cady Stanton defends the rights of women in her "Declaration of Sentiments and Resolutions," pointing always to the social injustices that she documents. Frederick Douglass speaks from the perspective of a former slave when he cries out against the injustice of an institution that existed in the Americas for hundreds of years. And a hundred years after Douglass, Reverend Martin Luther King Jr. sent his "Letter from Birmingham Jail," still questing justice for African Americans and freedom seekers everywhere. Part Two: Justice ends with "A Theory of Justice" by the most important modern philosopher of justice, John Rawls, who measured justice always by its effect on the neediest and least powerful segment of any society. All these writers place their views in the larger context of a universal dialogue on the subject of justice. When you write, you add your own voice to the conversation. By commenting on the selections, expressing and arguing a position, and pointing out contradictions or contrasts among texts, you are participating in the world of ideas.

Keep in mind that I prepared *A World of Ideas* for my own students, most of whom work their way through college and do not take the idea of an education lightly. For that reason, I felt I owed them the opportunity to encounter the very best minds I could put them in touch with. Anything less seemed to me to be a missed opportunity. I hope you, like so many other writing students, find this book both educational and inspiring.

CONTENTS

PART ONE

GOVERNMENT

– 13 –

VISUALIZING GOVERNMENT
EUGÈNE DELACROIX, Liberty Leading the People [IMAGE]
18

PART TWO

JUSTICE

– 135 –

PART THREE

THE INDIVIDUAL

– 245 –

VISUALIZING THE INDIVIDUAL

CASPAR DAVID FRIEDRICH, Wanderer Above the Sea of Fog [IMAGE]

250

who, like Buddha, will be totally individual and help us move onward toward enlightenment. As he says of hierarchical organizations, "the great danger, as with all institutions, is that the individual has the illusion of being an individual."

P A R T   F O U R

WEALTH AND POVERTY

– 339 –

VISUALIZING WEALTH AND POVERTY
HENRY O. TANNER, The Thankful Poor [IMAGE]
344

P A R T   F I V E

MIND

– 439 –

the individual and represent the needs of the group to which we belong.

Gardner, a contemporary psychologist, has a novel view of the mind that proposes seven distinct forms of human intelligence: linguistic, logical-mathematical, spatial, musical, bodily-kinesthetic, interpersonal, and intrapersonal.

The basic question Pinker asks is, what is intelligence? Then he proceeds to examine the machines that have acted intelligently by following rules that produce reliable information. He then outlines his computational theory of intelligence and links it to "thinking machines."

In his quest for insights into the nature of consciousness, Ramachandran examines some of the most unusual disorders of the mind, including syndromes that make one think family members are "imitations" of themselves. He asks, what is the sense of self, and how does language contribute to producing it?

PART SIX

NATURE

– 571 –

VISUALIZING NATURE

ASHER B. DURAND, Kindred Spirits [IMAGE]

576

A prominent figure in philosophy and politics during the reign of England's Elizabeth I, Bacon describes the obstacles that hinder human beings' efforts to understand the world around them and the mysteries of nature.

PART SEVEN

ETHICS AND MORALITY

– 683 –

VISUALIZING ETHICS AND MORALITY
JOSEPH WRIGHT OF DERBY, An Experiment on
a Bird in the Air Pump [IMAGE]
687

PART EIGHT

GENDER AND CULTURE

– 791 –

VISUALIZING GENDER AND CULTURE

MARY STEVENSON CASSATT, In The Loge [IMAGE]

796

In this excerpt from one of the first great works of feminism,
Wollstonecraft argues that the laws, property rights, and class
distinctions of her day are mechanisms of control that deny
women their liberty and demean their lives.

Mill, one of the most distinguished philosophers of his time, the
Victorian age, cries out against a social system that denies education and opportunity to women. He clarifies the subjection of
women in marriage and argues against wasting the talent of half
of society, talent that he says is in great demand in the modern
industrial age.

In this excerpt from A Room of One's Own, her book-length
essay on the role of women in history and society, Woolf imaginatively reconstructs the environment of Shakespeare's hypothetical sister and demonstrates how little opportunity she would
have had in the sixteenth century.

The anthropologist Margaret Mead attacks the idea that there is
a biological basis for what we may think of as a masculine or a
feminine temperament. She illustrates her argument with examples from a number of societies whose views about masculinity
and femininity are quite at odds with any that we might recognize in our own experience.

Because he wanted to study society at its most basic level, Lévi-
Strauss spent almost two years among Brazilian Indians who
had little or no contact with Europeans. He describes their political system and the responsibilities of the chief. He also describes
the gender-specific activities that prevailed in the Nambikwara
hunter-gatherer society.

EVALUATING IDEAS
An Introduction
to Critical Reading

The selections in this book demand a careful and attentive reading. The authors, whose works have changed the way we view our world, our institutions, and ourselves, make every effort to communicate their views with clarity and style. But their views are complex and subtle, and we must train ourselves to read them sensitively, responsively, and critically. Critical reading is basic for approaching the essays in this book. Indeed, it is fundamental for approaching any reading material that deserves serious attention.

Reading critically means reading actively: questioning the premises of the argument, speculating on the ways in which evidence is used, comparing the statements of one writer with those of another, and holding an inner dialogue with the author. These skills differ from the passive reception we employ when we watch television or read lightweight materials. Being an active, participating reader makes it possible for us to derive the most from good books.

Critical reading involves most of the following processes:

- *Prereading* Developing a sense of what the piece is about and what its general purposes seem to be.

- *Annotating* Using a pencil or a pen to mark those passages that seem important enough to return to later. Annotations establish a dialogue between you and the author.

- *Questioning* Raising issues that you feel need to be taken into consideration. These may be issues that you believe the author has treated either well or badly and that you feel are important. Questioning can be part of the annotation process.

- *Reviewing* Rereading your annotations and underlinings in order to grasp the entire "picture" of what you've just read. Sometimes

1

writing a summary of the piece as you review makes the meaning even clearer.

- *Forming your own ideas* Reviewing what you have read, evaluating the way that the writer presents the issues, and developing
  your own views on the issues. This is the final step.

THE PROCESS OF CRITICAL READING

Prereading

Before you read a particular selection, you may find it useful
to turn to the beginning of the part in which it appears. There you
will find an introduction discussing the broader issues and questions central to all the selections in the part. This may help you to
focus your thoughts and formulate your opinions as you read the
essays themselves.

Begin any selection in this book by reading its headnote. Each
headnote supplies historical background on the writer, sets the intellectual stage for the ideas discussed in the essay, and comments on the
writer's main points. The second part of each headnote introduces the
main rhetorical or stylistic methods that the writer uses to communicate his/her thoughts. In the process of reading the headnote, you will
develop an overview that helps prepare you for reading the essay.

This kind of preparation is typical of critical reading. It makes the
task of reading more delightful, more useful, and much easier. A review
of the headnote to Niccolò Machiavelli and part of his essay "The
Qualities of the Prince" will illustrate the usefulness of such preparation. This essay appears in Part One—"Government"—so the content
can already be expected to be concerned with styles of government.
The introduction to Machiavelli provides the following points, each
followed here by the number of the paragraph in which it appears:

Machiavelli was an Italian aristocrat in Renaissance Italy. (1)

Machiavelli describes the qualities necessary for a prince—that
is, any ruler—to maintain power. (2)

A weak Italy was prey to the much stronger France and Spain at
this time. (2)

Machiavelli recommends securing power by whatever means
necessary and maintaining it. (3)

His concern for moralizing or acting out of high moral principle
is not great. (3)

He supports questionable means of becoming and remaining prince. (3)

Machiavelli does not fret over the means used to achieve his ends and sometimes advocates repression, imprisonment, and torture. (3)

Machiavelli has been said to have a cynical view of human nature. (4)

His rhetorical method is to discuss both sides of an issue: cruelty and mercy, liberality and stinginess. (8)

He uses aphorisms to persuade the reader that he is saying something wise and true. (9)

With these observations in mind, the reader knows that the selection that follows will be concerned with governance in Renaissance Italy. The question of ends versus means is central to Machiavelli's discussion, and he does not idealize people and their general goodness. Yet because of Machiavelli's rhetorical methods, particularly his use of aphorism,[1] the reader can expect that Machiavelli's argument will be exceptionally persuasive.

Thus, as a critical reader, you will be well advised to keep track of these basic statements from the headnote. You need not accept all of them, but you should certainly be alert to the issues that will probably be central to your experience of the essay. Remember: it is just as reasonable to question the headnote as it is to question the essay itself.

Before reading the essay in detail, you might develop an overview of its meaning by scanning it quickly. In the case of "The Qualities of the Prince," note the subheadings, such as "On Those Things for Which Men, and Particularly Princes, Are Praised or Blamed." Checking each of the subheadings before you read the entire piece might provide you with a map or guide to the essay.

Each passage is preceded by two or three prereading questions. These are designed to help you keep two or three points in mind as you read. Each of these questions focuses your attention on an important idea or interpretation in the passage. For Machiavelli the questions are:

1. Why does Machiavelli praise skill in warfare in his opening pages? How does that skill aid a prince?
2. Is it better for a prince to be loved or to be feared?

---

[1]**aphorism** A short, pithy statement of truth.

In each case, a key element in Machiavelli's argument is the center of each question. By watching for the answer to these questions, you will find yourself focusing on some of the most important aspects of the passage.

Annotating and Questioning

As you read a text, your annotations establish a dialogue between you and the author. You can underline or highlight important statements that you feel help clarify the author's position. They may be statements to which you will want to refer later. Think of them as serving one overriding purpose: to make it possible for you to review the piece and understand its key points without having to reread it entirely.

Your dialogue with the author will be most visible in the margins of the essay, which is one reason the margins in this book are so generous. Take issue with key points or note your assent — the more you annotate, the more you free your imagination to develop your own ideas. My own methods involve notating both agreement and disagreement. I annotate thoroughly, so that after a quick second glance I know what the author is saying as well as what I thought of the essay when I read it closely. My annotations help me keep the major points fresh in my mind.

Annotation keeps track both of what the author says and of what our responses are. No one can reduce annotation to a formula — we all do it differently — but it is not a passive act. Reading with a pencil or a pen in hand should become second nature. Without annotations, you often have to reread entire sections of an essay to remember an argument that once was clear and understandable but after time has become part of the fabric of the prose and thus "invisible." Annotation is the conquest of the invisible; it provides a quick view of the main points.

When you annotate,

- Read with a pen or a pencil.
- Underline key sentences — for example, definitions and statements of purpose.
- Underline key words that appear often.
- Note the topic of paragraphs in the margins.
- Ask questions in the margins.
- Make notes in the margins to remind yourself to develop ideas later.

- Mark passages you might want to quote later.
- Keep track of points with which you disagree.

Some sample annotations follow, again from the second essay in the book, Niccolò Machiavelli's "The Qualities of the Prince." A sixteenth-century text in translation, *The Prince* is challenging to work with. My annotations appear in the form of underlinings and marginal comments and questions. Only the first few paragraphs appear here, but the entire essay is annotated in my copy of the book.

A Prince's Duty Concerning Military Matters

The prince's profession should be war.

A prince, therefore, must not have any other object nor any other thought, nor must he take anything as his profession but war, its institutions, and its discipline; because that is the only profession which befits one who commands; and it is of such importance that not only does it maintain those who were born princes, but many times it enables men of private station to rise to that position; and, on the other hand, it is evident that when princes have given more thought to personal luxuries than to arms, they have lost their state. And the first way to lose it is to neglect this art; and the way to acquire it is to be well versed in this art.

Examples

Francesco Sforza became Duke of Milan from being a private citizen because he was armed; his sons, since they avoided the inconveniences of arms, became private citizens after having been dukes. For, among the other bad effects it causes, being disarmed makes you despised; this is one of those infamies a prince should guard himself against, as will be treated below: for between an armed and an unarmed man there is no comparison whatsoever, and it is not reasonable for an armed man to obey an unarmed man willingly, nor that an unarmed man should be safe among armed servants; since, when the former is suspicious and the latter are contemptuous, it is impossible for them to work well together. And therefore, a prince who does not understand military matters, besides the other misfortunes already noted, cannot be esteemed by his own soldiers, nor can he trust them.

Being disarmed makes you despised. Is this true?

He must, therefore, never raise his thought from this exercise of war, and in peacetime he must train himself more than in time of war; this can be done in two ways: one by <u>action, the other by the mind</u>. And as far as actions are concerned, besides <u>keeping his soldiers well disciplined and trained,</u> he must always be out hunting, and must <u>accustom his body to hardships</u> in this manner; and he must also learn the nature of the terrain, and know how mountains slope, how valleys open, how plains lie, and understand the nature of rivers and swamps; and he should devote much attention to such activities. <u>Such knowledge is useful in two ways:</u> first, one learns to know one's own country and can better understand how to defend it; second, with the knowledge and experience of the terrain, one can easily comprehend the characteristics of any other terrain that it is necessary to explore for the first time; for the hills, valleys, plains, rivers, and swamps of Tuscany, for instance, have certain similarities to those of other provinces; so that by knowing the lay of the land in one province one can easily understand it in others. And a prince who lacks this ability lacks the most important quality in a leader; because this skill teaches you to find the enemy, choose a campsite, lead troops, organize them for battle, and besiege towns to your own advantage.

[There follow the examples of Philopoemon, who was always observing terrain for its military usefulness, and a recommendation that princes read histories and learn from them. Three paragraphs are omitted.]

Training:
action/mind

Knowledge of
terrain

Two benefits

On Those Things for Which Men, and Particularly Princes, Are Praised or Blamed

Now there remains to be examined what should be the <u>methods and procedures of a prince</u> in dealing with his subjects and friends. And because I know that many have written about this, I am afraid that by writing about it again I shall be thought of as presumptuous, since in discussing this material I depart radically from the procedures of others. But since my intention is to write something useful for anyone who understands it, it seemed more suitable to me to search after the effectual truth of the matter rather than its imagined one. And many writers have imagined for themselves republics and principalities that have never been seen nor known to exist in reality; for there is such a gap between how one lives and how one ought to live that anyone who abandons what is done for what ought to be done learns his ruin rather than his preservation: for a man who wishes to make a vocation of being good at all times will come to ruin among so many who are not good. Hence it is necessary for a prince who wishes to maintain his position to learn how not to be good, and to use this knowledge or not to use it according to necessity.

Those who are good at all times come to ruin among those who are not good.

Prince must learn how not to be good.

Leaving aside, therefore, the imagined things concerning a prince, and taking into account those that are true, I say that all men, when they are spoken of, and particularly princes, since they are placed on a higher level, are judged by some of these qualities which bring them either blame or praise. And this is why one is considered generous, another miserly (to use a Tuscan word, since "avaricious" in our language is still used to mean one who wishes to acquire by means of theft; we call "miserly" one who excessively avoids using what he has); one is considered a giver, the other rapacious; one cruel, another merciful; one treacherous, another faithful; one effeminate and cowardly, another bold and courageous; one humane, another haughty; one lascivious, another chaste; one trustworthy, another cunning; one harsh, another lenient; one serious, another frivolous; one religious, another unbelieving; and the like. And I know that everyone will admit that it would be a very praiseworthy thing to find in a prince, of the qualities mentioned above, those that are held to be good, but since it is neither possible to have them nor to observe them all completely, because human nature does not permit it, a prince must be prudent enough to know how to escape the bad reputation of those vices that would lose the state

Note the prince's reputation.

Prince must avoid reputation for the worst vices.

Some vices may be needed to hold the state. True?

for him, and must protect himself from those that will not lose it for him, if this is possible; but if he cannot, he need not concern himself unduly if he ignores these less serious vices. And, moreover, he need not worry about incurring the bad reputation of those vices without which it would be difficult to hold his state; since, carefully taking everything into account, one will discover that something which appears to be a virtue, if pursued, will end in his destruction; while some other thing which seems to be a vice, if pursued, will result in his safety and his well-being.

Some virtues may end in destruction.

Reviewing

The process of review, which takes place after a careful reading, is much more useful if you have annotated and underlined the text well. To a large extent, the review process can be devoted to accounting for the primary ideas that have been uncovered by your annotations and underlinings. For example, reviewing the Machiavelli annotations shows that the following ideas are crucial to Machiavelli's thinking:

- The prince's profession should be war, so the most successful princes are probably experienced in the military.
- If they do not pay attention to military matters, princes will lose their power.
- Being disarmed makes the prince despised.
- The prince should be in constant training.
- The prince needs a sound knowledge of terrain.
- Machiavelli says he tells us what is true, not what ought to be true.
- Those who are always good will come to ruin among those who are not good.
- To remain in power, the prince must learn how not to be good.
- The prince should avoid the worst vices in order not to harm his reputation.
- To maintain power, some vices may be necessary.
- Some virtues may end in destruction.

Putting Machiavelli's ideas in this raw form does an injustice to his skill as a writer, but annotation is designed to result in such summary statements. We can see that there are some constant themes, such as the insistence that the prince be a military person. As the headnote tells us, in Machiavelli's day Italy was a group of rival city-states, and France, a larger, united nation, was invading these states one by one. Machiavelli dreamed that one powerful prince, such as his favorite, Cesare Borgia, could fight the French and save Italy. He emphasized the importance of the military because he lived in an age in which war was a constant threat.

Machiavelli anticipates the complaints of pacifists—those who argue against war—by telling us that those who remain unarmed are despised. To demonstrate his point, he gives us examples of those who lost their positions as princes because they avoided being armed. He clearly expects these examples to be persuasive.

A second important theme pervading Machiavelli's essay is his view on moral behavior. For Machiavelli, being in power is much more important than being virtuous. He is quick to admit that vice is not desirable and that the worst vices will harm the prince's reputation. But he also says that the prince need not worry about the "less serious" vices. Moreover, the prince need not worry about incurring a bad reputation by practicing vices that are necessary if he wishes to hold his state. In the same spirit, Machiavelli tells us that there are some virtues that might lead to the destruction of the prince.

Forming Your Own Ideas

One of the most important reasons for critically reading the texts in this book is to enable you to develop your own positions on issues that these writers raise. Identifying and clarifying the main ideas is only the first step; the next step in critical reading is evaluating those ideas.

For example, you might ask whether Machiavelli's ideas have any relevance for today. After all, he wrote nearly five hundred years ago and times have changed. You might feel that Machiavelli was relevant strictly during the Italian Renaissance or, alternatively, that his principles are timeless and have something to teach every age. For most people, Machiavelli is a political philosopher whose views are useful anytime and anywhere.

If you agree with the majority, then you may want to examine Machiavelli's ideas to see whether you can accept them. Consider just two of those ideas and their implications:

- Should rulers always be members of the military? Should they always be armed? Should the ruler of a nation first demonstrate competence as a military leader?
- Should rulers ignore virtue and practice vice when it is convenient?

In his commentary on government, Lao-tzu offers different advice from Machiavelli because his assumptions are that the ruler ought to respect the rights of individuals. For Lao-tzu the waging of war is an annoying, essentially wasteful activity. Machiavelli, on the other hand, never questions the usefulness of war: to him, it is basic to government. As a critical reader, you can take issue with such an assumption, and in doing so you will deepen your understanding of Machiavelli.

If we were to follow Machiavelli's advice, then we would choose American presidents on the basis of whether or not they had been good military leaders. Among those we would not have chosen might be Thomas Jefferson, Abraham Lincoln, and Franklin Delano Roosevelt. Those who were high-ranking military men include George Washington, Ulysses S. Grant, and Dwight D. Eisenhower. If you followed Machiavelli's rhetorical technique of using examples to convince your audience, you could choose from either group to prove your case.

Of course, there are examples from other nations. It has been common since the 1930s to see certain leaders dressed in their military uniforms: Benito Mussolini (Italy), Adolf Hitler (Germany), Joseph Stalin (the Soviet Union), Idi Amin (Uganda), Muammar al-Qaddafi (Libya), Saddam Hussein (Iraq). These are all tyrants who tormented their citizens and their neighbors. That gives us something to think about. Should a president dress in full military regalia all the time? Is that a good image for the ruler of a free nation to project?

Do you want a ruler, then, who is usually virtuous but embraces vice when it is necessary? This is a very difficult question to answer. President Richard Nixon tried to hide the Watergate break-in scandal, President Ronald Reagan did not reveal the details of the Iran-Contra scandal, President Bill Clinton lied about his relations with Monica Lewinsky, and George W. Bush misrepresented intelligence to invade Iraq. Yet all these presidents are noted for important achievements while in office. How might Machiavelli have handled these problems differently? How much truthfulness do we expect from our presidents? How much do we deserve?

These are only a few of the questions that are raised by my annotations in the few pages from Machiavelli examined here. Many other issues could be uncovered by these annotations, and many more from subsequent pages of the essay. Critical reading can be a powerful means by which to open what you read to discovery and discussion.

Once you begin a line of questioning, the ways in which you think about a passage begin expanding. You find yourself with more ideas of your own that have grown in response to those you have been reading about. Reading critically, in other words, gives you an enormous return on your investment of time. If you have the chance to investigate your responses to the assumptions and underlying premises of passages such as Machiavelli's, you will be able to refine your thinking even further. For example, if you agree with Machiavelli that rulers should be successful military leaders for whom small vices may be useful at times, and you find yourself in a position to argue with someone who feels Machiavelli is mistaken in this view, then you will have a good opportunity to evaluate the soundness of your thinking. You will have a chance to see your own assumptions and arguments tested.

In many ways, this entire book is about such opportunities. The essays that follow offer you powerful ideas from great thinkers. They invite you to participate in their thoughts, exercise your own knowledge and assumptions, and arrive at your own conclusions. Basically, that is the meaning of education.

PART ONE

GOVERNMENT

Lao-tzu
Niccolò Machiavelli
Jean-Jacques Rousseau
Thomas Jefferson
José Ortega y Gasset
Carl Becker
Hannah Arendt

INTRODUCTION

He who exercises government by means of his virtue may be
compared to the north polar star, which keeps its place and all
the stars turn towards it.

–CONFUCIUS (551–479 B.C.)

When a government becomes powerful it is destructive,
extravagant and violent; it is an usurer which takes bread from
innocent mouths and deprives honorable men of their
substance, for votes with which to perpetuate itself.

–MARCUS TULLIUS CICERO (106–43 B.C.)

All the ills of mankind, all the tragic misfortunes that fill the
history books, all the political blunders, all the failures of the
great leaders have arisen merely from a lack of skill at dancing.

–MOLIÈRE (1622–1673)

Society in every state is a blessing, but Government, even in its
best state, is but a necessary evil; in its worst state, an intolerable
one.

–THOMAS PAINE (1737–1809)

No government can be long secure without formidable
opposition.

–BENJAMIN DISRAELI (1804–1881)

A government is the most dangerous threat to man's rights: it
holds a legal monopoly on the use of physical force against
legally disarmed victims.

–AYN RAND (1902–1982)

At the core of any idea of government is the belief that individuals need an organized allocation of authority to protect their well-being. However, throughout history the form of that allocation of authority has undergone profound shifts, and each successive type of government has inspired debates and defenses. The first civilizations in Mesopotamia and Egypt (4000–3000 B.C.) were theocracies ruled by a high priest. Gradually these political systems evolved into monarchies in which a king whose role was separate from that of the religious leaders held power. During the sixth century B.C. the Greek city-state Athens developed the first democratic system wherein male citizens (but not women or slaves) could elect a body of leaders. As these forms of government developed, so too did the concept of government as the center of law and administration. However, governments and ideas of governments (actual or ideal) have not followed a straight path. History has witnessed constant

14

oscillations between various forms and functions of government, from tyrannies to republics. In turn, these governments and their relation to the individual citizen have been the focus of many great thinkers.

In this section, the thinkers represented have concentrated on both the role and form of government. Lao-tzu reflects on the ruler who would, by careful management, maintain a happy citizenry. Machiavelli places the survival of the prince above all other considerations of government and, unlike Lao-tzu, ignores the concerns and rights of the individual. For Machiavelli, power is the issue, and maintaining it is the sign of good government. Rousseau's emphasis on the social contract focuses on the theory that citizens voluntarily submit to governance in the hope of gaining greater personal freedom.

Whereas governing well concerns most of these thinkers, the forms of government concern others. Thomas Jefferson struggled with the monarchical form of government, as did Rousseau before him, and envisioned a republic that would serve the people. Kings were a threatened species in eighteenth-century Europe, and with Jefferson's aid, they became extinct in the United States. Hannah Arendt was convinced that the totalitarian governments of the twentieth century needed concentration camps in order to practice total domination.

Lao-tzu, whose writings provide the basis for Taoism, one of three major Chinese religions, was interested primarily in political systems. His work, the *Tao-te Ching*, has been translated loosely as "The Way of Power." One thing that becomes clear from reading his work—especially the selections presented here—is his concern for the well-being of the people in any government. He does not recommend specific forms of government (monarchic, representative, democratic) or advocate election versus the hereditary transfer of power. But he does make it clear that the success of the existing forms of government (in his era, monarchic) depends on good relations between the leader and the people. He refers to the chief of state as Master or Sage, implying that one obligation of the governor is to be wise. One expression of that wisdom is the willingness to permit things to take their natural course. His view is that the less the Master needs to do—or perhaps the less government needs to intervene—the happier the people will be.

Niccolò Machiavelli was a pragmatic man of the Renaissance in Italy. As a theoretician and as a member of the political court, he understood government from the inside and carefully examined its philosophy. Because his writings stress the importance of gaining and holding power at any cost, Machiavelli's name has become synonymous with political cunning. However, a careful reading of his work as a reflection of the instability of his time shows that his advice to wield power ruthlessly derived largely from his fear that a weak prince would lose the city-state of Florence to France or to another powerful, plundering nation. His commitment to a powerful prince is based on his view that in the long run strength will guarantee the peace and happiness of the citizen for whom independence is otherwise irrelevant. Therefore, Machiavelli generally ignores questions concerning the comfort and rights of the individual.

In contrast, Jean-Jacques Rousseau is continually concerned with the basic questions of personal freedom and liberty. A fundamental principle in "The Origin of Civil Society" is that the individual's agreement with the state is designed to increase the individual's freedoms, not to diminish them. Rousseau makes this assertion while at the same time admitting that the individual forfeits certain rights to the body politic in order to gain overall freedom. Moreover, Rousseau describes civil society as a body politic that expects its rulers—including the monarch—to behave in a way designed to benefit the people. Such a view in eighteenth-century France was revolutionary. The ruling classes at that time treated the people with great contempt, and the monarch rarely gave any thought to the well-being of the common people. Rousseau's advocacy of a republican form of government in which the monarch served the people was a radical view and would find its ultimate expression decades later in the French Revolution.

Thomas Jefferson's views were also radical for his time. Armed with the philosophy of Rousseau and others, his Declaration of Independence advocates the eradication of the monarch entirely. Not everyone in the colonies agreed with this view. Indeed, his political opponents, such as Alexander Hamilton and Aaron Burr, were far from certain such a view was correct. In fact, some efforts were made to install George Washington as king (he refused). In the Declaration of Independence, Jefferson reflects Rousseau's philosophy by emphasizing the right of the individual to "life, liberty, and the pursuit of happiness" and the obligation of government to serve the people by protecting those rights.

The Spanish philosopher José Ortega y Gasset was alert in 1930 to the threat of dangerous dictatorships developing in Italy, Spain, Germany, and Russia. He wrote at a time of worldwide economic collapse in which he saw the masses in Europe emerging from the aftermath of war and revolution, a condition that, he felt, threatened democracies only recently stabilized. His view is that the mass of people in a modern state cannot act on its own, but needs competent intellectual and moral leadership. Otherwise, the mass acts in a predictable fashion: much like a lynch mob. When that happens, the state forces society to serve the state, rather than have the state serve society.

Carl Becker's essay "Ideal Democracy" was written ten years later than Ortega's, while the world was still in the Great Depression. Becker saw democracy being threatened by dictatorships abroad and feared for the continued existence of democracy in the United States. The possibility of a world war was clear to Becker as he wrote, and he feared that with the rise of fascism and communism the prestige of democracy had suffered terribly. In his essay, Becker defines and clarifies the goals of a democracy and helps us understand its historical place in world governments.

The issues of freedom, justice, and individual rights were all virtually irrelevant in the totalitarian regimes that served as the focus of Hannah Arendt's work. Arendt argued that the fascist states, especially Nazi Germany, and the communist states, especially the Soviet Union, represented a form of government in which individual rights were sacrificed for the good of "the state." In "Total Domination," Arendt argues that the power of totalitarian states depends on the use of terror to enforce the state's ideology. The result is a form of government that eclipses the tyrannical extremes Rousseau and Jefferson sought to eradicate and exceeds even Machiavelli's imaginings of absolute power.

VISUALIZING GOVERNMENT

Eugène Delacroix (1798–1863) was considered the greatest of the romantic painters of France. His use of color and subject matter moved away from the earlier classicists who dominated the late eighteenth century. He painted subjects from recent history, such as *Massacre at Chios,* which expressed sympathy for the Greek cause in their war of independence from the Turks. His painting *The Barque of Dante* (1822) made him a controversial figure in France, so when he painted *Liberty Leading the People* in his early thirties, he was already a celebrity. There was no classical or mythic figure of liberty to use from ancient Greek or Roman history, so Delacroix looked back only as far as the French Revolution (1798) and in the process mythicized for all time the force of liberty and the responsibility of government to the people it serves.

His painting was a political document in itself. It presents a heroic female figure, the epitome of mythic Liberty — whose image in various manifestations appears on coins around the world — struggling with authority in an effort to achieve a truly representative government and surrounded by the common people of France.

EUGÈNE DELACROIX, *LIBERTY LEADING THE PEOPLE.* 1830.
Oil on canvas, 8'6" × 10'10". Louvre, Paris.

This painting became a rallying cry for Reformers around the world
and is widely reprinted in poster form throughout Europe and the
Western Hemisphere. It symbolizes the common cause people have
to overthrow dictatorship or tyranny. It also commemorates the revolutionary action of citizens who barricaded Parisian streets in their
fight against a government that they eventually overthrew.

Because of its powerful visual structure—with Liberty in the center, the tricolor flag of freedom above, and citizens of all social orders
and ages rallying to the cause—this painting may be considered the
most dramatic visual argument for democracy and independence of
Delacroix's time, or any time.

The Italian historian and art critic Giulio Carlo Argan declared
this the first political painting of modern art. It is an allegorical representation of the three-day revolution in July 1830 in which the
Bourbon king, Charles X, was overthrown. The Bourbons were the
family that ruled France prior to the French Revolution (1789). King
Louis XVI was executed during the Revolution and Napoleon became
emperor. After his defeat in 1814, Napoleon went into exile and the
victorious allies reinstated the throne for the Bourbons with the intention of their respecting a constitutional monarchy on the model of

England's. That worked under Louis XVIII, but when his brother Charles X took the throne, he said he would rather "hew wood" than be a king modeled after the king of England. His imperious ways undid most of the positive achievements of the French Revolution, and in 1830, the people rose and demanded his resignation.

The painting is both allegorical and realistic, but there has never been a suggestion that Delacroix represented a specific street or moment during the 1830 July Revolution, despite the suggestion that he himself was involved in the action. His point was that Liberty would come to the barricades wherever and whenever the people's struggle was just. The painting conspicuously includes middle and poorer classes of citizens as a way of emphasizing the people's movement to reject the autocratic government of the Bourbon king. Liberty, a powerful woman carrying the tricolor of the republic (which the Bourbons had abandoned) also carries a bayonetted musket indicating her willingness to fight for a republican form of government. Her Phrygian hat was a style worn often during the revolution of 1789 and itself symbolized liberty. She may also have been a model for the Statue of Liberty, a gift from France to the United States in 1886. The man with the top hat to the left may be a self-portrait of the artist, Delacroix, who was a member of la Garde nationale, or French National Guard, and whose studio was in the neighborhood where much of the fighting occurred. The boy with the two pistols is said to have been a representation from life.

The painting was purchased by the French government as a reminder of the Revolution for the post-Bourbon, "citizen king," Louis-Phillipe. It hung for a while in the palace, but its message of violence in the streets against the government finally condemned it to removal. It was later brought to the Louvre. The painting is massive, a fact apparent even in the accommodating Louvre, and it stands as a reminder that the people have a vested interest in government— that in modern times they cannot be ignored nor barred from speaking out. It is still one of the most visited paintings in the Louvre in Paris and one of the most reproduced of all modern paintings.

As you read the essays in this chapter, think about how Delacroix's painting, with its principle of government by and for the people at all costs, relates to each writer's philosophy of government. Following each selection a Seeing Connections question asks you to directly compare the writer's ideas with Delacroix's work.

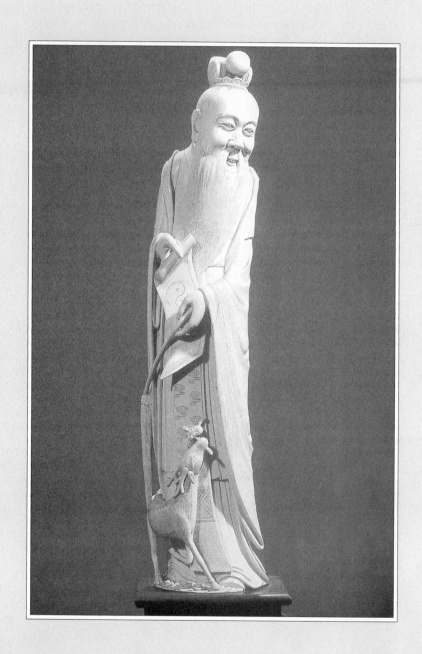

LAO-TZU
Thoughts from the Tao-te Ching

THE AUTHOR of the *Tao-te Ching* (in English often pronounced "dow deh jing") is unknown, although the earliest texts
ascribe the work to Lao-tzu (sixth century B.C.), whose name can
be translated as "Old Master." However, nothing can be said with
certainty about Lao-tzu (lou' dzu') as a historical figure. One tradition holds that he was named Li Erh and born in the state of Ch'u
in China at a time that would have made him a slightly older contemporary of Confucius (551–479 B.C.). Lao-tzu was said to have
worked in the court of the Chou dynasty for most of his life. When
he decided to leave the court to pursue a life of contemplation,
the keeper of the gate urged him to write down his thoughts before
he went into a self-imposed exile. Legend has it that he wrote the
Tao-te Ching and then left the state of Ch'u, never to be seen again.

Lao-tzu's writings offered a basis for Taoism, a religion officially
founded by Chang Tao-ling in about A.D. 150. However, the *Tao-te
Ching* is a philosophical document as much about good government
as it is about moral behavior. The term *Tao* cannot be easily understood or easily translated. In one sense it means "the way," but it
also means "the method," as in "the way to enlightenment" or "the
way to live." Some of the chapters of the *Tao-te Ching* imply that the
Tao is the allness of the universe, the ultimate reality of existence,
and perhaps even a synonym for God. The text is marked by numerous complex ambiguities and paradoxes. It constantly urges us to
look beyond ourselves, beyond our circumstances, and become one
with the Tao—even though it cannot tell us what the Tao is.

The *Tao-te Ching* has often been called a feminine treatise because it emphasizes the creative forces of the universe and frequently

From *Tao-te Ching*. Translated by Stephen Mitchell.

employs the imagery and metaphor of the womb—for example, "The Tao is called the Great Mother." The translator, Stephen Mitchell, translates some of the pronouns associated with the Master as "she," with the explanation that Chinese has no equivalent for the male- and female-gendered pronouns and that "of all the great world religions the teaching of Lao-tzu is by far the most female."

The teachings of Lao-tzu are the opposite of the materialist quest for power, dominance, authority, and wealth. Lao-tzu takes the view that possessions and wealth are leaden weights of the soul, that they are meaningless and trivial, and that the truly free and enlightened person will regard them as evil. Because of his antimaterialist view, his recommendations may seem ironic or unclear, especially when he urges politicians to adopt a practice of judicious inaction. Lao-tzu's advice to politicians is not to do nothing but to intercede only when it is a necessity and then only inconspicuously. Above all, Lao-tzu counsels avoiding useless activity: "the Master / acts without doing anything / and teaches without saying anything." Such a statement is difficult for modern westerners to comprehend, although it points to the concept of enlightenment, a state of spiritual peace and fulfillment that is central to the *Tao-te Ching*.

Lao-tzu's political philosophy minimizes the power of the state—especially the power of the state to oppress the people. Lao-tzu takes the question of the freedom of the individual into account by asserting that the wise leader will provide the people with what they need but not annoy them with promises of what they do not need. Lao-tzu argues that by keeping people unaware that they are being governed, the leader allows the people to achieve good things for themselves. As he writes, "If you want to be a great leader, / you must learn to follow the Tao. / Stop trying to control. / Let go of fixed plans and concepts, / and the world will govern itself" (Verse 57); or in contrast, "If a country is governed with repression, / the people are depressed and crafty" (Verse 58).

To our modern ears this advice may or may not sound sensible. For those who feel government can solve the problems of the people, it will seem strange and unwise. For those who believe that the less government the better, the advice will sound sane and powerful.

The Rhetoric of the *Tao-te Ching*

Traditionally, Lao-tzu is said to have written the *Tao-te Ching* as a guide for the ruling sage to follow. In other words, it is a handbook for politicians. It emphasizes the virtues that the ruler must possess, and in this sense the *Tao-te Ching* invites comparison with Machiavelli's efforts to instruct his ruler.

The visual form of the text is poetry, although the text is not metrical or image laden. Instead of thoroughly developing his ideas, Lao-tzu uses a traditional Chinese form that resembles the aphorism, a compressed statement weighty with meaning. Virtually every statement requires thought and reflection. Thus, the act of reading becomes an act of cooperation with the text.

One way of reading the text is to explore the varieties of interpretation it will sustain. The act of analysis requires patience and willingness to examine a statement to see what lies beneath the surface. Take, for example, one of the opening statements:

> The Master leads
> by emptying people's minds
> and filling their cores,
> by weakening their ambition
> and toughening their resolve.
> He helps people lose everything
> they know, everything they desire,
> and creates confusion
> in those who think that they know.

This passage supports a number of readings. One centers on the question of the people's desire. "Emptying people's minds" implies eliminating desires that lead the people to steal or compete for power. "Weakening their ambition" implies helping people direct their powers toward the attainable and useful. Such a text is at odds with Western views that support advertisements for expensive computers, DVD players, luxury cars, and other items that generate ambition and desire in the people.

In part because the text resembles poetry, it needs to be read with attention to innuendo, subtle interpretation, and possible hidden meanings. One of the rhetorical virtues of paradox is that it forces the reader to consider several sides of an issue. The resulting confusion yields a wider range of possibilities than would arise from a self-evident statement. Through these complicated messages, Lao-tzu felt he was contributing to the spiritual enlightenment of the ruling sage, although he had no immediate hope that his message would be put into action. A modern state might have a difficult time following Lao-tzu's philosophy, but many individuals have tried to attain peace and contentment by leading lives according to its principles.

PREREADING QUESTIONS:
WHAT TO READ FOR

The following prereading questions may help you anticipate key issues in the discussion of Lao-tzu's "Thoughts from the *Tao-te Ching*." Keeping them in mind during your first reading of the selection should help focus your attention.

- What is the Master's attitude toward action?
- The Tao is "the way"—how are we to understand its meaning? What does it mean to be in harmony with the Tao?
- According to Lao-tzu, why is moderation important in government?

Thoughts from the Tao-te Ching

3

If you oversteem great men,   1
people become powerless.
If you overvalue possessions,
people begin to steal.

The Master leads   2
by emptying people's minds
and filling their cores,
by weakening their ambition
and toughening their resolve.
He helps people lose everything
they know, everything they desire,
and creates confusion
in those who think that they know.

Practice not-doing,   3
and everything will fall into place.

17

When the Master governs, the people   4
are hardly aware that he exists.
Next best is a leader who is loved.
Next, one who is feared.
The worst is one who is despised.

If you don't trust the people,   5
you make them untrustworthy.

The Master doesn't talk, he acts.   6
When his work is done,
the people say, "Amazing:
we did it, all by ourselves!"

18

When the great Tao is forgotten,   7
goodness and piety appear.
When the body's intelligence declines,
cleverness and knowledge step forth.
When there is no peace in the family,
filial piety begins.
When the country falls into chaos,
patriotism is born.

19

Throw away holiness and wisdom,   8
and people will be a hundred times happier.
Throw away morality and justice,
and people will do the right thing.
Throw away industry and profit,
and there won't be any thieves.

If these three aren't enough,   9
just stay at the center of the circle
and let all things take their course.

26

The heavy is the root of the light.   10
The unmoved is the source of all movement.

Thus the Master travels all day   11
without leaving home.
However splendid the views,
she stays serenely in herself.

Why should the lord of the country   12
flit about like a fool?
If you let yourself be blown to and fro,

you lose touch with your root.
If you let restlessness move you,
you lose touch with who you are.

29

Do you want to improve the world?   13
I don't think it can be done.

The world is sacred.   14
It can't be improved.
If you tamper with it, you'll ruin it.
If you treat it like an object, you'll lose it.

There is a time for being ahead,   15
a time for being behind;
a time for being in motion,
a time for being at rest;
a time for being vigorous,
a time for being exhausted;
a time for being safe,
a time for being in danger.

The Master sees things as they are,   16
without trying to control them.
She lets them go their own way,
and resides at the center of the circle.

30

Whoever relies on the Tao in governing men   17
doesn't try to force issues
or defeat enemies by force of arms.
For every force there is a counterforce.
Violence, even well intentioned,
always rebounds upon oneself.

The Master does his job   18
and then stops.
He understands that the universe
is forever out of control,
and that trying to dominate events
goes against the current of the Tao.
Because he believes in himself,
he doesn't try to convince others.

Because he is content with himself,
he doesn't need others' approval.
Because he accepts himself,
the whole world accepts him.

31

Weapons are the tools of violence;   19
all decent men detest them.

Weapons are the tools of fear;   20
a decent man will avoid them
except in the direst necessity
and, if compelled, will use them
only with the utmost restraint.
Peace is his highest value.
If the peace has been shattered,
how can he be content?
His enemies are not demons,
but human beings like himself.
He doesn't wish them personal harm.
Nor does he rejoice in victory.
How could he rejoice in victory
and delight in the slaughter of men?

He enters a battle gravely,   21
with sorrow and with great compassion,
as if he were attending a funeral.

37

The Tao never does anything,   22
yet through it all things are done.

If powerful men and women   23
could center themselves in it,
the whole world would be transformed
by itself, in its natural rhythms.
People would be content
with their simple, everyday lives,
in harmony, and free of desire.

When there is no desire,   24
all things are at peace.

38

The Master doesn't try to be powerful;   25
thus he is truly powerful.
The ordinary man keeps reaching for power;
thus he never has enough.

The Master does nothing,   26
yet he leaves nothing undone.
The ordinary man is always doing things,
yet many more are left to be done.

The kind man does something,   27
yet something remains undone.
The just man does something,
and leaves many things to be done.
The moral man does something,
and when no one responds
he rolls up his sleeves and uses force.

When the Tao is lost, there is goodness.   28
When goodness is lost, there is morality.
When morality is lost, there is ritual.
Ritual is the husk of true faith,
the beginning of chaos.

Therefore the Master concerns himself   29
with the depths and not the surface,
with the fruit and not the flower.
He has no will of his own.
He dwells in reality,
and lets all illusions go.

46

When a country is in harmony with the Tao,   30
the factories make trucks and tractors.
When a country goes counter to the Tao,
warheads are stockpiled outside the cities.

There is no greater illusion than fear,   31
no greater wrong than preparing to defend yourself,
no greater misfortune than having an enemy.

Whoever can see through all fear   32
will always be safe.

53

The great Way is easy, 33
yet people prefer the side paths.
Be aware when things are out of balance.
Stay centered within the Tao.

When rich speculators prosper 34
while farmers lose their land;
when government officials spend money
on weapons instead of cures;
when the upper class is extravagant and irresponsible
while the poor have nowhere to turn—
all this is robbery and chaos.
It is not in keeping with the Tao.

57

If you want to be a great leader, 35
you must learn to follow the Tao.
Stop trying to control.
Let go of fixed plans and concepts,
and the world will govern itself.

The more prohibitions you have, 36
the less virtuous people will be.
The more weapons you have,
the less secure people will be.
The more subsidies you have,
the less self-reliant people will be.

Therefore the Master says: 37
I let go of the law,
and people become honest.
I let go of economics,
and people become prosperous.
I let go of religion,
and people become serene.
I let go of all desire for the common good,
and the good becomes common as grass.

58

If a country is governed with tolerance, 38
the people are comfortable and honest.
If a country is governed with repression,
the people are depressed and crafty.

When the will to power is in charge,
the higher the ideals, the lower the results.
Try to make people happy,
and you lay the groundwork for misery.
Try to make people moral,
and you lay the groundwork for vice.

39

Thus the Master is content
to serve as an example
and not to impose her will.
She is pointed, but doesn't pierce.
Straightforward, but supple.
Radiant, but easy on the eyes.

40

59

For governing a country well
there is nothing better than moderation.

41

The mark of a moderate man
is freedom from his own ideas.
Tolerant like the sky,
all-pervading like sunlight,
firm like a mountain,
supple like a tree in the wind,
he has no destination in view
and makes use of anything
life happens to bring his way.

42

Nothing is impossible for him.
Because he has let go,
he can care for the people's welfare
as a mother cares for her child.

43

60

Governing a large country
is like frying a small fish.
You spoil it with too much poking.

44

Center your country in the Tao
and evil will have no power.
Not that it isn't there,
but you'll be able to step out of its way.

45

Give evil nothing to oppose
and it will disappear by itself.

61

When a country obtains great power,
it becomes like the sea:
all streams run downward into it.
The more powerful it grows,
the greater the need for humility.
Humility means trusting the Tao,
thus never needing to be defensive.

A great nation is like a great man:
When he makes a mistake, he realizes it.
Having realized it, he admits it.
Having admitted it, he corrects it.
He considers those who point out his faults
as his most benevolent teachers.
He thinks of his enemy
as the shadow that he himself casts.

If a nation is centered in the Tao,
if it nourishes its own people
and doesn't meddle in the affairs of others,
it will be a light to all nations in the world.

65

The ancient Masters
didn't try to educate the people,
but kindly taught them to not-know.

When they think that they know the answers,
people are difficult to guide.
When they know that they don't know,
people can find their own way.

If you want to learn how to govern,
avoid being clever or rich.
The simplest pattern is the clearest.
Content with an ordinary life,
you can show all people the way
back to their own true nature.

66

All streams flow to the sea
because it is lower than they are.   53
Humility gives it its power.

If you want to govern the people,
you must place yourself below them.   54
If you want to lead the people,
you must learn how to follow them.

The Master is above the people,
and no one feels oppressed.   55
She goes ahead of the people,
and no one feels manipulated.
The whole world is grateful to her.
Because she competes with no one,
no one can compete with her.

67

Some say that my teaching is nonsense.
Others call it lofty but impractical.   56
But to those who have looked inside themselves,
this nonsense makes perfect sense.
And to those who put it into practice,
this loftiness has roots that go deep.

I have just three things to teach:
simplicity, patience, compassion.   57
These three are your greatest treasures.
Simple in actions and in thoughts,
you return to the source of being.
Patient with both friends and enemies,
you accord with the way things are.
Compassionate toward yourself,
you reconcile all beings in the world.

75

When taxes are too high,
people go hungry.   58
When the government is too intrusive,
people lose their spirit.

Act for the people's benefit. 59
Trust them; leave them alone.

80

If a country is governed wisely, 60
its inhabitants will be content.
They enjoy the labor of their hands
and don't waste time inventing
labor-saving machines.
Since they dearly love their homes,
they aren't interested in travel.
There may be a few wagons and boats,
but these don't go anywhere.
There may be an arsenal of weapons,
but nobody ever uses them.
People enjoy their food,
take pleasure in being with their families,
spend weekends working in their gardens,
delight in the doings of the neighborhood.
And even though the next country is so close
that people can hear its roosters crowing and its
    dogs barking,
they are content to die of old age
without ever having gone to see it.

QUESTIONS FOR CRITICAL READING

1. According to Lao-tzu, what must the ruler provide the people with if they are to be happy? See especially Verse 66.
2. To what extent does Lao-tzu concern himself with individual happiness?
3. How would you describe Lao-tzu's attitude toward the people?
4. Why does Lao-tzu think the world cannot be improved? See Verse 29.
5. Which statements made in this selection do you feel support a materialist view of experience? Can they be reconciled with Lao-tzu's overall thinking in the selection?
6. What are the limits and benefits of the expression: "Practice not-doing, / and everything will fall into place"? See Verse 3.
7. To what extent is Lao-tzu in favor of military action? What seem to be his views about the military? See Verse 31.
8. The term *Master* is used frequently in the selection. What can you tell about the character of the Master?

SUGGESTIONS FOR CRITICAL WRITING

1. The term *the Tao* is used often in this selection. Write a short essay that defines what Lao-tzu seems to mean by the term. If you were a politician and had the responsibility of governing a state, how would you follow the Tao as it is implied in Lao-tzu's statements? Is the Tao restrictive? Difficult? Open to interpretation? How well do you think it would work?

2. Write a brief essay that examines the following statements from the perspective of a young person today:

   > The more prohibitions you have,
   > the less virtuous people will be.
   > The more weapons you have,
   > the less secure people will be.
   > The more subsidies you have,
   > the less self-reliant people will be. (Verse 57)

   To what extent do you agree with these statements, and to what extent do you feel they are statements that have a political importance? Do people in the United States seem to agree with these views, or do they disagree? What are the most visible political consequences of our nation's position regarding these ideas?

3. Some people have asserted that the American political system benefits the people most when the following views of Lao-tzu are carefully applied:

   > Therefore the Master says:
   > I let go of the law,
   > and people become honest.
   > I let go of economics,
   > and people become prosperous.
   > I let go of religion,
   > and people become serene.
   > I let go of all desire for the common good,
   > and the good becomes common as grass. (Verse 57)

   In a brief essay, decide to what extent American leaders follow these precepts. Whether you feel they do or not, do you think that they should follow these precepts? What are the likely results of their being put into practice?

4. Some of the statements Lao-tzu makes are so packed with meaning that it would take pages to explore them. One example is "When they think that they know the answers, / people are difficult to guide." Take this statement as the basis of a short essay and, in reference to a personal experience, explain the significance of this statement.

5. What does Lao-tzu imply about the obligation of the state to the individual it governs and about the obligation of the individual to the state? Is one much more important than the other? Using the texts in this selection, establish what you feel is the optimum balance in the relationship between the two.

6. **CONNECTIONS**   Compare Lao-tzu's view of government with that of Machiavelli in the next selection. Consider what seem to be the ultimate purposes of government, what seem to be the obligations of the leader to the people being led, and what seems to be the main work of the state. What comparisons can you make between Lao-tzu's Master and Machiavelli's prince?

7. **SEEING CONNECTIONS**   How would Lao-tzu have described the action in Delacroix's *Liberty Leading the People* (p. 18)? Would he have been sympathetic to the efforts of the French people trying to remove an unpopular king in 1830? To what extent would he have approved of the representation of Liberty holding a musket with a bayonet? Which figure in the painting would Lao-tzu have felt the most sympathy for? What might Lao-tzu's message to Delacroix have been if it had been possible for him to communicate with the painter?

NICCOLÒ MACHIAVELLI
The Qualities of the Prince

NICCOLÒ MACHIAVELLI (1469–1527) was an aristocrat whose fortunes wavered according to the shifts in power in Florence. Renaissance Italy was a collection of powerful city-states, which were sometimes volatile and unstable. When Florence's famed Medici princes were returned to power in 1512 after eighteen years of banishment, Machiavelli did not fare well. He was suspected of crimes against the state and imprisoned. Even though he was not guilty, he had to learn to support himself as a writer instead of continuing his career in civil service.

His works often contrast two forces: luck (one's fortune) and character (one's virtues). His own character outlasted his bad luck in regard to the Medicis, and he was returned to a position of responsibility. *The Prince* (1513), his most celebrated work, was a general treatise on the qualities the prince (that is, ruler) must have to maintain his power. In a more particular way, it was directed at the Medicis to encourage them to save Italy from the predatory incursions of France and Spain, whose troops were nibbling at the crumbling Italian principalities and who would, in time, control much of Italy.

The chapters presented here contain the core of the philosophy for which Machiavelli became famous. His instructions to the prince are curiously devoid of any high-sounding moralizing or any encouragement to be good as a matter of principle. Instead, Machiavelli recommends a very practical course of action for the prince: secure power by direct and effective means. It may be that Machiavelli fully expects that the prince will use his power for good ends—certainly he does not recommend tyranny. But he also supports using questionable means to achieve the final end of becoming and remaining

From *The Prince*. Translated by Peter Bondanella and Mark Musa.

the prince. Although Machiavelli recognizes that there is often a conflict between the ends and the means used to achieve them, he does not fret over the possible problems that may accompany the use of "unpleasant" means, such as punishment of upstarts or the use of repression, imprisonment, and torture.

Through the years, Machiavelli's view of human nature has come under criticism for its cynicism. For instance, he suggests that a morally good person would not remain long in any high office because that person would have to compete with the mass of people, who, he says, are basically bad. Machiavelli constantly tells us that he is describing the world as it really is, not as it should be. Perhaps Machiavelli is correct, but people have long condemned the way he approves of cunning, deceit, and outright lying as means of staying in power.

The contrast between Machiavelli's writings and Lao-tzu's opinions in the *Tao-te Ching* is instructive. Lao-tzu's advice issues from a detached view of a universal ruler; Machiavelli's advice is very personal, embodying a set of directives for a specific prince. Machiavelli expounds upon a litany of actions that must be taken; Lao-tzu, on the other hand, advises that judicious inaction will produce the best results.

Machiavelli's Rhetoric

Machiavelli's approach is less poetic and more pragmatic than Lao-tzu's. Whereas Lao-tzu's tone is almost biblical, Machiavelli's is that of a how-to book, relevant to a particular time and a particular place. Yet, like Lao-tzu, Machiavelli is brief and to the point. Each segment of the discussion is terse and economical.

Machiavelli announces his primary point clearly, refers to historical precedents to support his point, and then explains why his position is the best one by appealing to both common sense and historical experience. When he suspects the reader will not share his view wholeheartedly, he suggests an alternate argument and then explains why it is wrong. This is a very forceful way of presenting one's views. It gives the appearance of fairness and thoroughness — and, as we learn from reading Machiavelli, he is very much concerned with appearances. His method also gives his work fullness, a quality that makes us forget how brief it really is.

Another of his rhetorical methods is to discuss opposite pairings, including both sides of an issue. From the first he explores a number of oppositions — the art of war and the art of life, liberality and stinginess, cruelty and clemency, the fox and the lion. The method may seem simple, but it is important because it employs two of the basic techniques of rhetoric—comparison and contrast.

The aphorism is another of Machiavelli's rhetorical weapons. An aphorism is a saying—a concise statement of a principle—that has been accepted as true. Familiar examples are "A penny saved is a penny earned" and "There is no fool like an old fool." Machiavelli tells us, "A man who wishes to make a vocation of being good at all times will come to ruin among so many who are not good."

Such definite statements have several important qualities. One is that they are pithy: they seem to say a great deal in a few words. Another is that they appear to contain a great deal of wisdom, in part because they are delivered with such certainty, and in part because they have the ring of other aphorisms that we accept as true. Because they sound like aphorisms, they gain a claim to (unsubstantiated) truth, and we tend to accept them much more readily than perhaps we should. This may be why the speeches of contemporary politicians (modern versions of the prince) are often sprinkled with such expressions and illustrates why Machiavelli's rhetorical technique is still reliable, still effective, and still worth studying.

PREREADING QUESTIONS:
WHAT TO READ FOR

The following prereading questions may help you anticipate key issues in the discussion of Niccolò Machiavelli's "The Qualities of the Prince." Keeping them in mind during your first reading of the selection should help focus your attention.

- Why does Machiavelli praise skill in warfare in his opening pages? How does that skill aid a prince?
- Is it better for a prince to be loved or to be feared?

The Qualities of the Prince

A Prince's Duty Concerning Military Matters

A prince, therefore, must not have any other object nor any other thought, nor must he take anything as his profession but war, its institutions, and its discipline; because that is the only profession which befits one who commands; and it is of such importance that not only does it maintain those who were born princes, but many times it enables men of private station to rise to that position; and, on the other hand, it is evident that when princes have given more thought to personal luxuries than to arms, they have lost their state. And the first way to lose it is to neglect this art; and the way to acquire it is to be well versed in this art.

Francesco Sforza[1] became Duke of Milan from being a private   2 citizen because he was armed; his sons, since they avoided the inconveniences of arms, became private citizens after having been dukes. For, among the other bad effects it causes, being disarmed makes you despised; this is one of those infamies a prince should guard himself against, as will be treated below: for between an armed and an unarmed man there is no comparison whatsoever, and it is not reasonable for an armed man to obey an unarmed man willingly, nor that an unarmed man should be safe among armed servants; since, when the former is suspicious and the latter are contemptuous, it is impossible for them to work well together. And therefore, a prince who does not understand military matters, besides the other misfortunes already noted, cannot be esteemed by his own soldiers, nor can he trust them.

He must, therefore, never raise his thought from this exercise of   3 war, and in peacetime he must train himself more than in time of war; this can be done in two ways: one by action, the other by the mind. And as far as actions are concerned, besides keeping his soldiers well disciplined and trained, he must always be out hunting, and must accustom his body to hardships in this manner; and he must also learn the nature of the terrain, and know how mountains slope, how valleys open, how plains lie, and understand the nature of rivers and swamps; and he should devote much attention to such activities. Such knowledge is useful in two ways: first, one learns to know one's own country and can better understand how to defend it; second, with the knowledge and experience of the terrain, one can easily comprehend the characteristics of any other terrain that it is necessary to explore for the first time; for the hills, valleys, plains, rivers, and swamps of Tuscany,[2] for instance, have certain similarities to those of other provinces; so that by knowing the lay of the land in one province one can easily understand it in others. And a prince who lacks this ability lacks the most important quality in a

---

[1] **Francesco Sforza (1401–1466)** Became duke of Milan in 1450. He was, like most of Machiavelli's examples, a skilled diplomat and soldier. His court was a model of Renaissance scholarship and achievement.

[2] **Tuscany** Florence is in the region of Italy known as Tuscany.

leader; because this skill teaches you to find the enemy, choose a campsite, lead troops, organize them for battle, and besiege towns to your own advantage.

Philopoemon, Prince of the Achaeans,[3] among the other praises 4 given to him by writers, is praised because in peacetime he thought of nothing except the means of waging war; and when he was out in the country with his friends, he often stopped and reasoned with them: "If the enemy were on that hilltop and we were here with our army, which of the two of us would have the advantage? How could we attack them without breaking formation? If we wanted to retreat, how could we do this? If they were to retreat, how could we pursue them?" And he proposed to them, as they rode along, all the contingencies that can occur in an army; he heard their opinions, expressed his own, and backed it up with arguments; so that, because of these continuous deliberations, when leading his troops no unforeseen incident could arise for which he did not have the remedy.

But as for the exercise of the mind, the prince must read histo- 5 ries and in them study the deeds of great men; he must see how they conducted themselves in wars; he must examine the reasons for their victories and for their defeats in order to avoid the latter and to imitate the former; and above all else he must do as some distinguished man before him has done, who elected to imitate someone who had been praised and honored before him, and always keep in mind his deeds and actions; just as it is reported that Alexander the Great imitated Achilles; Caesar, Alexander; Scipio, Cyrus.[4] And anyone who reads the life of Cyrus written by Xenophon then realizes how important in the life of Scipio that imitation was to his glory and how much, in purity, goodness, humanity, and generosity, Scipio conformed to those characteristics of Cyrus that Xenophon had written about.

Such methods as these a wise prince must follow, and never in 6 peaceful times must he be idle; but he must turn them diligently to

---

[3] **Philopoemon (252?–182 B.C.), Prince of the Achaeans** Philopoemon, from the city-state of Megalopolis, was a Greek general noted for skillful diplomacy. He led the Achaeans, a group of Greek states that formed the Achaean League, in several important expeditions, notably against Sparta. His cruelty in putting down a Spartan uprising caused him to be reprimanded by his superiors.

[4] **Cyrus (585?–529? B.C.)** Cyrus II (the Great), Persian emperor. Cyrus and the other figures featured in this sentence—Alexander the Great (356–323 B.C.); Achilles, hero of Homer's *Iliad;* Julius Caesar (100?–44 B.C.); and Scipio Africanus (236–184/3 B.C.), legendary Roman general—are all examples of politicians who were also great military geniuses. Xenophon (431–350? B.C.) was one of the earliest Greek historians; he chronicled the lives and military exploits of Cyrus and his son-in-law Darius.

his advantage in order to be able to profit from them in times of adversity, so that, when Fortune changes, she will find him prepared to withstand such times.

On Those Things for Which Men, and Particularly Princes, Are Praised or Blamed

Now there remains to be examined what should be the methods   7
and procedures of a prince in dealing with his subjects and friends. And because I know that many have written about this, I am afraid that by writing about it again I shall be thought of as presumptuous, since in discussing this material I depart radically from the procedures of others. But since my intention is to write something useful for anyone who understands it, it seemed more suitable to me to search after the effectual truth of the matter rather than its imagined one. And many writers have imagined for themselves republics and principalities that have never been seen nor known to exist in reality; for there is such a gap between how one lives and how one ought to live that anyone who abandons what is done for what ought to be done learns his ruin rather than his preservation: for a man who wishes to make a vocation of being good at all times will come to ruin among so many who are not good. Hence it is necessary for a prince who wishes to maintain his position to learn how not to be good, and to use this knowledge or not to use it according to necessity.

Leaving aside, therefore, the imagined things concerning a   8
prince, and taking into account those that are true, I say that all men, when they are spoken of, and particularly princes, since they are placed on a higher level, are judged by some of these qualities which bring them either blame or praise. And this is why one is considered generous, another miserly (to use a Tuscan word, since "avaricious" in our language is still used to mean one who wishes to acquire by means of theft; we call "miserly" one who excessively avoids using what he has); one is considered a giver, the other rapacious; one cruel, another merciful; one treacherous, another faithful; one effeminate and cowardly, another bold and courageous; one humane, another haughty; one lascivious, another chaste; one trustworthy, another cunning; one harsh, another lenient; one serious, another frivolous; one religious, another unbelieving; and the like. And I know that everyone will admit that it would be a very praiseworthy thing to find in a prince, of the qualities mentioned above, those that are held to be good, but since it is neither possible to have them nor to observe them all completely, because human nature does not permit

it, a prince must be prudent enough to know how to escape the bad reputation of those vices that would lose the state for him, and must protect himself from those that will not lose it for him, if this is possible; but if he cannot, he need not concern himself unduly if he ignores these less serious vices. And, moreover, he need not worry about incurring the bad reputation of those vices without which it would be difficult to hold his state; since, carefully taking everything into account, one will discover that something which appears to be a virtue, if pursued, will end in his destruction; while some other thing which seems to be a vice, if pursued, will result in his safety and his well-being.

On Generosity and Miserliness

Beginning, therefore, with the first of the above-mentioned   9
qualities, I say that it would be good to be considered generous; nevertheless, generosity used in such a manner as to give you a reputation for it will harm you; because if it is employed virtuously and as one should employ it, it will not be recognized and you will not avoid the reproach of its opposite. And so, if a prince wants to maintain his reputation for generosity among men, it is necessary for him not to neglect any possible means of lavish display; in so doing such a prince will always use up all his resources and he will be obliged, eventually, if he wishes to maintain his reputation for generosity, to burden the people with excessive taxes and to do everything possible to raise funds. This will begin to make him hateful to his subjects, and, becoming impoverished, he will not be much esteemed by anyone; so that, as a consequence of his generosity, having offended many and rewarded few, he will feel the effects of any slight unrest and will be ruined at the first sign of danger; recognizing this and wishing to alter his policies, he immediately runs the risk of being reproached as a miser.

A prince, therefore, unable to use this virtue of generosity in a   10
manner which will not harm himself if he is known for it, should, if he is wise, not worry about being called a miser; for with time he will come to be considered more generous once it is evident that, as a result of his parsimony, his income is sufficient, he can defend himself from anyone who makes war against him, and he can undertake enterprises without overburdening his people, so that he comes to be generous with all those from whom he takes nothing, who are countless, and miserly with all those to whom he gives nothing, who are few. In our times we have not seen great deeds accomplished except by those who were considered miserly; all others were done away

with. Pope Julius II,[5] although he made use of his reputation for generosity in order to gain the papacy, then decided not to maintain it in order to be able to wage war; the present King of France[6] has waged many wars without imposing extra taxes on his subjects, only because his habitual parsimony has provided for the additional expenditures; the present King of Spain,[7] if he had been considered generous, would not have engaged in nor won so many campaigns.

Therefore, in order not to have to rob his subjects, to be able to defend himself, not to become poor and contemptible, and not to be forced to become rapacious, a prince must consider it of little importance if he incurs the name of miser, for this is one of those vices that permits him to rule. And if someone were to say: Caesar with his generosity came to rule the empire, and many others, because they were generous and known to be so, achieved very high positions; I reply: you are either already a prince or you are on the way to becoming one; in the first instance such generosity is damaging; in the second it is very necessary to be thought generous. And Caesar was one of those who wanted to gain the principality of Rome; but if, after obtaining this, he had lived and had not moderated his expenditures, he would have destroyed that empire. And if someone were to reply: there have existed many princes who have accomplished great deeds with their armies who have been reputed to be generous; I answer you: a prince either spends his own money and that of his subjects or that of others; in the first case he must be economical; in the second he must not restrain any part of his generosity. And for that prince who goes out with his soldiers and lives by looting, sacking, and ransoms, who controls the property of others, such generosity is necessary; otherwise he would not be followed by his troops. And with what does not belong to you or to your subjects you can be a more liberal giver, as were Cyrus, Caesar, and Alexander; for spending the wealth of others does not lessen your reputation but adds to it; only the spending of your own is what harms you. And there is nothing that uses itself up faster than generosity, for as you employ it you lose the means of employing it, and you become either poor or despised or, in order to escape

11

---

[5] **Pope Julius II (1443–1513)** Giuliano della Rovere, pope from 1503 to 1513. Like many of the popes of the day, Julius II was also a diplomat and a general.

[6] **present King of France** Louis XII (1462–1515). He entered Italy on a successful military campaign in 1494.

[7] **present King of Spain** Ferdinand V (1452–1516). A studied politician; he and Queen Isabella (1451–1504) financed Christopher Columbus's voyage to the New World in 1492.

poverty, rapacious and hated. And above all other things a prince must guard himself against being despised and hated; and generosity leads you to both one and the other. So it is wiser to live with the reputation of a miser, which produces reproach without hatred, than to be forced to incur the reputation of rapacity, which produces reproach along with hatred, because you want to be considered as generous.

On Cruelty and Mercy and Whether It Is Better to Be Loved than to Be Feared or the Contrary

Proceeding to the other qualities mentioned above, I say that every   12
prince must desire to be considered merciful and not cruel; nevertheless, he must take care not to misuse this mercy. Cesare Borgia[8] was considered cruel; nonetheless, his cruelty had brought order to Romagna,[9] united it, restored it to peace and obedience. If we examine this carefully, we shall see that he was more merciful than the Florentine people, who, in order to avoid being considered cruel, allowed the destruction of Pistoia.[10] Therefore, a prince must not worry about the reproach of cruelty when it is a matter of keeping his subjects united and loyal; for with a very few examples of cruelty he will be more compassionate than those who, out of excessive mercy, permit disorders to continue, from which arise murders and plundering; for these usually harm the community at large, while the executions that come from the prince harm one individual in particular. And the new prince, above all other princes, cannot escape the reputation of being called cruel, since new states are full of dangers. And Virgil, through Dido, states: "My difficult condition and the newness of my rule make me act in such a manner, and to set guards over my land on all sides."[11]

Nevertheless, a prince must be cautious in believing and in act-   13
ing, nor should he be afraid of his own shadow; and he should proceed in such a manner, tempered by prudence and humanity, so

---

[8] **Cesare Borgia (1476–1507)** He was known for his brutality and lack of scruples, not to mention his exceptionally good luck. He was a firm ruler, son of Pope Alexander VI.

[9] **Romagna** Region northeast of Tuscany; includes the towns of Bologna, Ferrara, Ravenna, and Rimini. Borgia united it as his base of power in 1501.

[10] **Pistoia** (also known as Pistoria) A town near Florence, disturbed in 1501 by a civil war that could have been averted by strong repressive measures.

[11] The quotation is from the *Aeneid* (2.563–64), the greatest Latin epic poem, written by Virgil (70–19 B.C.). Dido, a woman general, ruled Carthage.

that too much trust may not render him imprudent nor too much distrust render him intolerable.

From this arises an argument: whether it is better to be loved than   14
to be feared, or the contrary. I reply that one should like to be both one and the other; but since it is difficult to join them together, it is much safer to be feared than to be loved when one of the two must be lacking. For one can generally say this about men: that they are ungrateful, fickle, simulators and deceivers, avoiders of danger, greedy for gain; and while you work for their good they are completely yours, offering you their blood, their property, their lives, and their sons, as I said earlier, when danger is far away; but when it comes nearer to you they turn away. And that prince who bases his power entirely on their words, finding himself stripped of other preparations, comes to ruin; for friendships that are acquired by a price and not by greatness and nobility of character are purchased but are not owned, and at the proper moment they cannot be spent. And men are less hesitant about harming someone who makes himself loved than one who makes himself feared because love is held together by a chain of obligation which, since men are a sorry lot, is broken on every occasion in which their own self-interest is concerned; but fear is held together by a dread of punishment which will never abandon you.

A prince must nevertheless make himself feared in such a man-   15
ner that he will avoid hatred, even if he does not acquire love; since to be feared and not to be hated can very well be combined; and this will always be so when he keeps his hands off the property and the women of his citizens and his subjects. And if he must take someone's life, he should do so when there is proper justification and manifest cause; but, above all, he should avoid the property of others; for men forget more quickly the death of their father than the loss of their patrimony. Moreover, the reasons for seizing their property are never lacking; and he who begins to live by stealing always finds a reason for taking what belongs to others; on the contrary, reasons for taking a life are rarer and disappear sooner.

But when the prince is with his armies and has under his com-   16
mand a multitude of troops, then it is absolutely necessary that he not worry about being considered cruel; for without that reputation he will never keep an army united or prepared for any combat. Among the praiseworthy deeds of Hannibal[12] is counted this: that,

---

[12] **Hannibal (247–183 B.C.)** An amazingly inventive military tactician who led the Carthaginian armies against Rome for more than fifteen years. He crossed the Alps from Gaul (France) in order to surprise Rome. He was noted for use of the ambush and for "inhuman cruelty."

having a very large army, made up of all kinds of men, which he commanded in foreign lands, there never arose the slightest dissention, neither among themselves nor against their prince, both during his good and his bad fortune. This could not have arisen from anything other than his inhuman cruelty, which, along with his many other abilities, made him always respected and terrifying in the eyes of his soldiers; and without that, to attain the same effect, his other abilities would not have sufficed. And the writers of history, having considered this matter very little, on the one hand admire these deeds of his and on the other condemn the main cause of them.

And that it be true that his other abilities would not have been   17
sufficient can be seen from the example of Scipio, a most extraordinary man not only in his time but in all recorded history, whose armies in Spain rebelled against him; this came about from nothing other than his excessive compassion, which gave to his soldiers more liberty than military discipline allowed. For this he was censured in the senate by Fabius Maximus,[13] who called him the corruptor of the Roman militia. The Locrians,[14] having been ruined by one of Scipio's officers, were not avenged by him, nor was the arrogance of that officer corrected, all because of his tolerant nature; so that someone in the senate who tried to apologize for him said that there were many men who knew how not to err better than they knew how to correct errors. Such a nature would have, in time, damaged Scipio's fame and glory if he had maintained it during the empire; but, living under the control of the senate, this harmful characteristic of his not only concealed itself but brought him fame.

I conclude, therefore, returning to the problem of being feared   18
and loved, that since men love at their own pleasure and fear at the pleasure of the prince, a wise prince should build his foundation upon that which belongs to him, not upon that which belongs to others: he must strive only to avoid hatred, as has been said.

How a Prince Should Keep His Word

How praiseworthy it is for a prince to keep his word and to live   19
by integrity and not by deceit everyone knows; nevertheless, one sees from the experience of our times that the princes who have accomplished great deeds are those who have cared little for keeping

---

[13]**Fabius Maximus (?–203 B.C.)** Roman general who fought Hannibal. He was jealous of the younger Roman general Scipio.

[14]**Locrians** Inhabitants of Locri, an Italian town settled by the Greeks in c. 680 B.C.

their promises and who have known how to manipulate the minds of men by shrewdness; and in the end they have surpassed those who laid their foundations upon honesty.

You must, therefore, know that there are two means of fighting: 20 one according to the laws, the other with force; the first way is proper to man, the second to beasts; but because the first, in many cases, is not sufficient, it becomes necessary to have recourse to the second. Therefore, a prince must know how to use wisely the natures of the beast and the man. This policy was taught to princes allegorically by the ancient writers, who described how Achilles and many other ancient princes were given to Chiron[15] the Centaur to be raised and taught under his discipline. This can only mean that, having a half-beast and half-man as a teacher, a prince must know how to employ the nature of the one and the other; and the one without the other cannot endure.

Since, then, a prince must know how to make good use of the   21 nature of the beast, he should choose from among the beasts the fox and the lion; for the lion cannot defend itself from traps and the fox cannot protect itself from wolves. It is therefore necessary to be a fox in order to recognize the traps and a lion in order to frighten the wolves. Those who play only the part of the lion do not understand matters. A wise ruler, therefore, cannot and should not keep his word when such an observance of faith would be to his disadvantage and when the reasons which made him promise are removed. And if men were all good, this rule would not be good; but since men are a sorry lot and will not keep their promises to you, you likewise need not keep yours to them. A prince never lacks legitimate reasons to break his promises. Of this one could cite an endless number of modern examples to show how many pacts, how many promises have been made null and void because of the infidelity of princes; and he who has known best how to use the fox has come to a better end. But it is necessary to know how to disguise this nature well and to be a great hypocrite and a liar: and men are so simpleminded and so controlled by their present necessities that one who deceives will always find another who will allow himself to be deceived.

I do not wish to remain silent about one of these recent   22 instances. Alexander VI[16] did nothing else, he thought about nothing else, except to deceive men, and he always found the occasion to do

---

[15] **Chiron** A mythical figure, a centaur (half man, half horse). Unlike most centaurs, he was wise and benevolent; he was also a legendary physician.

[16] **Alexander VI (1431–1503)** Roderigo Borgia, pope from 1492 to 1503. He was Cesare Borgia's father and a corrupt but immensely powerful pope.

this. And there never was a man who had more forcefulness in his oaths, who affirmed a thing with more promises, and who honored his word less; nevertheless, his tricks always succeeded perfectly since he was well acquainted with this aspect of the world.

Therefore, it is not necessary for a prince to have all of the above-mentioned qualities, but it is very necessary for him to appear to have them. Furthermore, I shall be so bold as to assert this: that having them and practicing them at all times is harmful; and appearing to have them is useful; for instance, to seem merciful, faithful, humane, forthright, religious, and to be so; but his mind should be disposed in such a way that should it become necessary not to be so, he will be able and know how to change to the contrary. And it is essential to understand this: that a prince, and especially a new prince, cannot observe all those things by which men are considered good, for in order to maintain the state he is often obliged to act against his promise, against charity, against humanity, and against religion. And therefore, it is necessary that he have a mind ready to turn itself according to the way the winds of Fortune and the changeability of affairs require him; and, as I said above, as long as it is possible, he should not stray from the good, but he should know how to enter into evil when necessity commands. 23

A prince, therefore, must be very careful never to let anything slip from his lips which is not full of the five qualities mentioned above: he should appear, upon seeing and hearing him, to be all mercy, all faithfulness, all integrity, all kindness, all religion. And there is nothing more necessary than to seem to possess this last quality. And men in general judge more by their eyes than their hands; for everyone can see but few can feel. Everyone sees what you seem to be, few perceive what you are, and those few do not dare to contradict the opinion of the many who have the majesty of the state to defend them; and in the actions of all men, and especially of princes, where there is no impartial arbiter, one must consider the final result.[17] Let a prince therefore act to seize and to maintain the state; his methods will always be judged honorable and will be praised by all; for ordinary people are always deceived by appearances and by the outcome of a thing; and in the world there is nothing but ordinary people; and there is no room for the few, while the many have a place to lean on. A certain prince[18] of the present day, whom I shall refrain from naming, preaches nothing but peace and faith, and to both one and the other he is entirely opposed; and 24

---

[17] The Italian original, *si guarda al fine*, has often been mistranslated as "the ends justify the means," something Machiavelli never wrote. [Translators' note]

[18] **A certain prince** Probably King Ferdinand V of Spain (1452–1516).

both, if he had put them into practice, would have cost him many times over either his reputation or his state.

On Avoiding Being Despised and Hated

But since, concerning the qualities mentioned above, I have 25 spoken about the most important, I should like to discuss the others briefly in this general manner: that the prince, as was noted above, should think about avoiding those things which make him hated and despised; and when he has avoided this, he will have carried out his duties and will find no danger whatsoever in other vices. As I have said, what makes him hated above all else is being rapacious and a usurper of the property and the women of his subjects; he must refrain from this; and in most cases, so long as you do not deprive them of either their property or their honor, the majority of men live happily; and you have only to deal with the ambition of a few, who can be restrained without difficulty and by many means. What makes him despised is being considered changeable, frivolous, effeminate, cowardly, irresolute; from these qualities a prince must guard himself as if from a reef, and he must strive to make everyone recognize in his actions greatness, spirit, dignity, and strength; and concerning the private affairs of his subjects, he must insist that his decision be irrevocable; and he should maintain himself in such a way that no man could imagine that he can deceive or cheat him.

That prince who projects such an opinion of himself is greatly 26 esteemed; and it is difficult to conspire against a man with such a reputation and difficult to attack him, provided that he is understood to be of great merit and revered by his subjects. For a prince must have two fears: one, internal, concerning his subjects; the other, external, concerning foreign powers. From the latter he can defend himself by his good troops and friends; and he will always have good friends if he has good troops; and internal affairs will always be stable when external affairs are stable, provided that they are not already disturbed by a conspiracy; and even if external conditions change, if he is properly organized and lives as I have said and does not lose control of himself, he will always be able to withstand every attack, just as I said that Nabis the Spartan[19] did. But concerning his subjects, when external affairs do not change, he has to fear that they may conspire secretly: the prince secures himself

---

[19] **Nabis the Spartan** Tyrant of Sparta from 207 to 192 B.C., routed by Philopoemon and the Achaean League.

from this by avoiding being hated or despised and by keeping the people satisfied with him; this is a necessary matter, as was treated above at length. And one of the most powerful remedies a prince has against conspiracies is not to be hated by the masses; for a man who plans a conspiracy always believes that he will satisfy the people by killing the prince; but when he thinks he might anger them, he cannot work up the courage to undertake such a deed; for the problems on the side of the conspirators are countless. And experience demonstrates that conspiracies have been many but few have been concluded successfully; for anyone who conspires cannot be alone, nor can he find companions except from amongst those whom he believes to be dissatisfied; and as soon as you have uncovered your intent to one dissatisfied man, you give him the means to make himself happy, since he can have everything he desires by uncovering the plot; so much is this so that, seeing a sure gain on the one hand and one doubtful and full of danger on the other, if he is to maintain faith with you he has to be either an unusually good friend or a completely determined enemy of the prince. And to treat the matter briefly, I say that on the part of the conspirator there is nothing but fear, jealousy, and the thought of punishment that terrifies him; but on the part of the prince there is the majesty of the principality, the laws, the defenses of friends and the state to protect him; so that, with the good will of the people added to all these things, it is impossible for anyone to be so rash as to plot against him. For, where usually a conspirator has to be afraid before he executes his evil deed, in this case he must be afraid, having the people as an enemy, even after the crime is performed, nor can he hope to find any refuge because of this.

One could cite countless examples on this subject; but I want to satisfy myself with only one which occurred during the time of our fathers. Messer Annibale Bentivoglio, prince of Bologna and grandfather of the present Messer Annibale, was murdered by the Canneschi[20] family, who conspired against him; he left behind no heir except Messer Giovanni,[21] then only a baby. As soon as this murder occurred, the people rose up and killed all the Canneschi. This came about because of the good will that the house of the Bentivoglio enjoyed in those days; this good will was so great that with Annibale dead, and there being no one of that family left in the city who could rule Bologna, the Bolognese people, having heard that in Florence there was one of the Bentivoglio blood who was believed

27

---

[20] **Canneschi** Prominent family in Bologna.
[21] **Giovanni Bentivoglio (1443–1508)** Former tyrant of Bologna. In sequence he was a conspirator against, then a conspirator with, Cesare Borgia.

until that time to be the son of a blacksmith, went to Florence to find him, and they gave him the control of that city; it was ruled by him until Messer Giovanni became of age to rule.

I conclude, therefore, that a prince must be little concerned 28 with conspiracies when the people are well disposed toward him; but when the populace is hostile and regards him with hatred, he must fear everything and everyone. And well-organized states and wise princes have, with great diligence, taken care not to anger the nobles and to satisfy the common people and keep them contented; for this is one of the most important concerns that a prince has.

QUESTIONS FOR CRITICAL READING

1. The usual criticism of Machiavelli is that he advises his prince to be unscrupulous. Find examples for and against this claim.
2. Why do you agree or disagree with Machiavelli when he asserts that the great majority of people are not good? Does our government assume that to be true too?
3. Politicians — especially heads of state — are the contemporary counterparts of the prince. To what extent should successful heads of modern states show skill in war? Is modern war similar to wars in Machiavelli's era? If so, in what ways?
4. Clarify the advice Machiavelli gives concerning liberality and stinginess. Is this still good advice?
5. Are modern politicians likely to succeed by following all or most of Machiavelli's recommendations? Why or why not?

SUGGESTIONS FOR CRITICAL WRITING

1. In speaking of the prince's military duties, Machiavelli says that "being disarmed makes you despised." Choose an example or instance to strengthen your argument for or against this position. Is it possible that in modern society being defenseless is an advantage?
2. Find evidence within this excerpt to demonstrate that Machiavelli's attitude toward human nature is accurate. Remember that the usual criticism of Machiavelli is that he is cynical — that he thinks the worst of people rather than the best. Find quotations from the excerpt that support either or both of these views; then use them as the basis for an essay analyzing Machiavelli's views on human nature.
3. By referring to current events and leaders — either local, national, or international — decide whether Machiavelli's advice to the prince is useful to the modern politician. Consider whether the advice is completely useless or completely reliable, or whether its value depends on specific

conditions. First state the advice, then show how it applies (or does not apply) to specific politicians, and finally critique its general effectiveness.

4. Probably the chief ethical issue raised by *The Prince* is the question of whether the desired ends justify the means used to achieve them. Write an essay in which you take a stand on this question. Begin by defining the issue: What does the concept "the ends justify the means" actually mean? What difficulties may arise when unworthy means are used to achieve worthy ends? Analyze Machiavelli's references to circumstances in which questionable means were (or should have been) used to achieve worthy ends. Use historical or personal examples to give your argument substance.

5. **CONNECTIONS**   One of Machiavelli's most controversial statements is: "A man who wishes to make a vocation of being good at all times will come to ruin among so many who are not good." How would Lao-tzu respond to this statement? How does the American political environment in the current decade support this statement? Under what conditions would such a statement become irrelevant?

6. **CONNECTIONS**   For some commentators, the prince that Machiavelli describes resembles the kind of ruler Hannah Arendt deplores in her essay "Total Domination." Examine Machiavelli's views in terms of how his principles would result in a form of government similar to that which Arendt describes. Is terror a legitimate weapon for Machiavelli's prince? How would Machiavelli rationalize the prince's use of terror, should it become necessary?

7. **SEEING CONNECTIONS**   How would Machiavelli respond to Delacroix's *Liberty Leading the People* (p. 18)? This painting represents a ragtag group of citizens armed and attempting to overthrow a "prince," King Charles X of France. The citizens did indeed cause Charles to abdicate in favor of Louis-Philippe, called "the Citizen King" because he was not part of the royal family of the Bourbons who had produced the modern kings of France. How does the event represented in the painting figure in Machiavelli's advice on how a prince should maintain power? Would Machiavelli have welcomed the idea of Liberty being the central figure in a painting like Delacroix's?

JEAN-JACQUES ROUSSEAU
The Origin of Civil Society

JEAN-JACQUES ROUSSEAU (1712–1778) was the son of Suzanne Bernard and Isaac Rousseau, a watchmaker in Geneva, Switzerland. Shortly after his birth, Rousseau's mother died, and a rash duel forced his father from Geneva. Rousseau was then apprenticed at age thirteen to an engraver, a master who treated him badly. He soon ran away from his master and found a home with a Catholic noblewoman who at first raised him as her son and then, when he was twenty, took him as her lover. In the process Rousseau converted from Calvinist Protestantism to Roman Catholicism. Eventually, he left Switzerland for Paris, where he won an important essay contest and became celebrated in society.

Over the course of his lifetime, Rousseau produced a wide variety of literary and musical works, including a novel, *Emile* (1762), an opera, *The Village Soothsayer* (1752), and an autobiography, *The Confessions* (published posthumously in 1789). *The Social Contract* (1762) was part of a never-completed longer work on political systems. In many ways Rousseau wrote in reaction to political thinkers such as Hugo Grotius and Thomas Hobbes, to whom he responds in the following selection. He contended that the Dutch philosopher and legal expert Grotius unquestioningly accepted the power of the aristocracy. He felt Grotius paid too much attention to what was rather than what ought to be. On the other hand, Hobbes, the English political philosopher, asserted that people had a choice of being free or being ruled. In other words, those who were members of civil society chose to give up their freedom and submit to the monarch's rule. Either they relinquished their freedom, or they removed themselves from civil society to live a brutish existence.

From *Social Contract: Essays by Locke, Hume, and Rousseau*. Translated by Gerald Hopkins.

Rousseau argued against Grotius by examining the way things ought to be. He argued against Hobbes by asserting that both the body politic and the monarch were sovereign and that when people created a civil society they surrendered their freedom to themselves as a group. If one person acted as sovereign or lawgiver, then that lawgiver had the responsibility of acting in accord with the will of the people. In a sense, this view parallels some of the views of Lao-tzu in the *Tao-te Ching*.

Popularly referred to as a defender of republicanism, Rousseau looked to the Republic of Geneva, his birthplace, as a model of government. He also idealized the generally democratic government of smaller Swiss cantons, such as Neuchatel, which used a form of town meeting where people gathered face-to-face to settle important issues. Ironically, Geneva put out a warrant for his arrest upon the publication of *The Social Contract* because although it praised Geneva's republicanism, it also condemned societies that depended on rule by a limited aristocracy. Unfortunately for Rousseau, at that time Geneva was governed by a small number of aristocratic families. Rousseau was deprived of his citizenship and could not return to his native home.

Similarly, Rousseau's controversial views were not easily received by those in power in France. After the publication of *Emile* offended the French Parliament, Rousseau was forced to abandon his comfortable rustic circumstances—living on country estates provided by patrons from the court—and spend the rest of his life in financial uncertainty. Ironically, in 1789, a decade after his death, Rousseau's philosophy was adopted by supporters of the French Revolution in their bloody revolt against the aristocracy.

Rousseau's Rhetoric

Rousseau's method is in many ways antagonistic: he establishes the views of other thinkers, counters them, and then offers his own ideas. An early example appears in the opening of paragraph 8: "Grotius denies that political power is ever exercised in the interests of the governed, and quotes the institution of slavery in support of his contention. His invariable method of arguing is to derive Right from Fact." Among other things, Rousseau expects his readers to know who Grotius was and what he said. He also expects his readers to agree that Grotius derives "Right from Fact" by understanding that the fact of monarchy justifies it as being right. As Rousseau tells us, that kind of circular reasoning is especially kind to tyrants because it justifies them by their existence.

Rousseau uses analysis and examination of detail as his main rhetorical approaches. Whether he examines the ideas of others or presents ideas of his own, he is careful to examine the bases of the argument and to follow the arguments to their conclusions. He does this very thoroughly in his section "Of Slavery," in which he demonstrates that slavery is unacceptable no matter which of the current arguments are used to support it, including the widely held view that it was justifiable to enslave captured soldiers on the grounds that they owed their lives to their captors.

Rousseau also makes careful use of aphorism and analogy. His opening statement, "Man is born free, and everywhere he is in chains," is an aphorism that has been often quoted. It is a powerful and perplexing statement. How do people who are born free lose their freedom? Is it taken from them, or do they willingly surrender it? Rousseau spends considerable time examining this point.

The use of analogy is probably most striking in his comparison of government with the family. The force of the analogy reminds us that the members of a family are to be looked after by the family. As he tells us beginning in paragraph 5, the family is the only natural form of society. But instead of stopping there, he goes on to say that children are bound to the father only as long as they need him. Once they are able to be independent, they dissolve the natural bond and "return to a condition of equal independence." This analogy differs from the existing popular view that the monarch was like the father in a family and the people like his children; in fact, the analogy works against the legitimacy of the traditional monarchy as it was known in eighteenth-century France.

Rousseau also refers to other writers, using a rhetorical device known as *testimony*: he paraphrases the views of other authorities and moves on to promote his own. But in referring to other writers, Rousseau is unusually clever. For example, in paragraph 10 he begins with the analogy of the shepherd as the ruler in this fashion: "Just as the shepherd is superior in kind to his sheep, so, too, the shepherds of men, or, in other words, their rulers, are superior in kind to their peoples. This, according to Philo, was the argument advanced by Caligula, the Emperor, who drew from the analogy the perfectly true conclusion that either Kings are Gods or their subjects brute beasts." Caligula was a madman and an emperor guilty of enormous cruelty; from his point of view it may have seemed true that kings were gods. But Rousseau, in citing this questionable authority, disputes the validity of the analogy.

He argues as well against the view that might makes right in "Of the Right of the Strongest." The value of the social contract, he explains, is to produce a society that is not governed by the mightiest and most ruthless and that permits those who are not mighty to live peacefully and unmolested. Thus, those who participate in the social contract give up certain freedoms but gain many more—among them the freedom not to be dominated by physical brutality.

Rousseau concentrates on the question of man in nature, or natural society. His view is that natural society is dominated by the strongest individuals but that at some point natural society breaks down. Thus, in order to guarantee the rights of those who are not the strongest, the political order must change. "Some form of association" is developed "for the protection of the person and property of each constituent member." By surrendering some freedom to the group as a whole—to "the general will"—the individuals in the group can expect to prosper more widely and to live more happily. According to Rousseau, the establishment of a social contract ensures the stability of this form of civil society.

PREREADING QUESTIONS: WHAT TO READ FOR

The following prereading questions may help you anticipate key issues in the discussion of Jean-Jacques Rousseau's "The Origin of Civil Society." Keeping them in mind as you read should help focus your attention.

- When Rousseau says, "Man is born free, and everywhere he is in chains," does he seem to be referring literally to slaves in chains, or more figuratively to people in general?

- How convincing is Rousseau when he claims that the oldest form of government is the family?

- The "Social Contract" is one of Rousseau's chief ideas. What does it seem to mean?

The Origin of Civil Society

Note

It is my wish to inquire whether it be possible, within the civil order, to 1 *discover a legitimate and stable basis of Government. This I shall do by considering human beings as they are and laws as they might be. I shall attempt, throughout my investigations, to maintain a constant connection between what right permits and interest demands, in order that no separation may be made between justice and utility. I intend to begin without first proving the importance of my subject. Am I, it will be asked, either prince or legislator that I take it upon me to write of politics? My answer is—No; and it is for that very reason that I have chosen politics as the matter of my book. Were I either the one or the other I should not waste my time in laying down what has to be done. I should do it, or else hold my peace.*

I was born into a free state and am a member of its sovereign body. 2 *My influence on public affairs may be small, but because I have a right to exercise my vote, it is my duty to learn their nature, and it has been for me a matter of constant delight, while meditating on problems of Government in general, to find ever fresh reasons for regarding with true affection the way in which these things are ordered in my native land.*

The Subject of the First Book

Man is born free, and everywhere he is in chains. Many a man 3 believes himself to be the master of others who is, no less than they, a slave. How did this change take place? I do not know. What can make it legitimate? To this question I hope to be able to furnish an answer.

Were I considering only force and the effects of force, I should 4 say: "So long as a People is constrained to obey, and does, in fact, obey, it does well. So soon as it can shake off its yoke, and succeeds in doing so, it does better. The fact that it has recovered its liberty by virtue of that same right by which it was stolen, means either that it is entitled to resume it, or that its theft by others was, in the first place, without justification." But the social order is a sacred right which serves as a foundation for all other rights. This right, however, since it comes not by nature, must have been built upon conventions. To discover what these conventions are is the matter of our inquiry. But, before proceeding further, I must establish the truth of what I have so far advanced.

Of Primitive Societies

The oldest form of society—and the only natural one—is the 5 family. Children remain bound to their father for only just so long as they feel the need of him for their self-preservation. Once that need ceases the natural bond is dissolved. From then on, the children, freed from the obedience which they formerly owed, and the father, cleared of his debt of responsibility to them, return to a condition of equal independence. If the bond remain operative it is no longer something imposed by nature, but has become a matter of deliberate choice. The family is a family still, but by reason of convention only.

This shared liberty is a consequence of man's nature. Its first law 6
is that of self-preservation: its first concern is for what it owes itself. As soon as a man attains the age of reason he becomes his own master, because he alone can judge of what will best assure his continued existence.

We may, therefore, if we will, regard the family as the basic model 7
of all political associations. The ruler is the father writ large: the people are, by analogy, his children, and all, ruler and people alike, alienate their freedom only so far as it is to their advantage to do so. The only difference is that, whereas in the family the father's love for his children is sufficient reward to him for the care he has lavished on them, in the State, the pleasure of commanding others takes its place, since the ruler is not in a relation of love to his people.

Grotius[1] denies that political power is ever exercised in the inter- 8
ests of the governed, and quotes the institution of slavery in support of his contention. His invariable method of arguing is to derive Right from Fact. It might be possible to adopt a more logical system of reasoning, but none which would be more favorable to tyrants.

According to Grotius, therefore, it is doubtful whether the term 9
"human race" belongs to only a few hundred men, or whether those few hundred men belong to the human race. From the evidence of his book it seems clear that he holds by the first of these alternatives, and on this point Hobbes[2] is in agreement with him. If this is so, then humanity is divided into herds of livestock, each with its "guardian" who watches over his charges only that he may ultimately devour them.

Just as the shepherd is superior in kind to his sheep, so, too, the 10
shepherds of men, or, in other words, their rulers, are superior in kind to their peoples. This, according to Philo,[3] was the argument advanced by Caligula,[4] the Emperor, who drew from the analogy the

---

[1] **Hugo Grotius (1583–1645)** A Dutch lawyer who spent some time in exile in Paris. His fame as a child prodigy was considerable; his book on the laws of war (*De jure belli ac Pacis*) was widely known in Europe.

[2] **Thomas Hobbes (1588–1679)** An Englishman known as a materialist philosopher who did not credit divine influence in politics. He became famous for *Leviathan*, a study of politics that treated the state as if it were a monster (leviathan) with a life of its own.

[3] **Philo (13? B.C.–A.D. 47?)** A Jew who absorbed Greek culture and who wrote widely on many subjects. His studies on Mosaic law were considered important.

[4] **Caligula (A.D. 12–41)** Roman emperor of uncertain sanity. He loved his sister Drusilla so much that he had her deified when she died. A military commander, he was assassinated by an officer.

perfectly true conclusion that either Kings are Gods or their subjects brute beasts.

The reasoning of Caligula, of Hobbes, and of Grotius is funda-   11
mentally the same. Far earlier, Aristotle,[5] too, had maintained that men are not by nature equal, but that some are born to be slaves, others to be masters.

Aristotle was right: but he mistook the effect for the cause.   12
Nothing is more certain than that a man born into a condition of slavery is a slave by nature. A slave in fetters loses everything — even the desire to be freed from them. He grows to love his slavery, as the companions of Ulysses grew to love their state of brutish transformation.[6]

If some men are by nature slaves, the reason is that they have   13
been made slaves *against* nature. Force made the first slaves: cowardice has perpetuated the species.

I have made no mention of King Adam or of the Emperor Noah,   14
the father of three great Monarchs[7] who divided up the universe between them, as did the children of Saturn,[8] whom some have been tempted to identify with them. I trust that I may be given credit for my moderation, since, being descended in a direct line from one of these Princes, and quite possibly belonging to the elder branch, I may, for all I know, were my claims supported in law, be even now the legitimate Sovereign of the Human Race.[9] However that may be, all will concur in the view that Adam was King of the World, as was Robinson Crusoe of his island, only so long as he was its only inhabitant, and the great advantage of empire held on such terms was that the Monarch, firmly seated on his throne, had no need to fear rebellions, conspiracy, or war.

---

[5] **Aristotle (384–322 B.C.)** A student of Plato; his philosophical method became the dominant intellectual force in Western thought.

[6] **state of brutish transformation** This sentence refers to the Circe episode in Homer's *Odyssey* (10, 12). Circe was a sorceress who, by means of drugs, enchanted men and turned them into swine. Ulysses (Latin name of Odysseus), king of Ithaca, is the central figure of the *Odyssey*.

[7] **the father of three great Monarchs** Adam in the Bible (Gen. 4:1–25) fathered Cain, Abel, Enoch, and Seth. Noah's sons, Shem, Ham, and Japheth, repopulated the world after the Flood (Gen. 6:9–9:19).

[8] **children of Saturn** Saturn is a mythic god associated with the golden age of Rome and with the Greek god Cronus. It is probably the children of Cronus — Zeus, Poseidon, Hades, Demeter, and Hera — referred to here.

[9] **Sovereign of the Human Race** Rousseau is being ironic; like the rest of us, he is descended from Adam (according to the Bible).

Of the Right of the Strongest

However strong a man, he is never strong enough to remain   15
master always, unless he transform his Might into Right, and Obedience into Duty. Hence we have come to speak of the Right of the
Strongest, a right which, seemingly assumed in irony, has, in fact,
become established in principle. But the meaning of the phrase has
never been adequately explained. Strength is a physical attribute, and
I fail to see how any moral sanction can attach to its effects. To yield
to the strong is an act of necessity, not of will. At most it is the result
of a dictate of prudence. How, then, can it become a duty?

Let us assume for a moment that some such Right does really exist.   16
The only deduction from this premise is inexplicable gibberish. For to
admit that Might makes Right is to reverse the process of effect and
cause. The mighty man who defeats his rival becomes heir to his Right.
So soon as we can disobey with impunity, disobedience becomes legitimate. And, since the Mightiest is always right, it merely remains for us
to become possessed of Might. But what validity can there be in a Right
which ceases to exist when Might changes hands? If a man be constrained by Might to obey, what need has he to obey by Duty? And if
he is not constrained to obey, there is no further obligation on him to
do so. It follows, therefore, that the word Right adds nothing to the
idea of Might. It becomes, in this connection, completely meaningless.

Obey the Powers that be. If that means Yield to Force, the precept   17
is admirable but redundant. My reply to those who advance it is that
no case will ever be found of its violation. All power comes from God.
Certainly, but so do all ailments. Are we to conclude from such an
argument that we are never to call in the doctor? If I am waylaid by a
footpad at the corner of a wood, I am constrained by force to give him
my purse. But if I can manage to keep it from him, is it my duty to
hand it over? His pistol is also a symbol of Power. It must, then, be
admitted that Might does not create Right, and that no man is under
an obligation to obey any but the legitimate powers of the State. And
so I continually come back to the question I first asked.

Of Slavery

Since no man has natural authority over his fellows, and since   18
Might can produce no Right, the only foundation left for legitimate
authority in human societies is Agreement.

If a private citizen, says Grotius, can alienate his liberty and   19
make himself another man's slave, why should not a whole people do
the same, and subject themselves to the will of a King? The argument
contains a number of ambiguous words which stand in need of

explanation. But let us confine our attention to one only—*alienate*. To alienate means to give or to sell. Now a man who becomes the slave of another does not give himself. He sells himself in return for bare subsistence, if for nothing more. But why should a whole people sell themselves? So far from furnishing subsistence to his subjects, a King draws his own from them, and from them alone. According to Rabelais,[10] it takes a lot to keep a King. Do we, then, maintain that a subject surrenders his person on condition that his property be taken too? It is difficult to see what he will have left.

It will be said that the despot guarantees civil peace to his sub- 20 jects. So be it. But how are they the gainers if the wars to which his ambition may expose them, his insatiable greed, and the vexatious demands of his Ministers cause them more loss than would any outbreak of internal dissension? How do they benefit if that very condition of civil peace be one of the causes of their wretchedness? One can live peacefully enough in a dungeon, but such peace will hardly, of itself, ensure one's happiness. The Greeks imprisoned in the cave of Cyclops[11] lived peacefully while awaiting their turn to be devoured.

To say that a man gives himself for nothing is to commit oneself 21 to an absurd and inconceivable statement. Such an act of surrender is illegitimate, null, and void by the mere fact that he who makes it is not in his right mind. To say the same thing of a whole People is tantamount to admitting that the People in question are a nation of imbeciles. Imbecility does not produce Right.

Even if a man can alienate himself, he cannot alienate his chil- 22 dren. They are born free, their liberty belongs to them, and no one but themselves has a right to dispose of it. Before they have attained the age of reason their father may make, on their behalf, certain rules with a view to ensuring their preservation and well-being. But any such limitation of their freedom of choice must be regarded as neither irrevocable nor unconditional, for to alienate another's liberty is contrary to the natural order, and is an abuse of the father's rights. It follows that an arbitrary government can be legitimate only on condition that each successive generation of subjects is free either to accept or to reject it, and if this is so, then the government will no longer be arbitrary.

When a man renounces his liberty he renounces his essential 23 manhood, his rights, and even his duty as a human being. There is no compensation possible for such complete renunciation. It is incompatible with man's nature, and to deprive him of his free will is to deprive his actions of all moral sanction. The convention, in short, which sets

---

[10]**François Rabelais (c. 1494–1553)** French writer, author of *Gargantua* and *Pantagruel,* satires on politics and religion.

[11]**cave of Cyclops** The cyclops is a one-eyed giant cannibal whose cave is the scene of one of Odysseus's triumphs in Homer's *Odyssey* (9).

up on one side an absolute authority, and on the other an obligation to obey without question, is vain and meaningless. Is it not obvious that where we can demand everything we owe nothing? Where there is no mutual obligation, no interchange of duties, it must, surely, be clear that the actions of the commanded cease to have any moral value? For how can it be maintained that my slave has any "right" against me when everything that he has is my property? His right being *my* right, it is absurd to speak of it as ever operating to my disadvantage.

Grotius, and those who think like him, have found in the fact of   24
war another justification for the so-called "right" of slavery. They argue that since the victor has a *right* to kill his defeated enemy, the latter may, if he so wish, ransom his life at the expense of his liberty, and that this compact is the more legitimate in that it benefits both parties.

But it is evident that this alleged *right* of a man to kill his enemies   25
is not in any way a derivative of the state of war, if only because men, in their primitive condition of independence, are not bound to one another by any relationship sufficiently stable to produce a state either of war or of peace. They are not *naturally* enemies. It is the link between *things* rather than between *men* that constitutes war, and since a state of war cannot originate in simple personal relations, but only in relations between things, private hostility between man and man cannot obtain either in a state of nature where there is no generally accepted system of private property, or in a state of society where law is the supreme authority.

Single combats, duels, personal encounters are incidents which   26
do not constitute a "state" of anything. As to those private wars which were authorized by the Ordinances of King Louis IX[12] and suspended by the Peace of God, they were merely an abuse of Feudalism—that most absurd of all systems of government, so contrary was it to the principles of Natural Right and of all good polity.

War, therefore, is something that occurs not between man and   27
man, but between States. The individuals who become involved in it are enemies only by accident. They fight not as men or even as citizens, but as soldiers: not as members of this or that national group, but as its defenders. A State can have as its enemies only other States, not men at all, seeing that there can be no true relationship between things of a different nature.

This principle is in harmony with that of all periods, and with   28
the constant practice of every civilized society. A declaration of war is a warning, not so much to Governments as to their subjects. The

---

[12] **King Louis IX (1214–1270)** King of France, also called St. Louis. He was looked upon as an ideal monarch.

foreigner—whether king, private person, or nation as a whole—who steals, murders, or holds in durance the subjects of another country without first declaring war on that country's Prince, acts not as an enemy but as a brigand. Even when war has been joined, the just Prince, though he may seize all public property in enemy territory, yet respects the property and possessions of individuals, and, in so doing, shows his concern for those rights on which his own laws are based. The object of war being the destruction of the enemy State, a commander has a perfect right to kill its defenders so long as their arms are in their hands: but once they have laid them down and have submitted, they cease to be enemies, or instruments employed by an enemy, and revert to the condition of men, pure and simple, over whose lives no one can any longer exercise a rightful claim. Sometimes it is possible to destroy a State without killing any of its subjects, and nothing in war can be claimed as a right save what may be necessary for the accomplishment of the victor's end. These principles are not those of Grotius, nor are they based on the authority of poets, but derive from the Nature of Things, and are founded upon Reason.

The Right of Conquest finds its sole sanction in the Law of the 29 Strongest. If war does not give to the victor the right to massacre his defeated enemies, he cannot base upon a nonexistent right any claim to the further one of enslaving them. We have the right to kill our enemies only when we cannot enslave them. It follows, therefore, that the right to enslave cannot be deduced from the right to kill, and that we are guilty of enforcing an iniquitous exchange if we make a vanquished foeman purchase with his liberty that life over which we have no right. Is it not obvious that once we begin basing the right of life and death on the right to enslave, and the right to enslave on the right of life and death, we are caught in a vicious circle? Even if we assume the existence of this terrible right to kill all and sundry, I still maintain that a man enslaved, or a People conquered, in war is under no obligation to obey beyond the point at which force ceases to be operative. If the victor spares the life of his defeated opponent in return for an equivalent, he cannot be said to have shown him mercy. In either case he destroys him, but in the latter case he derives value from his act, while in the former he gains nothing. His authority, however, rests on no basis but that of force. There is still a state of war between the two men, and it conditions the whole relationship in which they stand to one another. The enjoyment of the Rights of War presupposes that there has been no treaty of Peace. Conqueror and conquered have, to be sure, entered into a compact, but such a compact, far from liquidating the state of war, assumes its continuance.

Thus, in whatever way we look at the matter, the "Right" to 30 enslave has no existence, not only because it is without legal validity,

but because the very term is absurd and meaningless. The words
Slavery and *Right* are contradictory and mutually exclusive. Whether
we be considering the relation of one man to another man, or of an
individual to a whole People, it is equally idiotic to say—"You and I
have made a compact which represents nothing but loss to you and
gain to me. I shall observe it so long as it pleases me to do so—and
so shall you, until I cease to find it convenient."

That We Must Always Go Back
to an Original Compact

Even were I to grant all that I have so far refuted, the champions   31
of despotism would not be one whit the better off. There will always
be a vast difference between subduing a mob and governing a social
group. No matter how many isolated individuals may submit to the
enforced control of a single conqueror, the resulting relationship will
ever be that of Master and Slave, never of People and Ruler. The body
of men so controlled may be an agglomeration; it is not an association.
It implies neither public welfare nor a body politic. An individual may
conquer half the world, but he is still only an individual. His interests,
wholly different from those of his subjects, are private to himself.
When he dies his empire is left scattered and disintegrated. He is like
an oak which crumbles and collapses in ashes so soon as the fire consumes it.

"A People," says Grotius, "may give themselves to a king." His   32
argument implies that the said People were already a People before
this act of surrender. The very act of gift was that of a political group
and presupposed deliberation. Before, therefore, we consider the act
by which a People chooses their king, it were well if we considered
the act by which a People is constituted as such. For it necessarily precedes the other, and is the true foundation on which all Societies rest.

Had there been no original compact, why, unless the choice   33
were unanimous, should the minority ever have agreed to accept the
decision of the majority? What right have the hundred who desire a
master to vote for the ten who do not? The institution of the franchise is, in itself, a form of compact, and assumes that, at least once
in its operation, complete unanimity existed.

Of the Social Pact

I assume, for the sake of argument, that a point was reached in   34
the history of mankind when the obstacles to continuing in a state of
Nature were stronger than the forces which each individual could

employ to the end of continuing in it. The original state of Nature, therefore, could no longer endure, and the human race would have perished had it not changed its manner of existence.

Now, since men can by no means engender new powers, but 35 can only unite and control those of which they are already possessed, there is no way in which they can maintain themselves save by coming together and pooling their strength in a way that will enable them to withstand any resistance exerted upon them from without. They must develop some sort of central direction and learn to act in concert.

Such a concentration of powers can be brought about only as 36 the consequence of an agreement reached between individuals. But the self-preservation of each single man derives primarily from his own strength and from his own freedom. How, then, can he limit these without, at the same time, doing himself an injury and neglecting that care which it is his duty to devote to his own concerns? This difficulty, in so far as it is relevant to my subject, can be expressed as follows:

"Some form of association must be found as a result of which 37 the whole strength of the community will be enlisted for the protection of the person and property of each constituent member, in such a way that each, when united to his fellows, renders obedience to his own will, and remains as free as he was before." That is the basic problem of which the Social Contract provides the solution.

The clauses of this Contract are determined by the Act of Asso- 38 ciation in such a way that the least modification must render them null and void. Even though they may never have been formally enunciated, they must be everywhere the same, and everywhere tacitly admitted and recognized. So completely must this be the case that, should the social compact be violated, each associated individual would at once resume all the rights which once were his, and regain his natural liberty, by the mere fact of losing the agreed liberty for which he renounced it.

It must be clearly understood that the clauses in question can be 39 reduced, in the last analysis, to one only, to wit, the complete alienation by each associate member to the community of *all his rights*. For, in the first place, since each has made surrender of himself without reservation, the resultant conditions are the same for all: and, because they are the same for all, it is in the interest of none to make them onerous to his fellows.

Furthermore, this alienation having been made unreservedly, 40 the union of individuals is as perfect as it well can be, none of the associated members having any claim against the community. For should there be any rights left to individuals, and no common authority be empowered to pronounce as between them and the public, then each, being in some things his own judge, would soon claim to be so in all. Were that so, a state of Nature would still remain in being, the conditions of association becoming either despotic or ineffective.

In short, whoso gives himself to all gives himself to none. And, 41 since there is no member of the social group over whom we do not acquire precisely the same rights as those over ourselves which we have surrendered to him, it follows that we gain the exact equivalent of what we lose, as well as an added power to conserve what we already have.

If, then, we take from the social pact everything which is not 42 essential to it, we shall find it to be reduced to the following terms: "each of us contributes to the group his person and the powers which he wields as a person under the supreme direction of the general will, and we receive into the body politic each individual as forming an indivisible part of the whole."

As soon as the act of association becomes a reality, it substitutes 43 for the person of each of the contracting parties a moral and collective body made up of as many members as the constituting assembly has votes, which body receives from this very act of constitution its unity, its dispersed *self*, and its will. The public person thus formed by the union of individuals was known in the old days as a *City*, but now as the *Republic* or *Body Politic*. This, when it fulfills a passive role, is known by its members as *The State*, when an active one, as *The Sovereign People*, and, in contrast to other similar bodies, as a *Power*. In respect of the constituent associates, it enjoys the collective name of *The People*, the individuals who compose it being known as *Citizens* in so far as they share in the sovereign authority, as *Subjects* in so far as they owe obedience to the laws of the State. But these different terms frequently overlap, and are used indiscriminately one for the other. It is enough that we should realize the difference between them when they are employed in a precise sense.

Of the Sovereign

It is clear from the above formula that the act of association 44 implies a mutual undertaking between the body politic and its constituent members. Each individual comprising the former contracts, so to speak, with himself and has a twofold function. As a member of the sovereign people he owes a duty to each of his neighbors, and, as a Citizen, to the sovereign people as a whole. But we cannot here apply that maxim of Civil Law according to which no man can be held to an undertaking entered into with himself, because there is a great difference between a man's duty to himself and to a whole of which he forms a part.

Here it should be pointed out that a public decision which can 45 enjoin obedience on all subjects to their Sovereign, by reason of the double aspect under which each is seen, cannot, on the contrary, bind the sovereign in his dealings with himself. Consequently, it is against the nature of the body politic that the sovereign should impose upon himself a law which he cannot infringe. For, since he can regard himself under one aspect only, he is in the position of an individual entering into a contract with himself. Whence it follows that there is not, nor can be, any fundamental law which is obligatory for the whole body of the People, not even the social contract itself. This does not mean that the body politic is unable to enter into engagements with some other Power, provided always that such engagements do not derogate from the nature of the Contract; for the relation of the body politic to a foreign Power is that of a simple individual.

But the body politic, or Sovereign, in that it derives its being 46 simply and solely from the sanctity of the said Contract, can never bind itself, even in its relations with a foreign Power, by any decision which might derogate from the validity of the original act. It may not, for instance, alienate any portion of itself, nor make submission to any other sovereign. To violate the act by reason of which it exists would be tantamount to destroying itself, and that which is nothing can produce nothing.

As soon as a mob has become united into a body politic, any 47 attack upon one of its members is an attack upon itself. Still more important is the fact that, should any offense be committed against the body politic as a whole, the effect must be felt by each of its members. Both duty and interest, therefore, oblige the two contracting parties to render one another mutual assistance. The same individuals should seek to unite under this double aspect all the advantages which flow from it.

Now, the Sovereign People, having no existence, outside that of 48 the individuals who compose it, has, and can have, no interest at variance with theirs. Consequently, the sovereign power need give no guarantee to its subjects, since it is impossible that the body should wish to injure all its members, nor, as we shall see later, can it injure any single individual. The Sovereign, by merely existing, is always what it should be.

But the same does not hold true of the relation of subject to sov- 49 ereign. In spite of common interest, there can be no guarantee that the subject will observe his duty to the sovereign unless means are found to ensure his loyalty.

Each individual, indeed, may, as a man, exercise a will at vari- 50
ance with, or different from, that general will to which, as citizen, he contributes. His personal interest may dictate a line of action quite other than that demanded by the interest of all. The fact that his own existence as an individual has an absolute value, and that he is, by nature, an independent being, may lead him to conclude that what he owes to the common cause is something that he renders of his own free will; and he may decide that by leaving the debt unpaid he does less harm to his fellows than he would to himself should he make the necessary surrender. Regarding the moral entity constitut-ing the State as a rational abstraction because it is not a man, he might enjoy his rights as a citizen without, at the same time, fulfill-ing his duties as a subject, and the resultant injustice might grow until it brought ruin upon the whole body politic.

In order, then, that the social compact may not be but a vain 51
formula, it must contain, though unexpressed, the single undertak-ing which can alone give force to the whole, namely, that whoever shall refuse to obey the general will must be constrained by the whole body of his fellow citizens to do so: which is no more than to say that it may be necessary to compel a man to be free—freedom being that condition which, by giving each citizen to his country, guarantees him from all personal dependence and is the foundation upon which the whole political machine rests, and supplies the power which works it. Only the recognition by the individual of the rights of the community can give legal force to undertakings entered into between citizens, which, otherwise, would become absurd, tyrannical, and exposed to vast abuses.

Of the Civil State

The passage from the state of nature to the civil state produces a 52
truly remarkable change in the individual. It substitutes justice for instinct in his behavior, and gives to his actions a moral basis which formerly was lacking. Only when the voice of duty replaces physical impulse and when right replaces the cravings of appetite does the man who, till then, was concerned solely with himself, realize that he is under compulsion to obey quite different principles, and that he must now consult his reason and not merely respond to the prompt-ings of desire. Although he may find himself deprived of many advantages which were his in a state of nature, he will recognize that

he has gained others which are of far greater value. By dint of being exercised, his faculties will develop, his ideas take on a wider scope, his sentiments become ennobled, and his whole soul be so elevated, that, but for the fact that misuse of the new conditions still, at times, degrades him to a point below that from which he has emerged, he would unceasingly bless the day which freed him forever from his ancient state, and turned him from a limited and stupid animal into an intelligent being and a Man.

Let us reduce all this to terms which can be easily compared. 53 What a man loses as a result of the Social Contract is his natural liberty and his unqualified right to lay hands on all that tempts him, provided only that he can compass its possession. What he gains is civil liberty and the ownership of what belongs to him. That we may labor under no illusion concerning these compensations, it is well that we distinguish between natural liberty which the individual enjoys so long as he is strong enough to maintain it, and civil liberty which is curtailed by the general will. Between possessions which derive from physical strength and the right of the first-comer, and ownership which can be based only on a positive title.

To the benefits conferred by the status of citizenship might be 54 added that of Moral Freedom, which alone makes a man his own master. For to be subject to appetite is to be a slave, while to obey the laws laid down by society is to be free. But I have already said enough on this point, and am not concerned here with the philosophical meaning of the word *liberty*.

Of Real Property

Each individual member of the Community gives himself to it at 55 the moment of its formation. What he gives is the whole man as he then is, with all his qualities of strength and power, and everything of which he stands possessed. Not that, as a result of this act of gift, such possessions, by changing hands and becoming the property of the Sovereign, change their nature. Just as the resources of strength upon which the City can draw are incomparably greater than those at the disposition of any single individual, so, too, is public possession when backed by a greater power. It is made more irrevocable, though not, so far, at least, as regards foreigners, more legitimate. For the State, by reason of the Social Contract which, within it, is the basis of all Rights, is the master of all its members' goods, though, in its dealings with other Powers, it is so only by virtue of its rights as first occupier, which come to it from the individuals who make it up.

The Right of "first occupancy," though more real than the "Right   56
of the strongest," becomes a genuine right only after the right of property has been established. All men have a natural right to what is necessary to them. But the positive act which establishes a man's claim to any particular item of property limits him to that and excludes him from all others. His share having been determined, he must confine himself to that, and no longer has any claim on the property of the community. That is why the right of "first occu-pancy," however weak it be in a state of nature, is guaranteed to every man enjoying the status of citizen. In so far as he benefits from this right, he withholds his claim, not so much from what is another's, as from what is not specifically his.

In order that the right of "first occupancy" may be legalized, the   57
following conditions must be present. (1) There must be no one already living on the land in question. (2) A man must occupy only so much of it as is necessary for his subsistence. (3) He must take possession of it, not by empty ceremony, but by virtue of his inten-tion to work and to cultivate it, for that, in the absence of legal title, alone constitutes a claim which will be respected by others.

In effect, by according the right of "first occupancy" to a man's   58
needs and to his will to work, are we not stretching it as far as it will go? Should not some limits be set to this right? Has a man only to set foot on land belonging to the community to justify his claim to be its master? Just because he is strong enough, at one particular moment, to keep others off, can he demand that they shall never return? How can a man or a People take possession of vast territories, thereby excluding the rest of the world from their enjoyment, save by an act of criminal usurpation, since, as the result of such an act, the rest of humanity is deprived of the amenities of dwelling and subsistence which nature has provided for their common enjoyment? When Nuñez Balboa,[13] landing upon a strip of coast, claimed the Southern Sea and the whole of South America as the property of the crown of Castille, was he thereby justified in dispossessing its former inhabi-tants, and in excluding from it all the other princes of the earth? Grant that, and there will be no end to such vain ceremonies. It would be open to His Catholic Majesty[14] to claim from his Council

---

[13] **Nuñez Balboa (1475–1519)** Spanish explorer who discovered the Pacific Ocean.

[14] **His Catholic Majesty** A reference to the king of Spain, probably Ferdinand II of Aragon (1452–1516).

Chamber possession of the whole Universe, only excepting those portions of it already in the ownership of other princes.

One can understand how the lands of individuals, separate but contiguous, become public territory, and how the right of sovereignty, extending from men to the land they occupy, becomes at one real and personal—a fact which makes their owners more than ever dependent, and turns their very strength into a guarantee of their fidelity. This is an advantage which does not seem to have been considered by the monarchs of the ancient world, who, claiming to be no more than kings of the Persians, the Scythians, the Macedonians, seem to have regarded themselves rather as the rulers of men than as the masters of countries. Those of our day are cleverer, for they style themselves kings of France, of Spain, of England, and so forth. Thus, by controlling the land, they can be very sure of controlling its inhabitants.   59

The strange thing about this act of alienation is that, far from depriving its members of their property by accepting its surrender, the Community actually establishes their claim to its legitimate ownership, and changes what was formerly mere usurpation into a right, by virtue of which they may enjoy possession. As owners they are Trustees for the Commonwealth. Their rights are respected by their fellow citizens and are maintained by the united strength of the community against any outside attack. From ceding their property to the State—and thus, to themselves—they derive nothing but advantage, since they have, so to speak, acquired all that they have surrendered. This paradox is easily explained once we realize the distinction between the rights exercised by the Sovereign and by the Owner over the same piece of property, as will be seen later.   60

It may so happen that a number of men begin to group themselves into a community before ever they own property at all, and that only later, when they have got possession of land sufficient to maintain them all, do they either enjoy it in common or parcel it between themselves in equal lots or in accordance with such scale of proportion as may be established by the sovereign. However this acquisition be made, the right exercised by each individual over his own particular share must always be subordinated to the overriding claim of the Community as such. Otherwise there would be no strength in the social bond, nor any real power in the exercise of sovereignty.   61

I will conclude this chapter, and the present Book, with a remark which should serve as basis for every social system: that, so far from destroying natural equality, the primitive compact substitutes for it a moral and legal equality which compensates for all those physical inequalities from which men suffer. However unequal they may be   62 in bodily strength or in intellectual gifts, they become equal in the eyes of the law, and as a result of the compact into which they have entered.

QUESTIONS FOR CRITICAL READING

1. Examine Rousseau's analogy of the family as the oldest and only natural form of government. Do you agree that the analogy is useful and that its contentions are true? Which aspects of this natural form of government do not work to help us understand the basis of government?
2. Rousseau seems to accept the family as a patriarchal structure. How would his views change if he accepted it as a matriarchal structure? How would they change if he regarded each member of the family as absolutely equal in authority from birth?
3. What does it mean to reason from what is fact instead of from what is morally right?
4. What features of Rousseau's social contract are like those of a legal contract? How does a person contract to be part of society?
5. What distinctions can be made among natural, moral, and legal equality? Which kind of equality is most important to a social system?

SUGGESTIONS FOR CRITICAL WRITING

1. When Rousseau wrote, "Man is born free, and everywhere he is in chains," the institution of slavery was widely practiced and justified by many authorities. Today slavery has been generally abolished. How is this statement relevant to people's condition in society now? What are some ways in which people relinquish their independence or freedom?
2. Clarify the difference between your duty to yourself and your duty to society (your social structure—personal, local, national). Establish your duties in relation to each structure. How can these duties conflict with one another? How does the individual resolve the conflicts?
3. Do you agree with Rousseau when he says, "All men have a natural right to what is necessary to them"? What is necessary to all people, and in what sense do they have a right to what is necessary? Who should provide those necessities? Should necessities be provided for everyone or only for people who are unable to provide for themselves? If society will not provide these necessities, does the individual have the right to break the social contract by means of revolution?
4. What seems to be Rousseau's opinion regarding private property or the ownership of property? Beginning with paragraph 59, Rousseau distinguishes between monarchs with sovereignty over people and those with sovereignty over a region, such as France, Italy, or another country. What is Rousseau's view of the property that constitutes a state and who actually owns it? He mentions that the rights of individual owners

must give way to the rights of the community in general. What is your response to this view?

5. Rousseau makes an important distinction between natural liberty and civil liberty. People in a state of nature enjoy natural liberty, and when they bind themselves together into a body politic, they enjoy civil liberty. What are the differences? Define each kind of liberty as carefully as you can, and take a stand on whether you feel civil liberty or natural liberty is superior. How is the conflict between the two forms of liberty felt today?

6. **CONNECTIONS** Rousseau's thinking emphasizes the role played by the common people in any civil society. How does that emphasis compare with Machiavelli's thinking? Consider the attitudes each writer has toward the essential goodness of people and the essential responsibilities of the monarch or government leader. In what ways is Rousseau closer in thinking to Lao-tzu than to Machiavelli?

7. **SEEING CONNECTIONS** Rousseau could not have seen Delacroix's painting *Liberty Leading the People* (p. 18), but he would definitely have had a strong opinion about it if he had. Would he have thought the Liberty leading these people was natural liberty or civil liberty? What details in the painting convince you one way or the other? Would Rousseau have approved of the action going on in the painting or would he have condemned it? What are your reasons for believing this? Shape your essay as an argument defending a clear position.

THOMAS JEFFERSON
The Declaration of Independence

THOMAS JEFFERSON (1743–1826) authored one of the most memorable statements in American history: the Declaration of Independence. He composed the work in 1776 under the watchful eyes of Benjamin Franklin, John Adams, and the rest of the Continental Congress, which spent two and a half days going over every word. Although the substance of the document was developed in committee, Jefferson, because of the grace of his writing style, was selected to craft the actual wording.

Jefferson rose to eminence in a time of great political upheaval. By the time he took a seat in the Virginia legislature in 1769, the colony was already on the course toward revolution. His pamphlet "A Summary View of the Rights of British America" (1774) brought him to the attention of those who were agitating for independence and established him as an ardent republican and revolutionary. In 1779 he was elected governor of Virginia. After the Revolutionary War he moved into the national political arena as the first secretary of state (1790–1793). He then served as John Adams's vice president (1797–1801) and was himself elected president in 1800. Perhaps one of his greatest achievements during his two terms (1801–1809) in office was his negotiation of the Louisiana Purchase, in which the United States acquired from France 828,000 square miles of land west of the Mississippi for about $15 million.

One of the fundamental paradoxes of Jefferson's personal and political life has been his attitude toward slavery. Like most wealthy Virginians, Jefferson owned slaves. However, in 1784 he tried to abolish slavery in the western territories that were being added to the United States. His "Report on Government for the Western Territory" failed by one vote. Historians have pointed out that Jefferson probably had an affair with Sally Hemmings, a mixed-race slave, and fathered children with her.

However unclear his personal convictions, many of Jefferson's accomplishments, which extend from politics to agriculture and mechanical invention, still stand. One of the most versatile Americans of any generation, he wrote a book, *Notes on Virginia* (1782); designed and built Monticello, his famous homestead in Virginia; and in large part founded and designed the University of Virginia (1819).

Despite their revolutionary nature, the ideas Jefferson expressed in the Declaration of Independence were not entirely original. Rousseau's republican philosophies greatly influenced the work. When Jefferson states in the second paragraph that "all men are created equal, that they are endowed by their Creator with certain unalienable rights," he reflects Rousseau's emphasis on the political equality of men and on protecting certain fundamental rights (see Rousseau, beginning with para. 39, p. 67). Jefferson also wrote that "Governments are instituted among Men, deriving their just powers from the consent of the governed." This is one of Rousseau's primary points, although it was Jefferson who immortalized it in these words.

Jefferson's Rhetoric

Jefferson's techniques include the use of the periodic sentence, which was especially typical of the age. The first sentence of the Declaration of Independence is periodic—that is, it is long and carefully balanced, and the main point comes at the end. Such sentences are not popular today, although an occasional periodic sentence can still be powerful in contemporary prose. Jefferson's first sentence says (in paraphrase): *When one nation must sever its relations with a parent nation . . . and stand as an independent nation itself . . . the causes ought to be explained.* Moreover, the main body of the Declaration of Independence lists the "causes" that lead to the final and most important element of the sentence. Causal analysis was a method associated with legal thought and reflects Jefferson's training in eighteenth-century legal analysis. One understood things best when one understood their causes.

The periodic sentence demands certain qualities of balance and parallelism that all good writers should heed. The first sentence in paragraph 2 demonstrates both qualities. The balance is achieved by making each part of the sentence roughly the same length. The parallelism is achieved by linking words in deliberate repetition for effect (they are in italicized type in the following analysis). Note how the "truths" mentioned in the first clause are enumerated in the succession of noun clauses beginning with "that"; "Rights" are enumerated in the final clause:

> We hold these truths to be self-evident,
> > *that* all men are created equal,
> > *that* they are endowed by their Creator with certain inalienable Rights,
> > *that* among these are Life, Liberty and the pursuit of Happiness.

Parallelism is one of the greatest stylistic techniques available to a writer sensitive to rhetoric. It is a natural technique: many untrained writers and speakers develop it on their own. The periodicity of the sentences and the balance of their parallelism suggest thoughtfulness, wisdom, and control.

Parallelism creates a natural link to the useful device of enumeration, or listing. Many writers using this technique establish their purpose from the outset—"I wish to address three important issues . . ."—and then number them: "First, I want to say . . . Second . . . ," and so on. Jefferson devotes paragraphs 3 through 29 to enumerating the "causes" he mentions in paragraph 1. Each one constitutes a separate paragraph; thus, each has separate weight and importance. Each begins with "He" or "For" and is therefore in parallel structure. The technique of repetition of the same words at the beginning of successive lines is called *anaphora*. Jefferson's use of anaphora here is one of the best known and most effective in all literature. The "He" referred to is Britain's king George III (1738–1820), who is never mentioned by name. Congress is opposed not to a personality but to the sovereign of a nation that is oppressing the United States and a tyrant who is not dignified by being named. The "For" introduces grievous acts the king has given his assent to; these are offenses against the colonies.

However, Jefferson does not develop the causes in detail. We do not have specific information about what trade was cut off by the British, what taxes were imposed without consent, or how King George waged war or abdicated government in the colonies. Presumably, Jefferson's audience knew the details and was led by the twenty-seven paragraphs to observe how numerous the causes were. And all are serious; any one alone was enough cause for revolution. The effect of Jefferson's enumeration is to illustrate the patience of the colonies up to this point and to tell the world that the colonies have finally lost patience on account of the reasons listed. The Declaration of Independence projects the careful meditations and decisions of exceptionally calm, patient, and reasonable people.

PREREADING QUESTIONS: WHAT TO READ FOR

The following prereading questions may help you anticipate key issues in the discussion of Thomas Jefferson's Declaration of Independence. Keeping them in mind during your first reading of the selection should help focus your attention.

- Under what conditions may a people alter or abolish their government?

- Why does Jefferson consider King George a tyrant?

The Declaration of Independence

In Congress, July 4, 1776

The Unanimous Declaration of the Thirteen United States of America

When in the Course of human events, it becomes necessary for   1
one people to dissolve the political bands which have connected them with another, and to assume among the Powers of the earth, the separate and equal station to which the Laws of Nature and of Nature's God entitle them, a decent respect to the opinions of mankind requires that they should declare the causes which impel them to the separation.

We hold these truths to be self-evident, that all men are created   2
equal, that they are endowed by their Creator with certain inalienable Rights, that among these are Life, Liberty, and the pursuit of Happiness. That to secure these rights, Governments are instituted among Men, deriving their just powers from the consent of the governed. That whenever any Form of Government becomes destructive of these ends, it is the Right of the People to alter or to abolish it, and to institute new Government, laying its foundation on such principles and organizing its powers in such form, as to them shall seem most likely to effect their Safety and Happiness. Prudence, indeed, will dictate that Governments long established should not be changed for light and transient causes; and accordingly all experience hath shown, that mankind are more disposed to suffer, while evils are sufferable, than to right themselves by abolishing the forms to which they are accustomed. But when a long train of abuses and usurpations, pursuing

invariably the same Object evinces a design to reduce them under absolute Despotism, it is their right, it is their duty, to throw off such Government, and to provide new Guards for their future security.— Such has been the patient sufferance of these Colonies; and such is now the necessity which constrains them to alter their former Systems of Government. The history of the present King of Great Britain is a history of repeated injuries and usurpations, all having in direct object the establishment of an absolute Tyranny over these States. To prove this, let Facts be submitted to a candid world.

He has refused his Assent to Laws, the most wholesome and necessary for the public good. 3

He has forbidden his Governors to pass Laws of immediate and pressing importance, unless suspended in their operation till his Assent should be obtained; and when so suspended, he has utterly neglected to attend to them. 4

He has refused to pass other laws for the accommodation of large districts of people, unless those people would relinquish the right of Representation in the Legislature, a right inestimable to them and formidable to tyrants only. 5

He has called together legislative bodies at places unusual, uncomfortable, and distant from the depository of their Public Records, for the sole purpose of fatiguing them into compliance with his measures. 6

He has dissolved Representative Houses repeatedly, for opposing with manly firmness his invasions on the rights of the people. 7

He has refused for a long time, after such dissolutions, to cause others to be elected; whereby the Legislative Powers, incapable of Annihilation, have returned to the People at large for their exercise; the State remaining in the mean time exposed to all the dangers of invasion from without, and convulsions within. 8

He has endeavored to prevent the population of these States;[1] for that purpose obstructing the Laws for Naturalization of Foreigners; refusing to pass others to encourage their migration hither, and raising the conditions of new Appropriations of Lands. 9

He has obstructed the Administration of Justice, by refusing his Assent to Laws for establishing Judiciary Powers. 10

He has made Judges dependent on his Will alone, for the tenure of their offices, and the amount and payment of their salaries. 11

He has erected a multitude of New Offices, and sent hither swarms of Officers to harass our People, and eat out their substance. 12

---

[1] **prevent the population of these States** This meant limiting migration to the colonies, thus controlling their growth.

He has kept among us, in times of peace, Standing Armies with- 13
out the Consent of our legislature.

He has affected to render the Military independent of and supe- 14
rior to the Civil Power.

He has combined with others to subject us to a jurisdiction for- 15
eign to our constitution, and unacknowledged by our laws; giving
his Assent to their acts of pretended Legislation:

For quartering large bodies of armed troops among us: 16

For protecting them, by a mock Trial, from Punishment for any 17
Murders which they should commit on the Inhabitants of these
States:

For cutting off our Trade with all parts of the world: 18

For imposing taxes on us without our Consent: 19

For depriving us in many cases, of the benefits of Trial by Jury: 20

For transporting us beyond Seas to be tried for pretended 21
offenses:

For abolishing the free System of English Laws in a neighboring 22
Province, establishing therein an Arbitrary government, and enlarging
its Boundaries so as to render it at once an example and fit instrument for introducing the same absolute rule into these Colonies:

For taking away our Charters, abolishing our most valuable 23
Laws, and altering fundamentally the Forms of our Governments:

For suspending our own Legislatures, and declaring themselves 24
invested with Power to legislate for us in all cases whatsoever.

He has abdicated Government here, by declaring us out of his 25
Protection and waging War against us.

He has plundered our seas, ravaged our Coasts, burnt our 26
towns, and destroyed the lives of our people.

He is at this time transporting large armies of foreign mercenar- 27
ies to complete the works of death, desolation, and tyranny, already
begun with circumstances of Cruelty & perfidy scarcely paralleled in
the most barbarous ages, and totally unworthy the Head of a civilized nation.

He has constrained our fellow Citizens taken Captive on the 28
high Seas to bear Arms against their Country, to become the executioners of their friends and Brethren, or to fall themselves by their
Hands.

He has excited domestic insurrections amongst us, and has 29
endeavored to bring on the inhabitants of our frontiers, the merci-
less Indian Savages, whose known rule of warfare, is an undistin-
guished destruction of all ages, sexes, and conditions.

In every stage of these Oppressions We have Petitioned for 30
Redress in the most humble terms: Our repeated Petitions have been

answered only by repeated injury. A Prince, whose character is thus marked by every act which may define a Tyrant, is unfit to be the ruler of a free People.

Nor have We been wanting in attention to our British brethren. 31 We have warned them from time to time of attempts by their legislature to extend an unwarrantable jurisdiction over us. We have reminded them of the circumstances of our emigration and settlement here. We have appealed to their native justice and magnanimity, and we have conjured them by the ties of our common kindred to disavow these usurpations, which, would inevitably interrupt our connections and correspondence. They too have been deaf to the voice of justice and of consanguinity. We must, therefore, acquiesce in the necessity, which denounces our Separation, and hold them, as we hold the rest of mankind, Enemies in War, in Peace Friends.

We, therefore, the Representatives of the United States of Amer- 32 ica, in General Congress, Assembled, appealing to the Supreme Judge of the world for the rectitude of our intentions, do, in the Name, and by Authority of the good People of these Colonies, solemnly publish and declare, That these United Colonies are, and of Right ought to be Free and Independent States, that they are Absolved from all Allegiance to the British Crown, and that all political connection between them and the State of Great Britain, is and ought to be totally dissolved; and that as Free and Independent States, they have full Power to levy War, conclude Peace, contract Alliances, establish Commerce, and to do all other Acts and Things which Independent States may of right do. And for the support of this Declaration, with a firm reliance on the Protection of Divine Providence, we mutually pledge to each other our Lives, our Fortunes, and our sacred Honor.

QUESTIONS FOR CRITICAL READING

1. What laws of nature does Jefferson refer to in paragraph 1?
2. What do you think Jefferson feels is the function of government (para. 2)?
3. What does Jefferson say about women? Is there any way you can determine his views from reading this document? Does he appear to favor a patriarchal system?
4. Find at least one use of parallel structure in the Declaration (see p. 78 in the section on Jefferson's rhetoric for a description of parallelism). What key terms are repeated in identical or equivalent constructions, and to what effect?
5. Which causes listed in paragraphs 3 through 29 are the most serious? Are any trivial? Which ones are serious enough to cause a revolution?

6. What do you consider to be the most graceful sentence in the entire Declaration? Where is it placed in the Declaration? What purpose does it serve there?

7. In what ways does the king's desire for stable government interfere with Jefferson's sense of his own independence?

SUGGESTIONS FOR CRITICAL WRITING

1. Jefferson defines the inalienable rights of a citizen as "Life, Liberty, and the pursuit of Happiness." Do you think these are indeed inalienable rights? Answer this question by including some sentences that use parallel structure and repeat key terms in similar constructions. Be certain that you define each of these rights both for yourself and for our time.

2. Write an essay discussing what you feel the function of government should be. Include at least three periodic sentences (underline them). You may first want to establish Jefferson's view of government and then compare or contrast it with your own.

3. Jefferson envisioned a government that allowed its citizens to exercise their rights to life, liberty, and the pursuit of happiness. Has Jefferson's revolutionary vision been achieved in America? Begin with a definition of these three key terms: *life, liberty,* and *the pursuit of happiness.* Then, for each term use examples—drawn from current events, your own experience, American history—to take a clear and well-argued stand on whether the nation has achieved Jefferson's goal.

4. Slavery was legal in America in 1776, and Jefferson reluctantly owned slaves. He never presented his plan for gradual emancipation of the slaves to Congress because he realized that Congress would never approve it. But Jefferson and Franklin did finance a plan to buy slaves and return them to Africa, where in 1821 returning slaves founded the nation of Liberia. Agree or disagree with the following statement and defend your position: the ownership of slaves by the people who wrote the Declaration of Independence invalidates it. You may wish to read the relevant chapters on Jefferson and slavery in Merrill D. Peterson's *Thomas Jefferson and the New Nation* (1970).

5. What kind of government does Jefferson seem to prefer? In what ways would his government differ from that of the king he is reacting against? Is he talking about an entirely different system or about the same system but with a different kind of "prince" at the head? How would Jefferson protect the individual against the whim of the state, while also protecting the state against the whim of the individual?

6. **CONNECTIONS** Write an essay in which you examine the ways in which Jefferson agrees or disagrees with Lao-tzu's conception of human nature and of government. How does Jefferson share Lao-tzu's commitment to judicious inactivity? What evidence is there that the king subscribes to it? Describe the similarities and differences between Jefferson's views and those of Lao-tzu.

7. **CONNECTIONS**   What principles does Jefferson share with Jean-Jacques Rousseau? Compare the fundamental demands of the Declaration of Independence with Rousseau's conceptions of liberty and independence. How would Rousseau have reacted to this declaration?

8. **SEEING CONNECTIONS**   Jefferson wrote in 1776, thirteen years before the French Revolution and the execution of the French king. He was hardly thinking of overthrowing the British government, but rather he was merely establishing the United States as an independent nation. The citizens in Delacroix's *Liberty Leading the People* (p. 18) in 1830 were intent on ridding themselves of a king (as was Jefferson), not killing him. How likely is it that Jefferson might have taken this painting and used it as a poster for the American Revolution (assuming, of course, that it had been available at that time)? What details in the Declaration of Independence reinforce your belief that Jefferson would or would not have been comfortable with the painting?

JOSÉ ORTEGA Y GASSET
The Greatest Danger, the State

JOSÉ ORTEGA Y GASSET (1883–1955) was Spain's most important philosopher. He received his doctorate from Complutense University of Madrid in 1904 when he was barely twenty-one. He studied further in Germany at Berlin, Leipsig, and Marburg where he was influenced by a group of philosophers studying the work of Immanuel Kant (1724–1804), whose late work in metaphysics insisted on a "categorical imperative" that established a clear moral principle. When Ortega returned to Spain, he took a teaching job in 1909 only to be appointed professor of philosophy at the Complutense University of Madrid in 1910. Later, his essays on two major writers of the twentieth century, Marcel Proust and James Joyce, established him as an international figure and one of the most influential humanists in Spain.

Ortega was not only an academic. He also participated in the government of Spain in the early 1930s and was named civil governor of Madrid. When the civil war took hold in Spain and the lines were clearly drawn between Communists (called Republicans) and Fascists (called Nationalists) under Francisco Franco (1892–1975), Ortega—because of his position—refused to take sides. He left Spain and went into voluntary exile to protest the civil war and its outcome: the victory of the Fascist, or Nationalist, forces and the elevation of Franco as Spain's dictator.

Ortega settled in Portugal in 1945 when the war in Europe was over. Despite the oppressive rule of Franco, he returned to Madrid in 1948 and established the Institute of Humanities, where he worked relatively unharassed by the authorities. His writings ranged from literature to sociology to aesthetics. One of his earliest works, *Meditations on Quixote* (1914), examined the symbols of

---

From *The Revolt of the Masses*. Authorized translation from the Spanish.

Spanish writing, linking them to the Spanish people. In *Inverte-brate Spain* (1922), he challenged what he felt was the spineless leadership in the period following World War I. He pleaded for the establishment of a United States of Europe—a development that eventually took shape in the 1990s as the European Union.

One of his most influential books, *The Dehumanization of Art* (1925), insisted that modern art appeals to a special aesthetic sensi-bility. It is not the same sensibility that we bring to a view out our window of a lovely mountain. It is not the same sensibility that we bring to our observation of people in our lives. In Ortega's words, the artist cultivates "specifically aesthetic sentiments." These feel-ings are different from those that a person might express in an everyday human situation. Therefore, the feelings that we under-stand as human emotions may be of great importance to us in daily life but of little importance in contemplating a work of art.

His best-known book, *The Revolt of the Masses* (first published in 1930), contains a political theme. Ortega feared that democracy as it was developing in Europe had within it the seeds of tyranny by the masses. He saw such a threat in Russian communism and in the fascism of Italy. He also feared that rapid population growth and occupational specialization would rob people of a common cul-tural past and cultural identity. Such a condition made it easier for a tyranny by the masses to take over and to tolerate or even execute modern horrors, such as the concentration camps and extermination ovens of Nazi Germany.

Even before the Spanish civil war, Ortega had observed the growing power of postrevolutionary Russia, which suffered its own civil war from 1917 to 1922, and the rise in 1922 of Mussolini and his Blackshirts, thugs who imposed fascist rule on Italy. Even before that, Ortega had the example of the French Revolution when the masses of French citizens rose and massacred aristocrats and clergy and imposed a brutal rule over the nation. That revolution resulted in the elevation of Napoleon Bonaparte, who—as emperor—was essentially Europe's first total dictator and a predecessor of Franco, Hitler, Stalin, Mussolini, and a host of other lesser dictators across the globe.

Ortega's Rhetoric

In *The Revolt of the Masses* Ortega carries a basic message: he fears that the rise of the masses could result in a "tyranny of the majority." Early twentieth-century American journalists sometimes called it the threat of mob-ocracy. Ortega, in another section of his book, defines the minority as those who are qualified with special training, while the masses are those who are not qualified. Further, he is convinced that unless the masses are led by an intellectual and capable minority there will be disorder and confusion leading to events such as lynchings and violence. As he says, "When the mass acts on its own, it does so only in one way, for it has no other: it lynches. It is not altogether by chance that lynch law comes from America, for America is, in a fashion, the paradise of the masses" (para. 3).

Ortega condemned violence and rhetoric—saying, "To-day violence is the rhetoric of the period" (para. 3)—because he felt that the most common means of persuasion of his time was violence, such as was then being used in Russia and Italy and would soon be used in Germany and Spain. "Rhetoric is the cemetery of human realities," he continues, implying that people have ceased listening to reason and argument and have given themselves over to a mass movement that listens to nothing but the call for action.

Yet, Ortega's rhetoric is careful and powerful in its own way. His concern is for us to take a close look at the nature of the state and its powers over us. In this sense, he is sympathetic to the very issues that motivate Hannah Arendt in her examination of the power of the state (p. 121).

Ortega begins his essay with a simple definition: "the mass is that part which does not act of itself" (para. 1). He goes on to say that the nature of the mass is such that it must be directed by "superior minorities." This first paragraph explains the implications of these statements, which could easily be misunderstood. The ways in which the minority must be superior are implied; he does not specifically state them. His definition of the mass is simple enough; it is what we once called the "common man."

Ortega's method depends on definition and the examination of the elements of that definition. But it also depends on the analysis of examples and a review of some of the historical circumstances that might shed light on his concept of the revolution of the masses. In paragraph 5, he reviews the development of the modern state. European states were small and fragmented in the eighteenth century, while the industrialization of the nineteenth century produced more powerful and more populous states. Ortega specifically points to the emergence in the nineteenth century of a large middle class with talent and a skill for organization.

Using an extended metaphor (para. 5), Ortega talks about the "ship of State" and suggests that the metaphor was invented by the bourgeoisie because they felt a new "oceanic" power in the concept of nationhood. In his review of the history of the state, Ortega points to its early limitations in terms of soldiers, bureaucracy, and wealth. However, the revolutions of 1798 in France and 1848 in various European countries came at a time when the population was much larger than it had been in the Middle Ages or the Renaissance. By the mid-nineteenth century, in other words, the middle class had enlarged and the mass of people was vastly larger than at any earlier time.

The relationship between civilization and the state, which is its product, is another issue Ortega examines. His perception is that the mass, feeling it *is* the state, resists the "creative minority" in anything that disturbs the status quo. What Ortega feared most was that the state would overwhelm society—or, as he says, "Then the State gets the upper hand and society has to begin to live for the State" (para. 14). As an example, he points to the fascist government of Italy and Mussolini's declaration, "All for the State; nothing outside the State; nothing against the State" (para. 15). Then, Ortega paradoxically claims that Mussolini achieved his end by using precisely "the ideas and the forces he [was] combating: by liberal democracy." This is probably the most alarming part of his message.

PREREADING QUESTIONS: WHAT TO READ FOR

The following prereading questions may help you anticipate key issues in the discussion of Ortega y Gasset's "The Greatest Danger, the State." Keeping them in mind during your first reading of the selection should help focus your attention.

- Who is "the mass" and who is "the minority"?
- What are the dangers Ortega sees arising from the enlarged mass of modern society?
- How does the state threaten society?

The Greatest Danger, the State

In a right ordering of public affairs, the mass[1] is that part which   1
does not act of itself. Such is its mission. It has come into the world
in order to be directed, influenced, represented, organized—even in

_____
[1] **mass** The collective population.

order to cease being mass, or at least to aspire to this. But it has not come into the world to do all this by itself. It needs to submit its life to a higher court, formed of the superior minorities. The question as to who are these superior individuals may be discussed ad libitum,[2] but that without them, whoever they be, humanity would cease to preserve its essentials is something about which there can be no possible doubt, though Europe spend a century with its head under its wing, ostrich-fashion, trying if she can to avoid seeing such a plain truth. For we are not dealing with an opinion based on facts more or less frequent and probable, but on a law of social "physics," much more immovable than the laws of Newton's physics. The day when a genuine philosophy[3] once more holds sway in Europe—it is the one thing that can save her—that day she will once again realize that man, whether he like it or no, is a being forced by his nature to seek some higher authority. If he succeeds in finding it of himself, he is a superior man; if not, he is a mass-man and must receive it from his superiors.

For the mass to claim the right to act of itself is then a rebellion 2 against its own destiny, and because that is what it is doing at present, I speak of the rebellion of the masses. For, after all, the one thing that can substantially and truthfully be called rebellion is that which consists in not accepting one's own destiny, in rebelling against one's self. The rebellion of the archangel Lucifer would not have been less if, instead of striving to be God—which was not his destiny—he had striven to be the lowest of the angels—equally not his destiny. (If Lucifer had been a Russian, like Tolstoi,[4] he would perhaps have preferred this latter form of rebellion, none the less against God than the other more famous one.)

When the mass acts on its own, it does so only in one way, for it 3 has no other: it lynches. It is not altogether by chance that lynch law comes from America, for America is, in a fashion, the paradise of the masses. And it will cause less surprise, nowadays, when the masses triumph, that violence should triumph and be made the one *ratio*, the one doctrine. It is now some time since I called attention to this

---

[2] **ad libitum** As one desires.

[3] For philosophy to rule, it is not necessary that philosophers be the rulers—as Plato at first wished—nor even for rulers to be philosophers—as was his later, more modest, wish. Both these things are, strictly speaking, most fatal. For philosophy to rule, it is sufficient for it to exist; that is to say, for the philosophers to be philosophers. For nearly a century past, philosophers have been everything but that—politicians, pedagogues, men of letters, and men of science. [Ortega's note]

[4] **Count Leo Tolstoy (1828–1910)** Author of *War and Peace*.

advance of violence as a normal condition.[5] To-day it has reached its full development, and this is a good symptom, because it means that automatically the descent is about to begin. To-day violence is the rhetoric of the period, the empty rhetorician has made it his own. When a reality of human existence has completed its historic course, has been shipwrecked and lies dead, the waves throw it up on the shores of rhetoric, where the corpse remains for a long time. Rhetoric is the cemetery of human realities, or at any rate a Home for the Aged. The reality itself is survived by its name, which, though only a word, is after all at least a word and preserves something of its magic power.

But though it is not impossible that the prestige of violence as a   4
cynically established rule has entered on its decline, we shall still con-
tinue under that rule, though in another form. I refer to the gravest danger now threatening European civilization. Like all other dangers that threaten it, this one is born of civilization itself. More than that, it constitutes one of its glories: it is the State as we know it to-day. We are confronted with a replica of what we said . . . about science: the fertility of its principles brings about a fabulous progress, but this inevitably imposes specialization, and specialization threatens to strangle science.

The same thing is happening with the State. Call to mind what the   5
State was at the end of the eighteenth century in all European nations. Quite a small affair! Early capitalism and its industrial organizations, in which the new, rationalized technique triumphs for the first time, had brought a commencement of increase in society. A new social class appeared, greater in numbers and power than the pre-existing: the middle class. This astute middle class possessed one thing, above and before all: talent, practical talent. It knew how to organize and discipline, how to give continuity and consistency to its efforts. In the midst of it, as in an ocean, the "ship of State" sailed its hazardous course. The ship of State is a metaphor re-invented by the bourgeoisie, which felt itself oceanic, omnipotent, pregnant with storms. That ship was, as we said, a very small affair: it had hardly any soldiers, bureau-crats, or money. It had been built in the Middle Ages by a class of men very different from the bourgeois—the nobles, a class admirable for their courage, their gifts of leadership, their sense of responsibility. Without them the nations of Europe would not now be in existence. But with all those virtues of the heart, the nobles were, and always have been, lacking in virtues of the head. Of limited intelligence, sentimental, instinctive, intuitive—in a word, "irrational." Hence

---

[5] Vide *España Invertebrada,* 1912. [Ortega's note]

they were unable to develop any technique, a thing which demands rationalization. They did not invent gunpowder. Incapable of inventing new arms, they allowed the bourgeois, who got it from the East or somewhere else, to utilize gunpowder and automatically to win the battle against the warrior noble, the "caballero," stupidly covered in iron so that he could hardly move in the fight, and who had never imagined that the eternal secret of warfare consists not so much in the methods of defense as in those of attack, a secret which was to be rediscovered by Napoleon.[6]

As the State is a matter of technique—of public order and administration—the "ancien régime" reaches the end of the seventeenth century with a very weak State, harassed on all sides by a widespread social revolt. The disproportion between State power and social power at this time is such that, comparing the situation then with that of the time of Charlemagne,[7] the eighteenth-century State appears degenerate. The Carolingian State was of course much less powerful than the State of Louis XVI,[8] but, on the other hand, the society surrounding it was entirely lacking in strength.[9] The enormous disproportion between social strength and the strength of public power made possible the Revolution, the revolutions—up to 1848.

---

[6] We owe to Ranke this simple picture of the great historic change by which for the supremacy of the nobles is substituted the predominance of the bourgeois; but of course its symbolic geometric outlines require no little filling-in in order to be completely true. Gunpowder was known from time immemorial. The invention by which a tube was charged with it was due to someone in Lombardy. Even then it was not efficacious until the invention of the cast cannon-ball. The "nobles" used firearms to a small extent, but they were too dear for them. It was only the bourgeois armies, with their better economic organization, that could employ them on a large scale. It remains, however, literally true that the nobles, represented by the medieval type of army of the Burgundians, were definitely defeated by the new army, not professional but bourgeois, formed by the Swiss. Their primary force lay in the new discipline and the new rationalism of tactics. [Ortega's note]

[7] **Charlemagne or Charles the Great (742–814)** First of the medieval emperors.

[8] **Louis XVI (1754–1793)** King of France executed during the French Revolution.

[9] It would be worthwhile insisting on this point and making clear that the epoch of absolute monarchies in Europe has coincided with very weak States. How is this to be explained? Why, if the State was all-powerful, "absolute," did it not make itself stronger? One of the causes is that indicated, the incapacity—technical, organizing, bureaucratic—of the aristocracies of blood. But this is not enough. Besides that, it also happened that the absolute State and those aristocracies *did not want to aggrandize the State at the expense of society in general*. Contrary to the common belief, the absolute State instinctively respects society much more than our democratic State, which is more intelligent but has less sense of historic responsibility. [Ortega's note]

But with the Revolution the middle class took possession of public   7
power and applied their undeniable qualities to the State, and in little
more than a generation created a powerful State, which brought revolutions to an end. Since 1848, that is to say, since the beginning of
the second generation of bourgeois governments, there have been no
genuine revolutions in Europe. Not assuredly because there were no
motives for them, but because there were no means. Public power
was brought to the level of social power. *Good-bye for ever to Revo-*
lutions! The only thing now possible in Europe is their opposite: the
coup d'état.[10] Everything which in following years tried to look like
a revolution was only a coup d'état in disguise.

In our days the State has come to be a formidable machine   8
which works in marvelous fashion; of wonderful efficiency by reason of the quantity and precision of its means. Once it is set up in
the midst of society, it is enough to touch a button for its enormous
levers to start working and exercise their overwhelming power on
any portion whatever of the social framework.

The contemporary State is the easiest seen and best-known   9
product of civilization. And it is an interesting revelation when one
takes note of the attitude that mass-man adopts before it. He sees it,
admires it, knows that *there it is,* safeguarding his existence; but he
is not conscious of the fact that it is a human creation invented by
certain men and upheld by certain virtues and fundamental qualities
which the men of yesterday had and which may vanish into air to-
morrow. Furthermore, the mass-man sees in the State an anonymous power, and feeling himself, like it, anonymous, he believes
that the State is something of his own. Suppose that in the public
life of a country some difficulty, conflict, or problem presents itself,
the mass-man will tend to demand that the State intervene immediately and undertake a solution directly with its immense and unassailable resources.

This is the gravest danger that to-day threatens civilization: State   10
intervention; the absorption of all spontaneous social effort by the
State, that is to say, of spontaneous historical action, which in the long
run sustains, nourishes, and impels human destinies. When the mass
suffers any ill-fortune or simply feels some strong appetite, its great
temptation is that permanent, sure possibility of obtaining everything—
without effort, struggle, doubt, or risk—merely by touching a button
and setting the mighty machine in motion. The mass says to itself,
"*L'Etat, c'est moi,*"[11] which is a complete mistake. The State is the mass

---

[10] **coup d'état** Seizing the government, usually by military means.
[11] **"L'Etat, c'est moi"** "I am the State," attributed to Napoleon and Louis XIV.

only in the sense in which it can be said of two men that they are identical because neither of them is named John. The contemporary State and the mass coincide only in being anonymous. But the mass-man does in fact believe that he is the State, and he will tend more and more to set its machinery working on whatsoever pretext, to crush beneath it any creative minority which disturbs it—disturbs it in any order of things: in politics, in ideas, in industry.

The result of this tendency will be fatal. Spontaneous social   11
action will be broken up over and over again by State intervention; no new seed will be able to fructify. Society will have to live *for* the State, man *for* the governmental machine. And as, after all, it is only a machine whose existence and maintenance depend on the vital supports around it, the State, after sucking out the very marrow of society, will be left bloodless, a skeleton, dead with that rusty death of machinery, more gruesome than the death of a living organism.

Such was the lamentable fate of ancient civilization. No doubt the   12
imperial State created by the Julii and the Claudii[12] was an admirable machine, incomparably superior as a mere structure to the old republican State of the patrician families. But, by a curious coincidence, hardly had it reached full development when the social body began to decay.

Already in the times of the Antonines (second century), the State   13
overbears society with its anti-vital supremacy. Society begins to be enslaved, to be unable to live except *in the service of the State*. The whole of life is bureaucratized. What results? The bureaucratization of life brings about its absolute decay in all orders. Wealth diminishes, births are few. Then the State, in order to attend to its own needs, forces on still more the bureaucratization of human existence. This bureaucratization to the second power is the militarization of society. The State's most urgent need is its apparatus of war, its army. Before all the State is the producer of security (that security, be it remembered, of which the mass-man is born). Hence, above all, an army. The Severi,[13] of African origin, militarize the world. Vain task! Misery increases, women are every day less fruitful, even soldiers are lacking. After the time of the Severi, the army had to be recruited from foreigners.

Is the paradoxical, tragic process of Statism now realized? Soci-   14
ety, that it may live better, creates the State as an instrument. Then the State gets the upper hand and society has to begin to live for the

---

[12]**Julius Caesar and Tiberius Claudius Nero** Roman emperors and both dictators.
[13]**Severi** The Roman army of Emperor Septimus Severus (193–211).

State.[14] But for all that the State is still composed of the members of that society. But soon these do not suffice to support it, and it has to call in foreigners: first Dalmatians, then Germans. These foreigners take possession of the State, and the rest of society, the former populace, has to live as their slaves—slaves of people with whom they have nothing in common. That is what State intervention leads to: the people are converted into fuel to feed the mere machine which is the State. The skeleton eats up the flesh around it. The scaffolding becomes the owner and tenant of the house.

When this is realized, it rather confounds one to hear Mussolini   15
heralding as an astounding discovery just made in Italy, the formula: "All for the State; nothing outside the State; nothing against the State." This alone would suffice to reveal in Fascism a typical movement of mass-men. Mussolini found a State admirably built up—not by him, but precisely by the ideas and the forces he is combating: by liberal democracy. He confines himself to using it ruthlessly, and, without entering now into a detailed examination of his work, it is indisputable that the results obtained up to the present cannot be compared with those obtained in political and administrative working by the liberal State. If he has succeeded in anything it is so minute, so little visible, so lacking in substance as with difficulty to compensate for the accumulation of the abnormal powers which enable him to make use of that machine to its full extent.

Statism is the higher form taken by violence and direct action   16
when these are set up as standards. Through and by means of the State, the anonymous machine, the masses act for themselves. The nations of Europe have before them a period of great difficulties in their internal life, supremely arduous problems of law, economics, and public order. Can we help feeling that under the rule of the masses the State will endeavor to crush the independence of the individual and the group, and thus definitely spoil the harvest of the future?

A concrete example of this mechanism is found in one of the   17
most alarming phenomena of the last thirty years: the enormous increase in the police force of all countries. The increase of population has inevitably rendered it necessary. However accustomed we may be to it, the terrible paradox should not escape our minds that the population of a great modern city, in order to move about peaceably and attend to its business, necessarily requires a police force to regulate the circulation. But it is foolishness for the party of "law and order" to imagine that these "forces of public authority" created to

---

[14] Recall the last words of Septimus Severus to his sons: "Remain united, pay the soldiers, and take no heed of the rest." [Ortega's note]

preserve order are always going to be content to preserve the order that that party desires. Inevitably they will end by themselves defining and deciding on the order they are going to impose—which, naturally, will be that which suits them best.

It might be well to take advantage of our touching on this matter to observe the different reaction to a public need manifested by different types of society. When, about 1800, the new industry began to create a type of man—the industrial worker—more criminally inclined than traditional types, France hastened to create a numerous police force. Towards 1810 there occurs in England, for the same reasons, an increase in criminality, and the English suddenly realize that they have no police. The Conservatives are in power. What will they do? Will they establish a police force? Nothing of the kind. They prefer to put up with crime, as well as they can. "People are content to let disorder alone, considering it the price they pay for liberty." "In Paris," writes John William Ward,[15] "they have an admirable police force, but they pay dear for its advantages. I prefer to see, every three or four years, half a dozen people getting their throats cut in the Ratcliffe Road, than to have to submit to domiciliary visits, to spying, and to all the machinations of Fouché."[16] Here we have two opposite ideas of the State. The Englishman demands that the State should have limits set to it.

18

---

[15] **John William Ward (1781–1833)** British politician and the first Earl of Dudley. He served as Secretary of State for Foreign Affairs for one year.
[16] **Joseph Fouché (1763–1820)** Napoleon's chief of security, essentially a policeman.

QUESTIONS FOR CRITICAL READING

1. To what extent do you agree with Ortega regarding the rise in the number of police in modern industrialized society? In paragraph 18, Ortega contrasts two approaches to the state's dealing with crime and police. Which does your nation choose?
2. What does it mean for the state to get the upper hand and for society then to have to live for the state?
3. Do you agree that the "State's most urgent need is its apparatus of war, its army" (para. 13)?
4. Is your state, as you perceive it, stronger or weaker than your society?

SUGGESTIONS FOR CRITICAL WRITING

1. Ortega claims that when the mass operates on its own it has only one choice: it lynches. What evidence have you in terms of your

personal observation or your observation of events via the media, such as unfolded during Hurricane Katrina in New Orleans in 2005 or the Los Angeles riots in 1992, when people acted as a mass without leadership? Can you support Ortega's view, or do you find yourself rejecting it?

2. Assuming that Ortega is correct in saying that the mass needs to submit to a superior minority, what kind of minority would that have to be in order for you to be comfortable in such a state? Does Ortega seem to be describing a democratic state when he posits a superior minority? In what ways could a minority be superior? Is there any way to avoid producing a superior minority in society?

3. Is it true that when the mass takes control violence becomes the only truly persuasive force in the state? Have you seen any evidence that would support that view? Examine your perception of the state in terms of the persuasiveness of its message. What persuades you to be a good citizen? To what extent do you feel you serve the state? To what extent do you feel the state serves you? Do you sense that the mass has taken control of the state?

4. Ortega says that people are forced by nature to "seek some higher authority" and that those who find it in themselves are destined to be the superior minority, while those who do not find it are destined to be part of the mass. How reasonable is this view? Is it really clear that people naturally seek a higher authority? Do you think people need a higher authority in their lives? What would be an example of such an authority? How could people find it within themselves?

5. Why is the state the source of the greatest danger? What is Ortega fearful of in this selection? Do you find yourself in agreement with his concern that the state may at times enslave society? Does the state, as an abstract entity, naturally move toward asking us to serve it rather than assuming that it exists to serve us? What are the dangers here and how can you or your friends function in a way that would minimize the threat?

6. **CONNECTIONS** Andrew Carnegie, in his essay "The Gospel of Wealth?" (p. 387), also makes it clear that he thinks the general mass of citizens are better off if economic decisions are made for them by people who have succeeded economically. At first glance, Carnegie's and Ortega's beliefs might appear to be similar, but that is not the case. After carefully reading and analyzing Carnegie's essay, try to establish what the basic differences are between his views and those of Ortega.

7. **CONNECTIONS** After reading Carl Becker's "Ideal Democracy" (p. 101), can you clarify the anxiety that Ortega has regarding the tyranny of the majority? Does Becker warn us about the dangers of democracy in a way that helps make Ortega's fears understandable? The democratic governments of Italy and Germany were converted into tyrannical dictatorships with astonishing speed. Becker talks about democracy not doing well in a destitute society, which may explain in part the failure of those democracies. Does Ortega leave much room for economic concerns in his examination of the mass?

8. **SEEING CONNECTIONS**   How would Ortega describe the action in Delacroix's *Liberty Leading the People* (p. 18)? Is there a clear sense that the leadership of a superior minority is at work in the painting? Is there a clear sense that the mass of people is represented in the painting? Would Ortega have praised this painting or condemned it on moral grounds? Would he have thought of the action depicted as a revolution or a coup d'état?

CARL BECKER
Ideal Democracy

CARL LOTUS BECKER (1873–1945), a distinguished historian, was John Wendell Anderson Professor of History at Cornell University for most of his professional life. He was born in Iowa, in Blackhawk County, and studied at the University of Wisconsin–Madison, where he worked with one of the most distinguished and influential theorists of American history, Frederick Jackson Turner. Turner's theories about the effect of the frontier on shaping the development and character of the United States became central to the way historians viewed the nation's growth. Becker took his doctorate at Columbia University, where he worked with James Harvey Robinson, one of the founders of the movement known as "the new history."

The new history movement, of which Becker was one of the most notable members, broadened the meaning of history to include more than simply the political events of the past. The scientific, sociological, cultural, and intellectual achievements of society became central to historians as a result of Robinson's and Becker's work. Robinson and Becker established the New School for Social Research in New York City and Robinson became its first president.

Becker's early work focused on the beginnings of the U.S. experiment with democracy. He saw that the American Revolution was not only about independence but also about changing the basic form of government and abandoning the age-old institution of a king and court who governed without taking into account the will of the people. An early book, *The United States; an Experiment in Democracy* (1920), clarified his thinking on the nature of the Revolution and its purposes. He followed that with *The Declaration of Independence, a Study in the History of Political Ideas* (1922) and *The Struggle for Independence. Part 1: The Eve of the Revolution* (1926). The next

---

From *Modern Democracy*.

year he published *The Spirit of '76 and Other Essays*, with J. M. Clark and William E. Dodd.

Becker was president of the American Historical Association in 1931 when he delivered "Everyman His Own Historian," a speech that has resonated with historians ever since. In a very carefully reasoned discussion, Becker proposed a view that seemed heretical to most of his audience. What he suggested is that it is difficult to define history in a way that makes it as absolute and as specific as a fact. In his speech, he contrasts facts and interpretations of facts in such a manner as to conclude that everyone brings personal values, opinions, commitments, and views to all history and, thus, everyone conceives of history in his or her own way. History, in other words, is not absolute, but relative. This was a revolutionary view, anticipating some of the postmodern thought of our own time.

While his scholarly work centered on the founding of the United States, especially the philosophical underpinnings of the signatories of the Declaration of Independence and their commitment to the values that are expressed in that document, Becker's best-known work is *The Heavenly City of the Eighteenth-Century Philosophers* (1932).

The founders of the United States—such as Jefferson, Adams, Franklin, Hamilton, and others—were themselves eighteenth-century thinkers, so Becker's analysis of the thought, political and otherwise, of the French and English philosophers who established reason as their guide was central to his lifelong concerns for the American experiment. When he delivered the lectures at Yale University that eventually became his book on eighteenth-century philosophers, the world faced many menaces. In 1932, the Great Depression threatened the fate of all capitalist nations. Communism on one side and Fascism on another had both created dictatorships that endangered liberal thinkers everywhere. Both of these forces were vying for control of the political structure of the United States at the time of its greatest economic weakness.

Becker's intent in his book was to show how the philosophical roots of the American Revolution's determination to create a democracy were not only deep but also strong. The essentially humanistic thought of the eighteenth-century Enlightenment rejected the idea of a "city of God," as proposed in the Middle Ages, just as it rejected the idea of a golden age of Rome or Greece, as proposed in the Renaissance. The Enlightenment instead established reason as one's guide and a humanitarian principle as one's goal. *The Heavenly City of the Eighteenth-Century Philosophers* became widely known and is still read with considerable respect today.

"Ideal Democracy" is the first of three Page-Barbour lectures delivered at the University of Virginia in 1940 and gathered into a book simply titled *Modern Democracy* (1941). Faced with the prospect of a major European war, Becker had begun to rethink some of his positions as expressed in his speech to the American Historical Association and moved toward a less relativistic position. He felt that moral principles should be central to anyone's sense of history, just as they are central to anyone's conception of humanism. His views on ideal democracy are just that, ideal. He followed that lecture with others titled "The Reality" and "The Dilemma." He lived in difficult and threatening times, much like those of the eighteenth-century men who founded our nation.

Becker's Rhetoric

Becker uses a number of rhetorical approaches to clarify his views. The overarching technique is that of definition. His purpose in the entire lecture is to make evident the nature of democracy. He compares it with forms of government that depend on autocracy and the leadership of the few rather than the many. His definition of *democracy* concludes that "[a] democratic government has always meant one in which the citizens, or a sufficient number of them to represent more or less effectively the common will, freely act from time to time, and according to established forms, to appoint or recall the magistrates and to enact or revoke the laws by which the community is governed" (para. 5). But then, he ends Part I of the lecture with a cautionary observation about the fact that in "our time . . . democracy as thus defined has suffered an astounding decline in prestige" (para. 6). We suffer a rhetorical shock finding that once a definition has been produced we fear it may not define our present condition.

Among Becker's other devices is the rhetorical question. He asks at the end of Part I, "What are we to think of this sudden reversal in fortune and prestige? How explain it? What to do about it?" (para. 7). These are difficult questions and not necessarily answered by what follows. They are for us to ponder. Becker uses a form of enumeration by telling us that to survive democracy needs certain conditions, each of which he describes for us: the need for communication (para. 11), economic security (para. 12), industrial prosperity (para. 13), ending by saying, "Democracy is in some sense an economic luxury" (para. 13). Added to these conditions, Becker reminds us that the citizens themselves must possess qualities that make democracy work: they must be "capable of managing their own affairs" (para. 14); be able to reconcile conflicts of interest; be rational; and, finally, be "men of good will."

A further rhetorical device Becker uses is comparison, as when he compares a modern democracy with a Greek city-state, such as

Athens, the birthplace of modern democracy (para. 17). The comparison with a private association—which Athens is more like than is our nation—is crucial because the private association usually contains people of similar status, character, and ambitions because it is self-selective. In a Greek city-state, which was small by modern standards, the citizens were linked by ethnicity, clan, and family. But in a modern democracy diversity is the norm, especially in a nation such as the United States was when it was first born. Becker points out the general success of democracy in "new" countries, as opposed to countries like France, England, and Germany.

Using the topic circumstance, Becker reviews history in Part III of the lecture as a way of exploring the question of progress. He describes the inclination of people to postulate utopias, ideal worlds that contrast with the desperate reality they experience, a result, he says, of the pessimism that haunted pre-Christian Europe (para. 22). The achievement of the humanistic eighteenth century made the modern concept of progress possible. As he says, "the eighteenth-century world view, making man the measure of all things, mitigated if it did not destroy this sharp contrast between authority and obedience. God still reigned but he did not govern. He had, so to speak, granted his subjects a constitution and authorized them to interpret it as they would in the supreme court of reason" (para. 27).

Becker ends with testimonials from two authorities backing his basic views. First is a quotation from John Stuart Mill praising his own father's faith in reason as a guide to happiness (para. 30); that is followed by a comment from historian James Bryce clarifying his ideal democracy (para. 31).

It is not surprising that the very issues Becker worries over regarding an ideal democracy in 1941 are just as much of a concern today, despite the obvious changes in our material circumstances.

PREREADING QUESTIONS: WHAT TO READ FOR

The following prereading questions may help you anticipate key issues in the discussion of Carl Becker's "Ideal Democracy." Keeping them in mind during your first reading of the selection should help focus your attention.

- What is Becker's fullest definition of *democracy*?
- What conditions are necessary for a democratic form of government to flourish?
- What qualities must citizens of a democracy possess if democracy is to take root and survive?
- What are the aims and goals of good government, and how do they relate to the idea of democracy?

Ideal Democracy

I

I often find it difficult, when invited to speak before a university   1
audience, to hit upon a proper subject. But the invitation to deliver
the Page-Barbour lectures at the University of Virginia relieved me of
that difficulty: the invitation itself, automatically so to speak, conveniently laid the proper subject in my lap. For the University of Virginia
is inseparably associated with the name of its famous founder; and
no subject, it seemed to me, could be more appropriate for a historian on this occasion than one which had some connection with the
ideas or the activities of Thomas Jefferson.

Even so, you will rightly think, I had a sufficiently wide choice.   2
Jefferson entertained so many ideas, was engaged in so many activities! There was, indeed, scarcely anything of human interest that was
alien to his curious and far-ranging intelligence. Nevertheless, his
name is always associated with a certain general idea, a certain ideal.
In devising his own epitaph, Jefferson himself selected, out of all his
notable achievements, only three for which he wished to be especially
remembered. *Here was buried Thomas Jefferson, author of the Declaration
of American Independence, of the Statute of Virginia for Religious Freedom, and Father of the University of Virginia.* These were the things for
which he wished to be remembered. Taken together and in their
implications, they are the things for which he has been remembered:
that is to say, they conveniently symbolize that way of looking at man
and the life of man, that social philosophy, which we always think
of when we think of him. The word which best denotes this social
philosophy is democracy. I feel sure, therefore, that here, in this
famous center of learning, you will not think it inappropriate for me
to say something, something relevant if that be at all possible, about
democracy—a subject so close to Jefferson's heart and so insistently
present in all our minds today.

Democracy, like *liberty* or *science* or *progress,* is a word with which   3
we are all so familiar that we rarely take the trouble to ask what we
mean by it. It is a term, as the devotees of semantics say, which has
no "referent"—there is no precise or palpable thing or object which
we all think of when the word is pronounced. On the contrary, it is
a word which connotes different things to different people, a kind of
conceptual Gladstone bag which, with a little manipulation, can be
made to accommodate almost any collection of social facts we may
wish to carry about in it. In it we can as easily pack a dictatorship as
any other form of government. We have only to stretch the concept
to include any form of government supported by a majority of the
people, for whatever reasons and by whatever means of expressing
assent, and before we know it the empire of Napoleon, the Soviet

regime of Stalin, and the Fascist systems of Mussolini and Hitler are all safely in the bag. But if this is what we mean by democracy, then virtually all forms of government are democratic, since virtually all governments, except in times of revolution, rest upon the explicit or implicit consent of the people. In order to discuss democracy intelligently it will be necessary, therefore, to define it, to attach to the word a sufficiently precise meaning to avoid the confusion which is not infrequently the chief result of such discussions.

All human institutions, we are told, have their ideal forms laid   4 away in heaven, and we do not need to be told that the actual institutions conform but indifferently to these ideal counterparts. It would be possible then to define democracy either in terms of the ideal or in terms of the real form—to define it as government of the people, by the people, for the people; or to define it as government of the people, by the politicians, for whatever pressure groups can get their interests taken care of. But as a historian I am naturally disposed to be satisfied with the meaning which, in the history of politics, men have commonly attributed to the word—a meaning, needless to say, which derives partly from the experience and partly from the aspirations of mankind. So regarded, the term democracy refers primarily to a form of government, and it has always meant government by the many as opposed to government by the one—government by the people as opposed to government by a tyrant, a dictator, or an absolute monarch. This is the most general meaning of the word as men have commonly understood it.

In this antithesis there are, however, certain implications, always   5 tacitly understood, which give a more precise meaning to the term. Peisistratus,[1] for example, was supported by a majority of the people, but his government was never regarded as a democracy for all that. Caesar's power derived from a popular mandate, conveyed through established republican forms, but that did not make his government any the less a dictatorship. Napoleon called his government a democratic empire, but no one, least of all Napoleon himself, doubted that he had destroyed the last vestiges of the democratic republic. Since the Greeks first used the term, the essential test of democratic government has always been this: the souce of political authority must be and remain in the people and not in the ruler. A democratic government has always meant one in which the citizens, or a sufficient number of them to represent more or less effectively the common will, freely act from time to time, and according to established forms, to appoint or recall the magistrates and to enact or revoke the laws by which the

---

[1] **Peisistratus (605–525 B.C.)** In 560 B.C. made himself the tyrant of Athens.

community is governed. This I take to be the meaning which history has impressed upon the term democracy as a form of government. It is, therefore, the meaning which I attach to it in these lectures.

The most obvious political fact of our time is that democracy as thus defined has suffered an astounding decline in prestige. Fifty years ago it was not impossible to regard democratic government, and the liberties that went with it, as a permanent conquest of the human spirit. In 1886 Andrew Carnegie[2] published a book entitled *Triumphant Democracy*. Written without fear and without research, the book was not an achievement of the highest intellectual distinction perhaps; but the title at least expressed well enough the prevailing conviction—the conviction that democracy had fought the good fight, had won the decisive battles, and would inevitably, through its inherent merits, presently banish from the world the most flagrant political and social evils which from time immemorial had afflicted mankind. This conviction could no doubt be most easily entertained in the United States, where even the tradition of other forms of government was too remote and alien to color our native optimism. But even in Europe the downright skeptics, such as Lecky,[3] were thought to be perverse, and so hardheaded a historian as J. B. Bury[4] could proclaim with confidence that the long struggle for freedom of thought had finally been won.

I do not need to tell you that within a brief twenty years the prevailing optimism of that time has been quite dispelled. One European country after another has, willingly enough it seems, abandoned whatever democratic institutions it formerly enjoyed for some form of dictatorship. The spokesmen of Fascism and Communism announce with confidence that democracy, a sentimental aberration which the world has outgrown, is done for; and even the friends of democracy support it with declining conviction. They tell us that democracy, so far from being triumphant, is "at the cross roads" or "in retreat," and that its future is by no means assured. What are we to think of this sudden reversal in fortune and prestige? How explain it? What to do about it?

II

One of the presuppositions of modern thought is that institutions, in order to be understood, must be seen in relation to the conditions

---

[2] **Andrew Carnegie (1835–1919)** Scotch-born steel magnate, once the richest man in the world.

[3] **William Edward Hartpole Lecky (1838–1903)** Prominent Irish historian.

[4] **J. B. Bury (1861–1927)** Another prominent Irish historian.

of time and place in which they appear. It is a little difficult for us to look at democracy in this way. We are so immersed in its present fortunes that we commonly see it only as a "close-up," filling the screen to the exclusion of other things to which it is in fact related. In order to form an objective judgment of its nature and significance, we must therefore first of all get it in proper perspective. Let us then, in imagination, remove from the immediate present scene to some cool high place where we can survey at a glance five or six thousand years of history, and note the part which democracy has played in human civilization. The view, if we have been accustomed to take democratic institutions for granted, is a bit bleak and disheartening. For we see at once that in all this long time, over the habitable globe, the great majority of the human race has neither known nor apparently much cared for our favorite institutions.

Civilization was already old when democracy made its first notable 9 appearance among the small city-states of ancient Greece, where it flourished brilliantly for a brief century or two and then disappeared. At about the same time something that might be called democracy appeared in Rome and other Italian cities, but even in Rome it did not survive the conquest of the world by the Roman Republic, except as a form of local administration in the cities of the empire. In the twelfth and thirteenth centuries certain favorably placed medieval cities enjoyed a measure of self-government, but in most instances it was soon replaced by the dictatorship of military conquerors, the oligarchic control of a few families, or the encroaching power of autocratic kings. The oldest democracy of modern times is the Swiss Confederation, the next oldest is the Dutch Republic. Parliamentary government in England does not antedate the late seventeenth century, the great American experiment is scarcely older. Not until the nineteenth century did democratic government make its way in any considerable part of the world—in the great states of continental Europe, in South America, in Canada and Australia, in South Africa and Japan.

From this brief survey it is obvious that, taking the experience 10 of mankind as a test, democracy has as yet had but a limited and temporary success. There must be a reason for this significant fact. The reason is that democratic government is a species of social luxury, at best a delicate and precarious adventure which depends for success upon the validity of certain assumptions about the capacities and virtues of men, and upon the presence of certain material and intellectual conditions favorable to the exercise of these capacities and virtues. Let us take the material conditions first.

It is a striking fact that until recently democracy never flourished 11 except in very small states—for the most part in cities. It is true that in both the Persian and the Roman empires a measure of self-government was accorded to local communities, but only in respect to purely local affairs; in no large state as a whole was democratic government found to be practicable. One essential reason is that until recently the means of communication were too slow and uncertain to create the necessary solidarity of interest and similarity of information over large areas. The principle of representation was well enough known to the Greeks, but in practice it proved impracticable except in limited areas and for special occasions. As late as the eighteenth century it was still the common opinion that the republican form of government, although the best ideally, was unsuited to large countries, even to a country no larger than France. This was the view of Montesquieu,[5] and even of Rousseau.[6] The view persisted into the nineteenth century, and English conservatives, who were opposed to the extension of the suffrage in England, consoled themselves with the notion that the American Civil War would confirm it—would demonstrate that government by and for the people would perish, if not from off the earth at least from large countries. If their hopes were confounded the reason is that the means of communication, figuratively speaking, were making large countries small. It is not altogether fanciful to suppose that, but for the railroad and the telegraph, the United States would today be divided into many small republics maneuvering for advantage and employing war and diplomacy for maintaining an unstable balance of power.

If one of the conditions essential to the success of democratic government is mobility, ease of communication, another is a certain measure of economic security. Democracy does not flourish in communities on the verge of destitution. In ancient and medieval times democratic government appeared for the most part in cities, the centers of prosperity. Farmers in the early Roman Republic and in the Swiss Cantons were not wealthy to be sure, but equality of possessions and of opportunity gave them a certain economic security. In medieval cities political privilege was confined to the prosperous merchants and craftsmen, and in Athens and the later Roman Republic democratic government was found to be workable only on condition that the poor citizens were subsidized by the government or paid for attending the assemblies and the law courts. 12

In modern times democratic institutions have, generally speaking, been most successful in new countries, such as the United States, Canada, and Australia, where the conditions of life have been easy for the people; and in European countries more or less in proportion to their industrial prosperity. In European countries, indeed, there has 13

---

[5] **Montesquieu (1689–1755)** Important French thinker of the Enlightenment.
[6] **Jean-Jacques Rousseau (1712–1778)** French philosopher and political thinker of the Enlightenment (see p. 55).

been a close correlation between the development of the industrial revolution and the emergence of democratic institutions. Holland and England, the first countries to experience the industrial revolution, were the first also (apart from Switzerland, where certain peculiar conditions obtained) to adopt democratic institutions; and as the industrial revolution spread to France, Belgium, Germany, and Italy, these countries in turn adopted at least a measure of democratic government. Democracy is in some sense an economic luxury, and it may be said that in modern times it has been a function of the development of new and potentially rich countries, or of the industrial revolution which suddenly dowered Europe with unaccustomed wealth. Now that prosperity is disappearing round every next corner, democracy works less well than it did.

So much for the material conditions essential for the success of   14 democratic government. Supposing these conditions to exist, democratic government implies in addition the presence of certain capacities and virtues in its citizens. These capacities and virtues are bound up with the assumptions on which democracy rests, and are available only in so far as the assumptions are valid. The primary assumption of democratic government is that its citizens are capable of managing their own affairs. But life in any community involves a conflict of individual and class interests, and a corresponding divergence of opinion as to the measures to be adopted for the common good. The divergent opinions must be somehow reconciled, the conflict of interests somehow compromised. It must then be an assumption of democratic government that its citizens are rational creatures, sufficiently so at least to understand the interests in conflict; and it must be an assumption that they are men of good will, sufficiently so toward each other at least to make those concessions of individual and class interest required for effecting workable compromises. The citizens of a democracy should be, as Pericles[7] said the citizens of Athens were, if not all originators at least all sound judges of good policy.

These are what may be called the minimum assumptions and the   15 necessary conditions of democratic government anywhere and at any time. They may be noted to best advantage, not in any state, but in small groups within the state—in clubs and similar private associations of congenial and like-minded people united for a specific purpose. In such associations the membership is limited and select. The members are, or may easily become, all acquainted with each other. Everyone knows, or may easily find out, what is being done and who

---

[7] **Pericles (c. 495–429 B.C.)** Athenian hero of the Peloponnesian War and builder of the Acropolis.

is doing it. There will of course be differences of opinion, and there may be disintegrating squabbles and intrigues. But on the whole, ends and means being specific and well understood, the problems of government are few and superficial; there is plenty of time for discussion; and since intelligence and good will can generally be taken for granted there is the disposition to make reasonable concessions and compromises. The analogy must be taken for what it is worth. States may not be the mystical blind Molochs[8] of German philosophy, but any state is far more complex and intangible than a private association, and there is little resemblance between such associations and the democracies of modern times. Other things equal, the resemblance is closest in very small states, and it is in connection with the small city-states of ancient Greece that the resemblance can best be noted.

The Greek states were limited in size, not as is often thought   16
solely or even chiefly by the physiography of the country, but by some instinctive feeling of the Greek mind that a state is necessarily a natural association of people bound together by ties of kinship and a common tradition of rights and obligations. There must then, as Aristotle said, be a limit.

> For if the citizens of a state are to judge and distribute offices according to merit, they must know each other's characters; where they do not possess this knowledge, both the elections to offices and the decisions in the law courts will go wrong. Where the population is very large they are manifestly settled by haphazard, which clearly ought not to be. Besides, in overpopulous states foreigners and metics[9] will readily acquire citizenship, for who will find them out?

It obviously did not occur to Aristotle that metics and foreigners   17
should be free to acquire citizenship. It did not occur to him, or to any Greek of his time, or to the merchants of the self-governing medieval city, that a state should be composed of all the people inhabiting a given territory. A state was rather an incorporated body of people within, but distinct from, the population of the community.

Ancient and medieval democracies had thus something of the   18
character of a private association. They were, so to speak, purely pragmatic phenomena, arising under very special conditions, and regarded as the most convenient way of managing the affairs of people bound together by community of interest and for the achievement of specific ends. There is no suggestion in Aristotle that democracy (polity) is intrinsically a superior form of government, no suggestion that it derives from a special ideology of its own. If it rests upon any superiority other than convenience, it is the superiority which it shares with

---

[8] **Molochs** The forces of evil that demand obedience.
[9] **metics** Resident aliens.

any Greek state, that is to say, the superiority of Greek over barbarian civilization. In Aristotle's philosophy it is indeed difficult to find any clear-cut distinction between the democratic form of government and the state itself; the state, if it be worthy of the name, is always, what-ever the form of government, "the government of freemen and equals," and in any state it is always necessary that "the freemen who compose the bulk of the people should have absolute power in some things." In Aristotle's philosophy the distinction between good and bad in politics is not between good and bad types of government, but between the good and bad form of each type. Any type of government—monarchy, aristocracy, polity—is good provided the rulers aim at the good of all rather than at the good of the class to which they belong. From Aristotle's point of view neither democracy nor dictatorship is good or bad in itself, but only in the measure that it achieves, or fails to achieve, the aim of every good state, which is that "the inhabitants of it should be happy." It did not occur to Aristotle that democracy (polity), being in some special sense in harmony with the nature of man, was everywhere applicable, and therefore destined by fate or the gods to carry throughout the world a superior form of civilization.

It is in this respect chiefly that modern democracy differs from   19 earlier forms. It rests upon something more than the minimum assumptions. It is reinforced by a full-blown ideology which, by endowing the individual with natural and imprescriptible rights, sets the democratic form of government off from all others as the one which alone can achieve the good life. What then are the essential tenets of the modern democratic faith?

III

The liberal democratic faith, as expressed in the works of eigh-   20 teenth and early nineteenth-century writers, is one of the formulations of the modern doctrine of progress. It will be well, therefore, to note briefly the historical antecedents of that doctrine.

In the long history of man on earth there comes a time when he   21 remembers something of what has been, anticipates something that will be, knows the country he has traversed, wonders what lies beyond— the moment when he becomes aware of himself as a lonely, differen-tiated item in the world. Sooner or later there emerges for him the most devastating of all facts, namely, that in an indifferent universe which alone endures, he alone aspires, endeavors to attain, and attains only to be defeated in the end. From that moment his immediate experience ceases to be adequate, and he endeavors to project him-self beyond it by creating ideal worlds of semblance, Utopias of other time or place in which all has been, may be, or will be well.

In ancient times Utopia was most easily projected into the   22
unknown past, pushed back to the beginning of things—to the
time of P'an Ku[10] and the celestial emperors, to the Garden of Eden,
or the reign of King Chronos[11] when men lived like gods free from
toil and grief. From this happy state of first created things there had
obviously been a decline and fall, occasioned by disobedience and
human frailty, and decreed as punishment by fate or the angry gods.
The mind of man was therefore afflicted with pessimism, a sense of
guilt for having betrayed the divine purpose, a feeling of inadequacy
for bringing the world back to its original state of innocence and
purity. To men who felt insecure in a changing world, and helpless
in a world always changing for the worse, the future had little to
offer. It could be regarded for the most part only with resignation,
mitigated by individual penance or welldoing, or the hope of some
miraculous intervention by the gods, or the return of the god-like
kings, to set things right again, yet with little hope that from this setting right there would not be another falling away.

This pervasive pessimism was gradually dispelled in the Western   23
world, partly by the Christian religion, chiefly by the secular intellectual revolution occurring roughly between the fifteenth and the eighteenth centuries. The Christian religion gave assurance that the lost
golden age of the past would be restored for the virtuous in the future,
and by proclaiming the supreme worth of the individual in the eyes of
God enabled men to look forward with hope to the good life after
death in the Heavenly City. Meantime, the secular intellectual revolution, centering in the matter-of-fact study of history and science, gradually emancipated the minds of men from resignation to fate and the
angry gods. Accumulated knowledge of history, filling in time past
with a continuous succession of credible events, banished all lost
golden ages to the realm of myth, and enabled men to live without distress in a changing world since it could be regarded as not necessarily
changing for the worse. At the same time, a more competent observation and measurement of the action of material things disclosed an
outer world of nature, indifferent to man indeed, yet behaving, not as
the unpredictable sport of the gods, but in ways understandable to
human reason and therefore ultimately subject to man's control.

Thus the conditions were fulfilled which made it possible for men   24
to conceive of Utopia, neither as a lost golden age of the past nor as
a Heavenly City after death prepared by the gods for the virtuous, but
as a future state on earth of man's own devising. In a world of nature
that could be regarded as amenable to man's control, and in a world

---

[10] **P'an Ku** The first man in Chinese Taoist creation myths.
[11] **King Chronos** King of the lost island of Atlantis, according to Greek legend.

of changing social relations that need not be regarded as an inevitable decline and fall from original perfection, it was possible to formulate the modern doctrine of progress: the idea that, by deliberate intention and rational direction, men can set the terms and indefinitely improve the conditions of their mundane existence.

The eighteenth century was the moment in history when men   25 first fully realized the engaging implications of this resplendent idea, the moment when, not yet having been brought to the harsh appraisal of experience, it could be accepted with unclouded optimism. Never had the universe seemed less mysterious, more open and visible, more eager to yield its secrets to common-sense questions. Never had the nature of man seemed less perverse, or the mind of man more pliable to the pressure of rational persuasion. The essential reason for this confident optimism is that the marvels of scientific discovery disclosed to the men of that time a God who still functioned but was no longer angry. God the Father could be conceived as a beneficent First Cause who, having performed his essential task of creation, had withdrawn from the affairs of men, leaving them competently prepared and fully instructed for the task of achieving their own salvation. In one tremendous sentence Rousseau expressed the eighteenth-century world view of the universe and man's place in it. "Is it simple," he exclaimed, "is it natural that God should have gone in search of Moses in order to speak to Jean Jacques Rousseau?"

God had indeed spoken to Rousseau, he had spoken to all men,   26 but his revelation was contained, not in Holy Writ interpreted by Holy Church, but in the great Book of Nature which was open for all men to read. To this open book of nature men would go when they wanted to know what God had said to them. Here they would find recorded the laws of nature and of nature's God, disclosing a universe constructed according to a rational plan; and that men might read these laws aright they had been endowed with reason, a bit of the universal intelligence placed within the individual to make manifest to him the universal reason implicit in things and events. "Natural law," as Volney[12] so clearly and confidently put it, "is the regular and constant order of facts by which God rules the universe; the order which his wisdom presents to the sense and reason of men, to serve them as an equal and common rule of conduct, and to guide them, without distinction of race or sect, toward perfection and happiness." Thus God had devised a planned economy, and had endowed men with the capacity for managing it: to bring his ideas, his conduct, and his institutions into harmony with the universal laws of nature was man's simple allotted task.

---

[12] **Constantin-François de Chasseboeuf, comte de Volney (1757–1820)** French philosopher and historian.

At all times political theory must accommodate itself in some   27
fashion to the prevailing world view, and liberal-democratic political
theory was no exception to this rule. From time immemorial authority
and obedience had been the cardinal concepts both of the prevailing
world view and of political and social theory. From time immemorial
men had been regarded as subject to overruling authority—the
authority of the gods, and the authority of kings who were themselves gods, or descended from gods, or endowed with divine authority to rule in place of gods; and from time immemorial obedience to
such divine authority was thought to be the primary obligation of men.
Even the Greeks, who were so little afraid of their gods that they
could hobnob with them in the most friendly and engaging way,
regarded mortals as subject to them; and when they lost faith in the
gods they deified the state as the highest good and subordinated the
individual to it. But the eighteenth-century world view, making man
the measure of all things, mitigated if it did not destroy this sharp
contrast between authority and obedience. God still reigned but he
did not govern. He had, so to speak, granted his subjects a constitution and authorized them to interpret it as they would in the supreme
court of reason. Men were still subject to an overruling authority, but
the subjection could be regarded as voluntary because self-imposed,
and self-imposed because obedience was exacted by nothing more
oppressive than their own rational intelligence.

Liberal-democratic political theory readily accommodated itself   28
to this change in the world view. The voice of the people was now
identified with the voice of God, and all authority was derived from
it. The individual instead of the state or the prince was now deified and
endowed with imprescriptible rights; and since ignorance or neglect
of the rights of man was the chief cause of social evils, the first task
of political science was to define these rights, the second to devise a
form of government suited to guarantee them. The imprescriptible
rights of man were easily defined, since they were self-evident: "All
men are created equal, [and] are endowed by their Creator with certain inalienable rights, among which are life, liberty, and the pursuit
of happiness." From this it followed that all just governments would
remove those artificial restraints which impaired these rights, thereby
liberating those natural impulses with which God had endowed the
individual as a guide to thought and conduct. In the intellectual realm,
freedom of thought and the competition of diverse opinion would
disclose the truth, which all men, being rational creatures, would
progressively recognize and willingly follow. In the economic realm,
freedom of enterprise would disclose the natural aptitudes of each
individual, and the ensuing competition of interests would stimulate
effort, and thereby result in the maximum of material advantage for
all. Liberty of the individual from social constraint thus turned out to

be not only an inherent natural right but also a preordained natural mechanism for bringing about the material and moral progress of mankind. Men had only to follow reason and self-interest: something not themselves, God and Nature, would do whatever else was necessary for righteousness.

Thus modern liberal-democracy is associated with an ideology   29 which rests upon something more than the minimum assumptions essential to any democratic government. It rests upon a philosophy of universally valid ends and means. Its fundamental assumption is the worth and dignity and creative capacity of the individual, so that the chief aim of government is the maximum of individual self-direction, the chief means to that end the minimum of compulsion by the state. Ideally considered, means and ends are conjoined in the concept of freedom: freedom of thought, so that the truth may prevail; freedom of occupation, so that careers may be open to talent; freedom of self-government, so that no one may be compelled against his will.

In the possibility of realizing this ideal the prophets and protago-   30 nists of democracy exhibited an unquestioned faith. If their faith seems to us somewhat naive, the reason is that they placed a far greater reliance upon the immediate influence of good will and rational discussion in shaping the conduct of men than it is possible for us to do. This difference can be conveniently noted in a passage from the *Autobiography* of John Stuart Mill,[13] in which he describes his father's extraordinary faith in two things—representative government and complete freedom of discussion.

> So complete was my father's reliance on the influence of reason over the minds of mankind, whenever it was allowed to reach them, that he felt as if all would be gained if the whole population were taught to read, if all sorts of opinions were allowed to be addressed to them by word and writing, and if by means of the suffrage they could nominate a legislature to give effect to the opinions they adopted. He thought that when the legislature no longer represented a class interest, it would aim at the general interest, honestly and with adequate wisdom; since the people would be sufficiently under the guidance of educated intelligence, to make in general good choice of persons to represent them, and having done so to leave to those whom they had chosen a liberal discretion. Accordingly, aristocratic rule, the government of the few in any of its shapes, being in his eyes the only thing that stood between mankind and the administration of its affairs by the best wisdom to be found amongst them, was the object of his sternest disapprobation, and a democratic suffrage the principle article of his political creed.[14]

---

[13] **John Stuart Mill (1806–1873)** English philosopher and champion of utilitarianism, which aims to provide the greatest good to the greatest number.

[14] *Autobiography* (Columbia Press, 1924), p. 74. [Becker's note]

The beliefs of James Mill were shared by the little group of 31
Philosophical Radicals who gathered about him. They were, indeed,
the beliefs of all those who in the great crusading days placed their
hopes in democratic government as a panacea for injustice and
oppression. The actual working of democratic government, as these
devoted enthusiasts foresaw it, the motives that would inspire men
and the objects they would pursue in that ideal democracy which so
many honest men have cherished and fought for, have never been
better described than by James Bryce[15] in his *Modern Democracies*. In
this ideal democracy, says Bryce,

> the average citizen will give close and constant attention to public
> affairs, recognizing that this is his interest as well as his duty. He
> will try to comprehend the main issues of policy, bringing to them
> an independent and impartial mind, which thinks first not of its
> own but of the general interest. If, owing to inevitable differences of
> opinion as to what are the measures needed for the general welfare,
> parties become inevitable, he will join one, and attend its meetings,
> but will repress the impulses of party spirit. Never failing to come to
> the polls, he will vote for his party candidate only if satisfied by his
> capacity and honesty. He will be ready to . . . be put forward as a
> candidate for the legislature (if satisfied of his own competence),
> because public service is recognized as a duty. With such citizens as
> electors, the legislature will be composed of upright and capable
> men, single-minded in their wish to serve the nation. Bribery in
> constituencies, corruption among public servants, will have disap-
> peared. Leaders may not always be single-minded, nor assemblies
> always wise, nor administrators efficient, but all will be at any rate
> honest and zealous, so that an atmosphere of confidence and good
> will will prevail. Most of the causes that make for strife will be
> absent, for there will be no privileges, no advantages to excite jeal-
> ousy. Office will be sought only because it gives opportunity for
> useful public service. Power will be shared by all, and a career open
> to all alike. Even if the law does not—perhaps it cannot—prevent
> the accumulation of fortunes, these will be few and not inordinate,
> for public vigilance will close the illegitimate paths to wealth. All
> but the most depraved persons will obey and support the law, feel-
> ing it to be their own. There will be no excuse for violence, because
> the constitution will provide a remedy for every grievance. Equality
> will produce a sense of human solidarity, will refine manners, and
> increase brotherly kindness.[16]

Such is the ideal form of modern democracy laid away in heaven. 32
I do not need to tell you that its earthly counterpart resembles it but

---

[15]**James Bryce (1838–1922)** Irish historian who was a trustee for the
Carnegie trust in Scotland.

[16]I, 48. [Becker's note]

slightly. In the next lecture I shall discuss some of the circumstances that brought about so flagrant a discord between democracy as it was ideally projected and democracy as it actually functions today.

QUESTIONS FOR CRITICAL READING

1. Becker says freedom of thought and the competition of diverse opinions will reveal the truth. How important is such freedom of thought and diversity for the survival of a democracy?
2. If a primary assumption in a democracy is that people should be capable of managing their own affairs, what is a government's responsibility to those citizens who cannot do so?
3. From what you can tell of contemporary history, how important is "industrial prosperity" to the flourishing of democracy?
4. Most humans never experienced democracy and many today do not aspire to democracy. To what extent does that bring the concept of democracy into question?
5. In paragraph 3, Becker talks about "varieties" of democracies, including fascist Germany and the the Soviet "regime of Stalin." These governments seem to have been supported by a majority of their citizens. Were they then true democracies?
6. How true is it that "virtually all forms of government are democratic, since virtually all governments, except in times of revolution, rest upon the explicit or implicit consent of the people" (para. 3)?
7. Does the concept of an ideal democracy need to be viewed in relation to a specific time and place, such as our own time and place? If so, what contemporary issues help us define democracy differently from, say, Becker's definition?
8. Becker says that, given the circumstances of history, democracy "has as yet had but a limited and temporary success" (para. 10). What do you feel he means by this statement?

SUGGESTIONS FOR CRITICAL WRITING

1. Becker talks about the problems of the limitations of communication as having inhibited early democracies and having limited them to small self-contained city-states. How has the vast improvement in communications — by means of radio, television, telephone, and print media — helped to expand the concept of democracy and to make it possible on a global scale? Consider the effect of the Internet and the blogosphere on spreading or maintaining democracy. Will modern communications systems make democracy more widespread? Why?
2. Becker says, "Democracy does not flourish in communities on the verge of destitution" (para. 12). Examine the reports in a major newspaper or

newsmagazine and see to what extent your research validates or invalidates this view. Decide whether or not Becker's judgment is accurate or merely prejudiced against desperately poor communities.

3. The question of whether or not democracy has suffered a decline in prestige is still relevant, even though the times in which Becker wrote were quite different from ours. If you think that democracy has suffered a further decline in prestige, write a brief essay that sets out your views on why it has done so. If possible, suggest some ways in which democracy could restore its prestige in the world. Try using some of Becker's rhetorical devices: comparison, testimony, and definition.

4. Carefully examine Becker's lecture and consider each effort he makes to come to a satisfactory definition of *democracy*. How many separate definitions do you find, and how do they differ from one another? Using Becker's lecture as a starting point, and taking into account that more than sixty years have elapsed since he gave it, offer your own definition of *democracy*. Use examples from the way you see democracy working today in different countries and different situations. Do you find democracy at work in the institutions you have a daily experience with, such as church, school, businesses, corporations, and clubs?

5. In paragraphs 8, 9, and 10, Becker reviews the historical record concerning the existence and success of democracy over a considerable sweep of history. He concludes that democracy has had a "limited and temporary success." After considering his ideas, do you feel that democracy may in fact become unsuccessful again, as it did in Athens? Why should you or any citizen fear that democracy might fail? What might be done to help prevent such a failure?

6. **CONNECTIONS** Andrew Carnegie in *The Gospel of Wealth* (p. 387) would praise Becker's view that suggests democracy would not work in a destitute society. To what extent would Carnegie agree with Becker about the virtue and character of democracy? How might Carnegie wish to amend any of Becker's definitions? Becker was a noted liberal and Carnegie a noted conservative. How do their views affect their respective attitudes toward the ideal of democracy? Carnegie is mentioned specifically by Becker in paragraph 6, so it is clear that Becker took Carnegie's views into consideration.

7. **SEEING CONNECTIONS** Given the fact that Becker was a very careful student of the American Revolution, what do you think he might have written about Delacroix's *Liberty Leading the People* (p. 18)? Write a brief essay that attempts to define the action represented in the painting in terms of promoting democracy. Consider, especially, the imagery that points toward a democratic revolution rather than a military coup or takeover.

HANNAH ARENDT
Total Domination

HANNAH ARENDT (1906–1975) was born and educated in Germany, earning her doctorate from the University of Heidelberg when she was twenty-two years old. She left Germany for Paris after Hitler came to power in 1933 and early in the development of Nazi ideology. In New York City she worked with Jewish relief groups and in 1940 married Heinrich Bluecher, a professor of philosophy. Arendt joined the faculty of the University of Chicago in 1963 and then taught as a visiting professor at a number of universities, eventually settling at the New School for Social Research in New York.

The Origins of Totalitarianism, from which this selection is excerpted, was first published in 1951 and solidified Arendt's reputation as an important political philosopher. She began work on the book in 1945, after Nazism was defeated in Europe, and finished most of it by 1949, during the period of growing tension between the United States and the Soviet Union that began the Cold War. Much of the book analyzes the politics of ideology in fascist and communist countries. Arendt went on to write a number of other influential works, such as *The Human Condition* (1958) and *Crises of the Republic* (1972), both of which address the problems she saw connected with a decline in moral values in modern society. One of her most controversial books, *Eichmann in Jerusalem* (1963), examines Adolf Eichmann, head of the Gestapo's Jewish section, who was tried and executed in Jerusalem. She observed that the nature of Eichmann's evil was essentially banal—that his crime involved going along with orders without taking the time to assess them critically. Her last work, *The Life of the Mind,* was not completed, although two of its planned three volumes were published posthumously in 1978.

From *The Origins of Totalitarianism.*

"Total Domination" is part of one of the last chapters in *The Origins of Totalitarianism*. The first part of the book sets forth a brief history of modern anti-Semitism because the rise of totalitarianism in Germany was based in large part on Hitler's belief that the Aryan race was biologically and morally more evolved than all other races. In this selection Arendt shows how the totalitarian state derives its power from propagating a set of ideas, or ideology, such as the view that one race is superior to all others. Once that premise is accepted, she demonstrates, then any and all atrocities against people of other races can be permitted and promoted.

In two instances, describing the ideology of German fascism and the ideology of Soviet communism, Arendt demonstrates the ways in which the uncritical acceptance of an ideology provides the core of power for totalitarian states. In the case of Germany, racism led to the theory that if some races are inferior and debased then they must be destroyed for the good of humanity—a theory that was put into brutal practice by the Nazis. Arendt shows how this view derives from a misunderstanding of Darwin's theories of the survival of the fittest (see Darwin's "Natural Selection," p. 597). In the case of the Soviet Union, totalitarianism depended on the "scientific" theory of history put forth by Karl Marx (see Marx's "Communist Manifesto," p. 359) that insisted on class struggle and the need of the most "progressive class" to destroy the less progressive classes. Marx was referred to as the "Darwin of history" in part because his views reflected the same scientific logic as Darwin's theories of biology. According to Arendt, both the Nazi and communist totalitarian regimes claimed those laws of biology or history as the justification for their own brutal acts of terror.

Arendt's Rhetoric

Arendt is a careful rhetorician. She works in a logical fashion to analyze basic principles to see how they control the outcome of events. In this case, the outcome is the totalitarian institution of the concentration camp in which human dignity is destroyed. For the totalitarian government, the terror and torment of concentration camps demonstrate "that everything is possible" (para. 1), even though it might seem impossible to reduce a person to a thing. Total domination, as she states, is designed to reduce the diversity and complexity of humanity to a single reaction to terror and pain.

Interestingly, Arendt can find no economic virtue in maintaining huge numbers of people in concentration camps. Occasionally in the Soviet Union, inmates' labor was of value, but some 60 percent or more of the inmates died under the harsh labor conditions. In Nazi Germany the work done in the concentration camps was of such poor quality that it usually had to be done again. Further, during World War II, German resources that might have been used to fight the war were diverted to the concentration camps, which functioned as extermination centers even while Germany reeled under potential defeat. In other words, the concentration camps were self-defeating in every important way except that they demonstrated to a populace that total domination was possible.

One important rhetorical principle at work in this essay is the essential definition of total domination by the process of describing the circumstances of the concentration camps as well as the rationale for their construction. The Nazis knew, and Hitler had already trumpeted the news to the world in his book *Mein Kampf* (My Struggle), that if a lie was big enough, large numbers of people would believe it even if it stood against common sense. "The Big Lie" has become a common principle of modern political science. Likewise, if the enormity of the crime is great enough, it is not likely that people will believe it actually occurred. Therefore, it should not have been a surprise that the few people who had escaped the camps before the war were not believed. They told their stories, but even future victims of the camps refused to believe they existed. Western governments thought the accounts of the concentration camps were monstrous exaggerations.

Throughout the book from which this passage comes, Arendt insists that the essence of totalitarianism is terror and that without it the totalitarian state collapses. The concentration camps are the "laboratories" in which absolute terror dominates and that represent total domination. Individual liberty and freedom are erased by the terror of total domination, and in this sense the values that Rousseau and Jefferson argue for are irrelevant. In some states, such as the one Machiavelli imagined (p. 37), terror might be useful for controlling the opposition, but in the totalitarian state it controls everyone. As Arendt states, "a victory of the concentration-camp system would mean the same inexorable doom for human beings as the use of the hydrogen bomb would mean the doom of the human race" (para. 14).

PREREADING QUESTIONS: WHAT TO READ FOR

The following prereading questions may help you anticipate key issues in the discussion of Hannah Arendt's "Total Domination." Keeping them in mind during your first reading of the selection should help focus your attention.

- What is the role of terror in the totalitarian state?
- Why is total domination necessary in a totalitarian state?
- What happens to human beings in concentration camps?

Total Domination

The concentration and extermination camps of totalitarian 1
regimes serve as the laboratories in which the fundamental belief of
totalitarianism that everything is possible is being verified. Compared
with this, all other experiments are secondary in importance —
including those in the field of medicine whose horrors are recorded
in detail in the trials against the physicians of the Third Reich —
although it is characteristic that these laboratories were used for
experiments of every kind.

Total domination, which strives to organize the infinite plurality 2
and differentiation of human beings as if all of humanity were just
one individual, is possible only if each and every person can be
reduced to a never-changing identity of reactions, so that each of
these bundles of reactions can be exchanged at random for any other.
The problem is to fabricate something that does not exist, namely, a
kind of human species resembling other animal species whose only
"freedom" would consist in "preserving the species." Totalitarian
domination attempts to achieve this goal both through ideological
indoctrination of the elite formations[1] and through absolute terror in
the camps; and the atrocities for which the elite formations are ruthlessly used become, as it were, the practical application of the ideological indoctrination — the testing ground in which the latter must
prove itself — while the appalling spectacle of the camps themselves
is supposed to furnish the "theoretical" verification of the ideology.

The camps are meant not only to exterminate people and degrade 3
human beings, but also serve the ghastly experiment of eliminating,
under scientifically controlled conditions, spontaneity itself as an
expression of human behavior and of transforming the human personality into a mere thing, into something that even animals are not;
for Pavlov's dog,[2] which, as we know, was trained to eat not when it
was hungry but when a bell rang, was a perverted animal.

---

[1] **elite formations** By this term Arendt seems to mean the SS men and camp
guards.

[2] **Pavlov's dog** Between 1898 and 1930, the Russian psychologist Ivan Petrovich
Pavlov (1849–1936) trained a dog to associate the sound of a ringing bell with food.
Eventually the dog's reflex was to salivate at the sound of the bell even when there was
no food.

Under normal circumstances this can never be accomplished, 4 because spontaneity can never be entirely eliminated insofar as it is connected not only with human freedom but with life itself, in the sense of simply keeping alive. It is only in the concentration camps that such an experiment is at all possible, and therefore they are not only "*la société la plus totalitaire encore réalisée*"[3] (David Rousset) but the guiding social ideal of total domination in general. Just as the stability of the totalitarian regime depends on the isolation of the fictitious world of the movement from the outside world, so the experiment of total domination in the concentration camps depends on sealing off the latter against the world of all others, the world of the living in general, even against the outside world of a country under totalitarian rule. This isolation explains the peculiar unreality and lack of credibility that characterize all reports from the concentration camps and constitute one of the main difficulties for the true understanding of totalitarian domination, which stands or falls with the existence of these concentration and extermination camps; for, unlikely as it may sound, these camps are the true central institution of totalitarian organizational power.

There are numerous reports by survivors. The more authentic 5 they are, the less they attempt to communicate things that evade human understanding and human experience—sufferings, that is, that transform men into "uncomplaining animals." None of these reports inspires those passions of outrage and sympathy through which men have always been mobilized for justice. On the contrary, anyone speaking or writing about concentration camps is still regarded as suspect; and if the speaker has resolutely returned to the world of the living, he himself is often assailed by doubts with regard to his own truthfulness, as though he had mistaken a nightmare for reality.

This doubt of people concerning themselves and the reality of 6 their own experience only reveals what the Nazis have always known: that men determined to commit crimes will find it expedient to organize them on the vastest, most improbable scale. Not only because this renders all punishments provided by the legal system inadequate and absurd; but because the very immensity of the crimes guarantees that the murderers who proclaim their innocence with all manner of lies will be more readily believed than the victims who tell the truth. The Nazis did not even consider it necessary to keep this discovery to themselves. Hitler circulated millions of copies of his book

---

[3]**la société . . . réalisée** "The most totalitarian society yet achieved." David Rousset (1912–1997) survived the concentration camps and wrote *The Other Kingdom* (1947) about his experience.

in which he stated that to be successful, a lie must be enormous—which did not prevent people from believing him as, similarly, the Nazis' proclamations, repeated *ad nauseam*,[4] that the Jews would be exterminated like bedbugs (*i.e.*, with poison gas), prevented anybody from *not* believing them.

There is a great temptation to explain away the intrinsically incredible by means of liberal rationalizations. In each one of us, there lurks such a liberal, wheedling us with the voice of common sense. The road to totalitarian domination leads through many intermediate stages for which we can find numerous analogies and precedents. The extraordinarily bloody terror during the initial stage of totalitarian rule serves indeed the exclusive purpose of defeating the opponent and rendering all further opposition impossible; but total terror is launched only after this initial stage has been overcome and the regime no longer has anything to fear from the opposition. In this context it has been frequently remarked that in such a case the means have become the end, but this is after all only an admission, in paradoxical disguise, that the category "the end justifies the means" no longer applies, that terror has lost its "purpose," that it is no longer the means to frighten people. Nor does the explanation suffice that the revolution, as in the case of the French Revolution, was devouring its own children, for the terror continues even after everybody who might be described as a child of the revolution in one capacity or another—the Russian factions, the power centers of party, the army, the bureaucracy—has long since been devoured. Many things that nowadays have become the specialty of totalitarian government are only too well known from the study of history. There have almost always been wars of aggression; the massacre of hostile populations after a victory went unchecked until the Romans mitigated it by introducing the *parcere subjectis*;[5] through centuries the extermination of native peoples went hand in hand with the colonization of the Americas, Australia, and Africa; slavery is one of the oldest institutions of mankind and all empires of antiquity were based on the labor of state-owned slaves who erected their public buildings. Not even concentration camps are an invention of totalitarian movements. They emerge for the first time during the Boer War,[6] at the beginning of the century, and

[4] **ad nauseam** To the point of sickness.

[5] ***parcere subjectis*** A Roman policy of lenience and mercy toward those they defeated.

[6] **Boer War (1899–1902)** The British established concentration camps in which some forty thousand people died during their war against the Transvaal and the Orange Free State—which were then controlled by the Boers, who were descended from earlier Dutch settlers—in what is now South Africa.

continued to be used in South Africa as well as India for "undesirable elements"; here, too, we first find the term "protective custody" which was later adopted by the Third Reich. These camps correspond in many respects to the concentration camps at the beginning of totalitarian rule; they were used for "suspects" whose offenses could not be proved and who could not be sentenced by ordinary process of law. All this clearly points to totalitarian methods of domination; all these are elements they utilize, develop, and crystallize on the basis of the nihilistic principle that "everything is permitted," which they inherited and already take for granted. But wherever these new forms of domination assume their authentically totalitarian structure they transcend this principle, which is still tied to the utilitarian motives and self-interest of the rulers, and try their hand in a realm that up to now has been completely unknown to us: the realm where "everything is possible." And, characteristically enough, this is precisely the realm that cannot be limited by either utilitarian motives or self-interest, regardless of the latter's content.

What runs counter to common sense is not the nihilistic principle that "everything is permitted," which was already contained in the nineteenth-century utilitarian conception[7] of common sense. What common sense and "normal people" refuse to believe is that everything is possible. We attempt to understand elements in present or recollected experience that simply surpass our powers of understanding. We attempt to classify as criminal a thing which, as we all feel, no such category was ever intended to cover. What meaning has the concept of murder when we are confronted with the mass production of corpses? We attempt to understand the behavior of concentration-camp inmates and SS-men psychologically, when the very thing that must be realized is that the psyche *can* be destroyed even without the destruction of the physical man; that, indeed, psyche, character, and individuality seem under certain circumstances to express themselves only through the rapidity or slowness with which they disintegrate. The end result in any case is inanimate men, *i.e.*, men who can no longer be psychologically understood, whose return to the psychologically or otherwise intelligibly human world closely resembles the resurrection of Lazarus.[8] All statements of common sense, whether of a psychological or sociological nature, serve only to encourage those who think it "superficial" to "dwell on horrors."

---

[7] **utilitarian conception** Utilitarianism, often known for its doctrine of the greatest good for the greatest number, was a nineteenth-century philosophy rooted in what people felt was essentially common sense.

[8] **Lazarus** From the Bible (John 11:18–48). Jesus, urged by Martha, resurrected Lazarus, who had been dead for four days.

If it is true that the concentration camps are the most consequen- 9
tial institution of totalitarian rule, "dwelling on horrors" would seem
to be indispensable for the understanding of totalitarianism. But recollection can no more do this than can the uncommunicative eyewitness
report. In both these genres there is an inherent tendency to run away
from the experience; instinctively or rationally, both types of writer
are so much aware of the terrible abyss that separates the world of the
living from that of the living dead, that they cannot supply anything
more than a series of remembered occurrences that must seem just
as incredible to those who relate them as to their audience. Only the
fearful imagination of those who have been aroused by such reports
but have not actually been smitten in their own flesh, of those who
are consequently free from the bestial, desperate terror which, when
confronted by real, present horror, inexorably paralyzes everything
that is not mere reaction, can afford to keep thinking about horrors.
Such thoughts are useful only for the perception of political contexts
and the mobilization of political passions. A change of personality of
any sort whatever can no more be induced by thinking about horrors than by the real experience of horror. The reduction of a man to
a bundle of reactions separates him as radically as mental disease
from everything within him that is personality or character. When,
like Lazarus, he rises from the dead, he finds his personality or character unchanged, just as he had left it.

Just as the horror, or the dwelling on it, cannot affect a change of 10
character in him, cannot make men better or worse, thus it cannot
become the basis of a political community or party in a narrower sense.
The attempts to build up a European elite with a program of intra-
European understanding based on the common European experience
of the concentration camps have foundered in much the same manner
as the attempts following the First World War to draw political conclusions from the international experience of the front generation.[9] In
both cases it turned out that the experiences themselves can communicate no more than nihilistic banalities. Political consequences such
as postwar pacifism, for example, derived from the general fear of war,
not from the experiences in war. Instead of producing a pacifism
devoid of reality, the insight into the structure of modern wars, guided
and mobilized by fear, might have led to the realization that the only
standard for a necessary war is the fight against conditions under
which people no longer wish to live — and our experiences with the
tormenting hell of the totalitarian camps have enlightened us only

---

[9] **the front generation** The generation that fought or experienced the fighting
in World War I (1914–1918).

too well about the possibility of such conditions. Thus the fear of concentration camps and the resulting insight into the nature of total domination might serve to invalidate all obsolete political differentiations from right to left and to introduce beside and above them the politically most important yardstick for judging events in our time, namely: whether they serve totalitarian domination or not.

In any event, the fearful imagination has the great advantage to dissolve the sophistic-dialectical[10] interpretations of politics which are all based on the superstition that something good might result from evil. Such dialectical acrobatics had at least a semblance of justification so long as the worst that man could inflict upon man was murder. But, as we know today, murder is only a limited evil. The murderer who kills a man—a man who has to die anyway—still moves within the realm of life and death familiar to us; both have indeed a necessary connection on which the dialectic is founded, even if it is not always conscious of it. The murderer leaves a corpse behind and does not pretend that his victim has never existed; if he wipes out any traces, they are those of his own identity, and not the memory and grief of the persons who loved his victim; he destroys a life, but he does not destroy the fact of existence itself.

The Nazis, with the precision peculiar to them, used to register their operations in the concentration camps under the heading "under cover of the night (*Nacht und Nebel*)." The radicalism of measures to treat people as if they had never existed and to make them disappear in the literal sense of the word is frequently not apparent at first glance, because both the German and the Russian system are not uniform but consist of a series of categories in which people are treated very differently. In the case of Germany, these different categories used to exist in the same camp, but without coming into contact with each other; frequently, the isolation between the categories was even stricter than the isolation from the outside world. Thus, out of racial considerations, Scandinavian nationals during the war were quite differently treated by the Germans than the members of other peoples, although the former were outspoken enemies of the Nazis. The latter in turn were divided into those whose "extermination" was immediately on the agenda, as in the case of the Jews, or could be expected in the predictable future, as in the case of the Poles, Russians, and Ukrainians, and into those who were not yet covered by instructions about such an overall "final solution," as in

---

[10] **sophistic-dialectical** Arendt seems to be referring to Marxist communist views that pit two mighty historical forces—like good and evil—against one another. Her point is that such a dialectic is artificial and dangerous.

the case of the French and Belgians. In Russia, on the other hand, we must distinguish three more or less independent systems. First, there are the authentic forced-labor groups that live in relative freedom and are sentenced for limited periods. Secondly, there are the concentration camps in which the human material is ruthlessly exploited and the mortality rate is extremely high, but which are essentially organized for labor purposes. And, thirdly, there are the annihilation camps in which the inmates are systematically wiped out through starvation and neglect.

The real horror of the concentration and extermination camps   13
lies in the fact that the inmates, even if they happen to keep alive, are more effectively cut off from the world of the living than if they had died, because terror enforces oblivion. Here, murder is as impersonal as the squashing of a gnat. Someone may die as the result of systematic torture or starvation, or because the camp is overcrowded and superfluous human material must be liquidated. Conversely, it may happen that due to a shortage of new human shipments the danger arises that the camps become depopulated and that the order is now given to reduce the death rate at any price. David Rousset called his report on the period in a German concentration camp "Les Jours de Notre Mort,"[11] and it is indeed as if there were a possibility to give permanence to the process of dying itself and to enforce a condition in which both death and life are obstructed equally effectively.

It is the appearance of some radical evil, previously unknown to   14
us, that puts an end to the notion of developments and transformations of qualities. Here, there are neither political nor historical nor simply moral standards but, at the most, the realization that something seems to be involved in modern politics that actually should never be involved in politics as we used to understand it, namely all or nothing—all, and that is an undetermined infinity of forms of human living-together, or nothing, for a victory of the concentration-camp system would mean the same inexorable doom for human beings as the use of the hydrogen bomb would mean the doom of the human race.

There are no parallels to the life in the concentration camps. Its   15
horror can never be fully embraced by the imagination for the very reason that it stands outside of life and death. It can never be fully reported for the very reason that the survivor returns to the world of the living, which makes it impossible for him to believe fully in his own past experiences. It is as though he had a story to tell of another planet, for the status of the inmates in the world of the living, where nobody is supposed to know if they are alive or dead, is such that it

---

[11] **Les Jours . . . Mort**   Literally, the days of our death.

is as though they had never been born. Therefore all parallels create confusion and distract attention from what is essential. Forced labor in prisons and penal colonies, banishment, slavery, all seem for a moment to offer helpful comparisons, but on closer examination lead nowhere.

Forced labor as a punishment is limited as to time and intensity. 16 The convict retains his rights over his body; he is not absolutely tortured and he is not absolutely dominated. Banishment banishes only from one part of the world to another part of the world, also inhabited by human beings; it does not exclude from the human world altogether. Throughout history slavery has been an institution within a social order; slaves were not, like concentration-camp inmates, withdrawn from the sight and hence the protection of their fellow-men; as instruments of labor they had a definite price and as property a definite value. The concentration-camp inmate has no price, because he can always be replaced; nobody knows to whom he belongs, because he is never seen. From the point of view of normal society he is absolutely superfluous, although in times of acute labor shortage, as in Russia and in Germany during the war, he is used for work.

The concentration camp as an institution was not established 17 for the sake of any possible labor yield; the only permanent economic function of the camps has been the financing of their own supervisory apparatus; thus from the economic point of view the concentration camps exist mostly for their own sake. Any work that has been performed could have been done much better and more cheaply under different conditions. Especially Russia, whose concentration camps are mostly described as forced-labor camps because Soviet bureaucracy has chosen to dignify them with this name, reveals most clearly that forced labor is not the primary issue; forced labor is the normal condition of all Russian workers, who have no freedom of movement and can be arbitrarily drafted for work to any place at any time. The incredibility of the horrors is closely bound up with their economic uselessness. The Nazis carried this uselessness to the point of open anti-utility when in the midst of the war, despite the shortage of building material and rolling stock, they set up enormous, costly extermination factories and transported millions of people back and forth. In the eyes of a strictly utilitarian world the obvious contradiction between these acts and military expediency gave the whole enterprise an air of mad unreality.

This atmosphere of madness and unreality, created by an appar- 18 ent lack of purpose, is the real iron curtain which hides all forms of concentration camps from the eyes of the world. Seen from outside, they and the things that happen in them can be described only in images drawn from a life after death, that is, a life removed from earthly purposes. Concentration camps can very aptly be divided into three types corresponding to three basic Western conceptions of a life after death: Hades, Purgatory, and Hell. To Hades correspond those relatively mild forms, once popular even in nontotalitarian countries, for getting undesirable elements of all sorts—refugees, stateless persons, the asocial, and the unemployed—out of the way; as DP camps,[12] which are nothing other than camps for persons who have become superfluous and bothersome, they have survived the war. Purgatory is represented by the Soviet Union's labor camps, where neglect is combined with chaotic forced labor. Hell in the most literal sense was embodied by those types of camp perfected by the Nazis, in which the whole of life was thoroughly and systematically organized with a view to the greatest possible torment.

All three types have one thing in common: the human masses   19 sealed off in them are treated as if they no longer existed, as if what happened to them were no longer of any interest to anybody, as if they were already dead and some evil spirit gone mad were amusing himself by stopping them for a while between life and death before admitting them to eternal peace.

----

[12] **DP camps** Displaced Persons camps. These camps were common in Europe after World War II.

QUESTIONS FOR CRITICAL READING

1. Why are concentrations camps described as "laboratories" for the totalitarian regime?
2. What is the importance of the concentration camps' goal of removing human spontaneity?
3. In what sense are the concentration camps "the true central institution of totalitarian organizational power" (para. 4)?
4. Arendt implies that the experience of the concentration camp has the effect of "a mental disease." Why would that be so?
5. How is murder different from the mass death that characterizes the concentration camps?
6. Why is the concentration camp "useful" to the totalitarian government?

SUGGESTIONS FOR CRITICAL WRITING

1. Examine the economic issues Arendt raises that are involved in the establishment and operation of concentration camps in a totalitarian state. Decide whether a totalitarian state, whose goal is to achieve total

domination, would be able to derive economic advantage from concentration camps. Why would this be an important issue? If there were a considerable economic advantage to maintaining concentration camps, would that fact make them any less terrifying?

2. Arendt reflected the fears of her own time in this essay. For her the most terrifying and immediate totalitarian governments were those of Nazi Germany and the Soviet Union. What evidence do you see in our contemporary world that might suggest totalitarianism is not completely "dead"? Do you perceive any threatening totalitarian governments anywhere in the world today? How do they seem to function and to interact with other nations?

3. Should you establish that a government is functioning as a totalitarian state today, do you feel it is a moral imperative that you do everything possible to overthrow that state? Would it be ethical and moral to go to war against such a state even if it did not immediately threaten you? Would it be ethical and moral for you to turn your back on a totalitarian state and ignore its operation so that it could achieve the kind of total domination Arendt describes?

4. **CONNECTIONS** How would Machiavelli interpret Arendt's discussion of ends and means in paragraph 8? Would Machiavelli have recommended concentration camps to his prince as a means of maintaining power? If a prince believed that concentration camps would be the means by which a state could achieve stability and power, would he be right in assuming that the stability and power thus achieved were worthwhile ends? Do you think Machiavelli would have accepted a totalitarian prince?

5. **CONNECTIONS** José Ortega y Gasset's "The Greatest Danger, the State" anticipates Arendt's discussion of total domination. Examine both essays for their similarity of concern regarding the threat of the state to society. According to Arendt, how many of Ortega's fears seem to have been borne out in the creation of the Nazi state? Be sure to rely on details from both essays to fashion your argument.

6. **SEEING CONNECTIONS** What would Arendt's position be regarding Delacroix's *Liberty Leading the People* (p. 18)? Would she have applauded the revolutionary action of the painting or would she have ridiculed it as being naive and insufficient to cope with a totalitarian state? Consider her position regarding the use of violence as well as José Ortega y Gasset's observations about the masses' tendency to employ violence.

PART TWO

JUSTICE

Marcus Tullius Cicero
Frederick Douglass
Henry David Thoreau
Elizabeth Cady Stanton
Martin Luther King Jr.
John Rawls

INTRODUCTION

If any one steal the property of a temple or of the court, he shall
be put to death, and also the one who receives the stolen thing
from him shall be put to death.
—HAMMURABI (1792–1750 B.C.)

Justice turns the scale, bringing to some learning through
suffering.
—AESCHYLUS (525–456 B.C.)

Spare me through your mercy, do not punish me through your
justice.
—ANSELM OF CANTERBURY (1033–1109)

The sentiment of justice is so natural, and so universally acquired
by all mankind, that it seems to be independent of all law, all
party, all religion.
—VOLTAIRE (1694–1778)

Where justice is denied, where poverty is enforced, where
ignorance prevails, and where any one class is made to feel that
society is in an organized conspiracy to oppress, rob, and degrade
them, neither persons nor property will be safe.
—FREDERICK DOUGLASS (1817–1895)

Justice must always question itself, just as society can exist only
by means of the work it does on itself and on its institutions.
—MICHEL FOUCAULT (1926–1984)

Ideas of justice have revolved historically around several closely
related concepts: moral righteousness, equity of treatment, and reciprocity of action. Justice is an element of interpersonal relations, but
philosophers usually link it to the individual's relationship to the
state. In the Western tradition, the Greek philosopher Plato (428–
347 B.C.) was the first to frame the concept of justice in terms of the
health of the state. In his work *The Republic* he defined justice both
as an overarching ideal and as a practical necessity for the functioning of a harmonious society. In his view, justice was served when
each stratum of society (philosopher-rulers, soldiers, and artisans
and workers) operated within its own sphere of action and did not
interfere with others.

Like Plato, the Greek philosopher Aristotle (384–322 B.C.)
viewed the general concept of justice as an important eternal quality that the individual should strive to uphold. He defined general
justice as the overarching goal of moral righteousness that ensures a
good society, legislative justice as the duty of the individual to

comply with the laws of the society (civic virtue), and particular justice as the duty of the judge to redress inequalities in personal transactions. In turn each of these forms of justice works to maintain the overarching ideals of political and economic justice and thus protect the society from collapse. Ironically, although political justice centers on the concept of freedom and liberty, in Aristotle's time warring states enslaved defeated warriors and their families. Aristotle justified this practice by asserting that basic inequalities between people rendered some people natural slaves.

In later centuries, philosophers such as Thomas Hobbes (English, 1588–1679) drew on Aristotle's theories of natural justice — the justice found in a state of nature where the strong always impose their will on the weak. However, Hobbes found that because people actually live in communities with a political structure that leads them to suffer or commit injustices, the concept of justice becomes essentially moral. Hobbes wrestled with the moral parameters of justice and finally concluded that it is impossible to form a universal concept of justice and that justice is whatever laws are most useful and expedient for society.

This tension between justice as a moral ideal and its manifestation in society as practical law has been a hallmark of its evolution as an idea. Indeed, as the writers in this section so eloquently reveal, the laws that are meant to ensure justice within a society often enforce deep injustices. All the authors in this section investigate the relationship between the individual (or group of individuals) and society in an attempt to come to an understanding of how laws contribute to just ends and the promotion of equality, or how they enforce unequal treatment. Some of these authors respond to the laws that have affected them directly, while others respond to concepts that they feel should be in place in order to guarantee justice to all people.

Cicero presents a dialogue with a character, Philus, whose assignment is to create an argument in favor of injustice. As a great rhetorician and orator, Cicero plays an interesting game in asking someone whose personal views are strongly in favor of justice to argue against it. The procedure is interesting for us because we can see more clearly the virtue of justice by examining in detail the arguments against it. Philus does a creditable job by relying on arguments already developed by another philosopher, Carneades. His appeal is to the strength of the state and the need for the individual to yield to collective values. The result is an argument for injustice that is dangerous because we might be convinced by it.

In the excerpt from his *Narrative of the Life of Frederick Douglass, an American Slave*, Douglass links the question of justice to the question of freedom. According to federal and state laws in the early nineteenth century that protected slavery in the South, Douglass was doomed to remain a slave until his dying day, unless his owner freed him or allowed him to purchase his freedom. In recording the circumstances of his life under a government that enforced slave laws — in both the North and the South — at the same time that it advocated independence, Douglass illustrates how deeply the injustice of slavery could damage the individual slave and slaveholder.

The question of how the individual should react in the face of unjust laws is taken up by Henry David Thoreau. He refused to pay taxes that would be used in a war against Mexico that he felt was dishonorable, realized that he would have to pay a penalty for his views, and was willing to do so. Thoreau makes a special plea to conscience as a way of dealing with injustice by requiring the individual to place conscience first and law second. His "Civil Disobedience" reminds us that we are the citizens of the nation and that we ought to make our own will known. Thoreau stresses that there is a price for doing what is right, but that all honest citizens must pay it.

Elizabeth Cady Stanton relies on the rhetorical device of parody in her Declaration of Sentiments and Resolutions. Modeled directly on Thomas Jefferson's Declaration of Independence, Stanton's appeal serves as a reminder that Jefferson spoke only of men's independence, not that of women. Her demands are no less reasonable than Jefferson's, and it is a source of embarrassment to her that she has to redress such an omission after so much time has elapsed since Jefferson's declaration was adopted.

Like Thoreau, Martin Luther King Jr. was also imprisoned for breaking a law his conscience deemed unjust. In his struggle against the Jim Crow laws enforcing segregation in the South, King acted on his belief that the individual can and should fight laws that treat members of society unjustly. King's *Letter from Birmingham Jail* provides a masterful and moving definition of what makes laws just or unjust. Furthermore, King develops the concept of nonviolent demonstration as a method by which the individual can protest unjust laws.

The modern thinker who has had the largest impact on discussion of the idea of justice is John Rawls. In his book *Theory of Justice*, he examines the ideas of Plato and Aristotle and defends the rights of the individual against the demands of the state in insisting on justice as fairness. In this selection from the book, which includes the main idea of his theory of justice, Rawls takes a view that differs from those of many practical thinkers. He feels that any just society will provide certain "Primary Goods," such as freedom, equality, and opportunity, to every citizen. He also feels that the justice of any law ought to be measured by its effect on the least advantaged citizens rather than the greatest number of citizens. His view is radical, and his argument in favor of it is carefully couched.

The writers in this section discuss justice and injustice as it is both conceived and experienced by individuals. They consider the needs of the state and the rights of the individual while they also probe the underlying concepts of justice in any society. Some writers are theoretical in their views, while others write about practical matters of justice as these affect people in their everyday lives. For us, the arguments these writers develop should help us understand the complexities of the idea of justice. There is no simple way to define justice, despite the fact that we ordinarily know injustice when we see it.

VISUALIZING JUSTICE

Justice is considered one of the four cardinal virtues as delineated by Plato in *The Republic*, the others being Courage, Wisdom, and Moderation. From the time of the ancient Greeks, and probably much earlier, artists created images that emblematized justice. Usually, justice is represented as a woman holding a balance that emphasizes equality and moderation. In some paintings or sculptures, she is also wearing a blindfold, indicating that she listens only to the evidence and does not take into account the social status of the plaintiff or the defendant. Luca Giordano's painting shows Justice triumphant, with plenty of approval from heavenly and earthly figures. In a sense, it is an exciting celebration involving heaven and earth.

Giordano's huge wall painting is carefully balanced, with figures on the right complementing figures on the left in a specific symmetrical arrangement. Even the curve of the ostrich's wing and neck helps give a sense of rhythm and balance to the lower portion of the painting. At the center, Justice sits holding a sword in her right hand and the typical balance, or scale, an ancient symbol of evenness and fairness, in her left. Above her are a number of angels: one sounding a note of triumph on a horn; another bringing a torch to illuminate injustice; and, in the center top, one who is armed and almost certainly represents St. Michael, known in the Renaissance as "l'homme armée," the armed man. According to the Bible, when he appeared to Adam and Eve, enacting God's justice by driving them out of the Garden of Eden after they had sinned, St. Michael appeared to them in armor with a sword and shield. Here he wields a spear and wears a light armored cuirass.

The ostrich and its eggs symbolize rebirth and light, thus suggesting associations with Christ. Pliny, the classical writer, accused the ostrich of hiding its head in the sand and being, thus, unable to

LUCA GIORDANO, *JUSTICE.* 1684–86.
Fresco, the Palazzo Medici-Riccardi, Florence, Italy.

see the truth. Giordano's ostrich, by contrast, stares at the heavens, clearly possessing a vision of the truth. To the far left of the ostrich, the leopard, the symbol of valor, is protecting Justice, as is the armed man seated below her. The figure wrapped with leopard skin, to the right of the ostrich, is invested with the power of the leopard. Some commentaries on Genesis contend that God used leopard

skins to clothe Adam and Eve when they recognized their naked-
ness. This symbolism connects the figure to the concept of heavenly
justice.

Justice is herself drawn from a model of Dike, the symbol of
moral justice in Greek society. The balance that she holds is symbolic
of her own even-temperedness, as can be seen from the calm expression on her face. Dike was a divinity whose job it was to punish
injustice wherever she found it and to closely oversee the work of
judges to be sure that justice was carried out. Justice in this painting
is the central figure, establishing her overarching importance for the
world.

The fact that weapons abound in Giordano's painting emphasizes the fact that he realized, as did his audience, that justice was
not automatic in society. It had to be enforced both in heaven and
on earth. As a primary virtue with Greek origins, justice connects
with Greek political ideals of democracy and fairness as well as individuality. Even the figures in heaven remind us that justice is not an
arbitrary human virtue, but rather that it is universal and permanent, a fixture of heaven and earth. The angel with the victory
wreath ready to be placed on Justice's head blows a military horn.
The small putto, or angel, next to Justice's sword, carries a fasces, a
bundle of wrapped rods, a symbol of the strength achieved by band-
ing heavenly forces together. St. Michael is noted in the Bible for his
military prowess in dispatching Satan and the fallen angels into hell,
thus there could be no more appropriate archangel assigned to the
protection of justice on earth.

The figure in the topmost left of the composition — a head with
what seems to be a crown of thorns (in contrast to Justice's laurel
wreath) — may be Jesus Christ. His judgment and punishment on
earth was not just. Rather it was a mockery of justice and thus a
reminder of how serious Giordano was about reminding us of the
importance of this most cardinal of virtues. If it is Christ looking on,
he is offering approval of Justice's having achieved a balance in the
Palazzo Medici-Riccardi.

This was a late painting in a very productive life. Giordano
(1634–1705) was born in Naples, where he eventually retired and
died. But he was especially popular in Spain in his early and middle
years. His work in churches, palaces, and elsewhere was abundant
and his reputation for speed and skill was widespread. His work is
plentiful even today in Naples, Italy, and Madrid and many other
cities in Spain. *Justice* was created as a fresco, a painting on a plas-
tered ceiling or wall, for a renowned Florentine palazzo that the
Marchese Riccardi had recently purchased and remodeled. Today it
is a public government building in Florence.

MARCUS TULLIUS CICERO
The Defense of Injustice

MARCUS TULLIUS CICERO (106–43 B.C.) lived in Rome during some of the empire's most turbulent times. He was a great writer and a legendary orator. His works, with some exceptions, have survived to modern times and are often cited by rhetoricians — those who study the art of persuasion and fine writing. His letters are collected in four volumes; his books include *De Amicitiae* (On Friendship), *De Officiis* (On Duty), *De Oratore* (The Orator), *De Senectute* (On Old Age), *Tusculan Disputations, On the Nature of the Gods,* and many more influential texts, including some interesting poetry.

These books were written in a characteristic style that has been described as Ciceronian, a reference to his fullness of expression, his sometimes decorative language, and his rhythmic flow. His elegance inspired many imitators, including some modern writers who read him only in translation. His reliance on dialogue in his serious works connects him with Plato, whose dialogues were well known in Rome. Often, Cicero included philosophical ideas taken from his reading of Plato and Aristotle, whom he may have read in Greek.

Cicero was not just a philosopher. He was a lawyer and a politician as well as one of the most eloquent of Romans during a period when political debate was conducted at a very high level in the Roman Senate. He was a fierce republican and wrote *On the Republic* to help foster ideas that would help maintain the Republic at a time when civil wars were threatening it. Cicero was close to Julius Caesar, who was victorious in a struggle against Pompey and others and became the equivalent of a dictator in Rome. Cicero urged Caesar to honor the republican ideals that he felt represented the highest values of justice of any government in Rome. He also realized that he might be in danger if Caesar were out of office.

From *On Government*. Translated by Michael Grant.

Cicero had spoken against Marc Antony, who came into a position of influence when Caesar was assassinated in 44 B.C. Cicero was not in the senate when Caesar was murdered, nor did he have any connections with Brutus and the conspirators, and for a short while he stayed away from Rome.

Eventually Marc Antony joined in a new triumvirate with Octavian, Caesar's adopted son. Cicero had been guilty of speaking about Octavian in such a way as to seem disloyal and perhaps dangerous. Despite the fact that Cicero supported Octavian, and that Octavian tried to protect him against his enemies, Cicero was marked as dangerous by Marc Antony because he had condemned Marc Antony's policies in his collection of political criticism called *Philippics*. Because his arguments against the triumvirate were so powerful, Cicero was captured and killed on December 7, 43 B.C. His head and hands were brought to Octavian in Rome as a symbolic gesture.

Cicero's Rhetoric

The selection that follows is from pieces he wrote on the nature of the state. It begins with a dialogue between two powerful speakers. Laelius challenges Philus to argue against justice and in praise of injustice. This is a typical approach among master rhetoricians, whose skills often permit them to argue either side of an issue with equal deftness. For many people this skill invalidates rhetoric because they see the disputants as having no fundamental interests to defend, instead behaving like lawyers who are willing to argue a case that they know is not worthy to be argued. However, in this situation Cicero is clever. He realizes that in the hands of a skillful rhetorician, the case against justice will do a great deal to reveal the qualities of justice that make it most valuable to society. Philus is chosen to make this argument in part because he has a reputation for being impeccably honest, is profoundly committed to justice, and is the last person one would connect with a speech against justice. Cicero tells us as much in an effort to convince us that Philus is playing the role of devil's advocate for injustice.

In a way perhaps designed to protect his own reputation, Philus tells us that he will argue by using the words and arguments of another important rhetorician, Carneades (c. 213–128 B.C.), who had a reputation for ridiculing "the best causes." Carneades was a skeptic philosopher who enjoyed dismantling what appeared to be the most secure arguments just to demonstrate that there was nothing one could absolutely believe without examination. Cicero hopes that, as powerful as Philus's speech may be, we will not accept his views as desirable. However, Philus makes such a remarkable case for injustice that, if we are not careful, we may end up accepting it.

Philus begins by reminding Laelius and us that justice is rare and valuable, "far more valuable than all the gold in the world" (para. 4). Once that is said, he launches into his argument for injustice by commenting on those people who have praised it and wondering whether there could be such a thing as natural justice. He reasons that justice must be unnatural and a creation of government because, unlike things in nature, it is not "the same thing to all human beings" (para. 6). In paragraph 7, he surveys different societies and points out the diversity of ideas on important subjects. Since there is no universal view of justice, it must be constructed by each government independently.

In paragraph 10, Philus tells us that justice has been interpreted differently over the ages. Justice is not one static thing; it changes over time and in different places because it is not—like trees, rocks, and colors—a natural thing that is perceptible to everyone. Justice may mean obeying the laws, but which laws should a person obey? If laws came from God or from nature they would be easy to follow. Philus says, "laws are *not* imposed on us by nature—or by our innate sense of justice. They are imposed by the fear of being penalized. In other words, human beings are not just, by nature, at all" (para. 12).

Some lines or pages are lost between paragraphs 13 and 14, and when Philus returns to his speech he begins describing the action of governments, comparing government by men "exploiting their wealth or noble birth" with government by "the people." He condemns the latter as a government in chaos, and in his analysis he arrives at the compromise Scipio recommends: a government with a single leader, but with the council of the nobles and with the voice of the people in evidence. This structure would balance the powers of three important groups and possibly produce justice.

In paragraph 16, Philus begins to offer us some frightening alternatives:

1. We can perform injustice and not suffer it ourselves;
2. We can both perform it and suffer it; or,
3. We can neither perform it nor suffer it.

He evaluates the choices and says the best one is to perform injustice and get away with it without suffering it ourselves. In paragraph 17, he slyly reveals that the current policy of Rome, and by implication all empires, is to conquer lands and take them from other people. If justice were the uppermost concern, Rome would be merciful to all people, but if that were true Rome would lose its empire.

Philus contrasts what he calls wisdom with justice. Everyday wisdom says that the empire must be preserved. But justice says that merciful behavior is right and all other behavior is wrong. Justice says people should not be conquered against their will; wisdom says that the empire cannot grow and be great unless weak people are conquered by the strong. In paragraph 19, Philus begins to examine the choices of an individual, and in paragraph 20, he unleashes his most powerful argument against justice. He offers a hypothetical argument: "Let us imagine that there are two men, one a paragon of virtue, fairness, justice, and honesty, and the other an outrageous ruffian." He asks: Which would we rather be, a good man who has been blinded, ruined, expelled, and beggared, or a bad man who receives all the world's blessings? Philus knows which we would choose.

Then, by process of analogy, he likens the condition of the individual to the condition of the state. "No country would not rather be an unjust master than a just slave" (para. 21). Unfortunately, much of Philus's speech is lost at this point, and Laelius ends the "experiment" by making some profound and direct statements that are designed to counter Philus's argument.

In paragraph 22, Laelius begins by talking about "true law," something Philus implied did not exist. Laelius defends the concept of a natural law that conforms to reason and is the same for everyone. "To invalidate this law is sinful," he says. He goes on to say in the next and final paragraph that "[t]here will not be one law at Rome, and another at Athens," by which he means that laws should be consistent from state to state. "Instead there will be one single, everlasting, immutable law, which applies to all nations and all times. The maker, and umpire, and proposer of this law will be God, the single master and ruler of us all."

PREREADING QUESTIONS: WHAT TO READ FOR

The following prereading questions may help you anticipate key issues in the discussion of Marcus Tullius Cicero's "The Defense of Injustice." Keeping them in mind during your first reading of the selection should help focus your attention.

- Why does Philus point out the differences in the ways people in other nations practice their religions?

- Which arguments for injustice are most persuasive?
- Which virtues of justice seem most important in light of Philus's argument?

The Defense of Injustice

LAELIUS: For the purposes of argument, see if you can offer a defense 1
of injustice!

PHILUS: What a fine cause you have handed over to me — to speak in 2
favor of evil!

LAELIUS: Yes, I can see what you have reason to fear. You are afraid 3
that, if you repeat the customary arguments against justice, you
might be supposed also to approve of them. Yet you yourself, I must
point out, stand for old-fashioned integrity and honor to an almost
unparalleled degree! And your habit of arguing on the other side — on
the grounds that you find it the easiest way to arrive at the truth — is
something with which we are quite familiar.

PHILUS: All right, then. In order to humor you, I will smear myself with 4
dirt, quite deliberately. For that is what people who are looking for
gold always feel that they have to do. So we who are looking for justice,
which is far more valuable than all the gold in the world, surely ought
to do the same, without shrinking from any hardship whatever.

But I only wish that since I am now going to make use of what 5
someone else has said, I could also use his own language! The man I
am referring to is Carneades.[1] For he, with his gift for sophistical
disputation, was quite accustomed to making the best causes sound
ridiculous! And so, after reviewing the arguments of Plato and Aristotle in favor of justice — a subject on which the latter filled four
large books[2] — what Carneades then proceeded to do was to refute
them! From Chrysippus[3] I did not expect anything substantial or
impressive. He uses his own peculiar method of argument, analyzing everything from a purely verbal rather than a factual point of
view.

These heroes acted correctly in exalting the virtue of justice, in 6
disrepair as it was. For justice, when it exists, is the most generous

---

[1] **Carneades (c. 213–128 B.C.)** North African skeptic philosopher known for
his teaching and public arguments. Known to the modern world through Cicero and
other writers.
[2] The four-book commentary on justice no longer exists.
[3] **Chrysippus (c. 280–207 B.C.)** A prominent Stoic philosopher.

and liberal of all virtues, loving itself less than it loves all the people in the world, and living for the benefit of others rather than of itself. In seating it, therefore, upon that heavenly throne, not far from wisdom itself, those philosophers were perfectly right. But one more thing has to be pointed out. They did not, evidently, lack the desire to exalt justice. For, if they had, what would have been their reason and purpose for writing at all? Nor did they lack the ability to do so, in which, indeed, they surpassed everyone else. Yet their enthusiasm and eloquence alike were undermined by a certain weakness. For the justice into which we are inquiring is not just something that naturally exists, but a quality that is created by those who are occupied in government. It cannot be merely natural, because if it was, justice and injustice would be the same thing to all human beings, like heat and cold, or bitter and sweet.

But that is not the case; on the contrary, beliefs on the subject vary enormously. If, for example, one could climb into Pacuvius's "chariot of winged snakes"[4] and drop in on many diverse nations and have a good look at them, one would find, first of all, that in Egypt, that most unchanging country of all in which the written records of the events of a vast series of centuries are preserved, a bull is considered a god—which the Egyptians call Apis. And numerous other monsters and animals of every kind are ranked among divinities and regarded as holy. That, to us, appears thoroughly alien. Here in Rome, on the other hand, as in Greece, splendid shrines can be seen, adorned with statues of deities in human form.

Yet the Persians have always considered that to be a blasphemous custom. Indeed, Xerxes I is said to have commanded that the temples of Athens should be burnt down, for this sole reason, that he considered it blasphemous to keep the gods shut up within walls, when they belong to the entire world. Indeed subsequently Philip II of Macedonia, who planned to attack the Persians, and Alexander III the Great,[5] who actually did so, quoted as their pretext their determination to avenge the Greek temples—which the Greeks had decided that they must never rebuild, so that later generations would always have before their eyes this visible memorial of Persian sacrilege.

Furthermore, a considerable number of peoples, unlike ourselves, have believed that the practice of human sacrifice is pious and thoroughly pleasing to the immortal gods. They include the

7

8

9

---

[4] **Pacuvius (c. 220–130 B.C.)** Cicero's favorite tragic poet. His work is quoted frequently in Cicero's works, but Pacuvius's plays exist only in fragments today.

[5] **Philip . . . Great** Philip II and Alexander the Great were rulers of Greece in the fourth century B.C., and Xerxes I was ruler of Persia in the fifth century B.C.

Taurians on the coast of the Euxine Sea, King Busiris of Egypt,[6] and the Gauls and the Carthaginians. Indeed, people's life-styles are sometimes so divergent that the Cretans and Aetolians consider banditry respectable. As for the Spartans, they declared, habitually, that any territory whatever that they could touch with their spears belonged to themselves! And the Athenians, too, swore oaths, in public, pronouncing that every piece of ground that produced olives or grain was their own property. The Gauls, however, consider it degrading to grow grain by manual labor. For that reason they take up arms so that they can go and reap other people's fields. But consider the customs that we—who are, of course, the most just of men!—habitually follow. What we do is to tell the Gauls across the Alps that they must not plant olives and vines, because we want to increase the value of our own. That, you might say, is prudent; "just" is not the word you could apply to it. One can see, from this example, that what is sensible is not always truly wise. Consider Lycurgus.[7] He invented a series of admirably wise and sensible laws. Yet he felt able to insist, all the same, that the lands of the rich should be cultivated by the poor as if they were slaves.

Moreover, if I wanted to describe the differing ideas of justice, 10 and the divergent institutions and customs and ways of life, that have prevailed, not only in various nations of the world, but even in this single city of our own, I could show you, also, that they have not remained the same, but have been changed in a thousand different ways. Take for example Manius Manilius here, our interpreter of the law. The advice that he generally gave you about women's legacies and inheritance when he was a young man, before the Voconian Law[8] was passed, was not at all the same advice as he would give you now. (Yet that law, I might add, was passed for the benefit of males, and is very unfair to women. For why should a woman not have money of her own? And why should a Vestal Virgin be permitted to have an heir, when her mother cannot? Nor can I see why, if a limit had to be set to the amount of property a woman could possess, the daughter of Publius Licinius Crassus Dives Mucianus,[9] provided that she were her father's only child, should be authorized by

---

[6] **Busiris** Legendary Egyptian king.

[7] **Lycurgus** Possibly legendary, Lycurgus was known as a lawgiver and founder of the Spartan constitution.

[8] **Voconian Law** A law enacted in 169 B.C. that prevented women from receiving inheritances. Cicero in *On Old Age* reports that he once spoke in favor of the law.

[9] **Mucianus (180–130 B.C.)** Roman politician.

law to own a hundred million *sesterces*, while three million is more than my own daughter is entitled to own.)[10] . . .

So laws, then, can vary considerably, and can be changed. If they 11
had all come from God, that would not be so. For, in that case, the
same laws would be applicable to all, and, besides, a man would not
be bound by one law at one time of his life and by another later on.
But what I ask, therefore, is this. Let us accept that it is the duty of a
just and good man to obey the laws. But *which* laws is he to obey? All
the different laws that exist?

There are difficulties here. Inconsistency, between laws, ought to 12
be impermissible, since it is contrary to what nature demands. But
the point is that laws are *not* imposed on us by nature—or by our
innate sense of justice. They are imposed by the fear of being penalized. In other words, human beings are not just, by nature, at all.

Let us reject, moreover, the argument that, although laws vary, 13
good men naturally follow the true, authentic path of justice, and
not merely what is thought to be just. That argument maintains that
what a good and just man does is to give everyone his due. (One
problem which arises in this connection is what, if anything, we are
to grant *dumb animals* as their due. Men of far from mediocre
caliber, indeed men of powerful learning such as Pythagoras and
Empedocles,[11] insist that identical standards of justice apply to all
living creatures, and declare that inexorable penalties await those
who ill-treat animals. To do them harm, in other words, seems to
them to be criminal.)[12]

PHILUS: Anyone who has the power of life and death over a people is 14
a despot—though they prefer to be known as kings, following the
example of Jupiter the Best.

When however, instead, a group of men seize the state by 15
exploiting their wealth or noble birth or some other resource, that is
a political upheaval, though they call themselves conservatives. If, on
the other hand, the people gain the supremacy, and the whole government is conducted according to their wishes, a state of affairs has
arisen which is hailed as liberty, but is, in fact, chaos. But when there
is a situation of mutual fear, with one person or one class fearing
another, then because nobody has sufficient confidence in his own
strength a kind of bargain is struck between the ordinary people and

---

[10] Several lines are missing from the original manuscript.
[11] **Pythagoras (582–507 B.C.) . . . Empedocles (493–433 B.C.)** Influential
Greek philosophers whose works were well known to Cicero.
[12] At this point some of the original manuscript is lost.

the men who are powerful. The result, in that case, is the mixed form of constitution which Scipio[13] recommends. Which means that weakness, not nature or good intention, is the mother of justice.

For we have to choose one of three things. We can perform injustice and not suffer it. Or we can both perform and suffer it. Or we can neither perform it nor suffer it. The most fortunate choice is the first, to perform injustice, if you can get away with it. The second best is neither to perform it nor suffer it. And the worst is to engage in an everlasting turmoil consisting of both performing it and suffering it.   16

Wisdom, as commonly understood, prompts us to increase our resources, to multiply our riches, to enlarge our frontiers. For the essential significance, surely, of those eulogistic words inscribed upon the monuments of our greatest generals, "he extended the boundaries of the empire," is that he had extended them by taking territory from someone else. That, then, is the teaching of "wisdom," that we should rule over as many subjects as possible, indulge in pleasures, hold on to power, be rulers and masters. But justice, on the other hand, demands that we should be merciful to all men, act in the interests of the entire human race, give everyone what they are entitled to, and never tamper with religious property or what belongs to the community or to private persons.   17

If you follow the dictates of what we call wisdom, then, you acquire wealth, power, resources, lofty status, military commands, and positions of supreme authority, whether you are a state or a private person. What we, however, are at present considering is the former of these two categories, the state, and so what is done by states assumes priority for our present purpose. True, the same standards of justice apply to states and individuals alike, but the former are what we now have to consider. In particular, not to mention other nations, it is clear enough that our own Roman people, whose history Scipio traced from its beginnings in yesterday's discussion, and whose empire is now world-wide, grew from the smallest to the greatest dimensions by wisdom, and not by justice.   18

When, however, one sets justice against wisdom in the way I have attempted to do here, the contrast is sometimes blurred by arguments that complicate the issue. The men who put these arguments forward understand very well how to argue; and their reasoning on the subject carries all the more impressive weight because, in the course of their investigation into how to find the good man (a man who himself should be open and frank), they, like him, refrain from using underhand, crafty, or dishonest methods of argument. What these philosophers do, then, is take a closer look at the "wise"   19

---

[13] **Scipio (185–129 B.C.)** Roman general.

man, and put forward the view that he is good not because goodness or justice automatically, or in themselves, offer him satisfaction, but, on the contrary, because a good man's life is free of fear, worry, anxiety, and peril, whereas bad men always have something to feel uneasy about, and the prospects of trials and penalties are never out of their sight. No benefit or reward gained by injustice, these thinkers add, is substantial enough to counterbalance perpetual fear, or the never-ending thought that some punishment or other is not far away.[14] . . .

Let us imagine that there are two men, one a paragon of virtue,   20 fairness, justice, and honesty, and the other an outrageous ruffian. And let us suppose that their country is so misguided that it believes that the good man is an evil, villainous criminal, and that the bad man, on the other hand, is a model of honorable propriety. Then let us go on to suppose that, since this is the unanimous opinion, the good man is attacked, seized, imprisoned, blinded, convicted, chained, branded, expelled, and beggared, so that everyone feels, quite rightly, that he is the most wretched man alive. Whereas the bad man, on the other hand, is praised, courted, and loved by one and all. Every kind of public office and military command is showered upon him, as well as riches and wealth from every quarter. To sum up, then, he will have the universal reputation of being the best man in the world, who deserves everything good that fortune can give him. Now, I ask you, who could be so mad as to doubt which of the two men he would prefer to be?

The same applies to states, just as much as to individuals. No   21 country would not rather be an unjust master than a just slave. I shall not range far ahead for the example I am going to quote. While I was consul, and you were on my council, the question of the treaty with Numantia came up before me. Everyone knew that treaties had been made already, by Quintus Pompeius and then by Gaius Hostilius Mancinus.[15] Mancinus, a good man, went so far as to favor the bill which I myself had proposed in accordance with a senatorial decree, even though he was to be the sufferer. Pompeius, on the other hand, fought back strongly against an equally critical resolution directed against himself. If you are looking for self-denial, honor, and integrity, those are the qualities that Mancinus displayed. But if you want rationality, good sense, and prudence, Pompeius wins.[16] . . .

---

[14] Some of the original manuscript is lost here.

[15] **Quintus Pompeius . . . Gaius Hostilius Mancinus** Roman consuls in 141 and 137 B.C.

[16] Much of Carneades' argument (which Philus relies upon) is missing here.

LAELIUS: True law is in keeping with the dictates both of reason and 22
of nature. It applies universally to everyone. It is unchanging and
eternal. Its commands are summons to duty, and its prohibitions
declare that nothing wrongful must be done. As far as good men are
concerned, both its commands and its prohibitions are effective;
though neither have any effect on men who are bad. To attempt to
invalidate this law is sinful. Nor is it possible to repeal any part of it,
much less to abolish it altogether. From its obligations neither Senate nor people can release us. And to explain or interpret it we need
no one outside our own selves.

There will not be one law at Rome, and another at Athens. There 23
will not be different laws now and in the future. Instead there will be
one single, everlasting, immutable law, which applies to all nations
and all times. The maker, and umpire, and proposer of this law will be
God, the single master and ruler of us all. If a man fails to obey God,
then he will be in flight from his own self, repudiating his own human
nature. As a consequence, even if he escapes the normal punishment
for wrongdoing, he will suffer the penalties of the gravest possible sort.

QUESTIONS FOR CRITICAL READING

1. Why does Laelius choose Philus to argue against justice?
2. Does arguing against a positive value help our understanding of that
   value's importance?
3. What is Philus's reputation and how does it affect his argument?
4. How do ideas of justice differ in the different lands Philus mentions?
5. On which side of this argument is Cicero himself?
6. To what extent is Philus a feminist?
7. Which of Laelius's statements in the final paragraphs of the selection
   seem weakest to you?
8. What are the strengths of Laelius's argument at the end of the selection?

SUGGESTIONS FOR CRITICAL WRITING

1. In paragraph 13, Philus reminds us that Pythagoras and Empedocles
   both insisted that "identical standards of justice apply to all living creatures." Do you feel that the question of justice applies to our treatment
   of animals? How would one construct an argument that took one side
   or the other of this argument? Is anyone making this argument in public today?

2. Philus says you can't have one law that everyone will obey. Make an argument in favor of maintaining one law for all people in all nations. Remember that different societies treat women in vastly different ways and, in effect, have one law for men and another for women. Some societies still tolerate slavery, and at one time slavery was maintained by law in many nations of the world. In Cicero's time, the citizens of any defeated nation could expect to become slaves. Slavery had been legal in the ancient world of both Rome and Greece.

3. In paragraph 15, Philus says that "weakness, not nature or good intention, is the mother of justice." Do you agree? Does our desire for justice arise from a sense of our own weakness? What differences may exist between the strong and the weak in terms of their attitude toward justice? Who needs justice more?

4. Philus mentions natural law or natural justice several times. He argues against there being any such law or justice. Develop an argument that defends the concept of natural law. What, for instance, might people living outside society in a natural setting hope for in terms of justice? What might their concept of justice be? How necessary would justice be in a state of nature?

5. Clarify what Philus means by the term "wisdom," which he introduces in paragraph 18. How do you understand his use of the term and how appropriate is the word "wisdom" for the ideas he describes? Would most people today regard the behavior he sketches out as an example of wisdom? Is it wisdom for you? What moral or ethical problems arise from Philus's concept of wisdom?

6. Philus asks you to make a choice between being one of two different men. He describes them in detail in paragraph 20. Which one would you rather be? Defend your choice by reference to your best understanding of justice. Would it be just for you to behave as you would, given the choices Philus gives you?

7. Philus gives us three choices in regard to injustice: 1. We can perform injustice and not suffer it ourselves; 2. We can both perform it and suffer it; or 3. We can neither perform it nor suffer it. He says the best choice is clearly the first. Do you think that is true? Do you think he feels it is true? Argue a case that supports one of these three choices, but that at the same time condemns the other two.

8. Aristotle warns us that it is dangerous to argue from analogy. But Philus makes his strongest points at the end of his argument when he compares the individual in paragraph 20 with the entire state in paragraph 21. How strong is his argument in the last paragraphs of his presentation? Basically, he tells us that strength creates its own justice and that the weak must go along with the strong. Is this what you understand as justice?

9. **CONNECTIONS**   Compare Philus's views of what justice is and how wisdom works in a political environment with the views of Henry David Thoreau in "Civil Disobedience." How do their views on justice differ and how do their views on just laws differ?

10. **SEEING CONNECTIONS** What concepts and ideas implied by Giordano's fresco *Justice* (p. 140) would Philus have used in an argument against justice? Philus talks about wisdom, one of the four cardinal virtues, but would he have conceived of justice as belonging with wisdom in that group? Would Philus see examples of natural law or natural justice in the painting? If so, what would he have made of them? How would he have defended his view that justice varies from place to place in light of the details in the painting?

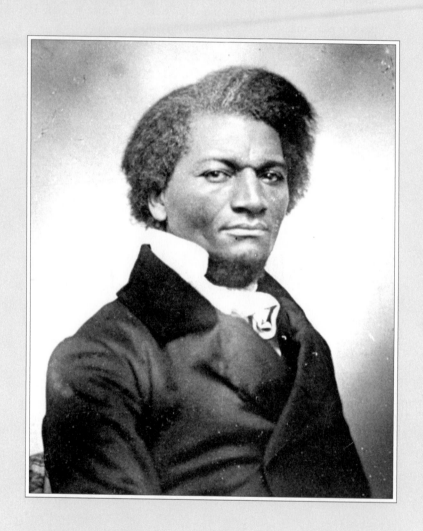

FREDERICK DOUGLASS
From *Narrative of the Life of Frederick Douglass, an American Slave*

FREDERICK DOUGLASS (1817–1895) was born into slavery in Maryland; he died not only a free man but also a man who commanded the respect of his country, his government, and hosts of supporters. Ironically, it was his owner's wife, Mrs. Hugh Auld, a Northerner, who helped Douglass learn to read and write. Until her husband forcefully convinced her that teaching slaves was "unlawful, as well as unsafe," Mrs. Auld taught Douglass enough so that he could begin his own education—and escape to freedom. Mrs. Auld eventually surpassed her husband in her vehement opposition to having Douglass read, leading Douglass to conclude that slavery had a negative effect on slave and slaveholder alike: both suffered the consequences of a political system that was inherently unjust.

The *Narrative* is filled with examples of the injustice of slavery. Douglass had little connection with his family. Separated from his mother, Harriet Bailey, Douglass never knew who his father was. In his *Narrative*, he records the beatings he witnessed as a slave, the conditions under which he lived, and the struggles he felt within himself to be a free man. Douglass himself survived brutal beatings and torture by a professional slave "breaker."

The laws of the time codified the injustices that Douglass and all American slaves suffered. The Fugitive Slave Act of 1793 tightened the hold on all slaves who had gone north in search of freedom. Federal marshals were enjoined to return slaves to their owners. The Underground Railroad helped so many runaway slaves find their way to Canada that a second Fugitive Slave Act was enacted in 1850 with stiff penalties for those who did not obey the law.

First published 1845; revised 1892.

In retaliation, many northern states enacted personal freedom laws to counter the Fugitive Slave Act. Eventually, these laws became central to the South's decision to secede. However, Douglass's fate, when he eventually escaped in 1838 by impersonating an African American seaman (using his papers to board ship), was not secure. Abolitionists in New York helped him find work in shipyards in New Bedford, Massachusetts. He changed his name from Auld to Douglass to protect himself, and he began his career as an orator in 1841 at an antislavery meeting in Nantucket.

To avoid capture after publication of an early version of his autobiography, Douglass spent two years on a speaking tour of Great Britain and Ireland (1845–1847). He then returned to the United States, bought his freedom, and rose to national fame as the founder and editor of the *North Star*, an abolitionist paper published in Rochester, New York. One of his chief concerns was for the welfare of the slaves who had managed to secure their freedom. When the Civil War began, there were no plans to free the slaves, but Douglass managed to convince President Lincoln that it would further the war effort to free them; in 1863, the president delivered the Emancipation Proclamation.

However, the years after the war and Lincoln's death were not good for freed slaves. Terrorist groups in both the North and the South worked to keep them from enjoying freedom, and training programs for former slaves that might have been effective were never fully instituted. During this time, Douglass worked in various capacities for the government—as assistant secretary of the Santo Domingo Commission, as an official in Washington, D.C., and as U.S. minister to Haiti (1889–1891). He was the first African American to become a national figure and to have influence with the government.

Douglass's Rhetoric

Douglass was basically self-taught, but he knew enough to read the powerful writers of his day. He was a commanding speaker in an age in which eloquence was valued and speakers were rewarded handsomely. This excerpt from the *Narrative*—Chapters 6, 7, and 8—is notable for its clear and direct style. The use of the first-person narrative is as simple as one could wish, yet the feelings projected are sincere and moving.

Douglass's structure is the chronological narrative, relating events in the order in which they occurred. He begins his story at the point of meeting a new mistress, a woman from whom he expected harsh treatment. Because she was new to the concept of slavery, however, she behaved in ways that were unusual, and

Douglass remarks on her initially kind attitude. Douglass does not interrupt himself with flashbacks or leaps forward in time but tells the story as it happened. At critical moments, he slows the narrative to describe people or incidents in unusual detail and lets the reader infer from these details the extent of the injustice he suffered.

By today's standards, Douglass's style may seem formal. His sentences are often longer than those of modern writers, although they are always carefully balanced and punctuated by briefer sentences. Despite his long paragraphs, heavy with example and description, after a century and a half his work remains immediate and moving. No modern reader will have difficulty responding to what Frederick Douglass has to say. His views on education are as accessible and as powerful now as when they were written.

PREREADING QUESTIONS: WHAT TO READ FOR

The following prereading questions may help you anticipate key issues in the discussion of the excerpt that follows from *Narrative of the Life of Frederick Douglass, an American Slave.* Keeping them in mind during your first reading of the selection should help focus your attention.

- How would learning to read and write help promote justice in Douglass's life?
- In what ways was Douglass aware of being treated unjustly?
- What concepts of justice did slaveholders seem to have? What form did justice take in their system?

From *Narrative of the Life of Frederick Douglass, an American Slave*

My new mistress proved to be all she appeared when I first met   1
her at the door, — a woman of the kindest heart and finest feelings. She had never had a slave under her control previously to myself, and prior to her marriage she had been dependent upon her own industry for a living. She was by trade a weaver; and by constant application to her business, she had been in a good degree preserved from the blighting and dehumanizing effects of slavery. I was utterly astonished at her goodness. I scarcely knew how to behave towards her. She was entirely unlike any other white woman I had ever seen. I could not approach her as I was accustomed to approach other

white ladies. My early instruction was all out of place. The crouch-
ing servility, usually so acceptable a quality in a slave, did not
answer when manifested toward her. Her favor was not gained by it;
she seemed to be disturbed by it. She did not deem it impudent or
unmannerly for a slave to look her in the face. The meanest slave
was put fully at ease in her presence, and none left without feeling
better for having seen her. Her face was made of heavenly smiles,
and her voice of tranquil music.

But, alas! this kind heart had but a short time to remain such.   2
The fatal poison of irresponsible power was already in her hands,
and soon commenced its infernal work. That cheerful eye, under the
influence of slavery, soon became red with rage; that voice, made all
of sweet accord, changed to one of harsh and horrid discord; and
that angelic face gave place to that of a demon.

Very soon after I went to live with Mr. and Mrs. Auld, she very   3
kindly commenced to teach me the A, B, C. After I had learned this,
she assisted me in learning to spell words of three or four letters.
Just at this point of my progress, Mr. Auld found out what was
going on, and at once forbade Mrs. Auld to instruct me further,
telling her, among other things, that it was unlawful, as well as
unsafe, to teach a slave to read. To use his own words, further, he
said, "If you give a nigger an inch, he will take an ell.[1] A nigger
should know nothing but to obey his master—to do as he is told to
do. Learning would *spoil* the best nigger in the world. Now," said he,
"if you teach that nigger (speaking of myself) how to read, there
would be no keeping him. It would forever unfit him to be a slave.
He would at once become unmanageable, and of no value to his
master. As to himself, it could do him no good, but a great deal of
harm. It would make him discontented and unhappy." These words
sank deep into my heart, stirred up sentiments within that lay slum-
bering, and called into existence an entirely new train of thought. It
was a new and special revelation, explaining dark and mysterious
things, with which my youthful understanding had struggled, but
struggled in vain. I now understood what had been to me a most
perplexing difficulty—to wit, the white man's power to enslave the
black man. It was a grand achievement, and I prized it highly. From
that moment, I understood the pathway from slavery to freedom. It
was just what I wanted, and I got it at a time when I the least
expected it. Whilst I was saddened by the thought of losing the aid of
my kind mistress, I was gladdened by the invaluable instruction
which, by the merest accident, I had gained from my master. Though
conscious of the difficulty of learning without a teacher, I set out

---

[1] **ell** A measure about a yard in length.

with high hope, and a fixed purpose, at whatever cost of trouble, to learn how to read. The very decided manner with which he spoke, and strove to impress his wife with the evil consequences of giving me instruction, served to convince me that he was deeply sensible of the truths he was uttering. It gave me the best assurance that I might rely with the utmost confidence on the results which, he said, would flow from teaching me to read. What he most dreaded, that I most desired. What he most loved, that I most hated. That which to him was a great evil, to be carefully shunned, was to me a great good, to be diligently sought; and the argument which he so warmly urged, against my learning to read, only served to inspire me with a desire and determination to learn. In learning to read, I owe almost as much to the bitter opposition of my master, as to the kindly aid of my mistress. I acknowledge the benefit of both.

I had resided but a short time in Baltimore before I observed a   4
marked difference, in the treatment of slaves, from that which I had witnessed in the country. A city slave is almost a freeman, compared with a slave on the plantation. He is much better fed and clothed, and enjoys privileges altogether unknown to the slave on the plantation. There is a vestige of decency, a sense of shame, that does much to curb and check those outbreaks of atrocious cruelty so commonly enacted upon the plantation. He is a desperate slaveholder, who will shock the humanity of his nonslaveholding neighbors with the cries of his lacerated slave. Few are willing to incur the odium attaching to the reputation of being a cruel master; and above all things, they would not be known as not giving a slave enough to eat. Every city slaveholder is anxious to have it known of him, that he feeds his slaves well; and it is due to them to say, that most of them do give their slaves enough to eat. There are, however, some painful exceptions to this rule. Directly opposite to us, on Philpot Street, lived Mr. Thomas Hamilton. He owned two slaves. Their names were Henrietta and Mary. Henrietta was about twenty-two years of age, Mary was about fourteen; and of all the mangled and emaciated creatures I ever looked upon, these two were the most so. His heart must be harder than stone, that could look upon these unmoved. The head, neck, and shoulders of Mary were literally cut to pieces. I have frequently felt her head, and found it nearly covered with festering sores, caused by the lash of her cruel mistress. I do not know that her master ever whipped her, but I have been an eyewitness to the cruelty of Mrs. Hamilton. I used to be in Mr. Hamilton's house nearly every day. Mrs. Hamilton used to sit in a large chair in the middle of the room, with a heavy cowskin always by her side, and scarce an hour passed during the day but was marked by the blood of one of these slaves. The girls seldom passed her without her saying, "Move

faster, you *black gip!*" at the same time giving them a blow with
the cowskin over the head or shoulders, often drawing the blood.
She would then say, "Take that, you *black gip!*"—continuing, "If you
don't move faster, I'll move you!" Added to the cruel lashings to
which these slaves were subjected, they were kept nearly half-
starved. They seldom knew what it was to eat a full meal. I have seen
Mary contending with the pigs for the offal thrown into the street. So
much was Mary kicked and cut to pieces, that she was oftener called
"*pecked*" than by her name.

    I lived in Master Hugh's family about seven years. During this   5
time, I succeeded in learning to read and write. In accomplishing
this, I was compelled to resort to various stratagems. I had no regular teacher. My mistress, who had kindly commenced to instruct me,
had, in compliance with the advice and direction of her husband,
not only ceased to instruct, but had set her face against my being
instructed by any one else. It is due, however, to my mistress to say
of her, that she did not adopt this course of treatment immediately.
She at first lacked the depravity indispensable to shutting me up in
mental darkness. It was at least necessary for her to have some training in the exercise of irresponsible power, to make her equal to the
task of treating me as though I were a brute.

    My mistress was, as I have said, a kind and tender-hearted   6
woman; and in the simplicity of her soul she commenced, when I
first went to live with her, to treat me as she supposed one human
being ought to treat another. In entering upon the duties of a slaveholder, she did not seem to perceive that I sustained to her the relation of a mere chattel, and that for her to treat me as a human being
was not only wrong, but dangerously so. Slavery proved as injurious
to her as it did to me. When I went there, she was a pious, warm,
and tender-hearted woman. There was no sorrow or suffering for
which she had not a tear. She had bread for the hungry, clothes for
the naked, and comfort for every mourner that came within her
reach. Slavery soon proved its ability to divest her of these heavenly
qualities. Under its influence, the tender heart became stone, and
the lamblike disposition gave way to one of tiger-like fierceness. The
first step in her downward course was in her ceasing to instruct me.
She now commenced to practice her husband's precepts. She finally
became even more violent in her opposition than her husband himself. She was not satisfied with simply doing as well as he had commanded; she seemed anxious to do better. Nothing seemed to make
her more angry than to see me with a newspaper. She seemed to
think that here lay the danger. I have had her rush at me with a face
made all up of fury, and snatch from me a newspaper, in a manner

that fully revealed her apprehension. She was an apt woman; and a little experience soon demonstrated, to her satisfaction, that education and slavery were incompatible with each other.

From this time I was most narrowly watched. If I was in a separate room any considerable length of time, I was sure to be suspected of having a book, and was at once called to give an account of myself. All this, however, was too late. The first step had been taken. Mistress, in teaching me the alphabet, had given me the *inch*, and no precaution could prevent me from taking the *ell*.

The plan which I adopted, and the one by which I was most successful, was that of making friends of all the little white boys whom I met in the street. As many of these as I could, I converted into teachers. With their kindly aid, obtained at different times and in different places, I finally succeeded in learning to read. When I was sent to errands, I always took my book with me, and by going one part of my errand quickly, I found time to get a lesson before my return. I used also to carry bread with me, enough of which was always in the house, and to which I was always welcome; for I was much better off in this regard than many of the poor white children in our neighborhood. This bread I used to bestow upon the hungry little urchins, who, in return, would give me that more valuable bread of knowledge. I am strongly tempted to give the names of two or three of those little boys, as a testimonial of the gratitude and affection I bear them; but prudence forbids;—not that it would injure me, but it might embarrass them; for it is almost an unpardonable offense to teach slaves to read in this Christian country. It is enough to say of the dear little fellows, that they lived on Philpot Street, very near Durgin and Bailey's ship-yard. I used to talk this matter of slavery over with them. I would sometimes say to them, I wished I could be as free as they would be when they got to be men. "You will be free as soon as you are twenty-one, *but I am a slave for life!* Have not I as good a right to be free as you have?" These words used to trouble them; they would express for me the liveliest sympathy, and console me with the hope that something would occur by which I might be free.

I was now about twelve years old, and the thought of being *a slave for life* began to bear heavily upon my heart. Just about this time, I got hold of a book entitled "The Columbian Orator." Every opportunity I got, I used to read this book. Among much of other interesting matter, I found in it a dialogue between a master and his slave. The slave was represented as having run away from his master three times. The dialogue represented the conversation which took place between them, when the slave was retaken the third time. In this dialogue, the whole argument in behalf of slavery was brought forward by the master, all of which was disposed of by the slave. The slave was made to say some very smart as well as impressive things in reply to his master—things which had the desired though unexpected effect; for the conversation resulted in the voluntary emancipation of the slave on the part of the master.

In the same book, I met with one of Sheridan's[2] mighty   10
speeches on and in behalf of Catholic emancipation. These were choice documents to me. I read them over and over again with unabated interest. They gave tongue to interesting thoughts of my own soul, which had frequently flashed through my mind, and died away for want of utterance. The moral which I gained from the dialogue was the power of truth over the conscience of even a slaveholder. What I got from Sheridan was a bold denunciation of slavery, and a powerful vindication of human rights. The reading of these documents enabled me to utter my thoughts, and to meet the arguments brought forward to sustain slavery; but while they relieved me of one difficulty, they brought on another even more painful than the one of which I was relieved. The more I read, the more I was led to abhor and detest my enslavers. I could regard them in no other light than a band of successful robbers, who had left their homes, and gone to Africa, and stolen us from our homes, and in a strange land reduced us to slavery. I loathed them as being the meanest as well as the most wicked of men. As I read and contemplated the subject, behold! that very discontentment which Master Hugh had predicted would follow my learning to read had already come, to torment and sting my soul to unutterable anguish. As I writhed under it, I would at times feel that learning to read had been a curse rather than a blessing. It had given me a view of my wretched condition, without the remedy. It opened my eyes to the horrible pit, but to no ladder upon which to get out. In moments of agony, I envied my fellow-slaves for their stupidity. I have often wished myself a beast. I preferred the condition of the meanest reptile to my own. Any thing, no matter what, to get rid of thinking! It was this everlasting thinking of my condition that tormented me. There was no getting rid of it. It was pressed upon me by every object within sight or hearing, animate or inanimate. The silver trump of freedom had roused my soul to eternal wakefulness. Freedom now appeared, to disappear no more forever. It was heard in every sound, and seen in every thing. It was ever present to torment

---

[2] **Richard Brinsley Sheridan (1751–1816)** Irish dramatist and orator. However, Douglass really refers to a speech by Daniel O'Connell (1775–1847) in favor of Irish Catholic emancipation.

me with a sense of my wretched condition. I saw nothing without seeing it, I heard nothing without hearing it, and felt nothing without feeling it. It looked from every star, it smiled in every calm, breathed in every wind, and moved in every storm.

I often found myself regretting my own existence, and wishing   11
myself dead; and but for the hope of being free, I have no doubt but that I should have killed myself, or done something for which I should have been killed. While in this state of mind, I was eager to hear any one speak of slavery. I was a ready listener. Every little while, I could hear something about the abolitionists.[3] It was some time before I found what the word meant. It was always used in such connections as to make it an interesting word to me. If a slave ran away and succeeded in getting clear, or if a slave killed his master, set fire to a barn, or did any thing very wrong in the mind of a slaveholder, it was spoken of as the fruit of *abolition.* Hearing the word in this connection very often, I set about learning what it meant. The dictionary afforded me little or no help. I found it was "the act of abolishing"; but then I did not know what was to be abolished. Here I was perplexed. I did not dare to ask any one about its meaning, for I was satisfied that it was something they wanted me to know very little about. After a patient waiting, I got one of our city papers, containing an account of the number of petitions from the north, praying for the abolition of slavery in the District of Columbia, and of the slave trade between the States. From this time I understood the words *abolition* and *abolitionist,* and always drew near when that word was spoken, expecting to hear something of importance to myself and fellow-slaves. The light broke in upon me by degrees. I went one day down on the wharf of Mr. Waters; and seeing two Irishmen unloading a scow of stone, I went, unasked, and helped them. When we had finished, one of them came to me and asked me if I were a slave. I told him I was. He asked, "Are ye a slave for life?" I told him that I was. The good Irishman seemed to be deeply affected by the statement. He said to the other that it was a pity so fine a little fellow as myself should be a slave for life. He said it was a shame to hold me. They both advised me to run away to the north; that I should find friends there, and that I should be free. I pretended not to be interested in what they said, and treated them as if I did not understand them; for I feared they might be treacherous. White men have been known to encourage slaves to escape, and then, to get the reward, catch them and return them to their masters. I was afraid that these seemingly good men might use me so; but I nevertheless

---

[3] **abolitionists** Those who actively opposed slavery.

remembered their advice, and from that time I resolved to run away. I looked forward to a time at which it would be safe for me to escape. I was too young to think of doing so immediately; besides, I wished to learn how to write, as I might have occasion to write my own pass. I consoled myself with the hope that I should one day find a good chance. Meanwhile, I would learn to write.

The idea as to how I might learn to write was suggested to me by being in Durgin and Bailey's ship-yard, and frequently seeing the ship carpenters, after hewing, and getting a piece of timber ready for use, write on the timber the name of that part of the ship for which it was intended. When a piece of timber was intended for the larboard side, it would be marked thus—"L." When a piece was for the starboard side, it would be marked thus—"S." A piece for the larboard side forward, would be marked thus—"L.F." When a piece was for starboard side forward, it would be marked thus—"S.F." For larboard aft, it would be marked thus—"L.A." For starboard aft, it would be marked thus—"S.A." I soon learned the names of these letters, and for what they were intended when placed upon a piece of timber in the ship-yard. I immediately commenced copying them, and in a short time was able to make the four letters named. After that, when I met with any boy who I knew could write, I would tell him I could write as well as he. The next word would be, "I don't believe you. Let me see you try it." I would then make the letters which I had been so fortunate as to learn, and ask him to beat that. In this way I got a good many lessons in writing, which it is quite possible I should never have gotten in any other way. During this time, my copy-book was the board fence, brick wall, and pavement; my pen and ink was a lump of chalk. With these, I learned mainly how to write. I then commenced and continued copying the Italics in Webster's Spelling Book, until I could make them all without looking on the book. By this time, my little Master Thomas had gone to school, and learned how to write, and had written over a number of copy-books. These had been brought home, and shown to some of our near neighbors, and then laid aside. My mistress used to go to class meeting at the Wilk Street meeting-house every Monday afternoon, and leave me to take care of the house. When left thus, I used to spend the time in writing in the spaces left in Master Thomas's copy-book, copying what he had written. I continued to do this until I could write a hand very similar to that of Master Thomas. Thus, after a long, tedious effort for years, I finally succeeded in learning how to write.

In a very short time after I went to live at Baltimore, my old master's youngest son Richard died; and in about three years and six months after his death, my old master, Captain Anthony, died, leaving only his son, Andrew, and daughter, Lucretia, to share his estate. He died while on a visit to see his daughter at Hillsborough. Cut off thus unexpectedly, he left no will as to the disposal of his property. It was therefore necessary to have a valuation of the property, that it might be equally divided between Mrs. Lucretia and Master Andrew. I was immediately sent for, to be valued with the other property. Here again my feelings rose up in detestation of slavery. I had now a new conception of my degraded condition. Prior to this, I had become, if not insensible to my lot, at least partly so. I left Baltimore with a young heart overborne with sadness, and a soul full of apprehension. I took passage with Captain Rowe, in the schooner *Wild Cat*, and, after a sail of about twenty-four hours, I found myself near the place of my birth. I had now been absent from it almost, if not quite, five years. I, however, remembered the place very well. I was only about five years old when I left it, to go and live with my old master on Colonel Lloyd's plantation; so that I was now between ten and eleven years old.

We were all ranked together at the valuation. Men and women, old and young, married and single, were ranked with horses, sheep, and swine. There were horses and men, cattle and women, pigs and children, all holding the same rank in the scale of being, and were all subjected to the same narrow examination. Silvery-headed age and sprightly youth, maids and matrons, had to undergo the same indelicate inspection. At this moment, I saw more clearly than ever the brutalizing effects of slavery upon both slave and slaveholder. 14

After the valuation, then came the division. I have no language to express the high excitement and deep anxiety which were felt among us poor slaves during this time. Our fate for life was now to be decided. We had no more voice in that decision than the brutes among whom we were ranked. A single word from the white men was enough—against all our wishes, prayers, and entreaties—to sunder forever the dearest friends, dearest kindred, and strongest ties known to human beings. In addition to the pain of separation, there was the horrid dread of falling into the hands of Master Andrew. He was known to us all as being a most cruel wretch,— a common drunkard, who had, by his reckless mismanagement and profligate dissipation, already wasted a large portion of his father's property. We all felt that we might as well be sold at once to the Georgia traders, as to pass into his hands; for we knew that that would be our inevitable condition,—a condition held by us all in the utmost horror and dread. 15

I suffered more anxiety than most of my fellow-slaves. I had known what it was to be kindly treated; they had known nothing of the kind. They had seen little or nothing of the world. They were in 16 very deed men and women of sorrow, and acquainted with grief. Their backs had been made familiar with the bloody lash, so that they had become callous; mine was yet tender; for while at Baltimore I got few whippings, and few slaves could boast of a kinder master and mistress than myself; and the thought of passing out of their hands into those of Master Andrew—a man who, but a few days before, to give me a sample of his bloody disposition, took my little brother by the throat, threw him on the ground, and with the heel of his boot stamped upon his head till the blood gushed from his nose and ears—was well calculated to make me anxious as to my fate. After he had committed this savage outrage upon my brother, he turned to me, and said that was the way he meant to serve me one of these days,—meaning, I suppose, when I came into his possession.

Thanks to a kind Providence, I fell to the portion of Mrs. Lucretia, and was sent immediately back to Baltimore, to live again in the family of Master Hugh. Their joy at my return equalled their sorrow at my departure. It was a glad day to me. I had escaped a worse fate than lion's jaws. I was absent from Baltimore, for the purpose of valuation and division, just about one month, and it seemed to have been six.   17

Very soon after my return to Baltimore, my mistress, Lucretia, died, leaving her husband and child, Amanda; and in a very short time after her death, Master Andrew died. Now all the property of my old master, slaves included, was in the hands of strangers,— strangers who had had nothing to do with accumulating it. Not a slave was left free. All remained slaves, from the youngest to the oldest. If any one thing in my experience, more than another, served to deepen my conviction of the infernal character of slavery, and to fill me with unutterable loathing of slaveholders, it was their base ingratitude to my poor old grandmother. She had served my old master faithfully from youth to old age. She had been the source of all his wealth; she had peopled his plantation with slaves; she had become a great grandmother in his service. She had rocked him in infancy, attended him in childhood, served him through life, and at his death wiped from his icy brow the cold death-sweat, and closed his eyes forever. She was nevertheless left a slave—a slave for life—a slave in the hands of strangers; and in their hands she saw her children, her grandchildren, and her great-grandchildren, divided, like so many sheep, without being gratified with the small privilege of a single word, as to their or her own destiny. And, to cap the climax of their base ingratitude and fiendish barbarity, my grandmother, who was now very old, having outlived my old master and all his   18 children, having seen the beginning and end of all of them, and her present owners finding she was of but little value, her frame already racked with the pains of old age, and complete helplessness fast stealing over her once active limbs, they took her to the woods, built her a little hut, put up a little mud-chimney, and then made her welcome to the privilege of supporting herself there in perfect loneliness; thus virtually turning her out to die! If my poor old grandmother now lives, she lives to suffer in utter loneliness; she lives to remember and mourn over the loss of children, the loss of grandchildren, and the loss of great-grandchildren. They are, in the language of the slave's poet, Whittier,[4] —

> Gone, gone, sold and gone
> To the rice swamp dank and lone,
> Where the slave-whip ceaseless swings,
> Where the noisome insect stings,
> Where the fever-demon strews
> Poison with the falling dews,
> Where the sickly sunbeams glare
> Through the hot and misty air: —
> > Gone, gone, sold and gone
> > To the rice swamp dank and lone,
> > From Virginia hills and waters —
> > Woe is me, my stolen daughters!

The hearth is desolate. The children, the unconscious children, who once sang and danced in her presence, are gone. She gropes her way, in the darkness of age, for a drink of water. Instead of the voices of her children, she hears by day the moans of the dove, and by night the screams of the hideous owl. All is gloom. The grave is at the door. And now, when weighed down by the pains and aches of old age, when the head inclines to the feet, when the beginning and ending of human existence meet, and helpless infancy and painful old age combine together — at this time, this most needful time, the time for the exercise of that tenderness and affection which children only can exercise towards a declining parent — my poor old grandmother, the devoted mother of twelve children, is left all alone, in yonder little hut, before a few dim embers. She stands — she sits — she staggers — she falls — she groans — she dies — and there are none of her children or grandchildren present, to wipe from her wrinkled brow the cold sweat of death, or to place

[4] **John Greenleaf Whittier (1807–1892)** New England abolitionist, journalist, and poet. The poem Douglass cites is "The Farewell" (1835).

beneath the sod her fallen remains. Will not a righteous God visit
for these things?

In about two years after the death of Mrs. Lucretia, Master   20
Thomas married his second wife. Her name was Rowena Hamilton.
She was the eldest daughter of Mr. William Hamilton. Master now
lived in St. Michael's. Not long after his marriage, a misunderstanding took place between himself and Master Hugh; and as a means of
punishing his brother, he took me from him to live with himself at
St. Michael's. Here I underwent another most painful separation. It,
however, was not so severe as the one I dreaded at the division of
property; for, during this interval, a great change had taken place in
Master Hugh and his once kind and affectionate wife. The influence
of brandy upon him, and of slavery upon her, had effected a disastrous change in the characters of both; so that, as far as they were
concerned, I thought I had little to lose by the change. But it was not
to them that I was attached. It was to those little Baltimore boys that
I felt the strongest attachment. I had received many good lessons
from them, and was still receiving them, and the thought of leaving
them was painful indeed. I was leaving, too, without the hope of ever
being allowed to return. Master Thomas had said he would never let
me return again. The barrier betwixt himself and brother he considered impassable.

I then had to regret that I did not at least make the attempt to   21
carry out my resolution to run away; for the chances of success are
tenfold greater from the city than from the country.

I sailed from Baltimore for St. Michael's in the sloop *Amanda*,   22
Captain Edward Dodson. On my passage, I paid particular attention
to the direction which the steamboats took to go to Philadelphia. I
found, instead of going down, on reaching North Point they went
up the bay, in a north-easterly direction. I deemed this knowledge of
the utmost importance. My determination to run away was again
revived. I resolved to wait only so long as the offering of a favorable
opportunity. When that came, I was determined to be off.

QUESTIONS FOR CRITICAL READING

1. Douglass describes Mrs. Auld as possessing "the fatal poison of irresponsible power" (para. 2). What precisely does he mean by this?
2. How does the absence of justice undermine the force of law?
3. Why did the slaveholders believe learning to read would spoil a slave?
4. What were the results of Douglass's learning to read?
5. How did the slaveholders regard their slaves? What differences does
   Douglass describe in their behavior?

SUGGESTIONS FOR CRITICAL WRITING

1. The society in which Douglass lived was governed by laws established by elected officials who had benefited from the writings of Cicero, Rousseau, and Jefferson, among others. How could the slaveholders in Maryland have conceived of their possession of slaves as an expression of justice?

2. What is the most important political issue raised in the essay? Douglass never talks about the law, but he implies a great deal about justice. What is the political truth regarding the laws in Maryland at this time? What seems to be the relationship between politics and justice in this essay? Do you think true justice was possible in this society?

3. One of the most constant defenses of the justness of slavery — even after the Civil War — was that it was for the good of the slaves. Even some of the freed slaves told interviewers in the 1930s that things had been better for them under slavery than they were during the Depression. How might Douglass have argued against this defense?

4. Douglass assures us that Mrs. Auld was "a kind and tender-hearted woman" (para. 6) when he first went to live with her but that her behavior soon came to resemble that of other slaveholders. How did her behavior alter, and what circumstances contributed to the change? Why does Douglass tell us about the change?

5. What, on the whole, is Douglass's attitude toward white people? Examine his statements about them, and establish as far as possible his feelings regarding their character. Is he bitter about his slavery experiences? Does he condemn the society that supported slavery as having been unjust?

6. How effective is the detailed description in this selection? Choose the best descriptive passages and analyze them for their effectiveness in context. What does Douglass hope to accomplish by lavishing so much attention on such description? How does his description help you better understand the concept of true justice?

7. **CONNECTIONS**   Which writer would Douglass have found most important in his quest for justice — Cicero, Thomas Jefferson, Henry David Thoreau, or Elizabeth Cady Stanton? Which would slaveholders have been most likely to agree with? What political ideals does Douglass seem to hold? What seems to be his concept of justice? To which writer does he seem to owe some of his views?

8. **CONNECTIONS**   Apply the definitions of totalitarianism put forth by Hannah Arendt (p. 121) to the American institution of slavery. How does Douglass's selection describe or reveal the form of governmental "justice" that allowed him to live as a slave?

9. **SEEING CONNECTIONS**   What specific visual details in Giordano's fresco *Justice* (p. 140) would have attracted Douglass's attention in his quest for justice? What would he have found most encouraging about the painting? What in the painting would have given him hope for a future in a just world?

HENRY DAVID THOREAU
Civil Disobedience

HENRY DAVID THOREAU (1817–1862) began keeping a journal when he graduated from Harvard in 1837. The journal was preserved and published, and it shows us the seriousness, determination, and elevation of moral values characteristic of all his work. He is best known for *Walden* (1854), a record of his departure from the warm congeniality of Concord, Massachusetts, and the home of his close friend Ralph Waldo Emerson (1803–1882), for the comparative "wilds" of Walden Pond, where he built a cabin, planted a garden, and lived simply. In *Walden,* Thoreau describes the deadening influence of ownership and extols the vitality and spiritual uplift that come from living close to nature. He also argues that civilization's comforts sometimes rob a person of independence, integrity, and even conscience.

Thoreau and Emerson were prominent among the group of writers and thinkers who were referred to as the Transcendentalists. They believed in something that transcended the limits of sensory experience—in other words, something that transcended materialism. Their philosophy was based on the works of Immanuel Kant (1724–1804), the German idealist philosopher; Samuel Taylor Coleridge (1772–1834), the English poet; and Johann Wolfgang von Goethe (1749–1832), the German dramatist and thinker. These writers praised human intuition and the capacity to see beyond the limits of common experience.

The Transcendentalists' philosophical idealism carried over into the social concerns of the day, expressing itself in works such as *Walden* and "Civil Disobedience," which was published with the title "Resistance to Civil Government" in 1849, a year after the publication of *The Communist Manifesto*. Although Thoreau all but

Originally published as "Resistance to Civil Government," 1849.

denies his idealism in "Civil Disobedience," it is obvious that after spending a night in the Concord jail, he realizes he cannot quietly accept his government's behavior in regard to slavery. He begins to feel that it is not only appropriate but imperative to disobey unjust laws.

In Thoreau's time the most flagrantly unjust laws were those that supported slavery. The Transcendentalists strongly opposed slavery and spoke out against it. Abolitionists in Massachusetts harbored escaped slaves and helped them move to Canada and freedom. The Fugitive Slave Act, enacted in 1850, the year after "Civil Disobedience" was published, made Thoreau a criminal because he refused to comply with Massachusetts civil authorities when in 1851 they began returning escaped slaves to the South as the law required.

"Civil Disobedience" was much more influential in the twentieth century than it was in the nineteenth. Mohandas Gandhi (1869–1948) claimed that while he was editor of an Indian newspaper in South Africa, it helped to inspire his theories of nonviolent resistance. Gandhi eventually implemented these theories against the British Empire and helped win independence for India. In the 1960s, Martin Luther King Jr. applied the same theories in the fight for racial equality in the United States. Thoreau's essay once again found widespread adherents among the many young men who resisted being drafted into the military to fight in Vietnam because they believed that the war was unjust.

"Civil Disobedience" was written after the Walden experience (which began on July 4, 1845, and ended on September 6, 1847). Thoreau quietly returned to Emerson's home and "civilization." His refusal in 1846 to pay the Massachusetts poll tax—a "per head" tax imposed on all citizens to help support what he considered an unjust war against Mexico—landed him in the Concord jail. He spent just one day and one night there—his aunt paid the tax for him—but the experience was so extraordinary that he began examining it in his journal.

Thoreau's Rhetoric

Thoreau maintained his journal throughout his life and eventually became convinced that writing was one of the few professions by which he could earn a living. He made more money, however, from lecturing on the lyceum circuit. The lyceum, a New England institution, was a town adult education program, featuring important speakers such as the very successful Emerson and foreign lecturers.

Admission fees were very reasonable, and in the absence of other popular entertainment, the lyceum was a major proving ground for speakers interested in promoting their ideas.

"Civil Disobedience" was first outlined in rough-hewn form in the journal, where the main ideas appear and where experiments in phrasing began. (Thoreau was a constant reviser.) Then in February 1848, Thoreau delivered a lecture on "Civil Disobedience" at the Concord Lyceum urging people of conscience to actively resist a government that acted badly. Finally, the piece was prepared for publication in *Aesthetic Papers*, an intellectual journal edited by Elizabeth Peabody (1804–1894), the sister-in-law of another important New England writer, Nathaniel Hawthorne (1804–1864). There it was refined again, and certain important details were added.

"Civil Disobedience" bears many of the hallmarks of the spoken lecture. For one thing, it is written in the first person and addresses an audience that Thoreau expects will share many of his sentiments but certainly not all his conclusions. His message is to some extent anarchistic, virtually denying an unjust government any authority or respect.

Modern political conservatives generally take his opening quote — "That government is best which governs least" — as a rallying cry against governmental interference in everyday affairs. Such conservatives usually propose reducing government interference by reducing the government's capacity to tax wealth for unpopular causes. In fact, what Thoreau opposes is simply any government that is not totally just, totally moral, and totally respectful of the individual.

The easiness of the pace of the essay also derives from its original form as a speech. Even such locutions as "But to speak practically and as a citizen" (para. 3) connect the essay with its origins. Although Thoreau was not an overwhelming orator — he was short and somewhat homely, an unprepossessing figure — he ensured that his writing achieved what some speakers might have accomplished by means of gesture and theatrics.

Thoreau's language is marked by clarity. He speaks directly to every issue, stating his own position and recommending the position he feels his audience, as reasonable and moral people, should accept. One impressive achievement in this selection is Thoreau's capacity to shape memorable, virtually aphoristic statements that remain "quotable" generations later, beginning with his own quotation from the words of John L. O'Sullivan: "That government is best which governs least." Thoreau calls it a motto, as if it belonged on the great seal of a government or on a coin. It contains an interesting and impressive rhetorical flourish—the device of repeating "govern" and the near rhyme of "best" with "least."

His most memorable statements show considerable attention to the rhetorical qualities of balance, repetition, and pattern. "The only obligation which I have a right to assume is to do at any time what I think right" (para. 4) uses the word *right* in two senses: first, as a matter of personal volition; second, as a matter of moral rectitude. One's right, in other words, becomes the opportunity to do right. "For it matters not how small the beginning may seem to be: what is once well done is done forever" (para. 21) also relies on repetition for its effect and balances the concept of a beginning with its capacity to reach out into the future. The use of the rhetorical device of *chiasmus*, a criss-cross relationship between key words, marks "Under a government which imprisons any unjustly, the true place for a just man is also a prison" (para. 22). Here is the pattern:

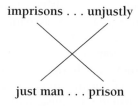

imprisons . . . unjustly

just man . . . prison

Such attention to phrasing is typical of speakers whose expressions must catch and retain the attention of listeners. Audiences do not have the advantage of referring to a text, so the words they hear must be forceful.

Thoreau relies also on analogy—comparing men with machines, people with plants, even the citizen with states considering secession from the Union. His analogies are effective and thus worth examining in some detail. He draws on the analysis of circumstance throughout the essay, carefully examining government actions to determine their qualities and their results. His questions include comments on politics (para. 1), on the Bible (para. 23), on Confucius (para. 24), and finally on his contemporary Daniel Webster (1782–1852) (para. 42), demonstrating a wide range of influences but avoiding the pedantic tone that can come from using quotations too liberally or from citing obscure sources. This essay is simple, direct, and uncluttered. Its enduring influence is in part due to the clarity and grace that characterize Thoreau's writing at its best. Its power derives from Thoreau's demand that citizens act on the basis of conscience.

PREREADING QUESTIONS: WHAT TO READ FOR

The following prereading questions may help you anticipate key issues in the discussion of Henry David Thoreau's "Civil Disobedience." Keeping them in mind during your first reading of the selection should help focus your attention.

- What kind of government does Thoreau feel would be most just?

- What is the individual's responsibility regarding supporting the government when it is wrong?

- How does Thoreau deal with unjust laws?

Civil Disobedience

I heartily accept the motto—"That government is best which governs least,"[1] and I should like to see it acted up to more rapidly and systematically. Carried out, it finally amounts to this, which also I believe—"That government is best which governs not at all"; and when men are prepared for it, that will be the kind of government which they will have. Government is at best but an expedient; but most governments are usually, and all governments are sometimes, inexpedient. The objections which have been brought against a standing army, and they are many and weighty, and deserve to prevail, may also at last be brought against a standing government. The standing army is only an arm of the standing government. The government itself, which is only the mode which the people have chosen to execute their will, is equally liable to be abused and perverted before the people can act through it. Witness the present Mexican war,[2] the work of comparatively a few individuals using the standing government as their tool; for in the outset the people would not have consented to this measure.

---

[1] **"... governs least"** John L. O'Sullivan (1813–1895) wrote in the *United States Magazine and Democratic Review* (1837) that "all government is evil, and the parents of evil.... The best government is that which governs least." Thomas Jefferson wrote, "That government is best which governs the least, because its people discipline themselves." Both comments echo the *Tao-te Ching*.

[2] **the present Mexican war (1846–1848)** The war was extremely unpopular in New England because it was an act of a bullying government anxious to grab land from a weaker nation. The United States had annexed Texas in 1845, precipitating a retaliation from Mexico.

This American government—what is it but a tradition, a recent 2
one, endeavoring to transmit itself unimpaired to posterity but each
instant losing some of its integrity? It has not the vitality and force of
a single living man; for a single man can bend it to his will. It is a
sort of wooden gun to the people themselves. But it is not the less
necessary for this; for the people must have some complicated
machinery or other, and hear its din, to satisfy that idea of government which they have. Governments show thus how successfully
men can be imposed on, even impose on themselves, for their own
advantage. It is excellent, we must all allow. Yet this government
never of itself furthered any enterprise but by the alacrity with
which it got out of its way. *It* does not keep the country free. *It* does
not settle the West. *It* does not educate. The character inherent in
the American people has done all that has been accomplished; and it
would have done somewhat more if the government had not sometimes got in its way. For government is an expedient by which men
would fain succeed in letting one another alone; and, as has been
said, when it is most expedient the governed are most let alone by it.
Trade and commerce, if they were not made of India-rubber, would
never manage to bounce over the obstacles which legislators are
continually putting in their way; and, if one were to judge these men
wholly by the effects of their actions and not partly by their intentions, they would deserve to be classed and punished with those
mischievous persons who put obstructions on the railroads.

But to speak practically and as a citizen, unlike those who call 3
themselves no-government men, I ask for, not at once no government, but *at once* a better government. Let every man make known
what kind of government would command his respect, and that will
be one step toward obtaining it.

After all, the practical reason why, when the power is once in 4
the hands of the people, a majority are permitted, and for a long
period continue, to rule is not because they are most likely to be in
the right, nor because this seems fairest to the minority but because
they are physically the strongest. But a government in which the
majority rule in all cases cannot be based on justice, even as far as
men understand it. Can there not be a government in which majorities do not virtually decide right and wrong but conscience?—in
which majorities decide only those questions to which the rule of
expediency is applicable? Must the citizen ever for a moment, or in
the least degree, resign his conscience to the legislator? Why has
every man a conscience then? I think that we should be men first
and subjects afterward. It is not desirable to cultivate a respect for
the law, so much as for the right. The only obligation which I have a

right to assume is to do at any time what I think right. It is truly
enough said that a corporation has no conscience; but a corporation
of conscientious men is a corporation *with* a conscience. Law never
made men a whit more just; and, by means of their respect for it,
even the well-disposed are daily made the agents of injustice. A
common and natural result of an undue respect for law is that you
may see a file of soldiers, colonel, captain, corporal, privates,
powder-monkeys,[3] and all, marching in admirable order over hill
and dale to the wars, against their wills, ay, against their common
sense and consciences, which makes it very steep marching indeed
and produces a palpitation of the heart. They have no doubt that it
is a damnable business in which they are concerned; they are all
peaceably inclined. Now, what are they? Men at all? or small mov-
able forts and magazines at the service of some unscrupulous man in
power? Visit the Navy-Yard,[4] and behold a marine, such a man as an
American government can make, or such as it can make a man with
its black arts—a mere shadow and reminiscence of humanity, a
man laid out alive and standing, and already, as one may say, buried
under arms with funeral accompaniments, though it may be—

> Not a drum was heard, not a funeral note,
> As his corse to the rampart we hurried;
> Not a soldier discharged his farewell shot
> O'er the grave where our hero we buried.[5]

The mass of men serve the state thus, not as men mainly, but as   5
machines, with their bodies. They are the standing army, and the
militia, jailers, constables, posse comitatus,[6] &c. In most cases there
is no free exercise whatever of the judgment or of the moral sense;
but they put themselves on a level with wood and earth and stones;
and wooden men can perhaps be manufactured that will serve the
purpose as well. Such command no more respect than men of straw
or a lump of dirt. They have the same sort of worth only as horses
and dogs. Yet such as these even are commonly esteemed good citizens. Others—as most legislators, politicians, lawyers, ministers,
and office-holders—serve the state chiefly with their heads; and, as
they rarely make any moral distinctions, they are as likely to serve

---

[3] **powder-monkeys** The boys who delivered gunpowder to cannons.

[4] **Navy-Yard** This is apparently the U.S. naval yard at Boston.

[5] These lines are from "Burial of Sir John Moore at Corunna" (1817) by the Irish
poet Charles Wolfe (1791–1823).

[6] **posse comitatus** Literally, the power of the county; the term means a law-
enforcement group made up of ordinary citizens.

the Devil, without *intending* it, as God. A very few, as heroes, patriots, martyrs, reformers in the great sense, and *men*, serve the state with their consciences also and so necessarily resist it for the most part; and they are commonly treated as enemies by it. A wise man will only be useful as a man and will not submit to be "clay" and "stop a hole to keep the wind away," but leave that office to his dust at least:

> I am too high-born to be propertied,
> To be a secondary at control,
> Or useful serving-man and instrument
> To any sovereign state throughout the world.[7]

He who gives himself entirely to his fellow-men appears to them useless and selfish; but he who gives himself partially to them is pronounced a benefactor and philanthropist.   6

How does it become a man to behave toward this American government today? I answer, that he cannot without disgrace be associated with it. I cannot for an instant recognize that political organization as *my* government which is the *slave's* government also.   7

All men recognize the right of revolution; that is, the right to refuse allegiance to, and to resist the government when its tyranny or its inefficiency are great and unendurable. But almost all say that such is not the case now. But such was the case, they think, in the Revolution of '75. If one were to tell me that this was a bad government because it taxed certain foreign commodities brought to its ports, it is most probable that I should not make an ado about it, for I can do without them. All machines have their friction; and possibly this does enough good to counterbalance the evil. At any rate, it is a great evil to make a stir about it. But when the friction comes to have its machine, and oppression and robbery are organized, I say let us not have such a machine any longer. In other words, when a sixth of the population of a nation which has undertaken to be the refuge of liberty are slaves, and a whole country is unjustly overrun and conquered by a foreign army and subjected to military law, I think that it is not too soon for honest men to rebel and revolutionize. What makes this duty the more urgent is the fact that the country so overrun is not our own, but ours is the invading army.   8

---

[7] **"clay," "stop a hole . . . wind away," I am too high-born . . .** These lines are from Shakespeare; the first is from *Hamlet*, V.i.226–27. The verse is from *King John*, V.ii.79–82.

Paley,[8] a common authority with many on moral questions, in his   9
chapter on the "Duty of Submission to Civil Government," resolves all
civil obligation into expediency; and he proceeds to say, "that so long
as the interest of the whole society requires it, that is, so long as the
established government cannot be resisted or charged without public inconveniency, it is the will of God that the established government be obeyed, and no longer. . . . This principle being admitted,
the justice of every particular case of resistance is reduced to a computation of the quantity of the danger and grievance on the one side,
and of the probability and expense of redressing it on the other." Of
this, he says, every man shall judge for himself. But Paley appears
never to have contemplated those cases to which the rule of expediency does not apply, in which a people, as well as an individual,
must do justice, cost what it may. If I have unjustly wrested a plank
from a drowning man, I must restore it to him though I drown
myself. This, according to Paley, would be inconvenient. But he that
would save his life, in such a case, shall lose it. This people must
cease to hold slaves and to make war on Mexico, though it cost them
their existence as a people.

In their practice, nations agree with Paley; but does anyone think   10
that Massachusetts does exactly what is right at the present crisis?

> A drab of state, a cloth-o'-silver slut,
> To have her train borne up, and her soul trail in the dirt.[9]

Practically speaking, the opponents to a reform in Massachusetts are
not a hundred thousand politicians at the South but a hundred thousand merchants and farmers here, who are more interested in commerce and agriculture than they are in humanity, and are not prepared
to do justice to the slave and to Mexico, cost what it may. I quarrel
not with far-off foes but with those who, near at home, co-operate
with, and do the bidding of, those far away, and without whom the
latter would be harmless. We are accustomed to say that the mass of
men are unprepared; but improvement is slow because the few are
not materially wiser or better than the many. It is not so important
that many should be as good as you as that there be some absolute

---

[8]**William Paley (1743–1805)** An English theologian who lectured widely on
moral philosophy. Paley is famous for *A View of the Evidences of Christianity* (1794).
"Duty of Submission to Civil Government Explained" is Chapter 3 of Book 6 of *The
Principles of Moral and Political Philosophy* (1785).
    [9]**A drab . . .** From Cyril Tourneur (1575?–1626), *Revenger's Tragedy* (1607),
IV.iv.70–72. "Drab" is an obsolete term for a prostitute. Thoreau quotes the lines to
imply that Massachusetts is a "painted lady" with a defiled soul.

goodness somewhere; for that will leaven the whole lump. There are thousands who are in opinion opposed to slavery and to the war who yet in effect do nothing to put an end to them; who, esteeming themselves children of Washington and Franklin, sit down with their hands in their pockets and say that they know not what to do, and do nothing; who even postpone the question of freedom to the question of free trade, and quietly read the prices-current along with the latest advices from Mexico after dinner and, it may be, fall asleep over them both. What is the price-current of an honest man and patriot today? They hesitate and they regret and sometimes they petition; but they do nothing in earnest and with effect. They will wait, well disposed, for others to remedy the evil, that they may no longer have it to regret. At most, they give only a cheap vote, and a feeble countenance and God-speed, to the right, as it goes by them. There are nine hundred and ninety-nine patrons of virtue to one virtuous man. But it is easier to deal with the real possessor of a thing than with the temporary guardian of it.

All voting is a sort of gaming, like checkers or backgammon,   11 with a slight moral tinge to it, a playing with right and wrong, with moral questions; and betting naturally accompanies it. The character of the voters is not staked. I cast my vote, perchance, as I think right; but I am not vitally concerned that that right should prevail. I am willing to leave it to the majority. Its obligation, therefore, never exceeds that of expediency. Even voting *for the right* is *doing* nothing for it. It is only expressing to men feebly your desire that it should prevail. A wise man will not leave the right to the mercy of chance, nor wish it to prevail through the power of the majority. There is but little virtue in the action of masses of men. When the majority shall at length vote for the abolition of slavery, it will be because they are indifferent to slavery, or because there is but little slavery left to be abolished by their vote. *They* will then be the only slaves. Only *his* vote can hasten the abolition of slavery who asserts his own freedom by his vote.

I hear of a convention to be held at Baltimore,[10] or elsewhere,   12 for the selection of a candidate for the Presidency, made up chiefly of editors, and men who are politicians by profession; but I think, what is it to any independent, intelligent, and respectable man what decision they may come to? Shall we not have the advantage of his wisdom and honesty nevertheless? Can we not count upon some

---

[10] **Baltimore** In 1848, the political environment was particularly intense; it was a seedbed for theoreticians of the Confederacy, which was only beginning to be contemplated seriously.

independent votes? Are there not many individuals in the country who do not attend conventions? But no: I find that the responsible man, so called, has immediately drifted from his position, and despairs of his country when his country has more reason to despair of him. He forthwith adopts one of the candidates thus selected as the only *available* one, thus proving that he is himself *available* for any purposes of the demagogue. His vote is of no more worth than that of any unprincipled foreigner or hireling native who may have been bought. O for a man who is a *man* and, as my neighbor says has a bone in his back which you cannot pass your hand through! Our statistics are at fault: the population has been returned too large. How many *men* are there to a square thousand miles in this country? Hardly one. Does not America offer any inducement for men to settle here? The American has dwindled into an Odd Fellow[11] — one who may be known by the development of his organ of gregariousness and a manifest lack of intellect and cheerful self-reliance; whose first and chief concern, on coming into the world, is to see that the Alms-houses are in good repair; and, before yet he has lawfully donned the virile garb, to collect a fund for the support of the widows and orphans that may be; who, in short, ventures to live only by the aid of the Mutual Insurance Company, which has promised to bury him decently.

It is not a man's duty, as a matter of course, to devote himself to the eradication of any, even the most enormous wrong; he may still properly have other concerns to engage him; but it is his duty, at least, to wash his hands of it and, if he gives it no thought longer, not to give it practically his support. If I devote myself to other pursuits and contemplations, I must first see, at least, that I do not pursue them sitting upon another man's shoulders. I must get off him first, that he may pursue his contemplations too. See what gross inconsistency is tolerated. I have heard some of my townsmen say, "I should like to have them order me out to help put down an insurrection of the slaves, or to march to Mexico — see if I would go"; and yet these very men have each directly by their allegiance and so indirectly, at least, by their money, furnished a substitute. The soldier is applauded who refuses to serve in an unjust war by those who do not refuse to sustain the unjust government which makes the war; is applauded by those whose own act and authority he disregards and sets at naught; as if the State were penitent to that degree that it hired one to scourge it

13

---

[11] **Odd Fellow** The Independent Order of Odd Fellows, a fraternal and benevolent secret society, founded in England in the eighteenth century and first established in the United States in 1819 in Baltimore.

while it sinned, but not to that degree that it left off sinning for a moment. Thus, under the name of Order and Civil Government, we are all made at last to pay homage to and support our own meanness. After the first blush of sin comes its indifference; and from immoral it becomes, as it were, *unmoral*, and not quite unnecessary to that life which we have made.

The broadest and most prevalent error requires the most disin- 14 terested virtue to sustain it. The slight reproach to which the virtue of patriotism is commonly liable, the noble are most likely to incur. Those who, while they disapprove of the character and measures of a government, yield to it their allegiance and support, are undoubtedly its most conscientious supporters, and so frequently the most serious obstacles to reform. Some are petitioning the State to dissolve the Union, to disregard the requisitions of the President. Why do they not dissolve it themselves—the union between themselves and the State—and refuse to pay their quota into its treasury? Do not they stand in the same relation to the State that the State does to the Union? And have not the same reasons prevented the State from resisting the Union which have prevented them from resisting the State?

How can a man be satisfied to entertain an opinion merely, and 15 enjoy *it*? Is there any enjoyment in it if his opinion is that he is aggrieved? If you are cheated out of a single dollar by your neighbor, you do not rest satisfied with knowing that you are cheated, or with saying that you are cheated, or even with petitioning him to pay you your due; but you take effectual steps at once to obtain the full amount and see that you are never cheated again. Action from principle, the perception and the performance of right, changes things and relations; it is essentially revolutionary and does not consist wholly with anything which was. It not only divides states and churches, it divides families; ay, it divides the *individual*, separating the diabolical in him from the divine.

Unjust laws exist: shall we be content to obey them, or shall 16 we endeavor to amend them and obey them until we have succeeded, or shall we transgress them at once? Men generally, under such a government as this, think that they ought to wait until they have persuaded the majority to alter them. They think that if they should resist the remedy would be worse than the evil. *It* makes it worse. Why is it not more apt to anticipate and provide for reform? Why does it not cherish its wise minority? Why does it cry and resist before it is hurt? Why does it not encourage its citizens to be on the alert to point out its faults and *do* better than it would have them? Why does it always crucify Christ and excommunicate

Copernicus and Luther[12] and pronounce Washington and Franklin rebels?

One would think that a deliberate and practical denial of its authority was the only offense never contemplated by government; else why has it not assigned its definite, its suitable and proportionate penalty? If a man who has no property refuses but once to earn nine shillings for the State, he is put in prison for a period unlimited by any law that I know, and determined only by the discretion of those who placed him there; but if he should steal ninety times nine shillings from the State, he is soon permitted to go at large again.

If the injustice is part of the necessary friction of the machine of government, let it go, let it go: perchance it will wear smooth — certainly the machine will wear out. If the injustice has a spring or a pulley or a rope or a crank exclusively for itself, then perhaps you may consider whether the remedy will not be worse than the evil; but if it is of such a nature that it requires you to be the agent of injustice to another, then I say break the law. Let your life be a counter friction to stop the machine. What I have to do is to see, at any rate, that I do not lend myself to the wrong which I condemn.

As for adopting the ways which the State has provided for remedying the evil, I know not of such ways. They take too much time, and a man's life will be gone. I have other affairs to attend to. I came into this world, not chiefly to make this a good place to live in, but to live in it, be it good or bad. A man has not everything to do, but something; and because he cannot do *everything*, it is not necessary that he should do *something* wrong. It is not my business to be petitioning the Governor or the Legislature any more than it is theirs to petition me; and if they should not hear my petition what should I do then? But in this case the State has provided no way: its very Constitution is the evil. This may seem to be harsh and stubborn and unconciliatory; but it is to treat with the utmost kindness and consideration the only spirit that can appreciate or deserves it. So is all change for the better, like birth and death, which convulse the body.

I do not hesitate to say that those who call themselves Abolitionists should at once effectually withdraw their support, both in person and property, from the government of Massachusetts, and not wait till they constitute a majority of one before they suffer the right to prevail through them. I think that it is enough if they have

17

18

19

20

---

[12]**Nicolaus Copernicus (1473–1543) and Martin Luther (1483–1546)** Copernicus revolutionized astronomy and the way humankind perceives the universe; Luther was a religious revolutionary who began the Reformation and created the first Protestant faith.

God on their side, without waiting for that other one. Moreover, any man more right than his neighbors constitutes a majority of one already.

I meet this American government or its representative, the State   21
government, directly and face to face once a year—no more—in the person of its tax-gatherer; this is the only mode in which a man situated as I am necessarily meets it; and it then says distinctly, Recognize me; and the simplest, the most effectual and, in the present posture of affairs, the indispensablest mode of treating with it on this head, of expressing your little satisfaction with and love for it, is to deny it then. My civil neighbor, the tax-gatherer, is the very man I have to deal with—for it is, after all, with men and not with parchment that I quarrel—and he has voluntarily chosen to be an agent of the government. How shall he ever know well what he is and does as an officer of the government, or as a man, until he is obliged to consider whether he shall treat me, his neighbor, for whom he has respect, as a neighbor and well-disposed man, or as a maniac and disturber of the peace, and see if he can get over this obstruction to his neighborliness without a ruder and more impetuous thought or speech corresponding with his action. I know this well, that if one thousand, if one hundred, if ten men whom I could name—if ten *honest* men only—ay, if *one* HONEST man in this State of Massachusetts, *ceasing to hold slaves*, were actually to withdraw from this copartnership and be locked up in the county jail therefor, it would be the abolition of slavery in America. For it matters not how small the beginning may seem to be: what is once well done is done forever. But we love better to talk about it: that we say is our mission. Reform keeps many scores of newspapers in its service but not one man. If my esteemed neighbor,[13] the State's ambassador, who will devote his days to the settlement of the question of human rights in the Council Chamber, instead of being threatened with the prisons of Carolina, were to sit down the prisoner of Massachusetts, that State which is so anxious to foist the sin of slavery upon her sister—though at present she can discover only an act of inhospitality to be the ground of a quarrel with her—the Legislature would not wholly waive the subject the following winter.

Under a government which imprisons any unjustly, the true place   22
for a just man is also a prison. The proper place today, the only place

---

[13] **esteemed neighbor** Thoreau refers to Samuel Hoar (1778–1856), a Massachusetts congressman, who went to South Carolina to protest that state's practice of seizing black seamen from Massachusetts ships and enslaving them. South Carolina threatened Hoar and drove him out of the state. He did not secure the justice he demanded.

which Massachusetts has provided for her freer and less desponding spirits is in her prisons, to be put out and locked out of the State by her own act, as they have already put themselves out by their principles. It is there that the fugitive slave and the Mexican prisoner on parole and the Indian come to plead the wrongs of his race should find them; on that separate but more free and honorable ground where the State places those who are not *with* her but *against* her— the only house in a slave State in which a free man can abide with honor. If any think that their influence would be lost there, and their voices no longer afflict the ear of the State, that they would not be as an enemy within its walls, they do not know by how much truth is stronger than error, nor how much more eloquently and effectively he can combat injustice who has experienced a little in his own person. Cast your whole vote, not a strip of paper merely, but your whole influence. A minority is powerless while it conforms to the majority; it is not even a minority then; but it is irresistible when it clogs by its whole weight. If the alternative is to keep all just men in prison or give up war and slavery, the State will not hesitate which to choose. If a thousand men were not to pay their tax-bills this year, that would not be a violent bloody measure, as it would be to pay them, and enable the State to commit violence and shed innocent blood. This is, in fact, the definition of a peaceable revolution, if any such is possible. If the tax-gatherer or any other public officer asks me, as one has done, "But what shall I do?" my answer is, "If you really wish to do anything, resign your office." When the subject has refused allegiance and the officer has resigned his office, then the revolution is accomplished. But even suppose blood should flow. Is there not a sort of blood shed when the conscience is wounded? Through this wound a man's real manhood and immortality flow out, and he bleeds to an everlasting death. I see this blood flowing now.

I have contemplated the imprisonment of the offender rather than the seizure of his goods—though both will serve the same purpose— because they who assert the purest right, and consequently are most dangerous to a corrupt State, commonly have not spent much time in accumulating property. To such the State renders comparatively small service, and a slight tax is wont to appear exorbitant, particularly if they are obliged to earn it by special labor with their hands. If there were one who lived wholly without the use of money, the State itself would hesitate to demand it of him. But the rich man—not to make any invidious comparison—is always sold to the institution which makes him rich. Absolutely speaking, the more money, the less virtue; for money comes between a man and his objects and obtains them for him; and it was certainly no great virtue to obtain it. It puts to rest many questions which he would otherwise be taxed

23

to answer; while the only new question which it puts is the hard but superfluous one, how to spend it. Thus his moral ground is taken from under his feet. The opportunities of living are diminished in proportion as what are called the "means" are increased. The best thing a man can do for his culture when he is rich is to endeavor to carry out those schemes which he entertained when he was poor. Christ answered the Herodians[14] according to their condition. "Show me the tribute-money," said he—and one took a penny out of his pocket—if you use money which has the image of Caesar on it, and which he has made current and valuable, that is, if *you are men of the State* and gladly enjoy the advantages of Caesar's government, then pay him back some of his own when he demands it; "Render therefore to Caesar that which is Caesar's, and to God those things which are God's"—leaving them no wiser than before as to which was which; for they did not wish to know.

When I converse with the freest of my neighbors, I perceive that whatever they may say about the magnitude and seriousness of the question, and their regard for the public tranquillity, the long and the short of the matter is that they cannot spare the protection of the existing government, and they dread the consequences to their property and families of disobedience to it. For my own part, I should not like to think that I ever rely on the protection of the State. But if I deny the authority of the State when it presents its tax-bill, it will soon take and waste all my property and so harass me and my children without end. This is hard. This makes it impossible for a man to live honestly, and at the same time comfortably, in outward respects. It will not be worth the while to accumulate property; that would be sure to go again. You must hire or squat somewhere and raise but a small crop and eat that soon. You must live within yourself and depend upon yourself always tucked up and ready for a start, and not have many affairs. A man may grow rich in Turkey even, if he will be in all respects a good subject of the Turkish government. Confucius[15] said: "If a state is governed by the principles of reason, poverty and misery are subjects of shame; if a state is not governed by the principles of reason, riches and honors are the subjects of shame." No; until I want the protection of Massachusetts to be extended to me in some distant Southern port, where my liberty is

24

---

[14] **Herodians** Followers of King Herod who were opposed to Jesus Christ (see Matt. 22:16).

[15] **Confucius (551–479 B.C.)** The most important Chinese religious leader. His *Analects* (collection) treated not only religious but moral and political matters as well.

endangered, or until I am bent solely on building up an estate at home by peaceful enterprise, I can afford to refuse allegiance to Massachusetts and her right to my property and life. It costs me less in every sense to incur the penalty of disobedience to the State than it would to obey. I should feel as if I were worth less in that case.

Some years ago the State met me in behalf of the Church and commanded me to pay a certain sum toward the support of a clergyman whose preaching my father attended, but never I myself. "Pay," it said, "or be locked up in the jail." I declined to pay. But, unfortunately, another man saw fit to pay it. I did not see why the schoolmaster should be taxed to support the priest, and not the priest the schoolmaster; for I was not the State's schoolmaster, but I supported myself by voluntary subscription. I did not see why the lyceum should not present its tax-bill and have the State to back its demand, as well as the Church. However, at the request of the selectmen, I condescended to make some such statement as this in writing: — "Know all men by these presents, that I, Henry Thoreau, do not wish to be regarded as a member of any incorporated society which I have not joined." This I gave to the town clerk; and he has it. The State, having thus learned that I did not wish to be regarded as a member of that church, has never made a like demand on me since; though it said that it must adhere to its original presumption that time. If I had known how to name them, I should then have signed off in detail from all the societies which I never signed on to; but I did not know where to find a complete list.

I have paid no poll-tax[16] for six years. I was put into a jail once on this account, for one night; and, as I stood considering the walls of solid stone, two or three feet thick, the door of wood and iron, a foot thick, and the iron grating which strained the light, I could not help being struck with the foolishness of that institution which treated me as if I were mere flesh and blood and bones, to be locked up. I wondered that it should have concluded at length that this was the best use it could put me to and had never thought to avail itself of my services in some way. I saw that if there was a wall of stone between me and my townsmen, there was a still more difficult one to climb or break through before they could get to be as free as I was. I did not for a moment feel confined, and the walls seemed a great waste of stone and mortar. I felt as if I alone of all my

---

[16] **poll-tax** A tax levied on every citizen living in a given area; *poll* means "head," so it is a tax per head. The tax Thoreau refers to, about $2, was used to support the Mexican War.

townsmen had paid my tax. They plainly did not know how to treat me but behaved like persons who are underbred. In every threat and in every compliment there was a blunder; for they thought that my chief desire was to stand the other side of that stone wall. I could not but smile to see how industriously they locked the door on my meditations, which followed them out again without let or hindrance, and *they* were really all that was dangerous. As they could not reach me, they had resolved to punish my body; just as boys, if they cannot come at some person against whom they have a spite, will abuse his dog. I saw that the State was half-witted, that it was timid as a lone woman with her silver spoons, and that it did not know its friends from its foes, and I lost all my remaining respect for it and pitied it.

Thus the State never intentionally confronts a man's sense, intel-   27
lectual or moral, but only his body, his senses. It is not armed with superior wit or honesty but with superior physical strength. I was not born to be forced. I will breathe after my own fashion. Let us see who is the strongest. What force has a multitude? They only can force me who obey a higher law than I. They force me to become like themselves. I do not hear of *men* being *forced* to live this way or that by masses of men. What sort of life were that to live? When I meet a government which says to me, "Your money or your life," why should I be in haste to give it my money? It may be in a great strait and not know what to do: I cannot help that. It must help itself; do as I do. It is not worth the while to snivel about it. I am not responsible for the successful working of the machinery of society. I am not the son of the engineer. I perceive that, when an acorn and a chestnut fall side by side, the one does not remain inert to make way for the other, but both obey their own laws and spring and grow and flourish as best they can till one, perchance, overshadows and destroys the other. If a plant cannot live according to its nature, it dies; and so a man.

The night in prison was novel and interesting enough. The prison-   28
ers in their shirt-sleeves were enjoying a chat and the evening air in the doorway when I entered. But the jailer said, "Come, boys, it is time to lock up"; and so they dispersed, and I heard the sound of their steps returning into the hollow apartments. My room-mate was introduced to me by the jailer as "a first-rate fellow and a clever man." When the door was locked, he showed me where to hang my hat and how he managed matters there. The rooms were whitewashed once a month; and this one, at least, was the whitest, most simply furnished, and probably the neatest apartment in the town. He naturally wanted to know where I came from and what brought me there; and when I had told him, I asked him in my turn how he came there, presuming him

to be an honest man, of course; and, as the world goes, I believe he was. "Why," said he, "they accuse me of burning a barn; but I never did it." As near as I could discover, he had probably gone to bed in a barn when drunk and smoked his pipe there; and so a barn burnt. He had the reputation of being a clever man, had been there some three months waiting for his trial to come on, and would have to wait as much longer; but he was quite domesticated and contented, since he got his board for nothing and thought that he was well treated.

He occupied one window, and I the other; and I saw that if one   29
stayed there long, his principal business would be to look out the win-
dow. I had soon read all the tracts that were left there and examined where former prisoners had broken out and where a grate had been sawed off and heard the history of the various occupants of that room; for I found that even here there was a history and a gossip which never circulated beyond the walls of the jail. Probably this is the only house in the town where verses are composed, which afterward printed in a circular form but not published. I was shown quite a long list of verses which were composed by some young men who had been detected in an attempt to escape, who avenged them-
selves by signing them.

I pumped my fellow-prisoner as dry as I could, for fear I should   30
never see him again; but at length he showed me which was my bed and left me to blow out the lamp.

It was like travelling into a far country, such as I had never   31
expected to behold, to lie there for one night. It seemed to me that I never had heard the town-clock strike before, nor the evening sounds of the village; for we slept with the windows open, which were inside the grating. It was to see my native village in the light of the Middle Ages, and our Concord was turned into a Rhine stream, and visions of knights and castles passed before me. They were the voices of old burghers that I heard in the streets. I was an involuntary spectator and auditor of whatever was done and said in the kitchen of the adjacent village-inn—a wholly new and rare experi-
ence to me. It was a closer view of my native town. I was fairly inside of it. I never had seen its institutions before. This is one of its peculiar institutions; for it is a shire town.[17] I began to comprehend what its inhabitants were about.

In the morning our breakfasts were put through the hole in the   32
door, in small oblong-square tin pans, made to fit, and holding a pint of chocolate, with brown bread and an iron spoon. When they

---

[17] **shire town** A county seat, which means the town had a court, county offices, and jails.

called for the vessels again, I was green enough to return what bread I had left; but my comrade seized it and said that I should lay that up for lunch or dinner. Soon after he was let out to work at haying in a neighboring field, whither he went every day, and would not be back till noon; so he bade me good-day, saying that he doubted if he should see me again.

When I came out of prison — for someone interfered and paid 33 that tax — I did not perceive that great changes had taken place on the common, such as he observed who went in a youth and emerged a tottering and gray-headed man; and yet a change had to my eyes come over the scene — the town and State and country — greater than any that mere time could effect. I saw yet more distinctly the State in which I lived. I saw to what extent the people among whom I lived could be trusted as good neighbors and friends; that their friendship was for summer weather only; that they did not greatly propose to do right; that they were a distinct race from me by their prejudices and superstitions, as the Chinamen and Malays are; that, in their sacrifices to humanity, they ran no risks, not even to their property; that, after all, they were not so noble but they treated the thief as he had treated them and hoped, by a certain outward observance and a few prayers, and by walking in a particular straight though useless path from time to time, to save their souls. This may be to judge my neighbors harshly; for I believe that many of them are not aware that they have such an institution as the jail in their village.

It was formerly the custom in our village, when a poor debtor 34 came out of jail, for his acquaintances to salute him, looking through their fingers, which were crossed to represent the grating of a jail window, "How do ye do?" My neighbors did not thus salute me but first looked at me and then at one another as if I had returned from a long journey. I was put into jail as I was going to the shoemaker's to get a shoe which was mended. When I was let out the next morning I proceeded to finish my errand, and having put on my mended shoe, joined a huckleberry party who were impatient to put themselves under my conduct; and in half an hour — for the horse was soon tackled — was in the midst of a huckleberry field on one of our high-est hills two miles off, and then the State was nowhere to be seen.

This is the whole history of "My Prisons." 35

I have never declined paying the highway tax, because I am as 36 desirous of being a good neighbor as I am of being a bad subject; and as for supporting schools I am doing my part to educate my fel-low countrymen now. It is for no particular item in the tax-bill that I refuse to pay it. I simply wish to refuse allegiance to the State, to withdraw and stand aloof from it effectually. I do not care to trace the course of my dollar, if I could, till it buys a man or a musket to shoot one with—the dollar is innocent—but I am concerned to trace the effects of my allegiance. In fact, I quietly declare war with the State, after my fashion, though I will still make what use and get what advantage of her I can, as is usual in such cases.

If others pay the tax which is demanded of me from a sympathy 37 with the State, they do but what they have already done in their own case, or rather they abet injustice to a greater extent than the State requires. If they pay the tax from a mistaken interest in the individual taxed, to save his property, or prevent his going to jail, it is because they have not considered wisely how far they let their private feelings interfere with the public good.

This, then, is my position at present. But one cannot be too much 38 on his guard in such a case, lest his action be biassed by obstinacy or an undue regard for the opinions of men. Let him see that he does only what belongs to himself and to the hour.

I think sometimes, Why, this people mean well; they are only 39 ignorant; they would do better if they knew how: why give your neighbors this pain to treat you as they are not inclined to? But I think again, this is no reason why I should do as they do or permit others to suffer much greater pain of a different kind. Again, I sometimes say to myself, When many millions of men, without heat, without ill will, without personal feeling of any kind, demand of you a few shillings only, without the possibility, such is their constitution, of retracting or altering their present demand, and without the possibility, on your side, of appeal to any other millions, why expose yourself to this overwhelming brute force? You do not resist cold and hunger, the winds and the waves, thus obstinately; you quietly submit to a thousand similar necessities. You do not put your head into the fire. But just in proportion as I regard this as not wholly a brute force but partly a human force, and consider that I have relations to those millions as to so many millions of men, and not of mere brute or inanimate things, I see that appeal is possible, first and instantaneously, from them to the Maker of them, and secondly, from them to themselves. But if I put my head deliberately into the fire, there is no appeal to fire or to the Maker of fire, and I have only myself to blame. If I could convince myself that I have any right to be satisfied with men as they are, and to treat them accordingly, and not according, in some respects, to my requisitions and expectations of what they and I ought to be, then, like a good Mussulman[18] and fatalist, I should endeavor to be satisfied with things as they are and say it is the will of God. And, above all, there is this difference

---

[18]**Mussulman** Muslim; a follower of the religion of Islam.

between resisting this and a purely brute or natural force, that I can resist this with some effect; but I cannot expect, like Orpheus,[19] to change the nature of the rocks and trees and beasts.

I do not wish to quarrel with any man or nation. I do not wish to   40
split hairs, to make fine distinctions, or set myself up as better than my neighbors. I seek rather, I may say, even an excuse for conforming to the laws of the land. I am but too ready to conform to them. Indeed, I have reason to suspect myself on this head; and each year, as the tax-gatherer comes round, I find myself disposed to review the acts and position of the general and State governments, and the spirit of the people, to discover a pretext for conformity.

> We must affect our country as our parents;
> And if at any time we alienate
> Our love or industry from doing it honor,
> We must respect effects and teach the soul
> Matter of conscience and religion,
> And not desire of rule or benefit.[20]

I believe that the State will soon be able to take all my work of this sort out of my hands, and then I shall be no better a patriot than my fellow-countrymen. Seen from a lower point of view, the Constitution, with all its faults, is very good; the law and the courts are very respectable; even this State and this American government are, in many respects, very admirable and rare things, to be thankful for, such as a great many have described them; but seen from a point of view a little higher, they are what I have described them; seen from a higher still, and the highest, who shall say what they are, or that they are worth looking at or thinking of at all?

However, the government does not concern me much, and I   41
shall bestow the fewest possible thoughts on it. It is not many moments that I live under a government, even in this world. If a man is thought-free, fancy-free, imagination-free, that which *is not* never for a long time appearing *to be* to him, unwise rulers or reformers cannot fatally interrupt him.

I know that most men think differently from myself; but those   42
whose lives are by profession devoted to the study of these or kindred subjects content me as little as any. Statesmen and legislators,

---

[19] **Orpheus** In Greek mythology, Orpheus was a poet whose songs were so plaintive that they affected animals, trees, and even stones.

[20] **We must affect . . .** From George Peele (1556–1596), *The Battle of Alcazar* (acted 1588–1589, printed 1594), II.ii. Thoreau added these lines in a later printing of the essay. They emphasize the fact that one is disobedient to the state as one is to a parent—with love and affection and from a cause of conscience. Disobedience is not taken lightly.

standing so completely within the institution, never distinctly and nakedly behold it. They speak of moving society but have no resting-place without it. They may be men of a certain experience and discrimination and have no doubt invented ingenious and even useful systems, for which we sincerely thank them; but all their wit and usefulness lie within certain not very wide limits. They are wont to forget that the world is not governed by policy and expediency. Webster[21] never goes behind government and so cannot speak with authority about it. His words are wisdom to those legislators who contemplate no essential reform in the existing government; but for thinkers, and those who legislate for all time, he never once glances at the subject. I know of those whose serene and wise speculations on this theme would soon reveal the limits of his mind's range and hospitality. Yet, compared with the cheap professions of most reformers, and the still cheaper wisdom and eloquence of politicians in general, his are almost the only sensible and valuable words, and we thank Heaven for him. Comparatively, he is always strong, original, and, above all, practical. Still his quality is not wisdom but prudence. The lawyer's truth is not Truth but consistency, or a consistent expediency. Truth is always in harmony with herself and is not concerned chiefly to reveal the justice that may consist with wrong-doing. He well deserves to be called, as he has been called, the Defender of the Constitution. There are really no blows to be given by him but defensive ones. He is not a leader but a follower. His leaders are the men of '87.[22] "I have never made an effort," he says, "and never propose to make an effort; I have never countenanced an effort, and never mean to countenance an effort, to disturb the arrangement as originally made, by which the various States came into the Union." Still thinking of the sanction which the Constitution gives to slavery, he says, "Because it was a part of the original compact—let it stand." Notwithstanding his special acuteness and ability, he is unable to take a fact out of its merely political relations and behold it as it lies absolutely to be disposed of by the intellect—what, for instance, it behooves a man to do here in America today with regard to slavery but ventures, or is driven, to make some such desperate answer as the following, while professing to speak absolutely, and as a private man—from which what new and singular code of social duties might be inferred? "The manner," says he, "in which the governments of those States where slavery exists are to regulate it, is for their own

---

[21] **Daniel Webster (1782–1852)** One of the most brilliant orators of his time. He was secretary of state from 1841 to 1843, which is why Thoreau thinks he cannot be a satisfactory critic of government.

[22] **men of '87** The men who framed the Constitution in 1787.

consideration, under their responsibility to their constituents, to the general laws of propriety, humanity, and justice, and to God. Associations formed elsewhere, springing from a feeling of humanity, or any other cause, have nothing whatever to do with it. They have never received any encouragement from me, and they never will."[23]

They who know of no purer sources of truth, who have traced   43
up its stream no higher, stand, and wisely stand, by the Bible and the Constitution, and drink at it there with reverence and humility; but they who behold where it comes trickling into this lake or that pool gird up their loins once more and continue their pilgrimage toward its fountain-head.

No man with a genius for legislation has appeared in America.   44
They are rare in the history of the world. There are orators, politicians, and eloquent men by the thousand; but the speaker has not yet opened his mouth to speak who is capable of settling the much-vexed questions of the day. We love eloquence for its own sake and not for any truth which it may utter or any heroism it may inspire. Our legislators have not yet learned the comparative value of free-trade and of freedom, of union, and of rectitude, to a nation. They have no genius or talent for comparatively humble questions of taxation and finance, commerce and manufacturers and agriculture. If we were left solely to the wordy wit of legislators in Congress for our guidance, uncorrected by the seasonable experience and the effectual complaints of the people, America would not long retain her rank among the nations. For eighteen hundred years, though perchance I have no right to say it, the New Testament has been written; yet where is the legislator who has wisdom and practical talent enough to avail himself of the light which it sheds on the science of legislation?

The authority of government, even such as I am willing to sub-   45
mit to — for I will cheerfully obey those who know and can do better than I, and in many things even those who neither know nor can do so well — is still an impure one: to be strictly just, it must have the sanction and consent of the governed. It can have no pure right over my person and property but what I concede to it. The progress from an absolute to a limited monarchy, from a limited monarchy to a democracy, is a progress toward a true respect for the individual. Even the Chinese philosopher[24] was wise enough to regard the individual as the basis of the empire. Is a democracy such as we know it the last improvement possible in government? Is it not possible to

---

[23] These extracts have been inserted since the Lecture was read. [Thoreau's note]

[24] **Chinese philosopher** Thoreau probably means Confucius.

take a step further towards recognizing and organizing the rights of man? There will never be a really free and enlightened State until the State comes to recognize the individual as a higher and independent power, from which all its own power and authority are derived, and treats him accordingly. I please myself with imagining a State at last which can afford to be just to all men and to treat the individual with respect as a neighbor; which even would not think it inconsistent with its own repose if a few were to live aloof from it, not meddling with it, nor embraced by it, who fulfilled all the duties of neighbors and fellow-men. A State which bore this kind of fruit and suffered it to drop off as fast as it ripened would prepare the way for a still more perfect and glorious State, which also I have imagined but not yet anywhere seen.

QUESTIONS FOR CRITICAL READING

1. How would you characterize the tone of Thoreau's address? Is he chastising his audience? Is he praising it? What opinion do you think he has of his audience?
2. Explain what Thoreau means when he says, "But a government in which the majority rule in all cases cannot be based on justice, even as far as men understand it" (para. 4).
3. How is injustice "part of the necessary friction of the machine of government" (para. 18)?
4. Why does Thoreau provide us with "the whole history of 'My Prisons'" (paras. 28–35)? Describe what being in jail taught Thoreau. Why do you think Thoreau reacted so strongly to being in a local jail for a single day?
5. Choose an example of Thoreau's use of irony, and comment on its effectiveness. (One example appears in para. 25.)
6. How might Thoreau view the responsibility of the majority to a minority within the sphere of government?
7. How clear are Thoreau's concepts of justice? On what are they based?
8. Is it possible that when Thoreau mentions "the Chinese philosopher" (para. 45) he means Lao-tzu? Would Lao-tzu agree that the individual is "the basis of the empire"?

SUGGESTIONS FOR CRITICAL WRITING

1. Thoreau insists, "Law never made men a whit more just" (para. 4). He introduces the concept of conscience as a monitor of law and government. Explain his views on conscience and the conscientious person. How can conscience help create justice? Why is it sometimes difficult for law to create justice?

2. Do you agree with Thoreau when he says, "All voting is a sort of gaming" (para. 11)? Examine his attitude toward elections and the relationship of elections to the kind of justice one can expect from a government.

3. Answer Thoreau's question: "Unjust laws exist: shall we be content to obey them, or shall we endeavor to amend them and obey them until we have succeeded, or shall we transgress them at once?" (para. 16). Thoreau reminds us that the law has been created by the majority and to disobey would put him in a minority—a "wise minority." Why should the wise minority have the right to disobey laws created by the majority?

4. In what ways was the United States government of Thoreau's time built on the individual or on the individual's best interests? In what way is our current government based on the individual's best interests? How can satisfying the individual's best interests be reconciled with satisfying the community's interest? Which would produce more justice?

5. Examine quotations from Thoreau that focus on justice for the individual, and write an essay that establishes the values of the government Thoreau describes. How might that government see its obligations to the governed? How would it treat matters of justice and moral issues? Describe Thoreau's view of the American government of his time in enough detail to give a clear sense of the essay to someone who has not read it.

6. Reread Thoreau's question in item 3 above. Answer it in an essay that focuses on issues that are significant to you. Be as practical and cautious as you feel you should be, and provide your own answer—not the one you feel Thoreau might have given. Then describe the forms that Thoreau's disobedience would be likely to take. What probably would be the limits of his actions?

7. **CONNECTIONS**   Thoreau admits (para. 41) that he is not very concerned with government because he does not have to pay much attention to it. His life goes on regardless of government. He also says that "[t]he authority of government . . . is still an impure one: to be strictly just, it must have the sanction and consent of the governed" (para. 45). How would Thomas Jefferson have reacted to Thoreau's attitudes toward government? Would he have agreed with Thoreau's view that it is essentially unimportant to the individual? Does Thoreau derive from Jefferson his view that the success of a government depends on the sanction of the governed? Or did Jefferson have a different idea about the relationship between the government and the governed?

8. **CONNECTIONS**   Thoreau was especially sympathetic to the plight of African American slaves and would likely have shared the views of Martin Luther King Jr. What advice might Thoreau have given King? Write an essay that applies the basic ideas of "Civil Disobedience" to the circumstances in which King found himself.

9. **SEEING CONNECTIONS**   Which painting would Thoreau have been most likely to include as an illustration in his essay: Delacroix's *Liberty*

Leading the People (p. 18) or Giordano's *Justice* (p. 140)? Although it is possible, it is unlikely that he saw either painting. Which one is most important for supporting Thoreau's concept of justice and civil duty? Use details from both paintings to support your argument. If you were to argue that he definitely saw one or the other of the paintings, which would it be?

ELIZABETH CADY STANTON
Declaration of Sentiments and Resolutions

ELIZABETH CADY STANTON (1815–1902) was exceptionally intelligent, and because her lawyer father was willing to indulge her gifts, she was provided the best education a woman in her time in America could expect. Born and raised in Johnstown, New York, she was one of six children, five girls and one boy, Eleazar, in whom all the hopes of the family rested. When Eleazar died after graduating from college, Elizabeth strove to replace him in the admiration of her father. She studied Greek so successfully that she was admitted as the only young woman in the local secondary school, where she demonstrated her abilities—which on the whole were superior to those of the boys with whom she studied.

Nonetheless, she did not win the esteem she hoped for. Her father, although he loved and cared for her, continually told her he wished she had been born a boy. In Johnstown, as elsewhere, women had few rights and rather low expectations. The question of education was a case in point: it was a profound exception for Elizabeth Cady to go to school with boys or even to study what they studied. She had no hopes of following in their paths because all the professions they aimed for were closed to women. This fact was painfully brought home to her when she finished secondary school. All the boys she studied with went on to Union College in Schenectady, but she was barred from attending the all-male institution. Instead, she attended the much inferior Troy Female Seminary, run by a pioneer of American education, Emma Willard (1787–1870).

Troy was as good a school as any woman in America could attend; yet it emphasized a great many traditional womanly

From the *History of Woman Suffrage*.

pursuits as well as the principles of Calvinism, which Elizabeth Cady came to believe were at the root of the problem women had in American society. In the 1830s, women did not have the vote; if they were married, they could not own property; and they could not sue for divorce no matter how ugly their marital situation. A husband expected a dowry from his wife, and he could spend it exactly as he wished: on gambling, carousing, or speculating. Not until 1848, the year of the Seneca Falls Convention, did New York pass laws to change this situation.

Elizabeth Cady married when she was twenty-four years old. Her husband, Henry Stanton, was a prominent abolitionist and journalist. He had little money, and the match was not entirely blessed by Elizabeth's father. In characteristic fashion she had the word *obey* struck from the marriage vows; thus she had trouble finding a preacher who would adhere to her wishes. And, preferring never to be known as Mrs. Stanton, she was always addressed as Elizabeth Cady Stanton.

Early on, the couple settled in Boston, where Elizabeth found considerable intellectual companionship and stimulation. Good servants made her household tasks minimal. But soon Henry Stanton's health demanded that they move to Seneca Falls, New York, where there were few servants of any caliber, and where there were few people of intellectual independence to stimulate her. Her lot in life became much like that of any housewife, and she could not abide it.

After a discussion at tea with a number of like-minded women, she proposed a woman's convention to discuss their situation. On July 14, 1848 (a year celebrated for revolutions in every major capital of Europe), the following notice appeared in the *Seneca County Courier*, a semiweekly journal:

SENECA FALLS CONVENTION

WOMAN'S RIGHTS CONVENTION.—A Convention to discuss the social, civil, and religious condition and rights of woman, will be held in the Wesleyan Chapel, at Seneca Falls, N.Y., on Wednesday and Thursday, the 19th and 20th of July, current; commencing at 10 o'clock A.M. During the first day the meeting will be exclusively for women, who are earnestly invited to attend. The public generally are invited to be present on the second day, when Lucretia Mott, of Philadelphia, and other ladies and gentlemen, will address the convention.

On the appointed day, less than a week after the notice, carriages and other vehicles tied up the streets around the Wesleyan Chapel with a large number of interested people. The first shock was that the chapel was locked, and the first order of business was for a man to climb through an open window to unlock the doors. The chapel was filled immediately, but not only with women. Many men were present, including Frederick Douglass, and the women decided that because they were already there, the men could stay.

The convention was a significant success, establishing a pattern that has been repeated frequently since. Elizabeth Cady Stanton, in her declaration, figured as a radical in the assembly, proposing unheard-of reforms such as granting women the vote, which most of the moderates in the assembly could not agree on. For a while the assembly wished to omit the question of the vote, but Stanton by presenting it as her first statement in the declaration, made it clear that without the right to vote on legislation and legislators, women would never be able to change the status quo. Eventually, with the help of Douglass and others, the convention accepted her position, and the women's movement in America was under way.

Stanton's Rhetoric

Because the Seneca Falls Declaration is modeled directly on Jefferson's Declaration of Independence, we cannot get a good idea of Stanton's rhetorical gifts. However, by relying on Jefferson, she exercised a powerful wit (for which her other writing is well known) by reminding her audience that when the Declaration of Independence was uttered, no thought was given to half its potential audience — women. Thus, the Seneca Falls Declaration is a parody, and it is especially effective in the way it parodies its model so closely.

The same periodic sentences, parallelism, and balance are used and largely to the same effect. She employed the same profusion of one-paragraph utterances and exactly the same opening for each of them. Stanton played a marvelous trick, however. In place of the tyrannical foreign King George — Jefferson's "He" — she has put the tyrant man. Because of the power of her model, her declaration gathers strength and ironically undercuts the model.

The most interesting aspect of Stanton's rhetorical structure has to do with the order in which she includes the abuses and wrongs that she asks to be made right. She begins with the vote, just as Jefferson began with the law. Both are essential to the entire argument, and both are the key to change. Whereas Jefferson demands an entirely new government, Elizabeth Cady Stanton ends by demanding the "equal participation" of women with men in the government they have already won.

PREREADING QUESTIONS:
WHAT TO READ FOR

The following prereading questions may help you anticipate key issues in the discussion of Elizabeth Cady Stanton's Declaration of Sentiments and Resolutions. Keeping them in mind during your first reading of the selection should help focus your attention.

- What power has man had over women, according to Stanton?
- What is Stanton's attitude toward just and unjust laws?

Declaration of Sentiments and Resolutions

Adopted by the Seneca Falls Convention, July 19–20, 1848

When, in the course of human events, it becomes necessary for one portion of the family of man to assume among the people of the earth a position different from that which they have hitherto occupied, but one to which the laws of nature and of nature's God entitle them, a decent respect to the opinions of mankind requires that they should declare the causes that impel them to such a course. 1

We hold these truths to be self-evident: that all men and women are created equal; that they are endowed by their Creator with certain inalienable rights; that among these are life, liberty, and the pursuit of happiness; that to secure these rights governments are instituted, deriving their just powers from the consent of the governed. Whenever any form of government becomes destructive of these ends, it is the right of those who suffer from it to refuse allegiance to it, and to insist upon the institution of a new government, laying its foundation on such principles, and organizing its powers in such form, as to them shall seem most likely to effect their safety and happiness. Prudence, indeed, will dictate that governments long established should not be changed for light and transient causes; and accordingly all experience hath shown that mankind are more disposed to suffer, while evils are sufferable, than to right themselves by abolishing the forms to which they were accustomed. But when a long train of abuses and unsurpations, pursuing invariably the same object, evinces a design to reduce them under absolute despotism, it is their duty to throw off such government, and to provide new guards for their future security. Such has been the patient sufferance of the 2 women under this government, and such is now the necessity which constrains them to demand the equal station to which they are entitled.

The history of mankind is a history of repeated injuries and usurpations on the part of man toward woman, having in direct object the establishment of an absolute tyranny over her. To prove this, let facts be submitted to a candid world. 3

He has never permitted her to exercise her inalienable right to the elective franchise. 4

He has compelled her to submit to laws, in the formation of which she had no voice. 5

He has withheld from her rights which are given to the most ignorant and degraded men — both natives and foreigners. 6

Having deprived her of this first right of a citizen, the elective franchise, thereby leaving her without representation in the halls of legislation, he has oppressed her on all sides. 7

He has made her, if married, in the eye of the law, civilly dead. 8

He has taken from her all right in property, even to the wages she earns. 9

He has made her, morally, an irresponsible being, as she can commit many crimes with impunity, provided they be done in the presence of her husband. In the covenant of marriage, she is compelled to promise obedience to her husband, he becoming to all intents and purposes, her master — the law giving him power to deprive her of her liberty, and to administer chastisement. 10

He has so framed the laws of divorce, as to what shall be the proper causes, and in case of separation, to whom the guardianship of the children shall be given, as to be wholly regardless of the happiness of women — the law, in all cases, going upon a false supposition of the supremacy of man, and giving all power into his hands. 11

After depriving her of all rights as a married woman, if single, and the owner of property, he has taxed her to support a government which recognizes her only when her property can be made profitable to it. 12

He has monopolized nearly all the profitable employments, and from those she is permitted to follow, she receives but a scanty remuneration. He closes against her all the avenues to wealth and distinction which he considers most honorable to himself. As a teacher of theology, medicine, or law, she is not known. 13

He has denied her the facilities for obtaining a thorough education, at colleges being closed against her. 14

He allows her in Church, as well as State, but a subordinate position, claiming Apostolic authority for her exclusion from the ministry, and, with some exceptions, from any public participation in the affairs of the Church. 15

He has created a false public sentiment by giving to the world a 16
different code of morals for men and women, by which moral delin-
quencies which exclude women from society, are not only tolerated,
but deemed of little account in man.

He has usurped the prerogative of Jehovah himself, claiming it 17
as his right to assign for her a sphere of action, when that belongs to
her conscience and to her God.

He has endeavored, in every way that he could, to destroy her 18
confidence in her own powers, to lessen her self-respect, and to
make her willing to lead a dependent and abject life.

Now, in view of this entire disfranchisement of one-half the people 19
of this country, their social and religious degradation—in view of the
unjust laws above mentioned, and because women do feel themselves
aggrieved, oppressed, and fraudulently deprived of their most sacred
rights, we insist that they have immediate admission to all the rights
and privileges which belong to them as citizens of the United States.

In entering upon the great work before us, we anticipate no 20
small amount of misconception, misrepresentation, and ridicule; but
we shall use every instrumentality within our power to effect our
object. We shall employ agents, circulate tracts, petition the State
and National legislatures, and endeavor to enlist the pulpit and the
press in our behalf. We hope this Convention will be followed by a
series of Conventions embracing every part of the country.

[The following resolutions were discussed by Lucretia Mott, 21
Thomas and Mary Ann McClintock, Amy Post, Catharine A. F. Steb-
bins, and others, and were adopted:]

WHEREAS, The great precept of nature is conceded to be, that "man 22
shall pursue his own true and substantial happiness." Blackstone[1] in
his Commentaries remarks, that this law of Nature being coeval[2] with
mankind, and dictated by God himself, is of course superior in obligation to any other. It is binding over all the globe, in all countries
and at all times; no human laws are of any validity if contrary to this,
and such of them as are valid, derive all their force, and all their
validity, and all their authority, mediately and immediately, from
this original; therefore,

Resolved, That such laws as conflict, in any way, with the true 23
and substantial happiness of woman, are contrary to the great

---

[1] **Sir William Blackstone (1723–1780)** The most influential of English scholars of the law. His *Commentaries of the Laws of England* (4 vols., 1765–1769) form the
basis of the study of law in England.
[2] **being coeval** Existing simultaneously.

precept of nature and of no validity, for this is "superior in obligation to any other."

Resolved, That all laws which prevent woman from occupying 24
such a station in society as her conscience shall dictate, or which
place her in a position inferior to that of man, are contrary to the
great precept of nature, and therefore of no force or authority.

Resolved, That woman is man's equal—was intended to be so 25
by the Creator, and the highest good of the race demands that she
should be recognized as such.

Resolved, That the women of this country ought to be enlight- 26
ened in regard to the laws under which they live, that they may no
longer publish their degradation by declaring themselves satisfied
with their present position, nor their ignorance, by asserting that they
have all the rights they want.

Resolved, That inasmuch as man, while claiming for himself 27
intellectual superiority, does accord to woman moral superiority, it
is pre-eminently his duty to encourage her to speak and teach, as
she has an opportunity, in all religious assemblies.

Resolved, That the same amount of virtue, delicacy, and refine- 28
ment of behavior that is required of woman in the social state,
should also be required of man, and the same transgressions should
be visited with equal severity on both man and woman.

Resolved, That the objection of indelicacy and impropriety, which 29
is so often brought against woman when she addresses a public
audience, comes with a very ill-grace from those who encourage, by
their attendance, her appearance on the stage, in the concert, or in
feats of the circus.

Resolved, That woman has too long rested satisfied in the circum- 30
scribed limits which corrupt customs and a perverted application of
the Scriptures have marked out for her, and that it is time she should
move in the enlarged sphere which her great Creator has assigned her.

Resolved, That it is the duty of the women of this country to 31
secure to themselves their sacred right to the elective franchise.

Resolved, That the equality of human rights results necessarily 32
from the fact of the identity of the race in capabilities and responsibilities.

Resolved, therefore, That, being invested by the Creator with the 33
same capabilities, and the same consciousness of responsibility for
their exercise, it is demonstrably the right and duty of woman, equally
with man, to promote every righteous cause by every righteous
means; and especially in regard to the great subjects of morals and
religion, it is self-evidently her right to participate with her brother
in teaching them, both in private and in public, by writing and by
speaking, by any instrumentalities proper to be used, and in any
assemblies proper to be held; and this being a self-evident truth

growing out of the divinely implanted principles of human nature, any custom or authority adverse to it, whether modern or wearing the hoary sanction of antiquity, is to be regarded as a self-evident falsehood, and at war with mankind.

[At the last session Lucretia Mott[3] offered and spoke to the fol-   34
lowing resolution:]

Resolved, That the speedy success of our cause depends upon   35
the zealous and untiring efforts of both men and women, for the
overthrow of the monopoly of the pulpit, and for the securing to
woman an equal participation with men in the various trades, professions, and commerce.

---

[3] **Lucretia Mott (1793–1880)** One of the founders of the 1848 convention at which these resolutions were presented. She was one of the earliest and most impor-tant of the feminists who struggled to proclaim their rights. She was also a promi-nent abolitionist.

QUESTIONS FOR CRITICAL READING

1. Stanton begins her declaration with a diatribe against the government. To what extent is the government responsible for the wrongs she enumerates?
2. Exactly what is Stanton taking issue with? What are the wrongs that have been done? Do they seem important to you?
3. How much of the effect of the selection depends upon the parody of the Declaration of Independence?
4. Which of the individual declarations is the most important? Which is the least important?
5. Are any of the declarations serious enough to warrant starting a revolu-tion?
6. Why do you think the suggestion that women deserve the vote was so hard to put across at the convention?

SUGGESTIONS FOR CRITICAL WRITING

1. Make a careful comparison between this declaration and Jefferson's Declaration of Independence. What are the similarities? What are the differences? Why would Stanton's declaration be particularly more distinguished because it is a parody of such a document? What weak-nesses might be implied because of the close resemblance?

2. Write an essay that is essentially a declaration in the same style Stanton uses. Choose a cause carefully and follow the same pattern that Stanton does in the selection. Establish the appropriate relationship between government and the cause you are interested in defending or promoting.

3. To what extent is it useful to petition a government to redress the centuries of wrongs done to women? Is it the government's fault that women were treated so badly? Is the government able to have a significant effect on helping to change the unpleasant circumstances of women? Is it appropriate or inappropriate for Stanton to attack government in her search for equality?

4. The Declaration of Independence was aimed at justifying a war. Is the question of war anywhere implied in Stanton's address? If war is not the question, what is? Is there any substitute for war in Stanton's essay?

5. Read down the list of declarations and resolutions that Stanton enumerates. Have all of these issues been dealt with in our times? Would such a declaration as this still be appropriate, or has the women's movement accomplished all its goals?

6. Examine the issues treated in paragraph 16, concerning "a different code of morals" for men and women. Explain exactly what Stanton meant by that expression, and consider how different things are today from what they were in Stanton's day.

7. **CONNECTIONS**   To what extent do you think Henry David Thoreau would have agreed with Stanton? What aspects of her declaration would he have found most useful for his own position? Would he have urged women to practice civil disobedience on behalf of women's rights, or would he have accepted the general point of view of his time and concerned himself only with the independence of men?

8. **SEEING CONNECTIONS**   What specific details in Giordano's fresco *Justice* (p. 140) would have given Stanton the most hope for justice for women in the future? Would she have been cheered more by the fact that justice seems to be as important in heaven as on earth or by the fact that justice is represented by the militant Greek female deity Dike? Would Stanton feel that Giordano had women's interests in mind when designing the elements of the painting?

MARTIN LUTHER KING JR.
Letter from Birmingham Jail

MARTIN LUTHER KING JR. (1929–1968) was the most influential civil rights leader in America for a period of more than fifteen years. He was an ordained minister with a doctorate in theology from Boston University. He worked primarily in the South, where he labored steadily to overthrow laws that promoted segregation and to increase the number of black voters registered in southern communities.

From 1958 to 1968, demonstrations and actions opened up opportunities for African Americans who in the South hitherto had been prohibited from sitting in certain sections of buses, using facilities such as water fountains in bus stations, and sitting at luncheon counters with whites. Such laws—unjust and insulting, not to mention unconstitutional—were not challenged by local authorities. Martin Luther King Jr., who became famous for supporting a program to integrate buses in Montgomery, Alabama, was asked by the Southern Christian Leadership Conference (SCLC) to assist in the fight for civil rights in Birmingham, Alabama, where an SCLC meeting was to be held.

King was arrested as the result of a program of sit-ins at luncheon counters and wrote the letter printed here to a group of clergymen who had criticized his position. King had been arrested before and would be arrested again—resembling Henry David Thoreau somewhat in his attitude toward laws that did not conform to moral justice.

King, like Thoreau, was willing to suffer for his views, especially when he found himself faced with punitive laws denying civil rights to all citizens. His is a classic case in which the officers of the government pled that they were dedicated to maintaining a stable civil society, even as they restricted King's individual rights. In 1963, many of the good people to whom King addressed this letter firmly believed that peace and order might be threatened by granting African Americans the true independence and freedom that King insisted were their rights and indeed were guaranteed under the Constitution. This is why King's letter objects to an injustice that was rampant in Frederick Douglass's time but inexcusable in the time of John F. Kennedy.

Eventually the causes King promoted were victorious. His efforts helped change attitudes in the South and spur legislation that has benefited all Americans. His views concerning nonviolence spread throughout the world, and by the early 1960s he had become famous as a man who stood for human rights and human dignity virtually everywhere. He won the Nobel Peace Prize in 1964.

Although King himself was nonviolent, his program left both him and his followers open to the threat of violence. The sit-ins and voter registration programs spurred countless bombings, threats, and murders by members of the white community. King's life was often threatened, his home bombed, his followers harassed. He was assassinated at the Lorraine Motel in Memphis, Tennessee, on April 4, 1968. But before he died he saw—largely through his own efforts, influence, and example—the face of America change.

King's Rhetoric

The most obvious rhetorical tradition King assumes in this important work is that of the books of the Bible that were originally letters, such as Paul's Epistle to the Ephesians and his several letters to the Corinthians. Many of Paul's letters were written while he was in prison in Rome, and he established a moral position that could inspire the citizens who received the letters. At the same time, Paul carried out the most important work of the early Christian church—spreading the word of Jesus to those who wished to be Christians but who needed clarification and encouragement.

It is not clear that the clergymen who received King's letter fully appreciated the rhetorical tradition he drew upon—but they were men who preached from the Bible and certainly should have understood it. The text itself alludes to the mission of Paul and to his communications to his people. King works with this rhetorical tradition not only because it is effective but because it resonates with the deepest aspect of his calling—spreading the gospel of Christ. Brotherhood and justice were his message.

King's tone is one of utmost patience with his critics. He seems bent on winning them over to his point of view, just as he seems confident that—because they are, like him, clergymen—their goodwill should help them see the justice of his views.

His method is that of careful reasoning, focusing on the substance of their criticism, particularly on their complaints that his actions were "unwise and untimely" (para. 1). King takes each of those charges in turn, carefully analyzes it against his position, and then follows with the clearest possible statement of his own views and why he feels they are worth adhering to. The "Letter from Birmingham Jail" is a model of close and reasonable analysis of a very complex situation. It succeeds largely because it remains concrete, treating one issue after another carefully, refusing to be caught up in passion or posturing. Above all, King remains grounded in logic, convinced that his arguments will in turn convince his audience.

PREREADING QUESTIONS: WHAT TO READ FOR

The following prereading questions may help you anticipate key issues in the discussion of Martin Luther King's "Letter from Birmingham Jail." Keeping them in mind during your first reading of the selection should help focus your attention.

- What kind of injustice did Martin Luther King find in Birmingham?
- Why was Martin Luther King disappointed in the white churches?

Letter from Birmingham Jail

April 16, 1963

My Dear Fellow Clergymen:[1]

While confined here in the Birmingham city jail, I came across   1
your recent statement calling my present activities "unwise and untimely." Seldom do I pause to answer criticism of my work and

---

[1] This response to a published statement by eight fellow clergymen from Alabama (Bishop C. C. J. Carpenter, Bishop Joseph A. Durick, Rabbi Hilton L. Grafman, Bishop Paul Hardin, Bishop Holan B. Harmon, the Reverend George M. Murray, the Reverend Edward V. Ramage, and the Reverend Earl Stallings) was composed under somewhat constricting circumstances. Begun on the margins of the newspaper in which the statement appeared while I was in jail, the letter was continued on scraps of writing paper supplied by a friendly Negro trusty, and concluded on a pad my attorneys were eventually permitted to leave me. Although the text remains in substance unaltered, I have indulged in the author's prerogative of polishing it for publication. [King's note]

ideas. If I sought to answer all the criticisms that cross my desk, my secretaries would have little time for anything other than such correspondence in the course of the day, and I would have no time for constructive work. But since I feel that you are men of genuine good will and that your criticisms are sincerely set forth, I want to try to answer your statement in what I hope will be patient and reasonable terms.

I think I should indicate why I am here in Birmingham, since you have been influenced by the view which argues against "outsiders coming in." I have the honor of serving as president of the Southern Christian Leadership Conference, an organization operating in every southern state, with headquarters in Atlanta, Georgia. We have some eighty-five affiliated organizations across the South, and one of them is the Alabama Christian Movement for Human Rights. Frequently we share staff, educational, and financial resources with our affiliates. Several months ago the affiliate here in Birmingham asked us to be on call to engage in a nonviolent direct-action program if such were deemed necessary. We readily consented, and when the hour came we lived up to our promise. So I, along with several members of my staff, am here because I was invited here. I am here because I have organizational ties here. 2

But more basically, I am in Birmingham because injustice is here. Just as the prophets of the eighth century B.C. left their villages and carried their "thus saith the Lord" far beyond the boundaries of their home towns, and just as the Apostle Paul left his village of Tarsus[2] and carried the gospel of Jesus Christ to the far corners of the Greco-Roman world, so am I compelled to carry the gospel of freedom beyond my own home town. Like Paul, I must constantly respond to the Macedonian call for aid.[3] 3

Moreover, I am cognizant of the interrelatedness of all communities and states. I cannot sit idly by in Atlanta and not be concerned about what happens in Birmingham. Injustice anywhere is a threat to justice everywhere. We are caught in an inescapable network of mutuality, tied in a single garment of destiny. Whatever affects one directly, affects all indirectly. Never again can we afford to live with the narrow, provincial, "outside agitator" idea. Anyone who lives inside the United States can never be considered an outsider anywhere within its bounds. 4

---

[2]**village of Tarsus** Birthplace of St. Paul (?–A.D. 67), in Asia Minor, present-day Turkey, close to Syria.

[3]**the Macedonian call for aid** The citizens of Philippi, in Macedonia (northern Greece), were among the staunchest Christians. Paul went to their aid frequently; he also had to resolve occasional bitter disputes within the Christian community there (see Phil. 2:2–14).

You deplore the demonstrations taking place in Birmingham. 5
But your statement, I am sorry to say, fails to express a similar concern for the conditions that brought about the demonstrations. I am
sure that none of you would want to rest content with the superficial
kind of social analysis that deals merely with effects and does not
grapple with underlying causes. It is unfortunate that demonstrations are taking place in Birmingham, but it is even more unfortunate that the city's white power structure left the Negro community
with no alternative.

In any nonviolent campaign there are four basic steps: collec- 6
tion of the facts to determine whether injustices exist; negotiation;
self-purification; and direct action. We have gone through all these
steps in Birmingham. There can be no gainsaying the fact that racial
injustice engulfs this community. Birmingham is probably the most
thoroughly segregated city in the United States. Its ugly record of
brutality is widely known. Negroes have experienced grossly unjust
treatment in the courts. There have been more unsolved bombings
of Negro homes and churches in Birmingham than in any other city
in the nation. These are the hard brutal facts of the case. On the
basis of these conditions, Negro leaders sought to negotiate with the
city fathers. But the latter consistently refused to engage in good-
faith negotiation.

Then, last September, came the opportunity to talk with leaders 7
of Birmingham's economic community. In the course of the negotia-
tions, certain promises were made by the merchants—for example,
to remove the stores' humiliating racial signs. On the basis of these
promises, the Reverend Fred Shuttlesworth and the leaders of the
Alabama Christian Movement for Human Rights agreed to a moratorium on all demonstrations. As the weeks and months went by, we
realized that we were the victims of a broken promise. A few signs,
briefly removed, returned; the others remained.

As in so many past experiences, our hopes had been blasted, 8
and the shadow of deep disappointment settled upon us. We had
no alternative except to prepare for direct action, whereby we
would present our very bodies as a means of laying our case before
the conscience of the local and the national community. Mindful of
the difficulties involved, we decided to undertake a process of self-
purification. We began a series of workshops on nonviolence, and
we repeatedly asked ourselves: "Are you able to accept blows without retaliating?" "Are you able to endure the ordeal of jail?" We
decided to schedule our direct-action program for the Easter season,
realizing that except for Christmas, this is the main shopping period
of the year. Knowing that a strong economic-withdrawal program
would be the by-product of direct action, we felt that this would be

the best time to bring pressure to bear on the merchants for the needed change.

Then it occurred to us that Birmingham's mayoral election was   9
coming up in March, and we speedily decided to postpone action until after election day. When we discovered that the Commissioner of Public Safety, Eugene "Bull" Connor, had piled up enough votes to be in the run-off, we decided again to postpone action until the day after the run-off so that the demonstrations could not be used to cloud the issues. Like many others, we waited to see Mr. Connor defeated, and to this end we endured postponement after postponement. Having aided in this community need, we felt that our direct-action program could be delayed no longer.

You may well ask, "Why direct action? Why sit-ins, marches,   10
and so forth? Isn't negotiation a better path?" You are quite right in calling for negotiation. Indeed, this is the very purpose of direct action. Nonviolent direct action seeks to create such a crisis and foster such a tension that a community which has constantly refused to negotiate is forced to confront the issue. It seeks so to dramatize the issue that it can no longer be ignored. My citing the creation of tension as part of the work of the nonviolent resister may sound rather shocking. But I must confess that I am not afraid of the word "tension." I have earnestly opposed violent tension, but there is a type of constructive, nonviolent tension which is necessary for growth. Just as Socrates[4] felt that it was necessary to create a tension in the mind so that individuals could rise from the bondage of myths and half truths to the unfettered realm of creative analysis and objective appraisal, so must we see the need for nonviolent gadflies to create the kind of tension in society that will help men rise from the dark depths of prejudice and racism to the majestic heights of understanding and brotherhood.

The purpose of our direct-action program is to create a situation   11
so crisis-packed that it will inevitably open the door to negotiation. I therefore concur with you in your call for negotiation. Too long has our beloved Southland been bogged down in a tragic effort to live in monologue rather than dialogue.

One of the basic points in your statement is that the action that I   12
and my associates have taken in Birmingham is untimely. Some have asked: "Why didn't you give the new city administration time to act?"

---

[4]**Socrates (470?–399 B.C.)** The "tension in the mind" King refers to is created by the question-answer technique known as the Socratic method. By posing questions at the beginning of the paragraph, King shows his willingness to share Socrates' rhetorical techniques. Socrates was imprisoned and killed for his civil disobedience (see paras. 21 and 25). He was the greatest of the Greek philosophers.

The only answer that I can give to this query is that the new Birmingham administration must be prodded about as much as the outgoing one, before it will act. We are sadly mistaken if we feel that the election of Albert Boutwell as mayor will bring the millennium[5] to Birmingham. While Mr. Boutwell is a much more gentle person than Mr. Connor, they are both segregationists, dedicated to maintenance of the status quo. I have hoped that Mr. Boutwell will be reasonable enough to see the futility of massive resistance to desegregation. But he will not see this without pressure from devotees of civil rights. My friends, I must say to you that we have not made a single gain in civil rights without determined legal and nonviolent pressure. Lamentably, it is an historical fact that privileged groups seldom give up their privileges voluntarily. Individuals may see the moral light and voluntarily give up their unjust posture; but, as Reinhold Niebuhr[6] has reminded us, groups tend to be more immoral than individuals.

We know through painful experience that freedom is never   13
voluntarily given by the oppressor; it must be demanded by the oppressed. Frankly, I have yet to engage in a direct-action campaign that was "well timed" in the view of those who have not suffered unduly from the disease of segregation. For years now I have heard the word "Wait!" It rings in the ear of every Negro with piercing familiarity. This "Wait" has almost always meant "Never." We must come to see, with one of our distinguished jurists, that "justice too long delayed is justice denied."[7]

We have waited for more than 340 years for our constitutional   14
and God-given rights. The nations of Asia and Africa are moving with jet-like speed toward gaining political independence, but we still creep at horse-and-buggy pace toward gaining a cup of coffee at a lunch counter. Perhaps it is easy for those who have never felt the stinging darts of segregation to say, "Wait." But when you have seen vicious mobs lynch your mothers and fathers at will and drown your sisters and brothers at whim; when you have seen hate-filled policemen curse, kick, and even kill your black brothers and sisters; when

---

[5] **the millennium** A reference to Revelation 20, according to which the second coming of Christ will be followed by one thousand years of peace, when the devil will be incapacitated. After this will come a final battle between good and evil, followed by the Last Judgment.

[6] **Reinhold Niebuhr (1892–1971)** Protestant American philosopher who urged church members to put their beliefs into action against social injustice. He urged Protestantism to develop and practice a code of social ethics and wrote in *Moral Man and Immoral Society* (1932) of the point King mentions here.

[7] **"justice too long delayed is justice denied"** Chief Justice Earl Warren's expression in 1954 was adapted from English writer Walter Savage Landor's phrase "Justice delayed is justice denied."

you see the vast majority of your twenty million Negro brothers smothering in an airtight cage of poverty in the midst of an affluent society; when you suddenly find your tongue twisted and your speech stammering as you seek to explain to your six-year-old daughter why she can't go to the public amusement park that has just been advertised on television, and see tears welling up in her eyes when she is told that Funtown is closed to colored children, and see ominous clouds of inferiority beginning to form in her little mental sky, and see her beginning to distort her personality by developing an unconscious bitterness toward white people; when you have to concoct an answer for a five-year-old son who is asking, "Daddy, why do white people treat colored people so mean?"; when you take a cross-country drive and find it necessary to sleep night after night in the uncomfortable corners of your automobile because no motel will accept you; when you are humiliated day in and day out by nagging signs reading "white" and "colored"; when your first name becomes "nigger," your middle name becomes "boy" (however old you are) and your last name becomes "John," and your wife and mother are never given the respected title "Mrs."; when you are harried by day and haunted by night by the fact that you are a Negro, living constantly at tiptoe stance, never quite knowing what to expect next, and are plagued with inner fears and outer resentments; when you are forever fighting a degenerating sense of "nobodiness" — then you will understand why we find it difficult to wait. There comes a time when the cup of endurance runs over, and men are no longer willing to be plunged into the abyss of despair. I hope, sirs, you can understand our legitimate and unavoidable impatience.

You express a great deal of anxiety over our willingness to break laws. This is certainly a legitimate concern. Since we so diligently urge people to obey the Supreme Court's decision of 1954 outlawing segregation in the public schools, at first glance it may seem rather paradoxical for us consciously to break laws. One may well ask: "How can you advocate breaking some laws and obeying others?" The answer lies in the fact that there are two types of laws: just and unjust. I would be the first to advocate obeying just laws. One has not only a legal but a moral responsibility to obey just laws. Conversely, one has a moral responsibility to disobey unjust laws. I would agree with St. Augustine[8] that "an unjust law is no law at all." 15

Now, what is the difference between the two? How does one determine whether a law is just or unjust? A just law is a manmade 16

---

[8] **St. Augustine (354–430)** Early bishop of the Christian Church who deeply influenced the spirit of Christianity for many centuries.

code that squares with the moral law or the law of God. An unjust law is a code that is out of harmony with the moral law. To put it in the terms of St. Thomas Aquinas:[9] An unjust law is a human law that is not rooted in eternal law and natural law. Any law that uplifts human personality is just. Any law that degrades human personality is unjust. All segregation statutes are unjust because segregation distorts the soul and damages the personality. It gives the segregator a false sense of superiority and the segregated a false sense of inferiority. Segregation, to use the terminology of the Jewish philosopher Martin Buber,[10] substitutes an "I-it" relationship for an "I-thou" relationship and ends up relegating persons to the status of things. Hence segregation is not only politically, economically, and sociologically unsound, it is morally wrong and sinful. Paul Tillich[11] has said that sin is separation. Is not segregation an existential expression of man's tragic separation, his awful estrangement, his terrible sinfulness? Thus it is that I can urge men to obey the 1954 decision of the Supreme Court, for it is morally right; and I can urge them to disobey segregation ordinances, for they are morally wrong.

Let us consider a more concrete example of just and unjust 17 laws. An unjust law is a code that a numerical or power majority group compels a minority group to obey but does not make binding on itself. This is *difference* made legal. By the same token, a just law is a code that a majority compels a minority to follow and that it is willing to follow itself. This is *sameness* made legal.

Let me give another explanation. A law is unjust if it is inflicted 18 on a minority that, as a result of being denied the right to vote, had no part in enacting or devising the law. Who can say that the legislature of Alabama which set up that state's segregation laws was democratically elected? Throughout Alabama all sorts of devious methods are used to prevent Negroes from becoming registered voters, and there are some counties in which, even though Negroes constitute a majority of the population, not a single Negro is registered. Can any

---

[9] **St. Thomas Aquinas (1225–1274)** The greatest of the medieval Christian philosophers and one of the greatest church authorities.

[10] **Martin Buber (1878–1965)** Jewish theologian. *I and Thou* (1923) is his most famous book.

[11] **Paul Tillich (1886–1965)** An important twentieth-century Protestant theologian who held that Christianity was reasonable and effective in modern life. Tillich saw sin as an expression of man's separation from God, from himself, and from his fellow man. King sees the separation of the races as a further manifestation of man's sinfulness. Tillich, who was driven out of Germany by the Nazis, stresses the need for activism and the importance of action in determining moral vitality, just as King does.

law enacted under such circumstances be considered democratically structured?

Sometimes a law is just on its face and unjust in its application. 19 For instance, I have been arrested on a charge of parading without a permit. Now, there is nothing wrong in having an ordinance which requires a permit for a parade. But such an ordinance becomes unjust when it is used to maintain segregation and to deny citizens the First Amendment privilege of peaceful assembly and protest.

I hope you are able to see the distinction I am trying to point out. 20 In no sense do I advocate evading or defying the law, as would the rabid segregationist. That would lead to anarchy. One who breaks an unjust law must do so openly, lovingly, and with a willingness to accept the penalty. I submit that an individual who breaks a law that conscience tells him is unjust, and who willingly accepts the penalty of imprisonment in order to arouse the conscience of the community over its injustice, is in reality expressing the highest respect for law.

Of course, there is nothing new about this kind of civil disobe- 21 dience. It was evidenced sublimely in the refusal of Shadrach, Meshach, and Abednego to obey the laws of Nebuchadnezzar,[12] on the ground that a higher moral law was at stake. It was practiced superbly by the early Christians, who were willing to face hungry lions and the excruciating pain of chopping blocks rather than submit to certain unjust laws of the Roman Empire. To a degree, academic freedom is a reality today because Socrates practiced civil disobedience. In our own nation, the Boston Tea Party represented a massive act of civil disobedience.

We should never forget that everything Adolf Hitler did in Ger- 22 many was "legal" and everything the Hungarian freedom fighters[13] did in Hungary was "illegal." It was "illegal" to aid and comfort a Jew in Hitler's Germany. Even so, I am sure that, had I lived in Germany at the time, I would have aided and comforted my Jewish brothers. If today I lived in a Communist country where certain principles dear to the Christian faith are suppressed, I would openly advocate disobeying that country's antireligious laws.

I must make two honest confessions to you, my Christian and 23 Jewish brothers. First, I must confess that over the past few years I

---

[12]**Nebuchadnezzar (c. 630–562 B.C.)** Chaldean king who twice attacked Jerusalem. He ordered Shadrach, Meshach, and Abednego to worship a golden image. They refused, were cast into a roaring furnace, and were saved by God (see Dan. 1:7–3:30).

[13]**Hungarian freedom fighters** The Hungarians rose in revolt against Soviet rule in 1956. Soviet forces put down the uprising with great force, which shocked the world. Many freedom fighters died, and many others escaped to the West.

have been gravely disappointed with the white moderate. I have almost reached the regrettable conclusion that the Negro's great stumbling block in his stride toward freedom is not the White Citizen's Counciler[14] or the Ku Klux Klanner, but the white moderate, who is more devoted to "order" than to justice; who prefers a negative peace which is the absence of tension to a positive peace which is the presence of justice; who constantly says, "I agree with you in the goal you seek, but I cannot agree with your methods of direct action"; who paternalistically believes he can set the timetable for another man's freedom; who lives by a mythical concept of time and who constantly advises the Negro to wait for a "more convenient season." Shallow understanding from people of good will is more frustrating than absolute misunderstanding from people of ill will. Lukewarm acceptance is much more bewildering than outright rejection.

24   I had hoped that the white moderate would understand that law and order exist for the purpose of establishing justice and that when they fail in this purpose they become the dangerously structured dams that block the flow of social progress. I had hoped that the white moderate would understand that the present tension in the South is a necessary phase of the transition from an obnoxious negative peace, in which the Negro passively accepted his unjust plight, to a substantive and positive peace, in which all men will respect the dignity and worth of human personality. Actually, we who engage in nonviolent direct action are not the creators of tension. We merely bring to the surface the hidden tension that is already alive. We bring it out in the open, where it can be seen and dealt with. Like a boil that can never be cured so long as it is covered up but must be opened with all its ugliness to the natural medicines of air and light, injustice must be exposed, with all the tension its exposure creates, to the light of human conscience and the air of national opinion, before it can be cured.

25   In your statement you assert that our actions, even though peaceful, must be condemned because they precipitate violence. But is this a logical assertion? Isn't this like condemning a robbed man because his possession of money precipitated the evil act of robbery? Isn't this like condemning Socrates because his unswerving commitment to truth and his philosophical inquiries precipitated the act by the misguided populace in which they made him drink hemlock?

---

[14]**White Citizen's Counciler** White Citizen's Councils organized in southern states in 1954 to fight school desegregation as ordered by the Supreme Court in May 1954. The councils were not as secret or violent as the Klan; they were also ineffective.

Isn't this like condemning Jesus because his unique God-consciousness and never-ceasing devotion to God's will precipitated the evil act of crucifixion? We must come to see that, as the federal courts have consistently affirmed, it is wrong to urge an individual to cease his efforts to gain his basic constitutional rights because the quest may precipitate violence. Society must protect the robbed and punish the robber.

I had also hoped that the white moderate would reject the myth 26 concerning time in relation to the struggle for freedom. I have just received a letter from a white brother in Texas. He writes: "All Christians know that the colored people will receive equal rights eventually, but it is possible that you are in too great a religious hurry. It has taken Christianity almost two thousand years to accomplish what it has. The teachings of Christ take time to come to earth." Such an attitude stems from a tragic misconception of time, from the strangely irrational notion that there is something in the very flow of time that will inevitably cure all ills. Actually, time itself is neutral; it can be used either destructively or constructively. More and more I feel that the people of ill will have used time much more effectively than have the people of good will. We will have to repent in this generation not merely for the hateful words and actions of the bad people, but for the appalling silence of the good people. Human progress never rolls in on wheels of inevitability; it comes through the tireless efforts of men willing to be co-workers with God, and without this hard work, time itself becomes an ally of the forces of social stagnation. We must use time creatively, in the knowledge that the time is always ripe to do right. Now is the time to make real the promise of democracy and transform our pending national elegy into a creative psalm of brotherhood. Now is the time to lift our national policy from the quicksand of racial injustice to the solid rock of human dignity.

You speak of our activity in Birmingham as extreme. At first I 27 was rather disappointed that fellow clergymen would see my nonviolent efforts as those of an extremist. I began thinking about the fact that I stand in the middle of two opposing forces in the Negro community. One is a force of complacency, made up in part of Negroes who, as a result of long years of oppression, are so drained of self-respect and a sense of "somebodiness" that they have adjusted to segregation; and in part of a few middle-class Negroes who, because of a degree of academic and economic security and because in some ways they profit by segregation, have become insensitive to the problems of the masses. The other force is one of bitterness and hatred, and it comes perilously close to advocating violence. It is expressed in the various black nationalist groups that are springing up across the nation, the largest and best known being Elijah Muhammad's

Muslim movement.[15] Nourished by the Negro's frustration over the continued existence of racial discrimination, this movement is made up of people who have lost faith in America, who have absolutely repudiated Christianity, and who have concluded that the white man is an incorrigible "devil."

I have tried to stand between these two forces, saying that we need emulate neither the "do-nothingism" of the complacent nor the hatred and despair of the black nationalist. For there is the more excellent way of love and nonviolent protest. I am grateful to God that, through the influence of the Negro church, the way of nonviolence became an integral part of our struggle.   28

If this philosophy had not emerged, by now many streets of the South would, I am convinced, be flowing with blood. And I am further convinced that if our white brothers dismiss as "rabble-rousers" and "outside agitators" those of us who employ nonviolent direct action, and if they refuse to support our nonviolent efforts, millions of Negroes will, out of frustration and despair, seek solace and security in black nationalist ideologies—a development that would inevitably lead to a frightening racial nightmare.[16]   29

Oppressed people cannot remain oppressed forever. The yearning for freedom eventually manifests itself, and that is what has happened to the American Negro. Something within has reminded him of his birthright of freedom, and something without has reminded him that it can be gained. Consciously or unconsciously, he has been caught up by the *Zeitgeist*,[17] and with his black brothers of Africa and his brown and yellow brothers of Asia, South America, and the Caribbean, the United States Negro is moving with a sense of great urgency toward the promised land of racial justice. If one recognizes this vital urge that has engulfed the Negro community, one should readily understand why public demonstrations are taking place. The Negro has many pent-up resentments and latent frustrations, and he must release them. So let him march; let him make prayer pilgrimages to   30

---

[15] **Elijah Muhammad's Muslim movement** The Black Muslim movement, which began in the 1920s but flourished in the 1960s under its leader, Elijah Muhammad (1897–1975). Among notable figures who became Black Muslims were the poet Amiri Baraka (b. 1934), the world champion prizefighter Muhammad Ali (b. 1942), and the controversial reformer and religious leader Malcolm X (1925–1965). King saw their rejection of white society (and consequently brotherhood) as a threat.

[16] **a frightening racial nightmare** The black uprisings of the 1960s in all major American cities, and the conditions that led to them, were indeed a racial nightmare. King's prophecy was quick to come true.

[17] ***Zeitgeist*** German word for the intellectual, moral, and cultural spirit of the times.

the city hall; let him go on freedom rides[18]—and try to understand why he must do so. If his repressed emotions are not released in nonviolent ways, they will seek expression through violence; this is not a threat but a fact of history. So I have not said to my people, "Get rid of your discontent." Rather, I have tried to say that this normal and healthy discontent can be channeled into the creative outlet of nonviolent direct action. And now this approach is being termed extremist.

But though I was initially disappointed at being categorized as an   31 extremist, as I continued to think about the matter I gradually gained a measure of satisfaction from the label. Was not Jesus an extremist for love: "Love your enemies, bless them that curse you, do good to them that hate you, and pray for them which despitefully use you, and persecute you." Was not Amos an extremist for justice: "Let justice roll down like waters and righteousness like an ever-flowing stream." Was not Paul an extremist for the Christian gospel: "I bear in my body the marks of the Lord Jesus." Was not Martin Luther an extremist: "Here I stand; I cannot do otherwise, so help me God." And John Bunyan: "I will stay in jail to the end of my days before I make a butchery of my conscience." And Abraham Lincoln: "This nation cannot survive half slave and half free." And Thomas Jefferson: "We hold these truths to be self-evident, that all men are created equal . . ."[19] So the question is not whether we will be extremists, but what kind of extremists we will be. Will we be extremists for hate or for love? Will we be extremists for the preservation of injustice or for the extension of justice? In that dramatic scene on Calvary's hill three men were crucified. We must never forget that all three were crucified for the same crime—the crime of extremism. Two were extremists for immorality, and thus fell below their environment. The other, Jesus Christ, was an extremist for love, truth, and goodness, and thereby rose above his environment. Perhaps the South, the nation, and the world are in dire need of creative extremists.

---

[18]**freedom rides** In 1961, the Congress of Racial Equality (CORE) organized rides of whites and blacks to test segregation in southern buses and bus terminals with interstate passengers. More than 600 federal marshals were needed to protect the riders, most of whom were arrested.

[19]**Amos, Old Testament prophet (eighth century B.C.); Paul (?–A.D. 67); Martin Luther (1483–1546); John Bunyan (1628–1688); Abraham Lincoln (1809–1865); and Thomas Jefferson (1743–1826)** These figures are all noted for religious, moral, or political innovations that changed the world. Amos was a prophet who favored social justice; Paul argued against Roman law; Luther began the Reformation of the Christian Church; Bunyan was imprisoned for preaching the gospel according to his own understanding; Lincoln freed America's slaves; Jefferson drafted the Declaration of Independence.

I had hoped that the white moderate would see this need. Per- 32
haps I was too optimistic; perhaps I expected too much. I suppose I
should have realized that few members of the oppressor race can
understand the deep groans and passionate yearnings of the
oppressed race, and still fewer have the vision to see that injustice
must be rooted out by strong, persistent, and determined action. I am
thankful, however, that some of our white brothers in the South have
grasped the meaning of this social revolution and committed themselves to it. They are still all too few in quantity, but they are big in
quality. Some—such as Ralph McGill, Lillian Smith, Harry Golden,
James McBride Dabbs, Ann Braden, and Sarah Patton Boyle—have
written about our struggle[20] in eloquent and prophetic terms. Others
have marched with us down nameless streets of the South. They have
languished in filthy, roach-infested jails, suffering the abuse and
brutality of policemen who view them as "dirty nigger-lovers." Unlike
so many of their moderate brothers and sisters, they have recognized
the urgency of the moment and sensed the need for powerful "action"
antidotes to combat the disease of segregation.

Let me take note of my other major disappointment. I have been 33
so greatly disappointed with the white church and its leadership. Of
course, there are some notable exceptions. I am not unmindful of the
fact that each of you has taken some significant stands on this issue. I
commend you, Reverend Stallings, for your Christian stand on this
past Sunday, in welcoming Negroes to your worship service on a
nonsegregated basis. I commend the Catholic leaders of this state for
integrating Spring Hill College several years ago.

But despite these notable exceptions, I must honestly reiterate 34
that I have been disappointed with the church. I do not say this as
one of those negative critics who can always find something wrong
with the church. I say this as a minister of the gospel, who loves the
church; who was nurtured in its bosom; who has been sustained by
its spiritual blessings and who will remain true to it as long as the
cord of life shall lengthen.

When I was suddenly catapulted into the leadership of the bus 35
protest in Montgomery, Alabama, a few years ago, I felt we would be
supported by the white church. I felt that the white ministers,
priests, and rabbis of the South would be among our strongest allies.
Instead, some have been outright opponents, refusing to understand

---

[20] **written about our struggle** These are all prominent southern writers who
expressed their feelings regarding segregation in the South. Some of them, like Smith
and Golden, wrote very popular books with a wide influence. Some, like McGill and
Smith, were severely rebuked by white southerners.

the freedom movement and misrepresenting its leaders; all too many others have been more cautious than courageous and have remained silent behind the anesthetizing security of stained-glass windows.

In spite of my shattered dreams, I came to Birmingham with the hope that the white religious leadership of this community would see the justice of our cause and, with deep moral concern, would serve as the channel through which our just grievances could reach the power structure. I had hoped that each of you would understand. But again I have been disappointed. . . .   36

There was a time when the church was very powerful—in the time when the early Christians rejoiced at being deemed worthy to suffer for what they believed. In those days the church was not merely a thermometer that recorded the ideas and principles of popular opinion; it was a thermostat that transformed the mores of society. Whenever the early Christians entered a town, the people in power became disturbed and immediately sought to convict the Christians for being "disturbers of the peace" and "outside agitators." But the Christians pressed on, in the conviction that they were "a colony of heaven," called to obey God rather than man. Small in number, they were big in commitment. They were too God-intoxicated to be "astronomically intimidated." By their effort and example they brought an end to such ancient evils as infanticide and gladiatorial contests.   37

Things are different now. So often the contemporary church is a weak, ineffectual voice with an uncertain sound. So often it is an archdefender of the status quo. Far from being disturbed by the presence of the church, the powerful structure of the average community is consoled by the church's silent—and often even vocal—sanction of things as they are.   38

But the judgment of God is upon the church as never before. If today's church does not recapture the sacrificial spirit of the early church, it will lose its authenticity, forfeit the loyalty of millions, and be dismissed as an irrelevant social club with no meaning for the twentieth century. Every day I meet young people whose disappointment with the church has turned into outright disgust.   39

Perhaps I have once again been too optimistic. Is organized religion too inextricably bound to the status quo to save our nation and the world? Perhaps I must turn my faith to the inner spiritual church, the church within the church, as the true *ekklesia*[21] and the   40

---

[21] **ekklesia** Greek word for "church" meaning not just the institution but the spirit of the church.

hope of the world. But again I am thankful to God that some noble souls from the ranks of organized religion have broken loose from the paralyzing chains of conformity and joined us as active partners in the struggle for freedom. They have left their secure congregations and walked the streets of Albany, Georgia, with us. They have gone down the highways of the South on torturous rides for freedom. Yes, they have gone to jail with us. Some have been dismissed from their churches, have lost the support of their bishops and fellow ministers. But they have acted in the faith that right defeated is stronger than evil triumphant. Their witness has been the spiritual salt that has preserved the true meaning of the gospel in these troubled times. They have carved a tunnel of hope through the dark mountain of disappointment.

I hope the church as a whole will meet the challenge of this decisive hour. But even if the church does not come to the aid of justice, I have no despair about the future. I have no fear about the outcome of our struggle in Birmingham, even if our motives are at present misunderstood. We will reach the goal of freedom in Birmingham and all over the nation, because the goal of America is freedom. Abused and scorned though we may be, our destiny is tied up with America's destiny. Before the pilgrims landed at Plymouth, we were here. Before the pen of Jefferson etched the majestic words of the Declaration of Independence across the pages of history, we were here. For more than two centuries our forebears labored in this country without wages; they made cotton king; they built the homes of their masters while suffering gross injustice and shameful humiliation—and yet out of a bottomless vitality they continued to thrive and develop. If the inexpressible cruelties of slavery could not stop us, the opposition we now face will surely fail. We will win our freedom because the sacred heritage of our nation and the eternal will of God are embodied in our echoing demands. 41

Before closing I feel impelled to mention one other point in your statement that has troubled me profoundly. You warmly commended the Birmingham police force for keeping "order" and "preventing violence." I doubt that you would have so warmly commended the police force if you had seen its dogs sinking their teeth into unarmed, nonviolent Negroes. I doubt that you would so quickly commend the policemen if you were to observe their ugly and inhumane treatment of Negroes here in the city jail; if you were to watch them push and curse old Negro women and young Negro girls; if you were to see them slap and kick old Negro men and young boys; if you were to observe them, as they did on two occasions, refuse to give us food because we wanted to sing our grace together. I cannot join you in your praise of the Birmingham police department. 42

It is true that the police have exercised a degree of discipline in   43
handling the demonstrators. In this sense they have conducted themselves rather "nonviolently" in public. But for what purpose? To preserve the evil system of segregation. Over the past few years I have
consistently preached that nonviolence demands that the means
we use must be as pure as the ends we seek. I have tried to make clear
that it is wrong to use immoral means to attain moral ends. But now I
must affirm that it is just as wrong, or perhaps even more so, to use
moral means to preserve immoral ends. Perhaps Mr. Connor and his
policemen have been rather nonviolent in public, as was Chief
Pritchett in Albany, Georgia, but they have used the moral means of
nonviolence to maintain the immoral end of racial injustice. As T. S.
Eliot[22] has said, "The last temptation is the greatest treason: To do
the right deed for the wrong reason."

I wish you had commended the Negro sit-inners and demonstra-   44
tors of Birmingham for their sublime courage, their willingness to suffer, and their amazing discipline in the midst of great provocation.
One day the South will recognize its real heroes. They will be the
James Merediths,[23] with the noble sense of purpose that enables them
to face jeering and hostile mobs, and with the agonizing loneliness
that characterizes the life of the pioneer. They will be old, oppressed,
battered Negro women, symbolized in a seventy-two-year-old woman
in Montgomery, Alabama, who rose up with a sense of dignity and
with her people decided not to ride segregated buses, and who
responded with ungrammatical profundity to one who inquired about
her weariness: "My feets is tired, but my soul is at rest." They will be
the young high school and college students, the young ministers of
the gospel and a host of their elders, courageously and nonviolently
sitting in at lunch counters and willingly going to jail for conscience's
sake. One day the South will know that when these disinherited children of God sat down at lunch counters, they were in reality standing
up for what is best in the American dream and for the most sacred values in our Judaeo-Christian heritage, thereby bringing our nation

---

[22] **Thomas Stearns Eliot (1888–1965)** Renowned as one of the twentieth
century's major poets, Eliot was born in the United States but in 1927 became a
British subject and a member of the Church of England. Many of his poems focused
on religious and moral themes. These lines are from Eliot's play *Murder in the Cathe-
dral*, about Saint Thomas à Becket (1118–1170), the archbishop of Canterbury, who
was martyred for his opposition to King Henry II.

[23] **the James Merediths** James Meredith (b. 1933) was the first black to
become a student at the University of Mississippi. His attempt to register for classes
in 1962 created the first important confrontation between federal and state authorities, when Governor Ross Barnett personally blocked Meredith's entry to the university. Meredith graduated in 1963 and went on to study law at Columbia University.

back to those great wells of democracy which were dug deep by the founding fathers in their formulation of the Constitution and the Declaration of Independence.

Never before have I written so long a letter. I'm afraid it is much 45 too long to take your precious time. I can assure you that it would have been much shorter if I had been writing from a comfortable desk, but what else can one do when he is alone in a narrow jail cell, other than write long letters, think long thoughts, and pray long prayers?

If I have said anything in this letter that overstates the truth and 46 indicates an unreasonable impatience, I beg you to forgive me. If I have said anything that understates the truth and indicates my having a patience that allows me to settle for anything less than brotherhood, I beg God to forgive me.

I hope this letter finds you strong in the faith. I also hope that cir- 47 cumstances will soon make it possible for me to meet each of you, not as an integrationist or a civil rights leader but as a fellow clergyman and a Christian brother. Let us all hope that the dark clouds of racial prejudice will soon pass away and the deep fog of misunderstanding will be lifted from our fear-drenched communities, and in some not too distant tomorrow the radiant stars of love and brotherhood will shine over our great nation with all their scintillating beauty.

> Yours in the cause of
> Peace and Brotherhood,
> MARTIN LUTHER KING, JR.

QUESTIONS FOR CRITICAL READING

1. Define "nonviolent direct action" (para. 2). In what areas of human experience is it best implemented? Is politics its best area of application? What are the four steps in a nonviolent campaign?
2. Do you agree that "law and order exist for the purpose of establishing justice" (para. 24)? Why? Describe how law and order either do or do not establish justice in your community. Compare notes with your peers.
3. King describes an unjust law as "a code that a numerical or power majority group compels a minority group to obey but does not make binding on itself" (para. 17). Devise one or two other definitions of an unjust law. What unjust laws currently on the books do you disagree with?
4. What do you think is the best-written paragraph in the essay? Why?
5. King cites "tension" in paragraph 10 and elsewhere as a beneficial force. Do you agree? What kind of tension does he mean?
6. In what ways was King an extremist (paras. 30–31)?

7. In his letter, to what extent does King consider the needs of women? Would he feel that issues of women's rights are unrelated to issues of racial equality?

8. According to King, how should a government function in relation to the needs of the individual? Does he feel, like Thoreau's "Chinese philosopher," that the empire is built on the individual?

SUGGESTIONS FOR CRITICAL WRITING

1. Write a brief letter protesting an injustice that you feel may not be entirely understood by people you respect. Clarify the nature of the injustice, the reasons that people hold an unjust view, and the reasons your views should be accepted. Consult King's letter, and use his techniques.

2. In paragraph 43, King says, "I have consistently preached that nonviolence demands that the means we use must be as pure as the ends we seek." What does he mean by this? Define the ends he seeks and the means he approves. Do you agree with him on this point? If you have read the selection from Machiavelli, contrast their respective views. Which view seems more reasonable to you?

3. The first part of the letter defends King's journey to Birmingham as a Christian to help his fellows gain justice. He challenges the view that he is an outsider, using such expressions as "network of mutuality" and "garment of destiny" (para. 4). How effective is his argument? Examine the letter for other expressions that justify King's intervention on behalf of his brothers and sisters. Using his logic, describe other social areas where you might be justified in acting on your own views on behalf of humanity. Do you expect your endeavors would be welcomed? Are there any areas where you think it would be wrong to intervene?

4. In paragraphs 15–22, King discusses two kinds of laws—those that are morally right and those that are morally wrong. Which laws did King regard as morally right? Which laws did he consider morally wrong? Analyze one or two current laws that you feel are morally wrong. Be sure to be fair in describing the laws and establishing their nature. Then explain why you feel they are morally wrong. Would you feel justified in breaking these laws? Would you feel prepared, as King was, to pay the penalties demanded of one who breaks the law?

5. Compare King's letter with sections of Paul's letters to the faithful in the New Testament. Either choose a single letter, such as the Epistle to the Romans, or select passages from Romans, the two letters to the Corinthians, the Galatians, the Ephesians, the Thessalonians, or the Philippians. How did Paul and King agree and disagree about brotherly love, the mission of Christ, the mission of the church, concern for the law, and the duties of the faithful? Inventory the New Testament letters and King's letter carefully for concrete evidence of similar or contrary positions.

6. **CONNECTIONS**   To what extent do Martin Luther King Jr.'s views about government coincide with those of Lao-tzu? Is there a legitimate comparison to be made between King's policy of nonviolent resistance and Lao-tzu's judicious inactivity? To what extent would King have agreed with Lao-tzu's views? Would Lao-tzu have supported King's position in his letter, or would he have interpreted events differently?

7. **CONNECTIONS**   King cites conscience as a guide to obeying just laws and defying unjust laws. How close is his position to that of Henry David Thoreau? Do you think that King had read Thoreau's "Civil Disobedience" as an important document regarding justice and injustice? Compare and contrast the positions of these two writers.

8. **SEEING CONNECTIONS**   The Reverend Martin Luther King Jr. may well have known Giordano's fresco *Justice* (p. 140). To what extent would he have found Giordano's concept of justice incomplete? To what extent would he have found Giordano's concept reassuring of his own personal views about the scope and importance of justice? Would King have agreed that justice is one of the four cardinal virtues? What might King have wanted to add to the painting to make it more complete for a modern viewer?

JOHN RAWLS
A Theory of Justice

JOHN RAWLS (1921–2002) was widely considered one of the
most distinguished moral philosophers of the second half of the
twentieth century. He was educated at Princeton University and
served in the 32nd Infantry Division in New Guinea and the Philip-
pines from 1943 to 1946. After returning to Princeton for his doctorate, he taught at Cornell, Oxford, Massachusetts Institute of Technology, and finally Harvard University, where he was Conant University
Professor, the highest-level professorship at the university.

Rawls began to work out the ideas that eventually formed his
most important book, *A Theory of Justice* (1971), in the 1950s, both
in his earliest articles and in his notes for his lectures and teaching.
He spent more than ten years refining his thinking on the subject,
and in the process began to attract the attention of other thinkers
concerned with problems of justice and equality. Much to his surprise, *A Theory of Justice* became a best-seller, and it has affected
the discourse in justice and politics so widely that contemporary
scholars cannot discuss these issues without paying homage to
Rawls's work. In essence, he changed the direction of thought away
from the utilitarian—a system of justice that benefits the greatest
number with the greatest good—to a system of justice based on
fairness, in which any social action must be measured by its effect
on the least advantaged people in the society. Rawls argued that if a
social action were to harm an individual, that action should be
avoided.

In *A Theory of Justice*, Rawls develops two basic ideas: the
"original position" and the "veil of ignorance." In what is called a
thought experiment similar to Plato's "The Allegory of the Cave"
(p. 447), Rawls proposes a version of a social contract much like

---

From *A Theory of Justice*.

Rousseau's (p. 55). However, the principles are different. In the "original position" concept, Rawls proposes an original starting point for a society in which the designers of the society make certain assumptions about the "Primary Goods"—freedom, equality, opportunity, wealth, powers, and income—that each person in the society must have. The planners of the society, much like Thomas Jefferson and those who constructed our Constitution, were to take into consideration all the desirable qualities important to a rational society. Then, to make things more interesting and fair, Rawls devised the concept of the "veil of ignorance" in which the planners and the members of the society made their decisions about the Primary Goods without knowing where they themselves would actually fall in the society in terms of their sex, race, birth, or talent. If they were kept ignorant of those facts, Rawls believed, their decisions would not be biased by personal circumstances. Rawls assumed that every individual was directed by self-interest first, so the "veil of ignorance" would prevent the creation of a social structure that would benefit only those who were deciding how justice would be allocated.

Above all, Rawls believed that justice must be fair and that the rights of the individual should never be sacrificed for the greater good of society. Personal freedom insofar as it did not impinge on the freedom of others was one of his most sacred values. Underlying all these ideas is the insistence that people are equal and should be treated equally.

One of Rawls's most controversial ideas is often referred to as the "difference principle." Rawls felt that any inequality produced by a social structure must be measured by its effect on the least advantaged people in the society. For instance, a tax structure that produced inequality of wealth in a community must be measured by its harmful or beneficial effect on those who are least wealthy, and not on the middle class or those with the most advantages. This position has been attacked in part because it seems to penalize those who have the talent to create wealth for themselves. Rawls responds by suggesting that the society he envisions can accept a certain amount of inequality of distribution of wealth, as long as it does not upset the equilibrium of the society. Exactly how this position is worked out in practice is not clear, but on a theoretical level it seems to suggest that a certain amount of unequal distribution of Primary Goods could result in an internal revolution, thus destroying the equilibrium of the society as a result of a perceived injustice. Justice cannot be fair if only a certain group has most of the wealth, opportunities, power, or income. Such a situation constitutes a loss of equilibrium.

Rawls's Rhetoric

Rawls is not considered a stylish writer; his purpose is not to convince us by means of a poetic or graceful style, but to present the basic ingredients of an argument. His approach is methodical in the sense that he begins with principles that are carefully defined, then moves on to show us how these principles would be applied and in what conditions they would be appropriate. In other words, this is a method that demands careful attention from the first sentences onward because everything flows from those early statements.

He begins by alluding to related theories, such as Jean-Jacques Rousseau's social contract, which suggests that people in a society agree to an unspoken contract that binds them to accept the conditions of the society or else leave. But Rawls ignores the bases of the contracts proposed by Rousseau and others, and by contrast alludes to principles that "free and rational persons concerned to further their own interests would accept in an initial position of equality as defining the fundamental terms of their association" (para. 1). Rawls ends his first paragraph with a statement of purpose and definition: "This way of regarding the principles of justice I shall call justice as fairness." This principle is fundamental to his argument.

Rawls develops the concept of the "original position" in the third paragraph: "This original position . . . is understood as a purely hypothetical situation characterized so as to lead to a certain conception of justice." Whereas Rousseau refers to a "state of nature" that may have existed in which people bound themselves to a society, Rawls attempts to formulate an ideal or hypothetical situation that conforms with views that he feels may guarantee fairness.

The fourth paragraph examines the idea that justice should guarantee fairness to everyone in the society. Rawls considers the nature of cooperation that naturally pertains to a social order in which people voluntarily and rationally decide to join. In paragraph 5, he addresses the question of interest, a term he uses to clarify the position of individuals in a just society. When he states that individuals are "rational and mutually disinterested" (para. 5), he means that individuals make decisions based on their own concerns, not those of others. A disinterested decision could only be made by someone who does not benefit from the outcome.

Rawls reminds us that those who are designing the social order from the original position must decide what "conception of justice as fairness" (para. 6) they will choose. To be sure, this is a difficult concept. The framers of the U.S. Constitution faced a similar prospect, and despite their concern with equality and fairness, they ignored the conditions of the least advantaged in their society: slaves. In the sixth paragraph, Rawls mentions the principle of utility, which means the utilitarian view that the best society provides the greatest good to the greatest number of people. In that view, the Constitution achieved a utilitarian end, but that does not satisfy Rawls because it ignores the rights of the least advantaged.

The seventh paragraph establishes the bedrock principles by which Rawls expects justice to be established. The planners of the society must assign "rights and duties" in an equal fashion. Economic inequities can be tolerated only if they benefit the least advantaged members of society. This is a difficult provision to implement—but not to implement it would mean failure to achieve a justice of fairness, which is the demand Rawls makes in his opening pages.

Several of the latter paragraphs examine what Rawls calls "the merit of the contract terminology" (para. 10) so that we will have as firm an understanding of the idea of the social contract as we can. This discussion reminds us that when members of a society agree to join a community, those members are expected to abide by an implied contract of behavior.

Rawls does not, in this introductory segment to *A Theory of Justice*, propose concrete judgments as to how justice as fairness would be established. In later sections of his book he undertakes the examination of certain aspects of a social order in which justice as fairness functions. Yet, throughout his book, his principles remain those of the philosopher, essentially abstract and ideal. Nonetheless, his ideas, like those of Plato in his *Republic*, have implications for any society that expects its members to respect those who administer justice, for when justice cannot be achieved in a society, dire consequences ensue.

PREREADING QUESTIONS: WHAT TO READ FOR

The following prereading questions may help you anticipate key issues in the discussion of John Rawls's "A Theory of Justice." Keeping them in mind during your first reading of the selection should help focus your attention.

- How does Rawls articulate his idea of "justice as fairness"?
- What are the "primary goods" that people in a society need?
- What is Rawls's attitude toward the least advantaged people in society?

A Theory of Justice

My aim is to present a conception of justice which generalizes and 1
carries to a higher level of abstraction the familiar theory of the social
contract as found, say, in Locke, Rousseau, and Kant.[1] In order to do
this we are not to think of the original contract as one to enter a particular society or to set up a particular form of government. Rather, the
guiding idea is that the principles of justice for the basic structure of
society are the object of the original agreement. They are the principles that free and rational persons concerned to further their own
interests would accept in an initial position of equality as defining the
fundamental terms of their association. These principles are to regulate all further agreements; they specify the kinds of social cooperation
that can be entered into and the forms of government that can be
established. This way of regarding the principles of justice I shall call
justice as fairness.

Thus we are to imagine that those who engage in social coopera- 2
tion choose together, in one joint act, the principles which are to
assign basic rights and duties and to determine the division of social
benefits. Men are to decide in advance how they are to regulate their
claims against one another and what is to be the foundation charter
of their society. Just as each person must decide by rational reflection
what constitutes his good, that is, the system of ends which it is rational for him to pursue, so a group of persons must decide once and
for all what is to count among them as just and unjust. The choice
which rational men would make in this hypothetical situation of
equal liberty, assuming for the present that this choice problem has
a solution, determines the principles of justice.

In justice as fairness the original position of equality corresponds 3
to the state of nature in the traditional theory of the social contract.
This original position is not, of course, thought of as an actual historical state of affairs, much less as a primitive condition of culture. It is
understood as a purely hypothetical situation characterized so as to

---

[1] As the text suggests, I shall regard Locke's *Second Treatise of Government*,
Rousseau's *The Social Contract*, and Kant's ethical works beginning with *The Foundations of the Metaphysics of Morals* as definitive of the contract tradition. For all of its
greatness, Hobbes's *Leviathan* raises special problems. A general historical survey is
provided by J. W. Gough, *The Social Contract*, 2nd ed. (Clarendon Press: Oxford,
1957), and Otto Gierke, *Natural Law and the Theory of Society*, trans. with an introduction by Ernest Barker (Cambridge University Press: Cambridge, 1934). A presentation of the contract view as primarily an ethical theory is to be found in G. R.
Grice, *The Grounds of Moral Judgment* (Cambridge University Press: Cambridge,
1967). [Rawls's note]

lead to a certain conception of justice.[2] Among the essential features of this situation is that no one knows his place in society, his class position or social status, nor does any one know his fortune in the distribution of natural assets and abilities, his intelligence, strength, and the like. I shall even assume that the parties do not know their conceptions of the good or their special psychological propensities. The principles of justice are chosen behind a veil of ignorance. This ensures that no one is advantaged or disadvantaged in the choice of principles by the outcome of natural chance or the contingency of social circumstances. Since all are similarly situated and no one is able to design principles to favor his particular condition, the principles of justice are the result of a fair agreement or bargain. For given the circumstances of the original position, the symmetry of everyone's relations to each other, this initial situation is fair between individuals as moral persons, that is, as rational beings with their own ends and capable, I shall assume, of a sense of justice. The original position is, one might say, the appropriate initial status quo, and thus the fundamental agreements reached in it are fair. This explains the propriety of the name "justice as fairness": it conveys the idea that the principles of justice are agreed to in an initial situation that is fair. The name does not mean that the concepts of justice and fairness are the same, any more than the phrase "poetry as metaphor" means that the concepts of poetry and metaphor are the same.

Justice as fairness begins, as I have said, with one of the most general of all choices which persons might make together, namely with the choice of the first principles of a conception of justice which is to regulate all subsequent criticism and reform of institutions. Then, having chosen a conception of justice, we can suppose that they are to choose a constitution and a legislature to enact laws, and so on, all in accordance with the principles of justice initially agreed upon. Our social situation is just if it is such that by this sequence of hypothetical agreements we would have contracted into the general system of rules which defines it. Moreover, assuming that the original position does determine a set of principles (that is, that a particular conception of justice would be chosen), it will then be true that whenever social

4

---

[2] Kant is clear that the original agreement is hypothetical. See *The Metaphysics of Morals*, pt. I (*Rechtslehre*), especially §§ 47, 52; and pt. II of the essay "Concerning the Common Saying: This May Be True in Theory but It Does Not Apply in Practice," in *Kant's Political Writings*, ed. Hans Reiss and trans. H. B. Nisbet (Cambridge University Press: Cambridge, 1970), 73–87. See Georges Vlachos, *La Pensée politique de Kant* (Presses Universitaires de France: Paris, 1962), 326–35; and J. G. Murphy, *Kant: The Philosophy of Right* (Macmillan: London, 1970), 109–12, 133–36, for a further discussion. [Rawls's note]

institutions satisfy these principles those engaged in them can say to one another that they are cooperating on terms to which they would agree if they were free and equal persons whose relations with respect to one another were fair. They could all view their arrangements as meeting the stipulations which they would acknowledge in an initial situation that embodies widely accepted and reasonable constraints on the choice of principles. The general recognition of this fact would provide the basis for a public acceptance of the corresponding principles of justice. No society can, of course, be a scheme of cooperation which men enter voluntarily in a literal sense; each person finds himself placed at birth in some particular position in some particular society, and the nature of this position materially affects his life prospects. Yet a society satisfying the principles of justice as fairness comes as close as a society can to being a voluntary scheme, for it meets the principles which free and equal persons would assent to under circumstances that are fair. In this sense its members are autonomous and the obligations they recognize self-imposed.

One feature of justice as fairness is to think of the parties in the 5
initial situation as rational and mutually disinterested. This does not mean that the parties are egoists, that is, individuals with only certain kinds of interests, say in wealth, prestige, and domination. But they are conceived as not taking an interest in one another's interests. They are to presume that even their spiritual aims may be opposed, in the way that the aims of those of different religions may be opposed. Moreover, the concept of rationality must be interpreted as far as possible in the narrow sense, standard in economic theory, of taking the most effective means to given ends. I shall modify this concept to some extent, but one must try to avoid introducing into it any controversial ethical elements. The initial situation must be characterized by stipulations that are widely accepted.

In working out the conception of justice as fairness one main 6
task clearly is to determine which principles of justice would be chosen in the original position. To do this we must describe this situation in some detail and formulate with care the problem of choice which it presents. . . . It may be observed, however, that once the principles of justice are thought of as arising from an original agreement in a situation of equality, it is an open question whether the principle of utility would be acknowledged. Offhand it hardly seems likely that persons who view themselves as equals, entitled to press their claims upon one another, would agree to a principle which may require lesser life prospects for some simply for the sake of a greater sum of advantages enjoyed by others. Since each desires to protect his interests, his capacity to advance his conception of the good, no one has a reason to acquiesce in an enduring loss for himself in order to bring

about a greater net balance of satisfaction. In the absence of strong
and lasting benevolent impulses, a rational man would not accept a
basic structure merely because it maximized the algebraic sum of
advantages irrespective of its permanent effects on his own basic
rights and interests. Thus it seems that the principle of utility is
incompatible with the conception of social cooperation among
equals for mutual advantage. It appears to be inconsistent with the
idea of reciprocity implicit in the notion of a well-ordered society.
Or, at any rate, so I shall argue.

I shall maintain instead that the persons in the initial situation   7
would choose two rather different principles: the first requires equality in the assignment of basic rights and duties, while the second
holds that social and economic inequalities, for example inequalities
of wealth and authority, are just only if they result in compensating
benefits for everyone, and in particular for the least advantaged members of society. These principles rule out justifying institutions on the
grounds that the hardships of some are offset by a greater good in the
aggregate. It may be expedient but it is not just that some should
have less in order that others may prosper. But there is no injustice in
the greater benefits earned by a few provided that the situation of
persons not so fortunate is thereby improved. The intuitive idea is
that since everyone's well-being depends upon a scheme of cooperation without which no one could have a satisfactory life, the division of
advantages should be such as to draw forth the willing cooperation of
everyone taking part in it, including those less well situated. Yet this
can be expected only if reasonable terms are proposed. The two principles mentioned seem to be a fair agreement on the basis of which
those better endowed, or more fortunate in their social position, neither of which we can be said to deserve, could expect the willing
cooperation of others when some workable scheme is a necessary
condition of the welfare of all.[3] Once we decide to look for a conception of justice that nullifies the accidents of natural endowment and
the contingencies of social circumstance as counters in quest for
political and economic advantage, we are led to these principles.
They express the result of leaving aside those aspects of the social
world that seem arbitrary from a moral point of view.

The problem of the choice of principles, however, is extremely   8
difficult. I do not expect the answer I shall suggest to be convincing
to everyone. It is, therefore, worth noting from the outset that justice
as fairness, like other contract views, consists of two parts: (1) an

---

[3] For the formulation of this intuitive idea I am indebted to Allan Gibbard.
[Rawls's note]

interpretation of the initial situation and of the problem of choice posed there, and (2) a set of principles which, it is argued, would be agreed to. One may accept the first part of the theory (or some variant thereof), but not the other, and conversely. The concept of the initial contractual situation may seem reasonable although the particular principles proposed are rejected. To be sure, I want to maintain that the most appropriate conception of this situation does lead to principles of justice contrary to utilitarianism and perfectionism, and therefore that the contract doctrine provides an alternative to these views. Still, one may dispute this contention even though one grants that the contractarian method is a useful way of studying ethical theories and of setting forth their underlying assumptions.

Justice as fairness is an example of what I have called a contract 9 theory. Now there may be an objection to the term "contract" and related expressions, but I think it will serve reasonably well. Many words have misleading connotations which at first are likely to confuse. The terms "utility" and "utilitarianism" are surely no exception. They too have unfortunate suggestions which hostile critics have been willing to exploit; yet they are clear enough for those prepared to study utilitarian doctrine. The same should be true of the term "contract" applied to moral theories. As I have mentioned, to understand it one has to keep in mind that it implies a certain level of abstraction. In particular, the content of the relevant agreement is not to enter a given society or to adopt a given form of government, but to accept certain moral principles. Moreover, the undertakings referred to are purely hypothetical: a contract view holds that certain principles would be accepted in a well-defined initial situation.

The merit of the contract terminology is that it conveys the idea 10 that principles of justice may be conceived as principles that would be chosen by rational persons, and that in this way conceptions of justice may be explained and justified. The theory of justice is a part, perhaps the most significant part, of the theory of rational choice. Furthermore, principles of justice deal with conflicting claims upon the advantages won by social cooperation; they apply to the relations among several persons or groups. The word "contract" suggests this plurality as well as the condition that the appropriate division of advantages must be in accordance with principles acceptable to all parties. The condition of publicity for principles of justice is also connoted by the contract phraseology. Thus, if these principles are the outcome of an agreement, citizens have a knowledge of the principles that others follow. It is characteristic of contract theories to stress the public nature of political principles. Finally there is the long tradition of the contract doctrine. Expressing the tie with this line of thought helps to define ideas and accords with natural piety. There are then several advantages in the use of the term "contract." With due precautions taken, it should not be misleading.

A final remark. Justice as fairness is not a complete contract the- 11
ory. For it is clear that the contractarian idea can be extended to the choice of more or less an entire ethical system, that is, to a system including principles for all the virtues and not only for justice. Now for the most part I shall consider only principles of justice and others closely related to them; I make no attempt to discuss the virtues in a systematic way. Obviously if justice as fairness succeeds reasonably well, a next step would be to study the more general view suggested by the name "rightness as fairness." But even this wider theory fails to embrace all moral relationships, since it would seem to include only our relations with other persons and to leave out of account how we are to conduct ourselves toward animals and the rest of nature. I do not contend that the contract notion offers a way to approach these questions which are certainly of the first importance; and I shall have to put them aside. We must recognize the limited scope of justice as fairness and of the general type of view that it exemplifies. How far its conclusions must be revised once these other matters are understood cannot be decided in advance.

QUESTIONS FOR CRITICAL READING

1. What is the "original position"? Why do you think Rawls named it so?
2. What personal qualities will people who are planning society in the original position need to have?
3. Rawls says the planners must be disinterested, or totally objective. How does the "veil of ignorance" help them achieve the desired level of objectivity?
4. Why is justice as fairness a desirable goal in society?
5. At the end of paragraph 3, Rawls states that justice and fairness are not the same thing. How does his example of distinguishing between poetry and metaphor explain his position?
6. Rawls states, "In justice as fairness the original position of equality corresponds to the state of nature in the traditional theory of the social contract" (para. 3). What does he mean by this, and what do the terms "state of nature" and "original position" mean to you?
7. One of the qualifications for people planning justice as fairness is that they be "rational and mutually disinterested." Why are these important qualities? How is justice as fairness harmed if the planners are not rational or if they operate only from self-interest?
8. In paragraph 6, Rawls suggests that rational planners would not conceive of a society that gave fewer opportunities to some people for the

sake of giving many more to others. Do you agree? Do you think our society operates on this rational principle?

9. What for you is the most important decision a society can make to help guarantee a justice of fairness?

SUGGESTIONS FOR CRITICAL WRITING

1. Keeping in mind that this selection is theoretical in nature and not a practical description of how justice should be applied in a society, offer a critique of the social order Rawls describes in which some people with the ability to make lots of money may have to share a great deal of it with others who make less. What is Rawls's position on such a situation? What is yours? How can you guarantee justice in a society that permits a small number of people to be extremely wealthy while many are relatively poor?

2. Rawls believes that justice must be fair. Do you feel that the system of justice under which we live is fair? Do you think that our system of justice is based on a workable conception of what fairness should be? Do you think justice should be fair? What prevents it from being so?

3. If you were one of the people given the job of designing a "conception of justice" for a society in which you would choose to live, what would you expect of that society in terms of fairness and justice? Can you possibly construct an ideal society without factoring in your own special circumstances, such as your gender, race, ethnicity, social status, level of privilege, or level of education? Rawls wants to factor those issues out of the process. Can you do that? Can anyone? If not, can any system of justice be fair?

4. The utilitarian position emphasizes a form of justice in which the greatest good for the greatest number of people dictates social decisions. Since the nineteenth century, this view, sometimes called the principle of utility, has been fairly dominant in Western democracies. However, Rawls condemns this view because it does not improve the condition of the least advantaged members of society. In fact, it may even harm such people. What is your position on Rawls's rejection of utility? How carefully must a society that values justice work to prevent enacting laws that might make worse the lives of the least advantaged?

5. One of the most important of the "Primary Goods" Rawls considers is equality. Construct an essay in which you define what you think social equality means, taking into consideration such individual differences as genetic makeup, health, intelligence, and physical attributes. How should differences in gender, sexual orientation, or physical prowess be considered in any society that values equality? Why is equality a desirable goal? How can it be achieved?

6. Many religions have taken considered positions on questions of equality. For example, in some synagogues and mosques, men and women

cannot worship together. Some religions hold that women are inferior by nature and therefore must be ruled entirely by their husbands or fathers. A religion may forbid women to work outside the home or discourage educating children of either sex beyond grade school. How should a society that values equality and religious freedom resolve conflicts when such fundamental beliefs intersect and clash?

7. **CONNECTIONS**   Thomas Jefferson was in a position similar to those figures Rawls imagines planning a social order based on justice as fairness. What elements of the Declaration of Independence seem to aim toward goals Rawls would find acceptable? Do you feel Jefferson would have shared Rawls's views about trying to avoid any social decisions that might harm the least advantaged citizen? Would Jefferson have had the most advantaged people in society make sacrifices in order to avoid harming the least advantaged? Would you?

8. **CONNECTIONS**   Rawls suggests that what he describes is not really a total contract theory. Turn to Jean-Jacques Rousseau's "The Origin of Civil Society" (p. 55) and try to see how close these two writers are in their view of how a society forms itself and what kind of implicit contract people make with each other when they decide to create and maintain a social order. How concerned is Rousseau with the concept of justice? How much do Rousseau and Rawls have in common regarding their sense of what society should be like?

9. **SEEING CONNECTIONS**   To what extent would Rawls be satisfied or dissatisfied with Giordano's fresco *Justice* (p. 140)? Would he feel that Giordano was as concerned about fairness as he? Would he feel that Giordano credited personal freedom as one of the chief elements of justice? Would he feel that Giordano was deeply concerned with the concept of equality among people or with the concept of protecting the weakest people in society? Would the fact that the painting decorated the palazzo of one of the wealthiest Florentines have affected Rawls's views? Would the fact that the former palazzo is now a public government building affect Rawls's views?

PART THREE

THE INDIVIDUAL

Ralph Waldo Emerson
Emile Durkheim
W. E. B. Du Bois
Ruth Benedict
Erich Fromm

INTRODUCTION

The life of humanity is so long, that of the individual so brief, that we often see only the ebb of the advancing wave and are thus discouraged. It is history that teaches us to hope.

—ROBERT E. LEE (1807–1870)

And while the law [of competition] may be sometimes hard for the individual, it is best for the race, because it ensures the survival of the fittest in every department.

—ANDREW CARNEGIE (1835–1919)

No army can withstand the strength of an idea whose time has come. An idea, to be suggestive, must come to the individual with the force of a revelation.

—WILLIAM JAMES (1842–1910)

The individual has always had to struggle to keep from being overwhelmed by the tribe. If you try it, you will be lonely often, and sometimes frightened. But no price is too high to pay for the privilege of owning yourself.

—FRIEDRICH NIETZSCHE (1844–1900)

Our power does not know liberty or justice. It is established on the destruction of the individual will.

—VLADIMIR LENIN (1870–1924)

And this I believe: that the free, exploring mind of the individual human is the most valuable thing in all the world. And this I would fight for: the freedom of the mind to take any direction it wishes, undirected. And this I must fight against: any idea, religion, or government which limits or destroys the individual.

—JOHN STEINBECK (1902–1968)

In classical times, the issue of the individual in society was not a central concern to most thinkers. Socrates may be among the most clearly individualistic figures in ancient Greece, but he paid with his life for his beliefs. He was accused of corrupting the youth because his teachings did not revere the official gods suitably. As a philosopher and an individualist, he did not abandon Athens as he might have in order to save his life but rather showed his essential approval of the social order of his time and submitted to his fate in a fashion that, according to Plato's account, was noble and heroic.

In Rome, there were many major figures who, according to Plutarch, changed history in profound ways, and we may account them as individuals even though they rarely had much to say about the individual in society. They were mostly concerned with keeping the

246

state in order or with changing their own status within the state. They were aware of the dangers of tyranny, and they understood the threats of the outlanders whom they kept under constant siege, but their concerns were for the preservation of society. Like the Greeks, they always felt the barbarians were at the gates and would destroy their society— as indeed they eventually did.

The Middle Ages in Europe were shaped by the absence of a central government similar to Rome's. Instead of a political power, European society was largely dominated by the Church of Rome, which itself diversified and broke into two divisions, with what we now call the Greek Orthodox Church serving the East. Again, the concern for the individual was not uppermost in the mind of the church, which was focused more on questions of sin and submission. The Reformation, which included the creation of the Protestant churches of Martin Luther and John Calvin in the sixteenth century, was an event of great importance to the development of modern individualism. But the other great theologians of the time considered political activity and ethical issues that were central to the survival of the church and the proper behavior of the individual in respect to honoring religious traditions. They did not comment extensively on the individual or individualism.

The emergence of theories about the individual came slowly to the fore in late-seventeenth-century Europe, but they were more pronounced in the eighteenth century during the period known as the Enlightenment, which lasted from the late 1680s to the late 1790s. During this period, thinkers such as Jean-Jacques Rousseau began to consider the individual in relation to society and to propose, among other things, that societies develop from the will of individuals and reflect the individuals within it. Rousseau's *Social Contract* was novel for the very reason that it begins its reflection not from an examination of the social order—as does the work of English philosopher Thomas Hobbes before him—but rather from the individual. Only after considering the rights and the influence of the individual does Rousseau begin talking about the structure of society.

Ralph Waldo Emerson, son of a cleric and himself a onetime minister at the Second Church in Boston, moved away from religious institutions after the death of his wife and a crisis of confidence in the rituals of the church he was serving. Because he was a gifted preacher, he was able to command an audience at the atheneums that dotted New England. His essays began to appear in magazines and eventually made him one of the most famous writers in America. He attacked conformity and the follow-the-leader style of thinking that he feared was becoming part of the then materialist society. He criticized a society that stifled individualism. His essay "Self-Reliance" places the responsibility for civil action and intellectual development in the hands of the individual and clarifies the need for the individual to act courageously and without self-interest. He constantly urges the individual with aphorisms such as "Trust thyself," "Trust thy emotion," and "To be great is to be misunderstood." His most famous quotation, "A foolish consistency is the hobgoblin of little minds," appears in this essay. His concern is that the individual must always practice self-reliance or else lose a sense of individualism. The power of this essay comes from its resemblance to an urgent war cry, and the message seems to have been picked up by all the authors following in this section.

The father of sociology, Emile Durkheim, wrote about individualism in France at a time when the entire nation was engaged in a decade-long debate over the falsely accused Alfred Dreyfus, an army captain convicted of treason. The country was split, and Durkheim, who as a sociologist usually studied social structure more closely than he studied the individuals within it, took a stand in defense of Dreyfus. He presents an argument, originally published in the press, attacking a prominent scholar who defended the army's position on the basis that it was only appropriate for the individual to sacrifice himself or herself for the greater good. Durkheim sees the reasoning of his opponent as bankrupt and worthless and presses forward in raising the value of the individual and individualism in the late nineteenth century. He goes so far as to challenge the special religious qualifications of his opponent and to declare that true individualism could be a new religion of humanity.

Once the most powerful intellectual voice of America's African American community, W. E. B. Du Bois took his doctorate in history from Harvard University, where he was the first African American to be granted a Ph.D. When he began his career, he turned to sociology and pressed forward to study the nature of the African American community as it had developed in both the North and the South. In his most famous book, *The Souls of Black Folk* (1903), Du Bois ostensibly writes an autobiography but in the process discusses the conditions under which African Americans lived. He centers things on himself by declaring that he is a problem, what he calls "the Negro Problem," and then goes on to ask what it feels like to be a problem. He then explores the "double-consciousness" of African Americans and how it affects their lives. His several earlier books on the sociology of the African American community inform his discussion of himself as a child in school and later as a man teaching school. For him, the individual is fragile and must be bolstered by courage and confidence.

One of the most famous anthropologists of the twentieth century, Ruth Benedict talks about a number of cultures that are unfamiliar to most modern students. Her work with Native American tribes— the Kwakiutl of the Pacific Northwest, the Zuni and Pueblo of the Southwest, as well as the Cheyenne and Plains Indians—permits her to explore the question of individualism in very different societies. What she demonstrates is that each culture has a set of norms that is often a "bad fit" for some individuals. The ways in which different cultures treat and value individuals who deviate from the norm is remarkable for its range of distinction. Benedict is a champion of cultural diversity and illustrates her discussion with numerous examples of how various individuals function in a society that does or doesn't tolerate aberrant behavior.

Erich Fromm is best known as a psychologist influenced by the writings of Karl Marx and Sigmund Freud. In *The Individual in the Chains of Illusion,* from which our excerpt is taken, Fromm clarifies the nature of his thought and explains how it varies from that of his great influences. Fromm is clearly concerned about the threat of the atomic bomb to the world at large. Like Emerson, he recommends disobedience as a virtue, especially in relation to an individual's refusal to press the button that would launch the atomic bomb. The threat of world destruction in 1962, when he wrote his book, was very serious. He points to the Fascist and Communist societies of the 1930s and 1940s that created political and ethical illusions eagerly adopted by huge numbers of people. Essentially, these societies crushed individualism in return for security and a sense of collective purpose that placed society first and the individual a distant second. Fromm goes so far as to praise Adam and Eve and Prometheus for having been disobedient because their actions essentially "made human evolution possible." He sees life as beginning with acts of disobedience and warns that if life were to end it would probably be the result of the obedience of someone who is merely "following orders." The illusion he discusses is caused by the security provided by the society that robs the individual of independence.

Interestingly, these essays seem to center on the question of conformity and the surrender of independence to social demands. Disobedience, which would seem on the surface to be an undesirable quality, becomes a central issue for most of these writers because they wish to promote the value of individuals who think for themselves and who do not fear taking a risk or living adventurously. Society is a powerful force with the potential to offer great satisfaction to its members, but the individual must always maintain the independence of mind and spirit that will keep society on a balanced track.

VISUALIZING THE INDIVIDUAL

The arts and literature have portrayed the individual in Western culture in many different ways. In some works, the individual is imagined as threatened, set apart, even confused, as in Shakespeare's famous character Hamlet. The seventeenth century seems to have been a watershed for individuality, producing Hamlet and a host of other figures, such as John Milton's Adam and Eve (in *Paradise Lost*), both of whom act individually rather than collectively and pay a

CASPAR DAVID FRIEDRICH, *WANDERER ABOVE THE SEA OF FOG.* CA. 1817–1818. Oil on canvas, 38 ½" × 29 ¼". Kunsthalle, Hamburg, Germany.

heavy price for their independence. For late-eighteenth-century romantics, even Milton's Satan in *Paradise Lost* was sometimes regarded as a hero rather than a villain simply because he stood up and rebelled against what he thought was a tyranny of control.

The romantics of the late eighteenth and early nineteenth centuries saw the individual as struggling against the forces of nature and society. With more and more advances in science and growing prosperity brought by the industrial revolution, the individual became ever more powerful and independent. The great romantic poets—like William Wordsworth, Samuel Taylor Coleridge, Percy Bysshe Shelley, and Lord Byron—portrayed themselves as independent of society and some of its norms. They sometimes lived as free spirits, often close to nature, but always intellectually liberated and often unencumbered by the usual sexual and marital constraints of their time. Their efforts were often transcendent, much as those of the transcendental writers were, of whom Ralph Waldo Emerson is one.

Caspar David Friedrich (1774–1840) was celebrated during his career as a landscape painter who specialized in portraying nature and the individual as an element within it. The people in his paintings were often small and almost insignificant in relation to the drama of the landscapes he chose to place them in. He aimed to portray a mood in many of his paintings, and in light of the many tragedies in his immediate family, some critics saw despair reflected in his work, especially in his later paintings. He suffered a stroke that largely disabled him in his last five years of life, but he continued painting. Many of his works include ruined chapels and churches, which were seen as emblems of his own insecurity about the value of religion in modern life. He was said to have perceived in his age a crisis in religious belief, which may have stemmed from his early upbringing as a Lutheran and his later despair at the death of so many close loved ones.

Wanderer Above the Sea of Fog was painted when Friedrich was about forty-three. In it we see a figure dressed in the clothes of a contemporary gentleman and carrying a walking stick, indicating that he scaled the heights with some effort to stand as he does on a craggy elevation, high in the mountains. He is conspicuously alone, and in staring across the landscape, he separates himself from us, the viewers, by looking away as if we did not exist. The sea of fog beneath his feet shows that he is vastly above the plains on which the majority of his fellow citizens live. He even stands above some of the distant mountains, over which he towers.

This has been an influential painting ever since it was first shown. For many viewers it is full of symbolic significance that indicates the force of the individual, not just in society, but in the entire world of nature. The individual in the painting is not a small or an insignificant figure but rather stands in the very center, dominating the most important space in the scene. His size, from foot to head, is the same as that of the preeminent crag on which he stands, and therefore he is presented not as a victim of the vision he sees but as a heroic figure with majesty over the visual scene. The fundamental visual layout of the painting is that of a pyramid, beginning at the bottom corners and culminating at the head of the individual, whose mind encompasses all.

The fog beneath the figure has sometimes been interpreted as emblematic of the uncertainty of the age, during which people had begun to question the nature of religion and the place of the individual in the world. The individual depicted dominates the space and looks over the fog, which is notably called a "sea," implying that he will have to navigate it in order to arrive at the conclusions that will place him in proper relation to heaven and earth.

As the individual looks forward, there are more mountains to scale, more challenges that he will accept and probably successfully negotiate, all by himself. His loneliness is not a negative value here because he is not so much lonely as he is singular. He depends on no one but himself. The sky above him is tinged with the reddening glow of a new day rather than with the sun-drenched clouds of a dramatic sunset. In a sense, the painting represents a new dawning of the individual in a modern world filled with uncertainty and profound challenges.

RALPH WALDO EMERSON
Self-Reliance

RALPH WALDO EMERSON (1803–1882) was the son of a Unitarian minister and part of a family that dates back to the Puritans. He was educated at Harvard College and, after a few years teaching at a girls' school in Boston, went to the Harvard Divinity School to prepare for the ministry. Although he became a popular preacher at the Second Church of Boston, ill health made it problematic for him to continue practicing as a minister. He left that post after a personal crisis of faith a few years after the death of his first wife (at age twenty).

He embarked on a tour of Europe in 1832–1833 and had the opportunity to meet a wide range of European intellectuals and romantics. William Wordsworth and Samuel Taylor Coleridge, the most prominent English romantic poets, and Thomas Carlyle, later author of *The French Revolution* (1837), were all figures who stimulated him and opened new intellectual worlds for his exploration. Emerson read widely in Eastern religion and philosophy as well as in Plato and other traditional philosophers.

When he returned from Europe, he rarely preached in church. He married again and had a family; his first wife's legacy enabled him to devote his time to reading and writing. His first major essay, *Nature* (1836), was published anonymously but later appeared in book form (1849) under his name. In this essay, he distilled the thoughts he had been collecting in his journals since college. He saw himself firmly positioned in nature and saw that nature reflected the mind of God. In this essay, he began to conceive of the idea of the Over-Soul, the "Universal Mind" that comprehends all things, and the idea then fed into his concept of the "transcendental man," the intuitive thinker who could, like Plato, see beyond surface materialism into the "true meaning" of the world. Transcendentalism became a movement in New England from the first publication of *Nature* until the beginning of the Civil War in 1860. It was basically a rejection of the intense emphasis of the eighteenth-century philosophers on pure reason. Rather, it proposed an intuitive understanding on the part of the individual to perceive directly the nature of things. Transcendentalism was never codified or made into a coherent philosophy because it was centered in the individual and was seen as an expression of the individual's direct apprehension of the divine spirit in nature.

Emerson's views concerning nature were both practical and spiritual. He saw four important values in nature that had profound importance for humankind. First, nature was the provider of materials for people's use; second, it provided a profound sense of beauty for the beholder; third, its elements constituted a "language" that the individual could "read" symbolically to promote understanding; and fourth, it represented a discipline in terms of the workings of the environment, all of which moved the individual closer to an understanding of the divine spirit. Some of Emerson's thinking in *Nature* benefited from his extensive reading in Indian and Asian literature and reflects some of its mystical attitudes.

Before *Nature* was released in book form, Emerson published "Self-Reliance" and other important essays in *Essays: First Series* (1841). Among the other essays in this volume are "History," "Spiritual Laws," "Love," "Friendship," "The Over-Soul," "Intellect," and "Art." These are the concerns of a man in his thirties and they sometimes reveal a brashness that is characteristic of youth empowered by great thoughts. These works were widely read throughout New England, Great Britain, and much of the rest of the English-speaking world. Emerson was able to make a comfortable living by going on the lecture circuit, commanding a considerable audience wherever he went. He was one of a remarkable number of "star lecturers" who became famous for speeches delivered in atheneums throughout the United States as well as in public halls elsewhere.

Emerson was deeply involved in the abolition movement in the United States, and he was also involved in the intellectual life around him. He knew Margaret Fuller and her social-living experiment, Brook Farm. Henry David Thoreau was a very close friend and associate, not just in terms of their sharing transcendental ideas, but in terms of their being neighbors. Thoreau for a time lived with Emerson. Louisa May Alcott, Jones Very, William Hawthorne, and many other American literary notables were his friends and sometimes his inspiration.

The ideas in "Self-Reliance" were not abstract to Emerson. He often went his own way and sometimes paid a price for doing so. For example, he delivered one of his most famous lectures to the Divinity School at Harvard in 1838. Now called the "Divinity School Address," this lecture is essentially an attack on all formal religious institutions and a call for the individual to perceive the spirit of divinity intuitively. Religious experience was more important to him than religion itself. As a result of this address, for thirty years Harvard refused to let him speak there.

Emerson's Rhetoric

Emerson was an energetic speaker and an enormously popular preacher when he held his post in Boston. His public addresses were always well attended and his work, when published, reached a wide audience for decades after his death. Indeed, readers have found "Self-Reliance" to be a compelling and important document worth passing on to generation after generation.

One of Emerson's rhetorical skills in "Self-Reliance" is to give the impression that he has an intimate relationship with the reader. He writes in the first person — "I read the other day . . ." — in a conversational tone that puts the reader at ease. Clearly, there is a certain level of formality that identifies the style as writing of the mid nineteenth century, even though Emerson feels he is being colloquial and easy. He is speaking to an educated audience who is likely to know the figures to whom he alludes; in this sense, he speaks to a less diverse audience than would a modern speaker.

However, under the easy tone is a considerable urgency, an argument that he pursues almost ruthlessly to convince the reader of the importance of self reliance. What appears on the following pages is the first part of "Self-Reliance," where Emerson develops that argument. In later sections of his essay (which do not appear here), he advises *how* one can be self-reliant, but the real force of the essay is in this first section, where all of his rhetorical powers are in evidence.

The first paragraphs of the essay are devoted to praising youth. Most of what is said in the first three paragraphs speaks directly to young men — a consequence of the age, in which he expected self-reliance to apply mainly to men. Today, we interpret his message as addressed to women as well. In paragraph 4, Emerson reminds us of the power of the infant to speak out and control the space it inhabits — and while not self-reliant, it is self-proclaiming. The following paragraph centers on the boy as he grows into a man, with the lesson that the young are less likely to be conformists than those in middle age. In other words, we begin as individualists and only later grow into being conformists.

Following paragraphs treat specific subjects that impinge on the individual's liberty. Paragraph 7 considers, among other things, charity: What does the individual owe to others, especially the poor? The power of virtues, which may seem to hamper the individual, is regarded in paragraph 8, in which Emerson reminds us that he plans to go in his own direction because, for some people, "virtues are penances." Paragraph 10 examines conformity, particularly the type demanded by a party, political or otherwise. Conformity then yields to consistency, beginning with paragraph 12, and leads to one of the most famous lines in the essay: "A foolish consistency is the hobgoblin of little minds . . . " (para. 14). In paragraph 16, however, we find a consistency that is not foolish: the practice of honor, about which he says, "Honor is venerable . . . because it is no ephemeris." In other words, it is permanent and not insubstantial. The selection ends with a review of individual characters: people whose independence and self-reliance not only changed them but also changed the world.

One of Emerson's special rhetorical skills is his reliance on aphorisms, forceful statements that are more claims than facts. They are so forcefully put that they seem convincing all by themselves. Here are a few examples:

"[A]ll history resolves itself very easily into the biography of a few stout and earnest persons." (para. 17)

"Trust thyself . . . ." (para. 3)

"Trust your emotion." (para. 13)

"To be great is to be misunderstood." (para. 14)

Nowhere does Emerson provide any evidence for these claims, nor does he seem even inclined to do so. He expects us to accept his statements without qualification except insofar as he may himself provide it. In some cases, he offers claims that, when examined, are immediately seen as false, if not unreasonable. For instance, he claims in the first paragraph that Moses, Plato, and Milton "set at naught books and traditions," whereas all were deeply involved in books (Genesis, *The Republic, Paradise Lost*) while still managing to modify tradition without stepping outside what was understood as the traditions of their time. Emerson's point, of course, is that these figures are great because they imprinted their times with new ideas and set forth to change institutions and societies.

Part of what makes this essay so forceful is our own understanding of how conformity robs us of our individualism. It is especially compelling to young readers whose self-confidence and energy propel them to trust themselves and question the power of institutions and authorities who might wish to force them into patterns not of their own choosing.

PREREADING QUESTIONS: WHAT TO READ FOR

The following prereading questions may help you anticipate key issues in Ralph Waldo Emerson's discussion of "Self-Reliance." Keeping them in mind during your first reading of the selection should help focus your attention.

- What does it mean to "[t]rust thyself"?
- How does the example of the child and young person encourage us to be self-reliant?
- Why does Emerson insist that we must become nonconformists?
- In what sense does Emerson make self-reliance an essential ingredient of individualism?

Self-Reliance

Ne te quaesiveris extra.[1]

Man is his own star, and the soul that can
Render an honest and a perfect man,
Command all light, all influence, all fate,
Nothing to him falls early or too late.
Our acts our angels are, or good or ill,
Our fatal shadows that walk by us still.
—EPILOGUE TO BEAUMONT AND FLETCHER'S
  Honest Man's Fortune

Cast the bantling[2] on the rocks,
Suckle him with the she-wolf's teat:
Wintered with the hawk and fox,
Power and speed be hands and feet.

I read the other day some verses written by an eminent painter[3] which were original and not conventional. Always the soul hears an admonition in such lines, let the subject be what it may. The sentiment they instill is of more value than any thought they may contain. To believe your own thought, to believe that what is true for you in

---

[1] *Ne . . . extra* Do not seek yourself outside yourself. (Latin)

[2] **Cast the bantling** Emerson's lines. A bantling is an abandoned child.

[3] **eminent painter** Washington Allston (1779–1843), a romantic landscape painter and poet who lived in Cambridge, Massachusetts.

your private heart, is true for all men — that is genius. Speak your latent conviction and it shall be the universal sense; for always the inmost becomes the outmost — and our first thought is rendered back to us by the trumpets of the Last Judgment. Familiar as the voice of the mind is to each, the highest merit we ascribe to Moses, Plato, and Milton, is that they set at naught books and traditions, and spoke not what men but what they thought. A man should learn to detect and watch that gleam of light which flashes across his mind from within, more than the lustre of the firmament of bards and sages. Yet he dismisses without notice his thought, because it is his. In every work of genius we recognize our own rejected thoughts: they come back to us with a certain alienated majesty. Great works of art have no more affecting lesson for us than this. They teach us to abide by our spontaneous impression with good humored inflexibility than most when the whole cry of voices is on the other side. Else, to-morrow a stranger will say with masterly good sense precisely what we have thought and felt all the time, and we shall be forced to take with shame our own opinion from another.

There is a time in every man's education when he arrives at the conviction that envy is ignorance; that imitation is suicide; that he must take himself for better, for worse, as his portion; that though the wide universe is full of good, no kernel of nourishing corn can come to him but through his toil bestowed on that plot of ground which is given to him to till. The power which resides in him is new in nature, and none but he knows what that is which he can do, nor does he know until he has tried. Not for nothing one face, one character, one fact makes much impression on him, and another none. It is not without preestablished harmony, this sculpture in the memory. The eye was placed where one ray should fall, that it might testify of that particular ray. Bravely let him speak the utmost syllable of his confession. We but half express ourselves, and are ashamed of that divine idea which each of us represents. It may be safely trusted as proportionate and of good issues, so it be faithfully imparted, but God will not have his work made manifest by cowards. It needs a divine man to exhibit any thing divine. A man is relieved and gay when he has put his heart into his work and done his best; but what he has said or done otherwise, shall give him no peace. It is a deliverance which does not deliver. In the attempt his genius deserts him; no muse befriends; no invention, no hope.

Trust thyself: every heart vibrates to that iron string. Accept the place the divine Providence has found for you; the society of your contemporaries, the connexion of events. Great men have always done so and confided themselves childlike to the genius of their age, betraying their perception that the Eternal was stirring at their heart, working through their hands, predominating in all their being. And we are now men, and must accept in the highest mind the same transcendent destiny; and not pinched in a corner, not cowards fleeing before a revolution, but redeemers and benefactors, pious aspirants to be noble clay plastic under the Almighty effort, let us advance and advance on Chaos and the Dark.

What pretty oracles nature yields us on this text in the face and   4
behavior of children, babes, and even brutes. That divided and rebel mind, that distrust of a sentiment because our arithmetic has computed the strength and means opposed to our purpose, these have not. Their mind being whole, their eye is as yet unconquered, and when we look in their faces, we are disconcerted. Infancy conforms to nobody: all conform to it, so that one babe commonly makes four or five out of the adults who prattle and play to it. So God has armed youth and puberty and manhood no less with its own piquancy and charm, and made it enviable and gracious and its claims not to be put by, if it will stand by itself. Do not think the youth has no force because he cannot speak to you and me. Hark! in the next room, who spoke so clear and emphatic? Good Heaven! it is he! it is that very lump of bashfulness and phlegm which for weeks has done nothing but eat when you were by, that now rolls out these words like bell-strokes. It seems he knows how to speak to his contemporaries. Bashful or bold, then, he will know how to make us seniors very unnecessary.

The nonchalance of boys who are sure of a dinner, and would dis-   5
dain as much as a lord to do or say aught to conciliate one, is the healthy attitude of human nature. How is a boy the master of society; independent, irresponsible, looking out from his corner on such people and facts as pass by, he tries and sentences them on their merits, in the swift summary way of boys, as good, bad, interesting, silly, eloquent, troublesome. He cumbers himself never about consequences, about interests: he gives an independent, genuine verdict. You must court him: he does not court you. But the man is, as it were, clapped into jail by his consciousness. As soon as he has once acted or spoken with éclat, he is a committed person, watched by the sympathy or the hatred of hundreds whose affections must now enter into his account. There is no Lethe[4] for this. Ah, that he could pass again into his neutral, godlike independence! Who can thus lose all pledge, and having observed, observe again from the same unaffected, unbiased, unbribable, unaffrighted innocence, must always be formidable, must always engage the poet's and the man's regards. Of such an immortal youth the force would be felt. He would utter opinions on all passing affairs, which being seen to be not private but necessary, would sink like darts into the ear of men, and put them in fear.

----

[4]**Lethe** The river of forgetfulness in classical mythology.

6

These are the voices which we hear in solitude, but they grow faint and inaudible as we enter into the world. Society everywhere is in conspiracy against the manhood of every one of its members. Society is a joint-stock company in which the members agree for the better securing of his bread to each shareholder, to surrender the liberty and culture of the eater. The virtue in most request is conformity. Self-reliance is its aversion. It loves not realities and creators, but names and customs.

Whoso would be a man must be a nonconformist. He who 7 would gather immortal palms must not be hindered by the name of goodness, but must explore if it be goodness. Nothing is at last sacred but the integrity of our own mind. Absolve you to yourself, and you shall have the suffrage of the world. I remember an answer which when quite young I was prompted to make to a valued adviser who was wont to importune me with the dear old doctrines of the church. On my saying, What have I to do with the sacredness of traditions, if I live wholly from within? my friend suggested — "But these impulses may be from below, not from above." I replied, "They do not seem to me to be such; but if I am the devil's child, I will live then from the devil." No law can be sacred to me but that of my nature. Good and bad are but names very readily transferable to that or this; the only right is what is after my constitution, the only wrong what is against it. A man is to carry himself in the presence of all opposition as if everything were titular and ephemeral but he. I am ashamed to think how easily we capitulate to badges and names, to large societies and dead institutions. Every decent and well-spoken individual affects and sways me more than is right. I ought to go upright and vital, and speak the rude truth in all ways. If malice and vanity wear the coat of philanthropy, shall that pass? If an angry bigot assumes this bountiful cause of Abolition, and comes to me with his last news from Barbadoes,[5] why should I not say to him, "Go love thy infant; love thy wood-chopper: be good-natured and modest: have that grace; and never varnish your hard, uncharitable ambition with this incredible tenderness for black folk a thousand miles off. Thy love afar is spite at home." Rough and graceless would be such greeting, but truth is handsomer than the affectation of love. Your goodness must have some edge to it—else it is none. The doctrine of hatred must be preached as the counteraction of the doctrine of love when that pules and whines. I shun father and mother and wife and brother, when my genius calls me. I would write on the lintels of the door-post, *Whim.* I hope it is somewhat better than whim at last, but we cannot spend the day in explanation. Expect me not to show cause why I seek or why I exclude

---

[5] **Barbadoes** Barbados, where slavery was abolished in 1834.

company. Then, again, do not tell me, as a good man did to-day, of my obligation to put all poor men in good situation. Are they *my* poor? I tell thee, thou foolish philanthropist, that I grudge the dollar, the dime, the cent I give to such men as do not belong to me and to whom I do not belong. There is a class of persons to whom by all spiritual affinity I am bought and sold; for them I will go to prison, if need be; but your miscellaneous popular charities; the education at college of fools; the building of meeting-houses to the vain end to which many now stand; alms to sots; and the thousandfold Relief Societies— though I confess with shame I sometimes succumb and give the dollar, it is a wicked dollar which by-and-by I shall have the manhood to withhold.

Virtues are in the popular estimate rather the exception than the rule. There is the man *and* his virtues. Men do what is called a good action, as some piece of courage or charity, much as they would pay a fine in expiation of daily non-appearance on parade. Their works are done as an apology or extenuation of their living in the world—as invalids and the insane pay a high board. Their virtues are penances. I do not wish to expiate, but to live. My life is not an apology, but a life. It is for itself and not for a spectacle. I much prefer that it should be of a lower strain, so it be genuine and equal, than that it should be glittering and unsteady. I wish it to be sound and sweet, and not to need diet and bleeding.[6] My life should be unique; it should be an alms, a battle, a conquest, a medicine. I ask primary evidence that you are a man, and refuse this appeal from the man to his actions. I know that for myself it makes no difference whether I do or forbear those actions which are reckoned excellent. I cannot consent to pay for a privilege where I have intrinsic right. Few and mean as my gifts may be, I actually am, and do not need for my own assurance or the assurance of my fellows any secondary testimony.

What I must do, is all that concerns me, not what the people think. This rule, equally arduous in actual and in intellectual life, may serve for the whole distinction between greatness and meanness. It is the harder, because you will always find those who think they know what is your duty better than you know it. It is easy in the world to live after the world's opinion; it is easy in solitude to live after our own; but the great man is he who in the midst of the crowd keeps with perfect sweetness the independence of solitude.

The objection to conforming to usages that have become dead to you, is, that it scatters your force. It loses your time and blurs the impression of your character. If you maintain a dead church, contribute

8

9

10

---

[6]**bleeding** A generally applied medical technique, especially for fever.

to a dead Bible-Society, vote with a great party either for the Government or against it, spread your table like base housekeepers—under
all these screens, I have difficulty to detect the precise man you are.
And, of course, so much force is withdrawn from your proper life. But
do your thing, and I shall know you. Do your work, and you shall reinforce yourself. A man must consider what a blind-man's-buff is this
game of conformity. If I know your sect, I anticipate your argument. I
hear a preacher announce for his text and topic the expediency of one
of the institutions of his church. Do I not know beforehand that not
possibly can he say a new and spontaneous word? Do I not know that
with all this ostentation of examining the grounds of the institution,
he will do no such thing? Do I not know that he is pledged to himself
not to look but at one side; the permitted side, not as a man, but as a
parish minister? He is a retained attorney, and these airs of the bench
are the emptiest affectation. Well, most men have bound their eyes
with one or another handkerchief, and attached themselves to some
one of these communities of opinion. This conformity makes them not
false in a few particulars, authors of a few lies, but false in all particulars. Their every truth is not quite true. Their two is not the real two,
their four not the real four: so that every word they say chagrins us,
and we know not where to begin to set them right. Meantime nature
is not slow to equip us in the prison-uniform of the party to which we
adhere. We come to wear one cut of face and figure, and acquire by
degrees the gentlest asinine expression. There is a mortifying experience
in particular which does not fail to wreak itself also in the general history; I mean, "the foolish face of praise,"[7] the forced smile which we put
on in company where we do not feel at ease in answer to conversation
which does not interest us. The muscles, not spontaneously moved, but
moved by a low usurping willfulness, grow tight about the outline of
the face and make the most disagreeable sensation, a sensation of
rebuke and warning which no brave young man will suffer twice.

For non-conformity the world whips you with its displeasure. 11
And therefore a man must know how to estimate a sour face. The
bystanders look askance on him in the public street or in the friend's
parlor. If this aversation had its origin in contempt and resistance like
his own, he might well go home with a sad countenance; but the
sour faces of the multitude, like their sweet faces, have no deep
cause—disguise no god, but are put on and off as the wind blows,
and a newspaper directs. Yet is the discontent of the multitude more
formidable than that of the senate and the college. It is easy enough
for a firm man who knows the world to brook the rage of the cultivated

---

[7] **"the . . . praise"** Alexander Pope (1688–1744), from "Epistle to Dr. Arbuthnot,"
line 212.

classes. Their rage is decorous and prudent, for they are timid as being very vulnerable themselves. But when to their feminine rage the indignation of the people is added, when the ignorant and the poor are aroused, when the unintelligent brute force that lies at the bottom of society is made to growl and mow, it needs the habit of magnanimity and religion to treat it godlike as a trifle of no concernment.

The other terror that scares us from self-trust is our consistency; 12 a reverence for our past act or word, because the eyes of others have no other data for computing our orbit than our past acts, and we are loath to disappoint them.

But why should you keep your head over your shoulder? Why 13 drag about this monstrous corpse of your memory, lest you contradict somewhat you have stated in this or that public place? Suppose you should contradict yourself; what then? It seems to be a rule of wisdom never to rely on your memory alone, scarcely even in acts of pure memory, but bring the past for judgment into the thousand-eyed present, and live ever in a new day. Trust your emotion. In your metaphysics you have denied personality to the Deity: yet when the devout motions of the soul come, yield to them heart and life, though they should clothe God with shape and color. Leave your theory as Joseph his coat in the hand of the harlot, and flee.[8]

A foolish consistency is the hobgoblin of little minds, adored by 14 little statesmen and philosophers and divines. With consistency a great soul has simply nothing to do. He may as well concern himself with his shadow on the wall. Out upon your guarded lips! Sew them up with packthread, do. Else, if you would be a man, speak what you think to-day in words as hard as cannon balls, and to-morrow speak what to-morrow thinks in hard words again, though it contradict every thing you said to-day. Ah, then, exclaim the aged ladies, you shall be sure to be misunderstood. Misunderstood! It is a right fool's word. Is it so bad then to be misunderstood? Pythagoras was misunderstood, and Socrates, and Jesus, and Luther, and Copernicus, and Galileo, and Newton, and every pure and wise spirit that ever took flesh. To be great is to be misunderstood.

I suppose no man can violate his nature. All the sallies of his 15 will are rounded in by the law of his being as the inequalities of Andes and Himalayas are insignificant in the curve of the sphere. Nor does it matter how you gauge and try him. A character is like an acrostic or Alexandrian stanza—read it forward, backward, or across, it still spells the same thing. In this pleasing contrite wood-life which God allows me, let me record day by day my honest

---

[8]**harlot, and flee** Joseph left his cloak behind as he fled from the temptress, Potiphar's wife (Genesis 39:12).

thought without prospect or retrospect, and, I cannot doubt, it will be found symmetrical, though I mean it not, and see it not. My book should smell of pines and resound with the hum of insects. The swallow over my window should interweave that thread or straw he carries in his bill into my web also. We pass for what we are. Character teaches above our wills. Men imagine that they communicate their virtue or vice only by overt actions and do not see that virtue or vice emit a breath every moment.

Fear never but you shall be consistent in whatever variety of actions, so they be each honest and natural in their hour. For of one will, the actions will be harmonious, however unlike they seem. These varieties are lost sight of when seen at a little distance, at a little height of thought. One tendency unites them all. The voyage of the best ship is a zigzag line of a hundred tacks. This is only microscopic criticism. See the line from a sufficient distance, and it straightens itself to the average tendency. Your genuine action will explain itself and will explain your other genuine actions. Your conformity explains nothing. Act singly, and what you have already done singly, will justify you now. Greatness always appeals to the future. If I can be great enough now to do right and scorn eyes, I must have done so much right before, as to defend me now. Be it how it will, do right now. Always scorn appearances, and you always may. The force of character is cumulative. All the foregone days of virtue work their health into this. What makes the majesty of the heroes of the senate and the field, which so fills the imagination? The consciousness of a train of great days and victories behind. There they all stand and shed a united light on the advancing actor. He is attended as by a visible escort of angels to every man's eye. That is it which throws thunder into Chatham's voice, and dignity into Washington's port, and America into Adams's eye.[9] Honor is venerable to us because it is no ephemeris. It is always ancient virtue. We worship it to-day, because it is not of to-day. We love it and pay it homage, because it is not a trap for our love and homage, but is self-dependent, self-derived, and therefore of an old immaculate pedigree, even if shown in a young person.

I hope in these days we have heard the last of conformity and consistency. Let the words be gazetted[10] and ridiculous henceforward. Instead of the gong for dinner, let us hear a whistle from the Spartan[11]

16

17

---

[9] **Chatham . . . eye** Reference to British parliamentarian William Pitt (1708–1778), Earl of Chatham, and presidents George Washington (1732–1799) and John Adams (1735–1826).

[10] **gazetted** Published.

[11] **Spartan** The Spartans were a highly disciplined warrior society in ancient Greece.

fife. Let us bow and apologize never more. A great man is coming to eat at my house. I do not wish to please him: I wish that he should wish to please me. I will stand here for humanity, and though I would make it kind, I would made it true. Let us affront and reprimand the smooth mediocrity and squalid contentment of the times, and hurl in the face of custom, and trade, and office, the fact which is the upshot of all history, that there is a great responsible Thinker and Actor moving wherever moves a man; that a true man belongs to no other time or place, but is the center of things. Where he is, there is nature. He measures you, and all men, and all events. You are constrained to accept his standard. Ordinarily every body in society reminds us of somewhat else or of some other person. Character, reality, reminds you of nothing else. It takes place of the whole creation. The man must be so much that he must make all circumstances indifferent — put all means into the shade. This all great men are and do. Every true man is a cause, a country, and an age; requires infinite spaces and numbers and time fully to accomplish his thought—and posterity seem to follow his steps as a procession. A man Caesar is born, and for ages after, we have a Roman Empire. Christ is born, and millions of minds so grow and cleave to his genius, that he is confounded with virtue and the possible of man. An institution is the lengthened shadow of one man; as, the Reformation, of Luther; Quakerism, of Fox; Methodism, of Wesley; Abolition, of Clarkson. Scipio,[12] Milton called "the height of Rome"; and all history resolves itself very easily into the biography of a few stout and earnest persons.

---

[12] **Reformation . . . Scipio** Founders of institutions: Martin Luther (1483–1546), George Fox (1624–1691), John Wesley (1703–1791), Thomas Clarkson (1760–1846), and Scipio Africanus (237–183 B.C.).

QUESTIONS FOR CRITICAL READING

1. Is it genius to "believe your own thought, to believe that what is true for you in your private heart, is true for all men" (para. 1)? How many people do you know who fit this description?
2. Emerson says that we quickly submit to special societies and dead institutions. How correct is he in your case?
3. Emerson says, "I shun father and mother and wife and brother, when my genius calls me" (para. 7). To what extent is this desirable behavior?
4. Must the individual become self-reliant?
5. Is conformity as much a problem in the twenty-first century as it was in the nineteenth century?
6. What is the difference between a foolish consistency and a consistency that you approve?

7. Emerson refuses to contribute funds for "the education at college of fools" (para. 7). Is he right in withholding his philanthropy, as he suggests in paragraph 8?

8. In paragraph 11, Emerson refers to the "bottom of society." What does he seem to mean by this expression? What do you mean by it?

SUGGESTIONS FOR CRITICAL WRITING

1. One of Emerson's aphorisms is "For non-conformity the world whips you with its displeasure" (para. 11). He does not provide evidence to support his claim. Can you support it from your personal experience? How does your immediate society treat the nonconformist? How difficult is it to be a nonconformist in the society in which you live? Is a college environment more likely or less likely to tolerate or reward nonconformity? Are you a nonconformist?

2. What are the chief elements in a person's struggle to become an individual? Examine each important element found in the essay; then add any further elements that you think Emerson may have omitted. He emphasizes self-trust, nonconformity, and independence of thought, among other qualities of behavior. Which ones are most important to your sense of developing your own individualism?

3. Emerson essentially makes his case by proclamation. He offers no evidence and basically argues no case. He just says things need to be the way he says they need to be. However, some of what he recommends may be socially destructive. Examine his most important claims about the way the individual must behave and argue against his views by demonstrating how much damage they would do to the society you live in today.

4. Emerson does not mention the term *peer pressure*, but if he lived today, he might do so. What role does peer pressure play in the quest for self-reliance? Using the rhetorical techniques of "Self-Reliance," add a large section to the essay on the role of peer pressure as it affects those who wish to become independent. Use examples from your own experience or the experiences of others.

5. In paragraph 15, Emerson says, "I suppose no man can violate his nature." This statement presupposes a philosophy regarding humanity that needs to be examined. What could Emerson mean by the expression "his nature"? How much does our society seem to believe that people have a distinct nature that directs their behavior? If Emerson is right about this statement, how can he expect someone to follow the dictates of "Self-Reliance" if they are against that person's nature?

6. **CONNECTIONS** Emerson refers to Plato in his essay and was deeply influenced by Plato's thought, especially his view that the world we see is not the "real" world as it exists in heaven. Read Plato's "The Allegory of the Cave" (p. 447) and decide just how much of his ideas Emerson incorporates in "Self-Reliance." How much in agreement are these two great thinkers? Is Plato talking about self-reliance without using the term?

7. **SEEING CONNECTIONS**   Write an essay from Emerson's point of view in which you interpret Caspar David Friedrich's *Wanderer Above the Sea of Fog* (p. 250) symbolically. What, for Emerson, would the crag on which the wanderer stands represent in society? What has the wanderer achieved in order to reach the top of the crag? To what extent would Emerson think the wanderer self-reliant? What do the distant objects in the painting seem to account for in relation to Emerson's essay?

EMILE DURKHEIM
Individualism and the Intellectuals

EMILE DURKHEIM (1858–1917), the father of modern sociology, established a science and an area of academic study that did not exist formally before he began his work. He was born in Lorraine, in eastern France, into a family that had traditionally trained its sons as rabbis. Durkheim's father, grandfather, and great-grandfather were rabbis, but Durkheim was not as personally religious as they, and in deciding to go in a different direction, he eventually became convinced that religions were more interesting for their organizing structures than for their divinity. He ended his life an agnostic, although he was always part of the Jewish community in France.

His early years were spent in Lycée Louis-le-Grand, the most demanding secondary school in Paris, which prepared him for the most prestigious college in that city, the École Normale Supérieure. This college had produced most of France's intellectuals since its founding during the First Republic in the 1790s. Durkheim was not an especially dazzling student, but while there, he met some of the young people who were destined to become the greatest philosophers and scholars of his day. After graduation, he studied for a time in Germany then returned and began teaching at the Université Bordeaux, where he established the first department of sociology in Europe. In 1902, he moved to the Sorbonne in Paris where, later appointed professor of education and sociology, he remained for the rest of his career.

Durkheim's mature work in sociology is interesting in its emphasis on social structures, especially the nature of the restrictions that social orders do or do not place on their members. His

Originally published as "L'individualisme et les intellectuels," *Revue bleue,* 4e série, 10 (1898): 7–13. Translated by Mark Traugott.

approach was not through the individual because, unlike Rousseau, he did not think of a social structure as resulting from the nature of the individuals that comprised it, but rather he thought of the structure as possessing unique qualities that had specific effects on the individual. For example, Durkheim studied religious groups and saw that the Protestant social order was very different from the Catholic social order. Protestantism, because of its many different forms and its wider range of beliefs, was looser in its structure than Catholicism, which held to much more specific beliefs ranging somewhat closer to moral absolutism. Despite what he says in this essay, Durkheim generally held that individuals in any social system were "insatiable" in their needs and demands and that the job of the social structure was to place limits on them so as to make sure the social order cohered and functioned successfully.

His most important studies concerned suicide in society. His research into the suicide rates of various social groups led him to believe that suicide was less a problem of individuals than one of societies. Highly regulated societies produce one kind of suicide, while less regulated societies produce another. During his research, Durkheim proposed a theory of *anomie*, a form of restlessness and lack of direction. Anomie is a condition of the society, not of the individual, and it implies a loss of moral certainty and a change in the system of norms that guide the society. Anomic suicide, he says, happens in societies in which a clear sense of norms is missing. Egoistic, or individualistic, suicide occurs when the individual finds himself detached from society and its norms. Durkheim's theory was frequently cited during the 1960s and 1970s in the United States, a period during which easy access to effective birth control and a youth who embraced "sex, drugs, and rock and roll" brought the moral and political values of the previous generation into question.

The titles of his most important books give us an idea of the range of his thoughts and interests: *The Division of Labor in Society* (1893), in which he first develops the concept of anomie; *The Rules of Sociological Method* (1895), in which he rejects the utilitarian view of society and its reliance on the greatest good for the greatest number; *Suicide: A Study in Sociology* (1897); and *The Elementary Forms of Religious Life* (1912).

Durkheim was treated with some suspicion during World War I because he was a Jew with a German name; however, he enthusiastically supported the French effort in a number of ways. His only son, Andre, himself a promising sociologist, was killed retreating from Serbia with allied French forces in 1915, and the shock and sadness weighed upon Durkheim and eventually resulted in his sickness. He died in November 1917, at the age of fifty-nine.

Durkheim's Rhetoric

The background for this impassioned polemic on the virtues of individualism (despite Durkheim's basic views about social structures) centers on the conviction of Alfred Dreyfus (1859–1935) for treason for purportedly spying for the Germans in 1894. Dreyfus was a captain in the French army and was sentenced to life on Devil's Island. The French nation was split for almost ten years between the Dreyfusards and the anti-Dreyfusards. What eventually became apparent was that the French high command found that another officer was the traitor, and they forged documents to bolster the conviction of Dreyfus. The French army refused to admit the truth because it would have made their procedures look bad in the public's eye. Durkheim published this essay in a magazine in 1898 in support of Dreyfus, who was eventually brought back from Devil's Island in 1899 and later restored to his rank in 1906.

Durkheim argues here against another French intellectual, Ferdinand Brunetière, a prominent Catholic scholar teaching at the École Normale Supérieure. Brunetière argued that the honor of the French army was at stake and that it was only reasonable that Dreyfus sacrifice himself for France—the principle being that the good of the social order trumps individualism. The question of innocence was less important than the preservation of the integrity of the institution of the army and French society. In other words, the individual must give way to the mass for the greater good. The greatest French author then living, Émile Zola (1840–1902), had also written a scathing polemic against the army and all those who condemned Dreyfus. It was his voice that startled the nation, brought him into court in a case that he won, and made the Dreyfus affair the most celebrated question of the age. Brunetière attacked individualistic intellectuals who refused to respect the greater good of the nation in favor of championing a single figure who ought to be glad to be sacrificed for the greater good.

Interestingly, Durkheim maintains his own form of argument by not mentioning Dreyfus or Brunetière. For one thing, everyone in his audience in 1898 knew exactly who he was talking about, and his strategy connects his statements about individualism less to a current event than to the general question of how the individual relates to the social order.

Durkheim begins with the question of the rights of the individual and how they relate to the "present age." Then he begins to define the terms of individualism (para. 4) that will guide him through the rest of the essay. He characterizes Brunetière's concept of the individual as being based in utilitarianism, providing the greatest good for the greatest number. Durkheim was antagonistic to the utilitarians and made his reputation by refuting their view of social structure. Herbert Spencer (1820–1903), a very influential British philosopher, took a scientific attitude toward social structures, but unlike Durkheim, he saw society as a product of the individuals that comprised it, and he further saw that societies evolved in a Darwinian fashion. It was Spencer, not Darwin, who coined the phrase "the survival of the fittest," and its application to societies and other phenomena followed. Durkheim dispatches him with an insult, claiming that Spencer is "morally . . . impoverished" (para. 4) and insisting that his views of the individual are essentially dismissed. He lumps Spencer with Brunetière and the utilitarians. Both, he feels, are no longer relevant, just as he dismisses Rousseau for similar reasons. Rousseau's sense of the social contract, Durkheim feels, is unreasonable because Rousseau sees the will of the society as appropriate because it averages out all the individuals in society. That will not do for Durkheim, who, in an uncharacteristic statement, finally declares that the individual is virtually sacred and must be recognized as such. He says, "It is humanity which is worthy of respect and sacred" (para. 10), just before he begins to introduce religion into the discussion.

His last section focuses on "the moral unity of the country" (para. 13) and moves on to a consideration of religion, which, as he says, is supposed to provide a moral basis for the community. In paragraph 16, he attacks Brunetière's position, which is based on his views of religion, by reminding him and us that the origins of Christianity centered on individualism and the inner life of the individual. He contrasts the external rites and ceremonies of religion as Brunetière knows it with the modern individual, for whom "[t]he very center of moral life was thus transported from the external to the internal, and the individual was thus elevated to be sovereign judge of his own conduct, accountable only to himself and to his God" (para. 16). Durkheim concludes by establishing that his concept of individualism is congruent with fundamental Christian morality.

He reminds us that individualism and intellectualism go together, asserting that "Yes, it is quite true that individualism implies a certain intellectualism; for freedom of thought is the first of the freedoms" (para. 11).

PREREADING QUESTIONS:
WHAT TO READ FOR

The following prereading questions may help you to anticipate key issues in Emile Durkheim's "Individualism and the Intellectuals." Keeping them in mind during your first reading of the selection should help focus your attention.

- What are some possible definitions of *individualism* on either side of the argument?
- How does Durkheim see the relationship of the individual to society?
- On what grounds does Durkheim connect individualism to religion?
- Ultimately, what is the relation of intellectualism to individualism?

Individualism and the Intellectuals

The question that has so painfully divided our country for the past six months is in the process of being transformed: originally a simple factual question, it has been generalized little by little. The recent intervention of a well-known man of letters[1] has greatly contributed to this result. It seems that the moment has arrived to renew in a brilliant move a polemic which was bogged down in repetitiveness. This is why, instead of resuming once again the discussion of facts, we have passed on, in a single bound, to the level of principles: it is the mental state of the "intellectuals,"[2] the basic ideas they profess, and no longer the details of their reasoning which are being attacked. If they obstinately refuse "to bend their logic before the word of an army general," it is evidently because they presume the right to decide the question for themselves; it is because they place their reason above authority, because the rights of the individual seem to them inalienable. It is therefore their individualism which has determined their schism. But then, it is said, if we wish to restore peace in our minds and to prevent the return of similar discord, this individualism must be fought tooth and nail. This inexhaustible source of internal division must be dried up once and for all. And so a veritable crusade has begun against this public scourge, against "this great sickness of the present age." 1

---

[1] See the article by Ferdinand Brunetière, "Après le procès," *Revue des deux mondes,* 15 March 1898. [Durkheim's note]

[2] Let us note in passing that this very convenient word has in no way the impertinent sense that has so maliciously been attributed to it. The intellectual is not a man who has a monopoly on intelligence; there is no social function for which intelligence is not necessary. But there are those where it is, at one and the same time, both the means and the end, the agent and the goal. In them, intelligence is used to extend intelligence, that is to say, used to enrich it with new knowledge, ideas, or sensations. It thus constitutes the whole of these professions (the arts and sciences), and it is in order to express this peculiarity that the man who consecrates himself to them has quite naturally come to be called an intellectual. [Durkheim's note]

We gladly accept the debate in these terms. We also believe that the controversies of yesterday only gave superficial expression to a more profound disagreement, and that opinion was divided far more over a question of principle than over a question of fact. Let us therefore leave aside the arguments over circumstances which have been exchanged on both sides. Let us forget the matter itself and the sad spectacles we have witnessed. The problem before us goes infinitely beyond the present incidents and must be distinguished from them.

2

There is one ambiguity that must be cleared up before all else.

3

In order to prosecute individualism more easily, they confuse it with the strict utilitarianism and the utilitarian egoism of Spencer[3] and the economists. But that is to make the contest too easy. It is indeed an easy game to denounce as an ideal without grandeur this crass commercialism which reduces society to nothing more than a vast apparatus of production and exchange. For it is exceedingly clear that all communal life is impossible without the existence of interests superior to those of the individual. We quite agree that nothing is more deserved than that such doctrines be considered anarchical. But what is inadmissable is that they should reason as though this form of individualism were the only one which existed or was even possible. Quite the contrary—it is more and more becoming a rarity and an exception. The practical philosophy of Spencer is morally so impoverished that it can hardly claim any adherents anymore. As for the economists, though they formerly allowed themselves to be seduced by the simplicity of this theory, for some time they have sensed the necessity of tempering the rigor of their primitive orthodoxy and of opening themselves to more generous sentiments. Molinari[4] is just about alone in France in remaining intractable, and I do not believe he has exercised a great influence on the ideas of our epoch. In truth, if individualism had no other representatives, it would be quite useless thus to move heaven and earth to combat an enemy who is in the process of quietly dying a natural death.

4

But there exists another sort of individualism which is less easily overcome. It has been professed, for the past century, by the vast majority of thinkers: this is the individualism of Kant[5] and Rousseau,[6]

5

---

[3] **Herbert Spencer (1820–1903)** Utilitarian philosopher who applied Darwinism to sociology.

[4] **Gustave de Molinari (1819–1912)** Laissez-faire liberal French economist.

[5] **Immanuel Kant (1724–1804)** Influential Enlightenment philosopher and author of *Critique of Pure Reason.*

[6] **Jean-Jacques Rousseau (1712–1778)** Major French Enlightenment philosopher and author of *The Social Contract.*

of the idealists—the one which the Declaration of the Rights of Man attempted, more or less happily, to formulate and which is currently taught in our schools and has become the basis of our moral catechism. They hope to deal a blow to this form of individualism by striking instead at the former type; but this one is profoundly different, and the criticisms which apply to the one could hardly suit the other. Far from making personal interest the objective of conduct, this one sees in all personal motives the very source of evil. According to Kant, I am sure of acting properly only if the motives which determine my behavior depend not on the particular circumstances in which I find myself, but on my humanity in the abstract. Inversely, my actions are bad when they can be logically justified only by my favored position or by my social condition, by my class or caste interests, by my strong passions, and so on. This is why immoral conduct can be recognized by the fact that it is closely tied to the actor's individuality and cannot be generalized without manifest absurdity. In the same way, if, according to Rousseau, the general will, which is the basis of the social contract, is infallible, if it is the authentic expression of perfect justice, it is because it is the sum of all individual wills; it follows that it constitutes a sort of impersonal average from which all individual considerations are eliminated, because, being divergent and even antagonistic, they neutralize each other and cancel each other out.[7] Thus, for both these men, the only moral ways of acting are those which can be applied to all men indiscriminately; that is, which are implied in the general notion of "man."

Here we have come a long way from that apotheosis of well-being and private interest, from that egoistic cult of the self for which utilitarian individualism has been rightly criticized. Quite the contrary, according to these moralists, duty consists in disregarding all that concerns us personally, all that derives from our empirical individuality, in order to seek out only that which our humanity requires and which we share with all our fellowmen. This ideal so far surpasses the level of utilitarian goals that it seems to those minds who aspire to it to be completely stamped with religiosity. This human person (*personne humaine*), the definition of which is like the touchstone which distinguishes good from evil, is considered sacred in the ritual sense of the word. It partakes of the transcendent majesty that churches of all time lend to their gods; it is conceived of as being invested with that mysterious property which creates a void about sacred things, which removes them from vulgar contacts and withdraws them from common circulation. And the

6

---

[7] See Rousseau, *The Social Contract,* book 1; book 2, chapter 3. [Durkheim's note]

respect which is given it comes precisely from this source. Whoever makes an attempt on a man's life, on a man's liberty, on a man's honor, inspires in us a feeling of horror analogous in every way to that which the believer experiences when he sees his idol profaned. Such an ethic is therefore not simply a hygenic discipline or a prudent economy of existence; it is a religion in which man is at once the worshiper and the god.

But this religion is individualistic, since it takes man as its object 7 and since man is an individual by definition. What is more, there is no system whose individualism is more intransigent. Nowhere are the rights of the individual affirmed with greater energy, since the individual is placed in the ranks of sacrosanct objects; nowhere is the individual more jealously protected from encroachments from the outside, whatever their source. The doctrine of utility can easily accept all sorts of compromises without belying its fundamental axiom; it can admit of individual liberties' being suspended whenever the interest of the greater number requires that sacrifice. But no compromise is possible with a principle which is thus placed outside and above all temporal interests. There is no political reason which can excuse an attack upon the individual when the rights of the individual are above those of the state. If then, individualism is, in and of itself, the catalyst of moral dissolution, we should see it here manifest its antisocial essence. Now we understand the gravity of the question. For this eighteenth-century liberalism which is at bottom the whole object of the dispute is not simply a drawing-room theory, a philosophical construct; it has become a fact, it has penetrated our institutions and our mores, it has blended with our whole life, and if, truly, we had to give it up, we would have to recast our whole moral organization at the same stroke.

Now it is already a remarkable fact that all those theoreticians of 8 individualism are no less sensitive to the rights of the collectivity than to those of the individual. No one has insisted more strongly than Kant upon the supraindividual character of ethics and of law; he makes of them a sort of commandment that man must obey without any discussion simply because it is a commandment. And if he has sometimes been reproached for having exaggerated the autonomy of reason, one could equally well say, and not without foundation, that he placed at the base of his ethics an irrational act of faith and submission. Moreover, doctrines are judged above all by what they produce—that is, by the spirit of the doctrines to which they give birth. Now Kantianism gave rise to the ethics of Fichte,[8] which

---

[8]**Johann Gottlieb Fichte (1762–1814)** German idealist philosopher noted for his thoughts on self-awareness.

are already quite impregnated with socialism, and the philosophy of Hegel,[9] of whom Marx was the disciple. As for Rousseau, we know how his individualism is complemented by his authoritarian conception of society. Following him, the men of the Revolution,[10] even while promulgating the famous Declaration of Rights, made of France an indivisible and centralized entity. Perhaps we should see in the work of the Revolution above all a great movement of national concentration. Finally, the principal reason the idealists have fought against the utilitarian ethic is that it appeared to them incompatible with social necessities.

This eclecticism, it is said, is not without contradictions. To be sure, we do not dream of defending the way these different thinkers went about fusing these two aspects of their systems of thought. If, with Rousseau, we begin by making of the individual a sort of absolute which can and must suffice unto itself, it is evidently difficult then to explain how it was possible for the civil state to be established. But the present question is to know not whether this or that moralist succeeded in showing how these two tendencies are reconciled, but whether or not they are, in and of themselves, reconcilable. The reasons given for establishing their unity may be worthless, and yet this unity may be real; and already the fact that they generally coincide in the same minds leads us to believe that they go together; from all this, it follows that they must depend on a single social state of which they are probably only different aspects.   9

And, in fact, once we have stopped confusing individualism with its opposite—that is, with utilitarianism—all these supposed contradictions disappear like magic. This religion of humanity has everything it needs to speak to its faithful in a no less imperative tone than the religions it replaces. Far from limiting itself to flattering our instincts, it fixes before us an ideal which infinitely surpasses nature. For ours is not naturally a wise and pure reason which, purged of all personal motives, would legislate in the abstract its own conduct. Doubtless, if the dignity of the individual came from his personal characteristics, from the peculiarities which distinguish him from others, we might fear that it would shut him off in a sort of moral egoism which would make any solidarity impossible. But in reality he receives dignity from a higher source, one which he shares with all men. If he has a right to this religious respect, it is because he   10

---

[9] **Georg Wilhelm Friedrich Hegel (1770–1831)** German idealist philosopher known for his theory of dialectic in which opposite arguments form the basis of reasoning.

[10] **Revolution** French Revolution (1789–1799), the destruction of French aristocratic rule and an elevation of the common people.

partakes of humanity. It is humanity which is worthy of respect and sacred. Now it is not all in him. It is diffused among all his fellow-men and consequently he cannot adopt it as the aim of his conduct without being obliged to come out of himself and relate to others. The cult, of which he is at once both object and agent, does not address itself to the particular being which he is and which bears his name, but to the human person (*la personne humaine*) wherever it is to be found, and in whatever form it is embodied. Impersonal and anonymous, such an aim, then, soars far above all individual minds (*consciences particulières*) and can thus serve them as a rallying point. The fact that it is not alien to us (by the simple fact that it is human) does not prevent it from dominating us. Now, the only thing neces-sary for a society to be coherent is that its members have their eyes fixed on the same goal, concur in the same faith. But it is in no way necessary that the object of this common faith be unrelated to indi-vidual natures. After all, individualism thus extended is the glorifica-tion not of the self but of the individual in general. It springs not from egoism but from sympathy for all that is human, a broader pity for all sufferings, for all human miseries, a more ardent need to com-bat them and mitigate them, a greater thirst for justice. Is there not herein what is needed to place all men of good will in communion? Without doubt, it can happen that individualism is practiced in a completely different spirit. Some use it for their personal ends, as a means of disguising their egoism and of more easily escaping their duties to society. But this abusive exploitation of individualism proves nothing against it, just as the utilitarian falsehoods about reli-gious hypocrisy prove nothing against religion.

But I am anxious to come to the great objection. This cult of man has as its primary dogma the autonomy of reason and as its primary rite the doctrine of free inquiry. But, we are told, if all opin-ions are free, by what miracle will they be in harmony? If they are formed without mutual awareness and without having to take one another into account, how can they not be incoherent? Intellectual and moral anarchy would thus be the inevitable result of liberalism. Such is the argument, always refuted and always renewed, to which the eternal adversaries of reason periodically return with a persever-ance which nothing discourages, every time a momentary lassitude of the human spirit places it more at their mercy. Yes, it is quite true that individualism implies a certain intellectualism; for freedom of thought is the first of the freedoms. But where has it been seen to have as a consequence this absurd infatuation with oneself which shuts everyone up in his own feelings and creates a vacuum between intellects? What it requires is the right for each individual to know the things he legitimately can know. But it in no way consecrates some sort of right to incompetence. On a question on which I can form no knowledgeable opinion, it costs my intellectual independence nothing to follow more competent opinions. The collaboration of learned men is possible only thanks to this mutual deference; every science constantly borrows from its neighboring disciplines propositions that it accepts without further verification. However, my reason requires reasons before it bows before someone else's. Respect for authority is in no way incompatible with rationalism as long as the authority is rationally grounded.

This is why, when it comes to calling upon certain men to rally themselves to an opinion which is not their own, it is not enough, in order to convince them, to recall to them that commonplace of banal rhetoric that society is not possible without mutual sacrifices and without a certain spirit of subordination. The docility which is asked of them must still be justified for the particular case by demonstrating their incompetence. For if, on the contrary, it were one of those questions which, by definition, come under the jurisdiction of common judgment, a similar abdication would be contrary to all reason and, consequently, to their duty. To know whether a tribunal can be permitted to condemn an accused man without having heard his defense requires no special intelligence. It is a problem of practical ethics for which every man of good sense is competent and to which no one should be indifferent. If, therefore, in recent times, a certain number of artists, and especially scholars, believed they had to refuse to concur in a judgment whose legality appeared to them suspect, it was not because, in their capacity as chemists or philologists, as philosophers or historians, they attributed to themselves some sort of special privilege and a sort of eminent right of control over the thing being judged. It is because, being men, they intend to exercise all their human rights and retain before them a matter which is amenable to reason alone. It is true that they have shown themselves to be more jealous of that right than has the rest of the society; but it is simply because in consequence of their professional practices they take it more to heart. Since they are accustomed by the practice of the scientific method to reserve their judgment as long as they do not feel themselves enlightened, it is natural that they should yield less easily to the sway of the masses and the prestige of authority.

Not only is individualism not anarchical, but it henceforth is the only system of beliefs which can ensure the moral unity of the country.

We often hear it said today that religion alone can produce this harmony. This proposition, which modern prophets believe they must develop in mystic tones, is essentially a simple truism about which everyone can agree. For we know today that a religion does not necessarily imply symbols and rites, properly speaking, or temples and priests. This whole exterior apparatus is only the superficial part. Essentially, it is nothing other than a body of collective beliefs and practices endowed with a certain authority. As soon as a goal is pursued by an entire people, it acquires, in consequence of this unanimous adherence, a sort of moral supremacy which raises it far above private aims and thus gives it a religious character. From another viewpoint, it is apparent that a society cannot be coherent if there does not exist among its members a certain intellectual and moral community. However, after recalling once again this sociological truism, we have not gotten very far. For if it is true that religion is, in a sense, indispensable, it is no less certain that religions change—that the religion of yesterday could not be the religion of tomorrow. What is important therefore is to say what the religion of today should be.

Now everything converges in the belief that this religion of humanity, of which the individualistic ethic is the rational expression, is the only one possible. Hereafter, to what can the collective sensitivity cling? To the extent that societies become more voluminous and expand over vaster territories, traditions and practices, in order to accommodate themselves to the diversity of situations and to the mobility of circumstances, are obliged to maintain themselves in a state of plasticity and inconstancy which no longer offers enough resistance to individual variations. These variations, being less well restrained, are produced more freely and multiply; that is to say, everyone tends to go off in his own direction. At the same time, as a result of a more developed division of labor, each mind finds itself oriented to a different point on the horizon, reflecting a different aspect of the world, and consequently the contents of consciousness (conscience) differs from one person to another. Thus, we make our way, little by little, toward a state, nearly achieved as of now, where the members of a single social group will have nothing in common among themselves except their humanity, except the constitutive attributes of the human person (personne humaine) in general. This idea of the human person, given different nuances according to the diversity of national temperaments, is therefore the only idea which would be retained, unalterable and impersonal, above the changing torrent of individual opinions. And the feelings it awakens would be the only ones which could be found in almost every heart. The communion of spirits can no longer be based on definite rites and prejudices, since rites and prejudices are overcome by the course of events. Consequently, nothing remains which men can love and honor in common if not man himself. That is how man has become a god for man and why he can no longer create other gods without lying to himself. And since each of us incarnates something of humanity, each individual consciousness contains something divine and thus finds itself marked with a character which renders it sacred and inviolable to others. Therein lies all individualism; and that is what makes it a necessary doctrine. For in order to halt its advance it would be necessary to prevent men from differentiating themselves more and more from each other, to equalize their personalities, to lead them back to the old conformism of former times, to contain, as a result, the tendency for societies to become always more extended and more centralized, and to place an obstacle in the way of the unceasing progress of the division of labor. Such an enterprise, whether desirable or not, infinitely exceeds all human capability.

Moreover, what are we offered in place of this despised individualism? The merits of Christian morality are praised and we are discreetly invited to embrace them. But are we to ignore the fact that the originality of Christianity consisted precisely in a remarkable development of the individualistic spirit? Whereas the religion of the ancient city-state was quite entirely made of external practices, from which the spiritual was absent, Christianity demonstrated in its inner faith, in the personal conviction of the individual, the essential condition of piety. First, it taught that the moral value of acts had to be measured according to the intention, a preeminently inward thing which by its very nature escapes all external judgments and which only the agent could competently appraise. The very center of moral life was thus transported from the external to the internal, and the individual was thus elevated to be sovereign judge of his own conduct, accountable only to himself and to his God. Finally, in consumating the definitive separation of the spiritual and the temporal, in abandoning the world to the disputes of men, Christ delivered it at once to science and to free inquiry. This explains the rapid progress made by the scientific spirit from the day when Christian societies were established. Individualism should not, then, be denounced as the enemy which must be combated at any cost! We combat it only to return to it, so impossible is it to escape it. We can oppose to it only itself; but the whole question is to know its proper bounds and whether there is some advantage in disguising it beneath symbols. Now if it is as dangerous as we are told, how can it become inoffensive or beneficial by simply having its true nature dissimulated with the help of metaphors? And looking at it from another point of view, if this restrained individualism which is Christianity was necessary eighteen centuries ago, there is a good chance that a more fully developed individualism is indispensable today. For things have changed. It is therefore a singular error to present the individualistic ethic as the antagonist of Christian morality. Quite the contrary—the former derived from the latter. By attaching ourselves to the first, we do not deny our past; we only continue it.

QUESTIONS FOR CRITICAL READING

1. What are some of the forms of individualism described in the opening paragraphs of the essay?
2. In paragraph 3, Durkheim says he needs to clear up an ambiguity. What kind of ambiguity does he seem to be referring to? Why is it not easier for us to determine what it is?
3. Durkheim's opponent says, in paragraph 1, that the intellectuals' problem is that "they obstinately refuse 'to bend their logic before the word of an army general.'" Why does that annoy Durkheim?
4. Must the intellectual subscribe to individualism?
5. Is conformity an issue in this argument, as it has been in other essays in this section?
6. Why is individualism threatened by "crass commercialism which reduces society to nothing more than a vast apparatus of production and exchange" (para. 4)?
7. Is Durkheim acting reasonably when he criticizes the utilitarian attitude that supports "individual liberties' being suspended whenever the interest of the greater number requires that sacrifice" (para. 7)?
8. How convincing is Durkheim when he discusses individualism as a "religion of humanity" (para. 15)?

SUGGESTIONS FOR CRITICAL WRITING

1. Durkheim says that no society can be coherent "if there does not exist among its members a certain intellectual and moral community" (para. 14). Examine this statement and, if you agree with it, establish what you think makes your community coherent. You may wish to begin by defining both your society and the idea of coherence. Do you contribute to the intellectual and moral community of which you are a part? Do your relatives and your friends contribute to it? What might happen to your society if intellectuals did not take part in an active way?
2. Durkheim says that "religion is, in a sense, indispensable" (para. 14). Do you feel that religion is indispensable to help form a moral base for the norms of your society? How would you argue against someone who feels that religion is unimportant to the functioning of a modern society? What important points that Durkheim makes would help bolster your argument? What points would weaken your argument?
3. The basis of utilitarianism is the desire to provide the greatest good to the greatest number of people in any society. Egoism is frowned upon and even the concept of motive is irrelevant if the outcome is good. Durkheim interprets this philosophy as disregarding the individual because the individual must give way to the greater good for all. Research the basic tenets of utilitarianism and argue for or against Durkheim's position.

4. Durkheim complains that one of the aphorisms regarding society is that it is not possible to have a society without "mutual sacrifices and without a certain spirit of subordination" (para. 12). Is he correct in his view? What sacrifices are expected of everyone in our society? Within your own specific social group are you expected to make sacrifices? Is subordination a requirement in the social order that you are part of? Do such sacrifices actually inhibit individualism?

5. What kind of "individual ethic" could be developed in the "religion of humanity" (para. 15) that Durkheim recommends? Most religions provide an ethical code that exists outside the individual and is impressed upon the individual. What does it mean to consider the divinity within each individual? Is it really possible for the individual to conceive an ethic without being just an ordinary egoist? Argue this question from whichever angle you feel is most persuasive.

6. **CONNECTIONS**   Durkheim, like many authors in this book, constantly refers to other major thinkers. One of them, Rousseau, is also represented in this text in the section on government (Part One). After reading Rousseau and Durkheim with an eye toward their positions on the individual, how do you view Durkheim's critique of Rousseau? What is the major difference between their thoughts? Which of these thinkers is most convincing to you?

7. **SEEING CONNECTIONS**   The individual standing on a crag in Caspar David Friedrich's *Wanderer Above the Sea of Fog* (p. 250) is clearly not for that moment part of a social order. However, he could never have arrived as he did without having started from a society that provided him with the ambition to stand as he does above the heights. How does this individual fit into Durkheim's views of the responsibility of the individual intellectual? What kind of society do you imagine this figure has left behind? Is he the "human person (*personne humaine*)" (para. 15) who Durkheim applauds late in his essay?

W. E. B. DU BOIS
Of Our Spiritual Strivings

WILLIAM EDWARD BURGHARDT DU BOIS (1868–1963), born in Great Barrington, Massachusetts, grew to become one of the nation's premier African American intellectuals. He was a prominent teacher, writer, and lecturer involved with the earliest foundation of the National Association for the Advancement of Colored People (NAACP) as well as the powerful Harlem Renaissance, whose great writers—among them Langston Hughes, Countee Cullen, Jean Toomer, and Zora Neale Hurston—as well as musicians and artists, considered him an essential force. Although he was a powerful influence in these and other movements in the African American community, he had a prickly personality and was sometimes described as distant and "above it all." His preference for the "high culture" of Beethoven and other classical composers over the jazz of 1920s Harlem is a case in point. His views were intellectually elevated and serious throughout his life.

His origins were relatively humble. His mother was a maid and his father did not stay with the family. She had a stroke at a relatively young age and left Du Bois to help support them with part-time jobs. His family helped and so did some neighbors, but it was always difficult to get by. Fortunately, his education in Great Barrington was very good, and his teachers recognized, as did he himself, that he was an unusually bright student. They placed him in the classical program leading to a college degree. Like many important people, he grew up with a sense of destiny, and many of his school fellows recognized that in him. After graduating from high school in 1885, he went to Fisk University in Nashville, Tennessee. Fisk was established in 1865 to educate freed African Americans, and his time there gave Du Bois not only his first taste

From *The Souls of Black Folk.*

of the segregated South but also his first experiences in a predominantly African American community. His years in Nashville later inspired his novel *Darkwater* (1921).

After graduating from Fisk in three years, Du Bois went to Harvard and stayed to earn his Ph.D. in history in 1895, the first Harvard doctorate awarded to an African American. He published his dissertation, *The Suppression of the African Slave Trade to the United States of America: 1638–1870* (1896). While working on his doctorate, Du Bois studied for a time at the University of Berlin. When at Harvard he had met many important modern thinkers, such as William James and George Santayana, and in Germany he was influenced by scholars such as Gustav von Schmoller in the relatively new science of sociology. He began his teaching at Wilberforce University in Ohio but soon moved to the University of Pennsylvania and published several important books in the field of sociology: *The Study of the Negro Problems* (1898), *The Philadelphia Negro* (1899), *The Negro in Business* (1899), and a few years later his most famous book, the more personal *The Souls of Black Folk* (1903).

Most of these books were written while Du Bois was teaching at Atlanta University, where he stayed for ten years. His project during this time was to write definitive studies of the sociology of African Americans. *The Souls of Black Folk* attracted attention because one of its chapters essentially challenges the received opinions of Booker T. Washington, then a major influence on African American education. Du Bois criticized him for basically accepting segregation and the status quo in the South and insisted that blacks should strive for full social and political equality. While Booker T. Washington seemed to preach a doctrine of people raising themselves up by their bootstraps, Du Bois developed a view of what he called "The Talented Tenth," a group of black intellectuals who he felt would lead African Americans to realize their potential. Ultimately, his dispute made Du Bois visible to a larger community and led eventually to his cofounding the NAACP.

Du Bois was editor of the major publication of the NAACP, *Crisis,* and made considerable efforts to publish the finest African American writers in America. But he also used *Crisis* as a personal pulpit to express his views about racial issues. He repeatedly affirmed that there was no fundamental physical difference between the races and that a doctrine of equality must be practiced in America. In *Crisis,* Du Bois was able to reach a large audience of primarily African American readers, and his subjects ranged from religion to politics and beyond. He took sides in every major debate of the period and was considered a "preceptor" to the African American community. Like African American intellectuals of today, Du Bois was looked to for his opinion on things as distinct as the Russo-Japanese War, the Russian Revolution, Marcus Garvey's "back to Africa" campaign, and blues and jazz. In the late 1930s, he visited Nazi Germany and protested the treatment of Jews, which he said was a crime against civilization. He was a noted Zionist in part as a result of his experiences in Germany.

His influence waned during the late 1920s and through the Depression-era 1930s in part because he disapproved of much of the artistic work of the Harlem Renaissance, which itself went into decline during the Great Depression. He was seen to be old-school and out of step with younger writers. However, Du Bois remained a major force in American intellectual life. He continued publishing novels and books, such as *Black Reconstruction in America, 1860–1880* (1935), *Black Folk, Then and Now* (1939), and *I Take My Stand for Peace* (1951). During the McCarthy Communist witch-hunt era of the early 1950s, Du Bois's international connections brought him under suspicion and his passport was suspended. Because he had, since the beginning of the century, been involved in Pan-African and other international congresses with uncertain political goals, he was suspected of being a Communist sympathizer and found himself limited in his movements. Eventually, in 1961, the president of the newly independent Ghana invited Du Bois to come and help create an encyclopedia of Africana. Just before Du Bois left America, he conspicuously joined the American Communist Party, accepted Ghanian citizenship, and with his wife moved to Accra, where he died in 1963.

Du Bois's Rhetoric

Reprinted below is the first selection, or chapter, in *The Souls of Black Folk*, a work Du Bois admitted he expected to be read primarily by white Americans. Its tone is even, reasoned, and comprehensive. It begins with the lyrics of what he calls a Sorrow Song, a legacy of slavery. Then the overarching subject of the entire selection is introduced in a subtle way: it is "the Negro Problem." But Du Bois introduces the term not in relation to all African Americans but in relation to himself as an individual. As he asks in the opening paragraph, "How does it feel to be a problem?" This is a rhetorical question (one of many) that is never answered quite directly, yet it is explored in considerable detail.

In paragraph 2, Du Bois explores the question by applying it specifically to his experiences as a young schoolboy in Great Barrington, Massachusetts. He has said elsewhere that he grew up without a sense that he was profoundly different from others but that in grade school a new girl who had moved into the community refused to exchange greeting cards—a classroom project—with him because he was black. From that moment, he began to realize that he was shut off from much of the world by what he called a "vast veil." The metaphor of the veil is powerfully revisited throughout the essay.

The absolute personal approach of the essay gives way quickly to consideration of a collective question that helps him position himself in the world. Du Bois is, after all, a sociologist, not a psychologist, and his focus soon becomes an analysis of "the Negro Problem" as experienced by African Americans in 1903. As he says, "One ever feels his two-ness—an American, a Negro" (para. 3), and he goes on to say that this sense of "double-consciousness" is in part at the heart of the problem as felt in the African American community. "The history of the American Negro is the history of this strife . . ." (para. 4).

Du Bois then steps back to review history with a special focus on the search for freedom: "few men ever worshiped Freedom with half such unquestioning faith as did the American Negro for two centuries" (para. 6). His emphasis in his analysis is not as much on the condition of slavery as on the condition following Reconstruction in which the freed people were given little opportunity and little chance to succeed. Without education, training, or experience in business and with a shattered family structure, they were expected to compete with wealthy, trained, and well-educated landowners whose family money and wide connections gave them a terribly unequal advantage. In addition, in 1876, the Republican president, Rutherford B. Hayes, essentially ended Reconstruction and permitted the South to institute the Jim Crow laws that severely limited voting and other civil rights of African Americans. As Du Bois says, "A people thus handicapped ought not to be asked to race with the world, but rather allowed to give all its time and thought to its own social problems" (para. 10).

In following paragraphs, Du Bois examines the role of prejudice and the resultant humiliation working in American society. Part of his discussion centers on education and its positive effects. He was a professor while he wrote this book, and his lifelong commitment to education as a force to emancipate all people is clearly evident as he closes the discussion. He centers on "[w]ork, culture, liberty— all these we need, not singly but together" (para. 12) in a passage that indicates the movement of his views from those of an individual schoolboy in the opening paragraphs to a pursuit of "that vaster ideal that swims before the Negro people, the ideal of human brotherhood, gained through the unifying ideal of Race" (para. 12).

PREREADING QUESTIONS: WHAT TO READ FOR

The following prereading questions may help you anticipate key issues in W. E. B. Du Bois's "Of Our Spiritual Strivings." Keeping them in mind during your first reading of the selection should help focus your attention.

- How does it feel to be a "problem"?
- What is the nature of the double-consciousness Du Bois discusses?
- Why does Du Bois focus so intently on the topic of freedom in the middle of the essay?
- What are the chief handicaps Du Bois sees in the history of African Americans?

Of Our Spiritual Strivings

O water, voice of my heart, crying in the sand,
　All night long crying with a mournful cry,
As I, lie and listen, and cannot understand
　　The voice of my heart in my side or the voice of the sea,
　O water, crying for rest, is it I, is it I?
　　All night long the water is crying to me.

Unresting water, there shall never be rest
　Till the last moon droop and the last tide fail,
And the fire of the end begin to burn in the west;
　　And the heart shall be weary and wonder and cry like the sea,
　All life long crying without avail,
　　As the water all night long is crying to me.

　　　　　　　　　　　　　　　 — ARTHUR SYMONS

Between me and the other world there is ever an unasked ques- 1
tion: unasked by some through feelings of delicacy; by others
through the difficulty of rightly framing it. All, nevertheless, flutter
round it. They approach me in a half-hesitant sort of way, eye me
curiously or compassionately, and then, instead of saying directly,
How does it feel to be a problem? they say, I know an excellent
colored man in my town; or, I fought at Mechanicsville; or, Do not

these Southern outrages make your blood boil? At these I smile, or am interested, or reduce the boiling to a simmer, as the occasion may require. To the real question, How does it feel to be a problem? I answer seldom a word.

And yet, being a problem is a strange experience—peculiar even 2 for one who has never been anything else, save perhaps in babyhood and in Europe. It is in the early days of rollicking boyhood that the revelation first bursts upon one, all in a day, as it were. I remember well when the shadow swept across me. I was a little thing, away up in the hills of New England, where the dark Housatonic winds between Hoosac and Taghkanic to the sea. In a wee wooden school-house, something put it into the boys' and girls' heads to buy gorgeous visiting-cards—ten cents a package—and exchange. The exchange was merry, till one girl, a tall newcomer, refused my card—refused it peremptorily, with a glance. Then it dawned upon me with a certain suddenness that I was different from the others; or like, mayhap, in heart and life and longing, but shut out from their world by a vast veil. I had thereafter no desire to tear down that veil, to creep through; I held all beyond it in common contempt, and lived above it in a region of blue sky and great wandering shadows. That sky was bluest when I could beat my mates at examination-time, or beat them at a foot-race, or even beat their stringy heads. Alas, with the years all this fine contempt began to fade; for the worlds I longed for, and all their dazzling opportunities, were theirs, not mine. But they should not keep these prizes, I said; some, all, I would wrest from them. Just how I would do it I could never decide: by reading law, by healing the sick, by telling the wonderful tales that swam in my head—some way. With other black boys the strife was not so fiercely sunny: their youth shrunk into tasteless sycophancy, or into silent hatred of the pale world about them and mocking distrust of everything white; or wasted itself in a bitter cry, Why did God make me an outcast and a stranger in mine own house? The shades of the prison-house closed round about us all: walls strait and stubborn to the whitest, but relentlessly narrow, tall, and unscalable to sons of night who must plod darkly on in resigna-tion, or beat unavailing palms against the stone, or steadily, half hopelessly, watch the streak of blue above.

After the Egyptian and Indian, the Greek and Roman, the Teuton 3 and Mongolian, the Negro is a sort of seventh son, born with a veil, and gifted with second-sight in this American world—a world which yields him no true self-consciousness, but only lets him see himself through the revelation of the other world. It is a peculiar sensation, this double-consciousness, this sense of always looking at one's self through the eyes of others, of measuring one's soul by the tape of a world that looks on in amused contempt and pity. One ever feels his twoness—an American, a Negro; two souls, two thoughts, two unreconciled strivings; two warring ideals in one dark body, whose dogged strength alone keeps it from being torn asunder.

The history of the American Negro is the history of this strife— this longing to attain self-conscious manhood, to merge his double self into a better and truer self. In this merging he wishes neither of the older selves to be lost. He would not Africanize America, for America has too much to teach the world and Africa. He would not bleach his Negro soul in a flood of white Americanism, for he knows that Negro blood has a message for the world. He simply wishes to make it possible for a man to be both a Negro and an American, without being cursed and spit upon by his fellows, without having the doors of Opportunity closed roughly in his face.

This, then, is the end of his striving: to be a co-worker in the kingdom of culture, to escape both death and isolation, to husband and use his best powers and his latent genius. These powers of body and mind have in the past been strangely wasted, dispersed, or forgotten. The shadow of a mighty Negro past flits through the tale of Ethiopia the Shadowy and of Egypt the Sphinx. Throughout history, the powers of single black men flash here and there like falling stars, and die sometimes before the world has rightly gauged their brightness. Here in America, in the few days since Emancipation, the black man's turning hither and thither in hesitant and doubtful striving has often made his very strength to lose effectiveness, to seem like absence of power, like weakness. And yet it is not weakness—it is the contradiction of double aims. The double-aimed struggle of the black artisan—on the one hand to escape white contempt for a nation of mere hewers of wood and drawers of water, and on the other hand to plough and nail and dig for a poverty-stricken horde—could only result in making him a poor craftsman, for he had but half a heart in either cause. By the poverty and ignorance of his people, the Negro minister or doctor was tempted toward quackery and demagogy; and by the criticism of the other world, toward ideals that made him ashamed of his lowly tasks. The would-be black savant was confronted by the paradox that the knowledge his people needed was a twice-told tale to his white neighbors, while the knowledge which would teach the white world was Greek to his own flesh and blood. The innate love of harmony and beauty that set the ruder souls of his people a-dancing and a-singing raised but confusion and doubt in the soul of the black artist; for the beauty revealed to him was the soul-beauty of a race which his larger audience despised, and he could not articulate the message of another people. This waste of double aims, this seeking to satisfy two unreconciled ideals, has wrought sad havoc with

the courage and faith and deeds of ten thousand thousand people—
has sent them often wooing false gods and invoking false means of
salvation, and at times has even seemed about to make them ashamed
of themselves.

Away back in the days of bondage they thought to see in one 6
divine event the end of all doubt and disappointment; few men ever
worshiped freedom with half such unquestioning faith as did the
American Negro for two centuries. To him, so far as he thought and
dreamed, slavery was indeed the sum of all villainies, the cause of all
sorrow, the root of all prejudice; emancipation was the key to a
promised land of sweeter beauty than ever stretched before the eyes
of wearied Israelites. In song and exhortation swelled one refrain—
Liberty; in his tears and curses the God he implored had Freedom in
his right hand. At last it came—suddenly, fearfully, like a dream.
With one wild carnival of blood and passion came the message in his
own plaintive cadences:

> Shout, O children!
> Shout, you're free!
> For God has bought your liberty!

Years have passed away since then—ten, twenty, forty; forty 7
years of national life, forty years of renewal and development, and yet
the swarthy spectre sits in its accustomed seat at the Nation's feast. In
vain do we cry to this our vastest social problem:

> Take any shape but that, and my firm nerves
> Shall never tremble!

The Nation has not yet found peace from its sins; the freedman has
not yet found in freedom his promised land. Whatever of good may
have come in these years to change, the shadow of a deep disappointment rests upon the Negro people—a disappointment all the
more bitter because the unattained ideal was unbounded save by the
simple ignorance of a lowly people.

The first decade was merely a prolongation of the vain search for 8
freedom, the boon that seemed ever barely to elude their grasp—like
a tantalizing will-o'-the-wisp, maddening and misleading the headless
host. The holocaust of war, the terrors of the Ku-Klux Klan, the lies
of carpet-baggers, the disorganization of industry, and the contradictory advice of friends and foes, left the bewildered serf with no new
watch-word beyond the old cry for freedom. As the time flew, however, he began to grasp a new idea. The ideal of liberty demanded
for its attainment powerful means, and these the Fifteenth Amendment gave him. The ballot, which before he had looked upon as a
visible sign of freedom, he now regarded as the chief means of gaining

and perfecting the liberty with which war had partially endowed him. And why not? Had not votes made war and emancipated millions? Had not votes enfranchised the freedmen? Was anything impossible to a power that had done all this? A million black men started with renewed zeal to vote themselves into the kingdom. So the decade flew away, the revolution of 1876 came, and left the half-free serf weary, wondering, but still inspired. Slowly but steadily, in the following years, a new vision began gradually to replace the dream of political power—a powerful movement, the rise of another ideal to guide the unguided, another pillar of fire by night after a clouded day. It was the ideal of "book-learning"; the curiosity, born of compulsory ignorance, to know and test the power of the cabalistic letters of the white man, the longing to know. Here at last seemed to have been discovered the mountain path to Canaan; longer than the highway of Emancipation and law, steep and rugged, but straight, leading to heights high enough to overlook life.

Up the new path the advance guard toiled, slowly, heavily, 9 doggedly; only those who have watched and guided the faltering feet, the misty minds, the dull understandings, of the dark pupils of these schools know how faithfully, how piteously, this people strove to learn. It was weary work. The cold statistician wrote down the inches of progress here and there, noted also where here and there a foot had slipped or someone had fallen. To the tired climbers, the horizon was ever dark, the mists were often cold, the Canaan was always dim and far away. If, however, the vistas disclosed as yet no goal, no resting-place, little but flattery and criticism, the journey at least gave leisure for reflection and self-examination; it changed the child of Emancipation to the youth with dawning self-consciousness, self-realization, self-respect. In those somber forests of his striving his own soul rose before him, and he saw himself—darkly as through a veil; and yet he saw in himself some faint revelation of his power, of his mission. He began to have a dim feeling that, to attain his place in the world, he must be himself, and not another. For the first time he sought to analyze the burden he bore upon his back, that dead-weight of social degradation partially masked behind a half-named Negro problem. He felt his poverty; without a cent, without a home, without land, tools, or savings, he had entered into competition with rich, landed, skilled neighbors. To be a poor man is hard, but to be a poor race in a land of dollars is the very bottom of hardships. He felt the weight of his ignorance—not simply of letters, but of life, of business, of the humanities; the accumulated sloth and shirking and awkwardness of decades and centuries shackled his hands and feet. Nor was his burden all poverty and ignorance. The red stain of bastardy, which two centuries of systematic legal defilement of Negro women had stamped upon his race, meant not only the loss of ancient African chastity, but also the hereditary weight of a mass of corruption from white adulterers, threatening almost the obliteration of the Negro home.

A people thus handicapped ought not to be asked to race with the world, but rather allowed to give all its time and thought to its own social problems. But alas! while sociologists gleefully count his bastards and his prostitutes, the very soul of the toiling, sweating black man is darkened by the shadow of a vast despair. Men call the shadow prejudice, and learnedly explain it as the natural defense of culture against barbarism, learning against ignorance, purity against crime, the "higher" against the "lower" races. To which the Negro cries Amen! and swears that to so much of this strange prejudice as is founded on just homage to civilization, culture, righteousness, and progress, he humbly bows and meekly does obeisance. But before that nameless prejudice that leaps beyond all this he stands helpless, dismayed, and well-nigh speechless; before that personal disrespect and mockery, the ridicule and systematic humiliation, the distortion of fact and wanton license of fancy, the cynical ignoring of the better and the boisterous welcoming of the worse, the all-pervading desire to inculcate disdain for everything black, from Toussaint[1] to the devil—before this there rises a sickening despair that would disarm and discourage any nation save that black host to whom "discouragement" is an unwritten word. 10

But the facing of so vast a prejudice could not but bring the inevitable self-questioning, self-disparagement, and lowering of ideals which ever accompany repression and breed in an atmosphere of contempt and hate. Whisperings and portents came borne upon the four winds: Lo! we are diseased and dying, cried the dark hosts; we cannot write, our voting is vain; what need of education, since we must always cook and serve? And the Nation echoed and enforced this self-criticism, saying: Be content to be servants, and nothing more; what need of higher culture for half-men? Away with the black man's ballot, by force or fraud—and behold the suicide of a race! Nevertheless, out of the evil came something of good—the more careful adjustment of education to real life, the clearer perception of the Negroes' social responsibilities, and the sobering realization of the meaning of progress. 11

So dawned the time of *Sturm und Drang:* storm and stress today rocks our little boat on the mad waters of the world-sea; there is within and without the sound of conflict, the burning of body and rending of 12

---

[1] **Toussaint Louverture (1743–1803)** Born a slave, led a successful revolution in Haiti in 1797.

soul; inspiration strives with doubt, and faith with vain questionings. The bright ideals of the past—physical freedom, political power, the training of brains and the training of hands—all these in turn have waxed and waned, until even the last grows dim and overcast. Are they all wrong—all false? No, not that, but each alone was over-simple and incomplete—the dreams of a credulous race-childhood, or the fond imaginings of the other world which does not know and does not want to know our power. To be really true, all these ideals must be melted and welded into one. The training of the schools we need today more than ever—the training of deft hands, quick eyes and ears, and above all the broader, deeper, higher culture of gifted minds and pure hearts. The power of the ballot we need in sheer self-defense—else what shall save us from a second slavery? Freedom, too, the long-sought, we still seek—the freedom of life and limb, the freedom to work and think, the freedom to love and aspire. Work, culture, liberty—all these we need, not singly but together, not suc-cessively but together, each growing and aiding each, and all striving toward that vaster ideal that swims before the Negro people, the ideal of human brotherhood, gained through the unifying ideal of race; the ideal of fostering and developing the traits and talents of the Negro, not in opposition to or contempt for other races, but rather in large conformity to the greater ideals of the American Republic, in order that some day on American soil two world-races may give each to each those characteristics both so sadly lack. We the darker ones come even now not altogether empty-handed: there are today no truer exponents of the pure human spirit of the Declaration of Indepen-dence than the American Negroes; there is no true American music but the wild sweet melodies of the Negro slave; the American fairy tales and folklore are Indian and African; and, all in all, we black men seem the sole oasis of simple faith and reverence in a dusty desert of dollars and smartness. Will America be poorer if she replace her brutal dyspeptic blundering with light-hearted but determined Negro humil-ity? or her coarse and cruel wit with loving jovial good-humor? or her vulgar music with the soul of the Sorrow Songs?

Merely a concrete test of the underlying principles of the great 13 republic is the Negro Problem, and the spiritual striving of the freed-men's sons is the travail of souls whose burden is almost beyond the measure of their strength, but who bear it in the name of an historic race, in the name of this the land of their fathers' fathers, and in the name of human opportunity.

And now what I have briefly sketched in large outline let me on 14 coming pages tell again in many ways, with loving emphasis and deeper detail, that men may listen to the striving in the souls of black folk.

QUESTIONS FOR CRITICAL READING

1. What does Du Bois seem to mean by his reference to being "born with a veil" (para. 3)?
2. How does "double-consciousness" interfere with "true self-consciousness"?
3. Why did Du Bois live "above it all" when he was a young man?
4. What does Du Bois have to say about the "doors of Opportunity" (para. 4)?
5. What could Du Bois have meant by "the unifying ideal of race" (para. 12)?
6. Which American ideals does Du Bois hold most dear?
7. Why did Du Bois have a sense of triumph when he bested his school-mates at exam time?

SUGGESTIONS FOR CRITICAL WRITING

1. To what extent does Du Bois seem to feel that he is a "problem"? He begins by pointing to his childhood and ends by discussing broad swaths of American history. What is the nature of the problem that he describes and how reasonable does he think it is to consider him an individual problem? How does he describe the "Negro Problem" that he treats in the heart of his essay? What is the individual's role in the "problem" as he affirms it?
2. What seem to be the ideals Du Bois struggles for in terms of promoting education? Why is education so important to him and to his sense of ini-tiating change in the racial circumstances of 1903? What will education achieve for the individual? How limiting is experience of life without a formal education? How important is education in achieving the goals he set forth even now, more than a hundred years after he wrote the essay?
3. Is Du Bois evenhanded in his treatment of all races in this essay? Does he admit to failings and achievements in all races equally? Would his views be as acceptable to Americans today as they were in 1903? What has changed in the national dialogue about race that would make Du Bois seem prophetic? What would make him seem outdated? Argue the case for his being as relevant today as he was in his own time, or argue that he is out-of-date and that things have changed so much that his vision of freedom has been achieved.
4. Du Bois said that he expected most readers of his book to be white Americans. He wrote much later in *Crisis* primarily for black Americans. Take any section of the essay and rewrite it as you imagine Du Bois might have had he in mind only black Americans as his readers. How would his tone have changed? How would his argument have changed?
5. **CONNECTIONS**   Frederick Douglass and W. E. B. Du Bois had in common their love of freedom and their avid appetite for education. Construct an imaginary dialogue between Douglass and Du Bois having each respond to these questions:

    a. How does the lack of education affect any group of people?
    b. What can education achieve for any social group that cannot be achieved otherwise?

    c. Has the freedom warranted by the Emancipation Proclamation been achieved?

    d. Have the conditions of African Americans improved since Du Bois wrote?

6. The crisis of the individual is central to this essay: presented first in Du Bois's description of the effect of prejudice against him when he was a schoolboy, but even more significantly in his description of the "double-consciousness" that confuses us when we see ourselves only through "the revelation of the other world" (para. 3). How is your sense of self affected by the way other people see you? Do you experience confusion of the kind Du Bois does?

7. **SEEING CONNECTIONS** Relying on the evidence and claims Du Bois provides in paragraphs 8 and 9, construct an argument that defends the position that Du Bois not only is likely to have seen reproductions of Caspar David Friedrich's *Wanderer Above the Sea of Fog* (p. 250) but that he is likely to have imagined himself as the figure in the painting. What images in these paragraphs particularly imply that Du Bois had the painting in mind when he wrote? What biographical details suggest that he may well have seen the original painting? If he were the figure in this painting, what would he see that would make him take the positions he espouses in the last paragraphs of his essay?

RUTH BENEDICT
The Individual and
the Pattern of Culture

AFTER RUTH BENEDICT (1887–1948) graduated from Vassar
College with her Phi Beta Kappa key, she traveled abroad and then
studied for a time at the New School for Social Research in New York
City. She became seriously interested in cultural studies after taking
Elsie Clews Parsons's course on the ethnology of the sexes. Admitted
to study anthropology at Columbia University under the supervision
of Franz Boas (1858–1942), she received her Ph.D. in 1923 and
became a faculty member at Columbia, where she remained for the
rest of her career. In 1948, she was promoted to full professor, the
first woman on the political science faculty to achieve that rank.

She is renowned for her work with native North Americans and
for her many distinguished books, such as *The Concept of the
Guardian Spirit in North America* (1923); *Tales of the Cochiti Indians*
(1931); *Patterns of Culture* (1934); *Race, Science, and Politics* (1940);
and *The Chrysanthemum and the Sword* (1946), a postwar study of
Japan. Like Boas, the leading anthropologist of his time, Benedict
insisted that cultures are not determined by race, biology, or geography but instead grow individually in response to their own personal
experiences and history, developing traditions that make them distinct in behavior.

Benedict discusses culture in terms of the individual; which is to
say, she sees the normal behavior of specific cultures as possessing
some of the psychological qualities of the individual and treats these
differences as analogous to the differences among individuals. Her
research permitted her to describe in detail the cultures of the
Kwakiutl Indians of the Northwest, the Zuni and Pueblo of the
Southwest, the Mescalero Apache, the Dobu of New Guinea, and

From *Patterns of Culture*.

various Native American groups in California. One of her great purposes in writing *Patterns of Culture* was to point out the extraordinary diversity among cultures and, specifically, to show that individuals are products of their culture just as their culture is the product of individuals.

One of her constant interests is in the ways that any given culture treats individuals whose personal gifts are not the ones the culture most values. She demonstrates that certain personal qualities, such as leadership ability, will be highly valued in some cultures and totally rejected in others. Moreover, "abnormal" individuals are treated very differently in cultures around the world. What is acceptable in our culture, especially the need to gather more and more possessions, is totally rejected in many cultures as abnormal and undesirable. Benedict soon recognized that cultural diversity is a reality that our culture must accept and understand, a lesson that is still worth learning.

This selection, which is the last chapter of her most influential book, *Patterns of Culture,* discusses the role of the individual in any culture. She tries to dispel the contention that there is a natural antagonism between the individual and society. Society may restrict absolute freedom through laws and regulations, but as she says, a society is not its laws. Its laws are not as restrictive as are some of the patterns of behavior generally accepted by the society. Society is created by individuals and expresses the ideals of individuals, even when it may restrict those whose gifts are not highly valued by that society. The individual, she explains, does not exist independently of the culture but rather is a product of the culture.

Some of her discussion veers toward psychiatry, as when she discusses the ways in which different cultures deal with neurotic individuals. She points out in her discussion of the Kwakiutl that desirable behavior in their culture would appear psychotic in others. She also maintains that there have been cultures whose most dignified and powerful people have been essentially pathological in their behavior. She singles out the actions of the American Puritan community in the seventeenth and eighteenth centuries, when, while claiming to pronounce the voice of God, members pilloried the innocent and burned women as witches at the stake. Her argument in favor of understanding the diversity of cultures is made clear in this brief selection.

Benedict's Rhetoric

Benedict's chief rhetorical device is that of comparison, offering descriptions of different practices in different cultures. Because she has chosen cultures very distinct from one another, her comparisons stand out with unusual clarity. Her own style of writing is also marked by a clarity that is welcome in an academic writer.

Her opening section focuses on the relationship between society and the individual, and she uses the practice of balancing two values against one another throughout the essay. She begins with an effort to establish her position: that there is no necessary antagonism between the individual and society. Her reasoning is based on an analysis of the relationship of the individual to society and the society's customs and laws, which she sees as the expression of the individuals who make up the society. As she says, where else can the qualities that comprise society come from except from individuals?

Benedict sees that the vast majority of individuals in any society will follow the patterns of that society as given. No matter where one is born, she says, the individual is malleable enough to assume the values and exhibit the behaviors that are normal in that culture. It is the nature of people to be "plastic to the molding force of the society into which they are born" (para. 8). In paragraph 9, however, Benedict begins a long discussion of those individuals who do not fit perfectly in their society and who are treated in a variety of ways by different cultures.

The following section of the essay develops by the use of example and sometimes by the use of comparison of one example with another. Benedict cites some examples of unusual (to us) behavior of certain Native American groups, especially in the case of violent behavior, even murder, and the resultant victim's demand for restitution. She then discusses psychotic behavior in various cultures and how individuals displaying such behavior are treated.

Certain individuals will be "denied validity" by their society, so Benedict begins in paragraph 18 talking about the attributes that make individuals "different" and how they are treated. As she says, there are some "persons who are put outside the pale of society" (para. 20). In Dobu society, a man who was "naturally friendly" and kind was thought to be a simpleton because he did not fit the pattern of behavior thought to be essential in New Guinea. The point she makes is that this man's behavior would be valued in our culture, so we cannot begin to think in terms of absolutes when it comes to the desired behavior of the individual.

Examples of "aberrant behavior" follow. Homosexuals, for example, have been valued rather than reviled in many cultures, including that of ancient Greece. In North American Indian tribes, some men dressed as women and performed women's duties while still hunting with the men. These figures, called *berdache*, were valuable because they commanded two sets of skills. Trance is another pattern of behavior that has been highly valued in some societies and in Western society in years past. The individual who has intense spiritual experiences and goes into a trance is highly valued in some cultures but marginalized in others.

In paragraph 36, Benedict makes reference to a literary figure, Don Quixote, as an example of an individual whose cultural standards are those of a bygone age—in this case, the age of chivalry—and whose values make him seem silly or unhinged in the modern times in which he lived. Her observations lead her to consider the options of those individuals who do not fit neatly into their own culture. She ends the essay with a consideration of American culture as she knew it in 1934 and points to the culture of the Puritans in which the most abnormal people were in control, making the normal people seem aberrant.

Benedict concludes with a peculiar kind of individual. It is the person who is "culturally encouraged" by his society, a profound egoist who embodies the values of his culture to such an extent that he becomes tyrannical in enforcing them. Thus, she points to two extremes of behavior in individuals in any culture and how they affect the lives of others.

PREREADING QUESTIONS: WHAT TO READ FOR

The following prereading questions may help you anticipate key issues in Ruth Benedict's "The Individual and the Pattern of Culture." Keeping them in mind during your first reading of the selection should help focus your attention.

- Is society antagonistic toward the individual?
- What is the effect of any culture on the behavior of those born into it?
- What kinds of individuals are treated as being beyond the pale of society?
- What, finally, does Benedict say about cultural diversity?

The Individual and the Pattern of Culture

The large corporate behavior we have discussed is nevertheless   1
the behavior of individuals. It is the world with which each person
is severally presented, the world from which he must make his

individual life. Accounts of any civilization condensed into a few dozen pages must necessarily throw into relief the group standards and describe individual behavior as it exemplifies the motivations of that culture. The exigencies of the situation are misleading only when this necessity is read off as implying that he is submerged in an overpowering ocean.

There is no proper antagonism between the role of society and that   2
of the individual. One of the most misleading misconceptions due to this nineteenth-century dualism was the idea that what was subtracted from society was added to the individual and what was subtracted from the individual was added to society. Philosophies of freedom, political creeds of laissez-faire,[1] revolutions that have unseated dynasties, have been built on this dualism. The quarrel in anthropological theory between the importance of the culture pattern and of the individual is only a small ripple from this fundamental conception of the nature of society.

In reality, society and the individual are not antagonists. His culture   3
provides the raw material of which the individual makes his life. If it is meager, the individual suffers; if it is rich, the individual has the chance to rise to his opportunity. Every private interest of every man and woman is served by the enrichment of the traditional stores of his civilization. The richest musical sensitivity can operate only within the equipment and standards of its tradition. It will add, perhaps importantly, to that tradition, but its achievement remains in proportion to the instruments and musical theory which the culture has provided. In the same fashion a talent for observation expends itself in some Melanesian tribe upon the negligible borders of the magico-religious field. For a realization of its potentialities it is dependent upon the development of scientific methodology, and it has no fruition unless the culture has elaborated the necessary concepts and tools.

The man in the street still thinks in terms of a necessary antago-   4
nism between society and the individual. In large measure this is because in our civilization the regulative activities of society are singled out, and we tend to identify society with the restrictions the law imposes upon us. The law lays down the number of miles per hour that I may drive an automobile. If it takes this restriction away, I am by that much the freer. This basis for a fundamental antagonism between society and the individual is naive indeed when it is extended as a basic philosophical and political notion. Society is only incidentally and in certain situations regulative, and law is not equivalent to the social order. In the simpler homogeneous cultures collective habit

---

[1] **laissez-faire** To do as you will; noninterference, particularly in business affairs.

or custom may quite supersede the necessity for any development of formal legal authority. American Indians sometimes say: "In the old days, there were no fights about hunting grounds or fishing territories. There was no law then, so everybody did what was right." The phrasing makes it clear that in their old life they did not think of themselves as submitting to a social control imposed upon them from without. Even in our civilization the law is never more than a crude implement of society, and one it is often enough necessary to check in its arrogant career. It is never to be read off as if it were the equivalent of the social order.

Society in its full sense as we have discussed it in this volume is never an entity separable from the individuals who compose it. No individual can arrive even at the threshold of his potentialities without a culture in which he participates. Conversely, no civilization has in it any element which in the last analysis is not the contribution of an individual. Where else could any trait come from except from the behavior of a man or a woman or a child? 5

It is largely because of the traditional acceptance of a conflict between society and the individual, that emphasis upon cultural behavior is so often interpreted as a denial of the autonomy of the individual. The reading of Sumner's *Folkways*[2] usually rouses a protest at the limitations such an interpretation places upon the scope and initiative of the individual. Anthropology is often believed to be a counsel of despair which makes untenable a beneficent human illusion. But no anthropologist with a background of experiences of other cultures has ever believed that individuals were automatons, mechanically carrying out the decrees of their civilization. No culture yet observed has been able to eradicate the differences in the temperaments of the persons who compose it. It is always a give-and-take. The problem of the individual is not clarified by stressing the antagonism between culture and the individual, but by stressing their mutual reinforcement. This rapport is so close that it is not possible to discuss patterns of culture without considering specifically their relation to individual psychology. 6

We have seen that any society selects some segment of the arc of possible human behavior, and in so far as it achieves integration its institutions tend to further the expression of its selected segment and to inhibit opposite expressions. But these opposite expressions are the congenial responses, nevertheless, of a certain proportion of the carriers of the culture. We have already discussed the reasons for believing that this selection is primarily cultural and not biological. 7

[2] **Folkways** Book by William Graham Sumner (1840–1910), an important sociologist and advocate of laissez-faire economics.

We cannot, therefore, even on theoretical grounds imagine that all the congenial responses of all its people will be equally served by the institutions of any culture. To understand the behavior of the individual, it is not merely necessary to relate his personal life-history to his endowments, and to measure these against an arbitrarily selected normality. It is necessary also to relate his congenial responses to the behavior that is singled out in the institutions of his culture.

The vast proportion of all individuals who are born into any   8 society always and whatever the idiosyncrasies of its institutions, assume, as we have seen, the behavior dictated by that society. This fact is always interpreted by the carriers of that culture as being due to the fact that their particular institutions reflect an ultimate and universal sanity. The actual reason is quite different. Most people are shaped to the form of their culture because of the enormous malleability of their original endowment. They are plastic to the molding force of the society into which they are born. It does not matter whether, with the Northwest Coast, it requires delusions of self-reference, or with our own civilization the amassing of possessions. In any case the great mass of individuals take quite readily the form that is presented to them.

They do not all, however, find it equally congenial, and those   9 are favored and fortunate whose potentialities most nearly coincide with the type of behavior selected by their society. Those who, in a situation in which they are frustrated, naturally seek ways of putting the occasion out of sight as expeditiously as possible are well served in Pueblo culture. Southwest institutions, as we have seen, minimize the situations in which serious frustration can arise, and when it cannot be avoided, as in death, they provide means to put it behind them with all speed.

On the other hand, those who react to frustration as to an insult   10 and whose first thought is to get even are amply provided for on the Northwest Coast. They may extend their native reaction to situations in which their paddle breaks or their canoe overturns or to the loss of relatives by death. They rise from their first reaction of sulking to thrust back in return, to "fight" with property or with weapons. Those who can assuage despair by the act of bringing shame to others can register freely and without conflict in this society, because their proclivities are deeply channeled in their culture. In Dobu those whose first impulse is to select a victim and project their misery upon him in procedures of punishment are equally fortunate.

It happens that none of the three cultures we have described   11 meets frustration in a realistic manner by stressing the resumption of the original and interrupted experience. It might even seem that in the case of death this is impossible. But the institutions of many cultures nevertheless attempt nothing less. Some of the forms the restitution takes are repugnant to us, but that only makes it clearer that in cultures where frustration is handled by giving rein to this potential behavior, the institutions of that society carry this course to extraordinary lengths. Among the Eskimo, when one man has killed another, the family of the man who has been murdered may take the murderer to replace the loss within its own group. The murderer then becomes the husband of the woman who has been widowed by his act. This is an emphasis upon restitution that ignores all other aspects of the situation—those which seem to us the only important ones; but when tradition selects some such objective it is quite in character that it should disregard all else.

Restitution may be carried out in mourning situations in ways that are less uncongenial to the standards of Western civilization. Among certain of the Central Algonkian Indians south of the Great Lakes the usual procedure was adoption. Upon the death of a child a similar child was put into his place. The similarity was determined in all sorts of ways: often a captive brought in from a raid was taken into the family in the full sense and given all the privileges and the tenderness that had originally been given to the dead child. Or quite as often it was the child's closest playmate, or a child from another related settlement who resembled the dead child in height and features. In such cases the family from which the child was chosen was supposed to be pleased, and indeed in most cases it was by no means the great step that it would be under our institutions. The child had always recognized many "mothers" and many homes where he was on familiar footing. The new allegiance made him thoroughly at home in still another household. From the point of view of the bereaved parents, the situation had been met by a restitution of the status quo that existed before the death of their child. 12

Persons who primarily mourn the situation rather than the lost individual are provided for in these cultures to a degree which is unimaginable under our institutions. We recognize the possibility of such solace, but we are careful to minimize its connection with the original loss. We do not use it as a mourning technique, and individuals who would be well satisfied with such a solution are left unsupported until the difficult crisis is past. 13

There is another possible attitude toward frustration. It is the precise opposite of the Pueblo attitude, and we have described it among the other Dionysian[3] reactions of the Plains Indians. Instead of trying 14

---

[3] **Dionysian** Reference to the Greek god of wine, Dionysius, pointing to the high emotion and passion of the Plains Indians.

to get past the experience with the least possible discomfiture, it finds relief in the most extravagant expression of grief. The Indians of the plains capitalized the utmost indulgences and exacted violent demonstrations of emotion as a matter of course.

In any group of individuals we can recognize those to whom 15 these different reactions to frustration and grief are congenial: ignoring it, indulging it by uninhibited expression, getting even, punishing a victim, and seeking restitution of the original situation. In the psychiatric records of our own society, some of these impulses are recognized as bad ways of dealing with the situation, some as good. The bad ones are said to lead to maladjustments and insanities, the good ones to adequate social functioning. It is clear, however, that the correlation does not lie between any one "bad" tendency and abnormality in any absolute sense. The desire to run away from grief, to leave it behind at all costs, does not foster psychotic behavior where, as among the Pueblos, it is mapped out by institutions and supported by every attitude of the group. The Pueblos are not a neurotic people. Their culture gives the impression of fostering mental health. Similarly, the paranoid attitudes so violently expressed among the Kwakiutl are known in psychiatric theory derived from our own civilization as thoroughly "bad"; that is, they lead in various ways to the breakdown of personality. But it is just those individuals among the Kwakiutl who find it congenial to give the freest expression to these attitudes who nevertheless are the leaders of Kwakiutl society and find greatest personal fulfillment in its culture.

Obviously, adequate personal adjustment does not depend 16 upon following certain motivations and eschewing others. The correlation is in a different direction. Just as those are favored whose congenial responses are closest to that behavior which characterizes their society, so those are disoriented whose congenial responses fall in that arc of behavior which is not capitalized by their culture. These abnormals are those who are not supported by the institutions of their civilization. They are the exceptions who have not easily taken the traditional forms of their culture.

For a valid comparative psychiatry, these disoriented persons who 17 have failed to adapt themselves adequately to their cultures are of first importance. The issue in psychiatry has been too often confused by starting from a fixed list of symptoms instead of from the study of those whose characteristic reactions are denied validity in their society.

The tribes we have described have all of them their non- 18 participating "abnormal" individuals. The individual in Dobu who was thoroughly disoriented was the man who was naturally friendly and found activity an end in itself. He was a pleasant fellow who did not seek to overthrow his fellows or to punish them. He worked for anyone who asked him, and he was tireless in carrying out their commands. He was not filled by a terror of the dark like his fellows, and he did not, as they did, utterly inhibit simple public responses of friendliness toward women closely related, like a wife or sister. He often patted them playfully in public. In any other Dobuan this was scandalous behavior, but in him it was regarded as merely silly. The village treated him in a kindly enough fashion, not taking advantage of him or making a sport of ridiculing him, but he was definitely regarded as one who was outside the game.

The behavior congenial to the Dobuan simpleton has been made   19
the ideal in certain periods of our own civilization, and there are still vocations in which his responses are accepted in most Western communities. Especially if a woman is in question, she is well provided for even today in our mores, and functions honorably in her family and community. The fact that the Dobuan could not function in his culture was not a consequence of the particular responses that were congenial to him, but of the chasm between them and the cultural pattern.

Most ethnologists have had similar experiences in recognizing   20
that the persons who are put outside the pale of society with contempt are not those who would be placed there by another culture. Lowie[4] found among the Crow Indians of the plains a man of exceptional knowledge of his cultural forms. He was interested in considering these objectively and in correlating different facets. He had an interest in genealogical facts and was invaluable on points of history. Altogether he was an ideal interpreter of Crow life. These traits, however, were not those which were the password to honor among the Crow. He had a definite shrinking from physical danger, and bravado was the tribal virtue. To make matters worse he had attempted to gain recognition by claiming a war honor which was fraudulent. He was proved not to have brought in, as he claimed, a picketed horse from the enemy's camp. To lay false claim to war honors was a paramount sin among the Crow, and by the general opinion, constantly reiterated, he was regarded as irresponsible and incompetent.

Such situations can be paralleled with the attitude in our civiliza-   21
tion toward a man who does not succeed in regarding personal possessions as supremely important. Our hobo population is constantly fed by those to whom the accumulation of property is not a sufficient motivation. In case these individuals ally themselves with the hoboes,

---

[4]**Robert H. Lowie (1883–1957)** American anthropologist born in Vienna who helped shape the academic discipline.

public opinion regards them as potentially vicious, as indeed because of the asocial situation into which they are thrust they readily become. In case, however, these men compensate by emphasizing their artistic temperament and become members of expatriated groups of petty artists, opinion regards them not as vicious but as silly. In any case they are unsupported by the forms of their society, and the effort to express themselves satisfactorily is ordinarily a greater task than they can achieve.

The dilemma of such an individual is often most successfully   22
solved by doing violence to his strongest natural impulses and accepting the role the culture honors. In case he is a person to whom social recognition is necessary, it is ordinarily his only possible course. One of the most striking individuals in Zuñi had accepted this necessity. In a society that thoroughly distrusts authority of any sort, he had a native personal magnetism that singled him out in any group. In a society that exalts moderation and the easiest way, he was turbulent and could act violently upon occasion. In a society that praises a pliant personality that "talks lots"—that is, that chatters in a friendly fashion—he was scornful and aloof. Zuñi's only reaction to such personalities is to brand them as witches. He was said to have been seen peering through a window from outside, and this is a sure mark of a witch. At any rate, he got drunk one day and boasted that they could not kill him. He was taken before the war priests who hung him by his thumbs from the rafters till he should confess to his witchcraft. This is the usual procedure in a charge of witchcraft. However, he dispatched a messenger to the government troops. When they came, his shoulders were already crippled for life, and the officer of the law was left with no recourse but to imprison the war priests who had been responsible for the enormity. One of these war priests was probably the most respected and important person in recent Zuñi history, and when he returned after imprisonment in the state penitentiary he never resumed his priestly offices. He regarded his power as broken. It was a revenge that is probably unique in Zuñi history. It involved, of course, a challenge to the priesthoods, against whom the witch by his act openly aligned himself.

The course of his life in the forty years that followed this defi-   23
ance was not, however, what we might easily predict. A witch is not barred from his membership in cult groups because he has been condemned, and the way to recognition lay through such activity. He possessed a remarkable verbal memory and a sweet singing voice. He learned unbelievable stores of mythology, of esoteric ritual, of cult songs. Many hundreds of pages of stories and ritual poetry were taken down from his dictation before he died, and he regarded his songs as much more extensive. He became indispensable in ceremonial life and before he died was the governor of Zuñi. The congenial

bent of his personality threw him into irreconcilable conflict with his society, and he solved his dilemma by turning an incidental talent to account. As we might well expect, he was not a happy man. As governor of Zuñi, and high in his cult groups, a marked man in his community, he was obsessed by death. He was a cheated man in the midst of a mildly happy populace.

It is easy to imagine the life he might have lived among the Plains   24
Indians, where every institution favored the traits that were native to him. The personal authority, the turbulence, the scorn, would all have been honored in the career he could have made his own. The unhappiness that was inseparable from his temperament as a success-ful priest and governor of Zuñi would have had no place as a war chief of the Cheyenne; it was not a function of the traits of his native endowment but of the standards of the culture in which he found no outlet for his native responses.

The individuals we have so far discussed are not in any sense   25
psychopathic. They illustrate the dilemma of the individual whose congenial drives are not provided for in the institutions of his cul-ture. This dilemma becomes of psychiatric importance when the behavior in question is regarded as categorically abnormal in a soci-ety. Western civilization tends to regard even a mild homosexual as an abnormal. The clinical picture of homosexuality stresses the neu-roses and psychoses to which it gives rise, and emphasizes almost equally the inadequate functioning of the invert and his behavior. We have only to turn to other cultures, however, to realize that homosexuals have by no means been uniformily inadequate to the social situation. They have not always failed to function. In some societies they have even been especially acclaimed. Plato's *Republic*[5] is, of course, the most convincing statement of the honorable estate of homosexuality. It is presented as a major means to the good life, and Plato's high ethical evaluation of this response was upheld in the customary behavior of Greece at that period.

The American Indians do not make Plato's high moral claims for   26
homosexuality, but homosexuals are often regarded as exceptionally able. In most of North America there exists the institution of the *berdache,* as the French called them. These men-women were men who at puberty or thereafter took the dress and the occupations of women. Sometimes they married other men and lived with them. Sometimes they were men with no inversion, persons of weak sexual endowment who chose this role to avoid the jeers of the women. The berdaches were never regarded as of first-rate supernatural power, as

---

[5] **Plato's Republic** Plato's description of the ideal society written c. 360 B.C.

similar men-women were in Siberia, but rather as leaders in women's occupations, good healers in certain diseases, or, among certain tribes, as the genial organizers of social affairs. They were usually, in spite of the manner in which they were accepted, regarded with a certain embarrassment. It was thought slightly ridiculous to address as "she" a person who was known to be a man and who, as in Zuñi, would be buried on the men's side of the cemetery. But they were socially placed. The emphasis in most tribes was upon the fact that men who took over women's occupations excelled by reason of their strength and initiative and were therefore leaders in women's techniques and in the accumulation of those forms of property made by women. One of the best known of all the Zuñis of a generation ago was the man-woman We-wha, who was, in the words of his friend, Mrs. Stevenson, "certainly the strongest person in Zuñi, both mentally and physically." His remarkable memory for ritual made him a chief personage on ceremonial occasions, and his strength and intelligence made him a leader in all kinds of crafts.

The men-women of Zuñi are not all strong, self-reliant person- 27
ages. Some of them take this refuge to protect themselves against their inability to take part in men's activities. One is almost a simpleton, and one, hardly more than a little boy, has delicate features like a girl's. There are obviously several reasons why a person becomes a berdache in Zuñi, but whatever the reason, men who have chosen openly to assume women's dress have the same chance as any other person to establish themselves as functioning members of the society. Their response is socially recognized. If they have native ability, they can give it scope; if they are weak creatures, they fail in terms of their weakness of character, not in terms of their inversion.

The Indian institution of the berdache was most strongly devel- 28
oped on the plains. The Dakota had a saying, "fine possessions like a berdache's," and it was the epitome of praise for any woman's household possessions. A berdache had two strings to his bow, he was supreme in women's techniques, and he could also support his *ménage* by the man's activity of hunting. Therefore no one was richer. When especially fine beadwork or dressed skins were desired for ceremonial occasions, the berdache's work was sought in preference to any other's. It was his social adequacy that was stressed above all else. As in Zuñi, the attitude toward him is ambivalent and touched with malaise in the face of a recognized incongruity. Social scorn, however, was visited not upon the berdache but upon the man who lived with him. The latter was regarded as a weak man who had chosen an easy berth instead of the recognized goals of their culture; he did not contribute to the household, which was already a model for all households through the sole efforts of the

berdache. His sexual adjustment was not singled out in the judgment that was passed upon him, but in terms of his economic adjustment he was an outcast.

When the homosexual response is regarded as a perversion, however, the invert is immediately exposed to all the conflicts to which aberrants are always exposed. His guilt, his sense of inadequacy, his failures, are consequences of the disrepute which social tradition visits upon him; and few people can achieve a satisfactory life unsupported by the standards of the society. The adjustments that society demands of them would strain any man's vitality, and the consequences of this conflict we identify with their homosexuality. 29

Trance is a similar abnormality in our society. Even a very mild mystic is aberrant in Western civilization. In order to study trance or catalepsy within our own social groups, we have to go to the case histories of the abnormal. Therefore the correlation between trance experience and the neurotic and psychotic seems perfect. As in the case of the homosexual, however, it is a local correlation characteristic of our century. Even in our own cultural background other eras give different results. In the Middle Ages when Catholicism made the ecstatic experience the mark of sainthood, the trance experience was greatly valued, and those to whom the response was congenial, instead of being overwhelmed by a catastrophe as in our century, were given confidence in the pursuit of their careers. It was a validation of ambitions, not a stigma of insanity. Individuals who were susceptible to trance, therefore, succeeded or failed in terms of their native capacities, but since trance experience was highly valued, a great leader was very likely to be capable of it. 30

Among primitive peoples, trance and catalepsy have been honored in the extreme. Some of the Indian tribes of California accorded prestige principally to those who passed through certain trance experiences. Not all of these tribes believed that it was exclusively women who were so blessed, but among the Shasta this was the convention. Their shamans were women, and they were accorded the greatest prestige in the community. They were chosen because of their constitutional liability to trance and allied manifestations. One day the woman who was so destined, while she was about her usual work, fell suddenly to the ground. She had heard a voice speaking to her in tones of the greatest intensity. Turning, she had seen a man with drawn bow and arrow. He commanded her to sing on pain of being shot through the heart by his arrow, but under the stress of the experience she fell senseless. Her family gathered. She was lying rigidly, hardly breathing. They knew that for some time she had had dreams of a special character which indicated a shamanistic calling, dreams of escaping grizzly bears, falling off cliffs or trees, or of being 31 surrounded by swarms of yellow-jackets. The community knew therefore what to expect. After a few hours the woman began to moan gently and to roll about upon the ground, trembling violently. She was supposed to be repeating the song which she had been told to sing and which during the trance had been taught her by the spirit. As she revived, her moaning became more and more clearly the spirit's song until at last she called out the name of the spirit itself, and immediately blood oozed from her mouth.

When the woman had come to herself after the first encounter   32 with her spirit, she danced that night her first initiatory shaman's dance. For three nights she danced, holding herself by a rope that was swung from the ceiling. On the third night she had to receive in her body her power from the spirit. She was dancing, and as she felt the approach of the moment she called out, "He will shoot me, he will shoot me." Her friends stood close, for when she reeled in a kind of cataleptic seizure, they had to seize her before she fell or she would die. From this time on she had in her body a visible materialization of her spirit's power, an icicle-like object which in her dances thereafter she would exhibit, producing it from one part of her body and returning it to another part. From this time on she continued to validate her supernatural power by further cataleptic demonstrations, and she was called upon in great emergencies of life and death, for curing and for divination and for counsel. She became, in other words, by this procedure a woman of great power and importance.

It is clear that, far from regarding cataleptic seizures as blots upon   33 the family escutcheon and as evidences of dreaded disease, cultural approval had seized upon them and made of them the pathway to authority over one's fellows. They were the outstanding characteristic of the most respected social type, the type which functioned with most honor and reward in the community. It was precisely the cataleptic individuals who in this culture were singled out for authority and leadership.

The possible usefulness of "abnormal" types in a social structure,   34 provided they are types that are culturally selected by that group, is illustrated from every part of the world. The shamans of Siberia dominate their communities. According to the ideas of these peoples, they are individuals who by submission to the will of the spirits have been cured of a grievous illness—the onset of the seizures—and have acquired by this means great supernatural power and incomparable vigor and health. Some, during the period of the call, are violently insane for several years; others irresponsible to the point where they have to be constantly watched lest they wander off in the snow and freeze to death; others ill and emaciated to the point of death, sometimes with bloody sweat. It is the shamanistic practice which constitutes their cure, and the extreme exertion of a Siberian séance leaves them, they claim, rested and able to enter immediately upon a similar performance. Cataleptic seizures are regarded as an essential part of any shamanistic performance. . . .

It is clear that culture may value and make socially available   35 even highly unstable human types. If it chooses to treat their peculiarities as the most valued variants of human behavior, the individuals in question will rise to the occasion and perform their social roles without reference to our usual ideas of the types who can make social adjustments and those who cannot. Those who function inadequately in any society are not those with certain fixed "abnormal" traits, but may well be those whose responses have received no support in the institutions of their culture. The weakness of these aberrants is in great measure illusory. It springs, not from the fact that they are lacking in necessary vigor, but that they are individuals whose native responses are not reaffirmed by society. They are, as Sapir[6] phrases it, "alienated from an impossible world."

The person unsupported by the standards of his time and place   36 and left naked to the winds of ridicule has been unforgettably drawn in European literature in the figure of Don Quixote. Cervantes turned upon a tradition still honored in the abstract the limelight of a changed set of practical standards, and his poor old man, the orthodox upholder of the romantic chivalry of another generation, became a simpleton. The windmills with which he tilted were the serious antagonists of a hardly vanished world, but to tilt with them when the world no longer called them serious was to rave. He loved his Dulcinea in the best traditional manner of chivalry, but another version of love was fashionable for the moment, and his fervor was counted to him for madness.

These contrasting worlds which, in the primitive cultures we   37 have considered, are separated from one another in space, in modern Occidental history more often succeed one another in time. The major issue is the same in either case, but the importance of understanding the phenomenon is far greater in the modern world where we cannot escape if we would from the succession of configurations in time. When each culture is a world in itself, relatively stable like the Eskimo culture, for example, and geographically isolated from all others, the issue is academic. But our civilization must deal with cultural standards that go down under our eyes and new ones that arise from a shadow upon the horizon. We must be willing to take account of changing normalities even when the question is of the morality in which we

---

[6]**Edward Sapir (1884–1939)** American linguist and sociologist.

were bred. Just as we are handicapped in dealing with ethical problems so long as we hold to an absolute definition of morality, so we are handicapped in dealing with human society so long as we identify our local normalities with the inevitable necessities of existence.

No society has yet attempted a self-conscious direction of the 38 process by which its new normalities are created in the next generation. Dewey[7] has pointed out how possible and yet how drastic such social engineering would be. For some traditional arrangements it is obvious that very high prices are paid, reckoned in terms of human suffering and frustration. If these arrangements presented themselves to us merely as arrangements and not as categorical imperatives, our reasonable course would be to adapt them by whatever means to rationally selected goals. What we do instead is to ridicule our Don Quixotes, the ludicrous embodiments of an outmoded tradition, and continue to regard our own as final and prescribed in the nature of things.

In the meantime the therapeutic problem of dealing with our 39 psychopaths of this type is often misunderstood. Their alienation from the actual world can often be more intelligently handled than by insisting that they adopt the modes that are alien to them. Two other courses are always possible. In the first place, the misfit individual may cultivate a greater objective interest in his own preferences and learn how to manage with greater equanimity his deviation from the type. If he learns to recognize the extent to which his suffering has been due to his lack of support in a traditional ethos, he may gradually educate himself to accept his degree of difference with less suffering. Both the exaggerated emotional disturbances of the manic-depressive and the seclusion of the schizophrenic add certain values to existence which are not open to those differently constituted. The unsupported individual who valiantly accepts his favorite and native virtues may attain a feasible course of behavior that makes it unnecessary for him to take refuge in a private world he has fashioned for himself. He may gradually achieve a more independent and less tortured attitude toward his deviations and upon this attitude he may be able to build an adequately functioning existence.

In the second place, an increased tolerance in society toward its 40 less usual types must keep pace with the self-education of the patient. The possibilities in this direction are endless. Tradition is as neurotic as any patient; its overgrown fear of deviation from its fortuitous standards conforms to all the usual definitions of the psychopathic. This fear does not depend upon observation of the limits within which

---

[7]**John Dewey (1859–1952)** American philosopher with whom Benedict studied. He was one of the founders of American pragmatism.

conformity is necessary to the social good. Much more deviation is allowed to the individual in some cultures than in others, and those in which much is allowed cannot be shown to suffer from their peculiarity. It is probable that social orders of the future will carry this tolerance and encouragement of individual difference much further than any cultures of which we have experience.

The American tendency at the present time leans so far to the opposite extreme that it is not easy for us to picture the changes that such an attitude would bring about. Middletown is a typical example of our usual urban fear of seeming in however slight an act different from our neighbors. Eccentricity is more feared than parasitism. Every sacrifice of time and tranquility is made in order that no one in the family may have any taint of nonconformity attached to him. Children in school make their great tragedies out of not wearing a certain kind of stockings, not joining a certain dancing-class, not driving a certain car. The fear of being different is the dominating motivation recorded in Middletown. 41

The psychopathic toll that such a motivation exacts is evident in every institution for mental diseases in our country. In a society in which it existed only as a minor motive among many others, the psychiatric picture would be a very different one. At all events, there can be no reasonable doubt that one of the most effective ways in which to deal with the staggering burden of psychopathic tragedies in America at the present time is by means of an educational program which fosters tolerance in society and a kind of self-respect and independence that is foreign to Middletown and our urban traditions. 42

Not all psychopaths, of course, are individuals whose native responses are at variance with those of their civilization. Another large group are those who are merely inadequate and who are strongly enough motivated so that their failure is more than they can bear. In a society in which the will-to-power is most highly rewarded, those who fail may not be those who are differently constituted, but simply those who are insufficiently endowed. The inferiority complex takes a great toll of suffering in our society. It is not necessary that sufferers of this type have a history of frustration in the sense that strong native bents have been inhibited; their frustration is often enough only the reflection of their inability to reach a certain goal. There is a cultural implication here, too, in that the traditional goal may be accessible to large numbers or to very few, and in proportion as success is obsessive and is limited to the few, a greater and greater number will be liable to the extreme penalties of maladjustment. 43

To a certain extent, therefore, civilization in setting higher and possibly more worthwhile goals may increase the number of its abnormals. But the point may very easily be overemphasized, for very 44 small changes in social attitudes may far outweigh this correlation. On the whole, since the social possibilities of tolerance and recognition of individual difference are so little explored in practice, pessimism seems premature. Certainly other quite different social factors which we have just discussed are more directly responsible for the great proportion of our neurotics and psychotics, and with these other factors civilizations could, if they would, deal without necessary intrinsic loss.

We have been considering individuals from the point of view of   45 their ability to function adequately in their society. This adequate functioning is one of the ways in which normality is clinically defined. It is also defined in terms of fixed symptoms, and the tendency is to identify normality with the statistically average. In practice this average is one arrived at in the laboratory, and deviations from it are defined as abnormal.

From the point of view of a single culture this procedure is very   46 useful. It shows the clinical picture of the civilization and gives considerable information about its socially approved behavior. To generalize this as an absolute normal, however, is a different matter. As we have seen, the range of normality in different cultures does not coincide. Some, like Zuñi and the Kwakiutl, are so far removed from each other that they overlap only slightly. The statistically determined normal on the Northwest Coast would be far outside the extreme boundaries of abnormality in the Pueblos. The normal Kwakiutl rivalry contest would only be understood as madness in Zuñi, and the traditional Zuñi indifference to dominance and the humiliation of others would be the fatuousness of a simpleton in a man of noble family on the Northwest Coast. Aberrant behavior in either culture could never be determined in relation to any least common denominator of behavior. Any society, according to its major preoccupations, may increase and intensify even hysterical, epileptic, or paranoid symptoms, at the same time relying socially in a greater and greater degree upon the very individuals who display them.

This fact is important in psychiatry because it makes clear   47 another group of abnormals which probably exists in every culture: the abnormals who represent the extreme development of the local cultural type. This group is socially in the opposite situation from the group we have discussed, those whose responses are at variance with their cultural standards. Society, instead of exposing the former group at every point, supports them in their furthest aberrations. They have a license which they may almost endlessly exploit. For this reason these persons almost never fall within the scope of any contemporary psychiatry. They are unlikely to be described even in the most careful manuals of the generation that fosters them. Yet from the point of view of another generation or culture they are ordinarily the most bizarre of the psychopathic types of the period.

The Puritan divines of New England in the eighteenth century were the last persons whom contemporary opinion in the colonies regarded as psychopathic. Few prestige groups in any culture have been allowed such complete intellectual and emotional dictatorship as they were. They were the voice of God. Yet to a modern observer it is they, not the confused and tormented women they put to death as witches, who were the psychoneurotics of Puritan New England. A sense of guilt as extreme as they portrayed and demanded both in their own conversion experiences and in those of their converts is found in a slightly saner civilization only in institutions for mental diseases. They admitted no salvation without a conviction of sin that prostrated the victim, sometimes for years, with remorse and terrible anguish. It was the duty of the minister to put the fear of hell into the heart of even the youngest child, and to exact of every convert emotional acceptance of his damnation if God saw fit to damn him. It does not matter where we turn among the records of New England Puritan churches of this period, whether to those dealing with witches or with unsaved children not yet in their teens or with such themes as damnation and predestination, we are faced with the fact that the group of people who carried out to the greatest extreme and in the fullest honor the cultural doctrine of the moment are by the slightly altered standards of our generation the victims of intolerable aberrations. From the point of view of a comparative psychiatry they fall in the category of the abnormal. [48]

In our own generation extreme forms of ego-gratification are culturally supported in a similar fashion. Arrogant and unbridled egoists as family men, as officers of the law and in business, have been again and again portrayed by novelists and dramatists, and they are familiar in every community. Like the behavior of Puritan divines, their courses of action are often more asocial than those of the inmates of penitentiaries. In terms of the suffering and frustration that they spread about them there is probably no comparison. There is very possibly at least as great a degree of mental warping. Yet they are entrusted with positions of great influence and importance and are as a rule fathers of families. Their impress both upon their own children and upon the structure of our society is indelible. They are not described in our manuals of psychiatry because they are supported by every tenet of our civilization. They are sure of themselves in real life in a way that is possible only to those who are oriented to the points of the compass laid down in their own culture. Nevertheless a future psychiatry may well ransack our novels and letters and public [49] records for illumination upon a type of abnormality to which it would not otherwise give credence. In every society it is among this very group of the culturally encouraged and fortified that some of the most extreme types of human behavior are fostered.

Social thinking at the present time has no more important task 50 before it than that of taking adequate account of cultural relativity. In the fields of both sociology and psychology the implications are fundamental, and modern thought about contacts of peoples and about our changing standards is greatly in need of sane and scientific direction. The sophisticated modern temper has made of social relativity, even in the small area which it has recognized, a doctrine of despair. It has pointed out its incongruity with the orthodox dreams of permanence and ideality and with the individual's illusions of autonomy. It has argued that if human experience must give up these, the nutshell of existence is empty. But to interpret our dilemma in these terms is to be guilty of an anachronism. It is only the inevitable cultural lag that makes us insist that the old must be discovered again in the new, that there is no solution but to find the old certainty and stability in the new plasticity. The recognition of cultural relativity carries with it its own values, which need not be those of the absolutist philosophies. It challenges customary opinions and causes those who have been bred to them acute discomfort. It rouses pessimism because it throws old formulae into confusion, not because it contains anything intrinsically difficult. As soon as the new opinion is embraced as customary belief, it will be another trusted bulwark of the good life. We shall arrive then at a more realistic social faith, accepting as grounds of hope and as new bases for tolerance the coexisting and equally valid patterns of life which mankind has created for itself from the raw materials of existence.

QUESTIONS FOR CRITICAL READING

1. Benedict says that most people born into a culture assume the behavior dictated by that culture. How true is this in your experience?
2. Our culture is described as a civilization given to amassing possessions. What evidence have you that would support this view?
3. What is the modern equivalent of the trance as described in paragraph 30? Is it acceptable in our society?
4. To what extent is the will to power highly rewarded in our society? Is it desirable behavior?
5. Benedict talks extensively about normality. How would you define normal behavior in our society?
6. What kinds of behavior tend to mark an individual as being "outside the pale of society"?

7. How well is deviation from the norm accepted in your immediate social circle? What kinds of people are ridiculed?

8. Which of the examples of aberrant behavior do you find most difficult to treat as "normal"?

SUGGESTIONS FOR CRITICAL WRITING

1. When Benedict said there was no necessary antagonism between society and the individual, it was 1934. Write an essay that either supports or contradicts her view in regard to society of the twenty-first century. Use her technique of presenting examples, with a discussion of each and its relevance, to evaluate the question of social antagonism. Is the individual free from the oppression of society?

2. In paragraph 37, Benedict discusses morality. She says, "We must be willing to take account of changing normalities even when the question is of the morality in which we were bred." She resists an "absolute definition of morality" in "dealing with human society." Using the moral values established by your parents and your grandparents, can you delineate the ways that the definition of *morality* has changed? What cultural differences do you see between your culture and that of your parents and older relatives? To what extent would your attitudes toward morality clash with theirs? Is there any way to tell which attitude is better? Argue your case on either side of the issue.

3. Your culture appears to expect certain actions from you, certain daily performances, certain patterns of behavior. In a brief essay, explain which behaviors valued by your society are most easy for you to assume. Which do you find most congenial? Which do you find very difficult to accept? Are you, as an individual, mostly supported by the expectations of your culture or not?

4. Describe in detail, with examples of the kind that Benedict uses, the culture you observed in secondary school. What kinds of behaviors were rewarded and what kinds were condemned? Was that culture a product of the individuals in your society or was it somehow imposed by society without the approval of the individuals? Did you find yourself able to develop as an individual in that culture, or were you unwillingly shaped by it?

5. Compare the ways homosexuals are treated in the societies Benedict mentions (paras. 25–29) with the way homosexuals are treated in your culture. Think not only in terms of the society in general in your region of the country but also of the smaller society in which you daily find yourself. Is your culture comparable in its attitudes and acceptance of homosexuals to the cultures Benedict tells about? Be sure to use examples to bolster your views.

6. **CONNECTIONS** What profound disagreements do you find between the ideas of cultural diversity in Benedict's essay and the ideas of self-reliance in Ralph Waldo Emerson's essay (p. 255)? What would Emerson have agreed with in Benedict's essay and what would he have

found intolerable? Construct an argument that defends Benedict's essay from the presumptions of individuality that are present in "Self-Reliance." Contrast Benedict's clarification of the nature of culture with Emerson's essential disregard for culture. How would Benedict respond to the discussion that Emerson offers on the powers of conformity of society and the need of the individual to be a nonconformist?

7. **SEEING CONNECTIONS**   What kind of an example would Benedict make of the figure in Caspar David Friedrich's *Wanderer Above the Sea of Fog* (p. 250)? How would the man in the painting fit into any of the patterns of culture Benedict discusses? Would she have thought him abnormal, not fitting into his own culture, or would she have thought him an egoist and therefore a major leader in his culture? What details in the painting support your views?

ERICH FROMM
The Individual in the Chains of Illusion

ERICH FROMM (1900–1980), born into a rabbinic family in Frankfurt, Germany, earned his Ph.D. at Heidelberg University at the age of twenty-two; after establishing himself as an important psychoanalyst, he left Nazi Germany in 1934. He lectured from 1934 to 1939 at the New School for Social Research and at Columbia University from 1940 to 1941. He later took an academic appointment at Bennington College and lectured at Yale University. In 1951, he joined the faculty at the National University of Mexico. From 1957 to 1961, he was a professor at Michigan State University, and from 1962 until his retirement in 1965, he was a professor at New York University, dividing his time between New York and Mexico City. In 1974, he left New York for Muralto, Switzerland, where he died a few days before his eightieth birthday.

His interest in politics and sociology led him to apply psychoanalytic theory to a wide range of important subjects. His first major book, *Escape from Freedom* (1941), revealed some of the anxieties people associate with freedom and set out to explain why totalitarian societies, such as those in Germany, Italy, and Japan at that time, were so enthusiastically accepted. His concern for the fate of the individual was very much in evidence in that book.

Early in his career, he was considered a follower of Sigmund Freud's views about the importance of sexuality in human behavior. However, he soon became an innovator and revised Freud's theories in a number of areas. He emphasized the social structure rather than the unconscious as a key force in shaping the individual's character, noting that human beings, unlike other animals, are not entirely driven by instincts. Humans employ "reason, imagination, and self-awareness" throughout their lives. Fromm taught that the important

---

From *Beyond the Chains of Illusion.*

elements in an individual's life—the environment, the socioeco-
nomic circumstances, and especially the family — shape the character
of the individual. He also explained that character traits inherent in
individuals—such as promptness and neatness—satisfy the needs
of the prevalent economic community. Such traits may change as the
needs of society change because society helps shape the individual.

Among his later views, Fromm held that character is dominated
by two forces: necrophilia (love of death) and biophilia (love of life).
All personalities have both these qualities: what is important is
which of these forces is dominant in the individual. The personality
dominated by necrophilia may evidence sadomasochistic behavior,
the desire to dominate and hurt others. Such behavior, which Fromm
sees as a perversion, is linked to early childhood experiences.
Biophilia, the opposite of necrophilia, is marked by a love of life
and a respect for living things. The health of the individual is
linked to a well-developed sense of biophilia.

Of his many books, the most well known are *The Sane Society*
(1955), *The Art of Loving* (1956), *Social Humanism* (1965), *The
Nature of Man* (1968), and the posthumously published *Of Disobedience and Other Essays* (1984). The book from which the following
selection comes was Fromm's effort at an autobiography clarifying
his relationship to the two greatest influences in his life: Karl Marx
and Sigmund Freud. *Beyond the Chains of Illusion: My Encounter
with Marx and Freud* (1962) reveals that he found Marx to be a
humanist at heart and that his theories had little or no relationship
to the Communist dictatorship practiced by Soviet Russia under
Stalin. His exploration of love in *The Art of Loving* was instrumental in his tempering the extreme aspects of Freud's thinking.

The selection that follows is not autobiographical in the sense
that it tells us about Fromm's life, but rather it contains some primary discussion of his thought late in life. He is obviously concerned
about the threat of atomic annihilation and the role of the individual
in humanity's effort to preserve the planet from total destruction.

Fromm's Rhetoric

The opening of the selection reviews the past, especially the
history of the years in which Fromm was himself aware of social
events. He concentrates on the devastation of the First World War
and the way it essentially changed the thoughts of many in Western
society. Despite the resistance of many powerful social organizations, the war erupted partly due to an overemphasis on nationalism
rather than an emphasis on the concept of human sharing and over-
riding human needs. Fromm sees that Marx had forewarned society

of a growing and dangerous nationalism, which is why he proposed a Socialist International that transcended national borders much like the Catholic Church. Fromm remained always a humanist and saw in the terror of the First World War an oppression of the individual by special-interest groups who seemed to love death more than life. Ultimately, he demonstrates that both world wars (Fromm was on the German side in 1914 but not in 1939) operated under illusions that were politically promoted to rob the individual of independent thought.

Beginning with paragraph 5, Fromm points to a ray of hope, the United Nations, and the concept of one world. But he also emphasizes the factors at work when he was writing. In place of the nation—or perhaps prior to concerns of the nation—the individual was becoming subsumed under the powers of the "organization." Like Emerson, Fromm is concerned with excessive conformity and picks up the Emersonian theme of disobedience in paragraphs 9 and 10 in which he goes so far as to say, "If the capacity for disobedience constituted the beginning of human history, obedience might cause the end of human history" (para. 10). He then examines the principle of obedience in our modern industrial world. If atomic weapons are to be deployed and used to destroy some or all of civilization, some single individual has to be obedient in order to press the buttons. It is that individual Fromm most wants to have learned the best principles of disobedience. Although he does not mention this point, it is clear that in our own time we hear frequently of military atrocities for which the explanation is usually that an individual was "merely following orders." Fromm wrote this book in 1962 after the Nuremberg trials of the Nazi leaders, although he is careful not to connect his view with any specific historical event. Instead he remains generalized, pointing to crimes of modern warfare that specifically targeted civilians, a practice that became widespread on the part of all combatants.

Fromm's concern for the United Nations leads him to think about the concept of one world, but at the heart of that concept he sees "One Man," the individual who "transcends the narrow limits of his nation and who experiences every human being as a neighbor, rather than as a barbarian" (para. 18). Like most writers of his generation, and like Emerson before him, Fromm uses the term *man* to mean all of us, men and women alike. Fromm's concept of the One Man is linked to the Buddha, who was himself singular in his behavior and thought, because he sees the Buddha as a lover of life. The One Man implies a virtually religious love of life and thus a step toward "constructing a new humanity" (para. 21).

Moving on from the concerns of the nation and the nationalism that Fromm feels is the basis of the barbarism of warfare, he discusses the effect of all "hierarchically organized bureaucracy," in which he includes not just religious and public institutions but also all large organizations. The danger of the large organization is that it treats the individual as a "cog in this machine" (para. 8). And the great danger, as with all institutions, is that the individual has the illusion of being an individual, while in fact the concern for security robs the individual of independence and risk taking. Fromm's purpose here is to expose the illusion so that we can achieve our own individuality.

Throughout the essay, Fromm's humanism is always at the heart of his thought. He begins thinking about the atomic age, but he ends with the symmetry and hope of ushering in the "Age of Man." His greatest hope is for a renaissance of humanism and a mastery of the technology that would otherwise, if permitted, essentially control rather than empower us. As he says, Western society has always maintained hope as one of its most important values. Fromm's hope is that the individual will eventually emerge and help change society.

PREREADING QUESTIONS:
WHAT TO READ FOR

The following prereading questions may help you anticipate key issues in Erich Fromm's discussion of *The Individual in the Chains of Illusion*. Keeping them in mind during your first reading of the selection should help focus your attention.

- What moral principles were violated in World Wars I and II?

- How does the idea of disobedience function in achieving a humane society?

- How does a "hierarchically organized bureaucracy" produce the illusion of being an individual?

- What is the "new obedience" in our culture?

The Individual in the Chains of Illusion

It is difficult to know to what extent a man born in 1900 can convey his experience to people born after 1914, or after 1929, or after 1945. I selected these dates, of course, intentionally. Anyone who was, like myself, at least fourteen years of age when the First World War broke out still experienced part of the solid, secure world of the nineteenth century. To be sure, if he was born as the son of a middle-class family with all necessities and quite a few luxuries provided, he experienced a much more comfortable aspect of this prewar period than if he had been born into a poor family. Yet even for the majority of the population, and especially for the working class, the end of the last and the beginning of the present century were a tremendous improvement over the conditions of existence even fifty years earlier, and they were filled with hope for a better future.

It is difficult for the generations born after 1914 to appreciate to 2 what extent this war shattered the foundations of Western civilization. This war broke out against the will of everybody, yet with the connivance of most participants or, rather, of special interest groups in each country which exercised sufficient pressure to make the war possible. By and large, Europeans, after almost one hundred years without major and catastrophic wars, and almost fifty years after the German-French war, were prone to think that "it can't happen." The powerful Socialist International seemed to be resolved to prevent war. The antiwar and pacifist movement was a potent force. But even the governments, whether that of the Czar, of the Kaiser, or of France and England, seemed to be resolved to avoid war. Yet it did happen. Reason and decency seemed suddenly to have left Europe. The same socialist leaders who only months before had pledged themselves to international solidarity now hurled at each other the vilest nationalistic epithets. The nations that had known and admired each other suddenly broke out in a mad paroxysm of hate. The British became cowardly mercenaries to the Germans; the Germans became vile Huns to their enemies; the music of Bach and Mozart became tainted; French words in the German language were ostracized. Not only that, but the moral rule against the killing of civilians was broken. Both sides bombed helpless cities and killed women and children; it was mainly the lack of development in aviation that restricted the scope and intensity of these raids. But the fate of the soldiers was equally in contrast to all demands of humanity. Millions on both sides were forced to attack the enemy trenches and were killed in the process, although it should have been clear that such tactics had become futile. But perhaps worst of all, the slaughter was based on a lie. The Germans were persuaded that they were fighting for freedom, and so were their Western enemies. When the chips were down, especially when, after 1916, a possibility for peace arose, both sides refused to settle because both insisted on gaining the territories for which the war was really being fought—regardless of the cost. At one point millions of men recognized the great deception. They rebelled against those who forced them to continue the slaughter, in Russia and Germany successfully, in France sporadically, by means of mutinies which were severely punished by the generals.

What had happened? The belief in continuing progress and peace 3 had been shattered, moral principles which had seemed secure were violated. The unthinkable had happened. Yet hope had not disappeared. After the first step in brutalization, hope arose again in the minds of men. It is important to understand this because nothing is more characteristic of Western history than the principle of hope which had governed it for two thousand years.

As I said before, the First World War shattered this hope but did not yet destroy it. Men rallied their energies and tried to take up the task where it had been interrupted in 1914. Many believed that the League of Nations would bring about the beginning of a new era of peace and reason; others, that the Russian Revolution would overcome its Czarist heritage and would develop into a true humanist-socialist society; aside from this, people in the capitalist countries believed that their system would follow a straight line of economic progress. The years between 1929 and 1933 shattered what was left of these hopes. The capitalist system showed that it was not capable of preventing unemployment and misery for a large part of the population. In Germany the people permitted Hitler to come to power and thus began a regime of archaic irrationality and ruthless cruelty. In Russia, after Stalin had transformed the revolution into a conservative state capitalism, he initiated a system of terror which was as ruthless, or more so, than that of the Nazis. While all this was happening, the approaching World War was already becoming visible on the horizon. The brutalization which had begun in 1914, which had been followed by the systems of Stalin and Hitler, now came to its full fruition. The Germans initiated it by their air attacks on Warsaw, Amsterdam, and Coventry. The Western allies followed by their attacks on Cologne, Hamburg, Leipzig, Tokyo, and finally, with the dropping of the atomic bomb on Hiroshima and Nagasaki. In hours or minutes, hundred thousands of men, women, and children were killed in one city, and all this with few scruples and hardly any remorse. Indiscriminate destruction of human life had become a legitimate means for attaining political goals. The process of increasing brutalization had done its work. Each side brutalizes the other, following the logic "if he is inhuman I must (and can) be inhuman too."

The war ended, and there arose a new flicker of hope, of which the foundation of the United Nations was a symbol. But soon after the end of the war the brutalization continued. The weapons of destruction became ever more powerful; now both sides are able to destroy at least half of each other's population (including most of their educated populations) in one day. Yet the consideration of the possibility of such mass destruction has become commonplace. Many on both sides are fighting to prevent the final act of madness; groups of men and women who follow the tradition of science, of humanism, and of hope. But millions have succumbed to the process of brutalization, and many more are just apathetic, and escape into the trivialities of the day.

The loss of hope and the increasing brutalization are, unfortu- 6
nately, not the only evils that have befallen Western civilization since
1914. Another cause for the deterioration of Western civilization is
connected precisely with its greatest achievements. The industrial revolution has led to a degree of material production which has given
the vast majority of the peoples of the West a standard of living
which would have seemed unthinkable to most observers a hundred
years ago. However, the satisfaction of real and legitimate needs has
changed into the creation and satisfaction of a powerful drive, namely,
"commodity hunger." Just as depressed individuals often are seized
by a compelling desire to buy things or in other cases to eat, modern
man has a greedy hunger for possessing and using new things, a
hunger which he rationalizes as an expression of his wish for a better life. He claims that the things he buys, if they are not directly
enriching to life, help him to save time. Yet he does not know what
to do with the time he saves, and spends one part of his income to
kill the time he is so proud of having saved.

We see this phenomenon most clearly in the richest country of 7
the world, in the United States. But it is quite clear that the trend in
all other countries is the same. The goal everywhere has become
maximal production and maximal consumption. The criterion of
progress is seen in the figures for consumption. This holds true for
the capitalist countries as well as for the Soviet Union. In fact, the
rivalry between the two systems seems to center around the question of which can produce a higher level of consumption, rather than
a better life. As a result, man in the industrialized countries trans-
forms himself more and more into a greedy, passive consumer. Things
are not provided to serve the perfection of man, but man has become
the servant of things, as a producer and as a consumer.

The industrial system has had very unfortunate effects in still 8
another direction. The method of production has changed considerably since the beginning of this century. Production, as well as distribution, is organized in big corporations which employ hundreds of
thousands of workers, clerks, engineers, salesmen, etc. They are managed by a hierarchically organized bureaucracy, and each person turns
into a small—or large—cog in this machine. He lives under the illusion of being an individual—while he has turned into a thing. As a
result, we observe an increasing lack of adventurousness, individualism, willingness to make decisions and take risks. The goal is security,
to be part of the big powerful machine, to be protected by it, and to
feel strong in the symbiotic connection with it. All studies and observation of the younger generation show the same picture: the trend to
look for *safe* jobs, not to be concerned so much with high income but
rather with satisfactory retirement provisions; the tendency to marry
young and to shift quickly from the haven of the parental family to the

haven of matrimony; cliché thinking, conformity, and obedience to the anonymous authority of public opinion and of the accepted patterns of feeling.

From the fight against the authority of Church, State, and family which characterize the last centuries, we have come back full circle to a new obedience; but this obedience is not one to autocratic persons, but to the organization. The "organization man" is not aware that he obeys; he believes that he only conforms with what is rational and practical. Indeed, disobedience has become almost extinct in the society of organization men, regardless of their ideology. Yet one must remember that the capacity for disobedience is as great a virtue as the capacity for obedience. One must remember that, according to the Hebrew and Greek myths, human history began with an act of disobedience. Adam and Eve, living in the Garden of Eden, were still part of nature, as the fetus is in the womb of the mother. Only when they dared to disobey an order were their eyes opened; they recognized each other as strangers and the world outside as strange and hostile. Their act of disobedience broke the primary bond with nature and made them individuals. Disobedience was the first act of freedom, the beginning of human history. Prometheus,[1] stealing the fire of the gods, is another disobedient dissenter. "I would rather be chained to this rock than be the obedient servant of the gods," he said. His act of stealing the fire is his gift to men, thus laying the very basis for civilization. He, like Adam and Eve, was punished for his disobedience; yet he, like them, has made human evolution possible. Man has continued to evolve by acts of disobedience not just in the sense that his *spiritual* development was possible only because there have been men who dared to say "no" to the powers that be in the name of their conscience or of their faith. His *intellectual* development was also dependent on the capacity for being disobedient, disobedient to the authorities who tried to muzzle new thoughts, and to the authority of long-established opinions which declared change to be nonsense.

If the capacity for disobedience constituted the beginning of human history, obedience might cause the end of human history. I am not speaking symbolically or poetically. There is the possibility that the human race will destroy itself and all life on earth within the next ten to fifteen years. There is no rationality or sense in it. But the fact is that while we are living technically in the atomic age, the majority of men live emotionally still in the Stone Age, including

9

10

---

[1] **Prometheus** In Greek mythology, a Titan who disobeyed the gods and gave man fire. He was punished by being tied to a pillar and suffering his liver to be eaten by an eagle in the day and then having it restored each evening.

most of those who are in power. If mankind commits suicide, it will be because people will obey those who command them to push the deadly buttons, because they will obey the archaic passions of fear, hate, and greed; because they will obey obsolete clichés of state sovereignty and national honor. The Soviet leaders talk much about revolution, and we in the "free world" talk much about freedom. Yet they discourage disobedience in the Soviet Union explicitly and by force—and we in the free world implicitly and by the more subtle methods of persuasion. There is a difference, and this difference becomes clear if we consider that this praise of disobedience could hardly be published in the Soviet Union while it can be published in the United States. Yet I believe that we are in great danger of being converted into complete organization men, and that means, eventually, into political totalitarianism, unless we regain the capacity to be disobedient and to learn how to doubt.

There is one other aspect of the present situation which I mentioned briefly in the beginning of this book but with which I must now deal more extensively: the problem of a renaissance of humanistic experience.   11

Sociologically it is easy to see that the evolution of the human race has led from small units like the clan and the tribe through city-states, national states, to world states and world cultures, like the Hellenistic, Roman, Islamic, and modern Western civilization. Yet the difference, as far as human experience is concerned, is not as fundamental as it may seem. The member of the primitive tribe differentiates sharply between the member of his group and the outsider. There are moral laws governing the members of the group, and without such laws no group could exist. But these laws do not apply to the "stranger." When groups grow in size, more people cease to be "strangers" and become "neighbors." Yet in spite of the quantitative change, qualitatively the distinction between the neighbor and the stranger remains. A stranger is not human, he is a barbarian, he is even not fully understandable.   12

Long before the human race was on the verge of becoming *One World,* socially and economically, its most advanced thinkers had visualized a new human experience, that of *One Man.* The Buddha[2] thought of man as man, as men having the same structure, the same problems, and the same answers, without regard to culture and race. The Old Testament visualized man as being one, bearing the likeness of the One God; the prophets visualized the day when the nations "shall beat their swords into plowshares, and their spears   13

---

[2] **Gautama Siddhartha, the Buddha (563?–483? B.C.)** Founder of Buddhism.

into pruninghooks"; [when] "nation shall not lift up sword against nation, neither shall they learn war any more" (Isaiah 2). They visualized the day when there will be no more "favorite" nations. "In that day shall there be a highway out of Egypt of Assyria, and the Assyrian shall come into Egypt and the Egyptian into Assyria. . . . In that day shall Israel be the third with Egypt and with Assyria, even a blessing in the midst of the land: whom the Lord of hosts shall bless saying, Blessed be Egypt my people, and Assyria the work of my hands, and Israel mine inheritance" (Isaiah 19).

Christianity created the concept that the Son of Man became the 14 Son of God — and God himself. Not this or that man, but Man. The Roman Church was a *Catholic* church precisely because it was a supranational, universal church. Classic Greek and Roman thinking arrived independently from Judaeo-Christian thought at the concept of One Man and of natural law rooted in the rights of man, rather than in the necessities of a nation or a state. Antigone[3] sacrifices her life in defense of universal human (natural) law against state law. Zenon[4] had the vision of a universal commonwealth. The Renaissance and Enlightenment enriched the Greek and Judaeo-Christian traditions and developed them further, in humanistic rather than in theological terms. Kant[5] constructed a moral principle valid for all men and outlined the possibility of eternal peace. Schiller[6] wrote (September 27, 1788): "The state is only a result of human forces, only a work of our thoughts, but man is the force of the source itself and the creator of the thought." In *Don Carlos,*[7] Posa speaks "as the deputy of all humanity whose heart beats/For all mankind; his passion was/The world and future generations."

The most complete and profound expression of this humanism 15 appears in the thought of Goethe.[8] His Iphigenia speaks in the voice of humanity, as the classic Antigone did. When the Barbarian king asks her:

> And dost thou think
> That the uncultured Scythian will attend
> The voice of truth and of humanity
> Which Atreus, the Greek, heard not?

---

[3] **Antigone** In Sophocles' tragedy *Antigone,* the title character disobeys King Creon by burying her brother Polyneices, who as a traitor was denied a proper burial.

[4] **Zenon (474–491)** Emperor of the East and a tyrant.

[5] **Immanuel Kant (1724–1804)** Major eighteenth-century philosopher.

[6] **Friedrich Schiller (1759–1855)** German poet, philosopher, and dramatist.

[7] **Don Carlos** Schiller's play (1787) in which Posa gives an important speech on personal freedom.

[8] **Johann Wolfgang von Goethe (1749–1832)** Greatest German writer and dramatist of his time. The passage is from a letter dated March 15, 1799.

she answers:

> 'Tis heard
> By everyone, born 'neath whatever clime,
> Within whose bosom flows the stream of life
> Pure and unhindered.

Goethe wrote (in 1799): "At a time when everybody is busy erecting new Fatherlands, the Fatherland of the man who thinks without prejudice and can rise above his time is nowhere and everywhere."

But in spite of the ideas which the greatest representatives of Western culture held, history took a different path. Nationalism killed humanism. The nation and its sovereignty became the new idols to which the individual succumbed. 16

In the meantime, however, the world has changed. The revolution of the colonial peoples, communication by air, the radio, etc., have shrunk the globe to the proportions of one continent or, rather, one state as they existed one hundred years ago. The One World which is in the process of being born is, however, not one world because of the friendly and brotherly relations that exist among its various parts, but rather because of the fact that missiles can carry death and destruction to almost any part of the world in a matter of hours. The one world is *one,* so far, inasmuch as it is one potential battlefield, rather than a new system of world citizenship. We live in one world, yet in his feelings and thoughts contemporary man still lives in the nation state. His loyalties are still primarily to sovereign states and not to the human race. This anachronism can only lead to disaster. It is a situation similar to that of the religious wars before religious tolerance and coexistence became an accepted principle of European life. 17

If the One World is not to destroy itself, it needs a new kind of man—a man who transcends the narrow limits of his nation and who experiences every human being as a neighbor, rather than as a barbarian; a man who feels at home in the world. 18

Why is this step so difficult? Man's life begins in the womb. Even after birth he is still part of mother, just as primitive man was part of nature. He becomes increasingly aware of himself as separate from others, yet he is deeply drawn to the security and safety of his past. He is afraid of emerging fully as an individual. Mother, the tribe, the family—they all are "familiar." The stranger, the one who is not familiar through the bonds of blood, customs, food, language, is suspected of being dangerous. 19

This attitude toward the "stranger" is inseparable from the attitude toward oneself. As long as any fellow being is experienced as fundamentally different from myself, as long as he remains a stranger, I remain a stranger to myself too. When I experience myself fully, then 20

I recognize that I am the same as any other human being, that I am the child, the sinner, the saint, the one who hopes and the one who despairs, the one who can feel joy and the one who can feel sadness. I discover that only the thought concepts, the customs, the surface are different, and that the human substance is the same. I discover that I am everybody, and that I discover myself in discovering my fellow man, and vice versa. In this experience I discover what humanity is; I discover the One Man.

Until now the One Man may have been a luxury, since the One 21 World had not yet emerged. Now the One Man must emerge if the One World is to live. Historically speaking, this may be a step comparable with the great revolution which was constituted by the step from the worship of many gods to the One God—or the One No-God. This step was characterized by the idea that man must cease to serve idols, be they nature or the work of his own hands. Man has never yet achieved this aim. He changed the name of his idols and continued serving them. Yet he changed. He made some progress in understanding himself, and tremendous progress in understanding nature. He developed his reason and approached the frontiers of becoming fully human. Yet in this process he developed such destructive powers that he may destroy civilization before the last step is taken toward constructing a new humanity.

Indeed, we have a rich heritage which waits for its realization. 22 But in contrast to the men of the eighteenth and nineteenth centuries who had an unfailing belief in the continuity of progress, we visualize the possibility that, instead of progress, we may create barbarism or our total destruction. The alternative of socialism or barbarism has become frighteningly real today, when the forces working toward barbarism seem to be stronger than those working against it. But it is not the "socialism" of managerial totalitarianism which will save the world from barbarism. It is the renaissance of humanism, the emergence of a new West which employs its new technical powers for the sake of man, rather than using man for the sake of things; it is a new society in which the norms for man's unfolding govern the economy, rather than the social and political process being governed by blind and anarchic economic interests.

In this struggle for a humanist renaissance Marx's and Freud's 23 ideas are important guideposts. Marx had a much deeper insight into the nature of the social process, and he was much more independent than Freud of the social and political ideologies of his time. Freud had a deeper insight into the nature of the process of human thought, affects, and passions, even though he did not transcend the principles of bourgeois society. They both have given us the intellectual tools to break through the sham of rationalization and ideologies, and to penetrate to the core of individual and social reality.

Regardless of the shortcomings of their respective theories, they 24
have removed mystifying veils which covered over human reality;
they have laid the foundations for a new Science of Man; and this
new science is badly needed if the Age of Man is to be ushered in—
if, to speak with Emerson, things are to cease riding mankind, and if
man is to be put into the saddle.

QUESTIONS FOR CRITICAL READING

1. Is it true that many depressed individuals have a compelling desire to
   buy something or to eat something? How does this fit in with Fromm's
   illusion of the individual?
2. To what extent do you think people in our culture have continued to
   be "greedy, passive consumer[s]"? Why is such behavior a problem?
3. Fromm says the goal "everywhere has become maximal production and
   maximal consumption" (para. 7). That may have been true in 1962, but
   is it true today?
4. Why might obedience cause the end of human history?
5. What are Fromm's views on education (see paras. 9 and 10)?
6. Fromm talks often of *humanism*. What does he seem to mean by the
   term?
7. Fromm connects disobedience with doubt. What do they have in common and why would doubt be important to the development of the
   individual?
8. What kind of individual would the "One Man" Fromm discusses be like
   (beginning in para. 13)?

SUGGESTIONS FOR CRITICAL WRITING

1. In discussing the development of society, Fromm suggests that there are
   moral laws that any group must hold to in order not to be destroyed
   from within. However, he also points out that traditionally these moral
   laws have not always applied to people who are outside the group. Using
   what you know of the political activities of nations or world groups,
   defend or attack Fromm's view. What evidence can you bring to bear on
   the question? Have things changed in this regard since 1962?
2. In paragraph 10, Fromm says "that while we are living technically in the
   atomic age, the majority of men live emotionally still in the Stone Age,
   including most of those who are in power." Relying on the headlines in
   newspapers or on Internet reports of political activity, attack or defend
   his views in that paragraph in terms of their importance to and relevance
   for the society in which you live. What actions—including those of
   people around you—suggest that people are living in an "emotional"
   Stone Age?
3. Are you concerned that you might, when you leave college and go to
   work, become a complete "organization man [or woman]"? What will

the expectations of your employer be when you get your first job? Do you think it is possible for you to be a genuine individual and also to fit into the structure of a modern corporation? What work experience have you had so far that suggests one pattern or the other? Is it possible that Fromm is wrong and that things have changed so much since 1962 that the concept of the "organization man" is passé?

4. Fromm is almost offhand in declaring that disobedience is a first act of freedom. Keeping in mind that all of us are urged to be obedient from our early years onward, why would Fromm say that we should be disobedient? And what kind of disobedience is he talking about—and not talking about? Obviously, disobedient people (especially children) are often a pain and are considered undesirable. What, then, is he really driving at when he counsels you to be disobedient? Can you follow his suggestion?

5. "Nationalism killed humanism," Fromm says in paragraph 16. This is an underlying issue throughout the essay. What, in your estimation, does he mean by this expression? Why are these two ideologies antagonistic? Consider the historical information in the beginning of the essay to help you define *nationalism* in Fromm's view. Is nationalism still an issue in our modern society or are there signs that it is beginning to recede in favor of larger global interests? What, then, is meant by *humanism*?

6. Fromm balances two forces against one another: necrophilia, love of death, against biophilia, love of life. He sees these as political forces, especially when he reviews the actions of dictators and nations that wage irrational war against others. In a brief essay, establish clearly the definition of each of these terms, using at least one example of the behavior of people devoted to either force. Then show how these forces have been at work in your own time. Use news reports or personal examples to make your point.

7. **CONNECTIONS**   Fromm refers directly to Emerson in the last paragraph of his essay, indicating that he has read and understood him. What are the main points of agreement between Emerson's "Self-Reliance" and Fromm's *The Individual in the Chains of Illusion*? What evidence is there in Fromm's essay that convinces you that he did or did not read Emerson's "Self-Reliance"? Are there important points that separate Fromm's basic views from those of Emerson? Write a comparative essay that gives a greater understanding of these essays when considered together than would be possible if each was analyzed individually.

8. **SEEING CONNECTIONS**   Write an essay in which you answer the question, In Caspar David Friedrich's *Wanderer Above the Sea of Fog* (p. 250), is the major figure standing on the crag a good representation of Fromm's "One Man," the man who can see things clearly, can understand himself, can seek adventure, can take risks and make decisions rather than be passive and molded by the organization? Fromm doubtless knew this painting. What evidence of humanist values would he have seen in it? What elements in the composition convince you of your views? Is there any sense in which the figure could be seen as an "organization man"?

PART FOUR

WEALTH AND POVERTY

Adam Smith

Karl Marx

Andrew Carnegie

John Kenneth Galbraith

Robert B. Reich

INTRODUCTION

Wealth and poverty: the one is the parent of luxury and
indolence, and the other of meanness and viciousness, and
both of discontent.

—PLATO (428–347 B.C.)

What difference does it make how much you have? What you do
not have amounts to much more.

—SENECA (4 B.C.–A.D. 65)

Great eagerness in the pursuit of wealth, pleasure, or honor, cannot
exist without sin.

—DESIDERIUS ERASMUS (1466–1536)

In any country where talent and virtue produce no advancement,
money will be the national god. Its inhabitants will either have to
possess money or make others believe that they do. Wealth will
be the highest virtue, poverty the greatest vice.

—DENIS DIDEROT (1713–1784)

Poverty in itself does not make men into a rabble; a rabble is
created only when there is joined to poverty a disposition of mind,
an inner indignation against the rich, against society, against the
government.

—GEORG WILHELM FRIEDRICH HEGEL (1770–1831)

Animals struggle with each other for food or for leadership, but
they do not, like human beings, struggle with each other for that
that stands for food or leadership: such things as our paper
symbols of wealth (money, bonds, titles), badges of rank to wear
on our clothes, or low-number license plates, supposed by some
people to stand for social precedence.

—S. I. HAYAKAWA (1906–1992)

Ancient writers talk about wealth in terms of a surplus of necessary
or desirable goods and products. After the invention of coins—which
historians attribute to the Lydians, whose civilization flourished in the
eastern Mediterranean region from 800 to 200 B.C.—wealth also
became associated with money. However, the relationship of wealth
to money has long been debated. According to Aristotle, people mis-
understand wealth when they think of it as "only a quantity of coin."
For him, money was useful primarily as a means of representing and
purchasing goods but was not sustaining in and of itself.

Writers like Aristotle have argued that wealth benefits the state
by ensuring stability, growth, security, and cultural innovations and
that it benefits the individual by providing leisure time, mobility, and

luxury. Most societies, however, have struggled with the problems caused by unequal distribution of wealth, either among individuals or between citizens and the state. The Spartan leader Lycurgus is said to have tackled the problem in the ninth century B.C. by convincing the inhabitants of the Greek city-state of Sparta that they needed to redistribute their wealth. Land and household goods were redistributed among the citizens, and Lycurgus was hailed as a hero. However, Lycurgus's model has not been the norm in subsequent civilizations, and questions about the nature of wealth and its role and distribution in society have persisted.

The selections in this section present ideas on wealth and poverty from a variety of perspectives. Adam Smith begins by tracing the natural evolution of wealth from farming to trade. Karl Marx expounds on what he feels are the corrosive effects of excessive wealth on the individual and on the problems caused by unequal distribution of wealth between laborers and business owners. John Kenneth Galbraith and Robert B. Reich further investigate the problems that an unequal distribution of wealth poses for society as a whole.

Adam Smith was known originally as a moral philosopher with a professorship at Glasgow, but he wrote at a time of extraordinary expansion in Great Britain. As industrial power grew in the late eighteenth century, England became more wealthy and began to dominate trade in important areas of commerce. In his own mind, Smith's interest in wealth may have been connected with his studies in morality, or it may have grown from his considerable curiosity about a broad range of subjects. Regardless, he produced one of the century's most important and extensive books on economics, *The Wealth of Nations*. It is still consulted by economists today.

Smith's "Of the Natural Progress of Opulence" is an attempt to understand the "natural" steps to wealth. Smith posits an interesting relationship between the country, where food and plants, such as cotton and flax, supply the necessities of life, and the city, which produces no food but takes the surplus from the country and turns it into manufactured goods. Smith's ideas concerning this process center on surplus. The farmers produce more than they can consume, and therefore they can market their goods to the city. The city takes some of the goods from the farmers and turns them into manufactured products, which can be sold back to the people in the country. When there is a surplus of manufactured goods, they can be sold abroad. That process can produce wealth—on a grand scale.

Karl Marx's *Communist Manifesto* clarifies the relationship between a people's condition and the economic system in which they live. Marx saw that capitalism provided opportunities for the wealthy and powerful to take advantage of labor. He argued that because labor cannot efficiently sell its product, management can keep labor in perpetual economic bondage.

Marx knew poverty firsthand, but one of his close associates, Friedrich Engels, who collaborated on portions of the *Manifesto*, was the son of a factory owner and so was able to observe closely how the rich can oppress the poor. For both of them, the economic system of capitalism produced a class struggle between the rich (bourgeoisie) and the laboring classes (proletariat).

In an effort to avoid anything like a class struggle between the rich and the poor, Andrew Carnegie wrote *The Gospel of Wealth*, defending not only the economic system that permitted a few people to amass great wealth but also praising it for being the highest expression of civilization. Carnegie dismisses communism as a failed system and cites Darwinian theories as supporting the laws of competition and accumulation that permitted men like him to possess vast fortunes. His proposal is that such men should give their wealth back to the community for its benefit in the form of institutions that would contribute to "the improvement of the race." Moreover, the rich should give their money away while they are living so that they can clearly guide their gifts in the directions they feel are most important. Carnegie, for example, concentrated on building public libraries throughout the United States and Canada, while founding a university and supporting others rather generously.

John Kenneth Galbraith's selection, "The Position of Poverty," dates from the middle of the twentieth century and addresses an issue that earlier thinkers avoided: the question of poverty. It is not that earlier writers were unaware that poverty existed—most mention it in passing—but their main concern was the accumulation and preservation of wealth. Galbraith, in his study of the economics of contemporary America, also focuses on wealth; the title of his most famous book is *The Affluent Society* (1958; rev. 1998). He, however, points toward something greater than the issue of attaining affluence. His concern is with the allocation of the wealth that American society has produced. His fears that selfishness and waste will dominate the affluent society have led him to write about what he considers the most important social issue related to economics: poverty and its effects. If Smith was correct in seeing wealth as appropriate subject matter for economic study, then Galbraith has pointed to the opposite of wealth as being equally worthy of close examination.

Robert B. Reich, a lecturer at Harvard University until he was appointed secretary of labor in the first Clinton administration, has taught courses in economics and published widely. His 1991 book *The Work of Nations* echoes the title of Adam Smith's eighteenth-century masterpiece of capitalist theory, *The Wealth of Nations*. Although Reich's views on labor are distinct from Smith's, his essay focuses on labor with the same intensity Smith brings to money. His views consider how worldwide economic developments will affect labor in the next decades. According to Reich, labor falls into three groups—routine workers, in-person servers, and symbolic analysts—each of which will fare differently in the coming years.

Most of these theorists agree that a healthy economy can relieve the misery and suffering of a population. Most agree that wealth and plenty are preferable to impoverishment and want. But some are also concerned with the effects of materialism and greed on the spiritual life of a nation. Galbraith sees a society with enormous power to bring about positive social change and the capacity to make positive moral decisions. But, for all his optimism, Galbraith reminds us that we have made very little progress in an area of social concern that has been a focus of thought and action for a generation.

VISUALIZING WEALTH AND POVERTY

Some of the most famous images associated with wealth are por-traits, often photographs of great industrialists and financiers such as Andrew Carnegie and J. P. Morgan. They are imposing figures in their business attire, staring straight at the viewer as if daring us to say a single word to them. Some renderings seem aware of their own mightiness. Others affect a brotherly kindness, allowing their wealth to reveal itself through the Renaissance furniture, rich Oriental rugs, and art masterpieces depicted with them.

Newspaper images of wealthy individuals usually include one or more possessions associated with their opulent lifestyles. Movie stars stand beside their Bentleys, real-estate tycoons are profiled next to their grandest buildings, playboys show up on their yachts, and inventors pose near their jet planes. Wealth has many faces, com-municated by just as many images, and we see them constantly in magazines aimed at both the rich and the less rich. Lifestyles of the rich are visible on television shows, in films, and even on YouTube.

Images of the poor, on the other hand, are different. Very few are images that attempt to maintain the dignity of the poor. Usually images of poverty show suffering people from remote parts of the globe; such imagery often accompanies requests for money to relieve that poverty. In the 1890s, the vast majority of Americans lived on farms and were what we would today describe as poor. Yet the poor maintained a sense of dignity that was recognized by all. Families stood by one another and helped relieve any sense of desperation

HENRY O. TANNER, *THE THANKFUL POOR.* 1894.
Oil on canvas. Collection of William H. and Camille O. Cosby.

caused by impoverishment. Poverty in the cities took a different form. The photographs by Jacob Riis (1849–1914) of the tenements on the Lower East Side of New York were among the most powerful images of genuine poverty that Americans might see in the early years of the twentieth century. Some of the neighborhoods he photographed were so crime-ridden that even police would not venture in.

One of the most remarkable portraits of the poor dates to the era of Andrew Carnegie. It portrays an older man and a young boy who appears to be his grandson, preparing to have dinner. The only source of light in the room seems to come from the window, which brings the wall alive with color. The two figures are poised, apparently saying grace before eating.

Henry Osawa Tanner (1859–1937) was born in Pittsburgh, Pennsylvania, where his father was a minister in the African Methodist Episcopal Church. When he was seven, his family moved to Philadelphia. He decided on his profession after watching an artist painting in a nearby park when he was thirteen. Tanner, a clearly talented painter, enrolled in the prestigious Pennsylvania Academy of Fine Arts in 1880 where he was a student of one of America's greatest painters, Thomas Eakins (1844–1916). Eakins recognized Tanner's ability and encouraged him. He also painted Tanner's portrait around the turn of the century, something he did for very few of his students.

Tanner often went to the Philadelphia Zoo to sketch animals to use in his early paintings. Professionals told him that he could sell animal paintings, so he painted several. But his primary subject matter was religious scenes, often from the Bible. Paintings such as *The Resurrection of Lazarus* and *The Good Shepherd* made his reputation. However, racism in Philadelphia, heightened by the northern migration of freed African Americans from the Carolinas, was such that Tanner felt pained and dismayed. He decided in 1891 to live in Paris and study there. In France, his race was of little or no concern and he found it more and more difficult to return to the United States.

In 1893, while back in the United States for a short time, he painted his most famous work, *The Banjo Lesson*. It portrays a man carefully instructing what seems to be his grandson on how to play the instrument. The two figures in that painting may have been the same that appear in *The Thankful Poor*. Tanner died on May 25, 1937, in Paris.

The Thankful Poor shows a small family at dinner, with sparkling plates, a stoneware water pitcher, a plate with a fish and what seems to be a portion of chicken. Tanner did not paint this family in a fashion that evokes a sense of pity for their poverty—in part because, while they may be poor, they are not impoverished. They have a home, they have furniture and food, and they have each other. The reverence with which they approach their meal is such that one cannot help but respect their dignity and wonder what their conversation was while they ate together. The structure of the painting weights the action to the lower left diagonal half of the composition. If one were to draw a line from the upper left corner to the lower right, all the important information regarding the older man appears to the left, while the image of the young boy appears to the right. General darkness is more powerful near the older man, while the light reflecting from the wall illuminates the young boy, as if to suggest that life may be brighter for him than for the older man. In this sense it is visually a hopeful painting.

ADAM SMITH
Of the Natural Progress of Opulence

ADAM SMITH (1723–1790) was born in Kirkcaldy on the eastern coast of Scotland. He attended Glasgow University and received a degree from Oxford, after which he gave a successful series of lectures on rhetoric in his hometown. This resulted in his appointment as professor of logic at Glasgow in 1751. A year later, he moved to a professorship in moral philosophy that had been vacated by Thomas Craggie, one of his former teachers. He held this position for twelve years. Smith's early reputation was built entirely on his work in moral philosophy, which included theology, ethics, justice, and political economy.

In many ways Adam Smith's views are striking in their modernity; in fact, his work continues to inform our understanding of current economic trends. His classic and best-known book, *An Inquiry into the Nature and Causes of the Wealth of Nations* (1776), examines the economic system of the modern nation that has reached, as England had, the commercial level of progress. According to Smith, a nation has to pass through a number of levels of culture—from hunter-gatherer to modern commercial—on its way to becoming modern. In this sense, he was something of an evolutionist in economics.

Wealth of Nations is quite different in both tone and concept from Smith's earlier success, *Theory of Moral Sentiments* (1759). The earlier work postulates a social order based, in part, on altruism—an order in which individuals aid one another—whereas *Wealth of Nations* asserts that the best economic results are obtained when individuals work for their own interests and their

From *An Inquiry into the Nature and Causes of the Wealth of Nations.*

own gain. This kind of effort, Smith assures us, results in the general improvement of a society because the industry of the individual benefits everyone in the nation by producing more wealth; the greater the wealth of the nation, the better the lot of every individual in the nation.

There is no question that Smith was an ardent capitalist who felt an almost messianic need to spread the doctrine of capitalism. He maintained throughout his life that *Wealth of Nations* was one with his writings on moral and social issues and that when his work was complete it would encompass the basic elements of any society.

In "Of the Natural Progress of Opulence," Smith outlines a microcosm of the progress of capitalism as he understood it. His purpose is to establish the steps by which a nation creates its wealth and the steps by which a region becomes wealthy. For the most part, he is interested in the development of capitalism in Great Britain, including his native Scotland. His perspective includes the natural developments that he observed in his own time in the late eighteenth century as well as developments that he could imagine from earlier times. Because he wrote and published his book just before the American Revolution and the subsequent industrial revolution, his primary concerns are farming and agriculture. In earlier sections of *Wealth of Nations*, Smith focused on metal—silver and gold—as a measure of wealth, then later on corn (by which he usually meant wheat or barley) as a measure of wealth. In this selection, he is more emphatic about land as a convenient instrument of wealth.

His primary point is related to what he sees as a natural progression. People in the country have land on which they plant crops, which they sell, in part, to people in the town. The people in the town, lacking land but possessing skills such as weaving, building, and the like, create a market for the goods from the country. They take the product of the land and, with the surplus beyond their daily needs for food and sustenance, manufacture useful goods. In turn, they sell the desirable goods to people in the country, and both manage to accumulate wealth in the process. In this view the manufactures of the town are important but by no means as essential as the food that sustains the nation. Indeed, Smith regards surplus production as the key to the move toward wealth, which accumulates into opulence.

It is interesting that Smith does not emphasize the trade of goods among nations. He does emphasize the fact that the interchange between the country and the town in England also has a counterpart in international trade. However, Smith seems a bit uneasy in contemplating the usefulness of international trade as a means to accumulate wealth. Land, he reminds the reader, is secure, controllable, and not likely to yield to the whimsy of foul winds, leaky ships, or dishonest foreign merchants. One realizes that regardless of what he might say in praise of other possibilities, Smith himself would likely prefer a life in the country on a spread of his own land, collecting rent from tenants who produce food and flax and other goods that help him accumulate wealth.

Smith's Rhetoric

Adam Smith is widely regarded as one of the most influential economic thinkers of the eighteenth century. His *Wealth of Nations* is a gigantic book with many complex arguments regarding the nature of money and the role of capital in trade. This selection is a relatively straightforward statement regarding what he feels is the usual progress that all nations experience in the creation and accumulation of wealth. However, the normal eighteenth-century paragraph is much longer than those of today. By the same token, the normal eighteenth-century sentence is more complex in structure than we are used to today. For that reason, many readers will pause for reflection as they read Smith's work.

Still, his sentences are ultimately clear and direct. His opening sentence, for example, is a mighty declaration: "The great commerce of every civilized society, is that carried on between the inhabitants of the town and those of the country." In this sentence Smith makes a clear pronouncement, a statement about *every* society. Such a sweeping generalization is likely to invite attack and skepticism, but he feels totally secure in his assertion and proceeds to argue his position point by point.

On a more modest note, when Smith says, "Upon equal, or nearly equal profits, most men will choose to employ their capitals rather in the improvement and cultivation of land, than either in manufactures or in foreign trade" (para. 3), he expects the reader to see the simple wisdom of trusting the land and distrusting instruments of trade. However, many readers—even in his own time—would see this sentence as revealing a personal preference rather than a general rule. Even in the eighteenth century, many merchants were growing rich by ignoring land and trusting trade on the high seas.

Smith's view on this issue reflects an aspect of his conservatism, a stance that remains recognizably conservative even by today's standards. Nevertheless, his principles have guided traders as well as farmers for more than two hundred years. In his time, the workers in agriculture outnumbered workers in manufactures by a factor of eighty or ninety. But today, workers in agriculture have decreased progressively since the industrial revolution. Now, as a result of more efficient farming methods, only two or three people out of a hundred work on farms producing food and other goods. It would be interesting to know how Smith might react to this dramatic shift in occupations.

In helping the reader to work through his argument, Smith includes inset "summaries" of the content of each paragraph. For paragraph 2, he includes two insets. The first—"*The cultivation of the country must be prior to the increase of the town,*"—alerts the reader to look for his explanation of why this claim is true. The second inset—"*though the town may sometimes be distant from the country from which it derives its subsistence.*"—helps readers focus on the implications of distances from agriculture and manufacture for the local population. Those who grow corn nearest the city will make more money than those who live at a distance and must pay for its transportation to market. It is interesting to note that later ages developed relatively inexpensive means of transport—such as canals and railroads—to even out the cost of carriage in relation to fixed prices.

Smith depends on the clear, step-by-step argument to hold the attention of his reader. He establishes and examines each major point, clarifies his own position, then moves on to the next related point. For example, he talks about nations with uncultivated land, or large areas of land, and how the procedure he outlines works. Then he introduces the situation of a nation that has no uncultivated land available, or land available only at very high cost. Under such circumstances, people will turn to manufacture but not rely on selling their products locally. In those conditions, they will risk foreign sales.

It is also worth noting that when Smith talks about the American colonies, he reminds the reader that there is plenty of land for people to work. As a result, little or no manufacture is produced for sale abroad. He sees this as an indication that the Americans are fiercely independent, demanding land of their own so as to guarantee that they will have adequate sustenance in the future. Throughout the selection Smith establishes a clear sense of the progress of nations toward the accumulation of wealth, and he provides the reader with a blueprint for financial success.

PREREADING QUESTIONS: WHAT TO READ FOR

The following prereading questions may help you anticipate key issues in the discussion of Adam Smith's "Of the Natural Progress of Opulence." Keeping them in mind during your first reading of the selection should help focus your attention.

- What is the nature of the commerce between the country and the town?
- What does Smith think is the natural order of things in the development of commerce?

Of the Natural Progress of Opulence

The great commerce is that between town and country, which is obviously advantageous to both.

The great commerce of every civilized society, is that carried on between the inhabitants of the town and those of the country. It consists in the exchange of rude for manufactured produce, either immediately, or by the intervention of money, or of some sort of paper which represents money. The country supplies the town with the means of subsistence, and the materials of manufacture. The town repays this supply by sending back a part of the manufactured produce to the inhabitants of the country. The town, in which there neither is nor can be any reproduction of substances, may very properly be said to gain its whole wealth and subsistence from the country. We must not, however, upon this account, imagine that the gain of the town is the loss of the country. The gains of both are mutual and reciprocal, and the division of labor is in this, as in all other cases, advantageous to all the different persons employed in the various occupations into which it is subdivided. The inhabitants of the country purchase of the town a greater quantity of manufactured goods, with the produce of a much smaller quantity of their own labor, than they must have employed had they attempted to prepare them themselves. The town affords a market for the surplus produce of the country, or what is over and above the maintenance of the cultivators, and it is there that the inhabitants of the country exchange it for something else which is in demand among them. The greater the number and revenue of the inhabitants of the town, the more extensive is the market which it affords to those of the country; and the more extensive that market, it is always the more advantageous to a great number. The corn which grows within a mile of the town, sells there for the same price with that which comes from twenty miles distance. But the price of the latter must, generally, not only pay the expence of raising and bringing it to market, but afford too the ordinary profits of agriculture to the farmer. The proprietors and cultivators of the country, therefore, which lies in the neighborhood of the town, over and above the ordinary profits of agriculture, gain, in the price of what they sell, the whole value of the carriage of the like produce that is brought from more distant parts, and they save, besides, the whole value of this carriage in the price of what they buy. Compare the cultivation of the lands in the neighborhood of any considerable town, with that of those which lie at some distance from it, and you will easily satisfy yourself how much the country is benefited by the commerce of the town. Among all the absurd speculations that have been propagated concerning the balance of trade, it has never been pretended that either the country loses by its commerce with the town, or the town by that with the country which maintains it.

The cultivation of the country must be prior to the increase of the town,

As subsistence is, in the nature of things, prior to conveniency and luxury, so the industry which procures the former, must necessarily be prior to that which ministers to the latter. The cultivation and improvement of the country, therefore, which affords subsistence, must, necessarily, be prior to the increase of the town, which furnishes only the means of conveniency and luxury. It is the surplus produce of the country only, or what is over and above the maintenance of the cultivators, that constitutes the subsistence of the town, which can therefore increase only with the increase of this surplus produce. The town, indeed, may not always derive its whole subsistence from the country in its neighborhood, or even from the territory to which it belongs, but from very distant countries; and this,

though the town may sometimes be distant from the country

from which it derives its subsistence.

though it forms no exception from the general rule, has occasioned considerable variations in the progress of opulence in different ages and nations.

That order of things which necessity imposes 3 in general, though not in every particular country, is, in every particular country, promoted by the natural inclinations of man. If human institutions had never thwarted those natural inclinations, the towns could no-where have increased beyond what the improvement and cultivation of the territory in which they were situated could support; till such time, at least, as the whole of that territory was completely cultivated and improved. Upon equal, or nearly equal profits, most men will choose to employ their capitals rather in the improvement and cultivation of land, than either in manufactures or in foreign trade. The man who employs his capital in land, has it more under his view and command, and his fortune is much less liable to accidents, than that of the trader, who is obliged frequently to commit it, not only to the winds and the waves, but to the more uncertain elements of human folly and injustice, by giving great credits in distant countries to men, with whose character and situation he can seldom be thoroughly acquainted. The capital of the landlord, on the contrary, which is fixed in the improvement of his land, seems to be as well secured as the nature of human affairs can admit of. The beauty of the country besides, the pleasures of a country life, the tranquillity of mind which it promises, and wherever the injustice of human laws does not disturb it, the independency which it really affords, have charms that more or less attract every body; and as to cultivate the ground was the original destination of man, so in every stage of his existence he seems to retain a predilection for this primitive employment.

This order of things is favored by the natural preference of man for agriculture.

Cultivators require the assistance of artificers, who settle together and form a village,

Without the assistance of some artificers, 4 indeed, the cultivation of land cannot be carried on, but with great inconveniency and continual interruption. Smiths, carpenters, wheel-wrights, and plough-wrights, masons, and bricklayers, tanners, shoemakers, and tailors, are people, whose service the farmer has frequent occasion for. Such *and their employment augments with the improvement of the country.*

artificers too stand, occasionally, in need of the assistance of one another; and as their residence is not, like that of the farmer, necessarily tied down to a precise spot, they naturally settle in the neighborhood of one another, and thus form a small town or village. The butcher, the brewer, and the baker, soon join them, together with many other artificers and retailers, necessary or useful for supplying their occasional wants, and who contribute still further to augment the town. The inhabitants of the town and those of the country are mutually the servants of one another. The town is a continual fair or market, to which the inhabitants of the country resort in order to exchange their rude for manufactured produce. It is this commerce which supplies the inhabitants of the town both with the materials of their work, and the means of their subsistence. The quantity of the finished work which they sell to the inhabitants of the country, necessarily regulates the quantity of the materials and provisions which they buy. Neither their employment nor subsistence, therefore, can augment, but in proportion to the augmentation of the demand from the country for finished work; and this demand can augment only in proportion to the extension of improvement and cultivation. Had human institutions, therefore, never disturbed the natural course of things, the progressive wealth and increase of the towns would, in every political society, be consequential, and in proportion to the improvement and cultivation of the territory or country.

In the American colonies an artificer who has acquired sufficient stock becomes a planter instead of manufacturing for distant sale,

In our North American colonies, where uncultivated land is still to be had upon easy terms, no manufactures for distant sale have ever yet been established in any of their towns. When an artificer has acquired a little more stock than is necessary for carrying on his own business in supplying the neighboring country, he does not, in North America, attempt to establish with it a manufacture for more distant sale, but employs it in the purchase and improvement of uncultivated land. From artificer he becomes planter, and neither the large wages nor the easy subsistence which that country affords to artificers, can bribe him rather to work   5 for other people than for himself. He feels that an artificer is the servant of his customers, from whom he derives his subsistence; but that a planter who cultivates his own land, and derives his necessary subsistence from the labor of his own family, is really a master, and independent of all the world.

as in countries where no uncultivated land can be procured.

In countries, on the contrary, where there is either no uncultivated land, or none that can be had upon easy terms, every artificer who has acquired more stock than he can employ in the occasional jobs of the neighborhood, endeavors to prepare work for more distant sale. The smith erects some sort of iron, the weaver some sort of linen or woollen manufactory. Those different manufactures come, in process of time, to be gradually subdivided, and thereby improved and refined in a great variety of ways, which may easily be conceived, and which it is therefore unnecessary to explain any further. 6

Manufactures are naturally preferred to foreign commerce.

In seeking for employment to a capital, manufactures are, upon equal or nearly equal profits, naturally preferred to foreign commerce, for the same reason that agriculture is naturally preferred to manufactures. As the capital of the landlord or farmer is more secure than that of the manufacturer, so the capital of the manufacturer, being at all times more within his view and command, is more secure than that of the foreign merchant. In every period, indeed, of every society, the surplus part both of the rude and manufactured produce, or that for which there is no demand at home, must be sent abroad in order to be exchanged for something for which there is some demand at home. But whether the capital, which carries this surplus produce abroad, be a foreign or a domestic one, is of very little importance. If the society has not acquired sufficient capital both to cultivate all its lands, and to manufacture in the completest manner the whole of its rude produce, there is even a considerable advantage that that rude produce should be exported by a foreign capital, in order that the whole stock of the society may be employed in more useful purposes. The wealth of ancient Egypt, that of China and Indostan, sufficiently demonstrate 7 that a nation may attain a very high degree of opulence, though the greater part of its exportation trade be carried on by foreigners. The progress of our North American and West Indian colonies would have been much less rapid, had no capital but what belonged to themselves been employed in exporting their surplus produce.

So the natural course of things is first agriculture, then manufactures, and finally foreign commerce.

According to the natural course of things, therefore, the greater part of the capital of every growing society is, first, directed to agriculture, afterwards to manufactures, and last of all to foreign commerce. This order of things is so very natural, that in every society that had any territory, it has always, I believe, been in some degree observed. Some of their lands must have been cultivated before any considerable towns could be established, and some sort of coarse industry of the manufacturing kind must have been carried on in those towns, before they could well think of employing themselves in foreign commerce.

But this order has been in many respects inverted.

But though this natural order of things must have taken place in some degree in every such society, it has, in all the modern states of Europe, been, in many respects, entirely inverted. The foreign commerce of some of their cities has introduced all their finer manufactures, or such as were fit for distant sale; and manufactures and foreign commerce together, have given birth to the principal improvements of agriculture. The manners and customs which the nature of their original government introduced, and which remained after that government was greatly altered, necessarily forced them into this unnatural and retrograde order.

QUESTIONS FOR CRITICAL READING

1. How does manufacture eventually help agriculture?
2. Why is it more important to cultivate land than foreign trade?
3. What is special about the civilizations of Egypt, China, and Indostan?
4. Why did the American and West Indian colonies grow so rapidly?
5. In unpopulated countries, what is the natural way people treat the land?
6. How do the town manufactures profit from the country's surplus goods?
7. What is an artificer?

SUGGESTIONS FOR CRITICAL WRITING

1. Explain how you know that Smith favors country living over town life. What seems to be his opinion of each way of living?

2. Explain what Smith means by "subsistence is, in the nature of things, prior to conveniency and luxury, so the industry which procures the former, must necessarily be prior to that which ministers to the latter" (para. 2). Smith makes this claim several times. Is he correct even today?

3. Examine Smith's discussion and write an essay that takes issue with his conclusions. Base your argument on the changes that have occurred in world economy since Smith's time. How have things changed economically to render his arguments less valid or less applicable?

4. In paragraph 3, Smith talks about the "natural inclinations of man." What are they? What relevance do they have to Smith's argument? Have man's "natural inclinations" changed substantially since Smith wrote *Wealth of Nations*?

5. Smith says, "The town affords a market for the surplus produce of the country" (para. 1). What does he mean by this statement? Is it still true today? What are the implications of this statement for the theories that Smith attempts to establish? Why is a surplus essential for his theory on the natural progress of opulence to be persuasive?

6. **CONNECTIONS** Examine Thomas Jefferson's Declaration of Independence (p. 77) for issues that relate well to the questions that Smith raises. What are the economic and capitalist underpinnings of Jefferson's statements? In what ways does Jefferson agree or disagree with Smith's concepts of the development of opulence?

7. **CONNECTIONS** Smith is the most important theorist of capitalism prior to the twentieth century. How do his ideas contrast with Karl Marx's views (p. 359) about capitalism and how capitalists work? What would Marx take issue with in Smith's argument? What can you tell about the nature of capitalism in the worlds of Adam Smith in 1776 and of Karl Marx in 1850?

8. **CONNECTIONS** How does Robert B. Reich's analysis of the "new economy" (p. 419) alter the basic wisdom of Smith's views on the natural progress of an economy's development from agriculture to manufactures to foreign trade? What novelties in the "new economy" alter your view of Smith's theory?

9. **SEEING CONNECTIONS** Smith talks extensively about land, agriculture, and manufacturing. Were he to see *The Thankful Poor* (p. 344), what would he have imagined the people in Tanner's painting did for a living? Would he have thought they owned land? Would he have thought they worked in agriculture? Or would he have thought they worked in manufacturing? What evidence in the painting might suggest one or another of these possibilities? Smith is concerned with the production of wealth and tries to help people understand how to do it. What would his advice to the old man and the young boy be? What would he have said about the likelihood of these people achieving wealth?

KARL MARX
The Communist Manifesto

KARL MARX (1818–1883) was born in Germany to Jewish parents who converted to Lutheranism. A scholarly man, Marx studied literature and philosophy, ultimately earning a doctorate in philosophy at the University of Jena. After being denied a university position, however, he turned to journalism to earn a living.

Soon after beginning his journalistic career, Marx came into conflict with Prussian authorities because of his radical social views, and after a period of exile in Paris he moved to Brussels. After several more moves, Marx found his way to London, where he finally settled in absolute poverty; his friend Friedrich Engels (1820–1895) contributed money to prevent Marx and his family from starving. During this time in London, Marx wrote the books for which he is famous while also writing for and editing newspapers. His contributions to the *New York Daily Tribune* number over three hundred items between the years 1851 and 1862.

Marx is best known for his theories of socialism, as expressed in *The Communist Manifesto* (1848)—which, like much of his important work, was written with Engels's help—and in the three-volume *Das Kapital* (*Capital*), the first volume of which was published in 1867. In his own lifetime, he was not well known, nor were his ideas widely debated. Yet he was part of an ongoing movement composed mainly of intellectuals. Vladimir Lenin (1870–1924) was a disciple whose triumph in the Russian Revolution of 1917 catapulted Marx to the forefront of world thought. Since 1917, Marx's thinking has been scrupulously analyzed, debated, and argued. Capitalist thinkers have found him unconvincing, whereas Communist thinkers have found him a prophet and keen analyst of social structures.

Translated by Samuel Moore. Part III of *The Communist Manifesto*, "Socialist and Communist Literature," is omitted here.

In England, Marx's studies centered on the concept of an ongoing class struggle between those who owned property—the bourgeoisie—and those who owned nothing but whose work produced wealth—the proletariat. Marx was concerned with the forces of history, and his view of history was that it is progressive and, to an extent, inevitable. This view is prominent in *The Communist Manifesto*, particularly in Marx's review of the overthrow of feudal forms of government by the bourgeoisie. He thought it inevitable that the bourgeoisie and the proletariat would engage in a class struggle, from which the proletariat would emerge victorious. In essence, Marx took a materialist position. He denied the providence of God in the affairs of humans and defended the view that economic institutions evolve naturally and that, in their evolution, they control the social order. Thus, communism was an inevitable part of the process, and in the *Manifesto* he worked to clarify the reasons for its inevitability.

One of Marx's primary contentions was that capital is "not a personal, it is a social power" (para. 78). Thus, according to Marx, the "past dominates the present" (para. 83) because the accumulation of past capital determines how people will live in the present society. Capitalist economists, however, see capital as a personal power, but a power that, as John Kenneth Galbraith might say, should be used in a socially responsible way.

Marx's Rhetoric

The selection included here omits one section, the least important for the modern reader. The first section has a relatively simple rhetorical structure that depends on comparison. The title, "Bourgeois and Proletarians," tells us that the section will clarify the nature of each class and then go on to make some comparisons and contrasts. These concepts were by no means as widely discussed or thought about in 1848 as they are today, so Marx is careful to define his terms. At the same time, he establishes his theories regarding history by making further comparisons with class struggles in earlier ages.

Marx's style is simple and direct. He moves steadily from point to point, establishing his views on the nature of classes, on the nature of bourgeois society, and on the questions of industrialism and its effects on modern society. He considers wealth, worth, nationality, production, agriculture, and machinery. Each point is addressed in turn, usually in its own paragraph.

The organization of the next section, "Proletarians and Communists" (paras. 60–133), is not, despite its title, comparative in nature. Rather, with the proletariat defined as the class of the future, Marx tries to show that the Communist cause is the proletarian cause. In the process, Marx uses a clever rhetorical strategy. He assumes that he is addressed by an antagonist—presumably a bourgeois or a proletarian who is in sympathy with the bourgeoisie. He then proceeds to answer each popular complaint against communism. He shows that it is not a party separate from other workers' parties (para. 61). He clarifies the question of abolishing existing property relations (paras. 68–93). He emphasizes the antagonism between capital and wage labor (para. 76); he discusses the disappearance of culture (para. 94); he clarifies the questions of the family (paras. 98–100) and of the exploitation of children (para. 101). He brings up the new system of public education (paras. 102–4). He raises the touchy issue of the "community of women" (paras. 105–10), as well as the charge that Communists want to abolish nations (paras. 111–15). He brushes aside religion (para. 116). When he is done with the complaints, he gives us a rhetorical signal: "But let us have done with the bourgeois objections to Communism" (para. 126).

The rest of the second section contains a brief summary, and then Marx presents his ten-point program (para. 131). The structure is simple, direct, and effective. In the process of answering the charges against communism, Marx is able to clarify exactly what it is and what it promises. In contrast to his earlier arguments, the ten points of his communist program seem clear, easy, and (again by contrast) almost acceptable. Although the style is not dashing (despite a few memorable lines), the rhetorical structure is extraordinarily effective for the purposes at hand.

In the last section (paras. 135–45), in which Marx compares the Communists with other reform groups such as those agitating for redistribution of land and other agrarian reforms, he indicates that the Communists are everywhere fighting alongside existing groups for the rights of people who are oppressed by their societies. As Marx says, "In short, the Communists everywhere support every revolutionary movement against the existing social and political order of things" (para. 141). Nothing could be a more plain and direct declaration of sympathies.

PREREADING QUESTIONS: WHAT TO READ FOR

The following prereading questions may help you anticipate key issues in the discussion of Karl Marx's *Communist Manifesto*. Keeping them in mind during your first reading of the selection should help focus your attention.

- What is the economic condition of the bourgeoisie? What is the economic condition of the proletariat?

- How does the expanding world market for goods affect national identity?

- What benefits does Marx expect communism to provide the proletariat?

The Communist Manifesto

A specter is haunting Europe—the specter of Communism. All the Powers of old Europe have entered into a holy alliance to exorcise this specter; Pope and Czar, Metternich[1] and Guizot,[2] French Radicals[3] and German police-spies. 1

Where is the party in opposition that has not been decried as communistic by its opponents in power? Where the Opposition that has not hurled back the branding reproach of Communism against the more advanced opposition parties, as well as against its reactionary adversaries? 2

Two things result from this fact. 3

I. Communism is already acknowledged by all European Powers to be itself a Power. 4

II. It is high time that Communists should openly, in the face of the whole world, publish their views, their aims, their tendencies, and meet this nursery tale of the specter of Communism with a Manifesto of the party itself. 5

To this end, Communists of various nationalities have assembled in London and sketched the following Manifesto, to be published in the English, French, German, Italian, Flemish, and Danish languages. 6

---

[1] **Prince Klemens von Metternich (1773–1859)** Foreign minister of Austria (1809–1848), who had a hand in establishing the peace after the final defeat in 1815 of Napoleon (1769–1821); Metternich was highly influential in the crucial Congress of Vienna (1814–1815).

[2] **François Pierre Guizot (1787–1874)** Conservative French statesman, author, and philosopher. Like Metternich, he was opposed to communism.

[3] **French Radicals** Actually middle-class liberals who wanted a return to a republic in 1848 after the eighteen-year reign of Louis-Philippe (1773–1850), the "citizen king."

Bourgeois and Proletarians[4]

The history of all hitherto existing society is the history of class   7
struggles.

Freeman and slave, patrician and plebeian, lord and serf, guild-   8
master and journeyman, in a word, oppressor and oppressed, stood in
constant opposition to one another, carried on uninterrupted, now
hidden, now open fight, a fight that each time ended, either in a revolutionary re-constitution of society at large, or in the common ruin of
the contending classes.

In the earlier epochs of history we find almost everywhere a   9
complicated arrangement of society into various orders, a manifold
gradation of social rank. In ancient Rome we have patricians, knights,
plebeians, slaves; in the Middle Ages, feudal lords, vassals, guild-
masters, journeymen, apprentices, serfs; in almost all of these classes,
again, subordinate gradations.

The modern bourgeois society that has sprouted from the ruins of   10
feudal society, has not done away with class antagonisms. It has but
established new classes, new conditions of oppression, new forms of
struggle in place of the old ones.

Our epoch, the epoch of the bourgeoisie, possesses, however, this   11
distinctive feature; it has simplified the class antagonisms. Society as a
whole is more and more splitting up into two great hostile camps, into
two great classes directly facing each other: Bourgeoisie and Proletariat.

From the serfs of the Middle Ages sprang the chartered burghers   12
of the earliest towns. From these burgesses the first elements of the
bourgeoisie were developed.

The discovery of America, the rounding of the Cape,[5] opened   13
up fresh ground for the rising bourgeoisie. The East Indian and
Chinese markets, the colonization of America, trade with the
colonies, the increase in the means of exchange and in commodities
generally, gave to commerce, to navigation, to industry, an impulse
never before known, and thereby, to the revolutionary element in
the tottering feudal society, a rapid development.

The feudal system of industry, under which industrial production   14
was monopolized by closed guilds, now no longer sufficed for the

---

[4] By bourgeois is meant the class of modern Capitalists, owners of the means of
social production and employers of wage labor. By proletarians, the class of modern
wage laborers who, having no means of production of their own, are reduced to selling their labor-power in order to live. [Engels's note]

[5] **the Cape** The Cape of Good Hope, at the southern tip of Africa. This was a
main sea route for trade with India and the Orient. Europe profited immensely from
the opening up of these new markets in the sixteenth century.

growing wants of the new market. The manufacturing system took its place. The guild-masters were pushed on one side by the manufacturing middle-class: division of labor between the different corporate guilds vanished in the face of division of labor in each single workshop.

Meantime the markets kept ever growing, the demand ever rising. Even manufacture no longer sufficed. Thereupon, steam and machinery revolutionized industrial production. The place of manufacture was taken by the giant, Modern Industry, the place of the industrial middle-class, by industrial millionaires, the leaders of whole industrial armies, the modern bourgeois. 15

Modern industry has established the world-market, for which the discovery of America paved the way. This market has given an immense development to commerce, to navigation, to communication by land. This development has, in its turn, reacted on the extension of industry; and in proportion as industry, commerce, navigation, railways extended, in the same proportion the bourgeoisie developed, increased its capital, and pushed into the background every class handed down from the Middle Ages. 16

We see, therefore, how the modern bourgeoisie is itself the product of a long course of development, of a series of revolutions in the modes of production and of exchange. 17

Each step in the development of the bourgeoisie was accompanied by a corresponding political advance of that class. An oppressed class under the sway of the feudal nobility, an armed and self-governing association in the medieval commune,[6] here independent urban republic (as in Italy and Germany), there taxable "third estate"[7] of the monarchy (as in France), afterwards, in the period of manufacture proper, serving either the semi-feudal or the absolute monarchy as a counterpoise against nobility, and, in fact, corner stone of the great monarchies in general, the bourgeoisie has at last, since the establishment of Modern Industry and of the world-market, conquered for itself, in the modern representative State, exclusive political sway. The executive of the modern State is but a committee for managing the common affairs of the whole bourgeoisie. 18

The bourgeoisie, historically, has played a most revolutionary part. 19

The bourgeoisie, wherever it has got the upper hand, has put an end to all feudal, patriarchal, idyllic relations. It has pitilessly torn asunder the motley feudal ties that bound man to his "natural superiors," and has left no other nexus between man and man than 20

---

[6] **the medieval commune** Refers to the growth in the eleventh century of towns whose economy was highly regulated by mutual interest and agreement.

[7] **"third estate"** The clergy was the first estate, the aristocracy the second estate, and the bourgeoisie the third estate.

naked self-interest, than callous "cash payment." It has drowned the most heavenly ecstasies of religious fervor,[8] of chivalrous enthusiasm, of Philistine sentimentalism, in the icy water of egotistical calculation. It has resolved personal worth into exchange value, and in place of the numberless indefeasible chartered freedoms, has set up that single, unconscionable freedom—Free Trade. In one word, for exploitation, veiled by religious and political illusions, it has substituted naked, shameless, direct, brutal exploitation.

The bourgeoisie has stripped of its halo every occupation hith- 21
erto honored and looked up to with reverent awe. It has converted the physician, the lawyer, the priest, the poet, the man of science, into its paid wage laborers.

The bourgeoisie has torn away from the family its sentimental 22
veil, and has reduced the family relation to a mere money relation.

The bourgeoisie has disclosed how it came to pass that the brutal 23
display of vigor in the Middle Ages, which reactionists so much admire, found its fitting complement in the most slothful indolence. It has been the first to show what man's activity can bring about. It has accomplished wonders far surpassing Egyptian pyramids, Roman aqueducts, and Gothic cathedrals; it has conducted expeditions that put in the shade all former Exoduses of nations and crusades.

The bourgeoisie cannot exist without constantly revolutionizing 24
the instruments of production, and thereby the relations of production, and with them the whole relations of society. Conservation of the old modes of production in unaltered form was, on the contrary, the first condition of existence for all earlier industrial classes. Constant revolutionizing of production, uninterrupted disturbance of all social conditions, everlasting uncertainty and agitation distinguish the bourgeois epoch from all earlier ones. All fixed, fast frozen relations, with their train of ancient and venerable prejudices and opinions, are swept away, all new formed ones become antiquated before they can ossify. All that is solid melts into the air, all that is holy is profaned, and man is at last compelled to face with sober senses, his real conditions of life, and his relations with his kind.

The need of a constantly expanding market for its products 25
chases the bourgeoisie over the whole surface of the globe. It must

---

[8] **religious fervor** This and other terms in this sentence contain a compressed historical observation. "Religious fervor" refers to the Middle Ages; "chivalrous enthusiasm" refers to the rise of the secular state and to the military power of knights; "Philistine sentimentalism" refers to the development of popular arts and literature in the sixteenth, seventeenth, and eighteenth centuries. "Philistine" refers to those who were generally uncultured, that is, the general public. "Sentimentalism" is a code word for the encouragement of emotional response rather than rational thought.

nestle everywhere, settle everywhere, establish connections everywhere.

The bourgeoisie has through its exploitation of the world-market   26
given a cosmopolitan character to production and consumption in
every country. To the great chagrin of reactionists, it has drawn from
under the feet of industry the national ground on which it stood. All
old-established national industries have been destroyed or are daily
being destroyed. They are dislodged by new industries, whose introduction becomes a life and death question for all civilized nations,
by industries that no longer work up indigenous raw material, but
raw material drawn from the remotest zones; industries whose
products are consumed, not only at home, but in every quarter of
the globe. In place of the old wants, satisfied by the productions
of the country, we find new wants, requiring for their satisfaction
the products of distant lands and climes. In place of the old local
and national seclusion and self-sufficiency, we have intercourse in
every direction, universal interdependence of nations. And as in
material, so also in intellectual production. The intellectual creations
of individual nations become common property. National onesided-
ness and narrowmindedness become more and more impossible,
and from the numerous national and local literatures there arises a
world-literature.

The bourgeoisie, by the rapid improvement of all instruments of   27
production, by the immensely facilitated means of communication,
draws all, even the most barbarian nations into civilization. The
cheap prices of its commodities are the heavy artillery with which it
batters down all Chinese walls, with which it forces the barbarians'
intensely obstinate hatred of foreigners to capitulate. It compels all
nations, on pain of extinction, to adopt the bourgeois mode of production; it compels them to introduce what it calls civilization into their
midst, i.e., to become bourgeois themselves. In a word, it creates a
world after its own image.

The bourgeoisie has subjected the country to the rule of the   28
towns. It has created enormous cities, has greatly increased the
urban population as compared with the rural and has thus rescued a
considerable part of the population from the idiocy of rural life. Just
as it has made the country dependent on the towns, so it has made
barbarian and semi-barbarian countries dependent on civilized
ones, nations of peasants on nations of bourgeois, the East on the
West.

The bourgeoisie keeps more and more doing away with the   29
scattered state of the population, of the means of production, and
of property. It has agglomerated population, centralized means of

production, and has concentrated property in a few hands. The necessary consequence of this was political centralization. Independent, or but loosely connected provinces, with separate interests, laws, governments, and systems of taxation, became lumped together in one nation, with one government, one code of laws, one national class interest, one frontier, and one customs tariff.

The bourgeoisie, during its rule of scarce one hundred years, 30 has created more massive and more colossal productive forces than have all preceding generations together. Subjection of Nature's forces to man, machinery, application of chemistry to industry and agriculture, steam-navigation, railways, electric telegraphs, clearing of whole continents for cultivation, canalization of rivers, whole populations conjured out of the ground—what earlier century had even a presentiment that such productive forces slumbered in the lap of social labor?

We see then: the means of production and of exchange on whose 31 foundation the bourgeoisie built itself up, were generated in feudal society. At a certain stage in the development of these means of production and of exchange, the conditions under which feudal society produced and exchanged, the feudal organization of agriculture and manufacturing industry, in one word, the feudal relations of property became no longer compatible with the already developed productive forces; they became so many fetters. They had to burst asunder; they were burst asunder.

Into their place stepped free competition, accompanied by a 32 social and political constitution adapted to it, and by the economical and political sway of the bourgeois class.

A similar movement is going on before our own eyes. Modern 33 bourgeois society with its relations of production, of exchange and of property, a society that has conjured up such gigantic means of production and of exchange, is like the sorcerer, who is no longer able to control the powers of the nether world whom he has called up by his spells. For many a decade past, the history of industry and commerce is but the history of the revolt of modern productive forces against modern conditions of production, against the property relations that are the conditions for the existence of the bourgeoisie and of its rule. It is enough to mention the commercial crises that by their periodical return put on its trial, each time more threateningly, the existence of the entire bourgeois society. In these crises a great part not only of the existing products, but also of the previously created productive forces, are periodically destroyed. In these crises there breaks out an epidemic that, in all earlier epochs, would have seemed an absurdity— the epidemic of overproduction. Society suddenly finds itself put back into a state of momentary barbarism; it appears as if a famine, a universal war of devastation, had cut off the supply of every means of subsistence; industry and commerce seem to be destroyed; and why? Because there is too much civilization, too much means of subsistence, too much industry, too much commerce. The productive forces at the disposal of society no longer tend to further the development of the conditions of the bourgeois property; on the contrary, they have become too powerful for these conditions by which they are fettered, and as soon as they overcome these fetters they bring disorder into the whole of bourgeois society, endanger the existence of bourgeois property. The conditions of bourgeois society are too narrow to comprise the wealth created by them. And how does the bourgeoisie get over these crises? On the one hand by enforced destruction of a mass of productive forces; on the other, by the conquest of new markets, and by the more thorough exploitation of the old ones. That is to say, by paving the way for more extensive and more destructive crises, and by diminishing the means whereby crises are prevented.

The weapons with which the bourgeoisie felled feudalism to the ground are now turned against the bourgeoisie itself. 34

But not only has the bourgeoisie forged the weapons that bring death to itself; it has also called into existence the men who are to wield those weapons—the modern working class—the proletarians. 35

In proportion as the bourgeoisie, i.e., capital, is developed, in the same proportion is the proletariat, the modern working class, developed, a class of laborers who live only so long as they find work, and who find work only so long as their labor increases capital. These laborers, who must sell themselves piecemeal, are a commodity, like every other article of commerce, and are consequently exposed to all the vicissitudes of competition, to all the fluctuations of the market. 36

Owing to the extensive use of machinery and to division of labor, the work of the proletarians has lost all individual character, and, consequently, all charm for the workman. He becomes an appendage of the machine, and it is only the most simple, most monotonous and most easily acquired knack that is required of him. Hence, the cost of production of a workman is restricted almost entirely to the means of subsistence that he requires for his maintenance, and for the propagation of his race. But the price of a commodity, and also of labor, is equal to its cost of production. In proportion, therefore, as the repulsiveness of the work increases the wage decreases. Nay more, in proportion as the use of machinery and division of labor increases, in the same proportion the burden of toil increases, whether by prolongation of the working hours, by 37 increase of the work enacted in a given time, or by increased speed of the machinery, etc.

Modern industry has converted the little workshop of the patri-   38
archal master into the great factory of the industrial capitalist. Masses of laborers, crowded into factories, are organized like soldiers. As privates of the industrial army they are placed under the command of a perfect hierarchy of officers and sergeants. Not only are they the slaves of the bourgeois class and of the bourgeois state, they are daily and hourly enslaved by the machine, by the overlooker, and, above all, by the individual bourgeois manufacturer himself. The more openly this despotism proclaims gain to be its end and aim, the more petty, the more hateful and the more embittering it is.

The less the skill and exertion or strength implied in manual   39
labor, in other words, the more modern industry becomes developed, the more is the labor of men superseded by that of women. Differences of age and sex have no longer any distinctive social validity for the working class. All are instruments of labor, more or less expensive to use, according to their age and sex.

No sooner is the exploitation of the laborer by the manufacturer,   40
so far at an end, that he receives his wages in cash, than he is set upon by the other portions of the bourgeoisie, the landlord, the shopkeeper, the pawnbroker, etc.

The lower strata of the middle class—the small trades-people,   41
shopkeepers and retired tradesmen generally, the handicraftsmen, and peasants—all these sink gradually into the proletariat, partly because their diminutive capital does not suffice for the scale on which Modern Industry is carried on, and is swamped in the competition with the large capitalists, partly because their specialized skill is rendered worthless by new methods of production. Thus the proletariat is recruited from all classes of the population.

The proletariat goes through various stages of development.   42
With its birth begins its struggle with the bourgeoisie. At first the contest is carried on by individual laborers, then by the workpeople of a factory, then by the operatives of one trade, in one locality, against the individual bourgeois who directly exploits them. They direct their attacks not against the bourgeois conditions of production, but against the instruments of production themselves; they destroy imported wares that compete with their labor, they smash to pieces machinery, they set factories ablaze, they seek to restore by force the vanished status of the workman of the Middle Ages.

At this stage the laborers still form an incoherent mass scattered   43
over the whole country, and broken up by their mutual competition. If anywhere they unite to form more compact bodies, this is

not yet the consequence of their own active union, but of the union of the bourgeoisie, which class, in order to attain its own political ends, is compelled to set the whole proletariat in motion, and is moreover yet, for a time, able to do so. At this stage, therefore, the proletarians do not fight their enemies, but the enemies of their enemies, the remnants of absolute monarchy, the landowners, the non-industrial bourgeois, the petty bourgeoisie. Thus the whole historical movement is concentrated in the hands of the bourgeoisie, every victory so obtained is a victory for the bourgeoisie.

But with the development of industry the proletariat not only increases in number; it becomes concentrated in greater masses, its strength grows and it feels that strength more. The various interests and conditions of life within the ranks of the proletariat are more and more equalized, in proportion as machinery obliterates all distinctions of labor, and nearly everywhere reduces wages to the same low level. The growing competition among the bourgeois, and the resulting commercial crisis, make the wages of the workers even more fluctuating. The unceasing improvement of machinery, ever more rapidly developing, makes their livelihood more and more precarious; the collisions between individual workmen and individual bourgeois take more and more the character of collisions between two classes. Thereupon the workers begin to form combinations (Trades' Unions)[9] against the bourgeois; they club together in order to keep up the rate of wages; they found permanent associations in order to make provision beforehand for these occasional revolts. Here and there the contest breaks out into riots. 44

Now and then the workers are victorious, but only for a time. The real fruit of their battle lies not in the immediate result but in the ever-expanding union of workers. This union is helped on by the improved means of communication that are created by modern industry, and that places the workers of different localities in contact with one another. It was just this contact that was needed to centralize the numerous local struggles, all of the same character, into one national struggle between classes. But every class struggle is a political struggle. And that union, to attain which the burghers of the Middle Ages with their miserable highways, required centuries, the modern proletarians, thanks to railways, achieve in a few years. 45

This organization of the proletarians into a class, and consequently into a political party, is continually being upset again by the 46

---

[9] **combinations (Trades' Unions)** The labor movement was only beginning in 1848. It consisted of trades' unions that started as social clubs but soon began agitating for labor reform. They represented an important step in the growth of socialism in Europe.

competition between the workers themselves. But it ever rises up again, stronger, firmer, mightier. It compels legislative recognition of particular interests of the workers by taking advantage of the divisions among the bourgeoisie itself. Thus the ten hours' bill in England[10] was carried.

Altogether collisions between the classes of the old society further, in many ways, the course of development of the proletariat. The bourgeoisie finds itself involved in a constant battle. At first with the aristocracy; later on, with those portions of the bourgeoisie itself whose interests have become antagonistic to the progress of industry; at all times, with the bourgeoisie of foreign countries. In all these battles it sees itself compelled to appeal to the proletariat, to ask for its help, and thus, to drag it into the political arena. The bourgeoisie itself, therefore, supplies the proletariat with its own elements of political and general education; in other words, it furnishes the proletariat with weapons for fighting the bourgeoisie.   47

Further, as we have already seen, entire sections of the ruling classes are, by the advance of industry, precipitated into the proletariat, or are at least threatened in their conditions of existence. These also supply the proletariat with fresh elements of enlightenment and progress.   48

Finally, in times when the class struggle nears the decisive hour, the process of dissolution going on within the ruling class—in fact, within the whole range of an old society—assumes such a violent, glaring character that a small section of the ruling class cuts itself adrift and joins the revolutionary class, the class that holds the future in its hands. Just as, therefore, at an earlier period, a section of the nobility went over to the bourgeoisie, so now a portion of the bourgeoisie goes over to the proletariat, and in particular, a portion of the bourgeois ideologists, who have raised themselves to the level of comprehending theoretically the historical movements as a whole.   49

Of all the classes that stand face to face with the bourgeoisie today the proletariat alone is a really revolutionary class. The other classes decay and finally disappear in the face of Modern Industry; the proletariat is its special and essential product.   50

The lower middle class, the small manufacturer, the shopkeeper, the artisan, the peasant, all these fight against the bourgeoisie, to save from extinction their existence as fractions of the   51

---

[10] **the ten hours' bill in England** This bill (1847) was an important labor reform. It limited the working day for women and children in factories to only ten hours, at a time when it was common for some people to work sixteen hours a day. The bill's passage was a result of political division, not of benevolence on the managers' part.

middle class. They are therefore not revolutionary, but conservative. Nay, more; they are reactionary, for they try to roll back the wheel of history. If by chance they are revolutionary, they are so only in view of their impending transfer into the proletariat; they thus defend not their present, but their future interests; they desert their own standpoint to place themselves at that of the proletariat.

The "dangerous class," the social scum, that passively rotting   52
mass thrown off by the lowest layers of old society, may, here and there, be swept into the movement by a proletarian revolution; its conditions of life, however, prepare it far more for the part of a bribed tool of reactionary intrigue.

In the conditions of the proletariat, those of the old society at large   53
are already virtually swamped. The proletarian is without property; his relation to his wife and children has no longer anything in common with the bourgeois family relations; modern industrial labor, modern subjection to capital, the same in England as in France, in America as in Germany, has stripped him of every trace of national character. Law, morality, religion, are to him so many bourgeois prejudices, behind which lurk in ambush just as many bourgeois interests.

All the preceding classes that got the upper hand sought to for-   54
tify their already acquired status by subjecting society at large to their conditions of appropriation. The proletarians cannot become masters of the productive forces of society, except by abolishing their own previous mode of appropriation, and thereby also every other previous mode of appropriation. They have nothing of their own to secure and to fortify; their mission is to destroy all previous securities for and insurances of individual property.

All previous historical movements were movements of minori-   55
ties, or in the interest of minorities. The proletarian movement is the self-conscious, independent movement of the immense majority. The proletariat, the lowest stratum of our present society, cannot stir, cannot raise itself up without the whole superincumbent strata of official society being sprung into the air.

Though not in substance, yet in form, the struggle of the prole-   56
tariat with the bourgeoisie is at first a national struggle. The prole-tariat of each country must, of course, first of all settle matters with its own bourgeoisie.

In depicting the most general phases of the development of the   57
proletariat, we traced the more or less veiled civil war, raging within existing society, up to the point where that war breaks out into open revolution, and where the violent overthrow of the bourgeoisie, lays the foundations for the sway of the proletariat.

Hitherto every form of society has been based, as we have   58
already seen, on the antagonism of oppressing and oppressed classes.

But in order to oppress a class, certain conditions must be assured to it under which it can, at least, continue its slavish existence. The serf, in the period of serfdom, raised himself to membership in the commune, just as the petty bourgeois, under the yoke of feudal absolutism, managed to develop into a bourgeois. The modern laborer, on the contrary, instead of rising with the progress of industry, sinks deeper and deeper below the conditions of existence of his own class. He becomes a pauper, and pauperism develops more rapidly than population and wealth. And here it becomes evident that the bourgeoisie is unfit any longer to be the ruling class in society, and to impose its conditions of existence upon society as an over-riding law. It is unfit to rule, because it is incompetent to assure an existence to its slave within his slavery, because it cannot help letting him sink into such a state that it has to feed him, instead of being fed by him. Society can no longer live under this bourgeoisie; in other words, its existence is no longer compatible with society.

The essential condition for the existence, and for the sway of the 59
bourgeois class, is the formation and augmentation of capital; the condition for capital is wage labor. Wage labor rests exclusively on competition between the laborers. The advance of industry, whose involuntary promoter is the bourgeoisie, replaces the isolation of the laborers, due to competition, by their involuntary combination, due to association. The development of Modern Industry, therefore, cuts from under its feet the very foundation on which the bourgeoisie produces and appropriates products. What the bourgeoisie therefore produces, above all, are its own grave diggers. Its fall and the victory of the proletariat are equally inevitable.

Proletarians and Communists

In what relation do the Communists stand to the proletarians as 60
a whole?

The Communists do not form a separate party opposed to other 61
working class parties.

They have no interests separate and apart from those of the pro- 62
letariat as a whole.

They do not set up any sectarian principles of their own, by 63
which to shape and mold the proletarian movement.

The Communists are distinguished from the other working class 64
parties by this only: 1. In the national struggles of the proletarians of the different countries, they point out and bring to the front the common interests of the entire proletariat, independently of all nationality. 2. In the various stages of development which the struggle of the

working class against the bourgeoisie has to pass through, they always and everywhere represent the interests of the movement as a whole.

The Communists, therefore, are on the one hand practically the   65
most advanced and resolute section of the working class parties of every country, that section which pushes forward all others; on the other hand, theoretically, they have over the great mass of the proletariat the advantage of clearly understanding the line of march, the conditions, and the ultimate general results of the proletarian movement.

The immediate aim of the Communists is the same as that of all   66
the other proletarian parties: formation of the proletariat into a class, overthrow of the bourgeois of supremacy, conquest of political power by the proletariat.

The theoretical conclusions of the Communists are in no way   67
based on ideas or principles that have been invented or discovered by this or that would-be universal reformer.

They merely express, in general terms, actual relations springing   68
from an existing class struggle, from a historical movement going on under our very eyes. The abolition of existing property relations is not at all a distinctive feature of Communism.

All property relations in the past have continually been subject to   69
historical change consequent upon the change in historical conditions.

The French Revolution, for example, abolished feudal property   70
in favor of bourgeois property.

The distinguishing feature of Communism is not the abolition   71
of property generally, but the abolition of bourgeois property. But modern bourgeois private property is the final and most complete expression of the system of producing and appropriating products, that is based on class antagonism, on the exploitation of the many by the few.

In this sense, the theory of the Communists may be summed up   72
in the single sentence: abolition of private property.

We Communists have been reproached with the desire of abol-   73
ishing the right of personally acquiring property as the fruit of a man's own labor, which property is alleged to be the groundwork of all personal freedom, activity and independence.

Hard won, self-acquired, self-earned property! Do you mean the   74
property of the petty artisan and of the small peasant, a form of property that preceded the bourgeois form? There is no need to abolish that; the development of industry has to a great extent already destroyed it, and is still destroying it daily.

Or do you mean modern bourgeois private property?   75

But does wage labor create any property for the laborer? Not a   76
bit. It creates capital, i.e., that kind of property which exploits wage

labor, and which cannot increase except upon condition of getting a new supply of wage labor for fresh exploitation. Property, in its present form, is based on the antagonism of capital and wage labor. Let us examine both sides of this antagonism.

To be a capitalist is to have not only a purely personal, but a 77 social status in production. Capital is a collective product, and only by the united action of many members, nay, in the last resort, only by the united action of all members of society, can it be set in motion.

Capital is therefore not a personal, it is a social power. 78

When, therefore, capital is converted into common property, 79 into the property of all members of society, personal property is not thereby transformed into social property. It is only the social character of the property that is changed. It loses its class character.

Let us now take wage labor. 80

The average price of wage labor is the minimum wage, i.e., that 81 quantum of the means of subsistence which is absolutely requisite to keep the laborer in bare existence as a laborer. What, therefore, the wage laborer appropriates by means of his labor, merely suffices to prolong and reproduce a bare existence. We by no means intend to abolish this personal appropriation of the products of labor, an appropriation that is made for the maintenance and reproduction of human life, and that leaves no surplus wherewith to command the labor of others. All that we want to do away with is the miserable character of this appropriation, under which the laborer lives merely to increase capital and is allowed to live only in so far as the interests of the ruling class require it.

In bourgeois society, living labor is but a means to increase 82 accumulated labor. In Communist society accumulated labor is but a means to widen, to enrich, to promote the existence of the laborer.

In bourgeois society, therefore, the past dominates the present; 83 in Communist society the present dominates the past. In bourgeois society, capital is independent and has individuality, while the living person is dependent and has no individuality.

And the abolition of this state of things is called by the bour- 84 geois abolition of individuality and freedom! And rightly so. The abolition of bourgeois individuality, bourgeois independence and bourgeois freedom is undoubtedly aimed at.

By freedom is meant, under the present bourgeois conditions of 85 production, free trade, free selling and buying.

But if selling and buying disappears, free selling and buying dis- 86 appears also. This talk about free selling and buying, and all the other "brave words" of our bourgeoisie about freedom in general have a meaning, if any, only in contrast with restricted selling and buying, with the fettered traders of the Middle Ages, but have no meaning when opposed to the Communistic abolition of buying and selling, of the bourgeois conditions of production, and of the bourgeoisie itself.

You are horrified at our intending to do away with private prop-   87
erty. But in your existing society private property is already done away with for nine-tenths of the population; its existence for the few is solely due to its non-existence in the hands of those nine-tenths. You reproach us, therefore, with intending to do away with a form of property, the necessary condition for whose existence is the non-existence of any property for the immense majority of society.

In one word, you reproach us with intending to do away with   88
your property. Precisely so: that is just what we intend.

From the moment when labor can no longer be converted into   89
capital, money, or rent, into a social power capable of being monopolized, i.e., from the moment when individual property can no longer be transformed into bourgeois property, into capital, from that moment, you say, individuality vanishes.

You must, therefore, confess that by "individual" you mean no   90
other person than the bourgeois, than the middle-class owner of property. This person must, indeed, be swept out of the way and made impossible.

Communism deprives no man of the power to appropriate the   91
products of society: all that it does is to deprive him of the power to subjugate the labor of others by means of such appropriation.

It has been objected that upon the abolition of private property   92
all work will cease and universal laziness will overtake us.

According to this, bourgeois society ought long ago to have   93
gone to the dogs through sheer idleness; for those of its members who work acquire nothing, and those who acquire anything do not work. The whole of this objection is but another expression of the tautology:[11] that there can no longer be any wage labor when there is no longer any capital.

All objections urged against the Communistic mode of produc-   94
ing and appropriating material products have, in the same way, been urged against the Communistic modes of producing and appropriating intellectual products. Just as, to the bourgeois, the disappearance of class property is the disappearance of production itself, so the disappearance of class culture is to him identical with the disappearance of all culture.

That culture, the loss of which he laments, is, for the enormous   95
majority, a mere training to act as a machine.

---

[11] **tautology** A statement whose two parts say essentially the same thing. The second half of the previous sentence is a tautology.

But don't wrangle with us so long as you apply, to our intended 96 abolition of bourgeois property, the standard of your bourgeois notions of freedom, culture, law, etc. Your very ideas are but the outgrowth of the conditions of your bourgeois production and bourgeois property, just as your jurisprudence is but the will of your class made into a law for all, a will whose essential character and direction are determined by the economical conditions of existence of your class.

The selfish misconception that induces you to transform into 97 eternal laws of nature and of reason the social forms springing from your present mode of production and form of property—historical relations that rise and disappear in the progress of production—this misconception you share with every ruling class that has preceded you. What you see clearly in the case of ancient property, what you admit in the case of feudal property, you are of course forbidden to admit in the case of your own bourgeois form of property.

Abolition of the family! Even the most radical flare up at this 98 infamous proposal of the Communists.

On what foundation is the present family, the bourgeois family, 99 based? On capital, on private gain. In its completely developed form this family exists only among the bourgeoisie. But this state of things finds its complement in the practical absence of the family among the proletarians, and in public prostitution.

The bourgeois family will vanish as a matter of course when its 100 complement vanishes, and both will vanish with the vanishing of capital.

Do you charge us with wanting to stop the exploitation of chil- 101 dren by their parents? To this crime we plead guilty.

But, you will say, we destroy the most hallowed of relations 102 when we replace home education by social.

And your education! Is not that also social, and determined by 103 the social conditions under which you educate; by the intervention, direct or indirect, of society by means of schools, etc.? The Communists have not invented the intervention of society in education; they do but seek to alter the character of that intervention, and to rescue education from the influence of the ruling class.

The bourgeois clap-trap about the family and education, about 104 the hallowed correlation of parent and child, become all the more disgusting, the more, by the action of Modern Industry, all family ties among the proletarians are torn asunder and their children transformed into simple articles of commerce and instruments of labor.

But you Communists would introduce community of women, 105 screams the whole bourgeoisie chorus.

The bourgeois sees in his wife a mere instrument of production. 106 He hears that the instruments of production are to be exploited in

common, and, naturally, can come to no other conclusion, than that
the lot of being common to all will likewise fall to the women.

He has not even a suspicion that the real point aimed at is to do   107
away with the status of women as mere instruments of production.

For the rest, nothing is more ridiculous than the virtuous indig-   108
nation of our bourgeois at the community of women which, they
pretend, is to be openly and officially established by the Communists.
The Communists have no need to introduce community of women, it
has existed almost from time immemorial.

Our bourgeois, not content with having the wives and daughters   109
of their proletarians at their disposal, not to speak of common prostitutes, take the greatest pleasure in seducing each others' wives.

Bourgeois marriage is in reality a system of wives in common, and   110
thus, at the most, what the Communists might possibly be reproached
with, is that they desire to introduce, in substitution for a hypocritically
concealed, an openly legalized community of women. For the rest, it is
self-evident that the abolition of the present system of production must
bring with it the abolition of the community of women springing from
that system, i.e., of prostitution both public and private.

The Communists are further reproached with desiring to abolish   111
countries and nationalities.

The working men have no country. We cannot take from them   112
what they don't possess. Since the proletariat must first of all acquire
political supremacy, must rise to be the leading class of the nation,
must constitute itself the nation, it is, so far, itself national, though
not in the bourgeois sense of the word.

National differences and antagonisms between peoples are daily   113
more and more vanishing, owing to the development of the bourgeoisie, to freedom of commerce, to the world-market, to uniformity
in the mode of production and in the conditions of life corresponding thereto.

The supremacy of the proletariat will cause them to vanish still   114
faster. United action, of the leading civilized countries at least, is one
of the first conditions for the emancipation of the proletariat.

In proportion as the exploitation of one individual by another is   115
put an end to, the exploitation of one nation by another will also be put
an end to. In proportion as the antagonism between classes within
the nation vanishes, the hostility of one nation to another will come
to an end.

The charges against Communism made from a religious, a   116
philosophical, and generally, from an ideological standpoint, are not
deserving of serious examination.

Does it require deep intuition to comprehend that man's ideas,   117
views, and conceptions, in one word, man's consciousness, changes

with every change in the conditions of his material existence, in his social relations and in his social life?

What else does the history of ideas prove than that intellectual 118 production changes in character in proportion as material production is changed? The ruling ideas of each age have ever been the ideas of its ruling class.

When people speak of ideas that revolutionize society they do but 119 express the fact that within the old society the elements of a new one have been created, and that the dissolution of the old ideas keeps even pace with the dissolution of the old conditions of existence.

When the ancient world was in its last throes the ancient religions 120 were overcome by Christianity. When Christian ideas succumbed in the eighteenth century to rationalist ideas, feudal society fought its death battle with the then revolutionary bourgeoisie. The ideas of religious liberty and freedom of conscience merely gave expression to the sway of free competition within the domain of knowledge.

"Undoubtedly," it will be said, "religious, moral, philosophical, 121 and judicial ideas have been modified in the course of historical development. But religion, morality, philosophy, political science, and law, constantly survived this change.

"There are, besides, eternal truths such as Freedom, Justice, etc., 122 that are common to all states of society. But Communism abolishes eternal truths, it abolishes all religion and all morality, instead of constituting them on a new basis; it therefore acts in contradiction to all past historical experience."

What does this accusation reduce itself to? The history of all 123 past society has consisted in the development of class antagonisms, antagonisms that assumed different forms at different epochs.

But whatever form they may have taken, one fact is common to 124 all past ages, viz., the exploitation of one part of society by the other. No wonder, then, that the social consciousness of past ages, despite all the multiplicity and variety it displays, moves within certain common forms, or general ideas, which cannot completely vanish except with the total disappearance of class antagonisms.

The Communist revolution is the most radical rupture with tra- 125 ditional property relations; no wonder that its development involves the most radical rupture with traditional ideas.

But let us have done with the bourgeois objections to Com- 126 munism.

We have seen above that the first step in the revolution by the 127 working class is to raise the proletariat to the position of ruling class, to win the battle of democracy.

The proletariat will use its political supremacy to wrest, by 128 degrees, all capital from the bourgeoisie, to centralize all instruments

of production in the hands of the State, i.e., of the proletariat organized as a ruling class; and to increase the total productive forces as
rapidly as possible.

Of course, in the beginning, this cannot be effected except by   129
means of despotic inroads on the rights of property, and on the conditions of bourgeois production; by means of measures, therefore,
which appear economically insufficient and untenable, but which in
the course of the movement outstrip themselves, necessitate further
inroads upon the old social order, and are unavoidable as a means of
entirely revolutionizing the mode of production.

These measures will of course be different in different countries.   130

Nevertheless in the most advanced countries the following will   131
be pretty generally applicable:

1. Abolition of property in land and application of all rents of land
   to public purposes.

2. A heavy progressive or graduated income tax.

3. Abolition of all right of inheritance.

4. Confiscation of the property of all emigrants and rebels.

5. Centralization of credit in the hands of the State, by means of a
   national bank with State capital and an exclusive monopoly.

6. Centralization of the means of communication and transport in
   the hands of the State.

7. Extension of factories and instruments of production owned by
   the State; the bringing into cultivation of waste lands, and the
   improvement of the soil generally in accordance with a common
   plan.

8. Equal liability of all to labor. Establishment of industrial armies,
   especially for agriculture.

9. Combination of agriculture with manufacturing industries; gradual abolition of the distinction between town and country by a
   more equable distribution of the population over the country.

10. Free education for all children in public schools. Abolition of
    children's factory labor in its present form. Combination of edu-
    cation with industrial production, etc., etc.

When, in the course of development, class distinctions have dis-   132
appeared, and all production has been concentrated in the hands of
a vast association of the whole nation, the public power will lose its
political character. Political power, properly so called, is merely the
organized power of one class for oppressing another. If the proletariat
during its contest with the bourgeoisie is compelled, by the force of
circumstances, to organize itself as a class, if, by means of a revolution,
it makes itself the ruling class, and, as such, sweeps away by force

the old conditions of production, then it will, along with these conditions, have swept away the conditions for the existence of class antagonism, and of classes generally, and will thereby have abolished its own supremacy as a class.

In place of the old bourgeois society, with its classes and class   133
antagonisms, we shall have an association in which the free development of each is the condition for the free development of all. . . .

Position of the Communists in Relation to the Various Existing Opposition Parties

[The preceding section] has made clear the relations of the Com-   134
munists to the existing working class parties, such as the Chartists in England and the Agrarian Reforms[12] in America.

The Communists fight for the attainment of the immediate aims,   135
for the enforcement of the momentary interests of the working class; but in the movement of the present they also represent and take care of the future of that movement. In France the Communists ally themselves with the Social-Democrats[13] against the conservative and radical bourgeoisie, reserving, however, the right to take up a critical position in regard to phrases and illusions traditionally handed down from the great Revolution.

In Switzerland they support the Radicals,[14] without losing sight of   136
the fact that this party consists of antagonistic elements, partly of Democratic Socialists, in the French sense, partly of radical bourgeois.

In Poland they support the party that insists on an agrarian rev-   137
olution, as the prime condition for national emancipation, that party which fomented the insurrection of Cracow in 1846.[15]

In Germany they fight with the bourgeoisie whenever it acts in   138
a revolutionary way, against the absolute monarchy, the feudal squirearchy, and the petty bourgeoisie.

---

[12] **Agrarian Reforms** Agrarian reform was a very important issue in America after the Revolution. The Chartists were a radical English group established in 1838; they demanded political and social reforms. They were among the more violent revolutionaries of the day. Agrarian reform, or redistribution of the land, was slow to come, and the issue often sparked violence between social classes.

[13] **Social-Democrats** In France in the 1840s, a group that proposed the ideal of labor reform through the establishment of workshops supplied with government capital.

[14] **Radicals** By 1848, European Radicals, taking their name from the violent revolutionaries of the French Revolution (1789–1799), were a nonviolent group content to wait for change.

[15] **the insurrection of Cracow in 1846** Cracow was an independent city in 1846. The insurrection was designed to join Cracow with Poland and to further large-scale social reforms.

But they never cease for a single instant to instill into the work-   139
ing class the clearest possible recognition of the hostile antagonism
between bourgeoisie and proletariat, in order that the German workers may straightway use, as so many weapons against the bourgeoisie,
the social and political conditions that the bourgeoisie must necessarily introduce along with its supremacy, and in order that, after
the fall of the reactionary classes in Germany, the fight against the
bourgeoisie itself may immediately begin.

The Communists turn their attention chiefly to Germany,   140
because that country is on the eve of a bourgeois revolution,[16] that
is bound to be carried out under more advanced conditions of
European civilization, and with a more developed proletariat, than
that of England was in the seventeenth and of France in the eighteenth century, and because the bourgeois revolution in Germany
will be but the prelude to an immediately following proletarian
revolution.

In short, the Communists everywhere support every revolution-   141
ary movement against the existing social and political order of things.

In all these movements they bring to the front, as the leading   142
question in each, the property question, no matter what its degree of
development at the time.

Finally, they labor everywhere for the union and agreement of   143
the democratic parties of all countries.

The Communists disdain to conceal their views and aims. They   144
openly declare that their ends can be attained only by the forcible
overthrow of all existing social conditions. Let the ruling classes
tremble at a Communistic revolution. The proletarians have nothing
to lose but their chains. They have a world to win.

Working men of all countries, unite!   145

---

[16]**on the eve of a bourgeois revolution** Ferdinand Lassalle (1825–1864)
developed the German labor movement and was in basic agreement with Marx, who
was nevertheless convinced that Lassalle's approach was wrong. The environment in
Germany seemed appropriate for revolution, in part because of its fragmented political structure and in part because no major revolution had yet occurred there.

QUESTIONS FOR CRITICAL READING

1. Begin by establishing your understanding of the terms *bourgeois* and
   proletarian. Does Marx make a clear distinction between the terms? Are
   such terms applicable to American society today? Which of these
   groups, if any, do you feel that you belong to?

2. Marx makes the concept of social class fundamental to his theories. Can "social class" be easily defined? Are social classes evident in our society? Are they engaged in a struggle of the sort Marx assumes to be inevitable?
3. What are Marx's views about the value of work in the society he describes? What is his attitude toward wealth?
4. Marx says that every class struggle is a political struggle. Do you agree?
5. Examine the first part. Which class gets more paragraphs—the bourgeoisie or the proletariat? Why?
6. Is the modern proletariat a revolutionary class?
7. Is Marx's analysis of history clear? Try to summarize his views on the progress of history.
8. Is capital a social force, or is it a personal force? Do you think of your savings (either now or in the future) as belonging to you alone or as in some way belonging to your society?
9. What, in Marx's view, is the responsibility of wealthy citizens?

SUGGESTIONS FOR CRITICAL WRITING

1. Defend or attack Marx's statement: "The executive of the modern State is but a committee for managing the common affairs of the whole bourgeoisie" (para. 18). Is this generally true? Take three "affairs of the whole bourgeoisie" and test each one in turn.
2. Examine Marx's statements regarding women. Refer especially to paragraphs 39, 98, 105, and 110. Does he imply that his views are in conflict with those of his general society? After you have a list of his statements, see if you can establish exactly what he is recommending. Do you approve of his recommendations?
3. Marx's program of ten points is listed in paragraph 131. Using the technique that Marx himself uses—taking each point in its turn, clarifying the problems with the point, and finally deciding for or against the point—evaluate his program. Which points do you feel are most beneficial to society? Which are detrimental to society? What is your overall view of the general worth of the program? Do you think it would be possible to put such a program into effect?
4. All Marx's views are predicated on the present nature of property ownership and the changes that communism will institute. He claims, for example, that a rupture with property relations "involves the most radical rupture with traditional ideas" (para. 125). And he discusses in depth his proposal for the rupture of property relations (paras. 68–93). Clarify traditional property relations—what can be owned and by whom—and then contrast with these the proposals Marx makes. Establish your own views as you go along. Include your reasons for taking issue or expressing agreement with Marx. What kinds of property relations do you see around you? What kinds are most desirable for a healthy society?

5. What is the responsibility of the state toward the individual in the kind of economic circumstances that Marx describes? How can the independence of individuals who have amassed great wealth and wish to operate freely be balanced against the independence of those who are poor and have no wealth to manipulate? What kinds of abuse are possible in such circumstances, and what remedies can a state achieve through altering the economic system? What specific remedies does Marx suggest? Are they workable?

6. Do you feel that Marx's suggestions are desirable? Or that they are likely to produce the effects he desires? Critics sometimes complain about Marx's misunderstanding of human nature. Do you feel he has an adequate understanding of human nature? What do you see as impediments to the full success of his program?

7. How accurate is Marx's view of the bourgeoisie? He identifies the bourgeoisie with capital and capitalists. He also complains that the bourgeoisie has established a world market for goods and by doing so has destroyed national and regional identities. Examine his analysis in paragraphs 22–36 in terms of what you see happening in the economic world today and decide whether or not his ideas about how the bourgeoisie functions still apply and ring true. Did Marx foresee the problems of globalization that incited protests and riots such as those aimed at the World Bank, the World Trade Organization, and the International Monetary Fund during the last years of the twentieth century into the early part of the twenty-first century?

8. **CONNECTIONS** Marx's philosophy differs from that of Robert B. Reich. How would Marx respond to Reich's analysis (p. 419) of the future of labor in the next few decades? Would Marx see signs of a coming class struggle in the distinctions Reich draws between the routine workers, the in-person servers, and the symbolic analysts? Does Reich's essay take any of Marx's theories into account?

9. **CONNECTIONS** For Marx, there is no more antagonistic figure of capitalism than Andrew Carnegie. Carnegie himself condemns communism as a failed system, while Marx condemns capitalism as a system designed to keep the rich rich and the poor poor. Imagine that Marx read *The Gospel of Wealth* and decided to counter it with an argument written as a letter to the editor of a major newspaper. What would be the basis of his attack, and how might he structure his letter? Consider Marx's own techniques in defending communism against the bourgeoisie (paras. 60 onward) as you go about constructing the argument against Carnegie.

10. **SEEING CONNECTIONS** Marx would obviously have seen the old man and the young boy in Tanner's *The Thankful Poor* (p. 344) as belonging to the proletariat. To what extent would this painting have alarmed and annoyed Marx? What evidence would it have given him to support his views about the evils of capitalism? What evidence in the painting might have weakened his views? How would he have

reacted to the implied piety in the painting and the thankfulness in the title? Would Marx have approved of the figures being thankful? To whom would he say they are thankful—and why would he think they express thanks, given their economic situation? Would Marx have praised Tanner for painting this scene, or would he have condemned him?

ANDREW CARNEGIE
The Gospel of Wealth

ANDREW CARNEGIE (1835–1919) was a truly self-made man. Born in Scotland, he immigrated with his family to Allegheny, Pennsylvania, when he was thirteen. He went right to work in a cotton mill where he labored twelve hours a day, six days a week, for $1.20. Three years later, he became a messenger boy for $2.20 a week for the local telegraph company in Pittsburgh. His connection with the telegraph company and his self-taught mastery of telegraphy proved fortuitous. This was a cutting-edge technology at the time and it intersected another cutting-edge industry next to which the telegraph wires were strung, the railroads. In 1853, Thomas A. Scott, the president of the Pennsylvania Railroad employed him as his assistant for $35 per month. His rise through the company was rapid after that.

Through the help of Scott, Carnegie invested money successfully then reinvested his profits in sleeping cars for the railroad. That led to his buying out part of the company that made the cars. Because his investments were so successful, he was able to move into the iron and iron products industry, manufacturing components for bridges and railroad tracks. By the time the Civil War began, Carnegie had amassed a considerable amount of capital: the key to his later success. During the war, Scott appointed Carnegie superintendent of military transport and the Union telegraph lines, which had to be kept up to speed for communication between Washington and the field commanders.

Late in the war, Carnegie invested $40,000 in property in Pennsylvania that yielded petroleum, and profits from that venture led him to move into the steel business in response to the need for cannon, shells, armor, and other military products. Because he had

Originally published as "Wealth" in the *North American Review*, June 1889.

put some of his investment money into iron companies before the war, he was positioned to make considerable profits. After the end of the war, Carnegie saw an opportunity to expand his business by replacing older wooden railroad bridges with steel and iron bridges, further building his fortune. It was then, in the 1870s, that he began to conceive of what was to become in 1892 the Carnegie Steel Company, one of the largest companies in the nation. Before that, however, he had purchased huge fields of iron ore around Lake Superior, so he was positioned as a supplier as well as a manufacturer of steel and iron.

Carnegie was a published author and expressed interest in improving his education and in meeting important literary and philosophical people such as Matthew Arnold (1822–1888), whom he admired, and Herbert Spencer (1820–1903), who became a very important influence on his thinking. Spencer was a utilitarian philosopher who was known as a social Darwinist. Spencer coined the phrase "the survival of the fittest" and applied it to the social sphere. Carnegie found Spencer's views totally congenial since he felt that there were superior people (he said "men") who were indeed the fittest in any economy and who deserved to profit from a laissez-faire economy and to rise in society. He was one of those men.

Carnegie was a serious reader and a lover of music. Late in life, he built and named Carnegie Hall in New York, which he designed specifically for concerts. Moreover, part of his success was due to his personal charm and grace, qualities that permitted him to travel in the highest social circles of his day. He also expressed a strong concern in helping working people educate themselves and enjoy the pleasures of art and music. Even in his thirties, he began to conceive his ultimate plan of giving away his fortune and had already begun giving some of his money away to public programs.

His operations in the steel industry, however, were not as obviously benevolent as his programs to benefit the public. He ruthlessly cut wages for skilled and unskilled workers because he thought that the greater his profits the more money he would have to give away and that he could do more good with that money than his workers could. His purpose was to serve the greatest good for the greatest number. In 1892, his workers held a strike at Homestead Steel that lasted 143 days. Carnegie was in Scotland most of this time, and his next in command, Henry Clay Frick, ordered Pinkerton guards to drive out the workers, who were then replaced with immigrants. There was violence and ten men were killed. After that incident, Carnegie's reputation was never the same.

He sold his holdings in 1901 to the banker J. P. Morgan for $480 million, which in today's money would be about $10.6 billion.

Morgan told Carnegie that he was probably the richest man in the world, which may have been true. The only other man at that time who could claim that title was John D. Rockefeller. Carnegie retired at sixty-six and began giving his money away in earnest, a sum ultimately amounting to 350 million dollars. He founded Carnegie Mellon University in Pittsburgh, gave considerable sums to Scottish universities and to his hometown in Scotland, and established pension funds for his workers at Homestead and at universities. In small towns and cities throughout the United States and Canada, he is remembered for having built free public libraries, very few of which existed before he began his program. He built 2,509 libraries in all before he ended his project in 1917. Carnegie was not a religious man, preferring to think of himself as more influenced by science and learning, but he did commission a large number of pipe organs to be installed in churches, ostensibly because he approved of the music they would play.

Interestingly, Carnegie challenged the great holders of fortunes in his day to give their money away while they were still living, as he was planning to do. However, other than John D. Rockefeller, few of them followed his lead. Many established philanthropies after their deaths, but they did not have the pleasure of seeing their wealth perform public service.

Carnegie's Rhetoric

One of the first rhetorical notes is the use of the word *Gospel* in the title. Originally the essay was titled "Wealth," but when it was quickly reprinted to be distributed more widely *Gospel* was added. The effect is to impart an almost divine authority to the text because it echoes the gospels of the New Testament and seems then to connect to the teachings of Jesus. Originally, *gospel* meant "good news," and Carnegie certainly thought his concepts here were the best news he could provide.

The organization of the essay is clear enough. Carnegie begins by posing a problem: "The problem of our age is the proper administration of wealth." This profound declaration focuses our attention, but in 1889 we might have felt that it was not the only, nor the most important, problem of the age. Being hyperbolic in that fashion simply forces us to put aside other considerations and attend to the problem of the "contrast between the palace of the millionaire and the cottage of the laborer" (para. 1). We might expect Carnegie to be critical of this unequal distinction, but instead he says that this is the natural result of civilization. By contrast, the home of the leader of the Sioux is much the same as the most ordinary Indian, and thus Carnegie tacitly implies that the Sioux are not civilized. Hidden in his discussion is the assumption that there is a form of Darwinian evolution at work that has produced a "progress of the race," a theme he touches on constantly, and that the modern industrial leader, such as Carnegie himself, is an example of the "fittest" in society.

Carnegie's Darwinism derives from the teaching of Herbert Spencer and was enthusiastically adopted by other leaders who amassed astonishing fortunes in the years during and after the Civil War. It surfaces in specific rhetorical flourishes that center on the idea of laws of nature that are inevitable and, for Carnegie, desirable. In paragraph 6, Carnegie introduces the "law of competition" and sees it as one of the most beneficial laws because it concentrates wealth into the hands of the few. The few then create capital and capital is what makes civilization the beautiful thing it is in his eyes. In paragraph 7, Carnegie talks about "the Law of Accumulation of Wealth, and the Law of Competition" and admits that, although the laws may be imperfect in some ways, "they are, nevertheless, like the highest type of man, the best and most valuable of all that humanity has yet accomplished." In the next paragraph, he refers to these as "the laws upon which civilization is founded," leaving the reader no other option than to accept his view.

Another crucial issue that Carnegie treats and develops throughout the essay is his concept of individualism. He contrasts the individualism of capitalism with the collectivism of communism, a movement that had been discussed throughout the second half of the nineteenth century. Individualism produced the wealth of the nation, according to Carnegie. It was responsible for the achievements of men like him. He treats it as a sacred principle in itself, although he does not declare it a law, as he does the laws of accumulation and distribution.

After praising the system that has produced so much wealth, he then condemns those who would make a religion of wealth. His main point is that fortunes such as his are only in trust, to be disbursed for the public good. Of course, he is the person to decide what the public should have: parks, works of art, public institutions, and other benefits "in the forms best calculated to do them lasting good" (para. 22). The community gets the benefit, but the philanthropist administers "it for the community far better than it could or would have done for itself" (para. 23).

Carnegie praises wealth, but condemns charity. He cites an example of a wealthy man who gave a handout to a stranger on the street and claims that what that man did was "probably one of the most selfish and very worst actions of his life" (para. 20). "Indiscriminate charity" is to be condemned because "[o]f every thousand dollars spent in so-called charity to-day, it is probable that $950 is unwisely spent." Charity only goes to those who can help themselves, and as he says, those who can help themselves rarely need assistance. Charity, he fears, only encourages "the slothful, the drunken, the unworthy."

Among the remarkable experiences Carnegie had in his philanthropic years was his singular effort to help support the Tuskegee Institute, a traditionally African American college in Alabama associated with its founder, Booker T. Washington (1856–1915). Carnegie and Washington worked together on a number of projects, among them the founding of the National Negro Business League. Carnegie was a major contributor to the early development of Tuskegee and an enthusiastic friend of Washington's, whose views regarding self-improvement much resembled his own.

Carnegie died in Lenox, Massachusetts, in 1919, and the bulk of his remaining wealth went to the Carnegie Corporation and continued his program of public funding.

PREREADING QUESTIONS:
WHAT TO READ FOR

The following prereading questions may help you anticipate key issues in the discussion of Andrew Carnegie's *The Gospel of Wealth*. Keeping them in mind during your first reading of the selection should help focus your attention.

- What does Carnegie see as the problem of "our age"?
- Why does Carnegie accept the great gap between the wealth of the millionaire and the relative poverty of the laborer?
- What laws does Carnegie feel are at work in society to help produce great wealth?
- What is the highest obligation of the person who has amassed a great fortune?

The Gospel of Wealth

The problem of our age is the proper administration of wealth, 1 so that the ties of brotherhood may still bind together the rich and poor in harmonious relationship. The conditions of human life have not only been changed, but revolutionized, within the past few hundred years. In former days there was little difference between the dwelling, dress, food, and environment of the chief and those of his retainers. The Indians are to-day where civilized man then was. When visiting the Sioux, I was led to the wigwam of the chief. It was just like the others in external appearance, and, even within, the difference was trifling between it and those of the poorest of his braves. The contrast between the palace of the millionaire and the cottage of the laborer with us to-day measures the change which has come with civilization.

This change, however, is not to be deplored, but welcomed as   2 highly beneficial. It is well, nay, essential for the progress of the race, that the houses of some should be homes for all that is highest and best in literature and the arts, and for all the refinements of civilization, rather than that none should be so. Much better this great irregularity than universal squalor. Without wealth there can be no Maecenas.[1] The "good old times" were not good old times. Neither master nor servant was as well situated then as to-day. A relapse to old conditions would be disastrous to both—not the least so to him who serves—and would sweep away civilization with it. But whether the change be for good or ill, it is upon us, beyond our power to alter, and therefore to be accepted and made the best of. It is a waste of time to criticize the inevitable.

It is easy to see how the change has come. One illustration will   3 serve for almost every phase of the cause. In the manufacture of products we have the whole story. It applies to all combinations of human industry, as stimulated and enlarged by the inventions of this scientific age. Formerly articles were manufactured at the domestic hearth or in small shops which formed part of the household. The master and his apprentices worked side by side, the latter living with the master, and therefore subject to the same conditions. When these apprentices rose to be masters, there was little or no change in their mode of life, and they, in turn, educated in the same routine succeeding apprentices. There was, substantially, social equality, and even political equality, for those engaged in industrial pursuits had then little or no political voice in the State.

But the inevitable result of such a mode of manufacture was   4 crude articles at high prices. To-day the world obtains commodities of excellent quality at prices which even the generation preceding this would have deemed incredible. In the commercial world similar causes have produced similar results, and the race is benefited

---

[1] **Gaius Maecenus (c. 74–8 B.C.)** Wealthy patron to great Roman authors.

thereby. The poor enjoy what the rich could not before afford. What were the luxuries have become the necessaries of life. The laborer has now more comforts than the farmer had a few generations ago. The farmer has more luxuries than the landlord had, and is more richly clad and better housed. The landlord has books and pictures rarer, and appointments more artistic, than the King could then obtain.

The price we pay for this salutary change is, no doubt, great. 5 We assemble thousands of operatives in the factory, in the mine, and in the counting-house, of whom the employer can know little or nothing, and to whom the employer is little better than a myth. All intercourse between them is at an end. Rigid Castes are formed, and, as usual, mutual ignorance breeds mutual distrust. Each Caste is without sympathy for the other, and ready to credit anything disparaging in regard to it. Under the law of competition, the employer of thousands is forced into the strictest economies, among which the rates paid to labor figure prominently, and often there is friction between the employer and the employed, between capital and labor, between rich and poor. Human society loses homogeneity.

The price which society pays for the law of competition, like the 6 price it pays for cheap comforts and luxuries, is also great; but the advantages of this law are also greater still, for it is to this law that we owe our wonderful material development, which brings improved conditions in its train. But, whether the law be benign or not, we must say of it, as we say of the change in the conditions of men to which we have referred: it is here; we cannot evade it; no substitutes for it have been found; and while the law may be sometimes hard for the individual, it is best for the race, because it insures the survival of the fittest in every department. We accept and welcome, therefore, as conditions to which we must accommodate ourselves, great inequality of environment, the concentration of business, industrial and commercial, in the hands of a few, and the law of competition between these, as being not only beneficial, but essential for the future progress of the race. Having accepted these, it follows that there must be great scope for the exercise of special ability in the merchant and in the manufacturer who has to conduct affairs upon a great scale. That this talent for organization and management is rare among men is proved by the fact that it invariably secures for its possessor enormous rewards, no matter where or under what laws or conditions. The experienced in affairs always rate the MAN whose services can be obtained as a partner as not only the first consideration, but such as to render the question of his capital scarcely worth considering, for such men soon create capital; while, without the special talent required, capital soon takes wings. Such men become interested in firms or corporations using millions; and estimating only simple interest to be made upon the capital invested, it is inevitable that their income must exceed their expenditures, and that they must accumulate wealth. Nor is there any middle ground which such men can occupy, because the great manufacturing or commercial concern which does not earn at least interest upon its capital soon becomes bankrupt. It must either go forward or fall behind: to stand still is impossible. It is a condition essential for its successful operation that it should be thus far profitable, and even that, in addition to interest on capital, it should make profit. It is a law that men possessed of this peculiar talent for affairs, under the free play of economic forces, must of necessity soon be in receipt of more revenue than can be judiciously expended upon themselves; and this law is as beneficial for the race as the others.

Objections to the foundations upon which society is based are   7 not in order, because the condition of the race is better with these than it has been with any others which have been tried. Of the effect of any new substitutes proposed we cannot be sure. The Socialist or Anarchist who seeks to overturn present conditions is to be regarded as attacking the foundation upon which civilization itself rests, for civilization took its start from the day that the capable, industrious workman said to his incompetent and lazy fellow, "If thou dost not sow, thou shalt not reap," and thus ended primitive Communism by separating the drones from the bees. One who studies this subject will soon be brought face to face with the conclusion that upon the sacredness of property civilization itself depends—the right of the laborer to his hundred dollars in the savings-bank, and equally the legal right of the millionaire to his millions. To those who propose to substitute Communism for this intense Individualism the answer, therefore, is: the race has tried that. All progress from that barbarous day to the present time has resulted from its displacement. Not evil, but good, has come to the race from the accumulation of wealth by those who have the ability and energy that produce it. But even if we admit for a moment that it might be better for the race to discard its present foundation, Individualism—that it is a nobler ideal that man should labor, not for himself alone, but in and for a brotherhood of his fellows, and share with them all in common, realizing Swedenborg's[2] idea of Heaven, where, as he says, the angels derive their happiness, not from laboring for self, but for each other—even admit all this, and a sufficient

---

[2] **Emanuel Swedenborg (1688–1771)** A spiritual awakening late in life made him believe he could speak with angels and visit heaven and hell. His book *Heaven and Hell* (1758) was widely read in the nineteenth century and is still influential.

answer is, This is not evolution, but revolution. It necessitates the changing of human nature itself—a work of aeons, even if it were good to change it, which we cannot know. It is not practicable in our day or in our age. Even if desirable theoretically, it belongs to another and long-succeeding sociological stratum. Our duty is with what is practicable now; with the next step possible in our day and generation. It is criminal to waste our energies in endeavoring to uproot, when all we can profitably or possibly accomplish is to bend the universal tree of humanity a little in the direction most favorable to the production of good fruit under existing circumstances. We might as well urge the destruction of the highest existing type of man because he failed to reach our ideal as to favor the destruction of Individualism, Private Property, the Law of Accumulation of Wealth, and the Law of Competition; for these are the highest results of human experience, the soil in which society so far has produced the best fruit. Unequally or unjustly, perhaps, as these laws sometimes operate, and imperfect as they appear to the Idealist, they are, nevertheless, like the highest type of man, the best and most valuable of all that humanity has yet accomplished.

We start, then, with a condition of affairs under which the best 8 interests of the race are promoted, but which inevitably gives wealth to the few. Thus far, accepting conditions as they exist, the situation can be surveyed and pronounced good. The question then arises— and, if the foregoing be correct, it is the only question with which we have to deal—What is the proper mode of administering wealth after the laws upon which civilization is founded have thrown it into the hands of the few? And it is of this great question that I believe I offer the true solution. It will be understood that *fortunes* are here spoken of, not moderate sums saved by many years of effort, the returns from which are required for the comfortable maintenance and education of families. This is not *wealth,* but only *competence,* which it should be the aim of all to acquire.

There are but three modes in which surplus wealth can be dis- 9 posed of. It can be left to the families of the decedents; or it can be bequeathed for public purposes; or, finally, it can be administered during their lives by its possessors. Under the first and second modes most of the wealth of the world that has reached the few has hitherto been applied. Let us in turn consider each of these modes. The first is the most injudicious. In monarchical countries, the estates and the greatest portion of the wealth are left to the first son, that the vanity of the parent may be gratified by the thought that his name and title are to descend to succeeding generations unimpaired. The condition of this class in Europe to-day teaches the futility of such hopes or ambitions. The successors have become impoverished through their follies or from the fall in the value of land. Even in Great Britain the strict law of entail[3] has been found inadequate to maintain the status of an hereditary class. Its soil is rapidly passing into the hands of the stranger. Under republican institutions the division of property among the children is much fairer, but the question which forces itself upon thoughtful men in all lands is: Why should men leave great fortunes to their children? If this is done from affection, is it not misguided affection? Observation teaches that, generally speaking, it is not well for the children that they should be so burdened. Neither is it well for the state. Beyond providing for the wife and daughters moderate sources of income, and very moderate allowances indeed, if any, for the sons, men may well hesitate, for it is no longer questionable that great sums bequeathed oftener work more for the injury than for the good of the recipients. Wise men will soon conclude that, for the best interests of the members of their families and of the state, such bequests are an improper use of their means.

It is not suggested that men who have failed to educate their sons   10
to earn a livelihood shall cast them adrift in poverty. If any man has seen fit to rear his sons with a view to their living idle lives, or, what is highly commendable, has instilled in them the sentiment that they are in a position to labor for public ends without reference to pecuniary considerations, then, of course, the duty of the parent is to see that such are provided for in *moderation*. There are instances of millionaires' sons unspoiled by wealth, who, being rich, still perform great services in the community. Such are the very salt of the earth, as valuable as, unfortunately, they are rare; still it is not the exception, but the rule, that men must regard, and, looking at the usual result of enormous sums conferred upon legatees, the thoughtful man must shortly say, "I would as soon leave to my son a curse as the almighty dollar," and admit to himself that it is not the welfare of the children, but family pride, which inspires these enormous legacies.

As to the second mode, that of leaving wealth at death for public   11
uses, it may be said that this is only a means for the disposal of wealth, provided a man is content to wait until he is dead before it becomes of much good in the world. Knowledge of the results of legacies bequeathed is not calculated to inspire the brightest hopes of much posthumous good being accomplished. The cases are not few in which the real object sought by the testator is not attained, nor are they few in which his real wishes are thwarted. In many cases the

---

[3] **Law of entail** A law designed to restrict inheritance to only the heirs of the family who owns the property.

bequests are so used as to become only monuments of his folly. It is well to remember that it requires the exercise of not less ability than that which acquired the wealth to use it so as to be really beneficial to the community. Besides this, it may fairly be said that no man is to be extolled for doing what he cannot help doing, nor is he to be thanked by the community to which he only leaves wealth at death. Men who leave vast sums in this way may fairly be thought men who would not have left it at all had they been able to take it with them. The memories of such cannot be held in grateful remembrance, for there is no grace in their gifts. It is not to be wondered at that such bequests seem so generally to lack the blessing.

12   The growing disposition to tax more and more heavily large estates left at death is a cheering indication of the growth of a salutary change in public opinion. The State of Pennsylvania now takes— subject to some exceptions—one-tenth of the property left by its citizens. The budget presented in the British Parliament the other day proposes to increase the death-duties; and, most significant of all, the new tax is to be a graduated one. Of all forms of taxation, this seems the wisest. Men who continue hoarding great sums all their lives, the proper use of which for public ends would work good to the community, should be made to feel that the community, in the form of the state, cannot thus be deprived of its proper share. By taxing estates heavily at death the state marks its condemnation of the selfish millionaire's unworthy life.

13   It is desirable that nations should go much further in this direction. Indeed, it is difficult to set bounds to the share of a rich man's estate which should go at his death to the public through the agency of the state, and by all means such taxes should be graduated, beginning at nothing upon moderate sums to dependents, and increasing rapidly as the amounts swell, until of the millionaire's hoard, as of Shylock's,[4] at least

> —The other half
> Comes to the privy coffer of the state.

This policy would work powerfully to induce the rich man to attend to the administration of wealth during his life, which is the end that society should always have in view, as being that by far most fruitful for the people. Nor need it be feared that this policy would sap the root of enterprise and render men less anxious to accumulate, for to the class whose ambition it is to leave great fortunes and be talked

---

[4] **Shylock** The moneylender and title character in Shakespeare's *The Merchant of Venice*.

about after their death, it will attract even more attention, and, indeed, be a somewhat nobler ambition to have enormous sums paid over to the state from their fortunes.

There remains, then, only one mode of using great fortunes; but   14 in this we have the true antidote for the temporary unequal distribution of wealth, the reconciliation of the rich and the poor—a reign of harmony—another ideal, differing, indeed, from that of the Communist in requiring only the further evolution of existing conditions, not the total overthrow of our civilization. It is founded upon the present most intense individualism, and the race is prepared to put it in practice by degrees whenever it pleases. Under its sway we shall have an ideal state, in which the surplus wealth of the few will become, in the best sense, the property of the many, because administered for the common good, and this wealth, passing through the hands of the few, can be made a much more potent force for the elevation of our race than if it had been distributed in small sums to the people themselves. Even the poorest can be made to see this, and to agree that great sums gathered by some of their fellow-citizens and spent for public purposes, from which the masses reap the principal benefit, are more valuable to them than if scattered among them through the course of many years in trifling amounts.

If we consider what results flow from the Cooper Institute,[5] for   15 instance, to the best portion of the race in New York not possessed of means, and compare these with those which would have arisen for the good of the masses from an equal sum distributed by Mr. Cooper in his lifetime in the form of wages, which is the highest form of distribution, being for work done and not for charity, we can form some estimate of the possibilities for the improvement of the race which lie embedded in the present law of the accumulation of wealth. Much of this sum, if distributed in small quantities among the people, would have been wasted in the indulgence of appetite, some of it in excess, and it may be doubted whether even the part put to the best use, that of adding to the comforts of the home, would have yielded results for the race, as a race, at all comparable to those which are flowing and are to flow from the Cooper Institute from generation to generation. Let the advocate of violent or radical change ponder well this thought.

We might even go so far as to take another instance, that of   16 Mr. Tilden's bequest of five millions of dollars for a free library in the city of New York, but in referring to this one cannot help saying

---

[5] **Cooper Institute** Now Cooper Union, founded in 1858 by Peter Cooper as a free school for the sciences and the arts.

involuntarily, How much better if Mr. Tilden[6] had devoted the last years of his own life to the proper administration of this immense sum; in which case neither legal contest nor any other cause of delay could have interfered with his aims. But let us assume that Mr. Tilden's millions finally become the means of giving to New York a noble public library, where the treasures of the world contained in books will be open to all forever, without money and without price. Considering the good of that part of the race which congregates in and around Manhattan Island, would its permanent benefit have been better promoted had these millions been allowed to circulate in small sums through the hands of the masses? Even the most strenuous advocate of Communism must entertain a doubt upon this subject. Most of those who think will probably entertain no doubt whatever.

Poor and restricted are our opportunities in this life; narrow our horizon; our best work most imperfect; but rich men should be thankful for one inestimable boon. They have it in their power during their lives to busy themselves in organizing benefactions from which the masses of their fellows will derive lasting advantage, and thus dignify their own lives. The highest life is probably to be reached, not by such imitation of the life of Christ as Count Tolstoi[7] gives us, but, while animated by Christ's spirit, by recognizing the changed conditions of this age, and adopting modes of expressing this spirit suitable to the changed conditions under which we live; still laboring for the good of our fellows, which was the essence of his life and teaching, but laboring in a different manner. 17

This, then, is held to be the duty of the man of Wealth: first, to set an example of modest, unostentatious living, shunning display or extravagance; to provide moderately for the legitimate wants of those dependent upon him; and after doing so to consider all surplus revenues which come to him simply as trust funds, which he is called upon to administer, and strictly bound as a matter of duty to administer in the manner which, in his judgment, is best calculated to produce the most beneficial results for the community—the man of wealth thus becoming the mere agent and trustee for his poorer brethren, bringing to their service his superior wisdom, experience, and ability to administer, doing for them better than they would or could do for themselves. 18

---

[6] **Samuel Tilden (1814–1886)** He bequeathed $4 million to found the New York Public Library after he died. His will was contested and only $3 million was given to found the library.

[7] **Leo Tolstoy (1828–1910)** Author of *War and Peace* and *Anna Karenina.* Tolstoy lived a spare and simple life in his old age.

We are met here with the difficulty of determining what are   19
moderate sums to leave to members of the family; what is modest,
unostentatious living; what is the test of extravagance. There must be
different standards for different conditions. The answer is that it is as
impossible to name exact amounts or actions as it is to define good
manners, good taste, or the rules of propriety; but, nevertheless, these
are verities, well known although undefinable. Public sentiment is
quick to know and to feel what offends these. So in the case of wealth.
The rule in regard to good taste in the dress of men or women applies
here. Whatever makes one conspicuous offends the canon. If any
family be chiefly known for display, for extravagance in home, table,
equipage, for enormous sums ostentatiously spent in any form upon
itself—if these be its chief distinctions, we have no difficulty in estimating its nature or culture. So likewise in regard to the use or abuse
of its surplus wealth, or to generous, free-handed cooperation in good
public uses, or to unabated efforts to accumulate and hoard to the last,
whether they administer or bequeath. The verdict rests with the best
and most enlightened public sentiment. The community will surely
judge, and its judgments will not often be wrong.

The best uses to which surplus wealth can be put have already   20
been indicated. Those who would administer wisely must, indeed, be
wise, for one of the serious obstacles to the improvement of our race is
indiscriminate charity. It were better for mankind that the millions of
the rich were thrown into the sea than so spent as to encourage the
slothful, the drunken, the unworthy. Of every thousand dollars spent
in so-called charity to-day, it is probable that $950 is unwisely spent;
so spent, indeed, as to produce the very evils which it proposes to
mitigate or cure. A well-known writer of philosophic books admitted
the other day that he had given a quarter of a dollar to a man who
approached him as he was coming to visit the house of his friend. He
knew nothing of the habits of this beggar; knew not the use that
would be made of this money, although he had every reason to suspect that it would be spent improperly. This man professed to be a
disciple of Herbert Spencer;[8] yet the quarter-dollar given that night
will probably work more injury than all the money which its thought-
less donor will ever be able to give in true charity will do good. He
only gratified his own feelings, saved himself from annoyance—and
this was probably one of the most selfish and very worst actions of his
life, for in all respects he is most worthy.

In bestowing charity, the main consideration should be to help   21
those who will help themselves; to provide part of the means by

---

[8] **Herbert Spencer (1820–1903)** British philosopher who applied Darwinian
theories of evolution to the social sciences.

which those who desire to improve may do so; to give those who desire to rise the aids by which they may rise; to assist, but rarely or never to do all. Neither the individual nor the race is improved by alms-giving. Those worthy of assistance, except in rare cases, seldom require assistance. The really valuable men of the race never do, except in cases of accident or sudden change. Every one has, of course, cases of individuals brought to his own knowledge where temporary assistance can do genuine good, and these he will not overlook. But the amount which can be wisely given by the individual for individuals is necessarily limited by his lack of knowledge of the circumstances connected with each. He is the only true reformer who is as careful and as anxious not to aid the unworthy as he is to aid the worthy, and, perhaps, even more so, for in alms-giving more injury is probably done by rewarding vice than by relieving virtue.

The rich man is thus almost restricted to following the examples   22 of Peter Cooper, Enoch Pratt of Baltimore, Mr. Pratt of Brooklyn, Senator Stanford,[9] and others, who know that the best means of benefiting the community is to place within its reach the ladders upon which the aspiring can rise—parks, and means of recreation, by which men are helped in body and mind; works of art, certain to give pleasure and improve the public taste; and public institutions of various kinds, which will improve the general condition of the people— in this manner returning their surplus wealth to the mass of their fellows in the forms best calculated to do them lasting good.

Thus is the problem of Rich and Poor to be solved. The laws of   23 accumulation will be left free; the laws of distribution free. Individualism will continue, but the millionaire will be but a trustee for the poor; intrusted for a season with a great part of the increased wealth of the community, but administering it for the community far better than it could or would have done for itself. The best minds will thus have reached a stage in the development of the race in which it is clearly seen that there is no mode of disposing of surplus wealth creditable to thoughtful and earnest men into whose hands it flows save by using it year by year for the general good. This day already dawns. But a little while, and although, without incurring the pity of their fellows, men may die sharers in great business enterprises from which their capital cannot be or has not been withdrawn, and is left chiefly at death for public uses, yet the man who dies leaving behind him millions of available wealth, which was his to administer during life, will pass away "unwept, unhonored, and unsung," no matter to

---

[9] **Peter Cooper (1791–1883), Enoch Pratt (1808–1896), Charles Pratt (1830–1891), Leland Stanford (1824–1893)** All were prominent millionaires and eventual philanthropists, three of whom founded universities.

what uses he leaves the dross which he cannot take with him. Of such as these the public verdict will then be: "The man who dies thus rich dies disgraced."

Such, in my opinion, is the true Gospel concerning Wealth, obe-   24
dience to which is destined some day to solve the problem of the Rich and the Poor, and to bring "Peace on earth, among men Good-Will."

QUESTIONS FOR CRITICAL READING

1. What do you see as the problem of wealth in this age?
2. What were the conditions of production in the age prior to Carnegie's (para. 3)?
3. What was wrong with the products of the age prior to Carnegie's?
4. What is the law of competition? Is it still at work today? Is it a law?
5. Is conformity an important issue for Carnegie? Is he for or against it?
6. How great are the inequalities of wealth in this country today?
7. Why does Carnegie take a hard line on charity? What is your view on charity today?
8. In paragraph 7, Carnegie refers to the "highest existing type of man." Who do you think he is referring to? Who would you mean if you used that term?

SUGGESTIONS FOR CRITICAL WRITING

1. Is it true that today the "poor enjoy what the rich could not before afford" (para. 4)? What do the poor enjoy today that the rich could not have enjoyed in 1889? To what extent are the things and conditions the poor enjoy now the result of the laws of competition and accumulation that Carnegie says operate in our civilization and make such enjoyment possible? If you feel that Carnegie is right in his contention about the production of benefits for the poor, do you then feel yourself inclined to agree with Carnegie in general?
2. What would Carnegie say about the great inequalities of wealth in this country today? In his time about 1 percent of the population controlled half the wealth. Today it is about 3 percent. The only person in the United States whose wealth could compare with Carnegie's is Bill Gates, and his fortune is about half of Carnegie's in today's dollars. Would Carnegie feel things are getting better or that conditions are so different that there is no comparison with his age? What would his advice be to those with great wealth today?
3. One of Carnegie's important ideas is that societies evolve in the manner that life on earth evolves. He uses the term "survival of the fittest" (para. 6) and lauds the system in economics that permits competition to weed out the weak and reward the strong. Social Darwinism, which is the theory Carnegie talks about, was very popular in the late 1800s.

Learn what you can about the idea and determine whether or not Carnegie is following the main line of social Darwinism or if he is changing the idea to suit himself. After you have done some research, ask the question, Is Carnegie right in what he proposes for the progress of civilization?

4. In paragraphs 6 and 7, Carnegie explains what kind of person will rise to great wealth, enumerating that person's qualities and establishing that such persons are rare enough to be worthy of great reward. He also argues against any criticism of his point of view by talking about how communism would be detrimental to society. He says, "Not evil, but good, has come to the race from the accumulation of wealth by those who have the ability and energy that produce it" (para. 7). Examine his arguments in these paragraphs and decide whether or not he is correct and explain why.

5. Carnegie gave away most of his wealth to support projects he felt would benefit the community. He built over 2,500 libraries, endowed many parks, and gave money to universities and other foundations that he thought would "improve the race." Assuming that you had unlimited wealth to give away, what would your priorities be? Do you approve of Carnegie's priorities, or do you feel they are not appropriate for today's communities? What would you want your wealth to achieve in our world?

6. **CONNECTIONS** Individualism is one of Carnegie's most important themes. He sees the individualism of capitalism as the driving energy behind prosperity and the improvement of civilization. Is his view of individualism similar to that of Ralph Waldo Emerson (p. 255)? Would his view of individualism be coherent with Emile Durkheim's (p. 271) when he says that the law of competition is "sometimes hard for the individual, [but] it is best for the race" (para. 6)? To what extent does Carnegie seem in or out of sympathy with the writers in the section on "The Individual" in this book?

7. **SEEING CONNECTIONS** Imagine that Carnegie saw Tanner's *The Thankful Poor* (p. 344) in a museum. What would have been his reaction to the man and boy portrayed in the painting? How would they fit into his thinking about charity and individualism? Would he have felt these people deserved support? To whom would he think they owe thanks, and for what? Considering Carnegie's connection with Tuskegee Institute, how might he have regarded the simplicity and the reverence with which the older man and the young boy approach the basic act of sharing a meal? Would he have seen this as having a religious subtext, or would he have seen it simply as an economic statement? In another essay, "The Advantages of Poverty," Carnegie complains that the wealthy are estranged from their children because of tutors, nannies, and boarding schools. What "advantages of poverty" would he see in this painting?

JOHN KENNETH GALBRAITH
The Position of Poverty

JOHN KENNETH GALBRAITH (1908–2006) was born in Canada but became an American citizen in 1937. He grew up on a farm in Ontario and received his first university degree in agricultural science. This background may have contributed to the success of his many books on subjects such as economics, the State Department, Indian art, and government, which have always explained complex concepts with a clarity easily grasped by laypeople. Sometimes he has been criticized for oversimplifying issues, but on the whole, he has made a brilliant success of writing with wit and humor about perplexing and sometimes troubling issues.

Galbraith was professor of economics at Harvard University for many years. During the presidential campaigns of Adlai Stevenson in 1952 and 1956, he assisted the Democrats as a speechwriter and economics adviser. He performed the same tasks for John F. Kennedy in 1960. Kennedy appointed Galbraith ambassador to India, a post that he maintained for a little over two years, including the period during which India and China fought a border war. His experiences in India resulted in *Ambassador's Journal: A Personal Account of the Kennedy Years* (1969). Kennedy called Galbraith his finest ambassadorial appointment.

Galbraith's involvement with politics was somewhat unusual for an academic economist at that time. It seems to have stemmed from strongly held personal views on the social issues of his time. One of the most important contributions of his best-known and probably most significant book, *The Affluent Society* (1958; rev. eds. 1969, 1976, 1998), was its analysis of America's economic ambitions. He pointed out that at that time the economy was entirely focused on the

From *The Affluent Society*.

measurement and growth of the gross national product. Economists and government officials concentrated on boosting output, a goal that he felt was misdirected because it would result in products that people really did not need and that would not benefit them. Creating artificial needs for things that had no ultimate value, and building in a "planned obsolescence," seemed to him to be wasteful and ultimately destructive.

Galbraith suggested that America concentrate on genuine needs and satisfy them immediately. He was deeply concerned about the environment and suggested that clean air was a priority that should take precedence over industry. He supported development of the arts and stressed the importance of improving housing across the nation. His effort was directed at trying to help Americans change certain basic values by giving up the pursuit of useless consumer novelties and substituting a program of genuine social development. The commitment to consumer products as the basis of the economy naturally argued against a redirection of effort toward the solution of social problems.

Galbraith is so exceptionally clear in his essay that little commentary is needed to establish its importance. He is insightful in clarifying two kinds of poverty: case poverty and insular poverty. Case poverty is restricted to an individual and his or her family and often seems to be caused by alcoholism, ignorance, mental deficiency, discrimination, or specific disabilities. It is an individual, not a group, disorder. Insular poverty affects a group in a given area—an "island" within the larger society. He points to poverty in Appalachia and in the slums of major cities, where most of the people in those "islands" are at or below the poverty level. Insular poverty is linked to the environment, and its causes are somehow derived from that environment.

Galbraith's analysis is perceptive and influential, and although little or no progress has been made in solving the problem of poverty since 1959, he assures us that there are steps that can be taken to help eradicate it. Such steps demand the nation's will, however, and he warns that the nation may lack the will. He also reasons that because the poor are a minority, few politicians make their plight a campaign issue. Actually, in this belief he is wrong. Kennedy in 1960, Lyndon Johnson in 1964, and Jimmy Carter in 1976 made programs for the poor central among their governmental concerns. Because of the war in Vietnam and other governmental policies, however, the 1960s and early 1970s were a time of staggering inflation, wiping out any of the advances the poor had made.

Galbraith's Rhetoric

The most important rhetorical achievement of the piece is its style. This is an example of the elevated plain style: a clear, direct, and basically simple approach to language that only occasionally admits a somewhat learned vocabulary—as in the use of a very few words such as *opulent, unremunerative,* and *ineluctable.* Most of the words he uses are ordinary ones.

He breaks the essay into five carefully numbered sections. In this way he highlights its basic structure and informs us that he has clearly separated its elements into related groups so that he can speak directly to aspects of his subject rather than to the entire topic. This rhetorical technique of division contributes to clarity and confers a sense of authority on the writer.

Galbraith relies on statistical information that the reader can examine if necessary. This information is treated in the early stages of the piece as a prologue. Once such information has been given, Galbraith proceeds in the manner of a logician establishing premises and deriving the necessary conclusions. The subject is sober and sobering, involving issues that are complex, uncertain, and difficult, but the style is direct, confident, and essentially simple. This is the secret of the success of the book from which this selection comes. *The Affluent Society* has been translated into well over a dozen languages and has been a best-seller around the globe, and fifty years after its first publication it remains an influential book. Its fundamental insights are such that it is likely to be relevant to the economy of the United States for generations to come.

PREREADING QUESTIONS: WHAT TO READ FOR

The following prereading questions may help you anticipate key issues in the discussion of John Kenneth Galbraith's "The Position of Poverty." Keeping them in mind during your first reading of the selection should help focus your attention.

- Why is modern poverty different from that of a century ago?
- What is case poverty?
- What is insular poverty?

The Position of Poverty

"The study of the causes of poverty," Alfred Marshall observed at   1
the turn of the century, "is the study of the causes of the degradation
of a large part of mankind." He spoke of contemporary England as
well as of the world beyond. A vast number of people both in town
and country, he noted, had insufficient food, clothing, and house-
room; they were: "Overworked and undertaught, weary and care-
worn, without quiet and without leisure." The chance of their
succor, he concluded, gave to economic studies "their chief and
their highest interest."[1]

No contemporary economist would be likely to make such an   2
observation about the United States. Conventional economic discourse makes obeisance to the continued existence of some poverty.
"We must remember that we still have a great many poor people." In
the nineteen-sixties, poverty promised, for a time, to become a subject of serious political concern. Then the Vietnam war came and the
concern evaporated or was displaced. For economists of conventional mood, the reminders that the poor still exist are a useful way
of allaying uneasiness about the relevance of conventional economic
goals. For some people, wants must be synthesized. Hence, the
importance of the goods to them is not *per se* very high. So much
may be conceded. But others are far closer to physical need. And
hence we must not be cavalier about the urgency of providing them
with the most for the least. The sales tax may have merit for the
opulent, but it still bears heavily on the poor. The poor get jobs
more easily when the economy is expanding. Thus poverty survives
in economic discourse partly as a buttress to the conventional economic wisdom.

The privation of which Marshall spoke was, going on to a cen-   3
tury ago, the common lot at least of all who worked without special
skill. As a general affliction, it was ended by increased output which,
however imperfectly it may have been distributed, nevertheless
accrued in substantial amount to those who worked for a living. The
result was to reduce poverty from the problem of a majority to that
of a minority. It ceased to be a general case and became a special
case. It is this which has put the problem of poverty into its peculiar
modern form.

---

[1] *Principles of Economics,* 8th ed. (London: Macmillan, 1927), pp. 2–4. [Galbraith's
note] Alfred Marshall (1842–1924) was an English economist whose *Principles of
Economics* (1890) was long a standard text and is still relied on by some economists
for its theories of costs, values, and distribution.

II

For poverty does survive. In part, it is a physical matter; those afflicted have such limited and insufficient food, such poor clothing, such crowded, cold, and dirty shelter that life is painful as well as comparatively brief. But just as it is far too tempting to say that, in matters of living standards, everything is relative, so it is wrong to rest everything on absolutes. People are poverty-stricken when their income, even if adequate for survival, falls radically behind that of the community. Then they cannot have what the larger community regards as the minimum necessary for decency; and they cannot wholly escape, therefore, the judgment of the larger community that they are indecent. They are degraded for, in the literal sense, they live outside the grades or categories which the community regards as acceptable.

Since the first edition of this book appeared, and one hopes however slightly as a consequence, the character and dimension of this degradation have become better understood. There have also been fulsome promises that poverty would be eliminated. The performance on these promises has been less eloquent.

The degree of privation depends on the size of the family, the place of residence—it will be less with given income in rural areas than in the cities—and will, of course, be affected by changes in living costs. One can usefully think of deprivation as falling into two broad categories. First, there is what may be called *case* poverty. This one encounters in every community, rural or urban, however prosperous that community or the times. Case poverty is the poor farm family with the junk-filled yard and the dirty children playing in the bare dirt. Or it is the gray-black hovel beside the railroad tracks. Or it is the basement dwelling in the alley.

Case poverty is commonly and properly related to some characteristic of the individuals so afflicted. Nearly everyone else has mastered his or her environment; this proves that it is not intractable. But some quality peculiar to the individual or family involved— mental deficiency, bad health, inability to adapt to the discipline of industrial life, uncontrollable procreation, alcohol, discrimination involving a very limited minority, some educational handicap unrelated to community shortcoming, or perhaps a combination of several of these handicaps—has kept these individuals from participating in the general well-being.

Second, there is what may be called *insular* poverty—that which manifests itself as an "island" of poverty. In the island, everyone or nearly everyone is poor. Here, evidently, it is not easy to explain matters by individual inadequacy. We may mark individuals down as intrinsically deficient in social performance; it is not proper or even wise so to characterize an entire community. The people of the island have been frustrated by some factor common to their environment.

Case poverty exists. It has also been useful to those who have needed a formula for keeping the suffering of others from causing suffering to themselves. Since this poverty is the result of the deficiencies, including the moral shortcomings, of the persons concerned, it is possible to shift the responsibility to them. They are worthless and, as a simple manifestation of social justice, they suffer for it. Or, at a somewhat higher level of social perception and compassion, it means that the problem of poverty is sufficiently solved by private and public charity. This rescues those afflicted from the worst consequences of their inadequacy or misfortune; no larger social change or reorganization is suggested. Except as it may be insufficient in its generosity, the society is not at fault. 9

Insular poverty yields to no such formulas. In earlier times, when agriculture and extractive industries were the dominant sources of livelihood, something could be accomplished by shifting the responsibility for low income to a poor natural endowment and thus, in effect, to God. The soil was thin and stony, other natural resources absent and hence the people were poor. And, since it is the undoubted preference of many to remain in the vicinity of the place of their birth, a homing instinct that operates for people as well as pigeons, the people remained in the poverty which heaven had decreed for them. It is an explanation that is nearly devoid of empirical application. Connecticut is very barren and stony and incomes are very high. Similarly Wyoming. West Virginia is well watered with rich mines and forests and the people are very poor. The South is much favored in soil and climate and similarly poor and the very richest parts of the South, such as the Mississippi-Yazoo Delta, have long had a well-earned reputation for the greatest deprivation. Yet so strong is the tendency to associate poverty with natural causes that even individuals of some modest intelligence will still be heard, in explanation of insular poverty, to say, "It's basically a poor country." "It's a pretty barren region." 10

Most modern poverty is insular in character and the islands are the rural and urban slums. From the former, mainly in the South, the southern Appalachians and Puerto Rico, there has been until recent times a steady flow of migrants, some white but more black, to the latter. Grim as life is in the urban ghetto, it still offers more hope, income, and interest than in the rural slum. 11

The most important characteristic of insular poverty is forces, common to all members of the community, that restrain or prevent participation in economic life at going rates of return. These restraints are several. Race, which acts to locate people by their color rather than by the proximity to employment, is obviously one. So are poor educational facilities. (And this effect is further exaggerated 12 when the poorly educated, endemically a drug on the labor market, are brought together in dense clusters by the common inadequacy of the schools available to blacks and the poor.) So is the disintegration of family life in the slum which leaves households in the hands of women. Family life itself is in some measure a manifestation of affluence. And so, without doubt, is the shared sense of helplessness and rejection and the resulting demoralization which is the product of the common misfortune.

The most certain thing about this poverty is that it is not reme-   13 died by a general advance in income. Case poverty is not remedied because the specific individual inadequacy precludes employment and participation in the general advance. Insular poverty is not directly alleviated because the advance does not remove the specific frustrations of environment to which the people of these areas are subject. This is not to say that it is without effect. If there are jobs outside the ghetto or away from the rural slum, those who are qualified, and not otherwise constrained, can take them and escape. If there are no such jobs, none can escape. But it remains that advance cannot improve the position of those who, by virtue of self or environment, cannot participate.

III

With the transition of the very poor from a majority to a com-   14 parative minority position, there has been a change in their political position. Any tendency of a politician to identify himself with those of the lowest estate usually brought the reproaches of the well-to-do. Political pandering and demagoguery were naturally suspected. But, for the man so reproached, there was the compensating advantage of alignment with a large majority. Now any politician who speaks for the very poor is speaking for a small and generally inarticulate minority. As a result, the modern liberal politician regularly aligns himself not with the poverty-ridden members of the community but with the far more numerous people who enjoy the far more affluent income of (say) the modern trade union member or the intellectual. Ambrose Bierce, in *The Devil's Dictionary*, called poverty "a file provided for the teeth of the rats of reform."[2] It is so no longer. Reform now concerns itself with the needs of people who are relatively well-to-do—whether the comparison be with their own past or with those who are really at the bottom of the income ladder.

---

[2] **Ambrose Bierce (1842–1914)** A southern American writer noted for satirical writings such as the one quoted.

In consequence, a notable feature of efforts to help the very 15 poor is their absence of any very great political appeal.[3] Politicians have found it possible to be indifferent where they could not be derisory. And very few have been under a strong compulsion to support these efforts.

The concern for inequality and deprivation had vitality only 16 so long as the many suffered while a few had much. It did not survive as a decisive political issue in a time when the many had much even though others had much more. It is our misfortune that when inequality declined as an issue, the slate was not left clean. A residual and in some ways rather more hopeless problem remained.

IV

An affluent society that is also both compassionate and rational 17 would, no doubt, secure to all who needed it the minimum income essential for decency and comfort. The corrupting effect on the human spirit of unearned revenue has unquestionably been exaggerated as, indeed, have the character-building values of hunger and privation. To secure to each family a minimum income, as a normal function of the society, would help ensure that the misfortunes of parents, deserved or otherwise, were not visited on their children. It would help ensure that poverty was not self-perpetuating. Most of the reaction, which no doubt would be adverse, is based on obsolete attitudes. When poverty was a majority phenomenon, such action could not be afforded. A poor society, as this essay has previously shown, had to enforce the rule that the person who did not work could not eat. And possibly it was justified in the added cruelty of applying the rule to those who could not work or whose efficiency was far below par. An affluent society has no similar excuse for such rigor. It can use the forthright remedy of providing income for those without. Nothing requires such a society to be compassionate. But it no longer has a high philosophical justification for callousness.

The notion that income is a remedy for indigency has a certain 18 forthright appeal.[4] It would also ease the problems of economic management by reducing the reliance on production as a source of

---

[3] This was true of the Office of Economic Opportunity—the so-called poverty program—and was ultimately the reason for its effective demise. [Galbraith's note]

[4] As earlier noted, in the first edition the provision of a guaranteed income was discussed but dismissed as "beyond reasonable hope." [Galbraith's note]

income. The provision of such a basic source of income must henceforth be the first and the strategic step in the attack on poverty.

But it is only one step. In the past, we have suffered from the supposition that the only remedy for poverty lies in remedies that allow people to look after themselves—to participate in the economy. Nothing has better served the conscience of people who wished to avoid inconvenient or expensive action than an appeal, on this issue, to Calvinist precept—"The only sound way to solve the problem of poverty is to help people help themselves." But this does not mean that steps to allow participation and to keep poverty from being self-perpetuating are unimportant. On the contrary. It requires that the investment in children from families presently afflicted be as little below normal as possible. If the children of poor families have first-rate schools and school attendance is properly enforced; if the children, though badly fed at home, are well nourished at school; if the community has sound health services, and the physical well-being of the children is vigilantly watched; if there is opportunity for advanced education for those who qualify regardless of means; and if, especially in the case of urban communities, housing is ample and housing standards are enforced, the streets are clean, the laws are kept, and recreation is adequate—then there is a chance that the children of the very poor will come to maturity without inhibiting disadvantage. In the case of insular poverty, this remedy requires that the services of the community be assisted from outside. Poverty is self-perpetuating partly because the poorest communities are poorest in the services which would eliminate it. To eliminate poverty efficiently, we must, indeed, invest more than proportionately in the children of the poor community. It is there that high-quality schools, strong health services, special provision for nutrition and recreation are most needed to compensate for the very low investment which families are able to make in their own offspring.

The effect of education and related investment in individuals is to help them overcome the restraints that are imposed by their environment. These need also to be attacked even more directly—by giving the mobility that is associated with plentiful, good, and readily available housing, by provision of comfortable, efficient, and economical mass transport, by making the environment pleasant and safe, and by eliminating the special health handicaps that afflict the poor.

Nor is case poverty entirely resistant to such remedies. Much can be done to treat those characteristics which cause people to reject or be rejected by the modern industrial society. Educational deficiencies can be overcome. Mental deficiencies can be treated. Physical handicaps can be remedied. The limiting factor is not a lack of knowledge of what can be done. Overwhelmingly, it is a shortage of money.

V

It will be clear that, to a remarkable extent, the remedy for   22
poverty leads to the same requirements as those for social balance.
The restraints that confine people to the ghetto are those that result
from insufficient investment in the public sector. And the means to
escape from these constraints and to break their hold on subsequent
generations just mentioned—better nutrition and health, better
education, more and better housing, better mass transport, an environment more conducive to effective social participation—all, with
rare exceptions, call for massively greater investment in the public
sector. In recent years, the problems of the urban ghetto have been
greatly discussed but with little resultant effect. To a certain extent,
the search for deeper social explanations of its troubles has been
motivated by the hope that these (together with more police) might
lead to solutions that would somehow elide the problem of cost. It is
an idle hope. The modern urban household is an extremely expensive thing. We have not yet taken the measure of the resources that
must be allocated to its public tasks if it is to be agreeable or even
tolerable. And first among the symptoms of an insufficient allocation is the teeming discontent of the modern ghetto.

A further feature of these remedies is to be observed. Their con-   23
sequence is to allow of participation in the economic life of the
larger community—to make people and the children of people who
are now idle productive. This means that they will add to the total
output of goods and services. We see once again that even by its
own terms the present preoccupation with the private sector of the
economy as compared with the whole spectrum of human needs is
inefficient. The parallel with investment in the supply of trained and
educated manpower discussed above will be apparent.

But increased output of goods is not the main point. Even to the   24
most intellectually reluctant reader, it will now be evident that
enhanced productive efficiency is not the motif of this volume. The
very fact that increased output offers itself as a by-product of the
effort to eliminate poverty is one of the reasons. No one would
be called upon to write at such length on a problem so easily solved
as that of increasing production. The main point lies elsewhere.
Poverty—grim, degrading, and ineluctable—is not remarkable in
India. For relatively few, the fate is otherwise. But in the United
States, the survival of poverty is remarkable. We ignore it because
we share with all societies at all times the capacity for not seeing
what we do not wish to see. Anciently this has enabled the noble-
man to enjoy his dinner while remaining oblivious to the beggars
around his door. In our own day, it enables us to travel in comfort

through the South Bronx and into the lush precincts of midtown Manhattan. But while our failure to notice can be explained, it cannot be excused. "Poverty," Pitt[5] exclaimed, "is no disgrace but it is damned annoying." In the contemporary United States, it is not annoying but it is a disgrace.

---

[5] **William Pitt, the Younger (1759–1806)** British prime minister from 1783 to 1801 and, briefly, again in 1804 and 1805.

QUESTIONS FOR CRITICAL READING

1. What is the fundamental difference between the attitude Alfred Marshall held toward the poor (para. 1) and the attitude contemporary economists hold?
2. Galbraith avoids a specific definition of poverty because he says it changes from society to society. How would you define poverty as it exists in our society? What are its major indicators?
3. According to Galbraith, what is the relationship of politics to poverty?
4. What, according to this essay, seem to be the causes of poverty?
5. Clarify the distinctions Galbraith makes between case poverty and insular poverty. Are they reasonable distinctions?
6. Does Galbraith oversimplify the issues of poverty in America?
7. Galbraith first published this piece in 1958. How much have attitudes toward poverty changed since then? What kinds of progress seem to have been made toward eradicating poverty?

SUGGESTIONS FOR CRITICAL WRITING

1. In paragraph 4, Galbraith says, "People are poverty-stricken when their income, even if adequate for survival, falls radically behind that of the community. Then they cannot have what the larger community regards as the minimum necessary for decency; and they cannot wholly escape, therefore, the judgment of the larger community that they are indecent. They are degraded for, in the literal sense, they live outside the grades or categories which the community regards as acceptable." Examine what he says here, and explain what he means. Is this an accurate description of poverty? How would you amend it? If you accept his description of poverty, what public policy would you recommend to deal with it? What would be the consequences of accepting Galbraith's description?
2. Galbraith points out some anomalies of poverty and place. For example, he notes that West Virginia is rich in resources but that its people have been notable for their poverty. Connecticut, on the other hand, is poor in resources, with stony, untillable land, yet its people

have been notable for their wealth. Some economists have also pointed out that when the Americas were settled, South America had gold, was home to lush tropics that yielded food and fruit for the asking, and held the promise of immense wealth. North America had a harsh climate, stubborn soil conditions, and dense forests that needed clearing. Yet North America has less poverty now than does South America. Write a brief essay in which you consider whether what is said above is too simplified to be useful. If it is not, what do you think is the reason for the economic distinctions that Galbraith and others point out?

3. What personal experiences have you had with poverty? Are you familiar with examples of case poverty? If so, describe them in such a way as to help others understand them. What causes produced the poverty? What is the social situation of the people in your examples? How might they increase their wealth?

4. Examine the newspapers for the last several days, and look through back issues of magazines such as *Time, Newsweek,* the *New Republic,* the *New Leader,* or *U.S. News & World Report.* How many stories does each devote to the question of poverty? Present a survey of the views you find, and compare them with Galbraith's. How much agreement or disagreement is there? Would the level of the nation's concern with poverty please Galbraith?

5. Write a brief essay about current political attitudes toward poverty. If possible, gather some recent statements made by politicians. Analyze them to see how closely they tally with Galbraith's concerns and views. Do any specific politicians act as spokespeople for the poor?

6. Galbraith says that poverty has undergone a dramatic change in our society: once most people were poor and only a few were affluent, and now most people are affluent and only a few are poor. Is Galbraith correct in this assessment? Interview your parents and grandparents and their friends to establish or disprove the validity of Galbraith's claim, and then explain what you feel are the problems the poor face as a result of their minority status. If possible, during your interviews ask what feelings your parents and their friends have about the poor. What feelings do you have? Are they shared by your friends?

7. **CONNECTIONS**   What might Karl Marx (p. 359) say in reaction to Galbraith's definition of poverty and his terms for case poverty and insular poverty? Should Galbraith have examined the role of the bourgeoisie in creating, maintaining, or ignoring poverty? Galbraith wrote the original version of this piece during the 1950s, while world communism was at its height. How might he have accommodated the issues that Marx felt were most important for the working person?

8. **CONNECTIONS**   Galbraith certainly read Andrew Carnegie's *The Gospel of Wealth* (p. 387). What do you think his criticisms of Carnegie might be? Would he have agreed with Carnegie's praise of the laws of competition and accumulation? What alternatives or modifications might Galbraith have suggested to Carnegie? Would Galbraith have approved Carnegie's views on the proper distribution of wealth? How

would Galbraith have responded to Carnegie's assurances that his program of philanthropy would heal the rift between the rich and the poor classes? Argue Galbraith's case either in praise of Carnegie's ideas and theories or in condemnation of them. Use specific points from Carnegie and critique them using Galbraith's principles.

9. **SEEING CONNECTIONS**   Tanner's *The Thankful Poor* (p. 344) is not a painting Galbraith was likely to have seen in his lifetime, but if he had, would he think of the people depicted as examples of case poverty or of insular poverty? What evidence within the painting points to one or the other of these causes? Would Galbraith have had more or less sympathy than Carnegie for the condition of the older man and the young boy? How would Galbraith have reacted to the thankfulness expressed in the title of the painting? What would he have thought the chances were of the young boy growing up and out of poverty? Is it possible that Galbraith would not have thought of these people as examples of poverty? If not, what would his view be?

ROBERT B. REICH
Why the Rich Are Getting Richer and the Poor, Poorer

ROBERT B. REICH (b. 1946), Professor of Public Policy at the Goldman School of Public Policy at the University of California at Berkeley, who served as secretary of labor in the first Clinton administration, holds a graduate degree from Yale Law School, and, unlike his former colleagues in the John F. Kennedy School of Government at Harvard, he does not hold a Ph.D. in economics. Nonetheless, he has written numerous books on economics and has been a prominent lecturer for more than a dozen years. Reich's books include *The Future of Success: Working and Living in the New Economy* (2000); *Reason: Why Liberals Will Win the Battle for America* (2004); and *Supercapitalism: The Transformation of Business, Democracy, and Everyday Life* (2007). All of these have been best-sellers, something unusual for an academic concerned with economics. *Locked in the Cabinet* (1997) is a memoir of his four years as secretary of labor. *The Work of Nations* (1991), from which this essay comes, is the distillation of many years' analysis of modern economic trends.

As a college student, Reich was an activist but not a radical. In 1968, he was a Rhodes scholar, studying at Oxford University with Bill Clinton and a number of others who became influential American policymakers. Reich is a specialist in policy studies — that is, the relationship of governmental policy to the economic health of the nation. Unlike those who champion free trade and unlimited expansion, Reich questions the existence of free trade by pointing to the effect of government taxation on business enterprise. Taxation — like many governmental policies regarding immigration, tariffs, and money supply — directly shapes the behavior of most

From *The Work of Nations*.

companies. Reich feels that government must establish and execute an industrial policy that will benefit the nation.

Even though organized labor groups, such as industrial unions, have rejected much of his theorizing about labor, Reich has developed a reputation as a conciliator who can see opposite sides of a question and resolve them. He is known for his denunciation of mergers, lawsuits, takeovers, and other deals that he believes simply churn money around rather than produce wealth. He feels that such maneuvers enrich a few predatory people but do not benefit labor in general—and, indeed, that the debt created by such deals harms labor in the long run.

In *The Next American Frontier* (1983), Reich insists that government, unions, and businesses must cooperate to create a workable program designed to improve the economy. Trusting to chance and free trade, he argues, will not work in the current economy. He also has said that the old assembly-line methods must give way to what he calls "flexible production," involving smaller, customized runs of products for specific markets.

Reich's *The Work of Nations* (1991), whose title draws on Adam Smith's classic *The Wealth of Nations* (1776), examines the borderless nature of contemporary corporations. Multinational corporations are a reality, and as he points out in the following essay, their flexibility makes it possible for them to thrive by moving manufacturing plants from nation to nation. The reasons for moving are sometimes connected to lower wages but more often are connected to the infrastructure of a given nation. Reliable roads, plentiful electricity, well-educated workers, low crime rates, and political stability are all elements that make a location attractive to a multinational corporation.

Reich's Rhetoric

The structure of "Why the Rich Are Getting Richer and the Poor, Poorer" is built on a metaphor: that of boats rising or falling with the tide. As Reich notes, "All Americans used to be in roughly the same economic boat" (para. 2), and when the economic tide rose, most people rose along with it. However, today "national borders no longer define our economic fates"; Reich therefore views Americans today as being in different boats, depending on their role in the economy, and his essay follows the fates of three distinct kinds of workers.

Examining the routine worker, he observes, "The boat containing routine producers is sinking rapidly" (para. 3). As he demonstrates, the need for routine production has declined in part because of improvements in production facilities. Much labor-intensive work has been replaced by machines. Modern factories often scramble to locate in places where production costs are lowest. People in other nations work at a fraction of the hourly rate of American workers, and because factories are relatively cheap to establish, they can be easily moved.

Reich continues the boat metaphor with "in-person servers." The boat that carries these workers, he says, "is sinking as well, but somewhat more slowly and unevenly" (para. 20). Workers in restaurants, retail outlets, car washes, and other personal service industries often work part-time and have few health or other benefits. Their jobs are imperiled by machines as well, although not as much as manufacturing jobs are. Although the outlook for such workers is buoyed by a declining population, which will reduce competition for their jobs, increased immigration may cancel this benefit.

Finally, Reich argues that the "vessel containing America's symbolic analysts is rising" (para. 28). This third group contains the population that identifies and solves problems and brokers ideas. "Almost everyone around the world is buying the skills and insights of Americans who manipulate oral and visual symbols" (para. 33). Engineers, consultants, marketing experts, publicists, and those in entertainment fields all manage to cross national boundaries and prosper at a rate that is perhaps startling. As a result of an expanding world market, symbolic analysts do not depend only on the purchasing power of routine and in-service workers. Instead, they rely on the same global web that dominates the pattern of corporate structure.

Reich's essay follows the fate of these three groups in turn to establish the pattern of change and expectation that will shape America's economic future. His metaphor is deftly handled, and he includes details, examples, facts, and careful references to support his position.

PREREADING QUESTIONS: WHAT TO READ FOR

The following prereading questions may help you anticipate key issues in the discussion of Robert B. Reich's "Why the Rich Are Getting Richer and the Poor, Poorer." Keeping them in mind during your first reading of the selection should help focus your attention.

- Why and how does an individual's position in the world economy depend on the function he/she performs in it?

- What are "routine producers"? What will be their fate in the future?

- Who are the "symbolic analysts" in our economy? How does one become a symbolic analyst?

Why the Rich Are Getting Richer and the Poor, Poorer

The division of labor is limited by the extent of the market.
—ADAM SMITH
An Inquiry into the Nature
and Causes of the Wealth of Nations (1776)

Regardless of how your job is officially classified (manufactur-   1
ing, service, managerial, technical, secretarial, and so on), or the
industry in which you work (automotive, steel, computer, advertising, finance, food processing), your real competitive position in the
world economy is coming to depend on the function you perform in
it. Herein lies the basic reason why incomes are diverging. The fortunes of routine producers are declining. In-person servers are also
becoming poorer, although their fates are less clear-cut. But symbolic analysts—who solve, identify, and broker new problems—
are, by and large, succeeding in the world economy.

All Americans used to be in roughly the same economic boat.   2
Most rose or fell together as the corporations in which they were
employed, the industries comprising such corporations, and the
national economy as a whole became more productive—or languished. But national borders no longer define our economic fates.
We are now in different boats, one sinking rapidly, one sinking
more slowly, and the third rising steadily.

The boat containing routine producers is sinking rapidly.   3
Recall that by midcentury routine production workers in the
United States were paid relatively well. The giant pyramidlike
organizations at the core of each major industry coordinated their
prices and investments—avoiding the harsh winds of competition
and thus maintaining healthy earnings. Some of these earnings, in
turn, were reinvested in new plant and equipment (yielding ever-
larger-scale economies); another portion went to top managers and
investors. But a large and increasing portion went to middle managers and production workers. Work stoppages posed such a
threat to high-volume production that organized labor was able to
exact an ever-larger premium for its cooperation. And the pattern
of wages established within the core corporations influenced the
pattern throughout the national economy. Thus the growth of a
relatively affluent middle class, able to purchase all the wondrous
things produced in high volume by the core corporations.

But, as has been observed, the core is rapidly breaking down 4
into global webs which earn their largest profits from clever
problem-solving, -identifying, and brokering. As the costs of transporting standard things and of communicating information about
them continue to drop, profit margins on high-volume, standardized production are thinning, because there are few barriers to
entry. Modern factories and state-of-the-art machinery can be
installed almost anywhere on the globe. Routine producers in the
United States, then, are in direct competition with millions of routine producers in other nations. Twelve thousand people are added
to the world's population every hour, most of whom, eventually,
will happily work for a small fraction of the wages of routine producers in America.[1]

The consequence is clearest in older, heavy industries, where 5
high-volume, standardized production continues its ineluctable move
to where labor is cheapest and most accessible around the world.
Thus, for example, the Maquiladora factories cluttered along the
Mexican side of the U.S. border in the sprawling shanty towns of
Tijuana, Mexicali, Nogales, Agua Prieta, and Ciudad Juárez—factories
owned mostly by Americans, but increasingly by Japanese—in which
more than a half million routine producers assemble parts into finished goods to be shipped into the United States.

The same story is unfolding worldwide. Until the late 1970s, 6
AT&T had depended on routine producers in Shreveport, Louisiana,
to assemble standard telephones. It then discovered that routine producers in Singapore would perform the same tasks at a far lower
cost. Facing intense competition from other global webs, AT&T's
strategic brokers felt compelled to switch. So in the early 1980s they
stopped hiring routine producers in Shreveport and began hiring
cheaper routine producers in Singapore. But under this kind of pressure for ever-lower high-volume production costs, today's Singa-
porean can easily end up as yesterday's Louisianan. By the late
1980s, AT&T's strategic brokers found that routine producers in
Thailand were eager to assemble telephones for a small fraction of
the wages of routine producers in Singapore. Thus, in 1989, AT&T
stopped hiring Singaporeans to make telephones and began hiring
even cheaper routine producers in Thailand.

---

[1] The reader should note, of course, that lower wages in other areas of the
world are of no particular attraction to global capital unless workers there are sufficiently productive to make the labor cost of producing *each unit* lower there than in
higher-wage regions. Productivity in many low-wage areas of the world has
improved due to the ease with which state-of-the-art factories and equipment can be
installed there. [Reich's note]

The search for ever-lower wages has not been confined to heavy   7
industry. Routine data processing is equally footloose. Keypunch
operators located anywhere around the world can enter data into
computers, linked by satellite or transoceanic fiber-optic cable, and
take it out again. As the rates charged by satellite networks continue
to drop, and as more satellites and fiber-optic cables become available (reducing communication costs still further), routine data processors in the United States find themselves in ever more direct
competition with their counterparts abroad, who are often eager to
work for far less.

By 1990, keypunch operators in the United States were earning,   8
at most, $6.50 per hour. But keypunch operators throughout the rest
of the world were willing to work for a fraction of this. Thus, many
potential American data-processing jobs were disappearing, and the
wages and benefits of the remaining ones were in decline. Typical
was Saztec International, a $20-million-a-year data-processing firm
headquartered in Kansas City, whose American strategic brokers contracted with routine data processors in Manila and with American-
owned firms that needed such data-processing services. Compared
with the average Philippine income of $1,700 per year, data-entry
operators working for Saztec earn the princely sum of $2,650. The
remainder of Saztec's employees were American problem-solvers
and -identifiers, searching for ways to improve the worldwide system
and find new uses to which it could be put.[2]

By 1990, American Airlines was employing over 1,000 data pro-   9
cessors in Barbados and the Dominican Republic to enter names and
flight numbers from used airline tickets (flown daily to Barbados
from airports around the United States) into a giant computer bank
located in Dallas. Chicago publisher R. R. Donnelley was sending
entire manuscripts to Barbados for entry into computers in preparation for printing. The New York Life Insurance Company was dispatching insurance claims to Castleisland, Ireland, where routine
producers, guided by simple directions, entered the claims and
determined the amounts due, then instantly transmitted the computations back to the United States. (When the firm advertised in
Ireland for twenty-five data-processing jobs, it received six hundred
applications.) And McGraw-Hill was processing subscription renewal
and marketing information for its magazines in nearby Galway.
Indeed, literally millions of routine workers around the world were
receiving information, converting it into computer-readable form,

---

[2] John Maxwell Hamilton, "A Bit Player Buys into the Computer Age," *New York Times Business World,* December 3, 1989, p. 14. [Reich's note]

and then sending it back—at the speed of electronic impulses—whence it came.

The simple coding of computer software has also entered into world commerce. India, with a large English-speaking population of technicians happy to do routine programming cheaply, is proving to be particularly attractive to global webs in need of this service. By 1990, Texas Instruments maintained a software development facility in Bangalore, linking fifty Indian programmers by satellite to TI's Dallas headquarters. Spurred by this and similar ventures, the Indian government was building a teleport in Poona, intended to make it easier and less expensive for many other firms to send their routine software design specifications for coding.[3]

This shift of routine production jobs from advanced to developing nations is a great boon to many workers in such nations who otherwise would be jobless or working for much lower wages. These workers, in turn, now have more money with which to purchase symbolic-analytic services from advanced nations (often embedded within all sorts of complex products). The trend is also beneficial to everyone around the world who can now obtain high-volume, standardized products (including information and software) more cheaply than before.

But these benefits do not come without certain costs. In particular the burden is borne by those who no longer have good-paying routine production jobs within advanced economies like the United States. Many of these people used to belong to unions or at least benefited from prevailing wage rates established in collective bargaining agreements. But as the old corporate bureaucracies have flattened into global webs, bargaining leverage has been lost. Indeed, the tacit national bargain is no more.

Despite the growth in the number of new jobs in the United States, union membership has withered. In 1960, 35 percent of all nonagricultural workers in America belonged to a union. But by 1980 that portion had fallen to just under a quarter, and by 1989 to about 17 percent. Excluding government employees, union membership was down to 13.4 percent.[4] This was a smaller proportion even than in the early 1930s, before the National Labor Relations Act created a legally protected right to labor representation. The drop in membership has been accompanied by a growing number of

10

11

12

13

---

[3] Udayan Gupta, "U.S.-Indian Satellite Link Stands to Cut Software Costs," *Wall Street Journal,* March 6, 1989, p. B2. [Reich's note]

[4] *Statistical Abstract of the United States* (Washington, D.C.: U.S. Government Printing Office, 1989), p. 416, table 684. [Reich's note]

collective bargaining agreements to freeze wages at current levels, reduce wage levels of entering workers, or reduce wages overall. This is an important reason why the long economic recovery that began in 1982 produced a smaller rise in unit labor costs than any of the eight recoveries since World War II — the low rate of unemployment during its course notwithstanding.

Routine production jobs have vanished fastest in traditional 14 unionized industries (autos, steel, and rubber, for example), where average wages have kept up with inflation. This is because the jobs of older workers in such industries are protected by seniority; the youngest workers are the first to be laid off. Faced with a choice of cutting wages or cutting the number of jobs, a majority of union members (secure in the knowledge that there are many who are junior to them who will be laid off first) often have voted for the latter.

Thus the decline in union membership has been most striking 15 among young men entering the work force without a college education. In the early 1950s, more than 40 percent of this group joined unions; by the late 1980s, less than 20 percent (if public employees are excluded, less than 10 percent).[5] In steelmaking, for example, although many older workers remained employed, almost half of all routine steelmaking jobs in America vanished between 1974 and 1988 (from 480,000 to 260,000). Similarly with automobiles: during the 1980s, the United Auto Workers lost 500,000 members — one-third of their total at the start of the decade. General Motors alone cut 150,000 American production jobs during the 1980s (even as it added employment abroad). Another consequence of the same phenomenon: the gap between the average wages of unionized and nonunionized workers widened dramatically — from 14.6 percent in 1973 to 20.4 percent by end of the 1980s.[6] The lesson is clear. If you drop out of high school or have no more than a high school diploma, do not expect a good routine production job to be awaiting you.

Also vanishing are lower- and middle-level management jobs 16 involving routine production. Between 1981 and 1986, more than 780,000 foremen, supervisors, and section chiefs lost their jobs through plant closings and layoffs.[7] Large numbers of assistant

---

[5] Calculations from Current Population Surveys by L. Katz and A. Revenga, "Changes in the Structure of Wages: U.S. and Japan," National Bureau of Economic Research, September 1989. [Reich's note]

[6] U.S. Department of Commerce, Bureau of Labor Statistics, "Wages of Unionized and Non-Unionized Workers," various issues. [Reich's note]

[7] U.S. Department of Labor, Bureau of Labor Statistics, "Reemployment Increases Among Displaced Workers," BLS News, USDL 86–414, October 14, 1986, table 6. [Reich's note]

division heads, assistant directors, assistant managers, and vice presidents also found themselves jobless. GM shed more than 40,000 white-collar employees and planned to eliminate another 25,000 by the mid-1990s.[8] As America's core pyramids metamorphosed into global webs, many middle-level routine producers were as obsolete as routine workers on the line.

As has been noted, foreign-owned webs are hiring some   17 Americans to do routine production in the United States. Philips, Sony, and Toyota factories are popping up all over—to the self-congratulatory applause of the nation's governors and mayors, who have lured them with promises of tax abatements and new sewers, among other amenities. But as these ebullient politicians will soon discover, the foreign-owned factories are highly automated and will become far more so in years to come. Routine production jobs account for a small fraction of the cost of producing most items in the United States and other advanced nations, and this fraction will continue to decline sharply as computer-integrated robots take over. In 1977 it took routine producers thirty-five hours to assemble an automobile in the United States; it is estimated that by the mid-1990s, Japanese-owned factories in America will be producing finished automobiles using only eight hours of a routine producer's time.[9]

The productivity and resulting wages of American workers who   18 run such robotic machinery may be relatively high, but there may not be many such jobs to go around. A case in point: in the late 1980s, Nippon Steel joined with America's ailing Inland Steel to build a new $400 million cold-rolling mill fifty miles west of Gary, Indiana. The mill was celebrated for its state-of-the-art technology, which cut the time to produce a coil of steel from twelve days to about one hour. In fact, the entire plant could be run by a small team of technicians, which became clear when Inland subsequently closed two of its old cold-rolling mills, laying off hundreds of routine workers. Governors and mayors take note: your much-ballyhooed foreign factories may end up employing distressingly few of your constituents.

Overall, the decline in routine jobs has hurt men more than   19 women. This is because the routine production jobs held by men in high-volume metal-bending manufacturing industries had paid higher wages than the routine production jobs held by women in

---

[8] *Wall Street Journal,* February 16, 1990, p. A5. [Reich's note]

[9] Figures from the International Motor Vehicles Program, Massachusetts Institute of Technology, 1989. [Reich's note]

textiles and data processing. As both sets of jobs have been lost, American women in routine production have gained more equal footing with American men—equally poor footing, that is. This is a major reason why the gender gap between male and female wages began to close during the 1980s.

The second of the three boats, carrying in-person servers, is sinking as well, but somewhat more slowly and unevenly. Most in-person servers are paid at or just slightly above the minimum wage and many work only part-time, with the result that their take-home pay is modest, to say the least. Nor do they typically receive all the benefits (health care, life insurance, disability, and so forth) garnered by routine producers in large manufacturing corporations or by symbolic analysts affiliated with the more affluent threads of global webs.[10] In-person servers are sheltered from the direct effects of global competition and, like everyone else, benefit from access to lower-cost products from around the world. But they are not immune to its indirect effects.

For one thing, in-person servers increasingly compete with former routine production workers, who, no longer able to find well-paying routine production jobs, have few alternatives but to seek in-person service jobs. The Bureau of Labor Statistics estimates that of the 2.8 million manufacturing workers who lost their jobs during the early 1980s, fully one-third were rehired in service jobs paying at least 20 percent less.[11] In-person servers must also compete with high school graduates and dropouts who years before had moved easily into routine production jobs but no longer can. And if demographic predictions about the American work force in the first decades of the twenty-first century are correct (and they are likely to be, since most of the people who will comprise the work force are already identifiable), most new entrants into the job market will be black or Hispanic men, or women—groups that in years past have possessed relatively weak technical skills. This will result in an even larger number of people crowding into in-person services. Finally, in-person servers will be competing with growing numbers of immigrants, both legal and illegal, for whom in-person services will comprise the most accessible jobs. (It is estimated that between

20

21

---

[10] The growing portion of the American labor force engaged in in-person services, relative to routine production, thus helps explain why the number of Americans lacking health insurance increased by at least 6 million during the 1980s. [Reich's note]

[11] U.S. Department of Labor, Bureau of Labor Statistics, "Reemployment Increases Among Disabled Workers," October 14, 1986. [Reich's note]

the mid-1980s and the end of the century, about a quarter of all workers entering the American labor force will be immigrants.[12])

Perhaps the fiercest competition that in-person servers face comes from labor-saving machinery (much of it invented, designed, fabricated, or assembled in other nations, of course). Automated tellers, computerized cashiers, automatic car washes, robotized vending machines, self-service gasoline pumps, and all similar gadgets substitute for the human beings that customers once encountered. Even telephone operators are fast disappearing, as electronic sensors and voice simulators become capable of carrying on conversations that are reasonably intelligent and always polite. Retail sales workers—among the largest groups of in-person servers—are similarly imperiled. Through personal computers linked to television screens, tomorrow's consumers will be able to buy furniture, appliances, and all sorts of electronic toys from their living rooms—examining the merchandise from all angles, selecting whatever color, size, special features, and price seem most appealing, and then transmitting the order instantly to warehouses from which the selections will be shipped directly to their homes. So, too, with financial transactions, airline and hotel reservations, rental car agreements, and similar contracts, which will be executed between consumers in their homes and computer banks somewhere else on the globe.[13]

Advanced economies like the United States will continue to generate sizable numbers of new in-person service jobs, of course, the automation of older ones notwithstanding. For every bank teller who loses her job to an automated teller, three new jobs open for aerobics instructors. Human beings, it seems, have an almost insatiable desire for personal attention. But the intense competition nevertheless ensures that the wages of in-person servers will remain relatively low. In-person servers—working on their own, or else dispersed widely amid many small establishments, filling all sorts of personal-care niches—cannot readily organize themselves into labor unions or create powerful lobbies to limit the impact of such competition.

In two respects, demographics will work in favor of in-person servers, buoying their collective boat slightly. First, as has been noted, the rate of growth of the American work force is slowing. In particular, the number of young workers is shrinking. Between 1985 and

22

23

24

---

[12] Federal Immigration and Naturalization Service, *Statistical Yearbook* (Washington, D.C.: U.S. Government Printing Office, 1986, 1987). [Reich's note]

[13] See Claudia H. Deutsch, "The Powerful Push for Self-Service," *New York Times*, April 9, 1989, section 3, p. 1. [Reich's note]

1995, the number of the eighteen- to twenty-four-year-olds will have declined by 17.5 percent. Thus, employers will have more incentive to hire and train in-person servers whom they might previously have avoided. But this demographic relief from the competitive pressures will be only temporary. The cumulative procreative energies of the postwar baby-boomers (born between 1946 and 1964) will result in a new surge of workers by 2010 or thereabouts.[14] And immigration—both legal and illegal—shows every sign of increasing in years to come.

Next, by the second decade of the twenty-first century, the   25 number of Americans aged sixty-five and over will be rising precipitously, as the baby-boomers reach retirement age and live longer. Their life expectancies will lengthen not just because fewer of them will have smoked their way to their graves and more will have eaten better than their parents, but also because they will receive all sorts of expensive drugs and therapies designed to keep them alive— barely. By 2035, twice as many Americans will be elderly as in 1988, and the number of octogenarians is expected to triple. As these decaying baby-boomers ingest all the chemicals and receive all the treatments, they will need a great deal of personal attention. Millions of deteriorating bodies will require nurses, nursing-home operators, hospital administrators, orderlies, home-care providers, hospice aides, and technicians to operate and maintain all the expensive machinery that will monitor and temporarily stave off final disintegration. There might even be a booming market for euthanasia specialists. In-person servers catering to the old and ailing will be in strong demand.[15]

One small problem: the decaying baby-boomers will not have   26 enough money to pay for these services. They will have used up their personal savings years before. Their Social Security payments will, of course, have been used by the government to pay for the previous generation's retirement and to finance much of the budget deficits of the 1980s. Moreover, with relatively fewer young Americans in the population, the supply of housing will likely exceed the demand, with the result that the boomers' major investments— their homes—will be worth less (in inflation-adjusted dollars) when they retire than they planned for. In consequence, the huge cost of

---

[14] U.S. Bureau of the Census, Current Population Reports, Series P-23, no. 138, tables 2-1, 4-6. See W. Johnson, A. Packer, et al., *Workforce 2000: Work and Workers for the 21st Century* (Indianapolis: Hudson Institute, 1987). [Reich's note]

[15] The Census Bureau estimates that by the year 2000, at least 12 million Americans will work in health services—well over 6 percent of the total work force. [Reich's note]

caring for the graying boomers will fall on many of the same people who will be paid to care for them. It will be like a great sump pump: in-person servers of the twenty-first century will have an abundance of health-care jobs, but a large portion of their earnings will be devoted to Social Security payments and income taxes, which will in turn be used to pay their salaries. The net result: no real improvement in their standard of living.

The standard of living of in-person servers also depends, indi-   27
rectly, on the standard of living of the Americans they serve who are engaged in world commerce. To the extent that these Americans are richly rewarded by the rest of the world for what they contribute, they will have more money to lavish upon in-person services. Here we find the only form of "trickle-down" economics that has a basis in reality. A waitress in a town whose major factory has just been closed is unlikely to earn a high wage or enjoy much job security; in a swank resort populated by film producers and banking moguls, she is apt to do reasonably well. So, too, with nations. In-person servers in Bangladesh may spend their days performing roughly the same tasks as in-person servers in the United States, but have a far lower standard of living for their efforts. The difference comes in the value that their customers add to the world economy.

Unlike the boats of routine producers and in-person servers,   28
however, the vessel containing America's symbolic analysts is rising. Worldwide demand for their insights is growing as the ease and speed of communicating them steadily increases. Not every symbolic analyst is rising as quickly or as dramatically as every other, of course; symbolic analysts at the low end are barely holding their own in the world economy. But symbolic analysts at the top are in such great demand worldwide that they have difficulty keeping track of all their earnings. Never before in history has opulence on such a scale been gained by people who have earned it, and done so legally.

Among symbolic analysts in the middle range are American sci-   29
entists and researchers who are busily selling their discoveries to global enterprise webs. They are not limited to American customers. If the strategic brokers in General Motors' headquarters refuse to pay a high price for a new means of making high-strength ceramic engines dreamed up by a team of engineers affiliated with Carnegie Mellon University in Pittsburgh, the strategic brokers of Honda or Mercedes-Benz are likely to be more than willing.

So, too, with the insights of America's ubiquitous management   30
consultants, which are being sold for large sums to eager entrepreneurs in Europe and Latin America. Also, the insights of America's energy consultants, sold for even larger sums to Arab sheikhs. American

design engineers are providing insights to Olivetti, Mazda, Siemens, and other global webs; American marketers, techniques for learning what worldwide consumers will buy; American advertisers, ploys for ensuring that they actually do. American architects are issuing designs and blueprints for opera houses, art galleries, museums, luxury hotels, and residential complexes in the world's major cities; American commercial property developers, marketing these properties to worldwide investors and purchasers.

Americans who specialize in the gentle art of public relations are in demand by corporations, governments, and politicians in virtually every nation. So, too, are American political consultants, some of whom, at this writing, are advising the Hungarian Socialist Party, the remnant of Hungary's ruling Communists, on how to salvage a few parliamentary seats in the nation's first free election in more than forty years. Also at this writing, a team of American agricultural consultants is advising the managers of a Soviet farm collective employing 1,700 Russians eighty miles outside Moscow. As noted, American investment bankers and lawyers specializing in financial circumnavigations are selling their insights to Asians and Europeans who are eager to discover how to make large amounts of money by moving large amounts of money. 31

Developing nations, meanwhile, are hiring American civil engineers to advise on building roads and dams. The present thaw in the Cold War will no doubt expand these opportunities. American engineers from Bechtel (a global firm notable for having employed both Caspar Weinberger and George Shultz for much larger sums than either earned in the Reagan administration) have begun helping the Soviets design and install a new generation of nuclear reactors. Nations also are hiring American bankers and lawyers to help them renegotiate the terms of their loans with global banks, and Washington lobbyists to help them with Congress, the Treasury, the World Bank, the IMF, and other politically sensitive institutions. In fits of obvious desperation, several nations emerging from communism have even hired American economists to teach them about capitalism. 32

Almost everyone around the world is buying the skills and insights of Americans who manipulate oral and visual symbols—musicians, sound engineers, film producers, makeup artists, directors, cinematographers, actors and actresses, boxers, scriptwriters, songwriters, and set designers. Among the wealthiest of symbolic analysts are Steven Spielberg, Bill Cosby, Charles Schulz, Eddie Murphy, Sylvester Stallone, Madonna, and other star directors and performers—who are almost as well known on the streets of Dresden and Tokyo as in the Back Bay of Boston. Less well rewarded but no 33 less renowned are the unctuous anchors on Turner Broadcasting's Cable News, who appear daily, via satellite, in places ranging from Vietnam to Nigeria. Vanna White is the world's most-watched game-show hostess. Behind each of these familiar faces is a collection of American problem-solvers, -identifiers, and brokers who train, coach, advise, promote, amplify, direct, groom, represent, and otherwise add value to their talents.[16]

There are also the insights of senior American executives who   34 occupy the world headquarters of global "American" corporations and the national or regional headquarters of global "foreign" corporations. Their insights are duly exported to the rest of the world through the webs of global enterprise. IBM does not export many machines from the United States, for example. Big Blue makes machines all over the globe and services them on the spot. Its prime American exports are symbolic and analytic. From IBM's world headquarters in Armonk, New York, emanate strategic brokerage and related management services bound for the rest of the world. In return, IBM's top executives are generously rewarded.

The most important reason for this expanding world market   35 and increasing global demand for the symbolic and analytic insights of Americans has been the dramatic improvement in worldwide communication and transportation technologies. Designs, instructions, advice, and visual and audio symbols can be communicated more and more rapidly around the globe, with ever-greater precision and at ever-lower cost. Madonna's voice can be transported to billions of listeners, with perfect clarity, on digital compact discs. A new invention emanating from engineers in Battelle's laboratory in Columbus, Ohio, can be sent almost anywhere via modem, in a form that will allow others to examine it in three dimensions through enhanced computer graphics. When face-to-face meetings are still required—and videoconferencing will not suffice—it is relatively easy for designers, consultants, advisers, artists, and executives to board supersonic jets and, in a matter of hours, meet directly with their worldwide clients, customers, audiences, and employees.

With rising demand comes rising compensation. Whether in   36 the form of licensing fees, fees for service, salaries, or shares in final profits, the economic result is much the same. There are also

---

[16] In 1989, the entertainment business summoned to the United States $5.5 billion in foreign earnings—making it among the nation's largest export industries, just behind aerospace. U.S. Department of Commerce, International Trade Commission, "Composition of U.S. Exports," various issues. [Reich's note]

nonpecuniary rewards. One of the best-kept secrets among symbolic analysts is that so many of them enjoy their work. In fact, much of it does not count as work at all, in the traditional sense. The work of routine producers and in-person servers is typically monotonous; it causes muscles to tire or weaken and involves little independence or discretion. The "work" of symbolic analysts, by contrast, often involves puzzles, experiments, games, a significant amount of chatter, and substantial discretion over what to do next. Few routine producers or in-person servers would "work" if they did not need to earn the money. Many symbolic analysts would "work" even if money were no object.

At midcentury, when America was a national market dominated   37
by core pyramid-shaped corporations, there were constraints on the earnings of people at the highest rungs. First and most obviously, the market for their services was largely limited to the borders of the nation. In addition, whatever conceptual value they might contribute was small relative to the value gleaned from large scale — and it was dependent on large scale for whatever income it was to summon. Most of the problems to be identified and solved had to do with enhancing the efficiency of production and improving the flow of materials, parts, assembly, and distribution. Inventors searched for the rare breakthrough revealing an entirely new product to be made in high volume; management consultants, executives, and engineers thereafter tried to speed and synchronize its manufacture, to better achieve scale efficiencies; advertisers and marketers sought then to whet the public's appetite for the standard item that emerged. Since white-collar earnings increased with larger scale, there was considerable incentive to expand the firm; indeed, many of America's core corporations grew far larger than scale economies would appear to have justified.

By the 1990s, in contrast, the earnings of symbolic analysts   38
were limited neither by the size of the national market nor by the volume of production of the firms with which they were affiliated. The marketplace was worldwide, and conceptual value was high relative to value added from scale efficiencies.

There had been another constraint on high earnings, which   39
also gave way by the 1990s. At midcentury, the compensation awarded to top executives and advisers of the largest of America's core corporations could not be grossly out of proportion to that of low-level production workers. It would be unseemly for executives who engaged in highly visible rounds of bargaining with labor unions, and who routinely responded to government requests to moderate prices, to take home wages and benefits wildly in

excess of what other Americans earned. Unless white-collar executives restrained themselves, moreover, blue-collar production workers could not be expected to restrain their own demands for higher wages. Unless both groups exercised restraint, the government could not be expected to forbear from imposing direct controls and regulations.

At the same time, the wages of production workers could not be   40
allowed to sink too low, lest there be insufficient purchasing power in the economy. After all, who would buy all the goods flowing out of American factories if not American workers? This, too, was part of the tacit bargain struck between American managers and their workers.

Recall the oft-repeated corporate platitude of the era about the   41
chief executive's responsibility to carefully weigh and balance the interests of the corporation's disparate stakeholders. Under the stewardship of the corporate statesman, no set of stakeholders—least of all white-collar executives—was to gain a disproportionately large share of the benefits of corporate activity; nor was any stakeholder— especially the average worker—to be left with a share that was disproportionately small. Banal though it was, this idea helped to maintain the legitimacy of the core American corporation in the eyes of most Americans, and to ensure continued economic growth.

But by the 1990s, these informal norms were evaporating, just   42
as (and largely because) the core American corporation was vanishing. The links between top executives and the American production worker were fading: an ever-increasing number of subordinates and contractees were foreign, and a steadily growing number of American routine producers were working for foreign-owned firms. An entire cohort of middle-level managers, who had once been deemed "white collar," had disappeared; and, increasingly, American executives were exporting their insights to global enterprise webs.

As the American corporation itself became a global web almost   43
indistinguishable from any other, its stakeholders were turning into a large and diffuse group, spread over the world. Such global stakeholders were less visible, and far less noisy, than national stakeholders. And as the American corporation sold its goods and services all over the world, the purchasing power of American workers became far less relevant to its economic survival.

Thus have the inhibitions been removed. The salaries and   44
benefits of America's top executives, and many of their advisers and consultants, have soared to what years before would have been unimaginable heights, even as those of other Americans have declined.

QUESTIONS FOR CRITICAL READING

1. What are symbolic analysts? Give some examples from your own experience.
2. What is the apparent relationship between higher education and an educated worker's prospects for wealth?
3. To what extent do you agree or disagree with Reich's description and analysis of routine workers and in-service workers?
4. If Reich's analysis is correct, which gender or social groups are likely to be most harmed by modern economic circumstances in America? Which are most likely to become wealthy? Why?
5. Are symbolic analysts inherently more valuable to our society than routine or in-service workers? Why do symbolic analysts command so much more wealth?
6. Which of the three groups Reich mentions do you see as having the greatest potential for growth in the next thirty years?

SUGGESTIONS FOR CRITICAL WRITING

1. Judging from the views that Reich holds about decreasing job opportunities for all three groups of workers, how will increased immigration affect the American economy? Is immigration a hopeful sign? Is it a danger to the economy? How do most people seem to perceive the effect of increased immigration?
2. To what extent do you think Reich is correct about the growing wealth of symbolic analysts? He says, "Never before in history has opulence on such a scale been gained by people who have earned it, and done so legally" (para. 28). Do you see yourself as a symbolic analyst? How do you see your future in relation to the three economic groups Reich describes?
3. Reich says, "Few routine producers or in-person servers would 'work' if they did not need to earn the money. Many symbolic analysts would 'work' even if money were no object" (para. 36). Is this true? Examine your own experience—along with the experience of others you know—and defend or attack this view. How accurate do you consider Reich to be in his analysis of the way various workers view their work?
4. Describe the changes that have taken place in the American economy since 1960, according to this essay. How have they affected the way Americans work and the work that Americans can expect to find? How have your personal opportunities been broadened or narrowed by the changes? Do you feel the changes have been good for the country or not? Why?
5. Reich's view of the great success of Japanese corporations and of their presence as manufacturing giants in the United States and elsewhere is largely positive. He has pointed out elsewhere that Honda and other

manufacturers in the United States provide jobs and municipal income that would otherwise go to other nations. What is your view of the presence of large Japanese corporations in the United States? What is your view of other nations' manufacturing facilities in the United States?

6. Why are the rich getting richer and the poor, poorer? Examine the kinds of differences between the rich and the poor that Reich describes. Is the process of increasing riches for the rich and increasing poverty for the poor inevitable, or will it begin to change in the near future?

7. **CONNECTIONS**   Karl Marx (p. 359) warns against globalism in the economy in part because it harms local industry and damages local styles and customs. How would Reich counter those fears? Is it clear that Reich approves of the new economy he describes, or does he accept globalism as a form of economic evolution? Would he be likely to agree with Andrew Carnegie (p. 387) that the laws of competition and accumulation operate in the new economy at least as forcefully as they did in Carnegie's time? Does he in any way seem approving of Marx's theories?

8. **CONNECTIONS**   Reich examines what seems to be a new form for the economy now that free trade is essentially a reality and major foreign nations—like Japan, China, and India—are creating enormous wealth while Western industrial nations are losing industries and jobs to those countries. How would Reich respond to Adam Smith's (p. 347) concepts of how a nation produces wealth? What are the differences Reich sees in the current economy as compared with that of Smith's time? Would he feel that any of Smith's principles regarding land, agriculture, and manufactures applies to our new economy? Establish Reich's position regarding Smith's basic theories.

9. **SEEING CONNECTIONS**   Where do the two people in Tanner's *The Thankful Poor* (p. 344) fit in Reich's concept of the new economy? What would Reich say about them if he were to include them in his discussion? What details in the painting might Reich point to as significant of the new economy? Keeping in mind that the painting was made in 1894, is it possible that Reich would simply say that these people have nothing to do with current economic conditions? Or would he say that the painting represents what will happen to many of the working poor in the United States? What evidence from the painting and from your understanding of the principles of wealth and poverty helps you draw your conclusions?

PART FIVE

MIND

Plato
René Descartes
Sigmund Freud
Carl Jung
Howard Gardner
Steven Pinker
V. S. Ramachandran

INTRODUCTION

We are shaped by our thoughts; we become what we think.
When the mind is pure, joy follows like a shadow that never
leaves.
> —SIDDHĀRTHA GAUTAMA, THE BUDDHA (563–483 B.C.)

That in the soul which is called the mind is, before it thinks, not
actually any real thing.
> —ARISTOTLE (384–322 B.C.)

Distinctions drawn by the mind are not necessarily equivalent to
distinctions in reality.
> —ST. THOMAS AQUINAS (1225–1274)

Consciousness is the perception of what passes in a man's own
mind. Can another man perceive that I am conscious of any
thing, when I perceive it not myself? No man's knowledge here
can go beyond his experience.
> —JOHN LOCKE (1632–1704)

The difference in mind between man and the higher animals,
great as it is, is one of degree and not of kind.
> —CHARLES DARWIN (1809–1882)

The computer takes up where psychoanalysis left off. It takes the
ideas of a decentered self and makes it more concrete by
modeling mind as a multiprocessing machine.
> —SHERRY TURKLE (b. 1948)

Ideas about the nature of the human mind have abounded
throughout history. Philosophers and scientists have sought to discern the mind's components and functions and have distinguished
humans from other animals according to the qualities associated
with the mind, such as reason and self-awareness. The ancient
Greeks formulated the concept of the psyche (from which we derive
the term *psychology*) as the center of consciousness and reason as well
as emotions. During the Renaissance, René Descartes (1596–1650)
concluded *Cogito ergo sum* ("I think, therefore I am") and proposed
that the mind was the source of human identity and that reason was
the key to comprehending the material world. Influenced by
Descartes, John Locke (1632–1704) developed a theory of the mind
as a *tabula rasa*, or blank slate, that was shaped entirely by external
experiences. The selections in this section further explore these
questions about the nature of the mind and its relationship to consciousness, knowledge, intellect, and the other means by which we
work to understand ourselves and our world.

440

The first selection, by Plato, contains one of the seminal ideas about the nature of the mind. Plato posited that the world of sensory experience is not the real world and that our senses are in fact incapable of experiencing reality. In Plato's view, reality is an ideal that exists only in an environment that is somewhat akin to the concept of heaven. He suggested that people are born with knowledge of that reality. The infant, in other words, possesses the ideas of reality to start with, having gained them from heaven and retaining them in memory. For Plato, education was the process by which students regained such "lost" memories and made them part of their conscious understanding. Although he never uses the terms *conscious* and *unconscious* in describing the mind, Plato's views foreshadow the later theories of psychologists such as William James (1842–1910), Sigmund Freud, and Carl Jung.

René Descartes wrote in an age that was influenced by a revival of attention to Greek philosophers. His views were consistent in some ways with those of Plato and Aristotle, especially in the quest for a form of certainty in knowledge on which all thought could be based. His primary motive was to prove the existence of God, which he felt he could do if he could establish one absolute truth on which to build a clear argument. His solution was *Cogito ergo sum*, which translates as "I think, therefore I am." Having established his own existence without a doubt, he was able to move toward a defensible proof of the existence of God. However, in the process of developing his argument, he introduced a long-lasting idea that influenced thought for many years: that the mind and the body are separate entities. The mind/body split had been apparent in the work of earlier writers, but it never had such a forceful champion as in Descartes. His influence has continued to modern times despite the current view that the mind and body are much more closely integrated than earlier investigators had assumed.

One of the best-known results of Freud's study of dreams is his conclusion that all people suffer from an Oedipus complex when they are extremely young. Freud explains that Oedipus, thinking he was escaping his fate, killed his father and married his mother, both of whom were strangers to him. Freud takes this familiar Greek myth and explores its significance in the lives of very young children, showing that it is common for them to wish to do away with their parent of the same sex and have their opposite-sex parent all to themselves. As people grow older, both the memory and the desire to follow through on this feeling are repressed and forgotten. They become part of our unconscious and, in some cases, may resurface in the form of guilt. As adults we know that such feelings are completely unacceptable, and the guilt that results can create psychological illness.

Carl Jung began his studies with Freud's views of the content of the unconscious, but one of his analyses led him in a novel direction. He concluded that some of the content of the unconscious mind could not have begun in the conscious mind because it was not the product of the individual's conscious experience. Jung reasoned that certain images present in the unconscious were common to all members of a culture. He called these images *archetypal* because they seemed fundamental and universal, such as the archetype of the father and the archetype of the mother. He then hypothesized that part of the mind's content is derived from cultural history. Unlike Freud, Jung saw the unconscious as containing images that represent deep instinctual longings belonging to an entire culture, not just to the individual.

Howard Gardner's interest is in intelligence, which he approaches from a pluralist point of view. His idea of seven distinct intelligences, as opposed to the conventional views represented by standardized IQ tests, is at once traditional and revolutionary. In drawing on the model of ancient Greek education, he urges us to examine the virtues of all seven forms of intelligence and not rely on the logical-mathematical model that dominates contemporary education. Gardner notes that certain forms of intelligence are culturally linked, but he leaves open the question of whether they are gender linked.

The question of whether or not there can be a thinking machine is only one aspect of Steven Pinker's discussion of how the mind works. He considers the basic issues of what thought is, how information affects our concept of thought and mind, and how some of the mysteries of consciousness complicate our understanding of the mind. He discusses computers and their computational powers, deriving one of his primary ideas: the computational theory of mind. He introduces some new terms, such as *mentalese,* which is the basic language of thought that permits us to transform sensory experience into a mental event. He uses the term to describe the way the outside world becomes a mental experience to form a "data representation" allowing us to combine observations in what seems to be an infinite range of possibilities. He illustrates his principle in a detailed examination of the word *elk.*

Taking a different approach, V. S. Ramachandran examines unusual states of mind caused by one or another form of brain disorder or disease. He talks about victims of Capgras syndrome, who are able to recognize a close friend or relative but assume that person is an impostor out to trick them. Those with Cotard's syndrome are certain they are dead and nothing one can say to them will change their minds. Ramachandran describes a range of experiments that reveal specific areas of brain function and praises modern brain imaging technology that permits observation of mental activity in the physical locale in which it takes place. He introduces a novel term, *qualia,* which means the mental apprehension of something like redness or sweetness. Qualia are mental events in response to external stimuli. In his search for the nature of the "self," Ramachandran points out that there can be no self without qualia nor can there be qualia without a self to apprehend it. His effort is to move us as closely as he can to understanding the nature of consciousness, even if it is only to make us aware of how profound a mystery it is.

These essays approach the problem of mind from different positions and are concerned with different questions of consciousness, thought, limitation, and intelligence. They raise some of the most basic questions concerning the mind, such as, What are its components? What can it know? What should we most value in its function? In answering these questions, each essay provides us with ideas that provoke more thought and still more questions.

VISUALIZING THE MIND

Among the many art movements of the early twentieth century, surrealism is one of the most interesting and persistent in its effect upon the mind of the viewer. The movement began in France in the 1920s and produced a good number of lasting works. Part of the

SALVADOR DALÍ, *THE PERSISTENCE OF MEMORY.* 1931.
Oil on canvas, 9 1/2" × 13". Museum of Modern Art, New York.

inspiration for the artists was the work of Sigmund Freud, whose concept of the unconscious was a novelty early in the century and created wide-ranging controversy. William James had proposed the existence of the unconscious mind in the late nineteenth century, but Freud's work, with its emphasis on sexual urges that he insisted were present in everyone—even in those who did not know they possessed the urges—proposed that much of what we do and much of what we dream comes from the unconscious mind.

Even writers, such as James Joyce, were influenced by the theories of psychoanalysis and experimented with mixing reality with unreality in the manner of our dreams. Dreams became a source for considerable experimentation in the arts. Ideally, these works were created as a means of connecting us with our unconscious mind. Surrealism is powerful even today in part because our understanding of the intersection of psychology and everyday behavior is even stronger than it was in the 1910s. The technique of many of the surrealist painters is based on visual distortion, particularly of the kind that people experience when using powerful hallucinogenic drugs. Art produces the distortion without reliance on mind-changing substances.

Salvador Dalí (1904–1989) was an outrageous showman who constantly flaunted his eccentric sexual behavior and who promoted himself as the "bad boy" of art. His self-promotion worked extremely well and he remained a famous artist until his death. And while *The Persistence of Memory* is a very small painting, hardly larger than a piece of 8" × 11" paper, its impact has been significant both in the popular imagination and in the writings of authorities on art.

The painting shows a barren landscape with a bay, said to be Port Lligat in northeastern Spain, near where Dalí was born. The landscape is populated by watches that drape over a tree limb, over a rectangular object, and over a mysterious figure with long eyelashes resembling Dalí's own. A great many explanations for the painting have surfaced and doubtless many more will be proposed. Dalí himself said that he had been inspired by a dream, as he had been inspired in many of his other works. As he said, his dream paintings were designed to "stamp themselves indelibly on the mind." *The Persistence of Memory* has indeed achieved that end by becoming one of the most iconic images of the first part of the twentieth century.

The clocks in the painting all have different times on their faces; the one more or less "normal" clock is infested with ants. Some commentators have seen the clock imagery as the result of the influence of the theory of relativity of Albert Einstein (1879–1955), who won the Nobel Prize in 1921. Like Freud's theories, Einstein's quickly caught the imagination of the artistic community. They were struck by his theory that time is not absolute but varies according to the space/time plane on which it is measured. The idea of relativity was adopted by artists, although hardly understood in detail, in part because it was an alternative to thinking that the laws of the universe were absolutes, like the law of gravity. It gave artists room to maneuver imaginatively.

The figure in the center has been described as a self-portrait, a mass of brain cells, and as a representation of Dalí as a fetus. This interpretation depends on the idea that the fetus could take many shapes or forms and is thus surreal in this environment, but it also relies on Dalí's comment that he had a memory not only of having been in his mother's womb but also of having the classic Freudian oedipal complex in loving his mother. That may be the persistence of memory to which he alludes. Whether it is intended to represent a fetus or not, it seems to be intended as a self-portrait of sorts, but one that is intensely distorted.

An art historian, Mariel Jean, drew a connection between the painting and a child being told to stick out his tongue in a doctor's office. The French word *montrer* means "to show" and it is extremely close to *montre*, which means watch, while the word for tongue, *langue*, is cognate to *langueur* or *languid*, as in drooping, tired, exhausted. The watches in the painting are drooping, exhausted, and because none of them are in agreement, they are essentially timeless. The idea of timelessness is reinforced by the massive stone cliffs, themselves the product of eons, jutting out into the bay. The only clue to the real time is the tree, which, leafless, assures us only that the painting is set in the fall of the year. By playing with Einstein's assurance that time is relative, Dalí's painting may imply that timelessness means there is no time, that it has become extinct, or that time is only part of our imagination and can be stretched much the way the watches are stretched. Whatever the painting implies, it has been seen as a powerful dream vision ever since it was first shown.

PLATO
The Allegory of the Cave

PLATO (428–347 B.C.) was born into an aristocratic, probably Athenian, family and educated according to the best precepts available. He eventually became a student of Socrates and later involved himself closely with Socrates' work and teaching. Plato was not only Socrates' finest student but also the one who immortalized Socrates in his works. Most of Plato's works are philosophical essays in which Socrates speaks as a character in a dialogue with one or more students or listeners.

Both Socrates and Plato lived in turbulent times. In 404 B.C. Athens was defeated by Sparta, and its government was taken over by tyrants. Political life in Athens became dangerous. Plato felt, however, that he could effect positive change in Athenian politics — until Socrates was tried unjustly for corrupting the youth of Athens and sentenced to death in 399 B.C. After that, Plato withdrew from public life and devoted himself to writing and to the academy he founded in an olive grove in Athens. The academy endured for almost a thousand years, which tells us how greatly Plato's thought was valued.

Although it is not easy to condense Plato's views, he may be said to have held the world of sense perception to be inferior to the world of ideal entities that exist only in a pure spiritual realm. These ideals, or forms, Plato argued, are perceived directly by everyone before birth and then dimly remembered here on earth. But the memory, dim as it is, enables people to understand what the senses perceive, despite the fact that the senses are unreliable and their perceptions imperfect.

This view of reality has long been important to philosophers because it gives a philosophical basis to antimaterialistic thought.

From *The Republic*. Translated and glossed by Benjamin Jowett.

It values the spirit first and frees people from the tyranny of sensory perception and sensory reward. In the case of love, Plato held that Eros leads individuals to revere the body and its pleasures; but the thrust of his teaching is that the body is a metaphor for spiritual delights. Plato maintains that the body is only a starting point, which eventually can lead to both spiritual fulfillment and the appreciation of true beauty.

On the one hand, "The Allegory of the Cave" is a discussion of politics: *The Republic*, from which it is taken, is a treatise on justice and the ideal government. On the other hand, it has long stood as an example of the notion that if we rely on our perceptions to know the truth about the world, then we will know very little about it. In order to live ethically, it is essential to know what is true and, therefore, what is important beyond the world of sensory perception.

Plato's allegory has been persuasive for centuries and remains at the center of thought that attempts to counter the pleasures of the sensual life. Most religions aim for spiritual enlightenment and praise the qualities of the soul, which lies beyond perception. Thus, it comes as no surprise that Christianity and other religions have developed systems of thought that bear a close resemblance to Plato's. Later refinements of his thought, usually called Neo-Platonism, have been influential even into modern times.

Plato's Rhetoric

Two important rhetorical techniques are at work in the following selection. The first and more obvious—at least on one level— is the device of the allegory, a story in which the characters and situations actually represent people and situations in another context. It is a difficult technique to sustain, although Aesop's fables were certainly successful in using animals to represent people and their foibles. The advantage of the technique is that a complex and sometimes unpopular argument can be fought and won before the audience realizes that an argument is under way. The disadvantage of the technique is that the terms of the allegory may only approximate the situation it represents; thus, the argument may fail to be convincing.

The second rhetorical technique Plato uses is the dialogue. In fact, this device is a hallmark of Plato's work; indeed, most of his writings are called dialogues. The *Symposium, Apology, Phaedo, Crito, Meno,* and most of his famous works are written in dialogue form. Usually in these works Socrates is speaking to a student or a friend about highly abstract issues, asking questions that require simple answers. Slowly, the questioning proceeds to elucidate the answers to complex issues.

This question-and-answer technique basically constitutes the Socratic method. Socrates analyzes the answer to each question, examines its implications, and then asserts the truth. The method works partly because Plato believes that people do not learn things but remember them. That is, people originate from heaven, where they knew the truth; they already possess knowledge and must recover it by means of the dialogue. Socrates' method is ideally suited to that purpose.

Beyond these techniques, however, we must look at Plato's style. It is true that he is working with difficult ideas, but his style is so clear, simple, and direct that few people would have trouble understanding what he is saying. Considering the influence this work has had on world thought, and the reputation Plato had earned by the time he wrote *The Republic*, its style is remarkably plain and accessible. Plato's respect for rhetoric and its proper uses is part of the reason he can express himself with such impressive clarity.

PREREADING QUESTIONS: WHAT TO READ FOR

The following prereading questions may help you anticipate key issues in the discussion of Plato's "The Allegory of the Cave." Keeping them in mind during your first reading of the selection should help focus your attention.

- In what ways are we like the people in the cave looking at shadows?

- Why is the world of sensory perception somewhat illusory?

- For Plato, what is the difference between the upper world and the lower world?

The Allegory of the Cave

SOCRATES,
GLAUCON. *The
den, the prison-
ers: the light at
a distance;*

And now, I said, let me show in a figure how   1
far our nature is enlightened or unenlightened:—
Behold! human beings living in an underground
den, which has a mouth open towards the light and

reaching all along the den; here they have been from their childhood, and have their legs and necks chained so that they cannot move, and can only see before them, being prevented by the chains from turning round their heads. Above and behind them a fire is blazing at a distance, and between the fire and the prisoners there is a raised way; and you will see, if you look, a low wall built along the way, like the screen which marionette players have in front of them, over which they show the puppets.

I see.   2

the low wall, and the moving figures of which the shadows are seen on the opposite wall of the den.

And do you see, I said, men passing along the   3 wall carrying all sorts of vessels, and statues and figures of animals made of wood and stone and various materials, which appear over the wall? Some of them are talking, others silent.

You have shown me a strange image, and they   4 are strange prisoners.

Like ourselves, I replied; and they see only   5 their own shadows, or the shadows of one another, which the fire throws on the opposite wall of the cave?

True, he said; how could they see anything but   6 the shadows if they were never allowed to move their heads?

And of the objects which are being carried in   7 like manner they would only see the shadows?

Yes, he said.   8

And if they were able to converse with one   9 another, would they not suppose that they were naming what was actually before them?

Very true.   10

The prisoners would mistake the shadows for realities.

And suppose further that the prison had an   11 echo which came from the other side, would they not be sure to fancy when one of the passers-by spoke that the voice which they heard came from the passing shadow?

No question, he replied.   12

To them, I said, the truth would be literally   13 nothing but the shadows of the images.

That is certain.   14

And now look again, and see what will naturally   15 follow if the prisoners are released and disabused

of their error. At first, when any of them is liberated and compelled suddenly to stand up and turn
his neck round and walk and look towards the
light, he will suffer sharp pains; the glare will distress him, and he will be unable to see the realities of which in his former state he had seen the
shadows; and then conceive someone saying to
him, that what he saw before was an illusion, but
that now, when he is approaching nearer to being
and his eye is turned towards more real existence,
he has a clearer vision—what will be his reply?
And you may further imagine that his instructor is
pointing to the objects as they pass and requiring
him to name them,—will he not be perplexed?
Will he not fancy that the shadows which he formerly saw are truer than the objects which are now
shown to him?

*And when
released, they
would still
persist in
maintaining
the superior
truth of the
shadows.*

Far truer.   16

And if he is compelled to look straight at the   17
light, will he not have a pain in his eyes which will
make him turn away to take refuge in the objects of
vision which he can see, and which he will conceive to be in reality clearer than the things which
are now being shown to him?

True, he said.   18

And suppose once more, that he is reluctantly   19
dragged up a steep and rugged ascent, and held
fast until he is forced into the presence of the sun
himself, is he not likely to be pained and irritated?
When he approaches the light his eyes will be dazzled, and he will not be able to see anything at all
of what are now called realities.

*When dragged
upwards, they
would be
dazzled by
excess of light.*

Not all in a moment, he said.   20

He will require to grow accustomed to the   21
sight of the upper world. And first he will see the
shadows best, next the reflections of men and other
objects in the water, and then the objects themselves; then he will gaze upon the light of the moon
and the stars and the spangled heaven; and he will
see the sky and the stars by night better than the
sun or the light of the sun by day?

Certainly.   22

Last of all he will be able to see the sun, and   23
not mere reflections of him in the water, but he

At length they will see the sun and understand his nature.

will see him in his own proper place, and not in another; and he will contemplate him as he is.

Certainly.   24

He will then proceed to argue that this is he   25
who gives the season and the years, and is the guardian of all that is in the visible world, and in a certain way the cause of all things which he and his fellows have been accustomed to behold?

Clearly, he said, he would first see the sun and   26
then reason about him.

And when he remembered his old habitation,   27
and the wisdom of the den and his fellow prison-

They would then pity their old companions of the den.

ers, do you not suppose that he would felicitate himself on the change, and pity them?

Certainly, he would.   28

And if they were in the habit of conferring   29
honors among themselves on those who were quickest to observe the passing shadows and to remark which of them went before, and which fol-lowed after, and which were together; and who were therefore best able to draw conclusions as to the future, do you think that he would care for such honors and glories, or envy the possessors of them? Would he not say with Homer,

Better to be the poor servant of a poor master,

and to endure anything, rather than think as they do and live after their manner?

Yes, he said, I think that he would rather suffer   30
anything than entertain these false notions and live in this miserable manner.

Imagine once more, I said, such an one coming   31
suddenly out of the sun to be replaced in his old situation; would he not be certain to have his eyes full of darkness?

To be sure, he said.   32

But when they returned to the den, they would see much worse than those who had never left it.

And if there were a contest, and he had to   33
compete in measuring the shadows with the pris-oners who had never moved out of the den, while his sight was still weak, and before his eyes had become steady (and the time which would be needed to acquire this new habit of sight might be very considerable), would he not be ridiculous? Men would say of him that up he went and down

he came without his eyes; and that it was better not even to think of ascending; and if any one tried to loose another and lead him up to the light, let them only catch the offender, and they would put him to death.

No question, he said.   34

The prison is the world of sight, the light of the fire is the sun.

This entire allegory, I said, you may now 35 append, dear Glaucon, to the previous argument; the prison house is the world of sight, the light of the fire is the sun, and you will not misapprehend me if you interpret the journey upwards to be the ascent of the soul into the intellectual world according to my poor belief, which, at your desire, I have expressed—whether rightly or wrongly God knows. But, whether true or false, my opinion is that in the world of knowledge the idea of good appears last of all, and is seen only with an effort; and, when seen, is also inferred to be the universal author of all things beautiful and right, parent of light and of the lord of light in this visible world, and the immediate source of reason and truth in the intellectual; and that this is the power upon which he who would act rationally either in public or private life must have his eye fixed.

I agree, he said, as far as I am able to understand you.   36

Moreover, I said, you must not wonder that 37 those who attain to this beatific vision are unwilling to descend to human affairs; for their souls are ever hastening into the upper world where they desire to dwell; which desire of theirs is very natural, if our allegory may be trusted.

Yes, very natural.   38

Nothing extraordinary in the philosopher being unable to see in the dark.

And is there anything surprising in one who 39 passes from divine contemplations to the evil state of man, misbehaving himself in a ridiculous manner; if, while his eyes are blinking and before he has become accustomed to the surrounding darkness, he is compelled to fight in courts of law, or in other places, about the images or the shadows of images of justice, and is endeavoring to meet the conceptions of those who have never yet seen absolute justice?

Anything but surprising, he replied.   40

The eyes may be blinded in two ways, by excess or by defect of light.

Anyone who has common sense will remember   41
that the bewilderments of the eyes are of two kinds,
and arise from two causes, either from coming out
of the light or from going into the light, which is
true of the mind's eye, quite as much as of the bodily eye; and he who remembers this when he sees
anyone whose vision is perplexed and weak, will
not be too ready to laugh; he will first ask whether
that soul of man has come out of the brighter life,
and is unable to see because unaccustomed to the
dark, or having turned from darkness to the day
is dazzled by excess of light. And he will count the
one happy in his condition and state of being, and
he will pity the other; or, if he have a mind to laugh
at the soul which comes from below into the light,
there will be more reason in this than in the
laugh which greets him who returns from above
out of the light into the den.

That, he said, is a very just distinction.   42

The conversion of the soul is the turning round the eye from darkness to light.

But then, if I am right, certain professors of   43
education must be wrong when they say that they
can put a knowledge into the soul which was not
there before, like sight into blind eyes.

They undoubtedly say this, he replied.   44

Whereas, our argument shows that the power   45
and capacity of learning exists in the soul already;
and that just as the eye was unable to turn from
darkness to light without the whole body, so too
the instrument of knowledge can only by the
movement of the whole soul be turned from the
world of becoming into that of being, and learn by
degrees to endure the sight of being, and of the
brightest and best of being, or in other words, of
the good.

Very true.   46

And must there not be some art which will   47
effect conversion in the easiest and quickest manner; not implanting the faculty of sight, for that
exists already, but has been turned in the wrong
direction, and is looking away from the truth?

Yes, he said, such an art may be presumed.   48

And whereas the other so-called virtues of the 49
soul seem to be akin to bodily qualities, for even
when they are not originally innate they can be

The virtue of wisdom has a divine power which may be turned either towards good or towards evil.

implanted later by habit and exercise, the virtue of wisdom more than anything else contains a divine element which always remains, and by this conversion is rendered useful and profitable; or, on the other hand, hurtful and useless. Did you never observe the narrow intelligence flashing from the keen eye of a clever rogue—how eager he is, how clearly his paltry soul sees the way to his end; he is the reverse of blind, but his keen eyesight is forced into the service of evil, and he is mischievous in proportion to his cleverness?

Very true, he said.   50

But what if there had been a circumcision of   51
such natures in the days of their youth; and they had been severed from those sensual pleasures, such as eating and drinking, which, like leaden weights, were attached to them at their birth, and which drag them down and turn the vision of their souls upon the things that are below—if, I say, they had been released from these impediments and turned in the opposite direction, the very same faculty in them would have seen the truth as keenly as they see what their eyes are turned to now.

Very likely.   52

Neither the uneducated nor the over-educated will be good servants of the State.

Yes, I said; and there is another thing which is   53
likely, or rather a necessary inference from what has preceded, that neither the uneducated and uninformed of the truth, nor yet those who never make an end of their education, will be able ministers of State; not the former, because they have no single aim of duty which is the rule of all their actions, private as well as public; nor the latter, because they will not act at all except upon compulsion, fancying that they are already dwelling apart in the islands of the blessed.

Very true, he replied.   54

Then, I said, the business of us who are the   55
founders of the State will be to compel the best minds to attain that knowledge which we have already shown to be the greatest of all—they must continue to ascend until they arrive at the good; but when they have ascended and seen enough we must not allow them to do as they do now.

Men should
ascend to the
upper world,
but they should
also return to
the lower.

What do you mean?   56

I mean that they remain in the upper world: 57
but this must not be allowed; they must be made to
descend again among the prisoners in the den, and
partake of their labors and honors, whether they
are worth having or not.

But is not this unjust? he said; ought we to give   58
them a worse life, when they might have a better?

You have again forgotten, my friend, I said, the   59
intention of the legislator, who did not aim at making any one class in the State happy above the rest;
the happiness was to be in the whole State, and he
held the citizens together by persuasion and necessity, making them benefactors of the State, and
therefore benefactors of one another; to this end he
created them, not to please themselves, but to be
his instruments in binding up the State.

True, he said, I had forgotten.   60

The duties of
philosophers.

Observe, Glaucon, that there will be no injus-   61
tice in compelling our philosophers to have a care
and providence of others; we shall explain to them
that in other States, men of their class are not
obliged to share in the toils of politics: and this is
reasonable, for they grow up at their own sweet
will, and the government would rather not have
them. Being self-taught, they cannot be expected to
show any gratitude for a culture which they have
never received. But we have brought you into the
world to be rulers of the hive, kings of yourselves
and of the other citizens, and have educated you
far better and more perfectly than they have been
educated, and you are better able to share in the
double duty. Wherefore each of you, when his turn
comes, must go down to the general underground
abode, and get the habit of seeing in the dark.

Their
obligations to
their country
will induce
them to take
part in her
government.

When you have acquired the habit, you will see ten
thousand times better than the inhabitants of the
den, and you will know what the several images
are, and what they represent, because you have
seen the beautiful and just and good in their truth.
And thus our State, which is also yours, will be a
reality, and not a dream only, and will be administered in a spirit unlike that of other States, in
which men fight with one another about shadows

only and are distracted in the struggle for power, which in their eyes is a great good. Whereas the truth is that the State in which the rulers are most reluctant to govern is always the best and most quietly governed, and the State in which they are most eager, the worst.

Quite true, he replied.   62

And will our pupils, when they hear this,   63
refuse to take their turn at the toils of State, when they are allowed to spend the greater part of their time with one another in the heavenly light?

They will be willing but not anxious to rule.

Impossible, he answered; for they are just   64
men, and the commands which we impose upon them are just; there can be no doubt that every one of them will take office as a stern necessity, and not after the fashion of our present rulers of State.

The statesman must be provided with a better life than that of a ruler; and then he will not covet office.

Yes, my friend, I said; and there lies the   65
point. You must contrive for your future rulers another and a better life than that of a ruler, and then you may have a well-ordered State; for only in the State which offers this, will they rule who are truly rich, not in silver and gold, but in virtue and wisdom, which are the true blessings of life. Whereas if they go to the administration of public affairs, poor and hungering after their own private advantage, thinking that hence they are to snatch the chief good, order there can never be; for they will be fighting about office, and the civil and domestic broils which thus arise will be the ruin of the rulers themselves and of the whole State.

Most true, he replied.   66

And the only life which looks down upon the   67
life of political ambition is that of true philosophy. Do you know of any other?

Indeed, I do not, he said.   68

QUESTIONS FOR CRITICAL READING

1. What is the relationship between Socrates and Glaucon? Are they equal in intellectual authority? Are they concerned with the same issues?

2. How does the allegory of the prisoners in the cave watching shadows on a wall relate to us today? What shadows do we see, and how do they distort our sense of what is real?

3. Are we prisoners in the same sense that Plato's characters are?

4. If Plato is right that the material world is an illusion, how would too great a reliance on materialism affect ethical decisions?

5. What ethical issues, if any, are raised by Plato's allegory?

6. In paragraph 49, Plato states that the virtue of wisdom "contains a divine element." What is "a divine element"? What does this statement seem to mean? Do you agree with Plato?

7. What distinctions does Plato make between the public and the private? Would you make the same distinctions (see paras. 53–55)?

SUGGESTIONS FOR CRITICAL WRITING

1. Analyze the allegory of the cave for its strengths and weaknesses. Consider what the allegory implies for people living in a world of the senses and for what might lie behind that world. To what extent are people like (or unlike) the figures in the cave? To what extent is the world we know like the cave?

2. Socrates ends the dialogue by saying that rulers of the state must be able to look forward to a better life than that of being rulers. He and Glaucon agree that only one life "looks down upon the life of political ambition"—"that of true philosophy" (para. 67). What is the life of true philosophy? Is it superior to that of governing (or anything else)? How would you define its superiority? What would its qualities be? What would its concerns be? Would you be happy leading such a life?

3. In what ways would depending on the material world for one's highest moral values affect ethical behavior? What is the connection between ethics and materialism? Write a brief essay that defends or attacks materialism as a basis for ethical action. How can people aspire to the good if they root their greatest pleasures in the senses? What alternatives do modern people have if they choose to base their actions on nonmaterialistic, or spiritual, values? What are those values? How can they guide our ethical behavior? Do you think they should?

4. In paragraph 61, Socrates outlines a program that would assure Athens of having good rulers and good government. Clarify exactly what the program is, what its problems and benefits are, and how it could be put into action. Then decide whether the program would work. You may consider whether it would work for our time, for Socrates' time, or both. If possible, use examples (hypothetical or real) to bolster your argument.

5. Socrates states unequivocally that Athens should compel the best and the most intelligent young men to be rulers of the state. Review his reasons for saying so, consider what his concept of the state is, and then take a stand on the issue. Is it right to compel the best and most

intelligent young people to become rulers? If so, would it be equally proper to compel those well suited for the professions of law, medicine, teaching, or religion to follow those respective callings? Would an ideal society result if all people were forced to practice the calling for which they had the best aptitude?

6. **CONNECTIONS** Plato has a great deal to say about goodness as it relates to government. Compare his views with those of Lao-tzu (p. 21) and Niccolò Machiavelli (p. 37). Which of those thinkers would Plato have agreed with most? In comparing these three writers and their political views, consider the nature of goodness they required in a ruler. Do you think that we hold similar attitudes today in our expectations for the goodness of our government?

7. **CONNECTIONS** Plato is concerned with the question of how we know what we know. Francis Bacon in "The Four Idols" (p. 579) is concerned with the same question, although he poses it in different terms. Examine the fundamental issues each author raises. How well do these thinkers agree on basic issues? To what extent, for example, does Bacon warn us to beware the evidence of our senses? To what extent is Bacon concerned about getting to the truth as Plato is?

8. **SEEING CONNECTIONS** How would Plato have used Salvador Dalí's *The Persistence of Memory* (p. 443) to help defend his view that what we perceive through our senses is not a form of reality? Would he have felt the images in the painting belong to the upper world or the lower world? If he were to interpret the images in the painting as a portrait of a dream experience, would he then have felt the world of dreams was similar to the world of those chained in the cave? Or would he have felt the painting itself was a record of yet another "reality" that was illusory?

RENÉ DESCARTES
Fourth Meditation: Of Truth and Error

RENÉ DESCARTES (1596–1650), credited with founding modern philosophy, was educated in Jesuit schools in France, beginning with Jesuit college at La Flèche, which was established by the king for the education of the brightest children of the upper classes. In time he came to reject certain principles of his education and developed his Method, the intellectual system expounded in his *Discourse on the Method of Rightly Conducting One's Reason and Seeking Truth in the Sciences* (1637). This work was followed by *Meditations on First Philosophy* (1641), which discuss the "first philosophy"—the nature of God.

For many thinkers *Discourse on Method* represents the beginning of the end of the domination of Aristotle and the scholastics. The scholastic philosophers (churchmen teaching throughout Europe) followed Aristotle and St. Thomas Aquinas in a rigid system governed by rules of logic. Although sensory evidence was sometimes relied upon, the final authority was the church. Descartes wished on the contrary to substitute the authority of his own reasoning in his investigations into the nature of truth.

His discovery of Method came to him suddenly in 1619 in a "blinding flash" of insight. Seeing the need for a unity of thought in science, he realized that the step-by-step proofs used by geometricians could be employed in all aspects of science. In "Discourse Two" he explains the four rules of his Method and ends with a summary of his insight into geometry:

> The first was never to accept anything as true that I did not know to be evidently so: that is to say, carefully to avoid precipitancy and prejudice, and to include in my judgements nothing more

From *Discourse on Method and the Meditations.* Translated by F. E. Sutcliffe.

than what presented itself so clearly and so distinctly to my mind
that I might have no occasion to place it in doubt.

The second, to divide each of the difficulties that I was
examining into as many parts as might be possible and necessary
in order best to solve it.

The third, to conduct my thoughts in an orderly way, beginning with the simplest objects and the easiest to know, in order to
climb gradually, as by degrees, as far as the knowledge of the most
complex, and even supposing some order among those objects
which do not precede each other naturally.

And the last, everywhere to make such complete enumera-
tions and such general reviews that I would be sure to have omitted nothing.

These long chains of reasonings, quite simple and easy,
which geometers are accustomed to using to teach their most difficult demonstrations, had given me cause to imagine that everything which can be encompassed by man's knowledge is linked in
the same way, and that, provided only that one abstains from
accepting any for true which is not true, and that one always
keeps the right order to one thing to be deduced from that which
precedes it, there can be nothing so distant that one does not
reach it eventually, or so hidden that one cannot discover it.

Descartes insisted that if each step of the inquiry were free
from error, the darkest secrets of nature could be discovered. What
he needed once he established this principle was an unassailable
position from which to begin. That first point reached, his chain of
reasoning could stretch to the stars; without it, true knowledge was
impossible. Descartes describes that point in *Discourse on Method*.
It contains the most famous catchphrase in philosophy: "*Cogito,
ergo sum*" (I think, therefore I am). After rejecting many other possible points of departure, Descartes hit upon the statement that
was for him unassailable: if he thought about something, then he
knew that he must exist, that he was a "thing that thinks," and that
he could not be deceived about the fact that he thought. After
establishing this basic truth, he moved toward a proof of the existence of God that did not depend on sensory evidence. It is sometimes described as an intuitive proof, because it depends on a chain
of reasoning that starts neither from observation nor from an outside authority.

Descartes was influenced by the skepticism of Michel Eyquem
de Montaigne (1533–1592), who, in his essays, accepted the view
that certainty was impossible because the senses were unreliable
and the very existence of the individual unprovable. In the latter
part of the sixteenth century, the discovery of important classical

texts—especially Sextus Empiricus's translation of the work of the ancient Greek philosopher Pyrrho—was enormously influential in Europe because they cast doubt on all things. The fracturing of the Christian Church into several sects called into question the most authoritative truths of all, most notably when Martin Luther challenged the authority of the church on the question of the truth. Doubt and uncertainty were therefore part of a crisis in European thought. Descartes worked out his theories a hundred years after Luther, and with the publication of *Discourse on Method* he seemed to have begun to offer a way out of the crisis.

Ironically, Descartes's reliance on intuitive chains of reasoning did not work in his favor in scientific investigations of the kind we now rely upon. He was uncomfortable with evidence gathered by the senses—what is now called *empirical evidence*—and therefore made little contribution to the development of modern science. However, he did not hold science back. He especially admired Galileo (1564–1642), the most renowned scientist of his time.

Another legacy of Descartes is the body-mind split. He states in *Fourth Meditation* that he is aware of the distinctions between his body and his mind and sees them as different in certain essentials. Eventually, he postulates that the mind's existence may not depend on the body. Such a view was widely developed in poetry and literature and is for some critics a lamentable fact.

Descartes's Rhetoric

The *Fourth Meditation: Of Truth and Error* is structured in a simple fashion by aiming to solve a single problem: how to avoid error and arrive at the truth. In his earlier work, *The Discourse on Method* (1637), Descartes had already proved his own existence and the existence of God, and the *Fourth Meditation* limits its focus entirely to himself and to God.

Because this is a meditation, it is not rigidly structured but seems to simply follow a path from uncertainty to certainty by ruling out specific issues and pondering those that remain. It follows the pattern of Method mentioned earlier. We also are given the impression that the work took only a single day to conceive, which may indeed be true. Descartes continues some of his investigation into the observations of phenomena but only enough to rule them out when considering error and truth. Instead, he concentrates on the nature of God and the qualities God gave him and how he must use them. He reflects on free will in a manner that seems, by today's standards, oversimplified. But for him will is a key force in producing error.

Apart from setting out on the familiar path of moving from simple to complex, building each point on the conclusion reached before, Descartes uses only a few rhetorical devices. One is enumeration (paras. 3 and 4) in which he says God would not deceive him and that God gave him the faculty of judgment, which if used properly will help find the truth. In addition, Descartes uses a simplified form of logic by which he establishes a point, contrasts it with another point, then draws a conclusion that seems to naturally follow from the basic principle he feels he has established.

Underlying some of his examination is a basic dichotomy: discerning the true from the false. Other oppositions support this dichotomy: God and Descartes; mind and body; presence and negativity. The negative is important because it helps Descartes explain error not as something real, but as a defect, an absence of something. One of the definitions of evil is "the absence of good," which then makes evil a nothing and thus easier to explain. While he conducts his meditation on error and truth, Descartes reminds us that in earlier writings he has pledged to be the one who doubts. He posits his critical mind as the examiner of how the mind works, how free will informs the mind, how the senses inform the mind, and how judgment produces decisions. However, as much as he doubts, Descartes is a true seventeenth-century thinker and feels he has definitely proved the existence of God and, along with proof of his own existence, has found an unassailable position from which to argue.

PREREADING QUESTIONS: WHAT TO READ FOR

The following prereading questions may help you anticipate key issues in the discussion of René Descartes's *Fourth Meditation: Of Truth and Error.* Keeping them in mind during your first reading of the selection should help focus your attention.

- How does Descartes describe the nature of God?

- What does Descartes seem to mean by saying he is placed "midway between God and nothing" (para. 4)?

- What qualities does Descartes perceive in himself that may lead him toward error?

- What role does knowledge play in Descartes's effort to bring his meditation to a conclusion?

Fourth Meditation: Of Truth and Error

I have so accustomed myself these past days to detach my mind   1
from the senses, and I have so accurately observed that there are very
few things one can know with certainty about corporeal objects, that
there are many more things which are known to us about the human
mind, and many more still about God himself, that I shall now turn
my mind away without difficulty from the consideration of sensible
or imaginable things, in order to bring it to bear on those which,
being disengaged from all matter, are purely intelligible.

And certainly the idea I have of the human mind, inasmuch as it   2
is a thinking thing, and not extended in length, breadth, and depth,
and does not participate in anything that pertains to the body, is
incomparably more distinct than the idea of any corporeal object.
And when I consider that I doubt, that is to say, that I am an incomplete and dependent being, the idea of a complete and independent
being, that is to say of God, presents itself to my mind with such
distinctness and clearness, and, from the fact alone that this idea is
found in me, or that I, who possess this idea, am or exist, I conclude
so evidently that God exists, and that my existence depends entirely
on him in each moment of my life, that I do not think that the
human mind can know anything with more clearness and certainty.
Already, then, I seem to discover a path that will lead us from the
contemplation of the true God, in whom all the treasures of knowledge and wisdom are contained, to the knowledge of the other
things in the universe.

For, in the first place, I recognize that it is impossible that he   3
should ever deceive me, since in all fraud and deceit is to be found a
certain imperfection; and although it may seem that to be able to
deceive is a mark of subtlety or power, yet the desire to deceive
bears evidence without doubt of weakness or malice, and, accordingly, cannot be found in God.

Secondly, I am aware in myself of a certain power of judgment,   4
which undoubtedly I have received from God, in the same way as all
the other things which I possess; and as he would not wish to
deceive me, it is certain that he has not given to me a power such
that I can ever be in error, if I use it properly. And there would
remain no doubt of this truth, if one could not, it seems, draw from
it the conclusion that, in consequence, I can never be mistaken; for,
if I owe everything I possess to God, and if he has not given me
power in order to fall into error, it seems that I can never be mistaken. And, in truth, when I think only of God, I discover in myself
no cause of error or falsehood; but then afterwards, returning to

myself, experience tells me that I am nevertheless subject to an infinity of errors. And seeking the cause of these more closely, I observe that it is not only a real and positive idea of God or of a supremely perfect being which presents itself to my mind, but also, so to speak, a certain negative idea of nothing, that is to say of that which is infinitely distant from all sort of perfection; and that I am, as it were, midway between God and nothing, or placed in such a way between the supreme being and non-being, that there is, in truth, nothing in me which can lead me into error, in so far as a sovereign being has produced me; but that if I consider myself as participating in some way in nothing or non-being, that is to say in so far as I am not myself the sovereign being, I find myself exposed to an infinity of deficiencies, so that I must not be surprised if I make mistakes.

Thus I discern that error, as such, is not something real which depends on God, but that it is simply a defect; and accordingly, that in order to fall into error I do not need some power given me specially by God to this end, but that my being mistaken arises from the fact that the power which God has given me of discerning the true from the false is not infinite in me.   5

However, this does not yet altogether satisfy me; for error is not a pure negation, that is to say, is not the simple deficiency or lack of some perfection which is not due to me, but rather it is a deprivation of some knowledge which it seems I ought to possess. And, considering the nature of God, it does not seem possible to me that he should have given me any faculty not perfect in its kind, that is to say, which lacks some perfection due to it; for if it is true that the more expert the worker, the more perfect and accomplished the works which come from his hands, what being shall we imagine has been produced by the supreme Creator of all things, that is not perfect and complete in all its parts? And assuredly there is no doubt that God could have created me in such a way that I should never fall into error; it is certain too that he always wills what is best: Is it more advantageous then, for me to be deceived than not to be deceived?   6

Considering this more attentively, the first thought that occurs to me is that I must not be surprised if my intelligence is not capable of understanding why God does what he does, and that thus I have no reason to doubt his existence merely because I see perhaps from experience many other things without being able to understand why or how God has produced them. For, knowing already that my nature is extremely weak and limited, and that God's nature, on the contrary, is immense, incomprehensible, and infinite, I no longer have difficulty in recognizing that there is an infinity of things in his power, the causes of which are beyond the range of my mind. And   7 this reason alone is sufficient to persuade me that the whole class of final causes[1] is of no use in physical or natural things; for it does not seem to me that I can, without temerity, seek to discover the impenetrable ends of God.

In addition it further occurs to me, that one must not consider a single creature separately, when one seeks to inquire into the perfection of God's works, but generally all creatures together. For the same thing that might, perhaps, with some reason, seem very imperfect if quite alone, may be very perfect in its nature if it is looked upon as part of the whole universe. And although, since I resolved to doubt everything, I have known with certainty only my own existence, and that of God, nevertheless, after having recognized the infinite power of God, I cannot deny that he may have produced many other beings, or at least that he can produce them, so that I exist and occupy a place in the world as a part of the total number of beings in the universe.

Whereupon, examining myself more closely, and considering what my errors are which alone bear witness to the existence of imperfection in me, I see that they depend on the concurrence of two causes, namely, the power I have of knowing things, and the power of choice, or free will, that is to say, of my understanding, and of my will. For by understanding alone I neither affirm nor deny anything, but merely conceive the ideas of things, which I can affirm or deny. Now, in considering it thus precisely, it can be said that there is never to be found any error in it provided that one takes the word *error* in its proper signification. And although there may perhaps be an infinity of things in the world of which I have no idea in my understanding, it cannot be said on that account that my understanding is deprived of these ideas, as of something which is due to its nature, but only that it does not have them, because, in truth, there is no reason which can prove that God should have given me a greater and more ample faculty of knowing than he actually has; and, however skillful and accomplished a workman I imagine him to be, I must not, on that account, think that he should have put into each of his works all the perfections he can put in some. Nor, moreover, can I complain that God has not given me a free will, or a will sufficiently ample and perfect, since, indeed, I am conscious of possessing a will so ample and extended as not to be enclosed in any limits. And what seems to me here to be very remarkable is that, of all the other faculties in me, there is none so perfect and extended that I do not clearly conceive that it could be

---

[1] **final causes** Logical term for the purpose of things.

even greater and more perfect. For, to give an example, if I consider the faculty of understanding which is in me, I find that it is of a very small extent, and greatly limited, and at the same time form the idea of another similar faculty, much more ample and even infinite; and from the mere fact that I can form the idea of it, I know without difficulty that it pertains to the nature of God. In the same way, if I examine my memory, or imagination, or any other faculty, I find none which is not very small and limited, and in God immense and infinite. It is will alone that I experience to be so great in me that I conceive the idea of no other as more ample and more extended; so that it is my will principally which tells me that I bear the image and resemblance of God. For, although the will is incomparably greater in God than in me, both from the point of view of the knowledge and power, which, being joined with it, make it stronger and more efficacious, and of its object inasmuch as it extends to infinitely more things, nevertheless it does not appear to me greater, if I consider it in itself formally and precisely. For the power of the will consists only in our being able to do a thing, or not to do it (that is to say, to affirm or deny, to pursue or to flee) or rather only, when affirming or denying, pursuing or fleeing the things our understanding proposes to us, in our acting in such a way that we are not conscious that any external force is constraining us. For, in order that I may be free, it is not necessary for me to be indifferent to the choice between one or other of two contraries; but rather, the more I lean towards one, either because I know clearly that the good and the true are in it, or because God so disposes my mind from within the more freely do I make my choice and embrace it. And indeed divine grace and natural knowledge, far from diminishing my freedom, increases it rather, and strengthens it. So that the indifference I feel when I am not inclined to one side rather than to another by the weight of any reason, is the lowest degree of freedom, and reveals a defect of knowledge rather than a perfection of will; for if I always knew clearly what is true and good, I should never have difficulty in deciding which judgment and which choice I should make, and thus I should be entirely free without ever being indifferent.

From all this I perceive that neither the power of willing which I 10 have received from God is in itself the cause of my errors, for it is very ample and perfect of its kind; nor is the power of understanding or conceiving, for, conceiving nothing except by means of the faculty which God has given me, without doubt all that I conceive I conceive correctly, and it is impossible for me to be deceived in it. Whence, then, arise my errors? From this fact alone, that the will being much more ample and extended than the understanding, I do not contain it within the same limits, but extend it also to things I do not understand, and the will being of itself indifferent to such things, very easily goes astray and chooses the bad instead of good, or the false instead of the true, which results in my falling into error or sinning.

For example, when inquiring these last few days whether any- 11 thing existed in the world, and finding that, from the very fact that I was examining this question, it followed most clearly that I existed myself, I could not help judging that what I conceived so clearly was true; not that I was forced to this conclusion by any external cause, but simply because the great clarity of my understanding was followed by a great inclination in my will; and I was led to believe with all the more freedom as I was the less indifferent. On the other hand, at the moment I not only know I exist, inasmuch as I am a thinking being, but also a certain idea of corporeal nature is presented to my mind which makes me doubt whether the thinking nature which is in me, or rather by which I am what I am, is different from this corporeal nature, or whether both are merely one and the same thing. And here I suppose that I do not yet know of any reason which persuades me one way or the other; from which it follows that it is a matter of complete indifference to me which of the two conclusions to deny or to affirm or even to abstain from giving any judgment at all on the matter.

And this indifference extends not only to things of which the 12 understanding has no knowledge, but generally also to all those which it does not discover with perfect clarity at the moment the will is deliberating on them; for, however probable the conjectures may be which make me inclined to form a judgment on something, the mere knowledge that these are only conjectures and not certain and indubitable reasons, suffices to cause me to judge the opposite. This is something which I have experienced sufficiently during the last few days, when I laid down as false all I had held hitherto to be very true, merely because I noticed that one could have some doubts about it.

But if I abstain from giving my judgment on a thing when I do 13 not conceive it clearly and distinctly enough, it is evident that I act rightly and am not deceived; but if I decide to deny or affirm it, then I no longer make use as I should of my free will; and if I affirm what is false, it is evident that I am deceived, and even though I judge according to the truth, it is only by chance, and I am none the less at fault and misuse my free will; for the natural light teaches us that the knowledge of the understanding must always precede the determination of the will. And it is in this wrong use of free will that is found the privation which constitutes the form of error. Privation, I say, is found in the operation, in so far as it comes from me, but it is not in the faculty that I have received from God, nor in the operation, in so far as it depends on him. For I have indeed no cause to complain that God has not given me a greater power of intelligence, or a greater natural light than he has, for it is of the nature of a finite understanding not to understand an infinity of things, and of the nature of a created understanding to be finite; but I have every reason to thank him, in that, having never owed me anything, he has nevertheless given me the few perfections which I possess; and I am far indeed from conceiving such unjust sentiments as to imagine that he has unjustly taken away or withheld the other perfections he has not given me. I have no reason, moreover, to complain of his having given me a will more extensive than my understanding, since, as the will consists of only one and, as it were, an indivisible thing, it appears that it is of such a nature that nothing could be taken away from it without destroying it; and indeed the more extensive it is, the more I should thank the goodness of him who gave it to me. And finally also I must not complain that God concurs with me in forming the acts of the will, that is to say the judgments, in which I am in error, because those acts are entirely true and absolutely good, in so far as they depend on God; and there is, as it were, more perfection in my nature in that I am able to form them, than if I were not. As for privation, in which alone consists the formal reason of error and sin, it has no need of the concurrence of God, since it is not a thing or a being, and if it is referred back to God as to its cause, it should not be called privation, but only negation, according to the meaning given to these words by the Schoolmen.[2]

For, in truth, it is not an imperfection in God, that he has given me the freedom to give my judgment, or to withhold it, concerning things of which he has not put a clear and distinct knowledge into my understanding; but undoubtedly it is an imperfection in me that I do not use it well, and give my judgment rashly on things which I perceive only obscurely and confusedly.   14

I see, nevertheless, that it would have been easy for God to have arranged matters in such a way that I should never be deceived, although I still remained free, and with a limited knowledge, namely, by giving to my understanding a clear and distinct knowledge of all the things on which I should ever have to deliberate, or merely by so deeply engraving in my memory the resolution never to judge anything without conceiving it clearly and distinctly, that I should never forget it. And I well observe that inasmuch as I consider myself alone, as if there were only me in the world, I should have been much more   15

---

[2] **Schoolmen** Catholic scholastic philosophers.

perfect than I am, if God had created me in such a way that I never fell into error. But I cannot therefore deny that it is not in some way a greater perfection in the universe taken as a whole that some of its parts are not exempt from defect, than if they are all alike. And I have no right to complain if God, having put me in the world, has not wished to put me at the level of the most noble and perfect things; indeed, I have reason to be satisfied that, if he has not given me the virtue of not falling into error by the first means that I set out above, which depends on a clear and evident knowledge of everything on which I can deliberate, he has at least left in my power the other means, which is to retain firmly the resolve never to give my judgment on things the truth of which is not clearly known to me. For although I know this weakness in my nature which makes it impossible for me to keep my mind continually fixed on the same thought, I can all the same, by attentive and oft-repeated meditation, imprint it so strongly in my memory that I never fail to recall it every time I have need to, and I can acquire in this way the habit of not falling into error. And, in so far as it is in this that the greatest and principal perfection of man consists, I consider that I have gained not a little by this Meditation, in having discovered the cause of falsity and error.

And certainly there can be no other cause than that which I 16 have explained; for every time that I so restrain my will within the limits of my knowledge that it makes no judgment except on things which are clearly and distinctly represented to it by the understanding, I cannot be in error; because every clear and distinct conception is undoubtedly something real and positive, and therefore cannot originate from nothing, but must necessarily have God as its author, God, I say, who, being supremely perfect, cannot be the cause of any error; and consequently one must conclude that such a conception or such a judgment is true.

Besides, I have not only learnt today what I must avoid in order 17 to escape error, but also what I must do in order to arrive at knowledge of the truth. For certainly I shall reach truth if I fix my attention sufficiently on all the things I conceive perfectly, and if I separate them from others which I apprehend only confusedly and obscurely, which, from now on, I shall take great care to do.

QUESTIONS FOR CRITICAL READING

1. How does Descartes feel he has proved his own existence (para. 11)?
2. Why is it important to note that understanding is finite (para. 13)?
3. What limitations make it impossible for Descartes to fully understand the intentions of God?

4. Must understanding precede "the determination of the will" (para. 13)?
5. Descartes firmly resolves "never to give my judgment on things the truth of which is not clearly known to me" (para. 15). How would this help him avoid error?
6. What kinds of errors does Descartes seem to worry about most?
7. How important are the uses of knowledge in avoiding error?
8. Doubt seems to be a virtue in this meditation. Why?

SUGGESTIONS FOR CRITICAL WRITING

1. A meditation is a brief focused consideration of a major issue which can be reflected upon over a period of time. Descartes's question was how to avoid error and reach the truth using one's mind to reason out all the details. Write a brief meditation on a question that is on your mind. For example, you might meditate on the question of whether it is moral to eat other animals, or whether the United States (or any country) should use torture in interrogating suspected terrorists, or whether you possess free will or not.
2. When Descartes talks about understanding and the impossibility of imperfection in God, he says God has given him the capacity for judgment, to give or to withhold, but that the imperfection that leads to error is in himself, not in the God-given gift. He also says God could have arranged things so that Descartes could never be deceived and that he would still be free. How true do you think this statement is? Could one be truly free if one could never be deceived? If you have personal experiences to bring to bear on this question, introduce them.
3. Descartes says, "[R]eturning to myself, experience tells me that I am nevertheless subject to an infinity of errors" (para. 4). Just as he is very personal in his discussion of truth and error, you may also be aware of your own "infinity of errors." What kinds of errors of understanding do you recall having made, what judgments did they affect, and how did your exercise of will express itself on others? Write a brief meditation on the nature of your errors and how you might have avoided them.
4. In describing the mind, Descartes insists right away that it "does not participate in anything that pertains to the body" (para. 2). In other words, the mind is one thing, and the body is another. How well do you think Descartes substantiates his claim? How would you argue against his view? How could you help support his view that the mind and body are separate? Why is it important to distinguish between the body and the mind?
5. In several places, Descartes tells us that he has proved the existence of God. Explain how he has done this and what evidence he is relying on as he presents his findings. To what extent are you convinced of his views? Why would a seventeenth-century philosopher feel the need to prove the existence of God to his readers? Do you think he makes several references to the existence of God because he fears readers don't

believe him? Do you think readers today need to be told that God exists more than readers in his time did? Would modern readers welcome his views?

6. Descartes never points to evidence that requires substantiation by sensory experience. He draws all of his conclusions by intellectual means, with no reference to experience drawn from the senses. He does this because it permits him to avoid errors introduced by faulty sensory observation. How effective do you feel his method of reasoning is and how much more or less effective would it be if he were to introduce experience drawn from nature?

7. **CONNECTIONS** Steven Pinker (p. 525) disagrees with Descartes on many basic points. How would Pinker critique this meditation? What would be his chief criticisms of Descartes's proof of the existence of God or of his assertion that the mind "does not participate in anything that pertains to the body" (para. 2)? Does Pinker use a similar method of argument—avoiding sensory evidence—to that of Descartes?

8. **SEEING CONNECTIONS** Descartes may have seen some paintings with distortions similar to those in Dalí's *The Persistence of Memory* (p. 443), although he certainly knew nothing about modern surrealism. On the other hand, he also thought that dreams were an important avenue to understanding. In another essay he said, "Whether we are awake or asleep, we should never let ourselves be persuaded except on the evidence of our reason." How would Descartes's reason interpret this painting if it had come to him in a dream? Of what would Descartes's reason "persuade" him regarding the connection between the mind and the body or the mind and the world of sensory experience?

SIGMUND FREUD
The Oedipus Complex

SIGMUND FREUD (1856–1939) is, in the minds of many, the founder of modern psychiatry. He developed the psychoanalytic method: the examination of the mind using dream analysis, the analysis of the unconscious through free association, and the correlation of findings with attitudes toward sexuality and sexual development. His theories changed the way people treated neurosis and most other mental disorders. Today we use terms he either invented or championed, such as *psychoanalysis, penis envy, Oedipus complex,* and *wish-fulfillment.*

Freud was born in Freiberg, Moravia (now Pribor in the Czech Republic), and moved to Vienna, Austria, when he was four. He pursued a medical career and soon began exploring neurology, which stimulated him to begin his psychoanalytic methods. *The Interpretation of Dreams* (1899) is one of his first important books. It was followed in rapid succession by a number of groundbreaking studies: *The Psychopathology of Everyday Life* (1904), *Three Essays on the Theory of Sexuality* (1905), *Totem and Taboo* (1913), *Beyond the Pleasure Principle* (1920), and *Civilization and Its Discontents* (1930). Freud's personal life in Vienna was essentially uneventful until he was put under house arrest by the Nazis in 1938 because he was Jewish. He was released and then moved to London, where he died the following year.

As a movement, psychoanalysis shocked most of the world by postulating a superego, which establishes high standards of personal behavior; an ego, which corresponds to the apparent personality; an id, which includes the deepest primitive forces of life; and an unconscious, into which thoughts and memories we cannot face are repressed or sublimated. The origin of much mental illness, the

---

From *The Interpretation of Dreams*. Translated by James Strachey.

theory presumes, lies in the inability of the mind to find a way to sublimate—to express in harmless and creative ways—the painful thoughts that have been repressed. Dreams and unconscious actions sometimes act as releases or harmless expressions of these thoughts and memories.

As Freud states in *The Interpretation of Dreams*, the unconscious works in complex ways to help us cope with feelings and desires that our superego deems unacceptable. Dreams are mental events, not necessarily connected to physical events. The repression of important emotions, a constant process, often results in dreams that express repressed feelings in a harmless and sometimes symbolic way. In a sense, dreams help us maintain our mental health.

Further, dreams are a primary subject matter of psychoanalysis because they reveal a great deal about the unconscious mind, especially the material that we repress from our consciousness. His discussion of the Oedipus complex, which follows, is a classic case in point. Most people found Freud's theory of the Oedipus complex very compelling once they began to understand the details of its expression. Freud assumed that when we are infants we love our opposite-sex parent and hate our same-sex parent. These feelings of love and hate change as we grow, but they can still linger and cause neurotic behavior. Because these feelings are repressed into the unconscious, we are not aware of them as adults.

Freud's Rhetoric

This selection comes from a section of *The Interpretation of Dreams* in which Freud discusses what he calls "typical dreams." It is here that he speaks directly about his theory of the Oedipus complex and links it specifically with two major pieces of Western literature. *Oedipus Rex* by Sophocles (496–406 B.C.) and *Hamlet* by William Shakespeare (1564–1616) are tragedies in which some of the unconscious desires of the hero to marry his mother are either carried out, as in *Oedipus Rex*, or strongly hinted at, as in *Hamlet*.

Freud realizes that many readers will not be convinced that such a compulsion exists. He explains, however, that because most young people outgrow the compulsion and thereafter repress it, most adults are unaware of their own oedipal feelings.

The rhetorical strategy of introducing two classic dramatic works that are centuries apart and demonstrating what they have in common is effective in helping the reader understand that the psychological condition Freud refers to is not unknown to Western culture. His analysis of his patients' dreams has helped dredge up the original content and the connection with the oedipal urge, thus freeing them of a sense of guilt and a need for self-punishment. Paragraphs 2–6 detail the story of King Oedipus and the strange way in which he eventually married his mother and thus brought a plague upon his land. Freud's point is that this ancient text reveals an aspect of the inner nature of the human mind that has not changed for many thousands of years.

As he tells us, his patients have dreams of intercourse with parents and then feel such torrents of guilt and shame that they sometimes become neurotic. The fact that Oedipus severely punishes himself at the end of the play corresponds with the sense of guilt that Freud's patients experience. Hamlet is even more severely punished and suffers even more psychological anguish throughout the play, even though he never commits incest with his mother. The power of thought is enough. Hamlet is described as "a pathologically irresolute character which might be classed as neurasthenic" (para. 7). In other words, he could have benefited from Freud's psychoanalysis.

Freud uses these two great plays as examples of his theories because he sees them as imaginative constructs that work out the repressed feelings people have always had. They are similar to dreams in that they are written by poets; and poets who rely on inspiration have traditionally drawn on the unconscious. Because these two tragedies are so important to Western literature, they have a special value that no minor literature could have. Consequently, they have been enormously convincing to those interested in the way the mind works. What Freud has done with these works is to hold them up as a mirror. In that mirror one can see quite clearly the evidence for the Oedipus complex that would be totally invisible in any self-examination. It is one of Freud's great rhetorical achievements.

In paragraph 8, Freud makes some other observations about the dreams some of his patients have had in which they imagined themselves killing their parents. This is such a horrible idea for most people that Freud is surprised that our internal censor permits such dreams to occur. His theory is that the thought is so monstrous that the dream censor "is not armed to meet" it (para. 8). His analysis suggests that worry about a parent may disguise the unconscious wish that the parent should die. Freud mentions "our explanation of dreams in general" (para. 8), by which he means that dreams are wish-fulfillments. If that is true, those who dream about killing a parent are likely to be deeply upset and may make themselves neurotic by their own sense of guilt.

Though most people go through an infantile oedipal stage, they usually grow out of it early in life. Freud suggests, however, that those who do not grow out of it may need psychoanalytic help.

PREREADING QUESTIONS:
WHAT TO READ FOR

The following prereading questions may help you anticipate key issues in the discussion of Sigmund Freud's "The Oedipus Complex." Keeping them in mind during your first reading of the selection should help focus your attention.

- What, exactly, is the Oedipus complex ?
- How does the Oedipus complex express itself in dreams?
- How do *Oedipus Rex* and *Hamlet* illustrate the Oedipus complex?

The Oedipus Complex

In my experience, which is already extensive, the chief part in   1
the mental lives of all children who later become psychoneurotics is played by their parents. Being in love with the one parent and hating the other are among the essential constituents of the stock of psychical impulses which is formed at that time and which is of such importance in determining the symptoms of the later neurosis. It is not my belief, however, that psychoneurotics differ sharply in this respect from other human beings who remain normal—that they are able, that is, to create something absolutely new and peculiar to themselves. It is far more probable—and this is confirmed by occasional observations on normal children—that they are only distinguished by exhibiting on a magnified scale feelings of love and hatred to their parents which occur less obviously and less intensely in the minds of most children.

This discovery is confirmed by a legend that has come down to   2
us from classical antiquity: a legend whose profound and universal power to move can only be understood if the hypothesis I have put forward in regard to the psychology of children has an equally universal validity. What I have in mind is the legend of King Oedipus and Sophocles' drama which bears his name.

Oedipus, son of Laïus, King of Thebes, and of Jocasta, was   3
exposed as an infant because an oracle had warned Laïus that the still
unborn child would be his father's murderer. The child was rescued,
and grew up as a prince in an alien court, until, in doubts as to his origin, he too questioned the oracle and was warned to avoid his home
since he was destined to murder his father and take his mother in marriage. On the road leading away from what he believed was his home,
he met King Laïus and slew him in a sudden quarrel. He came next to
Thebes and solved the riddle set him by the Sphinx who barred his
way. Out of gratitude the Thebans made him their king and gave him
Jocasta's hand in marriage. He reigned long in peace and honor, and
she who, unknown to him, was his mother bore him two sons and
two daughters. Then at last a plague broke out and the Thebans made
enquiry once more of the oracle. It is at this point that Sophocles'
tragedy opens. The messengers bring back the reply that the plague
will cease when the murderer of Laïus has been driven from the land.

> But he, where is he? Where shall now be read
> The fading record of this ancient guilt?

The action of the play consists in nothing other than the process of
revealing, with cunning delays and ever-mounting excitement—a
process that can be likened to the work of a psychoanalysis—that
Oedipus himself is the murderer of Laïus, but further that he is the
son of the murdered man and of Jocasta. Appalled at the abomina-
tion which he has unwittingly perpetrated, Oedipus blinds himself
and forsakes his home. The oracle has been fulfilled.

Oedipus Rex is what is known as a tragedy of destiny. Its tragic   4
effect is said to lie in the contrast between the supreme will of the
gods and the vain attempts of mankind to escape the evil that threatens them. The lesson which, it is said, the deeply moved spectator
should learn from the tragedy is submission to the divine will and
realization of his own impotence. Modern dramatists have accordingly tried to achieve a similar tragic effect by weaving the same contrast into a plot invented by themselves. But the spectators have
looked on unmoved while a curse or an oracle was fulfilled in spite
of all the efforts of some innocent man: later tragedies of destiny
have failed in their effect.

If *Oedipus Rex* moves a modern audience no less than it did the   5
contemporary Greek one, the explanation can only be that its effect
does not lie in the contrast between destiny and human will, but is to
be looked for in the particular nature of the material on which that
contrast is exemplified. There must be something which makes a voice
within us ready to recognize the compelling force of destiny in the
Oedipus, while we can dismiss as merely arbitrary such dispositions as

are laid down in *Die Ahnfrau*[1] or other modern tragedies of destiny. And a factor of this kind is in fact involved in the story of King Oedipus. His destiny moves us only because it might have been ours—because the oracle laid the same curse upon us before our birth as upon him. It is the fate of all of us, perhaps, to direct our first sexual impulse towards our mother and our first hatred and our first murderous wish against our father. Our dreams convince us that that is so. King Oedipus, who slew his father Laïus and married his mother Jocasta, merely shows us the fulfillment of our own childhood wishes. But, more fortunate than he, we have meanwhile succeeded, in so far as we have not become psychoneurotics, in detaching our sexual impulses from our mothers and in forgetting our jealousy of our fathers. Here is one in whom these primaeval wishes of our childhood have been fulfilled, and we shrink back from him with the whole force of the repression by which those wishes have since that time been held down within us. While the poet, as he unravels the past, brings to light the guilt of Oedipus, he is at the same time compelling us to recognize our own inner minds, in which those same impulses, though suppressed, are still to be found. The contrast with which the closing Chorus leaves us confronted—

> . . . Fix on Oedipus your eyes,
> Who resolved the dark enigma, noblest champion and most wise.
> Like a star his envied fortune mounted beaming far and wide:
> Now he sinks in seas of anguish, whelmed beneath a raging tide . . .

—strikes as a warning at ourselves and our pride, at us who since our childhood have grown so wise and so mighty in our own eyes. Like Oedipus, we live in ignorance of these wishes, repugnant to morality, which have been forced upon us by Nature, and after their revelation we may all of us well seek to close our eyes to the scenes of our childhood.[2]

---

[1] **Die Ahnfrau** Franz Grillparzer (1791–1872) wrote *Die Ahnfrau* (The Ancestress).

[2] [*Footnote added* 1914:] None of the findings of psychoanalytic research has provoked such embittered denials, such fierce opposition—or such amusing contortions—on the part of critics as this indication of the childhood impulses towards incest which persist in the unconscious. An attempt has even been made recently to make out, in the face of all experience, that the incest should only be taken as "symbolic."—Ferenczi (1912) has proposed an ingenious "over-interpretation" of the Oedipus myth, based on a passage in one of Schopenhauer's letters.—[*Added* 1919:] Later studies have shown that the "Oedipus complex," which was touched upon for the first time in the above paragraphs in the *Interpretation of Dreams*, throws a light of undreamt-of importance on the history of the human race and the evolution of religion and morality. (See my *Totem and Taboo*, 1912–13.) [Freud's notes]

There is an unmistakable indication in the text of Sophocles'   6
tragedy itself that the legend of Oedipus sprang from some primaeval
dream-material which had as its content the distressing disturbance
of a child's relation to his parents owing to the first stirrings of sexuality. At a point when Oedipus, though he is not yet enlightened, has
begun to feel troubled by his recollection of the oracle, Jocasta con-
soles him by referring to a dream which many people dream, though,
as she thinks, it has no meaning:

> Many a man ere now in dreams hath lain
> With her who bare him. He hath least annoy
> Who with such omens troubleth not his mind.

To-day, just as then, many men dream of having sexual relations with
their mothers, and speak of the fact with indignation and astonishment. It is clearly the key to the tragedy and the complement to the
dream of the dreamer's father being dead. The story of Oedipus is the
reaction of the imagination to these two typical dreams. And just as
these dreams, when dreamt by adults, are accompanied by feelings of
repulsion, so too the legend must include horror and self-punishment.
Its further modification originates once again in a misconceived secondary revision of the material, which has sought to exploit it for theological purposes. The attempt to harmonize divine omnipotence with
human responsibility must naturally fail in connection with this
subject-matter just as with any other.

Another of the great creations of tragic poetry, Shakespeare's   7
Hamlet, has its roots in the same soil as *Oedipus Rex*. But the changed
treatment of the same material reveals the whole difference in the mental life of these two widely separated epochs of civilization: the secular
advance of repression in the emotional life of mankind. In the *Oedipus*
the child's wishful fantasy that underlies it is brought into the open and
realized as it would be in a dream. In *Hamlet* it remains repressed;
and—just as in the case of a neurosis—we only learn of its existence
from its inhibiting consequences. Strangely enough, the overwhelming
effect produced by the more modern tragedy has turned out to be
compatible with the fact that people have remained completely in the
dark as to the hero's character. The play is built up on Hamlet's hesitations over fulfilling the task of revenge that is assigned to him; but its
text offers no reasons or motives for these hesitations and an immense
variety of attempts at interpreting them have failed to produce a result.
According to the view which was originated by Goethe[3] and is still the

---

[3]**Johann Wolfgang von Goethe (1749–1832)** One of Germany's greatest
writers.

prevailing one to-day, Hamlet represents the type of man whose power of direct action is paralyzed by an excessive development of his intellect. (He is "sicklied o'er with the pale cast of thought.") According to another view, the dramatist has tried to portray a pathologically irresolute character which might be classed as neurasthenic. The plot of the drama shows us, however, that Hamlet is far from being represented as a person incapable of taking any action. We see him doing so on two occasions: first in a sudden outburst of temper, when he runs his sword through the eaves-dropper behind the arras, and secondly in a premeditated and even crafty fashion, when, with all the callousness of a Renaissance prince, he sends the two courtiers to the death that had been planned for himself. What is it, then, that inhibits him in fulfilling the task set him by his father's ghost? The answer, once again, is that it is the peculiar nature of the task. Hamlet is able to do anything—except take vengeance on the man who did away with his father and took that father's place with his mother, the man who shows him the repressed wishes of his own childhood realized. Thus the loathing which should drive him on to revenge is replaced in him by self-reproaches, by scruples of conscience, which remind him that he himself is literally no better than the sinner whom he is to punish. Here I have translated into conscious terms what was bound to remain unconscious in Hamlet's mind; and if anyone is inclined to call him a hysteric, I can only accept the fact as one that is implied by my interpretation. The distaste for sexuality expressed by Hamlet in his conversation with Ophelia fits in very well with this: the same distaste which was destined to take possession of the poet's mind more and more during the years that followed, and which reached its extreme expression in *Timon of Athens*. For it can of course only be the poet's own mind which confronts us in Hamlet. I observe in a book on Shakespeare by Georg Brandes (1896) a statement that *Hamlet* was written immediately after the death of Shakespeare's father (in 1601), that is, under the immediate impact of his bereavement and, as we may well assume, while his child-hood feelings about his father had been freshly revived. It is known, too, that Shakespeare's own son who died at an early age bore the name of "Hamnet," which is identical with "Hamlet." Just as *Hamlet* deals with the relation of a son to his parents, so *Macbeth* (written at approximately the same period) is concerned with the subject of childlessness. But just as all neurotic symptoms, and, for that matter, dreams, are capable of being "over-interpreted" and indeed need to be, if they are to be fully understood, so all gen-uinely creative writings are the product of more than a single motive and more than a single impulse in the poet's mind, and are open to more than a single interpretation. In what I have written I have only attempted to interpret the deepest layer of impulses in the mind of the creative writer.[4]

I cannot leave the subject of typical dreams of the death of loved relatives, without adding a few more words to throw light on their significance for the theory of dreams in general. In these dreams we find the highly unusual condition realized of a dream-thought formed by a repressed wish entirely eluding censorship and passing into the dream without modification. There must be special factors at work to make this event possible, and I believe that the occurrence of these dreams is facilitated by two such factors. Firstly, there is no wish that seems more remote from us than this one: "we couldn't even *dream*"—so we believe—of wishing such a thing. For this reason the dream-censorship is not armed to meet such a monstrosity, just as Solon's[5] penal code contained no punishment for parricide. Secondly, in this case the repressed and unsuspected wish is particularly often met half-way by a residue from the previous day in the form of a *worry* about the safety of the person concerned. This worry can only make its way into the dream by availing itself of the corresponding wish; while the wish can disguise itself behind the worry that has become active during the day. We may feel inclined to think that things are simpler than this and that one merely carries on during the night and in dreams with what one has been turning over in one's mind during the day; but if so we shall be leaving dreams of the death of people of whom the dreamer is fond completely in the air and without any connection with our explanation of dreams in general, and we shall thus be clinging quite unnecessarily to a riddle which is perfectly capable of solution.

It is also instructive to consider the relation of these dreams to anxiety-dreams. In the dreams we have been discussing, a repressed wish has found a means of evading censorship—and the distortion which censorship involves. The invariable concomitant is that painful feelings are experienced in the dream. In just the same way

---

[4] [*Footnote added* 1919:] The above indications of a psychoanalytic explanation of *Hamlet* have since been amplified by Ernest Jones and defended against the alternative views put forward in the literature of the subject. [*Added* 1930:] Incidentally, I have in the meantime ceased to believe that the author of Shakespeare's works was the man from Stratford. [*Added* 1919:] Further attempts at an analysis of *Macbeth* will be found in a paper of mine [Freud, 1916*d*] and in one by Jekels (1917). [Freud's notes]

[5] **Solon (638–558 B.C.)** Greek known as the law giver. His ideas on law continue to influence us today.

anxiety-dreams only occur if the censorship has been wholly or partly overpowered; and, on the other hand, the overpowering of the censorship is facilitated if anxiety has already been produced as an immediate sensation arising from somatic[6] sources. We can thus plainly see the purpose for which the censorship exercises its office and brings about the distortion of dreams: it does so *in order to prevent the generation of anxiety or other forms of distressing affect.*

---

[6]**somatic** Having to do with the physical body.

QUESTIONS FOR CRITICAL READING

1. What role do parents play in the lives of those who become neurotics?
2. Do psychoneurotics differ substantially from normal people?
3. What does Freud expect his example of *Oedipus Rex* to call up in the mind of the reader?
4. What is a tragedy of destiny?
5. In what ways are all of us like Oedipus?
6. How is literature related to dreams, according to Freud?
7. Why do dreams sometimes need to be overinterpreted?
8. How does censorship operate in dreams?

SUGGESTIONS FOR CRITICAL WRITING

1. Most adults have absolutely no awareness of having had an oedipal period in their infancy. However, you may have observed oedipal behavior in young children. If so, describe how the children behaved and if possible describe how they have grown up and whether they have left the oedipal stage behind. Do your observations help to bolster Freud's views, or do they help to weaken them?
2. Describe in as much detail as possible any anxiety dreams you may have had. Often anxiety dreams are repetitive and recurrent. What are the circumstances in which you find yourself in your dream? What worries you most in the dream? What threatens you most? How does the dream resolve itself? Does the dream provoke guilt or shame? How would you interpret the dream in the light of what you have read here?
3. If you find yourself unable to remember your dreams, interview some friends and "collect" dreams from them. Ask them for dreams that make them feel uneasy — anxiety dreams. Have them write down their dreams and then ask them to talk about events in their waking life that preceded the dreams. See if there are contributing events or anticipations in the mind of the dreamers that would lead them to have anxiety

dreams. See, too, if there are any patterns to dreams of different people. Are there any "typical dreams" shared by your friends?

4. What are your typical dreams? Try to write them out as if they were plays. Identify characters, setting, and time, and then write the dialogue and stage directions that would give a good approximation of the content of the dreams. Do not censor your dreams or try to "overanalyze" them (despite Freud's recommendation). Do your best to make the dreams clear in their expression. Does this approach make your dreams any more meaningful to you? Explain.

5. Does your reading of *Hamlet* help to bear out Freud's theory that suggests Hamlet is suffering from an Oedipus complex? What is his relationship to his mother? How does she regard him? Is his killing of King Claudius an act of parricide? Is Hamlet's punishment warranted? Argue for or against Freud's view of the play.

6. In paragraph 6, Freud states, "There is an unmistakable indication in the text of Sophocles' tragedy itself that the legend of Oedipus sprang from some primaeval dream-material." Examine his evidence for this claim and decide yourself whether this seems a reasonable conclusion.

7. Most horror films involve monstrous actions and severe punishment. Is it possible that one of the functions of horror films is to reveal some of the inner nature of our minds somewhat the way *Oedipus Rex* and *Hamlet* do? Choose a favorite film and analyze it in terms of its revealing hidden desires that might trouble us if we felt them consciously and acted on them in life.

8. **CONNECTIONS** Plato's concerns in "The Allegory of the Cave" (p. 447) point to a level of reality that humans cannot reach because of the limitations of sensory apprehension. Is it also true that the dream world represents a level of reality that is impossible to reach because of the limitations of the conscious waking mind? Which part of the mind—the conscious or the unconscious—does Freud seem to regard as primary in his discussion of the Oedipus complex? Is there the sense that he regards one or the other as possessing a greater "reality"? How do his views fit with those of Plato?

9. **SEEING CONNECTIONS** Dalí explicitly called attention to his personal Oedipus complex, describing his love for his mother and implying that the fetal figure in the center of *The Persistence of Memory* (p. 443) was a self-portrait. Dalí may never have experienced psychoanalysis, "the talking cure," but he did express himself very openly in his painting. Would Freud have thought this painting might have helped Dalí achieve some kind of cure, or approach some kind of resolution, of his oedipal fixations? Freud was much more influenced by words than by visual art, but with an obvious connection to his own theories, could the painting have been an important factor in psychoanalysis? How might Freud have interpreted it?

CARL JUNG
The Personal and the Collective Unconscious

CARL GUSTAV JUNG (1875–1961), Freud's most famous disciple, was a Swiss physician who collaborated with Freud from 1907 to 1912, when the two argued about the nature of the unconscious. Jung's *Psychology of the Unconscious* (1912) posits an unconscious that is composed of more than the ego, superego, and id. According to Jung, an additional aspect of the unconscious is a collection of archetypal images that can be inherited by members of the same group. Experience clarifies these images, but the images in turn direct experience.

In one of his essays on the collective unconscious, Jung asserts that the great myths express the archetypes of actions and heroes stored in the unconscious by elucidating them for the individual and society. These archetypes represent themselves in mythic literature in images, such as the great father or the great mother, or in patterns of action, such as disobedience and self-sacrifice. They transcend social barriers and exemplify themselves similarly in most people in any given cultural group. For Jung, the individual must adapt to the archetypes that reveal themselves in the myths in order to be psychically healthy.

Like Freud, Jung postulates a specific model of the way the mind works: he claims the existence not only of a conscious mind—which all of us can attest to from experience and common sense—but also of an unconscious component to the mind. He argues that we are unaware of the content of our unconscious mind except, perhaps, in dreams (which occur when we are unconscious), which Freud and others insist speak to us in symbols rather than in direct language.

From *The Basic Writings of C. G. Jung.* Translated by Cary F. Baynes.

Jung also acknowledges the symbolic nature of the unconscious but disagrees with the source of the content of the unconscious mind.

In "The Personal and the Collective Unconscious" (1916), Jung describes the pattern of psychological transference that most psychoanalysts experience with their patients. In the case presented here, the patient's problems were associated with her father, and the transference was the normal one of conceiving of the doctor—in this case, Jung—in terms of the father. When this transference occurs, the patient often is cured of the problems that brought her to the psychoanalyst, but in this case the transference was incomplete. Jung offers a detailed analysis of the dreams that revealed the problems with the transference and describes the intellectual state of the woman whose dreams form the basis of the discussion. She is intelligent, conscious of the mechanism of transference, and careful about her own inner life. Yet the dream that Jung analyzes had a content that he could not relate to her personal life.

In an attempt to explain his inability to analyze the woman's dream strictly in terms of her personal life, Jung reexamines Freud's definition of the unconscious. As Jung explains Freud's view, the unconscious is a repository for material that is produced by the conscious mind and later repressed so as not to interfere with the function of the conscious mind. Thus, painful memories and unpleasant fears are often repressed and rarely become problems because they are sublimated—transformed into harmless activity, often dreams—and released. According to Freud, the material in the unconscious mind develops solely from personal experience.

Jung, however, argues that personal experiences form only part of the individual's unconscious, what he calls the "personal unconscious" (para. 17). For the patient in this essay, the images in the dream that he and the patient at first classified as a transference dream (in which the doctor became the father/lover figure) had qualities that could not be explained fully by transference. Instead, the dream seemed to represent a primordial figure, a god. From this, Jung develops the view that such a figure is cultural in nature and not personal. Nothing in the patient's life pointed to her concern for a god of the kind that developed in her dream. Jung proposes that the images that constituted the content of her dream were not a result of personal experience or education but, instead, were inherited. Jung defines this portion of the unconscious as the "collective unconscious" (para. 19).

Jung's theories proved unacceptable to Freud. After their collaboration ended, Jung studied the world's myths and mythic systems, including alchemy and occult literature. In them he saw many of the archetypal symbols that he felt were revealed in dreams—including symbolic quests, sudden transformations, dramatic or threatening landscapes, and images of God. His conclusions were that this literature, most or all of which was suppressed or rejected by modern religions such as Christianity, was a repository for the symbols of the collective unconscious—at least of Western civilization and perhaps of other civilizations.

Jung's Rhetoric

Like Freud, Jung tells a story. His selection is a narrative beginning with a recapitulation of Freud's view of the unconscious. Jung tells us that according to the conventional view, the contents of the unconscious have passed "the threshold of consciousness" (para. 2): in other words, they were once in the conscious mind of the individual. However, Jung also asserts that "the unconscious also contains components that have *not yet* reached the threshold of consciousness" (para. 3). At least two questions arise from this assertion: What is that content, and where did it come from?

Jung then provides the "example" (para. 5) of the woman whose therapy he was conducting. He tells us, as one would tell a story, about the woman's treatment and how such treatment works in a general sense. He explains the phenomenon of transference, claiming that "a successful transference can . . . cause the whole neurosis to disappear" (para. 5). Near the end of this patient's treatment he analyzed her dreams and found something he did not expect. He relates the narrative of the dream (para. 10), which includes the image of a superhuman father figure in a field of wheat swaying in the wind. From this he concludes that the image of the dream is not the doctor/father/lover figure that is common to transference—and that the patient was thoroughly aware of—but something of an entirely different order. He connects it to an archetype of God and proceeds to an analysis that explains the dream in terms of a collective unconscious whose content is shared by groups of people rather than created by the individual alone.

Jung's rhetorical strategy here is an argument proceeding from both example and analysis. The example is given in detail, along with enough background to make it useful to the reader. Then the example is narrated carefully, and its content is examined through a process of analysis familiar to those in psychiatry.

Some of the material in this selection is relatively challenging because Jung uses technical language and occasionally obscure references. However, the simplicity of the technique of narrative, telling a story of what happened, makes the selection intelligible, even though it deals with highly complex and controversial ideas.

PREREADING QUESTIONS:
WHAT TO READ FOR

The following prereading questions may help you anticipate key issues
in the discussion of Carl Jung's "The Personal and the Collective Unconscious." Keeping them in mind during your first reading of the selection
should help focus your attention.

- What are some of the contents of the unconscious?

- What is the difference between the personal and the collective unconscious?

The Personal and
the Collective Unconscious

In Freud's view, as most people know, the contents of the   1
unconscious are limited to infantile tendencies which are repressed
because of their incompatible character. Repression is a process that
begins in early childhood under the moral influence of the environment and lasts throughout life. Through analysis the repressions are
removed and the repressed wishes made conscious.

According to this theory, the unconscious contains only those   2
parts of the personality which could just as well be conscious and
are in fact suppressed only through upbringing. Although from one
point of view the infantile tendencies of the unconscious are the
most conspicuous, it would nonetheless be incorrect to define or
evaluate the unconscious entirely in these terms. The unconscious
has still another side to it: it includes not only repressed contents,
but also all psychic material that lies below the threshold of consciousness. It is impossible to explain the subliminal nature of all
this material on the principle of repression; otherwise, through the
removal of repressions, a man would acquire a phenomenal memory
which would thenceforth forget nothing.

We therefore emphatically say that in addition to the repressed   3
material the unconscious contains all those psychic components that
have fallen below the threshold, including subliminal sense perceptions. Moreover we know, from abundant experience as well as
for theoretical reasons, that the unconscious also contains components that have *not yet* reached the threshold of consciousness.

These are the seeds of future conscious contents. Equally we have reason to suppose that the unconscious is never at rest in the sense of being inactive, but is continually engaged in grouping and regrouping its contents. Only in pathological cases can this activity be regarded as completely autonomous; normally it is coordinated with the conscious mind in a compensatory relationship.

It is to be assumed that all these contents are personal in so far   4 as they are acquired during the individual's life. Since this life is limited, the number of acquired contents in the unconscious must also be limited. This being so, it might be thought possible to empty the unconscious either by analysis or by making a complete inventory of unconscious contents, on the ground that the unconscious cannot produce anything more than is already known and accepted in the conscious mind. We should also have to infer, as already indicated, that if one could stop the descent of conscious contents into the unconscious by doing away with repression, unconscious productivity would be paralyzed. This is possible only to a very limited extent, as we know from experience. We urge our patients to hold fast to repressed contents that have been re-associated with consciousness, and to assimilate them into their plan of life. But this procedure, as we may daily convince ourselves, makes no impression on the unconscious, since it calmly continues to produce dreams and fantasies which, according to Freud's original theory, must arise from personal repressions. If in such cases we pursue our observations systematically and without prejudice, we shall find material which, although similar in form to the previous personal contents, yet seems to contain allusions that go far beyond the personal sphere.

Casting about in my mind for an example to illustrate what I   5 have just said, I have a particularly vivid memory of a woman patient with a mild hysterical neurosis which, as we expressed it in those days, had its principal cause in a "father complex." By this we wanted to denote the fact that the patient's peculiar relationship to her father stood in her way. She had been on very good terms with her father, who had since died. It was a relationship chiefly of feeling. In such cases it is usually the intellectual function that is developed, and this later becomes the bridge to the world. Accordingly our patient became a student of philosophy. Her energetic pursuit of knowledge was motivated by her need to extricate herself from the emotional entanglement with her father. This operation may succeed if her feelings can find an outlet on the new intellectual level, perhaps in the formation of an emotional tie with a suitable man, equivalent to the former tie. In this particular case, however, the transition refused to take place, because the patient's feelings remained suspended, oscillating between her father and a man who was not altogether suitable. The progress of her life was thus held up, and that inner disunity so characteristic of a neurosis promptly made its appearance. The so-called normal person would probably be able to break the emotional bond in one or the other direction by a powerful act of will, or else — and this is perhaps the more usual thing — he would come through the difficulty unconsciously, on the smooth path of instinct, without ever being aware of the sort of conflict that lay behind his headaches or other physical discomforts. But any weakness of instinct (which may have many causes) is enough to hinder a smooth unconscious transition. Then all progress is delayed by conflict, and the resulting stasis of life is equivalent to a neurosis. In consequence of the standstill, psychic energy flows off in every conceivable direction, apparently quite uselessly. For instance, there are excessive innervations of the sympathetic system, which lead to nervous disorders of the stomach and intestines; or the vagus (and consequently the heart) is stimulated; or fantasies and memories, uninteresting enough in themselves, become overvalued and prey on the conscious mind (mountains out of molehills). In this state a new motive is needed to put an end to the morbid suspension. Nature herself paves the way for this, unconsciously and indirectly, through the phenomenon of the transference (Freud). In the course of treatment the patient transfers the father imago[1] to the doctor, thus making him, in a sense, the father, and in the sense that he is *not* the father, also making him a substitute for the man she cannot reach. The doctor therefore becomes both a father and a kind of lover — in other words, the object of conflict. In him the opposites are united, and for this reason he stands for a quasi-ideal solution of the conflict. Without in the least wishing it, he draws upon himself an overvaluation that is almost incredible to the outsider, for to the patient he seems like a savior or a god. This way of speaking is not altogether so laughable as it sounds. It is indeed a bit much to be a father and lover at once. Nobody could possibly stand up to it in the long run, precisely because it is too much of a good thing. One would have to be a demigod at least to sustain such a role without a break, for all the time one would have to be the giver. To the patient in the state of transference, this provisional solution naturally seems ideal, but only at first; in the end she comes to a standstill that is just as bad as the neurotic conflict was. Fundamentally, nothing has yet happened that might lead to a real solution. The conflict has merely been

---

[1] **imago** Idealized image of a person.

transferred. Nevertheless a successful transference can—at least temporarily—cause the whole neurosis to disappear, and for this reason it has been very rightly recognized by Freud as a healing factor of first-rate importance, but, at the same time, as a provisional state only, for although it holds out the possibility of a cure, it is far from being the cure itself.

This somewhat lengthy discussion seemed to me essential if my example was to be understood, for my patient had arrived at the state of transference and had already reached the upper limit where the standstill begins to make itself disagreeable. The question now arose: What next? I had of course become the complete savior, and the thought of having to give me up was not only exceedingly distasteful to the patient, but positively terrifying. In such a situation "sound common sense" generally comes out with a whole repertory of admonitions: "you simply must," "you really ought," "you just cannot," etc. So far as sound common sense is, happily, not too rare and not entirely without effect (pessimists, I know, exist), a rational motive can, in the exuberant feeling of health you get from transference, release so much enthusiasm that a painful sacrifice can be risked with a mighty effort of will. If successful—and these things sometimes are—the sacrifice bears blessed fruit, and the erstwhile patient leaps at one bound into the state of being practically cured. The doctor is generally so delighted that he fails to tackle the theoretical difficulties connected with this little miracle.

If the leap does not succeed—and it did not succeed with my patient—one is then faced with the problem of severing the transference. Here "psychoanalytic" theory shrouds itself in a thick darkness. Apparently we are to fall back on some nebulous trust in fate: somehow or other the matter will settle itself. "The transference stops automatically when the patient runs out of money," as a slightly cynical colleague once remarked to me. Or the ineluctable demands of life make it impossible for the patient to linger on in the transference—demands which compel the involuntary sacrifice, sometimes with a more or less complete relapse as a result. (One may look in vain for accounts of such cases in the books that sing the praises of psychoanalysis!)

To be sure, there are hopeless cases where nothing helps; but there are also cases that do not get stuck and do not inevitably leave the transference situation with bitter hearts and sore heads. I told myself, at this juncture with my patient, that there must be a clear and respectable way out of the impasse. My patient had long since run out of money—if indeed she ever possessed any—but I was curious to know what means nature would devise for a satisfactory way out of the transference deadlock. Since I never imagined that I was blessed with that "sound common sense" which always knows exactly what to do in every tangled situation, and since my patient knew as little as I, I suggested to her that we could at least keep an eye open for any movements coming from a sphere of the psyche uncontaminated by our superior wisdom and our conscious plannings. That meant first and foremost her dreams.

Dreams contain images and thought associations which we do   9
not create with conscious intent. They arise spontaneously without our assistance and are representatives of a psychic activity withdrawn from our arbitrary will. Therefore the dream is, properly speaking, a highly objective, natural product of the psyche, from which we might expect indications, or at least hints, about certain basic trends in the psychic process. Now, since the psychic process, like any other life process, is not just a causal sequence, but is also a process with a teleological orientation,[2] we might expect dreams to give us certain indicia about the objective causality as well as about the objective tendencies, because they are nothing less than self-portraits of the psychic life process.

On the basis of these reflections, then, we subjected the dreams   10
to a careful examination. It would lead too far to quote word for word all the dreams that now followed. Let it suffice to sketch their main character: the majority referred to the person of the doctor, that is to say, the actors were unmistakably the dreamer herself and her doctor. The latter, however, seldom appeared in this natural shape, but was generally distorted in a remarkable way. Sometimes his figure was of supernatural size, sometimes he seemed to be extremely aged, then again he resembled her father, but was at the same time curiously woven into nature, as in the following dream: *Her father (who in reality was of small stature) was standing with her on a hill that was covered with wheat fields. She was quite tiny beside him, and he seemed to her like a giant. He lifted her up from the ground and held her in his arms like a little child. The wind swept over the wheat fields, and as the wheat swayed in the wind, he rocked her in his arms.*

From this dream and from others like it I could discern various   11
things. Above all I got the impression that her unconscious was holding unshakably to the idea of my being the father-lover, so that the fatal tie we were trying to undo appeared to be doubly strengthened. Moreover one could hardly avoid seeing that the unconscious placed a special emphasis on the supernatural, almost "divine" nature

---

[2] **teleological orientation** Possessing a sense of design; directed toward an end or purpose.

of the father-lover, thus accentuating still further the overvaluation occasioned by the transference. I therefore asked myself whether the patient had still not understood the wholly fantastic character of her transference, or whether perhaps the unconscious could never be reached by understanding at all, but must blindly and idiotically pursue some nonsensical chimera. Freud's idea that the unconscious can "do nothing but wish," Schopenhauer's[3] blind and aimless Will, the gnostic demi-urge who in his vanity deems himself perfect and then in the blindness of his limitation creates something lamentably imperfect — all these pessimistic suspicions of an essentially negative background to the world and the soul came threateningly near. And indeed there would be nothing to set against this except a well-meaning "you ought," reinforced by a stroke of the ax that would cut down the whole phantasmagoria for good and all.

But as I turned the dreams over and over in my mind, there   12 dawned on me another possibility. I said to myself: it cannot be denied that the dreams continue to speak in the same old metaphors with which our conversations have made both doctor and patient sickeningly familiar. But the patient has an undoubted understanding of her transference fantasy. She knows that I appear to her as a semidivine father-lover, and she can, at least intellectually, distinguish this from my factual reality. Therefore the dreams are obviously reiterating the conscious standpoint minus the conscious criticism, which they completely ignore. They reiterate the conscious contents, not *in toto*, but insist on the fantastic standpoint as opposed to "sound common sense."

I naturally asked myself what was the source of this obstinacy   13 and what was its purpose? That it must have some purposive meaning I was convinced, for there is no truly living thing that does not have a final meaning, that can in other words be explained as a mere leftover from antecedent facts. But the energy of the transference is so strong that it gives one the impression of a vital instinct. That being so, what is the purpose of such fantasies? A careful examination and analysis of the dreams, especially of the one just quoted, revealed a very marked tendency — in contrast to conscious criticism, which always seeks to reduce things to human proportions — to endow the person of the doctor with superhuman attributes. He had to be gigantic, primordial, huger than the father, like the wind that sweeps over the earth — was he then to be made into a god? Or, I said to myself, was it rather the case that the unconscious was trying to *create* a god out of the person of the doctor, as it were to free a

---

[3] **Arthur Schopenhauer (1788–1860)** German pessimistic philosopher.

vision of God from the veils of the personal, so that the transference to the person of the doctor was no more than a misunderstanding on the part of the conscious mind, a stupid trick played by "sound common sense"? Was the urge of the unconscious perhaps only apparently reaching out towards the person, but in a deeper sense towards a god? Could the longing for a god be a *passion* welling up from our darkest, instinctual nature, a passion unswayed by any outside influences, deeper and stronger perhaps than the love for a human person? Or was it perhaps the highest and truest meaning of that inappropriate love we call transference, a little bit of real *Gottesminne*,[4] that has been lost to consciousness ever since the fifteenth century?

No one will doubt the reality of a passionate longing for a human   14 person; but that a fragment of religious psychology, an historical anachronism, indeed something of a medieval curiosity—we are reminded of Mechtild of Magdeburg[5]—should come to light as an immediate living reality in the middle of the consulting room, and be expressed in the prosaic figure of the doctor, seems almost too fantastic to be taken seriously.

A genuinely scientific attitude must be unprejudiced. The sole   15 criterion for the validity of an hypothesis is whether or not it possesses an heuristic—i.e., explanatory—value. The question now is, can we regard the possibilities set forth above as a valid hypothesis? There is no a priori[6] reason why it should not be just as possible that the unconscious tendencies have a goal beyond the human person, as that the unconscious can "do nothing but wish." Experience alone can decide which is the more suitable hypothesis.

This new hypothesis was not entirely plausible to my very critical   16 patient. The earlier view that I was the father-lover, and as such presented an ideal solution of the conflict, was incomparably more attractive to her way of feeling. Nevertheless her intellect was sufficiently clear to appreciate the theoretical possibility of the new hypothesis. Meanwhile the dreams continued to disintegrate the person of the doctor and swell them to ever vaster proportions. Concurrently with this there now occurred something which at first I alone perceived, and with the utmost astonishment, namely a kind of subterranean undermining of the transference. Her relations with a certain friend deepened perceptibly, notwithstanding the fact that consciously she still clung to the transference. So that when the time came for leaving

---

[4] ***Gottesminne*** Love of God.
[5] **Mechtild of Magdeburg (1207–1282)** Thirteenth-century German mystic, writer, and saint.
[6] **a priori** Based on theory rather than on experiment or evidence.

me, it was no catastrophe, but a perfectly reasonable parting. I had the privilege of being the only witness during the process of severance. I saw how the transpersonal control point developed—I cannot call it anything else—a *guiding function* and step by step gathered to itself all the former personal overvaluations; how, with this afflux of energy, it gained influence over the resisting conscious mind without the patient's consciously noticing what was happening. From this I realized that the dreams were not just fantasies, but self-representations of unconscious developments which allowed the psyche of the patient gradually to grow out of the pointless personal tie.

This change took place, as I showed, through the unconscious   17 development of a transpersonal control point; a virtual goal, as it were, that expressed itself symbolically in a form which can only be described as a vision of God. The dreams swelled the human person of the doctor to superhuman proportions, making him a gigantic primordial father who is at the same time the wind, and in whose protecting arms the dreamer rests like an infant. If we try to make the patient's conscious, and traditionally Christian, idea of God responsible for the divine image in the dreams, we would still have to lay stress on the distortion. In religious matters the patient had a critical and agnostic attitude, and her idea of a possible deity had long since passed into the realm of the inconceivable, i.e., had dwindled into a complete abstraction. In contrast to this, the god-image of the dreams corresponded to the archaic conception of a nature demon, something like Wotan.[7] *Theos to pneûma,* "God is spirit," is here translated back into its original form where *pneûma* means "wind": God is the wind, stronger and mightier than man, an invisible breath-spirit. As in the Hebrew *ruach,* so in Arabic *ruh* means breath and spirit. Out of the purely personal form the dreams developed an archaic god-image that is infinitely far from the conscious idea of God. It might be objected that this is simply an infantile image, a childhood memory. I would have no quarrel with this assumption if we were dealing with an old man sitting on a golden throne in heaven. But there is no trace of any sentimentality of that kind; instead, we have a primitive conception that can correspond only to an archaic mentality. These primitive conceptions, of which I have given a large number of examples in my *Symbols of Transformation,* tempt one to make, in regard to unconscious material, a distinction very different from that between "preconscious" and "unconscious" or "subconscious" and "unconscious." The justification for these distinctions need not be discussed here. They have a

---

[7] **Wotan** Supreme God; character in Richard Wagner's *Ring* cycle of operas.

definite value and are worth refining further as points of view. The fundamental distinction which experience has forced upon me merely claims the value of a further point of view. From what has been said it is clear that we have to distinguish in the unconscious a layer which we may call the *personal unconscious*. The materials contained in this layer are of a personal nature in so far as they have the character partly of acquisitions derived from the individual's life and partly of psychological factors which could just as well be conscious. It is readily understandable that incompatible psychological elements are liable to repression and therefore become unconscious; but on the other hand we also have the possibility of making and keeping the repressed contents conscious, once they have been recognized. We recognize them as personal contents because we can discover their effects, or their partial manifestation, or their specific origin in our personal past. They are the integral components of the personality, they belong to its inventory, and their loss to consciousness produces an inferiority in one or the other respect—an inferiority, moreover, that has the psychological character not so much of an organic mutilation or an inborn defect as of a want which gives rise to a feeling of moral resentment. The sense of moral inferiority always indicates that the missing element is something which, one feels, should not be missing, or which could be made conscious if only one took enough trouble. The feeling of moral inferiority does not come from a collision with the generally accepted and, in a sense, arbitrary moral law, but from the conflict with one's own self which, for reasons of psychic equilibrium, demands that the deficit be redressed. Whenever a sense of moral inferiority appears, it shows that there is not only the demand to assimilate an unconscious component, but also the possibility of assimilating it. In the last resort it is a man's moral qualities which force him, either through direct recognition of the necessity to do so, or indirectly through a painful neurosis, to assimilate his unconscious self and to keep himself fully conscious. Whoever progresses along this road of realizing the unconscious self must inevitably bring into consciousness the contents of the personal unconscious, thus widening the scope of his personality. I should add at once that this "widening" primarily concerns the moral consciousness, one's self-knowledge, for the unconscious contents that are released and brought into consciousness by analysis are usually unpleasant—which is precisely why these wishes, memories, tendencies, plans, etc. were repressed. These are the contents that are brought to light in much the same way by a thorough confession, though to a much more limited extent. The rest comes out as a rule in dream analysis. It is often very interesting to watch how the dreams fetch up the essential points, bit by bit and with the nicest choice. The total material that is added to consciousness causes a considerable widening of the horizon, a deepened self-knowledge which, more than anything else, is calculated to humanize a man and make him modest. But even self-knowledge, assumed by all wise men to be the best and most efficacious, has different effects on different characters. We make very remarkable discoveries in this respect in practical analysis, but I shall deal with this question in the next chapter.

As my example of the archaic idea of God shows, the uncon-   18 scious seems to contain other things besides personal acquisitions and belongings. My patient was quite unconscious of the derivation of "spirit" from "wind," or of the parallelism between the two. This content was not the product of her thinking, nor had she ever been taught it. The critical passage in the New Testament was inaccessible to her—*to pneûma pneî hopou thelei*[8]—since she knew no Greek. If we must take it as a wholly personal acquisition, it might be a case of so-called cryptomnesia,[9] the unconscious recollection of a thought which the dreamer had once read somewhere. I have nothing against such a possibility in this particular case; but I have seen a sufficient number of other cases—many of them are to be found in the book mentioned above—where cryptomnesia can be excluded with certainty. Even if it were a case of cryptomnesia, which seems to me very improbable, we should still have to explain what the predisposition was that caused just this image to be retained and later, as Semon puts it, "ecphorated" (*ekphoreîn*, Latin *efferre*, "to produce"). In any case, cryptomnesia or no cryptomnesia, we are dealing with a genuine and thoroughly primitive god image that grew up in the unconscious of a civilized person and produced a living effect—an effect which might well give the psychologist of religion food for reflection. There is nothing about this image that could be called personal: it is a wholly collective image, the ethnic origin of which has long been known to us. Here is an historical image of worldwide distribution that has come into existence again through a natural psychic function. This is not so very surprising, since my patient was born into the world with a human brain which presumably still functions today much as it did of old. We are dealing with a reactivated archetype, as I have elsewhere called these primordial images. These ancient images are restored to life by the

---

[8] *to pneûma pneî hopou thelei* the wind blows where it wishes (John 3:8).

[9] Cf. Théodore Flournoy, *Des Indes à la planète Mars: Étude sur un cas de somnambulisme avec glossolalie* (Paris and Geneva, 1900; trans. by D. B. Vermilye as *From India to the Planet Mars*, New York, 1900), and Jung, "Psychology and Pathology of So-called Occult Phenomena," *Coll. Works*, Vol. 1, pp. 81ff. [Jung's note]

primitive, analogical mode of thinking peculiar to dreams. It is not a question of inherited ideas, but of inherited thought patterns.

In view of these facts we must assume that the unconscious con-   19 tains not only personal, but also impersonal, collective components in the form of inherited categories or archetypes. I have therefore advanced the hypothesis that at its deeper levels the unconscious possesses collective contents in a relatively active state. That is why I speak of the collective unconscious.

QUESTIONS FOR CRITICAL READING

1. What is Jung's view of the relationship of the unconscious mind to the conscious mind? How does it compare to Freud's?
2. What is repression? Why does repression work as it does?
3. How does transference work in psychoanalytic treatment? Is it a good thing or not?
4. What is unusual about Jung's patient's dream? What about it can he not fit into a normal pattern of transference?
5. What is the distinction between the personal unconscious and the collective unconscious?
6. Do you agree that "Dreams contain images and thought associations which we do not create with conscious intent" (para. 9)? Why or why not?

SUGGESTIONS FOR CRITICAL WRITING

1. Jung talks about common sense and its limitations. For some people, common sense denies the existence of an unconscious mind. Relying on Jung, your own personal experiences, and any other sources you choose, defend the existence of an unconscious mind. At the same time, do your best to explain the content of the unconscious and why it is important to the individual.
2. With reference to your own dreams, argue for or against the belief that dreams are products of the conscious mind. Have you had dreams whose content did not pass the "threshold" of your conscious mind?
3. Although the adult Jung was not religious, as the son of a Swiss pastor he was well acquainted with religion. In paragraph 13, Jung asserts that his patient's dream reveals a fundamental human longing for God. As he puts it, "Could the longing for a god be a *passion* welling up from our darkest, instinctual nature?" Examine the possibility that such a psychological phenomenon has affected your attitude toward religion and religious belief.

4. Jung suggests that mythic literature maintains some of the images that make up the collective unconscious of a group of people. Select a myth (consult Ovid's *Metamorphosis*, Grimm's fairy tales, or the Greek myths, or choose a pattern of mythic behavior repeated in popular films) and analyze the instinctual longing it represents for us. What does the myth reveal about our culture?

5. **CONNECTIONS**   Jung was a follower of Freud until he eventually broke from him. The break was not altogether friendly, and the feelings between the two—on professional matters—were often strained. Compare Jung's approach to the subject of the unconscious with Freud's. In what respects do they differ? In what ways are their methods either compatible or incompatible with each other? Do you find Jung's methods more or less useful than Freud's? Explain why.

6. **CONNECTIONS**   In "Natural Selection" (p. 597), Charles Darwin suggests that as humans developed over a long period of time they may have continued many traditions that began early in history. How would Darwin's ideas help reinforce the concept of an unconscious that might transcend the ages and thus become part of our collective "memory" gathered through eons of evolution? Would Jung have found Darwin's ideas congenial, or would he have discounted them? Does he show any evidence of having been influenced by Darwin? Explain.

7. **SEEING CONNECTIONS**   Would Jung consider Dalí's *The Persistence of Memory* (p. 443) to be an example of the personal or of the collective "memory"? Given what Jung says of the collective unconscious, and considering that Dalí stated the painting developed from a dream, do you feel this painting validates or invalidates Jung's theories? What elements in the painting most satisfy Jung's requirements for understanding the collective unconscious? Is it likely that Dalí somehow represented the collective unconscious in this painting and that as a result the painting quickly became world famous? Or is the collective unconscious irrelevant to the painting?

HOWARD GARDNER
A Rounded Version: The Theory of Multiple Intelligences

HOWARD GARDNER (b. 1943), Hobbs Professor of Cognition and Education at the Harvard Graduate School of Education, is codirector of Harvard's Project Zero, a program dedicated to improving education in schools by emphasizing creativity in thinking and problem solving. By emphasizing the arts and the newer electronic technologies associated with learning, the program cultivates a "culture of thinking" in the classroom as opposed to a culture of rote learning. Gardner has received a MacArthur Foundation award (1981), which supported his research for five years, and has won a number of important awards in the field of education, including the Grawemeyer Award in Education (1990), given for the first time to an American. Among his many books are *Leading Minds: An Anatomy of Leadership* (1995) and *Extraordinary Minds: Portraits of Exceptional Individuals and an Examination of Our Extraordinariness* (1997).

Perhaps the most important and best-known product of Project Zero is the theory of multiple intelligences, which Gardner first published in *Frames of Mind* (1983). (His more recent book, *Intelligence Reframed: Multiple Intelligence for the 21st Century* [1999], offers a revisitation and more detailed elaboration on multiple intelligence theory and its application.) In *Frames of Mind*, he noted that the general attitude toward intelligence centers on the IQ (intelligence quotient) test that Alfred Binet (1857–1911) devised. Binet believed that intelligence is measurable and that IQ tests result in numerical scores that are reliable indicators of a more or less permanent basic intelligence. Gardner offered several objections to that

From *Multiple Intelligences: The Theory in Practice*.

view. One was that IQ predictors might point to achievement in schools and colleges but not necessarily to achievement in life. For example, students with middling scores performed at extraordinary levels in business, politics, and other walks of life, whereas high-achieving students often settled for middling careers. The reports on high-performing executives indicated a considerable intelligence at work, but it was not necessarily the kind of intelligence that could be measured by the Binet tests.

Gardner also was intrigued by findings that local regions of the brain controlled specific functions of the mind. For example, studies had established that certain regions of the brain were specialized for language functions, whereas others were specialized for physical movement, music, mathematics, and other skills. When those portions of the brain suffered damage, as with stroke or accident, the functions for which they were specialized were adversely affected. These observations, which were plentiful in the work of neurologists during and after World War II, led Gardner to propose the existence of a variety of intelligences rather than only one.

As he explains in the following essay from his book *Multiple Intelligences: The Theory in Practice* (1993), his studies led him to propose seven distinct intelligences. The first is linguistic, which naturally includes language. This intelligence applies not only to learning languages but also to using language well—as, for example, in the case of poets and writers. The second is logical-mathematical, which refers to the applications of mathematics and of logical reasoning. Our society uses these verbal-mathematical forms of intelligence as the practical measure of intelligence: the SATs, for instance, depend almost entirely on measuring these forms.

Gardner adds five more forms of intelligence. Spatial intelligence concerns the ways in which we perceive and imagine spatial relations. Some people, such as architects and sculptors, are clearly more gifted than others at imagining space. Musical intelligence is seen as distinct from other forms of intelligence if only because some people, such as child prodigies, are apparently born with superior musical abilities. Bodily-kinesthetic intelligence shows up in dancers and athletes, like Mikhail Baryshnikov and Jackie Joyner-Kersee, who perform extraordinarily with their bodies. But bodily-kinesthetic intelligence also applies to detailed physical work, such as the manipulations necessary for the work of surgeons, dentists, and craftspeople, such as weavers, potters, metal-workers, and jewelers.

Finally, Gardner also defines two kinds of personal intelligence that are difficult to isolate and study but that he feels must be regarded as forms of intelligence. Interpersonal intelligence concerns the way we get along with other people. People with high interpersonal intelligence might be salespeople, teachers, politicians, or evangelists. They respond to others and are sensitive to their needs and their concerns. They understand cooperation, compromise, and respect for other people's views. The second kind of personal intelligence—intrapersonal—refers to how one understands oneself. The self-knowledge to recognize one's strengths and weaknesses and to avoid an inflated sense of self-importance constitutes a high degree of intrapersonal intelligence.

Gardner sees all these intelligences working together in the individual. As he says, when one of them dominates, the individual can appear freakish, as in the person with autism who easily multiplies huge numbers in his head but cannot relate to other human beings. Because the individual must nurture all these intelligences to develop into a complete person, Gardner is working to revise educational practices to reflect all varieties of intelligence.

Greeks in the time of Plato and Aristotle seem to have understood much of what Gardner says. They included music and dance, for example, in the curriculum of their schools. They developed linguistic and interpersonal skills in the teaching of rhetoric and made logic and mathematics central to their teaching. One of Socrates' most famous statements, in fact—"Know thyself"—admonishes us to develop intrapersonal intelligence.

Gardner's Rhetoric

Rather than open the essay by describing the multiple intelligences, Gardner starts with a dramatic scene and a hypothetical story. He describes two eleven-year-old children who take an IQ test and then are regarded in special ways by their teachers: one is expected to do well in school, the other is expected to do less well. The expectations are met. But years later the student with the lower IQ is vastly more successful in business than the student who scored higher. Why is this so? The rest of the essay answers that implied rhetorical question.

One of the most important devices Gardner relies on is enumeration. He has seven different kinds of intelligence to discuss and takes each one in turn. The reader is not aware of a special range of importance to the seven forms of intelligence: the first, musical intelligence, is not necessarily the most important or the first to be recognized in an individual. Bodily-kinesthetic is not necessarily less important because it comes after musical intelligence. By placing logical-mathematical intelligence in the middle of the sequence, Gardner suggests that this form of intelligence, which our society traditionally treats as first in importance, should take its place beside a range of intelligences that are all more or less equal in value.

Just as important as the use of enumeration is Gardner's use of parallelism in the structure of each of the intelligences he enumerates. For each he offers a subhead that identifies the specific intelligence and then a "sketch with a thumbnail biography" that helps establish the nature of the intelligence. Then Gardner discusses the details of each intelligence and suggests ways in which it may relate to other forms of intelligence. This method has the advantage of extreme clarity. Likewise, paralleling examples and quotations in describing each intelligence makes the point over and over and ultimately produces a convincing argument without the appearance of argument.

Gardner makes another important rhetorical decision regarding the size and nature of the paragraphs. Modern readers, conditioned by newspapers and magazines, expect paragraphs to be short and direct. Gardner's paragraphs reflect a decision to communicate with a general reading audience rather than an audience of specialists or specially educated readers. For that reason, a single subject may sometimes be discussed in two or more adjacent paragraphs, with the paragraph break acting as a "breather" (see paras. 19–20 and 22–23).

All these rhetorical devices aid the reader in absorbing complex material. Gardner's primary efforts in this essay are to facilitate communication. He keeps his language simple, his sentences direct, and his paragraphs brief. For the modern reader, this is a recipe for understanding.

PREREADING QUESTIONS: WHAT TO READ FOR

The following prereading questions may help you anticipate key issues in the discussion of Howard Gardner's "A Rounded Version: The Theory of Multiple Intelligences." Keeping them in mind during your first reading of the selection should help focus your attention.

- What constitutes an intelligence, according to Gardner?
- What is the most compelling evidence for the theory of multiple intelligences?

A Rounded Version: The Theory of Multiple Intelligences

Coauthored by Joseph Walters

Two eleven-year-old children are taking a test of "intelligence."   1
They sit at their desks laboring over the meanings of different words,
the interpretation of graphs, and the solutions to arithmetic problems. They record their answers by filling in small circles on a single
piece of paper. Later these completed answer sheets are scored objectively: the number of right answers is converted into a standardized
score that compares the individual child with a population of children of similar age.

The teachers of these children review the different scores. They   2
notice that one of the children has performed at a superior level; on all
sections of the test, she answered more questions correctly than did
her peers. In fact, her score is similar to that of children three to four
years older. The other child's performance is average—his scores
reflect those of other children his age.

A subtle change in expectations surrounds the review of these test   3
scores. Teachers begin to expect the first child to do quite well during
her formal schooling, whereas the second should have only moderate
success. Indeed these predictions come true. In other words, the test
taken by the eleven-year-olds serves as a reliable predictor of their
later performance in school.

How does this happen? One explanation involves our free use of   4
the word "intelligence": the child with the greater "intelligence" has
the ability to solve problems, to find the answers to specific questions,
and to learn new material quickly and efficiently. These skills in turn
play a central role in school success. In this view, "intelligence" is a
singular faculty that is brought to bear in any problem-solving situation. Since schooling deals largely with solving problems of various
sorts, predicting this capacity in young children predicts their future
success in school.

"Intelligence," from this point of view, is a general ability that is   5
found in varying degrees in all individuals. It is the key to success in
solving problems. This ability can be measured reliably with standardized pencil-and-paper tests that, in turn, predict future success
in school.

What happens after school is completed? Consider the two indi-   6
viduals in the example. Looking further down the road, we find that
the "average" student has become a highly successful mechanical

engineer who has risen to a position of prominence in both the professional community of engineers as well as in civic groups in his
community. His success is no fluke—he is considered by all to be a
talented individual. The "superior" student, on the other hand, has
had little success in her chosen career as a writer; after repeated rejec-
tions by publishers, she has taken up a middle management position
in a bank. While certainly not a "failure," she is considered by her
peers to be quite "ordinary" in her adult accomplishments. So what
happened?

This fabricated example is based on the facts of intelligence test-   7
ing. IQ tests predict school performance with considerable accuracy,
but they are only an indifferent predictor of performance in a profession after formal schooling.[1] Furthermore, even as IQ tests measure
only logical or logical-linguistic capacities, in this society we are nearly
"brain-washed" to restrict the notion of intelligence to the capacities
used in solving logical and linguistic problems.

To introduce an alternative point of view, undertake the fol-   8
lowing "thought experiment." Suspend the usual judgment of what
constitutes intelligence and let your thoughts run freely over the
capabilities of humans—perhaps those that would be picked out
by the proverbial Martian visitor. In this exercise, you are drawn to
the brilliant chess player, the world-class violinist, and the champion athlete; such outstanding performers deserve special consideration. Under this experiment, a quite different view of *intelligence*
emerges. Are the chess player, violinist, and athlete "intelligent" in
these pursuits? If they are, then why do our tests of "intelligence"
fail to identify them? If they are not "intelligent," what allows them
to achieve such astounding feats? In general, why does the contemporary construct "intelligence" fail to explain large areas of human
endeavor?

In this chapter we approach these problems through the theory   9
of multiple intelligences (MI). As the name indicates, we believe that
human cognitive competence is better described in terms of a set of
abilities, talents, or mental skills, which we call "intelligences." All
normal individuals possess each of these skills to some extent; individuals differ in the degree of skill and in the nature of their combination. We believe this theory of intelligence may be more humane
and more veridical[2] than alternative views of intelligence and that it

---

[1] Jencks, C. (1972). *Inequality.* New York: Basic Books. [Gardner's note]
[2] **veridical** Telling the truth.

more adequately reflects the data of human "intelligent" behavior. Such a theory has important educational implications, including ones for curriculum development.

What Constitutes an Intelligence?

The question of the optimal definition of intelligence looms large in our inquiry. Indeed, it is at the level of this definition that the theory of multiple intelligences diverges from traditional points of view. In a traditional view, intelligence is defined operationally as the ability to answer items on tests of intelligence. The inference from the test scores to some underlying ability is supported by statistical techniques that compare responses of subjects at different ages; the apparent correlation of these test scores across ages and across different tests corroborates the notion that the general faculty of intelligence, g, does not change much with age or with training or experience. It is an inborn attribute or faculty of the individual.   10

Multiple intelligences theory, on the other hand, pluralizes the traditional concept. An intelligence entails the ability to solve problems or fashion products that are of consequence in a particular cultural setting or community. The problem-solving skill allows one to approach a situation in which a goal is to be obtained and to locate the appropriate route to that goal. The creation of a *cultural* product is crucial to such functions as capturing and transmitting knowledge or expressing one's views or feelings. The problems to be solved range from creating an end for a story to anticipating a mating move in chess to repairing a quilt. Products range from scientific theories to musical compositions to successful political campaigns.   11

MI theory is framed in light of the biological origins of each problem-solving skill. Only those skills that are universal to the human species are treated. Even so, the biological proclivity to participate in a particular form of problem solving must also be coupled with the cultural nurturing of that domain. For example, language, a universal skill, may manifest itself particularly as writing in one culture, as oratory in another culture, and as the secret language of anagrams in a third.   12

Given the desire of selecting intelligences that are rooted in biology, and that are valued in one or more cultural settings, how does one actually identify an "intelligence"? In coming up with our list, we consulted evidence from several different sources: knowledge about normal development and development in gifted individuals;   13 information about the breakdown of cognitive skills under conditions of brain damage; studies of exceptional populations, including prodigies, idiots savants, and autistic children; data about the evolution of cognition over the millennia; cross-cultural accounts of cognition; psychometric studies, including examinations of correlations among tests; and psychological training studies, particularly measures of transfer and generalization across tasks. Only those candidate intelligences that satisfied all or a majority of the criteria were selected as bona fide intelligences. A more complete discussion of each of these criteria for an "intelligence" and the seven intelligences that have been proposed so far, is found in *Frames of Mind.*[3] This book also considers how the theory might be disproven and compares it to competing theories of intelligence.

In addition to satisfying the aforementioned criteria, each intelligence must have an identifiable core operation or set of operations. As a neutrally based computational system, each intelligence is activated or "triggered" by certain kinds of internally or externally presented information. For example, one core of musical intelligence is the sensitivity to pitch relations, whereas one core of linguistic intelligence is the sensitivity to phonological features.   14

An intelligence must also be susceptible to encoding in a symbol system—a culturally contrived system of meaning, which captures and conveys important forms of information. Language, picturing, and mathematics are but three nearly worldwide symbol systems that are necessary for human survival and productivity. The relationship of a candidate intelligence to a human symbol system is no accident. In fact, the existence of a core computational capacity anticipates the existence of a symbol system that exploits that capacity. While it may be possible for an intelligence to proceed without an accompanying symbol system, a primary characteristic of human intelligence may well be its gravitation toward such an embodiment.   15

The Seven Intelligences

Having sketched the characteristics and criteria of an intelligence, we turn now to a brief consideration of each of the seven intelligences. We begin each sketch with a thumbnail biography of a   16

---

[3] Gardner, H. (1983). *Frames of Mind: The Theory of Multiple Intelligences.* New York: Basic Books. [Gardner's note]

person who demonstrates an unusual facility with that intelligence. These biographies illustrate some of the abilities that are central to the fluent operation of a given intelligence. Although each biography illustrates a particular intelligence, we do not wish to imply that in adulthood intelligences operate in isolation. Indeed, except for abnormal individuals, intelligences always work in concert, and any sophisticated adult role will involve a melding of several of them. Following each biography we survey the various sources of data that support each candidate as an "intelligence."

Musical Intelligence

> When he was three years old, Yehudi Menuhin was smuggled into the San Francisco Orchestra concerts by his parents. The sound of Louis Persinger's violin so entranced the youngster that he insisted on a violin for his birthday and Louis Persinger as his teacher. He got both. By the time he was ten years old, Menuhin was an international performer.[4]

Violinist Yehudi Menuhin's musical intelligence manifested itself   17
even before he had touched a violin or received any musical training. His powerful reaction to that particular sound and his rapid progress on the instrument suggest that he was biologically prepared in some way for that endeavor. In this way evidence from child prodigies supports our claim that there is a biological link to a particular intelligence. Other special populations, such as autistic children who can play a musical instrument beautifully but who cannot speak, underscore the independence of musical intelligence.

A brief consideration of the evidence suggests that musical skill   18
passes the other tests for an intelligence. For example, certain parts of the brain play important roles in perception and production of music. These areas are characteristically located in the right hemisphere, although musical skill is not as clearly "localized," or located in a specifiable area, as language. Although the particular susceptibility of musical ability to brain damage depends on the degree of training and other individual differences, there is clear evidence for "amusia" or loss of musical ability.

Music apparently played an important unifying role in Stone   19
Age (Paleolithic) societies. Birdsong provides a link to other species. Evidence from various cultures supports the notion that music is a

---

[4] Menuhin, Y. (1977). *Unfinished Journey*. New York: Knopf. [Gardner's note]

universal faculty. Studies of infant development suggest that there is a "raw" computational ability in early childhood. Finally, musical notation provides an accessible and lucid symbol system.

In short, evidence to support the interpretation of musical ability [20] as an "intelligence" comes from many different sources. Even though musical skill is not typically considered an intellectual skill like mathematics, it qualifies under our criteria. By definition it deserves consideration; and in view of the data, its inclusion is empirically justified.

Bodily-Kinesthetic Intelligence

Fifteen-year-old Babe Ruth played third base. During one game his team's pitcher was doing very poorly and Babe loudly criticized him from third base. Brother Mathias, the coach, called out, "Ruth, if you know so much about it, YOU pitch!" Babe was surprised and embarrassed because he had never pitched before, but Brother Mathias insisted. Ruth said later that at the very moment he took the pitcher's mound, he KNEW he was supposed to be a pitcher and that it was "natural" for him to strike people out. Indeed, he went on to become a great major league pitcher (and, of course, attained legendary status as a hitter).[5]

Like Menuhin, Babe Ruth was a child prodigy who recognized [21] his "instrument" immediately upon his first exposure to it. This recognition occurred in advance of formal training.

Control of bodily movement is, of course, localized in the motor [22] cortex, with each hemisphere dominant or controlling bodily movements on the contra-lateral side. In right-handers, the dominance for such movement is ordinarily found in the left hemisphere. The ability to perform movements when directed to do so can be impaired even in individuals who can perform the same movements reflexively or on a nonvoluntary basis. The existence of specific *apraxia*[6] constitutes one line of evidence for a bodily-kinesthetic intelligence.

The evolution of specialized body movements is of obvious [23] advantage to the species, and in humans this adaptation is extended through the use of tools. Body movement undergoes a clearly defined developmental schedule in children. And there is little question of its

---

[5] Connor, A. (1982). *Voices from Cooperstown*. New York: Collier. (Based on a quotation taken from *The Babe Ruth Story*, Babe Ruth & Bob Considine. New York: Dutton, 1948.) [Gardner's note]

[6] **apraxia** A neurological disorder characterized by an inability to execute purposeful movements despite having the desire or physical ability to do so.

universality across cultures. Thus it appears that bodily-kinesthetic "knowledge" satisfies many of the criteria for an intelligence.

The consideration of bodily-kinesthetic knowledge as "problem   24 solving" may be less intuitive. Certainly carrying out a mime sequence or hitting a tennis ball is not solving a mathematical equation. And yet, the ability to use one's body to express an emotion (as in a dance), to play a game (as in a sport), or to create a new product (as in devising an invention) is evidence of the cognitive features of body usage. The specific computations required to solve a particular bodily-kinesthetic *problem*, hitting a tennis ball, are summarized by Tim Gallwey:

> At the moment the ball leaves the server's racket, the brain calculates approximately where it will land and where the racket will intercept it. This calculation includes the initial velocity of the ball, combined with an input for the progressive decrease in velocity and the effect of wind and after the bounce of the ball. Simultaneously, muscle orders are given: not just once, but constantly with refined and updated information. The muscles must cooperate. A movement of the feet occurs, the racket is taken back, the face of the racket kept at a constant angle. Contact is made at a precise point that depends on whether the order was given to hit down the line or cross-court, an order not given until after a split-second analysis of the movement and balance of the opponent.
>
> To return an average serve, you have about one second to do this. To hit the ball at all is remarkable and yet not uncommon. The truth is that everyone who inhabits a human body possesses a remarkable creation.[7]

Logical-Mathematical Intelligence.   In 1983 Barbara McClintock   25 won the Nobel Prize in medicine or physiology for her work in microbiology. Her intellectual powers of deduction and observation illustrate one form of logical-mathematical intelligence that is often labeled "scientific thinking." One incident is particularly illuminating. While a researcher at Cornell in the 1920s McClintock was faced one day with a problem: while *theory* predicted 50-percent pollen sterility in corn, her research assistant (in the "field") was finding plants that were only 25- to 30-percent sterile. Disturbed by this discrepancy, McClintock left the cornfield and returned to her office, where she sat for half an hour, thinking:

> Suddenly I jumped up and ran back to the (corn) field. At the top of the field (the others were still at the bottom) I shouted "Eureka, I

---

[7] Gallwey, T. (1976). *Inner Tennis*. New York: Random House. [Gardner's note]

have it! I know what the 30% sterility is!" . . . They asked me to prove it. I sat down with a paper bag and a pencil and I started from scratch, which I had not done at all in my laboratory. It had all been done so fast; the answer came and I ran. Now I worked it out step by step—it was an intricate series of steps—and I came out with [the same result]. [They] looked at the material and it was exactly as I'd said it was; it worked out exactly as I had diagrammed it. Now, why did I know, without having done it on paper? Why was I so sure?[8]

This anecdote illustrates two essential facts of the logical- 26 mathematical intelligence. First, in the gifted individual, the process of problem solving is often remarkably rapid—the successful scientist copes with many variables at once and creates numerous hypotheses that are each evaluated and then accepted or rejected in turn.

The anecdote also underscores the *nonverbal* nature of the intelli- 27 gence. A solution to a problem can be constructed *before* it is articulated. In fact, the solution process may be totally invisible, even to the problem solver. This need not imply, however, that discoveries of this sort—the familiar "Aha!" phenomenon—are mysterious, intuitive, or unpredictable. The fact that it happens more frequently to some people (perhaps Nobel Prize winners) suggests the opposite. We interpret this as the work of the logical-mathematical intelligence.

Along with the companion skill of language, logical-mathematical 28 reasoning provides the principal basis for IQ tests. This form of intelligence has been heavily investigated by traditional psychologists, and it is the archetype of "raw intelligence" or the problem-solving faculty that purportedly cuts across domains. It is perhaps ironic, then, that the actual mechanism by which one arrives at a solution to a logical-mathematical problem is not as yet properly understood.

This intelligence is supported by our empirical criteria as well. 29 Certain areas of the brain are more prominent in mathematical calculation than others. There are idiots savants who perform great feats of calculation even though they remain tragically deficient in most other areas. Child prodigies in mathematics abound. The development of this intelligence in children has been carefully documented by Jean Piaget and other psychologists.

Linguistic Intelligence

At the age of ten, T. S. Eliot created a magazine called "Fireside" to which he was the sole contributor. In a three-day period during his winter vacation, he created eight complete issues. Each one included

---

[8]Keller, E. (1983). *A Feeling for the Organism* (p. 104). Salt Lake City: W. H. Freeman. [Gardner's note]

poems, adventure stories, a gossip column, and humor. Some of this material survives and it displays the talent of the poet.[9]

As with the logical intelligence, calling linguistic skill an "intelli-   30
gence" is consistent with the stance of traditional psychology. Linguistic intelligence also passes our empirical tests. For instance, a specific area of the brain, called "Broca's Area," is responsible for the production of grammatical sentences. A person with damage to this area can understand words and sentences quite well but has difficulty putting words together in anything other than the simplest of sentences. At the same time, other thought processes may be entirely unaffected.

The gift of language is universal, and its development in chil-   31
dren is strikingly constant across cultures. Even in deaf populations where a manual sign language is not explicitly taught, children will often "invent" their own manual language and use it surreptitiously! We thus see how an intelligence may operate independently of a specific input modality or output channel.

Spatial Intelligence

Navigation around the Caroline Islands in the South Seas is accomplished without instruments. The position of the stars, as viewed from various islands, the weather patterns, and water color are the only sign posts. Each journey is broken into a series of segments; and the navigator learns the position of the stars within each of these segments. During the actual trip the navigator must envision mentally a reference island as it passes under a particular star and from that he computes the number of segments completed, the proportion of the trip remaining, and any corrections in heading that are required. The navigator cannot *see* the islands as he sails along; instead he maps their locations in his mental "picture" of the journey.[10]

Spatial problem solving is required for navigation and in the use   32
of the notational system of maps. Other kinds of spatial problem solving are brought to bear in visualizing an object seen from a different angle and in playing chess. The visual arts also employ this intelligence in the use of space.

Evidence from brain research is clear and persuasive. Just as the   33
left hemisphere has, over the course of evolution, been selected as

---

[9] Soldo, J. (1982). Jovial juvenilia: T. S. Eliot's first magazine. *Biography*, 5, 25–37. [Gardner's note]

[10] Gardner, H. (1983). *Frames of Mind: The Theory of Multiple Intelligences*. New York: Basic Books. [Gardner's note]

the site of linguistic processing in right-handed persons, the right hemisphere proves to be the site most crucial for spatial processing. Damage to the right posterior regions causes impairment of the ability to find one's way around a site, to recognize faces or scenes, or to notice fine details.

Patients with damage specific to regions of the right hemi-   34 sphere will attempt to compensate for their spacial deficits with linguistic strategies. They will try to reason aloud, to challenge the task, or even make up answers. But such nonspatial strategies are rarely successful.

Blind populations provide an illustration of the distinction   35 between the spatial intelligence and visual perception. A blind person can recognize shapes by an indirect method: running a hand along the object translates into length of time of movement, which in turn is translated into the size of the object. For the blind person, the perceptual system of the tactile modality parallels the visual modality in the seeing person. The analogy between the spatial reasoning of the blind and the linguistic reasoning of the deaf is notable.

There are few child prodigies among visual artists, but there are   36 idiots savants such as Nadia.[11] Despite a condition of severe autism, this preschool child made drawings of the most remarkable representational accuracy and finesse.

Interpersonal Intelligence.   With little formal training in special   37 education and nearly blind herself, Anne Sullivan began the intimidating task of instructing a blind and deaf seven-year-old Helen Keller. Sullivan's efforts at communication were complicated by the child's emotional struggle with the world around her. At their first meal together, this scene occurred:

> Annie did not allow Helen to put her hand into Annie's plate and take what she wanted, as she had been accustomed to do with her family. It became a test of wills—hand thrust into plate, hand firmly put aside. The family, much upset, left the dining room. Annie locked the door and proceeded to eat her breakfast while Helen lay on the floor kicking and screaming, pushing and pulling at Annie's chair. [After half an hour] Helen went around the table looking for her family. She discovered no one else was there and that bewildered her. Finally, she sat down and began to

---

[11] Selfe, L. (1977). *Nadia: A Case of Extraordinary Drawing in an Autistic Child.* New York: Academic Press. [Gardner's note]

eat her breakfast, but with her hands. Annie gave her a spoon. Down on the floor it clattered, and the contest of wills began anew.[12]

Anne Sullivan sensitively responded to the child's behavior. She wrote home: "The greatest problem I shall have to solve is how to discipline and control her without breaking her spirit. I shall go rather slowly at first and try to win her love."

38

In fact, the first "miracle" occurred two weeks later, well before the famous incident at the pumphouse. Annie had taken Helen to a small cottage near the family's house, where they could live alone. After seven days together, Helen's personality suddenly underwent a profound change—the therapy had worked:

39

> My heart is singing with joy this morning. A miracle has happened! The wild little creature of two weeks ago has been transformed into a gentle child.[13]

It was just two weeks after this that the first breakthrough in Helen's grasp of language occurred; and from that point on, she progressed with incredible speed. The key to the miracle of language was Anne Sullivan's insight into the *person* of Helen Keller.

40

Interpersonal intelligence builds on a core capacity to notice distinctions among others; in particular, contrasts in their moods, temperaments, motivations, and intentions. In more advanced forms, this intelligence permits a skilled adult to read the intentions and desires of others, even when these have been hidden. This skill appears in a highly sophisticated form in religious or political leaders, teachers, therapists, and parents. The Helen Keller–Anne Sullivan story suggests that this interpersonal intelligence does not depend on language.

41

All indices in brain research suggest that the frontal lobes play a prominent role in interpersonal knowledge. Damage in this area can cause profound personality changes while leaving other forms of problem solving unharmed—a person is often "not the same person" after such an injury.

42

Alzheimer's disease, a form of presenile dementia, appears to attack posterior brain zones with a special ferocity, leaving spatial, logical, and linguistic computations severely impaired. Yet, Alzheimer's patients will often remain well groomed, socially proper, and continually

43

---

[12] Lash, J. (1980). *Helen and Teacher: The Story of Helen Keller and Anne Sullivan Macy* (p. 52). New York: Delacorte. [Gardner's note]

[13] Lash (p. 54). [Gardner's note]

apologetic for their errors. In contrast, Pick's disease, another variety of presenile dementia that is more frontally oriented, entails a rapid loss of social graces.

Biological evidence for interpersonal intelligence encompasses two additional factors often cited as unique to humans. One factor is the prolonged childhood of primates, including the close attachment to the mother. In those cases where the mother is removed from early development, normal interpersonal development is in serious jeopardy. The second factor is the relative importance in humans of social interaction. Skills such as hunting, tracking, and killing in prehistoric societies required participation and cooperation of large numbers of people. The need for group cohesion, leadership, organization, and solidarity follows naturally from this. 44

Intrapersonal Intelligence. In an essay called "A Sketch of the Past," written almost as a diary entry, Virginia Woolf discusses the "cotton wool of existence"—the various mundane events of life. She contrasts this "cotton wool" with three specific and poignant memories from her childhood: a fight with her brother, seeing a particular flower in the garden, and hearing of the suicide of a past visitor: 45

> These are three instances of exceptional moments. I often tell them over, or rather they come to the surface unexpectedly. But now for the first time I have written them down, and I realize something that I have never realized before. Two of these moments ended in a state of despair. The other ended, on the contrary, in a state of satisfaction.
>
> The sense of horror (in hearing of the suicide) held me powerless. But in the case of the flower, I found a reason; and was thus able to deal with the sensation. I was not powerless.
>
> Though I still have the peculiarity that I receive these sudden shocks, they are now always welcome; after the first surprise, I always feel instantly that they are particularly valuable. And so I go on to suppose that the shock-receiving capacity is what makes me a writer. I hazard the explanation that a shock is at once in my case followed by the desire to explain it. I feel that I have had a blow; but it is not, as I thought as a child, simply a blow from an enemy hidden behind the cotton wool of daily life; it is or will become a revelation of some order; it is a token of some real thing behind appearances; and I make it real by putting it into words.[14]

[14] Woolf, V. (1976). *Moments of Being* (pp. 69–70). Sussex: The University Press. [Gardner's note]

This quotation vividly illustrates the intrapersonal intelligence — 46
knowledge of the internal aspects of a person: access to one's own
feeling life, one's range of emotions, the capacity to effect discrimi-
nations among these emotions and eventually to label them and to
draw upon them as a means of understanding and guiding one's
own behavior. A person with good intrapersonal intelligence has a
viable and effective model of himself or herself. Since this intelligence is the most private, it requires evidence from language, music,
or some other more expressive form of intelligence if the observer is
to detect it at work. In the above quotation, for example, linguistic
intelligence is drawn upon to convey intrapersonal knowledge; it
embodies the interaction of intelligences, a common phenomenon
to which we will return later.

We see the familiar criteria at work in the intrapersonal intelli- 47
gence. As with the interpersonal intelligence, the frontal lobes play a
central role in personality change. Injury to the lower area of the
frontal lobes is likely to produce irritability or euphoria; while injury
to the higher regions is more likely to produce indifference, listlessness, slowness, and apathy—a kind of depressive personality. In such
"frontal-lobe" individuals, the other cognitive functions often remain
preserved. In contrast, among aphasics who have recovered sufficiently to describe their experiences, we find consistent testimony:
while there may have been a diminution of general alertness and
considerable depression about the condition, the individual in no way
felt himself to be a different person. He recognized his own needs,
wants, and desires and tried as best he could to achieve them.

The autistic child is a prototypical example of an individual with 48
impaired intrapersonal intelligence; indeed, the child may not even
be able to refer to himself. At the same time, such children often
exhibit remarkable abilities in the musical, computational, spatial, or
mechanical realms.

Evolutionary evidence for an intrapersonal faculty is more diffi- 49
cult to come by, but we might speculate that the capacity to transcend the satisfaction of instinctual drives is relevant. This becomes
increasingly important in a species not perennially involved in the
struggle for survival.

In sum, then, both interpersonal and intrapersonal faculties 50
pass the tests of an intelligence. They both feature problem-solving
endeavors with significance for the individual and the species.
Interpersonal intelligence allows one to understand and work with
others; intrapersonal intelligence allows one to understand and work
with oneself. In the individual's sense of self, one encounters a melding

of inter- and intrapersonal components. Indeed, the sense of self emerges as one of the most marvelous of human inventions—a symbol that represents all kinds of information about a person and that is at the same time an invention that all individuals construct for themselves.

Summary: The Unique Contributions of the Theory

As human beings, we all have a repertoire of skills for solving 51 different kinds of problems. Our investigation has begun, therefore, with a consideration of these problems, the contexts they are found in, and the culturally significant products that are the outcome. We have not approached "intelligence" as a reified[15] human faculty that is brought to bear in literally any problem setting; rather, we have begun with the problems that humans *solve* and worked back to the "intelligences" that must be responsible.

Evidence from brain research, human development, evolution, 52 and cross-cultural comparisons was brought to bear in our search for the relevant human intelligences: a candidate was included only if reasonable evidence to support its membership was found across these diverse fields. Again, this tack differs from the traditional one: since no candidate faculty is *necessarily* an intelligence, we could choose on a motivated basis. In the traditional approach to "intelligence," there is no opportunity for this type of empirical decision.

We have also determined that these multiple human faculties, 53 the intelligences, are to a significant extent *independent*. For example, research with brain-damaged adults repeatedly demonstrates that particular faculties can be lost while others are spared. This independence of intelligences implies that a particularly high level of ability in one intelligence, say mathematics, does not require a similarly high level in another intelligence, like language or music. This independence of intelligences contrasts sharply with traditional measures of IQ that find high correlations among test scores. We speculate that the usual correlations among subtests of IQ tests come about because all of these tasks in fact measure the ability to respond rapidly to items of a logical-mathematical or linguistic sort; we believe that these correlations would be substantially reduced if

---

[15] **reified** Regarding an abstraction (e.g., intelligence) as if it were a concrete thing.

one were to survey in a contextually appropriate way the full range of human problem-solving skills.

Until now, we have supported the fiction that adult roles depend   54
largely on the flowering of a single intelligence. In fact, however, nearly every cultural role of any degree of sophistication requires a combination of intelligences. Thus, even an apparently straightforward role, like playing the violin, transcends a reliance on simple musical intelligence. To become a successful violinist requires bodily-kinesthetic dexterity and the interpersonal skills of relating to an audience and, in a different way, choosing a manager; quite possibly it involves an intrapersonal intelligence as well. Dance requires skills in bodily-kinesthetic, musical, interpersonal, and spatial intelligences in varying degrees. Politics requires an interpersonal skill, a linguistic facility, and perhaps some logical aptitude. Inasmuch as nearly every cultural role requires several intelligences, it becomes important to consider individuals as a collection of aptitudes rather than as having a singular problem-solving faculty that can be measured directly through pencil-and-paper tests. Even given a relatively small number of such intelligences, the diversity of human ability is created through the differences in these profiles. In fact, it may well be that the "total is greater than the sum of the parts." An individual may not be particularly gifted in any intelligence; and yet, because of a particular combination or blend of skills, he or she may be able to fill some niche uniquely well. Thus it is of paramount importance to assess the particular combination of skills that may earmark an individual for a certain vocational or avocational niche.

QUESTIONS FOR CRITICAL READING

1. In the heading preceding paragraph 10, Gardner asks, "What Constitutes an Intelligence?" After reading this essay, how would you answer that question? How effectively does Gardner answer it?
2. What is the relation of culture to intelligence? See paragraph 11.
3. Why does society value logical-mathematical intelligence so highly? Do you feel it is reasonable to do so? Why?
4. What relationship do you see between intelligence and problem solving? What relationship do you see between education and problem solving?
5. Do you think that education can enhance these seven forms of intelligence? What evidence can you cite that intelligence is not fixed but can be altered by experience?
6. Why is it important "to assess the particular combination of skills that may earmark an individual" (para. 54)?

SUGGESTIONS FOR CRITICAL WRITING

1. Gardner says that his theory of MI (multiple intelligences) was shaped by his observations of "the biological origins of each problem-solving skill" (para. 12). Why is this important to his theory? How has he connected each of the intelligences to a biological origin? What biological issues are not fully accounted for in the theory of multiple intelligences?

2. In which of these seven forms of intelligence do you excel? Describe your achievements in these forms by giving specific examples that help your reader relate your abilities to the intelligences you have cited. Now that you have identified your primary intelligences, what implications do they suggest for your later life?

3. Gardner is keenly interested in reforming education in light of his theory of multiple intelligences. How could education be altered to best accommodate the seven forms of intelligence? What would be done differently in schools? Who would benefit from the differences you propose? How would society in general benefit from those differences?

4. Describe a problem-solving situation that requires two or more of the intelligences that Gardner describes. If possible, draw your example from your own experience or the experience of someone you know. Describe how the several intelligences work together to help solve the problem.

5. In some discussions of the forms of intelligence, commentators add an eighth—the naturalist's ability to recognize fine distinctions and patterns in the natural world. What might be the biological origin for that intelligence? In what cultural context might that intelligence be crucial? Do you feel that there is such an intelligence as represented by the naturalist or that it is included in other forms of intelligence?

6. **CONNECTIONS**   What relationship do you see between Plato's discussion of the soul and Gardner's discussion of intelligence? See paragraphs 41–55 in Plato's essay (p. 447). Which of Gardner's intelligences does Socrates seem to favor in Plato's dialogue?

7. **CONNECTIONS**   Gardner mentions problem-solving situations that require several kinds of intelligence. Examine René Descartes's *Fourth Meditation* (p. 461) for its problem-solving approach on avoiding error and reaching the truth. How would his entire strategy fit into Gardner's scheme? Would Gardner say he is using more than one kind of intelligence, or would he find that Descartes is using only one kind? On what basic principles do you think Descartes might have agreed with Gardner? And on what basic principles would Gardner have agreed with Descartes?

8. **SEEING CONNECTIONS**   What kinds of intelligence would Gardner say went into Salvador Dalí's *The Persistence of Memory* (p. 443)? How does each contribute to the painting and how would Gardner be likely to respond to the painting? Is there any special kind of intelligence that would come into play just for the purpose of enjoying the painting? Is

there any form of intelligence evident in the painting that Gardner has not taken into consideration? What special forms of intelligence seem to be connected with artistic products of the unconscious? Does intelligence of any kind have anything to do with dreams? Does it have anything to do with paintings and art?

STEVEN PINKER
Thinking Machines

STEVEN PINKER (b. 1954), a Canadian American, is the Johnstone Family Professor of Psychology at Harvard University, where he also earned his Ph.D. His undergraduate degree was from McGill University in Montreal, Canada. He was a very popular professor at the Massachusetts Institute of Technology from 1982 to 2003, teaching at the Center for Brain and Cognitive Sciences. His early work focused on problems of language and language acquisition. He was interested in how children learn language apparently intuitively and how they learn the rules of grammar, especially as evidenced in their choice of regular and irregular verbs. For instance, if *bring* were a regular verb it would be conjugated as *bring, brang, brung,* but it is irregular and follows the pattern *bring, brought, brought*. These patterns illustrate two mental faculties necessary for proper conjugation: the ability to follow the rules of verb change and to use memory to modify the rules of verb change. How children learn the difference is one of the questions Pinker posed in his first two books about problems of language acquisition and what they tell us about the workings of the mind.

One of Pinker's most important theories concerns the evolutionary nature of the language "instinct." Sometimes described as an evolutionary psychologist, he holds that language is a biological adaptation shaped by natural selection, on the model of Darwin's theories of evolution. This is in disagreement with the ideas of several prominent language scholars, but Pinker's theories have affected the work of numerous writers and scholars in language studies who strongly agree with him. The selection that follows presents an introduction to the second of his most important theories: the computational model of thinking.

From *How the Mind Works*.

Learnability and Cognition: The Acquisition of Argument Structure (1991) is one of Pinker's early studies of cognition and an important contribution to the relatively young science of cognitive studies. A gifted writer and communicator, Pinker successfully appeals to a general audience—several of his popular books have become best-sellers. *The Language Instinct* (1994) followed his early research and technical writing on language acquisition. He proposed that language is not just mental but also biological—that it represents an evolutionary adaptation of our species. Thus, as other linguisticians have suggested, language is built-in in some biological fashion. *How the Mind Works* (1997), from which the following selection is drawn, takes into account various features of mental qualities, moving from language to questions of perception, artificial intelligence, and many other considerations. In the opening of his book, he admits, "First, we don't understand how the mind works." Thus, he begins with a note of humility and honesty and admits that his theories may be wrong but that even if wrong they can push forward the body of knowledge we have about the mind. *Words and Rules: The Ingredients of Language* (1999) further addresses the questions of language that have interested him and his readers. *The Blank Slate: The Modern Denial of Human Nature* (2002) begins his discussion of the details of what we think of as human nature, and *The Stuff of Thought: Language as a Window into Human Nature* (2007) connects his observations with language studies and examines how they intersect with government, ethics, and the emotions.

Pinker has won numerous awards for his books and has been honored for excellence in teaching. He has been granted six honorary doctorates from almost as many nations, indicating the wider range of his work's influence in psychology. He has also had his share of controversy, especially when he defended Harvard's then-president Lawrence Summers, who suggested that there might be a biological explanation for the gender gap in mathematics and the sciences.

Pinker's Rhetoric

Pinker uses all the rhetorical skills of a seasoned teacher. He poses innumerable rhetorical questions—not all of which he answers. He summarizes his points as he moves carefully toward definitions that will satisfy the needs of his argument. He also poses his argument in a nonthreatening way, so the reader is largely unaware that Pinker is arguing a position. In other words, he is not contentious and does not threaten the reader or make the reader think that he has any expectation of changing the reader's mind.

Enumeration, another favorite technique of Pinker's, appears early in the essay—listing criteria for judging whether or not an alien possesses intelligence—and again later—posing the four formats of data representation.

But the foremost rhetorical device Pinker uses is example. Pinker makes some important observations about the way the mind works and then illustrates his ideas with concrete examples drawn from experience or reason. His opening paragraphs introduce a popular television show that influenced him in his youth, *The Twilight Zone.* The show, introduced by science-fiction writer Rod Serling, was important to Pinker because it enacted some of the hypothetical situations that psychologists could not reproduce in the lab. What is central to the episode he cites is the question of whether "a mechanical device" could be constructed that could "duplicate human intelligence." This is the focus of the entire selection, which poses the questions, "What makes intelligence possible?" and "What makes consciousness possible?" Pinker does not try to answer the second question in his essay, but he makes every effort to answer the first.

His second popular example is Lily Tomlin's *The Search for Intelligent Life in the Universe* (1991), a comic sketch that leads Pinker to the question of what it would take for an alien to be considered intelligent. Here, Pinker begins to lay the groundwork for his theory of the computational model of thinking by establishing that certain prerequisites exist for our assumption that an alien is behaving rationally. The most important is that the alien must be perceived as behaving in relation to a system of rules (like grammar) even if the observer does not know what the rules are. Here, too, enumeration helps make the point. First, there must be a set of rules; second, the rules must help in "pursuing something in the face of obstacles" (para. 8); third, the alien must be able to achieve the goal in different ways, depending on the obstacles. Pinker gives examples from two different writers, one contemporary and one a classic psychologist.

In paragraph 10, Pinker summarizes his point in the form of a definition: "Intelligence, then, is the ability to attain goals in the face of obstacles by means of decisions based on rational (truth-obeying) rules." Once this definition is accepted, Pinker then rejects behaviorism as a theory of mind and considers the idea of common sense. In paragraph 16, he questions whether the soul is a kind of ghost or spirit in the flesh of the brain, again using examples, such as the wooden puppet Pinocchio, while at the same time surveying a variety of theories.

Ultimately, he states that intelligence does not come from a spirit or special substance—like Pinocchio's magic wood—but rather from information. And once he has made that point, he moves toward an explanation of the computational model of thinking, which depends on many sources of data, demonstrating that the kinds of computations our minds make can be duplicated by machines. His example is a computer that calculates much faster than we can and that performs many functions that we think of as purely mental, such as storing and manipulating data. As a result of describing machines performing thought functions—machines that think—he compares the mind with the software that runs a computer, saying the mind evolved many subroutines and repetitive functions in response to biological adaptations honed by natural selection.

Finally, we realize that there is much left out of the theory, despite Pinker's assurance that thinking machines exist and mirror the function of our brains. He does not approach the question of consciousness or even ask whether or not a thinking machine might somehow learn to possess self-awareness and produce consciousness. As Pinker has said elsewhere, at this time the question of a thinking machine is a problem, but the question of consciousness is a mystery.

PREREADING QUESTIONS: WHAT TO READ FOR

The following prereading questions may help you anticipate key issues in the discussion of Steven Pinker's "Thinking Machines." Keeping them in mind during your first reading of the selection should help focus your attention.

- What do rules have to do with intelligence?
- How does Pinker define intelligence?
- What does a thinking machine do?
- What is the computational theory of mind?

Thinking Machines

Like many baby boomers, I was first exposed to problems in   1
philosophy by traveling through another dimension, a dimension not only of sight and sound but of mind, taking a journey into a wondrous land whose boundaries are that of imagination. I am referring to *The Twilight Zone*, the campy television series by Rod

Serling[1] that was popular during my childhood. Philosophers often try to clarify difficult concepts using thought experiments, outlandish hypothetical situations that help us explore the implications of our ideas. *The Twilight Zone* actually staged them for the camera.

One of the first episodes was called "The Lonely." James Corry is   2
serving a fifty-year sentence in solitary confinement on a barren asteroid nine million miles from Earth. Allenby, the captain of a supply ship that services the asteroid, takes pity on him and leaves a crate containing "Alicia," a robot that looks and acts like a woman. At first Corry is repulsed, but of course he soon falls deeply in love. A year later Allenby returns with the news that Corry has been pardoned and he has come to get him. Unfortunately Corry can take only fifteen pounds of gear, and Alicia weighs more than that. When Corry refuses to leave, Allenby reluctantly pulls out a gun and shoots Alicia in the face, exposing a tangle of smoking wires. He tells Corry, "All you're leaving behind is loneliness." Corry, devastated, mutters, "I must remember that. I must remember to keep that in mind."

I still remember my horror at the climax, and the episode was   3
much discussed in my pre-teen critics' circle. (Why didn't he just take her head? asked one commentator.) Our pathos came both from sympathy with Corry for his loss and from the sense that a sentient being had been snuffed out. Of course the directors had manipulated the audience by casting a beautiful actress rather than a heap of tin cans to play Alicia. But in evoking our sympathies they raised two vexing questions. Could a mechanical device ever duplicate human intelligence, the ultimate test being whether it could cause a real human to fall in love with it? And if a humanlike machine could be built, would it actually be *conscious* — would dismantling it be the act of murder we felt we had witnessed on the small screen?

The two deepest questions about the mind are "What makes   4
intelligence possible?" and "What makes consciousness possible?" With the advent of cognitive science, intelligence has become intelligible. It may not be too outrageous to say that at a very abstract level of analysis the problem has been solved. But consciousness or sentience, the raw sensation of toothaches and redness and saltiness and middle C, is still a riddle wrapped in a mystery inside an enigma. When asked what consciousness *is*, we have no better answer than Louis Armstrong's when a reporter asked him what jazz is: "Lady, if you have to ask, you'll never know." But even consciousness is not as

---

[1] **Rod Serling (1924–1975)** American screenwriter and host of *The Twilight Zone*, a sci-fi television show.

thoroughgoing a mystery as it used to be. *Parts* of the mystery have been pried off and turned into ordinary scientific problems. In this chapter I will first explore what intelligence is, how a physical being like a robot or a brain could achieve it, and how our brains do achieve it. Then I will turn to what we do and do not understand about consciousness.

The Search for Intelligent Life in the Universe

The Search for Intelligent Life in the Universe is the title of a stage   5
act by the comedian Lily Tomlin, an exploration of human follies and foibles. Tomlin's title plays on the two meanings of "intelligence": aptitude (as in the famous tongue-in-cheek definition of intelligence as "whatever IQ tests measure"), and rational, humanlike thought. The second meaning is the one I am writing about here.

We may have trouble defining intelligence, but we recognize it   6
when we see it. Perhaps a thought experiment can clarify the concept. Suppose there was an alien being who in every way looked different from us. What would it have to do to make us think it was intelligent? Science-fiction writers, of course, face this problem as part of their job; what better authority could there be on the answer? The author David Alexander Smith[2] gave as good a characterization of intelligence as I have seen when asked by an interviewer, "What makes a good alien?"

> One, they have to have intelligent but impenetrable responses to situations. You have to be able to observe the alien's behavior and say, "I don't understand the rules by which the alien is making its decisions, but the alien is acting rationally by some set of rules." . . .
> The second requirement is that they have to care about something. They have to want something and pursue it in the face of obstacles.

To make decisions "rationally," by some set of rules, means to   7
base the decisions on some grounds of truth: correspondence to reality or soundness of inference. An alien who bumped into trees or walked off cliffs, or who went through all the motions of chopping a tree but in fact was hacking at a rock or at empty space, would not seem intelligent. Nor would an alien who saw three predators enter a cave and two leave and then entered the cave as if it were empty.

These rules must be used in service of the second criterion,   8
wanting and pursuing something in the face of obstacles. If we had no fix on what a creature wanted, we could not be impressed when

---

[2] **David Alexander Smith (b. 1953)** American sci-fi novelist.

it did something to attain it. For all we know, the creature may have *wanted* to bump into a tree or bang an ax against a rock, and was brilliantly accomplishing what it wanted. In fact, without a specification of a creature's goals, the very idea of intelligence is meaningless. A toadstool could be given a genius award for accomplishing, with pinpoint precision and unerring reliability, the feat of sitting exactly where it is sitting. Nothing would prevent us from agreeing with the cognitive scientist Zenon Pylyshyn[3] that rocks are smarter than cats because rocks have the sense to go away when you kick them.

Finally, the creature has to use the rational rules to attain the   9
goal in different ways, depending on the obstacles to be overcome. As William James[4] explained:

> Romeo wants Juliet as the filings want the magnet; and if no obstacles intervene he moves toward her by as straight a line as they. But Romeo and Juliet, if a wall be built between them, do not remain idiotically pressing their faces against the opposite sides like the magnet and filings with the card. Romeo soon finds a circuitous way, by scaling the wall or otherwise, of touching Juliet's lips directly. With the filings the path is fixed; whether it reaches the end depends on accidents. With the lover it is the end which is fixed; the path may be modified indefinitely.

Intelligence, then, is the ability to attain goals in the face of   10
obstacles by means of decisions based on rational (truth-obeying) rules. The computer scientists Allen Newell and Herbert Simon[5] fleshed this idea out further by noting that intelligence consists of specifying a goal, assessing the current situation to see how it differs from the goal, and applying a set of operations that reduce the difference. Perhaps reassuringly, by this definition human beings, not just aliens, are intelligent. We have *desires*, and we pursue them using *beliefs*, which, when all goes well, are at least approximately or probabilistically true.

An explanation of intelligence in terms of beliefs and desires is   11
by no means a foregone conclusion. The old theory of stimulus and response from the school of behaviorism held that beliefs and desires have nothing to do with behavior — indeed, that they are as unscientific as banshees and black magic. Humans and animals emit a response to a stimulus either because it was earlier paired with a reflexive trigger for that response (for example, salivating to a bell

---

[3]**Zenon Pylyshyn (b. 1937)** Canadian professor of cognitive science at Rutgers University.
    [4]**William James (1842–1910)** One of the great American psychologists.
    [5]**Allen Newell (1927–1992) and Herbert Simon (1916–2001)** Cognitive psychologists at Carnegie Mellon University.

that was paired with food) or because the response was rewarded in the presence of that stimulus (for example, pressing a bar that delivers a food pellet). As the famous behaviorist B. F. Skinner[6] said, "The question is not whether machines think, but whether men do."

Of course, men and women do think; the stimulus-response the-   12
ory turned out to be wrong. Why did Sally run out of the building? Because she believed it was on fire and did not want to die. Her flee-ing was not a predictable response to some stimulus that can be objectively described in the language of physics and chemistry. Per-haps she left when she saw smoke, but perhaps she left in response to a phone call telling her that the building was on fire, or to the sight of arriving fire trucks, or to the sound of a fire alarm. But none of these stimuli would *necessarily* have sent her out, either. She would *not* have left if she knew that the smoke was from an English muffin in a toaster, or that the phone call was from a friend practicing lines for a play, or that someone had pulled the alarm switch by accident or as a prank, or that the alarms were being tested by an electrician. The light and sound and particles that physicists can measure do not lawfully predict a person's behavior. What does predict Sally's behavior, and predict it well, is whether she *believes* herself to be in danger. Sally's beliefs are, of course, related to the stimuli impinging on her, but only in a tortuous, circuitous way, mediated by all the rest of her beliefs about where she is and how the world works. And Sally's behavior depends just as much on whether she *wants* to escape the danger—if she were a volunteer firefighter, or suicidal, or a zealot who wanted to immolate herself to draw attention to a cause, or had children in the day-care center upstairs, you can bet she would not have fled.

Skinner himself did not pigheadedly insist that measurable   13
stimuli like wavelengths and shapes predicted behavior. Instead, he defined stimuli by his own intuitions. He was perfectly happy call-ing "danger"—like "praise," "English," and "beauty"—a kind of stimulus. That had the advantage of keeping his theory in line with reality, but it was the advantage of theft over honest toil. We under-stand what it means for a device to respond to a red light or a loud noise—we can even build one that does—but humans are the only devices in the universe that respond to danger, praise, English, and beauty. The ability of a human to respond to something as physi-cally nebulous as praise is part of the puzzle we are trying to solve,

---

[6] **B. F. Skinner (1904–1990)** Harvard professor and one of the most influential psychologists of his time. He believed behavior in response to stimuli gave insight into the nature of the workings of the mind.

not part of the solution to the puzzle. Praise, danger, English, and all the other things we respond to, no less than beauty, are in the eye of the beholder, and the eye of the beholder is what we want to explain. The chasm between what can be measured by a physicist and what can cause behavior is the reason we must credit people with beliefs and desires.

In our daily lives we all predict and explain other people's behavior from what we think they know and what we think they want. Beliefs and desires are the explanatory tools of our own intuitive psychology, and intuitive psychology is still the most useful and complete science of behavior there is. To predict the vast majority of human acts—going to the refrigerator, getting on the bus, reaching into one's wallet—you don't need to crank through a mathematical model, run a computer simulation of a neural network, or hire a professional psychologist; you can just ask your grandmother. 14

It's not that common sense should have any more authority in psychology than it does in physics or astronomy. But this part of common sense has so much power and precision in predicting, controlling, and explaining everyday behavior, compared to any alternative ever entertained, that the odds are high that it will be incorporated in some form into our best scientific theories. I call an old friend on the other coast and we agree to meet in Chicago at the entrance of a bar in a certain hotel on a particular day two months hence at 7:45 P.M. I predict, he predicts, and everyone who knows us predicts that on that day at that time we will meet up. And we do meet up. That is amazing! In what other domain could laypeople—or scientists, for that matter—predict, months in advance, the trajectories of two objects thousands of miles apart to an accuracy of inches and minutes? And do it from information that can be conveyed in a few seconds of conversation? The calculus behind this forecasting is intuitive psychology: the knowledge that I *want* to meet my friend and vice versa, and that each of us *believes* the other will be at a certain place at a certain time and *knows* a sequence of rides, hikes, and flights that will take us there. No science of mind or brain is ever likely to do better. That does not mean that the intuitive psychology of beliefs and desires is itself a science, but it suggests that scientific psychology will have to explain how a hunk of matter, such as a human being, can have beliefs and desires and how the beliefs and desires work so well. 15

The traditional explanation of intelligence is that human flesh is suffused with a non-material entity, the soul, usually envisioned as some kind of ghost or spirit. But the theory faces an insurmountable problem: How does the spook interact with solid matter? How does 16 an ethereal nothing respond to flashes, pokes, and beeps and get arms and legs to move? Another problem is the overwhelming evidence that the mind is the activity of the brain. The supposedly immaterial soul, we now know, can be bisected with a knife, altered by chemicals, started or stopped by electricity, and extinguished by a sharp blow or by insufficient oxygen. Under a microscope, the brain has a breathtaking complexity of physical structure fully commensurate with the richness of the mind.

Another explanation is that mind comes from some extraordi-   17
nary form of matter. Pinocchio was animated by a magical kind of wood found by Geppetto that talked, laughed, and moved on its own. Alas, no one has ever discovered such a wonder substance. At first one might think that the wonder substance is brain tissue. Darwin wrote that the brain "secretes" the mind, and recently the philosopher John Searle[7] has argued that the physico-chemical properties of brain tissue somehow produce the mind just as breast tissue produces milk and plant tissue produces sugar. But recall that the same kinds of membranes, pores, and chemicals are found in brain tissue throughout the animal kingdom, not to mention in brain tumors and cultures in dishes. All of these globs of neural tissue have the same physico-chemical properties, but not all of them accomplish humanlike intelligence. Of course, *something* about the tissue in the human brain is necessary for our intelligence, but the physical properties are not sufficient, just as the physical properties of bricks are not sufficient to explain architecture and the physical properties of oxide particles are not sufficient to explain music. Something in the *patterning* of neural tissue is crucial.

Intelligence has often been attributed to some kind of energy   18
flow or force field. Orbs, luminous vapors, auras, vibrations, magnetic fields, and lines of force figure prominently in spiritualism, pseudoscience, and science-fiction kitsch. The school of Gestalt psychology[8] tried to explain visual illusions in terms of electromagnetic force fields on the surface of the brain, but the fields were never found. Occasionally the brain surface has been described as a continuous vibrating medium that supports holograms or other wave interference patterns, but that idea, too, has not panned out. The hydraulic model, with its psychic pressure building up, bursting out, or being diverted through alternative channels, lay at the center of Freud's theory and can be

---

[7]**John Searle (b. 1932)** Professor of philosophy at the University of California, Berkeley.

[8]**Gestalt psychology** German school of thought that emphasizes the overall image formed by the mind as opposed to a step-by-step or part-by-part analysis of visual experience.

found in dozens of everyday metaphors: anger welling up, letting off steam, exploding under the pressure, blowing one's stack, venting one's feelings, bottling up rage. But even the hottest emotions do not literally correspond to a buildup and discharge of energy (in the physicist's sense) somewhere in the brain. . . .

A problem with all these ideas is that even if we *did* discover 19 some gel or vortex or vibration or orb that spoke and plotted mischief like Geppetto's log, or that, more generally, made decisions based on rational rules and pursued a goal in the face of obstacles, we would still be faced with the mystery of *how* it accomplished those feats.

No, intelligence does not come from a special kind of spirit or 20 matter or energy but from a different commodity, *information*. Information is a correlation between two things that is produced by a lawful process (as opposed to coming about by sheer chance). We say that the rings in a stump carry information about the age of the tree because their number correlates with the tree's age (the older the tree, the more rings it has), and the correlation is not a coincidence but is caused by the way trees grow. Correlation is a mathematical and logical concept; it is not defined in terms of the stuff that the correlated entities are made of.

Information itself is nothing special; it is found wherever causes 21 leave effects. What is special is information *processing*. We can regard a piece of matter that carries information about some state of affairs as a symbol; it can "stand for" that state of affairs. But as a piece of matter, it can do other things as well — physical things, whatever that kind of matter in that kind of state can do according to the laws of physics and chemistry. Tree rings carry information about age, but they also reflect light and absorb staining material. Footprints carry information about animal motions, but they also trap water and cause eddies in the wind.

Now here is an idea. Suppose one were to build a machine with 22 parts that are affected by the physical properties of some symbol. Some lever or electric eye or tripwire or magnet is set in motion by the pigment absorbed by a tree ring, or the water trapped by a footprint, or the light reflected by a chalk mark, or the magnetic charge in a bit of oxide. And suppose that the machine then causes something to happen in some other pile of matter. It burns new marks onto a piece of wood, or stamps impressions into nearby dirt, or charges some other bit of oxide. Nothing special has happened so far; all I have described is a chain of physical events accomplished by a pointless contraption.

Here is the special step. Imagine that we now try to interpret the 23 newly arranged piece of matter using the scheme according to which the original piece carried information. Say we *count* the newly burned wood rings and interpret them as the age of some tree at some time, even though they were not caused by the growth of any tree. And let's say that the machine was carefully designed so that the interpretation of its new markings made sense—that is, so that they carried information about something in the world. For example, imagine a machine that scans the rings in a stump, burns one mark on a nearby plank for each ring, moves over to a smaller stump from a tree that was cut down at the same time, scans its rings, and sands off one mark in the plank for each ring. When we count the marks on the plank, we have the age of the first tree at the time that the second one was planted. We would have a kind of *rational* machine, a machine that produces true conclusions from true premises—not because of any special kind of matter or energy, or because of any part that was itself intelligent or rational. All we have is a carefully contrived chain of ordinary physical events, whose first link was a configuration of matter that carries information. Our rational machine owes its rationality to two properties glued together in the entity we call a symbol: a symbol carries information, and it causes things to happen. (Tree rings correlate with the age of the tree, and they can absorb the light beam of a scanner.) When the caused things themselves carry information, we call the whole system an information processor, or a computer.

Now, this whole scheme might seem like an unrealizable hope. What guarantee is there that *any* collection of thingamabobs can be arranged to fall or swing or shine in just the right pattern so that when their effects are interpreted, the interpretation will make sense? (More precisely, so that it will make sense according to some prior law or relationship we find interesting; any heap of stuff can be given a contrived interpretation after the fact.) How confident can we be that some machine will make marks that actually correspond to some meaningful state of the world, like the age of a tree when another tree was planted, or the average age of the tree's offspring, or anything else, as opposed to being a meaningless pattern corresponding to nothing at all? 24

The guarantee comes from the work of the mathematician Alan Turing.[9] He designed a hypothetical machine whose input symbols and output symbols could correspond, depending on the details of the machine, to any one of a vast number of sensible interpretations. The machine consists of a tape divided into squares, a read-write head that can print or read a symbol on a square and move the tape 25

---

[9] **Alan Turing (1912–1954)** British mathematician who built an early computer.

in either direction, a pointer that can point to a fixed number of tickmarks on the machine, and a set of mechanical reflexes. Each reflex is triggered by the symbol being read and the current position of the pointer, and it prints a symbol on the tape, moves the tape, and/or shifts the pointer. The machine is allowed as much tape as it needs. This design is called a Turing machine.

What can this simple machine do? It can take in symbols standing for a number or a set of numbers, and print out symbols standing for new numbers that are the corresponding value for any mathematical function that can be solved by a step-by-step sequence of operations (addition, multiplication, exponentiation, factoring, and so on—I am being imprecise to convey the importance of Turing's discovery without the technicalities). It can apply the rules of any useful logical system to derive true statements from other true statements. It can apply the rules of any grammar to derive well-formed sentences. The equivalence among Turing machines, calculable mathematical functions, logics, and grammars, led the logician Alonzo Church[10] to conjecture that *any* well-defined recipe or set of steps that is guaranteed to produce the solution to some problem in a finite amount of time (that is, any algorithm) can be implemented on a Turing machine.   26

What does this mean? It means that to the extent that the world obeys mathematical equations that can be solved step by step, a machine can be built that simulates the world and makes predictions about it. To the extent that rational thought corresponds to the rules of logic, a machine can be built that carries out rational thought. To the extent that a language can be captured by a set of grammatical rules, a machine can be built that produces grammatical sentences. To the extent that thought consists of applying *any* set of well-specified rules, a machine can be built that, in some sense, thinks.   27

Turing showed that rational machines—machines that use the physical properties of symbols to crank out new symbols that make some kind of sense—are buildable, indeed, easily buildable. The computer scientist Joseph Weizenbaum once showed how to build one out of a die, some rocks, and a roll of toilet paper. In fact, one doesn't even need a huge warehouse of these machines, one to do sums, another to do square roots, a third to print English sentences, and so on. One kind of Turing machine is called a universal Turing machine. It can take in a *description* of any other Turing machine printed on its tape   28

---

[10] **Alonzo Church (1903–1995)** American mathematician; he taught at Princeton and was Alan Turing's dissertation adviser.

and thereafter mimic that machine exactly. A single machine can be programmed to do anything that any set of rules can do.

Does this mean that the human brain is a Turing machine? Certainly not. There are no Turing machines in use anywhere, let alone in our heads. They are useless in practice: too clumsy, too hard to program, too big, and too slow. But it does not matter. Turing merely wanted to prove that *some* arrangement of gadgets could function as an intelligent symbol-processor. Not long after his discovery, more practical symbol-processors were designed, some of which became IBM and Univac mainframes and, later, Macintoshes and PCs. But all of them were equivalent to Turing's universal machine. If we ignore size and speed, and give them as much memory storage as they need, we can program them to produce the same outputs in response to the same inputs.   29

Still other kinds of symbol-processors have been proposed as models of the human mind. These models are often simulated on commercial computers, but that is just a convenience. The commercial computer is first programmed to emulate the hypothetical mental computer (creating what computer scientists call a virtual machine), in much the same way that a Macintosh can be programmed to emulate a PC. Only the virtual mental computer is taken seriously, not the silicon chips that emulate it. Then a program that is meant to model some sort of thinking (solving a problem, understanding a sentence) is run on the virtual mental computer. A new way of understanding human intelligence has been born. . . .   30

Natural Computation

Why should you buy the computational theory of mind? Because it has solved millennia-old problems in philosophy, kicked off the computer revolution, posed the significant questions of neuroscience, and provided psychology with a magnificently fruitful research agenda.   31

Generations of thinkers have banged their heads against the problem of how mind can interact with matter. As Jerry Fodor[11] has put it, "Self-pity can make one weep, as can onions." How can our intangible beliefs, desires, images, plans, and goals reflect the world around us and pull the levers by which we, in turn, shape the world? Descartes became the laughingstock of scientists centuries after him (unfairly)   32

---

[11]**Jerry Fodor (b. 1935)** American philosopher, cognitive scientist, and professor of philosophy at Rutgers University.

because he proposed that mind and matter were different kinds of stuff that somehow interacted in a part of the brain called the pineal gland. The philosopher Gilbert Ryle[12] ridiculed the general idea by calling it the Doctrine of the Ghost in the Machine (a phrase that was later co-opted for book titles by the writer Arthur Koestler[13] and the psychologist Stephen Kosslyn and for an album title by the rock group The Police). Ryle and other philosophers argued that mentalistic terms such as "beliefs," "desires," and "images" are meaningless and come from sloppy misunderstandings of language, as if someone heard the expression "for Pete's sake" and went around looking for Pete. Simpatico behaviorist psychologists claimed that these invisible entities were as unscientific as the Tooth Fairy and tried to ban them from psychology.

And then along came computers: fairy-free, fully exorcised 33 hunks of metal that could not be explained without the full lexicon of mentalistic taboo words. "Why isn't my computer printing?" "Because the program doesn't *know* you replaced your dot-matrix printer with a laser printer. It still *thinks* it is *talking to* the dot-matrix and is *trying* to print the document by *asking* the printer to *acknowledge* its *message*. But the printer doesn't *understand* the message; it's *ignoring* it because it *expects* its input to begin with '%!' The program *refuses* to *give up control* while it *polls* the printer, so you have to *get the attention* of the *monitor* so that it can *wrest control* back from the program. Once the program *learns* what printer is connected to it, they can *communicate*." The more complex the system and the more expert the users, the more their technical conversation sounds like the plot of a soap opera.

Behaviorist philosophers would insist that this is all just loose 34 talk. The machines aren't really understanding or trying anything, they would say; the observers are just being careless in their choice of words and are in danger of being seduced into grave conceptual errors. Now, what is wrong with this picture? The *philosophers* are accusing the *computer scientists* of fuzzy thinking? A computer is the most legalistic, persnickety, hard-nosed, unforgiving demander of precision and explicitness in the universe. From the accusation you'd think it was the befuddled computer scientists who call a philosopher when their computer stops working rather than the other way around. A better explanation is that computation has finally demystified mentalistic terms. Beliefs are inscriptions in

---

[12] **Gilbert Ryle (1900–1976)** British philosopher and sharp critic of Descartes.
[13] **Arthur Koestler (1905–1983)** Hungarian writer and naturalized British subject; a noted anticommunist; author of the novel *Darkness at Noon* (1940).

memory, desires are goal inscriptions, thinking is computation, perceptions are inscriptions triggered by sensors, trying is executing operations triggered by a goal.

(You are objecting that we humans *feel* something when we   35
have a belief or a desire or a perception, and a mere inscription lacks the power to create such feelings. Fair enough. But try to separate the problem of explaining intelligence from the problem of explaining conscious feelings. So far I'm trying to explain intelligence; we'll get to consciousness later in the chapter.)

The computational theory of mind also rehabilitates once and for   36
all the infamous homunculus. A standard objection to the idea that thoughts are internal representations (an objection popular among scientists trying to show how tough-minded they are) is that a representation would require a little man in the head to look at it, and the little man would require an even littler man to look at the representations inside him, and so on, ad infinitum. But once more we have the spectacle of the theoretician insisting to the electrical engineer that if the engineer is correct his workstation must contain hordes of little elves. Talk of homunculi is indispensable in computer science. Data structures are read and interpreted and examined and recognized and revised all the time, and the subroutines that do so are unashamedly called "agents," "demons," "supervisors," "monitors," "interpreters," and "executives." Why doesn't all this homunculus talk lead to an infinite regress? Because an internal representation is not a lifelike photograph of the world, and the homunculus that "looks at it" is not a miniaturized copy of the entire system, requiring its entire intelligence. That indeed would have explained nothing. Instead, a representation is a set of symbols corresponding to *aspects* of the world, and each homunculus is required only to react in a few circumscribed ways to some of the symbols, a feat far simpler than what the system as a whole does. The intelligence of the system emerges from the activities of the not-so-intelligent mechanical demons inside it. The point, first made by Jerry Fodor in 1968, has been succinctly put by Daniel Dennett:[14]

> Homunculi are *bogeymen* only if they duplicate *entire* the talents they are rung in to explain. . . . If one can get a team or committee of *relatively* ignorant, narrow-minded, blind homunculi to produce the intelligent behavior of the whole, this is progress. A flow chart is typically the organizational chart of a committee of homunculi (investigators, librarians, accountants, executives); each box specifies a homunculus by prescribing a function *without saying how it is*

---

[14] **Daniel Dennett (b. 1942)** American philosopher of the mind teaching at Tufts University.

accomplished (one says, in effect: put a little man in there to do the job). If we then look closer at the individual boxes we see that the function of each is accomplished by subdividing it via another flow chart into still smaller, more stupid homunculi. Eventually this nesting of boxes within boxes lands you with homunculi so stupid (all they have to do is remember whether to say yes or no when asked) that they can be, as one says, "replaced by a machine." One *discharges* fancy homunculi from one's scheme by organizing armies of idiots to do the work.

. . . Another sign that the computational theory of mind is on   37
the right track is the existence of artificial intelligence: computers that perform humanlike intellectual tasks. Any discount store can sell you a computer that surpasses a human's ability to calculate, store and retrieve facts, draft drawings, check spelling, route mail, and set type. A well-stocked software house can sell you programs that play excellent chess and that recognize alphabetic characters and carefully pronounced speech. Clients with deeper pockets can buy programs that respond to questions in English about restricted topics, control robot arms that weld and spray-paint, and duplicate human expertise in hundreds of areas such as picking stocks, diagnosing diseases, prescribing drugs, and troubleshooting equipment breakdowns. In 1996 the computer Deep Blue defeated the world chess champion Gary Kasparov[15] in one game and played him to a draw in two others before losing the match, and it is only a matter of time before a computer defeats a world champion outright. Though there are no Terminator-class robots, there are thousands of smaller-scale artificial intelligence programs in the world, including some hidden in your personal computer, car, and television set. And progress continues.

These low-key successes are worth pointing out because of the   38
emotional debate over What Computers Will-Soon/Won't-Ever Do. One side says robots are just around the corner (showing that the mind is a computer); the other side says it will never happen (showing that it isn't). The debate seems to come right out of the pages of Christopher Cerf and Victor Navasky's[16] *The Experts Speak:*

> Well-informed people know it is impossible to transmit the voice over wires and that were it possible to do so, the thing would be of no practical value.
>
> —Editorial, *The Boston Post,* 1865

---

[15] **Gary Kasparov (b. 1963)** Russian chess champion with the highest rating of all time.

[16] **Christopher Cerf (b. 1941)** American author; **Victor Navasky (b. 1932)** Professor of journalism at Columbia University and former editor of the *Nation.* Together they published *The Experts Speak* (1984).

Fifty years hence . . . [w]e shall escape the absurdity of growing a
whole chicken in order to eat the breast or wing, by growing
these parts separately under a suitable medium.
                                              —Winston Churchill, 1932

Heavier-than-air flying machines are impossible.
                              —Lord Kelvin, pioneer in thermodynamics and
                                 electricity, 1895

[By 1965] the deluxe open-road car will probably be 20 feet long,
powered by a gas turbine engine, little brother of the jet engine.
            —Leo Cherne, editor-publisher of The Research Institute of
                 America, 1955

Man will never reach the moon, regardless of all future scientific
advances.
                      —Lee Deforest, inventor of the vacuum tube, 1957

Nuclear powered vacuum cleaners will probably be a reality
within ten years.
                —Alex Lewyt, manufacturer of vacuum cleaners, 1955

The one prediction coming out of futurology that is undoubt-   39
edly correct is that in the future today's futurologists will look silly.
The ultimate attainments of artificial intelligence are unknown, and
will depend on countless practical vicissitudes that will be discovered only as one goes along. What is indisputable is that computing
machines can be intelligent.

Scientific understanding and technological achievement are   40
only loosely connected. For some time we have understood much
about the hip and the heart, but artificial hips are commonplace
while artificial hearts are elusive. The pitfalls between theory and
application must be kept in mind when we look to artificial intelligence for clues about computers and minds. The proper label for the
study of the mind informed by computers is not Artificial Intelligence but Natural Computation.

The computational theory of mind has quietly entrenched itself in   41
neuroscience, the study of the physiology of the brain and nervous
system. No corner of the field is untouched by the idea that information processing is the fundamental activity of the brain. Information
processing is what makes neuroscientists more interested in neurons
than in glial cells, even though the glia take up more room in the
brain. The axon (the long output fiber) of a neuron is designed, down
to the molecule, to propagate information with high fidelity across
long separations, and when its electrical signal is transduced to a
chemical one at the synapse (the junction between neurons), the

physical format of the information changes while the information itself remains the same. And as we shall see, the tree of dendrites (input fibers) on each neuron appears to perform the basic logical and statistical operations underlying computation. Information-theoretic terms such as "signals," "codes," "representations," "transformations," and "processing" suffuse the language of neuroscience.

Information processing even defines the legitimate questions of   42 the field. The retinal image is upside down, so how do we manage to see the world right-side up? If the visual cortex is in the back of the brain, why doesn't it feel like we are seeing in the back of our heads? How is it possible that an amputee can feel a phantom limb in the space where his real limb used to be? How can our experience of a green cube arise from neurons that are neither colored green nor in the shape of a cube? Every neuroscientist knows that these are pseudo-questions, but why? Because they are about properties of the brain that make no difference to the transmission and processing of information.

If a scientific theory is only as good as the facts it explains and   43 the discoveries it inspires, the biggest selling point for the computational theory of mind is its impact on psychology. Skinner and other behaviorists insisted that all talk about mental events was sterile speculation; only stimulus-response connections could be studied in the lab and the field. Exactly the opposite turned out to be true. Before computational ideas were imported in the 1950s and 1960s by Newell and Simon and the psychologists George Miller and Donald Broadbent,[17] psychology was dull, dull, dull. The psychology curriculum comprised physiological psychology, which meant reflexes, and perception, which meant beeps, and learning, which meant rats, and memory, which meant nonsense syllables, and intelligence, which meant IQ, and personality, which meant personality tests. Since then psychology has brought the questions of history's deepest thinkers into the laboratory and has made thousands of discoveries, on every aspect of the mind, that could not have been dreamed of a few decades ago.

The blossoming came from a central agenda for psychology set   44 by the computational theory: discovering the form of mental representations (the symbol inscriptions used by the mind) and the processes (the demons) that access them. Plato said that we are trapped inside a

---

[17] **George Armitage Miller (b. 1920)** Professor of psychology at Princeton and founder of the Center for Cognitive Studies at Harvard. **Donald Broadbent (1926–1993)** One of Britain's first cognitive scientists.

cave and know the world only through the shadows it casts on the wall. The skull is our cave, and mental representations are the shadows. The information in an internal representation is all that we can know about the world. Consider, as an analogy, how *external* representations work. My bank statement lists each deposit as a single sum. If I deposited several checks and some cash, I cannot verify whether a particular check was among them; that information was obliterated in the representation. What's more, the *form* of a representation determines what can easily be inferred from it, because the symbols and their arrangement are the only things a homunculus stupid enough to be replaced by a machine can respond to. Our representation of numbers is valuable because addition can be performed on the numbers with a few dronelike operations: looking up entries in the addition table and carrying digits. Roman numerals have not survived, except as labels or decorations, because addition operations are far more complicated with them, and multiplication and division operations are practically impossible.

Pinning down mental representations is the route to rigor in psychology. Many explanations of behavior have an airy-fairy feel to them because they explain psychological phenomena in terms of other, equally mysterious psychological phenomena. Why do people have more trouble with this task than with that one? Because the first one is "more difficult." Why do people generalize a fact about one object to another object? Because the objects are "similar." Why do people notice this event but not that one? Because the first event is "more salient." These explanations are scams. Difficulty, similarity, and salience are in the mind of the beholder, which is what we should be trying to explain. A computer finds it more difficult to remember the gist of *Little Red Riding Hood* than to remember a twenty-digit number; you find it more difficult to remember the number than the gist. You find two crumpled balls of newspaper to be similar, even though their shapes are completely different, and find two people's faces to be different, though their shapes are almost the same. Migrating birds that navigate at night by the stars in the sky find the positions of the constellations at different times of night quite salient; to a typical person, they are barely noticeable.

But if we hop down to the level of representations, we find a firmer sort of entity, which can be rigorously counted and matched. If a theory of psychology is any good, it should predict that the representations required by the "difficult" task contain more symbols (count 'em) or trigger a longer chain of demons than those of the "easy" task. It should predict that the representations of two "similar" things have more shared symbols and fewer nonshared symbols than the representations of "dissimilar" things. The "salient" entities should

45

46

have different representations from their neighbors; the "nonsalient" entities should have the same ones.

Research in cognitive psychology has tried to triangulate on the   47
mind's internal representations by measuring people's reports, reaction times, and errors as they remember, solve problems, recognize objects, and generalize from experience. The way people generalize is perhaps the most telltale sign that the mind uses mental representations, and lots of them.

Suppose it takes a while for you to learn to read a fancy new   48
typeface, festooned with curlicues. You have practiced with some words and are now as quick as you are for any other typeface. Now you see a familiar word that was not in your practice set—say, *elk*. Do you have to relearn that the word is a noun? Do you have to relearn how to pronounce it? Relearn that the referent is an animal? What the referent looks like? That it has mass and breathes and suckles its young? Surely not. But this banal talent of yours tells a story. Your knowledge about the word *elk* could not have been connected directly to the physical shapes of printed letters. If it had, then when new letters were introduced, your knowledge would have no connection to them and would be unavailable until you learned the connections anew. In reality, your knowledge must have been connected to a node, a number, an address in memory, or an entry in a mental dictionary representing the abstract word *elk,* and that entry must be neutral with respect to how it is printed or pronounced. When you learned the new typeface, you created a new visual trigger for the letters of the alphabet, which in turn triggered the old *elk* entry, and everything hooked up to the entry was instantly available, without your having to reconnect, piece by piece, everything you know about elks to the new way of printing *elk*. This is how we know that your mind contains mental representations specific to abstract entries for words, not just the shapes of the words when they are printed.

These leaps, and the inventory of internal representations they   49
hint at, are the hallmark of human cognition. If you learned that *wapiti* was another name for an elk, you could take all the facts connected to the word *elk* and instantly transfer them to *wapiti,* without having to solder new connections to the word one at a time. Of course, only your zoological knowledge would transfer; you would not expect *wapiti* to be *pronounced* like *elk*. That suggests you have a level of representation specific to the concepts behind the words, not just the words themselves. Your knowledge of facts about elks hangs off the concept; the words *elk* and *wapiti* also hang off the concept; and the spelling *e-l-k* and pronunciation [ɛlk] hang off the word *elk*.

We have moved upward from the typeface; now let's move 50 downward. If you had learned the typeface as black ink on white paper, you wouldn't have to relearn it for white ink on red paper. This unmasks a representation for visual edges. Any color abutting any other color is seen as an edge; edges define strokes; an arrangement of strokes makes up an alphanumeric character.

The various mental representations connected with a concept like 51 an elk can be shown in a single diagram, sometimes called a semantic network, knowledge representation, or propositional database.

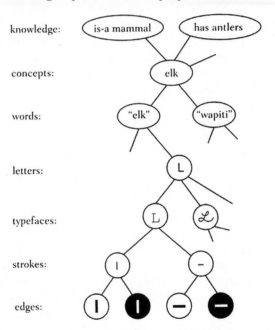

This is a fragment of the immense multimedia dictionary, encyclopedia, and how-to manual we keep in our heads. We find these layers upon layers of representations everywhere we look in the mind. Say I asked you to print the word *elk* in any typeface you wanted, but with your left hand (if you are a righty), or by writing it in the sand with your toe, or by tracing it with a penlight held in your teeth. The printing would be messy but recognizable. You might have to practice to get the motions to be smoother, but you would not have to relearn the strokes composing each letter, let alone the alphabet or the spelling of every English word. This transfer of skill must tap into a level of representation for motor control that specifies a geometric trajectory, not the muscle contractions or limb movements that accomplish it. The trajectory would be translated into actual motions by lower-level control programs for each appendage.

Or recall Sally escaping from the burning building earlier in this 52 chapter. Her desire must have been couched as the abstract representation flee-from-danger. It could not have been couched as run-from-smoke, because the desire could have been triggered by signs other than smoke (and sometimes smoke would not trigger it), and her flight could have been accomplished by many kinds of action, not just running. Yet her behavioral response was put together for the first time there and then. Sally must be modular: one part of her assesses danger, another decides whether to flee, yet another figures out how to flee.

The combinatorics of mentalese, and of other representations 53 composed of parts, explain the inexhaustible repertoire of human thought and action. A few elements and a few rules that combine them can generate an unfathomably vast number of different representations, because the number of possible representations grows exponentially with their size. Language is an obvious example. Say you have ten choices for the word to begin a sentence, ten choices for the second word (yielding a hundred two-word beginnings), ten choices for the third word (yielding a thousand three-word beginnings), and so on. (Ten is in fact the approximate geometric mean of the number of word choices available at each point in assembling a grammatical and sensible sentence.) A little arithmetic shows that the number of sentences of twenty words or less (not an unusual length) is about 10^{20}: a one followed by twenty zeros, or a hundred million trillion, or a hundred times the number of seconds since the birth of the universe. I bring up the example to impress you not with the vastness of language but with the vastness of thought. Language, after all, is not scat-singing: every sentence expresses a distinct idea. (There are no truly synonymous sentences.) So in addition to whatever ineffable thoughts people might have, they can entertain something like a hundred million trillion different effable thoughts.

The combinatorial immensity of thinkable structures is found in 54 many spheres of human activity. The young John Stuart Mill was alarmed to discover that the finite number of musical notes, together with the maximum practical length of a musical piece, meant that the world would soon run out of melodies. At the time he sank into this melancholy, Brahms, Tchaikovsky, Rachmaninoff, and Stravinsky had not yet been born, to say nothing of the entire genres of ragtime, jazz, Broadway musicals, electric blues, country and western, rock and roll, samba, reggae, and punk. We are unlikely to have a melody shortage anytime soon because music is combinatorial: if each note of a melody can be selected from, say, eight notes on average, there are 64 pairs of notes, 512 motifs of three notes, 4,096 phrases of four notes, and so on, multiplying out to trillions and trillions of musical pieces.

Our everyday ease in generalizing our knowledge is one class of   55
evidence that we have several kinds of data representations inside
our heads. Mental representations also reveal themselves in the psychology laboratory. With clever techniques, psychologists can catch a
mind in the act of flipping from representation to representation. A
nice demonstration comes from the psychologist Michael Posner[18]
and colleagues. Volunteers sit in front of a video screen and see pairs
of letters flashed briefly: A A, for example. They are asked to press
one button if the letters are the same, another button if they are different (say, A B). Sometimes the matching letters are both uppercase
or both lowercase (A A or a a); that is, they are physically identical.
Sometimes one is uppercase and one is lowercase (A a or a A); they
are the same letter of the alphabet, but physically different. When
the letters are physically identical, people press the buttons more
quickly and accurately than when they are physically different, presumably because the people are processing the letters as visual forms
and can simply match them by their geometry, template-style. When
one letter is A and the other letter is a, people have to convert them
into a format in which they are equivalent, namely "the letter *a*"; this
conversion adds about a tenth of a second to the reaction time. But
if one letter is flashed and the other follows seconds later, it doesn't
matter whether they were physically identical or not; A-then-A is as
slow as A-then-a. Quick template-matching is no longer possible.
Apparently after a few seconds the mind automatically converts a
visual representation into an alphabetic one, discarding the information about its geometry.

Such laboratory legerdemain has revealed that the human brain   56
uses at least four major formats of representation. One format is the
visual image, which is like a template in a two-dimensional, picturelike mosaic. Another is a phonological representation, a stretch of
syllables that we play in our minds like a tape loop, planning out the
mouth movements and imagining what the syllables sound like. This
stringlike representation is an important component of our short-term
memory, as when we look up a phone number and silently repeat it
to ourselves just long enough to dial the number. Phonological short-
term memory lasts between one and five seconds and can hold from
four to seven "chunks." (Short-term memory is measured in chunks
rather than sounds because each item can be a label that points to a
much bigger information structure in long-term memory, such as the

---

[18]**Michael Posner (b. 1936)** Professor of psychology at the University of Oregon
and an expert on attention.

content of a phrase or sentence.) A third format is the grammatical representation: nouns and verbs, phrases and clauses, stems and roots, phonemes and syllables, all arranged into hierarchical trees. In *The Language Instinct* I explained how these representations determine what goes into a sentence and how people communicate and play with language.

The fourth format is mentalese, the language of thought in which 57 our conceptual knowledge is couched. When you put down a book, you forget almost everything about the wording and typeface of the sentences and where they sat on the page. What you take away is their content or gist. (In memory tests, people confidently "recognize" sentences they never saw if they are paraphrases of the sentences they did see.) Mentalese is the medium in which content or gist is captured; I used bits of it in the bulletin board of the production system that identified uncles, and in the "knowledge" and "concept" levels of the semantic network shown in the last diagram. Mentalese is also the mind's lingua franca,[19] the traffic of information among mental modules that allows us to describe what we see, imagine what is described to us, carry out instructions, and so on. This traffic can actually be seen in the anatomy of the brain. The hippocampus and connected structures, which put our memories into long-term storage, and the frontal lobes, which house the circuitry for decision making, are not directly connected to the brain areas that process raw sensory input (the mosaic of edges and colors and the ribbon of changing pitches). Instead, most of their input fibers carry what neuroscientists call "highly processed" input coming from regions one or more stops downstream from the first sensory areas. The input consists of codes for objects, words, and other complex concepts.

. . . The payoff for the long discussion of mental computation 58 and mental representation I have led you through is, I hope, an understanding of the complexity, subtlety, and flexibility that the human mind is capable of *even if* it is nothing but a machine, nothing but the on-board computer of a robot made of tissue. We don't need spirits or occult forces to explain intelligence. Nor, in an effort to look scientific, do we have to ignore the evidence of our own eyes and claim that human beings are bundles of conditioned associations, puppets of the genes, or followers of brutish instincts. We can have both the agility and discernment of human thought *and* a mechanistic framework in which to explain it.

---

[19] **lingua franca** Italian phrase meaning the current most widely used language for commerce.

QUESTIONS FOR CRITICAL READING

1. What kinds of data representation do we have in our heads?
2. What leaps are the hallmark of human cognition (paras. 48–49)?
3. What is the importance of "combinatorics" for establishing the inexhaustibility of human thought (para. 53)?
4. What is a thinking machine? Can a machine think?
5. How convinced are you that information is the commodity of thought?
6. What is the computational theory of mind (paras. 31–41)?
7. What is the traditional explanation of intelligence (para. 16)?
8. What is meant by the term *mentalese* (paras. 53–57)?

SUGGESTIONS FOR CRITICAL WRITING

1. How convinced are you that the computer is a thinking machine? Examine the argument that Pinker presents, particularly early in the essay, and establish the points that you can accept and the points that you cannot accept. What is your view on the question of what thinking is and how we define it? How does your definition differ from Pinker's?
2. Examining your own circumstances and your own experiences as an intelligent person, either validate, invalidate, or qualify Pinker's definition of *intelligence* in paragraph 10. What is the importance of rules, obstacles, and goals? Are these things that describe or define intelligence? What further qualities would you expect to find in an alien before you determined that it was intelligent?
3. Go through the essay and pick out the four or five most important examples Pinker uses and decide which ones are (1) most interesting and (2) most convincing as illustrations of the point at hand. Where do his examples generally come from? Why are they appropriate to the situation? Are they themselves a mark of "thinking" or "intelligence"? Decide with careful analysis which are strongest and which are weakest and why. Do you feel that the use of examples is as powerful a tool of persuasion as Pinker does?
4. What, for you, makes a good alien? Imagine that an alien ship were to land somewhere near you. What would the alien look like, and how would the alien's thought processes—if the alien had any—express themselves? If intelligence is a result of evolution and natural selection, and if the alien came here with a group onboard the ship, is it likely that the alien's intelligence would resemble ours?
5. Pinker associates rational procedures with thinking. Rational procedures follow special rules that are understood by the thinker and as a result they are identified as thinking itself. How comfortable are you with this method of defining thought? This is the basis of Pinker's computational theory of mind. Explain his theory as if you were writing to someone who had never read this essay; then offer your critique

of the theory. If you accept the theory, you must accept the fact that machines think. Is that your position?

6. **CONNECTIONS**   In this essay and in other works, Pinker often criticizes René Descartes, even when he says that Descartes has sometimes been unfairly criticized. What would Pinker's chief criticisms of Descartes's *Fourth Meditation* (p. 461) be? If Descartes could critique Pinker's views on the way the mind works and on the question of intelligence, what would his chief arguments be? What would he find most unacceptable when dealing with Pinker's theories of evolutionary biology? Would he have accepted Pinker's theory of a thinking machine?

7. **SEEING CONNECTIONS**   Memory is one of the processes that Pinker feels is essential in children's acquisition of language. Phonological memory is one of the four "major formats of representation" that the human brain uses in order to process data. Another is "the visual image, which is like a template in a two-dimensional, picturelike mosaic" (para. 56). Without turning again to Dalí's *The Persistence of Memory* (p. 443), write a careful description of the painting relying only on your memory. Use only words (no sketches) and try to include all the elements and their relationships. In the process, decide whether or not Pinker would think of this painting as a template for memory, thought, or intelligence.

V. S. RAMACHANDRAN
Neuroscience — The New Philosophy

VILAYANUR S. RAMACHANDRAN (b. 1951) comes from a distinguished family in Tamil Nadu, India, one that includes a number of uncles who were scientists and parents who nurtured his talent by giving him a fine microscope when he was eleven. His mother also gave him a chemistry set when he was in Bangkok British School in Thailand, where he lived as a young boy. His teachers in that school also supported his curiosity and gave him materials for his experiments. He earned his M.D. at Stanley Medical College in Madras, India, and then went to Trinity College, Cambridge, for his Ph.D. in neuroscience. His earliest work is in the field of visual studies and the neurophysics of visuality, a topic that still interests him. His work in neuroscience has moved into many other areas, including probing the mysteries of consciousness.

Ramachandran's views take into consideration the processes of evolution that he feels have shaped the human brain to produce the highly complex responses it makes to the world around it. He constantly questions the evolutionary advantage of these responses, such as the expression of emotions as well as their repression. As he discusses mental events, he frequently makes references to specific regions of the brain because, as he explains, even in the last twenty years great advances have been made in brain imaging. We now know where in the brain certain activities associated with thought take place. We also know that areas of the brain communicate with each other in highly systematic forms. As a result, Ramachandran sometimes refers to some of the functions of the brain as mechanisms, and part of his interest is seeing what happens when these mechanisms are confounded and short-circuited.

From *A Brief Tour of Human Consciousness: From Imposter Poodles to Purple Numbers*.

Ramachandran is director of the Center for Brain and Cognition and a professor with the psychology department and neurosciences program at the University of California, San Diego, and an adjunct professor of biology at the Salk Institute. He has won many honors for his work and has been named one of the one hundred most prominent people to watch in the twenty-first century. He has published almost two hundred articles in scholarly journals, including invited articles in *Scientific American.* Among his books are *Phantoms in the Brain: Probing the Mysteries of the Human Mind* (1998), with coauthor Sandra Blakeslee; *The Encyclopedia of the Human Brain* (editor-in-chief, 2002); *The Emerging Mind* (2003); *A Brief Tour of Human Consciousness: From Impostor Poodles to Purple Numbers* (2005), from which the following selection comes; and *The Man with the Phantom Twin: Adventures in the Neuroscience of the Human Brain* (2008).

Ramachandran is an international figure who has appeared on important television shows in the United States on PBS and in England on the BBC. He has given numerous invited lectures around the world, including at the Library of Congress, the Getty Museum, McGill University, and the Massachusetts Institute of Technology, as well as in Chennai and New Delhi, India, and at the Royal Society, London.

Ramachandran's Rhetoric

The bulk of Ramachandran's essay concerns the nature of consciousness, although his approach is not direct. He begins with a number of anomalies, mental states that are not normal and some of which might be thought of as akin to madness. He explores several syndromes that are mystifying in nature, and in the process he tries first to define them by describing the observable symptoms and then by proposing a possible explanation through a discussion of the segments of the brain that seem to be involved. He follows with an interpretation that helps explain the basic functions of the brain.

He discusses Capgras syndrome (paras. 18–21), a condition in which a person with a brain lesion sees a member of his family, or a close friend, but is certain that this person is an imitation, not the real person. Even more strange is Cotard's syndrome (paras. 22–26), a condition in which a person is certain that he or she is dead. No amount of reasoning by someone else can change such a person's mind. Then Ramachandran discusses a much more common disorder, schizophrenia (paras. 29–37). Throughout all this discussion, he searches for explanations for the expressions of these disorders by consulting what he calls "basic brain mechanisms." While he conducts this investigation, Ramachandran maintains a sense of humor, occasionally inserting sly jokes. For example, he hypothesizes that schizophrenics can tickle themselves and make themselves laugh, although he says the experiment has not yet been conducted.

One of his most obvious rhetorical devices is to introduce examples that help clarify the sometimes complex discussion. Most of these examples are actually experiments, so they have the cachet of science, which helps to make them more relevant and to make them more persuasive. Enumeration is another common device. For example, he sees five "defining characteristics" of the self in the discussion of one important aspect of consciousness (para. 41). He uses these five points to try to circumscribe the problem because the problem of the self is close to a mystery except insofar as he is able to break it down into intelligible parts. Admitting that the answer to his question, "What exactly is meant by the 'self'?" is difficult to approach, he offers three ways that it can be apprehended by neuroscience (para. 45).

Another point near the end of the essay involves an ancient idea that was current in the early Renaissance: the homunculus—the Latin word for "little man," like a tiny spirit that makes things work. When he begins to discuss qualia (sensory representations like redness) in paragraph 49, he relies on the idea of a "second brain" to explain how qualia, crucial elements in the search for the self, convert into computational functions and ultimately into thinking. Ramachandran is almost embarrassed by discussing the homunculus, but he suggests that some combination of brain functions developed through evolution may actually emulate what we might think of as a homunculus directing the brain and creating the mind.

Elsewhere, Ramachandran asks rhetorically, "What is consciousness? This really breaks down into two questions: The first is the nature of qualia—how does the awareness of sensations like bitter, or painful, or red arise from the activity of neurons? The second: How does the sense of self—the person who experiences qualia—arise?" In paragraph 39, he poses another rhetorical question: "[H]ow does the flux of ions in little bits of jelly—the neurons — in our brains give rise to the redness of red, the flavor Marmite or paneer tikka masala or wine? Matter and mind seem so utterly unlike each other." This is another way of talking about the mind-body split that confounded Descartes and other philosophers. The discussion of qualia leads him directly to considerations of what our sense of self derives from and what its qualities are. As he says, if there were no "self," there could be no qualia.

One interesting, if minor, consideration at the end of the essay concerns the use of language in thinking and in communications, which to an extent produces self-awareness, something that is not common in many animals. The question he poses is whether or not the concept of qualia and the concept of self-awareness, or consciousness, is limited to humans or, perhaps, to primates. His discussion of "conjectures," the ability of the mind to imagine wholly unreal images, such as unicorns, suggests that our processing of qualia and our imagination are unique, since it is highly unlikely that other apes can create such an image in their minds even if they know what a horse is.

Ramachandran admits that the problem of clarifying the nature of self is by no means accomplished yet. If it were, he says, he would have submitted an article immediately and then he would be the most famous scientist in the world. So the upshot is that his work simply tries to move closer to an understanding of how a mental experience can exist in a material object like the brain and, even more remarkable, how that experience can be part of a system that we clearly perceive to be our special nature, our self. Uncovering consciousness is the most intriguing problem in neuroscience and its solution is yet to come.

PREREADING QUESTIONS: WHAT TO READ FOR

The following prereading questions may help you anticipate key issues in the discussion of V. S. Ramachandran's "Neuroscience — The New Philosophy." Keeping them in mind during your first reading of the selection should help focus your attention.

- How does imaging help us understand the function of the brain?
- How does current research affect our view of free will?
- What are qualia and how do they relate to a sense of self?
- What are Capgras syndrome, Cotard's syndrome, and schizophrenia?

Neuroscience— The New Philosophy

All of philosophy consists of unlocking, exhuming, and recanting
what's been said before, and then getting riled up about it.
                                               –V. S. RAMACHANDRAN

The main theme . . . so far has been the idea that the study of   1
patients with neurological disorders has implications far beyond the
confines of medical neurology, implications even for the humanities,
for philosophy, maybe even for aesthetics and art. . . . I would like
to continue this theme and take up the challenge of mental illness.
The boundary between neurology and psychiatry is becoming
increasingly blurred and it is only a matter of time before psychiatry
becomes just another branch of neurology. I shall also touch on a
few philosophical issues such as free will and the nature of self.

There have traditionally been two different approaches to mental   2
illness. The first one tries to identify chemical imbalances, changes in
transmitters and receptors in the brain, and attempts to correct these
changes using drugs. This approach has revolutionized psychiatry
and has been phenomenally successful. Patients who used to be put
in straitjackets or locked up can now lead relatively normal lives.
The second approach we can loosely characterize as the so-called
Freudian approach. It assumes that most mental illness arises from
early upbringing. I'd like to propose a third approach which is radically different from either of these but which, in a sense, comple-
ments them both.

To understand the origins of mental illness it is not enough   3
merely to say that some transmitter has changed in the brain. We
need to know how that change produces the bizarre symptoms that it
does—why certain patients have certain symptoms and why those
symptoms are different for different types of mental illness. I will
attempt to explain the symptoms of mental illness in terms of what is
known about function, anatomy, and neural structures in the brain.
And I will suggest that many of these symptoms and disorders seem
less bizarre when viewed from an evolutionary standpoint, that is
from a Darwinian perspective. I also propose to give this discipline a
new name—evolutionary neuro-psychiatry.

Let us begin with the classic example of what most people con-   4
sider to be a purely mental disorder or psychological disturbance—
hysteria. *Hysteria* is used here in its strict medical sense, as opposed
to the everyday notion of a person shouting and screaming. In the
strictly medical sense, a hysteric is a patient who suddenly experiences

blindness or develops a paralysis of an arm or a leg, but who has no neurological deficits that could be responsible for his or her condition: a brain MR scan reveals that the brain is apparently completely normal, there are no identifiable lesions, no apparent damage. So the symptoms are dismissed as being purely psychological in origin.

However, recent brain-imaging studies using PET scans and functional Magnetic Resonance [fMR] imaging have dramatically changed our understanding of hysteria. Using PET scans and fMR, we can now find what parts of the brain are active or inactive when a patient performs a specific action or engages in a specific mental process. For example, when we do mental arithmetic, the left angular gyrus usually exhibits activity. Or if I were to prick you with a needle and cause pain, another part of your brain would light up. We can then conclude that the particular brain region that lights up is somehow involved in mediating that function.

If you were to wiggle your finger, a PET scan would reveal that two areas of your brain light up. One is called the motor cortex, which is actually sending messages to execute the appropriate sequence of muscle twitches to move your finger, but there is another area in front of it called the pre-motor cortex that *prepares* you to move your finger.

John Marshall, Chris Frith, Richard Frackowiak, Peter Halligan, and others[1] tried this experiment on a hysterically paralyzed patient. When he tried to move his leg, the motor area failed to light up even though he claimed to be genuinely intending to move his leg. The reason he was unable to is that another area was simultaneously lighting up: the anterior cingulate and the orbito-frontal lobes. It's as if this activity in the anterior cingulate and orbito-frontal cortex was inhibiting or vetoing the hysterical patient's attempt to move his leg. This makes sense, because the anterior cingulate and orbito-frontal cortex are intimately linked to the limbic[2] emotional centers in the brain, and we know that hysteria originates from some emotional trauma that is somehow preventing him from moving his "paralyzed" leg.

Of course, all this doesn't explain exactly why hysteria occurs, but now we at least know where to look. In the future it might be possible to use a brain scan to distinguish genuine hysterics from malingerers or fraudulent insurance claimants. And it does prove that one of the oldest "psychological" disturbances — one that Freud studied — has a specific and identifiable organic cause. (Actually, an

5

6

7

8

---

[1] **Chris Frith (b. 1942) . . . and others** Neuropsychologists in Britain.
[2] **limbic** Limbic system or the deep structure of the brain associated with long-term memory, emotion, and personality.

important control is missing in this experiment: no one has yet obtained a brain scan from a genuine malingerer.)

We can think of hysteria as a disorder of "free will," and free   9
will is a topic that both psychologists and philosophers have been preoccupied with for over two thousand years.

Several decades ago the American neurosurgeon Benjamin Libet   10
and the German physiologist Hans Kornhuber were experimenting on volunteers exercising free will, instructing subjects to, for example, wiggle a finger at any time of their own choosing within a ten-minute period. A full three-quarters of a second *before* the finger movement the researchers picked up a scalp EEG potential, which they called the "readiness potential," even though the subject's sensation of consciously willing the action coincided almost exactly with the actual onset of finger movement. This discovery caused a flurry of excitement among philosophers interested in free will. For it seemed to imply that the brain events monitored by the EEG kick in almost a second before there is any sensation of "willing" the finger movement, even though your *subjective* experience is that your will caused the finger movement! But how can your will be the cause if the brain commands begin a second earlier? It's almost as though your brain is really in charge and your "free will" is just a post-hoc[3] rationalization—a delusion, almost—like King Canute[4] thinking he could control the tides or an American president believing that he is in charge of the whole world.

This alone is strange enough, but what if we add another twist to   11
the experiment. Imagine I'm monitoring your EEG while you wiggle your finger. Just as Kornhuber and Libet did, I will see a readiness potential a second before you act. But suppose I display the signal on a screen in front of you so that you can *see* your free will. Every time you are about to wiggle your finger, supposedly using your own free will, the machine will tell you a second in advance! What would you now experience? There are three logical possibilities. (1) You might experience a sudden loss of will, feeling that the machine is controlling you, that you are a mere puppet, and that free will is just an illusion. You may even become paranoid as a result, like schizophrenics who think their actions are controlled by aliens or implants (I'll return to this later). (2) You might think that it does not change your sense of free will one iota, preferring to believe that the machine has some sort of spooky paranormal precognition by which

---

[3] **post-hoc** Latin for "after this."
[4] **King Canute (c. 990–1035)** Viking king of England, Denmark, Norway, and part of Sweden who, according to legend, tricked his courtiers into believing that he could control the tides.

it is able to predict your movements accurately. (3) You might con-
fabulate, or rearrange the experienced sequence mentally in order to
cling to your sense of freedom; you might deny the evidence of your
eyes and maintain that your sensation of will preceded the machine's
signal, not vice versa.

At this stage this is still a "thought experiment"—technically it   12
is hard to get a feedback EEG signal on each trial, but we are trying
to get around this obstacle. Nevertheless, it is important to note that
one can do experiments that have direct relevance to broad philosophical issues such as free will—a field in which my colleagues Pat
Churchland, Dan Wegner, and Dan Dennett[5] have all made valuable
contributions.

Leaving aside this "thought experiment" for the moment, let's   13
return to the original observation on the readiness potential with its
curious implication that the brain events are kicking in a second or so
before any actual finger movement, even though conscious intent to
move the finger coincides almost exactly with the wiggle. Why might
this be happening? What might the evolutionary rationale be?

The answer is, I think, that there is an inevitable neural delay   14
before the signal arising in one part of the brain makes its way
through the rest of the brain to deliver the message: "wiggle your
finger." (A televisual equivalent is the sound delay experienced when
conducting an interview via satellite.) Natural selection has ensured
that the subjective sensation of willing is delayed deliberately to coincide not with the onset of the brain commands but with the actual
execution of the command by your finger.

And this in turn is important because it means that the subjec-   15
tive sensations which accompany brain events must have an evolutionary purpose. For if that were not the case, if they merely
accompanied brain events, as so many philosophers believe (this is
called epiphenomenalism[6])—in other words, if the subjective sensation of willing is like a shadow that accompanies us as we move
but is not causal in making us move—then why would evolution
bother delaying the signal so that it coincides with our movement?

So we have a paradox: on the one hand, the experiment shows   16
that free will is illusory: it cannot be causing the brain events because
the events kick in a second earlier. But on the other hand, the delay
must have some function, otherwise why would the delay have

[5]**Patricia Churchland (b. 1943)** Canadian philosopher at the University of
California; **Daniel Wegner (b. c. 1943)** Psychology professor at Harvard University; **Daniel Dennett (b. 1942)** Philosopher of mind at Tufts University.
   [6]**epiphenomenalism** A philosophy of mind asserting that mental states do
not have any effect on the physical world.

evolved? Yet if it *does* have a function, what could it be other than moving (in this case) the finger? Perhaps our very notion of causation requires a radical revision . . . as happened in quantum mechanics.

Other types of "mental" illness can also be approached, perhaps, through brain imaging. Take the case of pain: when someone is jabbed with a needle, there is usually activity in many regions of the brain, but especially in the insula[7] and in the anterior cingulate. The former structure seems to be involved in sensing the pain and the latter in giving pain its aversive quality. So when the pathways leading from the insula to the anterior cingulate are severed, the patient can feel the pain, but it doesn't hurt—a paradoxical syndrome called pain asymbolia. This leads me to wonder about the image on the brain of a masochist who derives pleasure from pain, or a patient with Lesch–Nyhan syndrome who "enjoys" mutilating himself. The insula would be activated, of course, but would the anterior cingulate also light up? Or, given, especially, the sexual overtones of masochism, a region concerned with pleasure, such as the nucleus accumbens, septum, or hypothalamic nuclei? At what stage in processing do the "pain/pleasure" labels get switched? (I am reminded of the masochist from Ipswich who loved taking ice cold showers at four in the morning and therefore didn't.)   17

. . . I mentioned the Capgras delusion, sometimes seen in patients who have sustained a head injury, in which sufferers start claiming that someone they both recognize and know well—such as their mother—is an imposter.   18

The theoretical explanation for Capgras syndrome is that the connection between the visual areas and the emotional core of the brain, the limbic system and the amygdala,[8] has been cut by the accident. So when the patient looks at his mother, since the visual areas in the brain concerned with recognizing faces is not damaged, he is able to say that she *looks* like his mother. But there is no emotion, because the wire taking that information to the emotional centers is cut, so he tries to rationalize this by believing her to be an imposter.   19

How can this theory be tested? Well, it is possible to measure the gut-level emotional reaction that someone has to a visual stimulus— or any stimulus—by measuring the extent to which they sweat. When any of us sees something exciting, emotionally important, the neural activation cascades from the visual centers to the emotional centers in the brain and we begin to sweat in order to dissipate the heat that we   20

---

[7] **insula** Insula, anterior cingulate, and other specific terms refer to anatomical segments of the brain.

[8] **amygdala** Frontal brain locale associated with the limbic system.

are going to generate from exercise, from action (feeding, fleeing, fighting, or sex). This effect can be measured by placing two electrodes on a person's skin to track changes in skin resistance—when skin resistance falls, we call it a galvanic skin response. Familiar or nonthreatening objects or people produce no galvanic skin response because they generate no emotional arousal. But if you look at a lion or a tiger, or—as it turns out—your mother, a huge galvanic skin response occurs. Believe it or not, every time you see your mother, you sweat! (And you don't even have to be Jewish.)

But we found that this doesn't happen in Capgras patients, sup-   21
porting the idea that there has been a disconnection between vision and emotion.

There exists an even more bizarre disorder, Cotard's syndrome,   22
in which the patient starts claiming he or she is dead. I suggest that this is similar to Capgras except that instead of vision alone being disconnected from the emotional centers in the brain, all the senses become disconnected from the emotional centers. So that nothing in the world has any emotional significance, no object or person, no tactile sensation, no sound—nothing—has emotional impact. The only way in which a patient can interpret this complete emotional desolation is to believe that he or she is dead. However bizarre, this is the only interpretation that makes sense to him; the reasoning gets distorted to accommodate the emotions. If this idea is correct we would expect no galvanic responses in a Cotard's patient whatever the stimulus.

The delusion of Cotard's is notoriously resistant to intellectual   23
correction. For example, a man will agree that dead people cannot bleed; then, if pricked with a needle, he will express amazement and conclude that the dead *do* bleed after all, instead of giving up his delusion and inferring that he is alive. Once a delusional fixation develops, all contrary evidence is warped to accommodate it. Emotion seems to override reason rather than the other way around. (Of course, this is true of most of us to some extent. I have known many an otherwise rational and intelligent person who believes the number 13 to be unlucky or who won't walk under a ladder.)

Capgras and Cotard's are both rare syndromes, but there is   24
another disorder, a sort of mini-Cotard's, that is much more commonly seen in clinical practice. This disorder is known as derealization and depersonalization, and is found in acute anxiety, panic attacks, depression, and other dissociative states. Suddenly the world seems completely unreal—like a dream. The patient feels like a zombie.

I believe such feelings involve the same circuitry as Capgras and   25
Cotard's. In nature, an opossum when chased by a predator will suddenly lose all muscle tone and play dead, hence the phrase "playing

possum." This is a good strategy for the opossum because (a) any movement will encourage the predatory behavior of the carnivore and (b) carnivores usually avoid carrion, which might be infected. Following the lead of Martin Roth, Mauricio Sierra, and German Berrios,[9] I suggest that derealization and depersonalization, and other dissociative states, are examples of playing possum in the emotional realm and that this is an evolutionary adaptive mechanism.

There is a well-known story of the explorer David Livingstone   26 being attacked by a lion. He saw his arm being mauled but felt no pain or even fear. He felt detached from it all, as if he were watching events from a distance. The same thing can happen to soldiers in battle or to a woman being raped. During such dire emergencies, the anterior cingulate in the brain, part of the frontal lobes, becomes extremely active. This inhibits or temporarily shuts down the amygdala and other limbic emotional centers, so temporarily suppressing potentially disabling emotions such as anxiety and fear. But at the same time, the anterior cingulate activation generates extreme alertness and vigilance in preparation for any appropriate defensive reaction that might be required.

In an emergency, this James Bond–like combination of shutting   27 down emotions ("nerves of steel") while being hypervigilant is useful, keeping us out of harm's way. It is better to do nothing than to engage in some sort of erratic behavior. But what if the same mechanism is accidentally triggered by chemical imbalances or brain disease, when there is no emergency? A person looks at the world, is intensely alert, hypervigilant, but the world has become completely devoid of emotional meaning because the limbic system has been shut down. There are only two possible ways to interpret this strange predicament, this paradoxical state of mind. Either "the world isn't real"—derealization—or "I am not real"—depersonalization.

Epileptic seizures originating in this part of the brain can also   28 produce these dreamlike states of derealization and depersonalization. Intriguingly, we know that during a seizure, when the patient is experiencing derealization, there is no galvanic skin response to anything. Following the seizure, skin response returns to normal. All of which supports the hypothesis that we have been considering.

Probably the disorder most commonly associated with the word   29 "madness" is schizophrenia. Schizophrenics do indeed exhibit bizarre symptoms. They hallucinate, often hearing voices. They become delusional, thinking they're Napoleon or Ramachandran.

---

[9] **Martin Roth (1917–2006), Mauricio Sierra, and German Berrios** Professors of psychiatry at Cambridge University.

They are convinced the government has planted devices in their brain to monitor their thoughts and actions. Or that aliens are controlling them.

Psycho-pharmacology has revolutionized our ability to treat   30
schizophrenia, but the question remains: Why do schizophrenics behave as they do? I'd like to speculate on this, based on some work my colleagues and I have done on anosognosia (denial of illness) — which results from right-hemisphere lesions—and some very clever speculations by Chris Frith, Sarah Blakemore, and Tim Crow.[10] Their idea is that, unlike normal people, schizophrenics cannot tell the difference between their own internally generated images and thoughts and perceptions that are evoked by real things outside.

If I conjure up a mental picture of a clown in front of me, I don't   31
confuse it with reality partly because my brain has access to the internal command I gave. I am expecting to visualize a clown, and that is what I see. It is not an hallucination. But if the "expectation" mechanism in my brain that does this becomes faulty, then I would be unable to tell the difference between a clown I'm imagining and a clown I'm actually seeing there. In other words, I would believe that the clown was real. I would hallucinate, and be unable to differentiate between fantasy and reality.

Similarly, I might momentarily entertain the thought that it   32
would be nice to be Napoleon, but in a schizophrenic this momentary thought becomes a full-blown delusion instead of being vetoed by reality.

What about the other symptoms of schizophrenia—alien con-   33
trol, for example? A normal person knows that he moves of his or her own free will, and can attribute the movement to the fact that the brain has sent the command "move." If the mechanism that monitors intention and compares it with performance is flawed, a more bizarre interpretation is likely to result, such as that body movements are controlled by aliens or brain implants, which is what paranoid schizophrenics claim.

How do you test a theory like this? Here is an experiment for   34
you to try: using your right index finger, tap repeatedly your left index finger, keeping your left index finger steady and inactive. Notice how you feel the tapping mainly on the left finger, very little on the right finger. That is because the brain has sent a command from the left hemisphere to the right hand saying "move." It has alerted the sensory areas of the brain to expect some touch signals

---

[10]**Tim Crow** British psychiatrist specializing in schizophrenia; **Sarah Blakemore** Cognitive neuroscientist at University College, London.

on the right hand. Your left hand, however, is perfectly steady, so the taps upon it come as something of a surprise. This is why you feel more sensation in the immobile finger, even though the tactile input to both fingers is exactly the same. (If you change hands, you will find that the results are reversed.)

Following our theory, I predict that if a schizophrenic were to try this experiment, he would feel the sensations equally in both fingers since he is unable to differentiate between internally generated actions and externally generated sensory stimuli. It's a five-minute experiment—yet no one has ever tried it. 35

Or imagine that you are visualizing a banana on a blank white screen in front of you. While you are doing this, if I secretly project a very low-contrast physical image of the banana on the screen, your threshold for detecting this real banana will be elevated—presumably even your normal brain tends to get confused between a very dim real banana and one which you imagine. This surprising result is called the "Perky effect" and one would predict that it would be amplified enormously in schizophrenics. 36

Another simple yet untried experiment: as you know, you can't tickle yourself. That is because your brain knows you're sending the command. Prediction: a schizophrenic will laugh when he tickles himself. 37

Even though the behavior of many patients with mental illness seems bizarre, we can now begin to make sense of the symptoms using our knowledge of basic brain mechanisms. Mental illness might be thought of as disturbances of consciousness and of self, two words that conceal great depths of ignorance. Let me try to summarize my own view of consciousness. There are really two problems here—the problem of the subjective sensations or qualia and the problem of the self. The problem of qualia is the more difficult. 38

The qualia question is, how does the flux of ions in little bits of jelly—the neurons—in our brains give rise to the redness of red, the flavor of Marmite or paneer tikka masala or wine? Matter and mind seem so utterly unlike each other. One way out of this dilemma is to think of them really as two different ways of describing the world, each of which is complete in itself. Just as we can describe light as made up either of particles or as waves—and there's no point in asking which description is correct, because they both are, even though the two seem utterly dissimilar—the same may be true of mental and physical events in the brain. 39

But what about the self, the last remaining great mystery in science and something that everybody is interested in? Obviously self and qualia are two sides of the same coin. You can't have free-floating sensations or qualia with no one to experience them and you can't 40 have a self completely devoid of sensory experiences, memories, or emotions. (As we saw in Cotard's syndrome, when sensations and perceptions lose all their emotional significance and meaning, the result is a dissolution of self.)

What exactly is meant by the "self"? Its defining characteristics   41
are fivefold. First of all, continuity: a sense of an unbroken thread running through the whole fabric of our experience with the accompanying feeling of past, present, and future. Second, and closely related, is the idea of unity or coherence of self. In spite of the diversity of sensory experiences, memories, beliefs, and thoughts, we each experience ourselves as one person, as a unity.

Third is a sense of embodiment or ownership—we feel our-   42
selves anchored to our bodies. Fourth, a sense of agency, what we call free will, being in charge of our own actions and destinies. I can wiggle my finger but I can't wiggle my nose or your finger.

Fifth, and most elusive of all, the self, almost by its very nature,   43
is capable of reflection—of being aware of itself. A self that's unaware of itself is an oxymoron.

Any or all of these different aspects of self can be differentially   44
disturbed in brain disease, which leads me to believe that the self comprises not just one thing, but many. Like "love" or "happiness," we use one word, *self*, to lump together many different phenomena. For example, if I stimulate your right parietal cortex with an electrode (while you're conscious and awake), you will momentarily feel that you are floating near the ceiling, watching your own body down below. You have an out-of-the-body experience. The embodiment of self—one of the axiomatic foundations of your self—is temporarily abandoned. And this is true of all of those aspects of self I listed above. Each of them can be selectively affected in brain disease.

Keeping this in mind, I see three ways in which the problem of   45
self might be tackled by neuroscience. First, maybe the problem of self is a straightforward empirical one. Maybe there is a single, very elegant, Archimedes-type Eureka! solution to the problem, just as DNA[11] base-pairing was the solution to the riddle of heredity. I think this is unlikely, but I could be wrong.

Second, given my earlier remarks about the self, the notion of   46
the self as being defined by a set of attributes—embodiment, agency, unity, continuity—maybe we will succeed in explaining each of these attributes individually in terms of what is going on in the brain. Then the problem of what the self is will vanish, or at least recede

---

[11] **DNA** Deoxyribonucleic acid; it gives essential information to genes in all living things.

into the background, just as scientists no longer speak of vital spirits or ask what "life" is. (We recognize that life is a word loosely applied to a collection of processes — DNA replication and transcription, Krebs cycle,[12] Lactic acid cycle, etc., etc.)

Third, maybe the solution to the problem of the self is not a   47
straightforward empirical one. It may instead require a radical shift in perspective, the sort of thing that Einstein did when he rejected the assumption that things can move at arbitrarily high velocities. When we finally achieve such a shift in perspective, we may be in for a big surprise and find that the answer was staring at us all along. I don't want to sound like a New Age guru, but there are curious parallels between this idea and the Hindu philosophical (albeit somewhat nebulous) view that there is no essential difference between self and others, or that the self is an illusion.

Of course, I have no clue what the solution to the problem of   48
self is, what the shift in perspective might be. If I did I would dash off a paper to *Nature* today, and overnight I'd become the most famous scientist alive. But, just for fun, I'll have a crack at describing what the solution might look like.

I will begin with qualia. It seems quite obvious that qualia must   49
have evolved to fulfill a specific biological function — they cannot be mere by-products (an "epiphenomenon") of neural activity. In 1997 I suggested that sensory representations that are themselves devoid of qualia might acquire qualia in the process of being economically encoded or "prepared" into manageable chunks as they are delivered to a central executive structure higher up in the brain. The result is a higher order representation that serves new computational goals. Let us call this second, higher-order, representation a metarepresentation. (Though I feel a bit uncomfortable using the prefix *meta*, which is often employed as a disguise for fuzzy thinking — especially among social scientists.) One could think of this metarepresentation almost as a second "parasitic" brain — or at least a set of processes — that has evolved in us humans to create a more economical description of the rather more automatic processes that are being carried out in the first brain. Ironically this idea implies that the so-called homunculus fallacy — the notion of a "little man in the brain watching a movie screen filled with qualia" — isn't really a fallacy. In fact, what I am calling a metarepresentation bears an uncanny resemblance to the homunculus that philosophers take so much delight in debunking. I suggest that the homunculus is simply either the

---

[12] **Krebs cycle** A series of metabolic reactions in the living cell that convert carbohydrates, fats, or proteins into energy.

metarepresentation itself, or another brain structure that emerged later in evolution for creating metarepresentations, and that it is either unique to us humans or considerably more sophisticated than a "chimpunculus." (Bear in mind, though, that it doesn't have to be a single new structure—it could be a set of novel functions that involves a distributed network. Ideas similar to this have also been foreshadowed by David Darling, Derek Bickerton, Marvin Minsky,[13] and many others, although usually invoked for reasons other than the ones I consider here.)

But what is the purpose of creating such a metarepresentation? Clearly it cannot be just a copy or duplicate of the first—that would serve no purpose. Just like the first representation itself, the second one serves to emphasize or highlight certain aspects of the first in order to create tokens that facilitate novel styles of subsequent computation, either for internally juggling symbols sequentially ("thought") or for communicating ideas to others through a one-dimensional sound stream ("language"). Indeed, if you combine abstraction . . . with sequential symbol juggling you get "thinking"—a hallmark of our species. 50

Once this line was crossed in evolution the brain became capable of generating what Karl Popper[14] would call "conjectures"; it could tentatively try out novel—even absurd—juxtapositions of perceptual tokens just to see what would happen. It's a moot point whether an ape can conjure up a visual image of a horse it has just seen, but it is unlikely that it can visualize a horse with a horn—a unicorn—or imagine a cow with wings—something humans can do effortlessly. 51

These ideas lead to an interesting question. Are qualia and self-awareness unique to humans or are they present in other primates? And to what extent do they depend on language? Vervet monkeys in the wild have specific calls to warn their companions about different predators. A "tree snake" call will send them scurrying down to the ground and a "terrestrial leopard" call will send them climbing higher up the tree. But the caller doesn't *know* that it is warning the others; vervet monkeys have no introspective consciousness—which, as we have seen, probably requires another part of the brain (perhaps linked to aspects of language) to generate a representation of the earlier sensory representation (a metarepresentation) of the 52

<hr>

[13] **David Darling (b. 1953)** English astronomer and science writer; **Derek Bickerton (b. 1926)** Professor emeritus of linguistics at the University of Hawaii; **Marvin Minsky (b. 1927)** Professor of computer science at the Massachusetts Institute of Technology and pioneer of artificial intelligence.
[14] **Karl Popper (1902–1994)** Austrian philosopher of science.

snake or leopard. We could teach a monkey that a pig is dangerous by administering a mild electric shock whenever the pig appears. But what if that monkey were put back in the treetops and a pig lifted on to an adjoining branch? I predict that the monkey would become agitated but not be capable of generating the "snake" cry to warn the other monkeys to climb down; i.e., to start using it as a verb. It is very likely that only humans are capable of the kind of consciousness of one's qualia and of the limits on one's capabilities— "will power"—that this would require.

QUESTIONS FOR CRITICAL READING

1. What are the five characteristics of "self" (para. 41)?
2. How might neuroscience tackle the problem of self (paras. 45–47)?
3. What are qualia (para. 39)?
4. How does the self relate to qualia? Can there be qualia without a self?
5. How has your thinking about your sense of self been altered by this essay?
6. How is the sense of self affected by brain disease (para. 44)?
7. Why are people with Cotard's syndrome so resistant to reason (para. 23)?
8. How does the phenomenon of sweat help neurologists (para. 20)?

SUGGESTIONS FOR CRITICAL WRITING

1. Review Ramachandran's fivefold requirements for determining "self." As a person who possesses a sense of self, analyze his categories of "embodiment, agency, unity, continuity" (para. 46) and connect your own sense of self to these concepts. Then go further by discussing in detail the qualities that you are convinced are specific to your sense of self. What is the self and how do you know you have one? If you became brain damaged, would your sense of self be changed or would your brain adapt to the injury?
2. Ramachandran discusses qualia in some depth. What exactly does he mean by qualia and how do qualia affect our view of the mind (para. 39)? Make a list of the qualia that Ramachandran mentions and then add qualia that you are aware of. Ramachandran asserts that qualia help give insight into self because if there is no self there can be no qualia. Is this true? Examine his reasoning on this point and offer either a validation of his thinking or propose an alternative view. If a computer can recognize qualia, does it have a self?
3. The discussion of free will in paragraphs 9–11 suggests that neuroscience intersects with philosophy because the question of free will has been a philosophical problem for hundreds of years and more. What

does Ramachandran have to say about free will? Does he imply that brain research has made it unimportant, or is it in fact even more important than the philosophers thought? Explain the significance of the brain imaging that shows a "readiness potential" and what that ultimately means for our sense of having free will.

4. In light of the information in this essay, would you say with certainty that you or your friends possess free will? What about people who exhibit some of the syndromes that Ramachandran describes? Do schizophrenics possess free will? Would they possess truly free will if they were being treated with psychoactive drugs? Do people on powerful "recreational" mind-altering drugs possess free will? Is it possible that everyone has a mild form of one or another of the mental syndromes that control behavior? If so, then what is the meaning of free will in modern society?

5. What is hysteria? Ramachandran begins his description in paragraph 4. What is his definition and what are the characteristics of a hysteric? What is the general understanding of the term as reported to you when you quiz people you know? When you quiz the general public? After you have a detailed poll of public opinion, research the more clinical use of the term. How does this research affect your understanding of the term? Have you ever witnessed a hysteric or known someone who experienced hysteria?

6. **CONNECTIONS** Clarify the concept of the homunculus (para. 49) by referring to the extensive discussion in Steven Pinker's "Thinking Machines" (p. 525). What does Pinker say about the concept, and what does Ramachandran say? Would Pinker agree with any of the points Ramachandran raises? To what extent does Ramachandran understand the issues that have been raised about the homunculus as it relates to the operation of the mind? What do you think are the main qualities of the homunculus theory that should be taken seriously? When you sit and think about yourself, or even praise or criticize yourself or your nature, who praises or criticizes whom? Do you need to invent the concept of the homunculus to answer that question?

7. **SEEING CONNECTIONS** Ramachandran does not discuss memory in this essay, but he does discuss various syndromes that imply a disconnect between certain normally functioning areas of the brain. If he were to examine Dalí's *The Persistence of Memory* (p. 443) as if it were the product of a diseased brain, what kind of syndrome might he have to invent to explain the bizarre elements in the painting? What would the "Dalí syndrome" tell us about brain function? Might Ramachandran reasonably assume that the painting is evidence of brain damage? Describe the connections between the parts of the brain that might be most seriously affected by this "syndrome."

PART SIX

NATURE

Francis Bacon
Charles Darwin
Rachel Carson
Stephen Jay Gould
Michio Kaku
Francis Fukuyama

INTRODUCTION

If there be light, then there is darkness; if cold, heat; if height, depth; if solid, fluid; if hard, soft; if rough, smooth; if calm, tempest; if prosperity, adversity; if life, death.
—PYTHAGORAS (c. 580–c. 500 B.C.)

The life of a man in a state of nature is solitary, poor, nasty, brutish, and short.
—THOMAS HOBBES (1588–1679)

Nature and nature's laws lay hid in the night.
God said, Let Newton be! and all was light!
—ALEXANDER POPE (1688–1744)

Some see nature all ridicule and deformity . . . and some scarce see nature at all. But to the eyes of the man of imagination, nature is imagination itself.
—WILLIAM BLAKE (1757–1827)

The old question of whether there is design is idle. The real question is what is the world, whether or not it have a designer—and that can be revealed only by the study of all nature's particulars.
—WILLIAM JAMES (1842–1910)

There are no accidents, only nature throwing her weight around. Even the bomb merely releases energy that nature has put there. Nuclear war would be just a spark in the grandeur of space. Nor can radiation "alter" nature: she will absorb it all. After the bomb, nature will pick up the cards we have spilled, shuffle them, and begin her game again.
—CAMILLE PAGLIA (b. 1947)

Ideas of nature—of the world that exists outside human invention—have formed the core of human inquiry since the beginning of society. Early civilizations viewed nature as a willfully creative and destructive force and structured their religions around gods and goddesses who personified components of the natural world. For example, many early Egyptian and Greek religions worshiped a sun god, such as Ra or Apollo, and performed rituals meant to gain the favor of these gods.

This affiliation of nature with divine forces was gradually joined by a new approach: scientific inquiry. The basic premise of scientific inquiry was that the physical world could be understood through careful observation and described through consistent and logical rules. Lucretius, a prominent Roman thinker who lived during the first century B.C., wrote one of the first treatises on natural science. In his work *On the Nature of Things*, he argued that nature should be viewed in purely materialistic terms and that the universe was composed of minute pieces of matter, or "atoms." During the Renaissance the pursuit of a scientific understanding of the world culminated with Nicolaus Copernicus's (1473–1543) heliocentric (sun-centered) model of the universe. In the seventeenth century Sir Isaac Newton (1642–1727) further developed these methods of objective observation while formulating his laws of physics. Although nature was still believed to be the creation of a divine force, its workings were gradually becoming more and more accessible to human understanding. In the process, humans began to reevaluate their own place in nature.

The six writers in this section offer various ideas on nature, from the origin of life to the structure of the universe. Many of their theories were contended in their time and continue to be debated and rethought, but they share the underlying mission of deciphering the forces that shape our world and our lives.

At the time Francis Bacon wrote, before the advent of sophisticated scientific instruments, most scientists relied on their five senses and their theoretical preconceptions to investigate the workings of the world around them. In "The Four Idols," Bacon raises questions about these modes of scientific inquiry by asking, What casts of mind are essential to gaining knowledge? What prevents us from understanding nature clearly? By thus critiquing traditional presumptions and methods of investigation, Bacon challenges his readers to examine nature with new mental tools.

In "Natural Selection," Charles Darwin proposes a theory that is still controversial today. While on a voyage around South America on HMS *Beagle*, Darwin observed remarkable similarities in the structures of various animals. He approached these discoveries with the advantages of a good education, a deep knowledge of the Bible and theology (he was trained as a minister), and a systematic and inquiring mind. Ultimately, he developed his theories of evolution to explain the significance of resemblances he detected among his scientific samples of insects and flowers and other forms of life. Explaining the nature of nature forms the underpinnings of Darwin's work.

Rachel Carson's "The Sunless Sea" is a masterpiece of description and exploration. Carson gives us a view of the darkest depths of the ocean, a span of almost half the world where there has never been any sunlight at all. Scientists originally thought that without sunlight there could be no life, but Carson points out that not only were they wrong but also that life in the deep is incredibly abundant, beyond what anyone could have imagined. As a result of her early writing on the ocean, more and more attention has been paid to the very issues she raised. Now, much more is known about the deepest parts of the ocean because new submersible robots have made it possible to explore miles below the surface. Her own research demonstrated that there were numerous mysteries in the ocean depths, particularly involving the different forms of life at different depths of the ocean. Carson whets our appetite to know more about the least-explored area of the planet.

Stephen Jay Gould, in "Nonmoral Nature," examines the results of the kind of thinking that Bacon deplored in the seventeenth century but that nevertheless flourished in the nineteenth century. Interpreting the world of nature as if it were fashioned by someone with the same prejudices as the Victorian scientist—usually also a minister—led people to see good and evil in animal and insect behavior. Even today most of us see the world in such terms. To Gould, however, moral issues relate to people—not to, say, dolphins or sharks. For him, thinking like a naturalist means achieving detachment: how we approach the evidence before us, in other words, is as important as what we actually observe. Gould wants us to give up anthropomorphic ways of interpreting evidence in favor of a more rational approach. As he demonstrates, this is not easy to achieve.

Puzzling out the most current thinking in theoretical physics requires speculation that borders on what Michio Kaku calls craziness. One of the craziest theories concerns dark matter, a form of matter in the universe that cannot be seen or touched. Yet according to the calculations of physicists and astronomers, more than 90 percent of the universe may be made up of dark matter. In "The Mystery of Dark Matter," Kaku explains that were it not for the existence of dark matter, our galaxy would spin apart and the universe itself would not hold together. In passing, Kaku alludes to another theory that contradicts common sense: the superstring theory. Instead of postulating hard particles at the heart of the atom, Kaku suggests that the smallest entities in the atom are vibrating strings of energy. This theory not only explains why there are so many particles but also resolves the inherent contradictions between the two great theories in modern physics, quantum theory and the theory of relativity.

"Genetic Engineering" is the product of nonscientist Francis Fukuyama, a political philosopher concerned about the potential for altering not just the genes of an individual or even a family but of an entire population. Fukuyama talks about cloning and designer babies as well as the ongoing practice of aborting unwanted children, such as those with deformities, profound disorders, or an unpopular gender, which in Asia currently targets girls as undesirable. All of these types of genetic "engineering" have grave consequences and raise moral and ethical questions. Cloning and genetic manipulation have crucial technical limitations at the moment, but as Fukuyama points out, they may become practical realities relatively soon. Then, he fears, we will face a serious problem. If people can alter "the genetic patrimony of mankind," then there is a chance that human nature itself will be altered. If it is, then our political values of justice, law, and government could be altered as well. In other words, genetic engineering can change the world.

Although Francis Bacon probably would not understand the astonishing theories that the other writers in this section discuss, he would appreciate the methods they used to reason about their hypotheses and to establish their conclusions. All these writers are joined in their desire to understand the workings of nature and in their profound respect for the questions that remain.

VISUALIZING NATURE

Kindred Spirits, by Asher Durand (1796–1886), was commissioned by a businessman who presented it to William Cullen Bryant (1794–1878), the American poet who had written a moving poetic tribute to Thomas Cole (1801–1848), one of the most famous artists of the Hudson River school. Durand himself was also known for his magnificent landscapes, which — like all the Hudson River school paintings — celebrated the vastness and power of nature. The figures poised on a large rock near the center of the painting are Bryant standing next to Cole, who holds his sketch pad and a recorder, which presumably he will use to play a tune celebrating nature.

Durand was born in Maplewood, New Jersey, shortly after the American Revolution, and exempt from working on the family farm due to his poor health, he apprenticed himself to an engraver and became celebrated for producing an engraved copy of the Declaration of Independence in 1823. Slowly, he shifted his interests to oil painting and portraits. When Thomas Cole became his mentor, they joined in painting the Adirondacks, the Catskills, and upstate New York near the Hudson River. Luman Reed, a mutual friend, became Durand's patron and urged him to paint landscapes, while Jonathan Sturgis, Reed's son-in-law, ultimately commissioned *Kindred Spirits*. With Cole's death, Durand became the most important painter of the Hudson River school.

ASHER B. DURAND, *KINDRED SPIRITS*. 1849.
Oil on canvas, 44" × 36" (112 × 91.4 cm).
Bentonville, Crystal Bridges Museum of American Art.
Photo: Crystal Bridges Museum.

The title, *Kindred Spirits*, was derived from a line in one of John Keats's (1795–1821) short lyric poems:

> O Solitude! if I must with thee dwell,
> Let it not be among the jumbled heap
> Of murky buildings: climb with me the steep, —
> Nature's observatory — whence the dell,
> In flowery slopes, its river's crystal swell,

May seem a span; let me thy vigils keep
'Mongst boughs pavilioned, where the deer's swift leap
Startles the wild bee from the foxglove bell.
But though I'll gladly trace these scenes with thee,
Yet the sweet converse of an innocent mind,
Whose words are images of thoughts refined,
Is my soul's pleasure; and it sure must be
Almost the highest bliss of human-kind,
When to thy haunts two kindred spirits flee.

Durand depicts his friends Bryant and Cole in a rich natural environment with a rocky declivity before them, large trees beside them, and a running river beneath them. Because of the season, there are no flowers and, curiously, no animals except for three birds: two in flight on the right side of the painting, one below on a tree limb. Durand seems to imply that Bryant and Cole are geniuses soaring above, while he sits below and records their communion in the wilderness.

What we see in the painting is a breathtaking view of incomparable loveliness, showing nature's elegance and the beauty of its design. The great cliffs on the right imply, not just the power of nature, but the power of the ages, as this gorge in the Catskill Mountains must have taken eons to create. Bryant and Cole are in conversation regarding the wonders around them. Cole, we imagine, discusses the view and the beauty he sees in contemplation of making a painting. But Bryant, a famous poet and a major pantheist who saw God in every feature of nature, may be receiving the inspiration for his own poem *A Forest Hymn*, which begins:

The groves were God's first temples. Ere man learned
To hew the shaft, and lay the architrave,
And spread the roof above them, — ere he framed
The lofty vault, to gather and roll back
The sound of anthems; in the darkling wood,
Amidst the cool and silence, he knelt down,
And offered to the Mightiest solemn thanks
And supplication.

With these lines in mind, Durand produced a painting that shows the nurturance of man in a setting void of a single piece of his handiwork. The humans in the painting are framed by nature and represent a small part of the grandeur, which may be Durand's way of taking Bryant's pantheistic views into account. Nature is grand; people are slight, even those who are thought of as exceptional geniuses. Interestingly, Keats's poem has none of the pantheistic implications of Bryant's, so we don't know whether Durand's views coincide with Bryant's or not.

FRANCIS BACON
The Four Idols

FRANCIS BACON, Lord Verulam (1561–1626), lived during one of the most exciting times in history. Among his contemporaries were the essayist Michel Eyquem de Montaigne; the playwrights Christopher Marlowe and William Shakespeare; the adventurer Sir Francis Drake; and Queen Elizabeth I, in whose reign Bacon held several high offices. He became lord high chancellor of England in 1618 but fell from power in 1621 through a complicated series of events, among which was his complicity in a bribery scheme. His so-called crimes were minor, but he paid dearly for them. His book *Essayes* (1597) was exceptionally popular during his lifetime, and when he found himself without a proper job, he devoted himself to what he declared to be his own true work: writing about philosophy and science.

His purpose in *Novum Organum* (The new organon), published in 1620, was to replace the old organon, or instrument of thought, Aristotle's treatises on logic and thought. Despite Aristotle's pervasive influence on sixteenth- and seventeenth-century thought—his texts were used in virtually all schools and colleges—Bacon thought that Aristotelian deductive logic produced error. In *Novum Organum* he tried to set the stage for a new attitude toward logic and scientific inquiry. He proposed a system of reasoning usually referred to as induction. This quasi-scientific method involves collecting and listing observations from nature. Once a mass of observations is gathered and organized, Bacon believed, the truth about what is observed will become apparent.

Bacon is often mistakenly credited with having invented the scientific method of inquiring into nature; but although he was right about the need for collecting and observing, he was wrong

---

From *Novum Organum*. Translated by Francis Headlam and R. L. Ellis.

about the outcome of such endeavors. After all, one could watch an infinite number of apples (and oranges, too) fall to the ground without ever having the slightest sense of why they do so. What Bacon failed to realize—and he died before he could become scientific enough to realize it—is the creative function of the scientist as expressed in the hypothesis. The hypothesis—an educated guess about why something happens—must be tested by the kinds of observations Bacon recommended.

Nonetheless, "The Four Idols" is a brilliant work. It does establish the requirements for the kind of observation that produces true scientific knowledge. Bacon despaired of any thoroughly objective inquiry in his own day, in part because no one paid attention to the ways in which the idols, limiting preconceptions, strangled thought, observation, and imagination. He realized that the would-be natural philosopher was foiled even before he began. Bacon was a farsighted man. He was correct about the failures of science in his time; and he was correct, moreover, in his assessment that advancement would depend on sensory perception and on aids to perception, such as microscopes and telescopes. The real brilliance of "The Four Idols" lies in Bacon's focus not on what is observed but on the instrument of observation—the human mind. Only when the instrument is freed of error can we rely on its observations to reveal the truth.

Bacon's Rhetoric

Bacon was trained during the great age of rhetoric, and his prose (even though in this case it is translated from Latin) shows the clarity, balance, and organization that characterize the prose writing of seventeenth-century England. The most basic device Bacon uses is enumeration: stating clearly that there are four idols and implying that he will treat each one in turn.

Enumeration is one of the most common and most reliable rhetorical devices. The listener hears a speaker say "I have only three things I want to say today" and is alerted to listen for all three, while feeling secretly grateful that there are only three. When encountering complex material, the reader is always happy to have such "road signs" as "The second aspect of this question is . . ."

"The Four Idols," after a three-paragraph introduction, proceeds with a single paragraph devoted to each idol, so that we have an early definition of each and a sense of what to look for. Paragraphs 8–16 cover only the issues related to the Idols of the Tribe: the problems all people have simply because they are people. Paragraphs 17–22 consider the Idols of the Cave: those particular fixations individuals have because of their special backgrounds or limitations. Paragraphs 23–26 address the questions related to Idols of the Marketplace, particularly those that deal with the way people misuse words and abuse definitions. The remainder of the selection treats the Idols of the Theater, which relate entirely to philosophic systems and preconceptions—all of which tend to narrow the scope of research and understanding.

Enumeration is used within each of these groups of paragraphs as well. Bacon often begins a paragraph with such statements as "There is one principal . . . distinction between different minds" (para. 19). Or he says, "The idols imposed by words on the understanding are of two kinds" (para. 24). The effect is to ensure clarity where confusion could easily reign.

As an added means of achieving clarity, Bacon sets aside a single paragraph—the last—to summarize the main points that he has made, in the order in which they were made.

Within any section of this selection, Bacon depends on observation, example, and reason to make his points. When he speaks of a given idol, he defines it, gives several examples to make it clearer, discusses its effects on thought, and then dismisses it as dangerous. He then goes on to the next idol. Where appropriate, in some cases he names those who are victims of a specific idol. In each case he tries to be thorough, explanatory, and convincing.

Not only is this work a landmark in thought; it is also, because of its absolute clarity, a beacon. We can still benefit from its light.

PREREADING QUESTIONS: WHAT TO READ FOR

The following prereading questions may help you anticipate key issues in the discussion of Francis Bacon's "The Four Idols." Keeping them in mind during your first reading of the selection should help focus your attention.

- What are the four idols?
- Why do the four idols make it difficult for us to see the truth?
- What are some chief characteristics of human understanding?

The Four Idols

The idols[1] and false notions which are now in possession of the   1
human understanding, and have taken deep root therein, not only
so beset men's minds that truth can hardly find entrance, but even
after entrance obtained, they will again in the very instauration[2] of
the sciences meet and trouble us, unless men being forewarned of
the danger fortify themselves as far as may be against their assaults.

There are four classes of idols which beset men's minds. To these   2
for distinction's sake I have assigned names—calling the first class
Idols of the Tribe; the second, *Idols of the Cave;* the third, *Idols of the Marketplace;* the fourth, *Idols of the Theater.*

The formation of ideas and axioms by true induction[3] is no   3
doubt the proper remedy to be applied for the keeping off and clearing away of idols. To point them out, however, is of great use; for
the doctrine of idols is to the interpretation of nature what the doctrine of the refutation of sophisms[4] is to common logic.

The *Idols of the Tribe* have their foundation in human nature   4
itself, and in the tribe or race of men. For it is a false assertion that
the sense of man is the measure of things. On the contrary, all perceptions as well of the sense as of the mind are according to the
measure of the individual and not according to the measure of the
universe. And the human understanding is like a false mirror,
which, receiving rays irregularly, distorts and discolors the nature of
things by mingling its own nature with it.

The *Idols of the Cave* are the idols of the individual man. For   5
everyone (besides the errors common to human nature in general)
has a cave or den of his own, which refracts[5] and discolors the light
of nature; owing either to his own proper and peculiar nature; or to
his education and conversation with others; or to the reading of books,

---

[1] **idols** By this term Bacon means phantoms or illusions. The Greek philosopher Democritus spoke of *eidola,* tiny representations of things that impressed
themselves on the mind (see note 21).

[2] **instauration** Institution.

[3] **induction** Bacon championed induction as the method by which new
knowledge is developed. As he saw it, induction involved a patient gathering and
categorizing of facts in the hope that a large number of them would point to the
truth. As a process of gathering evidence from which inferences are drawn, induction is contrasted with Aristotle's method, *deduction,* according to which a theory is
established and the truth deduced. Deduction places the stress on the authority of
the expert; induction places the stress on the facts themselves.

[4] **sophisms** Apparently intelligent statements that are wrong; false wisdom.

[5] **refracts** Deflects, bends back, alters.

and the authority of those whom he esteems and admires; or to the differences of impressions, accordingly as they take place in a mind preoccupied and predisposed or in a mind indifferent and settled; or the like. So that the spirit of man (according as it is meted out to different individuals) is in fact a thing variable and full of perturbation,[6] and governed as it were by chance. Whence it was well observed by Heraclitus[7] that men look for sciences in their own lesser worlds, and not in the greater or common world.

There are also idols formed by the intercourse and association of 6 men with each other, which I call *Idols of the Marketplace,* on account of the commerce and consort of men there. For it is by discourse that men associate; and words are imposed according to the apprehension of the vulgar.[8] And therefore the ill and unfit choice of words wonderfully obstructs the understanding. Nor do the definitions or explanations wherewith in some things learned men are wont[9] to guard and defend themselves, by any means set the matter right. But words plainly force and overrule the understanding, and throw all into confusion and lead men away into numberless empty controversies and idle fancies.

Lastly, there are idols which have immigrated into men's minds 7 from the various dogmas of philosophies, and also from wrong laws of demonstration.[10] These I call *Idols of the Theater;* because in my judgment all the received systems[11] are but so many stage-plays, representing worlds of their own creation after an unreal and scenic fashion. Nor is it only of the systems now in vogue, or only of the ancient sects and philosophies, that I speak; for many more plays of the same kind may yet be composed and in like artificial manner set forth; seeing that errors the most widely different have nevertheless causes for the most part alike. Neither again do I mean this only of entire systems, but also of many principles and axioms in science, which by tradition, credulity, and negligence, have come to be received.

But of these several kinds of idols I must speak more largely and 8 exactly, that the understanding may be duly cautioned.

---

[6] **perturbation** Uncertainty, disturbance. In astronomy, the motion caused by the gravity of nearby planets.

[7] **Heraclitus (535?–475? B.C.)** Greek philosopher who believed that there was no reality except in change; all else was illusion. He also believed that fire was the basis of all the world and that everything we see is a transformation of it.

[8] **vulgar** Common people.

[9] **wont** Accustomed.

[10] **laws of demonstration** Bacon may be referring to Aristotle's logical system of syllogism and deduction.

[11] **received systems** Official or authorized views of scientific truth.

The human understanding is of its own nature prone to sup-   9
pose the existence of more order and regularity in the world than
it finds. And though there be many things in nature which are singular and unmatched, yet it devises for them parallels and conjugates and relatives[12] which do not exist. Hence the fiction that all
celestial bodies move in perfect circles; spirals and dragons being
(except in name) utterly rejected. Hence too the element of fire
with its orb is brought in, to make up the square with the other
three which the sense perceives. Hence also the ratio of density[13] of
the so-called elements is arbitrarily fixed at ten to one. And so on of
other dreams. And these fancies affect not dogmas only, but simple
notions also.

The human understanding when it has once adopted an opin-   10
ion (either as being the received opinion or as being agreeable to
itself) draws all things else to support and agree with it. And though
there be a greater number and weight of instances to be found on
the other side, yet these it either neglects and despises, or else by
some distinction sets aside and rejects; in order that by this great
and pernicious predetermination the authority of its former conclusions may remain inviolate. And therefore it was a good answer that
was made by one who when they showed him hanging in a temple a
picture of those who had paid their vows as having escaped ship-
wreck, and would have him say whether he did not now acknowledge
the power of the gods—"Ay," asked he again, "but where are they
painted that were drowned after their vows?" And such is the way of
all superstition, whether in astrology, dreams, omens, divine judgments, or the like; wherein men having a delight in such vanities,
mark the events where they are fulfilled, but where they fail, though
this happen much oftener, neglect and pass them by. But with far
more subtlety does this mischief insinuate itself into philosophy and
the sciences; in which the first conclusion colors and brings into conformity with itself all that come after, though far sounder and better.
Besides, independently of that delight and vanity which I have
described, it is the peculiar and perpetual error of the human intellect

---

[12] **parallels and conjugates and relatives** A reference to the habit of assuming that phenomena are regular and ordered, consisting of squares, triangles, circles,
and other regular shapes.

[13] **ratio of density** The false assumption that the relationship of mass or weight
to volume was ten to one. This is another example of Bacon's complaint, establishing
a convenient regular "relative," or relationship.

to be more moved and excited by affirmatives than by negatives; whereas it ought properly to hold itself indifferently disposed towards both alike. Indeed, in the establishment of any true axiom, the negative instance is the more forcible of the two.

The human understanding is moved by those things most which strike and enter the mind simultaneously and suddenly, and so fill the imagination; and then it feigns and supposes all other things to be somehow, though it cannot see how, similar to those few things by which it is surrounded. But for that going to and fro to remote and heterogeneous instances, by which axioms are tried as in the fire,[14] the intellect is altogether slow and unfit, unless it be forced thereto by severe laws and overruling authority.

The human understanding is unquiet; it cannot stop or rest, and still presses onward, but in vain. Therefore it is that we cannot conceive of any end or limit to the world, but always as of necessity it occurs to us that there is something beyond. Neither again can it be conceived how eternity has flowed down to the present day; for that distinction which is commonly received of infinity in time past and in time to come can by no means hold; for it would thence follow that one infinity is greater than another, and that infinity is wasting away and tending to become finite. The like subtlety arises touching the infinite divisibility of lines,[15] from the same inability of thought to stop. But this inability interferes more mischievously in the discovery of causes:[16] for although the most general principles in nature ought to be held merely positive, as they are discovered, and cannot with

---

[14] **tried as in the fire** Trial by fire is a figure of speech representing thorough, rigorous testing even to the point of risking what is tested. An axiom is a statement of apparent truth that has not yet been put to the test of examination and investigation.

[15] **infinite divisibility of lines** This gave rise to the paradox of Zeno, the Greek philosopher of the fifth century B.C. who showed that it was impossible to get from one point to another because one had to pass the midpoint of the line determined by the two original points, and then the midpoint of the remaining distance, and then of that remaining distance, down to an infinite number of points. By using accepted truths to "prove" an absurdity about motion, Zeno actually hoped to prove that motion itself did not exist. This is the "subtlety," or confusion, Bacon says is produced by the "inability of thought to stop."

[16] **discovery of causes** Knowledge of the world was based on four causes: efficient (who made it?), material (what is it made of?), formal (what is its shape?), and final (what is its purpose?). The scholastics concentrated their thinking on the first and last, whereas the "middle causes," related to matter and shape, were the proper subject matter of science because they alone yielded to observation. (See para. 34.)

truth be referred to a cause; nevertheless, the human understanding being unable to rest still seeks something prior in the order of nature. And then it is that in struggling towards that which is further off, it falls back upon that which is more nigh at hand; namely, on final causes: which have relation clearly to the nature of man rather than to the nature of the universe, and from this source have strangely defiled philosophy. But he is no less an unskilled and shallow philosopher who seeks causes of that which is most general, than he who in things subordinate and subaltern[17] omits to do so.

The human understanding is no dry light, but receives an infusion   13 from the will and affections;[18] whence proceed sciences which may be called "sciences as one would." For what a man had rather were true he more readily believes. Therefore he rejects difficult things from impatience of research; sober things, because they narrow hope; the deeper things of nature, from superstition; the light of experience, from arrogance and pride, lest his mind should seem to be occupied with things mean and transitory; things not commonly believed, out of deference to the opinion of the vulgar. Numberless in short are the ways, and sometimes imperceptible, in which the affections color and infect the understanding.

But by far the greatest hindrance and aberration of the human   14 understanding proceeds from the dullness, incompetency, and deceptions of the senses; in that things which strike the sense outweigh things which do not immediately strike it, though they be more important. Hence it is that speculation commonly ceases where sight ceases; insomuch that of things invisible there is little or no observation. Hence all the working of the spirits[19] enclosed in tangible bodies lies hid and unobserved of men. So also all the more subtle changes of form in the parts of coarser substances (which they commonly call alteration, though it is in truth local motion through exceedingly small spaces) is in like manner unobserved. And yet unless these two things just mentioned be searched out and brought to light, nothing great can be achieved in nature, as far as the production of works is concerned. So again the essential nature of our common air, and of all bodies less dense than air (which are very many) is almost unknown. For the sense by itself is a thing infirm and erring; neither can instruments for enlarging or sharpening the senses do much; but all the truer kind of interpretation of nature is

---

[17] **subaltern** Lower in status.
[18] **will and affections** Human free will and emotional needs and responses.
[19] **spirits** The soul or animating force.

effected by instances and experiments fit and apposite;[20] wherein the sense decides touching the experiment only, and the experiment touching the point in nature and the thing itself.

The human understanding is of its own nature prone to abstrac- 15 tions and gives a substance and reality to things which are fleeting. But to resolve nature into abstractions is less to our purpose than to dissect her into parts; as did the school of Democritus,[21] which went further into nature than the rest. Matter rather than forms should be the object of our attention, its configurations and changes of configuration, and simple action, and law of action or motion; for forms are figments of the human mind, unless you will call those laws of action forms.

Such then are the idols which I call *Idols of the Tribe;* and which 16 take their rise either from the homogeneity of the substance of the human spirit,[22] or from its preoccupation, or from its narrowness, or from its restless motion, or from an infusion of the affections, or from the incompetency of the senses, or from the mode of impression.

The *Idols of the Cave* take their rise in the peculiar constitution, 17 mental or bodily, of each individual; and also in education, habit, and accident. Of this kind there is a great number and variety; but I will instance those the pointing out of which contains the most important caution, and which have most effect in disturbing the clearness of the understanding.

Men become attached to certain particular sciences and specula- 18 tions, either because they fancy themselves the authors and inventors thereof, or because they have bestowed the greatest pains upon them and become most habituated to them. But men of this kind, if they betake themselves to philosophy and contemplations of a general character, distort and color them in obedience to their former fancies; a thing especially to be noticed in Aristotle,[23] who made his natural philosophy[24] a mere bondservant to his logic, thereby rendering

---

[20] **apposite** Appropriate; well related.

[21] **Democritus (460?–370? B.C.)** Greek philosopher who thought the world was composed of atoms. Bacon felt such "dissection" to be useless because it was impractical. Yet Democritus's concept of the *eidola,* the mind's impressions of things, may have contributed to Bacon's idea of "the idol."

[22] **human spirit** Human nature.

[23] **Aristotle (384–322 B.C.)** Greek philosopher whose *Organon* (system of logic) dominated the thought of Bacon's time. Bacon sought to overthrow Aristotle's hold on science and thought.

[24] **natural philosophy** The scientific study of nature in general—biology, zoology, geology, etc.

it contentious and well nigh useless. The race of chemists[25] again out of a few experiments of the furnace have built up a fantastic philosophy, framed with reference to a few things; and Gilbert[26] also, after he had employed himself most laboriously in the study and observation of the loadstone, proceeded at once to construct an entire system in accordance with his favorite subject.

There is one principal and, as it were, radical distinction 19 between different minds, in respect of philosophy and the sciences, which is this: that some minds are stronger and apter to mark the differences of things, others to mark their resemblances. The steady and acute mind can fix its contemplations and dwell and fasten on the subtlest distinctions: the lofty and discursive mind recognizes and puts together the finest and most general resemblances. Both kinds however easily err in excess, by catching the one at gradations, the other at shadows.

There are found some minds given to an extreme admiration of 20 antiquity, others to an extreme love and appetite for novelty; but few so duly tempered that they can hold the mean, neither carping at what has been well laid down by the ancients, nor despising what is well introduced by the moderns. This however turns to the great injury of the sciences and philosophy; since these affectations of antiquity and novelty are the humors[27] of partisans rather than judgments; and truth is to be sought for not in the felicity of any age, which is an unstable thing, but in the light of nature and experience, which is eternal. These factions therefore must be abjured,[28] and care must be taken that the intellect be not hurried by them into assent.

Contemplations of nature and of bodies in their simple form 21 break up and distract the understanding, while contemplations of nature and bodies in their composition and configuration overpower and dissolve the understanding: a distinction well seen in the school of Leucippus[29] and Democritus as compared with the other philosophies. For that school is so busied with the particles that it hardly attends to the structure; while the others are so lost in admiration of the structure that they do not penetrate to the

---

[25] **chemists** Alchemists had developed a "fantastic philosophy" from their experimental attempts to transmute lead into gold.

[26] **William Gilbert (1544–1603)** English scientist who studied magnetism and codified many laws related to magnetic fields. He was particularly ridiculed by Bacon for being too narrow in his researches.

[27] **humors** Used in a medical sense to mean a distortion caused by imbalance.

[28] **abjured** Renounced, sworn off, repudiated.

[29] **Leucippus (fifth century B.C.)** Greek philosopher; teacher of Democritus and inventor of the atomistic theory. His works survive only in fragments.

simplicity of nature. These kinds of contemplation should therefore be alternated and taken by turns; that so the understanding may be rendered at once penetrating and comprehensive, and the inconveniences above mentioned, with the idols which proceed from them, may be avoided.

Let such then be our provision and contemplative prudence for keeping off and dislodging the *Idols of the Cave,* which grow for the most part either out of the predominance of a favorite subject, or out of an excessive tendency to compare or to distinguish, or out of partiality for particular ages, or out of the largeness or minuteness of the objects contemplated. And generally let every student of nature take this as a rule—that whatever his mind seizes and dwells upon with peculiar satisfaction is to be held in suspicion, and that so much the more care is to be taken in dealing with such questions to keep the understanding even and clear.

But the *Idols of the Marketplace* are the most troublesome of all: idols which have crept into the understanding through the alliances of words and names. For men believe that their reason governs words; but it is also true that words react on the understanding; and this it is that has rendered philosophy and the sciences sophistical and inactive. Now words, being commonly framed and applied according to the capacity of the vulgar, follow those lines of division which are most obvious to the vulgar understanding. And whenever an understanding of greater acuteness or a more diligent observation would alter those lines to suit the true divisions of nature, words stand in the way and resist the change. Whence it comes to pass that the high and formal discussions of learned men end oftentimes in disputes about words and names; with which (according to the use and wisdom of the mathematicians) it would be more prudent to begin, and so by means of definitions reduce them to order. Yet even definitions cannot cure this evil in dealing with natural and material things; since the definitions themselves consist of words, and those words beget others: so that it is necessary to recur to individual instances, and those in due series and order; as I shall say presently when I come to the method and scheme for the formation of notions and axioms.[30]

The idols imposed by words on the understanding are of two kinds. They are either names of things which do not exist (for as there are things left unnamed through lack of observation, so likewise are there names which result from fantastic suppositions and to which nothing in reality responds), or they are names of things which exist, but yet confused and ill-defined, and hastily and

22

23

24

---

[30] **notions and axioms** Conceptions and definitive statements of truth.

irregularly derived from realities. Of the former kind are Fortune, the Prime Mover, Planetary Orbits, Element of Fire, and like fictions which owe their origin to false and idle theories.[31] And this class of idols is more easily expelled, because to get rid of them it is only necessary that all theories should be steadily rejected and dismissed as obsolete.

But the other class, which springs out of a faulty and unskillful   25 abstraction, is intricate and deeply rooted. Let us take for example such a word as *humid,* and see how far the several things which the word is used to signify agree with each other; and we shall find the word *humid* to be nothing else than a mark loosely and confusedly applied to denote a variety of actions which will not bear to be reduced to any constant meaning. For it both signifies that which easily spreads itself round any other body; and that which in itself is indeterminate and cannot solidize; and that which readily yields in every direction; and that which easily divides and scatters itself; and that which easily unites and collects itself; and that which readily flows and is put in motion; and that which readily clings to another body and wets it; and that which is easily reduced to a liquid, or being solid easily melts. Accordingly when you come to apply the word—if you take it in one sense, flame is humid; if in another, air is not humid; if in another, fine dust is humid; if in another, glass is humid. So that it is easy to see that the notion is taken by abstraction only from water and common and ordinary liquids, without any due verification.

There are however in words certain degrees of distortion and   26 error. One of the least faulty kinds is that of names of substances, especially of lowest species and well-deduced (for the notion of *chalk* and of *mud* is good, of *earth* bad);[32] a more faulty kind is that of actions, as *to generate, to corrupt, to alter;* the most faulty is of qualities (except such as are the immediate objects of the sense), as *heavy, light, rare, dense,* and the like. Yet in all these cases some notions are of necessity a little better than others, in proportion to the greater variety of subjects that fall within the range of the human sense.

But the *Idols of the Theater* are not innate, nor do they steal into   27 the understanding secretly, but are plainly impressed and received

---

[31] **idle theories** These are things that cannot be observed and thus do not exist. Fortune is fate; the Prime Mover is God or some "first" force; the notion that planets orbited the sun was considered as "fantastic" as these others or as the idea that everything was made up of fire and its many permutations.

[32] **earth bad** Chalk and mud were useful in manufacture; hence they were terms of approval. *Earth* is used here in the sense we use *dirt,* as in "digging in the dirt."

into the mind from the play-books of philosophical systems and the perverted rules of demonstration.[33] To attempt refutations in this case would be merely inconsistent with what I have already said: for since we agree neither upon principles nor upon demonstrations, there is no place for argument. And this is so far well, inasmuch as it leaves the honor of the ancients untouched. For they are no wise disparaged—the question between them and me being only as to the way. For as the saying is, the lame man who keeps the right road outstrips the runner who takes a wrong one. Nay, it is obvious that when a man runs the wrong way, the more active and swift he is the further he will go astray.

But the course I propose for the discovery of sciences is such as   28
leaves but little to the acuteness and strength of wits, but places all wits[34] and understandings nearly on a level. For as in the drawing of a straight line or perfect circle, much depends on the steadiness and practice of the hand, if it be done by aim of hand only, but if with the aid of rule or compass, little or nothing; so is it exactly with my plan. But though particular confutations[35] would be of no avail, yet touching the sects and general divisions of such systems I must say something; something also touching the external signs which show that they are unsound; and finally something touching the causes of such great infelicity and of such lasting and general agreement in error; that so the access to truth may be made less difficult, and the human understanding may the more willingly submit to its purgation and dismiss its idols.

Idols of the Theater, or of systems, are many, and there can be   29
and perhaps will be yet many more. For were it not that now for many ages men's minds have been busied with religion and theology; and were it not that civil governments, especially monarchies, have been averse to such novelties, even in matters speculative; so that men labor therein to the peril and harming of their fortunes— not only unrewarded, but exposed also to contempt and envy; doubtless there would have arisen many other philosophical sects like to those which in great variety flourished once among the Greeks. For as on the phenomena of the heavens many hypotheses may be constructed, so likewise (and more also) many various dogmas may be set up and established on the phenomena of philosophy. And in the plays of this philosophical theater you may observe the same thing

---

[33] **perverted rules of demonstration** Another complaint against Aristotle's logic as misapplied in Bacon's day.

[34] **wits** Intelligence, powers of reasoning.

[35] **confutations** Specific counterarguments. Bacon means that he cannot offer particular arguments against each scientific sect; thus he offers a general warning.

which is found in the theater of the poets, that stories invented for the stage are more compact and elegant, and more as one would wish them to be, than true stories out of history.

In general, however, there is taken for the material of philoso-   30
phy either a great deal out of a few things, or a very little out of many things; so that on both sides philosophy is based on too narrow a foundation of experiment and natural history, and decides on the authority of too few cases. For the rational school of philosophers[36] snatches from experience a variety of common instances, neither duly ascertained nor diligently examined and weighed, and leaves all the rest to meditation and agitation of wit.

There is also another class of philosophers,[37] who having   31
bestowed much diligent and careful labor on a few experiments, have thence made bold to educe and construct systems; wresting all other facts in a strange fashion to conformity therewith.

And there is yet a third class,[38] consisting of those who out of   32
faith and veneration mix their philosophy with theology and traditions; among whom the vanity of some has gone so far aside as to seek the origin of sciences among spirits and genii.[39] So that this parent stock of errors—this false philosophy—is of three kinds: the sophistical, the empirical, and the superstitious. . . .

But the corruption of philosophy by superstition and an admix-   33
ture of theology is far more widely spread, and does the greatest harm, whether to entire systems or to their parts. For the human understanding is obnoxious to the influence of the imagination no less than to the influence of common notions. For the contentious and sophistical kind of philosophy ensnares the understanding; but this kind, being fanciful and tumid[40] and half poetical, misleads it more by flattery. For there is in man an ambition of the understanding, no less than of the will, especially in high and lofty spirits.

---

[36] **rational school of philosophers** Platonists who felt that human reason alone could discover the truth and that experiment was unnecessary. Their observation of experience produced only a "variety of common instances" from which they reasoned.

[37] **another class of philosophers** William Gilbert (1544–1603) experimented tirelessly with magnetism, from which he derived numerous odd theories. Though Gilbert was a true scientist, Bacon thought of him as limited and on the wrong track.

[38] **a third class** Pythagoras (c. 580–500 B.C.) was a Greek philosopher who experimented rigorously with mathematics and a tuned string. He is said to have developed the musical scale. His theory of reincarnation, or the transmigration of souls, was somehow based on his travels in India and his work with scales. The superstitious belief in the movement of souls is what Bacon complains of.

[39] **genii** Oriental demons or spirits; a slap at Pythagoras, who traveled in the Orient.

[40] **tumid** Overblown, swollen.

Of this kind we have among the Greeks a striking example in 34
Pythagoras, though he united with it a coarser and more cumbrous
superstition; another in Plato and his school,[41] more dangerous and
subtle. It shows itself likewise in parts of other philosophies, in the
introduction of abstract forms and final causes and first causes, with
the omission in most cases of causes intermediate, and the like.
Upon this point the greatest caution should be used. For nothing is
so mischievous as the apotheosis of error; and it is a very plague of
the understanding for vanity to become the object of veneration. Yet
in this vanity some of the moderns have with extreme levity
indulged so far as to attempt to found a system of natural philosophy on the first chapter of Genesis, on the book of Job, and other
parts of the sacred writings; seeking for the dead among the living:
which also makes the inhibition and repression of it the more
important, because from this unwholesome mixture of things
human and divine there arises not only a fantastic philosophy but
also an heretical religion. Very meet it is therefore that we be sober-
minded, and give to faith that only which is faith's. . . .

So much concerning the several classes of Idols, and their 35
equipage: all of which must be renounced and put away with a fixed
and solemn determination, and the understanding thoroughly freed
and cleansed; the entrance into the kingdom of man, founded on
the sciences, being not much other than the entrance into the kingdom of heaven, whereunto none may enter except as a little child.

---

[41] **Plato and his school** Plato's religious bent was further developed by Plotinus (A.D. 205–270) in his *Enneads*. Although Plotinus was not a Christian, his Neo-
Platonism was welcomed as a philosophy compatible with Christianity.

QUESTIONS FOR CRITICAL READING

1. Which of Bacon's idols is the most difficult to understand? Do your
   best to define it.
2. Which of these idols do we still need to worry about? Why? What dangers does it present?
3. What does Bacon mean by implying that our senses are weak (para. 14)?
   In what ways do you agree or disagree with that opinion?
4. Occasionally Bacon says something that seems a bit like an aphorism
   (see the introduction to Machiavelli, p. 37). Find at least one such
   expression in this selection. On examination, does the expression have
   as much meaning as it seems to have?
5. What kind of readers did Bacon expect for this piece? What clues does
   his way of communicating provide regarding the nature of his antici-
   pated readers?

SUGGESTIONS FOR CRITICAL WRITING

1. Which of Bacon's idols most seriously affects the way you as a person observe nature? Using enumeration, arrange the idols in order of their effect on your own judgment. If you prefer, you may write about the idol you believe is most effective in slowing investigation into nature.

2. Is it true, as Bacon says in paragraph 10, that people are in general "more moved and excited by affirmatives than by negatives"? Do we really stress the positive and deemphasize the negative in the conduct of our general affairs? Find at least three instances in which people seem to gravitate toward the positive or the negative in everyday situations. Try to establish whether Bacon has, in fact, described what is a habit of mind.

3. In paragraph 13, Bacon states that the "will and affections" enter into matters of thought. By this he means that our understanding of what we observe is conditioned by what we want and what we feel. Thus, when he says, "For what a man had rather were true he more readily believes," he tells us that people tend to believe what they want to believe. Test this statement by means of observation. Find out, for example, how many older people are convinced that the world is deteriorating, how many younger people feel that there is a plot on the part of older people to hold them back, how many women feel that men consciously oppress women, and how many men feel that feminists are not as feminine as they should be. What other beliefs can you discover that seem to have their origin in what people want to believe rather than in what is true?

4. Bacon's views on religion have always been difficult to define. He grew up in a very religious time, but his writings rarely discuss religion positively. In this work, he talks about giving "to faith that only which is faith's" (para. 34). He seems to feel that scientific investigation is something quite separate from religion. Examine the selection carefully to determine what you think Bacon's view on this question is. Then take a stand on the issue of the relationship between religion and science. Should science be totally independent of religious concerns? Should religious issues control scientific experimentation? What does Bacon mean when he complains about the vanity of founding "a system of natural philosophy on the first chapter of Genesis, on the book of Job, and other parts of the sacred writings" (para. 34)? "Natural philosophy" means biology, chemistry, physics, and science in general. Are Bacon's complaints justified? Would his complaints be relevant today?

5. **CONNECTIONS**   How has the reception of Charles Darwin's work been affected by a general inability of the public to see beyond Bacon's four idols? Read both Darwin's essay (p. 597) and that of Stephen Jay Gould (p. 635). Which of those two writers is more concerned with the lingering effects of the four idols? Do you feel that the effects have seriously affected people's beliefs regarding Darwinian theory?

6. **SEEING CONNECTIONS** *Kindred Spirits* (p. 576) represents William Cullen Bryant and Thomas Cole having a philosophical conversation in the wilderness of the Catskills. Would Bacon have approved their getting away from civilization to talk about philosophy, or would he have thought they were giving in to one of the four idols? What visual elements of the painting would Bacon have said were the "affirmatives" and what were the "negatives"? Do nature's visual affirmatives excite Durand, Bryant, and Cole more than the visual negatives do? What are nature's visual negatives?

CHARLES DARWIN
Natural Selection

CHARLES DARWIN (1809–1882) was trained as a minister in the Church of England, but he was also the grandson of one of England's greatest horticulturists, Erasmus Darwin. Partly as a way of putting off ordination in the church and partly because of his natural curiosity, Darwin found himself performing the functions of a naturalist on HMS *Beagle*, which was engaged in scientific explorations around South America during the years 1831 to 1836. Darwin's book *Journal of Researches into the Geology and Natural History of the Various Countries Visited by H. M. S. Beagle, 1832–36* (1839) details the experiences he had and offers some views of his self-education as a naturalist.

His journeys on the *Beagle* led him to note variations in species of animals he found in various separate locales, particularly between remote islands and the mainland. Varieties—his term for any visible (or invisible) differences in markings, coloration, size, or shape of appendages, organs, or bodies—were of some peculiar use, he believed, for animals in the environment in which he found them. He was not certain about the use of these varieties, and he did not know whether the changes that created the varieties resulted from the environment or from some chance operation of nature. Ultimately, he concluded that varieties in nature were caused by three forces: (1) natural selection, in which varieties occur spontaneously by chance but are then "selected for" because they are aids

---

From *On the Origin of Species by Means of Natural Selection*. This text is from the first edition, published in 1859. In the five subsequent editions, Darwin hedged more and more on his theory, often introducing material in defense against objections. The first edition is vigorous and direct; this edition jolted the worlds of science and religion out of their complacence. In later editions, this chapter was titled "Natural Selection; or, Survival of the Fittest."

to survival; (2) direct action of the environment, in which non-adaptive varieties do not survive because of climate, food conditions, or the like; and (3) the effects of use or disuse of a variation (for example, the short beak of a bird mentioned in para. 9). Darwin later regarded sexual selection, which figures prominently in this work, as less significant.

The idea of evolution—the gradual change of species through some kind of modification of varieties—had been in the air for many years when Darwin began his work. The English scientists W. C. Wells in 1813 and Patrick Matthew in 1831 had both proposed theories of natural selection, although Darwin was unaware of their work. Alfred Russel Wallace (1823–1913), a younger English scientist, revealed in 1858 that he was about to propose the same theory of evolution as was Darwin. They jointly published brief versions of their theories in 1858, and the next year Darwin rushed the final version of his book *On the Origin of Species by Means of Natural Selection* to press.

Darwin did not mention human beings as part of the evolutionary process in *On the Origin of Species*; because he was particularly concerned about the probable adverse reactions of theologians, he merely promised later discussion of that subject. It came in *The Descent of Man and Selection in Relation to Sex* (1871), the companion to *On the Origin of Species*.

When Darwin returned to England after completing his research on the *Beagle*, he supplemented his knowledge with information gathered from breeders of pigeons, livestock, dogs, and horses. This research, it must be noted, involved relatively few samples and was conducted according to comparatively unscientific practices. Yet although limited, it corresponded with his observations of nature. Humans could and did cause changes in species; Darwin's task was to show that nature—through the process of natural selection—could do the same thing.

The Descent of Man stirred up a great deal of controversy between the church and Darwin's supporters. Not since the Roman Catholic Church denied the fact that the earth went around the sun, which Galileo proved scientifically by 1632 (and was placed under house arrest for his pains), had there been a more serious confrontation between science and religion. Darwin was ridiculed by ministers and doubted by older scientists; but his views were stoutly defended by younger scientists, many of whom had arrived at similar conclusions. In the end, Darwin's views were accepted by the Church of England, and when he died in 1882 he was lionized and buried at Westminster Abbey in London. Only recently has controversy concerning his work arisen again.

Darwin's Rhetoric

Despite the complexity of the material it deals with, Darwin's writing is fluent, smooth, and stylistically sophisticated and keeps the reader engaged. Darwin's rhetorical method depends entirely on the yoking of thesis and demonstration. He uses definition frequently, but most often he uses testimony, gathering information and instances, both real and imaginary, from many different sources.

Interestingly enough, Darwin claimed that he used Francis Bacon's method of induction in his research, gathering evidence of many instances of a given phenomenon, from which the truth—or a natural law—emerges. In fact, Darwin did not quite follow this path. Like most modern scientists, he established a hypothesis after a period of observation, and then he looked for evidence that confirmed or refuted the hypothesis. He was careful to include examples that argued against his view, but like most scientists, he emphasized the importance of the supportive samples.

Induction plays a part in the rhetoric of this selection in that it is dominated by examples from bird breeding, birds in nature, domestic farm animals and their breeding, and botany, including the breeding of plants and the interdependence of certain insects and certain plants. Erasmus Darwin was famous for his work with plants, and it is natural that such observations would play an important part in his grandson's thinking.

The process of natural selection is carefully discussed, particularly in paragraph 8 and thereafter. Darwin emphasizes its positive nature and its differences from selection by human breeders. The use of comparison, which appears frequently in the selection, is most conspicuous in these paragraphs. He postulates a nature in which the fittest survive because they are best adapted for survival, but he does not dwell on the fate of those who are unfit individuals. It was left to later writers, often misapplying his theories, to do that.

PREREADING QUESTIONS: WHAT TO READ FOR

The following prereading questions may help you anticipate key issues in the discussion of Charles Darwin's "Natural Selection." Keeping them in mind during your first reading of the selection should help focus your attention.

- What is the basic principle of natural selection?
- How does "human" selection differ from nature's selection?

Natural Selection

How will the struggle for existence . . . act in regard to varia- 1
tion? Can the principle of selection, which we have seen is so potent
in the hands of man, apply in nature? I think we shall see that it can
act most effectually. Let it be borne in mind in what an endless
number of strange peculiarities our domestic productions, and, in a
lesser degree, those under nature, vary; and how strong the hereditary tendency is. Under domestication, it may be truly said that the
whole organization becomes in some degree plastic.[1] Let it be borne
in mind how infinitely complex and close-fitting are the mutual
relations of all organic beings to each other and to their physical
conditions of life. Can it, then, be thought improbable, seeing that
variations useful to man have undoubtedly occurred, that other variations useful in some way to each being in the great and complex
battle of life, should sometimes occur in the course of thousands of
generations? If such do occur, can we doubt (remembering that many
more individuals are born than can possibly survive) that individuals having any advantage, however slight, over others, would have
the best chance of surviving and or procreating their kind? On the
other hand, we may feel sure that any variation in the least degree
injurious would be rigidly destroyed. This preservation of favorable
variations and the rejection of injurious variations, I call Natural
Selection. Variations neither useful nor injurious would not be
affected by natural selection, and would be left a fluctuating element, as perhaps we see in the species called polymorphic.[2]

We shall best understand the probable course of natural selection 2
by taking the case of a country undergoing some physical change, for
instance, of climate. The proportional numbers of its inhabitants
would almost immediately undergo a change, and some species
might become extinct. We may conclude, from what we have seen
of the intimate and complex manner in which the inhabitants of
each country are bound together, that any change in the numerical
proportions of some of the inhabitants, independently of the change
of climate itself, would most seriously affect many of the others. If
the country were open on its borders, new forms would certainly
immigrate, and this also would seriously disturb the relations of
some of the former inhabitants. Let it be remembered how powerful
the influence of a single introduced tree or mammal has been shown

---

[1] **plastic** Capable of being shaped and changed.
[2] **species called polymorphic** Species that have more than one form over the
course of their lives, such as butterflies.

to be. But in the case of an island, or of a country partly surrounded by barriers, into which new and better adapted forms could not freely enter, we should then have places in the economy of nature which would assuredly be better filled up, if some of the original inhabitants were in some manner modified; for, had the area been open to immigration, these same places would have been seized on by intruders. In such case, every slight modification, which in the course of ages chanced to arise, and which in any way favored the individuals of any of the species, by better adapting them to their altered conditions, would tend to be preserved; and natural selection would thus have free scope for the work of improvement.

We have reason to believe . . . that a change in the conditions of 3
life, by specially acting on the reproductive system, causes or increases variability; and in the foregoing case the conditions of life are supposed to have undergone a change, and this would manifestly be favorable to natural selection, by giving a better chance of profitable variations occurring; and unless profitable variations do occur, natural selection can do nothing. Not that, as I believe, any extreme amount of variability is necessary; as man can certainly produce great results by adding up in any given direction mere individual differences, so could Nature, but far more easily, from having incomparably longer time at her disposal. Nor do I believe that any great physical change, as of climate, or any unusual degree of isolation to check immigration, is actually necessary to produce new and unoccupied places for natural selection to fill up by modifying and improving some of the varying inhabitants. For as all the inhabitants of each country are struggling together with nicely balanced forces, extremely slight modifications in the structure or habits of one inhabitant would often give it an advantage over others; and still further modifications of the same kind would often still further increase the advantage. No country can be named in which all the native inhabitants are now so perfectly adapted to each other and to the physical conditions under which they live, that none of them could anyhow be improved; for in all countries, the natives have been so far conquered by naturalized productions, that they have allowed foreigners to take firm possession of the land. And as foreigners have thus everywhere beaten some of the natives, we may safely conclude that the natives might have been modified with advantage, so as to have better resisted such intruders.

As man can produce and certainly has produced a great result 4
by his methodical and unconscious means of selection, what may not nature effect? Man can act only on external and visible characters; nature cares nothing for appearances, except in so far as they may be useful to any being. She can act on every internal organ,

on every shade of constitutional difference, on the whole machinery of life. Man selects only for his own good; Nature only for that of the being which she tends. Every selected character is fully exercised by her; and the being is placed under well-suited conditions of life. Man keeps the natives of many climates in the same country; he seldom exercises each selected character in some peculiar and fitting manner; he feeds a long and a short beaked pigeon on the same food; he does not exercise a long-backed or long-legged quadruped in any peculiar manner; he exposes sheep with long and short wool to the same climate. He does not allow the most vigorous males to struggle for the females. He does not rigidly destroy all inferior animals, but protects during each varying season, as far as lies in his power, all his productions. He often begins his selection by some half-monstrous form; or at least by some modification prominent enough to catch the eye, or to be plainly useful to him. Under nature, the slightest difference of structure or constitution may well turn the nicely balanced scale in the struggle for life, and so be preserved. How fleeting are the wishes and efforts of man! how short his time! and consequently how poor will his products be, compared with those accumulated by nature during whole geological periods. Can we wonder, then, that nature's productions should be far "truer" in character than man's productions; that they should be infinitely better adapted to the most complex conditions of life, and should plainly bear the stamp of far higher workmanship?

5   It may be said that natural selection is daily and hourly scrutinizing, throughout the world, every variation, even the slightest; rejecting that which is bad, preserving and adding up all that is good; silently and insensibly working, whenever and wherever opportunity offers, at the improvement of each organic being in relation to its organic and inorganic conditions of life. We see nothing of these slow changes in progress, until the hand of time has marked the long lapse of ages, and then so imperfect is our view into long past geological ages, that we only see that the forms of life are now different from what they formerly were.

6   Although natural selection can act only through and for the good of each being, yet characters and structures, which we are apt to consider as of very trifling importance, may thus be acted on. When we see leaf-eating insects green, and bark-feeders mottled-grey; the alpine ptarmigan white in winter, the red-grouse the color of heather, and the black-grouse that of peaty earth, we must believe that these tints are of service to these birds and insects in preserving them from danger. Grouse, if not destroyed at some period of their lives, would increase in countless numbers; they are known to suffer

largely from birds of prey; and hawks are guided by eyesight to their prey—so much so that on parts of the Continent[3] persons are warned not to keep white pigeons, as being the most liable to destruction. Hence I can see no reason to doubt that natural selection might be most effective in giving the proper color to each kind of grouse, and in keeping that color, when once acquired, true and constant. Nor ought we to think that the occasional destruction of an animal of any particular color would produce little effect; we should remember how essential it is in a flock of white sheep to destroy every lamb with the faintest trace of black. In plants, the down on the fruit and the color of the flesh are considered by botanists as characters of the most trifling importance; yet we hear from an excellent horticulturist, Downing,[4] that in the United States, smooth-skinned fruits suffer far more from a beetle, a curculio,[5] than those with down; that purple plums suffer far more from a certain disease than yellow plums; whereas another disease attacks yellow-fleshed peaches far more than those with other colored flesh. If, with all the aids of art, these slight differences make a great difference in cultivating the several varieties, assuredly, in a state of nature, where the trees would have to struggle with other trees and with a host of enemies, such differences would effectually settle which variety, whether a smooth or downy, a yellow or purple fleshed fruit, should succeed.

7   In looking at many small points of difference between species, which, as far as our ignorance permits us to judge, seem to be quite unimportant, we must not forget that climate, food, etc., probably produce some slight and direct effect. It is, however, far more necessary to bear in mind that there are many unknown laws of correlation[6] of growth, which, when one part of the organization is modified through variation and the modifications are accumulated by natural selection for the good of the being, will cause other modifications, often of the most unexpected nature.

8   As we see that those variations which under domestication appear at any particular period of life, tend to reappear in the offspring at the same period—for instance, in the seeds of the many

---

[3] **Continent** European continent; the contiguous land mass of Europe, which excludes the British Isles.

[4] **Andrew Jackson Downing (1815–1852)** American horticulturist and specialist in fruit and fruit trees.

[5] **curculio** A weevil.

[6] **laws of correlation** In certain plants and animals, one condition relates to another, as in the case of blue-eyed white cats, which are often deaf; the reasons are not clear but have to do with genes and their locations.

varieties of our culinary and agricultural plants; in the caterpillar and cocoon stages of the varieties of the silkworm; in the eggs of poultry, and in the color of the down of their chickens; in the horns of our sheep and cattle when nearly adult—so in a state of nature, natural selection will be enabled to act on and modify organic beings at any age, by the accumulation of profitable variations at that age, and by their inheritance at a corresponding age. If it profit a plant to have its seeds more and more widely disseminated by the wind, I can see no greater difficulty in this being effected through natural selection than in the cotton-planter increasing and improving by selection the down in the pods on his cotton-trees. Natural selection may modify and adapt the larva of an insect to a score of contingencies, wholly different from those which concern the mature insect. These modifications will no doubt effect, through the laws of correlation, the structure of the adult; and probably in the case of those insects which live only for a few hours, and which never feed, a large part of their structure is merely the correlated result of successive changes in the structure of their larvae. So, conversely, modifications in the adult will probably often affect the structure of the larva; but in all cases natural selection will ensure that modifications consequent on other modifications at a different period of life, shall not be in the least degree injurious: for if they became so, they would cause the extinction of the species.

Natural selection will modify the structure of the young in relation to the parent, and of the parent in relation to the young. In social animals it will adapt the structure of each individual for the benefit of the community, if each in consequence profits by the selected change. What natural selection cannot do is to modify the structure of one species, without giving it any advantage, for the good of another species; and though statements to this effect may be found in works of natural history, I cannot find one case which will bear investigation. A structure used only once in an animal's whole life, if of high importance to it, might be modified to any extent by natural selection; for instance, the great jaws possessed by certain insects, and used exclusively for opening the cocoon—or the hard tip to the beak of nestling birds, used for breaking the egg. It has been asserted that of the best short-beaked tumbler-pigeons, more perish in the egg than are able to get out of it; so that fanciers[7] assist in the act of hatching. Now, if nature had to make the beak of a full-grown pigeon very short for the bird's own advantage, the process of modification would be very slow, and there would be simultaneously the most

9

---

[7] **fanciers** Amateurs who raise and race pigeons.

rigorous selection of the young birds within the egg, which had the most powerful and hardest beaks, for all with weak beaks would inevitably perish; or, more delicate and more easily broken shells might be selected, the thickness of the shell being known to vary like every other structure.

Sexual Selection

Inasmuch as peculiarities often appear under domestication in one sex and become hereditarily attached to that sex, the same fact probably occurs under nature, and if so, natural selection will be able to modify one sex in its functional relations to the other sex, or in relation to wholly different habits of life in the two sexes, as is sometimes the case with insects. And this leads me to say a few words on what I call Sexual Selection. This depends, not on a struggle for existence, but on a struggle between the males for possession of the females; the result is not death to the unsuccessful competitor, but few or no offspring. Sexual selection is, therefore, less rigorous than natural selection. Generally, the most vigorous males, those which are best fitted for their places in nature, will leave most progeny. But in many cases, victory will depend not on general vigor, but on having special weapons, confined to the male sex. A hornless stag or spurless cock would have a poor chance of leaving offspring. Sexual selection by always allowing the victor to breed might surely give indomitable courage, length to the spur, and strength to the wing to strike in the spurred leg, as well as the brutal cock fighter,[8] who knows well that he can improve his breed by careful selection of the best cocks. How low in the scale of nature this law of battle descends, I know not; male alligators have been described as fighting, bellowing, and whirling round, like Indians in a wardance, for the possession of the females; male salmons have been seen fighting all day long; male stag-beetles often bear wounds from the huge mandibles[9] of other males. The war is, perhaps, severest between the males of polygamous animals,[10] and these seem oftenest provided with special weapons. The males of carnivorous animals are already well armed; though to them and to others, special means of defense may be given through means of sexual selection, as the mane to the lion, the shoulder-pad to the boar, and the hooked jaw to the male

10

---

[8]**brutal cock fighter** Cockfights were a popular spectator sport in England, especially for gamblers, but many people considered them a horrible brutality.

[9]**mandibles** Jaws.

[10]**polygamous animals** Animals that typically have more than one mate.

salmon; for the shield may be as important for victory as the sword or spear.

Among birds, the contest is often of a more peaceful character. All those who have attended to the subject believe that there is the severest rivalry between the males of many species to attract, by singing, the females. The rock-thrush of Guiana,[11] birds of paradise, and some others, congregate; and successive males display their gorgeous plumage and perform strange antics before the females, which standing by as spectators, at last choose the most attractive partner. Those who have closely attended to birds in confinement well know that they often take individual preferences and dislikes: thus Sir R. Heron[12] has described how one pied peacock was eminently attractive to all his hen birds. It may appear childish to attribute any effect to such apparently weak means: I cannot here enter on the details necessary to support this view; but if man can in a short time give elegant carriage and beauty to his bantams,[13] according to his standard of beauty, I can see no good reason to doubt that female birds, by selecting, during thousands of generations, the most melodious or beautiful males, according to their standard of beauty, might produce a marked effect. I strongly suspect that some well-known laws with respect to the plumage of male and female birds, in comparison with the plumage of the young, can be explained on the view of plumage having been chiefly modified by sexual selection, acting when the birds have come to the breeding age or during the breeding season; the modifications thus produced being inherited at corresponding ages or seasons, either by the males alone, or by the males and females; but I have not space here to enter on this subject.

Thus it is, as I believe, that when the males and females of any animal have the same general habits of life, but differ in structure, color, or ornament, such differences have been mainly caused by sexual selection; that is, individual males have had, in successive generations, some slight advantage over other males, in their weapons, means of defense, or charms; and have transmitted these advantages to their male offspring. Yet, I would not wish to attribute all such sexual differences to this agency: for we see peculiarities arising and becoming attached to the male sex in our domestic animals (as the wattle in male carriers, horn-like protuberances in the cocks of certain fowls, etc.), which we cannot believe to be either useful to the

---

[11] **Guiana** Formerly British Guiana, now Guyana, on the northeast coast of South America.

[12] **Sir Robert Heron (1765–1854)** English politician who maintained a menagerie of animals.

[13] **bantams** Cocks bred for fighting.

males in battle, or attractive to the females. We see analogous cases under nature, for instance, the tuft of hair on the breast of the turkey-cock, which can hardly be either useful or ornamental to this bird; indeed, had the tuft appeared under domestication, it would have been called a monstrosity.

Illustrations of the Action of Natural Selection

In order to make it clear how, as I believe, natural selection acts, 13 I must beg permission to give one or two imaginary illustrations. Let us take the case of a wolf, which preys on various animals, securing some by craft, some by strength, and some by fleetness; and let us suppose that the fleetest prey, a deer for instance, had from any change in the country increased in numbers, or that other prey had decreased in numbers, during that season of the year when the wolf is hardest pressed for food. I can under such circumstances see no reason to doubt that the swiftest and slimmest wolves would have the best chance of surviving, and so be preserved or selected, provided always that they retained strength to master their prey at this or at some other period of the year, when they might be compelled to prey on other animals. I can see no more reason to doubt this, than that man can improve the fleetness of his greyhounds by careful and methodical selection, or by that unconscious selection which results from each man trying to keep the best dogs without any thought of modifying the breed.

Even without any change in the proportional numbers of the 14 animals on which our wolf preyed, a cub might be born with an innate tendency to pursue certain kinds of prey. Nor can this be thought very improbable; for we often observe great differences in the natural tendencies of our domestic animals; one cat, for instance, taking to catch rats, another mice; one cat, according to Mr. St. John,[14] bringing home winged game, another hares or rabbits, and another hunting on marshy ground and almost nightly catching woodcocks or snipes. The tendency to catch rats rather than mice is known to be inherited. Now, if any slight innate change of habit or of structure benefited an individual wolf, it would have the best chance of surviving and of leaving offspring. Some of its young would probably inherit the same habits or structure, and by the repetition of this process, a new variety might be formed which would either supplant or coexist with the parent-form of wolf. Or, again, the wolves inhabiting

---

[14] **Charles George William St. John (1809–1856)** English naturalist whose book *Wild Sports and Natural History of the Highlands* was published in 1846.

a mountainous district, and those frequenting the lowlands, would naturally be forced to hunt different prey; and from the continued preservation of the individuals best fitted for the two sites, two varieties might slowly be formed. These varieties would cross and blend where they met; but to this subject of intercrossing we shall soon have to return. I may add, that, according to Mr. Pierce,[15] there are two varieties of the wolf inhabiting the Catskill Mountains in the United States, one with a light greyhound-like form, which pursues deer, and the other more bulky, with shorter legs, which more frequently attacks the shepherd's flocks.

Let us now take a more complex case. Certain plants excrete a   15
sweet juice, apparently for the sake of eliminating something injurious from their sap; this is effected by glands at the base of the stipules[16] in some Leguminosae, and at the back of the leaf of the common laurel. This juice, though small in quantity, is greedily sought by insects. Let us now suppose a little sweet juice or nectar to be excreted by the inner bases of the petals of a flower. In this case insects in seeking the nectar would get dusted with pollen, and would certainly often transport the pollen from one flower to the stigma of another flower. The flowers of two distinct individuals of the same species would thus get crossed; and the act of crossing, we have good reason to believe (as will hereafter be more fully alluded to), would produce very vigorous seedlings, which consequently would have the best chance of flourishing and surviving. Some of these seedlings would probably inherit the nectar-excreting power. Those individual flowers which had the largest glands or nectaries, and which excreted most nectar, would be oftenest visited by insects, and would be oftenest crossed; and so in the long-run would gain the upper hand. Those flowers, also, which had their stamens and pistils[17] placed, in relation to the size and habits of the particular insects which visited them, so as to favor in any degree the transportal of their pollen from flower to flower, would likewise be favored or selected. We might have taken the case of insects visiting flowers for the sake of collecting pollen instead of nectar; and as pollen is formed for the sole object of fertilization, its destruction appears a simple loss to the plant; yet if a little pollen were carried, at first occasionally and then habitually, by the pollen-devouring insects from flower to flower, and a cross thus effected, although

---

[15] **Mr. Pierce** Unidentified.

[16] **stipules** Spines at the base of a leaf.

[17] **stamens and pistils** Sexual organs of plants. The male and female organs appear together in the same flower.

nine-tenths of the pollen were destroyed, it might still be a great gain to the plant; and those individuals which produced more and more pollen, and had larger and larger anthers,[18] would be selected.

When our plant, by this process of the continued preservation or natural selection of more and more attractive flowers, had been rendered highly attractive to insects, they would, unintentionally on their part, regularly carry pollen from flower to flower; and that they can most effectually do this, I could easily show by many striking instances. I will give only one—not as a very striking case, but as likewise illustrating one step in the separation of the sexes of plants, presently to be alluded to. Some holly-trees bear only male flowers, which have four stamens producing rather a small quantity of pollen, and a rudimentary pistil; other holly-trees bear only female flowers; these have a full-sized pistil, and four stamens with shrivelled anthers, in which not a grain of pollen can be detected. Having found a female tree exactly sixty yards from a male tree, I put the stigmas[19] of twenty flowers, taken from different branches, under the microscope, and on all, without exception, there were pollen-grains, and on some a profusion of pollen. As the wind had set for several days from the female to the male tree, the pollen could not thus have been carried. The weather had been cold and boisterous, and therefore not favorable to bees; nevertheless every female flower which I examined had been effectually fertilized by the bees, accidentally dusted with pollen, having flown from tree to tree in search of nectar. But to return to our imaginary case: as soon as the plant had been rendered so highly attractive to insects that pollen was regularly carried from flower to flower, another process might commence. No naturalist doubts the advantage of what has been called the "physiological division of labor"; hence we may believe that it would be advantageous to a plant to produce stamens alone in one flower or on one whole plant, and pistils alone in another flower or on another plant. In plants under culture and placed under new conditions of life, sometimes the male organs and sometimes the female organs become more or less impotent; now if we suppose this to occur in ever so slight a degree under nature, then as pollen is already carried regularly from flower to flower, and as a more complete separation of the sexes of our plant would be advantageous on the principle of the division of labor, individuals with this tendency more and more increased, would be continually favored or selected, until at last a complete separation of the sexes would be effected.

16

---

[18] **anthers** That part of the stamen that contains pollen.
[19] **stigmas** Where the plant's pollen develops.

Let us now turn to the nectar-feeding insects in our imaginary   17
case: we may suppose the plant of which we have been slowly
increasing the nectar by continued selection, to be a common plant;
and that certain insects depended in main part on its nectar for food.
I could give many facts, showing how anxious bees are to save time;
for instance, their habit of cutting holes and sucking the nectar at
the bases of certain flowers, which they can, with a very little more
trouble, enter by the mouth. Bearing such facts in mind, I can see no
reason to doubt that an accidental deviation in the size and form of
the body, or in the curvature and length of the proboscis,[20] etc., far
too slight to be appreciated by us, might profit a bee or other insect,
so that an individual so characterized would be able to obtain its
food more quickly, and so have a better chance of living and leaving
descendants. Its descendants would probably inherit a tendency to a
similar slight deviation of structure. The tubes of the corollas[21] of
the common red and incarnate clovers (Trifolium pratense and
incarnatum) do not on a hasty glance appear to differ in length; yet
the hive-bee can easily suck the nectar out of the incarnate clover,
but not out of the common red clover, which is visited by humble-
bees[22] alone; so that whole fields of the red clover offer in vain an
abundant supply of precious nectar to the hive-bee. Thus it might
be a great advantage to the hive-bee to have a slightly longer or differently constructed proboscis. On the other hand, I have found by
experiment that the fertility of clover greatly depends on bees visiting and moving parts of the corolla, so as to push the pollen on to
the stigmatic surface. Hence, again, if humble-bees were to become
rare in any country, it might be a great advantage to the red clover to
have a shorter or more deeply divided tube to its corolla, so that the
hive-bee could visit its flowers. Thus I can understand how a flower
and a bee might slowly become, either simultaneously or one after
the other, modified and adapted in the most perfect manner to each
other, by the continued preservation of individuals presenting
mutual and slightly favorable deviations of structure.

I am well aware that this doctrine of natural selection, exempli-   18
fied in the above imaginary instances, is open to the same objections
which were at first urged against Sir Charles Lyell's noble views[23] on

---

[20] **proboscis** Snout.
[21] **corollas** Inner set of floral petals.
[22] **humble-bees** Bumblebees.
[23] **Sir Charles Lyell's noble views** Lyell (1797–1875) was an English geologist whose landmark work, *Principles of Geology* (1830–1833), Darwin read while on
the *Beagle*. The book inspired Darwin, and the two scientists became friends. Lyell
was shown portions of *On the Origin of Species* while Darwin was writing it.

"the modern changes of the earth, as illustrative of geology"; but we now very seldom hear the action, for instance, of the coast-waves, called a trifling and insignificant cause, when applied to the excavation of gigantic valleys or to the formation of the longest lines of inland cliffs. Natural selection can act only by the preservation and accumulation of infinitesimally small inherited modifications, each profitable to the preserved being; and as modern geology has almost banished such views as the excavation of a great valley by a single diluvial[24] wave, so will natural selection, if it be a true principle, banish the belief of the continued creation of new organic beings, or of any great and sudden modification in their structure.

---

[24] **diluvial** Pertaining to a flood. Darwin means that geological changes, such as those that caused the Grand Canyon, were no longer thought of as occurring instantly by flood (or other catastrophes) but were considered to have developed over a long period of time, as he imagines happened in the evolution of the species.

QUESTIONS FOR CRITICAL READING

1. Darwin's metaphor "battle of life" (para. 1) introduces issues that might be thought extraneous to a scientific inquiry. What is the danger of using such a metaphor? What is the advantage of doing so?
2. Many religious groups reject Darwin's concept of natural selection, but they heartily accept human selection in the form of controlled breeding. Why would there be such a difference between the two?
3. Do you feel that the theory of natural selection is a positive force? Could it be directed by divine power?
4. In this work, there is no reference to human beings in terms of the process of selection. How might the principles at work on animals also work on people? Do you think that Darwin assumes this?
5. When this chapter was published in a later edition, Darwin added to its title "Survival of the Fittest." What issues or emotions does that new title raise that "Natural Selection" does not?

SUGGESTIONS FOR CRITICAL WRITING

1. In paragraph 13, Darwin uses imaginary examples. Compare the value of his genuine examples and these imaginary ones. How effective is the use of imaginary examples in an argument? What requirements should an imaginary example meet to be forceful in an argument? Do you find Darwin's imaginary examples to be strong or weak?

2. From paragraph 14 on, Darwin discusses the process of modification of a species through its beginning in the modification of an individual. Explain, insofar as you understand the concept, how a species could be modified by a variation occurring in just one individual. In your explanation, use Darwin's rhetorical technique of the imaginary example.

3. Write an essay that takes as its thesis statement the following sentence from paragraph 18: "Natural selection can act only by the preservation and accumulation of infinitesimally small inherited modifications, each profitable to the preserved being." Be sure to examine the work carefully for other statements by Darwin that add strength, clarity, and meaning to this one. You may also employ the Darwinian device of presenting imaginary instances in your essay.

4. A controversy exists concerning the Darwinian theory of evolution. Explore the *Readers' Guide to Periodical Literature* (a reference you can find at your local or college library) and the Internet for up-to-date information on the creationist-evolutionist conflict in schools. Look up either or both terms to see what articles you can find. Define the controversy and take a stand on it. Use your knowledge of natural selection gained from this piece. Remember, too, that Darwin was trained as a minister of the church and was concerned about religious opinion.

5. When Darwin wrote this piece, he believed that sexual selection was of great importance in evolutionary changes in species. Assuming that this belief is true, establish the similarities between sexual selection in plants and animals and sexual selection, as you have observed it, in people. Paragraphs 10–12 discuss this issue. Darwin does not discuss selection in human beings, but it is clear that physical and stylistic distinctions between the sexes have some bearing on selection. Assuming that to be true, what qualities in people (physical and mental) are likely to survive? Why?

6. **CONNECTIONS**   Which of Francis Bacon's four idols (p. 579) would have made it most difficult for Darwin's contemporaries to accept the theory of evolution, despite the mass of evidence he presented? Do the idols interfere with people's ability to evaluate evidence?

7. **CONNECTIONS**   To what extent are Darwin's theories a threat to public morality? Consider Iris Murdoch's "Morality and Religion" (p. 729) and Friedrich Nietzsche's "Morality as Anti-Nature" (p. 713) in Part Seven. How do their ideas on morality relate to Darwin's ideas on the survival of the fittest? Some people in the mid nineteenth century feared that Darwin's theories could undermine religion and therefore religious codes of ethics and morality. Why do you think some people felt that way? Explain. Do you think such fears were legitimate? Why or why not?

8. **SEEING CONNECTIONS**   If Darwin were on the rock with William Cullen Bryant and Thomas Cole in Durand's *Kindred Spirits* (p. 576),

what would he have pointed to in the visual landscape as a means of forwarding his theories of natural selection? Given the opinions Bryant would likely have had, how difficult would it have been for Darwin to convince him and Cole (or Durand) of the reasonableness of Darwin's theories? Write an imaginary dialogue with all four characters contributing. Use specific visual elements in the painting as starting points.

RACHEL CARSON
The Sunless Sea

RACHEL CARSON (1907–1964) was educated at the Pennsylvania College for Women (now Chatham College) and Johns Hopkins University, where she received a master's degree in zoology in 1932. She continued her studies at the Marine Biological Laboratory of the Woods Hole Oceanographic Institute in Massachusetts. After teaching biology at the University of Maryland, Carson joined the Bureau of Fisheries (now the United States Fish and Wildlife Service) in 1936. She became editor-in-chief of its publications in 1949. Her first best-selling book on science, *The Sea Around Us* (1951), earned her a National Book Award, among many other prizes. In 1952 she left government service to devote herself to research and writing.

Although Rachel Carson was not a scientist, she was frequently praised for her science writing, which distinguished her from others in her field. She was a painstaking writer who, by her own admission, wrote late into the night and subjected her work to many revisions. In addition to magazine articles, she wrote a number of books, including *Under the Sea-Wind: A Naturalist's Picture of Ocean Life* (1941), *The Edge of the Sea* (1955), and *Silent Spring* (1962). She was eventually elected to the British Royal Society of Literature and the American Institute of Arts and Letters.

Her most successful book, *Silent Spring*, brought to the attention of the nation and the world the harmful effects of widespread use of pesticides. It sold more than 500,000 copies, which astonished Carson. The book had an enormous influence on the curtailment of the use of pesticides such as DDT, which had wreaked havoc on numerous species, especially birds. Only in recent years have some species begun to recover to normal populations.

From *The Sea Around Us.*

When she wrote *Silent Spring*, Carson realized that many scientists knew that the long-term effects of the pesticides they were developing would be devastating. The reason for their silence, according to Carson, was clear: the insecticide manufacturers supported entomologists with generous research grants, essentially "buying off" the very scientists who might have made a difference by informing the public about the dangers of spraying.

In *The Sea Around Us* (1951), Carson was not so much sounding an alarm as she was presenting a picture of a world that at the time was not known to the general public. Naturally, much has been discovered about the sea since the book's publication, but most of what Carson wrote is still quite relevant today. Indeed, when she wrote these pages she was a pioneer in oceanic ecology.

Carson's Rhetoric

Carson was praised for her ability to communicate matters of science to a wide audience. In college, she was an English major before she switched to biology; her rhetorical style, although not specifically literary in this essay, is characterized by careful writing, vivid description, and metaphors designed to move, as well as inform, her audience.

Her technique is straightforward. After establishing the expanse and depth of the world's oceans, Carson begins a survey of those who have tried to discover its secrets. She mentions William Beebe and Otis Barton, followed by French divers in the 1950s (she updated her details in a later edition of the book). She then goes through history to point to Sir John Ross in 1818, Edward Forbes in the 1850s, the surveying ship *Bulldog* in 1860, the *Challenger* in 1872—all to show that people had been gradually learning that life existed at depths that had seemed unlikely if not impossible.

Beginning in paragraph 10, Carson describes the contemporary situation in which a "'layer' of some sort" (para. 12) indicated that there were reflective bodies in the water that postwar sonic equipment was able to detect. But no one could identify what the layer consisted of. The likelihood, she suggests, is that the layer may be comprised of plankton or perhaps tiny squid that undulate upward toward the night sky, then downward away from daylight. In paragraphs 12–16, she describes attempts to observe the ocean depths and to discover what the "phantom bottom" (para. 13) actually was.

By paragraph 25 Carson has established that there are abundant sources of food at very deep levels of the ocean. Whales, seals, and other animals had been feeding at great depths for millions of years, so it should have been no surprise. Yet until recently there had been no way to study the truly great depths of the oceans. Paragraphs 26–30 examine the development and habits of whales and seals, reporting on their strange and unusual behavior. Paragraphs 31–34 examine the phenomenon of very high pressures experienced in the ocean's depths.

Then, surprisingly, she turns to the ocean lights that appear in depths that seemed to be entirely without light. In paragraphs 36–41 we find that fish of various sorts sometimes have vivid colors, although rays of light hardly reach their depths. Some aquatic species are luminescent, and others have only a sense of touch to inform them of their whereabouts. In paragraph 43 she states, "Pressure, darkness, and— we should have added only a few years ago—silence, are the conditions of life in the deep sea." She notes that military hydrophones— sound sensors planted throughout the oceans to detect submarines during World War II—picked up a wide variety of sounds emanating from many different species all through the oceans.

She ends her essay with some speculation on the age and range of the life in the depths of the seas, focusing on sharks, fossils, and fossil fish, such as the coelacanths, which were first discovered in 1938 after being assumed to have been extinct for 60 million years. Since the publication of her book, numerous other coelacanths have been fished from the sea, but they still remain mysterious animals.

Carson's rhetorical methods are marked by extensive description of historical explorations of the ocean, followed by a review of modern and contemporary reports of discovery and oceanic activity. Her capacity to describe the discoveries is part of her style and part of the appeal of this essay. She makes the information much more accessible by gathering it carefully and organizing it effectively, beginning with the earliest exploration, ending with the current understanding of explorers and scientists. To that she adds details concerning the life found at various levels of the deep. Here, too, she pauses to describe phenomena in detail so that we have a more tangible understanding of what is known about the darkest environments of the ocean.

PREREADING QUESTIONS: WHAT TO READ FOR

The following prereading questions may help you anticipate key issues in the discussion of Rachel Carson's "The Sunless Sea." Keeping them in mind during your first reading of the selection should help focus your attention.

- What had been known about the depths of the ocean in the nineteenth century?

- Which mysteries seem yet to be resolved?
- What had been learned about the ocean in Carson's time that had not been known before?

The Sunless Sea

Where great whales come sailing by,
Sail and sail, with unshut eye.
— MATTHEW ARNOLD

Between the sunlit surface waters of the open sea and the hid- 1
den hills and valleys of the ocean floor lies the least known region of
the sea. These deep, dark waters, with all their mysteries and their
unsolved problems, cover a very considerable part of the earth. The
whole world ocean extends over about three-fourths of the surface
of the globe. If we subtract the shallow areas of the continental
shelves and the scattered banks and shoals, where at least the pale
ghost of sunlight moves over the underlying bottom, there still
remains about half the earth that is covered by miles-deep, lightless
water, that has been dark since the world began.

This region has withheld its secrets more obstinately than any 2
other. Man, with all his ingenuity, has been able to venture only to its
threshold. Carrying tanks of compressed air, he can swim down to
depths of about 300 feet. He can descend about 500 feet wearing a
diving helmet and a rubberized suit. Only a few men in all the history
of the world have had the experience of descending, alive, beyond the
range of visible light. The first to do so were William Beebe[1] and Otis
Barton; in the bathysphere, they reached a depth of 3028 feet in the
open ocean off Bermuda, in the year 1934. Barton alone, in the summer of 1949, descended to a depth of 4500 feet off California, in a
steel sphere of somewhat different design; and in 1953 French divers
penetrated depths greater than a mile, existing for several hours in a
zone of cold and darkness where the presence of living man had
never before been known.

Although only a fortunate few can ever visit the deep sea, the pre- 3
cise instruments of the oceanographer, recording light penetration,
pressure, salinity, and temperature, have given us the materials with

---

[1]**William Beebe (1877–1962)** With Otis Barton (1899–?), was the first explorer
to reach depths of half a mile in the 1930s.

which to reconstruct in imagination these eerie, forbidding regions. Unlike the surface waters, which are sensitive to every gust of wind, which know day and night, respond to the pull of sun and moon, and change as the seasons change, the deep waters are a place where change comes slowly, if at all. Down beyond the reach of the sun's rays, there is no alternation of light and darkness. There is rather an endless night, as old as the sea itself. For most of its creatures, groping their way endlessly through its black waters, it must be a place of hunger, where food is scarce and hard to find, a shelterless place where there is no sanctuary from ever-present enemies, where one can only move on and on, from birth to death, through the darkness, confined as in a prison to his own particular layer of the sea.

They used to say that nothing could live in the deep sea. It was   4
a belief that must have been easy to accept, for without proof to the contrary, how could anyone conceive of life in such a place?

A century ago the British biologist Edward Forbes wrote: "As   5
we descend deeper and deeper into this region, the inhabitants become more and more modified, and fewer and fewer, indicating our approach to an abyss where life is either extinguished, or exhibits but a few sparks to mark its lingering presence." Yet Forbes urged further exploration of "this vast deep-sea region" to settle forever the question of the existence of life at great depths.

Even then the evidence was accumulating. Sir John Ross, during   6
his exploration of the arctic seas in 1818, had brought up from a depth of 1000 fathoms mud in which there were worms, "thus proving there was animal life in the bed of the ocean notwithstanding the darkness, stillness, silence, and immense pressure produced by more than a mile of superincumbent water."

Then from the surveying ship *Bulldog*, examining a proposed   7
northern route for a cable from Faroe to Labrador in 1860, came another report. The *Bulldog's* sounding line, which at one place had been allowed to lie for some time on the bottom at a depth of 1260 fathoms, came up with 13 starfish clinging to it. Through these starfish, the ship's naturalist wrote, "the deep has sent forth the long coveted message." But not all the zoologists of the day were prepared to accept the message. Some doubters asserted that the starfish had "convulsively embraced" the line somewhere on the way back to the surface.

In the same year, 1860, a cable in the Mediterranean was raised   8
for repairs from a depth of 1200 fathoms. It was found to be heavily encrusted with corals and other sessile[2] animals that had attached themselves at an early stage of development and grown to maturity

---

[2] **sessile** Attached directly at the base.

over a period of months or years. There was not the slightest chance that they had become entangled in the cable as it was being raised to the surface.

Then the *Challenger*, the first ship ever equipped for oceano-   9 graphic exploration, set out from England in the year 1872 and traced a course around the globe. From bottoms lying under miles of water, from silent deeps carpeted with red clay ooze, and from all the lightless intermediate depths, net-haul after net-haul of strange and fantastic creatures came up and were spilled out on the decks. Poring over the weird beings thus brought up for the first time into the light of day, beings no man had ever seen before, the *Challenger* scientists realized that life existed even on the deepest floor of the abyss.

The recent discovery that a living cloud of some unknown crea-   10 tures is spread over much of the ocean at a depth of several hundred fathoms below the surface is the most exciting thing that has been learned about the ocean for many years.

When, during the first quarter of the twentieth century, echo   11 sounding was developed to allow ships while under way to record the depth of the bottom, probably no one suspected that it would also provide a means of learning something about deep-sea life. But operators of the new instruments soon discovered that the sound waves, directed downward from the ship like a beam of light, were reflected back from any solid object they met. Answering echoes were returned from intermediate depths, presumably from schools of fish, whales, or submarines; then a second echo was received from the bottom.

These facts were so well established by the late 1930s that fish-   12 ermen had begun to talk about using their fathometers to search for schools of herring. Then the war brought the whole subject under strict security regulations, and little more was heard about it. In 1946, however, the United States Navy issued a significant bulletin. It was reported that several scientists, working with sonic equipment in deep water off the California coast, had discovered a wide-spread "layer" of some sort, which gave back an answering echo to the sound waves. This reflecting layer, seemingly suspended between the surface and the floor of the Pacific, was found over an area 300 miles wide. It lay from 1000 to 1500 feet below the surface. The discovery was made by three scientists, C. F. Eyring, R. J. Christensen, and R. W. Raitt, aboard the U.S.S. *Jasper* in 1942, and for a time this mysterious phenomenon, of wholly unknown nature, was called the ECR layer. Then in 1945 Martin W. Johnson, marine biologist of the Scripps Institution of Oceanography, made a further discovery which gave the first clue to the nature of the layer. Working aboard the vessel, *E. W. Scripps*, Johnson found that whatever sent back the echoes moved upward and downward in rhythmic fashion, being found near the surface at night, in deep water during the day. This discovery disposed of speculations that the reflections came from something inanimate, perhaps a mere physical discontinuity in the water, and showed that the layer is composed of living creatures capable of controlled movement.

From this time on, discoveries about the sea's "phantom bottom" came rapidly. With widespread use of echo-sounding instruments, it has become clear that the phenomenon is not something peculiar to the coast of California alone. It occurs almost universally in deep ocean basins—drifting by day at a depth of several hundred fathoms, at night rising to the surface, and again, before sunrise, sinking into the depths. 13

On the passage of the U.S.S. *Henderson* from San Diego to the Antarctic in 1947, the reflecting layer was detected during the greater part of each day, at depths varying from 150 to 450 fathoms, and on a later run from San Diego to Yokosuka, Japan, the *Henderson*'s fathometer again recorded the layer every day, suggesting that it exists almost continuously across the Pacific. 14

During July and August 1947, the U.S.S. *Nereus* made a continuous fathogram from Pearl Harbor to the Arctic and found the scattering layer over all deep waters along this course. It did not develop, however, in the shallow Bering and Chukchi seas. Sometimes in the morning, the *Nereus*'s fathogram showed two layers, responding in different ways to the growing illumination of the water; both descended into deep water, but there was an interval of twenty miles between the two descents. 15

Despite attempts to sample it or photograph it, no one is sure what the layer is, although the discovery may be made any day. There are three principal theories, each of which has its group of supporters. According to these theories, the sea's phantom bottom may consist of small planktonic shrimps, of fishes, or of squids. 16

As for the plankton theory, one of the most convincing arguments is the well-known fact that many plankton creatures make regular vertical migrations of hundreds of feet, rising toward the surface at night, sinking down below the zone of light penetration very early in the morning. This is, of course, exactly the behavior of the scattering layer. Whatever composes it is apparently strongly repelled by sunlight. The creatures of the layer seem almost to be held prisoner at the end—or beyond the end—of the sun's rays throughout the hours of daylight, waiting only for the welcome return of darkness 17 to hurry upward into the surface waters. But what is the power that repels; and what the attraction that draws them surfaceward once the inhibiting force is removed? Is it comparative safety from enemies that makes them seek darkness? Is it more abundant food near the surface that lures them back under cover of night?

Those who say that fish are the reflectors of the sound waves usually account for the vertical migrations of the layer as suggesting that the fish are feeding on planktonic shrimp and are following their food. They believe that the air bladder of a fish is, of all structures concerned, most likely from its construction to return a strong echo. There is one outstanding difficulty in the way of accepting this theory: we have no other evidence that concentrations of fish are universally present in the oceans. In fact, almost everything else we know suggests that the really dense populations of fish live over the continental shelves or in certain very definite determined zones of the open ocean where food is particularly abundant. If the reflecting layer is eventually proved to be composed of fish, the prevailing views of fish distribution will have to be radically revised.

The most startling theory (and the one that seems to have the fewest supporters) is that the layer consists of concentrations of squid, "hovering below the illuminated zone of the sea and awaiting the arrival of darkness in which to resume their raids into the plankton-rich surface waters." Proponents of this theory argue that squid are abundant enough, and of wide enough distribution, to give the echoes that have been picked up almost everywhere from the equator to the two poles. Squid are known to be the sole food of the sperm whale, found in the open oceans in all temperate and tropical waters. They also form the exclusive diet of the bottlenosed whale and are eaten extensively by most other toothed whales, by seals, and by many sea birds. All these facts argue that they must be prodigiously abundant.

It is true that men who have worked close to the sea surface at night have received vivid impressions of the abundance and activity of squids in the surface waters in darkness. Long ago Johan Hjort[3] wrote:

"One night we were hauling long lines on the Faroe slope, working with an electric lamp hanging over the side in order to see the line, when like lightning flashes one squid after another shot towards the light . . . In October 1902 we were one night steaming outside the slopes of the coast banks of Norway, and for many miles we could see the squids moving in the surface waters like luminous

[3]**Johan Hjort (1869–1948)** Norwegian marine biologist.

bubbles, resembling large milky white electric lamps being constantly lit and extinguished."[4]

Thor Heyerdahl[5] reports that at night his raft was literally bom- 22 barded by squids; and Richard Fleming says that in his oceanographic work off the coast of Panama it was common to see immense schools of squid gathering at the surface at night and leaping upward toward the lights that were used by the men to operate their instruments. But equally spectacular surface displays of shrimp have been seen, and most people find it difficult to believe in the ocean-wide abundance of squid.

Deep-water photography holds much promise for the solution 23 of the mystery of the phantom bottom. There are technical difficulties, such as the problem of holding a camera still as it swings at the end of a long cable, twisting and turning, suspended from a ship which itself moves with the sea. Some of the pictures so taken look as though the photographer has pointed his camera at a starry sky and swung it in an arc as he exposed the film. Yet the Norwegian biologist Gunnar Rollefson had an encouraging experience in correlating photography with echograms. On the research ship *Johan Hjort* off the Lofoten Islands, he persistently got reflection of sound from schools of fish in 20 to 30 fathoms. A specially constructed camera was lowered to the depth indicated by the echogram. When developed, the film showed moving shapes of fish at a distance, and a large and clearly recognizable cod appeared in the beam of light and hovered in front of the lens.

Direct sampling of the layer is the logical means of discovering 24 its identity, but the problem is to develop large nets that can be operated rapidly enough to capture swift-moving animals. Scientists at Woods Hole, Massachusetts, have towed ordinary plankton nets in the layer and have found that euphausiid[6] shrimps, glassworms, and other deep-water plankton are concentrated there; but there is still a possibility that the layer itself may actually be made up of larger forms feeding on the shrimps—too large or swift to be taken in the presently used nets. New nets may give the answer. Television is another possibility.

Shadowy and indefinite though they be, these recent indications 25 of an abundant life at mid-depths agree with the reports of the only

---

[4] From *The Depths of the Ocean*, by Sir John Murray and Johan Hjort, 1912 edition, Macmillan & Co., p. 649. [Carson's note]

[5] **Thor Heyerdahl (1914–2002)** Famous Norwegian explorer.

[6] **euphausiid** A small luminescent shrimp that migrates up and down in the ocean.

observers who have actually visited comparable depths and brought back eyewitness accounts of what they saw. William Beebe's impressions from the bathysphere were of a life far more abundant and varied than he had been prepared to find, although, over a period of six years, he had made many hundreds of net hauls in the same area. More than a quarter of a mile down, he reported aggregations of living things "as thick as I have ever seen them." At half a mile — the deepest descent of the bathysphere — Dr. Beebe recalled that "there was no instant when a mist of plankton . . . was not swirling in the path of the beam."

The existence of an abundant deep-sea fauna was discovered, probably millions of years ago, by certain whales and also, it now appears, by seals. The ancestors of all whales, we know by fossil remains, were land mammals. They must have been predatory beasts, if we are to judge by their powerful jaws and teeth. Perhaps in their foragings about the deltas of great rivers or around the edges of shallow seas, they discovered the abundance of fish and other marine life and over the centuries formed the habit of following them farther and farther into the sea. Little by little their bodies took on a form more suitable for aquatic life; their hind limbs were reduced to rudiments, which may be discovered in a modern whale by dissection, and the forelimbs were modified into organs for steering and balancing. 26

Eventually the whales, as though to divide the sea's food resources among them, became separated into three groups: the plankton-eaters, the fish-eaters, and the squid-eaters. The plankton-eating whales can exist only where there are dense masses of small shrimp or copepods to supply their enormous food requirements. This limits them, except for scattered areas, to Arctic and Antarctic waters and the high temperate latitudes. Fish-eating whales may find food over a somewhat wider range of ocean, but they are restricted to places where there are enormous populations of schooling fish. The blue water of the tropics and of the open ocean basins offers little to either of these groups. But that immense, square-headed, formidably toothed whale known as the cachalot or sperm whale discovered long ago what men have known for only a short time — that hundreds of fathoms below the almost untenanted surface waters of these regions there is an abundant animal life. The sperm whale has taken these deep waters for his hunting grounds; his quarry is the deep-water population of squids including the giant squid Architeuthis, which lives pelagically[7] at depths of 1500 feet or 27

---

[7] **pelagically** Living in the open ocean.

more. The head of the sperm whale is often marked with long stripes, which consist of a great number of circular scars made by the suckers of the squid. From this evidence we can imagine the battles that go on, in the darkness of the deep water, between these two huge creatures—the sperm whale with its 70-ton bulk, the squid with a body as long as 30 feet, and writhing, grasping arms extending the total length of the animal to perhaps 50 feet.

The greatest depth at which the giant squid lives is not defi- 28 nitely known, but there is one instructive piece of evidence about the depth to which sperm whales descend, presumably in search of the squids. In April 1932, the cable repair ship *All America* was investigating an apparent break in the submarine cable between Balboa in the Canal Zone and Esmeraldas, Ecuador. The cable was brought to the surface off the coast of Colombia. Entangled in it was a dead 45-foot male sperm whale. The submarine cable was twisted around the lower jaw and was wrapped around one flipper, the body, and the caudal flukes. The cable was raised from a depth of 540 fathoms, or 3240 feet.

Some of the seals also appear to have discovered the hidden 29 food reserves of the deep ocean. It has long been something of a mystery where, and on what, the northern fur seals of the eastern Pacific feed during the winter, which they spend off the coast of North America from California to Alaska. There is no evidence that they are feeding to any great extent on sardines, mackerel, or other commercially important fishes. Presumably four million seals could not compete with commercial fishermen for the same species without the fact being known. But there is some evidence on the diet of the fur seals, and it is highly significant. Their stomachs have yielded the bones of a species of fish that has never been seen alive. Indeed, not even its remains have been found anywhere except in the stomachs of seals. Ichthyologists say that this "seal fish" belongs to a group that typically inhabits very deep water, off the edge of the continental shelf.

How either whales or seals endure the tremendous pressure 30 changes involved in dives of several hundred fathoms is not definitely known. They are warm-blooded mammals like ourselves. Caisson disease, which is caused by the rapid accumulation of nitrogen bubbles in the blood with sudden release of pressure, kills human divers if they are brought up rapidly from depths of 200 feet or so. Yet, according to the testimony of whalers, a baleen whale, when harpooned, can dive straight down to a depth of half a mile, as measured by the amount of line carried out. From these depths, where it has sustained a pressure of half a ton on every inch of body, it returns almost immediately to the surface. The most plausible explanation is that, unlike the diver, who has air pumped to him while he is under water, the whale has in its body only the limited supply it carries down, and does not have enough nitrogen in its blood to do serious harm. The plain truth is, however, that we really do not know, since it is obviously impossible to confine a living whale and experiment on it, and almost as difficult to dissect a dead one satisfactorily.

At first thought it seems a paradox that creatures of such great 31 fragility as the glass sponge and the jellyfish can live under the conditions of immense pressure that prevail in deep water. For creatures at home in the deep sea, however, the saving fact is that the pressure inside their tissues is the same as that without, and as long as this balance is preserved, they are no more inconvenienced by a pressure of a ton or so than we are by ordinary atmospheric pressure. And most abyssal creatures, it must be remembered, live out their whole lives in a comparatively restricted zone, and are never required to adjust themselves to extreme changes of pressure.

But of course there are exceptions, and the real miracle of sea 32 life in relation to great pressure is not the animal that lives its whole life on the bottom, bearing a pressure of perhaps five or six tons, but those that regularly move up and down through hundreds or thousands of feet of vertical change. The small shrimps and other planktonic creatures that descend into deep water during the day are examples. Fish that possess air bladders, on the other hand, are vitally affected by abrupt changes of pressure, as anyone knows who has seen a trawler's net raised from a hundred fathoms. Apart from the accident of being captured in a net and hauled up through waters of rapidly diminishing pressures, fish may sometimes wander out of the zone to which they are adjusted and find themselves unable to return. Perhaps in their pursuit of food they roam upward to the ceiling of the zone that is theirs, and beyond whose invisible boundary they may not stray without meeting alien and inhospitable conditions. Moving from layer to layer of drifting plankton as they feed, they may pass beyond the boundary. In the lessened pressure of these upper waters the gas enclosed within the air bladder expands. The fish becomes lighter and more buoyant. Perhaps he tries to fight his way down again, opposing the upward lift with all the power of his muscles. If he does not succeed, he "falls" to the surface, injured and dying, for the abrupt release of pressure from without causes distension and rupture of the tissues.

The compression of the sea under its own weight is relatively 33 slight, and there is no basis for the old and picturesque belief that, at the deeper levels, the water resists the downward passage of objects from the surface. According to this belief, sinking ships, the bodies of drowned men, and presumably the bodies of the larger sea animals not consumed by hungry scavengers, never reach the bottom, but come to rest at some level determined by the relation of their own weight to the compression of the water, there to drift forever. The fact is that anything will continue to sink as long as its specific gravity is greater than that of the surrounding water, and all large bodies descend, in a matter of a few days, to the ocean floor. As mute testimony to this fact, we bring up from the deepest ocean basins the teeth of sharks and the hard ear bones of whales.

Nevertheless the weight of sea water—the pressing down of 34 miles of water upon all the underlying layers—does have a certain effect upon the water itself. If this downward compression could suddenly be relaxed by some miraculous suspension of natural laws, the sea level would rise about 93 feet all over the world. This would shift the Atlantic coastline of the United States westward a hundred miles or more and alter other familiar geographic outlines all over the world.

Immense pressure, then, is one of the governing conditions of 35 life in the deep sea; darkness is another. The unrelieved darkness of the deep waters has produced weird and incredible modifications of the abyssal fauna. It is a blackness so divorced from the world of the sunlight that probably only the few men who have seen it with their own eyes can visualize it. We know that light fades out rapidly with descent below the surface. The red rays are gone at the end of the first 200 or 300 feet, and with them all the orange and yellow warmth of the sun. Then the greens fade out, and at 1000 feet only a deep, dark, brilliant blue is left. In very clear waters the violet rays of the spectrum may penetrate another thousand feet. Beyond this is only the blackness of the deep sea.

In a curious way, the colors of marine animals tend to be related 36 to the zone in which they live. Fishes of the surface waters, like the mackerel and herring, often are blue or green; so are the floats of the Portuguese men-of-war and the azure-tinted wings of the swimming snails. Down below the diatom[8] meadows and the drifting sargassum weed, where the water becomes ever more deeply, brilliantly blue, many creatures are crystal clear. Their glassy, ghostly forms blend with their surroundings and make it easier for them to elude the ever-present, ever-hungry enemy. Such are the transparent hordes

---

[8]**diatom** One-celled algae that congregate in layers in the ocean.

of the arrowworms or glassworms, the comb jellies, and the larvae of many fishes.

At a thousand feet, and on down to the very end of the sun's rays, silvery fishes are common, and many others are red, drab brown, or black. Pteropods are a dark violet. Arrowworms, whose relatives in the upper layers are colorless, are here a deep red. Jellyfish medusae, which above would be transparent, at a depth of 1000 feet are a deep brown.   37

At depths greater than 1500 feet, all the fishes are black, deep violet, or brown, but the prawns wear amazing hues of red, scarlet, and purple. Why, no one can say. Since all the red rays are strained out of the water far above this depth, the scarlet raiment of these creatures can only look black to their neighbors.   38

The deep sea has its stars, and perhaps here and there an eerie and transient equivalent of moonlight, for the mysterious phenomenon of luminescence is displayed by perhaps half of all the fishes that live in dimly lit or darkened waters, and by many of the lower forms as well. Many fishes carry luminous torches that can be turned on or off at will, presumably helping them find or pursue their prey. Others have rows of lights over their bodies, in patterns that vary from species to species and may be a sort of recognition mark or badge by which the bearer can be known as friend or enemy. The deep-sea squid ejects a spurt of fluid that becomes a luminous cloud, the counterpart of the "ink" of his shallow-water relative.   39

Down beyond the reach of even the longest and strongest of the sun's rays, the eyes of fishes become enlarged, as though to make the most of any chance illumination of whatever sort, or they may become telescopic, large of lens, and protruding. In deep-sea fishes, hunting always in dark waters, the eyes tend to lose the "cones" or color-perceiving cells of the retina, and to increase the "rods," which perceive dim light. Exactly the same modification is seen on land among the strictly nocturnal prowlers which, like abyssal fish, never see the sunlight.   40

In their world of darkness, it would seem likely that some of the animals might have become blind, as has happened to some cave fauna. So, indeed, many of them have, compensating for the lack of eyes with marvelously developed feelers and long, slender fins and processes with which they grope their way, like so many blind men with canes, their whole knowledge of friends, enemies, or food coming to them through the sense of touch.   41

The last traces of plant life are left behind in the thin upper layer of water, for no plant can live below about 600 feet even in very clear water, and few find enough sunlight for their food-manufacturing activities below 200 feet. Since no animal can make its own food,   42 the creatures of the deeper waters live a strange, almost parasitic existence of utter dependence on the upper layers. These hungry carnivores prey fiercely and relentlessly upon each other, yet the whole community is ultimately dependent upon the slow rain of descending food particles from above. The components of this never-ending rain are the dead and dying plants and animals from the surface, or from one of the intermediate layers. For each of the horizontal zones or communities of the sea that lie, in tier after tier, between the surface and the sea bottom, the food supply is different and in general poorer than for the layer above. There is a hint of the fierce and uncompromising competition for food in the saber-toothed jaws of some of the small, dragonlike fishes of the deeper waters, in the immense mouths and in the elastic and distensible bodies that make it possible for a fish to swallow another several times its size, enjoying swift repletion after a long fast.

43 Pressure, darkness, and — we should have added only a few years ago — silence, are the conditions of life in the deep sea. But we know now that the conception of the sea as a silent place is wholly false. Wide experience with hydrophones and other listening devices for the detection of submarines has proved that, around the shore lines of much of the world, there is the extraordinary uproar produced by fishes, shrimps, porpoises, and probably other forms not yet identified. There has been little investigation as yet of sound in the deep, offshore areas, but when the crew of the *Atlantis* lowered a hydrophone into deep water off Bermuda, they recorded strange mewing sounds, shrieks, and ghostly moans, the sources of which have not been traced. But fish of shallower zones have been captured and confined in aquaria, where their voices have been recorded for comparison with sounds heard at sea, and in many cases satisfactory identification can be made.

44 During the Second World War the hydrophone network set up by the United States Navy to protect the entrance to Chesapeake Bay was temporarily made useless when, in the spring of 1942, the speakers at the surface began to give forth, every evening, a sound described as being like "a pneumatic drill tearing up pavement." The extraneous noises that came over the hydrophones completely masked the sounds of the passage of ships. Eventually it was discovered that the sounds were the voices of fish known as croakers, which in the spring move into Chesapeake Bay from their offshore wintering grounds. As soon as the noise had been identified and analyzed, it was possible to screen it out with an electric filter, so that once more only the sounds of ships came through the speakers.

45 Later in the same year, a chorus of croakers was discovered off the pier of the Scripps Institution at La Jolla. Every year from May

until late September the evening chorus begins about sunset, and "increases gradually to a steady uproar of harsh froggy croaks, with a background of soft drumming. This continues unabated for two to three hours and finally tapers off to individual outbursts at rare intervals." Several species of croakers isolated in aquaria gave sounds similar to the "froggy croaks," but the authors of the soft background drumming — presumably another species of croaker — have not yet been discovered.

One of the most extraordinarily widespread sounds of the   46 undersea is the crackling, sizzling sound, like dry twigs burning or fat frying, heard near beds of the snapping shrimp. This is a small, round shrimp, about half an inch in diameter, with one very large claw which it uses to stun its prey. The shrimp are forever clicking the two joints of this claw together, and it is the thousands of clicks that collectively produce the noise known as shrimp crackle. No one had any idea the little snapping shrimps were so abundant or so widely distributed until their signals began to be picked up on hydrophones. They have been heard over a broad band that extends around the world, between latitudes 35° N and 35° S (for example, from Cape Hatteras to Buenos Aires) in ocean waters less than 30 fathoms deep.

Mammals as well as fishes and crustaceans contribute to the   47 undersea chorus. Biologists listening through a hydrophone in an estuary of the St. Lawrence River heard "high-pitched resonant whistles and squeals, varied with the ticking and clucking sounds slightly reminiscent of a string orchestra tuning up, as well as mew-ing and occasional chirps." This remarkable medley of sounds was heard only while schools of the white porpoise were seen passing up or down the river, and so was assumed to be produced by them.

The mysteriousness, the eeriness, the ancient unchangingness of   48 the great depths have led many people to suppose that some very old forms of life — some "living fossils" — may be lurking undiscov-ered in the deep ocean. Some such hope may have been in the minds of the *Challenger* scientists. The forms they brought up in their nets were weird enough, and most of them had never before been seen by man. But basically they were modern types. There was nothing like the trilobites of Cambrian[9] time or the sea scorpions of the Silurian,[10] nothing reminiscent of the great marine reptiles that invaded the sea in the Mesozoic.[11] Instead, there were modern

---

[9] **Cambrian** Geologic period of 544–2500 million years ago.
[10] **Silurian** Geologic period of 438–505 million years ago.
[11] **Mesozoic** Geologic era of 98–286 million years ago.

fishes, squids, and shrimps, strangely and grotesquely modified, to be sure, for life in the difficult deep-sea world, but clearly types that have developed in rather recent geologic time.

Far from being the original home of life, the deep sea has proba- 49 bly been inhabited for a relatively short time. While life was developing and flourishing in the surface waters, along the shores, and perhaps in the rivers and swamps, two immense regions of the earth still forbade invasion by living things. These were the continents and the abyss. As we have seen, the immense difficulties of surviving on land were first overcome by colonists from the sea about 300 million years ago. The abyss, with its unending darkness, its crushing pressures, its glacial cold, presented even more formidable difficulties. Probably the successful invasion of this region—at least by higher forms of life—occurred somewhat later.

Yet in recent years there have been one or two significant hap- 50 penings that have kept alive the hope that the deep sea may, after all, conceal strange links with the past. In December 1938, off the southeast tip of Africa, an amazing fish was caught alive in a trawl— a fish that was supposed to have been dead for at least 60 million years! This is to say, the last known fossil remains of its kind date from the Cretaceous,[12] and no living example had been recognized in historic time until this lucky net-haul.

The fishermen who brought it up in their trawl from a depth of 51 only 40 fathoms realized that this five-foot, bright blue fish, with its large head and strangely shaped scales, fins, and tail, was different from anything that they ever caught before, and on their return to port they took it to the nearest museum, where it was christened Latimeria. It was identified as a coelacanth, or one of an incredibly ancient group of fishes that first appeared in the seas some 300 million years ago. Rocks representing the next 200 million and more years of earth history yielded fossil coelacanths; then, in the Cretaceous, the record of these fishes came to an end. After 60 million years of mysterious oblivion, one of the group, Latimeria, then appeared before the eyes of the South African fishermen, apparently little changed in structure from its ancient ancestors. But where had these fishes been in the meantime?

The story of the coelacanths did not end in 1938. Believing there 52 must be other such fish in the sea, an ichthyologist in South Africa, Professor J. L. B. Smith, began a patient search that lasted fourteen years before it was successful. Then, in December 1952, a second coelacanth was captured near the island of Anjouan, off the northwestern tip of Madagascar. It differed enough from Latimeria to be

---

[12] **Cretaceous** Geologic period of 65–208 million years ago.

placed in a separate genus, but like the first coelacanth known in modern times, it can tell us much of a shadowy chapter in the evolution of living things.

Occasionally a very primitive type of shark, known from its   53 puckered gills as a "frillshark," is taken in waters between a quarter of a mile and half a mile down. Most of these have been caught in Norwegian and Japanese waters—there are only about fifty preserved in the museums of Europe and America—but recently one was captured off Santa Barbara, California. The frillshark has many anatomical features similar to those of the ancient sharks that lived 25 to 30 million years ago. It has too many gills and too few dorsal fins for a modern shark, and its teeth, like those of fossil sharks, are three-pronged and briarlike. Some ichthyologists regard it as a relic derived from very ancient shark ancestors that have died out in the upper waters but, through this single species, are still carrying on their struggle for earthly survival, in the quiet of the deep sea.

Possibly there are other such anachronisms lurking down in these   54 regions of which we know so little, but they are likely to be few and scattered. The terms of existence in these deep waters are far too uncompromising to support life unless that life is plastic, molding itself constantly to the harsh conditions, seizing every advantage that makes possible the survival of living protoplasm in a world only a little less hostile than the black reaches of interplanetary space.

QUESTIONS FOR CRITICAL READING

1. How much of the earth has been "dark since the world began" (para. 1)?
2. What is a bathysphere?
3. Why did people think there was no life in the deep sea?
4. What were the earliest signs that there might be life in the great depths of the sea?
5. What is the ECR layer?
6. How did the "phantom bottom" behave?
7. Why was the squid theory so startling?
8. What does Carson tell us about whale behavior in the deep?

SUGGESTIONS FOR CRITICAL WRITING

1. Use the term *ocean depths* to perform an online search. Based on your findings, write an essay in which you update at least one aspect of Carson's essay. For example, what new discoveries have been made about the nature of the deep sea? What new technologies have been developed to aid in the explanation of the ocean floor?

2. What is known today about whales? How many species of whales are known to exist and how many are in peril of extinction or have become extinct? Use Carson's technique of reviewing what has been known historically about whales, and then bring us up to date with what is known today.

3. In three pages, summarize the most important points in Carson's essay. Assume that you are writing to someone who does not know much about the ocean and who knows nothing about Rachel Carson. What, for you, are the most impressive points that she makes and the points that should most concern the person for whom you are writing?

4. Jacques Cousteau is probably the most famous ocean explorer. What did he discover that would add to the information Carson details in "The Sunless Sea"? Was he able to solve any of the problems that Carson suggests remain to be solved? How important was his work to our understanding of the ocean? Explain.

5. **CONNECTIONS**   What are the similarities in the rhetorical techniques of Rachel Carson and Stephen Jay Gould (p. 635)? Consider their subject matter, their interest in mysteries, their concern for history, and their capacity for description. On what points about nature do they seem to differ? Would Gould be sympathetic to Carson's purposes in this essay? What might he have done differently?

6. **CONNECTIONS**   In paragraphs 26 and 27 Carson talks about some ways in which sea life changed over time. How would Darwin have reacted to what Carson describes? Does Carson seem to accept Darwin's views on the evolution of species, or is her research independent of Darwin? What contribution, if any, do you think she makes toward validating Darwin's theory that life evolves over time? Explain.

7. **SEEING CONNECTIONS**   What would most please Carson in Durand's portrait of nature in *Kindred Spirits* (p. 576)? Would she have been pleased that people were portrayed in this Catskill wilderness, or would she have been disturbed by their presence? What might she have told William Cullen Bryant and Thomas Cole if she could have spoken with them in 1871? What would she have urged Durand to change or alter in his painting if she could have spoken with him in 1871, knowing what she knew when she wrote "The Sunless Sea"? How would she have praised or criticized this portrait of nature? Might she have felt that the emphasis on beauty was misleading, or would she have felt that it would have encouraged preservation? How "green" is the painting?

STEPHEN JAY GOULD
Nonmoral Nature

STEPHEN JAY GOULD (1941–2002) was Alexander Agassiz professor of zoology, professor of geology, and curator of invertebrate paleontology in the Museum of Comparative Zoology at Harvard University, where his field of interest centered on the special evolutionary problems related to species of Bahamian snails. He decided to become a paleontologist when he was five years old, after he visited the American Museum of Natural History in New York City and first saw reconstructed dinosaurs.

Gould became well known for essays on science written with the clarity needed to explain complex concepts to a general audience and also informed by a superb scientific understanding. His articles for *Natural History* magazine have been widely quoted and collected in book form. His books have won both praise and prizes; they include *Ever Since Darwin* (1977), *The Panda's Thumb* (1980), *The Mismeasure of Man* (1981), *The Flamingo's Smile* (1985), *Bully for Brontosaurus* (1991), *Eight Little Piggies* (1993), *Dinosaur in a Haystack* (1995), *Full House: The Spread of Excellence from Plato to Darwin* (1996), and *Questioning the Millennium* (1997). In much of his writing, Gould pointed to the significance of the work of the scientist he most frequently cited, Charles Darwin. His books have been celebrated around the world, and in 1981 Gould won a MacArthur Fellowship—a stipend of more than $38,000 a year for five years that permitted him to do any work he wished.

"Nonmoral Nature" examines a highly controversial issue—the religious "reading" of natural events. Gould opposes the position of creationists who insist that the Bible's version of creation be taught in science courses as scientific fact. Moreover, he views the account of the creation in Genesis as religious, not scientific, and

From *Natural History*, vol. 91, no. 2, 1982.

points out that Darwin (who was trained as a minister) did not see a conflict between his theories and religious beliefs.

Gould's primary point in this selection is that the behavior of animals in nature—with ruthless and efficient predators inflicting pain on essentially helpless prey—has presented theologians with an exacting dilemma: If God is good and if creation reveals his goodness, why do nature's victims suffer?

Gould examines in great detail specific issues that plagued nineteenth-century theologians. One of these, the behavior of the ichneumon wasp, an efficient wasp that plants its egg in a host caterpillar or aphid, is his special concern. Gould describes the behavior of the ichneumon in detail to make it plain that the total mechanism of the predatory, parasitic animal is complex, subtle, and brilliant. The ichneumon paralyzes its host and then eats it from the inside out, taking care not to permit a victim to die until the last morsel is consumed. He also notes that because there are so many species of ichneumons, their behavior cannot be regarded as an isolated phenomenon.

It is almost impossible to read this selection without developing respect for the predator, something that was extremely difficult, if not impossible, for nineteenth-century theologians to do. Their problem, Gould asserts, was that they anthropomorphized the behavior of these insects. That is, they thought of them in human terms. The act of predation was seen as comparable to the acts of human thugs who toy with their victims, or as Gould puts it, the acts of executioners in Renaissance England who inflicted as much pain as possible on traitors before killing them. This model is the kind of lens through which the behavior of predators was interpreted and understood.

Instead of an anthropocentric—human-centered—view, Gould suggests a scientific view that sees the behavior of predators as sympathetically as that of victims. In this way, he asserts, the ichneumon—and nature—will be seen as nonmoral, and the act of predation seen as neither good nor evil. The concept of evil, he says, is limited to human beings. The world of nature is unconcerned with it, and if we apply morality to nature, we see nature as merely a reflection of our own beliefs and values. Instead, he wishes us to conceive of nature as he thinks it is, something apart from strictly human values.

Gould's Rhetoric

Gould's writing is distinguished for its clarity and directness. In this essay, he relies on the testimony of renowned authorities, establishing at once a remarkable breadth of interest and revealing considerably detailed learning about his subject. He explores a number of theories with sympathy and care, demonstrating their limits before offering his own views.

Because his field of interest is advanced biology, he runs the risk of losing the attention of the general reader. To avoid doing this, he could have oversimplified his subject, but he does not: he does not shrink from using Latin classifications to identify his subject matter, but he defines each specialized term when he first uses it. He clarifies each opposing argument and demonstrates, in his analysis, its limitations and potential.

Instead of using a metaphor to convince us of a significant fact or critical opinion, Gould "deconstructs" a metaphor that was once in wide use — that the animal world, like the human world, is ethical. He reveals the metaphor to us, shows how it has affected belief, and then asks us to reject it in favor of seeing the world as it actually is. Although acknowledging that the metaphor is inviting and can be irresistible, Gould says we must resist it.

Gould also makes widespread use of the rhetorical device of metonymy, in which a part of something stands for the whole. Thus, the details of nature, which is God's creation, are made to reflect the entirety, which is God. Therefore, the behavior of the ichneumon comes to stand for the nature of God; and because the ichneumon's behavior is adjudged evil by those who think that animal behavior is metaphorically like that of people, there is a terrible contradiction that cannot be rationalized by theological arguments.

Gould shows us just how difficult the problem of the theologian is. Then he shows us a way out. But his way out depends on the capacity to think in a new way, a change that some readers may not be able to achieve.

PREREADING QUESTIONS: WHAT TO READ FOR

The following prereading questions may help you anticipate key issues in the discussion of Stephen Jay Gould's "Nonmoral Nature." Keeping them in mind during your first reading of the selection should help focus your attention.

- What are the consequences of anthropomorphizing nature?
- What does it mean for nature to be nonmoral?

Nonmoral Nature

When the Right Honorable and Reverend Francis Henry, earl of   1
Bridgewater,[1] died in February, 1829, he left £8,000 to support a
series of books "on the power, wisdom, and goodness of God, as
manifested in the creation." William Buckland,[2] England's first official academic geologist and later dean of Westminster, was invited
to compose one of the nine Bridgewater Treatises. In it he discussed
the most pressing problem of natural theology: If God is benevolent
and the Creation displays his "power, wisdom, and goodness," then
why are we surrounded with pain, suffering, and apparently senseless cruelty in the animal world?

Buckland considered the depredation of "carnivorous races" as   2
the primary challenge to an idealized world in which the lion might
dwell with the lamb. He resolved the issue to his satisfaction by arguing that carnivores actually increase "the aggregate of animal enjoyment" and "diminish that of pain." The death of victims, after all, is
swift and relatively painless, victims are spared the ravages of decrepi-
tude and senility, and populations do not outrun their food supply to
the greater sorrow of all. God knew what he was doing when he made
lions. Buckland concluded in hardly concealed rapture:

> The appointment of death by the agency of carnivora, as the ordi-
> nary termination of animal existence, appears therefore in its main
> results to be a dispensation of benevolence; it deducts much from
> the aggregate amount of the pain of universal death; it abridges,
> and almost annihilates, throughout the brute creation, the misery
> of disease, and accidental injuries, and lingering decay; and
> imposes such salutary restraint upon excessive increase of num-
> bers, that the supply of food maintains perpetually a due ratio to
> the demand. The result is, that the surface of the land and depths
> of the waters are ever crowded with myriads of animated beings,
> the pleasures of whose life are co-extensive with its duration; and
> which throughout the little day of existence that is allotted to
> them, fulfill with joy the functions for which they were created.

We may find a certain amusing charm in Buckland's vision   3
today, but such arguments did begin to address "the problem of evil"

---

[1] **Reverend Francis Henry, earl of Bridgewater (1756–1829)** He was the
eighth and last earl of Bridgewater. He was also a naturalist and a Fellow at All Souls
College, Oxford, before he became earl of Bridgewater in 1823. On his death, he left
a fund to be used for the publication of the Bridgewater Treatises, essay discussions
of the moral implications of scientific research and discoveries.
[2] **William Buckland (1784–1856)** English clergyman and geologist. His
essay "Geology and Mineralogy" was a Bridgewater Treatise in 1836.

for many of Buckland's contemporaries—how could a benevolent God create such a world of carnage and bloodshed? Yet these claims could not abolish the problem of evil entirely, for nature includes many phenomena far more horrible in our eyes than simple predation. I suspect that nothing evokes greater disgust in most of us than slow destruction of a host by an internal parasite—slow ingestion, bit by bit, from the inside. In no other way can I explain why *Alien*, an uninspired, grade-C, formula horror film, should have won such a following. That single scene of Mr. Alien, popping forth as a baby parasite from the body of a human host, was both sickening and stunning. Our nineteenth-century forebears maintained similar feelings. Their greatest challenge to the concept of a benevolent deity was not simple predation—for one can admire quick and efficient butcheries, especially since we strive to construct them ourselves—but slow death by parasitic ingestion. The classic case, treated at length by all the great naturalists, involved the so-called ichneumon fly. Buckland had sidestepped the major issue.

The ichneumon fly, which provoked such concern among nat-   4
ural theologians, was a composite creature representing the habits of an enormous tribe. The Ichneumonoidea are a group of wasps, not flies, that include more species than all the vertebrates combined (wasps, with ants and bees, constitute the order Hymenoptera; flies, with their two wings—wasps have four—form the order Diptera). In addition, many related wasps of similar habits were often cited for the same grisly details. Thus, the famous story did not merely implicate a single aberrant species (perhaps a perverse leakage from Satan's realm), but perhaps hundreds of thousands of them—a large chunk of what could only be God's creation.

The ichneumons, like most wasps, generally live freely as adults   5
but pass their larval life as parasites feeding on the bodies of other animals, almost invariably members of their own phylum, Arthropoda. The most common victims are caterpillars (butterfly and moth larvae), but some ichneumons prefer aphids and others attack spiders. Most hosts are parasitized as larvae, but some adults are attacked, and many tiny ichneumons inject their brood directly into the egg of their host.

The free-flying females locate an appropriate host and then   6
convert it to a food factory for their own young. Parasitologists speak of ectoparasitism when the uninvited guest lives on the surface of its host, and endoparasitism when the parasite dwells within. Among endoparasitic ichneumons, adult females pierce the host with their ovipositor and deposit eggs within it. (The ovipositor, a thin tube extending backward from the wasp's rear end, may be many times as long as the body itself.) Usually, the host is not otherwise

inconvenienced for the moment, at least until the eggs hatch and the ichneumon larvae begin their grim work of interior excavation. Among ectoparasites, however, many females lay their eggs directly upon the host's body. Since an active host would easily dislodge the egg, the ichneumon mother often simultaneously injects a toxin that paralyzes the caterpillar or other victim. The paralysis may be permanent, and the caterpillar lies, alive but immobile, with the agent of its future destruction secure on its belly. The egg hatches, the helpless caterpillar twitches, the wasp larva pierces and begins its grisly feast.

Since a dead and decaying caterpillar will do the wasp larva no good, it eats in a pattern that cannot help but recall, in our inappropriate, anthropocentric interpretation, the ancient English penalty for treason—drawing and quartering, with its explicit object of extracting as much torment as possible by keeping the victim alive and sentient. As the king's executioner drew out and burned his client's entrails, so does the ichneumon larva eat fat bodies and digestive organs first, keeping the caterpillar alive by preserving intact the essential heart and central nervous system. Finally, the larva completes its work and kills its victim, leaving behind the caterpillar's empty shell. Is it any wonder that ichneumons, not snakes or lions, stood as the paramount challenge to God's benevolence during the heyday of natural theology?   7

As I read through the nineteenth- and twentieth-century literature on ichneumons, nothing amused me more than the tension between an intellectual knowledge that wasps should not be described in human terms and a literary or emotional inability to avoid the familiar categories of epic and narrative, pain and destruction, victim and vanquisher. We seem to be caught in the mythic structures of our own cultural sagas, quite unable, even in our basic descriptions, to use any other language than the metaphors of battle and conquest. We cannot render this corner of natural history as anything but story, combining the themes of grim horror and fascination and usually ending not so much with pity for the caterpillar as with admiration for the efficiency of the ichneumon.   8

I detect two basic themes in most epic descriptions: the struggles of prey and the ruthless efficiency of parasites. Although we acknowledge that we witness little more than automatic instinct or physiological reaction, still we describe the defenses of hosts as though they represented conscious struggles. Thus, aphids kick and caterpillars may wriggle violently as wasps attempt to insert their ovipositors. The pupa of the tortoise-shell butterfly (usually considered an inert creature silently awaiting its conversion from duckling to swan) may contort its abdominal region so sharply that   9 attacking wasps are thrown into the air. The caterpillars of *Hapalia*, when attacked by the wasp *Apanteles machaeralis*, drop suddenly from their leaves and suspend themselves in air by a silken thread. But the wasp may run down the thread and insert its eggs nonetheless. Some hosts can encapsulate the injected egg with blood cells that aggregate and harden, thus suffocating the parasite.

J.-H. Fabre,[3] the great nineteenth-century French entomologist, 10 who remains to this day the preeminently literate natural historian of insects, made a special study of parasitic wasps and wrote with an unabashed anthropocentrism about the struggles of paralyzed victims (see his books *Insect Life* and *The Wonders of Instinct*). He describes some imperfectly paralyzed caterpillars that struggle so violently every time a parasite approaches that the wasp larvae must feed with unusual caution. They attach themselves to a silken strand from the roof of their burrow and descend upon a safe and exposed part of the caterpillar:

> The grub is at dinner: head downwards, it is digging into the limp belly of one of the caterpillars. . . . At the least sign of danger in the heap of caterpillars, the larva retreats . . . and climbs back to the ceiling, where the swarming rabble cannot reach it. When peace is restored, it slides down [its silken cord] and returns to table, with its head over the viands and its rear upturned and ready to withdraw in case of need.

In another chapter, he describes the fate of a paralyzed cricket: 11

> One may see the cricket, bitten to the quick, vainly move its antennae and abdominal styles, open and close its empty jaws, and even move a foot, but the larva is safe and searches its vitals with impunity. What an awful nightmare for the paralyzed cricket!

Fabre even learned to feed some paralyzed victims by placing a 12 syrup of sugar and water on their mouthparts—thus showing that they remained alive, sentient, and (by implication) grateful for any palliation of their inevitable fate. If Jesus, immobile and thirsting on the cross, received only vinegar from his tormentors, Fabre at least could make an ending bittersweet.

The second theme, ruthless efficiency of the parasites, leads to 13 the opposite conclusion—grudging admiration for the victors. We learn of their skill in capturing dangerous hosts often many times larger than themselves. Caterpillars may be easy game, but the

---

[3] **Jean-Henri Fabre (1823–1915)** French entomologist whose patient study of insects earned him the nickname "the Virgil of Insects." His writings are voluminous and, at times, elegant.

psammocharid wasps prefer spiders. They must insert their ovipositors in a safe and precise spot. Some leave a paralyzed spider in its
own burrow. *Planiceps hirsutus*, for example, parasitizes a California
trapdoor spider. It searches for spider tubes on sand dunes, then
digs into nearby sand to disturb the spider's home and drive it out.
When the spider emerges, the wasp attacks, paralyzes its victim,
drags it back into its own tube, shuts and fastens the trapdoor, and
deposits a single egg upon the spider's abdomen. Other psam-
mocharids will drag a heavy spider back to a previously prepared
cluster of clay or mud cells. Some amputate a spider's legs to make
the passage easier. Others fly back over water, skimming a buoyant
spider along the surface.

Some wasps must battle with other parasites over a host's body.   14
Rhyssella curvipes can detect the larvae of wood wasps deep within
alder wood and drill down to its potential victims with its sharply
ridged ovipositor. *Pseudorhyssa alpestris*, a related parasite, cannot drill
directly into wood since its slender ovipositor bears only rudimentary cutting ridges. It locates the holes made by *Rhyssella*, inserts its
ovipositor, and lays an egg on the host (already conveniently paralyzed by *Rhyssella*), right next to the egg deposited by its relative. The
two eggs hatch at about the same time, but the larva of *Pseudorhyssa*
has a bigger head bearing much larger mandibles. *Pseudorhyssa* seizes
the smaller *Rhyssella* larva, destroys it, and proceeds to feast upon a
banquet already well prepared.

Other praises for the efficiency of mothers invoke the themes of   15
early, quick, and often. Many ichneumons don't even wait for their
hosts to develop into larvae, but parasitize the egg directly (larval
wasps may then either drain the egg itself or enter the developing
host larva). Others simply move fast. *Apanteles militaris* can deposit
up to seventy-two eggs in a single second. Still others are doggedly
persistent. *Aphidius gomezi* females produce up to 1,500 eggs and
can parasitize as many as 600 aphids in a single working day. In a
bizarre twist upon "often," some wasps indulge in polyembryony, a
kind of iterated supertwinning. A single egg divides into cells that
aggregate into as many as 500 individuals. Since some polyembry-
onic wasps parasitize caterpillars much larger than themselves and
may lay up to six eggs in each, as many as 3,000 larvae may develop
within, and feed upon, a single host. These wasps are endoparasites
and do not paralyze their victims. The caterpillars writhe back and
forth, not (one suspects) from pain, but merely in response to the
commotion induced by thousands of wasp larvae feeding within.

The efficiency of mothers is matched by their larval offspring. I   16
have already mentioned the pattern of eating less essential parts first,
thus keeping the host alive and fresh to its final and merciful dispatch.

After the larva digests every edible morsel of its victim (if only to prevent later fouling of its abode by decaying tissue), it may still use the outer shell of its host. One aphid parasite cuts a hole in the belly of its victim's shell, glues the skeleton to a leaf by sticky secretions from its salivary gland, and then spins a cocoon to pupate within the aphid's shell.

In using inappropriate anthropocentric language in this romp   17
through the natural history of ichneumons, I have tried to emphasize just why these wasps became a preeminent challenge to natural theology—the antiquated doctrine that attempted to infer God's essence from the products of his creation. I have used twentieth-century examples for the most part, but all themes were known and stressed by the great nineteenth-century natural theologians. How then did they square the habits of these wasps with the goodness of God? How did they extract themselves from this dilemma of their own making?

The strategies were as varied as the practitioners; they shared   18
only the theme of special pleading for an a priori doctrine[4]—they knew that God's benevolence was lurking somewhere behind all these tales of apparent horror. Charles Lyell[5] for example, in the first edition of his epochal *Principles of Geology* (1830–1833), decided that caterpillars posed such a threat to vegetation that any natural checks upon them could only reflect well upon a creating deity, for caterpillars would destroy human agriculture "did not Providence put causes in operation to keep them in due bounds."

The Reverend William Kirby,[6] rector of Barham and Britain's   19
foremost entomologist, chose to ignore the plight of caterpillars and focused instead upon the virtue of mother love displayed by wasps in provisioning their young with such care.

> The great object of the female is to discover a proper nidus for her
> eggs. In search of this she is in constant motion. Is the caterpillar
> of a butterfly or moth the appropriate food for her young? You see

---

[4] **an a priori doctrine** *A priori* means "beforehand," and Gould refers to those who approach a scientific situation with a preestablished view in mind. He is suggesting that such an approach prevents the kind of objectivity and fairness that scientific examination is supposed to produce.

[5] **Charles Lyell (1797–1875)** English geologist who established the glacial layers of the Eocene (dawn of recent), Miocene (less recent), and Pliocene (more recent) epochs during his excavations of Tertiary period strata in Italy. He was influential in urging Darwin to publish his theories. His work is still respected.

[6] **The Reverend William Kirby (1759–1850)** English specialist in insects. He was the author of a Bridgewater Treatise, *On the power, wisdom, and goodness of God, as manifested in the creation of animals, and in their history, habits, and instincts* (2 vols., 1835).

her alight upon the plants where they are most usually to be met with, run quickly over them, carefully examining every leaf, and, having found the unfortunate object of her search, insert her sting into its flesh, and there deposit an egg. . . . The active Ichneumon braves every danger, and does not desist until her courage and address have insured subsistence for one of her future progeny.

Kirby found this solicitude all the more remarkable because the   20
female wasp will never see her child and enjoy the pleasures of parenthood. Yet her love compels her to danger nonetheless:

> A very large proportion of them are doomed to die before their young come into existence. But in these the passion is not extinguished. . . . When you witness the solicitude with which they provide for the security and sustenance of their future young, you can scarcely deny to them love for a progeny they are never destined to behold.

Kirby also put in a good word for the marauding larvae, praising   21
them for their forbearance in eating selectively to keep their caterpillar prey alive. Would we all husband our resources with such care!

> In this strange and apparently cruel operation one circumstance is truly remarkable. The larva of the Ichneumon, though every day, perhaps for months, it gnaws the inside of the caterpillar, and though at last it has devoured almost every part of it except the skin and intestines, carefully all this time it avoids injuring the vital organs, as if aware that its own existence depends on that of the insect upon which it preys! . . . What would be the impression which a similar instance amongst the race of quadrupeds would make upon us? If, for example, an animal . . . should be found to feed upon the inside of a dog, devouring only those parts not essential to life, while it cautiously left uninjured the heart, arteries, lungs, and intestines—should we not regard such an instance as a perfect prodigy, as an example of instinctive forbearance almost miraculous? [The last three quotes come from the 1856, and last pre-Darwinian, edition of Kirby and Spence's *Introduction to Entomology*.]

This tradition of attempting to read moral meaning from nature   22
did not cease with the triumph of evolutionary theory after Darwin published *On the Origin of Species* in 1859—for evolution could be read as God's chosen method of peopling our planet, and ethical messages might still populate nature. Thus, St. George Mivart,[7] one

---

[7]**St. George Mivart (1827–1900)** English anatomist and biologist who examined the comparative anatomies of insect-eating and meat-eating animals. A convert to Roman Catholicism in 1844, he was unable to reconcile religious and evolutionary theories and was excommunicated from the Catholic Church in 1900.

of Darwin's most effective evolutionary critics and a devout Catholic, argued that "many amiable and excellent people" had been misled by the apparent suffering of animals for two reasons. First, however much it might hurt, "physical suffering and moral evil are simply incommensurable." Since beasts are not moral agents, their feelings cannot bear any ethical message. But secondly, lest our visceral sensitivities still be aroused, Mivart assures us that animals must feel little, if any, pain. Using a favorite racist argument of the time—that "primitive" people suffer far less than advanced and cultured people— Mivart extrapolated further down the ladder of life into a realm of very limited pain indeed: physical suffering, he argued,

> depends greatly upon the mental condition of the sufferer. Only during consciousness does it exist, and only in the most highly organized men does it reach its acme. The author has been assured that lower races of men appear less keenly sensitive to physical suffering than do more cultivated and refined human beings. Thus only in man can there really be any intense degree of suffering, because only in him is there that intellectual recollection of past moments and that anticipation of future ones, which constitute in great part the bitterness of suffering. The momentary pang, the present pain, which beasts endure, though real enough, is yet, doubtless, not to be compared as to its intensity with the suffering which is produced in man through his high prerogative of self-consciousness [from *Genesis of Species*, 1871].

It took Darwin himself to derail this ancient tradition—in that gentle way so characteristic of his radical intellectual approach to nearly everything. The ichneumons also troubled Darwin greatly and he wrote of them to Asa Gray[8] in 1860: 23

> I own that I cannot see as plainly as others do, and as I should wish to do, evidence of design and beneficence on all sides of us. There seems to me too much misery in the world. I cannot persuade myself that a beneficent and omnipotent God would have designedly created the Ichneumonidae with the express intention of their feeding within the living bodies of Caterpillars, or that a cat should play with mice.

---

[8] **Asa Gray (1810–1888)** America's greatest botanist. His works, which are still considered important, are *Structural Botany* (1879; originally published in 1842 as *Botanical Text-Book*), *The Elements of Botany* (1836), *How Plants Grow* (1858), and *How Plants Behave* (1872). Gray was a serious critic of Darwin and wrote a great number of letters to him, but he was also a firm believer in Darwinian evolution. Because he was also a well-known member of an evangelical Protestant faith, he was effective in countering religious attacks on Darwin by showing that there is no conflict between Darwinism and religion.

Indeed, he had written with more passion to Joseph Hooker[9] in 24 1856: "What a book a devil's chaplain might write on the clumsy, wasteful, blundering, low, and horribly cruel works of nature!"

This honest admission—that nature is often (by our standards) 25 cruel and that all previous attempts to find a lurking goodness behind everything represent just so much absurd special pleading— can lead in two directions. One might retain the principle that nature holds moral messages for humans, but reverse the usual perspective and claim that morality consists in understanding the ways of nature and doing the opposite. Thomas Henry Huxley[10] advanced this argument in his famous essay on *Evolution and Ethics* (1893):

> The practice of that which is ethically best—what we call goodness or virtue—involves a course of conduct which, in all respects, is opposed to that which leads to success in the cosmic struggle for existence. In place of ruthless self-assertion it demands self-restraint; in place of thrusting aside, or treading down, all competitors, it requires that the individual shall not merely respect, but shall help his fellows. . . . It repudiates the gladiatorial theory of existence. . . . Laws and moral precepts are directed to the end of curbing the cosmic process.

The other argument, more radical in Darwin's day but common 26 now, holds that nature simply is as we find it. Our failure to discern the universal good we once expected does not record our lack of insight or ingenuity but merely demonstrates that nature contains no moral messages framed in human terms. Morality is a subject for philosophers, theologians, students of the humanities, indeed for all thinking people. The answers will not be read passively from nature; they do not, and cannot, arise from the data of science. The factual state of the world does not teach us how we, with our powers for good and evil, should alter or preserve it in the most ethical manner.

Darwin himself tended toward this view, although he could not, 27 as a man of his time, thoroughly abandon the idea that laws of nature might reflect some higher purpose. He clearly recognized that the

---

[9]**Joseph Hooker (1817–1911)** English botanist who studied flowers in exotic locations such as Tasmania, the Antarctic, New Zealand, and India. He was, along with Charles Lyell, a friend of Darwin's and one of those who urged him to publish *On the Origin of Species*. He was the director of London's Kew Gardens from 1865 to 1885.

[10]**Thomas Henry Huxley (1825–1895)** English naturalist who, quite independent of organizations and formal support, became one of the most important scientists of his time. He searched for a theory of evolution that was based on a rigorous examination of the facts and found, in Darwin's work, the theory that he could finally respect. He was a strong champion of Darwin.

specific manifestations of those laws—cats playing with mice, and ichneumon larvae eating caterpillars—could not embody ethical messages, but he somehow hoped that unknown higher laws might exist "with the details, whether good or bad, left to the working out of what we may call chance."

Since ichneumons are a detail, and since natural selection is a law regulating details, the answer to the ancient dilemma of why such cruelty (in our terms) exists in nature can only be that there isn't any answer—and that the framing of the question "in our terms" is thoroughly inappropriate in a natural world neither made for us nor ruled by us. It just plain happens. It is a strategy that works for ichneumons and that natural selection has programmed into their behavioral repertoire. Caterpillars are not suffering to teach us something; they have simply been outmaneuvered, for now, in the evolutionary game. Perhaps they will evolve a set of adequate defenses sometime in the future, thus sealing the fate of ichneumons. And perhaps, indeed probably, they will not. 28

Another Huxley, Thomas's grandson Julian,[11] spoke for this position, using as an example—yes, you guessed it—the ubiquitous ichneumons: 29

> Natural selection, in fact, though like the mills of God in grinding slowly and grinding small, has few other attributes that a civilized religion would call divine. . . . Its products are just as likely to be aesthetically, morally, or intellectually repulsive to us as they are to be attractive. We need only think of the ugliness of *Sacculina* or a bladderworm, the stupidity of a rhinoceros or a stegosaur, the horror of a female mantis devouring its mate or a brood of ichneumon flies slowly eating out a caterpillar.

It is amusing in this context, or rather ironic since it is too serious to be amusing, that modern creationists accuse evolutionists of preaching a specific ethical doctrine called secular humanism and thereby demand equal time for their unscientific and discredited views. If nature is nonmoral, then evolution cannot teach any ethical theory at all. The assumption that it can has abetted a panoply of social evils that ideologues falsely read into nature from their beliefs— eugenics and (misnamed) social Darwinism prominently among them. Not only did Darwin eschew any attempt to discover an antireligious ethic in nature, he also expressly stated his personal bewilderment about such deep issues as the problem of evil. Just a few sentences after invoking the ichneumons, and in words that

---

[11]**Thomas's grandson Julian** Julian Huxley (1887–1975), an English biologist and a brother of the novelist Aldous Huxley.

express both the modesty of this splendid man and the compatibility, through lack of contact, between science and true religion, Darwin wrote to Asa Gray,

> I feel most deeply that the whole subject is too profound for the human intellect. A dog might as well speculate on the mind of Newton. Let each man hope and believe what he can.

QUESTIONS FOR CRITICAL READING

1. What does Gould reveal to us about the nature of insect life?
2. What scientific information does Gould provide that is most valuable in explaining how nature works?
3. What does it mean to anthropomorphize nature? What are some concrete results of doing so?
4. Describe the reaction you have to the process by which the ichneumon wasp parasitizes its host.
5. How might the behavior of the ichneumon wasp put at stake any genuine religious questions of today?
6. What counterassertions can you make to Gould's view that nature is nonmoral?

SUGGESTIONS FOR CRITICAL WRITING

1. In a brief essay, try to answer the question Gould examines in paragraph 1: "Why are we surrounded with pain, suffering, and apparently senseless cruelty in the animal world?"
2. Is the fact of such pain, suffering, and apparently senseless cruelty a religious issue? If so, in what way? If not, demonstrate why.
3. In paragraph 17, Gould describes natural theology as "the antiquated doctrine that attempted to infer God's essence from the products of his creation." Is this a reasonable description of natural theology as you understand it? What can a theology that bases its claims in an observation of nature assert about the essence of God? What kind of religion would support a theology that was based on the behavior of natural life, including ichneumons?
4. Gould points out that even after having established his theory of evolution, Darwin could not "thoroughly abandon the idea that laws of nature might reflect some higher purpose" (para. 27). Assuming that you agree with Darwin but also acknowledge the problems that Gould presents, clarify what the higher purpose of a nature such as Gould describes might be. Does Gould's description of the behavior of the ichneumon (or any other) predator in any way compromise the idea that nature has a higher purpose? Does Gould hold that it has a higher purpose?

5. **CONNECTIONS**   Compare this essay with Francis Bacon's "The Four Idols" (p. 579). What intellectual issues do the two essays share? What common ground do they share regarding attitudes toward science and religion? What might Bacon have decided about the ultimate ethical issues raised by a consideration of the ichneumon? Do you think that Bacon would have held the same views about the ichneumon's predatory powers as did the nineteenth-century theologians? That is, would he have conceived of nature in ethical/moral terms?

6. **CONNECTIONS**   Why would Gould's scientific subject matter involve issues of morality to a greater extent than, say, the subject matter of Francis Bacon (p. 579), Charles Darwin (p. 597), or Rachel Carson (p. 615)? Is it possible that the study of physics or chemistry is less fundamentally concerned with moral issues than the study of biology is? One result of Darwin's concerns is the possibility that apes and humans are related. Is this point less worthy of consideration from a moral viewpoint than the behavior of the ichneumon wasp? What are the major moral issues in science that you have observed from examining these writers?

7. **SEEING CONNECTIONS**   Gould's view of nature is definitely not similar to the view commonly held in the mid nineteenth century, when Durand painted *Kindred Spirits* (p. 576). The painting may also be seen as "anthropomorphizing" nature while representing its grandeur. Durand probably saw the two human figures of Bryant and Cole as benefiting from nature's "blessing" and beauty while also dominating nature, as is implied in Genesis. How would Gould have tried to correct their view of nature? What realities about the way nature functions would Gould have most wanted to tell them? Both Bryant and Cole were considered geniuses in their day. Would Gould have hesitated to attack their pietistic or pantheistic philosophies? What did Gould know that they did not?

MICHIO KAKU
The Mystery of Dark Matter

MICHIO KAKU (b. 1947) was born and raised in San Jose, California, received his undergraduate degree from Harvard, and returned to California for his Ph.D. in physics from Berkeley in 1972. Since 1973 he has been professor of theoretical physics at the City College and the Graduate Center of the City University of New York, publishing widely on superstring theory, supergravity, and string-field theory. He hosts a weekly national radio show on science called *Science Fantastic* that is carried by ninety radio stations in the United States. Kaku is deeply concerned about the practical ramifications of theoretical physics and has written several books on the dangers of nuclear war. He is active in groups that advocate disarmament.

"The Mystery of Dark Matter" is a chapter in his book entitled *Beyond Einstein* (1987, rev. 1995), written with Jennifer Trainer Thompson. In this work, Kaku attempts to explain the circumstances of modern physics, with a special look at efforts to resolve the conflicts between two important theories: quantum theory and the theory of relativity. Quantum theory explains the physics of atoms and small particles. The theory of relativity explains cosmic phenomena such as gravity and the universe. However, neither theory works in the other's sphere of influence. Hence a new theory is needed to resolve the problems: superstring theory, which postulates that instead of hard particles existing at the center of atoms "tiny strings of energy" vibrate at an infinite number of frequencies. These strings of energy are at the heart

From *Beyond Einstein*.

of atoms and consist of everything we know of as matter in the universe.

If superstring theory is correct, one of the tests will be a confirmation of the existence of—and perhaps an explanation of—dark matter. In this essay Kaku describes dark matter as matter that we know exists but that cannot be seen or perceived except in terms of its effect on other bodies, such as stars.

Because physics involves specialized, advanced mathematics, much of what Kaku says is simplified for a general audience. As a result we can understand the theories, but only in general terms. Therefore, without the mathematics, we must accept certain ideas at face value, making an effort to imagine, along with Kaku, how modern theories of physics work. Fortunately his coauthor, Jennifer Trainer Thompson, is able to spell out the very complex theories in a fashion that makes them as intelligible as possible for readers who are not experts in mathematics.

Some of the ideas in this essay are also developed in Kaku's best-selling *Hyperspace* (1994), which discusses the so-called crazy theories of contemporary physicists. Kaku tells us that modern research by contemporary physicists has produced a view of the natural world that virtually defies common sense, just as facts such as the earth's roundness (rather than flatness) and its movement around the sun (rather than the reverse) initially contradicted common sense. Unfortunately, common sense does not help us understand modern physics or the world of the atom. Because we cannot directly perceive the atom or the molecule, we require sophisticated equipment to make their nature evident. Interestingly, Francis Bacon insisted in *Novum Organum* that until better tools were developed, people would not be able to perceive the truth about the complexities of nature.

In an early chapter of *Hyperspace*, Kaku tells a story about being a young boy and watching fish in a small pond. He realized that for the carp, it was inconceivable that anything existed outside the water in which they swam. Their perceptions were limited entirely to the watery environment of their home. The same is true for people. Our environment may seem larger and more capacious than a pond, but we, like the carp, are limited in our perceptions. Plato realized this when he postulated his allegory of the cave and theorized that human beings' profoundly limited sensory apparatus prevents us from imagining experiences beyond what we know from our senses.

In "The Mystery of Dark Matter," Kaku discusses a phenomenon that similarly defies common sense. He explains that experiments and observations of a number of important astrophysicists through-out a period of more than twenty years have led physicists to con-clude that the universe is made up of more than the matter that we can perceive. Indeed, the best observations have suggested that as much as 90 percent of the universe may be made up of dark matter, even though this matter cannot be observed directly. If it were not so, theorists say, the galaxies would spin apart and the stars would drift into distant space, thereby cooling the universe to a tempera-ture that would lead to its death.

Kaku's Rhetoric

Jennifer Trainer Thompson, a nonphysicist, has worked on a number of Kaku's books meant for a general reading public, and she employs techniques common to contemporary journalism. She uses short paragraphs and intriguing subheads, such as "What Is the World Made Of?"; "How Much Does a Galaxy Weigh?"; and "Hot and Cold Dark Matter." These techniques help readers grasp the ideas that the research of Michio Kaku and other modern physicists has developed.

Because the essay offers a general overview of an interesting and elusive subject, Kaku provides a considerable amount of back-ground information. He tells us about the impact of the work of early mathematicians and physicists, some of whom developed the-ories that were far ahead of their times and who did not benefit from seeing their work validated. This technique is effective rhetori-cally, because it helps us understand the struggles of scientists on a human level. We feel sympathy for Vera Rubin, for example, who grew up wanting to be an astrophysicist and whose dreams were almost shattered by male scientists who tried to discourage her. Kaku gives insight into her struggles and demonstrates that much of what she thought was true has been borne out in contemporary observations. Kaku describes a number of other scientists who came up with "crazy" early theories, again helping us see the human side of the story.

The most important aspect of this essay's rhetoric involves the explanation of complex theories in terms that readers can grasp easily. Although we will not leave this essay with a full understand-ing of the complexities of dark matter, we will at least understand the problems that physicists face in trying to both describe how the universe works and postulate the existence of a kind of matter that seems to defy all common sense.

The following prereading questions may help you anticipate key issues in the discussion of Michio Kaku's "The Mystery of Dark Matter." Keeping them in mind during your first reading of the selection should help focus your attention.

- Why do physicists call it "dark matter"?
- What evidence tells us dark matter exists?
- What are the primary forces in the universe?

The Mystery of Dark Matter

With the cancellation of the SSC,[1] some commentators have publicly speculated that physics will "come to an end." Promising ideas such as the superstring theory, no matter how compelling and elegant, will never be tested and, hence, can never be verified. Physicists, however, are optimists. If evidence for the superstring theory cannot be found on the earth, then one solution is to leave the earth and go into outer space. Over the coming years, physicists will rely increasingly on cosmology to probe the inner secrets of matter and energy. Their laboratory will be the cosmos and the Big Bang itself.   1

Already, cosmology has given us several mysteries that may very well provide clues to the ultimate nature of matter. The first is dark matter, which makes up 90 percent of the universe. And the second is cosmic strings.   2

What Is the World Made Of?

One of the greatest achievements of twentieth-century science was the determination of the chemical elements of the universe. With only a little over one hundred elements, scientists could explain the trillions upon trillions of possible forms of matter, from DNA to animals to exploding stars. The familiar elements that made up the earth—such as carbon, oxygen, and iron—were the same as   3

---

[1] **SSC** An acronym for Superconducting Super Collider, a huge cyclotron designed to test the string theory of matter. It was canceled by the U.S. government in 1993.

the elements making up the distant galaxies. Analyzing the light taken from blazing stars billions of light-years from our galaxy, scientists found precisely the same familiar elements found in our own backyards, no more, no less.

Indeed, no new mysterious elements were found anywhere in   4
the universe. The universe was made of atoms and their subatomic constituents. That was the final word in physics.

But by the late twentieth century, an avalanche of new data has   5
confirmed that over 90 percent of the universe is made of an invisible form of unknown matter, or dark matter. The stars we see in the heavens, in fact, are now known to make up only a tiny fraction of the real mass of the universe.

Dark matter is a strange substance, unlike anything ever   6
encountered before. It has weight but cannot be seen. In theory, if someone held a clump of dark matter in their hand, it would appear totally invisible. The existence of dark matter is not an academic question, because the ultimate fate of the universe, whether it will die in a fiery Big Crunch or fade away in a Cosmic Whimper or Big Chill, depends on its precise nature.

High-mass subatomic vibrations predicted by the superstring   7
theory are a leading candidate for dark matter. Thus, dark matter may give us an experimental clue to probe the nature of the superstring. Even without the SSC, science may be able to explore the new physics beyond the Standard Model.

How Much Does a Galaxy Weigh?

The scientist who first suspected that there was something   8
wrong about our conception of the universe was Fritz Zwicky,[2] a Swiss-American astronomer at the California Institute of Technology. In the 1930s, he was studying the Coma cluster of galaxies, about 300 million light-years away, and was puzzled by the fact that they were revolving about each other so fast that they should be unstable. To confirm his suspicions, he had to calculate the mass of a galaxy. Since galaxies can contain hundreds of billion stars, calculating their weight is a tricky question.

There are two simple ways of making this determination. The   9
fact that these two methods gave startlingly different results has created the present crisis in cosmology.

---

[2] **Fritz Zwicky (1898–1974)** Swiss-American astronomer who studied supernovas (huge exploding stars) in distant galaxies.

First, we can count the stars. This may seem like an impossible   10
task, but it's really quite simple. We know the rough average density
of the galaxy, and then we multiply by the total volume of the
galaxy. (That's how, for example, we calculate the number of hairs
on the human head, and how we determine that blondes have fewer
hairs than brunettes.)

Furthermore, we know the average weight of the stars. Of course,   11
no one actually puts a star on a scale. Astronomers instead look for
binary star systems, where two stars rotate around each other. Once
we know the time it takes for a complete rotation, Newton's laws are
then sufficient to determine the mass of each star. By multiplying
the number of stars in a galaxy by the average weight of each star,
we get a rough number for the weight of the galaxy.

The second method is to apply Newton's laws directly on the   12
galaxy. Distant stars on a spiral arm of the galaxy, for example, orbit
around the galactic center at different rates. Furthermore, galaxies
and clusters of stars rotate around each other. Once we know the
time it takes for these various revolutions, we can then determine
the total mass of the galaxy using Newton's laws of motion.

Zwicky calculated the mass necessary to bind this cluster of galax-   13
ies by analyzing the rate at which they orbited around each other. He
found that this mass was twenty times greater than the actual mass of
the luminous stars. In a Swiss journal, Zwicky reported that there was a
fundamental discrepancy between these two results. He postulated that
there had to be some form of mysterious "dunkle Materie," or dark
matter, whose gravitational pull held this galactic cluster together.
Without this dark matter, the Coma galaxies should fly apart.

Zwicky was led to postulate the existence of dark matter   14
because of his unshakable belief that Newton's laws were correct out
to galactic distances. (This is not the first time that scientists predicted the presence of unseen objects based on faith in Newton's
laws. The planets Neptune and Pluto, in fact, were discovered
because the orbit of closer planets, such as Saturn, wobbled and
deviated from Newton's predictions. Rather than give up Newton's
laws, scientists simply predicted the existence of new outer planets.)

However, Zwicky's results were met with indifference, even hos-   15
tility, by the astronomical community. After all, the very existence of
galaxies beyond our own Milky Way galaxy had been determined
only nine years before by Edwin Hubble, so most astronomers were
convinced that his results were premature, that eventually they would
fade away as better, more precise observations were made.

So Zwicky's results were largely ignored. Over the years,   16
astronomers accidentally rediscovered them but dismissed them as

an aberration. In the 1970s, for example, astronomers using radio telescopes analyzed the hydrogen gas surrounding a galaxy and found that it rotated much faster than it should have, but discounted the result.

In 1973, Jeremiah Ostriker and James Peebles at Princeton University resurrected this theory by making rigorous theoretical calculations about the stability of a galaxy. Up to that time, most astronomers thought that a galaxy was very much like our solar system, with the inner planets traveling much faster than the outer planets. Mercury, for example, was named after the Greek god for speed since it raced across the heavens (traveling at 107,000 miles per hour). Pluto, on the other hand, lumbers across the solar system at 10,500 miles per hour. If Pluto traveled around the sun as fast as Mercury, then it would quickly fly into outer space, never to return. The gravitational pull of the sun would not be enough to hold on to Pluto.

However, Ostriker and Peebles showed that the standard picture of a galaxy, based on our solar system, was unstable; by rights, the galaxy should fly apart. The gravitational pull of the stars was not enough to hold the galaxy together. They then showed that a galaxy can become stable if it is surrounded by a massive invisible halo that holds the galaxy together and if 90 percent of its mass was actually in the halo in the form of dark matter. Their paper was also met with indifference.

But after decades of skepticism and derision, what finally turned the tide on dark matter was the careful, persistent results of astronomer Vera Rubin and her colleagues at the Carnegie Institution in Washington, D.C. The results of these scientists, who analyzed hundreds of galaxies, verified conclusively that the velocity of the outer stars in a galaxy did not vary much from that of the inner ones, contrary to the planets in our solar system. This meant that the outer stars should fly into space, causing the galaxy to disintegrate into billions of individual stars, unless held together by the gravitational pull of invisible dark matter.

Like the history of dark matter itself, it took several decades for Vera Rubin's lifetime of results to be recognized by the skeptical (and overwhelmingly male) astronomical community.

One Woman's Challenge

It has never been easy for a female scientist to be accepted by her male peers. In fact, at every step of the way, Dr. Rubin's career came perilously close to being derailed by male hostility. She first became interested in the stars in the 1930s as a ten-year-old child, gazing at the night sky over Washington, D.C., for hours at a time, even making detailed maps of meteor trails across the heavens.

Her father, an electrical engineer, encouraged her to pursue her   22
interest in the stars, even helping her build her first telescope at the age of fourteen and taking her to amateur astronomy meetings in Washington. However, the warm encouragement she felt inside her family contrasted sharply with the icy reception she received from the outside world.

When she applied to Swarthmore College, the admissions offi-   23
cer tried to steer her away from astronomy, to a more "ladylike" career of painting astronomical subjects. That became a standard joke around her family. She recalled, "Whenever anything went wrong for me at work, someone would say, 'Have you ever thought of a career in which you paint? . . . ' "[3]

When accepted at Vassar, she proudly told her high school   24
physics teacher in the hallway, who replied bluntly, "You'll do all right as long as you stay away from science." (Years later, she recalled, "It takes an enormous amount of self-esteem to listen to things like that and not be demolished.")[4]

After graduating from Vassar, she applied to graduate school at   25
Princeton, which had a world-renowned reputation in astronomy. However, she never even received the school's catalog, since Princeton did not accept female graduate students in astronomy until 1971.

She was accepted at Harvard, but declined the offer because she   26
had just gotten married to Robert Rubin, a physical chemist, and followed him to Cornell University, where the astronomy department consisted of just two faculty members. (After she declined, she got a formal letter back from Harvard, with the handwritten words scrawled on the bottom, "Damn you women. Every time I get a good one ready, she goes off and gets married.")[5]

Going to Cornell, however, was a blessing in disguise, since   27
Rubin took graduate courses in physics from two Nobel laureates in physics, Hans Bethe, who decoded the complex fusion reactions which energize the stars, and Richard Feynman, who renormalized quantum electrodynamics. Her master's thesis met head-on the hostility of a male-dominated world. Her paper, which showed that the faraway galaxies deviated from the uniform expansion of a simplified version of the Big Bang model, was rejected for publication

---

[3] Marcia Bartusiak, *Discover* (October 1990): 89. [Kaku's note]
[4] Alan Lightman and Roberta Brawer, *Origins: The Lives and Worlds of Modern Cosmologists* (Cambridge: Harvard University Press, 1990), 305. [Kaku's note]
[5] *Ibid.*, 288. [Kaku's note]

because it was too far-fetched for its time. (Decades later, her paper would be considered prophetic.)

But after receiving her master's degree from Cornell, Rubin found 28
herself an unhappy housewife. "I actually cried every time the *Astrophysical Journal* came into the house . . . nothing in my education had taught me that one year after Cornell my husband would be out doing his science and I would be home changing diapers."[6]

Nonetheless, Rubin struggled to pursue her childhood dream, 29
especially after her husband took a job in Washington. Taking nighttime classes, she received her Ph.D. from Georgetown University. In 1954, she published her Ph.D. thesis, a landmark study that showed that the distribution of the galaxies in the heavens was not smooth and uniform, as previously thought, but actually clumpy.

Unfortunately, she was years ahead of her time. Over the years, 30
she gained a reputation of being something of an eccentric, going against the prevailing prejudice of astronomical thought. It would take years for her ideas to gain the recognition they deserved.

Distressed by the controversy her work was generating, Rubin 31
decided to take a respite and study one of the most mundane and unglamorous areas of astronomy, the rotation of galaxies. Innocently enough, Rubin began studying the Andromeda galaxy, our nearest neighbor in space. She and her colleagues expected to find that the gas swirling in the outer fringes of the Andromeda galaxy was traveling much slower than the gas near the center. Like our own solar system, the speed of the gas should slow down as one went farther from the galactic nuclei.

Much to their surprise, they found that the velocity of the gas 32
was a constant, whether it was near the center or near the rim of the galaxy. At first, they thought this peculiar result was unique to the Andromeda galaxy. Then they systematically began to analyze hundreds of galaxies (two hundred galaxies since 1978) and found the same curious result. Zwicky had been right all along.

The sheer weight of their observational results could not be 33
denied. Galaxy after galaxy showed the same, flat curve. Because astronomy had become technically much more sophisticated since the time of Zwicky, it was possible for other laboratories to verify Rubin's numbers rapidly. The constancy of velocity of a rotating galaxy was now a universal fact of galactic physics. Dark matter was here to stay.

For her pioneering efforts, Vera Rubin was elected to the prestigious National Academy of Science in 1981. (Since it was founded 34

---

[6] Bartusiak, *Discover*, 90. [Kaku's note]

in 1863, only 75 women among the 3,508 scientists have been elected to the academy.)

Today, Rubin is still pained by how little progress female scientists   35
have made. Her own daughter has a Ph.D. in cosmic ray physics. When she went to Japan for an international conference, she was the only woman there. "I really couldn't tell that story for a long time without weeping," Rubin recalled, "because certainly in one generation, between her generation and mine, not an awful lot has changed."[7]

Not surprisingly, Rubin is interested in stimulating the interest   36
of young girls to pursue scientific studies. She has even written a children's book, entitled *My Grandmother Is an Astronomer.*

Bending Starlight

Since Rubin's original paper, even more sophisticated analyses of   37
the universe have shown the existence of the dark matter halo, which may be as much as six times the size of the galaxy itself. In 1986, Bodhan Paczynski of Princeton University realized that if the starlight from a distant star traveled by a nearby clump of dark matter, the dark matter might bend the starlight and act as a magnifying lens, making the star appear much brighter. In this way, by looking for dim stars that suddenly got brighter, the presence of dark matter could be detected. In 1994, two groups independently reported photographing such a stellar brightening. Since then, other teams of astronomers have joined in, hoping to find more examples of stellar brightening.

In addition, the bending of starlight by a distant galaxy can be   38
used as another way in which to calculate the galaxy's weight. Anthony Tyson and his colleagues at the AT&T Bell Laboratories have analyzed light rays from dim blue galaxies at the rim of the visible universe. This cluster of galaxies acts like a gravitational lens, bending the light from other galaxies. Photos of distant galaxies have confirmed that the bending is much more than expected, meaning that their weight comes from much more than the sum of their individual stars. Ninety percent of the mass of these galaxies turns out to be dark, as predicted.

Hot and Cold Dark Matter

While the existence of dark matter is no longer in dispute, its   39
composition is a matter of lively controversy. Several schools of thought have emerged, none of them very satisfactory.

---

[7] Lightman, *Origins*, 305. [Kaku's note]

First, there is the "hot dark matter" school, which holds that   40
dark matter is made of familiar lightweight subparticles such as neutrinos, which are notoriously difficult to detect. Since the total flux
of neutrinos filling up the universe is not well known, the universe
may be bathed in a flood of neutrinos, making up the dark matter of
the universe.

If the electron-neutrino, for example, is found to have a tiny   41
mass, then there is a chance that it may have enough mass to make
up the missing mass problem. (In February 1995, physicists at the
Los Alamos National Laboratory in New Mexico announced that
they had found evidence that the electron-neutrino has a tiny mass:
one-millionth the weight of an electron. However, this result must
still be verified by other laboratories before it is finally accepted by
other physicists.)

Then there is the "cold dark matter" school, which suspects that   42
dark matter is made of heavier, slow-moving, and much more exotic
subparticles. For the past decade, physicists have been looking for
exotic candidates that might make up cold dark matter. These particles have been given strange, whimsical names, such as "axions,"
named after a household detergent. Collectively, they are called
WIMPs, for "weakly interacting massive particles." (The skeptics
have retaliated by pointing out that a significant part of dark matter
may consist of familiar but dim forms of ordinary matter, such as
red dwarf stars, neutron stars, black holes, and Jupiter-sized planets.
Not to be outdone, they have called these objects MACHOs, for
"massive astrophysical compact halo objects." However, even the
proponents of MACHOs admit that, at best, they can explain only
20 percent of the dark matter problem. In late 1994, however, a version of the MACHO theory was dealt a blow when the Hubble Space
Telescope, scanning the Milky Way galaxy for red dwarf stars, found
far fewer of these dim stars than expected.)

But perhaps the most promising candidate for WIMPs are the   43
superparticles, or "sparticles" for short. Supersymmetry,[8] we remember, was first seen as a symmetry of particle physics in the superstring
theory. Indeed, the superstring is probably the only fully consistent
theory of superparticles.

---

[8]**supersymmetry** A mathematical theory that postulates the existence of a
"superpartner" for each physical particle discovered. Every particle has a spin and its
superparticle has a spin, sometimes the same, sometimes different. All particles are
either fermions (electrons, etc.) with a spin of $\frac{1}{2}$ or bosons (photons, etc.) with spins
from 0 to 2. Mathematical models match them with superpartners that can sometimes convert bosons into fermions. Fermions are the particles that make up all the
material world. Bosons make up gravity and light.

According to supersymmetry, every particle must have a super-   44
partner, with differing spin. The leptons (electrons and neutrinos)
for example, have spin $\frac{1}{2}$. Their superpartners are called "sleptons"
and have spin 0. Likewise, the superpartners of the quarks are called
"squarks" and also have spin 0.

Furthermore, the superpartner of the spin I photon (which   45
describes light) is called the "photino." And the superpartner of the
gluons (which holds the quarks together) is called "gluino."

The main criticism of sparticles is that we have never seen them   46
in the laboratory. At present, there is no evidence that these superparticles exist. However, it is widely believed that this lack of evidence
is only because our atom smashers are too feeble to create superparticles. In other words, their mass is simply too large for our atom
smashers to produce them.

Lack of concrete evidence has not, however, prevented physicists   47
from trying to use particle physics to explain the mysteries of dark
matter and cosmology. For example, one of the leading candidates
for the WIMP is the photino.

The cancellation of the SSC, therefore, does not necessarily   48
doom our attempts to verify the correctness of the superstring. Within
the next decade, it is hoped that the increased accuracy of our astronomical observations, with the deployment of a new generation of
telescopes and satellites, may narrow down the candidates for dark
matter. If dark matter turns out to be composed, at least in part, of
sparticles, belief in the superstring theory would receive an enormous boost.

How Will the Universe Die?

Last, dark matter may prove decisive in understanding the ulti-   49
mate fate of the universe. One persistent controversy has been the fate
of an expanding universe. Some believe that there is enough matter
and gravity to reverse its expansion. Others believe that the universe is
too low in density, so that the galaxies will continue their expansion,
until temperatures around the universe approach absolute zero.

At present, attempts to calculate the average density of the uni-   50
verse show the latter to be true: the universe will die in a Cosmic
Whimper or a Big Chill, expanding forever. However, this theory is
open to experimental challenges. Specifically, there might be enough
missing matter to boost the average density of the universe.

To determine the fate of the universe, cosmologists use the   51
parameter called "omega," which measures the matter density of the
universe. If omega is greater than one, then there is enough matter

in the universe to reverse the cosmic expansion, and the universe will begin to collapse until it reaches the Big Crunch.

However, if omega is less than one, then the gravity of the uni- 52 verse is too weak to change the cosmic expansion, and the universe will expand forever, until it reaches the near-absolute-zero temperatures of the Cosmic Whimper. If omega is equal to one, then the universe is balanced between these two scenarios, and the universe will appear to be perfectly flat, without any curvature. (For omega to equal one, the density of the universe must be approximately three hydrogen atoms per cubic meter.) Current astronomical data favors a value of .1 for omega, which is too small to reverse the cosmic expansion.

The leading modification of the Big Bang theory is the inflation- 53 ary universe, which predicts a value of omega of precisely 1. However, the visible stars in the heavens only give us 1 percent of the critical density. This is sometimes called the "missing mass" problem. (It is different from the dark matter problem, which was based on purely galactic considerations.) Dust, brown dwarfs, and nonluminous stars may boost this number a bit, but not by much. For example, the results from nucleosynthesis show that the maximum value of the density of this form of nonluminous matter cannot exceed 15 percent of the critical density.

Even if we add in the dark matter halos that surround the galaxies, 54 this only brings us up to 10 percent of the critical value. So the dark matter in halos cannot solve the missing mass problem by itself. . . .

QUESTIONS FOR CRITICAL READING

1. What is the Cosmic Whimper?
2. What are the qualities of dark matter? Why is it a "problem"?
3. How will cosmology help physicists understand more about "the inner secrets of matter and energy" (para. 1)?
4. When did scientists begin to notice "that there was something wrong about our conception of the universe" (para. 8)?
5. How do scientists count the stars?
6. What would make a galaxy like ours unstable enough to fly apart?
7. Which aspects of Kaku's presentation most defy common sense?

SUGGESTIONS FOR CRITICAL WRITING

1. In two pages, try to explain the nature of dark matter and the problems associated with it to a friend who has not read Kaku's essay and who does not have a technical background.

2. Why is it important to know how the universe will end? Which theory is more compelling, the Big Crunch or the Big Chill? Do your best to represent your view as the most likely view.

3. Kaku has written in both *Beyond Einstein* and *Hyperspace* about the superstring theory, which insists that at the heart of the atom is not a hard particle but a vibrating string of energy. Consult either of those books (or other discussions of the theory) and explain it in clear terms so that your classmates will understand it. What is your view of the likelihood of such a theory being accurate?

4. After conducting a search on the Internet for information on black holes, construct an essay that clarifies the nature of the black hole. Try to integrate this information with Kaku's theories about the ways in which a study of the cosmos will contribute to an understanding of the atom's inner workings. How does the behavior of black holes defy common sense? How does it help us understand the nature of the universe?

5. Kaku mentions the decision to abandon the superconducting super collider (SSC) in 1993. Do a search in both popular and scientific journals for a discussion of the promise and purpose of the SSC. Write an essay describing the reasons the SSC was originally planned and its construction begun, as well as the reasons why it was abandoned. The CERN Hadron Collider, which at 14 miles length is shorter than the one proposed by SSC, is now up and running at Geneva, Switzerland. Research the promise of CERN and report on the findings that scientists hope it will produce. How will those findings affect Kaku's primary concerns?

6. **CONNECTIONS** How does Plato's "The Allegory of the Cave" (p. 447) prepare us for reading the work of Kaku? What does Plato say about the human mind that has special relevance to Kaku's theories? In what ways would the four idols of Francis Bacon (p. 579) come into play in our efforts to make sense of the theories of physics that Kaku discusses?

7. **CONNECTIONS** To what extent could the concept of dark matter be compared with Carl Jung's views in "The Personal and the Collective Unconscious" (p. 487)? Is dark matter a metaphorical celestial unconscious? Since neither dark matter nor the unconscious can be perceived directly, and since both seem to be profoundly influential on our daily life, what ought we to think about the information that our senses gather? How far can we rely on our sensory apprehension? What are the limits of sense perception? What intellectual processes permit us to go beyond sensory perception?

8. **SEEING CONNECTIONS** The concept of dark matter would probably never have occurred to William Cullen Bryant and Thomas Cole in Durand's *Kindred Spirits* (p. 576); however, it is likely that they saw more in nature than meets the eye. The two figures in the painting

convey a sense of the spiritual quality of nature, and Durand's composition implies a beauty that transcends the simple arrangement of forms. What is it that Bryant, Cole, and Durand see in nature that is comparable to Kaku's dark matter? What is the unseen in nature that would have inspired the figures in the painting? Would Kaku have sympathized with their conclusions? Would you?

FRANCIS FUKUYAMA
Genetic Engineering

FRANCIS FUKUYAMA (b. 1952) is Bernard Schwartz Professor of International Political Economy and director of the International Development Program at the Paul H. Nitze School of Advanced International Studies of Johns Hopkins University, in Washington, D.C., where he lives. Fukuyama was known as a neoconservative political philosopher until the Iraq War changed his mind. Today he is more centrist in his thinking. Among his personal interests are photography and antique furniture restoration. His undergraduate degree was in classics from Cornell University, where he also studied political philosophy with Allan Bloom. He was awarded his doctorate in government from Harvard University.

In an early and provocative article in the *Guardian* (October 11, 2001), Fukuyama wrote, "And if we looked beyond liberal democracy and markets, there was nothing else towards which we could expect to evolve; hence the end of history. While there were retrograde areas that resisted that process, it was hard to find a viable alternative civilization that people actually wanted to live in after the discrediting of socialism, monarchy, fascism, and other types of authoritarianism." His statement, proclaiming the end of history, catapulted him to fame. Because he was widely misunderstood, he wrote a number of explanations that clarified his views. When he said that we had reached the end of history, what he meant was that the evolution of social governmental systems had reached its peak in liberal democratic governments.

Among Fukuyama's important books are *The End of History and the Last Man* (1992); *Trust: The Social Virtues and the Creation of Prosperity* (1995); *The Great Disruption: Human Nature and the Reconstitution of Social Order* (1999); *State-Building: Governance and World Order in the Twenty-first Century* (2004); and *America at the Crossroads: Democracy, Power, and the Neoconservative Legacy*

(2006). While most of these books concern various issues of governance and their effects on large populations, under the surface is a deeper issue: how human nature has adapted to varieties of governments and how human nature actually shapes governments. The democratic state with its market economy seems, to Fukuyama, to have evolved because of what we call human nature. It is basic to our needs.

Therefore, it is not surprising that in his book *Our Posthuman Future: Consequences of the Biotechnology Revolution* (2003) Fukuyama should be worried over the possibility that some biotechnological developments could actually threaten human nature and ultimately change it. Should that happen, then the governmental system that he feels is the most highly evolved will of necessity have to change and, perhaps, change in a direction that is dark and threatening. The selection that follows, "Genetic Engineering," comes from this book and explores the achievements of biotechnology's innovations in genetic analysis and genetic alterations. Some of the alterations that may have relevance to humans have already been put into production in foods and livestock. Fukuyama reasons that it may not be long before we know enough to apply some of that technology to humans.

What worries Fukuyama is that the potential for manipulating the genes in our cells, while seemingly limited at this moment, is growing at such a rapid pace that what we thought was impossible yesterday will be almost conventional tomorrow. The Human Genome Project, which partially decoded the genetic basis of life, was expected to take until 2010 or 2020 to achieve, but with high-speed computers aiding the research, the job was completed in 2003. Not all functions of all genes are fully understood, but the identification of some that control the onset of diseases is already helping people to make lifestyle choices to avoid transmitted or inherited disabling disorders. Fukuyama is not worried about those issues as much as he is the potential for genetic engineering to not only transform individuals but also their offspring. Already, people are deciding to have more male than female babies — which will eventually create huge gender imbalances in the population in Asia — and the possibility of engineering taller, slimmer, more intelligent, disease-resistant children seems not far in the future.

Human cloning is a technology that could be available as a practical method even sooner than the kinds of engineering that would alter behavior. However, there are a great many risks involved in cloning that may make it less viable for humans than it has been for livestock. It took many failures to produce Dolly, the first cloned sheep. Many individual sheep were born with severe defects, and the risk of producing a human with such defects will probably make progress on human cloning slow. As Fukuyama points out, there are many ethical issues involved in any of these technologies, but the ethicists may be slow in keeping up with scientific developments. As it is, the major issue now is the reluctance of scientists to experiment on humans with the same zeal with which they experiment on animals.

Fukuyama's Rhetoric

Because his subject is relatively complex, Fukuyama uses a number of technical terms that are unfamiliar to most readers. When he talks about the Human Genome Sequencing Consortium, he mentions a new field of study called *proteomics,* which he immediately explains as the study of the way genes produce proteins and how the proteins fold into the special shapes they need in order to function. Everywhere, Fukuyama offers definitions of terms and concepts that might not be familiar. Two terms related to the structure of the gene, *allele* and *telomere,* were defined earlier in his book. An allele is part of a pair of genes in which one is usually dominant and the other recessive. Inheriting the trait of blue eyes, for example, depends on linking two recessive genes, one from each parent. A telomere is a special tail end on a chromosome. Young people have very long telomeres, but as cells divide the telomere shortens. Observation shows that when there are no more telomeres, the individual dies. One problem with cloning is that, since it requires adult cells, the newly born infant may have shortened telomeres on its chromosomes and, thus, a significantly shortened life.

Fukuyama explains the technologies involved in genetic experimentation in a careful, patient fashion. He uses subheads, such as, "The Road to Designer Babies," when he calls attention to what people around the world want from modern genetic technology. He points out that right now if only those who can afford "designer babies" take advantage of the technology the impact on the "genetic patrimony of mankind" will be very small—virtually insignificant. However, he also points out that agricultural experimentation with genetic modification, including the introduction of non-species-specific genes, has already spread altered plants beyond the borders of controlled farmlands. Moreover, Fukuyama cautions that there is no way to tell what the long-term effects of genetic engineering will be in one, two, or even three generations. Gene interactions are so complex that no one can really predict the precise outcome of major genetic change.

The use of enumeration is common throughout the essay. There are, for example, three obstacles to human genetic engineering. The first he calls *complex causality* (para. 17), by which he means that it is not yet clear exactly what will be caused by any specific changes; the second is the danger of human experimentation and its obvious ethical problems; while the third has to do with the overall stability of human populations. The first two obstacles he demonstrates as real, solvable issues, but the third, which would involve changing "the genetic patrimony of mankind," he feels is unlikely, at least for now. He begins another series of cautions, however, in making two points. First, the speed with which technology permits powerful changes in biology might make it possible to alter human nature in the not-so-distant future. Second, Fukuyama reminds us that many drugs have been released without our knowing precisely what they do, and the chance exists that we will experiment with genetic engineering even if we do not know all the risks (para. 20).

Fukuyama's method is to explore in some depth each of the obstacles he cites, as in his discussion of eugenics (good genetic changes) and dysgenics (bad genetic changes) in paragraphs 21 and 22. Then as he ends the essay, he again resorts to enumeration by making two points: (1) "even if genetic engineering never materializes," the current progress in biotechnology will have profound effects on twenty-first-century politics and (2) even if it takes a hundred years for genetic engineering to affect human nature, "it is by far the most consequential of all future developments in biotechnology" (para. 29). His reasoning is that human nature is basic to our ideas of morality, justice, law, and the way we should live. If human nature changes, then all we know about our culture will change, too.

PREREADING QUESTIONS: WHAT TO READ FOR

The following prereading questions may help you anticipate key issues in the discussion of Francis Fukuyama's "Genetic Engineering." Keeping them in mind during your first reading of the selection should help focus your attention.

- What is genetic engineering?
- What are the problems with cloning humans?
- How might genetic engineering affect human nature in the future?
- What are designer babies?

Genetic Engineering

> All beings so far have created something beyond themselves; and
> do you want to be the ebb of this great flood and even go back to
> the beasts rather than overcome man? What is the ape to man? A
> laughingstock or a painful embarrassment. And man shall be just
> that for the overman: a laughingstock or a painful embarrassment.
> You have made your way from worm to man, and much in you is
> still worm. Once you were apes, and even now, too, man is more
> ape than any ape.
> —FRIEDRICH NIETZSCHE, *Thus Spoke Zarathustra*, 1.3

All of the consequences described in the preceding . . . may   1
come to pass without any further progress in the most revolutionary
biotechnology of all, genetic engineering. Today, genetic engineering
is used commonly in agricultural biotechnology to produce genetically modified organisms such as Bt corn (which produces its own
insecticide) or Roundup Ready soybeans (which are resistant to certain weed-control herbicides), products that have been the focus of
controversy and protest around the world. The next line of advance
is obviously to apply this technology to human beings. Human
genetic engineering raises most directly the prospect of a new kind
of eugenics,[1] with all the moral implications with which that word is
fraught, and ultimately the ability to change human nature.

Yet despite completion of the Human Genome Project, contem-   2
porary biotechnology is today very far from being able to modify
human DNA[2] in the way that it can modify the DNA of corn or beef
cattle. Some people would argue that we will never in fact achieve
this kind of capability and that the ultimate prospects for genetic
technology have been grossly overhyped both by ambitious scientists
and by biotechnology companies out for quick profits. Changing
human nature is neither possible, according to some, nor remotely
on the agenda of contemporary biotechnology. We need, then, a balanced assessment of what this technology can be expected to achieve,
and a sense of the constraints that it may eventually face.

The Human Genome Project was a massive effort, funded by   3
the United States and other governments, to decode the entire DNA
sequence of a human being, just as the DNA sequences of lesser creatures, like nematodes and yeast, had been decoded. DNA molecules
are the famous twisted, double-stranded sequences of four bases that

---

[1] **eugenics** Improving humans by genetic control.
[2] **DNA** Deoxyribonucleic acid, the basic building block of the gene.

make up each of the forty-six chromosomes contained in the nucleus of every cell in the body. These sequences constitute a digital code that is used to synthesize amino acids,[3] which are then combined to produce the proteins that are the building blocks of all organisms. The human genome consists of some 3 billion pairs of bases, a large percentage of which consists of noncoding, "silent" DNA. The remainder constitutes genes that contain the actual blueprints for human life.

The complete sequencing of the human genome was completed way ahead of schedule, in June 2000, in part because of competition between the official government-sponsored Human Genome Project and a similar effort by a private biotech company, Celera Genomics. The publicity surrounding this event sometimes suggested that scientists had decoded the genetic basis of life, but all the sequencing did was present the transcript of a book written in a language that is only partially understood. There is great uncertainty on such basic issues as how many genes are contained in human DNA. A few months after completion of the sequencing, Celera and the International Human Genome Sequencing Consortium released a study indicating that the number was 30,000 to 40,000 instead of the more than 100,000 previously estimated. Beyond genomics lies the burgeoning field of proteomics, which seeks to understand how genes code for proteins and how the proteins themselves fold into the exquisitely complex shapes required by cells.[4] And beyond proteomics there lies the unbelievably complex task of understanding how these molecules develop into tissues, organs, and complete human beings.

The Human Genome Project would not have been possible without parallel advances in the information technology required to record, catalog, search, and analyze the billions of bases making up human DNA. The merger of biology and information technology has led to the emergence of a new field, known as bioinformatics.[5] What will be possible in the future will depend heavily on the ability of computers to interpret the mind-boggling amounts of data generated by genomics and proteomics and to build reliable models of phenomena such as protein folding.

The simple identification of genes in the genome does not mean that anyone knows what it is they do. A great deal of progress has been made in the past two decades in finding the genes connected to cystic fibrosis, sickle-cell anemia, Huntington's chorea, Tay-Sachs disease, and the like. But these have all tended to be relatively simple

4

5

6

---

[3] **amino acids** Organic compounds that are essential building blocks of proteins.

[4] Carol Ezzell, "Beyond the Human Genome," *Scientific American* 283, no. 1 (July 2000): 64–69. [Fukuyama's note]

[5] Ken Howard, "The Bioinformatics Gold Rush," *Scientific American* 283, no. 1 (July 2000): 58–63 [Fukuyama's note]

disorders, in which the pathology can be traced to a wrong allele,[6] or coding sequence, in a single gene. Other diseases are caused by multiple genes that interact in complex ways: some genes control the expression (that is, the activation) of other genes, some interact with the environment in complex ways, some produce two or more effects, and some produce effects that will not be visible until late in the organism's life cycle.

When it comes to higher-order conditions and behaviors, such as intelligence, aggression, sexuality, and the like, we know nothing more today than that there is some degree of genetic causation, from studies in behavior genetics. We have no idea what genes are ultimately responsible, but suspect that the causal relationships are extraordinarily complex. In the words of Stuart Kauffman,[7] founder and chief scientific officer of BiosGroup, these genes are "some kind of parallel-processing chemical computer in which genes are continuously turning one another on and off in some vastly complex network of interaction. Cell-signaling pathways are linked to genetic regulatory pathways in ways we're just beginning to unscramble.[8]

The first step toward giving parents greater control over the genetic makeup of their children will come not from genetic engineering but with preimplantation genetic diagnosis and screening. In the future it should be routinely possible for parents to have their embryos automatically screened for a wide variety of disorders, and those with the "right" genes implanted in the mother's womb. Present-day medical technology, such as amniocentesis and sonograms, gives parents a certain degree of choice already, as when a fetus diagnosed with Down's syndrome is aborted, or when girl fetuses are aborted in Asia. Embryos have already been successfully screened for birth defects like cystic fibrosis.[9] Geneticist Lee Silver paints a future scenario in which a woman produces a hundred or so embryos, has them automatically analyzed for a "genetic profile," and then with a few clicks of the mouse selects the one that not only lacks alleles for single-gene disorders like cystic fibrosis, but also has enhanced characteristics, such as height, hair color, and intelligence.[10] The technologies to bring this about do not exist now but are on the way: a company

7

8

---

[6] **allele** One of a pair of genes for a trait, one dominant and one recessive.

[7] **Stuart Kauffman (b. 1939)** Professor of biochemistry at the University of Pennsylvania.

[8] Interview with Stuart A. Kauffman, "Forget In Vitro — Now It's 'In Silico,'" *Scientific American* 283, no. 1 (July 2000): 62–63. [Fukuyama's note]

[9] Gina Kolata, "Genetic Defects Detected in Embryos Just Days Old," *The New York Times*, September 24, 1992, p. A1. [Fukuyama's note]

[10] Lee M. Silver, *Remaking Eden: Cloning and Beyond in a Brave New World* (New York: Avon, 1998), pp 233–47. [Fukuyama's note]

called Affymetrix, for example, has developed a so-called DNA chip that automatically screens a DNA sample for various markers of cancer and other disorders.[11] Preimplantation diagnosis and screening does not require any ability to manipulate the embryo's DNA, but limits parental choice to the kind of variation that normally occurs through sexual reproduction.

The other technology that is likely to mature well before human genetic engineering is human cloning. Ian Wilmut's[12] success in creating the cloned sheep Dolly in 1997 provoked a huge amount of controversy and speculation about the possibility of cloning a human being from adult cells. President Clinton's request to the National Bioethics Advisory Commission for advice on this subject led to a study that recommended a ban on federal funding for human cloning research, a moratorium on such activities by private companies and concerns, and consideration by Congress of a legislative ban.[13] In lieu of a congressional ban, however, the attempt to clone a human being by a non–federally funded organization remains legal. There are reports that a sect called the Raelians[14] is trying to do just that,[15] as well as a well-publicized effort by Severino Antinori and Panos Zavos.[16] The technical obstacles to human cloning are substantially smaller than in the case of either preimplantation diagnosis or genetic engineering, and have mostly to do with the safety and ethicality of experimenting with human beings.

The Road to Designer Babies

The ultimate prize of modern genetic technology will be the "designer baby."[17] That is, geneticists will identify the "gene for" a characteristic like intelligence, height, hair color, aggression, or self-esteem and use this knowledge to create a "better" version of the child. The gene in question may not even have to come from a

---

[11] Ezzell (2000). [Fukuyama's note]

[12] **Ian Wilmut (b. 1944)** Head of the Department of Gene Expression at the Roslyn Institute in Scotland.

[13] National Bioethics Advisory Commission, *Cloning Human Beings* (Rockville, Md.: National Bioethics Advisory Commission, 1997). [Fukuyama's note]

[14] **Raelians** A UFO cult that claims to have privately cloned a human being.

[15] Margaret Talbot, "A Desire to Duplicate," *The New York Times Magazine*, February 4, 2001, pp. 40–68; Brian Alexander, "(You)2," *Wired*, February 2001, 122–35. [Fukuyama's note]

[16] **Severino Antinori (b. 1945)** Italian embryologist; **Panos Zavos (b. 1949)** American scientist who claims to have cloned a human embryo.

[17] Glenn McGee, *The Perfect Baby: A Pragmatic Approach to Genetics* (Lanham, Md.: Rowman and Littlefield, 1997). [Fukuyama's note]

human being. This is, after all, what happens in agricultural biotechnology. Bt corn, first developed by Ciba Seeds (now Novartis Seeds) and Mycogen Seeds in 1996, has an exotic gene inserted into its DNA that allows it to produce a protein from the *Bacillus thuringiensis* bacterium (hence the Bt designation) that is toxic to insect pests such as the European corn borer. The resulting plant is thus genetically modified to produce its own pesticide, and it hands down this characteristic to its offspring.

Doing the same thing to human beings is, of all of the technologies discussed in this [essay], the most remote. There are two ways by which genetic engineering can be accomplished: somatic[18] gene therapy and germ-line engineering. The first attempts to change the DNA within a large number of target cells, usually by delivering the new, modified genetic material by means of a virus or "vector." A number of somatic gene therapy trials have been conducted in recent years, with relatively little success. The problem with this approach is that the body is made up of trillions of cells; for the therapy to be effective, the genetic material of what amounts to millions of cells has to be altered. The somatic cells in question die with the individual being treated, if not before; the therapy has no lingering generational effects.   11

Germ-line engineering, by contrast, is what is done routinely in agricultural biotechnology and has been successfully carried out in a wide variety of animals. Modification of the germ line requires, at least in theory, changing only one set of DNA molecules, those in the fertilized egg, which will eventually undergo division and ramify into a complete human being. While somatic gene therapy changes only the DNA of somatic cells, and therefore affects only the individual who receives the treatment, germ-line changes are passed down to the individual's offspring. This has obvious attractions for the treatment of inherited diseases, such as diabetes.   12

Among other new technologies currently under study are artificial chromosomes that would add an extra chromosome to the forty-six natural ones; the chromosome could be turned on only when the recipient was old enough to give his or her informed consent and would not be inherited by descendants.[19] This technique would avoid the need to alter or replace genes in existing chromosomes. Artificial chromosomes might thus constitute a bridge between preimplantation screening and permanent modification of the germ line.   13

---

[18] **somatic** Belonging to the body.

[19] On the technology of artificial chromosomes, see John Campbell and Gregory Stock, "A Vision for Practical Human Germline Engineering," in Stock and Campbell, eds. (2000), pp. 9–16. [Fukuyama's note]

Before human beings can be genetically modified in this manner,   14
however, a number of steep obstacles need to be overcome. The first
has to do with the sheer complexity of the problem, which suggests
to some that any meaningful kind of genetic engineering for higher-
order behaviors will simply be impossible. We noted earlier that
many diseases are caused by the interaction of multiple genes; it is
also the case that a single gene has multiple effects. It was believed at
one time that each gene produced one messenger RNA,[20] which in
turn produced one protein. But if the human genome in fact contains
closer to 30,000 than 100,000 genes, then this model cannot hold
up, since there are far more than 30,000 proteins making up the
human body. This suggests that single genes play a role in producing
many proteins and therefore have multiple functions. The allele
responsible for sickle-cell anemia, for example, also confers resistance
to malaria, which is why it is common among blacks, who trace their
ancestry to Africa, where malaria was a major disease. Repairing the
gene for sickle-cell anemia might therefore increase susceptibility to
malaria, something that may not matter much for people in North
America but would harm carriers of the new gene in Africa. Genes
have been compared to an ecosystem, where each part influences
every other part: in the words of Edward O. Wilson, "in heredity as in
the environment, you cannot do just one thing. When a gene is
changed by mutation or replaced by another gene, unexpected and
possibly unpleasant side effects are likely to follow."[21]

The second major obstacle to human genetic engineering has   15
to do with the ethics of human experimentation. The National
Bioethics Advisory Commission raised the danger of human experimentation as the chief reason for seeking a short-term ban on
human cloning. It took nearly 270 failed attempts before Dolly was
successfully cloned.[22] While many of these failures came at the
implantation stage, nearly 30 percent of all animals that have been
cloned since then have been born with serious abnormalities. As
noted earlier, Dolly was born with shortened telomeres[23] and will
probably not live as long as a sheep born normally. One would presumably not want to create a human baby until one had a much
higher chance of success, and even then the cloning process might
produce defects that wouldn't show up for years.

---

[20] **messenger RNA** Ribonucleic acid that acts as a template for protein formation within the cell.

[21] Edward O. Wilson, "Reply to Fukuyama," *The National Interest,* no. 56 (Spring
1999): 35–37. [Fukuyama's note]

[22] Gina Kolata, *Clone: The Road to Dolly and the Path Ahead* (New York: William
Morrow, 1998), p. 27. [Fukuyama's note]

[23] **telomeres** Stabilizing DNA "tails" extending from chromosomes; they shorten
with aging.

The dangers that exist for cloning would be greatly magnified in   16
the case of genetic engineering, given the multiple causal pathways
between genes and their ultimate expression in the phenotype.[24]
The Law of Unintended Consequences would apply here in spades:
a gene affecting one particular disease susceptibility might have secondary or tertiary consequences that are unrecognized at the time
that the gene is reengineered, only to show up years or even a generation later.

The final constraint on any future ability to modify human   17
nature has to do with populations. Even if human genetic engineering overcomes these first two obstacles (that is, complex causality
and the dangers of human experimentation) and produces a successful designer baby, "human nature" will not be altered unless
such changes occur in a statistically significant way for the population as a whole. The Council of Europe has recommended the ban-
ning of germ-line engineering on the grounds that it would affect
the "genetic patrimony of mankind." This particular concern, as a
number of critics have pointed out, is a bit silly: the "genetic patrimony of mankind" is a very large gene pool containing many different alleles. Modifying, eliminating, or adding to those alleles on a
small scale will change an individual's patrimony but not the human
race's. A handful of rich people genetically modifying their children
for greater height or intelligence would have no effect on species-
typical height or IQ. Fred Iklé[25] argues that any future attempt to
eugenically improve the human race would be quickly overwhelmed
by natural population growth.[26]

Do these constraints on genetic engineering, then, mean that   18
any meaningful alteration of human nature is off the table for the
foreseeable future? There are several reasons to be cautious in coming to such a judgment prematurely.

The first has to do with the remarkable and largely unantici-   19
pated speed of scientific and technological developments in the life
sciences. In the late 1980s there was a firm consensus among geneticists that it was impossible to clone a mammal from adult somatic
cells, a view that came to an end with Dolly in 1997.[27] As recently as
the mid-1990s, geneticists were predicting that the Human Genome
Project would be completed sometime between 2010 and 2020; the

---

[24] **phenotype** The general appearance of any organism; W. French Anderson, "A New Front in the Battle against Disease," in Stock and Campbell, eds. (2000), p. 43. [Fukuyama's note]

[25] **Fred Iklé (b. 1924)** Distinguished Scholar at the Center for Strategic and International Studies, Washington, D.C.

[26] Fred Charles Iklé, "The Deconstruction of Death," *The National Interest*, no. 62 (Winter 2000/01): 91–92. [Fukuyama's note]

[27] Kolata (1998), pp. 120–56. [Fukuyama's note]

actual date by which the new, highly automated sequencing machines completed the work was July 2000. There is no way of predicting what kinds of shortcuts may appear in future years to reduce the complexity of the task ahead. For example, the brain is the archetype of a so-called complex adaptive system—that is, a system made up of numerous agents (in this case, neurons and other brain cells) following relatively simple rules that produce highly complex emergent behavior at a system level. Any attempt to model a brain using brute-force computation methods—one which tries to duplicate all of the billions of neuronal connections—is almost certainly bound to fail. A complex adaptive model, on the other hand, that seeks to model system-level complexity as an emergent property might have a much greater chance of succeeding. The same may be true for the interaction of genes.

That the multiple functions of genes and gene interactions are   20 highly complex does not mean that all human genetic engineering will be on hold until we fully understand them. No technology ever develops in this fashion. New drugs are invented, tested, and approved for use all the time without the manufacturers knowing exactly how they produce their effects. It is often the case in pharmacology that side effects go unrecognized, sometimes for years, or that a drug will interact with other drugs or conditions in ways that were totally unanticipated when it was first introduced. Genetic engineers will tackle simple problems first, and then work their way up the ladder of complexity. While it is likely that higher-order behaviors are the result of the complex interactions of many genes, we don't know that this is invariably the case. We may stumble on relatively simple genetic interventions that produce dramatic changes in behavior.

The issue of human experimentation is a serious obstacle to   21 rapid development of genetic engineering but by no means an insuperable one. As in drug testing, animals will bear most of the burden of risk at first. The kinds of risks acceptable in human trials will depend on projected benefits: a disease like Huntington's chorea, which produces a one-in-two chance of dementia and death in individuals and their offspring who carry the wrong allele, will be treated differently from an enhancement of muscle tone or breast size. The mere fact that there may be unanticipated or long-term side effects will not deter people from pursuing genetic remedies, any more than it has in earlier phases of medical development.

The question of whether the eugenic or dysgenic[28] effects of   22 genetic engineering could ever become sufficiently widespread to

---

[28] **dysgenic** Genetic changes that are undesirable in humans.

affect human nature itself is similarly an open one. Obviously, any form of genetic engineering that could have significant effects on populations would have to be shown to be desirable, safe, and relatively cheap. Designer babies will be expensive at first and an option only for the well-to-do. Whether having a designer baby will ever become cheap and relatively popular will depend on how rapidly technologies like preimplantation diagnosis come down the cost curve.

There are precedents, however, for new medical technologies having population-level effects as a result of millions of individual choices. One has to look no further than contemporary Asia, where a combination of cheap sonograms and easy access to abortion has led to a dramatic shifting of sex ratios. In Korea, for example, 122 boys were born in the early 1990s for every 100 girls, compared with a normal ratio of 105 to 100. The ratio in the People's Republic of China is only somewhat lower, at 117 boys for every 100 girls, and there are parts of northern India where ratios are even more skewed.[29] This has led to a deficit of girls in Asia that the economist Amartya Sen[30] at one point estimated to be 100 million.[31] In all of these societies, abortion for the purpose of sex selection is illegal; but despite government pressure, the desire of individual parents for a male heir has produced grossly lopsided sex ratios.

Highly skewed sex ratios can produce important social consequences. By the second decade of the twenty-first century, China will face a situation in which up to one-fifth of its marriage-age male population will not be able to find brides. It is hard to imagine a better formula for trouble, given the propensity of unattached young males to be involved in activities like risk-taking, rebellion, and crime.[32] There will be compensating benefits as well: the deficit of women will allow females to control the mating process more effectively, leading to more stable family life for those who can get married.

23

24

---

[29] Nicholas Eberstadt, "Asia Tomorrow, Gray and Male," *The National Interest* 53 (1998): 56–65, Terence H. Hull, "Recent Trends in Sex Ratios at Birth in China," *Population and Development Review* 16 (1990): 63–83; Chai Bin Park, "Preference for Sons, Family Size, and Sex Ratio: An Empirical Study in Korea," *Demography* 20 (1983): 333–52; and Barbara D. Miller, *The Endangered Sex: Neglect of Female Children in Rural Northern India* (Ithaca, N.Y., and London: Cornell University Press, 1981). [Fukuyama's note]

[30] **Amartya Sen (b. 1933)** Nobel Prize–winning economist and professor at Harvard.

[31] Elisabeth Croll, *Endangered Daughters: Discrimination and Development in Asia* (London: Routledge, 2001); and Ansley J. Coale and Judith Banister, "Five Decades of Missing Females in China," *Demography* 31 (1994): 459–79. [Fukuyama's note]

[32] Gregory S. Kavka, "Upside Risks," in Carl F. Cranor, ed., *Are Genes Us?: Social Consequences of the New Genetics* (New Brunswick, N.J.: Rutgers University Press, 1994), p. 160. [Fukuyama's note]

Nobody knows whether genetic engineering will one day become   25
as cheap and accessible as sonograms and abortion. Much depends
on what its benefits are assumed to be. The most common fear
expressed by present-day bioethicists is that only the wealthy will
have access to this kind of genetic technology. But if a biotechnology
of the future produces, for example, a safe and effective way to genetically engineer more intelligent children, then the stakes would
immediately be raised. Under this scenario it is entirely plausible that
an advanced, democratic welfare state would reenter the eugenics
game, intervening this time not to prevent low-IQ people from
breeding, but to help genetically disadvantaged people raise their IQs
and the IQs of their offspring.[33] It would be the state, under these circumstances, that would make sure that the technology became cheap
and accessible to all. And at that point, a population-level effect would
very likely emerge.

That human genetic engineering will lead to unintended conse-   26
quences and that it may never produce the kinds of effects some
people hope for are not arguments that it will never be attempted.
The history of technological development is littered with new technologies that produced long-term consequences that led to their
modification or even abandonment. For instance, no large hydroelectric projects have been undertaken anywhere in the developed
world for the past couple of generations, despite periodic energy
crises and rapidly growing demand for power.[34] The reason is that
since the burst of dam building that produced the Hetch Hetchy
Dam in 1923 and the Tennessee Valley Authority in the 1930s, an
environmental consciousness has arisen that began to weigh the
long-term environmental costs of hydroelectric power. When viewed
today, the quasi-Stalinist movies that were made celebrating the
heroic construction of Hoover Dam seem quaint in their glorification
of the human conquest of nature and their blithe disregard of ecological consequences.

Human genetic engineering is only the fourth pathway to the   27
future, and the most far-off stage in the development of biotechnology. We do not today have the ability to modify human nature in
any significant way, and it may turn out that the human race will
never achieve this ability. But two points need to be made.

---

[33] This scenario has been suggested by Charles Murray. See "Deeper into the
Brain," *National Review* 52 (2000): 46–49. [Fukuyama's note]

[34] There have been major new hydroelectric projects, such as the Three Gorges
Dam in China and the Ilisu Dam in Turkey, both of which have produced strong
opposition from developed countries for their likely effects on the environment and
on the populations in the floodplain, and, in the case of the Turkish dam, for the
antiquities that will be covered by the floodwaters. [Fukuyama's note]

First, even if genetic engineering never materializes, the first   28
three stages of development in biotechnology—greater knowledge
about genetic causation, neuropharmacology, and the prolongation
of life—will all have important consequences for the politics of the
twenty-first century. These developments will be hugely controversial because they will challenge dearly held notions of human equality and the capacity for moral choice; they will give societies new
techniques for controlling the behavior of their citizens; they will
change our understanding of human personality and identity; they
will upend existing social hierarchies and affect the rate of intellectual, material, and political progress; and they will affect the nature
of global politics.

The second point is that even if genetic engineering on a species   29
level remains twenty-five, fifty, or one hundred years away, it is by
far the most consequential of all future developments in biotechnology. The reason for this is that human nature is fundamental to our
notions of justice, morality, and the good life, and all of these will
undergo change if this technology becomes widespread. . . .

QUESTIONS FOR CRITICAL READING

1. Why is it important that the human genome sequencing finished
   ahead of schedule?
2. How has genetic engineering been used in agriculture?
3. What is "silent" DNA?
4. What is your view on "genetically disadvantaged people" (para. 25)?
5. How much do scientists know about what individual genes do?
6. What is the government's position on human cloning?
7. What are the main obstacles to the progress of genetic engineering in
   humans?
8. What might be the effect of genetic engineering on the "genetic patrimony of mankind" (para. 17)?
9. Nature "experimented" on the human genome for hundreds of thousands
   of years. Why should humans not experiment on the human genome?

SUGGESTIONS FOR CRITICAL WRITING

1. If it were possible to genetically engineer "designer babies," what qualities would you try to instill into your offspring? Which qualities do you
   think other people would wish to instill into their offspring? Would you
   want those qualities to appear only in your children, or would you set
   them up so the qualities would appear in their children as well? Do you
   feel your children would congratulate you on your choices?
2. Make a list of all the reasons in favor of creating "designer babies" and
   then make a list of all the reasons against creating "designer babies." If

you are able to discuss this point with others, include their opinions in your research. After you have done enough research, take your lists and argue one side or the other of the question, either in favor of people creating "designer babies" or against their doing so.

3. Review the general obstacles that Fukuyama feels will make it difficult for genetic engineering to be practical in the immediate future. Which obstacles do you feel are the most pressing and most powerful? Which of the obstacles is most likely to be truly decisive, either stopping the project entirely or positively contributing to genetic engineering?

4. Research the most recent discussions of DNA and RNA. Write an essay that explains what these important elements of genes do and how they were discovered. Imagine yourself writing to someone who has never heard of DNA and RNA and has no idea what they do. Consider the magnitude of the possibilities inherent in DNA and the complications or obstacles it may present for the future of genetic engineering. Explain the significance of DNA and RNA in modern biology.

5. In paragraph 13, Fukuyama describes a process of adding an additional chromosome to the human genes in some individuals. The extra chromosome would not actually affect the individual child until it was switched on at a certain age—somewhat like the hormonal changes at puberty or the graying of hair in old age. Would you approve of adding such a chromosome? If so, what would you want the chromosome to do?

6. **CONNECTIONS**   Find out what you can about "silent DNA" and consider whether or not it is the biological equivalent to the perplexing dark matter of physics that Michio Kaku talks about (p. 651). Each is a mystery in its own scientific area although each is observable by scientists. What might it mean that such mysteries persist despite advances in biology and astrophysics?

7. **CONNECTIONS**   Charles Darwin (p. 597) has a great deal to say about the changes that history witnesses in species. The question of genetic engineering is closely related to natural selection. However, it is really not natural selection, but rather human selection. What would Darwin say about the possibilities that Fukuyama discusses? What warnings might he issue to those who would make decisions about genetic engineering? How would the survival of the fittest figure in the decisions of what qualities designer babies and their offspring should have? Would Darwin feel genetic engineering was ethical or desirable?

8. **SEEING CONNECTIONS**   To what extent has Fukuyama taken into account the primary concerns that seem visually evident in Durand's *Kindred Spirits* (p. 576)? Does he seem to have a significant interest in the beauty of nature? Does he seem to have a significant interest in the spiritual values that moved William Cullen Bryant and Thomas Cole? How might Fukuyama's essay have been different if he shared the values of Durand, Bryant, and Cole?

PART SEVEN

ETHICS AND MORALITY

Aristotle

Friedrich Nietzsche

Iris Murdoch

Aldo Leopold

Peter Singer and Jim Mason

INTRODUCTION

A system of morality which is based on relative emotional values
is a mere illusion, a thoroughly vulgar conception which has
nothing sound in it and nothing true.

–SOCRATES (469–399 B.C.)

God considered not action, but the spirit of the action. It is the
intention, not the deed, wherein the merit or praise of the doer
consists.

–PETER ABELARD (1079–1142)

If men were born free, they would, so long as they remained free,
form no conception of good and evil.

–BARUCH SPINOZA (1632–1677)

All morality depends upon our sentiments; and when any action
or quality of the mind pleases us after a certain manner we say it
is virtuous; and when the neglect or nonperformance of it
displeases us after a like manner, we say that we lie under an
obligation to perform it.

–DAVID HUME (1711–1776)

There are no whole truths; all truths are half-truths. It is trying to
treat them as whole truths that plays the devil.

–ALFRED NORTH WHITEHEAD (1861–1947)

To set up as a standard of public morality a notion which can
neither be defined nor conceived is to open the door to every kind
of tyranny.

–SIMONE WEIL (1909–1943)

The establishment of ethical principles that translate into moral
behavior constitutes a major step forward for civilization. To be sure,
ancient civilizations maintained rules and laws governing behavior,
and in some cases those rules were written down and adhered to by
the majority of citizens. But the move that major religions made was
to go beyond simple rules or laws—to penetrate deeper layers of
emotion to make people want to behave well toward each other. The
writers and writings in this section have all examined the nature of
morality and have come to some interesting conclusions, focusing on
various aspects of the ethical nature of humankind.

Aristotle, in the fourth century B.C., wrote a treatise on ethics
aimed at instructing his son Nichomachus. The *Nichomachean Ethics*
is the single most famous ancient document that attempts to clarify
the nature of ethical behavior and its effect on the individual. In the

selection from the *Ethics* included here, Aristotle focuses on defining the good in life, not in the abstract, but in terms of the individual's obligation to participate in statecraft—what we might call politics. Aristotle also felt that in a democracy it is everyone's duty to understand the principles by which people can live happily and well. Once he has defined the good he proceeds to examine the nature of human happiness, and eventually he connects it to "virtuous conduct" (para. 23). In the process, he examines virtuous conduct in an effort to enlighten his son on the kind of behavior that is likely to reward him with the most happiness and the best life.

Aristotle emphasizes the soul over the body, in the sense that he emphasizes the spiritual over the material world. Reason, his guide, must be followed if we are to live well, but he realizes it is often disregarded. Therefore he discusses at some length the irrational aspects of our minds that affect behavior. In the final analysis, Aristotle argues for a reasonable approach to guiding the individual's behavior with respect for others.

Friedrich Nietzsche, a nineteenth-century philosopher and critic of all social institutions, approaches the question of ethics from a completely unexpected angle. In "Morality as Anti-Nature" he argues that the moral and ethical views of traditional religions are "anti-life." He believes religious injunctions stifle individuals' natural behaviors and promote values of death rather than of life. He speculates that religion condemns certain behaviors in order to protect those who are too weak to protect themselves, and that the strong, whom Nietzsche calls "Supermen," are condemned to obey commandments that rob them of the vitality of existence. His complaint is that religions punish everyone for the sins of the few because the few are weak and unable to control themselves. Nietzsche's views have been very influential in modern thought, especially during the last decades of the nineteenth and the whole of the twentieth century.

Iris Murdoch, one of the twentieth century's most distinguished writers, spent part of her life as an Oxford don teaching philosophy. Her major interests were ethics and morals; in "Morality and Religion" she addresses the question, Can there be morality without religion? Murdoch explores the issues of virtue and duty, both of which she sees as aspects of what we think of as moral behavior, and connects them with the ideals of institutional religion. She then goes on to examine guilt, usually thought of as a religious concept, and the question of sin. That leads her to consider how religion conceives of the struggle of good and evil, aiming as it does to conquer evil through moral behavior. But a paradox arises: If evil can be totally conquered, can there still be a system of morals or a behavior that needs to be called ethical? Murdoch's method is to keep us questioning basic issues until we begin to grasp their significance.

Because of his work as a professor of game management at the University of Wisconsin, Aldo Leopold began to think about the ways humans treat land and the resources associated with it. In a number of his books, he sketched out a view that ultimately became his philosophy of a land ethic. For most people land is a commodity, and for some it is a simple economic resource. Land is exploited in many ways, and in the past some of it was spoiled and abandoned. Things would have been different if Leopold's concepts had been put into practice. He wishes us to treat land in an ethical fashion. Just as we would think it unethical to harm each other, Leopold feels we must resist harming the land. Many of us have never thought about land use as an ethical issue, but Leopold's lifework has spawned a global movement that has taken the idea of a land ethic seriously.

Similarly, Peter Singer and Jim Mason, both famous for their work on animal liberation and animal rights, try to push the ethical frontier beyond just the interaction of humans. They see our general attitude toward eating meat as a form of speciesism. They insist that speciesism, the practice of elevating the values of one species — our own — over those of all others, is essentially unethical. It is like elevating one race or one gender over others in order to bestow privilege. They discuss the issue of dominion, a concept taken from the Bible, granting people control over all of the animals, insects, fish, and other living things — as well as the land — and the power to do whatever they wish with them, including killing, eradicating, and damaging soil, animals, and "pests." Although some thinkers have reinterpreted the biblical text about dominion to suggest responsible behavior, that revision has not altered the actions of those with economic interests who spoil land for profit. Singer and Mason also spend a great deal of time discussing factory farming and the ethics of eating meat, given the ways in which animals are treated. Ultimately, they encourage people to be conscientious omnivores by eating meat from animals that have been treated well and slaughtered painlessly. They recommend vegetarianism as the best ethical choice, but being a conscientious omnivore comes in second. What they demonstrate is that the concept of ethics and morality needs to be expanded beyond the limits of our own species.

Each of these selections offers insights into the ethical underpinnings of modern culture. They clarify the nature of the good and the moral. If humankind's ultimate goal is happiness, then the path to that goal must go through the precincts of ethical and moral behavior.

VISUALIZING ETHICS AND MORALITY

Joseph Wright of Derby (1734–1797) was born and raised in Derby (pronounced "darby"), England, and after a few years in Italy centered himself as an artist there and in Liverpool, England. He is thought to be the first great painter of the industrial revolution, painting the portraits of the important industrialists based in Liverpool. He also painted scenes from a variety of industrial and commercial sites, always looking for a moment of drama in the scene. He was particularly adept at chiaroscuro—the technique of balancing strongly contrasting lights and darks—often using a single light source to highlight profound juxtapositions between the action, usually at the center of the canvas, and the inaction, at the periphery.

Originally, the philosophical disciplines of aesthetics and ethics were closely related and considered together because they both involve the question of choice. Art involves making judgments and decisions about beauty and pleasure, while ethics involves making choices about behavior, moral or otherwise. Chiaroscuro in a narrative painting can be used to imply an impending ethical decision because the sharp representation of light and dark stands as an emblem for the choice between moral and immoral behavior.

JOSEPH WRIGHT OF DERBY, *AN EXPERIMENT ON A BIRD IN THE AIR PUMP.* 1768. Oil on canvas, 6' × 8'. The National Gallery of London.

Wright's paintings of blacksmiths' shops, iron forges, and other industrial sites often featured brilliant fires illuminating workers whose postures were reminiscent of Greek and Roman deities in classical paintings. Even the furnaces were suggestive of the furnace of Vulcan in Roman myth. But at the same time he was painting these pictures, Wright also painted *The Hermit Studying Anatomy* (1771–73) and *The Alchymist* (1771), depicting the title figure trying to change base metal into gold but instead discovering phosphorous, which produces the brilliant light in the scene. Alchemy was long discredited by this time, but it remained as a reminder that science was born from such practices and progressed slowly and through unexpected paths.

These paintings seem to be connected with Wright's occasional attendance at the Lunar Society in Birmingham, which tried to reconcile the religious and ethical resistance to the birth of science. His physician, Erasmus Darwin (1731–1802), of whom Wright painted a noted portrait, was one of the principal organizers of the society. The Lunar Society, which met regularly from 1765 to 1813, convened for dinner on the night of the full moon because the extra light made it easier for people to get home.

Commentators on Wright's work have speculated on the depth of his interest in either industrial progress or the development of science. They suggest that, while he may have been interested in both, he was also paying attention to the developments in the world in which he lived. In a sense, he was keeping up with the times.

Wright's most famous painting is *An Experiment on a Bird in the Air Pump* (1768), in the National Gallery in London. It portrays a traveling scientist who performs experiments in the homes of wealthy patrons who are interested in seeing what the latest scientific developments are. The air pump was still a novelty in Wright's time, but it is clear that this scientist is a showman, almost like a traveling magician, and therefore something of an entertainer. The experiment involves taking the air out of the glass bowl in which a white cockatoo has been placed. The process creates a vacuum, which will kill the bird, thus demonstrating that oxygen is essential to life.

The audience is the homeowner and his family members, all of whom have a distinct reaction to what is happening. The scientist apparently does not permit the bird to die, but stops the experiment just short of death. The scientist's assistant, the boy in the far right of the painting, seems about to lower a birdcage in which to place the revived cockatoo, whose wing is outstretched to show that it is animate again. The moon outside the window is an allusion to the Lunar Society, which promoted public education in the development of science.

The range of psychological responses to the experiment is wide. The older man at the lower right adopts the posture of a thoughtful philosopher pondering the circumstances of the scene. The young woman next to him cannot look because she cannot abide the death of the bird, while the man in front of her calls her attention to it with his pointing hand, as if saying everything is all right. The small girl near the center, in the brightest light, looks upward with a fearful expression. The man seated to the left is simply curious and dispassionate; perhaps he is the pragmatic homeowner. Next to him is a small boy who watches with intent expectation. The two young people to the far left are often described as lovers and are clearly much more interested in each other than in the experiment.

The light source comes from a lamp behind a beaker with a portion of a human skull in it, suggesting that the scientist has performed an earlier demonstration, perhaps of anatomy. Of course, like Yorick's skull in *Hamlet,* this detail implies the mortality of those in the room. The scientist seems to be staring directly out at us. His left hand is in the process of restoring the air to the bowl, while his right arm halts the action of the pump. The circular, gemlike composition of the lit portion is reminiscent of similarly lit religious paintings, perhaps commenting on the ultimate compatibility of religion and science.

ARISTOTLE
The Aim of Man

ARISTOTLE (384–322 B.C.) is the great inheritor of Plato's influence in philosophical thought. He was a student at the Academy of Plato in Athens from age seventeen to thirty-seven, and by all accounts he was Plato's most brilliant pupil. He did not agree with Plato on all issues, however, and seems to have broken with his master around the time of Plato's death (347 B.C.). In certain of his writings he is careful to disagree with the Platonists while insisting on his friendship with them. In the *Nichomachean Ethics*, for example, the most difficult section (omitted here) demonstrates that Plato is not correct in assuming that the good exists in some ideal form in a higher spiritual realm.

One interesting point concerning Aristotle's career is that when he became a teacher, his most distinguished student was Alexander the Great, the youthful ruler who spread Greek values and laws throughout the rest of the known world. Much speculation has centered on just what Aristotle might have taught Alexander about politics. The emphasis on statecraft and political goals in the *Nichomachean Ethics* suggests that it may have been a great deal. A surviving fragment of a letter from Aristotle to Alexander suggests that he advised Alexander to become the leader of the Greeks and the master of the barbarians.

The *Nichomachean Ethics* is a difficult document. Aristotle may have written it with an eye to tutoring his son, Nichomachus, but it is also meant to be read by those who have thought deeply about human ethical behavior. "The Aim of Man" treats most of the basic issues raised in the entire document. It is difficult primarily because it is so thoroughly abstract. Abstract reason was thought to be the highest form of reason because it is independent

From the *Nichomachean Ethics*. Translated by Martin Ostwald.

of sensory experience and because only human beings can indulge in it. Aristotle, whose studies included works on plants, physics, animals, law, rhetoric, and logic, to name only some subjects, reminds us often of what we have in common with the animal and vegetable worlds. But because he values abstract thought so much, his reasoning demands unusual attention from contemporary readers.

Moreover, because he wrote so much on scientific subjects — and, unlike Plato, emphasized the role of sensory perception in scientific matters — he is careful to warn that reasoning about humankind cannot entail the precision taken for granted in science. That warning is repeated several times in this selection. The study of humankind requires awareness of people's differences of background, education, habit, temperament, and other, similar factors. Such differences will impede the kinds of precision of definition and analysis taken for granted in other sciences.

Aristotle reveals an interesting Greek prejudice when he admits that the highest good for humankind is likely to be found in statecraft. He tells us that the well-ordered state — the pride of the Greek way of life — is of such noble value that other values must take second place to it. Because current thought somewhat agrees with this view, Aristotle sounds peculiarly modern in this passage. Unlike the Christian theorists of the Middle Ages, the theorists of the Islamic insurgence, or the theorists of the Judaic Scriptures, Aristotle does not put divinity or godliness first. He is a practical man whose concerns are with the life that human beings know here on earth. When he considers the question, for instance, of whether a man can be thought of as happy before he has died (tragedy can always befall the happy man), he is thoroughly practical and does not point to happiness in heaven as any substitute for happiness on earth.

Aristotle's Rhetoric

Even though Aristotle is the author of the single most influential treatise on rhetoric, this document does not have as eloquent a style as might be expected, which has suggested to some that the manuscript was taken from the lecture notes of a student. But, of course, he does use certain minor techniques that demonstrate his awareness of rhetorical effect. He makes careful use of aphorisms — for example, "One swallow does not make a spring" and "Perfect justice is noblest, health is best, / But to gain one's heart's desire is pleasantest" (para. 21).

In terms of style, Aristotle is at a disadvantage — or perhaps the modern world is — because he addresses an audience of those who have thought very deeply on the issues of human behavior, so that his style is elevated and complex. Fortunately, nothing he says here is beyond the grasp of the careful reader, although modern readers expect to be provided with a good many concrete examples to help them understand abstract principles. Aristotle purposely avoids using examples so as not to limit too sharply the truths he has to impart.

Aristotle's most prominent rhetorical technique is definition. His overall goal in this work is to define the aim of man. Thus, the first section of this work is entitled "Definition of the Good." In "Primacy of Statecraft" he begins to qualify various types of good. Later, he considers the relationship between good and happiness (paras. 8–9) and the various views concerning happiness and its definition (paras. 10–11). By then the reader is prepared for a "Functional Definition of Man's Highest Good" (paras. 12–18). He confirms his conclusions in the section entitled "Confirmation by Popular Beliefs" (paras. 19–22). After isolating happiness as the ultimate good, he devotes paragraphs 23–32 to its causes, its effects, and the events that will affect it, such as luck and human decision. The final section (paras. 33–39) constitutes an examination of the soul (the most human element) and its relationship to virtue; he begins that section by repeating, for the third time, his definition of happiness: "happiness is a certain activity of the soul in accordance with perfect virtue."

It could be said that, rhetorically speaking, the body of the work is an exploration and definition of the highest good.

PREREADING QUESTIONS: WHAT TO READ FOR

The following prereading questions may help you anticipate key issues in the discussion of Aristotle's "The Aim of Man." Keeping them in mind during your first reading of the selection should help focus your attention.

- How does Aristotle define the good?
- What is the relationship of the good to human happiness?
- What are the two kinds of human happiness Aristotle discusses?

The Aim of Man

Definition of the Good

Every art and every "scientific investigation," as well as every 1
action and "purposive choice," appears to aim at some good; hence
the good has rightly been declared to be that at which all things aim.
A difference is observable, to be sure, among the several ends: some
of them are activities, while others are products over and above the
activities that produce them. Wherever there are certain ends over
and above the actions themselves, it is the nature of such products
to be better than the activities.

As actions and arts and sciences are of many kinds, there must 2
be a corresponding diversity of ends: health, for example, is the aim
of medicine, ships of shipbuilding, victory of military strategy, and
wealth of domestic economics. Where several such arts fall under some
one faculty—as bridle-making and the other arts concerned with
horses' equipment fall under horsemanship, while this in turn along
with all other military matters falls under the head of strategy, and
similarly in the case of other arts—the aim of the master art is always
more choiceworthy than the aims of its subordinate arts, inasmuch
as these are pursued for its sake. And this holds equally good whether
the end in view is just the activity itself or something distinct from
the activity, as in the case of the sciences above mentioned.

Primacy of Statecraft

If in all our conduct, then, there is some end that we wish on its 3
own account, choosing everything else as a means to it; if, that is to
say, we do not choose everything as a means to something else (for
at that rate we should go on *ad infinitum*[1] and our desire would be
left empty and vain); then clearly this one end must be the good—
even, indeed, the highest good. Will not a knowledge of it, then,
have an important influence on our lives? Will it not better enable us
to hit the right mark, like archers who have a definite target to aim
at? If so, we must try to comprehend, in outline at least, what that
highest end is, and to which of the sciences or arts it belongs.

Evidently the art or science in question must be the most 4
absolute and most authoritative of all. Statecraft answers best to this
description; for it prescribes which of the sciences are to have a

---

[1] *ad infinitum* Endlessly; to infinity.

place in the state, and which of them are to be studied by the different classes of citizens, and up to what point; and we find that even the most highly esteemed of the arts are subordinated to it, e.g., military strategy, domestic economics, and oratory. So then, since statecraft employs all the other sciences, prescribing also what the citizens are to do and what they are to refrain from doing, its aim must embrace the aims of all the others; whence it follows that the aim of statecraft is man's proper good. Even supposing the chief good to be eventually the same for the individual as for the state, that of the state is evidently of greater and more fundamental importance both to attain and to preserve. The securing of even one individual's good is cause for rejoicing, but to secure the good of a nation or of a city-state[2] is nobler and more divine. This, then, is the aim of our present inquiry, which is in a sense the study of statecraft.

Two Observations on the Study of Ethics

Our discussion will be adequate if we are content with as much precision as is appropriate to the subject matter; for the same degree of exactitude ought no more to be expected in all kinds of reasoning than in all kinds of handicraft. Excellence and justice, the things with which statecraft deals, involve so much disagreement and uncertainty that they come to be looked on as mere conventions, having no natural foundation. The good involves a similar uncertainty, inasmuch as good things often prove detrimental: there are examples of people destroyed by wealth, of others destroyed by courage. In such matters, then, and starting from such premises as we do, we must be content with a rough approximation to the truth; for when we are dealing with and starting out from what holds good only "as a general rule," the conclusions that we reach will have the same character. Let each of the views put forward be accepted in this spirit, for it is the mark of an educated mind to seek only so much exactness in each type of inquiry as may be allowed by the nature of the subject matter. It is equally wrong to accept probable reasoning from a mathematician and to demand strict demonstrations from an orator. 5

A man judges well and is called a good judge of the things about which he knows. If he has been educated in a particular subject he is a good judge of that subject; if his education has been well-rounded he 6

---

[2] **city-state** Athens was an independent nation, a city-state (*polis*). Greece consisted of a great many independent states, which often leagued together in confederations.

is a good judge in general. Hence no very young man is qualified to attend lectures on statecraft; for he is inexperienced in the affairs of life, and these form the data and subject matter of statecraft. Moreover, so long as he tends to be swayed by his feelings he will listen vainly and without profit, for the purport of these [lectures] is not purely theoretical but practical. Nor does it make any difference whether his immaturity is a matter of years or of character: the defect is not a matter of time, but consists in the fact that his life and all his pursuits are under the control of his passions. Men of this sort, as is evident from the case of those we call incontinent,[3] do not turn their knowledge to any account in practice; but those whose desires and actions are controlled by reason will derive much profit from a knowledge of these matters.

So much, then, for our prefatory remarks about the student, the manner of inquiry, and the aim.   7

The Good as Happiness

To resume, then: since all knowledge and all purpose aims at some good, what is it that we declare to be the aim of statecraft; or, in other words, what is the highest of all realizable goods? As to its name there is pretty general agreement: the majority of men, as well as the cultured few, speak of it as happiness; and they would maintain that to live well and to do well are the same thing as to be happy. They differ, however, as to what happiness is, and the mass of mankind give a different account of it from philosophers. The former take it to be something palpable and obvious, like pleasure or wealth or fame; they differ, too, among themselves, nor is the same man always of one mind about it: when ill he identifies it with health, when poor with wealth; then growing aware of his ignorance about the whole matter he feels admiration for anyone who proclaims some grand ideal above his comprehension. And to add to the confusion, there have been some philosophers who held that besides the various particular good things there is an absolute good which is the cause of all particular goods. As it would hardly be worthwhile to examine all the opinions that have been entertained, we shall confine our attention to those that are most popular or that appear to have some rational foundation.   8

One point not to be overlooked is the difference between arguments that start from first principles[4] and arguments that lead up to   9

---

[3]**incontinent** Uncontrolled, in this case by reason.
[4]**first principles** Concepts such as goodness, truth, and justice. Arguments that lead to first principles usually begin with familiar, less abstract evidence.

first principles. Plato very wisely used to raise this question, and to ask whether the right way is from or toward first principles—as in the racecourse there is a difference between running from the judges to the boundary line and running back again. Granted that we must start with what is known, this may be interpreted in a double sense: as what is familiar to us or as what is intelligible in itself. Our own method, at any rate, must be to start with what is familiar to us. That is why a sound moral training is required before a man can listen intelligently to discussions about excellence and justice, and generally speaking, about statecraft. For in this field we must take as our "first principles" plain facts; if these are sufficiently evident we shall not insist upon the whys and wherefores. Such principles are in the possession of, or at any rate readily accessible to, the man with a sound moral training. As for the man who neither possesses nor can acquire them, let him hear the words of Hesiod:[5]

> Best is he who makes his own discoveries;
> Good is he who listens to the wise;
> But he who, knowing not, rejects another's wisdom
>   Is a plain fool.

Conflicting Views of Happiness

Let us now resume our discussion from the point at which we   10
digressed. What is happiness, or the chief good? If it is permissible to judge from men's actual lives, we may say that the mass of them, being vulgarians, identify it with pleasure, which is the reason why they aim at nothing higher than a life of enjoyment. For there are three outstanding types of life: the one just mentioned, the political, and, thirdly, the contemplative. "The mass of men" reveal their utter slavishness by preferring a life fit only for cattle; yet their views have a certain plausibility from the fact that many of those in high places share the tastes of Sardanapalus.[6] Men of superior refinement and active disposition, on the other hand, identify happiness

---

[5]*Works and Days*, II. 293–297. [Translator's note] **Hesiod (eighth century B.C.)** Well-known Greek author. His *Works and Days* is notable for its portraits of everyday shepherd life and for its moralizing fables. His *Theogony* is a description of the creation, widely taken as accurate in his day.

[6]An ancient Assyrian king to whom is attributed the saying, "Eat, drink, and be merry: nothing else is worth a snap of the fingers." [Translator's note] **Sardanapalus (d. 880 B.C.)** Noted for his slothful and decadent life. When it was certain that he was to die—the walls of his city had been breached by an opposing army—he had his wives, animals, and possessions burned with him in his palace.

with honor, this being more or less the aim of a statesman's life. It is evidently too superficial, however, to be the good that we are seeking; for it appears to depend rather on him who bestows than on him who receives it, while we may suspect the chief good to be something peculiarly a man's own, which he is not easily deprived of. Besides, men seem to pursue honor primarily in order to assure themselves of their own merit; at any rate, apart from personal acquaintances, it is by those of sound judgment that they seek to be appreciated, and on the score of virtue. Clearly, then, they imply that virtue is superior to honor: and so, perhaps, we should regard this rather than honor as the end and aim of the statesman's life. Yet even about virtue there is a certain incompleteness; for it is supposed that a man may possess it while asleep or during lifelong inactivity, or even while suffering the greatest disasters and misfortunes; and surely no one would call such a man happy, unless for the sake of a paradox. But we need not further pursue this subject, which has been sufficiently treated of in current discussions. Thirdly, there is the contemplative life, which we shall examine at a later point.

As for the life of money-making, it is something unnatural. 11 Wealth is clearly not the good that we are seeking, for it is merely useful as a means to something else. Even the objects above mentioned come closer to possessing intrinsic goodness than wealth does, for they at least are cherished on their own account. But not even they, it seems, can be the chief good, although much labor has been lost in attempting to prove them so. With this observation we may close the present subject.

Functional Definition of Man's Highest Good

Returning now to the good that we are seeking, let us inquire 12 into its nature. Evidently it is different in different actions and arts: it is not the same thing in medicine as in strategy, and so on. What definition of good will apply to all the arts? Let us say it is that for the sake of which all else is done. In medicine this is health, in the art of war victory, in building it is a house, and in each of the arts something different, although in every case, wherever there is action and choice involved, it is a certain end; because it is always for the sake of a certain end that all else is done. If, then, there is one end and aim of all our actions, this will be the realizable good; if there are several such ends, these jointly will be our realizable goods. Thus in a roundabout way the discussion has been brought back to the same point as before; which we must now try to explain more clearly.

As there is evidently a plurality of ends, and as some of these are   13
chosen only as means to ulterior ends (e.g., wealth, flutes, and
instruments in general), it is clear that not all ends are final.[7] But the
supreme good must of course be something final. Accordingly, if
there is only one final end, this will be the good that we are seeking;
and if there is more than one such end, the most complete and final
of them will be this good. Now we call what is pursued as an end in
itself more final than what is pursued as a means to something else;
and what is never chosen as a means we call more final than what is
chosen both as an end in itself and as a means; in fact, when a thing
is chosen always as an end in itself and never as a means we call it
absolutely final. Happiness seems, more than anything else, to answer
to this description: for it is something we choose always for its own
sake and never for the sake of something else; while honor, pleasure, reason, and all the virtues, though chosen partly for themselves
(for we might choose any one of them without heeding the result),
are chosen also for the sake of the happiness which we suppose they
will bring us. Happiness, on the other hand, is never chosen for the
sake of any of these, nor indeed as a means to anything else at all.

We seem to arrive at the same conclusion if we start from the   14
notion of self-sufficiency; for the final good is admittedly self-sufficient.
To be self-sufficient we do not mean that an individual must live in
isolation. Parents, children, wife, as well as friends and fellow citizens
generally, are all permissible; for man is by nature political. To be
sure, some limit has to be set to such relationships, for if they are
extended to embrace ancestors, descendants, and friends of friends,
we should go on *ad infinitum*. But this point will be considered later
on; provisionally we may attribute self-sufficiency to that which taken
by itself makes life choiceworthy and lacking in nothing. Such a thing
we conceive happiness to be. Moreover, we regard happiness as the
most choiceworthy of all things; nor does this mean that it is merely
one good thing among others, for if that were the case it is plain that
the addition of even the least of those other goods would increase its
desirability; since the addition would create a larger amount of good,
and of two goods the greater is always to be preferred. Evidently,
then, happiness is something final and self-sufficient, and is the end
and aim of all that we do.

---

[7]**not all ends are final** By *ends* Aristotle means purposes. Some purposes are
final—the most important; some are immediate—the less important. When a corporation contributes funds to Public Broadcasting, for example, its immediate purpose may be to fund a worthwhile program. Its final purpose may be to benefit from
the publicity gained from advertising.

But perhaps it will be objected that to call happiness the supreme   15
good is a mere truism, and that a clearer account of it is still needed.
We can give this best, probably, if we ascertain the proper function
of man. Just as the excellence and good performance of a flute player,
a sculptor, or any kind of artist, and generally speaking of anyone
who has a function or business to perform, lies always in that function, so man's good would seem to lie in the function of man, if he has
one. But can we suppose that while a carpenter and a cobbler each has
a function and mode of activity of his own, man qua man[8] has none,
but has been left by nature functionless? Surely it is more likely that
as his several members, eye and hand and foot, can be shown to have
each its own function, so man too must have a function over and
above the special functions of his various members. What will such
a function be? Not merely to live, of course: he shares that even with
plants, whereas we are seeking something peculiar to himself. We
must exclude, therefore, the life of nutrition and growth. Next comes
sentient[9] life, but this again is had in common with the horse, the
ox, and in fact all animals whatever. There remains only the "practical"[10] life of his rational nature; and this has two aspects, one of
which is rational in the sense that it obeys a "rational principle," the
other in the sense that it possesses and exercises reason. To avoid
ambiguity let us specify that by "rational" we mean the "exercise or
activity," not the mere possession, of reason; for it is the former that
would seem more properly entitled to the name. Thus we conclude
that man's function is an activity of the soul in conformity with, or
at any rate involving the use of, "rational principle."

An individual and a superior individual who belong to the same   16
class we regard as sharing the same function: a harpist and a good
harpist, for instance, are essentially the same. This holds true of any
class of individuals whatever; for superior excellence with respect to
a function is nothing but an amplification of that selfsame function:
e.g., the function of a harpist is to play the harp, while that of a good
harpist is to play it well. This being so, if we take man's proper function to be a certain kind of life, viz. an activity and conduct of the soul
that involves reason, and if it is the part of a good man to perform such
activities well and nobly, and if a function is well performed when it
is performed in accordance with its own proper excellence; we may
conclude that the good of man is an activity of the soul in accordance
with virtue, or, if there be more than one virtue, in accordance with

---

[8]**man qua man** Man as such, without reference to what he may be or do.

[9]**sentient** Knowing, aware, conscious.

[10]**"practical"** Aristotle refers to the actual practices that will define the ethical
nature of the individual.

the best and most perfect of them. And we must add, in a complete life. For one swallow does not make a spring, nor does one fine day; and similarly one day or brief period of happiness does not make a man happy and blessed.

So much, then, for a rough outline of the good: the proper procedure being, we may suppose, to sketch an outline first and afterwards to fill in the details. When a good outline has been made, almost anyone presumably can expand it and fill it out; and time is a good inventor and collaborator in this work. It is in just such a way that progress has been made in the various "human techniques,"[11] for filling in the gaps is something anybody can do.

But in all this we must bear constantly in mind our previous warning: not to expect the same degree of precision in all fields, but only so much as belongs to a given subject matter and is appropriate to a particular "type of inquiry." Both the carpenter and the geometer investigate the right angle, but in different ways: the one wants only such an approximation to it as will serve his work; the other, being concerned with truth, seeks to determine its essence or essential attributes. And so in other subjects we must follow a like procedure, lest we be so much taken up with side issues that we pass over the matter in hand. Similarly we ought not in all cases to demand the "reason why"; sometimes it is enough to point out the bare fact. This is true, for instance, in the case of "first principles"; for a bare fact must always be the ultimate starting point of any inquiry. First principles may be arrived at in a variety of ways: some by induction,[12] some by direct perception, some by a kind of habituation, and others in other ways. In each case we should try to apprehend them in whatever way is proper to them, and we should take care to define them clearly, because they will have a considerable influence upon the subsequent course of our inquiry. A good beginning is more than half of the whole inquiry, and once established clears up many of its difficulties.

Confirmation by Popular Beliefs

It is important to consider our ethical "first principle" not merely as a conclusion drawn from certain premises, but also in its relation to popular opinion; for all data harmonize with a true principle, but with a false one they are soon found to be discordant.

[11] **"human techniques"** Arts or skills; in a sense, technology.

[12] **induction** A process of reasoning based on careful observation and collection of details upon which theories are based. "A kind of habituation" may refer to a combination of intellectual approaches characteristic of an individual.

Now it has been customary to divide good things into three classes: external goods on the one hand, and on the other goods of the soul and goods of the body; and those of the soul we call good in the highest sense, and in the fullest degree. "Conscious actions," i.e., "active expressions of our nature," we take, of course, as belonging to the soul; and thus our account is confirmed by the doctrine referred to, which is of long standing and has been generally accepted by students of philosophy. . . .

We are in agreement also with those who identify happiness   20
with virtue or with some particular virtue; for our phrase "activity in accordance with virtue" is the same as what they call virtue. It makes quite a difference, however, whether we conceive the supreme good as the mere possession of virtue or as its employment—i.e., as a state of character or as its active expression in conduct. For a state of character may be present without yielding any good result, as in a man who is asleep or in some other way inactive; but this is not true of its active expression, which must show itself in action, indeed in good action. As at the Olympic games it is not merely the fairest and strongest that receive the victory wreath, but those who compete (since the victors will of course be found among the competitors), so in life too those who carry off the finest prizes are those who manifest their excellence in their deeds.

Moreover, the life of those active in virtue is intrinsically pleas-   21
ant. For besides the fact that pleasure is something belonging to the soul, each man takes pleasure in what he is said to love—the horse lover in horses, the lover of sights in public spectacles, and similarly the lover of justice in just acts, and more generally, the lover of virtue in virtuous acts. And while most men take pleasure in things which, as they are not truly pleasant by nature, create warring factions in the soul, the lovers of what is noble take pleasure in things that are truly pleasant in themselves. Virtuous actions are things of this kind; hence they are pleasant for such men, as well as pleasant intrinsically. The life of such men, therefore, requires no adventitious[13] pleasures, but finds its own pleasure within itself. This is further shown by the fact that a man who does not enjoy doing noble actions is not a good man at all: surely no one would call a man just who did not enjoy performing just actions, nor generous who did not enjoy performing generous actions, and so on. On this ground too, then, actions in conformity with virtue must be intrinsically pleasant. And certainly they are good as well as noble, and both in the highest degree, if the judgment of the good man is any criterion; for he will judge them as

---

[13] **adventitious** Unnecessary; superfluous.

we have said. It follows, therefore, that happiness is at once the best and noblest and pleasantest of things, and that these attributes are not separable as the inscription at Delos[14] pretends:

> Perfect justice is noblest, health is best,
> But to gain one's heart's desire is pleasantest.

For our best activities possess all of these attributes; and it is in our best activities, or in the best one of them, that we say happiness consists.

Nevertheless, happiness plainly requires external goods as well; 22 for it is impossible, or at least not easy, to act nobly without the proper equipment. There are many actions that can only be performed through such instruments as friends, wealth, or political influence; and there are some things, again, the lack of which must mar felicity, such as good birth, fine children, and personal comeliness: for the man who is repulsive in appearance, or ill-born, or solitary and childless does not meet the requirements of a happy man, and still less does one who has worthless children and friends, or who has lost good ones by death. As we have said, then, happiness seems to require the addition of external prosperity, and this has led some to identify it with "good fortune," just as others have made the opposite mistake of identifying it with virtue.

Sources of Happiness

For the same reason there are many who wonder whether happi- 23 ness is attained by learning, or by habituation or some other kind of training, or whether it comes by some divine dispensation,[15] or even by chance. Well, certainly if the gods do give any gifts to men we may reasonably suppose that happiness is god-given; indeed, of all human blessings it is the most likely to be so, inasmuch as it is the best of them all. While this question no doubt belongs more properly to another branch of inquiry, we remark here that even if happiness is not god-sent but comes as a result of virtue or some kind of learning or training, still it is evidently one of the most divine things in the world, because that which is the reward as well as the end and aim of virtuous conduct must evidently be of supreme excellence, something divine and most blessed. If this is the case, happiness must further be something that can be generally shared; for with the exception of

---

[14]**inscription at Delos** Delos is the island that once held the Athenian treasury. It was the birthplace of Apollo, with whom the inscription would be associated.
[15]**divine dispensation** A gift of the gods.

those whose capacity for virtue has been stunted or maimed, everyone will have the ability, by study and diligence, to acquire it. And if it is better that happiness should be acquired in this way than by chance, we may reasonably suppose that it happens so; because everything in nature is arranged in the best way possible—just as in the case of man-made products, and of every kind of causation, especially the highest. It would be altogether wrong that what is greatest and noblest in the world should be left to the dispensation of chance.

Our present difficulty is cleared up by our previous definition of   24 happiness, as a certain activity of the soul in accordance with virtue; whereas all other sorts of good are either necessary conditions of, or cooperative with and naturally useful instruments of this. Such a conclusion, moreover, agrees with the proposition we laid down at the outset: that the end of statecraft is the best of all ends, and that the principal concern of statecraft is to make the citizens of a certain character—namely, good and disposed to perform noble actions.

Naturally, therefore, we do not call an ox or a horse or any other   25 brute happy, since none of them is able to participate in conduct of this kind. For the same reason a child is not happy, since at his age he too is incapable of such conduct. Or if we do call a child happy, it is in the sense of predicting for him a happy future. Happiness, as we have said, involves not only a completeness of virtue but also a complete lifetime for its fulfillment. Life brings many vicissitudes and chance happenings, and it may be that one who is now prosperous will suffer great misfortunes in his old age, as is told of Priam[16] in the Trojan legends; and a man who is thus buffeted by fortune and comes to a miserable end can scarcely be called happy.

Happiness and the Vicissitudes of Fortune

Are we, then, to call no one happy while he lives? Must we, as   26 Solon[17] advises, wait to see his end? And if we accept this verdict, are we to interpret it as meaning that a man actually becomes happy only after he is dead? Would not this be downright absurd, especially for us who define happiness as a kind of vital activity? Or if we reject this interpretation, and suppose Solon to mean rather that it is only after death, when beyond the reach of further evil and calamity that a man can safely be said to have been happy during his life, there is still a

---

[16]**Priam** King of Troy in Homer's *Iliad*. He suffered a terrible reversal of fortune when Troy was defeated by the Greeks.

[17]**Solon (638–558 B.C.)** Greek lawgiver and one of Greece's earliest poets. He was one of the Seven Sages of Athens.

possible objection that may be offered. For many hold that both good and evil may in a certain sense befall a dead man (just as they may befall a living man even when he is unconscious of them)—e.g., honors and disgraces, and the prosperity or misfortune of his children and the rest of his descendants. And this presents a further problem: suppose a man to have lived to a happy old age, and to have ended as he lived, there are still plenty of reverses that may befall his descendants—some of them will perhaps lead a good life and be dealt with by fortune as they deserve, others not. (It is clear, too, that a man's relationship to his descendants admits of various degrees.) It would be odd, then, if the dead man were to change along with the fortunes of his descendants, becoming happy and miserable by turns; although, to be sure, it would be equally odd if the fortunes of his descendants did not affect him at all, even for a brief time.

But let us go back to our earlier question,[18] which may perhaps   27
clear up the one we are raising at present. Suppose we agree that we must look to the end of a man's life, and only then call him happy, not because he then *is* happy but because we can only then know him to have been so: Is it not paradoxical to have refused to call him happy during just the period when happiness was present to him? On the other hand, we are naturally loath to apply the term to living men, considering the vicissitudes to which they are liable. Happiness, we argue, must be something that endures without any essential change, whereas a living individual may experience many turns of fortune's wheel. Obviously if we judge by his changing fortunes we shall have to call the same man now happy now wretched, thereby regarding the happy man as a kind of chameleon and his happiness as built on no secure foundation; yet it surely cannot be right to regard a man's happiness as wholly dependent on his fortunes. True good and evil are not of this character; rather, as we have said, although good fortune is a necessary adjunct to a complete human life, it is virtuous activities that constitute happiness, and the opposite sort of activities that constitute its opposite.

The foregoing difficulty [that happiness can be judged of only   28
in retrospect] confirms, as a matter of fact, our theory. For none of man's functions is so permanent as his virtuous activities—indeed, many believe them to be more abiding even than a knowledge of the sciences; and of his virtuous activities those are the most abiding which are of highest worth, for it is with them that anyone blessed with supreme happiness is most fully and most continuously occupied, and hence never oblivious of. The happy man, then, will possess

---

[18] I.e., whether we are to call no one happy while he still lives. [Translator's note]

this attribute of permanence or stability about which we have been inquiring, and will keep it all his life; because at all times and in preference to everything else he will be engaged in virtuous action and contemplation, and he will bear the changes of fortune as nobly and in every respect as decorously as possible, inasmuch as he is truly good and "four-square beyond reproach."[19]

But the dispensations of fortune are many, some great, others small. Small ones do not appreciably turn the scales of life, but a multitude of great ones, if they are of the nature of blessings, will make life happier; for they add to life a grace of their own, provided that a man makes noble and good use of them. If, however, they are of an evil kind, they will crush and maim happiness, in that they bring pain and thereby hinder many of our natural activities. Yet true nobility shines out even here, if a multitude of great misfortunes be borne with calmness — not, to be sure, with the calmness of insensibility, but of nobility and greatness of soul.   29

If, as we have declared, it is our activities that give life its character, then no happy man can become miserable, inasmuch as he will never do what is hateful or base. For we hold that the truly good and wise man will bear with dignity whatever fortune sends, and will always make the best of his circumstances, as a good general makes the most effective use of the forces at his command, and a good shoemaker makes the best shoes out of the leather that is available, and so in the case of the other crafts. On this interpretation, the happy man can never become miserable — although of course he will not be blessed with happiness in the full sense of the word if he meets with such a fate as Priam's. At all events, he is not variable and always changing; for no ordinary misfortunes but only a multitude of great ones will dislodge him from his happy state, and should this occur he will not readily recover his happiness in a short time, but only, if at all, after a long period has run its course, during which he has achieved distinctions of a high order.   30

Is there any objection, then, to our defining a happy man as one whose activities are an expression of complete virtue, and who at the same time enjoys a sufficiency of worldly goods, not just for some limited period, but for his entire lifetime? Or perhaps we had better add the proviso that he shall be destined to go on living in this manner, and die as he has lived; for, whereas the future is obscure to   31

---

[19] A quotation from Simonides. [Translator's note] **Simonides (556?–469 B.C.)** Greek lyric poet who lived and wrote for a while in Athens. His works survive in a handful of fragments; this quotation is from fragment 5.

us, we conceive happiness to be an end, something altogether and in every respect final and complete. Granting all this, we may declare those living men to be "blessed with supreme happiness" in whom these conditions have been and are continuing to be fulfilled. Their blessedness, however, is of human order.

So much for our discussion of this question.   32

Derivation of the Two Kinds of Human Excellence

Since happiness is a certain activity of the soul in accordance with   33
perfect virtue, we must next examine the nature of virtue. Not only will such an inquiry perhaps clarify the problem of happiness; it will also be of vital concern to the true student of statecraft, whose aim is to make his fellow citizens good and law-abiding. The Cretan and Spartan lawgivers,[20] as well as such others as may have resembled them, exemplify this aim. And clearly, if such an inquiry has to do with statecraft, it will be in keeping with our original purpose to pursue it.

It goes without saying that the virtue we are to study is human   34
virtue, just as the good that we have been inquiring about is a human good, and the happiness a human happiness. By human virtue we mean virtue not of the body but of the soul, and by happiness too we mean an activity of the soul. This being the case, it is no less evident that the student of statecraft must have some knowledge of the soul, than that a physician who is to heal the eye or the whole body must have some knowledge of these organs; more so, indeed, in proportion as statecraft is superior to and more honorable than medicine. Now all physicians who are educated take much pains to know about the body. Hence as students of statecraft, too, we must inquire into the nature of the soul; but we must do so with reference to our own distinctive aim and only to the extent that it requires, for to go into minuter detail would be more laborious than is warranted by our subject matter.

We may adopt here certain doctrines about the soul that have   35
been adequately stated in our public discourses:[21] as that the soul may be distinguished into two parts, one of which is irrational while the other possesses reason. Whether these two parts are actually distinct like the parts of the body or any other divisible thing, or are

---

[20] **Cretan and Spartan lawgivers** Both Crete and Sparta were noted for their constitutions, based on the laws of Gortyn in Crete. These laws were aristocratic, not democratic as in Athens; they promoted a class system and a rigid code of personal behavior.

[21] **our public discourses** Aristotle may be referring to speeches at which the public is welcome, as opposed to his lectures to students.

distinct only in a logical sense, like convex and concave in the circumference of a circle, is immaterial to our present inquiry.

Of the irrational part, again, one division is apparently of a vegetative nature and common to all living things: I mean that which is the cause of nutrition and growth. It is more reasonable to postulate a vital faculty of this sort, present in all things that take nourishment, even when in an embryo stage, and retained by the full-grown organism, than to assume a special nutritive faculty in the latter. Hence we may say that the excellence belonging to this part of the soul is common to all species, and not specifically human: a point that is further confirmed by the popular view that this part of the soul is most active during sleep. For it is during sleep that the distinction between good men and bad is least apparent; whence the saying that for half their lives the happy are no better off than the wretched. This, indeed, is natural enough, for sleep is an inactivity of the soul in those respects in which the soul is called good or bad. (It is true, however, that to a slight degree certain bodily movements penetrate to the soul; which is the reason why good men's dreams are superior to those of the average person.) But enough of this subject: let us dismiss the nutritive principle, since it has by nature no share in human excellence. [36]

There seems to be a second part of the soul, which though irrational yet in some way partakes of reason. For while we praise the rational principle and the part of the soul that manifests it in the case of the continent and incontinent man alike, on the ground that it exhorts them rightly and urges them to do what is best; yet we find within these men another element different in nature from the rational element, and struggling against and resisting it. Just as ataxic limbs,[22] when we choose to move them to the right, turn on the contrary to the left, so it is with the soul: the impulses of the incontinent man run counter to his ruling part. The only difference is that in the case of the body we see what it is that goes astray, while in the soul we do not. Nevertheless the comparison will doubtless suffice to show that there is in the soul something besides the rational element, opposing and running counter to it. (In what sense the two elements are distinct is immaterial.) But this other element, as we have said, seems also to have some share in a rational principle: at any rate, in the continent man it submits to reason, while in the man who is at once temperate and courageous it is presumably all the more obedient; for in him it speaks on all matters harmoniously with the voice of reason. [37]

---

[22] **ataxic limbs** Aristotle refers to a nervous disorder of the limbs.

Evidently, then, the irrational part of the soul is twofold. There   38
is the vegetative element, which has no share in reason, and there is
the concupiscent,[23] or rather the appetitive element, which does in a
sense partake of reason, in that it is amenable and obedient to it: i.e.,
it is rational in the sense that we speak of "having *logos* of" [paying
heed to] father and friends, not in the sense of "having *logos* of"
[having a rational understanding of] mathematical truths. That this
irrational element is in some way amenable to reason is shown by
our practice of giving admonishment, and by rebuke and exhortation generally. If on this account it is deemed more correct to regard
this element as also possessing reason, then the rational part of the
soul, in turn, will have two subdivisions: the one being rational in
the strict sense as actually possessing reason, the other merely in the
sense that a child obeys its father.

Virtue, too, is differentiated in accordance with this division of   39
the soul: for we call some of the virtues intellectual and others moral:
wisdom, understanding, and sagacity being among the former, liberality and temperance among the latter. In speaking of a man's character
we do not say that he is wise or intelligent, but that he is gentle
or temperate; yet we praise the wise man too for the disposition he has
developed within himself, and praiseworthy dispositions we call
virtues.

---

[23]**concupiscent** Sexual; Aristotle corrects himself to refer to the general nature
of desire.

QUESTIONS FOR CRITICAL READING

1. Define the following terms: *good, virtue, honor, happiness, truth, soul, body.*
2. In the first paragraphs of the selection, Aristotle talks about aims and
   ends. What does he mean by these terms?
3. Do you feel that Aristotle's view of the relationship of virtue to happiness is as relevant today as he argued it was in his day?
4. What is Aristotle's attitude toward most people?
5. What characteristics can we assume about the audience for whom
   Aristotle writes?
6. In what senses is the selection modern? In what senses is it antique or
   dated?

SUGGESTIONS FOR CRITICAL WRITING

1. Aristotle discusses the virtuous life in this selection. How would you
   apply his views to your own life? What ethical issues is Aristotle pointing

us toward in this essay? To what extent does his guidance translate to modern life? Explain.

2. In his section on the primacy of statecraft, Aristotle makes a number of assertions regarding the relationship of the happiness of the individual to the welfare (or happiness) of the state. Clarify as much as possible the relationship of the individual's happiness to that of the state. How can a state be happy? Is the term relevant to anything other than an individual? Does Aristotle think that the individual's interests should be subservient to the state's?

3. In paragraph 15, Aristotle talks about the function of man. Relying on that discussion and other aspects of the work, write your own version of "The Function of Man." Be sure to use *man* as a collective term for both men and women. Once you have clarified the function of man, establish the connection between function and happiness. Is it true that the best-functioning person will be the happiest person? Aristotle implies that it is not enough to be, say, honorable or noble, but that one must act honorably or nobly. Is the implication true?

4. Take Aristotle's definition, "Happiness is a certain activity of the soul in accordance with perfect virtue." Define it in terms that are clear not only to you but also to your peers. Take care to include each part of the definition: "certain activity" (or lack of it), "soul" (which in modern terms may be "personality" or "psyche"), "in accordance with," "perfect virtue." You may rely on any parts of the selection that can be of help, but be sure to use the topic of definition to guide you through the selection. You certainly may disagree with Aristotle or amplify aspects of his definitions. In one sense, you will be defining *happiness* for yourself and your times.

5. In his "confirmation by popular beliefs" (para. 19 and following), Aristotle talks about the good. He mentions three classes of good, ranking them in order from lowest to highest: external goods, goods of the body, and goods of the soul. Using concrete examples, define each of these classes of good. Do you agree with Aristotle's order? Do you think that your peers agree with it? Where possible, give examples to help establish the validity of your opinion. Finally, do you think that our society in general puts the same value on these three classes of good that Aristotle does? Again, use examples where possible.

6. Analyze the following quotations from the selection, taking a stand on the question of whether or not Aristotle is generally correct in his assertion about the aim of man:

> It is in our best activities, or in the best one of them, that we say happiness consists. (para. 21)

> A man who does not enjoy doing noble actions is not a good man at all. (para. 21)

> Even supposing the chief good to be eventually the same for the individual as for the state, that of the state is evidently of greater and more fundamental importance both to attain and to preserve. (para. 4)

In life . . . those who carry off the finest prizes are those who manifest their excellence in their deeds. (para. 20)

If, as we have declared, it is our activities that give life its character, then no happy man can become miserable, inasmuch as he will never do what is hateful or base. (para. 30)

7. **CONNECTIONS** Write an essay in which you define happiness by comparing Aristotle's views with those in Jean-Jacques Rousseau's "The Origin of Civil Society" (p. 55) or in Thomas Jefferson's Declaration of Independence (p. 77). Compare their attitudes toward material and spiritual happiness as well as their attitudes toward political freedom and the need for possessions. What does Aristotle leave out that others feel is important?

8. **SEEING CONNECTIONS** The people in the household featured in Wright's *An Experiment on a Bird in the Air Pump* (p. 687) have obviously chosen to have the scientist come into their house to perform his experiments. How would observing this experiment have contributed to the happiness of those assembled in the painting? What is the nature of good in this painting? What role does virtue play in the painting? Considering the soul in psychological terms, what range of soulful experiences are present in the painting? Do they all contribute to ultimate happiness?

FRIEDRICH NIETZSCHE
Morality as Anti-Nature

FRIEDRICH NIETZSCHE (1844–1900), one of the most influential German philosophers, is the man who declared that God is dead (in *The Gay Science*, 1882). The statement came from his conviction that science had altered the balance between humans and nature, that psychology had begun to explain the unconscious mind, and that the commitment to religious belief of earlier times would give way. The result would be to leave people without a sense of hope or purpose unless they could create it for themselves. Like many historians and philosophers of the day, he feared that modern civilization itself was somehow hanging in the balance, and that unless people refashioned the spiritual energy that brought progress and prosperity, the foundations of society would collapse.

In some of his writing he characterized power as the driving force for most people. Two late works that have been influential in modern thought, *Daybreak: Reflections on Moral Prejudices* (1881) and *Thus Spoke Zarathustra* (1883–1885), begin to develop some of his most important thinking regarding what he called "the will to power." His solution to the problem of modernity was self-mastery, which he felt was the key to transcending the confusion of modern thought. Realizing that self-mastery was not an easy state to achieve, he called the man who could create his own moral and ethical values instead of blindly following conventional or societal standards "superman."

Nietzsche's personal life was difficult. Both his grandfathers were Lutheran ministers, and his paternal grandfather was a theological scholar whose book *Gamaliel* (1796) declared the permanency of Christianity. His father was also a Lutheran minister, but

From *The Twilight of the Idols* (1888) in *The Portable Nietzsche*. Translated by Walter Kaufmann.

he died when Friedrich was four years old. He and his younger sister had to leave their family home in the Prussian province of Saxony and live with relatives in Naumberg. When he was fourteen, he went to boarding school and prepared for the University of Bonn (1864), then the University of Leipzig (1865). His studies were in theology and philology—the study of the interpretation of primarily biblical and classical texts. He was also deeply fascinated by music—which he both played and composed—and eventually grew to love the music of Richard Wagner (1813–1883), which he felt expressed the spiritual realities of modern life.

Nietzsche's father died of an unspecified brain ailment. Nietzsche himself was ill much of his life. When he joined the army after university, he experienced a bad accident on a horse that left him weak and impaired. In 1870 during the Franco-Prussian War (1870–1871), Nietzsche served in a hospital unit and witnessed the carnage of war. He contracted illnesses in the wards that stayed with him for the rest of his life. He may have contracted syphilis either during this period or earlier, and in 1889 he began to show signs of brain sickness that made it necessary for him to be in a sanatorium. His mother and later his sister Elizabeth cared for him until his death.

Despite his short life, Nietzsche achieved much. In 1868, at the age of twenty-four, he became a professor of classical philology at the University of Basel in Switzerland. He published a considerable number of important and widely regarded books. *The Birth of Tragedy from the Spirit of Music* (1872), his first book, caught the eye of Wagner and helped establish Nietzsche's reputation. That book was an attempt to clarify the two basic religious forces in humankind: Apollonian intellectuality and Dionysian passion. Apollo was a god of conscience devoted to the arts and music. Dionysius, patron of Greek tragedy, was associated with vegetation, plentifulness, passion, and especially wine—and therefore inspiration. In 1873 Nietzsche published *Unfashionable Observations*, a critique of cultural critics. Before illness forced him to resign his professorship at the University of Basel in 1879, he published *Human, All-Too-Human* (1878), a collection of aphorisms—brief statements ranging from a single line to a page of text. This style, repeated in *Thus Spoke Zarathustra* and other works, became one of the hallmarks of his rhetorical approach. It gave him the appearance of a sage uttering wise sayings.

His production after leaving the university was not diminished. In 1882 he published one of his most impressive books, *The Gay Science*, which postulated an alternative to the Christian view that another world exists after death. His suggestion was known as "eternal recurrence," a view that says we are destined to live this life over and over again down to the slightest detail. The point of this observation was to make people take this life seriously enough to live it so well that they would not mind living it again. The concept of eternal recurrence influenced twentieth-century existentialists, who agreed that the way one lived life was the way one defined oneself.

The Genealogy of Morals (1887) was a critique of contemporary religion, especially Christianity. It emphasized his views about moral and ethical values and rejected the conventional views as being essentially based on an attack on our natural feelings and motives. A section of that book, "Beyond Good and Evil," attempts to neutralize those terms, which he sees as props of conventional religious thought.

The Twilight of the Idols: Or How One Philosophizes with a Hammer (1888), from which this selection is taken and one of his last books, is a careful attack on contemporary religious beliefs and an analysis of important philosophers such as Socrates and Plato as well as of more modern thinkers. Its title is a play on an opera by Wagner called *The Twilight of the Gods* and reveals his essential attitudes toward ethical values as maintained by most religions. Some of his basic views on ethics and morality are in evidence in the selection that follows.

Nietzsche's Rhetoric

"Morality as Anti-Nature" is a careful argument that attempts to prove that moral pronouncements by major religions are designed to stifle people's natural behaviors. According to Nietzsche, people give in to their natural, often destructive impulses because they are weak. Consequently, religions seek to enforce a moral code of conduct by threatening all people—even those who could easily control themselves—with damnation in the next world for any infraction of that code. Nietzsche regards passion as a good thing, but as he states in paragraph 1, "all the old moral monsters" agree that we must kill the passions. He opens by critiquing the Sermon on the Mount, reminding us that "it is said, for example, with particular reference to sexuality: 'If thy eye offend thee, pluck it out.' Fortunately, no Christian acts in accordance with this precept" (para. 1). This is a rhetorical salvo against many of his readers' standard views of religion.

He continues by demonstrating that religions prohibit various forms of sensuality in an effort to promote spirituality, stating,

"The spiritualization of sensuality is called *love*: it represents a great triumph over Christianity" (para. 5). This is an explosive statement, much like others he makes as he develops his argument. He then addresses another passion: hostility. This becomes an interesting political concept when he asserts that the success of the then German government, the Second Reich, depends on having enemies. As he states somewhat ironically in paragraph 5, "Another triumph is our spiritualization of *hostility*. It consists in a profound appreciation of the value of having enemies: in short, it means acting and thinking in the opposite way from that which has been the rule. The church always wanted the destruction of its enemies; we, we immoralists and Antichristians, find our advantage in this, that the church exists." His own writing in this selection demonstrates his position: he is opposed to conventional views of morals, and in order to clarify his own thoughts he needs to have the opposition of the church's views.

One of his rhetorical devices—in addition to the bald oppositional stance he takes in the opening of the selection—is the aphorism. He looks for opportunities to make a clear statement that capsulizes his views. The last sentence in paragraph 8 is an example: "Life has come to an end where the 'kingdom of God' begins." He describes himself as an immoralist—by which he means one who does not subscribe to conventional morals (but not one who acts immorally)—and states, "But we ourselves, we immoralists, are the answer" (para. 12). His most inflammatory aphorism is his last sentence: "Christianity is a metaphysics of the hangman" (para. 28). All this is rather shocking today; imagine what its effect was in 1888.

Among his less sensational rhetorical strategies is his careful enumeration of the elements of his argument. The first six sections examine specific details concerning the moral prohibitions of modern religions. His purpose here is to clarify his title, which he does in paragraph 8 when he states, "*Anti-natural* morality—that is, almost every morality which has so far been taught, revered, and preached—turns, conversely, *against* the instincts of life: it is *condemnation* of these instincts, now secret, now outspoken and impudent."

He then goes on to enumerate what he calls "The Four Great Errors": 1. the error of confusing cause and effect (paras. 13–15); 2. the error of false causality (paras. 16–18); 3. the error of imaginary causes (paras. 19–25); and 4. the error of free will (paras. 26–28). Each of these is treated carefully, sometimes with an example, but always with a clearly developed analysis.

Nietzsche offers modern readers a way of thinking that helps us avoid taking the views of Moses, Aristotle, Jesus, or Muhammad for granted. He provides modern thinkers with a challenge that many have gladly accepted.

PREREADING QUESTIONS: WHAT TO READ FOR

The following prereading questions may help you anticipate key issues in the discussion of Friedrich Nietzsche's "Morality as Anti-Nature." Keeping them in mind during your first reading of the selection should help focus your attention.

- What traditional moral views does Nietzsche attack?
- Why does Nietzsche think religious morals are anti-nature?
- What does Nietzsche say about the confusion of cause and effect?

Morality as Anti-Nature

1

All passions have a phase when they are merely disastrous, when   1
they drag down their victim with the weight of stupidity—and a later, very much later phase when they wed the spirit, when they "spiritualize" themselves. Formerly, in view of the element of stupidity in passion, war was declared on passion itself, its destruction was plotted; all the old moral monsters are agreed on this: *il faut tuer les passions.*[1] The most famous formula for this is to be found in the New Testament, in that Sermon on the Mount, where, incidentally, things are by no means looked at from a height. There it is said, for example, with particular reference to sexuality: "If thy eye offend thee, pluck it out." Fortunately, no Christian acts in accordance with this precept. *Destroying* the passions and cravings, merely as a preventive measure against their stupidity and the unpleasant consequences of this stupidity—today this itself strikes us as merely another acute form of stupidity. We no longer admire dentists who "pluck out" teeth so that they will not hurt any more.

---

[1] *il faut tuer les passions* One must kill the passions.

To be fair, it should be admitted, however, that on the ground   2
out of which Christianity grew, the concept of the "*spiritualization* of
passion" could never have been formed. After all the first church, as is
well known, fought *against* the "intelligent" in favor of the "poor in
spirit." How could one expect from it an intelligent war against passion? The church fights passion with excision in every sense: its practice, its "cure," is *castratism*.[2] It never asks: "How can one spiritualize,
beautify, deify a craving?" It has at all times laid the stress of discipline
on extirpation[3] (of sensuality, of pride, of the lust to rule, of avarice, of
vengefulness). But an attack on the roots of passion means an attack
on the roots of life: the practice of the church is *hostile to life*.

2

The same means in the fight against a craving—castration,   3
extirpation—is instinctively chosen by those who are too weak-willed,
too degenerate, to be able to impose moderation on themselves; by
those who are so constituted that they require *La Trappe*,[4] to use a
figure of speech, or (without any figure of speech) some kind of
definitive declaration of hostility, a *cleft* between themselves and the
passion. Radical means are indispensable only for the degenerate;
the weakness of the will—or, to speak more definitely, the inability
not to respond to a stimulus—is itself merely another form of degen-
eration. The radical hostility, the deadly hostility against sensuality,
is always a symptom to reflect on: it entitles us to suppositions concerning the total state of one who is excessive in this manner.

This hostility, this hatred, by the way, reaches its climax only   4
when such types lack even the firmness for this radical cure, for this
renunciation of their "devil." One should survey the whole history of
the priests and philosophers, including the artists: the most poisonous things against the senses have been said not by the impotent,
nor by ascetics,[5] but by the impossible ascetics, by those who really
were in dire need of being ascetics.

3

The spiritualization of sensuality is called *love*: it represents a great   5
triumph over Christianity. Another triumph is our spiritualization of
hostility. It consists in a profound appreciation of the value of having
enemies: in short, it means acting and thinking in the opposite way
from that which has been the rule. The church always wanted the

---

[2]**castratism** Cutting off.
[3]**extirpation** Rooting out.
[4]***La Trappe*** The Trappist order of monks. They do not speak.
[5]**ascetics** Those practicing extreme self-discipline, often hermits.

destruction of its enemies; we, we immoralists and Antichristians, find our advantage in this, that the church exists. In the political realm too, hostility has now become more spiritual—much more sensible, much more thoughtful, much more *considerate*. Almost every party understands how it is in the interest of its own self-preservation that the opposition should not lose all strength; the same is true of power politics. A new creation in particular—the new *Reich*,[6] for example—needs enemies more than friends: in opposition alone does it *feel* itself necessary, in opposition alone does it *become* necessary.

Our attitude to the "internal enemy" is no different: here too we   6
have spiritualized hostility; here too we have come to appreciate its value. The price of fruitfulness is to be rich in internal opposition; one remains young only as long as the soul does not stretch itself and desire peace. Nothing has become more alien to us than that desideratum[7] of former times, "peace of soul," the *Christian* desideratum; there is nothing we envy less than the moralistic cow and the fat happiness of the good conscience. One has renounced the *great* life when one renounces war.

In many cases, to be sure, "peace of soul" is merely a   7
misunderstanding—something else, which lacks only a more honest name. Without further ado or prejudice, a few examples. "Peace of soul" can be, for one, the gentle radiation of a rich animality into the moral (or religious) sphere. Or the beginning of weariness, the first shadow of evening, of any kind of evening. Or a sign that the air is humid, that south winds are approaching. Or unrecognized gratitude for a good digestion (sometimes called "love of man"). Or the attainment of calm by a convalescent who feels a new relish in all things and waits. Or the state which follows a thorough satisfaction of our dominant passion, the well-being of a rare repletion. Or the senile weakness of our will, our cravings, our vices. Or laziness, persuaded by vanity to give itself moral airs. Or the emergence of certainty, even a dreadful certainty, after long tension and torture by uncertainty. Or the expression of maturity and mastery in the midst of doing, creating, working, and willing—calm breathing, *attained* "freedom of the will." *Twilight of the Idols*—who knows? perhaps also only a kind of "peace of soul."

4

I reduce a principle to a formula. Every naturalism in morality—   8
that is, every healthy morality—is dominated by an instinct of life; some commandment of life is fulfilled by a determinate canon of

---

[6] **Reich** The Second Reich, 1871, founded by Wilhelm I as the German Empire.
[7] **desideratum** The thing that is desired.

"shalt" and "shalt not"; some inhibition and hostile element on the path of life is thus removed. *Anti-natural* morality—that is, almost every morality which has so far been taught, revered, and preached—turns, conversely, *against* the instincts of life: it is *condemnation* of these instincts, now secret, now outspoken and impudent. When it says, "God looks at the heart," it says No to both the lowest and the highest desires of life, and posits God as the *enemy of life*. The saint in whom God delights is the ideal eunuch. Life has come to an end where the "kingdom of God" begins.

5

Once one has comprehended the outrage of such a revolt against   9
life as has become almost sacrosanct in Christian morality, one has, fortunately, also comprehended something else: the futility, apparentness, absurdity, and *mendaciousness* of such a revolt. A condemnation of life by the living remains in the end a mere symptom of a certain kind of life: the question whether it is justified or unjustified is not even raised thereby. One would require a position *outside* of life, and yet have to know it as well as one, as many, as all who have lived it, in order to be permitted even to touch the problem of the *value* of life: reasons enough to comprehend that this problem is for us an unapproachable problem. When we speak of values, we speak with the inspiration, with the way of looking at things, which is part of life: life itself forces us to posit values; life itself values through us when we posit values. From this it follows that even that anti-natural morality which conceives of God as the counter-concept and condemnation of life is only a value judgment of life—but of what life? of what kind of life? I have already given the answer: of declining, weakened, weary, condemned life. Morality, as it has so far been understood—as it has in the end been formulated once more by Schopenhauer,[8] as "negation of the will to life"—is the very *instinct of decadence*, which makes an imperative of itself. It says: *"Perish!"* It is a condemnation pronounced by the condemned.

6

Let us finally consider how naive it is altogether to say: "Man   10
ought to be such and such!" Reality shows us an enchanting wealth of types, the abundance of a lavish play and change of forms—and some wretched loafer of a moralist comments: "No! Man ought to be different." He even knows what man should be like, this

---

[8]**Arthur Schopenhauer (1788–1860)** German philosopher who believed reality was nothing but senseless will, having no divine origin.

wretched bigot and prig: he paints himself on the wall and comments, "*Ecce homo!*"[9] But even when the moralist addresses himself only to the single human being and says to him, "You ought to be such and such!" he does not cease to make himself ridiculous. The single human being is a piece of *fatum*[10] from the front and from the rear, one law more, one necessity more for all that is yet to come and to be. To say to him, "Change yourself!" is to demand that everything be changed, even retroactively. And indeed there have been consistent moralists who wanted man to be different, that is, virtuous—they wanted him remade in their own image, as a prig: to that end, they *negated* the world! No small madness! No modest kind of immodesty!

Morality, insofar as it *condemns* for its own sake, and *not* out of regard for the concerns, considerations, and contrivances of life, is a specific error with which one ought to have no pity—an *idiosyncrasy of degenerates* which has caused immeasurable harm. 11

We others, we immoralists, have, conversely, made room in our hearts for every kind of understanding, comprehending, and *approving.* We do not easily negate; we make it a point of honor to be *affirmers.* More and more, our eyes have opened to that economy which needs and knows how to utilize all that the holy witlessness of the priest, of the *diseased* reason in the priest, rejects—that economy in the law of life which finds an advantage even in the disgusting species of the prigs, the priests, the virtuous. *What* advantage? But we ourselves, we immoralists, are the answer. 12

The Four Great Errors

1

The error of confusing cause and effect. There is no more dangerous error than that of mistaking the effect for the cause: I call it the real corruption of reason. Yet this error belongs among the most ancient and recent habits of mankind: it is even hallowed among us and goes by the name of "religion" or "morality." Every single sentence which religion and morality formulate contains it; priests and legislators of moral codes are the originators of this corruption of reason. 13

I give an example. Everybody knows the book of the famous Cornaro[11] in which he recommends his slender diet as a recipe for a 14

---

[9] *Ecce homo!* Behold this man!

[10] *fatum* Prophecy, declaration.

[11] **Luigi Cornaro (1467–1566)** Venetian who lived on a restricted diet. *The Sure and Certain Method of Attaining a Long and Healthful Life* (1550) was published when he was eighty-three.

long and happy life—a virtuous one too. Few books have been read so much; even now thousands of copies are sold in England every year. I do not doubt that scarcely any book (except the Bible, as is meet) has done as much harm, has *shortened* as many lives, as this well-intentioned *curiosum*. The reason: the mistaking of the effect for the cause. The worthy Italian thought his diet was the *cause* of his long life, whereas the precondition for a long life, the extraordinary slowness of his metabolism, the consumption of so little, was the cause of his slender diet. He was not free to eat little *or* much; his frugality was not a matter of "free will": he became sick when he ate more. But whoever is no carp not only does well to eat properly, but needs to. A scholar in our time, with his rapid consumption of nervous energy, would simply destroy himself with Cornaro's diet. *Crede experto.*[12]

2

The most general formula on which every religion and morality   15
is founded is: "Do this and that, refrain from this and that—then you will be happy! Otherwise . . ." Every morality, every religion, *is* this imperative; I call it the great original sin of reason, the *immortal unreason*. In my mouth, this formula is changed into its opposite— first example of my "revaluation of all values": a well-turned-out human being, a "happy one," *must* perform certain actions and shrinks instinctively from other actions; he carries the order, which he represents physiologically, into his relations with other human beings and things. In a formula: his virtue is the *effect* of his happiness. A long life, many descendants—this is not the wages of virtue; rather virtue itself is that slowing down of the metabolism which leads, among other things, also to a long life, many descendants—in short, to *Cornarism.* . . .

3

The error of a false causality. People have believed at all times that   16
they knew what a cause is; but whence did we take our knowledge— or more precisely, our faith that we had such knowledge? From the realm of the famous "inner facts," of which not a single one has so far proved to be factual. We believed ourselves to be causal in the act of willing: we thought that here at least we caught causality in the act. Nor did one doubt that all the antecedents of an act, its causes, were to be sought in consciousness and would be found there once sought—as "motives": else one would not have

---

[12] **Crede experto** Believe him who has tried!

been free and responsible for it. Finally, who would have denied that a thought is caused? that the ego causes the thought?

Of these three "inward facts" which seem to guarantee causality, the first and most persuasive is that of the will as cause. The conception of a consciousness ("spirit") as a cause, and later also that of the ego as cause (the "subject"), are only afterbirths: first the causality of the will was firmly accepted as given, as *empirical*.   17

Meanwhile we have thought better of it. Today we no longer believe a word of all this. The "inner world" is full of phantoms and will-o'-the-wisps: the will is one of them. The will no longer moves anything, hence does not explain anything either—it merely accompanies events; it can also be absent. The so-called *motive*: another error. Merely a surface phenomenon of consciousness, something alongside the deed that is more likely to cover up the antecedents of the deeds than to represent them. And as for the *ego!* That has become a fable, a fiction, a play on words: it has altogether ceased to think, feel, or will! . . .   18

4

The error of imaginary causes. To begin with dreams: *ex post facto*,[13] a cause is slipped under a particular sensation (for example, one following a far-off cannon shot)—often a whole little novel in which the dreamer turns up as the protagonist. The sensation endures meanwhile in a kind of resonance: it waits, as it were, until the causal instinct permits it to step into the foreground—now no longer as a chance occurrence, but as "meaning." The cannon shot appears in a *causal* mode, in an apparent reversal of time. What is really later, the motivation, is experienced first—often with a hundred details which pass like lightning—and the shot *follows*. What has happened? The representations which were *produced* by a certain state have been misunderstood as its causes.   19

In fact, we do the same thing when awake. Most of our general feelings—every kind of inhibition, pressure, tension, and explosion in the play and counterplay of our organs, and particularly the state of the *nervus sympathicus*[14]—excite our causal instinct: we want to have a reason for feeling this way or that—for feeling bad or for feeling good. We are never satisfied merely to state the fact that we feel this way or that: we admit this fact only—become conscious of it only—when we have furnished some kind of motivation. Memory, which swings into action in such cases, unknown to us, brings   20

---

[13]**ex post facto** After the fact.
[14]**nervus sympathicus** System of sympathetic nerves that gives us a "gut feeling."

up earlier states of the same kind, together with the causal interpretations associated with them—not their real causes. The faith, to be
sure, that such representations, such accompanying conscious processes, are the causes, is also brought forth by memory. Thus originates a habitual acceptance of a particular causal interpretation,
which, as a matter of fact, inhibits any investigation into the real
cause—even precludes it.

5

The psychological explanation of this. To derive something unknown   21
from something familiar relieves, comforts, and satisfies, besides giving
a feeling of power. With the unknown, one is confronted with danger,
discomfort, and care; the first instinct is to abolish these painful states.
First principle: any explanation is better than none. Since at bottom it
is merely a matter of wishing to be rid of oppressive representations,
one is not too particular about the means of getting rid of them: the
first representation that explains the unknown as familiar feels so good
that one "considers it true." The proof of pleasure ("of strength") as a
criterion of truth.

The causal instinct is thus conditional upon, and excited by,   22
the feeling of fear. The "why?" shall, if at all possible, not give the
cause for its own sake so much as for *a particular kind of cause*—
a cause that is comforting, liberating, and relieving. That it is something already familiar, experienced, and inscribed in the memory,
which is posited as a cause, that is the first consequence of this need.
That which is new and strange and has not been experienced before,
is excluded as a cause. Thus one searches not only for some kind of
explanation to serve as a cause, but for a particularly selected and
preferred kind of explanation—that which has most quickly and
most frequently abolished the feeling of the strange, new, and hitherto unexperienced: the *most habitual* explanations. Consequence:
one kind of positing of causes predominates more and more, is concentrated into a system, and finally emerges as *dominant*, that is, as
simply precluding other causes and explanations. The banker immediately thinks of "business," the Christian of "sin," and the girl of
her love.

6

The whole realm of morality and religion belongs under this concept of   23
imaginary causes. The "explanation" of *disagreeable* general feelings.
They are produced by beings that are hostile to us (evil spirits: the
most famous case—the misunderstanding of the hysterical as witches).
They are produced by acts which cannot be approved (the feeling of
"sin," of "sinfulness," is slipped under a physiological discomfort; one

always finds reasons for being dissatisfied with oneself). They are produced as punishments, as payment for something we should not have done, for what we should not have *been* (impudently generalized by Schopenhauer into a principle in which morality appears as what it really is—as the very poisoner and slanderer of life: "Every great pain, whether physical or spiritual, declares what we deserve; for it could not come to us if we did not deserve it." *World as Will and Representation* II, 666). They are produced as effects of ill-considered actions that turn out badly. (Here the affects, the senses, are posited as causes, as "guilty"; and physiological calamities are interpreted with the help of other calamities as "deserved.")

The "explanation" of *agreeable* general feelings. They are pro-   24
duced by trust in God. They are produced by the consciousness of good deeds (the so-called "good conscience"—a physiological state which at times looks so much like good digestion that it is hard to tell them apart). They are produced by the successful termination of some enterprise (a naive fallacy: the successful termination of some enterprise does not by any means give a hypochondriac or a Pascal[15] agreeable general feelings). They are produced by faith, charity, and hope—the Christian virtues.

In truth, all these supposed explanations are resultant states   25
and, as it were, translations of pleasurable or unpleasurable feelings into a false dialect: one is in a state of hope *because* the basic physiological feeling is once again strong and rich; one trusts in God *because* the feeling of fullness and strength gives a sense of rest. Morality and religion belong altogether to the *psychology of error*: in every single case, cause and effect are confused; or truth is confused with the effects of *believing* something to be true; or a state of consciousness is confused with its causes.

7

The error of free will. Today we no longer have any pity for the con-   26
cept of "free will": we know only too well what it really is—the foulest of all theologians' artifices, aimed at making mankind "responsible" in their sense, that is, *dependent upon them*. Here I simply supply the psychology of all "making responsible."

Wherever responsibilities are sought, it is usually the instinct of   27
wanting to judge and punish which is at work. Becoming has been deprived of its innocence when any being-such-and-such is traced back to will, to purposes, to acts of responsibility: the doctrine of the will has been invented essentially for the purpose of punishment,

---

[15]**Blaise Pascal (1623–1662)** French mathematician and scientist.

that is, because one wanted to impute guilt. The entire old psychology, the psychology of will, was conditioned by the fact that its originators, the priests at the head of ancient communities, wanted to create for themselves the right to punish—or wanted to create this right for God. Men were considered "free" so that they might be judged and punished—so that they might become *guilty:* consequently, every act had to be considered as willed, and the origin of every act had to be considered as lying within the consciousness (and thus the most fundamental counterfeit *in psychologicis* was made the principle of psychology itself).

Today, as we have entered into the reverse movement and we   28
immoralists are trying with all our strength to take the concept of guilt and the concept of punishment out of the world again, and to cleanse psychology, history, nature, and social institutions and sanctions of them, there is in our eyes no more radical opposition than that of the theologians, who continue with the concept of a "moral world-order" to infect the innocence of becoming by means of "punishment" and "guilt." Christianity is a metaphysics of the hangman.

QUESTIONS FOR CRITICAL READING

1. What does Nietzsche mean when he says that passions "drag down their victim" (para. 1)?
2. Why does he claim there is a war on the passions?
3. Why does Nietzsche make several references to stupidity in the opening paragraph?
4. Is there such a thing as a spiritualization of passion?
5. Why does Nietzsche consider moderation an important quality?
6. In what sense is love a spiritualization of sensuality?
7. What is "the internal enemy" (para. 6)?
8. Is there such a thing as "healthy morality" (para. 8)?
9. What is Nietzsche's view of the Ten Commandments?

SUGGESTIONS FOR CRITICAL WRITING

1. Assume you are writing for an audience that knows a bit about Nietzsche but has not read this selection. Write an essay in which you clarify Nietzsche's attitudes toward conventional morality and explain why he feels it is anti-nature. Also explain his attitude toward people who, because they have no self-control, cannot keep themselves from acting in degenerate ways.

2. Do you think Nietzsche is correct in assuming that morality is anti-nature? Use other texts from this section of the book in your argument to help you convince your readers. Be sure to define the term *anti-nature* as carefully as possible.

3. What might Nietzsche's moral views be? It is clear that he does not intend to behave unethically as a result of his analysis of the moral views he condemns. But he does not go into detail about the moral position he might take. He talks about affirming life. How would this translate into an ethical position and thus into a clear moral purpose in life? Do you think he plans to live a moral life, or will he just do as he pleases? Explain.

4. Assuming that Nietzsche is correct that conventional morality is against our natural expression of passions, argue a case that suggests that while he is correct, the truth is that people must be restricted in their natural expression. Which moral statements clearly recognize dangerous natural inclinations and restrict them? What benefits do these restrictions provide to the individual as well as to society as a whole? How might Nietzsche react to your argument?

5. Do you believe Nietzsche is accurate when he declares in paragraph 15 that "every religion and morality" is founded on a general principle of "Do this and that, refrain from this and that—then you will be happy!"? Is he simply misreading the teachings of religion? Write an essay in which you take issue with or agree with Nietzsche's premise and conclusions.

6. In paragraphs 19 and 20, Nietzsche discusses the "error of imaginary causes." Are there instances in your own life when you made the mistake of assigning imaginary causes to effects you observed? If your examples have a moral implication, be sure to clarify the nature of the error and decide whether or not your experience helps to reinforce Nietzsche's argument or weaken it.

7. **CONNECTIONS** How would Niccolò Machiavelli (p. 37) respond to Nietzsche's argument? Would he agree or disagree with Nietzsche about morals promoted by the church? What might Machiavelli, in light of reading Nietzsche, recommend as a moral path for the Prince? What would Nietzsche have to say about Machiavelli's Prince? Would he approve or disapprove of him? Why?

8. **SEEING CONNECTIONS** Taking several of the individuals who appear in Wright's painting *An Experiment on a Bird in the Air Pump* (p. 687), determine what you think their view of the moral situation in the experiment might be. Would any of them be concerned with whether or not the experiment was "anti-nature"? When Nietzsche talks about "the spiritualization of sensuality" do you think he would include the experience of watching this experiment run its course? To what extent would he think the experiment was a sensual activity? Would the characters in the painting think so?

IRIS MURDOCH
Morality and Religion

IRIS MURDOCH (1919–1999) was born in Dublin, Ireland, but her family soon moved to London, where she grew up. Most people know Murdoch as one of the most important novelists in English in the twentieth century. She wrote twenty-six novels that explore interesting aspects of philosophy and psychology. She once said that while she distrusted psychoanalysis, she felt that she was analyzing herself in her novels. Critics have considered her one of the most important literary figures of her time.

Her early schooling prepared her for a degree in Oxford in classics and philosophy. In the 1930s, she became a member of the Communist Party, but she soon rejected its principles and resigned from the party before World War II. During the war, she worked in the British Treasury offices, and afterwards she spent time in Belgium and Austria working with the United Nations Relief organization. Murdoch then spent a year trying to sort her life out. She had been given a scholarship to study at Vassar College, but could not get a visa because of her communist past. Eventually, in 1947, she accepted a studentship at Newnham College, Cambridge, to study philosophy under Ludwig Wittgenstein (1889–1951), one of the age's most influential philosophers. The next year she was elected Fellow of St. Anne's College, Oxford, and remained as a tutor (essentially a professor) until she retired in 1963 to write full time.

She won a number of important prizes for her literary work. Her novel *The Sea, The Sea* won Britain's most prestigious literary award, the Booker Prize, in 1978. The Divinity School at the University of Chicago honored her for "the religious depth of her novels" in 1992. Among the most important and interesting of her novels are *The Flight from the Enchanter* (1956), *The Red and the Green*

From *Metaphysics as a Guide to Morals.*

(1956), *The Black Prince* (1973), *The Sacred and Profane Love Machine* (1974), *The Book and the Brotherhood* (1987), and *The Green Knight* (1993).

In addition to novels, Murdoch also wrote a number of influential philosophical studies. Her first book, *Sartre, Romantic Rationalist* (1953), resulted from her meeting Jean-Paul Sartre (1905–1980) in the 1940s and her interest in existentialism. *The Sovereignty of Good and Other Concepts* (1967) is considered a work of first importance in moral studies. *Metaphysics as a Guide to Morals* (1992) developed from the Gifford Lectures she gave at the University of Edinburgh in 1981–82. Her last book, *Existentialists and Mystics: Writings on Philosophy and Literature* (1997), was published near the end of her life when she was suffering from the final stages of Alzheimer's disease.

Murdoch's impressive work *Metaphysics as a Guide to Morals*, from which the following selection is taken, deals with how we interpret and understand the nature of morals. One of the questions she addresses is whether there can be a true moral position outside the confines of religion. Murdoch weighs the arguments on both sides of the issue and lets her readers decide how to resolve them. She herself thrived on contradictions and saw them as energy for understanding.

Murdoch's Rhetoric

The first thing one notices about Murdoch's writing is that she relies on very long paragraphs. Each paragraph addresses a position on how religion and morality are related. She does not pose an overarching argument, but how religion affects what we think of as moral behavior is one of the issues she pursues.

Another aspect of her writing is her many references to philosophers such as Kant, Plato, Bentham, and Wittgenstein, and to historical events such as the Cultural Revolution in Mao's China and the murder of kulaks—wealthy farmers—in Stalin's Soviet Union. But these are not essential to our understanding of the issues she discusses.

She begins in paragraph 2 with a consideration of the nature of virtue, which she sees as "[t]he most evident bridge between morality and religion." Yet there are problems with the very idea of virtue, as she points out. For some people in the modern world, the word *virtue* has lost its positive meaning and is related to rigidity and priggishness. Moreover, it is not capable of being applied universally to people because "fear, misery, deprivation" (para. 2) will alter the nature of virtue in people who experience those conditions. Those who suffer from hunger or political oppression may not have much interest in conventional bourgeois theories of virtue. Therefore, Murdoch suggests, virtue may be a relative concept rather than a fixed idea.

In paragraph 3, she continues her discussion of virtue but adds the concept of duty, a sense of obligation that is understood in a social context. According to Murdoch, "Dutifulness could be an account of a morality with no hint of religion" (para. 3). In this extensive paragraph, Murdoch explores the idea of duty, connecting it to eighteenth-century principles of reason, showing that duty and reason fit together rather well. One understands one's duty to others, institutions, and nations, and one performs one's duty without religious intervention. Is that then a virtuous action? Is the performance of duty then irrelevant to the moral views of religion? As she says at the end of the paragraph, after exploring the issue it may be time to refer back to the "clear, rigid rules" of religions to find answers to these questions.

In paragraph 4, Murdoch contrasts secular idealism with religious belief. The question is whether one of these is more likely to produce moral good than the other. Is morality, she continually asks, dependent on religion, or can it be achieved outside religion? She points out a conundrum that continues in modern life: the criminal who constantly breaks the law and yet has a deep religious conviction. She criticizes religion indirectly by examining its non-rational elements, those of pure faith. But near the end of the paragraph she says, "Religion symbolizes high moral ideas which then travel with us and are more intimately and accessibly effective than the unadorned promptings of reason" (para. 4).

In paragraph 5, she begins to discuss the diary of Francis Kilvert (1840–1879), a simple clergyman who found in his rural community moments of intense beauty and moral uprightness. Kilvert is likened to another cleric, Julian of Norwich, who arrives at a deeply philosophical understanding when she holds a "little thing, the size of a hazel nut, which seemed to lie in the palm of my hand; and it was as round as any ball" (para. 5), and in it she saw a metaphor for the wholeness of creation, a sense that was at root a deep religious experience. Murdoch interprets this as a way of exhibiting "God's love for the world" (para. 5).

In paragraph 6, Murdoch proceeds to include religious philosophers such as Søren Kierkegaard (1813–1855), whose views on religion and morality are complex and not easily untangled. Her discussion reaches into the question of whether God exists and the Ontological Proof, a proof of God's existence that dates to the Middle Ages. The proof asserts that we can imagine a perfect being, God, and that because we can imagine it, it must exist because perfection is consistent only with actual existence. Murdoch puts it this way: "Guilt, especially deep apparently incurable guilt, can be one of the worst of human pains. To cure such an ill, because of human sin, God *must* exist" (para. 6).

In her final paragraph, Murdoch explores mysticism, which implies having a direct spiritual experience of God, achieved through prayer, religious discipline, fasting, or a variety of ascetic practices similar to meditation. As she says in her opening sentence, "Religion (even if 'primitive') is generally assumed to be in some sense moral. Mysticism is also assumed to be, by definition, moral" (para. 7). However, despite this assurance, she also points out that in some ages, such as the eighteenth-century Enlightenment period, "institutionalized religion [was] an enemy of morality, an enemy of freedom and free thought, guilty of cruelty and repression" (para. 7). In the remainder of this paragraph she attempts to work out some of the obvious conflicts inherent in these statements.

She ends with an interesting discussion of the relationship of two contradictory forces in the universe: good and evil. As she states in a rather paradoxical fashion: "Discord is essential to goodness" (para. 7). In other words, there can only be a concept of morality in an environment in which there is evil *and* goodness. Murdoch points out that "both morality and religion face the same insuperable difficulty": that if the goal of eradicating evil is achieved "the struggle, the need for devotion, would cease to be real. . . . If there is to be morality, there cannot altogether be an end to evil" (para. 7).

PREREADING QUESTIONS: WHAT TO READ FOR

The following prereading questions may help you anticipate key issues in the discussion of Iris Murdoch's "Morality and Religion." Keeping them in mind during your first reading of the selection should help focus your attention.

- How is the idea of virtue a bridge between religion and morality?
- In what senses do religion and morality seem to be different?
- Is morality impossible without religion?

Morality and Religion

In the background of many of these arguments lies a question   1
about the relation of morality to religion, the difference between
them, and the definition of religion. I have already suggested that
my whole argument can be read as moral philosophy. In any case
moral philosophy must include this dimension whether we call it
religion or not. Someone may say that there is only one way to
"acquire" religion and that is through being taught it as a small
child. You have to breathe it in. It is an ineffable attitude to the world
which cannot really be discussed. People who take up religion as
adults are merely playing at it, it remains at a level of illusion. So
someone could speak, being either a believer or an unbeliever. The
unbeliever might add that religion is imbibed in childhood, when it
forms part of the infantile child–parent relationship now well-
known to psychology; only religion, being a soothing drug, is less
easy to give up in later life.

The most evident bridge between morality and religion is the idea   2
of virtue. Virtue is still treated in some quarters as something precious
to be positively pursued; yet the concept has also faded, even tending
to fall apart between "idealism" and "priggishness." It may be seen as a
self-indulgent luxury. It has, perhaps has always had, many enemies.
Fear of a perverted ideology or of a too fervent "enthusiasm" may prevent a positive conception of virtue. Cynicism and materialism and
dolce vita[1] can occlude it, also fear, misery, deprivation, and loss of
concepts. Even in a religious context "personal spirituality" may be
something that has to be argued for. A utilitarian morality[2] may treat a
concern with becoming virtuous as a waste of energy which should be
transmitted directly to the alleviation of suffering. Of course numerous people are virtuous without thinking about it, and sages may say
that, if thought about, it may *ipso facto*[3] diminish. A saint may perhaps
be good by instinct and nature, though saintly figures are also revered
as reformed sinners. Perhaps the word itself begins to seem preten-
tious and old-fashioned.

An idea (concept) of virtue which need not be formally reflective   3
or clarified bears some resemblance to religion, so that one might say
either that it is a shadow of religion, or religion is a shadow of it. The

---

[1] *dolce vita* The sweet life; the irresponsible life.

[2] **utilitarian morality** Utilitarianism professed a creed of the greatest good for
the greatest number and would insist that any moral principle produce the greatest
happiness and the least pain for all involved.

[3] *ipso facto* By the very fact itself.

demand that we should be virtuous or try to become good is something that goes beyond explicit calls of duty. One can of course extend the idea of duty into the area of generalized goodness (virtuous living) by making it a duty always to have pure thoughts and good motives. For reasons I have suggested I would rather keep the concept of duty nearer to its ordinary sense as something fairly strict, recognizable, intermittent, so that we can say that there may be time off from the call of duty, but no time off from the demand of good. These are conceptual problems which are important in the building up of a picture; that is, an overall extension of the idea of duty would blur a valuable distinction, and undermine the particular function of the concept. Duty then I take to be formal obligation, relating to occasions where it can be to some extent clarified. ("Why go?" "I promised." "Why go?" "He's an old friend." "Why go?" "Well, it's somehow that sort of situation.") Duty may be easily performed without strain or reflection, but may also prompt the well-known experience of the frustration of desire together with a sense of necessity to act, wherein there is a proper place for the concept of *will*. Dutifulness could be an account of a morality with no hint of religion. The rational formality of moral maxims made to govern particular situations might make them seem like separated interrupted points of insight rather than like a light which always shines. This could be a picture of human life. Yet Kant[4] also portrays us as *belonging* at every second to the noumenal world of rationality and freedom, the separated pure source. We are orderly because duty is duty, yet also behind the exercise of it we might (surely, after all) glimpse the inspiring light of pure goodness which Kant calls Reason, and sometimes even God. Beyond all this we may picture a struggle in Kant's religious soul over the concept of Reason, so essential, yet so awkward. The rationality (Pure Reason) which enables us to deal with objects and causes *must* be related to that (Practical Reason) which enables us to deal with right and wrong. Well, the concept of truth can relate them. . . . Perhaps Kant felt no awkwardness — it is we who feel awkward, when we connect morality with love and desire. Certainly it does seem possible to set up a contrast between the dutiful man and the virtuous man which is different from the contrast between the dutiful man and the religious man. Here we may think of Christ saying render unto Caesar what is Caesar's. Duty as order, relating morals to politics. Good decent men lead orderly

---

[4]**Immanuel Kant (1724–1804)** German philosopher who linked pure reason and experiential knowledge. *Noumenal* is a Kantian term that refers to the unknowable world as it is in itself. According to Kant, we can only know the world as it appears to us, as a phenomenon. We can never know it as it is in itself, as a noumenon.

lives. It might also be said in this context that given the abysmal sinfulness of humans, only a strict list of rules can keep them from mutual destruction! The moral (or spiritual) life is both one and not one. There is the idea of a sovereign good, but there are also compartments, obligations, rules, aims, whose identity may have to be respected. These separate aspects or modes of behavior occasion some of the most difficult kinds of moral problems, as if we have to move between *styles*, or to change gear. We have to live a single moral existence, and also to retain the separate force of various kinds of moral vision. Jeanie Deans in Scott's novel[5] loves her sister, but cannot lie to save her life. Isabella in *Measure for Measure* will not save her brother by yielding her chastity to Angelo. Duty is one thing, love is another. These are dramatic examples; one can invent many more homely ones of the conflict of moral requirements of entirely different kinds, wherein one seems to have to choose between being two different kinds of person. This may be a choice between two paths in life, or it may be some everyday matter demanding an instant response. We tend to feel that these dissimilar demands and states of mind must somehow connect, there must be a deep connection, it must all somehow make a unified sense; this is a religious craving, God sees it all. What I earlier called axioms[6] are moral entities whose force must not be overcome by, or dissolved into, other moral streams: a requirement in liberal politics. Axioms may not "win" but must remain in consideration, a Benthamite[7] utilitarian conception of happiness must not, as a frequently relevant feature, be eroded by high-minded considerations about quality of happiness or by theories which make happiness invisible, or of course by political objectives. (The Cultural Revolution, the liquidation of the kulaks.[8]) Equally of course, degraded or evil pleasure cannot count as simple or silly happiness. Such complexities, involving conflicts of moral discernment and moral style, are with us always. So, "keeping everything in mind" is not an easy matter in morals. This may be an argument for clear rigid rules. Modern clerics who

---

[5] **Scott's novel** *The Heart of Mid-Lothian* (1818) by Sir Walter Scott (1771–1832).

[6] **axioms** Statements of truth, as in geometry.

[7] **Benthamite: Jeremy Bentham (1748–1832)** proposed a scheme of "private ethics" in which the aim of one's actions should be to cause the greatest pleasure and least pain. He was influential in developing English utilitarianism.

[8] **The Cultural Revolution . . . kulaks** The Cultural Revolution (1966–1976), begun by Mao Zedong (1893–1976), chairman of the Chinese Communist Party, was a period of political zealotry characterized by purges of intellectuals and anticommunists. The kulaks were relatively wealthy farmers who opposed Soviet collectivization of their land. Soviet leader Joseph Stalin (1879–1953) sought to execute or deport the kulaks, whom he maligned as "exploiters."

do not feel able to tell newly married couples to be virtuous, tell them to have a sense of humor. This shift is a telling case of a change of style.

Religious belief may be a stronger motive to good conduct   4 than non-religious idealism. Corrupt immoral persons (for instance hardened criminals) who cheerfully break all the "moral rules," may retain the religious images of their childhood which can, at some juncture, affect their conduct. This idea has been (not unsentimentally) dealt with in various novels and films. Indeed, this retention of images, and sensibility to images, might suggest the importance of a religious childhood. (Is it easier to get out of religion, or to get in?) Parents who have had such a childhood themselves, but have "given up religion," may often think along these lines. A kind of sensible well-meaning tolerance is involved here. But, a sterner breed may say, what about *truth*? Religion just *isn't true*. A religious man, even a goodish one, is spoilt and flawed by irrational superstitious convictions; and it is held to be ridiculous for lapsed parents to let their innocent children be tainted with beliefs which the parents know to be false. It is no use talking of a "good atmosphere," what is fundamentally at stake is *truth*. Such arguments come near to familiar problems of today. Is the non-religious good man so like the religious good man that it is merely some point of terminology or superficial style which is at issue? Orthodoxly religious people often tolerantly compliment the unbeliever by saying, "He is *really* a true Christian"; which may well annoy the unbeliever. More positively attempting a distinction to form part of a definition, it might be suggested that religion is a form of heightened consciousness (Matthew Arnold[9] said it was "morality touched by emotion"), it is intense and highly toned, it is about what is deep, what is holy, what is absolute, the emotional imaginative image-making faculties are engaged, the whole man is engaged. Every moment matters, there is no time off. High morality without religion is too abstract, high morality craves for religion. Religion symbolizes high moral ideas which then travel with us and are more intimately and accessibly effective than the unadorned promptings of reason. Religion suits the image-making human animal. Think what the image of Christ has done for us through centuries. Can such images *lie*? Do we not indeed adjust our attitudes to them, as time passes, so as to "make them true"? This continuous adjustment is an aspect of the history of religion.

---

[9]**Matthew Arnold (1822–1888)** Prominent English poet and social commentator.

I intended here, thinking about holiness and reverence, not the   5
exclusive property of believers, to quote from Francis Kilvert's[10]
Diary (begun in 1870). Kilvert was a parson in country parishes on
the Welsh border, a religious good man of simple faith. However, it
is difficult to quote from the Diary because of the transparent artless
lucidity of Kilvert's account of his days. Any particular quotation can
sound naive, or sentimental. "I went to see my dear little lover Mary
Tavener, the deaf and half dumb child. When I opened the door of
the poor crazy old cottage in the yard the girl uttered a passionate
inarticulate cry of joy and running to me flung her arms about my
neck and covered me with kisses." (12 June 1875.) "Old William
Price sat in his filthy den, unkempt, unshaven, shaggy and grey like
a wild beast, and if possible filthier than the den. I read to him
Faber's hymn of the Good Shepherd. He was much struck with it.
'That's what He has been telling me,' said the old man." (26 January
1872.) "The road was very still. No one seemed to be passing and
the birds sang late and joyfully in the calm mild evening as if they
thought it must be spring. A white mist gathered in the valley and
hung low along the winding course of the river mingled with the
rushing of the brooks, the distant voices of children at play came
floating at intervals across the river and near at hand a pheasant
screeched now and then and clapped its wings or changed his roost
from tree to tree like a man turning in bed before he falls asleep."
(27 January 1872.) Kilvert spent his days walking all over his territory, visiting everyone, noticing everything (people, animals, birds,
flowers) and describing it all in simple humble extremely readable
detail. "How delightful on these sweet summer evenings to wander
from cottage to cottage and farm to farm." It may be said that Kilvert
was lucky, but also that he deserved his luck. There is a serene light
and a natural kindly selfless love of people and of nature in what he
writes. He felt secure. He had faith. Wittgenstein[11] was struck by a
character in a play who seemed to him to feel safe, nothing that happened could harm him. Wittgenstein's "Ontological Proof" or "statement" (*Tractatus* 6.41) places the sense of the world outside the

---

[10] **Francis Kilvert (1840–1879)** English clergyman and diarist. Although after
his death his widow destroyed many of his notebooks, the remainder were discovered
by William Plomer (1903–1973), a South African writer, and published in 1938 and
1940.

[11] **Ludwig Wittgenstein (1889–1951)** Murdoch's philosophy professor. His
Tractatus approaches problems of language in describing philosophical ideas. His
concept of the "world outside of the world" implies that we imaginatively observe
the world outside itself, much as we observe ourselves. Thus the "little thing"
becomes an observable metaphor for a little world.

world, outside *all* of the contingent facts. Thinking of Wittgenstein's picture of the world (all the facts) as a self-contained sphere, a sort of steel ball, outside which ineffable value roams, we might look at something similar but different. "He showed me a little thing, the size of a hazel nut, which seemed to lie in the palm of my hand; and it was as round as any ball. I looked upon it with my eye of understanding, and thought 'What may this be?' I was answered in a general way thus: 'It is all that is made.' I wondered how long it could last, for it seemed as though it might suddenly fade away to nothing, it was so small. And I was answered in my understanding: 'It lasts and ever shall last, for God loveth it. And even so hath everything being, by the love of God.'" (Julian of Norwich,[12] *Revelations of Divine Love*, chapter 5.) Julian's showing, besides exhibiting God's love for the world, also indicates our absolute dependence as created things. We are nothing, we owe our being to something not ourselves. We are enlivened from a higher source.

Kierkegaard[13] would object to a moral–religious continuum.   6
We, existing individuals, therefore sinners, feel guilt, feel in need of salvation, to be reborn into a new being. "If any man be in Christ he is a new creature: old things are passed away, behold all things are become new." (2 Corinthians 5:17.) In Kierkegaard's version of Hegelian dialectic[14] it is not endlessly evolving toward totality, but is a picture of levels in the soul, or of different kinds of people, or of the pilgrimage of a particular person. The aesthetic individual is private, the ethical man, including the tragic hero, is public, the religious individual, the man of faith, is once more private. This dramatic triad also suggests the dangerous link between the two private stages, the aesthetic and the religious, so deeply unlike, so easily confused. The idea of repentance and leading a better cleansed and renewed life is a generally understood moral idea; and the, however presented, granting of absolution, God's forgiveness, keeps many people inside religion, or invites them to enter. Guilt, especially deep apparently incurable guilt, can be one of the worst of

---

[12]**Julian of Norwich (1332–1416?)** English mystic and writer. Her book *Revelations of Divine Love* recounts her mystical religious experiences.

[13]**Søren Kierkegaard (1813–1855)** Danish philosopher whose concept of "Either/Or" explored the choice between an ethical life or one that ignored ethics.

[14]**Hegelian dialectic** Postulates that the conflict of two opposites ultimately resolves itself through synthesis (a third option). Georg Wilhelm Friedrich Hegel (1770–1831), a German philosopher, has been enormously influential on all modern philosophers. He felt that humans experience a constant and irreconcilable conflict of reason and emotion.

human pains. To cure such an ill, because of human sin, God *must* exist. (As Norman Malcolm[15] suggested when discussing the Ontological Proof.) The condition of being changed and made anew is a general religious idea, sometimes appearing as magical instant salvation (as in suddenly "taking Christ as Saviour") or as the result of some lengthy ascesis.[16] Here salvation as spiritual change often goes with the conception of a *place* of purification and healing. (We light candles, we bring flowers, we go somewhere and kneel down.) This sense of a safe place is characteristic of religious imagery. Here the outer images the inner, and the inner images the outer. There is a literal place, the place of pilgrimage, the place of worship, the shrine, the sacred grove, there is also a psychological or spiritual place, a part of the soul. "Do not seek for God outside your soul." Religion provides a well-known well-tried procedure of rescue. Particularly in relation to guilt and remorse or the obsessions which can be bred from these, the *mystery* of religion (respected, intuited) is a source of spiritual energy. An orientation toward the good involves a reorientation of desire. Here a meeting with a good person may bring about a change of direction. If Plato had never met Socrates and experienced his death perhaps Western thinking might have been different. The mystical Christ too can be "met" with. (The idea of redemptive suffering is repugnant to some; but such suffering is everywhere around us, where the innocent suffers through love of the guilty.) Of course it may well be argued that there are sound unmysterious secular equivalents to these devices, there are many resources for the afflicted who may use their enlightened common sense, or go to their friends, doctors, therapists, psychoanalysts, social workers, take refuge in art or nature, or say (as the religious too may say) to hell with it all. Many people hate religion, with its terrible history and its irrationality, and would regard resort to religious rituals as a false substitute for real morals and genuine amendment of life. Judaism and Islam, who have avoided the path of image-making, and have revered the name of [God], avoid many of the problems which now beset Christianity. Buddhists live with the mystical Buddha in the soul. (Like Eckhart's[17] God and Christ in the soul.) The Hindu religion also has its philosophical mysticism above its numerous gods. Religion has been fundamentally mystical, and this becomes, in this age, more evident. So will the

---

[15]**Norman Malcolm (1911–1990)** American philosopher whose book *Ludwig Wittgenstein: A Memoir* is referenced in Murdoch's text.

[16]**ascesis** Ascetic behavior, such as fasting, celibacy, or becoming a hermit.

[17]**Johannes Eckhart (1260?–1327?)** German theologian who saw a unity in the soul and God: "the core of the soul and the core of God are one."

theologians invent new modes of speech, and will the churches fill with people who realize they do not need to believe in the supernatural?

Religion (even if "primitive") is generally assumed to be in some   7 sense moral. Mysticism is also assumed to be, by definition, moral. Thinkers of the Enlightenment however, and many since, have held, often rightly, that organized, institutionalized religion is an enemy of morality, an enemy of freedom and free thought, guilty of cruelty and repression. This has been so and in many quarters is so. There- fore the whole institution may be rationally considered to be dis- credited or outmoded. Many other influences from the past support such a line of thought. Kierkegaard saw Hegel as the enemy of reli- gion and of, *ipso facto*, the existing individual. The vast force of Hegel's thinking, followed up by Marx, is inimical to both. The Romantic Movement and the liberal political thinking which went with it have tended to look after the individual, and we associate high morality (idealism, selflessness, goodness) with many people in this century and the last who assumed that religion was *finished*. It must be agreed that, in very many ways, Western society has improved, become more tolerant, more free, more decently happy, in this period. It may also be agreed that with the decline of religious obser- vance and religious "consciousness" (the practice of prayer and the fear of God for instance), some aspects of moral conduct may decline also. (Of course this decline can have other causes.) How- ever that may be, Hegel and Marx, Nietzsche and Freud, have had influence. Virtues and values may give way to a more relaxed sense of determinism. There is a more "reasonable," ordinary, *available* rel- ativism and "naturalism" about. Hegel's *Geist*[18] is the energy which perpetually urges the ever-unsatisfied intellect (and so the whole of being) onward toward Absolute reality. Everything is relative, in- complete, not yet fully real, not yet fully true, dialectic is a continual reformulation. Such is the history of thought, of civilization, or of the "person" who, immersed in the process, is carried on toward some postulated self-consistent totality. Vaguely, such an image as something plausible may linger in the mind. I shall not discuss Hegel here, but look for a moment at a milder form of quasi- Hegelianism in F. H. Bradley's[19] *Appearance and Reality*. According to Bradley both morality and religion demand an unattainable unity. "Every separate aspect of the universe goes on to demand something

---

[18] **Geist** The reference is to Hegel's concept of the spirit/mind (geist). Hegel had three categories of spirit/mind: subjective, objective, and absolute. The absolute was reserved for contemplation of religion, fine arts, and philosophy.

[19] **F. H. Bradley (1846–1924)** English philosopher influenced by Hegel who emphasized the force of the mind over the physical world.

higher than itself." This is the dialectic, the overcoming of the in-complete, of appearance and illusion, the progress toward what is more true, more real, more harmoniously integrated. "And, like every other appearance, goodness implies that which, when carried out, must absorb it." Religion is higher than morality, being more unified, more expressive of a perfect wholeness. But both morality and religion face the same insuperable difficulty. Morality–religion believes in the reality of perfect good, and in the demand that good be victorious and evil destroyed. The postulated whole (good) is at once actually to be good, and at the same time to make itself good. Neither its perfect goodness nor its struggle may be degraded to an appearance (something incomplete and imperfect). But to unite these two aspects consistently is impossible. If the desired end were reached, the struggle, the need for devotion, would have ceased to be real. If there is to be morality, there cannot altogether be an end to evil. Discord is essential to goodness. Moral evil exists only in moral experience and that experience is essentially inconsistent. Morality desires unconsciously, with the suppression of evil, to become non-moral. It shrinks from this, yet it unknowingly desires the existence and perpetuity of evil. Morality, which makes evil, desires in evil to remove a condition of its own being; it labors to pass into a super-moral and therefore non-moral sphere. Moral–religious faith is make-believe: be sure that opposition to the good is overcome, but act as if it (the opposition) persists. "The religious consciousness rests on the felt unity of unreduced opposites."

QUESTIONS FOR CRITICAL READING

1. Can there be only one concept of virtue?
2. Why is virtue different from duty?
3. How is dutiful behavior different from religious behavior?
4. Does religion foster good behavior more than nonreligious idealism does?
5. How does guilt relate to morality?
6. Is religion essentially moral in nature?
7. Is high morality (idealism, selflessness, goodness) essentially religious?

SUGGESTIONS FOR CRITICAL WRITING

1. One question that underlies Murdoch's views is whether or not a high morality could ever be produced in a completely nonreligious environment. What is your view on this issue? What are the argu-ments in defense of religion as the essential producer of the high morality Murdoch points to in paragraph 7? Why might it be difficult

for such a high morality to be produced by secular means? In a non-religious context, what would ultimately support high morality?

2. One of Murdoch's assertions is that moral–religious views depend on the existence of evil, otherwise there can be no good behavior. This assertion is commonly made by those who insist on a Hegelian dialectic—a condition in which two opposites collide and a third force emerges. What would the world be like if there were no evil? Would moral behavior then be possible? Would immoral behavior be possible? Would all behavior be morally neutral? Explain.

3. What effects do poverty and the absence of opportunity have on individuals' senses of virtue? Do you agree with Murdoch that virtue "may be seen as a self-indulgent luxury" (para. 2)? Why or why not? Should bourgeois concepts of morality be applied to those without hope of change in their lives? Is morality dependent on social condition? Explain.

4. In paragraph 3 Murdoch states, "Dutifulness could be an account of a morality with no hint of religion." Do you agree? She is obviously tentative in her statement. Examine your own sense of duty and that of someone you know and decide how much duty—as well as the expression of dutiful acts—satisfies our concept of a true morality.

5. Murdoch implies at the end of paragraph 3 that certain political complexities suggest there might be a need to have "clear rigid rules" of behavior in order to establish a morality. She implies that even clerics are viewing contemporary moral standards as flexible, perhaps alterable in some circumstances. How do you feel? Should morality follow the "rules" approach of the Ten Commandments? Or is there a more flexible, "realistic" alternative? Explain.

6. What do you consider virtuous behavior? Try to be as specific as possible. Do you find it difficult to apply your virtues in everyday life? Why or why not? To what extent do you feel an individual's religious beliefs dictate his or her virtuousness? Is religious faith an accurate indicator of virtue? Why or why not? What is Murdoch's view of this issue?

7. **CONNECTIONS**   How would Friedrich Nietzsche (p. 713) approach a critique of the views that Murdoch explores in this essay? Where would his sympathies lie in relation to her discussion of the relationship of virtue to duty? Where would he stand on the controversies that suggest that organized religion inhibits rather than fosters morality? What points in Murdoch's argument would he most take issue with?

8. **CONNECTIONS**   Which of the selections in this section would most satisfy Murdoch's sense of the nature of morality and the relation of morality to religion? Who among these writers is most sympathetic to her views? Is she sympathetic to Aristotle's ideas in "The Aim of Man" (p. 691)? Does she share anything in common with Nietzsche in his "Morality as Anti-Nature" (p. 713)? Choose one and compare their views.

9. **SEEING CONNECTIONS**   Science and religion were somewhat at odds with each other when Wright painted *An Experiment on a Bird in the Air Pump* (p. 687). His association with Lunar Society members,

who tried to reconcile the two, led him to employ a visual composition often used in baroque religious paintings. What connection between science and morality seems to be implied in the painting? Does it seem similar to the connection Murdoch sees between morality and religion? Is it possible that the white bird in the bell jar is not a cockatoo but rather a dove and, therefore, conceivably a symbol for Christ? If that were the case, what would Murdoch be likely to say about the moral circumstance of the painting?

ALDO LEOPOLD
The Land Ethic

Aldo Leopold (1887–1948) was a powerful force in ecological and conservationist circles for many years, partly as the result of his major publication, *The Sand County Almanac,* which was in many ways the result of an experiment. In 1935, Leopold purchased an old farm in Baraboo, Wisconsin, in what was called the sand counties. The farm had been worn out through mismanagement of the land, and Leopold set himself the task of restoring it so that it would again be productive. Even though the *Almanac* was published one year after his death, the individual essays collected in the book had been read by many people during his lifetime. It has sold millions of copies and has been one of the most revered of modern writings on our relationship with our environment. It remains his gift to future generations. One of his most remembered statements is "A thing is right when it tends to preserve the integrity, stability, and beauty of the biotic community. It is wrong when it tends otherwise." For Leopold the biotic community included not just the land but all creatures and plants that it supports.

Leopold was born in Burlington, Iowa, then went to Lawrenceville School in New Jersey and on to Yale University School of Forestry, where he stayed to earn a master's degree in 1909. He spent nineteen years in the forest service in New Mexico and the Apache National Forest in Arizona, where he studied the ecology of the Southwest. He was transferred to Madison, Wisconsin, where he focused on game management. In 1928, he also began teaching at the University of Wisconsin, where he taught until his death.

In 1933, he published his first important book, *Game Management*, in which he detailed the methods by which wild game should be managed to keep their numbers in an optimum relationship to the land. In addition, he explained how to restore depleted game to their original habitat. As a result of this book, the University of Wisconsin School of Agriculture created the Department of Game

Management and appointed him its first professor. He was instrumental in founding the nation's first wilderness preserve and he worked constantly to help preserve wildlands and wildlife. As a professor, he wrote numerous articles in his field and worked tirelessly to help create the beginnings of the conservationist movement.

Those who know his work often compare him with Henry David Thoreau and the naturalist John Muir. Leopold is valued not only for the coherence and approachability of his writing but also for its beauty and occasional poetic qualities. Through his untiring efforts, he gave the ecological movement something of a thrust, and his writing essentially inspired a generation to look differently at the land that supported them.

Leopold's Rhetoric

Leopold has been praised for the clarity and simplicity of his writing. Although in this essay he uses an occasional technical term—such as *biota*, which means the land's entire system of life—his writing is direct, simple, and clearly structured. A first glance shows that his paragraphs tend to be much shorter than those of many of the writers of his time: in "The Land Ethic" several are only one sentence long and most consist of only three or four sentences.

The use of subheads, like "The Ecological Conscience" and "The Land Pyramid," helps us understand the focus of each section of the essay. Leopold usually begins with one or more definitions that establish immediately the subject at hand. In "The Ethical Sequence," he begins with two definitions of the same thing: "An ethic, ecologically, is a limitation on freedom of action in the struggle for existence. An ethic, philosophically, is a differentiation of social from antisocial conduct" (para. 4). He ends the section with another definition: "[e]thics are possibly a kind of community instinct in the making" (para. 9). In this definition he implies what he later says directly: the idea of ethics is functional in a community that places a high value on cooperation. He later explains that his concept of the land ethic simply extends the community to "include soils, waters, plants, and animals, or collectively: the land" (para. 11).

Another important device is the use of a summary at the end of certain sections. At the end of "The Ecological Conscience," Leopold sums up the situation in Wisconsin, where farmers were given directions and help in restoring their land to make it fertile again. He points out that economic self-interest is the dominant force motivating farmers to practice all that they were taught. Again and again, Leopold reminds us that education is not enough to ensure changes in land management because people will naturally respond to procedures that benefit them directly but usually will not to procedures that are indirect and do not produce a financial benefit. The ethics of land requires a sense of obligation, and as he says in his summary, "Obligations have no meaning without conscience" (para. 32).

In his summary for "Substitutes for a Land Ethic," he points out that government cannot be expected to perform all the required work for good land management. He says that "a system of conservation based solely on economic self-interest is hopelessly lopsided" (para. 45). A single-sentence paragraph, "An ethical obligation on the part of the private owner is the only visible remedy for these situations" (para. 46), ends the section. Paragraph 61 contains an enumerated summary of three main points, beginning with "1. That land is not merely soil." He has established that when he speaks of land he means land and everything that lives on it or depends on it, including all the plants and animals that have no economic benefit for farmers or others.

In "Land Health and the A-B Cleavage" Leopold establishes two positions about our attitude toward land. The first regards the land as a commodity, as soil; the second regards the land as "a biota," a complex system that includes all life as well as the soil. He sees the second approach as the most hopeful in finally producing a workable ethic if only because in that approach he "feels the stirrings of an ecological conscience" (para. 74).

The last section, "The Outlook," is itself a virtual summary. In it Leopold makes a plea for people not just to admire land but to value it "in the philosophical sense." In this section, he reviews many of his main points but does not suggest that things are hopeful: "[t]he case for a land ethic would appear hopeless but for the minority which is in obvious revolt against these 'modern' trends" (para. 85). Interestingly, in our time that minority has grown to enormous proportions. The green movement is an international force that is virtually global. Conservation movements have flourished in Europe, North America, and Asia and have gotten under way everywhere else. Leopold is looked to as a propelling force in changing the way we look at our environment.

PREREADING QUESTIONS: WHAT TO READ FOR

The following prereading questions may help you anticipate key issues in the discussion of Aldo Leopold's "The Land Ethic." Keeping them in mind during your first reading of the selection should help focus your attention.

- What is an ethic? What is a land ethic?
- Why is economic self-interest not sufficient motivation for preserving the land?
- What role do obligation and conscience play in constructing a land ethic?
- What does Leopold mean by the term *biota*?

The Land Ethic

When godlike Odysseus returned from the wars in Troy, he   1
hanged all on one rope a dozen slave girls of his household whom
he suspected of misbehavior during his absence.

This hanging involved no question of propriety. The girls were   2
property. The disposal of property was then, as now, a matter of
expediency, not of right and wrong.

Concepts of right and wrong were not lacking from Odysseus's   3
Greece: witness the fidelity of his wife through the long years before
at last his black-prowed galleys clove the wine-dark seas for home.
The ethical structure of that day covered wives, but had not yet been
extended to human chattels. During the three thousand years which
have since elapsed, ethical criteria have been extended to many
fields of conduct, with corresponding shrinkages in those judged by
expediency only.

The Ethical Sequence

This extension of ethics, so far studied only by philosophers, is   4
actually a process in ecological evolution. Its sequences may be
described in ecological as well as in philosophical terms. An ethic,
ecologically, is a limitation on freedom of action in the struggle for
existence. An ethic, philosophically, is a differentiation of social from
antisocial conduct. These are two definitions of one thing. The thing
has its origin in the tendency of interdependent individuals or groups
to evolve modes of cooperation. The ecologist calls these symbioses.[1]
Politics and economics are advanced symbioses in which the original
free-for-all competition has been replaced, in part, by cooperative
mechanisms with an ethical content.

---

[1] **symbioses** Relationships between interdependent organisms.

The complexity of cooperative mechanisms has increased with 5
population density, and with the efficiency of tools. It was simpler, for
example, to define the antisocial uses of sticks and stones in the days
of the mastodons than of bullets and billboards in the age of motors.

The first ethics dealt with the relation between individuals; the 6
Mosaic Decalogue[2] is an example. Later accretions dealt with the
relation between the individual and society. The Golden Rule tries
to integrate the individual to society; democracy to integrate social
organization to the individual.

There is as yet no ethic dealing with man's relation to land and to 7
the animals and plants which grow upon it. Land, like Odysseus's
slave girls, is still property. The land relation is still strictly economic,
entailing privileges but not obligations.

The extension of ethics to this third element in human environ- 8
ment is, if I read the evidence correctly, an evolutionary possibility
and an ecological necessity. It is the third step in a sequence. The
first two have already been taken. Individual thinkers since the days
of Ezekiel and Isaiah have asserted that the despoliation of land is
not only inexpedient but wrong. Society, however, has not yet
affirmed their belief. I regard the present conservation movement as
the embryo of such an affirmation.

An ethic may be regarded as a mode of guidance for meeting 9
ecological situations so new or intricate, or involving such deferred
reactions, that the path of social expediency is not discernible to the
average individual. Animal instincts are modes of guidance for the
individual in meeting such situations. Ethics are possibly a kind of
community instinct in the making.

The Community Concept

All ethics so far evolved rest upon a single premise: that the 10
individual is a member of a community of interdependent parts. His
instincts prompt him to compete for his place in the community,
but his ethics prompt him also to cooperate (perhaps in order that
there may be a place to compete for).

The land ethic simply enlarges the boundaries of the community 11
to include soils, waters, plants, and animals, or collectively: the land.

This sounds simple: Do we not already sing our love for and 12
obligation to the land of the free and the home of the brave? Yes, but
just what and whom do we love? Certainly not the soil, which we are

---

[2] **Mosaic Decalogue** The Ten Commandments.

sending helter-skelter downriver. Certainly not the waters, which we assume have no function except to turn turbines, float barges, and carry off sewage. Certainly not the plants, of which we exterminate whole communities without batting an eye. Certainly not the animals, of which we have already extirpated many of the largest and most beautiful species. A land ethic of course cannot prevent the alteration, management, and use of these "resources," but it does affirm their right to continued existence, and, at least in spots, their continued existence in a natural state.

In short, a land ethic changes the role of Homo sapiens from   13 conqueror of the land-community to plain member and citizen of it. It implies respect for his fellow members, and also respect for the community as such.

In human history, we have learned (I hope) that the conqueror   14 role is eventually self-defeating. Why? Because it is implicit in such a role that the conqueror knows, ex cathedra,[3] just what makes the community clock tick, and just what and who is valuable, and what and who is worthless, in community life. It always turns out that he knows neither, and this is why his conquests eventually defeat themselves.

In the biotic community, a parallel situation exists. Abraham   15 knew exactly what the land was for: it was to drip milk and honey into Abraham's mouth. At the present moment, the assurance with which we regard this assumption is inverse to the degree of our education.

The ordinary citizen today assumes that science knows what   16 makes the community clock tick; the scientist is equally sure that he does not. He knows that the biotic mechanism is so complex that its workings may never be fully understood.

That man is, in fact, only a member of a biotic team is shown by   17 an ecological interpretation of history. Many historical events, hitherto explained solely in terms of human enterprise, were actually biotic interactions between people and land. The characteristics of the land determined the facts quite as potently as the characteristics of the men who lived on it.

Consider, for example, the settlement of the Mississippi Valley.   18 In the years following the Revolution, three groups were contending for its control: the native Indian, the French and English traders, and the American settlers. Historians wonder what would have happened if the English at Detroit had thrown a little more weight into the Indian side of those tipsy scales which decided the outcome of the colonial migration into the cane lands of Kentucky. It is time now to

---

[3] **ex cathedra** Literally, "speaking from the chair," so speaking with great authority.

ponder the fact that the cane lands, when subjected to the particular mixture of forces represented by the cow, plow, fire, and ax of the pioneer, became bluegrass. What if the plant succession inherent in this dark and bloody ground had, under the impact of these forces, given us some worthless sedge, shrub, or weed? Would Boone and Kenton[4] have held out? Would there have been any overflow into Ohio, Indiana, Illinois, and Missouri? Any Louisiana Purchase? Any transcontinental union of new states? Any Civil War?

Kentucky was one sentence in the drama of history. We are commonly told what the human actors in this drama tried to do, but we are seldom told that their success, or the lack of it, hung in large degree on the reaction of particular soils to the impact of the particular forces exerted by their occupancy. In the case of Kentucky, we do not even know where the bluegrass came from—whether it is a native species, or a stowaway from Europe. 19

Contrast the cane lands with what hindsight tells us about the Southwest, where the pioneers were equally brave, resourceful, and persevering. The impact of occupancy here brought no bluegrass, or other plant fitted to withstand the bumps and buffetings of hard use. This region, when grazed by livestock, reverted through a series of more and more worthless grasses, shrubs, and weeds to a condition of unstable equilibrium. Each recession of plant types bred erosion; each increment to erosion bred a further recession of plants. The result today is a progressive and mutual deterioration, not only of plants and soils, but of the animal community subsisting thereon. The early settlers did not expect this: on the ciénegas[5] of New Mexico some even cut ditches to hasten it. So subtle has been its progress that few residents of the region are aware of it. It is quite invisible to the tourist who finds this wrecked landscape colorful and charming (as indeed it is, but it bears scant resemblance to what it was in 1848). 20

This same landscape was "developed" once before, but with quite different results. The Pueblo Indians settled the Southwest in pre-Columbian times, but they happened *not* to be equipped with range livestock. Their civilization expired, but not because their land expired. 21

In India, regions devoid of any sod-forming grass have been settled, apparently without wrecking the land, by the simple expedient of carrying the grass to the cow, rather than vice versa. (Was this the result of some deep wisdom, or was it just good luck? I do not know.) 22

---

[4] **Daniel Boone (1734–1820) and Simon Kenton (1755–1836)** Boone was an American pioneer remembered for his exploration and settlement of Kentucky. Kenton was a frontiersman and friend of Boone's.

[5] **ciénegas** Wetlands that support the Santa Fe River in New Mexico.

In short, the plant succession steered the course of history; the   23
pioneer simply demonstrated, for good or ill, what successions
inhered in the land. Is history taught in this spirit? It will be, once the
concept of land as a community really penetrates our intellectual life.

The Ecological Conscience

Conservation is a state of harmony between men and land. Despite   24
nearly a century of propaganda, conservation still proceeds at a snail's
pace; progress still consists largely of letterhead pieties and convention
oratory. On the back forty we still slip two steps backward for each
forward stride.

The usual answer to this dilemma is "more conservation educa-   25
tion." No one will debate this, but is it certain that only the *volume*
of education needs stepping up? Is something lacking in the *content*
as well?

It is difficult to give a fair summary of its content in brief form,   26
but, as I understand it, the content is substantially this: obey the law,
vote right, join some organizations, and practice what conservation
is profitable on your own land; the government will do the rest.

Is not this formula too easy to accomplish anything worthwhile? It   27
defines no right or wrong, assigns no obligation, calls for no sacrifice,
implies no change in the current philosophy of values. In respect of
land use, it urges only enlightened self-interest. Just how far will such
education take us? An example will perhaps yield a partial answer.

By 1930 it had become clear to all except the ecologically blind   28
that southwestern Wisconsin's topsoil was slipping seaward. In
1933 the farmers were told that if they would adopt certain remedial
practices for five years, the public would donate CCC[6] labor to
install them, plus the necessary machinery and materials. The offer
was widely accepted, but the practices were widely forgotten when
the five-year contract period was up. The farmers continued only
those practices that yielded an immediate and visible economic gain
for themselves.

This led to the idea that maybe farmers would learn more quickly   29
if they themselves wrote the rules. Accordingly the Wisconsin legislature in 1937 passed the Soil Conservation District Law. This said
to farmers, in effect: *We, the public, will furnish you free technical service and loan you specialized machinery, if you will write your own rules*

---

[6] **CCC** Civilian Conservation Corps.

for land use. Each county may write its own rules, and these will have the force of law. Nearly all the counties promptly organized to accept the proffered help, but after a decade of operation, *no county has yet written a single rule.* There has been visible progress in such practices as strip cropping, pasture renovation, and soil liming, but none in fencing woodlots against grazing, and none in excluding plow and cow from steep slopes. The farmers, in short, have selected those remedial practices which were profitable anyhow, and ignored those which were profitable to the community, but not clearly profitable to themselves.

When one asks why no rules have been written, one is told that the community is not yet ready to support them; education must precede rules. But the education actually in progress makes no mention of obligations to land over and above those dictated by self-interest. The net result is that we have more education but less soil, fewer healthy woods, and as many floods as in 1937.

The puzzling aspect of such situations is that the existence of obligations over and above self-interest is taken for granted in such rural community enterprises as the betterment of roads, schools, churches, and baseball teams. Their existence is not taken for granted, nor as yet seriously discussed, in bettering the behavior of the water that falls on the land, or in the preserving of the beauty or diversity of the farm landscape. Land-use ethics are still governed wholly by economic self-interest, just as social ethics were a century ago.

To sum up: we asked the farmer to do what he conveniently could to save his soil, and he has done just that, and only that. The farmer who clears the woods of a 75-percent slope, turns his cows into the clearing, and dumps its rainfall, rocks, and soil into the community creek, is still (if otherwise decent) a respected member of society. If he puts lime on his fields and plants his crops on contour, he is still entitled to all the privileges and emoluments of his Soil Conservation District. The district is a beautiful piece of social machinery, but it is coughing along on two cylinders because we have been too timid, and too anxious for quick success, to tell the farmer the true magnitude of his obligations. Obligations have no meaning without conscience, and the problem we face is the extension of the social conscience from people to land.

No important change in ethics was ever accomplished without an internal change in our intellectual emphasis, loyalties, affections, and convictions. The proof that conservation has not yet touched these foundations of conduct lies in the fact that philosophy and religion have not yet heard of it. In our attempt to make conservation easy, we have made it trivial.

Substitutes for a Land Ethic

When the logic of history hungers for bread and we hand out a   34
stone, we are at pains to explain how much the stone resembles
bread. I now describe some of the stones which serve in lieu of a
land ethic.

One basic weakness in a conservation system based wholly on   35
economic motives is that most members of the land community
have no economic value. Wildflowers and songbirds are examples.
Of the 22,000 higher plants and animals native to Wisconsin, it is
doubtful whether more than 5 percent can be sold, fed, eaten, or
otherwise put to economic use. Yet these creatures are members of
the biotic community, and if (as I believe) its stability depends on its
integrity, they are entitled to continuance.

When one of these noneconomic categories is threatened, and if   36
we happen to love it, we invent subterfuges to give it economic
importance. At the beginning of the century songbirds were supposed to be disappearing. Ornithologists jumped to the rescue with
some distinctly shaky evidence to the effect that insects would eat us
up if birds failed to control them. The evidence had to be economic
in order to be valid.

It is painful to read these circumlocutions today. We have no   37
land ethic yet, but we have at least drawn nearer the point of admitting that birds should continue as a matter of biotic right, regardless
of the presence or absence of economic advantage to us.

A parallel situation exists in respect of predatory mammals, rap-   38
torial birds, and fish-eating birds. Time was when biologists somewhat overworked the evidence that these creatures preserve the
health of game by killing weaklings, or that they control rodents for
the farmer, or that they prey only on "worthless" species. Here again,
the evidence had to be economic in order to be valid. It is only in
recent years that we hear the more honest argument that predators
are members of the community, and that no special interest has the
right to exterminate them for the sake of a benefit, real or fancied, to
itself. Unfortunately this enlightened view is still in the talk stage. In
the field the extermination of predators goes merrily on: witness the
impending erasure of the timber wolf by fiat of Congress, the Conservation Bureaus, and many state legislatures.

Some species of trees have been "read out of the party" by   39
economics-minded foresters because they grow too slowly, or have
too low a sale value to pay as timber crops: white cedar, tamarack,
cypress, beech, and hemlock are examples. In Europe, where
forestry is ecologically more advanced, the noncommercial tree
species are recognized as members of the native forest community,

to be preserved as such, within reason. Moreover some (like beech) have been found to have a valuable function in building up soil fertility. The interdependence of the forest and its constituent tree species, ground flora, and fauna is taken for granted.

Lack of economic value is sometimes a character not only of   40
species or groups, but of entire biotic communities: marshes, bogs, dunes, and "deserts" are examples. Our formula in such cases is to relegate their conservation to government as refuges, monuments, or parks. The difficulty is that these communities are usually interspersed with more valuable private lands; the government cannot possibly own or control such scattered parcels. The net effect is that we have relegated some of them to ultimate extinction over large areas. If the private owner were ecologically minded, he would be proud to be the custodian of a reasonable proportion of such areas, which add diversity and beauty to his farm and to his community.

In some instances, the assumed lack of profit in these "waste"   41
areas has proved to be wrong, but only after most of them had been done away with. The present scramble to reflood muskrat marshes is a case in point.

There is a clear tendency in American conservation to relegate to   42
government all necessary jobs that private landowners fail to perform. Government ownership, operation, subsidy, or regulation is now widely prevalent in forestry, range management, soil and watershed management, park and wilderness conservation, fisheries management, and migratory bird management, with more to come. Most of this growth in governmental conservation is proper and logical, some of it is inevitable. That I imply no disapproval of it is implicit in the fact that I have spent most of my life working for it. Nevertheless the question arises: What is the ultimate magnitude of the enterprise? Will the tax base carry its eventual ramifications? At what point will governmental conservation, like the mastodon, become handicapped by its own dimensions? The answer, if there is any, seems to be in a land ethic, or some other force which assigns more obligation to the private landowner.

Industrial landowners and users, especially lumbermen and   43
stockmen, are inclined to wail long and loudly about the extension of government ownership and regulation to land, but (with notable exceptions) they show little disposition to develop the only visible alternative: the voluntary practice of conservation on their own lands.

When the private landowner is asked to perform some unprof-   44
itable act for the good of the community, he today assents only with outstretched palm. If the act costs him cash this is fair and proper, but when it costs only forethought, open-mindedness, or time, the issue is at least debatable. The overwhelming growth of land-use subsidies

in recent years must be ascribed, in large part, to the government's own agencies for conservation education: the land bureaus, the agricultural colleges, and the extension services. As far as I can detect, no ethical obligation toward land is taught in these institutions.

To sum up: a system of conservation based solely on economic   45
self-interest is hopelessly lopsided. It tends to ignore, and thus eventually to eliminate, many elements in the land community that lack commercial value, but that are (as far as we know) essential to its healthy functioning. It assumes, falsely, I think, that the economic parts of the biotic clock will function without the uneconomic parts. It tends to relegate to government many functions eventually too large, too complex, or too widely dispersed to be performed by government.

An ethical obligation on the part of the private owner is the only   46
visible remedy for these situations.

The Land Pyramid

An ethic to supplement and guide the economic relation to land   47
presupposes the existence of some mental image of land as a biotic mechanism. We can be ethical only in relation to something we can see, feel, understand, love, or otherwise have faith in.

The image commonly employed in conservation education is "the   48
balance of nature." For reasons too lengthy to detail here, this figure of speech fails to describe accurately what little we know about the land mechanism. A much truer image is the one employed in ecology: the biotic pyramid. I shall first sketch the pyramid as a symbol of land, and later develop some of its implications in terms of land use.

Plants absorb energy from the sun. This energy flows through a   49
circuit called the *biota,* which may be represented by a pyramid consisting of layers. The bottom layer is the soil. A plant layer rests on the soil, an insect layer on the plants, a bird and rodent layer on the insects, and so on up through various animal groups to the apex layer, which consists of the larger carnivores.

The species of a layer are alike not in where they came from, or   50
in what they look like, but rather in what they eat. Each successive layer depends on those below it for food and often for other services, and each in turn furnishes food and services to those above. Proceeding upward, each successive layer decreases in numerical abundance. Thus, for every carnivore there are hundreds of his prey, thousands of their prey, millions of insects, uncountable plants. The pyramidal form of the system reflects this numerical progression from apex to base. Man shares an intermediate layer with the bears, raccoons, and squirrels which eat both meat and vegetables.

The lines of dependency for food and other services are called 51
food chains. Thus soil-oak-deer-Indian is a chain that has now been
largely converted to soil-corn-cow-farmer. Each species, including
ourselves, is a link in many chains. The deer eats a hundred plants
other than oak, and the cow a hundred plants other than corn. Both,
then, are links in a hundred chains. The pyramid is a tangle of chains
so complex as to seem disorderly, yet the stability of the system
proves it to be a highly organized structure. Its functioning depends
on the cooperation and competition of its diverse parts.

In the beginning, the pyramid of life was low and squat; the 52
food chains short and simple. Evolution has added layer after layer,
link after link. Man is one of thousands of accretions to the height
and complexity of the pyramid. Science has given us many doubts,
but it has given us at least one certainty: the trend of evolution is to
elaborate and diversify the biota.

Land, then, is not merely soil; it is a fountain of energy flowing 53
through a circuit of soils, plants, and animals. Food chains are the
living channels which conduct energy upward; death and decay
return it to the soil. The circuit is not closed; some energy is dissi-
pated in decay, some is added by absorption from the air, some is
stored in soils, peats, and long-lived forests; but it is a sustained circuit, like a slowly augmented revolving fund of life. There is always
a net loss by downhill wash, but this is normally small and offset by
the decay of rocks. It is deposited in the ocean and, in the course of
geological time, raised to form new lands and new pyramids.

The velocity and character of the upward flow of energy depend 54
on the complex structure of the plant and animal community, much as
the upward flow of sap in a tree depends on its complex cellular organization. Without this complexity, normal circulation would presumably not occur. Structure means the characteristic numbers, as well
as the characteristic kinds and functions, of the component species.
This interdependence between the complex structure of the land and
its smooth functioning as an energy unit is one of its basic attributes.

When a change occurs in one part of the circuit, many other parts 55
must adjust themselves to it. Change does not necessarily obstruct or
divert the flow of energy; evolution is a long series of self-induced
changes, the net result of which has been to elaborate the flow mechanism and to lengthen the circuit. Evolutionary changes, however, are
usually slow and local. Man's invention of tools has enabled him to
make changes of unprecedented violence, rapidity, and scope.

One change is in the composition of floras and faunas. The larger 56
predators are lopped off the apex of the pyramid; food chains, for the
first time in history, become shorter rather than longer. Domesticated
species from other lands are substituted for wild ones, and wild ones

are moved to new habitats. In this worldwide pooling of faunas and floras, some species get out of bounds as pests and diseases, others are extinguished. Such effects are seldom intended or foreseen; they represent unpredicted and often untraceable readjustments in the structure. Agricultural science is largely a race between the emergence of new pests and the emergence of new techniques for their control.

Another change touches the flow of energy through plants and 57 animals and its return to the soil. Fertility is the ability of soil to receive, store, and release energy. Agriculture, by overdrafts on the soil, or by too radical a substitution of domestic for native species in the superstructure, may derange the channels of flow or deplete storage. Soils depleted of their storage, or of the organic matter which anchors it, wash away faster than they form. This is erosion.

Waters, like soil, are part of the energy circuit. Industry, by pol- 58 luting waters or obstructing them with dams, may exclude the plants and animals necessary to keep energy in circulation.

Transportation brings about another basic change: the plants or 59 animals grown in one region are now consumed and returned to the soil in another. Transportation taps the energy stored in rocks, and in the air, and uses it elsewhere; thus we fertilize the garden with nitrogen gleaned by the guano birds from the fishes of seas on the other side of the equator. Thus the formerly localized and self-contained circuits are pooled on a worldwide scale.

The process of altering the pyramid for human occupation 60 releases stored energy, and this often gives rise, during the pioneering period, to a deceptive exuberance of plant and animal life, both wild and tame. These releases of biotic capital tend to becloud or postpone the penalties of violence.

This thumbnail sketch of land as an energy circuit conveys three 61 basic ideas:

1. That land is not merely soil.
2. That the native plants and animals kept the energy circuit open; others may or may not.
3. That man-made changes are of a different order than evolutionary changes, and have effects more comprehensive than is intended or foreseen.

These ideas, collectively, raise two basic issues: Can the land 62 adjust itself to the new order? Can the desired alterations be accomplished with less violence?

Biotas seem to differ in their capacity to sustain violent conver- 63 sion. Western Europe, for example, carries a far different pyramid than Caesar found there. Some large animals are lost; swampy forests have become meadows or plowland; many new plants and animals are introduced, some of which escape as pests; the remaining natives are greatly changed in distribution and abundance. Yet the soil is still there and, with the help of imported nutrients, still fertile; the waters flow normally; the new structure seems to function and to persist. There is no visible stoppage or derangement of the circuit.

Western Europe, then, has a resistant biota. Its inner processes 64 are tough, elastic, resistant to strain. No matter how violent the alterations, the pyramid, so far, has developed some new modus vivendi[7] which preserves its habitability for man, and for most of the other natives.

Japan seems to present another instance of radical conversion 65 without disorganization.

Most other civilized regions, and some as yet barely touched by 66 civilization, display various stages of disorganization, varying from initial symptoms to advanced wastage. In Asia Minor and North Africa diagnosis is confused by climatic changes, which may have been either the cause or the effect of advanced wastage. In the United States the degree of disorganization varies locally; it is worst in the Southwest, the Ozarks, and parts of the South, and least in New England and the Northwest. Better land uses may still arrest it in the less advanced regions. In parts of Mexico, South America, South Africa, and Australia a violent and accelerating wastage is in progress, but I cannot assess the prospects.

This almost worldwide display of disorganization in the land 67 seems to be similar to disease in an animal, except that it never culminates in complete disorganization or death. The land recovers, but at some reduced level of complexity, and with a reduced carrying capacity for people, plants, and animals. Many biotas currently regarded as "lands of opportunity" are in fact already subsisting on exploitative agriculture, i.e., they have already exceeded their sustained carrying capacity. Most of South America is overpopulated in this sense.

In arid regions we attempt to offset the process of wastage by 68 reclamation, but it is only too evident that the prospective longevity of reclamation projects is often short. In our own West, the best of them may not last a century.

The combined evidence of history and ecology seems to support 69 one general deduction: the less violent the man-made changes, the greater the probability of successful readjustment in the pyramid.

---

[7] **modus vivendi** A way of life.

Violence, in turn, varies with human population density; a dense population requires a more violent conversion. In this respect, North America has a better chance for permanence than Europe, if she can contrive to limit her density.

This deduction runs counter to our current philosophy, which   70
assumes that because a small increase in density enriched human life, than an indefinite increase will enrich it indefinitely. Ecology knows of no density relationship that holds for indefinitely wide limits. All gains from density are subject to a law of diminishing returns.

Whatever may be the equation for men and land, it is improb-   71
able that we as yet know all its terms. Recent discoveries in mineral and vitamin nutrition reveal unsuspected dependencies in the up circuit: incredibly minute quantities of certain substances determine the value of soils to plants, of plants to animals. What of the down circuit? What of the vanishing species, the preservation of which we now regard as an esthetic luxury? They helped build the soil; in what unsuspected ways may they be essential to its maintenance? Professor Weaver[8] proposes that we use prairie flowers to reflocculate[9] the wasting soils of the dust bowl; who knows for what purpose cranes and condors, otters and grizzlies may some day be used?

Land Health and the A-B Cleavage

A land ethic, then, reflects the existence of an ecological con-   72
science, and this in turn reflects a conviction of individual responsibility for the health of the land. Health is the capacity of the land for self-renewal. Conservation is our effort to understand and preserve this capacity.

Conservationists are notorious for their dissensions. Superficially   73
these seem to add up to mere confusion, but a more careful scrutiny reveals a single plane of cleavage common to many specialized fields. In each field one group (A) regards the land as soil, and its function as commodity production; another group (B) regards the land as a biota, and its function as something broader. How much broader is admittedly in a state of doubt and confusion.

In my own field, forestry, Group A is quite content to grow trees   74
like cabbages, with cellulose as the basic forest commodity. It feels no inhibition against violence; its ideology is agronomic. Group B, on the other hand, sees forestry as fundamentally different from agronomy

---

[8] **John Ernest Weaver (1884–1966)** Professor at the University of Nebraska and a specialist in prairie studies.

[9] **reflocculate** To help soil create lumps or masses.

because it employs natural species, and manages a natural environment rather than creating an artificial one. Group B prefers natural reproduction on principle. It worries on biotic as well as economic grounds about the loss of species like chestnut, and the threatened loss of the white pines. It worries about a whole series of secondary forest functions: wildlife, recreation, watersheds, wilderness areas. To my mind, Group B feels the stirrings of an ecological conscience.

In the wildlife field, a parallel cleavage exists. For Group A the basic commodities are sport and meat; the yardsticks of production are ciphers of take in pheasants and trout. Artificial propagation is acceptable as a permanent as well as a temporary recourse—if its unit costs permit. Group B, on the other hand, worries about a whole series of biotic side issues. What is the cost in predators of producing a game crop? Should we have further recourse to exotics? How can management restore the shrinking species, like prairie grouse, already hopeless as shootable game? How can management restore the threatened rarities, like trumpeter swan and whooping crane? Can management principles be extended to wildflowers? Here again it is clear to me that we have the same A-B cleavage as in forestry.

In the larger field of agriculture I am less competent to speak, but there seem to be somewhat parallel cleavages. Scientific agriculture was actively developing before ecology was born, hence a slower penetration of ecological concepts might be expected. Moreover the farmer, by the very nature of his techniques, must modify the biota more radically than the forester or the wildlife manager. Nevertheless, there are many discontents in agriculture which seem to add up to a new vision of "biotic farming."

Perhaps the most important of these is the new evidence that poundage or tonnage is no measure of the food value of farm crops; the products of fertile soil may be qualitatively as well as quantitatively superior. We can bolster poundage from depleted soils by pouring on imported fertility, but we are not necessarily bolstering food value. The possible ultimate ramifications of this idea are so immense that I must leave their exposition to abler pens.

The discontent that labels itself "organic farming," while bearing some of the earmarks of a cult, is nevertheless biotic in its direction, particularly in its insistence on the importance of soil flora and fauna.

The ecological fundamentals of agriculture are just as poorly known to the public as in other fields of land use. For example, few educated people realize that the marvelous advances in technique made during recent decades are improvements in the pump, rather than the well. Acre for acre, they have barely sufficed to offset the sinking level of fertility.

In all of these cleavages, we see repeated the same basic para-   80
doxes: man the conqueror *versus* man the biotic citizen; science the
sharpener of his sword *versus* science the searchlight on his universe; land the slave and servant *versus* land the collective organism.
Robinson's[10] injunction to Tristram may well be applied, at this
juncture, to Homo sapiens as a species in geological time:

> Whether you will or not
> You are a King, Tristram, for you are one
> Of the time-tested few that leave the world,
> When they are gone, not the same place it was.
> Mark what you leave.

The Outlook

It is inconceivable to me that an ethical relation to land can exist   81
without love, respect, and admiration for land, and a high regard for
its value. By value, I of course mean something far broader than
mere economic value; I mean value in the philosophical sense.

Perhaps the most serious obstacle impeding the evolution of a   82
land ethic is the fact that our educational and economic system is
headed away from, rather than toward, an intense consciousness of
land. Your true modern is separated from the land by many middle-
men, and by innumerable physical gadgets. He has no vital relation
to it; to him it is the space between cities on which crops grow. Turn
him loose for a day on the land, and if the spot does not happen to
be a golf links or a "scenic" area, he is bored stiff. If crops could be
raised by hydroponics instead of farming, it would suit him very
well. Synthetic substitutes for wood, leather, wool, and other natural
land products suit him better than the originals. In short, land is
something he has "outgrown."

Almost equally serious as an obstacle to a land ethic is the atti-   83
tude of the farmer for whom the land is still an adversary, or a
taskmaster that keeps him in slavery. Theoretically, the mechaniza-
tion of farming ought to cut the farmer's chains, but whether it
really does is debatable.

One of the requisites for an ecological comprehension of land is   84
an understanding of ecology, and this is by no means coextensive
with "education"; in fact, much higher education seems deliberately
to avoid ecological concepts. An understanding of ecology does not

---

[10]**Edwin Arlington Robinson (1869–1935)** New England poet. *Tristram* (1927)
was the third volume of a long poem on the Arthurian legends.

necessarily originate in courses bearing ecological labels; it is quite as likely to be labeled geography, botany, agronomy, history, or economics. This is as it should be, but whatever the label, ecological training is scarce.

The case for a land ethic would appear hopeless but for the   85 minority which is in obvious revolt against these "modern" trends.

The "key log" which must be moved to release the evolutionary   86 process for an ethic is simply this: quit thinking about decent land use as solely an economic problem. Examine each question in terms of what is ethically and esthetically right, as well as what is economically expedient. A thing is right when it tends to preserve the integrity, stability, and beauty of the biotic community. It is wrong when it tends otherwise.

It of course goes without saying that economic feasibility limits   87 the tether of what can or cannot be done for land. It always has and it always will. The fallacy the economic determinists have tied around our collective neck, and which we now need to cast off, is the belief that economics determines *all* land use. This is simply not true. An innumerable host of actions and attitudes, comprising perhaps the bulk of all land relations, is determined by the land users' tastes and predilections, rather than by his purse. The bulk of all land relations hinges on investments of time, forethought, skill, and faith rather than on investments of cash. As a land user thinketh, so is he.

I have purposely presented the land ethic as a product of social   88 evolution because nothing so important as an ethic is ever "written." Only the most superficial student of history supposes that Moses "wrote" the Decalogue; it evolved in the minds of a thinking community, and Moses wrote a tentative summary of it for a "seminar." I say tentative because evolution never stops.

The evolution of a land ethic is an intellectual as well as emo-   89 tional process. Conservation is paved with good intentions which prove to be futile, or even dangerous, because they are devoid of critical understanding either of the land, or of economic land use. I think it is a truism that as the ethical frontier advances from the individual to the community, its intellectual content increases.

The mechanism of operation is the same for any ethic: social   90 approbation for right actions: social disapproval for wrong actions.

By and large, our present problem is one of attitudes and imple-   91 ments. We are remodeling the Alhambra[11] with a steam shovel, and

---

[11] **Alhambra** Exquisitely detailed citadel built by the Moors in Granada, Spain, in 1248–1354.

we are proud of our yardage. We shall hardly relinquish the shovel, which after all has many good points, but we are in need of gentler and more objective criteria for its successful use.

QUESTIONS FOR CRITICAL READING

1. What is your definition of an *ethic*? What is a land ethic?
2. What is the point of Leopold's beginning the essay with the reference to Odysseus hanging his slave girls?
3. How does ethics relate to social cooperation? How does cooperation relate to land?
4. What does Leopold's concept of a land ethic include? Is it mainly for farmers?
5. What role did the land play in the settlement of the West?
6. How did the plant succession steer history (paras. 19–23)?
7. How did Wisconsin's farmers react to the government's offer of help to restore topsoil?
8. Are there genuine substitutes for a land ethic?

SUGGESTIONS FOR CRITICAL WRITING

1. To what extent do you think it's possible for our culture to establish the kind of land ethic that Leopold describes? How can people develop a conscience with regard to their use and abuse of the land? Leopold says that there is no chance of a land ethic being "written" down. What does he mean by this statement? Why is it important that such an ethic not be written down? Do you agree with Leopold on this matter? What are your ethical views on land and how are you putting them into action?
2. Leopold gives us an interesting example of a circumstance in which a noneconomic category was threatened—the disappearing songbirds. Examine his description of what happened (para. 36). Can you think of a similar program developed for the protection of something that has no economic value? When does aesthetics seem to be an appropriate substitute or cohort for ethics? Are there programs for saving flowers or wildlife that you think are similar to the one that Leopold describes?
3. In paragraph 40, Leopold talks about entire biota that are viewed as having no economic value. Examine your own ecological environment and identify at least one of those biotic communities: "marshes, bogs, dunes, and 'deserts'" (or vacant lots). What is the local consensus on these places? Do people value the biota or do they simply ignore it? Communicate with your local conservation boards and see what information you can obtain from them. Describe their efforts to preserve these biota. Include your own description of and feelings about these areas.
4. What should be the role of government in conservation practices? Leopold suggests that the government is usually given the tough unmanageable jobs and that it has too much to handle. What is the government

to do if people do not manage land wisely? What are the limits of its power? Do you agree with Leopold that education is not really up to the job of helping individuals do what needs to be done? Or has education changed substantially since 1948?

5. Do you believe that a system of conservation based on economic self-interest is doomed to failure? Or has the world finally begun to pay attention to the issues that most concern Leopold? The capitalist West has long assumed that economic self-interest will keep a kind of balance between those who conquer the land and those who become part of it. Have things changed in such a way as to make you more optimistic than Leopold was?

6. **CONNECTIONS**   Where would Friedrich Nietzsche (p. 713) or Iris Murdoch (p. 729) stand on the question of a system of ethics that was not specifically concerned with the interaction of communities of people? Would they look favorably on a system that includes concern for plants, animals, and insects? What are the religious implications of their ideas in relation to Leopold's? Would Leopold have found pleasure in reading the work of either of these philosophers, or would he have felt that their ideas were not relative to his concerns for the land?

7. **SEEING CONNECTIONS**   Imagine that the scientist giving the lecture in Wright's *An Experiment on a Bird in the Air Pump* (p. 687) agrees in all ways with Leopold. Write a version of his lecture to the assembled people, explaining the significance of his experiment on the bird. What is he trying to do in terms of awakening an ethical conscience in these people, and which of them do you think have begun to develop such a conscience? Which have not? What is the ethical situation in the painting, and how would Leopold interpret it?

Top photo: Peter Singer; bottom photo: Jim Mason

PETER SINGER AND JIM MASON
The Ethics of Eating Meat

PETER SINGER (b. 1946) AND JIM MASON (b. 1934) have long had profound concerns for animal rights and the ethical issues raised by the interrelationship of animals and people. They feel that any genuine system of ethics must address our moral relationship to animals just as scrupulously as it does our moral relationship to each other. Peter Singer, an Australian, was educated at the University of Melbourne and at Oxford University in England. For two years he was Radcliffe lecturer at Oxford, then he moved to New York University, and in 1977 returned to teach at Melbourne. Since 1999 he has been Ira W. DeCamp Professor of Bioethics at Princeton University. He is considered one of the most controversial of modern philosophers of ethics. He is also one of the most visible of modern philosophers, with books on animal rights, sociobiology, politics, and even philanthropy. His *What Should a Billionaire Give—and What Should You?* (2006) is his beginning foray into the question of philanthropy, the how and why of giving excess wealth away.

Jim Mason is an attorney who is also a journalist, author, lecturer, and editor. His concerns have paralleled those of Singer, focusing on animal rights. He grew up on a farm in Missouri and established an early understanding of animals and their behavior. He is best known for his 1980 book with Singer, *Animal Factories,* which details how animals raised for food are treated. He visited thousands of factory locations and photographed the conditions of confinement and mistreatment that are commonplace in the business of producing meat for our tables. His photographs are particularly disturbing to anyone who responds to evident pain and discomfort of animals.

Mason's book *An Unnatural Order: Roots of Our Destruction of Nature* (2005) attacks what he feels is the root of the problem of ethics in regard to animals. When he reviewed the historical record, he found the biblical declaration of "dominion" to be the cause of our

767

casual mistreatment of animals. The very first page of Genesis, the first book of the Bible, says, "And God said, Let us make man in our image, after our likeness: and let them have dominion over the fish of the sea, and over the fowl of the air, and over the cattle, and over all the earth, and over every creeping thing that creepeth upon the earth" (Genesis 1.26). Dominion has been taken to mean control, but neither the Bible nor commercial interests seem to have included the concept of responsibility toward or a sense of conscience about our treatment of living things. Mason, in his analysis, suggests that the biblical declaration of dominion was related to the shift in ancient cultural practices from matriarchal to patriarchal structures of religion and government. Whether this is true or not cannot be demonstrated, but it remains a central core of his analytic.

The question of dominion is not merely academic. It is employed by modern commercial and religious groups as a justification for ridding land of vermin and pests, as well as for damaging land and water sources for economic advantage. The concept is with us today and will be with us for some time.

Singer is also a controversial figure for his views of the relationships of humans and animals. To begin with, he feels there is no reason to privilege one species over any other. This statement alone is in our time what Galileo's discovery—that Earth was not the center of the universe—was in the Renaissance. It has brought religious and political forces against him because he places humans and animals on the same plane.

In his book *Practical Ethics* (1979; 1993), Singer has taken an unusually reasoned stand approving abortion within a certain limit of gestation. His stand is essentially utilitarian in that it takes into consideration the interests of those people involved in the pregnancy—the woman and the fetus—in terms of what their preferences are. He reasons that the woman has a preference and an understanding of pain but that up to the eighteenth week of gestation the fetus has no sense of preference and no understanding of pain. Therefore, if the woman wishes an abortion and times it properly, she may have one with no moral implications whatever. Naturally, this view has made Singer the target of attack and he has been called "the Doctor of Death" by his many critics.

One of his earliest books, *Animal Liberation: A New Ethics for Our Treatment of Animals* (1975), made him one of the best-known modern philosophers and led to a worldwide movement. The concern for animal rights is related to his work in this early book, and his theories of ethics in relation to animals developed from this beginning. His edited volume *In Defense of Animals* followed in 1985. *The Ethics of What We Eat: Why Our Food Choices Matter* (2005), with Jim Mason, provides the essay that follows, "The Ethics of Eating Meat."

Singer and Mason's Rhetoric

Singer and Mason use subheadings, as many contemporary writers do, especially those with a journalistic background. The selection that follows is the central part of a chapter that considers arguments on both sides of the issue of eating meat. As a result, the authors present the arguments of the opposition carefully; then they analyze the arguments and attempt to show their weaknesses in order to establish the arguments' fallibility. In the process of this approach, they present their claims and warrants carefully so as to represent their own argument in favor of either avoiding eating meat entirely or of being a conscientious omnivore (para. 46).

They have several interesting techniques for examining a contradictory argument. They show, for example, that while there may be distinctions between human and nonhuman animals, to claim that humans are superior depends on an argument that can be turned to prove one race or one gender is superior to the others. Turning the argument around is a powerful analytic that helps clarify the deep structure of any claim to truth. In paragraph 34, they examine an argument by the distinguished philosopher Roger Scruton, who has argued in favor of eating meat partly on the grounds that people are conscious, aware of themselves and their ambitions and hopes, and can see possibilities for future generations. Animals do not have these qualities and thus can be domesticated for food. Singer and Mason point out that babies and many brain-damaged individuals are essentially on the same level as the animals Scruton describes, and by his reasoning, they too could be a useful source of meat. By this time, Singer and Mason have already cited Jonathan Swift's "modest proposal" to serve up Irish one-year-olds as roasts on English tables. The argument collapses.

Starting in paragraph 39, Singer and Mason talk about the use of land to produce food, pointing to data that say an acre of land planted with crops will feed ten times the number of people that an acre of land given to grazing cattle will. Even the most humane of farms, like Polyface Farm that Michael Pollan praises for its careful treatment of animals, have their unpleasant aspects, as they demonstrate beginning with paragraph 41. Both Singer and Mason use the rhetorical device of developing paragraphs with testimony. In the case of their discussion of Polyface Farm, they derive the testimony directly from the farm itself (para. 41).

Much of the last part of the essay is devoted to establishing humane ways to treat farm animals destined for slaughter and eventually our table. They ask very clearly, "How humane is humane enough to eat?" (para. 44), and they suggest that the line between the humane and the inhumane treatment of animals destined for consumption is so vague that the only way to establish an absolutely clear ethical position is to abstain from eating them at all. The paragraphs that Singer and Mason devote to this issue are interesting because they include a powerful description of methods of slaughter, and therefore we can say that they are resorting to an emotional appeal in the middle of what seemed to be a thoroughly rational examination. Perhaps that is unavoidable — or perhaps we can say that if we are to talk about humane behavior then we need to consider how humane the treatment can be. It may not be humane enough. Conscientious omnivores, the authors decide at the end of the essay, may in fact be the best that they can hope for if they cannot convince everyone to be vegetarian.

PREREADING QUESTIONS: WHAT TO READ FOR

The following prereading questions may help you anticipate key issues in the discussion of Peter Singer and Jim Mason's "The Ethics of Eating Meat." Keeping them in mind during your first reading of the selection should help focus your attention.

- What is the prevailing Western ethic toward animals?
- What is the best argument in favor of eating meat?
- How do farmers go about humanely raising animals for food?
- What defines a conscientious omnivore? Is it possible to be one?

The Ethics of Eating Meat

Many people, like Jake Hillard and Lee Nierstheimer, eat what-   1
ever meat takes their fancy at the supermarket or in fast-food restaurants. Some, like Mary Ann Masarech and her daughters, make an effort to eat meat from humane and organic farms. Others, like the Farb family, eat no animal products at all. In this chapter we focus

solely on the impact these diets have on animals. What does ethics require of us with regard to eating animals and animal products? In this chapter, the ethics of what we eat become more philosophically complex.

Let's start with factory farming. We have seen how it inflicts   2
prolonged suffering on sows who spend most of their lives in crates that are too narrow for them to turn around in; on caged hens; on chickens kept in unnaturally large flocks, bred to grow too fast, and transported and killed in appalling conditions; on dairy cows who are regularly made pregnant and separated from their calves; and on beef cattle kept in bare dirt feedlots. Though we like and respect Jake and Lee and take into account the time and economic pressures on families with children, we think that buying factory-farm products is not the right thing to do.

You don't have to be a vegetarian to reach this conclusion.   3
Hugh Fearnley-Whittingstall[1] is the author of *The River Cottage Meat Book*—a large, glossy book devoted to the cooking and eating of meat. Yet he writes: "The vast majority of our food animals are now raised under methods that are systematically abusive. For them, discomfort is the norm, pain is routine, growth is abnormal, and diet is unnatural. Disease is widespread and stress is almost constant." Fearnley-Whittingstall lives in England, where laws protecting animals are much stricter than in the United States. American-style crates for sows or veal calves are illegal in Britain, and caged hens have at least 50 percent more space than many American hens are granted. Even so, he considers these conditions abusive to animals. Michael Pollan,[2] another meat eater, says that factory farms are designed on the principle that "animals are machines incapable of feeling pain" and that to support them requires "a willingness to avert your eyes" from the reality that animals can feel.

Roger Scruton,[3] a critic of animal rights and vigorous defender   4
of the traditional English sport of foxhunting in the years before Parliament banned it, lives on a farm in Wiltshire, where he raises animals for his own table. His attitude to animal rights is perhaps best

---

[1] **Hugh Fearnley-Whittingstall (b. 1965)** Chef on British television and an advocate of "real food"; Hugh Fearnley-Whittingstall, *The River Cottage Meat Book*, Hodder and Stoughton, London, 2004, p. 24. [Singer and Mason's note]

[2] **Michael Pollan (b. 1955)** American author of numerous books on food; Michael Pollan, "An Animal's Place," *New York Times Sunday Magazine,* November 10, 2002; see also Michael Pollan, *The Omnivore's Dilemma: A Natural History of Four Meals,* Penguin, New York, 2006. [Singer and Mason's note]

[3] **Roger Scruton (b. 1944)** British philosopher and leading aesthetician.

illustrated by the following incident, as reported by Sholto Byrnes, who visited him at his farm for an interview in the *Independent*:

> After a drink, we move through to begin lunch, components of which have been produced on the Scruton farm. "That's Singer," declares Roger, pointing at a plate of leftover sausages. Singer the pig, mischievously named after Peter Singer, the philosopher and animal-rights theorist, has been "ensausaged" personally by his former owner.[4]

Nevertheless, Scruton flatly rejects factory farming. "A true moral-   5
ity of animal welfare," he writes, "ought to begin from the premise that this way of treating animals is wrong."[5]

In America, those opposed to factory farming include Matthew   6
Scully, a former speech writer in George W. Bush's White House and the author of *Dominion: The Power of Man, the Suffering of Animals, and the Call to Mercy*. Although "animal rights" tend to be associated with those on the left, Scully makes a case for many of the same goals using arguments congenial to the Christian right. In Scully's view, even though God has given us "dominion" over the animals, we should exercise that dominion with mercy — and factory farming fails to do so. Scully's writings have found support from other conservatives, like Pat Buchanan, editor of the *American Conservative*, which gave cover-story prominence to Scully's essay "Fear Factories: The Case for Compassionate Conservatism — for Animals," and George F. Will, who used his *Newsweek* column to recommend Scully's book.[6]

No less a religious authority than Pope Benedict XVI has stated   7
that human "dominion" over animals does not justify factory farm-ing. When head of the Roman Catholic Church's Sacred Congrega-tion for the Doctrine of the Faith, the future pope condemned the "industrial use of creatures, so that geese are fed in such a way as to produce as large a liver as possible, or hens live so packed together that they become just caricatures of birds." This "degrading of living

---

[4] Sholto Byrnes, "Roger Scruton: The Patron Saint of Lost Causes," *Independent*, July 3, 2005, http://enjoyment.independent.co.uk/books/features/article296509.ece. [Singer and Mason's note]

[5] Roger Scruton, *Animal Rights and Wrongs*, 3rd ed., Claridge Press, 2003. [Singer and Mason's note]

[6] Matthew Scully, "Fear Factories: The Case for Compassionate Conservatism — for Animals," *American Conservative*, May 23, 2005; George F. Will, "What We Owe What We Eat," *Newsweek*, July 18, 2005; Matthew Scully, *Dominion: The Power of Man, the Suffering of Animals, and the Call to Mercy*, St. Martin's Press, New York, 2003. [Singer and Mason's note]

creatures to a commodity" seemed to him "to contradict the relationship of mutuality that comes across in the Bible."[7]

On this issue we agree with Scully, Buchanan, Will, Pollan, Fearnley-Whittingstall, Scruton, and Pope Benedict XVI: no one should be supporting the vast system of animal abuse that today produces most animal products in developed nations.   8

Unsound Defenses of Factory Farming

What possible arguments can there be in defense of factory farming? We will review some of them and show why they are unconvincing. First, it is sometimes said that we have no duties to animals, because they are incapable of having duties toward us. This has been argued by those who believe that the basis of ethics is some kind of contract, such as "I'll refrain from harming you, if you refrain from harming me."[8] Animals cannot agree to a contract and thus fall outside the sphere of morality. But so, on this view, do babies and those with permanent, severe intellectual disabilities. Do we really have no duties to them either? An even bigger problem for the contract view of ethics is that it cannot ground duties to future generations. We could save ourselves a lot of money and effort by storing radioactive waste from nuclear-power plants in containers designed to last no more than, say, 150 years. If we only have duties to those who have duties towards us, why would that be wrong? There is an old joke that goes, "Why should I do anything for posterity? What did posterity ever do for me?" The problem with contract theorists is that they don't get the joke.   9

Second, when ethical issues are raised about eating meat, many people use what might be called "the Benjamin Franklin defense." Franklin was for many years a vegetarian, until one day, while watching his friends fishing, he noticed that some of the fish they caught had eaten other fish. He then said to himself: "If you eat one another, I don't see why we may not eat you." The thought here may be that if a being treats others in a particular way, then humans are entitled to treat that being in an equivalent way. However, this does not follow as a matter of logic or ethics. Quite rightly, we do not normally take the behavior of animals as a model for how we may treat them. We   10

---

[7] Joseph Ratzinger, *God and the World: Believing and Living in Our Time. A Conversation with Peter Seewald.* San Francisco: St. Ignatius Press, 2002, p. 78. [Singer and Mason's note]

[8] See, for example, Peter Carruthers, *The Animals Issue: Moral Theory in Practice*, Cambridge University Press, Cambridge, 1992. [Singer and Mason's note]

would not, for example, justify tearing a cat to pieces because we had observed the cat tearing a mouse to pieces. Carnivorous fish don't have a choice about whether to kill other fish or not. They kill as a matter of instinct. Meanwhile, humans can choose to abstain from killing or eating fish and other animals.

Alternatively, the argument could be made that it is part of the   11 natural order that there are predators and prey, and so it cannot be wrong for us to play our part in this order. But this "argument from nature" can justify all kinds of inequities, including the rule of men over women and leaving the weak and the sick to fall by the wayside. Even if the argument were sound, however, it would work only for those of us still living in a hunter-gatherer society, for there is nothing at all "natural" about our current ways of raising animals. As for Franklin's argument about the fish who had eaten other fish, this is a selective use of an argument we would reject in other contexts. Franklin was a sufficiently acute observer of his own nature to recognize how selective he was being, because he admits that he hit upon his justification for eating the fish only after they were in the frying pan and had begun to smell "admirably well."[9]

Third, we have said that the suffering inflicted on animals by fac-   12 tory farming, transportation, and slaughter is unnecessary because— as the Farbs and many other vegan families demonstrate—there are alternatives to meat and other animal products that allow people to be healthy and well-nourished. It might be argued that food from animals is a central part of the standard Western diet and important, if not always central, to what people eat in many other cultures as well. Because animal products are so significant to us, and because we could not buy them as cheaply as we can now without factory farming, factory farming is justifiable despite the suffering it inflicts on animals. But when cultural practices are harmful, they should not be allowed to go unchallenged. Slavery was once part of the culture of the American South. Biases against women and against people of other races have been, and in some places still are, culturally significant. If a widespread cultural practice is wrong, we should try to change it.

It's true that the alternatives to factory farming we've examined,   13 whether Cyd Szymanski's eggs or Niman Ranch pork, are more expensive. Let's grant, too, that switching to a totally vegan diet is something that many people would find difficult, at least at first. But these assumptions are still insufficient to justify factory farming. The choice is not between business as usual and a vegan world. Without

---

[9] Benjamin Franklin, *Autobiograpy*, New York, Modern Library, 1950, p. 41. [Singer and Mason's note]

factory farming, families with limited means would be able to afford fewer animal products, but they would not have to stop buying them entirely. Nutritionists agree that most people in developed countries eat far more animal products than they need, and more than is good for their health. Spending the same amount of money and buying fewer animal products would therefore be a good thing, especially if those animal products came from animals free to walk around outside, which would make the meat less fatty, and if the reduced consumption in animal products were offset by increased consumption of fruit and vegetables. That is the recommendation of Hugh Fearnley-Whittingstall, and few people are more devoted to food than he is.

For perhaps a billion of the world's poorest people, hunger and   14 malnutrition are still a problem. But factory farming isn't going to solve that problem, for in developing countries the industry caters to the growing urban middle class, not the poor, who cannot afford to buy its products. In developing countries, factory-farming products are chosen for their taste and status, not for the consumer's good health. The world's largest and most comprehensive study of diet and disease has shown that in rural China, good health and normal growth are achieved on a diet that includes only one-tenth as much animal-based food as Americans eat. Increases in the consumption of animal products above that very low base are correlated with an increase in the "diseases of affluence": heart disease, obesity, diabetes, and cancer.[10]

The great suffering inflicted on animals by factory farming is not   15 outweighed by a possible loss in gastronomic satisfaction caused by the elimination of meat from animals raised on factory farms from the diet. The harder question is whether we should be vegan or at least vegetarian? To answer that question, we need to go beyond the rejection of unjustified suffering and ask whether it is wrong to kill animals—without suffering—for our food. We need to ask what moral status animals have, and what ethical standards should govern our treatment of them.

Ethics and Animals

The prevailing Western ethic assumes that human interests must   16 always prevail over the comparable interests of members of other species. Since the rise of the modern animal movement in the 1970s,

---

[10] T. Colin Campbell and Thomas Campbell, *The China Study: The Most Comprehensive Study of Nutrition Ever Conducted and the Startling Implications for Diet, Weight Loss and Long-Term Health*, Benbella, Dallas, TX, 2005. [Singer and Mason's note]

however, this ethic has been on the defensive. The argument is that, despite obvious differences between human and nonhuman animals, we share a capacity to suffer, and this means that they, like us, have interests. If we ignore or discount their interests simply on the grounds that they are not members of our species, the logic of our position is similar to that of the most blatant racists or sexists—those who think that to be white, or male, is to be inherently superior in moral status, irrespective of other characteristics or qualities.

The usual reply to this parallel between speciesism and racism   17 or sexism is to acknowledge that it is a mistake to think that whites are superior to other races, or that males are superior to women, but then to argue that humans really are superior to non-human animals in their capacity to reason and the extent of their self-awareness, while claiming that these are morally relevant characteristics. However, some humans—infants, and those with severe intellectual disabilities—have less ability to reason and less self-awareness than some non-human animals. So we cannot justifiably use these criteria to draw a distinction between all humans on the one hand and all non-human animals on the other.

In the eighteenth century, Jonathan Swift, the author of *Gulliver's*   18 *Travels*, made a "modest proposal" to deal with the "surplus" of the children of impoverished women in Ireland. "I have been assured," he wrote, "that a young healthy child well nursed is at a year old, a most delicious, nourishing, and wholesome food, whether stewed, roasted, baked, or boiled."[11] The proposal was, of course, a satire on British policy towards the Irish. But if we find this proposal shocking, our reaction shows that we do not really believe that the absence of an advanced ability to reason is sufficient to justify turning a sentient being into a piece of meat. Nor is it the potential of infants to develop these abilities that marks the crucial moral distinction, because we would be equally shocked by anyone who proposed the same treatment for humans born with serious and irreversible intellectual disabilities. But if, within our own species, we don't regard differences in intelligence, reasoning ability, or self-awareness as grounds for permitting us to exploit the being with lower capacities for our own ends, how can we point to the same characteristics to justify exploiting

---

[11]**Jonathan Swift (1667–1745)** Anglo-Irish satirist and dean of St. Patrick's, Dublin; Jonathan Swift, *A Modest Proposal for Preventing the Children of Poor People from Being a Burthen to Their Parents or Country, and for Making Them Beneficial to the Public*, first published 1729, reprinted in Tom Regan and Peter Singer, eds., *Animal Rights and Human Obligations*, Prentice-Hall, Englewood Cliffs, NJ, 1976, pp. 234–37. [Singer and Mason's note]

members of other species? Our willingness to exploit non-human animals is not something that is based on sound moral distinctions. It is a sign of "speciesism," a prejudice that survives because it is convenient for the dominant group, in this case not whites or males, but humans.

If we wish to maintain the view that no conscious human   19
beings, including those with profound, permanent intellectual disabilities, can be used in ways harmful to them solely as a means to another's end, then we are going to have to extend the boundaries of this principle beyond our own species to other animals who are conscious and able to be harmed. Otherwise we are drawing a moral circle around our own species, even when the members of our own species protected by that moral boundary are not superior in any morally relevant characteristics to many nonhuman animals who fall outside the moral circle. If we fail to expand this circle, we will be unable to defend ourselves against racists and sexists who want to draw the boundaries more closely around themselves.

Equal Consideration for Animals?

Those who defend our present treatment of animals often say   20
that the animal-rights movement would have us give animals the same rights as humans. This is obviously absurd—animals can't have equal rights to an education, to vote, or to exercise free speech. The kind of parity that most animal advocates want to extend to animals is not equal rights, but equal consideration of comparable interests. If an animal feels pain, the pain matters as much as it does when a human feels pain. Granted, the mental capacities of different beings will affect how they experience pain, how they remember it, and whether they anticipate further pain—and these differences can be important. But the pain felt by a baby is a bad thing, even if the baby is no more self-aware than, say, a pig, and has no greater capacities for memory or anticipation. Pain can be a useful warning of danger, so it is sometimes valuable, all things considered. But taken in themselves, unless there is some compensating benefit, we should consider similar experiences of pain to be equally undesirable, whatever the species of the being who feels the pain.

We have now progressed in our argument beyond the avoidance   21
of "unnecessary" suffering to the principle of equal consideration of interests, which tells us to give the same weight to the interests of non-human animals as we give to the similar interests of human beings. Let's see whether this principle can help us to decide whether eating meat is unethical.

Eating Meat: The Best Defense

The most thoughtful defenses of eating meat come from those   22
writers who are strongest in their condemnation of factory farming:
Michael Pollan, Hugh Fearnley-Whittingstall, and Roger Scruton.
Pollan's the *New York Times Sunday Magazine* essay "An Animal's
Place," begins with the line: "The first time I opened Peter Singer's
Animal Liberation, I was dining alone at the Palm, trying to enjoy a
ribeye steak cooked medium-rare." From there he goes on to
describe factory farming and acknowledge that we cannot justify
eating the food that this system produces. Pollan then juxtaposes his
grim account of modern industrial agriculture with a lyrical por-
trayal of Polyface Farm, spread over 550 acres of grass and forest in
Virginia's Shenandoah Valley. Here, Pollan tells us, "Joel Salatin and
his family raise six different food animals—cattle, pigs, chickens,
rabbits, turkeys, and sheep—in an intricate dance of symbiosis
designed to allow each species, in Salatin's words, 'to fully express
its physiological distinctiveness.'" We learn about Salatin's rotation
method: first cows graze on the pasture, then laying hens feast on
the grubs attracted by the cowpats, then sheep come and eat the
weeds that the cows and hens don't like. There are pigs, too, rooting
around in compost in a barn.

If we can recognize animal suffering in a factory farm, Pollan   23
says, "animal happiness is unmistakable too, and here I was seeing it
in abundance." That happiness ends, of course, when the animals
are killed, but for the rabbits and chickens, at least, that death is not
preceded by the terrifying experience of being trucked off to a
slaughterhouse. Salatin slaughters them on the farm. (He would like
to slaughter the cattle, pigs, and sheep on the premises, too, but the
U.S. Department of Agriculture will not let him.) Salatin's killing is
done on Saturday mornings, and anyone is welcome to come along
and watch. This leads Pollan to comment that if the walls of both
factory farms and slaughterhouses were made of glass, industrial
agriculture might be redeemed. Some people would become vegetarians, but others, forced to raise and kill animals in a place where
they can be watched, would do it with more consideration for the
animal, as well as for the eater. We would have "poultry farms
where chickens still go outside" and "hog farms where pigs live as
they did fifty years ago—in contact with the sun, the earth, and the
gaze of a farmer."

In the light of his experience at Polyface Farm, Pollan tells us that   24
to see the domestication of animals as "a form of enslavement or even
exploitation" is a mistake. It is, instead, "an instance of mutualism
between species" and an evolutionary, not a political, development.

Here Pollan may have been influenced by Stephen Budiansky's book *The Covenant of the Wild*.[12] Budiansky's argument is that domestication occurred when some species of animals began to hang around human settlements in order to eat waste or leftover food. Since the animals were edible—or perhaps gave milk and eggs that could be eaten—our ancestors encouraged them to stay around by providing food for them and protecting them from predators. The result has been the evolution of animal breeds that do well, in terms of species survival, by being domesticated. There would be far fewer chickens, pigs, and cattle in the world today if their ancestors had remained wild.

The entire story of domestication is speculative, but one thing is clear: Pollan describes it in a way that cannot be correct and uses it to suggest an ethical justification for our use of animals that it cannot support. He writes that "domestication happened when a small handful of especially opportunistic species discovered through Darwinian trial and error that they were more likely to survive and prosper in an alliance with humans than on their own." No mistake is more common, in accounts of evolutionary processes, than attributing purposiveness either to the process of evolution itself or to entities like genes or species, which are not capable of forming purpose at all. Species do not "discover" anything, through trial and error or in any other way. Individual animals survive and leave offspring, and others, with slightly different characteristics, do not. In this case, on Pollan's account, some animals were attracted to human settlements and were themselves sufficiently attractive to the humans to receive food and protection, while other animals were either not attracted to the human settlements or were not attractive to the humans. More of the offspring of those animals that were attracted and attractive survived and reproduced than was the case with those animals that were not attracted or not attractive.

Pollan then notes that "Cows, pigs, dogs, cats, and chickens have thrived, while their wild ancestors have languished" and that there are now only 10,000 wolves in North America, but 50 million dogs. From this he draws the conclusion that "From the animals' point of view, the bargain with humanity has been a great success, at least until our own time." But just as species are not capable of discovering anything, neither are they capable of making a bargain. Whether individual animals are capable of making a bargain is a separate question, but Pollan is surely not asserting that any individual animal ever consciously made a bargain with humans, to, for

25

26

[12] Stephen Budiansky, *The Covenant of the Wild*, HarperCollins, New York, 1992. [Singer and Mason's note]

example, trade her eggs or milk, or even his or her flesh, for a year or two's food and protection from predators.

Talk of bargains between humans and animals cannot justify   27
anything about how we treat animals today. There is, however, a better point that can be disentangled from Pollan's account of domestication. We can take Pollan to be arguing that since domestic animals have evolved to be what they now are through their symbiotic relationship with humans, their "characteristic form of life"—a phrase Pollan borrows from Aristotle—is one lived in domestication with humans, and that means—for chickens, pigs, cows, and sheep—a life on a farm or ranch. This is their nature, and the Good Life for them is one in which they can live, in accordance with their nature, on the Good Farm, until they are killed and eaten. The killing and eating is unavoidable, for without it neither farms, nor the animals on them, would exist at all.

Fearnley-Whittingstall's defense of meat-eating in *The River Cot-*   28
tage Meat Book is in some respects strikingly similar to that of Pollan, but it reaches this last point more directly. Fearnley-Whittingstall refers to Budiansky's *Covenant of the Wild* when explaining how "consensual domestication" came about—but he is careful to note that this kind of cooperation between species has nothing to do with individual consent and does not carry the moral implications of individual consent. His point is rather that the nature of farm animals has been shaped by their relationship with us, and they "can be healthy, contented, and even, at least in a sense that suits their species, fulfilled—for the duration of their short lives." Then he adds: "And I believe that these short, domesticated lives are, on balance, better than no lives at all." This gives us moral authority for eating them, but only if we buy from farmers who "embrace the notion of a contract with their meat animals" and "do all they can to uphold it, honorably, morally, and responsibly." *The River Cottage Meat Book* instructs its readers on how to find meat produced by the minority of farmers who do this.[13]

Questions About The Best Defense

Pollan's and Fearnley-Whittingstall's defenses of meat-eating are   29
essentially variants on one that is familiar to philosophers who have studied earlier debates about meat-eating. The argument occurs, for

---

[13] Hugh Fearnley-Whittingstall, *The River Cottage Meat Book*, Hodder and Stoughton, London, 2004, pp. 23–25. [Singer and Mason's note]

instance, in *Social Rights and Duties*, a collection of essays and lectures published in 1896 by the British essayist—and father of the novelist Virgina Woolf—Leslie Stephen. Stephen writes: "Of all the arguments for Vegetarianism none is so weak as the argument from humanity. The pig has a stronger interest than anyone in the demand for bacon. If all the world were Jewish, there would be no pigs at all." Henry Salt, an early advocate of animal rights, thought there was a philosophical fallacy at the core of Stephen's argument: "A person who is already in existence," Salt writes, "may feel that he would rather have lived than not, but he must first have the *terra firma* of existence to argue from; the moment he begins to argue as if from the abyss of the non-existent, he talks nonsense, by predicating good or evil, happiness or unhappiness, of that of which we can predicate nothing."[14]

Salt has drawn our attention to a deep issue that the argument   30
raises. We don't normally think of bringing people into existence as a way of benefiting them. When couples are uncertain about whether or not to have children, they tend to think of their own interests, or perhaps the interests of other existing people, rather than of the benefit they may be conferring on their future children by bringing them into existence—assuming that these children will come into existence in circumstances that make it likely that they will have good lives. But our ordinary way of thinking about such questions might be mistaken. Ask yourself if it would be wrong to bring a child into existence, knowing that the child suffered from a genetic defect that would make her life both brief and utterly miserable for every moment of her existence? Most people will answer "yes." Now consider bringing into existence a being who will lead a thoroughly satisfying life. Is that a good thing to do, other things being equal? If you answer this in the negative, you need to explain why it is wrong to bring a miserable being into existence, but not good to bring a happy or fulfilled being into existence. Sound explanations for this are extraordinarily difficult to find.

We will not attempt to resolve these challenging philosophical   31
questions here. Instead, we'll accept that, as long as a pig has a good life and a quick death, it is a good thing (or at least not a bad thing) for the pig that he or she exists. The argument, then, is that eating meat from farms that give pigs good lives cannot be bad for the pigs,

---

[14] **Henry Salt (1851–1939)** British prison reformer; Henry Salt, "The Logic of the Larder," first published in Henry Salt, *The Humanities of Diet*, The Vegetarian Society, Manchester, 1914, reprinted in Tom Regan and Peter Singer, *Animal Rights and Human Obligations*, Prentice-Hall, Englewood Cliffs, NJ, 1976, p. 186. [Singer and Mason's note]

since if no one ate meat, these pigs would not exist. To eat them, however, we have to kill them first, so killing them must be justifiable.

   Pollan seems to feel some discomfort about his own argument,   32
because he acknowledges that he has been using what is essentially
a utilitarian argument for meat-eating and then recalls that "utilitarians can also justify killing retarded orphans. Killing just isn't the
problem for them that it is for other people, including me." So he
goes back to Joel Salatin and asks him how he can bring himself to
kill a chicken. Salatin replies: "People have a soul. Animals don't.
It's a bedrock belief of mine. Unlike us, animals are not created in
God's image, so when they die, they just die." As Salatin's answer
reminds us, religions often reflect the speciesism of the human
beings who developed them. Pollan doesn't comment on Salatin's
answer. If he has objections to killing that go beyond utilitarian
arguments, he owes us an account of why these objections do not
apply to animals.

   Fearnley-Whittingstall has noticed that most meat eaters are   33
protected from thinking about the fact that animals are killed in
order to produce meat. He thinks this is wrong, and so he includes
in his book a double-page series of color photographs that begins
with him taking two of his beef cattle to slaughter, and then shows
them being killed, bled out, skinned, disemboweled, and sawn in
half. He reports that he watched the process itself and found it
"somewhat shocking," although he says that the process "does not
seem to me to cause much suffering" and did not make him feel
"angry, or sick, or guilty, or ashamed." It compares well, he argues,
with almost any other form of death for either a wild or a farmed
animal. But Fearnley-Whittingstall doesn't consider that his cattle,
like all the animals we eat, died while still very young. They might
have lived several more years before meeting one of these other
forms of death, years in which they matured, experienced sexual
intercourse, and, if they were females, cared for their children. We
humans, after all, are prepared to pass up many rapid and humane
forms of death in order to live a few more years, even if we are then
likely to die of a disease that causes us to suffer before we die.

   Scruton's background in philosophy leads him to put his   34
defense of killing animals for food on a more philosophical basis
than Pollan or Fearnley-Whittingstall. He writes: "Human beings are
conscious of their lives as their own; they have ambitions, hopes,
and aspirations." To be "cut short" before one's time is tragic,
because "human beings are fulfilled by their achievements and not
merely by their comforts." In contrast, animals like cattle do not
look forward to future achievements, nor do they seek to achieve

anything that will make their lives more fulfilling.[15] Scruton may be right about cattle, but his argument implies that it would be permissible to kill humans who, because of profound intellectual disabilities, are not conscious of their lives as their own and do not look forward to future achievements. Those who find this conclusion too shocking to accept cannot defend the killing of animals for meat on the grounds that animals lack the higher mental abilities that make it wrong to kill normal humans.

Drawing Conclusions

Suppose, though, that some people do accept this disturbing   35
conclusion and eat only humanely raised animals. Does that allow them an impregnable defense of their diet? Not quite. If there were no demand for bacon, nor for any other animal products, farms that now raise animals would convert to growing crops or else go out of business, and humans would replace animal protein with plant protein. Since, as we have seen, we can produce a specified amount of both protein and calories from a smaller area of land when we grow plant foods rather than animal foods, this change would release significant areas of land from agriculture or would render unnecessary the appropriation of more land for agriculture. If that land were allowed to return to forest, or in the case of existing wild habitat allowed to remain undisturbed, the total number of animals leading lives unconfined by factory farming would increase—for birds and animals are much more abundant in forests than on either cropland or pasture. In North America, for example, there are squirrels, chipmunks, racoons, rabbits, mice, and deer, as well as blackbirds, crows, cardinals, pigeons, sparrows, and starlings—to name just a few. In other countries the species that inhabit forests vary, as do the densities of individual birds and animals, which are highest in tropical forests.

Gaverick Matheny and Kai Chan have attempted to calculate the   36
overall net gain or loss of animal life that will result if people in developed countries should start to switch from their present heavily meat-based diet to one based on plant foods. By calculating the amount of land that could be allowed to return to forest or become

---

[15] Roger Scruton, "The Conscientious Carnivore" in Steve Sapontzis, ed., *Food for Thought: The Debate over Eating Meat*, Prometheus, Amherst, NY, 2004, p. 88. [Singer and Mason's note]

some other kind of natural habitat and the number of wild birds and animals who would live on that land, they conclude that even when meat is obtained from grazing cattle living decent lives, the number of animals living free of close confinement will be greater when we obtain protein from plant foods rather than from grazing cattle. The same is true for raising pigs, even if the pigs derive half of their food from waste. In the case of eggs and poultry, with the farming methods like those used at Polyface Farm, the balance may favor continued farming, but this depends on how much grain they need to be fed, in addition to what they can eat on pasture.[16]

Conscientious omnivores might reply that there is no reason to believe that land freed from agricultural use by a switch to a plant-based diet actually would be allowed to revert to wild habitat that could then support the increased number and diversity of animal life. Perhaps it would be bought up for suburban or industrial development. That may be true in some cases in developed countries, especially if the land is near a metropolitan or industrial area. But we should consider the globalized market that now exists for meat. The land no longer needed to produce meat for us may still be used to raise animals whose meat would then be available for export and therefore could slow the rate of forest clearance in, say, Brazil.   37

There are, of course, exceptions, where animals are raised on land unsuitable for growing crops, and the meat produced is too expensive to be exported. Raising lambs in the Welsh hills, for example, is a traditional form of husbandry that has existed for many centuries and makes use of land that could not otherwise produce food for humans. If the lives of the sheep are, on the whole, good ones, and they would not exist at all if the lambs were not killed and eaten, it can be argued that doing so has benefits, on the whole, for both human and animals.   38

Pollan also refers to a different argument for eating meat from grazing animals, which he owes to Steve Davis, an animal scientist at Oregon State University. According to Davis, we cannot avoid being responsible for killing animals, even if we are vegan. A tractor plowing a field to plant crops may crush field mice, and moles can be killed when their burrows are destroyed by the plow. Harvesting crops removes the ground cover in which small animals shelter, making it possible for predators to kill them. Applying pesticides   39

---

[16] Gaverick Matheny and Kai Chan, "Human Diets and Animal Welfare: The Illogic of the Larder," *Journal of Agricultural and Environmental Ethics*, vol. 18 (2005), pp. 579–94; and personal correspondence with Gaverick Matheny, April 2005. [Singer and Mason's note]

can kill birds. Davis then tries to calculate the number of animals killed by growing crops and the number killed by rearing beef cattle on pasture and argues that twice as many animals die per acre when growing crops as in pasture-reared beef production. He then concludes that if we are trying to kill as few animals as possible, we will do better to eat beef—as long as it is fed entirely on grass and not fattened on grain—than to follow a vegan diet.[17] Davis has, however, made a gross error in his calculations: he assumes that an acre of land will feed the same number of people irrespective of whether it is used to raise grass-fed beef or to grow crops. In fact, an acre of land used for crops will feed about ten times as many people as an acre of land used for grass-fed beef. When that difference is fed into the calculations, Davis's argument is turned on its head, and proves that vegans are indirectly responsible for killing only about a fifth as many animals as those who eat grass-fed beef.

Even if it is ethically acceptable to eat animals who have been   40 well-cared for during their lifetimes and then killed without experiencing pain or distress, for those unable to raise their own animals, it is difficult to be sure that the meat you buy comes from such animals. No farm gets more publicity for its exemplary treatment of animals than Polyface Farm. Pollan is not the only one to praise it. The "Style" section of the *New York Times* raved about it and called Joel Salatin, its owner, the "High Priest of the Pasture." Salatin's son has said that his father "has achieved almost godlike status in some circles."[18] But is Polyface really such a good place for animals? Rabbits on the farm are kept in small suspended wire cages. Chickens may be on grass, but instead of being free to roam, they are crowded into mobile wire pens. A review of sustainable-poultry systems by the National Sustainable Agriculture Information Service noted that with Salatin's pens "The confined space inside the pens makes bird welfare a concern" and that the crowding "can lead to pecking problems, because the birds lower in the pecking order cannot run away." Out of five sustainable-poultry systems investigated, the mobile wire pens were placed last for animal welfare, with a "poor to fair" rating. Herman Beck-Chenoweth, author of *Free Range Poultry Production and Marketing* and a poultry producer himself, calls

---

[17] Steven Davis, "The Least Harm Principle May Require that Humans Consume a Diet Containing Large Herbivores, Not a Vegan Diet," *Journal of Agricultural and Environmental Ethics*, vol. 16 (2003), pp. 387–94. [Singer and Mason's note]

[18] Todd Purdum, "High Priest of the Pasture," *New York Times Style Magazine*, Living, Spring 2005, pp. 76–79. The comment from Daniel Salatin about his father is taken from the 13th Annual Wisconsin Grazing Conference, February 14, 2005, www.grassworks.org/Conference/conference.htm. [Singer and Mason's note]

Salatin's way of raising chickens "a confinement system with a grass floor," adding that although it is "a big improvement over the broiler houses used by companies such as Tyson and Perdue . . . it is a confinement system just the same."[19]

There is also the question of slaughter. The U.S. Federal Meat   41
Inspection Act does not permit Salatin to sell meat from animals that he kills on his farm, so his pigs and cattle are trucked off to conventional slaughterhouses. The crowded transport is likely to be very stressful for them, and it is impossible to know how humanely they are actually slaughtered. Because chickens and rabbits are not covered by the Meat Inspection Act, Salatin can kill them on the farm, sparing them the ordeal of transportation and the strange and sometimes frightening environment of the slaughterhouse. Nevertheless, an account of the killing of chickens at Polyface Farm isn't reassuring:

> Slaughter begins promptly at 8:30 a.m. The goal is to be completely finished by 10:30 a.m. O'Connor, the least skilled of the workers, manhandles the first of thirty crates of birds from a stack on a tractor-drawn trailer outside the pavilion. The birds were taken off of feed and crated about twelve hours earlier so that their craws would be clear for slaughter. He grabs the birds by their feet. Wings flap. Eight white chickens are up-ended in the galvanized metal "killing cones" at the far end of the processing line. Razor-sharp boning knives flash in the early morning sun. The chickens' throats have been slit. Bright red blood flows down a metal trough and into a large plastic bucket. In a minute or so, the chickens are "bled out." They're moved on to the next station in the processing line. And a fresh batch of birds is inserted into the cones.[20]

As this account indicates, birds are crammed into crates with   42
seven other birds—probably including some more aggressive birds they would normally keep away from—and they stay there for twelve hours. Then they are grabbed by the "least skilled of the workers," and passed on, upside down, to other workers who will cut their throats—without any prior stunning. It seems that at Polyface, as elsewhere, it is economics, more than concern for animals, that determines how the animals are treated.

[19] See Herman Beck-Chenoweth, *Free-Range Poultry Production and Marketing*, Back40Books, Hartshorn, Missouri, 2001. The quote is taken from the same author's "Free Range, Pastured Poultry, Chicken Tractor—What's the Difference?" www.free-rangepoultry.com/compare.htm. [Singer and Mason's note]

[20] George Devault, "'Chicken Day' at the Farm of Many Faces," *The New Farm*, August 2002, www.newfarm.org/features/0802/chicken%20day/print.html. [Singer and Mason's note]

If there are grounds for concern about a farm so often admired, 43 many other supposedly "humane" farms are going to be worse. Not all, of course—we have described visits to some good ones in this book—at least, as far as we could tell from our brief visits. (We were not able to see how any of the animals from these farms were slaughtered.) In practice, as long as animals are commodities, raised for sale on a large scale in a competitive market situation, there will be conflicts between their interests and the economic interests of the producer, and the producer will always be under pressure to cut corners and reduce costs.

Psychological aspects of our choice of diet need to be considered 44 too. Just as farmers who start by raising animals "humanely" may slide into practices more profitable but less humane, so individuals may slide as well. How humane is humane enough to eat? The line between what conscientious omnivores can justify eating and what they cannot justify eating is vague. Since we are all often tempted to take the easy way out, drawing a clear line against eating animal products may be the best way to ensure that one eats ethically—and sticks to it.

The impact we will have on others is even more important. 45 Since factory farming inflicts a vast quantity of unjustifiable suffering on animals, persuading others to boycott it should be a high priority for anyone concerned about animals. In this respect, a broad brush-stroke may be better than a more finely tuned approach. Vegans and vegetarians draw clear lines by refusing to eat all, or some, animal products. Whenever they dine with others, that line is evident, and people are likely to ask them why they are not eating meat. That often leads to conversations that influence others, and so the good that we can do personally by boycotting factory farms can be multiplied by the number of others we influence to do the same. When conscientious omnivores eat meat, however, their dietary choices are less evident. On the plate, ham from a pig who led a happy life looks very much like ham from a factory-farmed pig. Thus the eating habits of the conscientious omnivore are likely to reinforce the common view that animals are things for us to use and unlikely to influence others to reconsider what they eat.

Where does all this leave the diet of conscientious omnivores? 46 Perhaps it's not, all things considered, the best possible diet, but the moral distance between the food choices made by conscientious omnivores and those made by most of the population is so great that it seems more appropriate to praise the conscientious omnivores for how far they have come, rather than to criticize them for not having gone further.

QUESTIONS FOR CRITICAL READING

1. What is speciesism? Is it avoidable?
2. Singer and Mason make a great deal of the capacity of animals to suffer pain. Why is that important to their argument?
3. What rights should animals share with humans?
4. Should farms become more like Polyface Farm? Would that solve the problem?
5. What is Michael Pollan's argument concerning the benefits to domesticated species versus those that remain wild?
6. To what extent are Singer and Mason convinced by Michael Pollan's argument?
7. Are the short lives of cattle bred for the market better than no lives at all? How does your answer satisfy or negate Singer and Mason's general complaints?
8. To what extent do you think animals are conscious of their lives? Are your pets more conscious than livestock?

SUGGESTIONS FOR CRITICAL WRITING

1. If you have experience with animals, especially with domesticated livestock, poultry, fish, or birds, how do you respond to Singer and Mason's suggestion that you refrain from eating meat? Does your personal experience have anything like the weight of an argument in helping to shape your behavior? Describe your experiences in detail and correlate them to the discussions that include references to Michael Pollan, Joel Salatin, and Roger Scruton. What would you say to these people if you had the chance to affect their views?
2. Joel Salatin (para. 32) says that he can bring himself to kill a chicken and serve it for dinner because "[p]eople have a soul. Animals don't. It's a bedrock belief of mine. Unlike us, animals are not created in God's image, so when they die, they just die." Do you agree with this view? Is the Bible clear on this point, or is Salatin simply rationalizing the situation to make himself feel more comfortable? Is it possible that this apparently religious comment is a disguise for everyday speciesism? What justifies your position on either side of this argument? If you owned a pet, would Salatin's argument be less convincing to you?
3. After reading this essay, do you find yourself prepared to change any of your eating habits? Do you think any of your friends might change their eating habits? Would adding more plant protein to and reducing animal protein in your diet be likely to please Singer and Mason? Would they be more pleased if you ate humanely treated animals? Would you be more comfortable? Do you think your health might be affected by changing your diet? Could you become a conscientious omnivore?
4. What is the weakest part of Singer and Mason's argument? They spend a great deal of time dissecting the arguments of those who support eating

meat. Are they wrong in how they deal with any of the experts they disagree with? Is Michael Pollan's argument not worth taking into consideration? Is there only one way to solve the ethical problem of eating animals? If you do not feel there is an ethical problem with eating animals, construct an argument that takes issue with Singer and Mason's.

5. Singer and Mason argue that an acre of land that will produce enough crops to feed ten people will only produce enough grazing cattle to feed one person. Considering the widespread famine and starvation in the world now and to come, wouldn't this be the most powerful ethical argument against eating meat? But would it not also be an ethical issue regarding only humans and not animals? What has this to do with establishing an ethical position regarding animals rather than humans? What argument against eating meat can you construct from the detail regarding the amount of food that can be produced from a single acre of land?

6. **CONNECTIONS**   Opposing the argument based on the notion of dominion is central to the views of Aldo Leopold (p. 745). What position would Leopold have taken on the question of eating meat? He clearly expresses concern for the biota on the land, although he says little or nothing about the treatment of animals. Yet, he sees, as do Singer and Mason, that the biblical passage that says mankind has dominion over the land and the animals gives a kind of license to people to use and abuse it as they will. What does Leopold have to say that will strengthen Singer and Mason's argument?

7. **SEEING CONNECTIONS**   What is the ethical situation in Wright's *An Experiment on a Bird in the Air Pump* (p. 687)? Consider two possible scenarios: (1) that after the experiment the bird will be cooked and mixed in a meat pie that all the onlookers will enjoy or (2) that the bird will be returned to the cage that the boy on the right is lowering. How would Singer and Mason construe either or both of these situations from an ethical standpoint?

PART EIGHT

GENDER AND CULTURE

Mary Wollstonecraft
John Stuart Mill
Virginia Woolf
Margaret Mead
Claude Lévi-Strauss
Germaine Greer

INTRODUCTION

Male and female represent the two sides of the great radical
dualism. But in fact they are perpetually passing into one another.
Fluid hardens to solid, solid rushes to fluid. There is no wholly
masculine man, no purely feminine woman.

— MARGARET FULLER (1810–1850)

Class, race, sexuality, gender, and all other categories by which
we categorize and dismiss each other need to be excavated from
the inside.

— DOROTHY ALLISON (b. 1949)

Male and female citizens, being equal in the eyes of the law,
must be equally admitted to all honors, positions, and public
employment according to their capacity and without other
distinctions besides those of their virtues and talents.

— OLYMPE DE GOUGES (1748–1793)

Every time we liberate a woman, we liberate a man.

— MARGARET MEAD (1901–1978)

Gender equality is more than a goal in itself. It is a precondition
for meeting the challenge of reducing poverty, promoting sustainable development, and building good governance.

— KOFI ANNAN (b. 1938)

Gender consciousness has become involved in almost every
intellectual field: history, literature, science, anthropology. There's
been an extraordinary advance.

— CLIFFORD GEERTZ (1926–2006)

For a long period of time, the question of gender appeared to
be a simple matter of society's assigning appropriate roles for men
and women, thus defining them in an important way in terms of
their gender. However, modern studies in anthropology over the
last 150 years have altered our view by demonstrating that gender
is largely a variable, cultural invention. Men and women are, these
studies tell us, shaped by the cultural environment into which they
are born. Their gender expectations may differ widely from what
we currently think of as appropriate in our culture.

The political unrest of the eighteenth century in the West insti-
gated profound changes in the way people thought about conventional
sex roles. Men like William Godwin (1756–1836) wrote extensively
about women's rights, beginning a movement that continues to this
day. Some nineteenth-century plays, such as Henrik Ibsen's *A Doll's
House,* simply reflected social changes and deep-seated concerns that

involved examining gender assumptions. The authors represented here, from philosophers to anthropologists to literary critics, examine the question of gender from a wide range of viewpoints spanning considerations that include women's rights, homosexual patterns in American Indian culture, and masculinity in our own culture.

Mary Wollstonecraft wrote in a time of extreme political change: when revolution was erupting in the American colonies in 1776 and in France in 1789. Kings and aristocrats were losing their heads, literally. Monarchies were giving way to republics. During this period democracy in its modern forms began to grace the lives of some, whereas tyranny oppressed others. Even though radical changes took place in some areas, a conservative backlash in England and elsewhere threatened to heighten oppression rather than expand freedom. Although Wollstonecraft is known today chiefly for her feminist works, she was also engaged in the radical political thought of the time. For example, her defense of the ideals of the French Revolution in *A Vindication of the Rights of Men* (1790) brought her work to the attention of other radical thinkers such as William Godwin (whom she later married), Thomas Paine, William Blake, and William Wordsworth.

Still, Wollstonecraft's name remains a keystone in the history of feminism. She went on to write one of the most important books of the late eighteenth century, *Vindication of the Rights of Woman* (1792), and is remembered most for her careful analysis of a society that did not value the gifts and talents of women. Her complaint is based on a theory of efficiency and economics: it is a waste to limit the opportunities of women. By making her appeal in this fashion she may have expected to gain the attention of the men who held power in late-eighteenth-century England. Some of them did listen. By the 1830s, at the height of the industrial revolution, women were often employed outside the home. However, they were frequently given the most wretched jobs (such as in mining) and were not accorded the kind of respect and opportunity that Wollstonecraft envisioned. They often became drudges in a process of industrial development that demeaned their humanity.

John Stuart Mill, born nine years after Wollstonecraft's death, was one of those men who began to take seriously the economic issues involved in the suppression of women in English and European societies. His prestige as a leading utilitarian philosopher gave him an audience of men who may have been more sympathetic to his views than they might have been to the views of a woman. As it was, Mill himself was deeply moved by the ideas of Harriet Taylor, an ardent champion of women's rights, whom he eventually married. Mill saw not only the waste to the productivity of the human race but also the moral incorrectness of treating half of that race as if it were not worthy, restricting its advancement by withholding higher education and economic opportunity.

In 1929, the novelist and essayist Virginia Woolf considered the question of how gifted women could hope to achieve important works if the current and historical patterns of oppression were to continue. Her book *A Room of One's Own* was addressed originally to a group of women studying at Cambridge in the two colleges reserved for them at the time. Woolf regarded these women appropriately as gifted, but she worried for their future because their opportunities in postwar England were quite limited. In a stroke of brilliance, Woolf demonstrates the pattern that oppresses gifted women by imagining for William Shakespeare an equally gifted sister named Judith and then tracing her probable development in sixteenth-century England. What chance would Judith have had to be a world-famous figure like her brother? Woolf's discussion is so lifelike and so well realized that it stands as a classic in modern feminist literature.

Margaret Mead brings a very different kind of authority to the gender question because it was one of her primary research topics when she lived among various tribal groups in Papua New Guinea. She is famous for having studied closely the sexual development of women in societies that had not been totally altered by contact with modern Europeans. She discovered that the roles thought appropriate to men and women in our society were not always the same in the Mundugumor (now Biwat) society, which demonstrated a considerable capacity for change. Mead warns against societies that standardize genders and adhere to rigid expectations. She cautions that individuals who do not have the temperaments that their society thinks gender appropriate will suffer great pain and frustration. Like Ruth Benedict, she points to the berdache, the "men-women" of the Plains Indians who were valued for their all-encompassing skills, which transcended sex roles.

The Belgian anthropologist Claude Lévi-Strauss also spent time living in a culture that was foreign to Western ways of thought. His purpose was to study the simplest society he could find to see what patterns of social organization are absolutely fundamental. The Nambikwara people of the Brazilian Amazon are hunter-gatherers whose political structure is recognizable to modern eyes. The role of the chief is similar to that of leaders in industrialized society. So, too, are some of the gender roles, although there seems to be a somewhat more relaxed attitude toward gender expectations.

Germaine Greer, a noted feminist, examines the modern vision of masculinity and carefully regards arguments that propose gender qualities as being natural and biological rather than cultural constructs. She questions the "scientific" basis of the role of biology and comes up with some surprising facts. More importantly, the bulk of her study examines the nature of masculinity as it is regarded in our culture. Then Greer proposes the ways masculinity is developed in the male starting from birth. Her views may be controversial, but they are verifiable by simple observation of our own experiences. The feminine role in creating masculinity is one of her last concerns, since she sees women as playing an uneasy part in producing and promoting the masculine ideal.

These essays represent a number of ways of looking at issues of gender. The stereotypical views that most people have in the modern industrialized world are brought into question by authors who work from a wide range of disciplines, bringing a considerable body of research and observation into the discussion. The one thing they have in common is that they urge us to rethink concepts of gender and to examine the role of societies in establishing gender expectations in all of us.

VISUALIZING GENDER AND CULTURE

When Mary Stevenson Cassatt (1844–1926) was born, society had few uncertainties regarding gender, relegating women to the home and family. But during and after the First World War, women began to follow Cassatt's example in choosing a career over a household. During Cassatt's lifetime, women fought for the vote in many countries: it was granted in Finland in 1906; in the United Kingdom, Canada, and Germany in 1918; and in the United States in 1920. Cassatt was a trendsetter and a gender rebel, although a gentle one.

She is known for having shocked her well-to-do parents by refusing to follow the ordinary path set for her as a young Philadelphia society woman. Instead of marriage or even a "sensible" career, she chose to be a painter. Her father was a wealthy banker of French ancestry, and for part of Cassatt's childhood the family lived in France and Germany. She visited London, Paris, and Berlin before she was ten years old, so at a young age, she had a broad understanding of the world. She had seen great art and great architecture. In Philadelphia, she studied art at the Pennsylvania Academy of Fine Arts from 1861 to 1865, learning the academic style of the day, which focused mainly on mythic and historic subject matter. When the American Civil War ended, she returned to Europe, traveling—usually by herself—from 1865 to 1870, something that women rarely did at that time. Her work was first shown at the Salon, France's annual art showcase, in 1868, but she returned to the United States during the Franco-Prussian War of 1870. She went back to Europe the next year and settled permanently in Paris in 1873.

MARY STEVENSON CASSATT, *IN THE LOGE*. 1878.
Oil on canvas, 32" × 26". Museum of Fine Arts, Boston.
The Hayden Collection—Charles Henry Hayden Fund. Photograph © Museum of Fine Arts, Boston.

Her career in painting put her in the company of the best of the French impressionists, who, like her, grew tired of the restrictions of the standard academic subject matter and style. She met Edgar Degas (1834–1917) in 1874 and found his approach to painting much more congenial. He introduced her to Édouard Manet, Claude Monet, Berthe Morisot, Camille Pissarro, Pierre-Auguste Renoir, and many more of the "new" painters. She showed with the impressionists four times between 1879 and 1886 and was one of only three women painters in the impressionist movement. She had her brother Alexander buy many important impressionist paintings and show them in the United States, where they were a great success. Her own work had a good reception in the United States as well, and she became known as the American impressionist painter.

Her style and subject matter varied from her early to her later work. After 1880, her signature subject matter was portraits of mothers and children, a subject that very few male painters explored. She admired the French impressionists' willingness to paint everyday scenes of ordinary people at work or at leisure. Her own work centered on people—often women engaged in daily activities in their homes. In a way, she was paying tribute to them. She rarely produced formal portraits and painted few landscapes.

In the Loge was the first of Cassatt's paintings to be shown in the United States. Because the critics had not yet seen and developed an understanding of impressionist paintings, they praised it as being a sketch rather than a finished work. But her painting was nonetheless a great success with the American public.

In the Loge is dominated by a black-garbed woman at the theater, looking through her opera glasses at someone or something we cannot see. To the upper left of the painting, a man leans from his box, looking through his opera glasses at the woman in the loge. They are at the Français theater, doing what people in public often do, looking to see who is there or contemplating a meeting of some kind. The woman's dress style reveals that they are at an afternoon performance.

One of the most subtle aspects of this painting is implied rather than specifically indicated. The two figures with the opera glasses are only part of an incomplete triangulation. The viewer wonders if the woman is looking critically at another woman to see if she is well dressed and attractive or if she is looking romantically at a man or another woman, contemplating a meeting. The man looking at her is straightforward: he's interested in the woman. But Cassatt has made the woman's situation purposely complex and ambiguous.

Modern French critics have proposed a theory of the gaze that places the power in a sexual relationship with the gazer, not the object of the gaze. Given the respective sizes of the gentleman and the woman, it is clear which of these gazers has the greater power in the composition of the painting. But there is yet another level to the concept of the gaze because, as we look at the painting and the figures within in it, we become part of the triangulation ourselves. We do not need opera glasses, so we are in a much more intimate relationship to these figures than they are to the ones they watch. How, then, are we to look at this woman? this man? What is our power relationship in viewing this painting?

MARY WOLLSTONECRAFT
Of the Pernicious Effects Which Arise from the Unnatural Distinctions Established in Society

MARY WOLLSTONECRAFT (1759–1797) was born into relatively modest circumstances, with a father whose heavy drinking and spending eventually ruined the family and left her and her sisters to support themselves. She became a governess, a teacher, and eventually a writer. Her views were among the most enlightened of her day, particularly regarding women and women's rights, giving her the reputation of being a very forward-looking feminist for her time, and even for ours. Her thinking, however, is comprehensive and not limited to a single issue.

She was known to the American patriot Thomas Paine (1737–1809), to Dr. Samuel Johnson (1709–1783), and to the English philosopher William Godwin (1756–1836), whom she eventually married. Her views on marriage were remarkable for her time; among other beliefs, she felt it unnecessary to marry a man in order to live happily with him. Her first liaison, with an American, Gilbert Imlay, gave her the opportunity to travel and learn something about commerce and capitalism at first hand. Her second liaison, with Godwin, brought her into the intellectual circles of her day. She married Godwin when she was pregnant, and died in childbirth. Her daughter, Mary, married the poet Percy Bysshe Shelley and wrote the novel *Frankenstein* (1818).

From *Vindication of the Rights of Woman.*

The excitement generated by the French Revolution (1789–1799) caused Wollstonecraft to react against the very conservative view put forward by the philosopher Edmund Burke. Her pamphlet *A Vindication of the Rights of Men* (1790) was well received. She followed it with *Vindication of the Rights of Woman* (1792), which was translated into French.

She saw feminism in political terms. The chapter reprinted here concentrates on questions of property, class, and law. As a person committed to the revolutionary principles of liberty, equality, and fraternity, Wollstonecraft linked the condition of women to the political and social structure of her society. Her aim was to point out the inequities in the treatment of women—which her society simply did not perceive—and to attempt to rectify them.

Wollstonecraft's Rhetoric

Mary Wollstonecraft wrote for an audience that did not necessarily appreciate brief, exact expression. Rather, they appreciated a more luxuriant and leisurely style than we use today. As a result, her prose can sometimes seem wordy to a modern audience. However, she handles imagery carefully (especially in the first paragraph) without overburdening her prose. She uses an approach that she calls "episodical observations" (para. 12). These are anecdotes—personal stories—and apparently casual cataloguings of thoughts on a number of related issues. She was aware that her structure was not tight, that it did not develop a specific argument, and that it did not force the reader to accept or reject her position. She also considered this a wise approach because it was obvious to her that her audience was completely prejudiced against her view. To attempt to convince them of her views was to invite total defeat.

Instead, she simply puts forward several observations that stand by themselves as examples of the evils she condemns. Even those who stand against her will see that there is validity to her claims; and they will not be so threatened by her argument as to become defensive before they have learned something new. She appeals always to the higher intellectual capacities of both men and women, directing her complaints, too, against both men and women. This balance of opinion, coupled with a range of thought-provoking examples, makes her views clear and convincing.

Also distinctive in this passage is the use of metaphor. The second sentence of paragraph 1 is particularly heavy with metaphor: "For it is in the most polished society that noisome reptiles and venomous serpents lurk under the rank herbage; and there is voluptuousness pampered by the still sultry air, which relaxes every good disposition before it ripens into virtue." The metaphor presents society as a garden in which the grass is decaying and dangerous serpents are lurking. Good disposition—character—is a plant that might ripen, but—continuing the metaphor—it ripens into virtue. A favorite source of metaphors for Wollstonecraft is drapery (dressmaking). When she uses one of these metaphors she is usually reminding the reader that drapery gives a new shape to things, that it sometimes hides the truth, and that it ought not to put a false appearance on what it covers.

One of her rhetorical techniques is that of literary allusion. By alluding to important literary sources—such as Greek mythology, William Shakespeare, Jean-Jacques Rousseau, and Samuel Johnson— she not only demonstrates her knowledge but also shows that she respects her audience, which she presumes shares the same knowledge. She does not show off by overquoting or by referring to very obscure writers. She balances her allusions perfectly, even transforming folk aphorisms into "homely proverbs" such as "whoever the devil finds idle he will employ."

Wollstonecraft's experiences with her difficult father gave her knowledge of gambling tables and card games, another source of allusions. She draws further on personal experience—shared by some of her audience—when she talks about the degradation felt by a woman of intelligence forced to act as a governess—a glorified servant—in a well-to-do family. Wollstonecraft makes excellent uses of these allusions, never overdoing them, always giving them just the right touch.

PREREADING QUESTIONS: WHAT TO READ FOR

The following prereading questions may help you anticipate key issues in the discussion of Mary Wollstonecraft's "Of the Pernicious Effects Which Arise from the Unnatural Distinctions Established in Society." Keeping them in mind during your first reading of the selection should help focus your attention.

- What are some of the pernicious effects that Wollstonecraft decries?

- What kinds of work are women fit for, in Wollstonecraft's view?

- What happens to people who are born to wealth and have nothing to do?

Of the Pernicious Effects Which Arise from the Unnatural Distinctions Established in Society

From the respect paid to property flow, as from a poisoned fountain, most of the evils and vices which render this world such a dreary scene to the contemplative mind. For it is in the most polished society that noisome reptiles and venomous serpents lurk under the rank herbage; and there is voluptuousness pampered by the still sultry air, which relaxes every good disposition before it ripens into virtue.

One class presses on another; for all are aiming to procure respect on account of their property: and property, once gained, will procure the respect due only to talents and virtue. Men neglect the duties incumbent on man, yet are treated like demi-gods; religion is also separated from morality by a ceremonial veil, yet men wonder that the world is almost, literally speaking, a den of sharpers or oppressors.

There is a homely proverb, which speaks a shrewd truth, that whoever the devil finds idle he will employ. And what but habitual idleness can hereditary wealth and titles produce? For man is so constituted that he can only attain a proper use of his faculties by exercising them, and will not exercise them unless necessity of some kind first set the wheels in motion. Virtue likewise can only be acquired by the discharge of relative duties; but the importance of these sacred duties will scarcely be felt by the being who is cajoled out of his humanity by the flattery of sycophants.[1] There must be more equality established in society, or morality will never gain ground, and this virtuous equality will not rest firmly even when founded on a rock, if one half of mankind be chained to its bottom by fate, for they will be continually undermining it through ignorance or pride.

It is vain to expect virtue from women till they are in some degree independent of men; nay, it is vain to expect that strength of natural affection which would make them good wives and mothers. Whilst they are absolutely dependent on their husbands they will be cunning, mean, and selfish, and the men who can be gratified by the fawning fondness of spaniel-like affection have not much delicacy, for love is not to be bought, in any sense of the words; its silken wings are

---

[1] **sycophants** Toadies or false flatterers.

instantly shrivelled up when anything beside a return in kind is sought. Yet whilst wealth enervates men, and women live, as it were, by their personal charms, how can we expect them to discharge those ennobling duties which equally require exertion and self-denial? Hereditary property sophisticates[2] the mind, and the unfortunate victims to it, if I may so express myself, swathed from their birth, seldom exert the locomotive faculty of body or mind; and, thus viewing everything through one medium, and that a false one, they are unable to discern in what true merit and happiness consist. False, indeed, must be the light when the drapery of situation hides the man, and makes him stalk in masquerade, dragging from one scene of dissipation to another the nerveless limbs that hang with stupid listlessness, and rolling round the vacant eye which plainly tells us that there is no mind at home.

I mean, therefore, to infer[3] that the society is not properly orga- 5 nized which does not compel men and women to discharge their respective duties, by making it the only way to acquire that countenance from their fellow-creatures which every human being wishes some way to attain. The respect, consequently, which is paid to wealth and mere personal charms, is a true north-east blast that blights the tender blossoms of affection and virtue. Nature has wisely attached affections to duties to sweeten toil, and to give that vigor to the exertions of reason which only the heart can give. But the affection which is put on merely because it is the appropriated insignia of a certain character, when its duties are not fulfilled, is one of the empty compliments which vice and folly are obliged to pay to virtue and the real nature of things.

To illustrate my opinion, I need only observe that when a woman 6 is admired for her beauty, and suffers herself to be so far intoxicated by the admiration she receives as to neglect to discharge the indispensable duty of a mother, she sins against herself by neglecting to cultivate an affection that would equally tend to make her useful and happy. True happiness, I mean all the contentment and virtuous satisfaction that can be snatched in this imperfect state, must arise from well regulated affections; and an affection includes a duty. Men are not aware of the misery they cause and the vicious weakness they cherish by only inciting women to render themselves pleasing; they do not consider that they thus make natural and artificial duties clash by sacrificing the comfort and respectability of a woman's life to voluptuous notions of beauty when in nature they all harmonize.

---

[2] **sophisticates** Ruins or corrupts.
[3] **infer** Imply.

Cold would be the heart of a husband, were he not rendered   7
unnatural by early debauchery, who did not feel more delight at seeing his child suckled by its mother, than the most artful wanton tricks
could ever raise; yet this natural way of cementing the matrimonial tie
and twisting esteem with fonder recollections, wealth leads women
to spurn. To preserve their beauty and wear the flowery crown of the
day, which gives them a kind of right to reign for a short time over the
sex, they neglect to stamp impressions on their husbands' hearts that
would be remembered with more tenderness when the snow on
the head began to chill the bosom than even their virgin charms. The
maternal solicitude of a reasonable affectionate woman is very interesting, and the chastened dignity with which a mother returns the
caresses that she and her child receive from a father who has been fulfilling the serious duties of his station, is not only a respectable but a
beautiful sight. So singular indeed are my feelings, and I have endeavored not to catch factitious[4] ones, that after having been fatigued with
the sight of insipid grandeur and the slavish ceremonies that with
cumbrous pomp supplied the place of domestic affections, I have
turned to some other scene to relieve my eye by resting it on the
refreshing green everywhere scattered by nature. I have then viewed
with pleasure a woman nursing her children, and discharging the
duties of her station with, perhaps, merely a servant maid to take off
her hands the servile part of the household business. I have seen her
prepare herself and children, with only the luxury of cleanliness, to
receive her husband, who returning weary home in the evening found
smiling babes and a clean hearth. My heart has loitered in the midst of
the group, and has even throbbed with sympathetic emotion, when
the scraping of the well known foot has raised a pleasing tumult.

Whilst my benevolence has been gratified by contemplating this   8
artless picture, I have thought that a couple of this description, equally
necessary and independent of each other, because each fulfilled the
respective duties of their station, possessed all that life could give.
Raised sufficiently above abject poverty not to be obliged to weigh the
consequence of every farthing they spend, and having sufficient to
prevent their attending to a frigid system of economy, which narrows
both heart and mind, I declare, so vulgar[5] are my conceptions, that I
know not what is wanted to render this the happiest as well as the
most respectable situation in the world, but a taste for literature, to
throw a little variety and interest into social converse, and some
superfluous money to give to the needy and to buy books. For it is not
pleasant when the heart is opened by compassion and the head active

-----

[4] **factitious** False.
[5] **vulgar** Common.

in arranging plans of usefulness, to have a prim urchin continually twitching back the elbow to prevent the hand from drawing out an almost empty purse, whispering at the same time some prudential maxim about the priority of justice.

Destructive, however, as riches and inherited honors are to the human character, women are more debased and cramped, if possible, by them than men, because men may still, in some degree, unfold their faculties by becoming soldiers and statesmen. 9

As soldiers, I grant, they can now only gather, for the most part, vainglorious laurels, whilst they adjust to a hair the European balance, taking especial care that no bleak northern nook or sound incline the beam.[6] But the days of true heroism are over, when a citizen fought for his country like a Fabricius[7] or a Washington, and then returned to his farm to let his virtuous fervor run in a more placid, but not a less salutary, stream. No, our British heroes are oftener sent from the gaming table than from the plough[8] and their passions have been rather inflamed by hanging with dumb suspense on the turn of a die, than sublimated by panting after the adventurous march of virtue in the historic page. 10

The statesman, it is true, might with more propriety quit the faro bank, or card table, to guide the helm, for he has still but to shuffle and trick.[9] The whole system of British politics, if system it may courteously be called, consisting in multiplying dependents and contriving taxes which grind the poor to pamper the rich; thus a war, or any wild goose chase, is, as the vulgar use the phrase, a lucky turn-up of patronage for the minister, whose chief merit is the art of keeping himself in place. It is not necessary then that he should have bowels for[10] the poor, so he can secure for his family the odd trick. Or should some show of respect, for what is termed with ignorant ostentation an Englishman's birthright, be expedient to bubble the gruff mastiff[11] that he has to lead 11

---

[6] **incline the beam** The metaphor is of the balance—the scale that representations of blind justice hold up. Wollstonecraft's point is that in her time soldiers fought to prevent the slightest changes in a balance of power that grew ever more delicate, not in heroic wars with heroic consequences.

[7] **Fabricius (fl. 282 B.C.)** Gaius Fabricius, a worthy Roman general and statesman known for resistance to corruption.

[8] **from the plough** Worthy Roman heroes were humble farmers, not gamblers.

[9] **shuffle and trick** The upper class spent much of its time gambling: faro is a high-stakes card game. Wollstonecraft is ironic when she says the statesman has "still but to shuffle and trick," but she connects the "training" of faro with the practice of politics in a deft, sardonic fashion. She is punning on the multiple meanings of *shuffle*—to mix up a deck of cards and to move oneself or one's papers about slowly and aimlessly—and *trick*—to win one turn of a card game and to do a devious deed.

[10] **bowels for** Feelings for; sense of pity.

[11] **to bubble the gruff mastiff** To fool even a guard dog.

by the nose, he can make an empty show very safely by giving his single voice and suffering his light squadron to file off to the other side. And when a question of humanity is agitated he may dip a sop in the milk of human kindness to silence Cerberus,[12] and talk of the interest which his heart takes in an attempt to make the earth no longer cry for vengeance as it sucks in its children's blood, though his cold hand may at the very moment rivet their chains by sanctioning the abominable traffic. A minister is no longer a minister than while he can carry a point which he is determined to carry. Yet it is not necessary that a minister should feel like a man, when a bold push might shake his seat.

But, to have done with these episodical observations, let me 12 return to the more specious slavery which chains the very soul of woman, keeping her forever under the bondage of ignorance.

The preposterous distinctions of rank, which render civilization a 13 curse by dividing the world between voluptuous tyrants and cunning envious dependents, corrupt, almost equally, every class of people, because respectability is not attached to the discharge of the relative duties of life, but to the station, and when the duties are not fulfilled the affections cannot gain sufficient strength to fortify the virtue of which they are the natural reward. Still there are some loopholes out of which a man may creep, and dare to think and act for himself; but for a woman it is a herculean task, because she has difficulties peculiar to her sex to overcome which require almost superhuman powers.

A truly benevolent legislator always endeavors to make it the 14 interest of each individual to be virtuous; and thus private virtue becoming the cement of public happiness, an orderly whole is consolidated by the tendency of all the parts towards a common center. But, the private or public virtue of woman is very problematical; for Rousseau, and a numerous list of male writers, insist that she should all her life be subjected to a severe restraint, that of propriety. Why subject her to propriety—blind propriety, if she be capable of acting from a nobler spring, if she be an heir of immortality? Is sugar always to be produced by vital blood? Is one half of the human species, like the poor African slaves, to be subject to prejudices that brutalize them, when principles would be a surer guard, only to sweeten the cup of man? Is not this indirectly to deny woman reason? For a gift is a mockery, if it be unfit for use.

Women are, in common with men, rendered weak and luxuri- 15 ous by the relaxing pleasures which wealth procures; but added to this they are made slaves to their persons, and must render them alluring that man may lend them his reason to guide their tottering

---

[12] **Cerberus** The guard dog of Hades, the Greek hell or underworld.

steps aright. Or should they be ambitious, they must govern their tyrants by sinister tricks, for without rights there cannot be any incumbent duties. The laws respecting woman, which I mean to discuss in a future part, make an absurd unit of a man and his wife,[13] and then, by the easy transition of only considering him as responsible, she is reduced to a mere cypher.[14]

The being who discharges the duties of its station is independent; and, speaking of women at large, their first duty is to themselves as rational creatures, and the next in point of importance, as citizens, is that which includes so many, of a mother. The rank in life which dispenses with their fulfilling this duty necessarily degrades them by making them mere dolls. Or, should they turn to something more important than merely fitting drapery upon a smooth block, their minds are only occupied by some soft platonic attachment; or, the actual management of an intrigue may keep their thoughts in motion; for when they neglect domestic duties, they have it not in their own power to take the field and march and counter-march like soldiers, or wrangle in the senate to keep their faculties from rusting.

I know that, as a proof of the inferiority of the sex, Rousseau has exultingly exclaimed, How can they leave the nursery for the camp![15] And the camp has by some moralists been termed the school of the most heroic virtues; though, I think, it would puzzle a keen casuist[16] to prove the reasonableness of the greater number of wars that have dubbed heroes. I do not mean to consider this question critically; because, having frequently viewed these freaks of ambition as the first natural mode of civilization, when the ground must be torn up, and the woods cleared by fire and sword, I do not choose to call them pests; but surely the present system of war has little connection with virtue of any denomination, being rather the school of *finesse* and effeminacy than of fortitude.

Yet if defensive war, the only justifiable war, in the present advanced state of society, where virtue can show its face and ripen amidst the rigors which purify the air on the mountain's top, were alone to be adopted as just and glorious, the true heroism of antiquity might again animate female bosoms. But fair and softly, gentle reader, male or female, do not alarm thyself, for though I have compared the character of a modern soldier with that of a civilized woman, I am

---

[13] **absurd unit of a man and his wife** In English law man and wife were legally one; the man spoke for both.

[14] **cypher** Zero.

[15] **leave the nursery for the camp!** Rousseau's *Émile* complains that women cannot leave a nursery to go to war.

[16] **casuist** One who argues closely, persistently, and sometimes unfairly.

not going to advise them to turn their distaff[17] into a musket, though I sincerely wish to see the bayonet converted into a pruning-hook. I only recreated an imagination, fatigued by contemplating the vices and follies which all proceed from a feculent[18] stream of wealth that has muddied the pure rills of natural affection, by supposing that society will some time or other be so constituted, that man must necessarily fulfill the duties of a citizen or be despised, and that while he was employed in any of the departments of civil life, his wife, also an active citizen, should be equally intent to manage her family, educate her children, and assist her neighbors.

But, to render her really virtuous and useful, she must not, if she 19 discharge her civil duties, want, individually, the protection of civil laws; she must not be dependent on her husband's bounty for her subsistence during his life or support after his death—for how can a being be generous who has nothing of its own? or virtuous, who is not free?

The wife, in the present state of things, who is faithful to her hus- 20 band, and neither suckles nor educates her children, scarcely deserves the name of a wife, and has no right to that of a citizen. But take away natural rights, and duties become null.

Women then must be considered as only the wanton solace of 21 men when they become so weak in mind and body that they cannot exert themselves, unless to pursue some frothy pleasure or to invent some frivolous fashion. What can be a more melancholy sight to a thinking mind than to look into the numerous carriages that drive helter-skelter about this metropolis in a morning full of pale-faced creatures who are flying from themselves. I have often wished, with Dr. Johnson,[19] to place some of them in a little shop with half a dozen children looking up to their languid countenances for support. I am much mistaken if some latent vigor would not soon give health and spirit to their eyes, and some lines drawn by the exercise of reason on the blank cheeks, which before were only undulated by dimples, might restore lost dignity to the character, or rather enable it to attain the true dignity of its nature. Virtue is not to be acquired even by speculation, much less by the negative supineness that wealth naturally generates.

Besides, when poverty is more disgraceful than even vice, is not 22 morality cut to the quick? Still to avoid misconstruction, though I consider that women in the common walks of life are called to fulfill

---

[17] **distaff** Instrument to wind wool in the act of spinning, notoriously a job only "fit for women."

[18] **feculent** Filthy, polluted; related to *feces*.

[19] **Dr. Samuel Johnson (1709–1784)** The greatest lexicographer and one of the most respected authors of England's eighteenth century. He was known to Mary Wollstonecraft and to her sister, Eliza, a teacher. The reference is to an item published in his *Rambler*, essay 85.

the duties of wives and mothers, by religion and reason, I cannot help lamenting that women of a superior cast have not a road open by which they can pursue more extensive plans of usefulness and independence. I may excite laughter by dropping a hint which I mean to pursue some future time, for I really think that women ought to have representatives, instead of being arbitrarily governed without having any direct share allowed them in the deliberations of government.

But, as the whole system of representation is now in this country only a convenient handle for despotism, they need not complain, for they are as well represented as a numerous class of hard-working mechanics, who pay for the support of royalty when they can scarcely stop their children's mouths with bread. How are they represented whose very sweat supports the splendid stud of an heir apparent, or varnishes the chariot of some female favorite who looks down on shame? Taxes on the very necessaries of life enable an endless tribe of idle princes and princesses to pass with stupid pomp before a gaping crowd, who almost worship the very parade which costs them so dear. This is mere gothic grandeur, something like the barbarous useless parade of having sentinels on horseback at Whitehall,[20] which I could never view without a mixture of contempt and indignation. 23

How strangely must the mind be sophisticated when this sort of state impresses it! But, till these monuments of folly are levelled by virtue, similar follies will leaven the whole mass. For the same character, in some degree, will prevail in the aggregate of society; and the refinements of luxury, or the vicious repinings,[21] of envious poverty, will equally banish virtue from society, considered as the characteristic of that society, or only allow it to appear as one of the stripes of the harlequin coat worn by the civilized man. 24

In the superior ranks of life every duty is done by deputies, as if duties could ever be waived, and the vain pleasures which consequent idleness forces the rich to pursue appear so enticing to the next rank that the numerous scramblers for wealth sacrifice everything to tread on their heels. The most sacred trusts are then considered as sinecures,[22] because they were procured by interest, and only sought to enable a man to keep *good company*. Women, in particular, all want to be ladies. Which is simply to have nothing to do, but listlessly to go they scarcely care where, for they cannot tell what. 25

But what have women to do in society? I may be asked, but to loiter with easy grace; surely you would not condemn them all to suckle 26

---

[20] **sentinels on horseback at Whitehall** This is a reference to the expensive demonstration of showmanship that continues to our day: the changing of the guard at Whitehall.

[21] **repinings** Discontent, fretting.

[22] **sinecures** Jobs with few duties but good pay.

fools and chronicle small beer![23] No. Women might certainly study
the art of healing, and be physicians as well as nurses. And midwifery,
decency seems to allot to them, though I am afraid the word midwife
in our dictionaries will soon give place to *accoucheur*,[24] and one proof
of the former delicacy of the sex be effaced from the language.

They might also study politics, and settle their benevolence on   27
the broadest basis; for the reading of history will scarcely be more
useful than the perusal of romances, if read as mere biography; if the
character of the times, the political improvements, arts, &c., be not
observed. In short, if it be not considered as the history of man; and
not of particular men, who filled a niche in the temple of fame, and
dropped into the black rolling stream of time, that silently sweeps
all before it, into the shapeless void called—eternity. For shape, can
it be called, "that shape hath none"?[25]

Business of various kinds they might likewise pursue, if they   28
were educated in a more orderly manner, which might save many from
common and legal prostitution. Women would not then marry
for a support, as men accept of places under government, and
neglect the implied duties; nor would an attempt to earn their own
subsistence—a most laudable one!—sink them almost to the level
of those poor abandoned creatures who live by prostitution. For are
not milliners and mantua-makers[26] reckoned the next class? The few
employments open to women, so far from being liberal, are menial;
and when a superior education enables them to take charge of the
education of children as governesses, they are not treated like the
tutors of sons, though even clerical tutors are not always treated in a
manner calculated to render them respectable in the eyes of their
pupils, to say nothing of the private comfort of the individual. But as
women educated like gentlewomen are never designed for the
humiliating situation which necessity sometimes forces them to fill,
these situations are considered in the light of a degradation; and
they know little of the human heart, who need to be told that nothing so painfully sharpens sensibility as such a fall in life.

Some of these women might be restrained from marrying by a   29
proper spirit or delicacy, and others may not have had it in their power
to escape in this pitiful way from servitude; is not that government
then very defective, and very unmindful of the happiness of one half of

---

[23] **chronicle small beer!** *Othello* (II.i. 158). This means to keep the household
accounts.

[24] *accoucheur* Male version of the female midwife.

[25] **"that shape hath none"** The reference is to *Paradise Lost* (II.667) by John
Milton (1608–1674); it is an allusion to death.

[26] **milliners and mantua-makers** Dressmakers, usually women (whereas
tailors were usually men).

its members, that does not provide for honest, independent women, by encouraging them to fill respectable stations? But in order to render their private virtue a public benefit, they must have a civil existence in the state, married or single; else we shall continually see some worthy woman, whose sensibility has been rendered painfully acute by undeserved contempt, droop like "the lily broken down by a plowshare."

It is a melancholy truth—yet such is the blessed effect of 30 civilization!—the most respectable women are the most oppressed; and, unless they have understandings far superior to the common run of understandings, taking in both sexes, they must, from being treated like contemptible beings, become contemptible. How many women thus waste life away the prey of discontent, who might have practiced as physicians, regulated a farm, managed a shop, and stood erect, supported by their own industry, instead of hanging their heads surcharged with the dew of sensibility, that consumes the beauty to which it at first gave lustre; nay, I doubt whether pity and love are so near akin as poets feign, for I have seldom seen much compassion excited by the helplessness of females, unless they were fair; then, perhaps pity was the soft handmaid of love, or the harbinger of lust.

How much more respectable is the woman who earns her own 31 bread by fulfilling any duty, than the most accomplished beauty!— beauty did I say?—so sensible am I of the beauty of moral loveliness, or the harmonious propriety that attunes the passions of a well regulated mind, that I blush at making the comparison; yet I sigh to think how few women aim at attaining this respectability by withdrawing from the giddy whirl of pleasure, or the indolent calm that stupefies the good sort of women it sucks in.

Proud of their weakness, however, they must always be pro- 32 tected, guarded from care, and all the rough toils that dignify the mind. If this be the fiat of fate, if they will make themselves insignificant and contemptible, sweetly to waste "life away," let them not expect to be valued when their beauty fades, for it is the fate of the fairest flowers to be admired and pulled to pieces by the careless hand that plucked them. In how many ways do I wish, from the purest benevolence, to impress this truth on my sex; yet I fear that they will not listen to a truth that dear-bought experience has brought home to many an agitated bosom, nor willingly resign the privileges of rank and sex for the privileges of humanity, to which those have no claim who do not discharge its duties.

Those writers are particularly useful, in my opinion, who make 33 man feel for man, independent of the station he fills, or the drapery of factitious sentiments. I then would fain[27] convince reasonable

---

[27] **fain** Happily, gladly.

men of the importance of some of my remarks; and prevail on them to weigh dispassionately the whole tenor of my observations. I appeal to their understandings; and, as a fellow-creature, claim, in the name of my sex, some interest in their hearts. I entreat them to assist to emancipate their companion, to make her a *help meet*[28] for them!

Would men but generously snap our chains, and be content   34 with rational fellowship instead of slavish obedience, they would find us more observant daughters, more affectionate sisters, more faithful wives, more reasonable mothers—in a word, better citizens. We should then love them with true affection, because we should learn to respect ourselves; and, the peace of mind of a worthy man would not be interrupted by the idle vanity of his wife, nor the babes sent to nestle in a strange bosom, having never found a home in their mother's.

---

[28] ***help meet***   Helper, helpmate.

QUESTIONS FOR CRITICAL READING

1. Who is the audience for Wollstonecraft's writing? Is she writing more for men than for women? Is it clear from what she says that she addresses an explicit audience with specific qualities?
2. Analyze paragraph 1 carefully for the use of imagery, especially metaphor. What are the effects of these images? Are they overdone?
3. Wollstonecraft begins by attacking property, or the respect paid to it. What does she mean? Does she sustain that line of thought throughout the piece?
4. In paragraph 12, Wollstonecraft speaks of the "bondage of ignorance" in which women are held. Clarify precisely what she means by that expression.
5. In paragraph 30, Wollstonecraft says that people who are treated as if they were contemptible will become contemptible. Is this a political or a psychological judgment?
6. What is the substance of Wollstonecraft's complaint concerning the admiration of women for their beauty?

SUGGESTIONS FOR CRITICAL WRITING

1. Throughout the piece Wollstonecraft attacks the unnatural distinctions made between men and women. Establish carefully what those unnatural distinctions are, why they are unnatural, and whether such distinctions persist to the present day. By contrast, establish what some natural distinctions between men and women are and whether Wollstonecraft has taken them into consideration.

2. References are made throughout the piece to prostitution and to the debaucheries of men. Paragraph 7 specifically refers to the "wanton tricks" of prostitutes. What is Wollstonecraft's attitude toward men in regard to sexuality and their attitudes toward women—both the women of the brothels and the women with whom men live? Find passages in the piece that you can quote and analyze in an effort to examine her views.

3. In paragraph 2, Wollstonecraft complains that "the respect due only to talents and virtue" is instead being given to people on account of their property. Further, she says in paragraph 9 that riches are "destructive . . . to the human character." Determine carefully, by means of reference to and analysis of specific passages, just what Wollstonecraft means by such statements. Then, use your own anecdotes or "episodical observations" to take a stand on whether these are views you yourself can hold for our time. Are riches destructive to character? Is too much respect paid to those who possess property? If possible, use metaphor or allusion—literary or personal.

4. In paragraph 4, Wollstonecraft speaks of "men who can be gratified by the fawning fondness of spaniel-like affection" from their women. Search through the essay for other instances of similar views and analyze them carefully. Establish exactly what the men she describes want their women to be like. Have today's men changed very much in their expectations? Why? Why not? Use personal observations where possible in answering this question.

5. The question of what roles women ought to have in society is addressed in paragraphs 26, 27, and 28. What are those roles? Why are they defined in terms of work? Do you agree that they are, indeed, the roles that women should assume? Would you include more roles? Do women in our time have greater access to those roles? Consider what women actually did in Wollstonecraft's time and what they do today.

6. **CONNECTIONS** Compare Wollstonecraft's views on the ways in which women are victims of prejudice with the views of Martin Luther King Jr. How much do women of Wollstonecraft's time have in common with the conditions of African Americans as described by King? What political issues are central to the efforts of both groups to achieve justice and equal opportunity? Might Wollstonecraft see herself in the same kind of struggle as King, or would she draw sharp distinctions?

7. **SEEING CONNECTIONS** Write a commentary on Cassatt's *In the Loge* (p. 796), assuming the views of Wollstonecraft. What would Wollstonecraft say about Cassatt's decision to become a professional painter and earn money through her work? How might she defend the choice of a career as a painter over other possible careers for Cassatt? How might Wollstonecraft interpret the scene presented in *In the Loge*? Would she see it as possibly sexual? Would she see the woman in the foreground as assuming a specific role in society? If so, would the role be one that would satisfy Wollstonecraft's view of how women should behave and be treated?

JOHN STUART MILL
The Subjection of Women

THE SON OF JAMES MILL, a distinguished philosopher and proponent of utilitarianism, John Stuart Mill (1806–1873) was educated by his father at home and restricted from associating with other children his age, except for those in his family. His education was remarkable. He was introduced to Greek when he was three and by the age of eight had read all of Herodotus and some of Plato in the original language. He went on to read the great Latin classics as a teenager. He praised his system of education in part because his father made him solve intellectual problems on his own, even if they were very difficult. The purpose of this education was to produce a philosopher who would carry on the work of utilitarians, like his father and Jeremy Bentham (1748–1832), whose views John Stuart Mill revised and elaborated on throughout his life.

Unfortunately, Mill suffered a nervous breakdown when he was twenty, essentially as a result of his not having had a relatively normal upbringing in a social circle larger than his family. But he recovered and went on to be a man of action as a member of Parliament, as a member of the British East India Company, and as one of the most influential thinkers of his time. He contributed important ideas in the area of logic and argument as well as in politics. His landmark work, *On Liberty* (1859), established a liberal position based on the "no harm" principle: people were free to do as they wished as long as they did no harm to anyone else. "The only part of the conduct of anyone, for which he is amenable to society, is that which concerns others. In the part which merely concerns himself, his independence is, of right, absolute. Over himself, over his own body and mind, the individual is sovereign." Mill established the priority of the individual over the collective, propounding a libertarian view that is still respected today.

From *The Subjection of Women*.

Mill's views in *Utilitarianism* (1863) modified the principles of his father and Bentham. Bentham's ideal was to achieve the greatest happiness for the greatest number of people. Mill's emphasis on individual freedom modified these views in several ways. One was that he advised wariness of a tyranny of the majority in which society could command behavior on the basis of what most people thought was right and proper action, thus restricting the happiness of some individuals. In another modification he qualified the kinds of happiness that should be sought after in life. Bentham treated all kinds of happiness as equal, while Mill gave priority to intellectual and spiritual happiness over physical happiness. As he wrote, "It is better to be a human being dissatisfied than a pig satisfied; better to be Socrates dissatisfied than a fool satisfied. And if the fool, or the pig, are of a different opinion, it is because they only know their own side of the question."

Another of his views, derived from his father's thinking, was called *associationism*. He felt that people were altered by their associations with ideas and others and that given the proper associations ordinary people could do unusual things. In modern terms, this would translate to the influence of the environment that shapes the intellectual, social, and familial values of the individual. The significance of this view was basic to his concerns regarding the subjection of women in nineteenth-century society. The prevalent male view was that women were innately unequal to men and, therefore, did not deserve to be given the rights and privileges of men. Mill knew that women were provided with an inferior education and an environment designed to prevent them from competing equally with men.

His views on the subjection of women were a natural outgrowth of his personal philosophy and that of his father, but they were reinforced by a long relationship with Harriet Taylor, a prominent feminist whom he married in 1851 while he was working for the British East India Company. She was clearly influential in his writing *On Liberty*, which was published the year after her death. Taylor was an extraordinary person in that her education was superior to most men and her arguments sharp and clear. They were friends for many years before they married.

The Subjection of Women (1869) was greeted with enormous controversy. Until 1870, a wife's property was owned by her husband; a wife had few grounds for divorce, while a husband had many; the children of a marriage belonged exclusively to the husband; a wife had no legal status independent of her husband; and no husband could be guilty of raping his wife. Mill wrote out of a sense of outrage for the obvious inequality that was tolerated by the majority and protected by the male legislative establishment.

Mill's Rhetoric

The section of *The Subjection of Women* that follows is less an argument than it is an examination of a simple question: "Would mankind be at all better off if women were free?" By and large Mill's focus here is on married women. He considers the question from several points of view. The consideration of justice illuminates the wife's perspective because the demands of justice clearly take her rights into account and suggest that since slavery has been abolished entirely it only follows that a wife should not be a slave in her own home. His exploration of this point is subtle, but thorough, in part because his audience knew the details of a wife's situation. The intended audience for his book seems to have been primarily educated men, which we surmise from the often quoted Latin—and even Greek—phrases, and thus Mill limited his influence to the privileged males of the "easy classes" and to a small number of atypically educated women.

One of his first concerns relates clearly to his views in *On Liberty* when he talks about the abuse of power. When one person has absolute power over another, he asks, what is the likely outcome? He points to the institution of slavery as an example of the tyranny of the individual and the complete abuse of power often visited upon slaves. The same situation exists in the institution of marriage in the Victorian period in which Mill lived. And it has not entirely been altered except in terms of the laws and the protection they sometimes give married women.

Another concern is more utilitarian and clearly an appeal to male readers who can see the advantages for their own economic interests and, perhaps, to men who can see the potential for the general advancement of learning: equal education for women. The effect of such education, combined with the opportunities of useful employment and advancement, would be to tap into the potential of that half of society that had influence only in the home. It is a terrible thing, he implies, to shut women away from free choice of employment. "Mental superiority of any kind is at present everywhere so much below the demand; there is such a deficiency of persons competent to do excellently anything which it requires any considerable amount of ability to do: that the loss to the world, by refusing to make use of one-half of the whole quantity of talent it possesses, is extremely serious" (para. 6). Among the advantages of giving women equal opportunity is "the stimulus that would be given to the intellect of men by the competition." It is interesting to see that he feels men would be improved by such competition instead of threatened by it.

A good deal of the essay is devoted to the topic of comparison: examining the differences between men and women. Mill describes the quality husbands have that tends toward the abuse of power: self-worship. "The self-worship of the monarch, or of the feudal superior, is matched by the self-worship of the male" (para. 4). For the self-worshiping male, his wife is merely a vassal, only a notch above a slave.

He describes women as having different interests from men, thus offering society an enlargement of understanding and influence. Mill praises the effect of "women's opinions" on men especially in his discussion of chivalry, which he describes as "the acme of the influence of women's sentiments on the moral cultivation of mankind" (para. 9). And, at the same time, he laments that chivalry has passed away, especially now that fighting as a primary activity for men has given way to business. The modern world has no room for the virtues of chivalry.

Mill's primary complaint about the behavior of women is that they pay much too much attention to charity. He feels that women's tendency to give money and services to the poor comes from their own unfree upbringing, when they were themselves given charity in anticipation of their marrying, rather than their becoming independent. Charity, Mill says, induces dependence and stifles the willingness and ability to do for oneself. It does more harm than good. However, apart from this warning, Mill supports the independence and freedom of women at a time when such an idea was virtually freakish.

PREREADING QUESTIONS: WHAT TO READ FOR

The following prereading questions may help you anticipate key issues in the discussion of John Stuart Mill's "The Subjection of Women." Keeping them in mind during your first reading of the selection should help focus your attention.

- What was the nature of the subjection of women in marriage? Who benefited from women's subjection?
- What are the primary effects of women on the character of males?
- What basic differences does Mill see between men and women in his time?
- What are the primary reasons for demanding the end of the subjection of women?

The Subjection of Women

There remains a question, not of less importance than those 1
already discussed, and which will be asked the most importunately
by those opponents whose conviction is somewhat shaken on the
main point. What good are we to expect from the changes proposed
in our customs and institutions? Would mankind be at all better off
if women were free? If not, why disturb their minds, and attempt to
make a social revolution in the name of an abstract right?

It is hardly to be expected that this question will be asked in 2
respect to the change proposed in the condition of women in marriage. The sufferings, immoralities, evils of all sorts, produced in
innumerable cases by the subjection of individual women to individual men, are far too terrible to be overlooked. Unthinking or uncan-
did persons, counting those cases alone which are extreme, or which
attain publicity, may say that the evils are exceptional; but no one
can be blind to their existence, nor, in many cases, to their intensity.
And it is perfectly obvious that the abuse of the power cannot be very
much checked while the power remains. It is a power given, or
offered, not to good men, or to decently respectable men, but to all
men; the most brutal, and the most criminal. There is no check but
that of opinion, and such men are in general within the reach of no
opinion but that of men like themselves. If such men did not brutally
tyrannize over the one human being whom the law compels to bear
everything from them, society must already have reached a paradisia-
cal state. There could be no need any longer of laws to curb men's
vicious propensities. Astraea[1] must not only have returned to earth,
but the heart of the worst man must have become her temple. The
law of servitude in marriage is a monstrous contradiction to all the
principles of the modern world, and to all the experience through
which those principles have been slowly and painfully worked out. It
is the sole case, now that negro slavery has been abolished, in which
a human being in the plenitude of every faculty is delivered up to the
tender mercies of another human being, in the hope forsooth that
this other will use the power solely for the good of the person subjected to it. Marriage is the only actual bondage known to our law.
There remain no legal slaves, except the mistress of every house.

It is not, therefore, on this part of the subject, that the question 3
is likely to be asked, *Cui bono?*[2] We may be told that the evil would

---

[1] **Astraea** The first Greek goddess of justice, innocence, and purity; she left earth
at the end of the Golden Age due to man's evilness.

[2] **Cui bono?** Latin, "Who benefits from it?"

outweigh the good, but the reality of the good admits of no dispute. In regard, however, to the larger question, the removal of women's disabilities—their recognition as the equals of men in all that belongs to citizenship—the opening to them of all honorable employments, and of the training and education which qualifies for those employments—there are many persons for whom it is not enough that the inequality has no just or legitimate defense; they require to be told what express advantage would be obtained by abolishing it.

To which let me first answer, the advantage of having the most   4 universal and pervading of all human relations regulated by justice instead of injustice. The vast amount of this gain to human nature, it is hardly possible, by any explanation or illustration, to place in a stronger light than it is placed by the bare statement, to any one who attaches a moral meaning to words. All the selfish propensities, the self-worship, the unjust self-preference, which exist among mankind, have their source and root in, and derive their principal nourishment from, the present constitution of the relation between men and women. Think what it is to a boy, to grow up to manhood in the belief that without any merit or any exertion of his own, though he may be the most frivolous and empty or the most ignorant and stolid of mankind, by the mere fact of being born a male he is by right the superior of all and every one of an entire half of the human race: including probably some whose real superiority to himself he has daily or hourly occasion to feel; but even if in his whole conduct he habitually follows a woman's guidance, still, if he is a fool, she thinks that of course she is not, and cannot be, equal in ability and judgment to himself; and if he is not a fool, he does worse—he sees that she is superior to him, and believes that, notwithstanding her superiority, he is entitled to command and she is bound to obey. What must be the effect on his character, of this lesson? And men of the cultivated classes are often not aware how deeply it sinks into the immense majority of male minds. For, among right-feeling and well-bred people, the inequality is kept as much as possible out of sight; above all, out of sight of the children. As much obedience is required from boys to their mother as to their father: they are not permitted to domineer over their sisters, nor are they accustomed to see these postponed to them, but the contrary; the compensations of the chivalrous feeling being made prominent, while the servitude which requires them is kept in the background. Well brought-up youths in the higher classes thus often escape the bad influences of the situation in their early years, and only experience them when, arrived at manhood, they fall under the dominion of facts as they really exist. Such people are little aware, when a boy is differently brought up, how early the notion of his inherent superiority to a girl arises in his mind; how it grows with his growth and strengthens with his strength; how it is inoculated by one schoolboy upon another; how early the youth thinks himself superior to his mother, owing her perhaps forbearance, but no real respect; and how sublime and sultan-like a sense of superiority he feels, above all, over the woman whom he honors by admitting her to a partnership of his life. Is it imagined that all this does not pervert the whole manner of existence of the man, both as an individual and as a social being? It is an exact parallel to the feeling of a hereditary king that he is excellent above others by being born a king, or a noble by being born a noble. The relation between husband and wife is very like that between lord and vassal, except that the wife is held to more unlimited obedience than the vassal was. However the vassal's character may have been affected, for better and for worse, by his subordination, who can help seeing that the lord's was affected greatly for the worse? Whether he was led to believe that his vassals were really superior to himself, or to feel that he was placed in command over people as good as himself, for no merits or labors of his own, but merely for having, as Figaro[3] says, taken the trouble to be born. The self-worship of the monarch, or of the feudal superior, is matched by the self-worship of the male. Human beings do not grow up from childhood in the possession of unearned distinctions, without pluming themselves upon them. Those whom privileges not acquired by their merit, and which they feel to be disproportioned to it, inspire with additional humility, are always the few, and the best few. The rest are only inspired with pride, and the worst sort of pride, that which values itself upon accidental advantages, not of its own achieving. Above all, when the feeling of being raised above the whole of the other sex is combined with personal authority over one individual among them; the situation, if a school of conscientious and affectionate forbearance to those whose strongest points of character are conscience and affection, is to men of another quality a regularly constituted Academy or Gymnasium for training them in arrogance and overbearingness; which vices, if curbed by the certainty of resistance in their intercourse with other men, their equals, break out towards all who are in a position to be obliged to tolerate them, and often revenge themselves upon the unfortunate

---

[3] **Figaro** Character critical of the aristocracy in Pierre-Augustin Caron de Beaumarchais's (1732–1799) plays *The Barber of Seville* and *The Marriage of Figaro.* Both were turned into operas.

wife for the involuntary restraint which they are obliged to submit to elsewhere.

The example afforded, and the education given to the senti- 5 ments, by laying the foundation of domestic existence upon a relation contradictory to the first principles of social justice, must, from the very nature of man, have a perverting influence of such magnitude, that it is hardly possible with our present experience to raise our imaginations to the conception of so great a change for the better as would be made by its removal. All that education and civilization are doing to efface the influences on character of the law of force, and replace them by those of justice, remains merely on the surface, as long as the citadel of the enemy is not attacked. The principle of the modern movement in morals and politics, is that conduct, and conduct alone, entitles to respect: that not what men are, but what they do, constitutes their claim to deference; that, above all, merit, and not birth, is the only rightful claim to power and authority. If no authority, not in its nature temporary, were allowed to one human being over another, society would not be employed in building up propensities with one hand which it has to curb with the other. The child would really, for the first time in man's existence on earth, be trained in the way he should go, and when he was old there would be a chance that he would not depart from it. But so long as the right of the strong to power over the weak rules in the very heart of society, the attempt to make the equal right of the weak the principle of its outward actions will always be an uphill struggle; for the law of justice, which is also that of Christianity, will never get possession of men's inmost sentiments; they will be working against it, even when bending to it.

The second benefit to be expected from giving to women the 6 free use of their faculties, by leaving them the free choice of their employments, and opening to them the same field of occupation and the same prizes and encouragements as to other human beings, would be that of doubling the mass of mental faculties available for the higher service of humanity. Where there is now one person qualified to benefit mankind and promote the general improvement, as a public teacher, or an administrator of some branch of public or social affairs, there would then be a chance of two. Mental superiority of any kind is at present everywhere so much below the demand; there is such a deficiency of persons competent to do excellently anything which it requires any considerable amount of ability to do; that the loss to the world, by refusing to make use of one-half of the whole quantity of talent it possesses, is extremely serious. It is true that this amount of mental power is not totally lost. Much of it is employed, and would in any case be employed, in domestic management, and in the few other occupations open to women; and from the remainder indirect benefit is in many individual cases obtained, through the personal influence of individual women over individual men. But these benefits are partial; their range is extremely circumscribed; and if they must be admitted, on the one hand, as a deduction from the amount of fresh social power that would be acquired by giving freedom to one-half of the whole sum of human intellect, there must be added, on the other, the benefit of the stimulus that would be given to the intellect of men by the competition; or (to use a more true expression) by the necessity that would be imposed on them of deserving precedency before they could expect to obtain it.

This great accession to the intellectual power of the species, and   7
to the amount of intellect available for the good management of its affairs, would be obtained, partly, through the better and more complete intellectual education of women, which would then improve *pari passu*[4] with that of men. Women in general would be brought up equally capable of understanding business, public affairs, and the higher matters of speculation, with men in the same class of society; and the select few of the one as well as of the other sex, who were qualified not only to comprehend what is done or thought by others, but to think or do something considerable themselves, would meet with the same facilities for improving and training their capacities in the one sex as in the other. In this way, the widening of the sphere of action for women would operate for good, by raising their education to the level of that of men, and making the one participate in all improvements made in the other. But independently of this, the mere breaking down of the barrier would of itself have an educational virtue of the highest worth. The mere getting rid of the idea that all the wider subjects of thought and action, all the things which are of general and not solely of private interest, are men's business, from which women are to be warned off—positively interdicted from most of it, coldly tolerated in the little which is allowed them—the mere consciousness a woman would then have of being a human being like any other, entitled to choose her pursuits, urged or invited by the same inducements as any one else to interest herself in whatever is interesting to human beings, entitled to exert the share of influence on all human concerns which belongs to an individual opinion, whether she attempted actual participation in them or not—this

---

[4]*pari passu* Latin, "in the same place."

alone would effect an immense expansion of the faculties of women, as well as enlargement of the range of their moral sentiments.

Besides the addition to the amount of individual talent available for the conduct of human affairs, which certainly are not at present so abundantly provided in that respect that they can afford to dispense with one-half of what nature proffers; the opinion of women would then possess a more beneficial, rather than a greater, influence upon the general mass of human belief and sentiment. I say a more beneficial, rather than a greater influence; for the influence of women over the general tone of opinion has always, or at least from the earliest known period, been very considerable. The influence of mothers on the early character of their sons, and the desire of young men to recommend themselves to young women, have in all recorded times been important agencies in the formation of character, and have determined some of the chief steps in the progress of civilization. Even in the Homeric age, αἰδώς towards the Τρωάδας ἑλκεσιπέπλους is an acknowledged and powerful motive of action in the great Hector.[5] The moral influence of women has had two modes of operation. First, it has been a softening influence. Those who were most liable to be the victims of violence, have naturally tended as much as they could towards limiting its sphere and mitigating its excesses. Those who were not taught to fight, have naturally inclined in favor of any other mode of settling differences rather than that of fighting. In general, those who have been the greatest sufferers by the indulgence of selfish passion, have been the most earnest supporters of any moral law which offered a means of bridling passion. Women were powerfully instrumental in inducing the northern conquerors to adopt the creed of Christianity, a creed so much more favorable to women than any that preceded it. The conversion of the Anglo-Saxons and of the Franks may be said to have been begun by the wives of Ethelbert and Clovis.[6] The other mode in which the effect of women's opinion has been conspicuous, is by giving a powerful stimulus to those qualities in men, which, not being themselves trained in, it was necessary for them that they should find in their protectors. Courage, and the military virtues generally, have at all times been greatly indebted to the desire which men felt of being admired by women: and the stimulus reaches far

8

---

[5]**Hector** Hector in *The Iliad* is concerned with what the women will think of him. The quote is from book 6, lines 441–43. Translated from the Greek, the first part of the quote means "a sense of shame," while the second part means "wearing long, flowing robes."

[6]**Ethelbert and Clovis** Pagan English kings who married Christian women and were converted.

beyond this one class of eminent qualities, since, by a very natural effect of their position, the best passport to the admiration and favor of women has always been to be thought highly of by men. From the combination of the two kinds of moral influence thus exercised by women, arose the spirit of chivalry: the peculiarity of which is, to aim at combining the highest standard of the warlike qualities with the cultivation of a totally different class of virtues— those of gentleness, generosity, and self-abnegation, towards the non-military and defenseless classes generally, and a special submission and worship directed towards women; who were distinguished from the other defenseless classes by the high rewards which they had it in their power voluntarily to bestow on those who endeavored to earn their favor, instead of extorting their subjection. Though the practice of chivalry fell even more sadly short of its theoretic standard than practice generally falls below theory, it remains one of the most precious monuments of the moral history of our race; as a remarkable instance of a concerted and organized attempt by a most disorganized and distracted society, to raise up and carry into practice a moral ideal greatly in advance of its social condition and institutions; so much so as to have been completely frustrated in the main object, yet never entirely inefficacious, and which has left a most sensible, and for the most part a highly valuable impress on the ideas and feelings of all subsequent times.

The chivalrous ideal is the acme of the influence of women's sentiments on the moral cultivation of mankind: and if women are to remain in their subordinate situation, it were greatly to be lamented that the chivalrous standard should have passed away, for it is the only one at all capable of mitigating the demoralizing influences of that position. But the changes in the general state of the species rendered inevitable the substitution of a totally different ideal of morality for the chivalrous one. Chivalry was the attempt to infuse moral elements into a state of society in which everything depended for good or evil on individual prowess, under the softening influences of individual delicacy and generosity. In modern societies, all things, even in the military department of affairs, are decided, not by individual effort, but by the combined operations of numbers; while the main occupation of society has changed from fighting to business, from military to industrial life. The exigencies of the new life are no more exclusive of the virtues of generosity than those of the old, but it no longer entirely depends on them. The main foundations of the moral life of modern times must be justice and prudence; the respect of each for the rights of every other, and the ability of each to take care of himself. Chivalry left without legal check all forms of wrong which reigned unpunished throughout society; it only encouraged a few to do right in preference to wrong, by the direction it gave to the instruments of praise and admiration. But the real dependence of morality must always be upon its penal sanctions—its power to deter from evil. The security of society cannot rest on merely rendering honor to right, a motive so comparatively weak in all but a few, and which on very many does not operate at all. Modern society is able to repress wrong through all departments of life, by a fit exertion of the superior strength which civilization has given it, and thus to render the existence of the weaker members of society (no longer defenseless but protected by law) tolerable to them, without reliance on the chivalrous feelings of those who are in a position to tyrannize. The beauties and graces of the chivalrous character are still what they were, but the rights of the weak, and the general comfort of human life, now rest on a far surer and steadier support; or rather, they do so in every relation of life except the conjugal.

At present the moral influence of women is no less real, but it is   10 no longer of so marked and definite a character: it has more nearly merged in the general influence of public opinion. Both through the contagion of sympathy, and through the desire of men to shine in the eyes of women, their feelings have great effect in keeping alive what remains of the chivalrous ideal—in fostering the sentiments and continuing the traditions of spirit and generosity. In these points of character, their standard is higher than that of men; in the quality of justice, somewhat lower. As regards the relations of private life it may be said generally, that their influence is, on the whole, encouraging to the softer virtues, discouraging to the sterner: though the statement must be taken with all the modifications dependent on individual character. In the chief of the greater trials to which virtue is subject in the concerns of life—the conflict between interest and principle—the tendency of women's influence is of a very mixed character. When the principle involved happens to be one of the very few which the course of their religious or moral education has strongly impressed upon themselves, they are potent auxiliaries to virtue: and their husbands and sons are often prompted by them to acts of abnegation which they never would have been capable of without that stimulus. But, with the present education and position of women, the moral principles which have been impressed on them cover but a comparatively small part of the field of virtue, and are, moreover, principally negative; forbidding particular acts, but having little to do with the general direction of the thoughts and purposes. I am afraid it must be said, that disinterestedness in the general conduct of life—the devotion of the energies to purposes which hold out no promise of private advantages to the family—is very seldom encouraged or supported by women's influence. It is small blame to them that they discourage objects of which they have not learnt to see the advantage, and which withdraw their men from them, and from the interests of the family. But the consequence is that women's influence is often anything but favorable to public virtue.

Women have, however, some share of influence in giving the tone to public moralities since their sphere of action has been a little widened, and since a considerable number of them have occupied themselves practically in the promotion of objects reaching beyond their own family and household. The influence of women counts for a great deal in two of the most marked features of modern European life—its aversion to war, and its addiction to philanthropy. Excellent characteristics both; but unhappily, if the influence of women is valuable in the encouragement it gives to these feelings in general, in the particular applications the direction it gives to them is at least as often mischievous as useful. In the philanthropic department more particularly, the two provinces chiefly cultivated by women are religious proselytism and charity. Religious proselytism at home, is but another word for embittering of religious animosities: abroad, it is usually a blind running at an object, without either knowing or heeding the fatal mischiefs—fatal to the religious object itself as well as to all other desirable objects—which may be produced by the means employed. As for charity, it is a matter in which the immediate effect on the persons directly concerned, and the ultimate consequence to the general good, are apt to be at complete war with one another: while the education given to women—an education of the sentiments rather than of the understanding—and the habit inculcated by their whole life, of looking to immediate effects on persons, and not to remote effects on classes of persons—make them both unable to see, and unwilling to admit, the ultimate evil tendency of any form of charity or philanthropy which commends itself to their sympathetic feelings. The great and continually increasing mass of unenlightened and shortsighted benevolence, which, taking the care of people's lives out of their own hands, and relieving them from the disagreeable consequences of their own acts, saps the very foundations of the self-respect, self-help, and self-control which are the essential conditions both of individual prosperity and of social virtue—this waste of resources and of benevolent feelings in doing harm instead of good, is immensely swelled by women's contributions, and stimulated by their influence. Not that this is a mistake

11

likely to be made by women, where they have actually the practical management of schemes of beneficence. It sometimes happens that women who administer public charities—with that insight into present fact, and especially into the minds and feelings of those with whom they are in immediate contact, in which women generally excel men—recognize in the clearest manner the demoralizing influence of the alms given or the help afforded, and could give lessons on the subject to many a male political economist. But women who only give their money, and are not brought face to face with the effects it produces, how can they be expected to foresee them? A woman born to the present lot of women, and content with it, how should she appreciate the value of self-dependence? She is not self-dependent; she is not taught self-dependence; her destiny is to receive everything from others, and why should what is good enough for her be bad for the poor? Her familiar notions of good are of blessings descending from a superior. She forgets that she is not free, and that the poor are; that if what they need is given to them unearned, they cannot be compelled to earn it: that everybody cannot be taken care of by everybody, but there must be some motive to induce people to take care of themselves; and that to be helped to help themselves, if they are physically capable of it, is the only charity which proves to be charity in the end.

These considerations show how usefully the part which women   12 take in the formation of general opinion, would be modified for the better by that more enlarged instruction, and practical conversancy with the things which their opinions influence, that would necessarily arise from their social and political emancipation. But the improvement it would work through the influence they exercise, each in her own family, would be still more remarkable.

It is often said that in the classes most exposed to temptation, a   13 man's wife and children tend to keep him honest and respectable, both by the wife's direct influence, and by the concern he feels for their future welfare. This may be so, and no doubt often is so, with those who are more weak than wicked; and this beneficial influence would be preserved and strengthened under equal laws; it does not depend on the woman's servitude, but is, on the contrary, diminished by the disrespect which the inferior class of men always at heart feel towards those who are subject to their power. But when we ascend higher in the scale, we come among a totally different set of moving forces. The wife's influence tends, as far as it goes, to prevent the husband from falling below the common standard of approbation of the country. It tends quite as strongly to hinder him from rising above it. The wife is the auxiliary of the common public opinion. A man who is married to a woman his inferior in intelligence, finds her a perpetual dead weight, or, worse than a dead weight, a drag, upon every aspiration of his to be better than public opinion requires him to be. It is hardly possible for one who is in these bonds, to attain exalted virtue. If he differs in his opinion from the mass—if he sees truths which have not yet dawned upon them, or if, feeling in his heart truths which they nominally recognize, he would like to act up to those truths more conscientiously than the generality of mankind—to all such thoughts and desires, marriage is the heaviest of drawbacks, unless he be so fortunate as to have a wife as much above the common level as he himself is.

For, in the first place, there is always some sacrifice of personal   14
interest required; either of social consequence, or of pecuniary means; perhaps the risk of even the means of subsistence. These sacrifices and risks he may be willing to encounter for himself; but he will pause before he imposes them on his family. And his family in this case means his wife and daughters; for he always hopes that his sons will feel as he feels himself, and that what he can do without, they will do without, willingly, in the same cause. But his daughters—their marriage may depend upon it: and his wife, who is unable to enter into or understand the objects for which these sacrifices are made—who, if she thought them worth any sacrifice, would think so on trust, and solely for his sake—who can participate in none of the enthusiasm or the self-approbation he himself may feel, while the things which he is disposed to sacrifice are all in all to her; will not the best and most unselfish man hesitate the longest before bringing on her this consequence? If it be not the comforts of life, but only social consideration, that is at stake, the burthen upon his conscience and feelings is still very severe. Whoever has a wife and children has given hostages to Mrs. Grundy.[7] The approbation of that potentate may be a matter of indifference to him, but it is of great importance to his wife. The man himself may be above opinion, or may find sufficient compensation in the opinion of those of his own way of thinking. But to the women connected with him, he can offer no compensation. The almost invariable tendency of the wife to place her influence in the same scale with social consideration, is sometimes made a reproach to women, and represented

---

[7]**Mrs. Grundy** Character in an eighteenth-century play who became the stereotype for a prude.

as a peculiar trait of feebleness and childishness of character in them: surely with great injustice. Society makes the whole life of a woman, in the easy classes, a continued self-sacrifice; it exacts from her an unremitting restraint of the whole of her natural inclinations, and the sole return it makes to her for what often deserves the name of a martyrdom, is consideration. Her consideration is inseparably connected with that of her husband, and after paying the full price for it, she finds that she is to lose it, for no reason of which she can feel the cogency. She has sacrificed her whole life to it, and her husband will not sacrifice to it a whim, a freak, an eccentricity; something not recognized or allowed for by the world, and which the world will agree with her in thinking a folly, if it thinks no worse! The dilemma is hardest upon that very meritorious class of men, who, without possessing talents which qualify them to make a figure among those with whom they agree in opinion, hold their opinion from conviction, and feel bound in honor and conscience to serve it, by making profession of their belief, and giving their time, labor, and means, to anything undertaken in its behalf. The worst case of all is when such men happen to be of a rank and position which of itself neither gives them, nor excludes them from, what is considered the best society; when their admission to it depends mainly on what is thought of them personally — and however unexceptionable their breeding and habits, their being identified with opinions and public conduct unacceptable to those who give the tone to society would operate as an effectual exclusion. Many a woman flatters herself (nine times out of ten quite erroneously) that nothing prevents her and her husband from moving in the highest society of her neighborhood — society in which others well known to her, and in the same class of life, mix freely — except that her husband is unfortunately a Dissenter, or has the reputation of mingling in low radical politics. That it is, she thinks, which hinders George from getting a commission or a place, Caroline from making an advantageous match, and prevents her and her husband from obtaining invitations, perhaps honors, which, for aught she sees, they are as well entitled to as some folks. With such an influence in every house, either exerted actively, or operating all the more powerfully for not being asserted, is it any wonder that people in general are kept down in that mediocrity of respectability which is becoming a marked characteristic of modern times?

There is another very injurious aspect in which the effect, not of 15 women's disabilities directly, but of the broad line of difference which those disabilities create between the education and character of a woman and that of a man, requires to be considered. Nothing can be more unfavorable to that union of thoughts and inclinations which is the ideal of married life. Intimate society between people radically dissimilar to one another, is an idle dream. Unlikeness may attract, but it is likeness which retains; and in proportion to the likeness is the suitability of the individuals to give each other a happy life. While women are so unlike men, it is not wonderful that selfish men should feel the need of arbitrary power in their own hands, to arrest *in limine*[8] the lifelong conflict of inclinations, by deciding every question on the side of their own preference. When people are extremely unlike, there can be no real identity of interest. Very often there is conscientious difference of opinion between married people, on the highest points of duty. Is there any reality in the marriage union where this takes place? Yet it is not uncommon anywhere, when the woman has any earnestness of character; and it is a very general case indeed in Catholic countries, when she is supported in her dissent by the only other authority to which she is taught to bow, the priest. With the usual barefacedness of power not accustomed to find itself disputed, the influence of priests over women is attacked by Protestant and Liberal writers, less for being bad in itself, than because it is a rival authority to the husband, and raises up a revolt against his infallibility. In England, similar differences occasionally exist when an Evangelical wife has allied herself with a husband of a different quality; but in general this source at least of dissension is got rid of, by reducing the minds of women to such a nullity, that they have no opinions but those of Mrs. Grundy, or those which the husband tells them to have. When there is no difference of opinion, differences merely of taste may be sufficient to detract greatly from the happiness of married life. And though it may stimulate the amatory propensities of men, it does not conduce to married happiness, to exaggerate by differences of education whatever may be the native differences of the sexes. If the married pair are well-bred and well-behaved people, they tolerate each other's tastes; but is mutual toleration what people look forward to, when they enter into marriage? These differences of inclination will naturally make their wishes different, if not restrained by affection or duty, as to almost all domestic questions which arise. What a difference there must be in the society which the two persons will wish to frequent, or be frequented by! Each will desire associates who share their own tastes: the persons agreeable to one, will be indifferent or positively disagreeable to the other; yet there can be none who are not common

---

[8] *in limine* Latin, "at the outset."

to both, for married people do not now live in different parts of the house and have totally different visiting lists, as in the reign of Louis XV.[9] They cannot help having different wishes as to the bringing up of the children: each will wish to see reproduced in them their own tastes and sentiments: and there is either a compromise, and only a half-satisfaction to either, or the wife has to yield—often with bitter suffering; and, with or without intention, her occult influence continues to counterwork the husband's purposes.

It would of course be extreme folly to suppose that these differ-   16 ences of feeling and inclination only exist because women are brought up differently from men, and that there would not be differences of taste under any imaginable circumstances. But there is nothing beyond the mark in saying that the distinction in bringing-up immensely aggravates those differences, and renders them wholly inevitable. While women are brought up as they are, a man and a woman will but rarely find in one another real agreement of tastes and wishes as to daily life. They will generally have to give it up as hopeless, and renounce the attempt to have, in the intimate associate of their daily life, that *idem velle, idem nolle,*[10] which is the recognized bond of any society that is really such: or if the man succeeds in obtaining it, he does so by choosing a woman who is so complete a nullity that she has no *velle* or *nolle* at all, and is as ready to comply with one thing as another if anybody tells her to do so. Even this calculation is apt to fail; dullness and want of spirit are not always a guarantee of the submission which is so confidently expected from them. But if they were, is this the ideal of marriage? What, in this case, does the man obtain by it, except an upper servant, a nurse, or a mistress? On the contrary, when each of two persons, instead of being a nothing, is a something; when they are attached to one another, and are not too much unlike to begin with; the constant partaking in the same things, assisted by their sympathy, draws out the latent capacities of each for being interested in the things which were at first interesting only to the other; and works a gradual assimilation of the tastes and characters to one another, partly by the insensible modification of each, but more by a real enriching of the two natures, each acquiring the tastes and capacities of the other in addition to its own. This often happens between two friends of the same sex, who are much associated in their daily life: and it would be a common, if not the commonest,

---

[9] **Louis XV (1710–1774)** King of France from 1715 until his death.
[10] ***idem velle, idem nolle*** Latin for "same likes, same dislikes."

case in marriage, did not the totally different bringing-up of the two sexes make it next to an impossibility to form a really well-assorted union. Were this remedied, whatever differences there might still be in individual tastes, there would at least be, as a general rule, complete unity and unanimity as to the great objects of life. When the two persons both care for great objects, and are a help and encouragement to each other in whatever regards these, the minor matters on which their tastes may differ are not all-important to them; and there is a foundation for solid friendship, of an enduring character, more likely than anything else to make it, through the whole of life, a greater pleasure to each to give pleasure to the other, than to receive it.

QUESTIONS FOR CRITICAL READING

1. Has modern society put an end to the subjection of women?
2. Do young men today grow up with the sense of their "inherent superiority to a girl"?
3. Do you agree that the rightful claim to power and authority should be given to merit and not to birth? How does gender figure into that equation?
4. What is the best argument for freeing women to compete with men for important jobs?
5. To what extent does Mill seem conscious of class differences between people?
6. How would women be changed by the proposals Mill makes here?
7. What was the chivalrous ideal? Is it still in effect in your immediate society?
8. Are you sympathetic to Mill's position regarding charity in paragraph 11?

SUGGESTIONS FOR CRITICAL WRITING

1. Mill says, "The main foundations of the moral life of modern times must be justice and prudence . . ." (para. 9). What is the relation of the moral life of modern times to the argument in favor of releasing women from subjection? How much progress do you see in your immediate environment in relation to freeing women? How do women and men seem to differ today from the descriptions of them in Mill's essay of 1869?
2. Research the chivalrous ideal and comment on Mill's understanding of it. Do you agree that the chivalrous ideal "is the acme of the influence of women's sentiments on the moral cultivation of mankind" (para. 9)?

Describe the positive and negative influences of that ideal, and then examine your own relationship with members of the opposite sex and determine whether or not that ideal is, however weakened, still in effect in modern times.

3. In paragraph 11, Mill says that women are not taught to be independent: "[s]he is not self-dependent; she is not taught self-dependence; her destiny is to receive everything from others. . . ." To what extent does that description still apply to women in our society or in other societies you know about? What are the impediments in modern life to women's development of self-dependence? Is Mill talking about the kind of self-reliance Ralph Waldo Emerson describes in his essay (p. 255)?

4. Examine the social implications of Mill's comments about an unequal marriage and its effect on a husband: "marriage is the heaviest of drawbacks, unless he be so fortunate as to have a wife as much above the common level as he himself is" (para. 13). What is the "common level," and what does his concern for level imply about his perception of society itself? Given his description of conditions in the Victorian era, what were the chances of an equal marriage taking place? What might be the results of a seriously unequal marriage?

5. Mill declares in paragraph 15 that "[i]ntimate society between people radically dissimilar to one another, is an idle dream. Unlikeness may attract, but it is likeness which retains. . . ." How realistic is this view? Does it seem to hold in modern life as much as Mill felt it held in his time? Has society changed so much that his view is now no longer reasonable, or have things essentially remained the same in this regard?

6. If you disagree with Mill on the question of women's subjugation, write an essay arguing against his key positions. You'll notice that Mill does not use example to bolster his argument. He uses probability and likelihood: men with power will abuse it, he says. Take the key points of his argument and turn them back on him using reason, example, and testimony. Be sure to avoid reducing his arguments to absurdity before you address them. Try to be as concrete and effective in your argument as possible. Then, see how many people you can convince.

7. **CONNECTIONS**   Write an essay comparing Mill's position on charity and philanthropy with the views of Andrew Carnegie (p. 387). Which views seem stronger? Which seem most compelling to you? Once you have clarified those views, decide exactly how John Kenneth Galbraith (p. 405) would argue either for or against Mill's position on charity. Would he have found Mill or Carnegie sympathetic, or would he have proposed counterarguments to their positions?

8. **SEEING CONNECTIONS**   Cassatt painted *In the Loge* (p. 796) less than ten years after Mill published *The Subjection of Women*. Imagine that Mill saw this painting in Cassatt's studio and offered his interpretation of the woman with the opera glasses to us in terms of her being in subjection or being free. What would he have said about this painting and the people who are represented in it? Would he have assumed

that the woman was married or single or widowed? Would he have praised her for appearing at the theater alone, or would he have felt she was going beyond the bounds of polite society? What would he have said about her class and the class of people represented in the painting? How would that have affected his attitude toward the woman or toward Cassatt, who—like him—lived independently in France?

VIRGINIA WOOLF
Shakespeare's Sister

Virginia Woolf (1882–1941), one of the most gifted of the modernist writers, was a prolific essayist and novelist in what came to be known as the Bloomsbury group, named after a section of London near the British Museum. Most members of the group were writers, such as E. M. Forster, Lytton Strachey, and the critic Clive Bell, and some were artists, such as Duncan Grant and Virginia Woolf's sister, Vanessa Bell. The eminent economist John Maynard Keynes was part of the group as well, along with a variety of other accomplished intellectuals.

Virginia Woolf published some of the most important works of the early twentieth century, including the novels *Jacob's Room* (1922), *Mrs. Dalloway* (1925), *To the Lighthouse* (1927), *Orlando* (1928), and *The Waves* (1931). Among her many volumes of nonfiction prose is *A Room of One's Own* (1929). In this book Woolf speculates on what life would have been like for an imaginary gifted sister of William Shakespeare.

In discussing the imaginary Judith Shakespeare, Woolf examines the circumstances common to women's lives during the Renaissance. For example, women had little or no say in their future. Unlike their male counterparts, they were not educated in grammar schools and did not learn trades that would enable them to make a living for themselves. Instead, they were expected to marry as soon as possible, even as young as thirteen or fourteen years of age, and begin raising a family of their own. When they did marry, their husbands were men selected by their parents; the wives essentially became the property of those men. Under English law a married couple was regarded as one entity, and that entity was spoken for only by the man. Similarly, the women of the period had few civil rights. As

---

From *A Room of One's Own*.

Woolf points out, the history books do not mention women very often, and when they do, it is usually to relate that wife beating was common and generally approved of in all classes of society.

As Woolf comments on the opportunities that women were denied during the Renaissance, she agrees with an unnamed bishop who said that no woman could have written Shakespeare's plays. Woolf explains that no woman could have had enough contact with the theater in those days to be received with anything but disdain and discourtesy. Women could not even act on stage in Shakespeare's time, much less write for it.

It would be all but impossible in a society of this sort to imagine a woman as a successful literary figure, much less as a popular playwright. After all, society excluded women, marginalizing them as insignificant—at least in the eyes of historians. Certainly women were mothers; as such, they bore the male children who went on to become accomplished and famous. However, without a trade or an education, women in Shakespeare's time were all but chattel slaves in a household.

In this setting, Woolf places a brilliant girl named Judith Shakespeare, a fictional character who, in Woolf's imaginative construction, had the same literary fire as her famous brother. How would she have tried to express herself? How would she have followed her talent? Woolf suggests the results would be depressing, and with good reason. No one would have listened to Judith; in all likelihood her life would have ended badly.

The women of Shakespeare's time mentioned in the history books are generally Elizabeths and Marys, queens and princesses whose power was inherent in their positions. Little is known, Woolf says, about the lives of ordinary middle-class women. In Woolf's time, historians were uninterested in such information. However, many recent books have included detailed research into the lives of people in the Elizabethan period. Studying journals, day-books (including budgets and planning), and family records, modern historians have found much more information than English historian George Trevelyan (to whom Woolf refers in her essay) drew on. In fact, it is now known that women's lives were more varied than even Woolf implies, but women still had precious few opportunities compared to men of the period.

Woolf's Rhetoric

This selection is the third chapter from *A Room of One's Own*; thus, it begins with a sentence that implies continuity with an earlier section. The context for the essay's opening is as follows: a male dinner guest has said something insulting to women at a dinner party, and Woolf wishes she could come back with some hard fact to contradict the insult. However, she has no hard fact, so her strategy is to construct a situation that is as plausible and as accurate as her knowledge of history permits. Lacking fact, the novelist Virginia Woolf relies on imagination.

As it turned out, Woolf's portrait of Judith Shakespeare is so vivid that many readers actually believed William Shakespeare had such a sister. Judith Shakespeare did not exist, however. Her fictional character enables Woolf to speculate on how the life of any talented woman would have developed given the circumstances and limitations imposed on all women at the time. In the process, Woolf tries to reconstruct the world of Elizabethan England and place Judith in it.

Woolf goes about this act of imagination with extraordinary deliberateness. Her tone is cool and detached, almost as if she were a historian herself. She rarely reveals contempt for the opinions of men who are dismissive of women, such as the unnamed bishop. Yet, we catch an edgy tone when she discusses his views on women in literature. On the other hand, when she turns to Mr. Oscar Browning, a professor who believed the best women in Oxford were inferior to the worst men, we see another side of Woolf. She reveals that after making his high-minded pronouncements, Mr. Browning returned to his quarters for an assignation with an illiterate stable boy. This detail is meant to reveal the true intellectual level of Mr. Browning, as well as his attitude toward women.

Woolf makes careful use of simile in such statements as "for fiction, imaginative work that is, is not dropped like a pebble upon the ground, as science may be; fiction is like a spider's web, attached ever so lightly perhaps, but still attached to life at all four corners" (para. 2). Later, she shows a highly efficient use of language: "to write a work of genius is almost always a feat of prodigious difficulty. . . . Dogs will bark; people will interrupt; money must be made; health will break down" (para. 11). For a woman—who would not even have had a room of her own in an Elizabethan household—the impediments to creating "a work of genius" were insurmountable.

One reason for Woolf's controlled and cool tone is that she wrote with the knowledge that most men were very conservative. In 1929, people would not read what she wrote if she became enraged on paper. They would turn the page and ignore her argument. Thus, her tone seems inviting and cautious, almost as if Woolf is portraying herself as conservative on women's issues and in agreement with men like the historian Trevelyan and the unnamed bishop. However, nothing could be further from the truth. Woolf's anger may seethe and rage beneath the surface, but she keeps the surface smooth enough for those who disagree with her to be lured on to read.

One of the interesting details of Woolf's style is her allusiveness. She alludes to the work of many writers—male writers such as John Keats; Alfred, Lord Tennyson; and Robert Burns; and women writers such as Jane Austen, Emily Brontë, and George Eliot. Woolf's range of reference is that of the highly literary person—which she was; yet the way in which she makes reference to other important writers is designed not to offend the reader. If the reader knows the references, then Woolf will communicate on a special shared level of understanding. If the reader does not know the references, there is nothing in Woolf's manner that makes it difficult for the reader to continue and understand her main points.

Woolf's rhetoric in this piece is singularly polite. She makes her points without rancor and alarm. They are detailed, specific, and in many ways irrefutable. What she feels she has done is nothing less than tell the truth.

PREREADING QUESTIONS:
WHAT TO READ FOR

The following prereading questions may help you anticipate key issues in the discussion of Virginia Woolf's "Shakespeare's Sister." Keeping them in mind during your first reading of the selection should help focus your attention.

- What was the expected role of women in Shakespeare's time?
- By what means could Shakespeare's imaginary sister have become a dramatist?

Shakespeare's Sister

It was disappointing not to have brought back in the evening some important statement, some authentic fact. Women are poorer than men because—this or that. Perhaps now it would be better to give up seeking for the truth, and receiving on one's head an avalanche of opinion hot as lava, discolored as dish-water. It would be better to draw the curtains; to shut out distractions; to light the lamp; to narrow the enquiry and to ask the historian, who records not opinions

but facts, to describe under what conditions women lived, not throughout the ages, but in England, say in the time of Elizabeth.

For it is a perennial puzzle why no woman wrote a word of   2
that extraordinary literature when every other man, it seemed, was
capable of song or sonnet. What were the conditions in which
women lived, I asked myself; for fiction, imaginative work that is, is
not dropped like a pebble upon the ground, as science may be; fiction is like a spider's web, attached ever so lightly perhaps, but still
attached to life at all four corners. Often the attachment is scarcely
perceptible; Shakespeare's plays, for instance, seem to hang there
complete by themselves. But when the web is pulled askew, hooked
up at the edge, torn in the middle, one remembers that these webs
are not spun in midair by incorporeal creatures, but are the work of
suffering human beings, and are attached to grossly material things,
like health and money and the houses we live in.

I went, therefore, to the shelf where the histories stand and   3
took down one of the latest, Professor Trevelyan's[1] *History of England*.
Once more I looked up Women, found "position of," and turned to
the pages indicated. "Wife-beating," I read, "was a recognized right of
man, and was practiced without shame by high as well as low. . . .
Similarly," the historian goes on, "the daughter who refused to marry
the gentleman of her parents' choice was liable to be locked up,
beaten, and flung about the room, without any shock being inflicted
on public opinion. Marriage was not an affair of personal affection,
but of family avarice, particularly in the 'chivalrous' upper classes. . . .
Betrothal often took place while one or both of the parties was in the
cradle, and marriage when they were scarcely out of the nurses'
charge." That was about 1470, soon after Chaucer's time. The next
reference to the position of women is some two hundred years later,
in the time of the Stuarts. "It was still the exception for women of
the upper and middle class to choose their own husbands, and
when the husband had been assigned, he was lord and master, so far
at least as law and custom could make him. Yet even so," Professor
Trevelyan concludes, "neither Shakespeare's women nor those of
authentic seventeenth-century memoirs, like the Verneys and the
Hutchinsons, seem wanting in personality and character." Certainly,
if we consider it, Cleopatra must have had a way with her; Lady
Macbeth, one would suppose, had a will of her own; Rosalind, one
might conclude, was an attractive girl. Professor Trevelyan is speaking no more than the truth when he remarks that Shakespeare's
women do not seem wanting in personality and character. Not being

---

[1] **Trevelyan: George Macaulay (1876–1962)** One of England's great historians. [Woolf's note]

a historian, one might go even further and say that women have burnt like beacons in all the works of all the poets from the beginning of time—Clytemnestra, Antigone, Cleopatra, Lady Macbeth, Phèdre, Cressida, Rosalind, Desdemona, the Duchess of Malfi, among the dramatists; then among the prose writers: Millamant, Clarissa, Becky Sharp, Anna Karenina, Emma Bovary, Madame de Guermantes—the names flock to mind, nor do they recall women "lacking in personality and character." Indeed, if woman had no existence save in the fiction written by men, one would imagine her a person of the utmost importance; very various; heroic and mean; splendid and sordid; infinitely beautiful and hideous in the extreme; as great as a man, some think even greater.[2] But this is woman in fiction. In fact, as Professor Trevelyan points out, she was locked up, beaten, and flung about the room.

A very queer, composite being thus emerges. Imaginatively she   4
is of the highest importance; practically she is completely insignificant. She pervades poetry from cover to cover; she is all but absent from history. She dominates the lives of kings and conquerors in fiction; in fact she was the slave of any boy whose parents forced a ring upon her finger. Some of the most inspired words, some of the most profound thoughts in literature fall from her lips; in real life she could hardly read, could scarcely spell, and was the property of her husband.

It was certainly an odd monster that one made up by reading the   5
historians first and the poets afterwards—a worm winged like an eagle; the spirit of life and beauty in a kitchen chopping up suet. But these monsters, however amusing to the imagination, have no existence in fact. What one must do to bring her to life was to think poetically and prosaically at one and the same moment, thus keeping in

---

[2] **even greater** "It remains a strange and almost inexplicable fact that in Athena's city, where women were kept in almost Oriental suppression as odalisques or drudges, the stage should yet have produced figures like Clytemnestra and Cassandra, Atossa and Antigone, Phèdre and Medea, and all the other heroines who dominate play after play of the 'misogynist' Euripides. But the paradox of this world where in real life a respectable woman could hardly show her face alone in the street, and yet on the stage a woman equals or surpasses a man, has never been satisfactorily explained. In modern tragedy the same predominance exists. At all events, a very cursory survey of Shakespeare's work (similarly with Webster, though not with Marlowe or Jonson) suffices to reveal how this dominance, this initiative of women, persists from Rosalind to Lady Macbeth. So too in Racine; six of his tragedies bear their heroines' names; and what male characters of his shall we set against Hermione and Andromaque, Bérénice and Roxane, Phèdre and Athalie? So again with Ibsen; what men shall we match with Solveig and Nora, Hedda and Hilda Wangel and Rebecca West?"—F. L. Lucas, *Tragedy*, pp. 114–15. [Woolf's note]

touch with fact—that she is Mrs. Martin, aged thirty-six, dressed in blue, wearing a black hat and brown shoes; but not losing sight of fiction either—that she is a vessel in which all sorts of spirits and forces are coursing and flashing perpetually. The moment, however, that one tries this method with the Elizabethan woman, one branch of illumination fails; one is held up by the scarcity of facts. One knows nothing detailed, nothing perfectly true and substantial about her. History scarcely mentions her. And I turned to Professor Trevelyan again to see what history meant to him. I found by looking at his chapter headings that it meant—

"The Manor Court and the Methods of Open-field Agriculture . . . 6
The Cistercians and Sheep-farming . . . The Crusades . . . The University . . . The House of Commons . . . The Hundred Years' War . . . The Wars of the Roses . . . The Renaissance Scholars . . . The Dissolution of the Monasteries . . . Agrarian and Religious Strife . . . The Origin of English Sea-power . . . The Armada . . ." and so on. Occasionally an individual woman is mentioned, an Elizabeth, or a Mary; a queen or a great lady. But by no possible means could middle-class women with nothing but brains and character at their command have taken part in any one of the great movements which, brought together, constitute the historian's view of the past. Nor shall we find her in any collection of anecdotes. Aubrey[3] hardly mentions her. She never writes her own life and scarcely keeps a diary; there are only a handful of her letters in existence. She left no plays or poems by which we can judge her. What one wants, I thought—and why does not some brilliant student at Newnham or Girton[4] supply it?— is a mass of information; at what age did she marry; how many children had she as a rule; what was her house like; had she a room to herself; did she do the cooking; would she be likely to have a servant? All these facts lie somewhere, presumably, in parish registers and account books; the life of the average Elizabethan woman must be scattered about somewhere, could one collect it and make a book of it. It would be ambitious beyond my daring, I thought, looking about the shelves for books that were not there, to suggest to the students of those famous colleges that they should rewrite history, though I own that it often seems a little queer as it is, unreal, lopsided; but why should they not add a supplement to history? calling it, of course, by some inconspicuous name so that women might

---

[3]**John Aubrey (1626–1697)** English antiquarian noted for his *Brief Lives*, biographical sketches of famous men.
[4]**Newnham or Girton** Two women's colleges founded at Cambridge in the 1870s. [Woolf's note] Newnham (1871) and Girton (1869) were the first women's colleges at Cambridge University.

figure there without impropriety? For one often catches a glimpse of them in the lives of the great, whisking away into the background, concealing, I sometimes think, a wink, a laugh, perhaps a tear. And, after all, we have lives enough of Jane Austen; it scarcely seems necessary to consider again the influence of the tragedies of Joanna Baillie upon the poetry of Edgar Allan Poe; as for myself, I should not mind if the homes and haunts of Mary Russell Mitford were closed to the public for a century at least. But what I find deplorable, I continued, looking about the bookshelves again, is that nothing is known about women before the eighteenth century. I have no model in my mind to turn about this way and that. Here am I asking why women did not write poetry in the Elizabethan age, and I am not sure how they were educated; whether they were taught to write; whether they had sitting-rooms to themselves; how many women had children before they were twenty-one; what, in short, they did from eight in the morning till eight at night. They had no money evidently; according to Professor Trevelyan they were married whether they liked it or not before they were out of the nursery, at fifteen or sixteen very likely. It would have been extremely odd, even upon this showing, had one of them suddenly written the plays of Shakespeare, I concluded, and I thought of that old gentleman, who is dead now, but was a bishop, I think, who declared that it was impossible for any woman, past, present, or to come, to have the genius of Shakespeare. He wrote to the papers about it. He also told a lady who applied to him for information that cats do not as a matter of fact go to heaven, though they have, he added, souls of a sort. How much thinking those old gentlemen used to save one! How the borders of ignorance shrank back at their approach! Cats do not go to heaven. Women cannot write the plays of Shakespeare.

Be that as it may, I could not help thinking, as I looked at the works of Shakespeare on the shelf, that the bishop was right at least in this; it would have been impossible, completely and entirely, for any woman to have written the plays of Shakespeare in the age of Shakespeare. Let me imagine, since facts are so hard to come by, what would have happened had Shakespeare had a wonderfully gifted sister, called Judith, let us say. Shakespeare himself went, very probably—his mother was an heiress—to the grammar school, where he may have learnt Latin—Ovid, Virgil, and Horace—and the elements of grammar and logic. He was, it is well known, a wild boy who poached rabbits, perhaps shot a deer, and had, rather sooner than he should have done, to marry a woman in the neighborhood, who bore him a child rather quicker than was right. That escapade sent him to seek his fortune in London. He had, it seemed, a taste for the theatre; he began by holding horses at the stage door. Very soon he got work in the theatre, became a successful actor, and lived at the hub of the universe, meeting everybody, knowing everybody, practicing his art on the boards, exercising his wits in the streets, and even getting access to the palace of the queen. Meanwhile his extraordinarily gifted sister, let us suppose, remained at home. She was as adventurous, as imaginative, as agog to see the world as he was. But she was not sent to school. She had no chance of learning grammar and logic, let alone of reading Horace and Virgil. She picked up a book now and then, one of her brother's perhaps, and read a few pages. But then her parents came in and told her to mend the stockings or mind the stew and not moon about with books and papers. They would have spoken sharply but kindly, for they were substantial people who knew the conditions of life for a woman and loved their daughter—indeed, more likely than not she was the apple of her father's eye. Perhaps she scribbled some pages up in an apple loft on the sly, but was careful to hide them or set fire to them. Soon, however, before she was out of her teens, she was to be betrothed to the son of a neighboring wool-stapler. She cried out that marriage was hateful to her, and for that she was severely beaten by her father. Then he ceased to scold her. He begged her instead not to hurt him, not to shame him in this matter of her marriage. He would give her a chain of beads or a fine petticoat, he said; and there were tears in his eyes. How could she disobey him? How could she break his heart? The force of her own gift alone drove her to it. She made up a small parcel of her belongings, let herself down by a rope one summer's night and took the road to London. She was not seventeen. The birds that sang in the hedge were not more musical than she was. She had the quickest fancy, a gift like her brother's, for the tune of words. Like him, she had a taste for the theatre. She stood at the stage door; she wanted to act, she said. Men laughed in her face. The manager—a fat, loose-lipped man—guffawed. He bellowed something about poodles dancing and women acting—no woman, he said, could possibly be an actress. He hinted—you can imagine what. She could get no training in her craft. Could she even seek her dinner in a tavern or roam the streets at midnight? Yet her genius was for fiction and lusted to feed abundantly upon the lives of men and women and the study of their ways. At last—for she was very young, oddly like Shakespeare the poet in her face, with the same grey eyes and rounded brows—at last Nick Greene, the actor-manager took pity on her; she found herself with child by that gentleman and so—who shall measure the heat and violence of the poet's heart when caught and tangled in a woman's body?—killed herself one winter's night and lies buried at some cross-roads where the omnibuses now stop outside the Elephant and Castle.[5]

That, more or less, is how the story would run, I think, if a woman in Shakespeare's day had had Shakespeare's genius. But for my part, I agree with the deceased bishop, if such he was—it is unthinkable that any woman in Shakespeare's day should have had Shakespeare's genius. For genius like Shakespeare's is not born among laboring, uneducated, servile people. It was not born in England among the Saxons and the Britons. It is not born today among the working classes. How, then, could it have been born among women whose work began, according to Professor Trevelyan, almost before they were out of the nursery, who were forced to it by their parents and held to it by all the power of law and custom? Yet genius of a sort must have existed among women as it must have existed among the working classes. Now and again an Emily Brontë or a Robert Burns[6] blazes out and proves its presence. But certainly it never got itself on to paper. When, however, one reads of a witch being ducked, of a woman possessed by devils, of a wise woman selling herbs, or even of a very remarkable man who had a mother, then, I think we are on the track of a lost novelist, a suppressed poet, of some mute and inglorious Jane Austen, some Emily Brontë who dashed her brains out on the moor or mopped and mowed about the highways crazed with the torture that her gift had put her to. Indeed, I would venture to guess that Anon, who wrote so many poems without signing them, was often a woman. It was a woman Edward Fitzgerald,[7] I think, suggested who made the ballads and the folk-songs, crooning them to her children, beguiling her spinning with them, or the length of the winter's night.

This may be true or it may be false—who can say?—but what is true in it, so it seemed to me, reviewing the story of Shakespeare's sister as I had made it, is that any woman born with a great gift in the sixteenth century would certainly have gone crazed, shot herself, or ended her days in some lonely cottage outside the village, half witch, half wizard, feared and mocked at. For it needs little skill in psychology to be sure that a highly gifted girl who had tried to use her gift for poetry would have been so thwarted and hindered by other people, so tortured and pulled asunder by her own contrary

---

[5] **Elephant and Castle** A bus stop in London. The name came from a local pub.
[6] **Emily Brontë (1818–1848)** wrote *Wuthering Heights*; **Robert Burns (1759–1796)** was a Scots poet; **Jane Austen (1775–1817)** wrote *Pride and Prejudice* and many other novels. All three wrote against very great odds.
[7] **Edward Fitzgerald (1809–1883)** British scholar, poet, and translator who wrote *The Rubaiyat of Omar Khayyam*.

instincts, that she must have lost her health and sanity to a certainty. No girl could have walked to London and stood at a stage door and forced her way into the presence of actor-managers without doing herself a violence and suffering an anguish which may have been irrational—for chastity may be a fetish invented by certain societies for unknown reasons—but were none the less inevitable. Chastity had then, it has even now, a religious importance in a woman's life, and has so wrapped itself round with nerves and instincts that to cut it free and bring it to the light of day demands courage of the rarest. To have lived a free life in London in the sixteenth century would have meant for a woman who was poet and playwright a nervous stress and dilemma which might well have killed her. Had she survived, whatever she had written would have been twisted and deformed, issuing from a strained and morbid imagination. And undoubtedly, I thought, looking at the shelf where there are no plays by women, her work would have gone unsigned. That refuge she would have sought certainly. It was the relic of the sense of chastity that dictated anonymity to women even so late as the nineteenth century. Currer Bell, George Eliot, George Sand,[8] all the victims of inner strife as their writings prove, sought ineffectively to veil themselves by using the name of a man. Thus they did homage to the convention, which if not implanted by the other sex was liberally encouraged by them (the chief glory of a woman is not to be talked of, said Pericles, himself a much-talked-of man), that publicity in women is detestable. Anonymity runs in their blood. The desire to be veiled still possesses them. They are not even now as concerned about the health of their fame as men are, and, speaking generally, will pass a tombstone or a signpost without feeling an irresistible desire to cut their names on it, as Alf, Bert or Chas. must do in obedience to their instinct, which murmurs if it sees a fine woman go by, or even a dog, Ce chien est à moi.[9] And, of course, it may not be a dog, I thought, remembering Parliament Square, the Sieges Allee and other avenues; it may be a piece of land or a man with curly black hair. It is one of the great advantages of being a woman that one can pass even a very fine negress without wishing to make an Englishwoman of her.

That woman, then, who was born with a gift of poetry in the six- 10 teenth century, was an unhappy woman, a woman at strife against herself. All the conditions of her life, all her own instincts, were hostile to the state of mind which is needed to set free whatever is in the brain.

---

[8]**Currer Bell (1816–1855), George Eliot (1819–1880), George Sand (1804–1876)** Masculine pen names for Charlotte Brontë, Mary Ann Evans, and Amandine-Aurore-Lucille Dudevant, three major novelists of the nineteenth century.

[9]**Ce chien est à moi** That's my dog.

But what is the state of mind that is most propitious to the act of creation, I asked. Can one come by any notion of the state that furthers and makes possible that strange activity? Here I opened the volume containing the Tragedies of Shakespeare. What was Shakespeare's state of mind, for instance, when he wrote *Lear* and *Antony and Cleopatra*? It was certainly the state of mind most favorable to poetry that there has ever existed. But Shakespeare himself said nothing about it. We only know casually and by chance that he "never blotted a line." Nothing indeed was ever said by the artist himself about his state of mind until the eighteenth century perhaps. Rousseau perhaps began it. At any rate, by the nineteenth century self-consciousness had developed so far that it was the habit for men of letters to describe their minds in confessions and autobiographies. Their lives also were written, and their letters were printed after their deaths. Thus, though we do not know what Shakespeare went through when he wrote *Lear,* we do know what Carlyle went through when he wrote the *French Revolution;* what Flaubert went through when he wrote *Madame Bovary;* what Keats[10] was going through when he tried to write poetry against the coming of death and the indifference of the world.

And one gathers from this enormous modern literature of con-   11
fession and self-analysis that to write a work of genius is almost always a feat of prodigious difficulty. Everything is against the likelihood that it will come from the writer's mind whole and entire. Generally material circumstances are against it. Dogs will bark; people will interrupt; money must be made; health will break down. Further, accentuating all these difficulties and making them harder to bear is the world's notorious indifference. It does not ask people to write poems and novels and histories; it does not need them. It does not care whether Flaubert finds the right word or whether Carlyle scrupulously verifies this or that fact. Naturally, it will not pay for what it does not want. And so the writer, Keats, Flaubert, Carlyle, suffers, especially in the creative years of youth, every form of distraction and discouragement. A curse, a cry of agony, rises from those books of analysis and confession. "Mighty poets in their misery dead"—that is the burden of their song. If anything comes through in spite of all this, it is a miracle, and probably no book is born entire and uncrippled as it was conceived.

But for women, I thought, looking at the empty shelves, these   12
difficulties were infinitely more formidable. In the first place, to have a room of her own, let alone a quiet room or a sound-proof room, was out of the question, unless her parents were exceptionally

---

[10] **Thomas Carlyle (1795–1881), Gustave Flaubert (1821–1880),** and **John Keats (1795–1821)** Important nineteenth-century writers, all men.

rich or very noble, even up to the beginning of the nineteenth century. Since her pin money, which depended on the good will of her father, was only enough to keep her clothed, she was debarred from such alleviations as came even to Keats or Tennyson or Carlyle, all poor men, from a walking tour, a little journey to France, from the separate lodging which, even if it were miserable enough, sheltered them from the claims and tyrannies of their families. Such material difficulties were formidable; but much worse were the immaterial. The indifference of the world which Keats and Flaubert and other men of genius have found so hard to bear was in her case not indifference but hostility. The world did not say to her as it said to them, Write if you choose; it makes no difference to me. The world said with a guffaw, Write? What's the good of your writing? Here the psychologists of Newnham and Girton might come to our help, I thought, looking again at the blank spaces on the shelves. For surely it is time that the effect of discouragement upon the mind of the artist should be measured, as I have seen a dairy company measure the effect of ordinary milk and Grade A milk upon the body of the rat. They set two rats in cages side by side, and of the two one was furtive, timid, and small, and the other was glossy, bold, and big. Now what food do we feed women as artists upon? I asked, remembering, I suppose, that dinner of prunes and custard. To answer that question I had only to open the evening paper and to read that Lord Birkenhead is of opinion—but really I am not going to trouble to copy our Lord Birkenhead's opinion upon the writing of women. What Dean Inge says I will leave in peace. The Harley Street specialist may be allowed to rouse the echoes of Harley Street with his vociferations without raising a hair on my head. I will quote, however, Mr. Oscar Browning, because Mr. Oscar Browning was a great figure in Cambridge at one time, and used to examine the students at Girton and Newnham. Mr. Oscar Browning was wont to declare "that the impression left on his mind, after looking over any set of examination papers, was that, irrespective of the marks he might give, the best woman was intellectually the inferior of the worst man." After saying that Mr. Browning went back to his rooms—and it is this sequel that endears him and makes him a human figure of some bulk and majesty—he went back to his rooms and found a stable-boy lying on the sofa—"a mere skeleton, his cheeks were cavernous and sallow, his teeth were black, and he did not appear to have the full use of his limbs. . . . 'That's Arthur' [said Mr. Browning]. 'He's a dear boy really and most high-minded.'" The two pictures always seem to me to complete each other. And happily in this age of biography the two pictures often do complete each other, so that we are able to interpret the opinions of great men not only by what they say, but by what they do.

But though this is possible now, such opinions coming from the   13
lips of important people must have been formidable enough even
fifty years ago. Let us suppose that a father from the highest motives
did not wish his daughter to leave home and become writer, painter,
or scholar. "See what Mr. Oscar Browning says," he would say; and
there was not only Mr. Oscar Browning; there was the *Saturday
Review;* there was Mr. Greg—the "essentials of a woman's being,"
said Mr. Greg emphatically, "are that *they are supported by, and they
minister to, men*"—there was an enormous body of masculine opinion
to the effect that nothing could be expected of women intellectually.
Even if her father did not read out loud these opinions, any girl could
read them for herself; and the reading, even in the nineteenth century, must have lowered her vitality, and told profoundly upon her
work. There would always have been that assertion—you cannot do
this, you are incapable of doing that—to protest against, to overcome. Probably for a novelist this germ is no longer of much effect;
for there have been women novelists of merit. But for painters it must
still have some sting in it; and for musicians, I imagine, is even now
active and poisonous in the extreme. The woman composer stands
where the actress stood in the time of Shakespeare. Nick Greene, I
thought, remembering the story I had made about Shakespeare's sister, said that a woman acting put him in mind of a dog dancing.
Johnson repeated the phrase two hundred years later of women
preaching. And here, I said, opening a book about music, we have
the very words used again in this year of grace, 1928, of women who
try to write music. "Of Mlle. Germaine Tailleferre one can only
repeat Dr. Johnson's dictum concerning a woman preacher, transposed into terms of music. 'Sir, a woman's composing is like a dog's
walking on his hind legs. It is not done well, but you are surprised
to find it done at all.'"[11] So accurately does history repeat itself.

Thus, I concluded, shutting Mr. Oscar Browning's life and   14
pushing away the rest, it is fairly evident that even in the nineteenth
century a woman was not encouraged to be an artist. On the contrary, she was snubbed, slapped, lectured, and exhorted. Her mind
must have been strained and her vitality lowered by the need of
opposing this, of disproving that. For here again we come within
range of that very interesting and obscure masculine complex which
has had so much influence upon the woman's movement; that deep-
seated desire, not so much that *she* shall be inferior as that *he* shall
be superior, which plants him wherever one looks, not only in front
of the arts, but barring the way to politics too, even when the risk to
himself seems infinitesimal and the suppliant humble and devoted.

---

[11] *A Survey of Contemporary Music*, Cecil Gray, p. 246. [Woolf's note]

Even Lady Bessborough, I remembered, with all her passion for politics, must humbly bow herself and write to Lord Granville Leveson-Gower: ". . . notwithstanding all my violence in politics and talking so much on that subject, I perfectly agree with you that no woman has any business to meddle with that or any other serious business, farther than giving her opinion (if she is ask'd)." And so she goes on to spend her enthusiasm where it meets with no obstacle whatsoever upon that immensely important subject, Lord Granville's maiden speech in the House of Commons. The spectacle is certainly a strange one, I thought. The history of men's opposition to women's emancipation is more interesting perhaps than the story of that emancipation itself. An amusing book might be made of it if some young student at Girton or Newnham would collect examples and deduce a theory—but she would need thick gloves on her hands, and bars to protect her of solid gold.

But what is amusing now, I recollected, shutting Lady 15 Bessborough, had to be taken in desperate earnest once. Opinions that one now pastes in a book labelled cock-a-doodle-dum and keeps for reading to select audiences on summer nights once drew tears, I can assure you. Among your grandmothers and great-grandmothers there were many that wept their eyes out. Florence Nightingale shrieked aloud in her agony.[12] Moreover, it is all very well for you, who have got yourselves to college and enjoy sitting-rooms—or is it only bed-sitting-rooms?—of your own to say that genius should disregard such opinions; that genius should be above caring what is said of it. Unfortunately, it is precisely the men or women of genius who mind most what is said of them. Remember Keats. Remember the words he had cut on his tombstone.[13] Think of Tennyson; think— but I need hardly multiply instances of the undeniable, if very unfortunate, fact that it is the nature of the artist to mind excessively what is said about him. Literature is strewn with the wreckage of men who have minded beyond reason the opinions of others.

And this susceptibility of theirs is doubly unfortunate, I thought, 16 returning again to my original enquiry into what state of mind is most propitious for creative work, because the mind of an artist, in order to achieve the prodigious effort of freeing whole and entire the work that is in him, must be incandescent, like Shakespeare's mind, I conjectured, looking at the book which lay open at *Antony and Cleopatra*. There must be no obstacle in it, no foreign matter unconsumed.

---

[12] *See Cassandra* by Florence Nightingale, printed in *The Cause*, by R. Strachey. [Woolf's note]

[13] **words . . . tombstone** "Here lies one whose name is writ on water." [Woolf's note]

For though we say that we know nothing about Shakespeare's   17
state of mind, even as we say that, we are saying something about
Shakespeare's state of mind. The reason perhaps why we know so
little of Shakespeare—compared with Donne or Ben Jonson or
Milton[14]—is that his grudges and spites and antipathies are hidden
from us. We are not held up by some "revelation" which reminds us
of the writer. All desire to protest, to preach, to proclaim an injury,
to pay off a score, to make the world the witness of some hardship
or grievance was fired out of him and consumed. Therefore his
poetry flows from him free and unimpeded. If ever a human being
got his work expressed completely, it was Shakespeare. If ever a
mind was incandescent, unimpeded, I thought, turning again to the
bookcase, it was Shakespeare's mind.

----

[14]**John Donne (1572–1631), Ben Jonson (1572/3–1637), John Milton
(1608–1674)** Three of the most important seventeenth-century poets.

QUESTIONS FOR CRITICAL READING

1. How did Elizabethan gender roles limit opportunities for women in
   the literary arts?
2. Why does Woolf begin by referring to an eminent historian?
3. Why does history treat sixteenth- and seventeenth-century women
   with so little notice?
4. What is Woolf's point regarding the behavior of Oscar Browning?
5. Why does Woolf worry over the relation of opinions to facts?
6. What is the difference between the way women are represented in history and the way they are depicted in fiction?
7. Why does Woolf have Judith Shakespeare become pregnant?

SUGGESTIONS FOR CRITICAL WRITING

1. Woolf says that a woman "born with a gift of poetry in the sixteenth century, was an unhappy woman, a woman at strife against herself" (para.
   10). What does it mean for a woman to be "at strife against herself"?
   What are the characteristics of such a strife, and what are its implications
   for the woman? In what ways would she be aware of such inner strife?
2. Look up brief biographies of the women writers who took men's names.
   Woolf lists three together: Currer Bell, George Eliot, and George Sand.
   What did they have in common? Why did they feel the need to use a
   man's name for their pseudonym? What did they do to avoid being
   stigmatized as women writers? Were they equally successful? Are they
   now considered feminist writers?
3. Woolf's view is that biology determines one's fate. She is explicitly
   speaking of the biology of the female in our culture, but how much do

you feel she attends to the entire range of gender? Margaret Mead (p. 855) talks about gender deviance and its effect upon the individual in a standardized society. Woolf's society was standardized, but she belonged to a subculture of intellectuals, the Bloomsbury group, that practiced many forms of deviant gender behavior. Would she have argued as strongly in support of deviant sexual behavior as she does for equal opportunities for Shakespeare's "sister"? What would her argument be? Present your case, using some of Woolf's rhetorical techniques.

4. Read the book from which this essay comes, *A Room of One's Own*. The last chapter discusses androgyny, the quality of possessing characteristics of both sexes. Woolf argues that perhaps a writer should not be exclusively male or female in outlook, but should combine both. How effective is her argument in that chapter? How much of an impact did the book have on your own views of feminism?

5. Explain why it is so important for a woman to have "a room of one's own." Obviously, the use of the word *room* stands for much more than a simple room with four walls and a door. What is implied in the way Woolf uses this term? Do you think this point is still valid for women in the twenty-first century? Why are so many women in any age denied the right to have "a room of one's own"?

6. Woolf says that "even in the nineteenth century a woman was not encouraged to be an artist. On the contrary, she was snubbed, slapped, lectured, and exhorted. Her mind must have been strained and her vitality lowered by the need of opposing this, of disproving that" (para. 14). Explain the implications of this statement, and decide whether it still describes the situation of many or most women. Use your personal experience where relevant, but consider the situations of any women you find interesting.

7. **CONNECTIONS** In what ways are Mary Wollstonecraft (p. 799) and Woolf in agreement about the waste of women's talents in any age? As you comment on this, consider, too, the ways in which these writers differ in their approach to discussing women and the ways in which women sometimes cooperate in accepting their own restrictions. Which of these writers is more obviously a modern feminist in your mind? Which of them is more convincing? Why?

8. **CONNECTIONS** Based on Woolf's attitudes in this essay, which of the male writers in this collection comes closest to supporting feminist views? Consider especially the work of Karl Marx, Martin Luther King Jr., Henry David Thoreau, and Erich Fromm. Which of their views seems most sympathetic to the problems Woolf considers here?

9. **SEEING CONNECTIONS** Woolf says that women artists were snubbed and ignored even in the nineteenth century. How would Woolf react to seeing Cassatt's *In the Loge* (p. 796) and learning that she was accepted by an important group of mostly male painters? Do some research on Cassatt, especially on her progress as a painter and her success in selling her work. Does Woolf's generalization hold true for Cassatt? Would Woolf have felt that the woman portrayed in Cassatt's painting was "in strife with herself" as a nineteenth-century woman?

MARGARET MEAD
Sex and Temperament

MARGARET MEAD (1901–1978), a student of Ruth Benedict's, received her Ph.D. in anthropology from Columbia University in 1929. She is renowned for her extensive fieldwork in the South Pacific, especially for her work on Manus, one of the Admiralty Islands, northwest of New Guinea. The fieldwork that she did in 1925 led to her doctoral dissertation and to the book that established her as one of the most visible and readable modern anthropologists, *Coming of Age in Samoa: A Psychological Study of Primitive Youth for Western Civilization* (1928). She learned seven indigenous languages and always used them with the people she studied and lived with so that she could think in their vernacular. Her experiences with the Manus spanned twenty-five years, some of which included a disastrous world war. She first lived with them in 1928, when she began the work that led her to write *Growing Up in New Guinea: A Comparative Study of Primitive Education* (1930).

Mead was married three times, as she tells us in her autobiography, *Blackberry Winter* (1972), which focuses on her early years. All three of her husbands were also anthropologists. With Gregory Bateson, to whom she was married from 1936 to 1950, she had her only child, a daughter. Later, Mead was romantically involved with yet another anthropologist, Rhoda Metraux, with whom she lived from 1955 until her death. She taught as an adjunct professor at Columbia University from 1954 to 1978 and took two years off to found the anthropology department at Fordham University in Lincoln Center, New York. Throughout these years, she was also involved with work in museums, particularly the American Museum of Natural History.

From *Sex and Temperament in Three Primitive Societies.*

Her primary research interests were the patterns of education of the young and the patterns of socialization of women and women's sexuality, particularly early sexual development. Mead asserted that cultural mores are relative and that there are many ways of working out the details of courtship, sex, marriage, and love. She consistently argued that there is no right way, suggesting rather that there are many ways, all of which are right within an individual culture.

Like Benedict, Mead emphasizes the psychological model of cultures, although the patterns she proposes are not quite comparable to the psychotic patterns that Benedict develops in relation to American Indians of the Northwest. To the dismay of some anthropologists, Mead also emphasizes the social, traditional, and historical aspects of a culture while concerning herself less with the biological or genetic. Recent critics have faulted Mead for this emphasis and have charged her with ignoring biological determinism in her research.

Near the end of her life, Mead was the most famous anthropologist in the United States. She wrote columns for popular magazines, published more than twenty books, and lectured widely to various audiences. Mead was popular, but she was also a careful and devoted scientist. Her work in the South Pacific still stands as a major contribution to our knowledge of how different cultures deal with basic social issues.

Mead's Rhetoric

Mead has the advantage of writing clearly and with a journalist's skill, focusing on the most interesting details. "Sex and Temperament" explores society's expectations regarding temperament rather than trying to convince the reader that one or another of the points of view is accurate. As she says in her opening paragraph, she is not interested in determining if there are "actual and universal differences between the sexes." Instead, she is concerned with the range of temperaments — "dominance, bravery, aggressiveness, objectivity, malleability" (para. 6) — that human beings can have and all the other temperamental qualities individuals can possess. Then, she goes on to explore whether any specific group of temperaments is explicitly limited to one sex or the other.

She admits that, at the beginning of her study, "[she] too had been accustomed to use in [her] thinking such concepts as 'mixed type,' to think of some men as having 'feminine' temperaments, of some women as having 'masculine' minds" (para. 6). In other words, she originally felt that there was a natural disposition of temperaments that was inbuilt depending on sex. Then, with her work among other cultures, her thinking began to change. Ultimately, she realized that each culture begins shaping individuals at birth to fit the patterns that it has determined as most desirable. As she says, there are several courses of action available to a society. One is to emphasize contrasting temperaments in boys and girls. Another is to de-emphasize differences and concentrate on individual talent and natural temperament in determining occupation and behavior, a condition that Mead seems to imply is in place in her own time. However, she is worried that we may "return to a strict regimentation of women" (para. 9) in the future. Society can also "admit that men and women are capable of being molded to a single pattern as easily as to a diverse one" (para. 11).

Interestingly, Mead offers a view that may not be a counterargument so much as a personal lament. She sees in societies in which men and women dress differently, behave differently, and are given different occupations a beautiful diversity that is lost when those distinctions are lost. She is careful to point out that standard biologically relevant distinctions—the difference in male strength and male height—are rendered vastly less significant in leveling the relationship of men and women today because the law has some of the same force that strength in battle had ages ago. Mead is balanced in her view, pointing to the behavior of societies as being responsible for the shaping of male and female standard temperaments.

Two of her rhetorical techniques are comparison and example. She frequently turns to her experience in the Arapesh or Mundugumor societies. She points to an instance in which the "sacrifice of sex-differences has meant a loss in complexity to the society" (para. 13) of the Mundugumor, and by implication, she seems to say that similar results either have happened or will happen in our own culture. Her discussion of the stereotyping of women and priests as always opposed to war demonstrates that this attitude has no basis in any "natural" endowments of either group. However, in any society in which such rigid temperamental qualities are educated into either sex, there will be a considerable number of rebels. She says that the greater the standardization of temperament, the greater will be the tendency to produce rebels.

She also exhibits considerable concern for individuals in society that places great emphasis on gender-related temperaments when those individuals do not themselves have the "proper" temperaments. These are people who do not fit the mold, who are not naturally disposed to the roles that society has established for them. When society is inflexible and makes it difficult for such individuals to express themselves, they endure a lifetime of frustration. Her concern extends even to those who are victims of birth, by which she means those born into nobility or into peasantry, with temperaments opposite to those that their society demands. She uses India, with its former caste system, as a specific example.

Mead proposes an experiment in which the temperamental distinctions that our society assumes are natural to men and women were linked to eye color instead of gender. She suggests attributing gentleness, nurturance, and submissiveness to blue-eyed people and arrogance, domination, and purposiveness to brown-eyed people. Thus, these qualities would not be gender linked. Interestingly, in some grade schools similar experiments with eye color were put into place to help young people understand the effect of sanctioned distinctions on people who did not fit the requirements of the group.

Mead's final suggestion is to avoid standardizing society or removing all of society's expectations. Instead, she suggests that society might learn to tolerate and accept the natural diversity within a population of many individuals with differing temperaments, some of whom fit society's expectations and some of whom do not. In any event, she celebrates diversity and sees that societies all have different ways of establishing desired temperaments but that they must make room for people who do not easily fit into sanctioned roles.

PREREADING QUESTIONS: WHAT TO READ FOR

The following prereading questions may help you anticipate key issues in the discussion of Margaret Mead's "Sex and Temperament." Keeping them in mind during your first reading of the selection should help focus your attention.

- What does Mead mean by *temperament*?
- What is a "standardized" society?
- What alternatives are there to a standardized society?
- Do all societies regard men and women as different in temperament?

Sex and Temperament

This study is not concerned with whether there are or are not 1 actual and universal differences between the sexes, either quantitative or qualitative. It is not concerned with whether women are more variable than men, which was claimed before the doctrine of evolution exalted variability, or less variable, which was claimed afterwards. It is not a treatise on the rights of women, nor an inquiry into the basis of feminism. It is, very simply, an account of how three primitive societies have grouped their social attitudes towards temperament about the very obvious facts of sex-difference. I studied this problem in simple societies because here we have the drama of civilization writ small, a social microcosm alike in kind, but different in size and magnitude, from the complex social structures of peoples who, like our own, depend upon a written tradition and upon the integration of a great number of conflicting historical traditions. Among the gentle mountain-dwelling Arapesh, the fierce cannibalistic Mundugumor, and the graceful head-hunters of Tchambuli, I studied this question. Each of these tribes had, as has every human society, the point of sex-difference to use as one theme in the plot of social life, and each of these three peoples has developed that theme differently. In comparing the way in which they have dramatized sex-difference, it is possible to gain a greater insight into what elements are social constructs, originally irrelevant to the biological facts of sex-gender.

Our own society makes great use of this plot. It assigns different 2 roles to the two sexes, surrounds them from birth with an expectation of different behavior, plays out the whole drama of courtship, marriage, and parenthood in terms of types of behavior believed to be innate and therefore appropriate for one sex or for the other. We know dimly that these roles have changed even within our history. Studies like Mrs. Putnam's *The Lady*[1] depict woman as an infinitely malleable lay figure upon which mankind has draped ever varying period-costumes, in keeping with which she wilted or waxed imperious, flirted or fled. But all discussions have emphasized not the relative social personalities assigned to the two sexes, but rather the superficial behavior-patterns assigned to women, often not even to all women, but only to women of the upper class. A sophisticated recognition that upper-class women were puppets of a changing tradition blurred rather than clarified the issue. It left untouched the roles assigned to men, who were conceived as proceeding along a special masculine road, shaping women to their fads and whims in womanliness. All discussion of the position of women, of the character and temperament of women, the enslavement or the emancipation of women, obscures the basic issue — the recognition that the cultural plot behind human relations is the way in which the roles of the two

---

[1] *The Lady: Studies of Certain Phases of Her History* Book by Emily James Putnam (1865–1944), the first woman dean of Barnard College, in New York City.

sexes are conceived, and that the growing boy is shaped to a local and special emphasis as inexorably as is the growing girl. . . .

. . . We know that human cultures do not all fall into one side or 3 the other of a single scale and that it is possible for one society to ignore completely an issue which two other societies have solved in contrasting ways. Because a people honor the old may mean that they hold children in slight esteem, but a people may also, like the Ba Thonga of South Africa, honor neither old people nor children; or, like the Plains Indians, dignify the little child and the grandfather; or, again, like the Manus and parts of modern America, regard children as the most important group in society. In expecting simple reversals—that if an aspect of social life is not specifically sacred, it must be specifically secular; that if men are strong, women must be weak—we ignore the fact that cultures exercise far greater license than this in selecting the possible aspects of human life which they will minimize, overemphasize, or ignore. And while every culture has in some way institutionalized the roles of men and women, it has not necessarily been in terms of contrast between the prescribed personalities of the two sexes, nor in terms of dominance or submission. With the paucity of material for elaboration, no culture has failed to seize upon the conspicuous facts of age and sex in some way, whether it be the convention of one Philippine tribe that no man can keep a secret, the Manus assumption that only men enjoy playing with babies, the Toda prescription of almost all domestic work as too sacred for women, or the Arapesh insistence that women's heads are stronger than men's. In the division of labor, in dress, in manners, in social and religious functioning—sometimes in only a few of these respects, sometimes in all—men and women are socially differentiated, and each sex, as a sex, forced to conform to the role assigned to it. In some societies, these socially defined roles are mainly expressed in dress or occupation, with no insistence upon innate temperamental differences. Women wear long hair and men wear short hair, or men wear curls and women shave their heads; women wear skirts and men wear trousers, or women wear trousers, and men wear skirts. Women weave and men do not, or men weave and women do not. Such simple tie-ups as these between dress and occupation and sex are easily taught to every child and make no assumptions to which a given child cannot easily conform.

It is otherwise in societies that sharply differentiate the behavior 4 of men and of women in terms which assume a genuine difference in temperament. Among the Dakota Indians of the Plains, the importance of an ability to stand any degree of danger or hardship was frantically insisted upon as a masculine characteristic. From the time that a boy was five or six, all the conscious educational effort of the household was bent towards shaping him into an indubitable male. Every tear, every timidity, every clinging to a protective hand or desire to continue to play with younger children or with girls, was obsessively interpreted as proof that he was not going to develop into a real man. In such a society it is not surprising to find the *berdache*,[2] the man who had voluntarily given up the struggle to conform to the masculine role and who wore female attire and followed the occupations of a woman. The institution of the *berdache* in turn served as a warning to every father; the fear that the son might become a *berdache* informed the parental efforts with an extra desperation, and the very pressure which helped to drive a boy to that choice was redoubled. The invert who lacks any discernible physical basis for his inversion has long puzzled students of sex, who when they can find no observable glandular abnormality turn to theories of early conditioning or identification with a parent of opposite sex. In the course of this investigation, we shall have occasion to examine the "masculine" woman and the "feminine" man as they occur in these different tribes, to inquire whether it is always a woman of dominating nature who is conceived as masculine, or a man who is gentle, submissive, or fond of children or embroidery who is conceived as feminine.

. . . [W]e shall be concerned with the patterning of sex-behavior 5 from the standpoint of temperament, with the cultural assumptions that certain temperamental attitudes are "naturally" masculine and others "naturally" feminine. In this matter, primitive people seem to be, on the surface, more sophisticated than we are. Just as they know that the gods, the food habits, and the marriage customs of the next tribe differ from those of their own people, and do not insist that one form is true or natural while the other is false or unnatural, so they often know that the temperamental proclivities which they regard as natural for men or for women differ from the natural temperaments of the men and women among their neighbors. Nevertheless, within a narrower range and with less of a claim for the biological or divine validity of their social forms than we often advance, each tribe has certain definite attitudes towards temperament, a theory of what human beings, either men or women or both, are naturally like, a norm in terms of which to judge and condemn those individuals who deviate from it.

Two of these tribes have no idea that men and women are dif- 6 ferent in temperament. They allow them different economic and

---

[2] **berdache** American Indian term for a man who dresses as a woman and does a woman's work.

religious roles, different skills, different vulnerabilities to evil magic and supernatural influences. The Arapesh believe that painting in color is appropriate only to men, and the Mundugumor consider fishing an essentially feminine task. But any idea that temperamental traits of the order of dominance, bravery, aggressiveness, objectivity, malleability, are inalienably associated with one sex (as opposed to the other) is entirely lacking. This may seem strange to a civilization which in its sociology, its medicine, its slang, its poetry, and its obscenity accepts the socially defined differences between the sexes as having an innate basis in temperament and explains any deviation from the socially determined role as abnormality of native endowment or early maturation. It came as a surprise to me because I too had been accustomed to use in my thinking such concepts as "mixed type," to think of some men as having "feminine" temperaments, of some women as having "masculine" minds. I set as my problem a study of the conditioning of the social personalities of the two sexes, in the hope that such an investigation would throw some light upon sex-differences. I shared the general belief of our society that there was a natural sex-temperament which could at the most only be distorted or diverted from normal expression. I was innocent of any suspicion that the temperaments which we regard as native to one sex might instead be mere variations of human temperament, to which the members of either or both sexes may, with more or less success in the case of different individuals, be educated to approximate.

· · ·

The knowledge that the personalities of the two sexes are socially produced is congenial to every program that looks forward towards a planned order of society. It is a two-edged sword that can be used to hew a more flexible, more varied society than the human race has ever built, or merely to cut a narrow path down which one sex or both sexes will be forced to march, regimented, looking neither to the right nor to the left. . . . 7

There are at least three courses open to a society that has realized the extent to which male and female personality are socially produced. Two of these courses have been tried before, over and over again, at different times in the long, irregular, repetitious history of the race. The first is to standardize the personality of men and women as clearly contrasting, complementary, and antithetical, and to make every institution in the society congruent with this standardization. If the society declared that woman's sole function was motherhood and the teaching and care of young children, it 8 could so arrange matters that every woman who was not physiologically debarred should become a mother and be supported in the exercise of this function. It could abolish the discrepancy between the doctrine that women's place is the home and the number of homes that were offered to them. It could abolish the discrepancy between training women for marriage and then forcing them to become the spinster supports of their parents.

Such a system would be wasteful of the gifts of many women   9
who could exercise other functions far better than their ability to bear children in an already overpopulated world. It would be wasteful of the gifts of many men who could exercise their special personality gifts far better in the home than in the market-place. It would be wasteful, but it would be clear. It could attempt to guarantee to each individual the role for which society insisted upon training him or her, and such a system would penalize only those individuals who, in spite of all the training, did not display the approved personalities. There are millions of persons who would gladly return to such a standardized method of treating the relationship between the sexes, and we must bear in mind the possibility that the greater opportunities open in the twentieth century to women may be quite withdrawn, and that we may return to a strict regimentation of women.

The waste, if this occurs, will be not only of many women, but   10
also of as many men, because regimentation of one sex carries with it, to greater or less degree, the regimentation of the other also. Every parental behest that defines a way of sitting, a response to a rebuke or a threat, a game, or an attempt to draw or sing or dance or paint, as feminine, is molding the personality of each little girl's brother as well as molding the personality of the sister. There can be no society which insists that women follow one special personality-pattern, defined as feminine, which does not do violence also to the individuality of many men.

Alternatively, society can take the course that has become espe-   11
cially associated with the plans of most radical groups: admit that men and women are capable of being molded to a single pattern as easily as to a diverse one, and cease to make any distinction in the approved personality of both sexes. Girls can be trained exactly as boys are trained, taught the same code, the same forms of expression, the same occupations. This course might seem to be the logic which follows from the conviction that the potentialities which different societies label as either masculine or feminine are really potentialities of some members of each sex, and not sex-linked at all. If this is accepted, is it not reasonable to abandon the kind of artificial standardizations of sex-differences that have been so long characteristic of European society, and admit that they are social fictions for which

we have no longer any use? In the world today, contraceptives make it possible for women not to bear children against their will. The most conspicuous actual difference between the sexes, the difference in strength, is progressively less significant. Just as the difference in height between males is no longer a realistic issue, now that lawsuits have been substituted for hand-to-hand encounters, so the difference in strength between men and women is no longer worth elaboration in cultural institutions.

In evaluating such a program as this, however, it is necessary to   12
keep in mind the nature of the gains that society has achieved in its most complex forms. A sacrifice of distinctions in sex-personality may mean a sacrifice in complexity. The Arapesh recognize a minimum of distinction in personality between old and young, between men and women, and they lack categories of rank or status. We have seen that such a society at the best condemns to personal frustration, and at the worst to maladjustment, all of those men and women who do not conform to its simple emphases. The violent person among the Arapesh cannot find, either in the literature, or in the art, or in the ceremonial, or in the history of his people, any expression of the internal drives that are shattering his peace of mind. Nor is the loser only the individual whose own type of personality is nowhere recognized in his society. The imaginative, highly intelligent person who is essentially in tune with the values of his society may also suffer by the lack of range and depth characteristic of too great simplicity. The active mind and intensity of one Arapesh boy whom I knew well was unsatisfied by the laissez-faire solutions, the lack of drama in his culture. Searching for some material upon which to exercise his imagination, his longing for a life in which stronger emotions would be possible, he could find nothing with which to feed his imagination but tales of the passionate outbursts of the maladjusted, outbursts characterized by a violent hostility to others that he himself lacked.

Nor is it the individual alone who suffers. Society is equally the   13
loser, and we have seen such an attenuation in the dramatic representations of the Mundugumor. By phrasing the exclusion of women as a protective measure congenial to both sexes, the Arapesh kept their *tamberan*[3] cult, with the necessary audiences of women. But the Mundugumor developed a kind of personality for both men and women to which exclusion from any part of life was interpreted as a deadly insult. And as more and more Mundugumor women have demanded and been given the right of initiation, it is not surprising

---

[3] *tamberan* A noise-making device such as a bull-horn used by the Arapesh in rituals that assert male solidarity and masculinity.

that the Mundugumor ceremonial life has dwindled, the actors have lost their audience, and one vivid artistic element in the life of the Mundugumor community is vanishing. The sacrifice of sex-differences has meant a loss in complexity to the society.

So in our own society. To insist that there are no sex-differences in a society that has always believed in them and depended upon them may be as subtle a form of standardizing personality as to insist that there are many sex-differences. This is particularly so in a changing tradition, when a group in control is attempting to develop a new social personality, as is the case today in many European countries. Take, for instance, the current assumption that women are more opposed to war than men, that any outspoken approval of war is more horrible, more revolting, in women than in men. Behind this assumption women can work for peace without encountering social criticism in communities that would immediately criticize their brothers or husbands if they took a similarly active part in peace propaganda. This belief that women are naturally more interested in peace is undoubtedly artificial, part of the whole mythology that considers women to be gentler than men. But in contrast let us consider the possibility of a powerful minority that wished to turn a whole society whole-heartedly towards war. One way of doing this would be to insist that women's motives, women's interests, were identical with men's, that women should take as bloodthirsty a delight in preparing for war as ever men do. The insistence upon the opposite point of view, that the woman as a mother prevails over the woman as a citizen at least puts a slight drag upon agitation for war, prevents a blanket enthusiasm for war from being thrust upon the entire younger generation. The same kind of result follows if the clergy are professionally committed to a belief in peace. The relative bellicosity of different individual clerics may be either offended or gratified by the prescribed pacific role, but a certain protest, a certain dissenting note, will be sounded in society. The dangerous standardization of attitudes that disallows every type of deviation is greatly reinforced if neither age nor sex nor religious belief is regarded as automatically predisposing certain individuals to hold minority attitudes. The removal of all legal and economic barriers against women's participating in the world on an equal footing with men may be in itself a standardizing move towards the wholesale stamping-out of the diversity of attitudes that is such a dearly bought product of civilization.

Such a standardized society, in which men, women, children, priests, and soldiers were all trained to an undifferentiated and coherent set of values, must of necessity create the kind of deviant that we found among the Arapesh and the Mundugumor, the individual who, regardless of sex or occupation, rebels because he is temperamentally unable to accept the one-sided emphasis of his culture. The individuals who were specifically unadjusted in terms of their psycho-sexual role would, it is true, vanish, but with them would vanish the knowledge that there is more than one set of possible values.

To the extent that abolishing the differences in the approved personalities of men and women means abolishing any expression of the type of personality once called exclusively feminine, or once called exclusively masculine, such a course involves a social loss. Just as a festive occasion is the gayer and more charming if the two sexes are dressed differently, so it is in less material matters. If the clothing is in itself a symbol, and a woman's shawl corresponds to a recognized softness in her character, the whole plot of personal relations is made more elaborate, and in many ways more rewarding. The poet of such a society will praise virtues, albeit feminine virtues, which might never have any part in a social Utopia that allowed no differences between the personalities of men and women. 16

To the extent that a society insists upon different kinds of personality so that one age-group or class or sex-group may follow purposes disallowed or neglected in another, each individual participant in that society is the richer. The arbitrary assignment of set clothing, set manners, set social responses, to individuals born in a certain class, of a certain sex, or of a certain color, to those born on a certain day of the week, to those born with a certain complexion, does violence to the individual endowment of individuals, but permits the building of a rich culture. The most extreme development of a society that has attained great complexity at the expense of the individual is historical India, based, as it was, upon the uncompromising association of a thousand attributes of behavior, attitude, and occupation with an accident of birth. To each individual there was given the security, although it might be the security of despair, of a set role, and the reward of being born into a highly complex society. 17

Furthermore, when we consider the position of the deviant individual in historical cultures, those who are born into a complex society in the wrong sex or class for their personalities to have full sway are in a better position than those who are born into a simple society which does not use in any way their special temperamental gifts. The violent women in a society that permits violence to men only, the strongly emotional member of an aristocracy in a culture that permits downright emotional expression only in the peasantry, the ritualistically inclined individual who is bred a Protestant in a country which has also Catholic institutions—each one of these can find expressed in some other group in the society the emotions that he or she is forbidden to manifest. He is given a certain kind of support by the mere 18 existence of these values, values so congenial to him and so inaccessible because of an accident of birth. For those who are content with a vicarious spectator-role, or with materials upon which to feast the creative imagination, this may be almost enough. They may be content to experience from the sidewalks during a parade, from the audience of a theatre or from the nave of a church, those emotions the direct expression of which is denied to them. The crude compensations offered by the moving pictures to those whose lives are emotionally starved are offered in subtler forms by the art and literature of a complex society to the individual who is out of place in his sex or his class or his occupational group.

Sex-adjustments, however, are not a matter of spectatorship, but   19
a situation in which the most passive individual must play some part if he or she is to participate fully in life. And while we may recognize the virtues of complexity, the interesting and charming plots that cultures can evolve upon the basis of accidents of birth, we may well ask: Is not the price too high? Could not the beauty that lies in contrast and complexity be obtained in some other way? If the social insistence upon different personalities for the two sexes results in so much confusion, so many unhappy deviants, so much disorientation, can we imagine a society that abandons these distinctions without abandoning the values that are at present dependent upon them?

Let us suppose that, instead of the classification laid down on   20
the "natural" bases of sex and race, a society had classified personality on the basis of eye-color. It had decreed that all blue-eyed people were gentle, submissive, and responsive to the needs of others, and all brown-eyed people were arrogant, dominating, self-centered, and purposive. In this case two complementary social themes would be woven together—the culture, in its art, its religion, its formal personal relations, would have two threads instead of one. There would be blue-eyed men, and blue-eyed women, which would mean that there were gentle, "maternal" women, and gentle, "maternal" men. A blue-eyed man might marry a woman who had been bred to the same personality as himself, or a brown-eyed woman who had been bred to the contrasting personality. One of the strong tendencies that makes for homosexuality, the tendency to love the similar rather than the antithetical persons, would be eliminated. Hostility between the two sexes as groups would be minimized, since the individual interests of members of each sex could be woven together in different ways, and marriages of similarity and friendships of contrast need carry no necessary handicap of possible psycho-sexual maladjustment. The individual would still suffer a mutilation of his temperamental preferences, for it would be the unrelated fact of eye-color that would determine the attitudes which he was educated to

show. Every blue-eyed person would be forced into submissiveness and declared maladjusted if he or she showed any traits that it had been decided were only appropriate to the brown-eyed. The greatest social loss, however, in the classification of personality on the basis of sex would not be present in this society which based its classification on eye-color. Human relations, and especially those which involve sex, would not be artificially distorted.

But such a course, the substitution of eye-color for sex as a basis   21 upon which to educate children into groups showing contrasting personalities, while it would be a definite advance upon a classification by sex, remains a parody of all the attempts that society has made through history to define an individual's role in terms of sex, or color, or date of birth, or shape of head.

However, the only solution of the problem does not lie between   22 an acceptance of standardization of sex-differences with the resulting cost in individual happiness and adjustment, and the abolition of these differences with the consequent loss in social values. A civilization might take its cues not from such categories as age or sex, race or hereditary position in a family line, but instead of specializing personality along such simple lines recognize, train, and make a place for many and divergent temperamental endowments. It might build upon the different potentialities that it now attempts to extirpate artificially in some children and create artificially in others.

Historically the lessening of rigidity in the classification of the   23 sexes has come about at different times, either by the creation of a new artificial category, or by the recognition of real individual differences. Sometimes the idea of social position has transcended sex-categories. In a society that recognizes gradations in wealth or rank, women of rank or women of wealth have been permitted an arrogance which was denied to both sexes among the lowly or the poor. Such a shift as this has been, it is true, a step towards the emancipation of women, but it has never been a step towards the greater freedom of the individual. A few women have shared the upper-class personality, but to balance this a great many men as well as women have been condemned to a personality characterized by subservience and fear. Such shifts as these mean only the substitution of one arbitrary standard for another. A society is equally unrealistic whether it insists that only men can be brave, or that only individuals of rank can be brave.

To break down one line of division, that between the sexes, and   24 substitute another, that between classes, is no real advance. It merely shifts the irrelevancy to a different point. And meanwhile, individuals born in the upper classes are shaped inexorably to one type of personality, to an arrogance that is again uncongenial to at least some of them, while the arrogant among the poor fret and fume beneath their training for submissiveness. At one end of the scale is the mild, unaggressive young son of wealthy parents who is forced to lead, at the other the aggressive, enterprising child of the slums who is condemned to a place in the ranks. If our aim is greater expression for each individual temperament, rather than any partisan interest in one sex or its fate, we must see these historical developments which have aided in freeing some women as nevertheless a kind of development that also involved major social losses.

The second way in which categories of sex-differences have   25
become less rigid is through a recognition of genuine individual gifts as they occurred in either sex. Here a real distinction has been substituted for an artificial one, and the gains are tremendous for society and for the individual. Where writing is accepted as a profession that may be pursued by either sex with perfect suitability, individuals who have the ability to write need not be debarred from it by their sex, nor need they, if they do write, doubt their essential masculinity or femininity. An occupation that has no basis in sex-determined gifts can now recruit its ranks from twice as many potential artists. And it is here that we can find a ground-plan for building a society that would substitute real differences for arbitrary ones. We must recognize that beneath the superficial classifications of sex and race the same potentialities exist, recurring generation after generation, only to perish because society has no place for them. Just as society now permits the practice of an art to members of either sex, so it might also permit the development of many contrasting temperamental gifts in each sex. It might abandon its various attempts to make boys fight and to make girls remain passive, or to make all children fight, and instead shape our educational institutions to develop to the full the boy who shows a capacity for maternal behavior, the girl who shows an opposite capacity that is stimulated by fighting against obstacles. No skill, no special aptitude, no vividness of imagination or precision of thinking would go unrecognized because the child who possessed it was of one sex rather than the other. No child would be relentlessly shaped to one pattern of behavior, but instead there should be many patterns, in a world that had learned to allow to each individual the pattern which was most congenial to his gifts.

Such a civilization would not sacrifice the gains of thousands of   26
years during which society has built up standards of diversity. The social gains would be conserved, and each child would be encouraged on the basis of his actual temperament. Where we now have patterns of behavior for women and patterns of behavior for men, we would then have patterns of behavior that expressed the interests

of individuals with many kinds of endowment. There would be ethical codes and social symbolisms, an art and a way of life, congenial to each endowment.

Historically our own culture has relied for the creation of rich   27 and contrasting values upon many artificial distinctions, the most striking of which is sex. It will not be by the mere abolition of these distinctions that society will develop patterns in which individual gifts are given place instead of being forced into an ill-fitting mold. If we are to achieve a richer culture, rich in contrasting values, we must recognize the whole gamut of human potentialities, and so weave a less arbitrary social fabric, one in which each diverse human gift will find a fitting place.

QUESTIONS FOR CRITICAL READING

1. What temperament traits do you have? Are they gender linked?
2. What problems face a society that has established rigid gender-linked expectations?
3. How are gender-linked temperament expectations reinforced by society?
4. How much of a range of difference in gender expectation has Mead found in other cultures?
5. Does our society expect different behavior from men than from women? Are those differences visible in daily behavior?
6. Is it possible for a society to mold similar behavior in men and women?
7. Why does Mead give us all the examples she does from other societies? Do you find them convincing?
8. What problems do people with the "wrong" temperaments face in a society?
9. Do you think gender-linked temperaments are biological and natural? Why or why not?

SUGGESTIONS FOR CRITICAL WRITING

1. Mead contends that gender-linked temperaments exist because a society has promoted and reinforced those distinctions. She suggests that gender-linked distinctions are not specifically biological. In a brief essay, summarize the key points of her argument and then, using your own observations and experiences, argue a case that either defends or attacks her position.
2. Which of the societies Mead refers to seems to have the best solution to dealing with what appear to be gender-linked temperaments? If possible, research that society and clarify the nature of its treatment of men and women. How does it treat men who seem "feminine" and women who seem "masculine" in temperament?

3. As best you can tell from this selection, what would Mead's ideal society be like in regard to the question of individual temperaments? Examine the passages in which she makes statements that you feel express her views and respond to them with your own analysis. Would her society satisfy the needs of our modern culture? Would it benefit a great many people, or would it benefit only the few? Is it a society in which you would be comfortable?

4. Drawing on your own experience, explain what you have observed about the way people you know treat "masculine women" and "feminine men." What has the culture done to those who mistreat such individuals? How do the individuals react? What price do they pay for the fact that their temperaments do not fit in with societal expectations? What price does the entire society pay for insisting on rigid patterns of behavior?

5. In paragraph 12, Mead begins an exploration of societies that erase sex differences between men and women. After describing those societies and the results of their decisions, Mead seems to be rethinking her position. She says, "The sacrifice of sex-differences has meant a loss in complexity to the society" (para. 13). Would our society lose complexity if sex differences were somehow erased? Or would the level of complexity remain the same or even increase?

6. **CONNECTIONS** To what extent does John Stuart Mill in his essay "The Subjection of Women" (p. 815) agree with or differ from Mead's concerns about gender-linked temperaments? What would he say to her suggestion that society could mold boys and girls to value whatever traits it chose? Would Mill have regarded a society that standardized temperament distinctions as representing a "tyranny of the majority"? How close are Mill's and Mead's thinking?

7. **SEEING CONNECTIONS** Would Mead feel that the figures in Cassatt's *In the Loge* (p. 796) were acting out in typical gender-linked fashion? Or would she have seen a shift from the expectations of Cassatt's time? What role do you think Cassatt's society would have expected of the woman in the painting? In what ways has that figure accepted that role? In what ways has she rejected it? Do you think she would be comfortable in our society? How might Mead interpret the principal female figure?

CLAUDE LÉVI-STRAUSS
Men, Women, and Chiefs

CLAUDE LÉVI-STRAUSS (b. 1908) was born in Brussels, Belgium, and studied philosophy and law at the Sorbonne in Paris. He graduated in 1932 and began to redirect his attentions toward anthropology. In 1935, he accepted a post in Brazil as a professor at the University of São Paolo. While there he visited the interior of the rain forest to study a number of indigenous groups; much of his research and writing is based on observations made during these stays, which lasted about two years. In contrast to Margaret Mead and Ruth Benedict, Lévi-Strauss did not especially like fieldwork and took care to do as little as possible. Nonetheless, his observations were keen, and his conclusions have inspired a generation of anthropologists.

"Men, Women, and Chiefs" comes from *Tristes Tropiques* (1955), which was later translated as *A World on the Wane* (1961). The book was the result of approximately two years of field studies among the Bororo, the Nambikwara, and the Tupi people in central Brazil. A highly personal work that has been described as both travel book and autobiography, it was originally conceived as a novel, but Lévi-Strauss decided to write it as nonfiction. The distinguished American essayist Susan Sontag described the book as "one of the great books of our century . . . rigorous, subtle, and bold in thought"; and Clifford Geertz, perhaps the most influential American anthropologist of his time, commented that it was "the best book ever written by an anthropologist." Essentially, it is a book about the way the mind works in which Lévi-Strauss permits his mind to explore numerous avenues of interest.

Among Lévi-Strauss's contributions to modern thought is his development of the concept of structuralism, which, although not

From *Tristes Tropiques*. Translated by John Russell.

easily summarized, is illustrated by his search for patterns of mind that represent basic, repeatable structures. The essence of his anthropological thinking concerns the patterns and combinations of human actions that may express themselves in a bewildering number of forms but which, when analyzed in depth, can be recognized as manifestations of basic structures that repeat themselves across cultures. Some of his work following *Structural Anthropology* (2 vols., 1958–1973) has developed these principles. For example, *The Raw and the Cooked* and *The Origin of Table Manners* (1964–1981), part of a multivolume project titled—in English—*Introduction to the Science of Mythology,* examine the basic structures of cooking and serving food.

"Men, Women, and Chiefs" alludes often to the work of Jean-Jacques Rousseau, whose theories of the social contract seemed to Lévi-Strauss to provide a model for the power structure of the society of the Nambikwara, the Brazilian tribe now living in the Amazon on protected lands. The Nambikwara were encountered first in 1770, but no extensive contact with European Brazilians took place until the early twentieth century, when telegraph lines were strung up near them. In 1907, the number of Nambikwara was estimated at close to ten thousand. By 1930, smallpox and measles had killed all but five hundred. In his discussion of their culture, dating from the late 1930s, Lévi-Strauss takes into account the effect of this loss on them, although he does not mention that in this selection.

Lévi-Strauss's Rhetoric

The general method Lévi-Strauss employs in his writing is posing a question—often not expressed directly, but implied. In the case of this selection, he seems to be asking several questions. One has to do with the origin and nature of power, a question that he sees as relevant to understanding the societal structure of the Nambikwara. He also sees this question as fundamental to most societies, which is why he quotes Rousseau and finds that *The Social Contract,* which made Rousseau famous, seems to be as much at work in the society of the Nambikwara as it is in the society of modern Brazil or France. Lévi-Strauss also asked an unstated question concerning the relationship between modern industrial societies and the most primitive and "simple" society that he could find to study. He never questions the term *primitive,* although today's anthropologists are not quick to use the term, since all societies that have survived into our time must be regarded as fully formed. Yet Lévi-Strauss's aim was to try to see what societies were like before what could be considered as the modern age. Did they share a similar structure socially and politically?

Another question concerns the basis of power in primitive society. He realizes that the chief has a great deal of power, even though he may live in the same way as the rest of his tribe. But he also has enormous responsibilities that—unlike the rest of the Nambikwara men, who do nothing unless directed by the chief—he must bear almost totally alone. Like Rousseau, Lévi-Strauss realizes that the stability of the immediate society depends on the consent of the governed. Power, Lévi-Strauss says, depends first on consent. Without it there can be no powerful chief. But in accord with the power the group gives over to the chief, the chief must himself act generously, conferring gifts on those most deserving in the group.

One difficult question without a ready answer is why anyone would want to be chief of the society Lévi-Strauss describes. Considering the attendant burdens, it is not a surprise that many men whom a departing chief may appoint simply turn down the job. One of the only visible distinctions that the chief has in the community is polygamy, the choice of several wives younger than his primary wife. Lévi-Strauss is not sure such a privilege is enough to reward a chief, but his description of the outright erotic playfulness of the chief and his youthful wives suggests that it may have powerful appeal. The result of the chief's selection of marriageable young women is that there are a number of men who cannot marry until late in life. Homosexual behavior, which is conventional among the Nambikwara, is one of the results of this practice.

Lévi-Strauss discusses the responsibilities of the chief: he must have good knowledge of the terrain; skill at finding food; the ability to negotiate with neighboring tribes; and the wisdom to decide exactly how far the group will travel, when it will rest, and when it will move. The chief makes all crucial decisions for the entire group, while the rest of the men do little or nothing until he directs their action. Lévi-Strauss uses comparison in describing the other men as indigent, which may be translated as lazy or perhaps uninvolved. They rely totally on the chief for direction in life.

Generosity and reciprocity are also key to the maintenance of power. Bestowing gifts, however small, on others is one way the chief has of keeping power. This compares to the behavior of powerful politicians in the industrialized world, which is one reason Lévi-Strauss emphasizes the point. The behavior of the Nambikwara resembles similar structural patterns of behavior in modern societies.

The role of the chief's first wife in Nambikwara society is what Lévi-Strauss calls "the normal role of the wife . . . in that she does the work usually attributed to her sex, looks after the children, does the cooking, and goes out to collect such food as she can" (para. 9). But the younger wives—who are described as "[b]oyish in appearance"—do not "obey the rules of the division of labor between the sexes, but do the work of either men or women" (para. 9). It is difficult from the selection to know whether when Lévi-Strauss talks about the normal roles of men and women he refers to the norm of the Nambikwara or the norm of his own society. It may be that he sees Nambikwara sex roles as a structural pattern replicated in 1950s industrialized nations.

Lévi-Strauss has a gift for narrative, although he does not rely on stories in this piece. Instead, he gives several examples of behavior that he witnessed, and once clarifying them in relation to the group, he offers occasional analysis. For instance, at the end of the selection, he meditates on why chiefs are chiefs, especially in a society that is as uncompetitive as the Nambikwara. Ultimately, Lévi-Strauss decides that maybe it is just a simple fact of psychology. Some people are born with an urge to lead, while others are not. As he says, "there are, in every group of human beings, men who, unlike their companions, love importance for its own sake" (para. 20).

PREREADING QUESTIONS: WHAT TO READ FOR

The following prereading questions may help you anticipate key issues in the discussion of Claude Lévi-Strauss's "Men, Women, and Chiefs." Keeping them in mind during your first reading of the selection should help focus your attention.

- What is the role of the chief?
- What are the two requisites of power?
- How do the Nambikwara practice polygamy?
- What forms of work do the women do in this society?

Men, Women, and Chiefs

The exceptional qualities manifested by both these chiefs   1
derived from the manner of their designation—for political power
is not hereditary among the Nambikwara. When a chief grows old,

falls ill, or feels that he can no longer shoulder his heavy burdens, he himself chooses his successor: "That one shall be chief . . ." But this autocracy is more apparent than real. We shall see later on how slender is the chief's authority; and in this matter, as in others, the final decision would seem to be preceded by an appeal to public opinion, so that the heir finally appointed is the man most acceptable to the majority. But the choice of the new chief is not dictated entirely by the wishes or preferences of the group; the leader-designate must be willing to take on the job and, not uncommonly, he answers with a violent: "No, I don't want to be chief!" A second choice must then be made. There does not, in fact, seem to be any great competition for power, and the chiefs whom I knew were more likely to complain of their heavy burdens and manifold responsibilities than to talk with pride of the chief's lofty position. What, in fact, are the chief's privileges, and what are his obligations?

Around the year 1560 Montaigne[1] met, in Rouen, three Brazilian Indians who had been brought back by some early navigator. What, he asked one of them, were the privileges of a chief ("king" was what he said) in their country? The Indian, himself a chief, said: "He's the first man to march off to war." Montaigne tells this story in his *Essays* and marvels at the proud definition. It was a matter, for me, of intense astonishment and admiration that I received the same reply, nearly four centuries later. The civilized countries do not show anything like the same constancy in their political philosophy! Striking as it is, the formula is not so fraught with meaning as the choice of the word for "chief" in Nambikwara language. *Uilikandé* seems to mean "the one who unites" or "the one who binds together," and it suggests that the Indian mentality is aware of the phenomenon which I have already underlined: that the chief is rather the cause of the group's wish to constitute itself as a group, than the effect of the need, felt by an already-existing group, for a central authority.

Personal prestige and the ability to inspire confidence are the foundations of power in Nambikwara society. Both are indispensable to the man who will be their guide in the adventurous, nomadic life of the dry season. For six or seven months the chief will be entirely responsible for the leadership of his band. He it is who organizes their departure, chooses their itinerary, and decrees where and for how long they will stop. He decides on the expeditions—hunting, fishing, collecting, scavenging—and he deals with relations with neighbor-bands. When the chief of a band is also the chief of a village

---

[1]**Michel Eyquem de Montaigne (1533–1592)** French Renaissance writer and author of *Essays* (1580).

(by this I mean a semi-permanent installation for use during the rainy season) his obligations go further. He determines the time and the place for the sedentary life. He supervises the gardens and says what crops are to be planted. More generally, he adapts his band's activities to the needs and possibilities of the season.

Where these manifold functions are concerned it should be said   4 at once that the chief cannot seek support either in clearly defined powers or in a publicly recognized authority. Consent lies at the origins of power, and consent also confers upon power its legitimacy. Bad conduct (from the Indians' point of view, needless to say) or marks of ill will on the part of one or two malcontents may throw the chief's whole program out of joint and threaten the well-being of his little community. Should this happen, the chief has no powers of coercion. He can disembarrass himself of undesirable elements only in so far as all the others are of the same mind as himself. And so he needs to be clever: and his cleverness is not so much that of an all-powerful sovereign as that of a politician struggling to maintain an uncertain majority. Nor does it suffice for him merely to keep his group together. They may live in virtual isolation during the nomadic season, but they never forget that neighbor-groups are not far away. The chief must not merely do well: he must try, and his group will expect him to try, to do better than the others.

How does the chief fulfill his obligations? The first and the main   5 instrument of his power is his generosity. Generosity is among most primitive peoples, and above all in America, an essential attribute of power. It has a role to play even in those elementary cultures where the notion of property consists merely in a handful of rudely fashioned objects. Although the chief does not seem to be in a privileged position, from the material point of view, he must have under his control surplus quantities of food, tools, weapons, and ornaments which, however trifling in themselves, are none the less considerable in relation to the prevailing poverty. When an individual, a family, or the band as a whole, wishes or needs something, it is to the chief that an appeal must be made. Generosity is, therefore, the first attribute to be expected of a new chief. It is a note which will be struck almost continuously; and from the nature, discordant or otherwise, of the sound which results the chief can judge of his standing with the band. His "subjects" make the most of all this: of that there can be no doubt. The chiefs were my best informers; and as I knew the difficulties of their position I liked to reward them liberally. Rarely, however, did any of my presents remain in their hands for more than a day or two. And when I moved on, after sharing for several weeks the life of any particular band, its members rejoiced in the acquisition of axes, knives, pearls, and so forth from my stores.

The chief, by contrast, was generally as poor, in material terms, as he had been when I arrived. His share, which was very much larger than the average allowance, had all been extorted from him. This often reduced the chief to a kind of despair. A chief who can say "No" in such situations is like a Prime Minister, in countries subject to parliamentary democracy, who can snap his fingers at a vote of confidence. A chief who can say: "I'll give no more! I've been generous long enough! Let someone else take a turn!" must really be sure of his authority if he is not to provoke a moment of grave crisis.

Ingenuity is generosity transposed to the level of the intellect. A 6 good chief gives proofs of his initiative and skill. He it is who prepares the poison for the arrows. He, likewise, who constructs the ball of wild rubber which is used on Nambikwara sports days. He must also be able to sing and dance, with a repertory large enough to amuse the band at any time and distract them from the monotony of their everyday life. These functions might easily make of him something of a shaman, and some chiefs do, in fact, combine the roles of warrior and witch-doctor. But mysticism in all its forms remains well in the background of Nambikwara life, and the gift of magic, when present, is merely one of the secondary attributes of command. It is more common for one person to assume the temporal and another the spiritual power. In this the Nambikwara differ from their neighbors, the Tupi-Kawahib, whose chiefs are also shamans much given to premonitory dreams, visions, trances, and the dissociation of personality.

But the skill and ingenuity of the Nambikwara chief are none 7 the less astonishing for being directed towards a more positive outlet. He must have a minute knowledge of the territories frequented by his band and by its neighbors: the hunting-grounds must have no secrets from him, and he must know just when each clump of wild fruit-trees will be ripe for plucking. Thus instructed, he can work out a rough itinerary for each of his neighbor-bands, whether friendly or hostile; and, as he needs to be constantly on the move, reconnoitering or exploring, he may well seem to be not so much leading his band as circling rapidly round it.

Apart from one or two men who have no real authority, but are 8 prepared to collaborate if paid to do so, the passivity of the band is in striking contrast to the dynamism of its leader. It is as if, having handed over to him certain advantages, they expect him to take entire charge of their interests and their security. This attitude was well displayed in the episode which I have already described of the journey on which, when we lost our way and had not enough food, the Indians lay down on the ground instead of going off to look for some, leaving it to the chief and his wives to remedy the situation as best they could.

I have often spoken of the chief's "wives." He is, practically   9
speaking, the only polygamist in the band: and this is both a conso-
lation, moral and sentimental, for the heavy burdens of office, and
one of the means of shouldering those burdens. With rare exceptions
the chief and the witch-doctor (when these functions are shared
between two men) are the only people to have more than one wife.
But this polygamy is of a special type: it is not plural marriage in the
strict sense, but rather a normal monogamous marriage to which are
added relationships of a different sort. The first wife fulfills the normal role of the wife in monogamous marriages, in that she does the
work usually attributed to her sex, looks after the children, does the
cooking, and goes out to collect such food as she can. Later unions,
though recognized as marriages, are of a different kind. The wives
come, to begin with, from a younger generation, and the first wife
addresses them as "daughter" or "niece." Nor do they obey the rules
of the division of labor between the sexes, but do the work of either
men or women, as they please. In camp, they regard "house-work"
as beneath them and live in idleness, either playing with children
nearer their own age, or making love with their husband, while the
first wife busies herself with the routine work of the home. But
when the chief goes hunting or exploring, or on some other masculine errand, his secondary wives go with him and give him both
physical and moral support. Boyish in appearance, and chosen from
the prettiest and healthiest girls of the group, they are, indeed, more
mistresses than wives, and he lives with them in an atmosphere of
amorous camaraderie which is in striking contrast to the conjugal
atmosphere of his first union.

Men and women do not as a rule bathe together, but the chief   10
can sometimes be seen in the river with his secondary wives, and
these occasions are marked by a great deal of splashing about,
horse-play, and jokes of every kind. In the evening he plays with
them. Sometimes the games are clearly erotic, and they roll about,
two, three, or even four together, closely entwined on the sand.
Sometimes they are more childish in tone: for instance the Wakle-
toçu chief and his two wives would lie on the ground in the shape of
a three-leafed clover, with their feet together in the middle, and
then, raising their legs in the air, would bring them together, clap-
ping the soles of their feet together in unison.

This form of polygamy represents, therefore, a normal monoga-   11
mous marriage, to which is added a pluralist variant of amorous
camaraderie. It is also an attribute of power, and has a functional
value in both the moral and the economic spheres. The wives generally live together in harmony, and, although the lot of the first wife
may seem thankless, she seems to feel, or at any rate to show, no

bitterness as she toils away while her husband and his little play-mates amuse themselves and, at times, go to the limits of erotic enjoyment, within sight and sound of her. This distinction between the original wife and her successors is not, in any case, immutable. It happens, though less often, that the first wife may join in the fun: nor is she in any way excluded from the lighter sides of family life. And the fact that she takes less part in their dalliances is balanced by the greater respect, and to some extent the obedience, which is owed to her by her youthful successors.

This system has serious consequences for the life of the group.   12 By withdrawing, as he does, a number of young girls from the nor-mal matrimonial cycle, the chief creates a disequilibrium between the number of young men and the number of available girls. The young men suffer most from this, for they are condemned either to remain single for years, or to ally themselves with widows or older women whose husbands have had enough of them.

The Nambikwara have, however, another way of resolving the   13 problem, and that is by homosexual relations or, as they call them, *tamindige kihandige:* "the loving lie." These relations, common among the younger men, are carried on with a publicity uncommon in the case of more normal relations. The partners do not go off into the bush, as they would with a partner of the opposite sex, but get down to it beside the camp-fire, much to the amusement of their neigh-bors. The incident provokes a joke or two, on the quiet, the rela-tions in question being regarded as childishness and of no serious account. It remains doubtful whether these exercises are carried to the point of complete satisfaction or whether, like much that goes on between husbands and wives among the Nambikwara, they are limited to sentimental outpourings and a certain amount of erotic fore-play.

Homosexual relations are only allowed between adolescent boys   14 who stand to one another in the relations of crossed cousins— cases, that is to say, in which one partner would normally marry the other's sister and is taking her brother as a provisional substitute. Whenever I asked an Indian about a relationship of this sort, the answer was always the same: "They are two cousins (or brothers-in-law) who make love together." Even when fully grown, the brothers-in-law are still very free in their ways, and it is not unusual to see two or three men, all married and the fathers of children, walking round in the evening with their arms round one another's waists.

The privilege of polygamy, which gives rise to these makeshift   15 arrangements, is clearly an important concession to the chief on the part of the entire group. How does he see it? The fact of being able to pick and choose among the prettiest young girls gives him great satisfaction—a satisfaction not so much physical, for reasons I have already given, as sentimental. But, above all, polygamy and its specific attributes are the means put by the group at the disposition of their chief in order to help him to carry out his duties. Were he alone, he could only with difficulty do more than the others. His secondary wives, freed, in virtue of their special status, from the normal bondage of their sex, can help and comfort him. They are both the reward and the instrument of power. Can we say, however, that from the Indian's point of view the reward is adequate? To get an answer to that, we must examine the question more generally and see what the Nambikwara band, if considered as an elementary social structure, has to teach us about the origins and function of power.

The evidence of the Nambikwara runs, to begin with, clean   16
counter to the ancient sociological theory, now temporarily resurrected by the psycho-analysts, according to which the primitive chief derives from a symbolical Father. This view goes on to assert that the forms of the State have developed, from this starting-point, on the analogy of family life. At the foundations of power in one of its most primitive forms, on the other hand, we have discerned a decisive phase which introduces, in relation to the phenomena of biology, quite a new element: this phase consists in the *giving of consent.* Consent is at the origins, and at the same time at the furthest limit, of power. What are in appearance one-sided relations (those existing, for instance, in a gerontocracy, an autocracy, or any other form of government) may arise among groups whose structure is already complex; but in forms of social organization as simple as the one I am now trying to describe they are inconceivable. In such cases, political relations may be reduced to a kind of arbitration between, on the one hand, the talents and authority of the chief and, on the other, the size, coherence, and good will of the group. All these factors exert a reciprocal influence upon one another.

I should like to be able to show how markedly, in this regard,   17
contemporary anthropology supports the theses of the eighteenth-century *philosophes.*[2] Doubtless Rousseau's schema differs from the quasi-contractual relations which obtain between the chief and his companions. Rousseau had in mind quite a different phenomenon—the renunciation by the individual of his own autonomy in the interests of the collective will. It is none the less true, however, that Rousseau and his contemporaries displayed profound sociological intuition when they realized that attitudes and elements of culture

---

[2] ***philosophes*** French thinkers prominent in the eighteenth century before the French Revolution. They included Jean-Jacques Rousseau.

such as are summed up in the words "contract" and "consent" are not secondary formations, as their adversaries (and Hume[3] in particular) maintained: they are the primary materials of social life, and it is impossible to imagine a form of political organization in which they are not present.

As a consequence of all this, it is clear that power is founded,   18 psychologically speaking, in consent. But in daily life it finds outlet in the game of oath and counter-oath which is played out by the chief and his companions. Another of the attributes of power is, in effect, the notion of reciprocity. The chief has power, but he must be generous. He has duties, but he can also have several wives. Between himself and the group there is a constantly adjusted equilibrium of oaths and privileges, services and responsibilities.

But in the case of marriage the whole thing goes one stage fur-   19 ther. By conceding to its chief the privilege of polygamy, the group exchanges the individual elements of security guaranteed by the rule of monogamy and receives in return the collective security which it expects from Authority. Each man receives his wife from another man, but the chief receives his several wives from the group as a group. In return, he offers to guarantee the group in times of danger or need; and this guarantee is offered not to the individuals whose daughters or sisters he marries, nor even to those who, as a result of this, will have to remain single. It is offered to the group as a group, for it is the group as a group which has suspended the common law to his personal advantage. These reflections may be of interest to any theoretical study of polygamy: but above all they remind us that the conception of the State as a system of guarantees, renewed after discussion of a national insurance system such as that put forward by Beveridge[4] and others, is not a purely modern development. It is a return to the fundamental nature of social and political organization.

Such is the group's point of view, where power is concerned.   20 What, now, is the chief's own attitude to his function as chief? From what motives does he accept an office which is not always a very pleasant one? The Nambikwara chief knows that his is a difficult role, and that it will take all he has to sustain it adequately. If, what is more, he does not succeed in continually enhancing his personal standing he may easily lose what he has taken months or years to acquire. That is why many men decline the position of power. But

---

[3] **David Hume (1711–1766)** Scottish philosopher and author of *A Treatise of Human Nature* (1739–1740).

[4] **William Henry Beveridge (1879–1963)** British economist responsible for Britain's recovery after World War II and for the formation of the British welfare state and the National Health Insurance program.

why is it that others accept it, and indeed go out of their way to get it? It is never easy to judge of psychological motives, and it becomes almost impossible to do so when the culture in question is so very different from our own. One can say, however, that the privilege of polygamy, however attractive from the sexual, social, and sentimental points of view, would not in itself be enough. Polygamous marriage is one of the technical conditions of power: as far as private satisfactions are concerned, it can offer only an auxiliary significance. Nor is that all: for when I call to mind the moral and psychological characteristics of the Nambikwara chiefs, and try to capture the fugitive nuances of their personality (these nuances cannot be analyzed scientifically, but where the experiment of friendship is concerned, or the intuitive feeling of human communication, they may be of great value), I am carried irresistibly forward to the following conclusion: that if there are chiefs, it is because there are, in every group of human beings, men who, unlike their companions, love importance for its own sake, take a delight in its responsibilities, and find rewards enough in those very burdens of public life from which their fellows shrink. Certainly these individual differences are developed and find outlet in a manner, and to a degree, which will itself differ from one culture to another. But the fact that they exist in a society so largely uncompetitive as that of the Nambikwara would suggest that their origin is not entirely social. Rather are they a part of that raw material of psychology in which every society somewhere finds it foundations. Men are not all alike, and even in primitive tribes, which sociologists have portrayed as crushed by all-powerful tradition, the differences between one man and another are noted as exactly, and exploited with as much pertinacity, as in what we call our "individualist" society.

This is, in another form, precisely the "miracle" of which Leibnitz[5] speaks, in connection with the American savages whose ways, as described by early travelers, taught him "never to mistake the hypotheses of political philosophy for demonstration." For my own part, I went to the ends of the earth in search of what Rousseau called "the barely perceptible advances of the earliest time." Beneath and beyond the veil of the all-too-learned laws of the Bororo and the Caduveo[6] I had gone in search of a state which, to quote once again from Rousseau, "no longer exists, perhaps may never have existed, and probably will never exist." "And yet," he goes on, "without an

21

---

[5] **Gottfried Leibnitz (1646–1716)** German mathematician and philosopher.

[6] **Bororo . . . Caduveo** Bororo was Lévi-Strauss's best informant in the Amazon; Caduveo were a people in the Brazilian highlands who had been exposed to European culture, which they rejected.

accurate idea of that state we cannot judge properly of our present situation." Myself luckier than he, I thought that I had come upon that state in a society then nearing its end. It would have been pointless for me to wonder whether or not it was a vestigial version of what Rousseau had in mind; whether traditional or degenerate, it brought me into contact with one of the most indigent of all conceivable forms of social and political organization. I had no need to go into its past history to discover what had maintained it at its rudimentary level—or what, as was more likely, had brought it thus far down. I had merely to focus my attention on the experiment in sociology which was being carried out under my nose.

But that "experiment" eluded me. I had been looking for a society   22
reduced to its simplest expression. The society of the Nambikwara had been reduced to the point at which I found nothing but human beings.

QUESTIONS FOR CRITICAL READING

1. How are chiefs chosen among the Nambikwara? Why are they always men?
2. What does the word *chief* mean in the Nambikwara language (para. 2)?
3. What was Montaigne told were the privileges of a chief when he spoke with Brazilian Indians in 1560? How much had those privileges changed by 1950?
4. How does Lévi-Strauss regard the gender-linked activities of the Nambikwara? Does he treat them as normal?
5. Would Lévi-Strauss expect to find a female chief among the Nambikwara? Would you?
6. What is the attitude of the chief's first wife toward his other wives?
7. What is the role of consent in preserving power in the Nambikwara society?
8. Why is the chief relatively poor in his society?

SUGGESTIONS FOR CRITICAL WRITING

1. In paragraph 2, Lévi-Strauss observes that with regard to the chief the group chooses to form because of his presence rather than seeking a chief because of "the effect of the need, felt by an already-existing group." Examine the discussion of the chief and the chief's roles in Nambikwara society and explain, based on the text, what Lévi-Strauss means by his comment. Does his description of the behavior of the chief bear out his observation, or do you think that already existent groups search for a chief? How does that dynamic work itself out in

modern society? Does a modern "chief" create a group, or does the group create a "chief"?

2. Lévi-Strauss says, "Personal prestige and the ability to inspire confidence are the foundations of power in Nambikwara society" (para. 3). Choose an organization that you have personal experience with and decide whether or not Lévi-Strauss's observation applies to that organization. Be detailed and as specific as possible in giving examples and evidence that support your view. You may choose a political or social organization, a local or national organization, or any other form of organization that you have been witness to. How many of the Nambikwara practices seem to be shared by the modern organization?

3. Lévi-Strauss makes it clear that the gender relationships in Nambikwara society are pretty well standardized, with women doing what he thinks of as typical women's work and men — if they work at all — doing typical men's work. Given the obvious distribution of services according to gender in this society, do you feel the Nambikwara would be truly liberated if gender responsibilities were changed? Would the Nambikwara be well served with a woman as chief? What reasons can you give for your stance?

4. Polygamy is usually patterned on one man having several wives rather than one woman having several husbands. That is the pattern in the political structure of the Nambikwara. Lévi-Strauss sees the Nambikwara as demonstrating some of the same patterns as modern societies do. Do modern politicians seem to follow the same pattern? (You may consult newspapers on this point.) The young wives of the Nambikwara chief behave more like mistresses, which may help connect this pattern to modern life. Is this pattern specifically gender linked, or would you expect women "chiefs" to emulate the Nambikwara male chief's pattern too?

5. What are the limits of the Nambikwaran chief's powers? Why is consent such an important feature of the maintenance of power? Given that consent is also an important element in any democratic society, do you feel that awarding consent is linked to gender in our society as it is in the Nambikwara? Would our society award consent to a woman leader? In what cases is that a normal practice? In what cases is it abnormal? Would our society award consent to a male or female homosexual, transvestite, or transsexual? What are the reasons given for our society to award or to withhold consent in these cases?

6. **CONNECTIONS** It seems fairly clear that Lévi-Strauss wrote this selection with Jean-Jacques Rousseau in mind. Read Rousseau's "The Origin of Civil Society" (p. 55) and compare his ideas with those of Lévi-Strauss in terms of what both think is the earliest social pattern and the earliest form of civil government. To what extent do you think Lévi-Strauss may have been affected by Rousseau's thinking regarding the origins of society before he began writing about the Nambikwara? Do you think Lévi-Strauss is being totally objective, or is he trying to find preexisting patterns?

7. **SEEING CONNECTIONS** Lévi-Strauss saw Cassatt's *In the Loge* (p. 796), probably in reproduction. He would have been aware of her reputation as an impressionist painter who focused on everyday activities of ordinary people, a focus he shared in his research in the Amazon rain forest. What patterns of behavior would he feel Cassatt reveals in her painting that would be likely to appear in most societies, including that of the Nambikwara? Is the question of power addressed in this painting? Lévi-Strauss talks about prestige, the ability to inspire confidence, the awarding of consent, and generosity as important qualities in the Nambikwara culture. Are those qualities in evidence in this painting? Would Lévi-Strauss think them as important in Cassatt's society? Would he credit her as an amateur anthropologist?

GERMAINE GREER
Masculinity

BORN IN MELBOURNE, Australia, in 1939, Germaine Greer
has long been considered a leading feminist even though she has
sometimes been critical of feminist politics. She taught English literature at the University of Sydney, where she earned an M.A. for a
thesis on the poetry of Lord Byron. Her thesis won her a Commonwealth Scholarship to get her Ph.D. in early English literature at
Cambridge, where she became a faculty member at the all-women's
Newnham College. She was controversial while at Cambridge, not
only for her outspoken feminism and racy language, but also for
her anarchist polemics and occasional pranks. After she earned her
doctorate in 1968, she married an Australian journalist, but the
marriage did not last. By the time she was thirty and her first
book, *The Female Eunuch* (1970), was published, she had become
an international celebrity. The book was a sensation and its success led her to leave behind her academic career temporarily and
become a public figure.

She traveled broadly after 1972, championing women's rights
in many countries, including Bangladesh where she wrote a story
on the women who were raped by soldiers during the war in that
country. She produced a comedy show on Granada television in
England and wrote for a number of underground magazines. In
1979, she accepted a professorship at the University of Tulsa and
founded the *Tulsa Studies in Women's Literature*. In 1989, she
returned to Newnham College, Cambridge, but left in 1996 over a
stand she took against offering a fellowship to Rachael Padman, a
transsexual, on the grounds that she had been born a man and that

From *The Whole Woman*.

Newnham was a college for women. The controversy was acrimo-
nious and stimulated considerable discussion in academic circles.
One attack on Greer was so disparaging that it was eventually
removed from Web sites for legal reasons. Today Greer teaches at
the University of Warwick, in Coventry, England.

Greer's argument in *The Female Eunuch* centered in large part
on examining the ways in which women are raised in contemporary society. She feels that they have been trained to be submissive
and yielding and have grown suspicious of their sexuality and
ashamed of their bodies. The nuclear family is an especially damaging environment for women, she feels. Such a position naturally
drew criticism from the conservative press, but it also attracted a
wide following among women who felt that Greer had awakened
them from a long sleep.

Her second book, *The Obstacle Race: The Fortunes of Women
Painters and Their Work* (1979), involved extensive research into
art and art history. In it she examines stories of women painters
whose work was attributed to men, including a number of famous
paintings whose value diminished critically and financially when
they were discovered to be the work of women. She explains, much
as Virginia Woolf does regarding women writers, how difficult it
has been for women artists to be taken seriously and to be properly
rewarded for the quality of their work. One chapter discusses what
she feels is the equivalent of aesthetic rape: the failure to preserve
the work of women, many of whose paintings were discarded or
lost to posterity.

Sex and Destiny (1984) continued her examination of sexual
issues in numerous communities, especially in the developing
world. Here, too, she sees the structure of the family as damaging
to women and their potential for growth. *The Change: Women,
Aging, and the Menopause* (1991) explored an aspect of feminism
rarely discussed and at the same time attacked hormone replace-
ment for menopausal women. Greer feels that women are bullied
into accepting procedures that will do them no good and that may
do them harm.

The Whole Woman (1999) supplies the selection that follows.
In a sense, this book picks up where *The Female Eunuch* left off
thirty years earlier. Greer sees that much has changed, but she
makes something of a rallying call, fearing that today's young
women may have given in to the pressures of popular culture that
require them to aspire to a role that is unhealthy for them to play.
As she says, women in 1970 were not starving and cutting themselves, so she is somewhat worried that the feminist movement is
backsliding.

Greer's Rhetoric

"Masculinity," one of the last chapters in her book, may seem out of place in a study of the whole woman, but it is appropriate as a contrast to the body of her argument. She presents her argument almost in the form of an anthropological study, essentially reporting what she has discovered about the nature of masculinity in our culture. One of her most interesting rhetorical devices is the use of strong short statements that almost take the form of a maxim or proverb:

"Masculinity is to maleness as femininity is to femaleness." (para. 1)

"Men do not only give orders; they also take orders." (para. 8)

"Masculinity requires the creation of dangerous situations, actual or symbolic." (para. 10)

"Masculinity is a system." (para. 12)

Each of these requires an examination and therefore a clear focus for understanding. Her device of interweaving quotations from both men and women regarding masculine behavior interrupts the discussion but adds the weight of outside testimony on her subject, similar to the list of quotations that opens this section on gender.

Greer begins by establishing that "masculinity is the cultural construct" (para. 1) of maleness in our society. Once she has made that point, she moves on to explain how society actually goes about constructing the idea of masculinity. Her strategy is effective in that, after making her declaration, she seems aware that her readers may take immediate issue with her and feel that masculinity is not cultural but rather biological. She then begins paragraph 2 with an analysis of a scientific study that seems to be a clear counterargument to her position. Research on people with Turner's syndrome — a condition in which males do not have the usual XY chromosome in their genes but only one X and females, instead of the XX chromosome, also have only one X. The result is that people with Turner's syndrome are classified as female, even if they do not have the biological capacity to have children.

The researchers who reported on the behavior of children with Turner's syndrome determined that single-X boys seemed feminine and single-X girls seemed masculine. But when Greer examined the data and the testing of these individuals she was able to see that the criteria the researchers used were essentially cultural and that the behavior of the single-X individuals was not conspicuously different from that of XX and XY individuals given similar tests. Thus, the biological argument suffers and Greer continues with her determination of how a culture constructs masculinity.

Greer begins with the first caretaker and discovers that a widely regarded study noted that boy babies are treated quite differently from girl babies. "The boy baby learns that he can have what he wants and quickly, the girl baby that she has to learn patience" (para. 4). Then she establishes the somewhat Freudian notion that the boy baby's first love affair is with his mother and that it is a success. But the girl baby's first love affair with her father is "inevitably a failure" (para. 5). The outcome is that "boys grow up convinced that they are lovable regardless of their appearance or their behavior."

Greer then launches into the body of her essay, tracing the cultural forces at work that help shape the masculine male. Her argument, using examples and some quotations, stays at a very basic level, describing the language and activities that ordain male behavior. At one point, she uses a metaphor when she describes the behavior of a group of males in terms of primate behavior: "grooming the silverback" (para. 9). After clarifying her position regarding the cultural influences on males, she briefly discusses how those influences not only produce the masculine male but also how women fit into the groups, such as corporations, that were originally constructed by masculine males.

The strength of her arguments lies first in her ability to balance her views against opposing ones and then in her ability to present what seem to be uncontroversial observations about the behavior of men that readers can verify or deny from their own experience. Ultimately, that is the test of her position on masculinity.

PREREADING QUESTIONS:
WHAT TO READ FOR

The following prereading questions may help you anticipate key issues in the discussion of Germaine Greer's "Masculinity." Keeping them in mind during your first reading of the selection should help focus your attention.

- Why is masculinity a cultural construct?
- What is the argument against masculinity being a cultural construct?
- How differently is a male baby raised from a female baby in our culture?
- How do male organizations help shape the masculine male?

Masculinity

Masculinity is to maleness as femininity is to femaleness. That is 1
to say that maleness is the natural condition, the sex if you like, and
masculinity is the cultural construct, the gender. Where once feminists talked of sex discrimination, they now usually refer to gender
roles, because the cultural construct is what can and should be
changed; sex, as a biological given, is less susceptible. The distinction is rather like the one to be found between the genotype, which
is what is written in the DNA, and the phenotype, which is how that
immense text is quoted in actuality. The potential of the genotype is
enormous; the phenotype is the finite creature that is all that can be
made of almost limitless possibility in a single lifespan in a single set
of circumstances.

> A man feels himself more of a man when he is imposing himself
> and making others the instruments of his will.
> —BERTRAND DE JOUVENEL, *Power*

In June 1997 a report in *Nature* argued that masculinity (as dis- 2
tinct from maleness) was genetic: David Skuse of the Institute of
Child Health and workers at the Wessex Regional Genetics Laboratory had been studying Turner's syndrome, which is a consequence
of being born with only the X of the final pair of chromosomes.
Though they have no uteri or ovaries, these single-X individuals are
classified as female. They usually grow up to be short in stature and
infertile. The researchers found that the single-X "girls" displayed
"masculine" characteristics in that they were insensitive, demanding,
and obtuse. The researchers explained this as a lack of the feminine
traits of intuition and sociability, on which girls usually score higher
than boys, the inference being that these were carried in the second
X. The single-X individuals who inherited their X from their mother
had more problems of social adjustment than the ones who inherited their X from their father. Peter McGuffin and Jane Scourfield of
the University of Wales Medical College welcomed the information.

> There has been a tendency to play down the possible role of biol-
> ogy in accounting for psychological differences between men and
> women. For the first time we have evidence about the location of
> a gene that plays a part, challenging the prevailing belief that gen-
> der differences are largely culturally determined.

If we look more closely at what the new information actually   3
amounted to, this interpretation seems rather too definite. The Skuse
team had graded eighty-eight Turner's syndrome individuals on an
unsociability questionnaire; those whose X chromosome came from
their fathers scored five out of a possible twenty-four, those whose X
came from their mothers scored nine, but this compares with scores
for a control population of four for the boys and two for the girls.
The Turner's syndrome children would appear to have rather more
serious socialization problems than normal XY boys who scored
closer to XX girls. An "unsociability" test that establishes a high of
twenty-four when the norm is between two and four would seem to
contain a number of significant variables; did the whole group of
single-X "girls" display the same or contrasting kinds of unsociability?
How much of the single-X truculence could have been explained by
differential treatment from carers and parents? And so on.

> He [President Clinton] embodies a masculine virility that has
> been under attack in the States for so long.
>   — KATIE ROIPHE

Despite all the hoo-ha, Skuse and his team had not proved that   4
masculine men are born. They had certainly not done nearly enough
to counter the vast amount of research on how they are made. That
process begins when the carer who thinks a child a boy readily offers
it food when it cries; the same carer, thinking a child a girl, will allow
it to cry longer and will soothe rather than feed it. This sounds preposterous but it has been proved in a famous series of experiments,
in which subjects were given wrapped-up infants and randomly told
that the infants were male or female. When told that female babies
were male, the subjects treated them as male, responding quickly to
their vociferations and interpreting them as demands for food. When
told that male babies were female, they let them cry longer and were
comparatively reluctant to offer them food. Observers of breast-
feeding have likewise observed that male babies are fed more often
and for longer at a time than female babies. Mothers perceive boy
babies as hungrier and as better feeders than girls; what this means is
probably that they enjoy feeding their boy babies more than they
enjoy feeding their girls, for whatever reason. We know less about
these mechanisms than we should because as little work has been
done on the psychology of breast-feeding as on every other aspect of
the well woman's function. The boy baby learns that he can have
what he wants and quickly, the girl baby that she has to
learn patience. Boy babies are cooed to on a different note. They are

potty-trained later. The sociability and intuitiveness that Skuse valued in XX girls is simply biddability by another name, and there is a
distinct possibility that it has its roots in the insecurity that the little
girl feels in her relationship with both her parents.

> Do you think that men are any good for anything? It seems to me
> that men are ruining the world.
>
> —NINA SIMONE, 1997

Then there is the vexed question of father-love versus mother-   5
love. Daughters will develop more self-confidence if their fathers are
encouraging and appreciative of their efforts, but fathers seldom give
such matters much attention and, if they do, usually demand objective verification of a daughter's merit before giving encouragement.
The self-confidence of boys, on the other hand, is reinforced by mothers' attention which is abundant and rarely conditional. Whether it be
because a girl's first love affair (with her father) is inevitably a failure
compared to a boy's effortless conquest of his mother, or the outcome
of interaction of more complex and mysterious causes, boys grow up
convinced that they are lovable regardless of their appearance or their
behavior. The saddest, smelliest, most shambling male individual still
imagines that women will find him attractive and is prepared to act on
the assumption. And he considers himself entitled to criticize any and
all aspects of a women's appearance as harshly as any other male.

Until comparatively recently both boys and girls were dressed   6
alike and looked alike until a boy was breeched and his hair cut into
a manly style. As long as his mother's milk was in him a boy was
expected to be girlish, a milksop; his tears were no shame to him.
The age at which induction into masculinity was to commence was
indeterminate and unstable, especially as mothers wept and railed at
the mere thought of giving their babies up to the brutality of schoolmasters, who were expected to teach them to bear pain without
flinching as a condition of teaching them anything else. Elizabeth
Barrett Browning[1] is thought to have exaggerated a tad in keeping her
son's blond curls trailing over his shoulders until he was almost in
his teens, by which time it was thought too late to make a man of
him. Though we might hope that schoolmaster brutality is a thing of
the past, comparatively young men have experienced extreme brutalization at the hands of schoolmasters. An article in *Loaded* magazine

---

[1] **Elizabeth Barrett Browning (1806–1861)** Author of *Sonnets from the
Portuguese.*

described teachers who punched boys in the stomach and hit them with sticks. This is one of them:

> A brick shithouse with a ruddy face and unusually thick eyebrows, he was an ex-army man with the morals of a housefly and a temper meaner than the Moscow winter. A man who might have been put on earth for the singular purpose of terrorizing each and every adolescent male under his charge.

The persistence of the expression "to make a man of [someone]"   7 is the best possible evidence of the deliberateness of the streamlining of the male person into the masculine man. Repeatedly the boy is told that he is about to be made a man of, especially when he joins some paramilitary organization, the scout movement, the cadets, the school officer training corps. At a slightly less belligerent level, he is encouraged to take part in team sports, to get used to rough and tumble and learn to take his punishment "like a man." If at all possible he will usually take as his model his father, present or absent, alive or dead. The primary virtue of masculinity for the young man is courage, manifested as stoicism in everyday vicissitudes and as belligerence

> My uncles would take me out just to learn how to fight and the lesson was, don't lose the fight or else your uncles are going to give you a hiding.
> — JONAH LOMU

when threatened. A man is supposed to be unflinching, hard in every sense. So he is taught to control his gestures, to keep his hands and arms still and his face expressionless. His body outline is to be contained and impermeable. Real men do not fuss or scurry. It is not women who have foisted this requirement upon men but other men, who prove their own hardness by constantly challenging other men to repeated trials of physical and mental strength. Women often connive at the process; some mothers will taunt their sons if they think them cowardly; some wives and sweethearts will incite their men to attack other men in their defense. Generally, however, though women make boys out of babies it is men who make men out of boys. Though in these enlightened times schoolteachers may encourage boys to express softer feelings, even to weep, in the schoolyard, on the playing field, and in the street, compensation for this erosion of masculinity is exacted with interest. Young males form groups behind dominant individuals and prove themselves by conflict with rival groups; at the same time they jockey for power and seniority within the group. The group may be nothing more macho than a cricket team but, even when the game is played in the correct sportsmanlike fashion, individuals are caught up in the drama of acquiring and losing prestige.

Men do not only give orders; they also take orders. A masculine   8
man's attention is focused upon his role in the various groups to which he belongs and from which he gains verification of self-worth. If he spends time with women it is partly or even mostly because he wants to demonstrate his prowess to his mates; he owes no loyalty to the women whatsoever. If it might improve his status he will surrender a woman with whom he has been intimate to another man and feel no qualm of jealousy. Young women are slow to grasp their irrelevance to the emotional center of a masculine man's life, mainly because young men are the emotional center of young women's lives. To be successful young men have to achieve a measure of respect from other men; this is the spring of all their behaviors, in the workplace and at play. They have to acquire a vast amount of lore, principally about sport, but also about cars and other boys' toys, subjects upon which girls are uninformed and stupid, and they have to keep it up to date, which requires attention. For a man who is not imposing physically there is the resort of humor; if he is amusing enough he will be caressed by the hard men he cannot emulate.

Wherever men are gathered together, in the pool hall, at a restau-   9
rant, you can see the wannabes waiting on the dominant males, studying their reactions, gauging when to defer and when to challenge. There

> Despite advances towards sexual equality, many men still feel embarrassed when they have to buy nappies. They fear people will think them henpecked husbands ordered by their wives to buy the nappies. Proudly placing a six-pack [of beer] alongside the nappies sends out the message that the man is really a he-man.
> —NICK GREEN, Tesco Clubcard manager

will always be one man who can silence the others with a look; most will defer, one may challenge or mock challenge, giving the leader a chance to strut his stuff, and there will be the junior males, who seek to ingratiate themselves by stepping and fetching, and grooming the silverback. The presence of women in such groups distracts the men from the work in hand—if they acknowledge women's presence; which they usually don't. The conversation is between males; when women make a contribution the men ignore it and respond to the last utterance by a male. Often the only woman present is the silent, smiling consort of the dominant male, who is gratified if his subordinates pay her an appropriate measure of attention. The kind of consort who is exhibited in this way is usually particularly decorative; the top honcho is pleased to see his henchmen afraid to catch her eye or speak to her, even as they dream of such executive totty for themselves.

Masculinity requires the creation of dangerous situations, actual   10
or symbolic. The myth that feeds masculinity is that every boy should become a strong and resolute warrior capable of defending his women and children from attack by other males. In stature he should be bigger than a woman, and more heavily muscled. As a U.S. Navy officer wrote in the *Navy Times* in July 1989:

> Warriors kill. If someone cannot kill, regardless of the reason, that individual is not a warrior. Men make the best warriors in comparison to women because men are better at killing in war.
>
> Women cannot compete in a battlefield as they cannot compete in professional sports against men. Women do not hold even one Olympic record for strength or speed. Women are weaker and slower on average as well. Strength, not weakness, wins battles and wars.

As a typical masculinist statement this deserves analysis. "Killing   11
in war" is here represented as a gendered activity, with the unstated inference that any man who is not good at "killing in war" is less of a man. The role of modern technology which, being inanimate, must be gender-free, is transferred to a mythical supermale who is good at killing not because he is equipped with devastatingly effective weaponry but because he is some kind of an athlete. Only a minute proportion of males will ever come within reach of an Olympic record, but the achievements of male record-holders empower all men. The implication that the weakest man must be stronger and faster than any woman whatsoever is obviously absurd. The ultimate effect of the myth of masculinity is to generate anxiety in the vast majority of men who cannot live up to it. The cult of masculinity drives many a man who knows himself to be unaggressive and timid to opt out of conventional manhood altogether. Masculinity run riot creates the situation it most dreads, the wholesale effeminization of men who cannot play its game.

Masculinity is a system. It is the complex of learned behaviors   12
and subtly coded interactions that forms the connective tissue of corporate society. Women who are inducted into masculinist hierarchies

are exported tissue, in constant danger of provoking an inflammatory response and summary rejection. The brokers of Wall Street are typical of a self-selecting masculinist elite in that they bond by sharing intensely transgressive experiences. Juniors will recommend themselves to the alpha males by persecuting underlings, and in particular, women. The men of one Wall Street brokerage firm used to hold drinking parties in the "boom-boom" room from which women were excluded. Any woman who dared to make a complaint about the incessant verbal abuse and physical harassment she was subjected to would be dealt with after hours in the boom-boom room, where a lavatory bowl hung from the ceiling. Fifty-year-old stockbroker Pamela Martens described Wall Street as "an old boy network where that barbaric aggressive behavior has to be cloned if you want to advance." The British Stock Exchange is no more civilized: a successful trader used to be known as a "big swinging dick" and women as either "babes," "mums" or, if they were thought to be at all feminist, "lesbians."

Female interlopers are often quite unaware of the intensity of   13 the inter-male negotiation and consolidation going on around them. When push comes to shove the guys repair to the men's room and plot their strategy. The woman who thinks her male colleagues are dealing with the case on its merits rather than as a pawn in a long-term power play will only remain in her position of eminence

> The time has come for all guys to come out of the locker room. Don't be ashamed of that fetid jockstrap and those toxic sweat socks. Leave that toilet seat up proudly! The time has come not only to live openly guy but to embrace the whole guy lifestyle.
>   – "GUY PRIDE," *Maxim Manifesto,* March 1997

as long as she serves their purposes. It is no accident that women inducted into male hierarchies so seldom identify with other women or advance the interests of other women. They wouldn't have risen so far in the organization if they did. The most obvious case of this mechanism at work was Margaret Thatcher,[2] imported into the Tory hierarchy as an irritant, only to prove strangely successful and so extend the men's tolerance to an unprecedented degree, and ultimately to be unceremoniously, ageistly, sexistly dumped.

---

[2] **Margaret Thatcher (b. 1925)** Prime minister of Great Britain 1979–1990.

According to Ken Auletta,[3] writing in the *New Yorker,* women   14
executives in the American entertainment business believe that
"women are better managers—more nurturing, more collegial,
more communicative, more instinctual—and that these strengths
mesh better with the corporate culture of teamwork and partnering
which is emblematic of the information age. And as women gain
authority, most of them believe, our movies, our music, our television, our software, and our other communications will improve."
The accompanying photograph showed twenty-four utterly con-
formist apparently pre-menopausal females; none wore glasses;
almost all were smiling, decorously rather than broadly; all wore lip-
stick, suits, and heels; all were carefully coifed; more than half were
blonde. If we have them to thank for the current state of entertainment, rotten as it is with the crudest misogyny, drunk as it is on
extravagant and trivialized violence, they must be a very curious
bunch of women. The old rule probably still holds good; if women
are running the front office, power must have taken refuge somewhere else. Insisting on women's management style as fundamentally softer and more accommodating is a very good way of ensuring
that power stays where it is, in the men's room.

---

[3] **Ken Auletta (b. 1942)** Author of eight books and a columnist for the *New
Yorker* magazine.

QUESTIONS FOR CRITICAL READING

1. At what age does induction into masculinity begin?
2. Do organizations like the Boy Scouts and the army try to make men
    out of boys? How?
3. To what extent do you think it is true that boy babies are raised differ-
    ently from girl babies?
4. What is a good definition of masculinity?
5. How do women survive in a masculine organization?
6. What is the significance of courage in the formation of the masculine male?
7. What does Greer mean when she says, "Real men do not fuss or scurry"
    (para. 7)?
8. Why is killing in war no longer a gendered activity?

SUGGESTIONS FOR CRITICAL WRITING

1. Greer says that as a result of the way he has been raised since baby-
    hood, "The saddest, smelliest, most shambling male individual still

imagines that women will find him attractive and is prepared to act on the assumption" (para. 5). Write an essay in which you either verify this statement — primarily from experience but possibly from news magazines, biographies, or a study of popular films or TV. If you disagree with Greer on this point, argue your own view carefully, using examples or observations.

2. In paragraph 12, Greer says, "Masculinity is a system. It is the complex of learned behaviors and subtly coded interactions that forms the connective tissue of corporate society." Interpreting "corporate society" to include any structured organization — gangs, fraternities, sororities, or student organizations — establish what you think the "learned behaviors and coded interactions" are that represent and produce the system and how that then produces masculinity. Are you in agreement with Greer, or do you feel you must argue against her?

3. To what extent do you feel that Greer thinks masculinity is a desirable quality in our society? Her statement about "[m]asculinity run riot" (para. 11) implies that there is a form of masculinity that does not run riot and that therefore may be acceptable behavior. Taking your cue from Greer, write a short essay that establishes exactly what qualities of masculinity you think are essential in your immediate society — and perhaps in society at large — for it to function properly. Would an absence of masculinity do our society irreparable harm?

4. Greer makes a great deal out of the expression "to make a man" of a boy. If you are male, describe your experiences with people or organizations that have tried to make a man of you. Do you value their efforts or do you find that they did you a disservice? If you are female, what have you observed in your male acquaintances regarding the effort people have made to make men of them? Did your acquaintances seem to change for the better or for the worse? What do you think it means to make a man of a boy? From your point of view, is it a good thing?

5. In paragraph 11, Greer says, "Masculinity run riot creates the situation it most dreads, the wholesale effeminization of men who cannot play its game." Does this observation seem true to you? Describe what you think Greer means by "[m]asculinity run riot." Is it possible to overdo masculinity? Can a man be too masculine? Why would masculinity "run riot" effeminize men? Would the "junior males" who "step and fetch it" in the "pool hall" or "restaurant" be effeminized men? What does Greer seem to mean by "effeminization"?

6. **CONNECTIONS** In paragraph 5, Greer discusses issues that sound particularly close to the Freudian view on the oedipal complex. How much in agreement with Freud does Greer seem to be? Compare her views with those of Freud in his essay "The Oedipus Complex" (p. 475). Although Freud insists that oedipal drives are totally unconscious for the individual, you may have witnessed either in literature or in your own experience the complex in action. Do you think it works the way Greer says it does? Is Greer being Freudian? Explain your reasoning on this point.

7. **SEEING CONNECTIONS**   Greer's book on female painters, *The Obstacle Race*, is more concerned with women who were disregarded and whose work was lost than it is with painters, such as Cassatt, who were successful in a man's world. Greer says women pay a price for being successful, as she describes in her final paragraphs. Research Cassatt's background and decide whether or not she fits the pattern Greer establishes for female painters. Then examine *In the Loge* (p. 796) with an eye to expressions of masculinity and femininity. Has Cassatt portrayed the woman in the loge as being more masculine than feminine in behavior? What details or visual structures in the painting seem classifiable as masculine or feminine? Are they all cultural constructs?

WRITING ABOUT IDEAS
An Introduction to Rhetoric

Writing about ideas has several functions. First, it helps make our thinking available to others for examination. The writers whose works are presented in this book benefited from their first readers' examinations and at times revised their work considerably as a result of such criticism. Writing about ideas also helps us to refine what we think—even without criticism from others—because writing is a self-instructional experience. We learn by writing in part because writing clarifies our thinking. When we think silently, we construct phrases and then reflect on them; when we speak, we both utter these phrases and sort them out in order to give our audience a tidier version of our thoughts. But spoken thought is difficult to sustain because we cannot review or revise what we said an hour earlier. Writing has the advantage of permitting us to expand our ideas, to work them through completely and possibly to revise in the light of later discoveries. It is by writing that we truly gain control over our ideas.

GENERATING TOPICS FOR WRITING

Filled with sophisticated discussions of important ideas, the selections in this volume endlessly stimulate our responses and our writing. Reading the works of great thinkers can also be chastening to the point of making us feel sometimes that they have said it all and there is no room for our own thoughts. However, the suggestions that follow will assist you in writing your response to the ideas of an important thinker.

Thinking Critically: Asking a Question. One of the most reliable ways to start writing is to ask a question and then to answer it. In many ways, that is what the writers in this book have done again and again. Ruth Benedict asked why "[t]he man in the street still thinks in terms of a necessary antagonism between society and the individual." She observes that people's concepts of society focus on restrictions rather than on opportunities, which gives her a chance to explore the question in depth. Adam Smith asked what the principles of accumulating wealth really were and proceeded to examine the economic system of his time in such detail that his views are still valued. He is associated with the capitalist system as firmly as Marx is with the communist system. John Kenneth Galbraith asked questions about why poverty existed in a prosperous nation such as the United States. John Rawls asked whether justice could be fair. Michio Kaku asked whether the theory of dark matter constituting 90 percent of the universe can be true. Such questioning is at the center of all critical thinking.

As a writer stimulated by other thinkers, you can use the same technique. For example, turn back to the Machiavelli excerpt annotated in "Evaluating Ideas: An Introduction to Critical Reading" (p. 5). All the annotations can easily be turned into questions. Any of the following questions, based on the annotations and our brief summary of the passage, could be the basis of an essay:

- Should a leader be armed?
- Is it true that an unarmed leader is despised?
- Will those leaders who are always good come to ruin among those who are not good?
- To remain in power, must a leader learn how not to be good?

One technique is to structure an essay around the answer to such a question. Another is to develop a series of questions and to answer each of them in various parts of an essay. Yet another technique is to use the question indirectly—by answering it, but not in an obvious way. In "Why the Rich Are Getting Richer and the Poor, Poorer," for example, Robert B. Reich answers a question we may not have asked. In the process he examines the nature of our current economy to see what it promises for different sectors of the population. His answer to the question concerns the shift in labor from manufacturing to information, revealing that "symbolic analysts" have the best opportunities in the future to amass wealth.

Many kinds of questions can be asked of a passage even as brief as the sample from Machiavelli. For one thing, we can limit ourselves to our annotations and go no further. But we also can reflect on larger issues and ask a series of questions that constitute a fuller inquiry. Out of that inquiry we can generate ideas for our own writing.

Two important ideas were isolated in our annotations. The first was that the prince must devote himself to war. In modern times, this implies that a president or other national leader must put matters of defense first—that a leader's knowledge, training, and concerns must revolve around warfare. Taking that idea in general, we can develop other questions that, stimulated by Machiavelli's selection, can be used to generate essays:

- Which modern leaders would Machiavelli support?
- Would Machiavelli approve of our current president?
- Do military personnel make the best leaders?
- Should our president have a military background?
- Could a modern state survive with no army or military weapons?
- What kind of a nation would we have if we did not stockpile nuclear weapons?

These questions derive from "The prince's profession should be war," the first idea that we isolated in the annotations. The next group of questions comes from the second idea, the issue of whether a leader can afford to be moral:

- Can virtues cause a leader to lose power?
- Is Machiavelli being cynical about morality, or is he being realistic (as he claims he is)? (We might also ask if Machiavelli uses the word *realistic* as a synonym for *cynical*.)
- Do most American leaders behave morally?
- Do most leaders believe that they should behave morally?
- Should our leaders be moral all the time?
- Which vices can we permit our leaders to have?
- Are there any vices we want our leaders to have?
- Which world leaders behave most morally? Are they the ones we most respect?
- Could a modern government govern well or at all if it were to behave morally in the face of immoral adversaries?

One reason for reading Machiavelli is to help us confront broad and serious questions. One reason for writing about these ideas is to help clarify our own positions on such important issues.

Using Suggestions for Writing. Every selection in this book is followed by a number of questions and a number of writing assignments. The questions are designed to help clarify the most important issues raised in the piece. Unlike the questions derived from annotation, their purpose is to stimulate a classroom discussion so that you can benefit from hearing others' thoughts on these issues. Naturally, subjects for essays can arise from such discussion, but the discussion is most important for refining and focusing your ideas. The writing assignments, on the other hand, are explicitly meant to provide a useful starting point for producing an essay of five hundred to one thousand words.

A sample suggestion for writing about Machiavelli follows:

> Machiavelli advises the prince to study history and reflect on the actions of great men. Do you support such advice? Machiavelli mentions a number of great leaders in his essay. Which leaders would you recommend a prince should study? How do you think Machiavelli would agree or disagree with your recommendations?

Like most of the suggestions for writing, this one can be approached in several ways. It can be broken down into three parts. The first question is whether it is useful to study, as Machiavelli does, the performance of past leaders. If you agree, then the second question asks you to name some leaders whose behavior you would recommend studying. If you do not agree, you can point to the performance of some past leaders and explain why their study would be pointless today. Finally, the third question asks how you think Machiavelli would agree or disagree with your choices.

To deal successfully with this suggestion for writing, you could begin by giving your reasons for recommending that a political leader study "the actions of great men." George Santayana once said, "Those who cannot remember the past are condemned to repeat it." That is, we study history in order not to have to live it over again. If you believe that a study of the past is important, the first part of an essay can answer the question of why such study could make a politician more successful.

The second part of the suggestion focuses on examples. In the sample from Machiavelli above, we omitted the examples, but in the complete essay they are very important for bringing Machiavelli's point home. Few things can convince as completely as examples, so the first thing to do is to choose several leaders to work with. If you have studied a world leader, such as Indira Gandhi, Winston Churchill, Franklin Delano Roosevelt, or Margaret Thatcher, you could use that figure as one of your examples. If you have not done so, then use the research library's sections on history and politics to find books or articles on one or two leaders and read them with an eye to establishing their usefulness for your argument. An Internet search can help you gather information efficiently. Consult the Internet resources created specially for this book at **www .bedfordstmartins.com/worldofideas**. The central question you would seek to answer is how a specific world leader could benefit from studying the behavior and conduct of a modern leader.

The third part of the suggestion for writing—how Machiavelli would agree or disagree with you—is highly speculative. It invites you to look through the selection to find quotations or comments that indicate probable agreement or disagreement on Machiavelli's part. You can base your argument only on what Machiavelli says or implies, and this means that you will have to reread his essay to find evidence that will support your view.

In a sense, this part of the suggestion establishes a procedure for working with the writing assignments. Once you clarify the parts of the assignment and have some useful questions to guide you, and once you determine what research, if any, is necessary, the next step is to reread the selection to find the most appropriate information to help you write your own essay. One of the most important activities in learning how to write from these selections is to reread while paying close attention to the annotations that you've made in the margins of the essays. It is one way in which reading about significant ideas differs from reading for entertainment. Important ideas demand reflection and reconsideration. Rereading provides both.

DEVELOPING IDEAS IN WRITING

Every selection in this book—whether by Francis Bacon or Margaret Mead, Frederick Douglass or Karl Marx—employs specific rhetorical techniques that help the author communicate important ideas. Each introduction identifies the special rhetorical techniques used by the writer, partly to introduce you to the way in which such techniques are used.

Rhetoric is a general term used to discuss effective writing techniques. For example, an interesting rhetorical technique that Machiavelli uses is illustration by example, usually to prove his points. Francis Bacon uses the technique of enumeration by partitioning his essay into four sections. Enumeration is especially useful when the writer wishes to be very clear or to cover a subject point by point, using each point to accumulate more authority in the discussion. Martin Luther King Jr. uses the technique of allusion, reminding the religious leaders who were his audience that St. Paul wrote similar letters to help early Christians better understand the nature of their faith. By alluding to the Bible and St. Paul, King effectively reminded his audience that they all were serving God.

A great many more rhetorical techniques may be found in these readings. Some of the techniques are familiar because many of us already use them, but we study them to understand their value and to use them more effectively. After all, rhetorical techniques make it possible for us to communicate the significance of important ideas. Many of the authors in this book would surely admit that the effect of their ideas actually depends on the way they are expressed, which is a way of saying that they depend on the rhetorical methods used to express them.

Methods of Development

Most of the rhetorical methods used in these essays are discussed in the introductions to the individual selections. Several represent exceptionally useful general techniques. These are methods of development and represent approaches to developing ideas that contribute to the fullness and completeness of an essay. You may think of them as techniques that can be applied to any idea in almost any situation. They can enlarge on the idea, clarify it, express it, and demonstrate its truth or effectiveness. Sometimes a technique may be direct, sometimes indirect. Sometimes it calls attention to itself, sometimes it works behind the scenes. Sometimes it is used alone, sometimes in conjunction with other methods. The most important techniques are explained and then illustrated with examples from the selections in the book.

Development by Definition.   Definition is essential for two purposes: to make certain that you have a clear grasp of your concepts and that you communicate a clear understanding to your reader. Definition goes far beyond the use of the dictionary in the manner of "According to Webster's, . . ." Such an approach is facile because complex ideas are not easily reduced to dictionary definitions. A more useful strategy is to offer an explanation followed by an example. Because some of the suggestions for writing that follow the selections require you to use definition as a means of writing about ideas, the following tips should be kept in mind:

- Definition can be used to develop a paragraph, a section, or an entire essay.
- It considers questions of function, purpose, circumstance, origin, and implications for different groups.
- Explanations and examples make all definitions more complete and effective.

Many of the selections are devoted almost entirely to the act of definition. For example, in "The Position of Poverty," John Kenneth Galbraith begins by defining the two kinds of poverty that he feels characterize the economic situation of the poor—case poverty and insular poverty. He defines case poverty in this paragraph:

> Case poverty is commonly and properly related to some characteristic of the individuals so afflicted. Nearly everyone else has mastered his environment; this proves that it is not intractable. But some quality peculiar to the individual or family involved— mental deficiency, bad health, inability to adapt to the discipline of industrial life, uncontrollable procreation, alcohol, discrimination involving a very limited minority, some educational handicap unrelated to community shortcoming, or perhaps a combination of several of these handicaps—has kept these individuals from participating in the general well-being. (para. 7)

When he begins defining insular poverty, however, he is unable to produce a neat single-paragraph definition. He first establishes that insular poverty describes a group of people alienated from the majority for any of many reasons. Next, he spends five paragraphs discussing what can produce such poverty—migration, racial prejudice, and lack of education. When working at the level of seriousness that characterizes his work, Galbraith shows us that definition works best when it employs full description and complex, detailed discussion.

An essay on the annotated selection from Machiavelli might define a number of key ideas. For example, to argue that Machiavelli is cynical in suggesting that his prince would not retain power if he acted morally, we would need to define what it means to be cynical and what moral behavior means in political terms. When we argue any point, it is important to spend time defining key ideas.

Martin Luther King Jr., in "Letter from Birmingham Jail," takes time to establish some key definitions so that he can speak forcefully to his audience:

> Let us consider a more concrete example of just and unjust laws. An unjust law is a code that a numerical or power majority group compels a minority group to obey but does not make binding on itself. This is *difference* made legal. By the same token, a just law is a code that a majority compels a minority to follow and that it is willing to follow itself. This is *sameness* made legal. (para. 17)

This is an adequate definition as far as it goes, but most serious ideas need more extensive definition than this passage gives us. And King does go further, providing what Machiavelli does in his essay: examples and explanations. Every full definition will profit from the extension of understanding that an explanation and example will provide. Consider this paragraph from King:

> Let me give another explanation. A law is unjust if it is inflicted on a minority that, as a result of being denied the right to vote, had

no part in enacting or devising the law. Who can say that the legislature of Alabama which set up that state's segregation laws was democratically elected? Throughout Alabama all sorts of devious methods are used to prevent Negroes from becoming registered voters, and there are some counties in which, even though Negroes constitute a majority of the population, not a single Negro is registered. Can any law enacted under such circumstances be considered democratically structured? (para. 18)

King makes us aware of the fact that definition is complex and capable of great subtlety. It is an approach that can be used to develop a paragraph or an essay.

Development by Comparison.   Comparison is a natural operation of the mind. We rarely talk for long about any topic without comparing it with something else. We are fascinated with comparisons between ourselves and others and come to know ourselves better as a result of such comparisons. Machiavelli, for example, compares the armed with the unarmed prince and shows us, by means of examples, the results of being unarmed.

Comparison usually includes the following:

- A definition of two or more elements to be compared (by example, explanation, description, or any combination of these),
- Discussion of shared qualities,
- Discussion of unique qualities,
- A clear reason for making the comparison.

Virginia Woolf's primary rhetorical strategy in "Shakespeare's Sister" is to invent a comparison between William Shakespeare and a fictional sister that he never had. Woolf's point is that if indeed Shakespeare had had a sister who was as brilliant and gifted as he was, she could not have become famous like her brother. The Elizabethan environment would have expected her to remain uneducated and to serve merely as a wife and mother. In the sixteenth century, men like William Shakespeare could go to London and make their fortune. Women, in comparison, were prisoners of social attitudes regarding their sex. As Woolf tells us,

He was, it is well known, a wild boy who poached rabbits, perhaps shot a deer, and had, rather sooner than he should have done, to marry a woman in the neighborhood, who bore him a child rather quicker than was right. That escapade sent him to seek his fortune in London. He had, it seemed, a taste for the theatre; he began by holding horses at the stage door. Very soon he got work in the theatre, became a successful actor, and lived at the

> hub of the universe, meeting everybody, knowing everybody,
> practicing his art on the boards, exercising his wits in the streets,
> and even getting access to the palace of the queen. Meanwhile his
> extraordinarily gifted sister, let us suppose, remained at home.
> She was as adventurous, as imaginative, as agog to see the world
> as he was. But she was not sent to school. She had no chance of
> learning grammar and logic, let alone of reading Horace and
> Virgil. She picked up a book now and then, one of her brother's
> perhaps, and read a few pages. But then her parents came in and
> told her to mend the stockings or mind the stew and not moon
> about with books and papers. (para. 7)

Woolf's comparison makes it clear that the social circumstances of
the life of a woman in Shakespeare's time worked so much against
her personal desires and ambitions that it would be all but impossible for her to achieve anything of distinction on the London stage—
or in any other venue in which men dominated. Even though a
woman was monarch in England, it was a man's world.

Development by Example. Examples make abstract ideas concrete. When Machiavelli talks about looking at history to learn political
lessons, he cites specific cases and brings them to the attention of his
audience, the prince. Thomas Jefferson in the Declaration of Independence devotes most of his text to examples of the unacceptable behavior of the English king toward the colonies. Elizabeth Cady Stanton
follows his lead and does the same, beginning her list of examples of
gender discrimination with the assertion that "The history of mankind
is a history of repeated injuries and usurpations on the part of man
toward woman, having in direct object the establishment of an
absolute tyranny over her. To prove this, let facts be submitted to a
candid world" (para. 3). Then she lists the facts just as did Jefferson.
Every selection in this book offers examples either to convince us of the
truth of a proposition or to deepen our understanding of a statement.

Examples need to be chosen carefully because the burden of
proof and of explanation and clarity often depends on them. When
the sample suggestion given earlier for writing on Machiavelli's essay
asks who among modern world leaders Machiavelli would approve,
it is asking for carefully chosen examples. When doing research for
an essay, it is important to be sure that your example or examples
really suit your purposes.

Examples can be used in several ways. One is to do as Charles
Darwin does and present a large number of examples that force
readers to a given conclusion. This indirect method is sometimes
time-consuming, but the weight of numerous examples can be effective. A second method, such as Machiavelli's, also can be effective.

By making a statement that is controversial or questionable and that can be tested by example, you can lead your audience to draw a reasonable conclusion.

When using examples, keep these points in mind:

- Choose a few strong examples that support your point.
- Be concrete and specific—naming names, citing events, and giving details where necessary.
- Develop each example as fully as possible, and point out its relevance to your position.

In some selections, such as Darwin's discussion of natural selection, the argument hinges entirely on examples, and Darwin cites one example after another. Stephen Jay Gould shows how a particular example, that of the parasitical ichneumon fly, causes certain philosophical difficulties for theologians studying biology and therefore for anyone who looks closely at nature. The ichneumon, which people find ugly, attacks caterpillars, which people find sympathetic. As Gould tells us, we tend to dislike the parasite and sympathize with its victim. But there is another side to this, a second theme:

> The second theme, ruthless efficiency of the parasites, leads to the opposite conclusion—grudging admiration for the victors. We learn of their skill in capturing dangerous hosts often many times larger than themselves. Caterpillars may be easy game, but the psammocharid wasps prefer spiders. They must insert their ovipositors in a safe and precise spot. Some leave a paralyzed spider in its own burrow. *Planiceps hirsutus*, for example, parasitizes a California trapdoor spider. It searches for spider tubes on sand dunes, then digs into nearby sand to disturb the spider's home and drive it out. When the spider emerges, the wasp attacks, paralyzes its victim, drags it back into its own tube, shuts and fastens the trapdoor, and deposits a single egg upon the spider's abdomen. Other psammocharids will drag a heavy spider back to a previously prepared cluster of clay or mud cells. Some amputate a spider's legs to make the passage easier. Others fly back over water, skimming a buoyant spider along the surface. (para. 13)

Gould's example demonstrates that there are two ways of thinking about the effectiveness of the parasitic psammocharid. The wasp does not always make its life easier by attacking defenseless prey; instead, it goes after big game spiders. Gould's description technique, emphasizing the wasp's risk of danger, forces readers to respect the daring and ingenuity of the parasite even if at first we would not think to do so.

Development by Analysis of Cause and Effect.   People are interested in causes. We often ask what causes something, as if understanding the cause will somehow help us accept the result. Yet cause and effect can be subtle. With definition, comparison, and example, we can feel that the connections between a specific topic and our main points are reasonable. With cause and effect, however, we need to reason out the cause. Be warned that development by analysis of cause and effect requires you to pay close attention to the terms and situations you write about. Because it is easy to be wrong about causes and effects, their relationship must be examined thoughtfully. After an event has occurred, only a hypothesis about its cause may be possible. In the same sense, if no effect has been observed, only speculation about outcomes with various plans of action may be possible. In both cases, reasoning and imagination must be employed to establish a relationship between cause and effect.

The power of the rhetorical method of development through cause and effect is such that you will find it in every section of this book, in the work of virtually every author. Keep in mind these suggestions for using it to develop your own thinking:

- Clearly establish in your own mind the cause and the effect you wish to discuss.

- Develop a good line of reasoning that demonstrates the relationship between the cause and the effect.

- Be sure that the cause-effect relationship is real and not merely apparent.

In studying nature, scientists often examine effects in an effort to discover causes. Darwin, for instance, sees the comparable structure of the skeletons of many animals of different species and makes every effort to find the cause of such similarity. His answer is a theory: evolution. Another theorist, Michio Kaku, informs us that 90 percent of the universe is composed of dark matter: "Dark matter is a strange substance, unlike anything ever encountered before. It has weight but cannot be seen. In theory, if someone held a clump of dark matter in their hand, it would appear totally invisible. The existence of dark matter is not an academic question, because the ultimate fate of the universe, whether it will die in a fiery Big Crunch or fade away in a Cosmic Whimper of Big Chill, depends on its precise nature" (para. 6). Having said that, he goes on to explain the cause and effect equation:

> However, Ostriker and Peebles showed that the standard picture of a galaxy, based on our solar system, was unstable; by rights, the galaxy should fly apart. The gravitational pull of the stars was not enough to hold the galaxy together. They then showed that a galaxy can become stable if it is surrounded by a massive invisible halo that holds the galaxy together and if 90 percent of its mass was actually in the halo in the form of dark matter. (para. 18)

In this case, Kaku reveals that on the basis of the observed effect—that the universe does not fall apart even though it seems that it should—a theory must be constructed to explain the cause of its remaining held together. That theory produces the very puzzling concept of dark matter.

Everywhere in this collection authors rely on cause and effect to develop their thoughts. Thomas Jefferson establishes the relationship between abuses by the British and America's need to sever its colonial ties. Karl Marx establishes the capitalist economic system as the cause of the oppression of the workers who produce the wealth enjoyed by the rich. John Kenneth Galbraith is concerned with the causes of poverty, which he feels is an anomaly in modern society. Henry David Thoreau establishes the causes that demand civil disobedience as an effect. John Stuart Mill believes traditional Western values support the subordination of women.

Development by Analysis of Circumstances.   Everything we discuss exists as certain circumstances. Traditionally, the discussion of circumstances has had two parts. The first examines what is possible or impossible in a given situation. Whenever you try to convince your audience to take a specific course of action, it is helpful to show that given the circumstances, no other action is possible. If you disagree with a course of action that people may intend to follow because none other seems possible, however, you may have to demonstrate that another is indeed possible.

The second part of this method of development analyzes what has been done in the past: if something was done in the past, then it may be possible to do it again in the future. A historical survey of a situation often examines circumstances.

When using the method of analysis of circumstances to develop an idea, keep in mind the following tips:

- Clarify the question of possibility and impossibility.

- Review past circumstances so that future ones can be determined.

- Suggest a course of action based on an analysis of possibility and past circumstances.

- Establish the present circumstances, listing them if necessary. Be detailed, and concentrate on facts.

Martin Luther King Jr. examines the circumstances that led to his imprisonment and the writing of "Letter from Birmingham Jail." He explains that "racial injustice engulfs this community," and he reviews the "hard brutal facts of the case." His course of action is clearly stated and reviewed. He explains why some demonstrations were postponed and why his organization and others have been moderate in demands and actions. But he also examines the possibility of using nonviolent action to help change the inequitable social circumstances that existed in Birmingham. His examination of past action goes back to the Bible and the actions of the Apostle Paul. His examination of contemporary action is based on the facts of the situation, which he carefully enumerates. He concludes his letter by inviting the religious leaders to whom he addresses himself to join him in a righteous movement for social change.

Machiavelli is also interested in the question of possibility, because he is trying to encourage his ideal prince to follow a prescribed pattern of behavior. As he constantly reminds us, if the prince does not do so, it is possible that he will be deposed or killed. Taken as a whole, "The Qualities of the Prince" is a recitation of the circumstances that are necessary for success in politics. Machiavelli establishes this in a single paragraph:

> Therefore, it is not necessary for a prince to have all of the above-mentioned qualities, but it is very necessary for him to appear to have them. Furthermore, I shall be so bold as to assert this: that having them and practicing them at all times is harmful; and appearing to have them is useful; for instance, to seem merciful, faithful, humane, forthright, religious, and to be so; but his mind should be disposed in such a way that should it become necessary not to be so, he will be able and know how to change to the contrary. And it is essential to understand this: that a prince, and especially a new prince, cannot observe all those things by which men are considered good, for in order to maintain the state he is often obliged to act against his promise, against charity, against humanity, and against religion. And therefore, it is necessary that he have a mind ready to turn itself according to the way the winds of Fortune and the changeability of affairs require him; and, as I said above, as long as it is possible, he should not stray from the good, but he should know how to enter into evil when necessity commands. (para. 23)

This is the essential Machiavelli, the Machiavelli who is often thought of as a cynic. He advises his prince to be virtuous but says that it is not always possible to be so. Therefore, the prince must learn how not to be good when "necessity commands." The circumstances, he tells us, always determine whether it is possible to be virtuous. A charitable reading of this passage must conclude that his advice is at best amoral.

Many of the essays in this collection rely on an analysis of circumstances. Frederick Douglass examines the circumstances of slavery and freedom. When Karl Marx reviews the changes in economic history in *The Communist Manifesto*, he examines the circumstances under which labor functions:

> The feudal system of industry, under which industrial pro-
> duction was monopolized by closed guilds, now no longer sufficed
> for the growing wants of the new market. The manufacturing sys-
> tem took its place. The guild-masters were pushed on one side by
> the manufacturing middle-class: division of labor between the dif-
> ferent corporate guilds vanished in the face of division of labor in
> each single workshop. (para. 14)

Robert B. Reich examines the circumstances of our contemporary economy. He determines, among other things, that the wages of
in-person servers—bank tellers, retail salespeople, restaurant
employees, and others—will continue to be low despite the great
demand for such workers. Not only are these workers easily
replaced, but automation has led to the elimination of jobs—including bank teller jobs made redundant by automatic tellers and by
banking with personal computers and routine factory jobs replaced
by automation. Under current circumstances, these workers will lose
out to the "symbolic analysts" who know how to make their specialized knowledge work for them and who cannot be easily replaced.

Development by Analysis of Quotations.   Not all the essays in
this collection rely on quotations from other writers, but many do.
"Letter from Birmingham Jail," for example, relies on quotations
from the Bible. In that piece, Martin Luther King Jr. implies his
analysis of the quotations because the religious leaders to whom he
writes know the quotations well. By invoking the quotations, King
gently chides the clergy, who ought to be aware of their relevance.
In a variant on using quotations, Robert B. Reich relies on information taken from various government reports. He includes the information in his text and supplies numerous footnotes indicating the
sources, which are usually authoritative and convincing.

When you use quotations, remember these pointers:

- Quote accurately, and avoid distorting the original context.
- Unless the quotation is absolutely self-evident, offer your own
  clarifying comments.
- To help your audience understand why you have chosen a specific quotation, establish its function in your essay.

When Germaine Greer undertakes her study of the social construction of masculinity, one of her most interesting rhetorical techniques is to use quotations from a number of sources that help to

make her case. For one thing, she sprinkles brief quotations through-out the essay, such as Bertrand de Jouvenel's "A man feels himself more of a man when he is imposing himself and making others the instruments of his will." She does not comment on these quotations, but simply inserts them for us to ponder. But she also uses some quotations that she then analyzes, such as the comment from a U.S. Navy officer that begins with "Warriors kill" (para. 10) and goes on to declare that men are warriors and women are not. Greer analyzes the paragraph and uses its own statements to deconstruct it and show that by its own terms women can function in the army as well as men can. Greer is an English professor and thus has considerable experience analyzing texts that make claims that cannot be substanti-ated. Her method of textual analysis is accepted practice among scholars and helps her convince the reader of her argument.

In his examination of our tendency to anthropomorphize nature, Stephen Jay Gould uses quotations to show that there is a considerable literature on his subject. He quotes from J. H. Fabre, a French entomologist, to show how Fabre "humanized" caterpillars and demon-strated sympathy for the paralyzed victims of the parasitic wasps that fed off them. On the other hand, Gould points out that an equally interesting group of thinkers was impressed by the wasps' capacity to provide for their offspring. To support the viewpoint that admires the wasp, Gould quotes extensively from the writing of the Reverend William Kirby and other scientists, including Darwin (see paras. 19–29). Although Gould interprets these paragraphs, they speak clearly for themselves and fit into his argument perfectly. He ends his essay with a quotation from Darwin about the relation of religion and evolution: "I feel most deeply that the whole subject is too profound for the human intellect. A dog might as well speculate on the mind of Newton. Let each man hope and believe what he can."

In your own writing you will find plenty of opportunity to cite passages from an author whose ideas have engaged your attention. In writing an essay in response to Machiavelli, Carl Jung, Germaine Greer, or any other author in the book, you may find yourself quot-ing and commenting in some detail on specific lines or passages. This is especially true if you find yourself disagreeing with a point. Your first job, then, is to establish what you disagree with — and usually it helps to quote, which is essentially a way of producing evidence.

Finally, it must be noted that only a few aspects of the rhetorical methods used by the authors in this book have been discussed here. Rhetoric is a complex art that needs fuller study. But the points raised here are important because they are illustrated in many of the texts you will read, and by watching them at work you can begin to learn to use them yourself. By using them you will be able to achieve in your writing the fullness and purposiveness that mark mature prose.

ESTABLISHING AN ARGUMENT

Most of the selections in this book are constructed as arguments, although they take a variety of forms. Some assume a hostile audience, some a friendly audience. Some assume their subject is controversial, some assume they are primarily uncovering the truth, and some are simply being informative by explaining something complex. Machiavelli's selection from *The Prince* argues for a strongman political leader. In her analysis of Nazism, Hannah Arendt argues that terror is necessary for the state to achieve total domination over the people. One of the most brilliant arguments in the book is Cicero's "The Defense of Injustice"—brilliant because his techniques, which are discussed carefully, almost convince us. Henry David Thoreau argues for civil disobedience as a means of achieving justice. It is one of the most powerful arguments for justice that any American has written. Martin Luther King Jr.'s "Letter from Birmingham Jail" is itself one of the premier arguments in favor of nonviolent action. Its presentation of reasoned argument is outstanding. Andrew Carnegie argues that the wealthy must give their money back to the community in their lifetimes so they can see that their money is well spent.

Karl Marx's *The Communist Manifesto* is still relevant long after the demise of communism. His arguments against globalization are probably the most telling for today's audience. John Kenneth Galbraith's argument in "The Position of Poverty" is that our economy must address the plight of the poor, not the "plight" of the rich. Robert B. Reich also addresses globalization and argues that the people who will prosper in our economy are the "symbolic analysts" who can interpret and master texts. Stephen Jay Gould argues against anthropomorphizing nature while Francis Fukuyama examines the arguments for and against genetic engineering of human beings. Aristotle argues in favor of the moral life as the good life, while Friedrich Nietzsche argues that moral codes of his time go against the forces of nature. Aldo Leopold argues that we must treat the land ethically, just as we treat each other ethically, and Peter Singer and Jim Mason argue that there may be no ethical justification for eating meat. John Stuart Mill argues against the subjection of women in modern society. Germaine Greer argues that "masculinity" is not determined biologically, but culturally.

Iris Murdoch conducts an experimental argument asking whether religion is essential for morality to be relevant. Can there be morality without religion? Virginia Woolf's famous argument regarding the opportunities for women in history centers on the lack of opportunities for Shakespeare's imaginary "gifted sister." Howard Gardner argues that there are many forms of intelligence that should be credited in our society. Charles Darwin uses masses of collected evidence to derive an argument in favor of natural selection and, thus, evolution.

Most of the selections use one or more of the three basic forms of argument. **Classical arguments** rely on facts and evidence as well as on logic and reasoning to convince the reader of a specific position. Cicero's argument for injustice is an example. He reviews other cultures and determines that the concept of what is just varies enormously, so from the contradictory facts, he cannot determine what is best. He then examines the evidence in two hypothetical situations in which justice operates differently and asks us to choose what is just. Henry David Thoreau refuses to support a government with which he does not agree, particularly when he sees it acting unjustly. As a result, he declares, "That government is best which governs not at all." But he realizes that such a government can exist only when people are so good and so just that they do not need a government.

The second common form, like classical argument, is designed to convince someone of a specific position on a subject. This form, known as the **Toulmin argument,** has three parts:

- Claim: what you are trying to prove (often contained in the thesis statement)
- Support: the data—facts, observations, or conditions—you use to prove your claim
- Warrant: an assumption or belief that underlies the claim and is taken for granted

Thomas Jefferson's claim is that America deserves to be independent from Britain. The extraordinary volume of support, or data, he presents demonstrates that King George III has become a tyrant and "is unfit to be the ruler of a free people." His warrant is the underlying belief that, "all men are created equal" and must be free, not victims of a tyranny. Jefferson has a great deal at stake here. He proposes rebellion and independence from a much more powerful nation and therefore must be convincing, especially to the Americans themselves, most of whom emigrated from Great Britain and felt they owed it allegiance. If other Americans were not convinced by his argument, his life was forfeit.

The third form, the **Rogerian argument,** differs in that it does not appear to try to convince an audience of a specific position that must be accepted. Instead, the Rogerian argument tries to find a common ground on the subject that most people would agree with. Thus, this kind of argument does not seem to be an argument at all. It usually functions by establishing basic positions that most people would find nonthreatening, and in the process, such arguments appear to be simple discussions. Claude Lévi-Strauss's "Men, Women, and Chiefs" aims to lay out the details of life in the Nambikwara culture, while not appearing to argue that "primitive" culture seems to reinforce the gender-linked patterns that exist in the Western culture of the 1950s. W. E. B. Du Bois in "Of Our Spiritual Strivings" tells us a great deal about his childhood and upbringing and does not appear to be arguing in favor of a position that we would object to. Yet he speaks of being made to feel that he is a "problem" because he is an African American and in the process argues against prejudice and restriction of opportunity.

Whatever the form, the structure of most argument will follow this pattern:

Beginning of an argument

- Identify the subject and its importance.
- Suggest (or imply) how you plan to argue your case.

Middle of an argument

- Explain the main points of your argument with accompanying evidence.
- Argue each point in turn with the analysis of evidence.
- Rebut arguments against your position.

Conclusion of an argument

- Review the claims basic to your argument.
- Summarize your arguments, what they imply, and what you then conclude.

The following sample essay, "The Qualities of the President," modeled on Machiavelli's "The Qualities of the Prince," is an example of a Rogerian argument. The author reviews examples of the behavior of various kinds of modern leaders and then develops common ground with the reader to foster agreement on the qualities that seem most desirable in a modern president. The writer is not confrontational and does not demand absolute agreement but instead offers an exploration of the subject while nonetheless driving to a reasonable conclusion.

A SAMPLE ESSAY

The following sample essay is based on the first several paragraphs of Machiavelli's "The Qualities of the Prince" that were annotated in "Evaluating Ideas: An Introduction to Critical Reading"
(pp. 5–8). The essay is based on the annotations and the questions
that were developed from them:

- Should a leader be armed?

- Is it true that an unarmed leader is despised?

- Will those leaders who are always good come to ruin among
  those who are not good?

- To remain in power, must a leader learn how not to be good?

Not all these questions are addressed in the essay, but they serve
as a starting point and a focus for writing. The methods of development that are discussed above form the primary rhetorical techniques of the essay, and each method that is used is labeled in
the margin. The sample essay does two things simultaneously: it
attempts to clarify the meaning of Machiavelli's advice, and then it
attempts to apply that advice to a contemporary circumstance. Naturally, the essay could have chosen to discuss only the Renaissance
situation that Machiavelli described, but to do so would have
required specialized knowledge of that period. In this sample essay
the questions prompted by the annotations serve as the basis of the
discussion.

The Qualities of the President

Introduction   Machiavelli's essay, "The Qualities of the Prince," has a number of
very worrisome points. The ones that worry me most have to do with the
question of whether it is reasonable to expect a leader to behave
virtuously. I think this is connected to the question of whether the
leader should be armed. Machiavelli emphasizes that the prince must be
armed or else face the possibility that someone will take over the
government. When I think about how that advice applies to modern
times, particularly in terms of how our president should behave, I find
Machiavelli's position very different from my own.

Circumstance   First, I want to discuss the question of being armed. That is where
Machiavelli starts, and it is an important concern. In Machiavelli's time,
the late fifteenth and early sixteenth centuries, it was common for men
to walk in the streets of Florence wearing a rapier for protection. The
possibility of robbery or even attack by rival political groups was great in

those days. Even if he had a bodyguard, it was still important for a prince to know how to fight and to be able to defend himself. Machiavelli seems to be talking only about self-defense when he recommends that the prince be armed. In our time, sadly, it too is important to think about protecting the president and other leaders.

Examples   In recent years there have been many assassination attempts on world leaders, and our president, John F. Kennedy, was killed in Dallas in 1963. His brother Robert was killed when he was campaigning for the presidency in 1968. Also in 1968 Martin Luther King Jr. was killed in Memphis because of his beliefs in racial equality. In the 1980s Pope John Paul II was shot by a would-be assassin, as was President Ronald Reagan. They both lived, but Indira Gandhi, the leader of India, was shot and killed in 1984. This is a frightening record. Probably even Machiavelli would have been appalled. But would his solution - -being armed - -have helped? I do not think so.

Cause/Effect   For one thing, I cannot believe that if the pope had a gun he would have shot his would-be assassin, Ali Acga. The thought of it is almost silly. Martin Luther King Jr., who constantly preached the value of nonviolence, logically could not have shot at an assailant. How could John F. Kennedy have returned fire at a sniper? Robert Kennedy had bodyguards, and both President Reagan and Indira Gandhi were protected by armed guards. The presence of arms obviously does not produce the desired effect: security. The only thing that can produce that is to reduce the visibility of a leader. The president could speak on television or, when he must appear in public, use a bulletproof screen. The opportunities for would-be assassins can be reduced. But the thought of an American president carrying arms is unacceptable.

Comparison   The question of whether a president should be armed is to some extent symbolic. Our president stands for America, and if he were to appear in press conferences or state meetings wearing a gun, he would give a symbolic message to the world: look out, we're dangerous. Cuba's Fidel Castro usually appears in a military uniform with a gun, and when he spoke at the United Nations in 1960, he was the first, and I think the only, world leader to wear a pistol there. I have seen pictures of Benito Mussolini and Adolf Hitler appearing in public in military uniform, but never in a business suit. The same is true of Libyan leader Muammar al-Qaddafi and Iraq's Saddam Hussein. Today when a president or a head of state is armed there is often reason to worry. The current leaders of

Russia usually wear suits, but Joseph Stalin always wore a military uniform. His rule in the Soviet Union was marked by the extermination of whole groups of people and the imprisonment of many more. We do not want an armed president.

Use of quotations

also

Yet Machiavelli plainly says, "among the other bad effects it causes, being disarmed makes you despised . . . for between an armed and an unarmed man there is no comparison whatsoever" (para. 2). The problem with this statement is that it is more relevant to the sixteenth century

Comparison

than to the twenty-first. In our time the threat of assassination is so great that being armed would be no sure protection, as we have seen in the case of the assassination of President Sadat of Egypt, winner of the Nobel Peace Prize. On the other hand, the pope, like Martin Luther King Jr., would never have appeared with a weapon, and yet it can hardly be said they were despised. If anything, the world's respect for them is enormous. America's president also commands the world's respect, as does the prime minister of Great Britain. Yet neither would ever think of being armed. If what Machiavelli said was true in the early 1500s, it is pretty clear that it is not true today.

Definition

All this basically translates into a question of whether a leader should be virtuous. I suppose the definition of <u>virtuous</u> would differ with different people, but I think of it as holding a moral philosophy that you try to live by. No one is ever completely virtuous, but I think a president ought to try to be so. That means the president ought to tell the truth, since that is one of the basic virtues. The cardinal virtues--which were the same in Machiavelli's time as in ours--are justice, prudence, fortitude, and temperance. In a president, the virtue of justice is absolutely a must, or else what America stands for is lost. We definitely want our president to be prudent, to use good judgment, particularly in this nuclear age, when acts of imprudence could get us blown up. Fortitude, the ability to stand up for what is right, is a must for our president. Temperance is also important; we do not want a drunk for a president, nor do we want anyone with excessive bad habits.

Conclusion

It seems to me that a president who was armed or who emphasized arms in the way Machiavelli appears to mean would be threatening injustice (the way Stalin did) and implying intemperance, like many armed world leaders. When I consider this issue, I cannot think of any vice that our president ought to possess at any time. Injustice, imprudence, cowardice, and intemperance are, for me, unacceptable. Maybe

Machiavelli was thinking of deception and lying as necessary evils, but they are a form of injustice, and no competent president--no president who was truly virtuous--would need them. Prudence and fortitude are the two virtues most essential for diplomacy. The president who has those virtues will govern well and uphold our basic values.

The range of this essay is controlled and expresses a viewpoint that is focused and coherent. This essay of about one thousand words illustrates each method of development discussed in the text and uses each one to further the argument. The writer disagrees with one of Machiavelli's positions and presents an argument based on personal opinion that is bolstered by example and by analysis of current political conditions as they compare with those of Machiavelli's time. A longer essay could have gone more deeply into issues raised in any single paragraph and could have studied more closely the views of a specific president, such as President Ronald Reagan, who opposed stricter gun control laws even after he was shot.

The range of the selections in this volume is great, constituting a significant introduction to important ideas in many areas. They are especially useful for stimulating our own thoughts and ideas. There is an infinite number of ways to approach a subject, but observing how writers apply rhetorical methods in their work is one way to begin our own development as writers. Careful analysis of each selection can guide our exploration of these writers, who encourage our learning and reward our study.

Acknowledgments

Text Credits

Hannah Arendt, "Total Domination." From *The Origins of Totalitarianism* by Hannah Arendt. Copyright © 1948, 1976 by Hannah Arendt. Reprinted by permission of George Borchardt, Inc., on behalf of the Literary Trust of Hannah Arendt Blucher.

Aristotle, "The Aim of Man." From *Nicomachean Ethics: Aristotle*, First Edition, by Ostwald Martin, translator. Copyright © 1962. Electronically reproduced by permission of Pearson Education, Inc., Upper Saddle River, NJ.

Carl Becker, "Ideal Democracy." Excerpts (4-5) from *Modern Democracy*. Also published in "Afterthoughts on Constitutions" in *Yale Review* XVII, 455. Copyright © 1941. Reprinted by permission of Yale University Press.

Ruth Benedict, "The Individual and the Patterns of Culture." Excerpts from *Patterns of Culture* by Ruth Benedict. Copyright 1934 by Ruth Benedict. Copyright © renewed 1961 by Ruth Valentine. Reprinted by permission of Houghton Mifflin Harcourt Publishing Company. All rights reserved.

Rachel Carson, "The Sunless Sea." From *The Sea Around Us* by Rachel Carson. Copyright © 1950 by Rachel L. Carson. Used by permission of Frances Collin, Trustee.

Cicero, "The Defense of Injustice." From *On Government* by Cicero, translated by Michael Grant (Penguin Classics, 1993). Copyright © Michael Grant Publications Ltd. 1993. Reprinted with permission from Penguin Group (UK).

Emile Durkheim, "The Individual and the Intellectuals." From *On Morality and Society: Selected Writings* by Emile Durkheim. Edited by Robert N. Bellah. © 1973 The University of Chicago Press. Originally published as "L'individualisme et les intellectuals," *Revue bleue*, 4e serie, 10 (1898): 7–13. Translated by Mark Traugott. Reprinted by permission of University of Chicago Press.

Sigmund Freud, "The Oedipus Complex." (Chapter III) from *Interpretation of Dreams, The Standard Edition of the Complete Psychological Works of Sigmund Freud*, Volume IV, pp. 122ff. Copyright © 1953. A.W. Freud et al. Reprinted by permission of Sigmund Freud Copyrights. Represented by Paterson Marsh Ltd., Literary & Copyright Agents.

Erich Fromm, "The Individual in the Chains of Illusion." Excerpts from *My Encounter with Marx and Freud* by Erich Fromm. Copyright © 1962 by Simon & Schuster, Inc. Copyright © renewed 1990 by The Estate of Erich Fromm. Copyright © 2006 Continuum USA. Reprinted by permission of Continuum International Publishing Group, Inc.

Francis Fukuyama, "Genetic Engineering." From *Our Posthuman Future: Consequences of the Biotechnology Revolution* by Francis Fukuyama. Copyright © 2002 Farrar, Straus & Giroux, LLC. Reprinted by permission of Farrar, Straus and Giroux LLC.

John Kenneth Galbraith, "The Position of Poverty." Excerpt from *The Affluent Society*, Fourth Edition. Copyright © 1958, 1969, 1976, and 1984 by John Kenneth Galbraith. Reprinted by permission of Houghton Mifflin Harcourt Publishing Company. All rights reserved.

Howard Gardner, "A Rounded Version: The Theory of Multiple Intelligences." From *Multiple Intelligences*. Copyright © 1993 by Howard Gardner. Reprinted by permission of Basic Books, a member of Perseus Books, LLC.

José Ortega y Gasset, "The Greatest Danger, the State." From *The Revolt of the Masses* by José Ortega y Gasset, authorized translation from the Spanish. Copyright 1932 by W.W. Norton & Company, Inc. Renewed © 1960 by Teresa Carey. Used by permission of W.W. Norton & Company, Inc.

Stephen Jay Gould, "Nonmoral Nature." From *Natural History*, February 1982, volume 9, #2. Copyright © 1982 Stephen Jay Gould. Reprinted with the permission of Rhonda Shearer, Director Art Science Research Laboratory.

Germaine Greer, "Masculinity." From *The Whole Woman* by Germaine Greer. Copyright © 1999 Germaine Greer. Used with permission of Alfred A. Knopf, a division of Random House, Inc.

Carl Jung, "The Personal and the Collective Unconscious." From *Psyche and Symbol* by C. G. Jung. Copyright © 1991 Princeton University Press. Reprinted by permission of Princeton University Press.

Michio Kaku, "The Mystery of Dark Matter." From *Beyond Einstein: The Cosmic Quest for the Theory of the Universe* by Michio Kaku. Copyright © 1987, 1995 by Michio Kaku and Jennifer Trainer Thompson. Reprinted by permission of the Stuart Krichevsky Literary Agency, Inc.

Martin Luther King Jr., "Letter from Birmingham Jail." Copyright 1963 by Martin Luther King Jr., copyright renewed 1991 by Coretta Scott King. Reprinted by arrangement with The Heirs to the Estate of Martin Luther King Jr., c/o Writers House Inc., as agent for the proprietor.

Lao-tzu, "Thoughts from the *Tao-te Ching*." Excerpts as submitted from *Tao-te Ching* by Lao-tzu, A New English Version, with Foreword and Notes by Stephen Mitchell. Translation copyright © 1988 by Stephen Mitchell. Reprinted by permission of HarperCollins Publishers, Inc.

Aldo Leopold, "The Land Ethic." From *A Sand County Almanac* by Aldo Leopold. Copyright © 1949 by Oxford University Press. © 1966 by Oxford University Press. Reprinted by permission of Oxford University Press.

Claude Lévi-Strauss, "Men, Women, and Chiefs." English Translation © 1973 by Jonathan Cape Ltd. Originally published in French as *Tristes Tropiques* by Claude Lévi-Strauss. Copyright © 1955 by Librairie Plon. Reprinted by permission of George Borchardt, Inc. for Librairie Plon.

Niccolò Machiavelli, excerpt (13 pages) from "The Prince," by Niccolò di Bernardo Machiavelli. Translated by Mark Musa and Peter Bondanella, from *The Portable Machiavelli*, edited by Peter Bondanella and Mark Musa. Translated by Mark Musa and Peter Bondanella. Copyright © 1979 by Viking Penguin, Inc. Used by permission of Viking Penguin, and a division of Penguin Group (USA) Inc.

Margaret Mead, "Sex and Temperament." Excerpts from *Three Primitive Societies* by Margaret Mead. Copyright © 1935 William Morrow & Company. Reprinted courtesy of The Institute for Intercultural Studies, Inc., New York.

Iris Murdoch, "Morality and Religion." From *Metaphysics As a Guide to Morals* by Iris Murdoch. Copyright © 1992 by Iris Murdoch. Used by permission of Penguin, a division of Penguin Group (USA) Inc. Published by Chatto & Windus (UK). Reprinted by permission of The Random House Group Ltd.

Friedrich Nietzsche, "Morality as Anti-Nature." From *The Portable Nietzsche* by Friedrich Nietzsche, edited by Walter Kaufmann, translated by Walter Kaufmann. Copyright © 1954 by The Viking Press. Renewed © 1982 by Viking Penguin, Inc. Used by permission of Viking Penguin, a division of Penguin Group (USA) Inc.

Steven Pinker, "Thinking Machines." From *How the Mind Works* by Steven Pinker, pp. 59–93. Copyright © 1997 by Steven Pinker. Used by permission of W.W. Norton & Company, Inc.

V. S. Ramachandran, "Neuroscience — The New Philosophy." From *A Brief Tour of Human Consciousness: From Impostor Poodles to Purple Numbers* by V. S. Ramachandran, pp. 82–101. Copyright © 2004. Reprinted by permission of Pearson Education, Inc.

John Rawls, "A Sense of Justice." From *A Theory of Justice* by John Rawls, pp. 362–367, Cambridge, Mass.: The Belknap Press of Harvard University Press. Copyright © 1971, 1999 by the President and Fellows of Harvard College. Reprinted by permission of the publisher.

Robert Reich, "Why the Rich Are Getting Richer and the Poor, Poorer." From *The Work of Nations* by Robert Reich. Copyright © 1991 by Robert B. Reich. Reprinted by permission of Alfred A. Knopf, a division of Random House, Inc.

Jean-Jacques Rousseau, "The Origin of Civil Society." Translated by Gerard Hopkins, from *Social Contract: Essays by Locke, Hume, and Rousseau* edited by Ernest Barker. Copyright © 1947. Reprinted with permission of Oxford University Press.

Peter Singer & Jim Mason, "The Ethics of Eating Meat." From *The Ethics of What We Eat: Why Our Food Choices Matter* by Peter Singer and Jim Mason, Rodale Press, New York, 2006. Reprinted by permission of the author.

Virginia Woolf, "Shakespeare's Sister." From *A Room of One's Own* by Virginia Woolf. Copyright © 1929 by Houghton Mifflin Harcourt Publishing Company. Renewed 1957 by Leonard Woolf. Reprinted by permission of the publisher.

Image Credits

[1.1] Page 18: Eugène Delacroix, *Liberty Leading the People*. Erich Lessing/Art Resource, NY. Louvre, Paris, France.

[1.2] Page 20: Lao-tzu, © Charles Walker/Topfoto/The Image Works.

[1.3] Page 36: Niccolò Machiavelli, © Topham/The Image Works.

[1.4] Page 54: Jean-Jacques Rousseau, ©Archivo Iconografico, S.A./CORBIS.

[1.5] Page 76: Thomas Jefferson, portrait: © ARPL/HIP/The Image Works.

[1.6] Page 86: José Ortega y Gasset, © Associated Press.

[1.7] Page 100: Carl Becker, Courtesy Division of Rare and Manuscript Collections, Carl A. Kroch Library, Cornell University.

[1.8] Page 120: Hannah Arendt, © Oscar White/CORBIS.

[2.1] Page 140: Luca Giordano, Fresco in the Medici Palace, Florence (The Triumph of Justice). Public domain image, courtesy The Yorck Project, *10,000 Masterpieces of Painting*, 2002.

[2.2] Page 142: Cicero, © The Art Archive/Museo Capitolino Rome/Dagli Orti.

[2.3] Page 156: Frederick Douglass, © AP/Wide World Photos.

[2.4] Page 172: Henry David Thoreau, © Hulton Archive/Getty Images.

[2.5] Page 200: Elizabeth Cady Stanton, © Bettmann/CORBIS.

[2.6] Page 210: Martin Luther King Jr., portrait © Bob Adelman/Magnum Photos.

[2.7] Page 232: John Rawls, Courtesy Harvard University.

[3.1] Page 250: Caspar David Friedrich, *Wanderer Above the Sea of Fog*, Bildarchiv Preussischer Kulturbesitz/Erich Lessing, Art Resource, NY. Hamburger Kunsthalle, Hamburg, Germany.

[3.2] Page 254: Ralph Waldo Emerson, © Hulton Archive/Getty Images.

[3.3] Page 270: Emile Durkheim, © The London Art Archive/Alamy.

[3.4] Page 286: W. E. B. Du Bois, © Hulton Archive/Getty Images.

[3.5] Page 300: Ruth Benedict, Special Collections, Vassar College Libraries.

[3.6] Page 324: Erich Fromm, © Bill Ray/Time & Life Pictures/Getty Images.

[4.1] Page 344: Henry Ossawa Tanner, *The Thankful Poor*, Art Resource, NY. Private Collection.

[4.2] Page 346: Adam Smith, © Hulton-Deutsch Collection/CORBIS.

[4.3] Page 358: Karl Marx, © AP/Wide World Photos.

[4.4] Page 386: Andrew Carnegie, © Hulton Archive/Getty Images.

[4.5] Page 404: John Kenneth Galbraith, © Time-Life Pictures/Getty Images.

[4.6] Page 418: Robert B. Reich, © Reuters/CORBIS.

[5.1] Page 443: Salvador Dalí, *The Persistence of Memory,* © 2010 Salvador Dalí, Gala-Salvador Dalí Foundation/Artists Rights Society (ARS), New York/Art Resource, NY. Digital Image © The Museum of Modern Art, New York, NY.

[5.2] Page 446: Plato, © Gianni Dagli Orti/CORBIS.

[5.3] Page 460: René Descartes, © Bettmann/CORBIS.

[5.4] Page 474: Sigmund Freud, © ARPL/HIP/The Image Works.

[5.5] Page 486: Carl Jung, © Hulton Archive/Getty Images.

[5.6] Page 502: Howard Gardner, © Time-Life Pictures/Getty Images.

[5.7] Page 524: Steven Pinker, © David Levenson/Getty Images.

[5.8] Page 552: V. S. Ramachandran, © Martin Pope/Telegraph UK/Zum.

[6.1] Page 576: Asher Durand, *Kindred Spirits.* Photo © Francis G. Mayer/CORBIS.

[6.2] Page 578: Francis Bacon, © ARPL/HIP/The Image Works.

[6.3] Page 596: Charles Darwin, © Bridgeman Art Library.

[6.4] Page 614: Rachel Carson, © Erich Hartmann/Magnum Photos.

[6.5] Page 634: Stephen Jay Gould, © Time-Life Pictures/Getty Images.

[6.6] Page 650: Michio Kaku, Courtesy Hyperspace Productions, Inc./mkaku.org.

[6.7] Page 666: Francis Fukuyama, © Ulf Andersen/Getty Images.

[7.1] Page 687: Joseph Wright, *An Experiment on a Bird in the Air Pump.* Art Resource, NY. National Gallery, London, Great Britain.

[7.2] Page 690: Aristotle, © The Art Archive/Museo Nazionale Romano, Rome/Dagli Orti.

[7.3] Page 712: Friedrich Nietzsche, © Bettmann/CORBIS.

[7.4] Page 728: Iris Murdoch, © Hulton Archive/Getty Images.

[7.5] Page 744: Aldo Leopold, Robert McCabe/Courtesy of the University of Wisconsin-Madison Archives.

[7.6 and 7.7] Page 766: Peter Singer & Jim Mason, Reprinted by arrangement with Rodale Inc. Photo copyright © Denise Applewhite/Princeton University (Peter Singer); Photo copyright © Cara M. Rea (Jim Mason).

[8.1] Page 796: *In the Loge,* 1878, Mary Stevenson Cassatt, American, 1844–1926. Oil on canvas, 81.28 × 66.04 cm (32 × 26 in.). Museum of Fine Arts, Boston. The Hayden Collection—Charles Henry Hayden Fund, 10.35.

[8.2] Page 798: Mary Wollstonecraft, © Hulton Archive/Getty Images.

[8.3] Page 814: John Stuart Mill, © Hulton Archive/Getty Images.

[8.4] Page 836: Virginia Woolf, © AP/Wide World Photos.

[8.5] Page 854: Margaret Mead, © Hulton Archive/Getty Images.

[8.6] Page 872: Claude Lévi-Strauss, © Martine Franck/Magnum Photos.

[8.7] Page 888: Germaine Greer, © John Hedgecoe/Topham/The Image Works.

INDEX OF
RHETORICAL TERMS